RACE RACISM AND AMERICAN LAW

Derrick A. Bell, Jr.

Professor of Law, Harvard University

LITTLE, BROWN AND COMPANY
Boston Toronto
1973

LIBRARY OF CONGRESS CATALOG CARD NO. 73-6407

THIRD PRINTING, 1975

Acknowledgment of permission to reprint previously published material appears on pages xxxv–xxxviii.

Published simultaneously in Canada
by Little, Brown & Company (Canada) Limited

PRINTED IN THE UNITED STATES OF AMERICA

This book is dedicated to all those who throughout America's history have risked its wrath to protest its faults. The photograph represents one such protest, and, perhaps, a prophecy:

The dramatic finale of an
Extraordinary achievement
Performed for a nation which
Had there been a choice
Would have chosen another, and
If given a chance
Will accept the achievement
And neglect the achievers.
Here, with simple gesture, they
Symbolize a people whose patience
With exploitation will expire with
The dignity and certainty
With which it has been endured . . .
Too long.

SUMMARY OF CONTENTS

CONTENTS

PART VI. RIGHT TO JUSTICE

APPENDIX

TABLE OF CASES

Italic type indicates principal cases.

PERMISSIONS

The excerpts from the following materials appear with the kind permission of the copyright holders.

Allport, Gordon, The Nature of Prejudice, 1954, Addison-Wesley, Reading, Mass., pp. 107, 109.

Alpert, The Origin of Slavery in the United States — The Maryland Precedent, 14 American Journal of Legal History 189, 194-195, 209-211 (1970).

Applebaum, H., Miscegenation Statutes: A Constitutional and Social Problem, 53 Georgetown Law Journal 49-50 (1964).

Bell, D., School Litigation Strategies for the 1970s: New Phases in the Continuing Quest for Quality Schools, 1970 Wisconsin Law Review 257, 290-292.

Bennett, Lerone, Before the Mayflower 189 (1961). Copyright by Johnson Publications.

Borden, Philip, Found Cumbering the Soil: Manifest Destiny and the Indian in the Nineteenth Century, 71-72, 79-80, 80-82, 83-84. From The Great Fear: Race in the Mind of America edited by Gary B. Nash and Richard Weiss. Copyright © 1970 by Gary B. Nash and Richard Weiss. Adapted and reprinted by permission of Holt, Rinehart and Winston, Inc.

Carter, Robert, The Warren Court and Desegregation, from The Warren Court: A Critical Analysis, R. Sayler, B. Boyer, R. Gooding, eds. (1969). Copyright by Chelsea House Publishers.

Christopher, W., The Constitutionality of the Voting Rights Act of 1965, Stanford Law Review 1-8 (1965). Copyright 1965 by the Board of Trustees of the Leland Stanford Junior University.

Cox, O., Caste, Class and Race, 526-527 (1948). Copyright © 1948 by Oliver Cromwell Cox. All rights reserved. By permission of Monthly Review Press.

Daynard, Test Case Litigation as a Source of Significant Social Change, 18 Catholic Lawyer 37, 38 (1972).

Dillard, I., The Emancipation Proclamation in the Perspective of Time, 23 Law in Transition 95-100. Published by the National Lawyers Guild.

Edmonds, Ron, Statement: Proceedings, National Policy Conference on Education for Blacks, pages 140-144 (April 1, 1972).

Finkelstein, Michael O. The Application of Statistical Decision Theory to the Jury Discrimination Cases, 80 Harvard Law Review 338 (1966). Copyright 1966 by the Harvard Law Review Association.

Fiss, Owen, The Charlotte-Mecklenburg Case — Its Significance for Northern School Desegregation, 38 University of Chicago Law Review 697, 699-703 (1971).

Franklin, J. H. From The Emancipation Proclamation by John Hope Franklin. Copyright © 1963 by John Hope Franklin. Reprinted by permission of Doubleday & Company, Inc., pages 138-140.

Franklin, J. H., History of Racial Segregation in the United States, Annals of the American Academy of Political and Social Science, Mar. 1956, Vol. 34, pp. 1-9.

Fried, Charles, Moral Causation, 77 Harvard Law Review 1258 (1964). Copyright 1964 by the Harvard Law Review Association.

Gould, William, Black Power in the Unions: The Impact Upon Collective Bargaining Relationships, 79 Yale Law Journal 46 (1963). Reprinted by permission of The Yale Law Journal Company and Fred B. Rothman & Company from The Yale Law Journal, Vol. 79, pp. 55, 63.

Greene, L., The Negro in Colonial New England 232-233, Columbia University Press, 1942.

Grier, W. H., and P. M. Cobbs. Excerpted from Chapter V, Marriage and Love, in Black Rage by William H. Grier and Price M. Cobbs, © 1968 by William H. Grier and Price M. Cobbs. Used by permission of Basic Books, Inc.

Hamilton, Charles V., Race and Education: A Search for Legitimacy, Harvard Educational Review 38, Fall 1968, 669-684. Copyright © 1968 by President and Fellows of Harvard College.

Harlan, Louis R., Desegregation in New Orleans Public Schools During Reconstruction, American Historical Review (April 1962).

Hill, The New Judicial Perception of Employment Discrimination — Litigation Under Title VII of the Civil Rights Act of 1964, 43 University of Colorado Law Review 243-247, 251-252 (1972).

Hoover, Robert, Statement: Proceedings, National Policy Conference on Education for Blacks, page 135 (April 1, 1972).

Jones, James E., Jr., The Promises of the 60's — The Reality of the 70's, 2 Black Law Journal 5, 10-11 (1972). Copyright © 1972, by The Black Law Journal, UCLA.

Jordan, W., White Over Black, 136-140, University of North Carolina Press and the Institute of Early American History and Culture.

Kardiner, A., and L. Ovesey, The Mark of Oppression: Explorations in the Personality of the American Negro 42-45 (1951).

King, M. L., Jr. From pp. 84-86, Letter From Birmingham Jail — April 16, 1963 — in Why We Can't Wait by Martin Luther King, Jr. Copyright © 1963 by Martin Luther King, Jr. Reprinted by permission of Harper & Row, Publishers, Inc.

Kirp, Community Control, Public Policy, and the Limits of Law, 68 Michigan Law Review 1355, 1365-1367, 1369-1370.

Kovel, J. From White Racism: A Psychohistory, by Joel Kovel. Copyright © 1970 by Joel Kovel. Reprinted by permission of Pantheon Books/A Division of Random House, Inc.

LeMelle, Tilden J., introduction to Richard Burkey, Racial Discrimination and Public Policy in the United States 38 (1971).

Lester, Julius, The Necessity of Separation, Ebony (Aug. 1970). Published by Johnson Publications.

Lines, Race and Learning: A Perspective On the Research, 11 Inequality in Education 26 (Mar. 1972). Reprinted with permission from Inequality in Education, the magazine of the Center for Law and Education at Harvard University.

Litwack, Leon F., North of Slavery 74, 75, 79, 113-117, 120-121, 168-170, 211-212, The University of Chicago Press, 1961. © 1961 by The University of Chicago.

Logan, Rayford W., and Michael R. Winston. From The Negro in the United States, Vol. II. © 1971 by Litton Educational Publishing, Inc. Reprinted by permission of Van Nostrand Reinhold Company.

Lynd, Staughton, Slavery and the Founding Fathers, from Black History 119-131, M. Drimmer ed. (1968).

Meier, August. Excerpted from Civil Rights Strategies for Negro Employment by August Meier in Employment, Race, and Poverty, edited by Arthur M. Ross and Herbert Hill, copyright © 1967 by Harcourt Brace Jovanovich, Inc. and reprinted with their permission.

Note, American Slavery and the Conflict of Laws, 71 Columbia Law Review 74, 87-98 (1971).

Note, The Federal Injunction as a Remedy for Unconstitutional Police Conduct. Reprinted by permission of The Yale Law Journal Company and Fred B. Rothman & Company from The Yale Law Journal, Vol. 78, p. 145.

Note, Racial Discrimination in Public Housing Site Selection, 23 Stanford Law Review 63 (1970). Copyright 1970 by the Board of Trustees of the Leland Stanford Junior University.

Note, Red, White and Grey: Equal Protection and the American Indian, 21 Stanford Law Review 1236 (1969). Copyright 1969 by the Board of Trustees of the Leland Stanford Junior University.

Note, The Responsibility of Local Zoning Authorities to Nonresident Indigents, 23 Stanford Law Review 774 (1971). Copyright 1971 by the Board of Trustees of the Leland Stanford Junior University.

Olson, Robert, Employment Discrimination Litigation: New Priorities in the Struggle for Black Equality, 6 Harvard Civil Rights–Civil Liberties Law Review 22-33 (1970). Reprinted by permission of Harvard Civil Rights–Civil Liberties Law Review, copyright 1970.

Pinderhughes, Charles A., Understanding Black Power: Processes and Proposals, 125 American Journal of Psychiatry 1552-57 (1969). Copyright 1969, the American Psychiatric Association.

Roper, Donald M., In Quest of Judicial Objectivity: The Marshall Court and the Legitimation of Slavery, 21 Stanford Law Review 532 (1969). Copyright 1969 by the Board of Trustees of the Leland Stanford Junior University.

Rosen, S. J. From The Law and Racial Discrimination in Employment, by Sanford Jay Rosen in Employment, Race, and Poverty, edited by Arthur M. Ross and Herbert Hill, copyright © 1967 by Harcourt Brace Jovanovich, Inc. and reprinted with their permission.

Ross, A. M. From The Negro in the American Economy, by Arthur M. Ross in Employment, Race and Poverty, edited by Arthur M. Ross and Herbert Hill, copyright © 1967 by Harcourt Brace Jovanovich, Inc. and reprinted with their permission.

Schuchter, Arnold, White Power, Black Freedom 36, 37 (1968). Published by Beacon Press.

Steel, Lewis M., Nine Men in Black Who Think White, N.Y. Times Magazine, October 13, 1968. © 1968 by the New York Times Company. Reprinted by permission.

Van Loon, E., Representative Government and Equal Protection: Securing Effective Voting Strength by the Use of Proportional Representation in At-Large Districts, 5 Harvard Civil Rights–Civil Liberties Law Review, 472, 473-487 (1970). Reprinted by permission of Harvard Civil Rights–Civil Liberties Law Review, copyright 1970.

Wish, H., Historian Looks at School Segregation, 16 Western Reserve Law Review 555, 569-570 (1965).

The photograph on p. v, of the 1968 Olympic victory of John Carlos and Tommie Smith, is reprinted by permission of United Press International.

PREFACE

Purpose

If the title has not alerted the reader, the photograph of the famous 1968 Olympic protest on the dedication page will have provided ample notice that this book is concerned with American racism initiated by whites against blacks, and seeks to determine to what extent that racism is reflected in the law.

American blacks, of course, are not the only victims of racism, but they are by far the largest and most active of the country's minorities, and thus the appropriate focus for a detailed study of the law and racism. Other groups have adopted strategies identified with black protests to oppose discrimination practiced against them. And even when they don't emulate black protest tactics, other minorities often benefit from legal precedents obtained by blacks. In fact, decisions protecting the right of blacks to nondiscriminatory juries and election districts, to due process in student disciplinary proceedings, and to noninterference by the state in associations designed to further antidiscrimination efforts, have served to extend the rights of the white majority in these areas.

But while the body of law is enormous and its impact substantial, it is apparent that, despite perennial expectations and hopes, racial problems and the impact they have on the law continue to grow in size, complexity and importance. Over the years, and particularly during the 1950s and 1960s, court decisions and statutes dealing with racial problems have received more public discussion, been more generally hailed and more roundly condemned, than those of any other area of judicial or legislative activity. And yet, for all the furor they caused and all the change in racial patterns and policies attributed to them, these "civil rights" cases and laws are today increasingly regarded as obsolete, and of little or no contemporary value.

Why do the hard-won decisions protecting basic rights of black citizens from racial discrimination become obsolete before they are effectively enforced? What factors stifle vigorous enforcement of laws which, in a nation dedicated to individual freedom, should never have been needed? Do civil rights cases and laws gained during the last two decades face the neglect, reversal and outright repeal which was the fate of the very similar measures fashioned to protect the rights of blacks during an earlier racial reconstruction period a century ago? As lawyers, can we advise blacks and other minorities to stake their futures on such laws?

These are the questions which determined the character of this book. They are intended to spark study and discussion of the materials at a scholarly level, but they should also reveal the more pragmatic approach lawyers must adopt as they attempt to solve problems and fashion legal remedies for black clients who, having won the symbols, seek the substance of equal opportunity.

The discussion of legal decisions involving racial issues is now a familiar part of many law school classes, not only in civil rights courses, but in contracts, property and other courses of the traditional law school curriculum where civil rights cases are used to give interest and "relevance." But such usage serves mainly the needs of the subject matter, and even in constitutional law classes there is little chance that the significance of racial decisions on racial problems can be examined. This casebook, the first devoted specifically to a study of racism in the law, is based on a belief, which has grown stronger during its writing, that reason and a great deal of neglected material justify a far closer examination of racial cases than most law students have received.

Structure

While racial injustices suffered by blacks and other nonwhite minorities in this country are interconnected and have a cumulative effect, for convenience the subject matter is organized into the classical categories: education, rights of citizenship (voting, use of public facilities, protest rights and sex and marriage), employment, housing and administration of justice (jury discrimination, criminal and civil remedies, etc.). The opening chapters review the history of racism in American law and the impact of racism on minority groups other than blacks; the pivotal third chapter, "Ending Racism Through Law," discusses the possibility that legal methods are inadequate to solve this problem, and examines both alternatives and outcomes if the law fails to eliminate discriminatory policies and practices.

If there was a "truth in titles" law, it would likely require that the name of this work be prefaced with the words "Selected Readings," for the statutes, regulations, cases and writings about race constitute a vast literature, the size of which — despite major and (perhaps) overzealous editing — far exceeds the limits of a single volume. For additional cases and materials, I heartily recommend a source to which I turned again and again: Volume II of Political and Civil Rights in the United States (T. Emerson, D. Haber, N. Dorsen, eds.), Little, Brown 1967. Supplements are published every few years. I have cited other more specific sources throughout the book. But those references are suggestive rather than exhaustive, in part to permit a broader than usual inclusion of nonlegal writing intended to illuminate consideration of racial issues and how lawmakers attempt to resolve them. The nonlegal materials should bring a greater sense of reality to this highly sensitized area of the law, where everyone has an opinion and almost no one, including the legally trained, says what he really thinks.

It is not that referral to these writings will serve as a substitute for legal expertise. Courts and law teachers still want to hear (or believe they do) the citation to a controlling case in point, the reference to an appropriate statute, and a tight, analytically sound argument that is as devoid as possible of any reference to the political, sociological and psychological pressures that will probably play a major part in the decision of a case. It is doubtful that any of us will change this very soon.

What I hope the nonlegal writings will do is provide the advantage of perspective for the lawyer whose profession requires that he deal with the law as it is. This, of course, is becoming increasingly difficult. It is likely, then, that for some, the nonlegal writings will make the task easier. For others, the thoughts contained in these writings may make the task impossible.

Style

Even with the omission of much valuable material and the editing of much that is included, teachers and students may find it difficult to cover comfortably, even in a fifteen-week (forty-five-hour) semester, the contents of a text with more than enough material for a full year course. Some teachers, especially those relying on the class discussion method, may decide to focus on a portion of the material, leaving the rest for supplemental reading. Indeed, an interesting and impressively rigorous seminar could be based on the materials in, say, Chapters One, Three and Seven. One or more of the other chapters covering voting, education, employment, housing or justice could be substituted for the protest problems in Chapter Seven as the "substantive" component of such a seminar.

On the other hand, those who structure the course around student presentations may assign all the readings with the expectation that major classroom discussion will be focused on those issues raised in the seventeen hypothetical problems which I have titled "Racism Hypos." These may be supplemented with other problems in follow-up lectures or discussions. While experienced teachers will have reservations about how many students will read materials not scheduled for class discussion, I have found that the nature of the readings and the interest brought to them by most students who select this course result in a much higher than average student follow-through on such assignments.

I think that student interest and understanding of this material will benefit if classroom discussion is structured around student presentation of arguments based on the Racism Hypos. There are an infinite number of ways this can be done. One basic format is as follows:

At an early class, students are urged to review the Racism Hypos and make tentative choices of those that interest them. Using these selections to the extent possible, the class is divided into "law firms" (one or two students per firm depending on class size), and each law firm is assigned to represent a party. Basic research on the assigned problem should be performed during the early weeks, at which time the class can follow the traditional lecture and discussion process while covering the materials in Part I, "The Development of Racism in American Law." At this time, scheduling of the presentations for the balance of the term should also be accomplished. Ideally, classes devoted to lecture and discussion should be interspersed with those devoted to student presentation of the Hypos.

In the presentations, a preannounced period of time is allocated to each law firm, the members of which attempt to make as convincing an argument as possible for their side of the case. The class will serve as judges (as an alternative, or in addition to the class, a revolving panel of student judges may be selected for this purpose), and students will be expected to interrupt the presentation with questions, comments, criticism, etc. Allocated times for argument should be strictly adhered to. In this regard, it is an advantage if the course can be scheduled for one and one-half hour sessions.

At the conclusion of each presentation, opportunity should be provided for a critique of the law firm's efforts and the issues contained in its arguments. It adds interest to take a hand vote as to which side should prevail, although student judges may handle this function. The winner will often be the law firm with the sympathetic position rather than that with the law on its side. But such results can be the basis for further discussion. It is also beneficial to have each student submit at the conclusion of the argument an unsigned critique of both law firms' strengths and weaknesses during the oral argument. This critique would include a general grade: "excellent," "very good," "good," "satisfactory," "unsatisfactory." Some teachers may wish to indicate that they will use these critiques in determining the students' grades for this portion of the course.

A further basis for grading can be a written opinion (the winning law firm writing the majority opinion and the losing law firm a dissent). Finally, on grades I have found that interest, preparation and participation in the course remain more stable if there is a final exam. This can be of the take-home variety and could be distributed perhaps two weeks before the end of the term.

Acknowledgments

While only one name appears on the cover, this book is the product of the work, encouragement and support provided by a number of individuals and organizations. For the much needed relief from my teaching duties, I wish to thank the Ford Foundation for its generous financial support. I left active practice to write, and the Harvard Law School and Dean Albert Sacks have done all one could ask to make available to me the school's impressive resources. My faculty colleagues, particularly Professors Gary Bellow, Andrew Kaufman, Frank Michelman and Alan Stone, have been generous with their time in reading various chapters of the book. I must thank Judge Robert L. Carter, who first convinced me to attempt this book. Judge A. Leon Higginbotham also offered generous encouragement, as did Professors William

Gould and Roger Kuhn and the teachers at several schools who used these materials in mimeographed form. Legal Defense Fund lawyers Norman J. Chachkin, William Robinson and Melvyn Leventhal helped keep me aware of late developments in the ever changing civil rights field.

Over the three years of the book's development, a long list of students have assisted with research, writing and citation checking. Susan Thorner has been outstanding, but there has been valuable work by Robert Graham, David Twedt, Pernila Stimley Brown, Weldon Rougeau, Stanley Langbein, neQiniso Abdullah, Glenn Lau Kee, James Wexler, Michael Klipper and Charles Hamilton.

I am afraid I subjected my faithful and ever effective secretary Susan Peterson to something like stenographic servitude during the preparation of this manuscript. My regards and thanks are slender reparations indeed for the skill, efficiency and never flagging optimism she brought to this project. The seemingly endless typing chores were shared by Ann Lightner and Judi Kaye. Ann Mendez and the staff at Little, Brown performed the onerous burden of editing the manuscript, substantially improving both clarity and form in the process. Errors that remain are the author's responsibility.

As every author knows, it is impossible to adequately acknowledge the sacrifices a wife and children must make so that authorship will be possible. Jewel and our three boys accepted the months of neglect with a stoicism and good grace that I fear is the unseen prerequisite of successful professional endeavor.

Derrick Bell

RACE, RACISM AND AMERICAN LAW

Part I
THE DEVELOPMENT OF RACISM IN AMERICAN LAW

1. SLAVERY AND AMERICAN LAW

INTRODUCTORY NOTE

"Twenty years after Columbus reached the New World, African Negroes, transported by Spanish, Dutch and Portuguese traders, were arriving in the Caribbean Islands. Almost all came as slaves. By 1600, there were more than half a million slaves in the Western Hemisphere.

"In Colonial America, the first Negroes landed at Jamestown in August, 1619. Within 40 years, Negroes had become a group apart, separated from the rest of the population by custom and law. Treated as servants for life, forbidden to intermarry with whites, deprived of their African traditions and dispersed among Southern plantations, American Negroes lost tribal, regional and family ties.

"Through massive importation, their numbers increased rapidly. By 1776, some 500,000 Negroes were held in slavery and indentured servitude in the United States. Nearly one of every six persons in the country was a slave." Rep. of Nat. Comm. on Civil Disorders, "Rejection and Protest: An Historical Sketch" 95 (1968).

Beginning with the early Colonial period and extending up to the time of the Civil War, there was a vast amount of litigation at both the state and federal levels involving blacks. In virtually all of the cases, blacks were the subjects and not the parties in the litigation. See H. Catterall, Judicial Cases Concerning American Slavery and the Negro, vols. I-V (1936). They were property subject to ownership; and the law, reflecting as it did then the prevailing belief in the inherent inferiority of all backs, experienced little difficulty in treating them as "chattels personal." K. Stampp, The Peculiar Institution 197-236 (1956).

There were, however, a number of cases, usually initiated by whites, in which the black sought his freedom. Often the case involved the drawing of a will or some other form of promise to emancipate the slave; not infrequently the key issue was whether the slave was entitled to his freedom under some variation of the common-law rule that masters who took slaves into a jurisdiction where slavery was not permitted lost all property rights in the slave.

By far the most famous of these cases was Dred Scott v. Sandford, 60 U.S. (19 How.) 393 (1857). The case raised the issue of whether the slave Dred Scott's temporary residence in free territory (Illinois) sufficed to free him under common-law principles. See infra at 36. The Supreme Court found that Scott was not a citizen of Missouri within the meaning of the Constitution and thus could not invoke the diversity jurisdiction of the federal courts. But rather than settle the case on this procedural ground, the Court reiterated former law that Scott's four-year residence in Illinois had not altered his slave status, and invalidated the Missouri Compromise of 1820 (dividing equally new states between slave and free) on the ground that it violated substantive rights in property under the Fifth Amendment's Due Process Clause.

In effect, the decision denied Congress the power to exclude slavery from any part of the unorganized western territories. The case, which gratuitously deprived blacks even in free states of rights of citizenship under the Constitution, is an example — often repeated — of how blacks become little more than pawns in litigation nominally concerning civil rights, but actually providing a forum for the resolution of competing interests of the white majority. Moreover, while the Dred Scott case had a devastating effect on Chief Justice Taney's reputation as a lawyer and a politician, his well-documented argument as to the status of black people in this country stands as an irrefutable testament to the extension of the nation's belief in the inferiority of blacks, and the degree to which those beliefs had been inculcated into the laws of the land.

A. THE DRED SCOTT CASE

DRED SCOTT v. SANDFORD
60 U.S. (19 How.) 393 (1857)

Mr. Chief Justice TANEY delivered the opinion of the court. . . .

The question is simply this: Can a negro, whose ancestors were imported into this country, and sold as slaves, become a member of the political community formed and brought into existence by the Constitution of the United States, and as such become entitled to all the rights, and privileges, and immunities, guarantied by that instrument to the citizen? One of which rights is the privilege of suing in a court of the United States in the cases specified in the Constitution.

It will be observed, that the plea applies to that class of persons only whose ancestors were negroes of the African race, and imported into this country, and sold and held as slaves. The only matter in issue before the court, therefore, is, whether the descendants of such slaves, when they shall be emancipated, or who are born of parents who had become free before their birth, are citizens of a State, in the sense in which the word citizen is used in the Constitution of the United States. And this being the only matter in dispute on the pleadings, the court must be understood as speaking in this opinion of that class only, that is, of those persons who are the descendants of Africans who were imported into this country, and sold as slaves.

[Blacks and Indians distinguished]

The situation of this population was altogether unlike that of the Indian race. The latter, it is true, formed no part of the colonial communities, and never amalgamated with them in social connections or in government. But although they were uncivilized, they were yet a free and independent people, associated together in nations or tribes, and governed by their own laws. Many of these political communities were situated in territories to which the white race claimed the ultimate right of dominion. But that claim was acknowledged to be subject to the right of the Indians to occupy it as long as they thought proper, and neither the English nor colonial Governments claimed or exercised any dominion over the tribe or nation by whom it was occupied, nor claimed the right to the possession of the territory, until the tribe or nation consented to cede it. These Indian Governments were regarded and treated as foreign Governments, as much so as if an ocean had separated the red man from the white; and their freedom has constantly been acknowledged, from the time of the first emigration to the English colonies to the present day, by the different Governments which succeeded each other. Treaties have been negotiated with them, and their alliance sought for in war; and the people who compose these Indian political communities have always been treated as foreigners not living under our Government. It is true that the course of events has brought the Indian tribes within the limits of the United States under subjection to the white race; and it has been found necessary, for their sake as well as our own, to regard them as in a state of pupilage, and to legislate to a certain extent over them and the territory they occupy. But they may, without doubt, like the subjects of any other foreign Government, be naturalized by the authority of Congress, and become citizens of a State, and of the United States; and if an individual should leave his nation or tribe, and take up his abode among the white population, he would be entitled to all the rights and privileges which would belong to an emigrant from any other foreign people.

We proceed to examine the case as presented by the pleadings.

[Blacks not intended to be U.S. citizens]

The words "people of the United States" and "citizens" are synonymous terms, and mean the same thing. They both describe the political body who, according to our republican institutions, form the sovereignty, and who hold the power and conduct the Government through their representatives. They are what we familiarly call the "sovereign people," and every citizen is one of this people, and a constituent member of this sovereignty. The question before us is, whether the class of persons described in the plea in abatement compose a portion of this people, and are constituent members of this sovereignty? We think they are not, and that they are not included, and were not intended to be included, under the word "citizens" in the Constitution, and can therefore claim none of the rights and privileges which that instrument provides for and secures to citizens of the United States. On the contrary, they were at that time considered as a subordinate and inferior class of beings, who had been subjugated by the dominant race, and, whether emancipated or not, yet remained subject to their authority, and had no rights or privileges but such as those who held the power and the Government might choose to grant them.

It is not the province of the court to decide upon the justice or injustice, the policy or impolicy, of these laws. The decision of that question belonged to the political or law-making power; to those who formed the sovereignty and framed the Constitution. The duty of the court is, to interpret the instrument they have framed, with the best lights we can obtain on the subject, and to administer it as we find it, according to its true intent and meaning when it was adopted.

[States can't confer national citizenship]

In discussing this question, we must not confound the rights of citizenship which a State may confer within its own limits, and the rights of citizenship as a member of the Union. It does not by any means follow, because he has all the rights and privileges of a citizen of a State, that he must be a citizen of the United States. He may have all of the rights and privileges of the citizen of a State, and yet not be entitled to the rights and privileges of a citizen in any other State. For, previous to the adoption of the Constitution of the United States, every State had the undoubted right to confer on whomsoever it pleased the character of citizen, and to endow him with all its rights. But this character of course was confined to the boundaries of the State, and gave him no rights or privileges in other States beyond those secured to him by the laws of nations and the comity of States. Nor have the several States surrendered the power of conferring these rights and privileges by adopting the Constitution of the United States. Each State may still confer them upon an alien, or any one it thinks proper, or upon any class or description of persons; yet he would not be a citizen in the sense in which that word is used in the Constitution of the United States, nor entitled to sue as such in one of its courts, nor to the privileges and immunities of a citizen in the other States. The rights which he would acquire would be restricted to the State which gave them. The Constitution has conferred on Congress the right to establish an uniform rule of naturalization, and this right is evidently exclusive, and has always been held by this court to be so. Consequently, no State, since the adoption of the Constitution, can by naturalizing an alien invest him with the rights and privileges secured to a citizen of a State under the Federal Government, although, so far as the State alone was concerned, he would undoubtedly be entitled to the rights of a citizen, and clothed with all the rights and immunities which the Constitution and laws of the State attached to that character.

It is very clear, therefore, that no State can, by any act or law of its own, passed since the adoption of the Constitution, introduce a new member into the political community created by the Constitution of the United States. It cannot make him a member of this community by making him a member of its own. And for the same reason it cannot introduce any person, or description of persons, who were not intended to be embraced in this new political family, which the Constitution brought into existence, but were intended to be excluded from it.

[U.S. owes blacks no rights and privileges]

The question then arises, whether the provisions of the Constitution, in relation to the personal rights and privileges to which the citizen of a State should be entitled, embraced the negro African race, at that time in this country, or who might afterwards be imported, who had then or should afterwards be made free in any State; and to put it in the power of a single State to make him a citizen of the United States, and endue him with the full rights of citizenship in every other State without their consent? Does the Constitution of the United States act upon him whenever he shall be made free under the laws of a State, and raised there to the rank of a citizen, and immediately clothe him with all the privileges of a citizen in every other State, and in its own courts?

The court think the affirmative of these propositions cannot be maintained. And if it cannot, the plaintiff in error could not be a citizen of the State of Missouri, within the meaning of the Constitution of the United States, and, consequently, was not entitled to sue in its courts.

It is true, every person, and every class and description of persons, who were at the time of the adoption of the Constitution recognised as citizens in the several States, became also citizens of this new political body; but none other; it was formed by them, and for them and their posterity, but for no one else. And the personal rights and privileges guarantied to citizens of this new sovereignty were intended to embrace those only who were then members of the several State communities, or who should afterwards by birthright or otherwise become members, according to the provisions of the Constitution and the principles on which it was founded. It was the union of those who were at that time members of distinct and separate political communities into one political family, whose power, for certain specified purposes, was to extend over the whole territory of the United States. And it gave to each citizen rights and privileges outside of his State which he did not before possess, and placed him in every other State upon a perfect equality with its own citizens as to rights of person and rights of property; it made him a citizen of the United States.

It becomes necessary, therefore, to determine who were citizens of the several States when the Constitution was adopted. And in order to do this, we must recur to the Governments and institutions of the thirteen colonies, when they separated from Great Britain and formed new sovereignties, and took their places in the family of independent nations. We must inquire who, at that time, were recognised as the people or citizens of a State, whose rights and liberties had been outraged by the English Government; and who declared their independence, and assumed the powers of Government to defend their rights by force of arms.

[Blacks have no rights as human beings]

In the opinion of the court, the legislation and histories of the times, and the language used in the Declaration of Independence, show, that neither the class of persons who had been imported as slaves, nor their descendants, whether they had become free or not, were then acknowledged as a part of the people, nor intended to be included in the general words used in that memorable instrument.

It is difficult at this day to realize the state of public opinion in relation to that unfortunate race, which prevailed in the civilized and enlightened portions of the world at the time of the Declaration of Independence, and when the Constitution of the United States was framed and adopted. But the public history of every European nation displays it in a manner too plain to be mistaken.

They had for more than a century before been regarded as beings of an inferior order, and altogether unfit to associate with the white race, either in social or political relations; and so far inferior, that they had no rights which the white man was bound to respect; and that the negro might justly and lawfully be reduced to slavery for his benefit.* He was bought and sold, and treated as an ordinary article of merchandise and traffic, whenever a profit could be made by it. This opinion was at that time fixed and universal in the civilized portion of the white race. It was regarded as an axiom in morals as well as in politics, which no one thought of disputing, or supposed to be open to dispute; and men in every grade and position in society daily and habitually acted upon it in their private pursuits, as well as in matters of public concern, without doubting for a moment the correctness of this opinion.

And in no nation was this opinion more firmly fixed or more uniformly acted upon than by the English Government and English people. They not only seized them on the coast of Africa, and sold them or held them in slavery for their own use; but they took them as ordinary articles of merchandise to every country where they could make a profit on them, and were far more extensively engaged in this commerce than any other nation in the world.

* It is this statement which, while comprising no part of the holding in the case, became the key quotation representating the impact of the case on blacks and whites. Frederick Douglass described the statement as a "historical fact." F. Douglass, Life and Times of Frederick Douglass 293 (1962).

The opinion thus entertained and acted upon in England was naturally impressed upon the colonies they founded on this side of the Atlantic. And, accordingly, a negro of the African race was regarded by them as an article of property, and held, and bought and sold as such, in every one of the thirteen colonies which united in the Declaration of Independence, and afterwards formed the Constitution of the United States. The slaves were more or less numerous in the different colonies, as slave labor was found more or less profitable. But no one seems to have doubted the correctness of the prevailing opinion of the time.

[Colonial legislation as proof of black inferiority]

The legislation of the different colonies furnishes positive and indisputable proof of this fact.

It would be tedious, in this opinion, to enumerate the various laws they passed upon this subject. It will be sufficient, as a sample of the legislation which then generally prevailed throughout the British colonies, to give the laws of two of them; one being still a large slaveholding State, and the other the first State in which slavery ceased to exist.

The province of Maryland, in 1717, (ch. 13, s. 5,) passed a law declaring "that if any free negro or mulatto intermarry with any white woman, or if any white man shall intermarry with any negro or mulatto woman, such negro or mulatto shall become a slave during life, excepting mulattoes born of white women, who, for such intermarriage, shall only become servants for seven years, to be disposed of as the justices of the county court, where such marriage so happens, shall think fit; to be applied by them towards the support of a public school within the said county. And any white man or white woman who shall intermarry as aforesaid, with any negro or mulatto, such white man or white woman shall become servants during the term of seven years, and shall be disposed of by the justices as aforesaid, and be applied to the uses aforesaid."

The other colonial law to which we refer was passed by Massachusetts in 1705, (chap. 6.) It is entitled "An act for the better preventing of a spurious and mixed issue." &c.; and it provides, that "if any negro or mulatto shall presume to smite or strike any person of the English or other Christian nation, such negro or mulatto shall be severely whipped, at the discretion of the justices before whom the offender shall be convicted."

And "that none of her Majesty's English or Scottish subjects, nor of any other Christian nation, within this province, shall contract matrimony with any negro or mulatto; nor shall any person, duly authorized to solemnize marriage, presume to join any such in marriage, on pain of forfeiting the sum of fifty pounds; one moiety thereof to her Majesty, for and towards the support of the Government within this province, and the other moiety to him or them that shall inform and sue for the same, in any of her Majesty's courts of record within the province, by bill, plaint, or information."

We give both of these laws in the words used by the respective legislative bodies, because the language in which they are framed, as well as the provisions contained in them, show, too plainly to be misunderstood, the degraded condition of this unhappy race. They were still in force when the Revolution began, and are a faithful index to the state of feeling towards the class of persons of whom they speak, and of the position they occupied throughout the thirteen colonies, in the eyes and thoughts of the men who framed the Declaration of Independence and established the State Constitutions and Governments. They show that a perpetual and impassable barrier was intended to be erected between the white race and the one which they had reduced to slavery, and governed as subjects with absolute and despotic power, and which they then looked upon as so far below them in the scale of created beings, that intermarriages between white persons and negroes or mulattoes were regarded as unnatural and immoral, and punished as crimes, not only in the parties, but in the person who joined them in marriage. And no distinction in this respect was made between the free negro or mulatto and the slave, but this stigma, of the deepest degradation, was fixed upon the whole race.

We refer to these historical facts for the purpose of showing the fixed opinions concerning that race, upon which the statesmen of that day spoke and acted. It is necessary to do this, in order to determine whether the general terms used in the Constitution of the United States, as to the rights of man and the rights of the people, was intended to include them, or to give them or their posterity the benefit of any of its provisions.

["All men created equal" does not include blacks]

The language of the Declaration of Independence is equally conclusive:

It begins by declaring that, "when in the course of human events it becomes necessary for one people to dissolve the political bands which have connected them with another, and to assume among the powers of the earth the separate and equal station to which the laws of nature and nature's God entitle them, a decent respect for the opinions of mankind requires that they should declare the causes which impel them to the separation."

It then proceeds to say: "We hold these truths to be self-evident: that all men are created equal; that they are endowed by their Creator with certain unalienable rights; that among them is life, liberty, and the pursuit of happiness; that to secure these rights, Governments are instituted, deriving their just powers from the consent of the governed."

The general words above quoted would seem to embrace the whole human family, and if they were used in a similar instrument at this day would be so understood. But it is too clear for dispute, that the enslaved African race were not intended to be included, and formed no part of the people who framed and adopted this declaration; for if the language, as understood in that day, would embrace them, the conduct of the distinguished men who framed the Declaration of Independence would have been utterly and flagrantly inconsistent with the principles they asserted; and instead of the sympathy of mankind, to which they so confidently appealed, they would have deserved and received universal rebuke and reprobation.

Yet the men who framed this declaration were great men — high in literary acquirements — high in their sense of honor, and incapable of asserting principles inconsistent with those on which they were acting. They perfectly understood the meaning of the language they used, and how it would be understood by others; and they knew that it would not in any part of the civilized world be supposed to embrace the negro race, which, by common consent, had been excluded from civilized Governments and the family of nations, and doomed to slavery. They spoke and acted according to the then established doctrines and principles, and in the ordinary language of the day, and no one misunderstood them. The unhappy black race were separated from the white by indelible marks, and laws long before established, and were never thought of or spoken of except as property, and when the claims of the owner or the profit of the trader were supposed to need protection.

[The Constitution as proof]

This state of public opinion had undergone no change when the Constitution was adopted, as is equally evident from its provisions and language.

The brief preamble sets forth by whom it was formed, for what purposes, and for whose benefit and protection. It declares that it is formed by the *people* of the United States; that is to say, by those who were members of the different political communities in the several States; and its great object is declared to be to secure the blessings of liberty to themselves and their posterity. It speaks in general terms of the *people* of the United States, and of *citizens* of the several States, when it is providing for the exercise of the powers granted or the privileges secured to the citizen. It does not define what description of persons are intended to be included under these terms, or who shall be regarded as a citizen, and one of the people. It uses them as terms so well understood, that no further description or definition was necessary.

But there are two clauses in the Constitution which point directly and specifically to the negro race as a separate class of persons, and show clearly that they were not regarded as a portion of the people or citizens of the Government then formed.

One of these clauses reserves to each of the thirteen States the right to import slaves until the year 1808, if it thinks proper. And the importation which it thus sanctions was unquestionably of persons of the race of which we are speaking, as the traffic in slaves in the United States had always been confined to them. And by the other provision the States pledge themselves to each other to maintain the right of property of the master, by delivering up to him any slave who may have escaped from his service, and be found within their respective territories. By the first above-mentioned clause, therefore, the right to purchase and hold this property is directly sanctioned and authorized for twenty years by the people who framed the Constitution. And by the second, they pledge themselves to maintain and uphold the right of the master in the manner specified, as long as the Government they then formed should endure. And these two provisions show, conclusively, that neither the description of persons therein referred to, nor their descendants, were embraced in any of the other provisions of the Constitution; for certainly these two clauses were not intended to confer on them or their posterity the blessings of liberty, or any of the personal rights so carefully provided for the citizen.

No one of that race had ever migrated to the United States voluntarily; all of them had been brought here as articles of merchandise. The number that had been emancipated at that time were but few in comparison with those held in slavery; and they were identified in the public mind with the race to which they belonged, and regarded as a part of the slave population rather than the free. It is obvious that they were not even in the minds of the framers of the Constitution when they were conferring special rights and privileges upon the citizens of a State in every other part of the Union.

[The condition of the black race]

Indeed, when we look to the condition of this race in the several States at the time, it is impossible to believe that these rights and privileges were intended to be extended to them.

It is very true, that in that portion of the Union where the labor of the negro race was found to be unsuited to the climate and unprofitable to the master, but few slaves were held at the time of the Declaration of Independence; and when the Constitution was adopted, it had entirely worn out in one of them, and measures had been taken for its gradual abolition in several others. But this change had not been produced by any change of opinion in relation to this race; but because it was discovered, from experience, that slave labor was unsuited to the climate and productions of these States: for some of the States, where it had ceased or nearly ceased to exist, were actively engaged in the slave trade, procuring cargoes on the coast of Africa, and transporting them for sale to those parts of the Union where their labor was found to be profitable, and suited to the climate and productions. And this traffic was openly carried on, and fortunes accumulated by it, without reproach from the people of the States where they resided. And it can hardly be supposed that, in the States where it was then countenanced in its worst form — that is, in the seizure and transportation — the people could have regarded those who were emancipated as entitled to equal rights with themselves.

And we may here again refer, in support of this proposition, to the plain and unequivocal language of the laws of the several States, some passed after the Declaration of Independence and before the Constitution was adopted, and some since the Government went into operation.

We need not refer, on this point, particularly to the laws of the present slaveholding States. Their statute books are full of provisions in relation to this class, in the same spirit with the Maryland law which we have before quoted. They have continued to treat them as an inferior class, and to subject them to strict police regulations, drawing a broad line of distinction between the citizen and the slave races, and legislating in relation to them upon the same principle which prevailed at the time of the Declaration of Independence. As relates to these States, it is too plain for argument, that they have never been regarded as a part of the people or citizens of the State, nor supposed to possess any political rights which the dominant race might not withhold or grant at their pleasure. And as long ago as 1822, the Court of Appeals of Kentucky decided that free negroes and mulattoes were not citizens within the meaning of the Constitution of the United States; and the correctness of this decision is recognised, and the same doctrine affirmed, in 1 Meigs's Tenn. Reports, 331.

And if we turn to the legislation of the States where slavery had worn out, or measures taken for its speedy abolition, we shall find the same opinions and principles equally fixed and equally acted upon.

[Blacks not citizens in nonslave states]

Thus, Massachusetts, in 1786, passed a law similar to the colonial one of which we have spoken. The law of 1786, like the law of 1705, forbids the marriage of any white person with any negro, Indian, or mulatto, and inflicts a penalty of fifty pounds upon any one who shall join them in marriage; and declares all such marriages absolutely null and void, and degrades thus the unhappy issue of the marriage by fixing upon it the stain of bastardy. And this mark of degradation was renewed, and again impressed upon the race, in the careful and deliberate preparation of their revised code published in 1836. This code forbids any person from joining in marriage any white person with any Indian, negro, or mulatto, and subjects the party who shall offend in this respect, to imprisonment, not exceeding six months, in the common jail, or to hard labor, and to a fine of not less than fifty nor more than two hundred dollars; and, like the law of 1786, it declares the marriage to be absolutely null and void. It will be seen that the punishment is increased by the code upon the person who shall marry them, by adding imprisonment to a pecuniary penalty.

So, too, in Connecticut. We refer more particularly to the legislation of this State, because it was not only among the first to put an end to slavery within its own territory, but was the first to fix a mark of reprobation upon the African slave trade. The law last mentioned was passed in October, 1788, about nine months after the State had ratified and adopted the present Constitution of the United States; and by that law it prohibited its own citizens, under severe penalties, from engaging in the trade, and declared all policies of insurance on the vessel or cargo made in the State to be null and void. But, up to the time of the adoption of the Constitution, there is nothing in the legislation of the State indicating any change of opinion as to the relative rights and position of the white and black races in this country, or indicating that it meant to place the latter, when free, upon a level with its citizens. And certainly nothing which would have led the slaveholding States to suppose, that

Connecticut designed to claim for them, under the new Constitution, the equal rights and privileges and rank of citizens in every other State.

The first step taken by Connecticut upon this subject was as early as 1774, when it passed an act forbidding the further importation of slaves into the State. But the section containing the prohibition is introduced by the following preamble:

"And whereas the increase of slaves in this State is injurious to the poor, and inconvenient."

This recital would appear to have been carefully introduced, in order to prevent any misunderstanding of the motive which induced the Legislature to pass the law, and places it distinctly upon the interest and convenience of the white population — excluding the inference that it might have been intended in any degree for the benefit of the other.

And in the act of 1784, by which the issue of slaves, born after the time therein mentioned, were to be free at a certain age, the section is again introduced by a preamble assigning a similar motive for the act. It is in these words:

"Whereas sound policy requires that the abolition of slavery should be effected as soon as may be consistent with the rights of individuals, and the public safety and welfare" — showing that the right of property in the master was to be protected, and that the measure was one of policy, and to prevent the injùry and inconvenience, to the whites, of a slave population in the State.

And still further pursuing its legislation, we find that in the same statute passed in 1774, which prohibited the further importation of slaves into the State, there is also a provision by which any negro, Indian, or mulatto servant, who was found wandering out of the town or place to which he belonged, without a written pass such as is therein described, was made liable to be seized by any one, and taken before the next authority to be examined and delivered up to his master — who was required to pay the charge which had accrued thereby. And a subsequent section of the same law provides, that if any free negro shall travel without such pass, and shall be stopped, seized, or taken up, he shall pay all charges arising thereby. And this law was in full operation when the Constitution of the United States was adopted, and was not repealed till 1797. So that up to that time free negroes and mulattoes were associated with servants and slaves in the police regulations established by the laws of the State.

And again, in 1833, Connecticut passed another law, which made it penal to set up or establish any school in that State for the instruction of persons of the African race not inhabitants of the State, or to instruct or teach in any such school or institution, or board or harbor for that purpose, any such person, without the previous consent in writing of the civil authority of the town in which such school or institution might be.

And it appears by the case of Crandall v. The State, reported in 10 Conn. Rep., 340, that upon an information filed against Prudence Crandall for a violation of this law, one of the points raised in the defence was, that the law was a violation of the Constitution of the United States; and that the persons instructed, although of the African race, were citizens of other States, and therefore entitled to the rights and privileges of citizens in the State of Connecticut. But Chief Justice Dagget, before whom the case was tried, held, that persons of that description were not citizens of a State, within the meaning of the word citizen in the Constitution of the United States, and were not therefore entitled to the privileges and immunities of citizens in other States.

The case was carried up to the Supreme Court of Errors of the State, and the question fully argued there. But the case went off upon another point, and no opinion was expressed on this question.

We have made this particular examination into the legislative and judicial action of Connecticut, because, from the early hostility it displayed to the slave trade on the coast of Africa, we may expect to find the laws of that State as lenient and favorable to the subject race as those of any other State in the Union; and if we find that at the time the Constitution was adopted, they were not even there raised to the rank of citizens, but were still held and treated as property, and the laws relating to them passed with reference altogether to the interest and convenience of the white race, we shall hardly find them elevated to a higher rank anywhere else.

A brief notice of the laws of two other States, and we shall pass on to other considerations.

By the laws of New Hampshire, collected and finally passed in 1815, no one was permitted to be enrolled in the militia of the State, but free white citizens; and the same provision is found in a subsequent collection of the laws, made in 1855. Nothing could more strongly mark the entire repudiation of the African race. The alien is excluded, because, being born in a foreign country, he cannot be a member of the community until he is naturalized. But why are the African race, born in the State, not permitted to share in one of the highest duties of the citizen? The answer is obvious; he is not, by the institutions and laws of the State, numbered among its people. He forms no part of the sovereignty of the State, and is not therefore called on to uphold and defend it.

Again, in 1822, Rhode Island, in its revised code, passed a law forbidding persons who were authorized to join persons in marriage, from joining in marriage any white person with any negro, Indian, or mulatto, under the penalty of two hundred dollars, and declaring all such marriages absolutely null and void; and the same law was again re-enacted in its revised code of 1844. So that, down to the last-mentioned period, the strongest mark of inferiority and degradation was fastened upon the African race in that State.

It would be impossible to enumerate and compress in the space usually allotted to an opinion of a court, the various laws, marking the condition of this race, which were passed from time to time after the Revolution, and before and since the adoption of the Constitution of the United States. In addition to those already referred to, it is sufficient to say, that Chancellor Kent, whose accuracy and research no one will question, states in the sixth edition of his Commentaries, (published in 1848, 2 vol., 258, note *b,*) that in no part of the country except Maine, did the African race, in point of fact, participate equally with the whites in the exercise of civil and political rights.

The legislation of the States therefore shows, in a manner not to be mistaken, the inferior and subject condition of that race at the time the Constitution was adopted, and long afterwards, throughout the thirteen States by which that instrument was framed; and it is hardly consistent with the respect due to these States, to suppose that they regarded at that time, as fellow-citizens and members of the sovereignty, a class of beings whom they had thus stigmatized; whom, as we are bound, out of respect to the State sovereignties, to assume they had deemed it just and necessary thus to stigmatize, and upon whom they had impressed such deep and enduring marks of inferiority and degradation; or, that when they met in convention to form the Constitution, they looked upon them as a portion of their constituents, or designed to include them in the provisions so carefully inserted for the security and protection of the liberties and rights of their citizens. It cannot be supposed that they intended to secure to them rights, and privileges, and rank, in the new political body throughout the Union, which every one of them denied within the limits of its own dominion. More especially, it cannot be believed that the large slaveholding States regarded them as included in the word citizens, or would have consented to a Constitution which might compel them to receive them in that character from another State. For if they were so received, and entitled to the privileges and immunities of citizens, it would exempt them from the operation of the special laws and from the police regulations which they considered to be necessary for their own safety. It would give to persons of the negro race, who were recognised as citizens in any one State of the Union, the right to enter every other State whenever they pleased, singly or in companies, without pass or passport, and without obstruction, to sojourn there as long as they pleased, to go where they pleased at every hour of the day or night without molestation, unless they committed some violation of law for which a white man would be punished; and it would give them the full liberty of speech in public and in private upon all subjects upon which its own citizens might speak; to hold public meetings upon political affairs, and to keep and carry arms wherever they went. And all of this would be done in the face of the subject race of the same color, both free and slaves, and inevitably producing discontent and insubordination among them, and endangering the peace and safety of the State.

It is impossible, it would seem, to believe that the great men of the slaveholding States, who took so large a share in framing the Constitution of the United States, and exercised so much influence in procuring its adoption, could have been so forgetful or regardless of their own safety and the safety of those who trusted and confided in them.

[Blacks can not be naturalized]

Besides, this want of foresight and care would have been utterly inconsistent with the caution displayed in providing for the admission of new members into this political family. For, when they gave to the citizens of each State the privileges and immunities of citizens in the several States, they at the same time took from the several States the power of naturalization, and confined that power exclusively to the Federal Government. No State was willing to permit another State to determine who should or should not be admitted as one of its citizens, and entitled to demand equal rights and privileges with their own people, within their own territories. The right of naturalization was therefore, with one accord, surrendered by the States, and confided to the Federal Government. And this power granted to Congress to establish an uniform rule of *naturalization* is, by the well-understood meaning of the word, confined to persons born in a foreign country, under a foreign Government. It is not a power to raise to the rank of a citizen any one born in the United States, who, from birth or parentage, by the laws of the country, belongs to an inferior and subordinate class. And when we find the States guarding themselves from the indiscreet or improper admission by other States of emigrants from other countries, by giving the power exclusively to Congress, we cannot fail to see that they could never have left with the States a much more important power — that is, the power of transforming into citizens a numerous class of persons, who in that character would be much more dangerous to the peace and safety of a large portion of the Union, than the few foreigners one of the States might improperly naturalize. The Constitution upon its adoption obviously took from the States all power by any subsequent legislation to introduce as a citizen into the political family of the United States any one, no matter where he was born, or what might be his character or condition; and it gave to Congress the power to confer this character upon those only who were born outside of the dominions of the United States. And no law of a State, therefore, passed since the Constitution was adopted, can give any right of citizenship outside of its own territory.

[Articles of Confederation as further evidence]

A clause similar to the one in the Constitution, in relation to the rights and immunities of citizens of one State in the other States, was contained in the Articles of Confederation. But there is a difference of language, which is worthy of note. The provision in the Articles of Confederation was, "that the *free inhabitants* of each of the States, paupers, vagabonds, and fugitives from justice, excepted, should be entitled to all the privileges and immunities of free citizens in the several States."

It will be observed, that under this Confederation, each State had the right to decide for itself, and in its own tribunals, whom it would acknowledge as a free inhabitant of another State. The term *free inhabitant,* in the generality of its terms, would certainly include one of the African race who had been manumitted. But no example, we think, can be found of his admission to all the privileges of citizenship in any State of the Union after these Articles were formed, and while they continued in force. And, notwithstanding the generality of the words "free inhabitants," it is very clear that, according to their accepted meaning in that day, they did not include the African race, whether free or not: for the fifth section of the ninth article provides that Congress should have the power "to agree upon the number of land forces to be raised, and to make requisitions from each State for its quota in proportion to the number of *white* inhabitants in such State, which requisition should be binding."

Words could hardly have been used which more strongly mark the line of distinction between the citizen and the subject; the free and the subjugated races. The latter were not even counted when the inhabitants of a State were to be embodied in proportion to its numbers for the general defence. And it cannot for a moment be supposed, that a class of persons thus separated and rejected from those who formed the sovereignty of the States, were yet intended to be included under the words "free inhabitants," in the preceding article, to whom privileges and immunities were so carefully secured in every State.

But although this clause of the Articles of Confederation is the same in principle with that inserted in the Constitution, yet the comprehensive word *inhabitant,* which might be construed to include an emancipated slave, is omitted; and the privilege is confined to *citizens* of the State. And this alteration in words would hardly have been made, unless a different meaning was intended to be conveyed, or a possible doubt removed. The just and fair inference is, that as this privilege was about to be placed under the protection of the General Government, and the words expounded by its tribunals, and all power in relation to it taken from the State and its courts, it was deemed prudent to describe with precision and caution the persons to whom this high privilege was given — and the word *citizen* was on that account substituted for the words *free inhabitant.* The word citizen excluded, and no doubt intended to exclude, foreigners who had not become citizens of some one of the States when the Constitution was adopted; and also every description of persons who were not fully recognised as citizens in the several States. This, upon any fair construction of the instruments to which we have referred, was evidently the object and purpose of this change of words.

To all this mass of proof we have still to add, that Congress has repeatedly legislated upon the same construction of the Constitution that we have given. Three laws, two of which were passed almost immediately after the Government went into operation, will be abundantly sufficient to show this. The two first are particularly worthy of notice, because many of the men who assisted in framing the Constitution, and took an active part in procuring its adoption, were then in the halls of legislation, and certainly understood what they meant when they used the words "people of the United States" and "citizen" in that well-considered instrument.

[The naturalization law]

The first of these acts is the naturalization law, which was passed at the second session of the first Congress, March 26, 1790, and confines the right of becoming citizens "*to aliens being free white persons.*"

Now, the Constitution does not limit the power of Congress in this respect to white persons. And they may, if they think proper, authorize the naturalization of any one, of any color, who was born under allegiance to another Government. But the language of the law above quoted, shows that citizenship at that time was perfectly understood to be confined to the white race; and that they alone constituted the sovereignty in the Government.

Congress might, as we before said, have authorized the naturalization of Indians, because they were aliens and foreigners. But, in their then untutored and savage state, no one would have thought of admitting them as citizens in a civilized community. And, moreover, the atrocities they had but recently committed, when they were the allies of Great Britain in the Revolutionary war, were yet fresh in the recollection of the people of the United States, and they were even then guarding themselves against the threatened renewal of Indian hostilities. No one supposed then that any Indian would ask for, or was capable of enjoying, the privileges of an American citizen, and the word white was not used with any particular reference to them.

Neither was it used with any reference to the African race imported into or born in this country; because Congress had no power to naturalize them, and therefore there was no necessity for using particular words to exclude them.

It would seem to have been used merely because it followed out the line of division which the Constitution has drawn between the citizen race, who formed and held the Government, and the African race, which they held in subjection and slavery, and governed at their own pleasure.

[The first militia law]

Another of the early laws of which we have spoken, is the first militia law, which was passed in 1792, at the first session of the second Congress. The language of this law is equally plain and significant with the one just mentioned. It directs that every "free able-bodied white male citizen" shall be enrolled in the militia. The word *white* is evidently used to exclude the African race, and the word "citizen" to exclude unnaturalized foreigners; the latter forming no part of the sovereignty, owing it no allegiance, and therefore under no obligation to defend it. The African race, however, born in the country, did owe allegiance to the Government, whether they were slave or free; but it is repudiated, and rejected from the duties and obligations of citizenship in marked language.

[Employees on U.S. ships]

The third act to which we have alluded is even still more decisive; it was passed as late as 1813, (2 Stat., 809,) and it provides: "That from and after the termination of the war in which the United States are now engaged with Great Britain, it shall not be lawful to employ, on board of any public or private vessels of the United States, any person or persons except citizens of the United States, *or* persons of color, natives of the United States."

Here the line of distinction is drawn in express words. Persons of color, in the judgment of Congress, were not included in the word citizens, and they are described as another and different class of persons, and authorized to be employed, if born in the United States.

[The City of Washington]

And even as late as 1820, (chap. 104, sec. 8,) in the charter to the city of Washington, the corporation is authorized "to restrain and prohibit the nightly and other disorderly meetings of slaves, free negroes, and mulattoes," thus associating them together in its legislation; and after prescribing the punishment that may be inflicted on the slaves, proceeds in the following words: "And to punish such free negroes and mulattoes by penalties not exceeding twenty dollars for any one offence; and in case of the inability of any such free negro or mulatto to pay any such penalty and cost thereon, to cause him or her to be confined to labor for any time not exceeding six calendar months." And in a subsequent part of the same section, the act authorizes the corporation "to prescribe the terms and conditions upon which free negroes and mulattoes may reside in the city."

This law, like the laws of the States, shows that this class of persons were governed by special legislation directed expressly to them, and always connected with provisions for the government of slaves, and not with those for the government of free white citizens. And after such an uniform course of legislation as we have stated, by the colonies, by the States, and by Congress, running through a period of more than a century, it would seem that to call persons thus marked and stigmatized, "citizens" of the United States, "fellow-citizens," a constituent part of the sovereignty, would be an abuse of terms, and not calculated to exalt the character of an American citizen in the eyes of other nations.

[The executive branch]

The conduct of the Executive Department of the Government has been in perfect harmony upon this subject with this course of legislation. The question was brought officially before the late William Wirt, when he was the Attorney General of the United States, in 1821, and he decided that the words "citizens of the United States" were used in the acts of Congress in the same sense as in the Constitution; and that free persons of color were not citizens, within the meaning of the Constitution and laws; and this opinion has been confirmed by that of the late Attorney General, Caleb Cushing, in a recent case, and acted upon by the Secretary of State, who refused to grant passports to them as "citizens of the United States."

[Limited citizenship rejected]

But it is said that a person may be a citizen, and entitled to that character, although he does not possess all the rights which may belong to other citizens; as, for example, the right to vote, or to hold particular offices; and that yet, when he goes into another State, he is entitled to be recognised there as a citizen, although the State may measure his rights by the rights which it allows to persons of a like character or class resident in the State, and refuse to him the full rights of citizenship.

This argument overlooks the language of the provision in the Constitution of which we are speaking.

Undoubtedly, a person may be a citizen, that is, a member of the community who form the sovereignty, although he exercises no share of the political power, and is incapacitated from holding particular offices. Women and minors, who form a part of the political family, cannot vote; and when a property qualification is required to vote or hold a particular office, those who have not the necessary qualification cannot vote or hold the office, yet they are citizens.

So, too, a person may be entitled to vote by the law of the State, who is not a citizen even of the State itself. And in some of the States of the Union foreigners not naturalized are allowed to vote. And the State may give the right to free negroes and mulattoes, but that does not make them citizens of the State, and still less of the United States. And the provision in the Constitution giving privileges and immunities in other States, does not apply to them.

Neither does it apply to a person who, being the citizen of a State, migrates to another State. For then he becomes subject to the laws of the State in which he lives, and he is no longer a citizen of the State from which he removed. And the State in which he resides may then, unquestionably, determine his *status* or condition, and place him among the class of persons who are not recognised as citizens, but belong to an inferior and subject race; and may deny him the privileges and immunities enjoyed by its citizens.

But so far as mere rights of person are concerned, the provision in question is confined to citizens of a State who are temporarily in another State without taking up their residence there. It gives them no political rights in the State, as to voting or holding office, or in any other respect. For a citizen of one State has no right to participate in the government of another. But if he ranks as a citizen in the State to which he belongs, within the meaning of the Constitution of the United States, then, whenever he goes into another State, the Constitution clothes him, as to the rights of person, with all the privileges and immunities which belong to citizens of the State. And if persons of the African race are citizens of a State, and of the United States, they would be entitled to all of these privileges and immunities in every State, and the State could not restrict them; for they would hold these privileges and immunities under the paramount authority of the Federal Government, and its courts would be bound to maintain and enforce them, the Constitution and laws of the State to the contrary notwithstanding. And if the States could limit or restrict them, or place the party in an inferior grade, this clause of the Constitution would be unmeaning, and could have no operation; and would give no rights to the citizen when in another State. He would have none but what the State itself chose to allow him. This is evidently not the construction or meaning of the clause in question. It guaranties rights to the citizen, and the State cannot withhold them. And these rights are of a character and would lead to consequences which make it absolutely certain that the African race were not included under the name of citizens of a State, and were not in the contemplation of the framers of the Constitution when these privileges and immunities were provided for the protection of the citizen in other States.

[Negroes are property]

The only two provisions which point to them and include them, treat them as property, and make it the duty of the Government to protect it: no other power, in relation to this race, is to be found in the Constitution; and as it is a Government of special, delegated, powers, no authority beyond these two provisions can be constitutionally exercised. The Government of the United States had no right to interfere for any other purpose but that of protecting the rights of the owner, leaving it altogether with the several States to deal with this race, whether emancipated or not, as each State may think justice, humanity, and the interests and safety of society, require. The States evidently intended to reserve this power exclusively to themselves.

No one, we presume, supposes that any change in public opinion or feeling, in relation to this unfortunate race, in the civilized nations of Europe or in this country, should induce the court to give to the words of the Constitution a more liberal construction in their favor than they were intended to bear when the instrument was framed and adopted. Such an argument would be altogether inadmissible in any tribunal called on to interpret it. If any of its provisions are deemed unjust, there is a mode prescribed in the instrument itself by which it may be amended; but while it remains unaltered, it must be construed now as it was understood at the time of its adoption. It is not only the same in words, but the same in meaning, and delegates the same powers to the Government, and reserves and secures the same rights and privileges to the citizen; and as long as it continues to exist in its present form, it speaks not only in the same words, but with the same meaning and intent with which it spoke when it came from the hands of its framers, and was voted on and adopted by the people of the United States. Any other rule of construction would abrogate the judicial character of this court, and make it the mere reflex of the popular opinion or passion of the day. This court was not created by the Constitution for such purposes. Higher and graver trusts have been confided to it, and it must not falter in the path of duty.

What the construction was at that time, we think can hardly admit of doubt. We have the language of the Declaration of Independence and of the Articles of Confederation, in addition to the plain words of the Constitution itself; we have the legislation of the different States, before, about the time, and since, the Constitution was adopted; we have the legislation of Congress, from the time of its adoption to a recent period; and we have the constant and uniform action of the Executive Department, all concurring together, and leading to the same result. And if anything in relation to the construction of the Constitution can be regarded as settled, it is that which we now give to the word "citizen" and the word "people."

And upon a full and careful consideration of the subject, the court is of opinion, that, upon the facts stated in the plea in abatement, Dred Scott was not a citizen of Missouri within the meaning of the Constitution of the United States, and not entitled as such to sue in its courts; and, consequently, that the Circuit Court had no jurisdiction of the case, and that the judgment on the plea in abatement is erroneous. . . .

NOTES

1. There were six concurring opinions and two dissents by Justices McLean and Curtis in the 241-page Dred Scott opinion. Justice Curtis differed with the majority on every major point, including Chief Justice Taney's gratuitous finding that not even free colored persons born within the states are citizens of those states and the United States.

2. Far from settling the slavery issue, the Dred Scott decision set off a storm of criticism of and acclaim for the case and the Court. Republican Senator Seward, in a major speech on the Senate floor, called the decision a "pro-slavery conspiracy." He concluded: "Dred Scott, who had played the hand of dummy in this interesting political game, unwittingly, yet to the complete satisfaction of his adversary, was voluntarily emancipated; and thus received from his master, as a reward, the freedom which the court had denied him as a right." Actually, in 1846 Scott had sought to purchase his and his family's freedom and was turned down. He then petitioned a local court for his freedom on the grounds of residence in Illinois and the Minnesota Territory. Scott and his family were manumitted in May 1857. He worked as a hotel porter in St. Louis, but died of tuberculosis a year later. V. Hopkins, Dred Scott's Case 10, 165, 167, 176 (1951).

3. A convention of blacks met in Philadelphia to denounce the Dred Scott decision. Bergman, The Chronological History of the Negro in America 212 (1969). But the very excessiveness of the decision's language likely spurred those opposed to slavery to redouble their efforts to abolish the institution. One writer maintains that Dred Scott was not the "classically worst" assertion of judicial supremacy, but was rather a "sincere" judicial effort to solve a nation-wrecking problem. He concludes: "The Court's fault, if it may be so described, lay in accepting the buck which Congress and the statesmen had passed, and in failing to anticipate the partisan, political use which its efforts could be made to serve." Mendelson, Dred Scott's Case — Reconsidered, 38 Minn. L. Rev. 16, 28 (1953). See also Corwin, The Dred Scott Decision in the Light of Contemporary Legal Doctrine, 17 Am. Hist. Rev. 52 (1911).

4. The understandable desire on the part of the legal profession to finally erase what Chief Justice Charles Evans Hughes called the Court's "self-inflicted wound" has resulted in the Dred Scott case's being the most frequently overturned decision in history. The final demise of Dred Scott has

been attributed to the following: (1) the Civil War — "The law of the case was lost in the maelstrom which engulfed North and South," A. Blaustein and C. Ferguson, Desegregation and the Law 85 (1957); (2) the Thirteenth Amendment, according to The Civil Rights Cases, 109 U.S. 3, 3 S. Ct. 18, 27 L. Ed. 835 (1883); (3) the Fourteenth Amendment, by H. Horowitz and K. Karst, Law, Lawyers and Social Change 102 (1969); (4) all three Civil War Amendments, by former Chief Justice Earl Warren: E. Warren, A Republic If You Can Keep It, 46 (1972); (5) Brown v. Board of Education, 347 U.S. 483, 74 S. Ct. 686, 98 L. Ed. 873 (1954), printed infra page 431, by Judge John Minor Wisdom in United States v. Jefferson County Board of Education, 372 F.2d 836, 873 (5th Cir. 1966), and (6) Jones v. Mayer Co., 392 U.S. 409, 88 S. Ct. 2186, 20 L. Ed. 2d 1189 (1968), printed infra page 626, by Larsen, The New Law of Race Relations, 1969 Wis. L. Rev. 470, 486. Professor Larsen believes that the Jones case, "by infusing new vitality both into the early Reconstruction statutes and into the Thirteenth Amendment, will prove to be the most far-reaching race relations case since the Civil War."

B. THE JUDICIAL APPROACH TO SLAVERY ISSUES

Slavery decisions almost uniformly favored the "peculiar institution" and gave precedence to the interests of slave owners over those of slaves seeking freedom through litigation. The constitutional provision protecting slavery certainly limited the Court's discretion in this field, but the decisions went beyond even constitutional requirements in what were apparently conscious efforts to protect all property rights, including those in humans.

The Dred Scott case is the definitive example of this judicial policy, but long before this famous decision in 1857, federal courts were upholding the prerogatives of a slave society in a whole series of cases. Many of these cases were decided during the period in which John Marshall was chief justice.

In the article excerpted below, Professor Roper paints the picture of a chief justice quite willing to sidestep the slavery issue, while securing the Court's position as constitutional arbiter in the federal system.

ROPER, IN QUEST OF JUDICIAL OBJECTIVITY: THE MARSHALL COURT AND THE LEGITIMATION OF SLAVERY

*21 Stan. L. Rev. 533-537 (1969)**

. . . On the surface . . . there seems to have been the potential for sharp divergence on slavery questions, but, overall, homogeneity triumphed over heterogeneity. In a series of four cases between 1806 and 1813, involving petitions for freedom filed by slaves, the Court consistently decided in favor

* Roper, In Quest of Judicial Objectivity: The Marshall Court and the Legitimation of Slavery, 21 Stan. L. Rev. 532 (1969). Copyright 1969 by the Board of Trustees of the Leland Stanford Junior University.

of the slave owner.[6] Not only were these cases well argued by counsel for the slaves, but one of them was decided in the face of a counter assertion about a rule of local law by the Justice most familiar with it, Gabriel Duvall of Maryland. In his first and last dissenting opinion in 25 years on the bench, Duvall in Queen v. Hepburn asserted that hearsay evidence had been accepted in Maryland "for many years" on petitions for freedom "if the fact is of such antiquity that living testimony cannot be procured. . . . To exclude hearsay in such cases would leave the party interested without remedy."[7] Marshall himself noted that hearsay evidence was admissible in "cases of pedigree, of prescription, of custom, and in some cases, of boundary."[8] Duvall argued: "It appears to me, that the reason for admitting hearsay evidence upon a question of freedom is much stronger than in cases of pedigree, or in controversies relative to the boundaries of land. It will be universally admitted that the right to freedom, is more important than the right of property."[9] Duvall's anguished admonition to give liberty priority over property rights, together with the other Justices' apparent disregard of his knowledge of Maryland law, reveals the strength of the Court's commitment to the preservation of property rights.

Concern for property rights was not, however, the only factor in shaping the slavery opinions. A paramount consideration for the Marshall Court, particularly for the Chief Justice, was to secure the Supreme Court's position as constitutional arbiter in the federal system. Since the Court's authority could easily be curtailed by congressional reduction of its appellate jurisdiction, it was essential to avoid unduly provoking Congress. Accordingly, the need to secure the Court's position counseled a policy of unanimity, to give the impression that there was no valid alternative to its position.[10]

Marshall's cautious approach to slavery questions is well-known. The year after antagonizing the establishment in Charleston by insisting on due process for slaves in the Denmark Vesey incident, William Johnson held that a South Carolina law regulating and restricting the movement of free Negro seamen conflicted with the commerce clause of the United States Constitution.[11] The protest following that decision caused Marshall to write Story of Johnson's plight, and of his own escape via a Falstaffian tactic from a similar situation. Virginia had a "twin brother," said Marshall, to the South Carolina law, and "a case has been brought before me in which I might have considered its constitutionality, had I chosen to do so; but it was not absolutely necessary,

6. Queen v. Hepburn, 11 U.S. (7 Cranch) 290 (1813); Wood v. Davis, 11 U.S. (7 Cranch) 271 (1812); Scott v. Negro Ben, 10 U.S. (6 Cranch) 3 (1810); Scott v. Negro London, 7 U.S. (3 Cranch) 324 (1806).

7. 11 U.S. (7 Cranch) at 298.

8. Id. at 296.

9. Id. at 298-99.

10. Roper, Judicial Unanimity and the Marshall Court — A Road to Reappraisal, 9 Am. J. Legal Hist. 118 (1965).

11. Elkison v. Deliesseline, 8 F. Cas. 493 (No. 4366) (C.C.S.C. 1823) [Printed infra, page 27].

and as I am not fond of butting a wall in sport, I escaped on the construction of the act."[12]

The hysteria that accompanied the slavery issue led members of Congress to overestimate grossly the Court's capacity to affect the institution of slavery, not to mention its desire to do so.[13] At any rate, the Court's fear of arousing the wrath of Congress was a further deterrent, as though one were necessary, to challenging slavery.

The Justices' individual feelings about slavery partly countered their concern for property rights and desire to avoid controversy. Over the years a majority of the Court was opposed to slavery, though the term antislavery has a tepid connotation when used of Marshall and his associates. Their opposition to slavery ranged from John McLean, who later sought to use the antislavery movement to foster his perpetual pursuit of the presidency, and Story on one end of the spectrum, to Marshall and Washington, who both wished that slavery would somehow go away, on the other end. Marshall's and Washington's sentiments were reflected in their involvement in the American Colonization Society.[14] But mild as this sentiment seems, the abhorrence of slavery expressed from the bench and in private indicates that consciences were touched.

Judicial objectivity was the approach evolved by the Marshall Court in slavery cases to resolve this conflict between the Justices' individual opposition to slavery and their concern for property rights and the institutional position of the Court. This can perhaps best be seen in the cases involving the slave trade. The Justices were more likely to express their feelings against the trade than their feelings against slavery itself, perhaps because the former were stronger and because there was less chance of upsetting a property right or antagonizing a slave holder. Before his appointment to the Court, Smith Thompson had been willing, as Secretary of the Navy, to establish a mutual right of search and seizure between Britain and the United States, since he believed that all previous measures had proved insufficient[15] to curb "this inhuman and disgraceful traffic."[16] In general the Court collectively and

12. Marshall was probably referring to his ruling in The Wilson v. United States, 30 F. Cas. 239 (No. 17,846) (C.C. Va. 1820). See I C. Warren, The Supreme Court in United States History 623-24 (rev. ed. 1947); letter from Marshall to Story, Sept. 26, 1823, excerpt in id. at 626.

13. I C. Warren, supra note 12, at 542-44, 621-28.

14. P. Staudenraus, The African Colonization Movement, 1816-1865, at 36, 70, 107 (1961). Justice Johnson differed with his colleagues on the Colonization Society. D. Morgan, supra note 5, at 135 n. 38 [1954].

In all fairness to Washington it has been observed that on circuit in Pennsylvania he generally read the Fugitive Slave Act of 1793 in such a way as to curtail its scope and effectiveness. W. Leslie, The Fugitive Slave Clause, 1787-1842: A Study in American Constitutional History and in the Conflict of Laws 309 (1946) (unpublished doctoral dissertation in University of Michigan Library).

15. 5 Memoirs of John Quincy Adams 217 (C. Adams ed. 1875).

16. Letter from Thompson to Commodore Oliver H. Perry, May 29, 1819, Secretary of the Navy, Private Letters, National Archives.

individually used the antislave-trade acts to reduce the slave traffic as much as possible.[17] It is not surprising, then, to find that a case involving the slave trade, The Antelope,[18] marked the outer limits of the Court's assault on slavery; at the same time, this case shows how moral indignation can influence the formulation of an opinion.

The facts of The Antelope are complicated. It is sufficient to say that a revenue cutter, off the coast of Florida, apprehended a vessel bearing approximately 280 Africans who, with few exceptions, had been seized from Portuguese and Spanish slave ships and were subsequently claimed by the vice-consuls of those nations.

The arguments of Francis Scott Key and Attorney General William Wirt made even Marshall realize that the case presented a conflict between "the sacred rights of liberty and of property."[19] This makes it tempting to read Marshall's opinion as choosing to favor the sacred right of property. Supporting that conclusion is Marshall's apparent disregard of an opinion delivered by Story on circuit. In United States v. La Jeune Eugénie[20] Story had decried the slave trade as

> repugnant to the great principles of Christian duty, the dictates of natural religion, the obligations of good faith and morality, and the eternal maxims of social justice. When any trade can be truly said to have these ingredients, it is impossible that it can be consistent with any system of law that purports to rest on the authority of reason or revelation. And it is sufficient to stamp any trade as interdicted by public law, when it can be justly affirmed, that it is repugnant to the general principles of justice and humanity.[21]

Counsel only hinted that the Court should follow Story's lead, and Marshall rejected the veiled invitation: "[I]t is not wonderful that public feeling should march somewhat in advance of strict law . . . . Indeed," he continued, in what seems to have been an admonishment to his close friend Story, "we ought not to be surprised, if, on this novel series of cases even courts of

17. See, e.g. The Josefa Segunda, 18 U.S. (5 Wheat.) 338 (1820). The admonition of the Court in that case that "in the execution of these laws, no vigilance can be excessive," id. at 357, went pretty much unheeded. See W. E. B. DuBois, The Suppression of the African Slave Trade to the United States of America, 1638-1870, at 129 (1896).

In its intolerance of the slave trade, the Marshall Court differed from its successor and was in accord with its own generation. For example, Samuel Nelson, who replaced Thompson on the Second Circuit (Vermont, Connecticut, and New York), failed to check the pro-slave trade rulings of Judge Samuel R. Betts of the southern district of New York as Thompson had done. W. Howard, American Slavers and the Federal Law, 1837-1862, at 161-69 (1963).

18. 23 U.S. (10 Wheat.) 66 (1825).

19. Id. at 114.

20. 26 F. Cas. 832 (No. 15,551) (C.C. Mass. 1822).

21. Id. at 846.

justice should, in some instances, have carried the principle of suppression farther than a more deliberate consideration of the subject would justify."[22]

But The Antelope came closer to adopting Story's La Jeune Eugénie position than to rejecting it. The circuit court for Georgia, on which William Johnson sat, was overruled on two of three points and was sustained on the third only because the Court was evenly divided. The opinion of the Court takes a position somewhere between that of Story in La Jeune Eugénie and Johnson's circuit court opinion. While Story had said that the slave trade was contrary to international law, Johnson wrote: "[H]owever revolting to humanity may be the reflection, the laws of any country on the subject of the slave trade are nothing more in the eyes of any other nation than a class of the trade laws of the nation that enacts them."[23] Splitting the difference was a vintage performance for Marshall. Had he been content simply to hold that international law did not prohibit the slave trade, it would have been sufficient to have followed the precedent of Sir William Scott.[24] But on reaching that point, Marshall characteristically, and gratuitously, went on. The slave trade was contrary to the law of nature: It is generally admitted "that every man has a natural right to the fruits of his own labor," and therefore "no other person can rightfully deprive him of those fruits, and appropriate them against his will."[25] The Court had divided on the question of whether or not there should be any restitution of the claims. But Marshall's opinion placated Story, probably Thompson, and possibly Duvall, sufficiently to prevent dissent. Yet without pressure from the moralist faction it is unlikely that Marshall would have drafted an opinion that by clear implication adopts the position that slavery can be maintained only by municipal law, because it is contrary to natural law.[26]

But the careful adherence to objectivity that characterized Johnson's circuit opinion pervades Marshall's in The Antelope: "[T]his court must not yield to feelings which might seduce it from the path of duty, and must obey the mandate of the law." And a few pages later Marshall asserts that when faced with the problem of determining whether the slave trade is contrary to international law, a jurist, unlike "a moralist," has to "search for its legal solution, in those principles of action which are sanctioned by the usages, the national acts, and the general assent, of that portion of the world of which he considers himself as a part, and to whose law the appeal is made."[27]

It is possible to discover a commitment to objectivity in Marshall's earlier slavery opinion. Queen v. Hepburn[28] involved a question of the impartiality

22. 23 U.S. (10 Wheat.) at 75-76, 116.

23. Quoted in D. Morgan, supra note 5, at 137.

24. The Louis, 2 Dodson 238 (1817), cited in 23 U.S. (10 Wheat.) at 342.

25. 23 U.S. (10 Wheat.) at 120.

26. This might be called the pseudo-Somersett doctrine. For a discussion of how Americans misinterpreted Lord Mansfield's Somersett ruling see Jerome Nadelhaft, The Somersett Case and Slavery: Myth, Reality, and Repercussions, 51 J. Negro Hist. 193 (1966).

27. 23 U.S. (10 Wheat.) at 114, 121.

28. 11 U.S. (7 Cranch) 290 (1813).

of a juror, as well as the dispute about the admissibility of hearsay evidence discussed above.[29] Marshall affirmed, as within the trial judge's discretion, a ruling barring a talesman from jury duty because he "avowed his detestation of slavery to be such, that in a doubtful case, he would find a verdict for the plaintiffs." In doing so, the Chief Justice alluded to the necessity of having jurors who "stand perfectly indifferent between the parties," although he did recognize that "[p]erhaps, on general and public questions, it is scarcely possible to avoid receiving some prepossessions . . . ."[30] On circuit in 1819, Marshall had commented: "The peculiar odium attached to the traffic, in which this vessel is alleged to have engaged, ought not to affect the legal questions which belong to the case."[31] So it was that the Chief Justice prepared himself for The Antelope. . . .*

ELKISON v. DELIESSELINE
8 F. Cas. 493 (No. 4366) (C.C.S.C. 1823)

[A South Carolina statute (typical of measures enacted by Southern states to discourage nonslave blacks from entering their territories and becoming — by their presence and status — disruptive forces) provided that "If any vessel (including those of the United States) shall come into any port or harbor of this state," bringing in any free colored persons, such persons are to become "absolute slaves" and, without even a trial, are to be sold. The statute vested the sheriff with absolute power to carry the law into effect, encouraging this performance by providing that he was to receive one half of the proceeds of the sale. The validity of this statute was challenged in an 1823 habeas corpus proceeding in Charleston before Supreme Court Justice William Johnson, who heard the case while "riding circuit."]

JOHNSON, Circuit Justice . . . .

. . . On the unconstitutionality of the law under which this man is confined, it is not too much to say, that it will not bear argument; and I feel myself sanctioned in using this strong language, from considering the course of reasoning by which it has been defended. Neither of the gentlemen has attempted to prove that the power therein assumed by the state can be exercised without clashing with the general powers of the United States to regulate commerce; but they have both strenuously contended, that ex necessitate it

29. See text accompanying notes 6-9 supra.

30. 11 U.S. (7 Cranch) at 297.

31. The Caroline, 5 F. Cas. 90, 91 (No. 2418) (C.C. Va. 1819).

* Roper does not make clear that Chief Justice Marshall, after completing his platitudes about the immorality of slavery, found that America did recognize the practice. He concluded:

"It follows, that a foreign vessel engaged in the African slave trade, captured on the high seas in time of peace, by an American cruiser, and brought in for adjudication, would be restored." 23 U.S. at 123.

Marshall then spent the balance of the opinion deciding how the slaves (one third of whom had died during the voyage) should be divided up among the competing claimants.

was a power which the state must and would exercise, and, indeed, Mr. Holmes concluded his argument with the declaration, that, if a dissolution of the Union must be the alternative, he was ready to meet it. Nor did the argument of Col. Hunt deviate at all from the same course. Giving it in the language of his own summary, it was this: South Carolina was a sovereign state when she adopted the constitution; a sovereign state cannot surrender a right of vital importance; South Carolina, therefore, either did not surrender this right, or still possesses the power to resume it, and whether it is necessary, or when it is necessary, to resume it, she is herself the sovereign judge. But it was not necessary to give this candid exposé of the grounds which this law assumes; for it is a subject of positive proof, that it is altogether irreconcilable with the powers of the general government; that it necessarily compromits the public peace, and tends to embroil us with, if not separate us from, our sister states; in short, that it leads to a dissolution of the Union, and implies a direct attack upon the sovereignty of the United States. . . .

The object of this law, and it has been so acknowledged in argument, is to prohibit ships coming into this port employing colored seamen, whether citizens or subjects of their own government or not. But if this state can prohibit Great Britain from employing her colored subjects (and she has them of all colors on the globe), or if at liberty to prohibit the employment of her subjects of the African race, why not prohibit her from using those of Irish or of Scottish nativity? If the color of his skin is to preclude the Lascar or the Sierra Leone seaman, why not the color of his eye or his hair exclude from our ports the inhabitants of her other territories? In fact it amounts to the assertion of the power to exclude the seamen of the territories of Great Britain, or any other nation, altogether. With regard to various friendly nations it amounts to an actual exclusion in its present form. Why may not the shipping of Morocco or of Algiers cover the commerce of France with this country, even at the present crisis? Their seamen are all colored, and even the state of Massachusetts might lately, and may perhaps now, expedite to this port a vessel with her officers black, and her crew composed of Nantucket Indians, known to be among the best seamen in our service. These might all become slaves under this act. If this law were enforced upon such vessels, retaliation would follow; and the commerce of this city, feeble and sickly, comparatively, as it already is, might be fatally injured. Charleston seamen, Charleston owners, Charleston vessels, might, eo nomine, be excluded from their commerce, or the United States involved in war and confusion. I am far from thinking that this power would ever be wantonly exercised, but these considerations show its utter incompatibility with the power delegated to congress to regulate commerce with foreign nations and our sister states.

Apply the law to the particular case before us, and the incongruity will be glaring. The offense, it will be observed, for which this individual is supposed to forfeit his freedom, is that of coming into this port in the ship Homer, in the capacity of a seaman. I say this is the whole of his offense; for I will not admit the supposition that he is to be burdened with the offense of the captain in not carrying him out of the state. He is himself shut up, he cannot go off; his removal depends upon another. It is true the sale of him is suspended upon the conviction of the captain, and the captain has the power to rescue him from slavery. But suppose the captain, as is very frequently the case, may find it his interest or his pleasure to get rid of him, and of the wages due him, his fate is suspended on the captain's caprice in this particular; but it is the exercise of the dispensing power in the captain, and nothing more. The seaman's crime is complete, and the forfeiture incurred by the single act of coming into port; and this even though driven into port by stress of weather, or forced by a power which he cannot control into a port for which he did not ship himself; the law contains no exception to meet such contingencies. The seaman's offense, therefore, is coming into the state in a ship or vessel; that of the captain consists in bringing him in, and not taking him out of the state, and paying all expenses. Now, according to the laws and treaties of the United States, it was both lawful for this seaman to come into this port, in this vessel, and for the captain to bring him in the capacity of a seaman; and yet these are the very acts for which the state law imposes these heavy penalties. Is there no clashing in this? It is in effect a repeal of the laws of the United States, pro tanto, converting a right into a crime.

But if the policy of this law was to keep foreign free persons of color from holding communion with our slaves, it certainly pursues a course altogether inconsistent with its object. One gentleman likened the importation of such persons to that of clothes infected with the plague, or of wild beasts from Africa; the other to that of fire-brands set to our own houses only to escape by the light. But surely if the penalty inflicted for coming here is in its effect that of being domesticated, by being sold here, then we ourselves inoculate our community with the plague; we ourselves turn loose the wild beast in our streets, and we put the fire-brand under our own houses. If there are evil persons abroad who would steal to this place in order to do us this mischief (and the whole provisions of this act are founded in that supposition), then this method of disposing of offenders by detaining them here presents the finest facilities in the world for introducing themselves lawfully into the very situation in which they would enjoy the best opportunities of pursuing their designs. Now, if this plea of necessity could avail at all against the constitution and laws of the United States, certainly that law cannot be pronounced necessary which may defeat its own ends; much less when other provisions of unexceptionable legality might be resorted to, which would operate solely to the end proposed, viz., the effectual exclusion of dangerous characters. . . .

Upon the whole, I am decidedly of the opinion that the third section of the state act now under consideration is unconstitutional and void, and that every arrest made under it subjects the parties making it to an action of trespass. . . .

THE AMISTAD CASE, 40 U.S. (15 Pet.) 518 (1841). In 1839, a group of blacks who had been carried from Africa to Cuba rebelled against the Spaniards who were carrying them, on board the Spanish schooner *L'Amistad,* from one point in Cuba to another. They sought to return to Africa, but landed eventually off Montauk Point, Long Island, New York, where they were apprehended by a United States warship and taken ashore to Connecticut. In the rebellion the blacks had killed one of the Spaniards. The two surviving Spaniards filed suits in admiralty claiming that the blacks were slaves and their property. They prayed for the return of the blacks either to themselves or to the Spanish Crown. The United States entered the case supporting the latter position, advising the Court that the Spanish minister had prayed for the return of the blacks to the Spaniards. The United States added that if the Court concluded that the blacks had been brought to this country from Africa in violation of United States law, then the Court should order their removal to the coast of Africa. The blacks denied that they were slaves, contending that they were free, native-born Africans and had been "unlawfully kidnapped," transported to Cuba and there sold to the Spaniards who now claimed them.

The Supreme Court, per Justice Story, held that neither were the blacks captured nor did they come to the United States properly under the laws of either the United States or of Spain, and that they, therefore, should not be returned. The United States, in urging the return of the blacks, relied on the ninth article of a treaty of 1819 with Spain, which provided that all "ships and merchandize, rescued out of the hands of any pirates or robbers," should be restored to the proprietors in the signatory state. To bring the case within the article, Justice Story said that three issues had to be resolved: first, whether the blacks were "within the description of merchandize"; second, whether there had been a rescue of them on the high seas; and third, whether the Spaniards on board, Ruiz and Montenez, were the true proprietors. The Court found that clearly under the law of Spain the blacks were not to be considered "merchandize" because they had been kidnapped in Africa and illegally transported to the island of Cuba: "If, then, these negroes are not slaves, but are kidnapped Africans, who, by the laws of Spain itself, are entitled to their freedom, and were kidnapped and illegally carried to Cuba, and illegally detained and restrained on board the Amistad; there is no pretence to say, that they are pirates or robbers. We may lament the dreadful acts, by which they asserted their liberty, and took possession of the Amistad, and endeavored to regain their native country; but they cannot be deemed pirates or robbers in the sense of the law of nations, or the treaty with Spain, or the laws of Spain itself; at least so far as those laws have been brought to our knowledge. . . ." 40 U.S. at 593-594. Justice Story said that the fact that the blacks were the property of the Spaniards did not alter the result. It was an established principle of the law of nations that documents such as those libelants possessed were but prima facie evidence of the fact they purported to state; they might always be impugnated for fraud, and nothing in the treaty of 1795 with Spain affected the Court's right to inquire into the veracity of the documents. Finally, "It is also a most important consideration in the present case, which ought not to be lost sight of, that, supposing these African negroes not to be slaves, but kidnapped, and free negroes, the treaty with Spain cannot be obligatory upon them; and the United States are bound to respect their rights as much as those of Spanish subjects." 40 U.S. at 595.

NOTES

1. Is it fair to conclude from the Elkison case that federal interest in an unencumbered commerce between the states and foreign countries was the pivotal concern leading to a decision in which black seamen were gratuitous beneficiaries?

2. In the famous Amistad case, the Supreme Court resisted strong political pressures and rendered a decision that recognized black slaves (whom the Court deemed to be "kidnapped Africans") as human beings with rights to life and liberty far superior to any such rights granted domestic blacks (slave or free) by the Constitution and federal law.

3. American fugitive slaves fared less well. The very next year, the Court, with Justice Story again writing for the Court, invalidated a state statute deemed an interference with the federal Fugitive Slave Act of 1793. Prigg v. Pennsylvania, 41 U.S. (16 Pet.) 539 (1842). Story found that the fugitive slave provision of the Constitution, Art. 4, §2, Clause 3, printed infra page 47, was "a fundamental article, without the adoption of which the Union could not have been formed" (41 U.S. at 611), and that any state legislation on the subject impeded the federal power.

4. This was not the last time that the Court of the federal government exhibited more concern for the rights of foreign blacks than for those who sought equality at home. Before desegregation, blacks often joked that to obtain service at any place of public accommodation, they need only don a turban and long robe. Does this phenomenon suggest strategies that might profitably be employed by contemporary black leadership?

SOMERSET v. STEWART, 98 Eng. Rep. 499 (K.B. 1772). The rule that permits emancipation of a slave brought by his master into nonslave territory can be traced to this case. Somerset, a slave, was brought to England from Virginia by his master, Stewart. When Stewart sought to force Somerset to Jamaica, a habeas corpus action was brought on Somerset's behalf. Stewart argued that, while slavery as such did not exist in England, the status of slavery was still recognized by English law. Lord Mansfield urged the parties to settle the matter by private agreement and continued the case on numerous occasions, to permit this. Finally, Mansfield ruled that slavery or "villeinage in gross" would not be recognized in England even if a man confessed himself a villein in open court. As to recognition of slavery existing in other jurisdictions, Mansfield concluded:

> So high an act of dominion must be recognized by the law of the country where

it is used. The power of a master over his slave has been extremely different in different countries. The state of slavery is of such a nature, that it is incapable of being introduced on any reasons, moral or political; but only positive law, which preserves its force long after the reasons, occasion, and time itself from whence it was created, is erased from memory: it's so odious, that nothing can be suffered to support it, but positive law. Whatever inconveniences, therefore, may follow from a decision, I cannot say this case is allowed or approved by the law of England; and therefore the black must be discharged. (98 Eng. Rep. at 510.)

NOTES

1. One writer argues that the Somerset decision was poorly reported and generally misconstrued to hold that Lord Mansfield had freed all 14,000 black slaves then in England, a result sought by Somerset's attorneys, but that the decision was limited to a finding that Stewart could not remove Somerset from England against his will in the absence of positive law. The broader interpretation of the decision was generally accepted in America, where its effect was to stimulate passage of fugitive slave legislation. The influence of the Somerset decision is reflected in the euphemistic clauses in the Northwest Ordinance, passed by Congress in July 1787, to the effect that, while slavery was to be barred from the territories, "any person escaping into the same, from whom labor or service is lawfully claimed in any one of the original states, such fugitive may be lawfully reclaimed and conveyed to the person claiming his or her labor or service. . . ." Article 6, and Art. 4, §2, Clause 3 of the Federal Constitution, the fugitive slave provision. Nadelhaft, The Somersett Case and Slavery: Myth, Reality, and Repercussions, 51 J. Negro Hist. 193 (1966).

2. After the decision in Somerset v. Stewart, the next and final steps in the abolition of slavery in England and the English colonies were taken by the legislature. Abolitionist activity intensified, and in 1807 Parliament outlawed the African slave trade. This enactment did not deal with the validity of slavery in the colonies; that was left for an act of Parliament in 1833.

3. While Lord Mansfield in 1772 was at least limiting the power of slave owners in England, Virginia (whose population of 200,000 slaves roughly equaled the white population) by the same year had passed thirty-three acts to prohibit the importation of slaves, all of which were uniformly rejected by England. Benjamin Franklin probably typified the reaction of many Americans to the Somerset decision when he wrote to a friend: "I have made a little extract . . . of the number of slaves imported and perishing with some close remarks on the hypocrisy of this country [England] which encourages such a detestable commerce by laws for promoting the Guinea trade, while it piqued itself on its virtue, love and liberty, and the equity of its courts, in setting free a single Negro." P. Bergman, The Chronological History of the Negro in America 46 (1969).

4. Just as conflicts based on the differing importance of slavery developed later between "slave" and "free" states in America, so the Somerset decision

created great consternation in English colonies whose economies depended on legal protection for slavery. One case growing out of this conflict was The Slave, Grace.

THE SLAVE, GRACE, 166 Eng. Rep. 179 (High Court of Admiralty, 1827). Mrs. Allan traveled to England in 1823, bringing with her a female attendant, Grace, by birth and servitude a slave; she returned to Antigua with Grace, who continued in service until August 8, 1825, when she was libeled in a Court of Admiralty and seized by a customs official as forfeited to the Crown for having been illegally imported as a slave in 1823. On appeal from a judgment for Mrs. Allan, Lord Stowell said that the foundation of the suit was Grace's right to be treated as a free person; the claim that she had such a right depended upon the argument that she became a free person merely by traveling to and residing in England. But the Court held that the suit failed in this foundation:

> I have looked with the utmost attention to discover, if possible, the foundation of her complaint — that she being a free person is treated as a slave. The truth of that complaint depends upon the nature of that freedom, if any, which she enjoyed before the institution of this suit; and I can find nothing that warrants any such assertion of a freedom so conferred. . . . If she depends upon such a freedom, conveyed by a mere residence in England, she complains of a violation of right which she possessed no longer than whilst she resided in England, but which had totally expired when that residence ceased and she was imported to Antigua. . . . (166 Eng. Rep. at 181.)

As to the opinion in Somerset v. Stewart, Lord Stowell questioned the view held by Lord Mansfield that slavery could be supported only by positive law:

> Far from me be the presumption of questioning any obiter dictum that fell from that great man upon that occasion; but I trust that I do not depart from the modesty that belongs to my situation, and I hope to my character, when I observe, that ancient custom is generally recognized as a just foundation of all law; that villenage of both kinds, which is said by some to be the prototype of slavery, had no other origin than ancient custom; that a great part of the common law itself in all its relations has little other foundation than the same custom. . . .

Lord Stowell expressed the view that the effect of the Somerset decision was limited to England. The Court exhibited considerable concern for the "public inconvenience" a judgment in favor of Grace could have: slaves could connive to have their masters take them to England for the purpose of procuring their freedom after they returned, which eventually might "establish a numerous population of free persons, not only extremely burdensome to the colony, but, from their sudden transition from slavery to freedom, highly dangerous to its peace and security." Lord Stowell warned that England should not abolish slavery, an evil for which the mother country was largely responsible, and leave it to the colonies to absorb the burdens of emancipation. English law, further, had protected the rights of the slave owners in the colonies, even after slavery had been abolished in England itself, so the opinion was not running counter to the antislavery trends in English law. Further change in the positions of slaves and slave owners in the colonies, he concluded, would have to come from Parliament.

Parliament in 1833 finally abolished slavery in the British colonies through "An Act for the Abolition of Slavery throughout the British colonies; for promoting the Industry of the manumitted Slaves; and for compensating the Persons hitherto entitled to the Services of such Slaves." 3 & 4 Will. 4, c. 73 (1833). The 1833 Act established a complex administrative procedure to ensure that emancipation would be gradual rather than abrupt. The measure reflected great concern that the slaves would not be prepared for sudden freedom, and even more concern with avoiding financial loss to their owners. Thus, guidelines for emancipation were established through which commissioners appointed by the King would regulate the payment of compensation to the former slave owners. As to the slaves, their status was changed to "apprenticed laborers," a status which was to continue until 1840. There seems to have been no provision establishing pay scales for the newly freed slaves during their apprenticeship, or otherwise ensuring that they would be more prepared for emancipation in 1840 than they would have been seven years before.

NOTE: THE NORTH ABOLISHES SLAVERY

In the Northern states, slavery was abolished by constitutional provision in Vermont (1777), Ohio (1802), Illinois (1818) and Indiana (1816); by a judicial decision in Massachusetts (1783); by constitutional interpretation in New Hampshire (1857); and by gradual abolition acts in Pennsylvania (1780), Rhode Island (1784), Connecticut (1784 and 1797), New York (1799 and 1817) and New Jersey (1804). L. Litwack, North of Slavery 3-20 (1961).

In varying degrees, abolition in the North was the result of several factors: idealism stemming from the Revolution, with its "rights of man" ideology; the lesser dependence of the Northern economy on a large labor force; its relatively small investment in slaves combined with the great hostility of the white laboring class to the competition of slaves; the fear of slave revolts, and a general belief that "inferior" blacks had no place in the new societies.

Even so, abolition was not accomplished without a major effort in most states, and idealism usually was the makeweight for a decision already based on more pragmatic grounds. As de Tocqueville observed, "In the United States people abolish slavery for the sake not of the Negroes but of the white men." A. de Tocqueville, Democracy in America 344 (Anchor Books ed. 1969). Vermont had only a few slaves, and its constitution explicitly outlawed slavery in 1777. Although New Hampshire also had but few slaves, a petition for freedom to the legislature in 1779 was considered "not ripe." Judicial interpretations of the state's 1783 constitution asserted the end of slavery, but confusion on the subject was not finally resolved until 1857, when a statute banned slavery.

In Massachusetts, efforts to specifically ban slavery in the constitution of 1780 failed, but the state's high court interpreted it to include such a provision in the famous Quock Walker case of 1783. According to Chief Justice William Cushing: "Although slavery had been tolerated in Massachusetts, it was incompatible with the new spirit 'favorable to the natural rights of mankind.'"

Where slavery was more firmly entrenched, as in Pennsylvania, Rhode Island, Connecticut, New York and New Jersey, the efforts of abolitionists met with more opposition. Each of these states adopted gradual abolition statutes designed to lessen the burden that abolition would place on the slave owner. In Pennsylvania, an act of March 1, 1780, c. 146, provided that no person born in the state after the date of enactment should be deemed a slave, but that such children would be considered as "indentured servants" of their parents' master until age twenty-eight. The statutes of the other states were quite similar. A. Zilversmit, The First Emancipation: The Abolition of Slavery in the North 4, 124-132 (1967).

Commenting on this nineteenth-century precedent for the "all deliberate speed" principle, one writer observed: "Freedom was thus conferred upon a future generation and the living were given merely the consolation of a free posterity." W. Jordan, White Over Black 345 (1968).

But freedom even for those blacks who were emancipated under these statutes left much to be desired.

The freedmen in New England, as in other English colonies, occupied an intermediate and inferior status, somewhat between that of a free white person and an indentured servant. This was in marked contrast to the free Negroes of colonial Brazil who, once liberated, are said to have been accorded social, and political rights enjoyed by other free persons. The status of the New England freedmen was much less favorable. Legally, their condition did not differ much from that of the slaves and they were usually included in the slave codes with Indian and Negro slaves. They could not vote, although they were taxed, could not serve on juries and were excluded from the militia in peace time. In lieu of military service they were compelled in Massachusetts (1707) to perform menial service on the parade ground or to labor on the roads. Legal punishments for free Negroes, however, were virtually the same as those for free white persons.

Economically the status of the free Negroes was inferior to that of the slaves. Whereas in slavery every type of employment was open to them, in freedom, faced with the combined competition of slaves, indentured servants and free white workmen, the freedmen were confined by circumstances largely to domestic service. Prejudice also contributed to their economic difficulties. A few Negroes found work on the farms, on trading and whaling vessels or in menial employments but only in the face of mounting hostility on the part of white workmen, who after the Revolution often manifested their antagonism by insulting and beating Negroes and in riots against them. Frequently forced into idleness because of their inability to find work, the freedmen were often stigmatized as a lazy and dissolute class. Socially, the freedmen were also faced with discrimination. In the towns they were confined largely to the alleys, near the docks or along the river fronts; they were not generally permitted to send their children to the public schools and on certain occasions were forbidden to appear in public places. Like the slaves, they were segregated in the churches and were buried in a separate corner of the graveyard. (L. Greene, The Negro in Colonial New England, 1620-1776, 332-333 (1942).)

Obviously, Northern states did not intend abolition of slavery to be equated with acceptance of blacks. "Until the post–Civil War era, in fact, most northern whites would maintain a careful distinction between granting Negroes legal protection — a theoretical right to life, liberty, and property — and political and social equality." L. Litwack, North of Slavery 15 (1961).

Northern states that abolished slavery generally also banned the importation of slaves for any purpose. Many applied the rule of Somerset v. Stewart to grant relief to those who petitioned for their freedom after having been brought into the states by their masters for more than short periods. Tracing the litigation in this area provides a worthwhile means of observing the extent to which the fate of blacks depended on the balance among competing white economic, political and social interests, all of which are reflected quite clearly in judicial decisions. As the following analysis reveals, Justice Story's Commentaries on the Conflict of Laws (1834), which was intended to bring order and rationality to the area, served mainly to justify decisions which thereafter were more openly based on parochial concerns.

NOTE, AMERICAN SLAVERY AND THE CONFLICT OF LAWS
71 Colum. L. Rev. 74, 87-98 (1971)

. . . Despite the strong philosophical and economic interests at stake, the judicial decisions rendered in slavery cases during the first four decades of the Constitution's history reveal a striking degree of consensus among the courts of both free and slave states. There was general agreement during this period that a non-fugitive slave could spend a limited period of time in a free state without the master's losing his property rights in the slave. There was not any general agreement, however, as to the limit to be placed on such a time period, and decisions in regard to this were not always consistent even within a single jurisdiction.[97] Nevertheless, the willingness of free states to recognize the bondage of slaves sojourning within their borders for limited periods of time, and the willingness of slave states to recognize the freedom acquired by former slaves who had remained beyond some time limit in a

97. See, e.g., the changing standard set by the Supreme Court of Missouri, discussed in the text accompanying notes 127-31 infra.

free state, was indicative of the accommodation which the states had reached and which was to last into the 1830's. There are a number of factors that seem to have promoted this early pattern of accommodation.

First, the accommodation seems to have arisen in part from the very ambivalence of the prevailing attitudes toward slavery. Before 1830, those who attacked slavery did so largely on the ground that it was a social blight, or an imperfection in a perfectible society, rather than on the ground that it was a positive evil. This position was not subjected to any vigorous counterattack by slaveholders, who generally were not prone to defend slavery on ideological grounds; their primary concern was merely to maintain their own legal right to own and control slaves. Furthermore, the failure of many nonslaveholders to accord to slaves (or free Negroes) the rights or privileges enjoyed by whites, along with a prevailing respect for property rights generally, prevented any effective opposition to slavery from being generated in the courts.[99] The concepts of "natural law" and the "law of nations" were weak weapons with which to attack the institution; as we have seen, even having granted that slavery was contrary to natural law (which many, even in the South, were willing to do), English law had already recognized the power of local law to sanction slavery.

. . .

A fourth factor promoting accommodation between slave and non-slave states was their shared legacy in certain vestiges of the Roman-European traditions of international law. The most important of these were the concepts of the "right" of transit and the recognition of status. The right of an individual to travel abroad without being molested, at least within states having amicable relationships with the state of the traveler's domicile, was widely recognized. Thus, a number of free states within the United States, particularly those that bordered on slave states and had frequent commerce with them, allowed a slaveowner to bring his slave into or through the state without the slave's status being affected, as long as the slaveowner did not intend to reside there or did not stay too long.[113] Similarly, slave states did not consider a slave to be free merely because he had accompanied his master on a brief journey to a free state. . . . [I]n American law, a slave, being recognized as such by the law of his domicile (determined by that of his master), was a slave in every other state. Furthermore, since a slave could not by himself change his domicile, the fact that he might have spent a number of years in a free state and intended to reside there did not in itself alter his domicile. The importance

99. But see Cushing, The Cushing Court and the Abolition of Slavery in Massachusetts: More Notes on the "Quock Walker Case," 5 Am. J. Legal Hist. 118 (1967), discussing a 1781 Massachusetts case in which it was unclear whether the slave was adjudged free on the ground that the state constitution's "free and equal under the laws" provision was applicable to Negroes, or merely on the ground that there had been a technical emancipation without an affirmation of real equality.

113. See Segall's Slaves, 3 Am. Jur. 404 (Ill. 1830); Willard v. Illinois, 5 Ill. (4 Scamm.) 461 (1843); see also Anderson v. Poindexter, 6 Ohio 475 (1856) (dictum).

given to the concept of status was evident in two principal situations. First, the courts of both slave and free states initially ruled that a slave was made free by accompanying his master to a free state only if the master established his residence there or intended to do so. If intent could be shown, no matter how short the stay,[117] it was generally held that the master had left the protection of his former domicile, and that the law of his new domicile would free the slave.[118] Second, slave states recognized the free status of a Negro who was validly held to be free by the laws of another state and held that slavery did not reattach upon return to the slave state. Thus, if a slave was either born[119] or bought[120] in a free state, his freedom was recognized even if he entered or returned to a slave state and even though his parents might still be considered slaves.[121] Similarly, slave states recognized foreign laws that operated to free slaves in certain situations.[122] Finally, if by local law or private contract certain modifications were made to a slave's status, the children were held to inherit this modified status from their mother. In Pleasants v. Pleasants,[123] the plaintiff's parents had been granted conditional freedom, which was to become effective upon their reaching the age of thirty. The plaintiff, born after the grant but before his mother became free, was held to have inherited the exact status of his mother at the time of his birth: conditional freedom to be effective when he reached the age of thirty.[124]

Finally, the courts during this period showed a willingness to search for solutions that would be agreeable to their neighbors, to their own citizens, and to sound legal principles. Among the states of Kentucky and Missouri, where slavery was permitted, and Illinois, where it was prohibited first by the Ordinance of 1787 and later by the state constitution,[125] geography and commerce made inevitable both a relatively large number of cases involving

117. Compare Wilson v. Melvin, 4 Mo. 592 (1837), where the stay in free soil was short but intent to remain was shown, with Louis v. Cabarrus, 4 La. 111 (1834), where the stay was comparatively long, but no intent to remain was proven.

118. E.g., Winny v. Whitesides, 1 Mo. 472 (1824); Bush's Representatives v. White, 19 Ky. 75 (1825).

119. E.g., Merry v. Tiffin, 1 Mo. 725 (1825); Gentry v. McMinnis, 33 Ky. 382 (1835); Merry v. Chexnaider, 10 Mart. (O.S.) 358 (La. 1830); Union Bank v. Benham, 23 Ala. 143 (1853).

120. E.g., Forsyth v. Nash, 2 Mart. (N.S.) 385 (La. 1816).

121. E.g., Union Bank of Tennessee v. Benham, 23 Ala. 143 (1853).

122. The majority of such cases involved a 1780 Pennsylvania law, which provided that any slave who was thereafter brought into the state and held there for six months would be free. The effect of this law was recognized in Violet v. Stephens, 16 Ky. (Litt. Sel. Cas.) 147 (1812); Barringtons v. Logan's Administrators, 32 Ky. (2 Dana) 432 (1834); Gentry v. McMinnis, 33 Ky. (3 Dana) 382 (1835); Spotts v. Gillaspie, 27 Va. (6 Rand.) 566 (1828). A Virginia statute restricting the importation of slaves on penalty of emancipation was similarly recognized in Stewart v. Oakes (Md. Ct. App. 1813), described in Davis v. Jacquin, 5 Har. & J. 100, 107 (Md. 1820).

123. 6 Va. (2 Call.) (1799).

124. The case was later overruled in Maria v. Surbaught, 23 Va. (2 Rand.) 228 (1834).

125. Ill. Const., art. VI, §1 (1818).

slaves and a need for amicable interstate relations. Slave state courts looked to the "spirit and object"[126] of free state constitutional provisions to determine whether the activity in question transgressed them.

Consonant with this attitude was the manner in which judicial discretion was exercised in making such determinations as the length of time a master had to remain in a free state before he could be said to have left the protection of his original domicile. A series of Missouri cases that turned upon the requisite length of time reveal considerable judicial flexibility; indeed, the Missouri court indicated that it would adopt an ad hoc approach when it stated that the length of time "cannot by any general rule be determined."[127] In an early case, the Missouri court, apparently treating change of domicile as the relevant test, had held that the length of time must indicate "an intention of making that place his residence, and that of his slave."[128] Five years later, however, the same court held that, to retain his right as owner of the slave, the master's reason for a stay in a free state must be "something more than convenience or ease, more like necessity . . . ." Anything less would forfeit the property interest in the slave.[129] The following year, the same court again based its decision on the existence of intent to remain.[130] In a still later case, the court stated that any "unnecessary delay" in a free state would cause the emancipation of a slave, even if the owner did not intend to remain there.[131] Certainly, one possible explanation of these variations is that they were attempts at an essentially political accommodation with Illinois, whose laws the vast majority of such cases involved. The Illinois cases show a similar accommodative tendency.[132] Thus, both the Missouri and Ilinois courts seem to have been acutely aware of each other's laws and decisions and to have been straining to reach amicable resolutions of their conflict of laws problems.

C. *The Period of Disintegration*

The nearly tacit accommodation between the courts of the North and the South did not endure. Beginning around 1830, and accelerating during the 1840's and 1850's, courts in both the North and the South took increasingly divergent attitudes toward the legal status of slavery, and they became increasingly less willing to accommodate the differing policies or laws of sister states.

The origins of this legal discord were numerous and complex. In part, the discord stemmed from a growing feeling among abolitionists in the North

126. LaGrange v. Chouteau, 2 Mo. 19, 20 (1828).

127. Julia v. McKinney, 3 Mo. 270 (1833).

128. Winny v. Whitesides, 1 Mo. 270 (1833).

129. Julia v. McKinney, 3 Mo. 270 (1833). The dissenting opinion stressed the need for proven intent.

130. Nat. v. Ruddle, 3 Mo. 400 (1834).

131. Rachel v. Walker, 4 Mo. 350 (1836).

132. Compare Julia v. McKinney, 3 Mo. 270 (1833) and Nat v. Ruddle, 3 Mo. 400 (1834), with Willard v. People, 5 Ill. (4 Scamm.) 461 (1843).

that slavery was an absolute and intolerable evil that should not be allowed to exist within the body politic. Rejecting the solution of Mansfield and Marshall — that slavery could exist wherever it was sanctioned by local law — abolitionists denounced as a "compromise with the devil" any doctrine or document (including the Constitution)[134] that permitted slavery to endure. In place of the ambivalence and tolerance of the "law of nations," the abolitionists appealed to a higher law which did not recognize the legitimacy of institutionalized evil, even when allowed by municipal law.

The anti-slavery movement exerted direct political pressure upon the South during the struggle over the alignment of the territories and the new states in the West. At the time of the Missouri Compromise of 1820, the slave and free states were evenly represented in the Senate, and the South was already outnumbered by the more populous North in the House of Representatives.[135] Thus, the alignment of the new states entering the Union was of considerable importance to the South, which feared legislative restrictions on slavery.

Meanwhile, the economics of slave-based agriculture encouraged cotton growers to expand westward in order to maintain profits. Soil exhaustion caused by non-diversified harvests, dependence upon an inefficient and unproductive labor force, the lack of a diversified economy, and the failure of indigenous industrialization contributed to the growing failure of the South to compete with the increasingly industrialized North and to the South's need to strengthen and to expand the slave system.

As a result, the South soon ceased to consider slavery as a necessary evil and began instead to defend the system as a positive good which was a necessary aspect of a valid and wholly defensible way of life. Political and economic pressure prompted southern leaders, as Calhoun put it in 1838, "to look into the nature and character of this great institution, and to correct any false impressions that even we had entertained in relation to it."[137] The consequent alienation between regions could hardly have failed to induce disagreements over choice of law rules to be applied in slavery cases. Furthermore, the growth of sectional antagonism coincided with an important development in conflict of laws theory that added fuel to the controversy.

In 1834, Justice Story published his Commentaries on the Conflict of Laws, with which, it has been said, "a new era began in the treatment of the subject."[138] . . .

Story discarded the notion of a "moral obligation" to observe the laws of other nations, on the ground that since "each nation must be the final judge for itself . . . . ,"[143] the grant of recognition to foreign laws expresses the will of a sovereign state, not the mandate of law.[144] He similarly rejected the Euro-

134. E.g., W. Phillips, The Constitution, A Pro-Slavery Compact (1844).

135. T. Bailey, The American Pageant 229-30 (1961).

137. Quoted in B. Wright, American Interpretations of Natural Law 228 (1931).

138. Lorenzen, Story's Commentaries on the Conflict of Laws — One Hundred Years After, 48 Harv. L. Rev. 15 (1934).

143. Id. at 43.

144. Id. at 47-48.

pean doctrine that laws fixing status should have universal recognition, using as an analogy, interestingly enough, the impossibility of admitting that a free state must recognize the status of a slave domiciled in a slave state.[145] On the subject of slavery itself, Story stated unequivocally:

> There is uniformity of opinion among foreign jurists, and foreign tribunals, in giving no effect to the state of slavery of a party, whatever it might have been in the country of his birth, or of that, in which he had been previously domiciled, unless it is also recognized by the laws of the country of his actual domicile, and where he is found, *and it is sought to be enforced.*[146]

Story's pronouncements proved to be a powerful influence on the resolution of conflicts arising in slavery cases, as evidenced by the new emphasis the courts placed upon the importance of territoriality and sovereign power. In Polydore v. Prince,[147] the court was called upon to decide whether a slave from Guadaloupe could bring action in a United States court. To the argument of the defendant's counsel that, since the plaintiff was a slave in Guadeloupe and without capacity to sue there, he should not have the capacity to sue in the United States, Judge Ware replied:

> The reasons upon which an action is denied him in the forum of his domicile are peculiar to that country, and have no application within another jurisdiction. The incapacity is created for causes that relate entirely to the domestic and internal policy of that country. As soon as he has passed beyond its territorial limits, the reason of his incapacity should cease also.[148]

Two Supreme Court cases decided a few years later further demolished the notion that any suprastate obligation demanded the recognition of slave status, thereby giving support to the notion that each state could deal with slaves and slavery as it wished. Prigg v. Pennsylvania[149] involved a Maryland slave who escaped into Pennsylvania. Prigg, an agent of the owner, found the slave and forcibly removed her to Maryland, thereby violating an 1826 Pennsylvania statute that prohibited the removal by force or fraud of a Negro or mulatto to another state for the purpose of keeping or selling him as a slave. The Pennsylvania Supreme Court affirmed his conviction, and Prigg appealed to the United States Supreme Court, arguing that the Pennsylvania statute was repugnant to the fugitive slave clause of the Constitution. The Court, in an opinion by Justice Story, accepted this argument, held the state law invalid, and reversed Prigg's conviction. But Story emphasized that slavery is

145. The analogy was probably borrowed from Saul v. Creditors, 5 Mart. (N.S.) 569 (La. 1827), an important conflicts case decided a few years before the publication of the Commentaries.

146. Story 165 (emphasis added).

147. 19 F. Cas. 950 (No. 11,257) (D. Me. 1837).

148. Id. at 952.

149. 41 U.S. (16 Pet.) 345 (1842).

a "mere municipal regulation" which no state is bound to recognize unless so restrained by the Constitution.[150] Later, in Strader v. Graham,[151] the Supreme Court refused to review a state's determination of the status of a non-fugitive slave found within its borders. The principal issue of law involved in the case was whether certain slaves who were owned by the Kentucky plaintiff and who, with their master's consent, had traveled to the free state of Ohio for temporary employment there as musicians, remained slaves upon their voluntary return to Kentucky. Plaintiff was seeking recovery in damages from the defendant who, some time after the return of the slaves to Kentucky, had aided in their escape to Canada. The state court had rendered judgment for the plaintiff, holding that the Negroes were indeed slaves at the time of their escape, since their status had not been affected by their sojourn in Ohio. The Supreme Court, in an opinion by Chief Justice Taney, dismissed the writ of error, holding that

> [e]very state has an undoubted right to determine the *status*, or domestic and social condition, of the persons domiciled within its territory; except in so far as the powers of the states in this respect are restrained, or duties and obligations imposed on them, by the Constitution of the United States. There is nothing in the Constitution of the United States that can in any degree control the law of Kentucky in this respect.[152]

Story had earlier been vehemently outspoken against slavery and he undoubtedly intended that his theories and decisions — and particularly the Prigg opinion — would free non-slave states from the constraint of recognizing foreign slaves within their borders. To a certain extent the notions that he advocated had that effect. Soon after the publication of the Commentaries, certain courts in the North began to grant freedom to slaves traveling with their owners' consent as soon as they entered the state. In the most commonly cited of these cases, Commonwealth v. Aves,[155] the material facts did not differ greatly from those in a number of border state cases where the courts — both slave and non-slave — had recognized the property rights of the owner. In Aves, however, the Supreme Judicial Court of Massachusetts emphasized territorial sovereignty, and held, citing the maxim volenti non fit injuria, that those who brought slaves into the state must accept the legal consequences.[156]

The Aves rationale was followed in Commonwealth v. Taylor,[157] and in

150. Id. at 395.

151. 51 U.S. (10 How.) 88 (1850).

152. Id. at 100. For the influence of Story on this case, see Catterall, Some Antecedents of the Dred Scott Case, 30 Amer. Hist. Rev. 56 (1924).

155. 35 Mass. (18 Pick.) 193 (1836).

156. The court, in dictum, said that its holding would not apply in a case where a traveler was forced to enter Massachusetts with a slave, as, for example, in case of a shipwreck. Id. at 225.

157. 44 Mass. (3 Met.) 72 (1841).

later cases decided by the courts of other northern states.[158] Furthermore, as sectional conflict became more intense, states that had earlier attempted to accommodate the interests of sister states began to refuse to recognize the enslaved status of anyone within their borders, even of those slaves merely passing through the state with their masters or fleeing in violation of Federal law. In Illinois, which had earlier, in Willard v. State, affirmed the right of slaveowners accompanied by their slaves to travel through the state without affecting the status of their slaves,[159] the state supreme court held in Rodney v. Illinois Central Railroad[160] that the state could not recognize any property right over a slave in Illinois. Suit had been brought against the railroad by a Missouri resident who alleged that the defendant had allowed the plaintiff's slave to use its facilities in effecting his escape. Following the dictum in Prigg v. Pennsylvania,[161] the state court held that a slave-owner could use no Illinois governmental functions to enforce his alleged property right.

> The law of Missouri, under which the negro owes service to the plaintiff, being repugnant to our law and the policy of our institutions, neither by the law of nations or the comity of States, can affect the condition of the fugitive slave in this State, or, within our jurisdiction, give the owner any property in or control over him.[162]

The conflict of laws doctrine urged by Justice Story soon revealed itself as a two-edged sword. When followed by courts of the North that shared Story's concept of morality, the doctrine could work to restrict slavery to its territorial origins. In the hands of judges with contrary interests, however, the doctrine could be used to deny freedom to slaves who might otherwise have been emancipated. Faced with the growing conflict with the North, a number of southern states refused to recognize either the permanent freedom of Negroes born in free states or the emancipating effects of a slave's prolonged residence in a free state. In some instances this refusal took the form of statutes adopted by state legislatures, such as the Louisiana statute which established that emancipation could not be effected by a slave's residence in another state.[163]

Frequently, however, this change was accomplished solely by judge-made law, as in Missouri, a state which had earlier been especially sensitive to its relations with neighboring Illinois. In Scott v. Emerson,[165] the state supreme

158. Hone v. Ammons, 14 Ill. 29 (1852); Anderson v. Poindexter, 6 Ohio 475 (1856); Lemmon v. New York, 20 N.Y. 562 (1860); In re Ralph, 1 Morris 1 (Iowa 1839); Jackson v. Bulloch, 12 Conn. 38 (1837).

159. Willard v. People, 5 Ill. (4 Scamm.) 461 (1843). It is interesting to note that the authors of the majority and the concurring opinions disagreed as to whether recognition of the right of transit was a duty under the law of nations or was discretionary at the will of the state.

160. 19 Ill. 42, 45 (1857).

161. See text accompanying notes 149-50 supra.

162. Id. at 44.

163. Cited in Eugenie v. Preval, 2 La. Ann. 180, 181 (1847).

165. 15 Mo. 576 (1852). Dred Scott, the plaintiff in the case, later became the center of national controversy in the case of Scott v. Sandford . . . .

court, despite a considerable body of case law precedent supporting a contrary result,[166] declared that a slave was not rendered free as a result of having spent four years in free areas. The court based its ruling in part on the decision in Strader v. Graham,[167] but also on the change in political climate:

> Times are not now as they were when the former decisions on this subject were made. Since then not only individuals but States have been possessed with a dark and fell spirit in relation to slavery, whose gratification is sought in the pursuit of measures, whose inevitable consequences must be the overthrow and destruction of the government. Under such circumstances it does not behoove the State of Missouri to show the least countenance to any measures which might gratify this spirit.[168]

In Kentucky, the state court of appeals made a similarly abrupt reversal. In 1848, the court, following its own precedents and the example of other slave states, had held that a former slave who had lived in Ohio for two years was free and his return to Kentucky would not cause his former status to reattach.[169] A year later, however, in Collins v. America,[170] the court refused to declare free a slave who had spent an indeterminate period of time in a free state with her master's consent, on the ground that

> [i]f the laws and Courts of Ohio may determine the condition of the slave while in that State, they cannot, by their own force or power, determine what shall be his condition when he has gone beyond their territorial jurisdiction.[171]

Later, the same court refused to recognize the validity of a declaration of freedom made in a habeas corpus proceeding in Pennsylvania, declaring that "by going to another state a resident subjects himself to its laws; but on return, his status is just as if he had never left."[172]

As the Civil War approached, cases involving conflict of laws questions sometimes became vehicles for vitriolic denunciation and political retaliation. In Mitchell v. Wells,[173] the Mississippi court, after a "careful review of the adjudications of this court" and in light of the "settled conviction that the

166. In a number of earlier cases, the Missouri supreme court had declared slaves who had accompanied their masters to free states for periods ranging from a few months to four years (Winny v. Whitesides, 1 Mo. 472 (1824); Rachel v. Walker, 4 Mo. 350 (1836) were free (Julia v. McKinney, 3 Mo. 270 (1833); Wilson v. Melvin, 4 Mo. 592 (1837)).

167. 51 U.S. (10 How.) 82 (1850).

168. 15 Mo. at 586.

169. Davis v. Tingle, 47 Ky. 539, 545-48 (1848).

170. 48 Ky. 565 (1849).

171. Id. at 571.

172. Maria v. Kirby, 51 Ky. 542 (1851).

173. 37 Miss. (8 George) 235 (1859).

interests of both races are best promoted by the institution of slavery as it exists among us,"[174] denied validity to a manumission effected in Ohio:

> If . . . our policy is opposed to the whole doctrine of negro emancipation, as at war with the interests and the happiness of both races, then, whatever tends to encourage emancipation, . . . or to establish the opposite policy, must be void, and should be so declared within the limits of Mississippi.[175]

The court asserted that Ohio had been so "afflicted with *negro-mania,*" so forgetful of her "constitutional obligations to the whole [white] race," that retaliation against her policy was justified.[176] . . .

C. THE POLITICAL APPROACH TO SLAVERY ISSUES

NOTE: SLAVERY AND THE FOUNDING FATHERS

By 1776, when the American Colonies were ready in the name of individual rights to rebel against English domination, slavery had been established for more than a century. The Revolutionary period thus revealed an increase in the general ambivalence of the white majority as to the status of blacks. Clearly, there was a contradiction between the recognition of individual rights demanded by white Americans for themselves and the suppression of those rights for blacks, free and slave, living in their midst. As Staughton Lynd concludes in his paper Slavery and the Founding Fathers, infra, the contradictions are best explained by the almost universal belief in Negro inferiority. In his original draft of the Declaration of Independence, Thomas Jefferson, a slaveholder himself, included a paragraph critical of King George's sanction of the slave trade. This was not merely an act of hypocrisy or a makeweight argument to justify the document as an effort to include blacks within the class petitioning for relief from English oppression. Rather, Virginia had long been concerned about the potential for revolt resulting from the sizable percentage of slaves in its population. Prior efforts to limit importation of slaves had been regularly rejected by England. Perhaps the section reflected what Jefferson considered just and what he believed would gain the support of those who professed the concept of liberty. However, at the insistence of Southern representatives in the Continental Congress, the key section on slavery contained in the following draft was struck from the declaration.

> He (George III) has incited treasonable insurrections of our fellow citizens, with the allurements of forfeiture and confiscation of our property.

174. Id. at 238.
175. Id. at 250.
176. Id. at 262.

> He has waged cruel war against human nature itself, violating its most sacred rights of life and liberty in the persons of a distant people who never offended him, captivating and carrying them into slavery in another hemisphere, or to incur miserable death in their transportation thither. This piratical warfare, the opprobrium of *infidel* powers, is the warfare of the *christian* King of Great-Britain. Determined to keep open a market where *men* should be bought and sold, he has prostituted his negative for suppressing every legislative attempt to prohibit or to restrain this execrable commerce. And that this assemblage of horrors might want no fact of distinguished die, he is now exciting those very people to rise in arms among us, and to purchase that liberty of which he has deprived them, by murdering the people on whom he also obtruded them: thus paying off former crimes committed against the *liberties* of one people with crimes which he urges them to commit against the *lives* of another. (The Declaration of Independence, original draft (1776), final draft printed in the Appendix infra.)

It was perhaps prophetic that the ringing, seemingly unequivocal words of the declaration — "We hold these Truths to be self-evident, that all Men are created equal" — in fact contained reservations; for Jefferson, their author, never deviated from his lifelong conviction that the Negro must be freed so as "to be removed beyond the reach of mixture" so that he would not stain "the blood of his master." W. Jordan, White Over Black 546 (1968).

During the eighteenth century, most of the colonies levied taxes on the importation of slaves and enjoyed a comfortable revenue from this source. But one by one, many of the colonies imposed statutory restrictions on the importation of slaves or banned the trade entirely. In the main, these statutes reflected the colonists' constant fear of slave insurrections. In the Northern colonies, the acts were also the result of the opposition of white immigrants to slave labor and, to some extent, the activities of abolitionists.

At the first Continental Congress meeting in 1774, efforts to halt the importation of slaves came to little, and, as already seen, the criticism of the slave traffic included in Jefferson's first draft of the Declaration of Independence was stricken. By the close of the Revolutionary War, the pressures to fully reopen the profitable African slave trade were great, particularly since, as a result of the fighting, the slaves, "by pillage, flight, and actual fighting, had become so reduced in numbers . . . that an urgent demand for more laborers was felt in the South." W. DuBois, The Suppression of the African Slave Trade 49 (1896).

There was virtually no action taken against the slave trade by the Congress of the Confederation. Indeed, the only legislative activity in regard to the trade prior to 1778 was taken by the individual states. During this period, Connecticut, Vermont, Pennsylvania, Delaware and Virginia had by law prohibited the further importation of slaves, and importation had practically ceased in all the New England and Middle states, including Maryland. W. DuBois, supra, 48-51.

The Founding Fathers, in establishing the framework of the new federal government, handled the question of slavery as an economic and political rather than a moral matter, particularly so in light of the sensitivity of Southern delegates, who would brook no interference with their institution. Even so, the delegates apparently recognized that slavery was, in the final analysis, incompatible with the doctrines of freedom and liberty that characterized this "Revolutionary Generation" at the close of the eighteenth century. As Professor Lynd points out in his article, and as the following relevant slavery provisions of the Constitution reflect, the delegates artfully avoided use of the term "slavery," referring instead to "persons" whom the states shall think it proper to import, or "persons" bound to service or labor.

Article I

Section 2. Clause 3. Representatives and direct Taxes shall be apportioned among the several States which may be included within this Union, according to their respective Numbers, which shall be determined by adding to the whole Number of free Persons, including those bound to Service for a Term of Years, and excluding Indians not taxed, three-fifths of all other Persons. . . .

Section 9. Clause 1. The Migration or Importation of such Persons as any of the States now existing shall think proper to admit, shall not be prohibited by the Congress prior to the Year one thousand eight hundred and eight, but a Tax or duty may be imposed on such Importations, not exceeding ten dollars for each Person. . . .

Article IV

Section 2. Clause 1. The Citizens of each State shall be entitled to all Privileges and Immunities of Citizens in the several States. . . .

Section 2. Clause 3. No person held to Service or Labour in one State, under the Laws thereof, escaping into another, shall, in Consequence of any Law or Regulation therein, be discharged from such Service or Labour, but shall be delivered up on Claim of the Party to whom such Service or Labour may be due.

LYND, SLAVERY AND THE FOUNDING FATHERS

Black History, 119-131 (M. Drimmer, ed. 1968)

This problem can be made more manageable by breaking it down into two separate questions. First, why did Southerners at the Convention agree to arm the Federal government with greater powers, powers that were ultimately turned against slavery? Second, why did Northerners at the Convention concur in the continuance of a system of labor which, they readily conceded, was flagrantly at odds with the principles of the American Revolution?

Each of these questions has a traditional answer. Southerners, it is said, did not fear to vest new powers in the federal government because sectional conflict was not yet acute in 1787. And Northerners, we are told, did not make an issue of slavery at the Convention because they were confident it would die away gradually of its own accord.

The bulk of the contemporary evidence does not support these familiar explanations.

Sectional conflict *was* already intense in 1787; indeed, Madison referred delegates to the previous votes of Congress for proof of his assertion that the Convention struggle was basically sectional. Diffuse and sporadic before the end of the War for Independence, sectional conflict congealed during the Critical Period into a straight-forward contest for national power.

. . .

A year later, all but four Southern delegates to the Constitutional Convention agreed to a Constitution vastly strengthening the powers of Congress. Why?

Once again, Madison gives us the clue. In nearly-identical letters to Jefferson, Randolph and Washington in the spring of 1787, Madison stated that if the South were to agree to strengthening Congress, the plan which gave each state one vote would have to be changed in the South's favor. Since the South (Madison assumed) was the more rapidly-growing section, this could be done by proportioning representation to numbers. Such a change would be "recommended to the Eastern States by the actual superiority of their populousness, and to the Southern by their expected superiority." In a word: the South would strengthen the national government if it could be assured of controlling it.

And so it fell out. Over and over again members of the Convention stated, as of something on which all agreed, that "as soon as the Southern & Western population should predominate, which must happen in a few years," the South would be compensated for any advantages wrung from it by the North in the mean time. Northerners insisted on equality of votes in the Senate because they feared what would happen when the South gained its inevitable (as they supposed) majority. "He must be short sighted indeed," declared King on July 12,

> who does not foresee that whenever the Southern States shall be more numerous than the Northern, they can & will hold a language that will awe them [the Northern States] into justice. If they threaten to separate now in case injury shall be done them, will their threats be less urgent or effectual, when force shall back their demands?

Gouverneur Morris echoed this gloomy prophecy the next day. "It has been said," Morris stated, "that N.C. [,] S.C. and Georgia only will in a little time have a majority of the people in America. They must in that case include the great interior Country, and every thing was to be apprehended from their getting the power into their hands." Morris said that the prospect would oblige him "to vote for ye. vicious principle of equality in the 2d. branch in order to provide some defense for the N. States agst. it."

The inclusion of slaves in apportioning representation, and the admission of new states represented in Congress on the same basis as the old states, were for the South alternative methods of implementing its expected numerical superiority. Farrand artificially separates these two questions, which were debated together in the crucial week of July 6 to 13. Nor is he correct in asserting that the adoption of the three-fifths formula for representation in the House was a foregone conclusion. The formula had previously been accepted only as a formula for taxation, and it was only as a formula for taxation that it appeared in the New Jersey plan. What was at issue in the Convention was whether the three-fifths formula should be extended to representation as well. The two applications were very different: as William Paterson and Luther Martin remarked, taxing slaves discouraged slavery, while giving them political representation rewarded it. Years later Rufus King stated that the three-fifths clause had been regarded as a great concession; at the Convention, once the crisis was passed, Charles Pinckney affirmed that the rule of representation in the House had been the "condition" of compromise on the rule of representation in the Senate.

The South was victorious in obtaining both the representation of slaves, and the admission of new states on a basis of equality with the old. These agreements were voted by the Convention on July 12 and 13. A circumstance much remarked in the nineteenth century was that on July 13 the Continental Congress in New York City, a body which just then had a decided majority of Southerners, passed the Northwest Ordinance banning slavery north of the Ohio River. Madison told Edward Coles, according to the latter, that the actions of the Convention and the Congress were coordinated parts of an overall compromise between the sections. "Many individuals were members of both bodies," Madison said,

> and thus were enabled to know what was passing in each — both sitting with closed doors and in secret sessions. The distracting question of slavery was agitating and retarding the labors of both, and led to conferences and inter-communications of the members, which resulted in a compromise by which the northern or anti-slavery portion of the country agreed to incorporate, into the Ordinance and Constitution, the provision to restore fugitive slaves; and this mutual and concurrent action was the cause of the similarity of the provision contained in both, and had its influence, in creating the great unanimity by which the Ordinance passed, and also in making the constitution the more acceptable to the slave holders.

Whether such a Compromise of 1787 took place, whether these were among the "several . . . political reasons" which (according to William Grayson) induced the Southern members of Congress to vote in 1787 for a ban on slavery they had rejected in 1784, remains probable but not proven. What is clear is that Southerners had good reason to consider the votes of the Convention on July 12 and 13 a clear-cut victory which held out hope of ultimate Southern control of the national government.

Thus slavery was written into the United States Constitution. In 1783 members of Congress had "been ashamed," in the phrase of Paterson, to use the word "slave" in framing the three-fifths formula. In wording the Constitution, the "peculiar scruples" of Northerners led them to omit the word "slave" so as to shield the new government from any "stain." These scruples, this shame, this sense of having somehow flawed the new fabric at its moment of inception, were summed up eloquently in Luther Martin's statement that a Revolution "grounded upon the preservation of *those rights* to which God and nature had entitled *us*, not in *particular*, but in *common* with *all the rest of mankind*" had ended by making a Constitution that was an "*insult to that God* . . . who views with equal eye the poor *African slave* and his *American master*."

Why did they do what they knew to be wrong?

Some Northern delegates at the Convention expressed the belief that Southerners would gradually abandon slavery, but it is difficult to imagine that they placed much confidence in that belief. The delegates of the Deep South were on their feet repeatedly stressing their intention to safeguard the peculiar institution. All knew that South Carolina had resumed slave importation at its pre-war rate. Jefferson, whose own state could not bring emancipation to a vote in the 1780's, wrote in 1786: "In Maryland and N. Carolina, a very few are disposed to emancipate. In S. Carolina and Georgia not the smallest symptom of it." Madison, who wrote Jefferson before the Convention that South Carolina would no doubt insist on a proviso "against any restraint from importing slaves," wrote him after the Convention that South Carolina and Georgia had been "inflexible on the point of slaves." And at the Convention, George Mason said: "The Western people are already calling out for slaves for their new lands; and will fill that Country with slaves if they can be got thro' S. Carolina and Georgia."

Why did the North acquiesce in this?

Even the most liberal of the Founding Fathers were unable to imagine a society in which whites and Negroes would live together as fellow-citizens. Honor and intellectual consistency drove them to favor abolition; personal distaste, to fear it. Jefferson said just this when he wrote: "Nothing is more certainly written in the book of fate, than that these people are to be free; nor is it less certain that the two races, equally free, cannot live in the same government." These were also the sentiments of Northerners like Otis, Franklin, and John Quincy Adams. Otis condemned slavery in the abstract, but also prided himself that North America was settled "not as the common people of England foolishly imagine, with a compound mongrel mixture of *English, Indian* and *Negro*, but with freeborn *British white subjects*." On the eve of his career as an abolitionist, John Quincy Adams praised Andrew Jackson for destroying the "motley tribe of black, white, and red combatants," the "parti-colored forces" of the "negro-Indian banditti" in Florida. As for Franklin, the future president of the Pennsylvania Abolition Society wrote in 1751:

> . . . the Number of purely white People in the World is proportionably very small. All Africa is black or tawny. Asia chiefly tawny. America (exclusive of the new Comers) wholly so. And in Europe, the Spaniards, Italians, French, Russians and Swedes, are generally of what we call a swarthy Complexion; as are the Germans

also, the Saxons only excepted, who with the English, make the principal Body of White People on the Face of the Earth. I could wish their Numbers were increased. And while we are, as I may call it, *Scouring* our Planet, by clearing America of Woods, and so making this Side of our Globe reflect a brighter Light to the Eyes of Inhabitants in Mars or Venus, why should we in the Sight of Superior Beings, darken its People? why increase the Sons of Africa, by Planting them in America, where we have so fair an Opportunity, by excluding all Blacks and Tawneys, of increasing the lovely White and Red?

A second reason why Northern liberals among the Fathers turned aside from an attack on slavery was their commitment to private property. Gouverneur Morris was the Convention's most outspoken opponent of slavery, the South Carolina delegates were its frankest defenders; but their identical assumptions about the place of property in society drove them to similar conclusions. Thus, in the Convention debates of July 5 and 6, Morris declared that "life and liberty were generally said to be of more value, than property," but that "an accurate view of the matter would nevertheless prove that property was the main object of Society." This was a view which the South Carolinians could only echo. What it came down to was, as Charles Cotesworth Pinckney put it, that "property in slaves should not be exposed to danger under a Govt. instituted for the protection of property." And so, while Morris stated on July 11 that if compelled to do injustice to human nature or the southern states, he must do it to the latter, that same evening he worked out the formula — proportioning representation to direct taxation — which proved a "bridge" to the three-fifths compromise; and in August it was he who proposed what he termed a "bargain" between North and South over slave importation.

Property, of course, induced the North to compromise in a more substantive way. As late as 1833, Madison could write that the good faith of the North was "sufficiently guarantied by the interest they have, as merchants, as ship owners, and as manufacturers, in preserving a Union with the slaveholding states." But apart from interest, the belief that private property was the indispensable foundation for personal freedom made it more difficult for Northerners to confront the fact of slavery squarely.

Unable to summon the moral imagination required to transcend race prejudice, unwilling to contemplate social experiments which impinged on private property, the Fathers, unhappily, ambivalently, confusedly, passed by on the other side. Their much-praised deistic coolness of temper could not help them here. The compromise of 1787 was a critical, albeit characteristic, failure of the American pragmatic intelligence.*

* Pursuant to the compromises worked out in the Constitutional Convention, the Second Congress enacted a fugitive slave law in 1793. The constitutionality of the act was upheld by the Supreme Court in Prigg v. Pennsylvania, 41 U.S. (16 Pet.) 539 (1842), referred to supra page 41. The act was amended and strengthened as part of the Missouri Compromise of 1850. See A. Blaustein and R. Zangrando, Civil Rights and the American Negro 127 (1968).

DILLARD, THE EMANCIPATION PROCLAMATION IN THE PERSPECTIVE OF TIME

23 Law in Transition, 95-100 (1963)

To know first what [the law] has been with respect to the Emancipation Proclamation we turn back to Lincoln's time. Almost up to the hour of its issuance, January 1, 1863, the Civil War President hoped an executive order freeing the slaves would not be necessary. True enough anti-slavery organizations had made a slogan of "Emancipation!" as early as 1816, and Lincoln himself had been revolted by the inhumanity to Negro men, women and children that he saw on his steamboat trip from Louisville to St. Louis in 1841. The miserable picture of uprooted slaves chained six and six together, like so many fish upon a trot-line, stayed in his mind's eye, "a continual torment to me." Recalling the sickening sight on the boat, he said: "If slavery is not wrong, nothing is wrong. I can not remember when I did not so think and feel." And when he served his term in Congress, 1847-1849, he saw a "sort of Negro-livery stable, where droves of Negroes were collected, temporarily kept, and finally taken to Southern markets, precisely like droves of horses." The traffic in human beings at the national capital was so distressing to the new Representative from the Illinois prairie that he sponsored a bill to pay slave owners in the District of Columbia a fair price for each slave freed.

But even though Lincoln denounced the Dred Scott decision in his 1858 campaign for the Senate against Douglas, and on the eve of the fateful election year of 1860 described slavery as "blowing out the moral lights around us," still he resisted the action of emancipation as long as he felt he safely could, and then he moved only under the whip of two years of fratricidal war. As President he first went back to his congressional proposal. He asked Congress for a resolution declaring that the Federal Government would "cooperate with any State which may adopt gradual abolishment of slavery, giving to such State pecuniary aid" as compensation "for the inconveniences public and private, produced by such change of system." Moreover, he underscored the economic aspect. Citing statistics as to population and military outlays, he said that "the current expenditures of this war would purchase, at fair valuation, all the slaves in any named State."

Meantime two field commanders, on their own initiative, took positions advanced beyond that of Lincoln on emancipation. General John C. Fremont, in the Western Department, and General David Hunter, in charge of the Department of the South, issued orders freeing slaves in areas of their military authority. Lincoln wrote to Fremont asking him to modify his proclamation to conform to Administration policy, but the soldier resisted until commanded publicly by Lincoln to do so, September 11, 1861. General Hunter's subsequent proclamation was declared void by Lincoln on May 19, 1862. The President, who took the position that the question of emancipation was political and not military, was denounced by the abolitionists for both revocations. Editor Greeley of the *New York Tribune*, a strong Lincoln supporter in 1860, was representative of those who believed that the President was not stern enough with the rebels, and who criticized him for himself driving "home the wedge intended to divide the Union."

But Lincoln's view was at one and the same time both more immediate and longer. His immediate concern was to win the war. His longer hope was to preserve the United States. And so he answered Greeley:

> I would save the Union. I would save it the shortest way under the Constitution. The sooner the national authority can be restored, the nearer the Union will be "the Union as it was." If there be those who would not save the Union unless they could at the same time save slavery, I do not agree with them. If there be those who would not save the Union unless they could at the same time destroy slavery, I do not agree with them. My paramount object in this struggle is to save the Union, and is not either to save or to destroy slavery. If I could save the Union without freeing any slave, I would do it; and if I could save it by freeing all the slaves, I would do it; and if I could save it by freeing some and leaving others alone, I would also do that. What I do about slavery and the colored race, I do because I do believe it helps to save the Union. I shall do less whenever I shall believe what I am doing hurts the cause, and I shall do more whenever I shall believe doing more will help the cause. I shall try to correct errors when shown to be errors, and I shall adopt new views so fast as they shall appear to be true views.
>
> I have here stated my purpose according to my view of official duty; and I intend no modification of my oft-expressed personal wish that all men everywhere could be free.

The joint resolution for compensated emancipation got through Congress in early 1862. Yet by that time hardly anyone was interested in the idea. Strict constructionists regarded the plan as unconstitutional while fervent abolitionists took the position that slave owners were not entitled to payment. Lincoln's appeal to the border States to grant freedom for a price was rejected by their combined delegations in Congress, 20 to 8. The most effective use of the idea of legislated emancipation came when Congress approved a measure freeing slaves in the District of Columbia and providing funds to send them abroad if deemed advisable.

As the dark year of 1862 wore on, Lincoln's position grew more difficult. The war dragged with the end not remotely in sight. Casualties and costs mounted. With an eye on the approaching mid-term congressional election, the heavily burdened Chief Executive received a delegation of church people from Chicago for the purpose of hearing their plea for outright, uncompensated emancipation of all slaves. How the wind was blowing could be told from his summary of his attitude: "I view the matter as a practical war measure, to be decided upon according to the advantages or disadvantages it may offer to the suppression of the rebellion."

Lincoln took his first major step toward emancipation, September 22, 1862. Issuing a preliminary proclamation, he declared that on January 1, 1863 he would announce the areas in which he would free the slaves as of that date. He was still playing for time, still hoping he could avoid the final, fateful stroke of the pen. But at the same time he was preparing himself to act in the light of military necessity. After what he called the "hundred days fair notice" during which the Confederates "could have turned it wholly aside, by simply again becoming good citizens of the United States," Lincoln was as good as his word. On the first day of the new year — the year that was to bring Chancellorsville, Fredericksburg, Gettysburg and Vicksburg — he signed the Emancipation Proclamation and declared it in effect. That it was a military act was clear from its terms. It was issued by the President in his constitutional capacity as Commander-in-Chief of the Army and the Navy. It liberated slaves only where the Confederates were in control. It did not include Tennessee or those areas in Virginia occupied by Union troops. It pledged that as the progress of the war made it possible, the freedmen would be accepted for service with the Northern forces.

Jefferson Davis retaliated by declaring that all free Negroes in the South would become slaves as would all free Negroes captured by the Confederate forces. Denunciation of Lincoln's Proclamation was to have been expected in the South, but not in the North to the degree that followed. Partly as a consequence of the preliminary proclamation of September 22, 1862, Lincoln's supporters lost heavily in the subsequent state and congressional elections. With critics of the President in charge of the Legislature at Springfield, Illinois, his home State went on record in strongest opposition to the Emancipation Proclamation. Only six days after Lincoln put his signature on the document the Illinois Legislature condemned his act "as unwarrantable in military as in civil law" and as "a gigantic usurpation, at once converting the war, professedly commenced by the administration, for the vindication of the authority of the Constitution, into the crusade for the sudden, unconditional and violent liberation" of Negro slaves. The Illinois resolution said also that freeing the slaves was "a result which would not only be a total subversion of the Federal Union but a revolution in the social organization of the Southern States, the immediate and remote, the present and far-reaching consequences of which to both races cannot be contemplated without the most dismal foreboding of horror and dismay."

Lincoln's Illinois soon corrected its record. The supporters of the President won the 1864 election and early in 1865 Illinois repealed its odious Black Laws and became the first State to ratify the proposed Thirteenth Amendment which declared slavery abolished and thus extended the Emancipation Proclamation throughout the United States and wrote it into the Constitution. But the newly won freedom was less than freedom inasmuch as the opportunity to use it was not also assured to the Negroes. And so the Fourteenth Amendment which made the Negro a citizen and protected his rights from abridgment by the States was submitted by Congress in 1866 and declared ratified by the required number of States in 1868. Then the Fifteenth Amendment which expressly guaranteed the Negro's right to vote was submitted in 1869 and declared a part of the Constitution the next year.*

QUESTIONS

1. As a legal matter, how many slaves were freed by the Emancipation Proclamation?

2. As the document was worded, and assuming that the fugitive slave acts remained enforceable in favor of slaveholding territories that did not join the rebellion, is it possible that a slave escaping from a state that seceded would gain his freedom if he reached a Northern state, while a slave from, say, West Virginia could be returned to slavery?

3. While, as indicated above, the legal effect of the Emancipation Proclamation on slavery was minimal, and its motivation based mainly on advantages to the Union cause, some historians maintain that its de facto importance for black people was nevertheless great. John Hope Franklin's writing set out below confirms this position. But why should a people oppressed under the nation's laws be spurred to action (theoretically always available to them) by an enactment that was itself basically impotent?

J. FRANKLIN, THE EMANCIPATION PROCLAMATION *138-140 (1963)*†

. . . Despite the fact that the President laid great stress on the issuance of the Proclamation as a military necessity, he did not entirely overlook the moral and humanitarian significance of the measure. And even in the document itself he gave some indication of his appreciation of this particular dimension that was, in time, to eclipse many other considerations. He said that the emancipation of the slaves was "sincerely believed to be an act of justice." This conception of emancipation could hardly be confined to the slaves in states or parts of states that were in rebellion against the United States on January 1, 1863. It must be recalled, moreover, that in the same sentence that he referred to emancipation as an "act of justice" he invoked "the considerate judgment of mankind and the gracious favor of Almighty God." This raised the Proclamation above the level of just another measure for the effective prosecution of the war. And, in turn, the war became more than a war to save the integrity and independence of the Union. It became also a war to promote the freedom of mankind.

Throughout the previous year the President had held to the view that

* See both preliminary and official versions of the Emancipation Proclamation in the Appendix.

† From the Emancipation Proclamation by John Hope Franklin. Copyright © 1963 by John Hope Franklin. Reprinted by permission of Doubleday & Company, Inc.

Negroes should be colonized in some other part of the world. And he advanced this view with great vigor wherever and whenever possible. He pressed the Cabinet and Congress to accept and implement his colonization views, and he urged Negroes to realize that it was best for all concerned that they should leave the United States. It is not without significance that Lincoln omitted from the Emancipation Proclamation any reference to colonization. It seems clear that the President had abandoned hope of gaining support for his scheme or of persuading Negroes to leave the only home they knew. Surely, moreover, it would have been a most incongruous policy as well as an ungracious act to have asked Negroes to perform one of the highest acts of citizenship — fighting for their country — and then invite them to leave. Thus, by inviting Negroes into the armed services and omitting all mention of colonization, the President indicated in the Proclamation that Negroes would enjoy a status that went beyond mere freedom. They were to be free persons, fighting for their *own* country, a country in which they were to be permitted to remain.

The impact of the Proclamation on slavery and Negroes was profound. Negroes looked upon it as a document of freedom, and they made no clear distinction between the areas affected by the Proclamation and those not affected by it. One has the feeling that the interest of the contrabands in Washington in seeing whether their home countries were excepted or included in the Proclamation was an academic interest so far as their own freedom was concerned. After all, they had proclaimed their own freedom and had put themselves beyond the force of the slave law or their masters. The celebration of the issuance of the Proclamation by thousands of Negroes in Norfolk illustrates the pervasive influence of the document. President Lincoln had said that Norfolk slaves were not emancipated by his Proclamation. Norfolk Negroes, however, ignored the exception and welcomed the Proclamation as the instrument of their own deliverance.

Slavery, in or out of the Confederacy, could not possibly have survived the Emancipation Proclamation. Slaves themselves, already restive under their yoke and walking off the plantation in many places, were greatly encouraged upon learning that Lincoln wanted them to be free. They proceeded to oblige him. There followed what one authority has called a general strike and another has described as widespread slave disloyalty throughout the Confederacy. Lincoln understood the full implications of the Proclamation. That is one of the reasons why he delayed issuing it as long as he did. Once the power of the government was enlisted on the side of freedom in one place, it could not successfully be restrained from supporting freedom in some other place. It was too fine a distinction to make. Not even the slaveholders in the excepted areas could make it. They knew, therefore, that the Emancipation Proclamation was the beginning of the end of slavery for them. Many of them did not like it, but the realities of the situation clearly indicated what the future had in store for them.

NOTE: THE RECONSTRUCTION ERA

The period from the end of the Civil War to 1877 saw the basic rights of blacks to citizenship established in law, but precious little accomplished to ensure their political and economic rights. Without the latter, the former proved, then as so often today, all but worthless.

The Freedmen's Bureau was established by Congress in 1865, and helped with some of the basic needs of the former slaves, but Thaddeus Stevens' plan to give land to blacks was never adopted. As Lerone Bennett recounts the history:

> . . . To Stevens, more than to any other man, the freedmen owed their undying faith in the magical phrase, "Forty Acres and a Mule." In and out of Congress, the crusty old Pennsylvanian demanded that large plantations be broken up and distributed to the freedmen in forty-acre lots. Congress refused to budge and Stevens, always a realist, admitted that the dream was stillborn. He was 74, old and gnarled like an oak tree, on the day he rose in the House and pronounced the eulogy. "In my youth," the Great Commoner said, "in my manhood, in my old age, I had fondly dreamed that when any fortunate chance should have broken up for a while the foundation of our institutions [that we would have] so remodeled all our institutions as to have freed them from every vestige of human oppression, of inequality of rights. . . . This bright dream has vanished 'like the baseless fabric of a vision.' "
>
> Charles Sumner made a similar fight in the Senate. When that body refused to countenance homes and land for the freedmen, Sumner the elegant Harvard man, the scholar, the orator, the passionate advocate of human freedom, went home and wept.
>
> There were tears, too, in South Carolina. When officials tried to reclaim land that had been distributed with temporary titles, the Negroes picked up stones and drove them away. General O. O. Howard, the head of the Freedmen's Bureau, went to South Carolina to explain the situation. The land had been given in good faith, but President Johnson had pardoned the owners and the land was to be returned to them. General Howard called a large assembly and stood on the platform looking out into the sea of black faces. He tried to say it, but the words wouldn't come. How does one tell a people that they have been taken *again*? To cover his confusion and shame, General Howard asked the people to sing him a song. One old woman on the edge of the crowd was up to the occasion. She opened her mouth and out came words tinged with insufferable sadness. "Nobody Knows The Trouble I've Seen." Howard, a gentle, one-armed humanitarian, broke down and wept. (L. Bennett, Before the Mayflower 189 (1961).)*

Must those relying on morality when seeking redress be prepared for disappointment, regardless of race, color or creed? Writing of the motivations and the performance of Germany in paying $820 million in reparations to Israel for the resettlement of five hundred thousand Jews, Arnold Schuchter concludes his review of the German reparations experience in language pro-

* Reprinted by permission of Johnson Publications.

viding a valuable message to blacks who — despite their increasing strength and militance — must call still on the morality of the majority:

> Moral commitment to redress of historic wrongs against humanness can be badly compromised in the political and legislative process by which moral commitment is translated into programs and financial support. Frequently, the nature of the compromise is not at all obvious and tends to be obscured by moral rhetoric. Often we only hear the "good" reason, while the "real" reason for political action that shows up in legislation contradicts that "good" reason. Consequently, we are caught off guard, and the legislative actions supposedly designed to correct social and political injustice actually result in greater injustice. Avoiding this outcome requires continuous and highly skilled scrutiny of the political and legislative process in order to catch contradictions between principle and outcome at the time of decision-making. Those who choose to assert their will to establish a radically different moral and political direction in America, to eradicate racism, segregation and social injustice, will have to institutionalize their commitment in a highly pragmatic and organized process of political surveillance, advocacy and action. (Schuchter, Reparations 243-244 (1970).).

The problem is, of course: Is it likely that minority groups will find it possible to follow Schuchter's advice? Isn't the difficulty in organizing powerless people the main reason why the Emancipation Proclamation experience has been repeated during the last one hundred years in subsequent civil rights laws and decisions?

To the extent that constitutional guarantees do not provide a shield against the political erosion of civil rights decisions and legislation, it will be well to examine the limitations of law as a vehicle for correcting racial injustices. This will be done in Chapter Three, following a brief examination in Chapter Two of how other "nonwhite" minorities have fared in this society.

2. AMERICAN RACISM AND OTHER "NONWHITES"

This book is concerned primarily with American racism initiated by whites against blacks, and seeks to determine to what extent that racism is reflected in the law. Blacks, however, are not the only victims of racial discrimination. History reveals that other minorities who were identifiably nonwhite — Indians, Chinese, Japanese, Mexicans — have suffered exploitation and discrimination in ways quite similar to those experienced by blacks and often for similar purposes. Of course the exploitation of these groups has not been less because Mexican-Americans are generally classified as "Caucasian," and Indians are sometimes so classified. The summaries and excerpts that follow are too brief to adequately convey the extent of racial discrimination experienced by these groups, but the coverage should suffice to permit a clearer understanding of the factors of racism, fear, hate, guilt and greed as they function in white America's relations with minorities.

A. THE INDIAN

BORDEN, FOUND CUMBERING THE SOIL: MANIFEST DESTINY AND THE INDIAN IN THE NINETEENTH CENTURY
The Great Fear: Race in the Mind of America 79-88 (*G. Nash and R. Weiss eds. 1970*)*

[Borden's essay traces pre–Civil War policy toward the Indian, which he describes as "Indian Removal."]

The early years of the nineteenth century, which saw the image of the Indian in the white mind take on characteristics of unmitigated savagery, were also years of tremendous confidence, optimism, individualism, and expansion in American life. The negative image of the Indian was dramatized against the background of a stridently nationalistic and expansive white culture. Until the issue of Negro slavery increasingly forced its way into the American mind, the national mood reflected the belief that the obstacles to reform were minor, that there was little Americans could not accomplish if they set their minds to it. The revivalist sects and renewed missionary vigor, as well as the numerous political action, utopian and religious community experiments testified to the restless optimism of American life and the belief

* From The Great Fear: Race in the Mind of America edited by Gary B. Nash and Richard Weiss. Copyright © 1970 by Gary B. Nash and Richard Weiss. Adapted and reprinted by permission of Holt, Rinehart and Winston, Inc.

that the perfect society could be built by virtuous individuals. Moreover, beginning with the era of large-scale expansion to the West following the War of 1812 and aided by developments in travel and communications, Americans began to feel that it was their ordained fate to inhabit the continent from east to west. By the mid-1840s the idea had a label — Manifest Destiny — and became an important part of American life and politics. Americans also possessed a sense of the inevitable progress of their civilization and its role in the world at large. There was little feeling for reds or blacks except as they presented obstacles to the idea of progress.

The negative image of the Indian and growing white self-confidence implied to many that the Indian, like the frontier itself, must be cleared in order to extend American values. Similarly, many believed that the progress of American civilization itself cured social ills. Unable to expand without confronting Indians, Americans rationalized their removal to remote places. Unable to cope with the complexities of reconciliation between the white and red races or to understand the physical needs and cultural qualities of the civilizations they opposed, Americans preferred to trust to the progress of time to solve the problem, or to hope that the problem would simply disappear.

. . .

Americans saw themselves as the inevitable inheritors of the continent. At best, the removal of Indians from their path was a way of buying time until Americans could afford to meet frontier racial problems. It was analogous to the desire of slave breeders and white liberals to solve southern racial problems by returning freed blacks to Africa. At worst, and despite its motives, removal had the effect of a genocidal attack upon Indians. Expansion and removal were factors in the same equation. Insofar as the former remained an unchallenged assumption, the Indian was foredoomed.

The unofficial policy of Indian removal antedated the official Indian Removal Act of 1830. It developed with the rapid expansion of the national domain. The earliest federal policy was cognizant of the Indian's plight. Henry Knox, Secretary of War under the Continental Congress and later in Washington's Cabinet, foresaw the need to deal fairly with the Indian as an alternative to destroying him. From time to time before the Louisiana Purchase, other national politicians attempted to interpret the commerce clause of the Constitution so as to regulate Indian trade and relations, especially where liquor was concerned. However, much of the official good will was negated because the power of enforcement often was left in the hands of local authorities. Through the early nineteenth century, the federal government continued to empower territorial governors to superintend Indian affairs. Because governors were often appointed in return for political services, were sometimes land speculators themselves, and determined their policies according to the needs of their white constituents, the most enlightened national policies would have been imperiled. Furthermore, national policy was benevolent only infrequently, and under the guise of securing the borders of the United States, treaties often were imposed on frontier Indian[s] by force.

The idea of removal began with Thomas Jefferson. The Louisiana Purchase tested Jefferson's Indian principles as it tested his Constitutional ones. The Purchase brought large numbers of Indian tribes under United States authority, and Jefferson early began to think in terms of transporting them across the Mississippi River for the good of all involved. Along with his Constitutional amendment enabling purchase, Jefferson submitted to Congress another amendment authorizing the purchase of several parcels of land then in Indian hands. Both failed. Jefferson instructed Indian agents to persuade tribes to move. When a Cherokee delegation "marched on Washington" in 1808 with the request that they be allowed to stay and purchase their lands from the government, Jefferson strongly voiced his preference for removal. Nevertheless, Jefferson, and Madison after him, took only tentative steps in the direction of removal. Neither was willing to commit force to the project of Indian relocation, although they sometimes tacitly sanctioned it among the territorial governors. This created an unpredictable policy and a series of potentially volatile border situations. Some governors, especially in the South, were moderate in Indian affairs. But others, like William Henry Harrison of the Indiana Territory, were unscrupulous in their land dealings and overbearing in their use of armed pressure. Thus, before the War of 1812, removal was an ideology but not an official policy. With local exceptions, it was not pushed vigorously. Red-white relations were not therefore calm. The increasing number of migrants, unchecked by federal restraints, frequently applied extralegal pressures on the Indians, who replied with violence of their own.

The War of 1812 was a turning point. American rhetoric of conquest and expansion, coupled with rising levels of tension in frontier areas made the Indian especially receptive to British promises of protection. Many tribes, though not all of them, joined the British. In return the British promised to protect Indians from American depredations and to establish an official and independent Indian state as a buffer between its more westerly holdings and the United States. But before the war concluded it became obvious that the British were both unwilling and unable to make good their pledges. In disillusionment, some Indians began slipping back to the American side or fading into political neutrality. In 1815, the Treaty of Ghent ending the war delivered the Indians into the hands of the Americans. With the postwar tide of migration to the West rising sharply, with American confidence growing, and with the need to detach the Indian from the British now ended, the national pressure for Indian removal intensified. Moreover, white Americans could now use Indian support for the British in the war as a justification for any kind of postwar policy.

[Borden states that the war created new heroes, like Andrew Jackson and William Henry Harrison, whose reputations were bound up in Indian fighting. Governors frequently campaigned on anti-Indian platforms, and Presidents

Monroe and Adams as well as the Congress became more receptive to large-scale Indian removal. Through one means or another, enough Indian removal treaties had been negotiated by the time of Jackson's inauguration to leave the area east of the Mississippi River largely free of Indians, and by the end of Monroe's presidency removal had become official government policy.

In 1823, Secretary of War John C. Calhoun sought the purchase of all Indian land in the East and the clearing of all lands west of the Mississippi. To further this policy, the Bureau of Indian Affairs was created. Jackson added coercion to the policy of Indian removal.]

. . . Heretofore the treaty process had called for agreement in principle between the government and Indians, followed by government purchase of Indian lands, provision of a new territory in which to settle, and assistance in moving. The Jackson administration regularized this process, but also unofficially sanctioned chicanery, intimidation, and bribery in land purchases, and inadequately funded removal procedures and provisions. The administration often left the process in the hands of military rather than civilian authorities. The result was sometimes outright destruction, as in the case of the Winnebagos; sometimes futile resistance, as in the case of the Sac and Fox; and sometimes decimation in moving, as in the case of the Creeks.

In formulating a policy, Jackson reacted to political pressure from the South, an area of strong support for his candidacy. In the South, the issue of Indian removal often was tied to land speculation, especially when the territories upon which the Indians were living were known to contain valuable minerals. Of the tribes that offered special problems in removal during Jackson's administration, only the Sac and Fox were in the North. The Creek, Choctaw, Chickasaw, and Cherokee nations all lived in the midst of southern civilization. The Seminoles also lived in the South, but in less habitable and cultivated regions.

Removal of the Cherokee was not the most brutal and bloody example of relocation but it represented best the marriage of frontier convenience and Indian myth. Jackson had based the rationale for his policy on the assumptions that Indians were savages, that cultivation defined land ownership, and that Indians were independent nations requiring treaty negotiation. According to each of these assumptions, the Cherokee should not have been removed. If by savages was meant a hunting society, or one practicing "pre-Christian" or bloody rites, the Cherokee were the least savage of American Indians. They had been the focus of intense missionary work and comprised a more largely — though unevenly — Christianized body than almost any other tribe. They were settled and pursued a farming existence. Furthermore, they had gathered many of the trappings of success in terms of the white work ethic: they held numerous black slaves, they possessed a school system of note, they were economically prosperous, they were peaceful.

The Cherokee were not unaware of their precarious position in the South. Foreseeing a fate similar to other southern tribes moved off their land by fraud and coercion, Cherokee leaders met on July 4, 1827, to draft a constitution as a separate nation. But the inauguration of Jackson, together with the discovery of gold on Cherokee land, doomed the tribe to the usual fate. The state of Georgia promptly passed laws nullifying all treaty obligations with the Indians and creating for the Cherokee a series of restrictive and humiliating laws similar to the Black Codes. Then it proceeded to open Cherokee territories to speculation. A Cherokee appeal to the Supreme Court in 1832 was heard by Justice John Marshall. Marshall dismissed the Cherokee claim, ruling that Indians could not sue in federal court. In a decision of the next year, however, Marshall upheld an earlier removal view. He insisted that as "domestic dependent nations," the Cherokee land claim must be treated with respect by the United States and that Georgia could not extend its jurisdiction by setting aside that of the United States or the Indian nation. Jackson refused to enforce the decision and in so doing invited intruders into Indian lands with government blessing.

Following the Marshall decision, the Jackson administration decided that for its legal protection and as an official mandate, the government needed Congressional approval of its policy of transferring Indians west. At Jackson's recommendation, Congress passed the Removal Act in 1830, thus formalizing government policy and providing a firmer framework for tribal relocation. Although it greatly accelerated the pace of resettlement, the law was an incident in the process of removal, not its starting point. What followed in the 1830s was a policy of land purchase, eviction, and resettlement for Indians. In this plan, land titles were extinguished and Indians from all areas of the East were pushed beyond the Mississippi. The policies of Jackson, and after him, Martin Van Buren, coupled with the ambiguity of the Marshall decisions and numerous "overlooked" private encroachments on Indian lands, led to several Indian wars in addition to general removal and to the division and reduction of some of the most "advanced" Indian tribes.

. . . To be sure, the willful deception practiced by the federal, state, and local governments in the 1830s in defrauding Creeks, the slaughters of the Black Hawk War of 1832, and, later, the incredible hardships of the Cherokee, Chicksaw, Choctaw, Creek, and Seminole, who died by the thousands on the "trail of tears" from the southeastern states to Oklahoma, did not go unprotested. Some eastern intellectuals, missionaries, and congressmen, while approving of the principle of removal for the protection of the Indian, were sickened by government excesses.* But their protest, no matter how prin-

* The forced western migration of the Creeks and Seminoles in the late 1830s and 1840s represented the conclusion of more than twenty years of warfare waged by the federal government to oust these Indians from the Everglades in Florida, where as early as 1730 escaping slaves had sought and found sanctuary. President Washington had tried to close the escape route in 1796 with a treaty binding the Creeks to return fugitive slaves. This treaty was later invoked by President Monroe, who in 1818 authorized military action to "punish" the Seminoles after American forces provoked several battles with the Seminoles and blacks. In what became the First Seminole War, General Andrew Jackson led a large expedition into Florida, where he killed one half of the 2400 exiles there, and emerged a military hero.

cipled, accepted many of the familiar assumptions about the Indian as an obstacle to civilization. Therefore they were ineffective intellectually, and in any case failed to touch the interest motives of the frontier. As stated by Lewis Cass, a territorial governor for eighteen years and Secretary of War under Jackson after 1831, according to the American way, the Indian had a right to be defrauded. His department, Cass explained, could offer the Indian no protection.

The policies of Indian removal were markedly successful for whites in the short run. They eliminated Indians from the states of the Union. But the problem of racial adjustment could not be solved by sending one party to the dispute away. Eventually whites and reds would have to come into contact again. When they did, the Indians would harbor bitter memories and deep hostility. Indians would not be so easily taken a second time. In effect, Indian removal left the problem of white adjustment to the existence of Indians for succeeding generations and administrations to solve.

[According to Borden, the stability in Indian affairs established in the Jacksonian period disappeared by 1848, when the Louisiana Purchase added almost a million and a quarter miles of land to the United States' domain.]

. . . The trickle of fortune seekers and speculators of the 1840s soon grew into a torrent of permanent settlers. In the decade of the 1850s, the population west of the Mississippi doubled. With the invasion of speculators, miners, ranchers, and farmers, the process of negotiation with tribal leaders for lands promised Indians *in perpetuum* began anew. On the near frontier and far, under the promises of new cessions and threats of war, Indians yielded up lands. In Kansas in the 1850s, Indians gave up almost nine-tenths of their territory. In California, in 1851 alone, 119 tribes were deprived of half their lands by a series of extortionate treaties.

Land hunger aside, there were other events contributing to the new wave of Indian misfortune before the Civil War. The first of these was disease. Four severe epidemics swept the plains between 1830 and 1860. The depopulation and debilitation they caused at a time when the number of whites in the West was multiplying impaired the ability of Indians to withstand the influx of homesteaders. A second factor was the intertribal rivalry generated among Indians by the relocation of eastern red men. The first invasion of the Plains Indians' territories and those of the more sedentary southwestern In-

The Second Seminole War raged for almost a decade after Spain ceded Florida to the United States in 1819. The government, while bound by treaty not to penetrate Indian lands, also was determined to enforce the Fugitive Slave Act. The result was the decision to "remove" the Indians to west of the Mississippi, and open Florida to settlement by slaveholders. Andrew Jackson, then president, was unsympathetic to Seminole resistance and sympathetic to slaveholders' petitions to accelerate the removal process. The long war that resulted was expensive (by 1838, some 900 Seminoles and 300 blacks had been removed at a cost of 20 million dollars), precipitating extended congressional debate quite similar to that experienced by the country during its involvement in the Vietnam conflict. The history of these events is set forth in F. Berry, Black Resistance — White Law 35-67 (1971).

dians in the 1830s and 1840s was by other Indians, not whites. Often the result was increased internal tension among western Indians who were warlike even before the newcomers' arrival. At first, it was white policy, not white presence, that forced Indians into a self-destructive situation.

[The Indians of the Plains were also adversely affected by the technological advance of white civilization. The railroads, which began pushing west in 1840 and receiving land grants from the government in the 1850s, facilitated white movement and led to more land speculation and preemption of property.

The white migration destroyed the buffalo herds, split tribes and fragmented Indian territory into smaller and smaller reserves. The constant uprooting and the necessity of adaption to new and hostile environments diminished the Indian population to about a third of its size in Colonial times.]

. . . Each new relocation brought the Indians to more isolated and less productive areas. The dwindling food supply and increased competition for it further eroded tribal independence. White diseases and liquor completed the cycle of destruction. By the time of the Civil War, not only had the territorial integrity of the Indian been threatened, but also his very survival. By the 1850s few tribes could get along without white technology, money, and amenities, so completely had their own cultures been transformed. Large numbers had been reduced to the status of indigent camp followers.

But, if some Indians hovered around the settlement camps and wagon trains to panhandle, others dogged them to kill. This posed a much more serious military problem than had eastern Indian aggression before the presidency of Andrew Jackson, although given the technical, economic, and population inequalities between white and red cultures, the eventual victory of white America was never in doubt. In the East, white population had usually been more dense. Often it was the Indian who was surrounded by hostile whites. Also, the distances necessary to move troops to the areas of conflict were relatively short. In the West, the problem was almost the opposite. The white population was sparse and its lines of communication were often delicate. In the era of the Civil War there were almost as many white settlements as there were available troops to protect them. The question of how to guard settlements was difficult. The best over-all policy for saving lives, as well as the most humane and logical, was federal control of expansion, and the first governmental response to the manifold problems of frontier expansion was a half-hearted attempt to restrain the pace of settlement. It did not work. Whites poured into the West with or without treaties, with or without government sanction, in spite of the warnings from Washington and the lack of legal justification. Unprepared and unwilling to employ force against migrating citizens, the federal government turned to the army, which settled the problem tactically. It devised a system of permanent forts, from which troops conducted periodic punitive raids against the Indians. Still, the awesome mobility of the Plains Indians often reduced the effectiveness of the policy. In the end, the military solution to the problem of racial adjustment of the 1850s and 1860s was no better than the removal policy of the Jacksonian era.

The fragmentation and instability of Indian life increased after the Civil War. With white homesteaders streaming in and more troops free to engage the Indians, the Indian war became a common feature of western history. The conflict between settlers and Indians in the 1860s and 1870s was simply the inevitable outcome of the history of the preceding years. The Indian response was shaped by the original removal, which led toward the annihilation of the Indian once the Mississippi River was crossed by white settlers. It was reinforced by the floods of white migrants who preempted the areas into which retreat was possible. For a half-century Indians had been under the most concentrated form of economic and cultural assault. The uprisings of the powerful southwestern tribes, the raids by the superior Sioux, and the pitiful flight of the sedentary Indians completed the pattern. Threatened with extinction, cut off from retreat, robbed of pride, the Indian assumed the role white men had earlier assigned to him — that of the savage attacker.

Each act of Indian resistance or reprisal was countered by increased force. By the decade of the 1870s, the sporadic outbursts in the mountain areas and farther west escalated into almost total confrontation. But with the exceptions of Indian victories which led to the closing of the Bozeman Trail in Montana in 1868, and the massacre of the troops of George A. Custer in 1876, all major battles were won by the United States Army. Numerous brutal raids by vigilante groups in retaliation for Indian murders and supply thefts magnified the effects of the major military victories. By the end of Reconstruction, the plains had been brought under white control. The year 1877 saw both the death of Crazy Horse, whose feared Ogalala Sioux tribes had formed one of the last, staunchest, and fiercest pockets of resistance, and the resignation of Chief Joseph of the Nez Percé to "fight no more, forever."

NOTE, RED, WHITE, AND GREY: EQUAL PROTECTION AND THE AMERICAN INDIAN

*21 Stan. L. Rev. 1236, 1238-1240 (1969)**

[This is a brief summary of the legislation and court decisions that helped shape the history of the American Indian.]

American Indian law developed in the context of the westward movement of white settlers onto Indian lands and is thus closely intertwined with the means used by whites to displace Indians. A cynic might suggest that federal Indian law was based on the separative premise when it was possible to move the Indians to other territory and on the assimilative premise when the land scarcity required that the Indian and his lands be brought into the totally alien private-property system of the white man, where the Indian could easily be dispossessed by such devices as inflated tax appraisals and long-term leases returning minimal rents.

The first major legislation dealing with Indian lands was the Indian Removal Act of 1830. This law, an application of the separative premise, authorized the President to negotiate treaties with the eastern tribes, exchanging their lands for land west of the Mississippi River and thus opening eastern territory for white settlement. Although the land exchange was to be arranged by treaty, the Cherokees and Seminoles refused to negotiate and the Army effected their removal.

Shortly after the passage of the Indian Removal Act, the Supreme Court was asked to determine the extent to which Indians were subject to federal and state law; guidelines for the resolution of these problems were set forth by Chief Justice Marshall in the Cherokee Indian cases of 1831 and 1832. In Cherokee Nation v. Georgia,[14] the Court faced the question whether it had jurisdiction over an action to enjoin the state of Georgia from enforcing its laws within the Cherokee territory. The Cherokee Nation had attempted to invoke the Court's original jurisdiction over controversies "between a State . . . and foreign States."[15] Chief Justice Marshall's opinion rejected the contention that the Cherokee Nation was a foreign state and instead characterized it as a "domestic dependent nation."[16] After deciding that the Court did not have jurisdiction over the Cherokee bill in equity, Marshall proceeded to characterize the precise nature of the relationship between the United States and the Indian tribes: "[The Indians] are in a state of pupilage. Their relation to the United States resembles that of a ward to his guardian."[17] From this dictum developed the wardship theory of Indian law.

In Worcester v. Georgia,[18] the second of the Cherokee Indian cases, the Court was called upon to decide whether the federal or state governments had paramount sovereignty over the Indian tribes. Worcester, a missionary residing within the boundaries of Cherokee territory in Georgia, was tried and convicted in the courts of that state for violating a statute that required all white persons to obtain a state license before taking up residence within the Cherokee Nation. Worcester contended that the Georgia law contravened the Constitution, treaties between the federal government and the Cherokee Nation, and statutes enacted by Congress pursuant to those treaties. The Supreme Court agreed. Chief Justice Marshall again wrote for the Court:

> The Cherokee nation, then, is a distinct community, occupying its own territory . . . in which the laws of Georgia can have no force, and which the citizens of Georgia have no right to enter, but with the assent of the Cherokees themselves, or in conformity with treaties and with the acts of congress. The whole intercourse between the United States and this nation is, by our constitution and laws, vested in the government of the United States.[19]

14. 30 U.S. (5 Pet.) I (1831).
15. U.S. Const. art. III, §2.
16. 30 U.S. (5 Pet.) at 17.
17. Id.
18. 31 U.S. (6 Pet.) 515 (1832).
19. Id. at 561. It is apparently bad form to cite this case without noting that President

By the 1880's, white settlers were pressing hard against the boundaries of western Indian reservations. That fact, combined with the rationale provided by social Darwinism, resulted in the General Allotment Act of 1887,[21] also known as the Dawes Act. This Act authorized the President, at his discretion, to allot individual parcels of reservation land to the inhabitants of that reservation and to declare the remaining undivided land surplus and open to white homesteaders.[22] The Act was assimilative in that it assumed that the Indian, with his own parcel of land, would aspire to the ideal of a successful family farm as did the white homesteader.

The General Allotment Act also provided that citizenship be granted to Indians who moved away from their tribal lands and "adopted the habits of civilized life"[24] and to allottees when they received their parcels. Citizenship had been conferred on some Indians by treaty and statute, but there were still a large number of Indians, most of them living on reservations, who were not citizens. This was remedied by the Indian Citizenship Act of 1924,[26] which, reflecting the assimilative premise dominant at that time, conferred citizenship on all Indians within the United States.

During the Roosevelt administration the separative premise again became dominant, as demonstrated by the passage of the Indian Reorganization Act of 1934,[27] which terminated the allotment process and attempted to increase and strengthen the Indian land base. By 1953, however, the pendulum had started to swing back toward the assimilative premise. This movement was most obviously manifested by efforts to terminate the special relationship that had developed between the federal government and the Indian tribes.

The present situation represents a compromise between the extremes of assimilation and separation; the individual Indian now has, in theory at least, a choice between alternative relationships to the rest of American society. Attempts are being made both to improve the status of reservation Indians and to ameliorate the transition process for Indians who wish to join the mainstream of American society. There has also been some movement toward greater participation by Indian groups in the national political process.

Jackson responded to the decision with the purported challenge: "John Marshall has made his decision; now let him enforce it." Sic sit.

21. Act of Feb. 8, 1887, ch. 119, 24 Stat. 388.

22. The proceeds from the sale of the "surplus" land were to be held in trust by the Treasury for the sole use of the tribe that had held the land. Id. §5, at 390. The land was sold at the homestead price of $2.50 per acre. It has been estimated that through the provisions of the General Allotment Act "the Indians were relieved of some ninety million acres, or almost two-thirds of their land base, between the years 1887 and 1930."

24. Act of Feb. 8, 1887, ch. 119, §6, 24 Stat. 390.

26. Act of June 2, 1924, ch. 233, 43 Stat. 253 (codified in 8 U.S.C. §1401(a)(2) (1964)).

27. Act of June 18, 1934, ch. 576, 48 Stat. 984. The main provisions of the Act were made applicable to Alaska by the Act of May 1, 1936, ch. 254, 49 Stat. 1250, and to Oklahoma by the Act of June 26, 1936, ch. 831, 49 Stat. 1967.

For a review of the more recent Indian legislation, see Lazarus, Title II of the 1968 Civil Rights Act: An Indian Bill of Rights, 45 N.D.L. Rev. 337 (1969); Note, The Indian, The Forgotten American, 81 Harv. L. Rev. 1818 (1968). A lengthy discussion of the effort to test in the Supreme Court Georgia's take-over of the Cherokees' lands is contained in Burke, The Cherokee Cases: A Study in Law, Politics, and Morality, 21 Stan. L. Rev. 500 (1969). In Of Utmost Good Faith, edited by Vine Deloria, Jr. (1971), the major treaties, statutes and judicial decisions affecting Indians are placed in their historical context with as much objectivity and detachment as the often shockingly cruel and unjust actions will permit.

The traditional myths concerning the winning of the West have been de-romanticized in much recent writing. The virtual eradication of the Western Indian is painfully detailed in D. Brown, Bury My Heart at Wounded Knee (1970). Indian politics — from the Indian's point of view — is surveyed with insight, wit and militance in V. Deloria, Custer Died For Your Sins (1969).

B. THE CHINESE

The Chinese were the first Asians to immigrate to California. They were made up primarily of laborers from Kwantung Province, who emigrated from China to escape the great hardship resulting from the Taiping Rebellion (1850-1864). The discovery of gold at Sutter's Mill in 1848 greatly increased the attractiveness of California to the Chinese. By 1879 the Chinese population of California exceeded 111,000. See S. Kung, Chinese in American Life 3, 30, 66 (1962). Much of the immigration was the product of the "coolie trade," an arrangement by which Chinese laborers were imported under "contracts" that amounted to a form of slavery. G. Barth, Bitter Strength 56-58 (1964).

The laborers quickly filled the existing labor vacuums in the state, and they provided an exceedingly cheap and efficient labor force. Responsible for the completion of such construction as the Central Pacific Railroad, they have been credited with much of California's subsequent prosperity. By 1860, however, they outnumbered the other immigrant groups in California, and had earned the animosity of white labor groups by being "too efficient." Kung, supra, at 68; C. McWilliams, Brothers Under the Skin 102 (1964 ed.).

The Democratic and Republican parties were evenly matched at this period, and the labor vote of California was crucial to them. A contest soon developed as to which party was more anti-Chinese. Not surprisingly, there was a correlation between the economic situation and the level of anti-Chinese agitation. McWilliams, supra, at 97-98, 103-104.

The California legislature passed laws and regulations which were designed specifically to create social and economic hardships for the Chinese. The statutes ranged from a "foreign miner's tax" to a "police tax" and a "cubic air" ordinance. Virtually all of these laws were eventually declared unconstitutional, including the San Francisco ordinance requiring operators of frame laundries to obtain a license. This law, which appeared fair on its face but which actually was applied only to Chinese, resulted in the famous equal protection decision, Yick Wo v. Hopkins.*

Two important court decisions, however, were the source of great trouble to the Chinese. In 1854 the California Supreme Court ruled that the laws of the state intentionally excluded all people of color from giving evidence in court either for or against a white person, and in 1867 a federal court held that the Chinese aliens were not eligible for naturalization. People v. Hall, 4 Cal. Rep. 399 (1854). To achieve their objective of excluding Asians, the anti-Chinese forces realized that federal action was necessary. As a result of their political pressure, a joint special committee was appointed by Congress to study the "Chinese problem" in California. This committee concluded, in an oft quoted report, that the presence of Chinese in California was advantageous to the capitalists but deleterious to the laboring classes. It also concluded that the intelligence of the Chinese was inferior to that of other races, including Negroes, and that coolies were men of vice; it recommended that they be denied naturalization and suffrage. Kung, supra, at 74. The Fifteen Passengers Bill, which limited to fifteen the number of immigrants that a ship could bring from China, was proposed and passed by Congress. It was vetoed, however, by the President, who considered it a violation of the Burlingame Treaty with China. This 1868 treaty did not give the Chinese the right to enter the United States (no treaty was needed for this purpose, since it was not until 1875 that Congress began to restrict immigration), but it recognized the "inalienable right" of man to change his home and allegiance as well as the "mutual advantage of the free migration of their citizens and subjects respectively from the one country to the other for purposes of curiosity, of trade, or as permanent residents." See M. Konvitz, The Alien and the Asiatic in American Law 5 (1946). This treaty was negotiated in 1880 to permit the United States to "regulate, limit, or suspend" the entrance of Chinese laborers, but "not to absolutely prohibit it." The power of interpretation was left to Congress, although it was provided that "the limitation or suspension shall be reasonable." Act of May 6, 1882, 22 Stat. 826.

The Chinese Exclusion Act of 1882 became the first exclusively racial immigration law. 22 Stat. 58. It was meant to carry into effect the treaty of 1880 by "suspending" the immigration of Chinese laborers for ten years. It provided, however, that the Chinese laborers who had been in the United States

* 118 U.S. 356, 6 S. Ct. 1064, 30 L. Ed. 220 (1886). See also United States v. Wong Kim Ark, 169 U.S. 649, 18 S. Ct. 456, 42 L. Ed. 890 (1898), establishing that a Chinese born in the United States is a citizen regardless of whether his parents are aliens or not. Ho Ah Kow v. Noonan, 12 F. Cas. 252 (No. 6,546) (C.C.D. Cal. 1876), invalidated the infamous "queue ordinance." Kung, Chinese in American Life at 22, explains that under this ordinance every male imprisoned in the county jail was required to have his hair cut to a uniform length of one inch from the scalp. As was well known, the custom of wearing queues was observed by practically every Chinese.

since 1880 or who were to come within ninety days of the act's passage had the right to depart from the United States and reenter with an identifying certificate. In 1884 it was established that these certificates were the only permissible evidence in establishing a right of reentry. Act of July 5, 1884, 23 Stat. 115.

The Scott Act of 1888 declared void all outstanding certificates (there were at least 20,000 of them), and barred from entering the United States again all Chinese laborers who had not reentered before its passage. Act of Sept. 13, 1888, 25 Stat. 476. The Supreme Court upheld this act in Chae Chan Ping v. United States, 130 U.S. 581, 9 S. Ct. 623, 32 L. Ed. 1068 (1889), the "Chinese Exclusion Case." Although the Court conceded that the act contravened the treaties made with China, it held that treaties are not superior, but equal, to acts of Congress, and therefore the last expression of sovereign will controlled. It ruled that the power to exclude aliens is incident to sovereignty, which is delegated by the Constitution. The Court also held that the vested property rights are unaffected by the abrogation of a treaty. It would be "most mischievous" if vested property rights could be so nullified.

The Geary Act of 1892 extended the suspension for an additional ten years, and in 1902 the suspension was converted into permanent exclusion. Act of May 5, 1892, 27 Stat. 25, 26; repealed, Dec. 17, 1943. The Act of 1892 provided that all Chinese laborers lawfully in the United States were required to obtain certificates of residence or to face deportation. The Chinese raised large sums of money to sponsor litigation challenging the constitutionality of the act, but the Supreme Court upheld the Geary Act. Fong Yue Ting v. United States, 149 U.S. 698, 13 S. Ct. 1016, 37 L. Ed. 905 (1893). The Court held that the determination of Congress was conclusive on the judiciary, and that the government has the inalienable right to expel all of any class of aliens, "absolutely or upon certain conditions, in war or in peace." In its opinion, the Court referred to the unassimilable character of the Chinese in the United States. In 1927, the Court found that no equal protection violation resulted from the exclusion of a child with some Chinese blood from white schools under state law. Gong Lum v. Rice, 275 U.S. 78, 48 S. Ct. 91, 72 L. Ed. 172 (1927).

The United States entered the Second World War as an ally of China, and, the wrath of the nation being turned on Japan, American hostility to the Chinese was reduced. This change of heart, together with a goodwill visit by Mme Chiang Kai-shek, led to the repeal of the exclusion acts, although not without strenuous opposition. The Act of 1943 repealed all previous exclusion acts and established a token quota of one hundred Chinese immigrants. Act of Dec. 17, 1943, 57 Stat. 600. This act was also a counter to Japanese propaganda against the United States. The Chinese gained the right of naturalization and were thus taken out of the category of citizens "ineligible for naturalization," a phrase used in discriminatory laws against Asians.

The law remained prejudicial, however, in that only Asians did not fall under the "national origins" system. A Chinese immigrant was put under the Chinese quota even though his national origin was English or Malayan.

In 1952 the Walter-McCarren Act was passed, over bitter debate and presidential veto. It still remains the basic immigration and naturalization law at the present time, although some far-reaching amendments have been made. Act of June 27, 1952, P.L. 82-414, 66 Stat. 163, 8 U.S.C. §§1101 et seq. See Higham, American Immigration Policy in Historical Perspective, 21 Law & Contemp. Prob. 235 (1956). The act retained the national origins system, but special racial quotas were established for Chinese and other Asians indigenous to a geographical Pacific triangle, drawn to include most Asian nations.

It was not until 1965 that an amendment to the 1952 Act eliminated the discrimination against Asians in the immigration laws. Act of Oct. 3, 1965, P.L. 89-236, 79 Stat. 911. Specifically, the 1965 Act abolished the special immigration restrictions relating to Asians and forbade discrimination because of race, sex, nationality, place of birth or place of residence. These amendments, as well as special provisions to allow Chinese immigrants to enter the country as refugees, have enabled the number of Chinese entering the United States to increase tremendously. Ironically, the sudden flow of immigrants has severely strained the social fabric of Chinese communities, to the point of disintegration, but this problem stems from a different source than the racial discrimination against immigrants — unless, of course, Chinatowns themselves are viewed as products of discrimination. See Chin, New York Chinatown Today: Community in Crisis, 1 Amerasia J. (March 1971).

Presently it appears that all the racial discrimination in the immigration and nationality laws has been eliminated. In a sense, the Chinese alien's problems have diffused, and have become a part of the general "alien's" problem.

As for the immigration laws as a whole, serious issues of due process and equal protection remain. See Gordon and Rosenfield, I Immigration Law (rev. 1970). Within the administration of the immigration laws there is much discretion available to the administrative agencies. The Department of State, which issues the visas to aliens, has almost complete control over the number of aliens entering, since there is no recourse from a consul's denial of a visa. Id.

Beyond problems of immigration, the Chinese in the United States are still widely thought to be intimately tied to China, and, as their history would seem to indicate, the discrimination which Americans of Chinese ancestry face is in large part determined by Americans' attitudes towards China.

C. THE JAPANESE

The Japanese, who in 1890 began immigrating in large numbers, arrived on the West Coast at one of the most inopportune periods in American history. Anti-Chinese feeling had reached its peak, and the hostilities which were generated were easily transferred to the new Asian arrivals. Japan stunned the world with her victory in the Russo-Japanese War of 1905, and the military strength which Japan had displayed aroused fears of a "yellow peril" in the United States. C. McWilliams, Brothers Under the Skin 142-143 (rev. ed. 1964).

In 1906 the San Francisco Board of Education, then controlled by the Labor party, decided to enforce an ordinance passed the previous year which would segregate the city's Asian children. "In the context of events, the School Board's action was highly, and intentionally, provocative." Protests were lodged in Washington, and President Theodore Roosevelt denounced the ordinance as a "wicked absurdity." McWilliams, supra, at 145.*

A suit by the Attorney General to enjoin the enforcement of the ordinance was never brought to trial, since President Roosevelt had negotiated the Gentlemen's Agreement (by which the Japanese government had agreed to restrict the flow of Japanese immigrants entering the United States), and the appeased school board agreed not to enforce the ordinance. California racists were not satisfied, however, and began to scream about a loophole in the agreement which allowed the importation of Japanese "picture brides." The fears of a Mongoloid invasion and contamination rose, and the Japanese immigrants, seeing this, petitioned the Japanese government not to allow any more Japanese women to come to the United States, in order to preserve the status quo of the Gentlemen's Agreement. Id. at 146.

But racism and exclusion need not take the form of exclusion acts; in 1913 California enacted "Alien Land Laws." Many states followed suit. The laws were designed to prevent Japanese immigrants from earning a living in agriculture, thereby driving them out of the state. The Japanese had filled the agricultural labor vacuum in California, and again their fault was that they were "too efficient" and provided stiff competition for other agricultural laborers. The first Alien Land Law was enacted in 1913, and its constitutionality was established during the following decade. Nevertheless, for a number of years prior to World War II, enforcement was only halfhearted. Legal loopholes, administrative inactivity and public indifference enabled Japanese aliens to circumvent many of the prohibitions. Although they were excluded from the labor movement and many businesses, their ingenuity and hard work nevertheless enabled the Japanese to do well in small farming and merchandizing.

But in the 1920s the Alien Land Laws did not seem sufficiently restrictive to many Americans, and in 1924 an exclusion act was passed. It was the

* This was in marked contrast to the reception given the protests of the then impotent Chinese government against discrimination. Over a period of years the Chinese government filed protest after protest with the State Department against the exclusion of previously admitted Chinese under the Scott Act of 1888, without receiving even an acknowledgment of its notes. By this time the American attitude toward China, as reflected in the legislation, was so hostile that many foreign offices assumed that the United States was trying to provoke a war with China. Id. at 95.

Quota Act of 1924, which excluded "aliens ineligible to citizenship." Act of May 26, 1924, 43 Stat. 153, 8 U.S.C. §§201 et seq. Japanese aliens were not to gain the right to citizenship until the Walter-McCarren Act of 1952. Since the Chinese were already excluded, the 1924 Act was obviously aimed at Japanese immigrants. Japan's sense of honor was greatly offended. She was still suffering from the Tokyo earthquake, and the exclusion act was viewed as the direct opposite of Japan's response to America's similar tragedy. (Japan had sent generous assistance to San Francisco in the aftermath of *its* earthquake, just before the San Francisco School Board incident.) This direct affront has been cited many times as one major factor enabling the military to gain the upper hand in the Japanese government, leading eventually to the Second World War. See W. Hosokawa, Nisei: The Quiet American 112-113 (1969).

When the United States declared war against Japan on December 8, 1941, all Japanese aliens were classified as "enemy aliens." On February 19, 1942, President Franklin Roosevelt issued Executive Order 9066, "giving authority to certain military commanders to prescribe military areas from which any or all persons may be excluded, and with respect to which the right to enter, remain in, or leave, shall be subject to the discretion of the military commander," who was Lieutenant General John L. DeWitt. Executive Order No. 9066, 7 Fed. Reg. 1407. Executive Order 9102 established the War Relocation Authority on March 18, 1942. Executive Order No. 9102, 7 Fed. Reg. 2165. Significantly enough, certain pressure groups — the Western Growers Protective Association, the American Legion, the Native Sons of the Golden West and various other groups — actively promoted the campaign to evacuate the Japanese. Some other pressure groups were the Grower-Shipper Vegetable Association, the Associated Farmers and the California Farm Bureau. Carey McWilliams has written:

> There is an irony about mass evacuation which has somehow escaped attention. The economic vulnerability of the Japanese on the West Coast made their removal possible and this vulnerability had been brought about largely by external pressures and discriminations. In Hawaii the Japanese were not nearly so vulnerable; indeed they were the mainstay of the economic life of the Islands and hence could not be evacuated. . . . Mass evacuation was not the product of wartime hysteria; it was the logical end-product, the goal, of a strategy of dominance which began forty years earlier and which was closely related to a similar strategy of American dominance in the Pacific. The resident Japanese were always the hostages of this larger strategy. (C. McWilliams, supra, at 164.)

Three cases were brought before the Supreme Court to test the constitutionality of the orders in three aspects: the curfew, the evacuation and the internment. The first case, Hirabyashi v. United States, 320 U.S. 81, 63 S. Ct. 1375, 87 L. Ed. 1774 (1943), presented the question whether the curfew restriction of March 24, 1942, adopted by General DeWitt, was based on an unconstitutional delegation by Congress of its legislative power, and whether it unconstitutionally discriminated between citizens of Japanese ancestry and those of other ancestries, in violation of the Fifth Amendment. The Court acknowledged the hardships imposed by the exclusion order on a large group of American citizens, but affirmed the validity of the restriction, stating:

> We cannot say that these facts and circumstances, considered in the particular war setting, could afford no ground for differentiating citizens of Japanese ancestry from other groups in the United States. . . . We cannot close our eyes to the fact, demonstrated by experience, that in time of war residents having ethnic affiliations with an invading enemy may be a greater source of danger than those of a different ancestry. (320 U.S. at 101.)

In Korematsu v. United States, 323 U.S. 214, 65 S. Ct. 193, 89 L. Ed. 194 (1944), the Court sustained the constitutionality of the evacuation order in a 6-to-3 decision. In Justice Murphy's dissenting opinion, DeWitt was quoted as saying before a congressional committee: "I don't want any of them here. They are a dangerous element. . . . It makes no difference whether he is an American citizen, he is still a Japanese. . . . But we must worry about the Japanese all the time until he is wiped off the map." 323 U.S. at 236.

The same day that the Korematsu case was decided, the Supreme Court also considered the case of Ex parte Endo, 323 U.S. 283, 65 S. Ct. 208, 89 L. Ed. 243 (1944), which tested the internment order. Endo sought release, on a writ of habeas corpus, from a War Relocation Authority camp. The Court upheld the writ, but only on extremely narrow grounds: that the detention was not authorized by the Congress or the President. The constitutional question was expressly avoided.

While the Japanese were interned, much of their property was confiscated, stolen or escheated. Little compensation was given. One writer reports:

> On July 2, 1948, President Truman signed into law the Japanese American Evacuation Claims Act. The evacuees were given until January 3, 1950, to file claims against the government. By that deadline they filed 23,689 claims asking a total of $131,949,176 — one third of the sum the Federal Reserve Bank had estimated they had lost. . . . In all, some $38,000,000 was paid out in evacuation claims — less than 10 cents for every dollar lost. Furthermore, claims were made on the basis of 1942 prices, and payment was made in inflated postwar dollars. In terms of reduced purchasing power, the evacuees were paid only a nickel in compensation for every dollar they had lost as a direct consequence of the evacuation. (Hosokawa, supra, at 445-447.)

In analyzing the overall effect of the wartime cases, Eugene Rostow has written:

> What the Supreme Court has done in these cases, especially in Korematsu v. U.S., is to increase the strength of the military in relation to civil government. It has

upheld an act of military power without a factual record in which the justification for the act was analyzed. Thus, it has created doubt as to the standards of responsibility to which the military power will be held. For the first time in American legal history, the Court has seriously weakened the protection of our basic civil right, the writ of habeas corpus. (The Japanese-American Cases — A Disaster, 54 Yale L.J. 489 (1945).)

See also M. Konvitz, The Alien and the Asiatic in American Law 244-276 (1946).

The ease with which federal authorities had succumbed to old wives' tales about Black Dragon societies, emperor worship, and sabotage cults endowed anti-Nipponism with an intellectual acceptability which it had not possessed during earlier periods. Moreover, the federal program for relocation of the Japanese in 1942 provided an unparalleled opportunity for the state governments to conduct investigations and to adopt plans for systematic discrimination against the Japanese upon their return.

Accordingly, both the California and Oregon legislatures amended their laws during the war years so as to provide for stricter control of Japanese land ownership, and in 1945 the Attorney General of California was given an appropriation to expedite investigation by the counties of Alien Land Law evasion. Upon ascertainment, the state, in conjunction with the county, was to institute escheat proceedings divided between state and county.

Such proceedings received judicial sanction by California courts, but were struck down by the Supreme Court in Oyama v. California, 332 U.S. 633, 68 S. Ct. 269, 92 L. Ed. 249 (1948). See The Alien Land Laws: A Reappraisal, 56 Yale L.J. 1017-1036 (1946-1947); Anti-Japanese Land Laws of California and Ten Other States, 35 Calif. L. Rev. 7 (1947). By a 6-to-3 decision, the Court ruled that the escheat action was unconstitutional because it was a denial of equal protection to the citizen-son, in whose name the alien father had placed his property. The Oyama case established the escheat action as unconstitutional. Later litigation voided the Alien Land Law.

In another important case, Takahashi v. Fish and Game Commission, 334 U.S. 410, 68 S. Ct. 1138, 92 L. Ed. 1478 (1948), the right of Issei (first-generation Japanese immigrants) to engage in commercial fishing was upheld by the Supreme Court. California had denied commercial fishing licenses to "aliens ineligible to citizenship" on the pretext that this was a conservation measure. The question presented was: Can California, consistently with the Constitution, use this federally created racial ineligibility for citizenship as a basis for barring Takahashi from earning his living as a commercial fisherman? The Supreme Court held that this violated the Equal Protection Clause and conflicted with the federal power to regulate immigration.

D. THE MEXICANS

In this summary, as in most discussions of problems involving Mexicans and discrimination, the term "Anglos" will refer to all those whose national origins are not Mexican, whose basic language is not Spanish nor any of the Spanish dialects spoken by those of Mexican origin, and whose cultural traditions do not derive from Mexico or the aggregate experience of Mexican-Americans in the borderlands. Because the primary social cleavage in the Southwest today is between "Anglos" and "Hispanos," the heterogeneity of Mexican-Americans is ignored by Anglos, and many ethnic groups are considered "Anglo" that in other areas of the country might be set apart. McWilliams, supra, at 114.

When the Mexican-American War ended in 1848, approximately 75,000 Spanish-speaking people lived in the borderlands that were now United States territory. In these areas (later to become the states of Texas, New Mexico, California, Arizona and Colorado), immigrants from the south had begun establishing settlements in the early 1500s. Santa Fe had been functioning as the capital of "Nuevo Santander" (the Spanish name for New Mexico) for some twenty years before Jamestown was established in 1607. Living in isolation on land that was as yet hardly penetrated by traders and explorers from the eastern states, the settlers had until the 1820s only infrequent contact with Anglos and this contact was not antagonistic.

The Southwest Territories passed from Spanish rule to Mexican sovereignty in 1821, when Mexico declared its independence from Spain. But Mexico experienced severe internal political problems for about the next twenty years, and these problems culminated with the secession of Texas from Mexico in 1836. Mexico considered the 1845 Act of Annexation, under which Congress allowed Texas to enter the Union, an act of war; armed conflict ensued in 1846.

The result of the Mexican-American War for the United States was the annexation of Texas and the rest of the Southwest. The Treaty of Guadalupe Hidalgo, signed on February 2, 1848, codified the secession and annexation of the Southwest. The treaty further guaranteed both the civil and property rights of the Mexicans who agreed to become American citizens. An estimated 75,000 Mexicanos accepted American citizenship, but as with other "nonwhite" Americans neither citizenship nor treaties provided protection. Certainly, the treaty failed to protect the Chicano.* The borderlands of Mexico, part of a country long regarded by many Americans as poor, degenerate and uncivilized, fell quickly to the surge of Anglos who immigrated there. The war with Mexico had left a heritage of hatred, hostility and contempt. The Anglos who flooded the Southwest had little appreciation for the

* "Chicano," a diminutive of "mejicano," was first used as a sobriquet, "given in sympathy and exasperation," for the refugees from the Mexican Revolution in the years following 1910. On the inspiration of Rudolfo "Corky" Gonzales, the militants have adopted it to "announce a distinct people, once suppressed but now reclaiming their integrity." Womack, The Chicanos, N.Y. Review of Books 12, 14 (Aug. 31, 1972). In the "barrio" (Mexican-American community) the word had long been used to distinguish Mexican-Americans from Mexican citizens.

economic, cultural and political history of the Chicanos, who fell victim to all the sufferings endured by a conquered people.

The pattern of oppression and discrimination that has characterized Anglo-Hispano relations for more than a century emerged in the course of westward expansion — in the determination of Anglos to take possession of the land. The pattern was reinforced when the demands of economic development created a need for cheap labor, which was easily filled by successive waves of immigrants from Mexico. In the competition for land and for control over other resources, the guarantees of cultural autonomy and property rights of the Spanish-speaking inhabitants contained in the Treaty of Guadalupe Hidalgo were forgotten.

The arrival of the transcontinental railroads created strong pressures for economic development, and increased the competition for control over the land. Mexican-Americans were disadvantaged in their struggle for survival not only by their small numbers — in 1860 they constituted only one tenth of the population of the Southwest as a whole — but also by the cultural and geographical isolation they had experienced for generations. The "Spanish Colonials," descendants of the earliest Spanish-speaking settlers, acted as a buffer group between more recent arrivals and the dominant Anglo culture; while they thus helped to soften the impact of an alien and antagonistic social environment, they also impeded the development of group consciousness and self-organization among the Chicano masses.

Protest was not lacking in the nineteenth century, but it was unsuccessful. Courtroom battles were lost, and the few organizations that fought for Mexican-American rights — the Knights of Labor, the Gorras Blancos — fought in vain. Womack, The Chicanos, N.Y. Review of Books 12 (Aug. 31, 1972). According to McWilliams, political participation was suppressed by such techniques as withholding statehood from Arizona and New Mexico until 1912 — until, that is, Anglos had achieved numerical superiority. In New Mexico, California and Texas, the native upper-class Hispanos collaborated with the Anglos and bought off the Chicano masses with favors and minor patronage. McWilliams, supra, at 134.

Organizing efforts were more successful after the Mexican Revolution of 1910, which produced a flood of new migrants — some 800,000 between 1910 and 1920. Economic conditions continued to favor the exploitation of cheap labor. The impact of federally financed irrigation of desert lands, which began in 1902 with the Reclamation Act, was felt in the mid-1920s, when changes in American eating habits created a great demand for fruits and vegetables, and new packaging methods made mass production feasible. One writer estimates that Mexican-Americans provided about 75 percent of the labor that grew these crops. In addition, most of the cotton field workers in Arizona, Texas and California, 60 percent of the mine workers, and 80 percent of the railroad workers in the western states between 1910 and 1930 were Mexican-Americans. Cohen, The Failure of the Melting Pot, in The Great Fear: Race in the Mind of America 150, G. Nash and R. Weiss, eds. (1970).

With the advent of "agri-business," the farm-village economy disintegrated, and the isolation that had militated against unity came to an end. In addition, self-perception was influenced by revolutionary foment in Mexico: a new pride and self-confidence was born out of identification with the Mexican Indian, rather than from spurious links with the Spanish heritage. The League of Latin American Citizens (LULAC), a "self-improvement" group, was established in 1927, and in 1928 and 1930 migrant workers, organized as the Confedracion de Uniones Obreras Mexicanas, staged strikes in southern California. "But the tougher the fights, the uglier the defeats; though LULAC citizened along, the Confederation was busted with tear gas and clubs." Womack, supra, at 13. Strikers were arrested or kidnapped and beaten by the growers' henchmen, and strike leaders were deported. Organized labor discriminated against the Mexican-American by excluding him from established unions and by creating ethnic wage differentials. The availability of "cheap Mexican labor" caused resentment among Anglos who could not exploit it for their own benefit. By the mid-1920s immigration laws were being enforced by "border patrols." Nevertheless, there were at least half a million entrants from Mexico between 1920 and 1929; this is a conservative estimate because there are no official records of illegal entrants, who may have numbered in the hundreds of thousands. Agitation increased during the Depression; nearly 500,000 Mexican-Americans, probably half of them American citizens, were deported.

World War II marked a turning point: the manpower shortage created by the war meant new opportunities for Chicanos, as did the postwar boom. But entry into higher echelons of the economy did not ensure an end to discrimination or vigilante action. On the contrary, Anglos reacted violently. Shortly after the "relocation" of Japanese-Americans, Californians directed their xenophobia at Mexican-Americans in a "Campaign of Terror" (Cohen, supra, at 153), which culminated in the "Zoot-Suit Riots" of June 1943. For a week, Anglo soldiers, policemen and civilians rampaged in the Mexican-American ghetto of Los Angeles, beating and stabbing their victims, many of whom were arrested.

Token social reform followed in the wake of economic progress. In 1947 segregated schools for Mexican-Americans were outlawed, in Westminster School District v. Mendez, 161 F.2d 774 (9th Cir. 1947); similar action was taken in Texas in 1948, Delgado v. Bastrop Independent School District, Civ. No. 388 (W.D. Texas, June 15, 1948), although a recent report indicates that segregation continues in that state. 7 Harv. Civ. Rights–Civ. Lib. L. Rev. 307 (1970). The Community Services Organization (founded in 1947) and the GI Forum (1948) were at once manifestations and catalysts of increasing self-awareness and self-assertiveness. By the early 1960s Chicanos were participating with some success in the political process. "Viva Kennedy" clubs brought out the Chicano vote for John F. Kennedy, and Mexican-American organizations helped to elect a few congressmen.

Militancy increased in the last decade in the wake of the civil rights movement. Some money became available to Chicano activists in 1964-1965 as a result of the War on Poverty, but the Delano grape strike undoubtedly had a greater impact on Chicanos and on American society at large. Activism has ranged from unionization of migrant workers to organization of Brown Beret self-defense units in the barrios and walkouts by high school students in protest against racist teachers and curricula. The rallying cry for protest is now *la raza* — "the people," in an exclusive sense. In the last few years the movement has dichotomized into "integrationist" and "separatist" branches. Internal ideological disputes may be a sign of success, or at least of increased self-confidence; Womack concludes that "altogether the Chicano movement is only another ethnic movement, at its bitterest a threat not to integrate which cannot stop the integration but which can wrest some reparations for the loss of old certainties." Womack, supra, at 15.

Response at the federal level has consisted of the Bilingual Education Act, 20 U.S.C. §§880(a) et seq. (1968), and the appointments by the Nixon administration of some thirty Chicanos to government posts. But the Mexican-American family still earns a median income of only two thirds that of Anglo families in the Southwest, and three million of the seven million Chicanos in that region are living at a subsistence level. Now about 80 percent urbanized, Chicanos are still crowded into "Mextown" ghettos. Federal law provides for the temporary importation of Mexicans to fill agricultural manpower needs, 7 U.S.C. §§1461 et seq.; there is thus a semipermanent pool of workers to be exploited. Womack, supra, at 14. Moreover, economic indices are not in themselves a sufficient measure of progress made and yet to be made. A California judge recently told a Mexican-American juvenile who had confessed to incest, "You are lower than an animal. . . . Mexican people, after 13 years of age, it's perfectly all right to go out and act like an animal. . . . We ought to . . . send you back to Mexico. . . . You . . . haven't the right to live in organized society — just miserable, lousy, rotten people." 115 Cong. Rec. 32358 (1969).

Not all courts have reflected so little sensitivity. For example, in a series of school cases, courts have recognized Mexican-American students as a cognizable ethnic group who have been the victims of segregated schools no less than blacks, and who are as entitled to the protection afforded by the Fourteenth Amendment and Title VI of the Civil Rights Act of 1964. A series of decisions requiring school boards to prepare desegregation plans specifically including Mexican as well as black children are reviewed infra in Chapter 9, Section B.

In addition to school desegregation, a federal court has recognized the right of predominantly Mexican-American school districts to share in state school appropriations on a rational basis. The case was brought by school children attending the Edgewood Independent School District in Bexar County, Texas, a district of near-total Mexican-American enrollment. The court found that the Texas public school financing structure was unconstitutional on the ground that the quality of the Mexican-American child's education should relate to the wealth of the state as a whole and not to the individual school district's real property tax reserve base. Rodriguez v. San Antonio Independent School District, 337 F. Supp. 280 (W.D. Tex. 1971), *rev'd*, 411 U.S. 1, 93 S. Ct. 1278 (1973).

Not surprisingly, the position of the Chicano in both earning power and employment is analogous to the deprivation and discrimination suffered in the area of education. The Mexican American Legal Defense and Educational Fund presently has initiated a number of lawsuits based on Title VII, the employment discrimination section of the Civil Rights Act of 1964. The group cites statistics showing that employment discrimination directed against the Chicano remains prevalent. In the Southwest the unemployment rate of Chicanos is twice that of Anglos, which, they maintain, does not reflect the true situation since chronically underemployed farm workers are not included in the statistics. In addition, in 1960, 79 percent of all Chicano workers held unskilled or semiskilled jobs.

Because of the long tradition of economic and social deprivation, the Chicano has been denied a basic opportunity to participate in the political process. In Beare v. Smith, 321 F. Supp. 1100 (S.D. Tex. 1971), a three-judge federal district court voided the Texas annual voter registration statute. Mexican-American plaintiffs pleaded and proved that the effect of the statute was to deprive them of equal protection of the law. Similarly, Garza v. Smith, 320 F. Supp. 131 (W.D. Tex. 1970), held unconstitutional Texas voter statutes which allowed aid to the physically handicapped voter but not to the illiterate voter. Since most illiterate voters in Texas are Chicano or black, these groups bore the brunt of the statutes, which were held to violate the Equal Protection Clause of the Fourteenth Amendment to the United States Constitution. Finally, in Graves v. Smith, 343 F. Supp. 704 (W.D. Tex. 1972), a three-judge federal district court found unconstitutional the Texas Legislature's system of reapportionment. In so doing the court cited both Beare, supra, and Garza, supra, and stated specifically in regard to Chicanos that: "This cultural and language impediment conjoined with the poll tax and the most restrictive voter registration procedures in the nation have operated to effectively deny Mexican Americans access to the political processes in Texas even longer than the Blacks were formally denied access by the white primary." 343 F. Supp. at 731.

NOTE: RACISM IN OTHER COUNTRIES

America has exported racism to the foreign territories that have come under its control, including the Philippines, Hawaii, Puerto Rico, Cuba and Hispaniola (Haiti and the Dominican Republic). See R. Weston, Racism in U.S. Imperialism (1972); II To Serve the Devil: Colonials and Sojourners (P. Jacobs, S. Landau, E. Pell, eds. 1971).

But racism is not a uniquely American outlook. South Africa's widely known policy of apartheid, aimed at complete physical and political separation of racial groups, is documented in detail in a special United Nations report, by Hernan Santa Cruz, Racial Discrimination (1971). The impact of racial prejudice on South African juries is discussed in E. Mittlebeeler, Race and Jury in South Africa, 14 Harv. L.J. 90 (1968). Santa Cruz also analyzes similar racist policies in Rhodesia, Namibia, and the Portuguese colonies in Africa (principally Angola and Mozambique). Great Britain's history of imperialism, which included intense involvement in the slave trade and the creation of segregated colonial societies, contributed to the growth of prejudice, which has been recently manifested in restrictive immigration laws and patterns of discrimination in housing and employment not dissimilar to those found in urban America. See W. Daniel, Racial Discrimination in England (1968); R. Hepple, Race, Jobs, and the Law in Britain (1968). Recent British civil rights legislation is discussed in A. Lester and G. Bindman, Race and the Law (1972) and compared with congressional enactments in D. Lasok, Some Aspects of Race Relations in the United Kingdom and the United States, 16 J. Pub. Law 376 (1967). A historical survey is also included in S. Hertz, Race Relations and the Law in Britain, 41 Temp. L.Q. 423 (1968), and R. Plender, Race Relations and the Law in Britain (1972). No comparable efforts to create equal civil rights have been made in Australia, where white settlers carried out a genocidal campaign against the indigenous aborigines and where until recently a "white Australia" immigration policy has prevailed. Racism: The Australian Experience, 2 vol. (F. Stevens, ed. 1971) is a comprehensive anthology of articles that attempts to diagnose the problem in historical and sociological terms.

The editors of Race Among Nations: A Conceptual Approach (G. Shepherd and T. LeMelle, eds. 1970) assert that insufficient attention has been paid to racism as a factor in modern international relations. The six essays in the volume suggest analytical approaches to the identification and evaluation of racism as a determinant in conflict and interaction among nations. Conversely, efforts have been made to bring the force of international law to bear on problems of domestic racism. The International Convention on the Elimination of All Forms of Racial Discrimination, 660 U.N.T.S. 195, which entered into force on January 4, 1969, sets up machinery for the reporting of the progress of signatories toward ending racism and for resolution of disputes involving internal discrimination. As of December 1971 there were fifty-nine parties to the agreement. The United States signed the convention, with a reservation that nothing in it should be construed to require or authorize governmental action incompatible with First Amendment rights, but has not ratified it.

An extensive bibliography of English-language materials on racism in the United States and other countries is found in Jost Delbrück, Die Rassenfrage als Problem des Völkerrechts und Nationaler Rechtsordnungen (1971) (The Question of Race as a Problem of International Law and National Legal Regulation).

3. ENDING RACISM THROUGH LAW

In many areas, despite attenuation compared to earlier times, color continues to limit the access of nonwhite Americans to opportunities and acceptance. The definitions and discussions of race and racism which follow should facilitate the making of tentative predictions as to the role law is likely to play during contemporary efforts to eliminate such racial discrimination. This discussion is important because so many judicial opinions dealing with racial subjects ignore available knowledge on the subject, while continuing to accept the myths about race — which are, of course, no less dangerous because their accuracy is assumed.

The first two chapters have presented a summary of the law's involvement in the enslavement of blacks, and in the exploitation and degradation of blacks and other large minority groups viewed by the white majority as non-Caucasian. The material should make clear that, until the last few decades, Chief Justice Taney's dictum that blacks "had no rights which the white man was bound to respect" expressed a basic truth about American race relations. But this truth is not merely of historical interest. The materials also provide a basis for discussion of the contemporary issue: to what extent has the complex of societal prejudices, fear, guilt and basic concern for majority self-interest served to perpetuate the accuracy of Chief Justice Taney's observation, despite the many laws, judicial decisions, and more enlightened attitudes that have marked recent decades?

To facilitate a continuing comparison between the past and the present, many of the chapters that follow will include historical writings focusing on the problems which are the subjects of those chapters. To further sharpen the discussion, this chapter contains material by sociologists and psychiatrists, as well as lawyers, seeking to define the meaning and importance of race in the society and to explain how the perception of race influences personal outlook, public policy and even constitutional law. Some of the writing is controversial and provocative. It suggests that even civil rights laws and decisions favoring blacks occur only when the interests of whites will be furthered — or at least not seriously threatened — thereby. Some of the authors question whether the equality blacks and other nonwhites seek can be attained through the law, and, if not, what alternative strategies are available, how they can be made effective, and if they fail, whether there are viable options for separate development of nonwhites as a people, either in this land or elsewhere.

None of these thoughts are new, but they are germane to a discussion of race, racism and American law. The writings that follow should provide a different viewpoint than most traditional legal writing as to the responsibility of race and racism for the survival of the nation's oldest and still most pressing domestic social problem.

A. DEFINING RACE AND RACISM

1. The Importance of Race

G. ALLPORT, THE NATURE OF PREJUDICE *106-108 (1954)**

There are several reasons why — especially in the past hundred years — "race" has become the core for the categorization of ideas about human differences.

1. Darwinism gave the picture of a species (e.g., dogs, cows, men) divided into distinct varieties of races. Though there are mongrel dogs and cows and mongrel men, the appealing idea that pure races are best took hold on popular imagination.

Some writers profess to see in Darwinism a kind of divine law, a cosmic and ultimate sanction for racial antagonism. Sir Arthur Keith, for example, argues that the preference for our own kind is inborn in the "tribal spirit . . . come down to us from the womb of time." Nature went to great length to provide against race mixture: "To make certain that they would play the great game of life as she intended . . . she put them [races] into colors."

2. Family inheritance is deeply impressive. If physical, physiological, mental, and temperamental traits run in families, why not in races — which are also groups characterized by common descent? This line of thinking overlooks the fact that certain family resemblances are the product not of inheritance but of learning. It also overlooks the fact that while a direct continuity of genes can be assumed in a biological family (changing, of course, through intermarriage in each generation), a race is a composite of so many families that it is far less unified in genetic composition.

3. There is proof of race in the very appearance of members of certain primary stocks, viz., the Negro, Mongolian, and Caucasian. It is not an accident that children's textbooks carry a list of supposed races as white, brown, yellow, red, and black. Color *seems* basic.

Yet expert opinion holds that very few genes are involved in the transmission of pigmentation, and that while color and a few other physical indications of race may run fairly true within a racial stock, they do not indicate the total inheritance of any given individual. It is said that not more than one percent of the genes involved in producing a person's inheritance are racially linked. Color is so linked, but there is no evidence that the genes determining

* G. Allport, The Nature of Prejudice, 1954, Addison-Wesley, Reading, Mass.

skin color are tied to genes determining mental capacity or moral qualities.

4. Even a fragment of visibility, however, focuses people's minds on the possibility that everything may be related to this fragment. A person's character is thought to tie in with his slant eyes, or a menacing aggressiveness is thought to be linked to dark color. Here is an instance of our common tendency to sharpen and exaggerate a feature that captures attention and to assimilate as much as possible to the visual category thus created.

5. Most people do not know the difference between race and ethnic group, between race and social caste, between nurture and nature. It makes for an economy of thought to ascribe peculiarities of appearance, custom, values, to race. It is simpler to attribute differences to heredity than to juggle all the complex social grounds for differences that exist.

The error becomes clear if we consider the case of the American Negro. Nothing seems plainer than the fact that he is a member of the black race. Yet one anthropologist estimates that probably less than one-fourth of the Negroes in America are of unmixed descent, and that in respect to alleged Negro physical traits, the average American Negro is as far from the pure Negroid type as he is from the average Caucasoid type. In short, the average American Negro is as much a white man as he is a black man. The label that we give is thus at least half purely social invention. Many times we apply it to people whose *race* is mostly white.

6. A subtle and attractive mystery surrounds the concept of "blood." There is a definiteness, an intimacy, a symbolic importance hovering around this shibboleth. Both family and racial pride focus on "blood." This symbolism has no support from science. Strictly speaking, all blood types are found in all races. Yet people who exalt "blood" do not know they are speaking in a metaphor; they think they are talking about scientific reality. Gunnar Myrdal, in writing about Negro-white relations in America, correctly saw that this mythical symbol had stark and solid consequences.

7. Race is a fashionable focus for the propaganda of alarmists and demagogues. It is the favorite bogey used by those who have something to gain, or who themselves are suffering from some nameless dread. Racists seem to be people who, out of their own anxieties, have manufactured the demon of race. One thinks of Gobineau, Chamberlain, Grant, Lothrop in this connection. These writers among others succeeded in alarming people and directing their attention to a fanciful diagnosis of the world's ills. Others, like Hitler, have found racism useful in distracting people from their own troubles, and providing them with an easy scapegoat.

An imaginative person can twist the concept of race in almost any way he wishes, and cause it to configurate and "explain" his prejudices. At the outbreak of the Civil War, for example, a Kentucky editor in the heat of partisanship clarified the whole situation to his satisfaction by arguing that it was now war to the death between two incompatible *races:* the pure rational Angles (the Southerners) and the decadent romantic Normans (the Northerners).

NOTES

1. The Allport excerpt is terse and perhaps too short to draw a distinction sharply between race and racism. What must be kept in mind, particularly during contemporary discussions of the inheritability of I.Q. and the relationship of intelligence to race (see, e.g., Jensen, How Much Can We Boast IQ and Scholastic Achievement? 39 Harv. Educ. Rev. 1 (1969), responses to which were published in subsequent issues of the Harvard Educational Review; Herrnstein, I.Q., Atlantic 43 (Dec. 1971); and Cohen, Does IQ Matter? 53 Commentary 51 (Apr. 1972)), is that most "blacks" have some white blood and considerably more "whites" are, in fact, part black than census figures indicate. And yet, as Professor Allport's work suggests, little of this reality is visible in commonly held notions about genetics, myths, culture and lineage which are so noticeable in the ways people talk and even think about the subject. How much of the racial metaphor is related to socioeconomic status? What is the relationship between racial identity as an aspect of self-concept and the difficulty of accepting the reality that the very idea of race is an arbitrary and myth-laden construct? For further reading, see The Concept of Race (A. Montagu, ed. 1964).

2. Paradoxically, the major precedent for the "separate but equal" doctrine, Plessy v. Ferguson, 163 U.S. 537, 16 S. Ct. 1138, 41 L. Ed. 256 (1896), summarized infra page 204, grew out of litigation in which Plessy was deemed black under Louisiana law even though "he was seven-eighths Caucasian, and his one-eighth African blood" was not discernible. He argued that the segregation statute requiring that he ride in the colored railroad coach deprived him of "the reputation of being white" and excluded him "from the friendship and companionship of the white man." Woodward, The Case of the Louisiana Traveler, in Quarrels That Have Shaped the Constitution 150, 152 (J. Garraty, ed. 1964).

3. During the era of "separate but equal," the problem of who was black and who was white created serious difficulties, and for carriers, a considerable amount of litigation was initiated by whites who, having been mistaken for blacks, were required to ride in segregated cars. In a typical case, Chicago R.I.&P. v. Allison, 120 Ark. 54, 178 S.W. 401 (1915), a white woman who was directed by a train conductor to the "colored" end of a segregated train coach, where she was required to ride three miles in about fifteen minutes, was held entitled to recover; but an award of $875 was found excessive, considering that there was no noise or misbehavior and that other whites were riding with the sole black in the coach. The court did find that a jury in estimating damage in such a case may consider the white woman's age, degree of refinement, and her mortification and humiliation, if any, as well as her fear and nervous shock.

Utilizing such a standard, a Texas court reversed as excessive a $1000 judgment obtained by a white woman who was compelled to ride sixty miles in a Negro coach. Missouri, K.&T. Ry. v. Ball, 25 Tex. Civ. App. 500, 61 S.W.

327 (1901). But a Kentucky court approved an award of $3750 for a white woman required to ride in a Negro car by a conductor who was insulting in his conduct and pushed her into the "colored" car, causing her nervous shock and anguish. Louisville and N.R.R. Co. v. Ritchel, 148 Ky. 701, 147 S.W. 411 (1912).

In a Virginia case, in which a jury awarded $400 to a white woman who rode ten to fifteen minutes in a segregated car with one black man and one black woman, there was testimony that in the presence of the conductor, a black woman who had known the plaintiff for fifteen or twenty years remarked, "Law, Miss Rosa, you are wrong," to which plaintiff replied: "I know I'm wrong. I'm not in my right place. I was raised with white people, and am white, and I'm going out of here." The conductor told her that she should keep her seat, that she had to stay somewhere and that there was plenty of room. Norfolk and W. Ry. v. Stone, 111 Va. 730, 69 S.E. 927 (1911).

4. Confusion over who is a Negro is still posed as a legal issue, but usually the context is deemed frivolous. Thus, an overworked Fifth Circuit was not amused when in 1972 a Florida school superintendent appealed from a district court school desegregation order because it contained no definition of what is a Negro. Calling it "a last gasp in the struggle against desegregation," the court noted that the Department of Health, Education and Welfare had defined Negroes as "persons considered by themselves, by the school or by the community to be of African or Negro origin." Perhaps the superintendent had read the railway cases reviewed above, but the court rejected his appeal, observing wearily: "The record indicates that in the past the School District has apparently had no difficulty identifying Negroes for the purposes of segregating them. For desegregation they can be identified with similar ease." United States v. Flagler County School District, 457 F.2d 1402 (5th Cir. 1972).

2. Defining Racism

A. DOWNS, RACISM IN AMERICA AND HOW TO COMBAT IT

United States Commission on Civil Rights 5-6 (1970)

Racism is one of those words that many people use, and feel strongly about, but cannot define very clearly. Those who suffer from racism usually interpret the word one way while others interpret it quite differently. This ambiguity is possible in part because the word refers to ideas that are very complicated and hard to pin down. Yet, before we can fully understand how racism works or how to combat its harmful effects we must first try to define it clearly even though such an attempt may be regarded as wrong by many.

Perhaps the best definition of *racism* is an operational one. This means that it must be based upon the way people actually behave, rather than upon logical consistency or purely scientific ideas. Therefore, racism may be viewed as *any attitude, action, or institutional structure which subordinates a person or group because of his or their color.* Even though "race" and "color" refer to two different kinds of human characteristics, in America it is the visibility of skin color — and of other physical traits associated with particular color or groups — that marks individuals as "targets" for subordination by members of the white majority. This is true of Negroes, Puerto Ricans, Mexican Americans, Japanese Americans, Chinese Americans, and American Indians. Specifically, white racism subordinates members of all these other groups primarily because they are not white in color, even though some are technically considered to be members of the "white race" and even view themselves as "whites."

As a matter of further explanation, racism is not just a matter of attitudes: actions and institutional structures, especially, can also be forms of racism. An "institutional structure" is any well-established, habitual, or widely accepted pattern of action or organizational arrangement, whether formal or informal. For example, the residential segregation of almost all Negroes in large cities is an "institutional structure." So is the widely used practice of denying employment to applicants with any nontraffic police record because this tends to discriminate unfairly against residents of low-income areas where police normally arrest young men for minor incidents that are routinely overlooked in wealthy suburbs.

Just being aware of someone's color or race, or even taking it into account when making decisions or in other behavior, is not necessarily racist. Racism occurs only when these reactions involve some kind of subordination. Thus, pride in one's black heritage, or Irish ancestry, is not necessarily racist.

Racism can occur even if the people causing it have no intention of subordinating others because of color, or are totally unaware of doing so. Admittedly, this implication is sure to be extremely controversial. Most Americans believe racism is bad. But how can anyone be "guilty" of doing something bad when he does not realize he is doing it? Racism can be a matter of *result* rather than *intention* because many institutional structures in America that most whites do not recognize as subordinating others because of color actually injure minority group members far more than deliberate racism.

The separation of races is not racism unless it leads to or involves subordination of one group by another (including subordination of whites by Negroes). Therefore, favoring the voluntary separation of races is not necessarily a form of racism. However, it would become racism if members of one group who wanted to cluster together tried to restrict the locational choices of members of some other group in order to achieve such clustering; for example, if whites tried to discourage Mexican Americans from moving into all-white neighborhoods or if a group of black students forced other black students to live in a specific dormitory. Furthermore, separation of groups is one of the oldest and most widespread devices for subordination in all socities. It is particularly effective in modern urbanized societies because it is extremely difficult, if not impossible, to provide different but truly equal opportunities and conditions for separated groups within an economically integrated society.

White racism exhibits itself in hundreds of ways in American society, and acts in hundreds of other ways that are not recognized by most citizens. Yet all of these can be usefully grouped into two basic categories: *overt racism,* and *indirect institutional subordination because of color.* (For convenience, the second category will be referred to as just *institutional subordination.*)

Overt racism is the use of color *per se* (or other visible characteristics related to color) as a subordinating factor. *Institutional subordination* is placing or keeping persons in a position or status of inferiority by means of attitudes, actions, or institutional structures which do not use color itself as the subordinating mechanism, but instead use other mechanisms indirectly related to color. Institutional subordination is particularly difficult to define clearly in a few words. The very essence of institutional subordination is its indirect nature, which often makes it hard to recognize. Furthermore, there are so many different forms of institutional subordination that it is difficult to include all of them in a single definition.

PINDERHUGHES, UNDERSTANDING BLACK POWER: PROCESSES AND PROPOSALS
125 Am. J. Psychiatry 1552-1557 (1969)

[In the course of an article explaining the psychological significance of the black power movement, psychiatrist Charles A. Pinderhughes indicates that racism is more than a political phenomenon based on economic self-interest. He asserts that the motivation to devalue nonwhites is far more basic than is generally assumed.]

People with power to influence social structure frequently are unconscious victims of pathogenic projections derived from the body image, which have been reinforced by the groups to which they belong. These basic psychological processes which generate false beliefs are shared by all people.

Hierarchy-Related Paranoia

Some false beliefs imputed to others depend upon whether they are viewed as "high-" or "low-type" people. "High-type" people are associated in the mind with the high part of the body, with the head, with thinking, with leadership, with what is taken in and believed, and with food. "Low-type" people are associated with the lower body, with the bottom, with the perineum, with what is excluded and expelled. Lower parties are often trained or molded by upper bodies and sent out on missions, often as expendables, as reflected in military and other hierarchical organizations. . . .

Color-related paranoia may also be associated with earliest infantile experience, since black is associated with absence of retinal stimulation and with darkness, mystery, and loss of contact with important persons. Regardless of the factors responsible for its development, white generally connotes the bright, the nobler, and the "good," while black connotes the sad, the gloomy, and the "evil." In addition to color, other physical characteristics may serve as vehicles for various forms of appearance-related paranoia.

Perception, Projection, and Paranoia

Understanding involves taking in, mulling over, appraising, and assimilating. A similarity to the process of digestion may be noted. In fact, each person's search for understanding begins in infancy with the taking of objects into the mouth, mouthing them, and then swallowing or ejecting them. Subsequently, the development of external sensory perception permits appraisal of objects without taking them into the body, although some stimuli from the object must enter and cause physiological change in the body in order for a perception to occur. These physiological changes (reflex, associative, cognitive, etc.) are then interpreted in terms of past experiences, so that each conscious perception represents an approximation or guess, based on past experience, which is attributed to the object by the psychological mechanism of projection.

Those perceptions associated with emotion are anchored deeply in body physiology through linkages with mental representations of significant persons, experiences, and body processes. For this reason, changing patterns of perception which are associated with strong emotion may be an unsettling or stormy process. Each individual tends to reinforce his beliefs by selectively focusing upon content which supports his own beliefs and by selectively ignoring content which undermines them. In this manner existing misinformation and delusions are perpetuated. All individuals retain in their personalities latent paranoid patterns.

Group-Related Paranoia

Accommodation to groups generally reactivates latent paranoid processes to varying degrees as members of a group learn to project the same interpretations to a given object or idea, while members of a different group may project different meanings upon the same object. Groups do not recognize delusions as long as all members believe them. They require group members to remain loyal and to use their reason and other faculties to support group delusions.

Persons perceived as similar to one's own kind are identified with, are valued highly, are trusted, are taken in . . . like food . . . like milk, are swallowed . . . are thought of as right and pure and white; they are associated with the "higher things in life" . . . with the head . . . and with the mind . . . and with persons who are above one . . . over one . . . with parents. Understanding literally means to stand under. *Understanding*, therefore, tends to take place between members of the same group by *introjection and identification.*

Persons seen as different are not taken in . . . are not seen as food . . . are seen as objects to keep out with vigilant defensiveness and suspicion. They are perceived as wrong, or inadequate, or sinister, and are rejected. If their appearance, culture, and behavior shows characteristics on which a low value is placed, they are associated further with low things, with the bottom . . . and with the buttocks and genitals. Between persons who are *not* members of the same group, understanding tends to take place by *projection,* rather than by introjection and identification.

Since repressed impulses are those which tend to be projected, and since all groups encourage in their members repression of impulses which threaten the group, these group-threatening motivations are commonly projected upon other groups. It is predictable, therefore, that members of differing groups will impute to one another the same or similar threatening motivations.

These group-related paranoid processes have not been considered pathological by psychiatrists. However, they are responsible for such extensive intrapsychic, interpersonal, and intergroup conflict, for so many misunderstandings, acts of violence, and deaths on a massive scale that psychiatrists may come to identify them as the most serious pathogenic factors in our era.

Segregation-Related Paranoia

Segregation-related paranoia offers additional problems in understanding for American blacks and whites. Any person or group that is segregated is associated in the mind, in the unconscious thinking processes, with any mental representations which are also segregated. Each individual learns to segregate out of public social interactions excreta, destructive aggression, and sexual feelings and thoughts. These, having been segregated, are in the unconscious mind associated with mental representations of segregated people. Each individual looking at a segregated group perceives, with a sense of reality, an association between the segregated group and dirty, smelly, destructive, and sexual sensations.

Thus hierarchy-related paranoia, appearance-related paranoia, segregation-related paranoia, and group-related paranoia — all of them unconscious and all derived from projections of the body image — combine to determine the perceptions we make and the constructions we create, whether they are objects or social structure. An individual's behavior is influenced by whether he perceives himself as "higher" or "lower," "darker" or "lighter," "free" or "restricted," a group member or an outsider; and the treatment accorded him depends upon how he is perceived on these four axes. These primitive immature thinking processes have eroded and undermined peoples' efforts toward mature behavior throughout the history of man. They may be regarded as physiological but pathogenic.

Expression of Group-Related Paranoias in American Social Structure

Alteration of Reality to Fit False Beliefs

The perception by whites of blacks as different, as less worthy and less human, led the developers of early American social structure to treat indentured blacks differently from indentured whites. For two centuries after the slave laws were initiated in the 1660s, blacks were defined as property of whites and their characteristics were coercively determined by the psychological projections of whites. Blacks were thereby altered to fit the false beliefs and interests of whites.

By disrupting the families and group structure of black people from diverse backgrounds, by maintaining authority and order among whites and preventing the development of authority and order among blacks, by developing deeply entrenched differences in psychology, education, living circumstances, behavior patterns, and even language, Americans structured the white group toward a pattern of characteristics viewed as superior and the black group toward a pattern of characteristics viewed as inferior. Whites were trained to aggrandize themselves, to love and respect themselves, to have initiative, narcissism, sense of entitlement, and to master external realities. Blacks were trained to surrender and sacrifice themselves, to trust others, to be simple and forthright, to love and respect others, to accept persecution, to devalue themselves, to defeat themselves, and to seek direction from others.

After emancipation in 1863, segregation laws and practices ensured that most descendants of slaves would continue to transfer to each new generation the slave culture caste which had been forced upon them. Although thought of as a group, they had no significant group structure, no unifying religion, no internal bonds, no internal authority, no power, and no organization to help them solve problems or take action in concert. These factors left black Americans, to a considerable degree, without personalities which could function independently and with fewer viable families or other cultural groups. These factors handicapped generations of blacks in competition for education, skills, property, influence, and power.

Correcting False Beliefs and Conditions Based Upon Them

In this context the Black Power movement is a massive sociotherapy, group therapy, and individual therapy movement whose advocates are attempting to develop more adaptive psychology, role relationships, and group structure for blacks by developing bonds, group formation, action in concert, internal cohesion, internal sense of authority, discipline, resources, independence, autonomy, initiative, and self-esteem for black people. Development of a more adaptive identity and culture and the generation of educational, economic, and political power are central. Black Power advocates press for a more open society, for more democratic institutions, for justice, for reparative programs, for more responsive interaction between black communities and the power structure affecting them, and for recognition of the limitations, pitfalls, and misuses of the intellect and reason so often worshiped in Western societies.

For many blacks the goal of the movement is to develop sufficient power to make possible behavior in line with conscience and with national and religious ethics, since white power used without conscience and black conscience without power result in continuation of an abusive and oppressive social order. What most whites perceive as an orderly American social system most blacks experience as unresponsive, unremitting, dehumanized, well-rationalized, quiet, courteous, institutionalized violence not unlike colonialism. Since influential and powerful persons and groups enjoy things as they are and are unwilling to change the society which they have opportunity to change, initiative for altering a destructive system and producing constructive change rests by default on the shoulders of the resourceless, powerless people who are better motivated though often ill-equipped for the task. . . .*

B. THE LIMITS OF LAW IN SOCIAL CHANGE

The Kerner Commission provoked an uproar across great segments of the country when it concluded: "Race prejudice has shaped our history decisively in the past . . . it now threatens to affect our future. White racism is essentially responsible for the explosive mixture which has been accumulating in our cities since the end of World War II." Nat. Advisory Comm'n on Civil Disorders 91 (1968).

In the main, blacks have looked to the courts to remedy those aspects of societal racism the practice of which contravenes constitutional protections or applicable statutory provisions. As the materials covered thus far reveal, resort to the courts has not always been a profitable means of combating racism; but, as the upcoming chapters will show, there is a long list of decisions, particularly since World War II, which seem to support an argument that reliance by blacks on the courts is not misplaced.

As will be shown in Chapter Seven, "The Right to Protest," most courts and probably a majority of the country believe that blacks should rely on the courts and abstain from violence and disruptive protests in their quest for racial justice. In the view of some, the idea that blacks should place utter faith on the judicial process is not only appropriate but necessary. Obviously adhering to this view, Justice Black again and again admonished blacks to use the courts and forsake the streets. Dissenting in Cox v. Louisiana, 379 U.S. 536, 584, 85 S. Ct. 453, 13 L. Ed. 2d 471 (1965), he warns:

> Minority groups in particular need always to bear in mind that the Constitution, while it requires States to treat all citizens equally and protect them in the exercise of rights granted by the Federal Constitution and laws, does not take away the State's power, indeed its duty, to keep order and to do justice according to law. Those who encourage minority groups to believe that the United States Constitution and federal laws give them a right to patrol and picket in the streets whenever they choose, in order to advance what they think to be a just and noble end, do no

* The psychiatric significance of racism is examined from the standpoint of the sensitive area of interracial sex in writings contained in Chapter Six. See also B. Bettelheim and M. Janowitz, Dynamics of Prejudice (1950).

service to those minority groups, their cause, or their country. I am confident from this record that this appellant violated the Louisiana statute because of a mistaken belief that he and his followers had a constitutional right to do so, because of what they believed were just grievances. But the history of the past 25 years if it shows nothing else shows that his group's constitutional and statutory rights have to be protected by the courts, which must be kept free from intimidation and coercive pressures of any kind. (379 U.S. at 584.)

Justice Black would withhold judicial relief against discrimination where protestors are disruptive and seek through pressure to bring about change which, he believes, only courts kept "free from intimidation and coercive pressures" are able to provide. But in Giles v. Harris, 189 U.S. 475, 23 S. Ct. 639, 47 L. Ed. 909 (1903), Justice Holmes recognized the limitations of judicial relief for a minority whose rights the majority is determined to destroy. In denying the petition of 6000 blacks seeking judicial enforcement of their franchise, Justice Holmes observed:

The bill imports that the great mass of the white population intends to keep the blacks from voting. To meet such an intent something more than ordering the plaintiff's name to be inscribed upon the lists of 1902 will be needed. If the conspiracy and the intent exist, a name on a piece of paper will not defeat them. Unless we are prepared to supervise the voting in that state by officers of the court, it seems to us that all the plaintiff could get from equity would be an empty form. Apart from damages to the individual, relief from a great political wrong, if done, as alleged, by the people of a state and the state itself, must be given by them or by the legislative and political department of the Government of the United States. (189 U.S. at 488.)

STEEL, NINE MEN IN BLACK WHO THINK WHITE
N.Y. Times Magazine, Oct. 13, 1968, p. 56

[In recent years, an increasing number of lawyers have been questioning whether many of the Supreme Court's civil rights decisions were not more beneficial to white image than to black rights. A major controversy was launched within the National Association for the Advancement of Colored People several years ago when staff attorney Lewis M. Steel published (without prior NAACP approval) an article critical of the civil rights decisions handed down during the fifteen years that Chief Justice Warren presided over the Court.]

Long before the Court undertook any serious review of its constitutional doctrines in the field of race relations, other American institutions were reevaluating their stands. During World War II and shortly thereafter, various agencies created machinery to make it appear that racial equality had become a part of our public policy. Thus, Presidential executive orders forbade racial discrimination by the recipients of Government contracts, the armed forces ordered the integration of military units and certain states enacted a variety of antidiscrimination laws. The reasons for these faint-hearted shifts in public policy have been discussed by the Advisory Commission and others. The war against Nazi Germany had raised the issue of racism and heightened the expectations of Negroes, who, because of labor shortages, were offered good jobs for the first time. Additionally, policy makers realized that the continuation of America's brand of apartheid could damage our standing with the newly emerging nations. Most important, black Americans came out of the war determined to fight for their rights at home.

Seen in the light of these pre-1954 shifts in attitude, the school-desegregation case did little more than bring the Court up to date. Until the 1954 decision, the gains won by Negroes were more in the nature of favors to be dispensed or withdrawn at the pleasure of the white overlords. Being gifts, not rights, these pre-1954 "reforms" stood as paper testaments only. Segregated Army units still fought in Korea; Negroes were still condemned to unequal job opportunities in defense plants and were openly segregated in the public schools of Northern states which had antisegregation laws.

In 1954, the Court was in a position to serve notice on the American people that equality was an absolute right of all citizens, that this right came before all other rights and that its further subversion could not be tolerated. By taking this stance, the Court could not only have gone a long way toward relieving its conscience but it could also have established itself as a true constitutional court, dedicated to an impartial search for just principles, irrespective of race.

Instead, the Court chose to act in the manner of the practical political reformer. Rather than ordering sweeping desegregation, it ordered another hearing. A year later, the Court ruled that the South did not have to desegregate its schools immediately, it merely had to do so "with all deliberate speed." Never in the history of the Supreme Court had the implementation of a constitutional right been so delayed or the creation of it put in such vague terms. The Court thereby made clear that it was a white court which would protect the interests of white America in the maintenance of stable institutions.

In essence, the Court considered the potential damage to white Americans resulting from the diminution of privilege as more critical than continued damage to the underprivileged. The Court found that public reasons — the offense to white sensibilities — existed to justify the delay in school desegregation. Worse still, it gave the primary responsibility for achieving educational equality to those who had established the segregated institutions.

This decision to delay integration and ignore racially discriminatory mechanisms was more shameful than the Court's 19th-century monuments to apartheid. For, by the mid-20th century, there was no basis on which the Court's nine educated men could justify a segregated society. Scientific racism had been discredited and America had been exposed to the full implications of racism in Nazi Germany.

Moreover, the United States had proclaimed itself the guarantor of freedom by taking up the sword against international Communism. From a judicial standpoint, crimes against humanity had been defined and punished at Nuremberg. American justices had shown themselves to be capable of harshness when judging another people guilty of ghettoizing and destroying an ethnic group. Their failure to take an equally strong position when reviewing the sins of their own countrymen — whose institutions, according to the Court itself, damaged "the hearts and minds" of Negro children "in a way unlikely ever to be undone" — will long remain as a blot on the record of American jurisprudence.

Unfortunately, however, the Court's treatment of public school desegregation was only the beginning of a pattern of conduct. Its handling of subsequent race cases indicates that it remains the Supreme Court of white America.

After its 1955 decision requiring "all deliberate speed," the Court did enter a series of decrees which slowly struck down segregation in public transportation and in public facilities and recreational areas. These decisions, however, were directed only at overt discriminatory practices in the Southern and border states.

[Mr. Steel then reviews the refusal of the Supreme Court to hear any of several Northern school cases raising the "de facto" issue during the 1960s. He suggests further that support for civil rights protests was quite limited — see excerpt printed infra page 394 — and is critical of the Court's failure to provide civil rights groups with relief against state court injunctions as in Cameron v. Johnson, printed infra page 310, and NAACP v. Overstreet, printed infra page 320.]

These decisional changes were achieved by an extremely simple expedient. The majority of the Supreme Court justices began to accept the protestations of good faith made by racist public officials, where only a few years earlier the majority had evinced a willingness to look beyond self-serving statements to ascertain the facts. Indeed, the Court has had dissenters who have vainly and loudly protested the majority's new anti-Negro attitude in the realization that such decisions mean a surrender to racists.

As the Court began to rule against Negroes seeking to reverse state convictions, it also decided that civil rights advocates could not seek relief from oppressive state prosecutions by removing their cases to the Federal courts; the justices were willing to assume the impartiality of courts which were strongholds of segregationists. By narrowing Federal jurisdiction, the Court achieved substantially the same effect as its predecessors did when they decided in the 19th century that laws intended to protect Negroes were unconstitutional.

Similarly, after developing rules that Negroes could not be excluded from juries, the Court negated much of its progress. In Swain v. Alabama, it upheld the right of Southern prosecutors to challenge and remove all Negroes while selecting a jury. The Court overlooked the fact that a Negro had never sat on a civil or criminal jury in the county in question and accepted at face value the prosecutor's declaration that he would allow Negroes to serve under certain circumstances.

Supporters of the Court's civil rights record can point only to the field of housing when seeking a pattern of pro-civil rights decisions, and the pattern fades when viewed critically. Since it struck down the judicial enforcement of restrictive covenants in land deeds in 1947, the Supreme Court has ruled favorably in California's Proposition 14 case and has upheld an 1866 law as a general prohibition against housing discrimination based upon race. The Proposition 14 case, decided in 1967, involved an amendment to the California Constitution which would have prohibited all state and local fair-housing laws and ordinances. The Court ruled this amendment unconstitutional. When, in the spring of this year, the Court upheld the 1866 law, it gave Negroes the right to sue individuals who refused to sell or rent property to them because of their race. Significantly, this ruling came after Congress had passed a fair-housing act. Once again, therefore, the Supreme Court, contrary to popular belief, was not the ground-breaker in racial reform. Moreover, neither the Proposition 14 case nor the endorsement of the 1866 law will significantly weaken ghetto walls. Most black Americans, having low incomes, will not be able to utilize these rulings, just as they were not able to profit much from the 1947 restrictive-covenant decision.

In 1967, the Supreme Court could have played a significant role in attacking ghetto housing. The case before it was Green Street Association v. Daley. The petitioners, Negro residents and a neighborhood association, complained that public officials in Chicago were using urban-renewal funds to create "a no-Negro buffer zone" around a white shopping center. In essence, the complaint alleged that the urban-renewal program, financed with public funds, was actually a program for Negro removal. The petitioners also said that the city was relocating Negroes only in ghetto areas, thus perpetuating housing segregation.

The complaint was dismissed by a Federal district court in Chicago and the decision affirmed by the circuit court. The Supreme Court, which could have ruled that these facts, if proved, would entitle the petitioners to relief under the 14th Amendment, declined to review the case. Again this year, when Negroes charged that highway construction in Nashville was being used to discriminate against the black community, the Supreme Court declined to review adverse lower-court decisions.

Favorable action in either of these cases would have done far more to aid the ordinary black man than all the other housing cases put together. For today, the effect of Government — local, state and Federal — on housing is far greater than that of individuals.

Those in the legal profession who defend the Court's record do so on the ground that the traditional relationship between the states and the Federal Government must be preserved. According to this theory, the liberties of all Americans are better preserved if the Federal Government is strictly limited in its right to oversee the affairs of the states; the restrictions, the theory says, prevent the creation of a monolithic centralized police state. According to these thinkers, an "activist" Supreme Court would be reliant on Federal power to enforce its writ in the states, thereby tipping an already precarious balance.

But what is this argument really worth? If basic civil rights can be denied on a systematic basis to any definable segment of the population, that segment is living in a police state. The justification of the Court's record presumes that constitutionally guaranteed freedoms should be analyzed from the point of view of the white American majority.

In effect, the argument is based on the premise that any threat, real or imagined, to the civil liberties of whites should be forestalled, even at the price of denying to black men the rights which may be hypothetically threatened by Federal intervention. For example, whites are afraid that *their* public school systems would be damaged by integration because black children attending segregated black schools perform at a lower academic level. Though the lower performance by Negroes has been brought about by the white community's treatment of Negroes as inferiors, integration has been delayed to save the white public schools at the further expense of black children.

Another argument in favor of judicial nonintervention is based upon the premise that in a democracy the people, through their legislatures, have the primary responsibility to redress grievances. This belief is also comforting only to the majority that completely controls the legislative process. . . .

In fields other than race relations, the Court has, to a much greater extent, acted without regard for popular opinion. Consider, for example, Supreme Court rulings in the fields of reapportionment, separation of church from state, obscenity, criminal law and the protection of Communists or others with unpopular political beliefs. In these areas, the Court has taken an active role in bringing about needed reforms. By and large, decisions in these fields have not been based upon a compromise between constitutional concepts and society's desire to preserve established institutions.

The reapportionment decisions show the differences in the handling of racial and nonracial cases. In cases involving only the one-man, one-vote principle applied to a political entity, the Court was not interested in the reasoning behind a challenged apportionment plan. It was enough that the power of some voters at the polls was diminished. But when Negroes began to challenge the use of gerrymandered districts or at-large elections to reduce the power of their votes, the Supreme Court backed away. For Negroes, it soon became clear, proof of the dilution of their votes was not sufficient; they also had to prove the subjective intent of legislators to limit their voting power.

A review of decisions affecting religion, obscenity and political belief also illustrates the differences between racial and nonracial cases. In first ruling that public-school authorities could not require the recitation of prayers in school and then broadening the scope of this ruling, the Court ignored massive outcries that it was ordaining a godless society. The pious — and America is a church-going country — were equally upset by a rash of decisions which effectively throttled the censor's authority to control what we read and see. Nor did the Court heed pleas that the necessity for the maintenance of law and order required the electronic invasion of homes and the use of confessions obtained before an accused could consult with a lawyer. Red-baiting was equally ineffective when the Court was faced with statutes and administrative fiats ostensibly designed to protect the United States against internal subversion. Supreme Court decisions in these fields demonstrate that public opinion need not influence the judicial interpretation of constitutional rights.

The Court has not been so bold in race relations. Since the Civil War, it has allowed itself to be swayed by the prejudices and mores of whites and, more recently, by their fears that equality for Negroes would adversely affect them. In the 19th century, an activist Supreme Court helped the Southern states defeat Congress's plan to rid this country of all the remnants of slavery. In recent years, a cautious Supreme Court has waltzed in time to the music of the white majority — one step forward, one step backward and sidestep, sidestep.

Each justice obviously has some effect on the direction of the Court's dance, so the power struggle over the appointment of a new Chief Justice cannot be entirely dismissed. However, the pattern of decisions in the field of civil rights indicates that it is not the thinking of individual justices, but the philosophy of the entire Court on civil rights that must be reoriented if the Court is to move out of the shadow of the 19th century.

Racial equality, of course, is dependent upon more than just Court decisions. Severe readjustments in political power and a redistribution of wealth must take place in order to avert catastrophic racial conflict. When the forces of reform are reduced to fighting for one judicial appointment to a Court that has inadequately interpreted the constitutional mandate of equality, it is evident that the advocates of the status quo are achieving their purpose no matter what the outcome of the power struggle.

DAYNARD, TEST CASE LITIGATION AS A SOURCE OF SIGNIFICANT SOCIAL CHANGE
18 Catholic Lawyer 37, 38 (1972)

The fact that a test case has produced a favorable judicial decision does not mean that the social change which the plaintiff or his attorney hoped thereby to achieve has in fact ensued. The "right to treatment" of a patient committed to a mental hospital, announced by Judge Bazelon in Rouse v. Cameron [373 F.2d 451 (D.C. Cir. 1966)], may well be a right without a remedy due to the failure of Congress to fund the hospital adequately, the lack of sufficient trained personnel or training facilities to properly staff mental hospitals, and the general inadequacy of treatment techniques. [The "remedy" of release, which is theoretically available in case of continuing failure to receive treatment, might be sufficient to coerce additional funding from Congress, but in many cases funding alone would not permit treatment.] The attempt which culminated in Shapiro v. Thompson [394 U.S. 618 (1969)], to guarantee subsistence welfare payments to migrants by striking down state welfare residency requirements may unintentionally have resulted in a lowering of the percentage of need which the previously most generous states are willing to pay. There are equally strong reasons to doubt that the Warren Court's cases which on paper give the accused a plethora of rights have in fact done much more than incite policemen to perjury and lower court judges to disingenuous decisions. [See Silverglate, Book Review, 84 Harv. L. Rev. 1748 (1971).] On the other hand, some cases, such as Brown v. Board of Education [347 U.S. 483 (1954)], may, by focusing public opinion on a social problem of which the case at bar is only a partial reflection, and by providing some impetus towards the solution of this broader problem make a contribution towards a social movement which cannot be measured by the specific changes ordered by the decision. Thus, any evaluation of how much change in social, economic, or political patterns has in fact resulted from even "successful" test case litigation would have to be based on a close empirical analysis, requiring extensive, imaginative, and costly data collection, not only of the extent to which the prescribed procedures have been implemented but also of other social changes, extrinsic to the prescribed procedures and to some extent unspecifiable in advance, which may dampen (or occasionally amplify) their effect.

LEMELLE IN R. BURKEY, RACIAL DISCRIMINATION AND PUBLIC POLICY IN THE UNITED STATES *38 (1971)*

. . . [O]ne may seriously question whether a society such as that of the United States is really capable of legislating and enforcing effective public policy to combat racial discrimination. Perhaps the most effective function of such legislation might be simply providing an aura of legitimacy for more direct political action to combat racial discrimination — particularly political action by the victims of the racial discrimination. . . . Whether a society in which racism has been internalized and institutionalized to the point of being an essential and inherently functioning component of that society — a culture from whose inception racial discrimination has been a regulative force for maintaining stability and growth and for maximizing other cultural values — whether such a society *of itself* can even legislate (let alone enforce) public policy to combat racial discrimination is most doubtful. The history of man offers no evidence of any society consciously legislating itself out of existence. To the contrary, radical cultural changes have occurred only after the demise of those societies stubbornly adhering to old values and their institutional representations. . . . A racist culture — can move to eradicate or make racism ineffective only when racism itself becomes a serious threat to the culture and its bearers. United States society, therefore, can legislate and enforce public policy to combat racial discrimination only when continued racial discrimination begins to be more a serious threat to the existing American culture than the useful regulator it has been.

NOTES

1. While Lewis Steel criticized the Warren Court for not going any further in support of black rights than white interests required, the Court has been severely attacked by a whole host of legal scholars who feel that many decisions went too far down an "egalitarian" road that should have been traversed — if at all — by the legislative branch. See A. Bickel, The Supreme Court and the Idea of Progress (1970); A. Bickel, The Least Dangerous Branch: The Supreme Court at the Bar of Politics, 247, 254 (1962); Wechsler, Toward Neutral Principles of Constitutional Law, 73 Harv. L. Rev. 1 (1959). Court of Appeals Judge J. Skelly Wright suggests that the Court's conservative critics are manifesting less an intellectual commitment to neutral principles of decision making than a general opposition to the Court's efforts to give recognition to the legitimate claims of powerless people. Wright, Professor Bickel, The Scholarly Tradition and the Supreme Court, 84 Harv. L. Rev. 769 (1971).

2. The limited effectiveness of test case litigation is well known, but Dr. Tilden W. LeMelle suggests that major social reform in the racial area is unlikely and may be impossible. Other writings support his position:

a. There is a pronounced reluctance to deal seriously with any major problems in this society, and when a problem persists (as it tends to do) for more than a few days,

> those who call attention to its continued existence are viewed as "going too far" and "causing the pendulum to swing the other way." We can make war on poverty, but shrink from the extensive readjustments required to stop breeding it. Once a law is passed, the commission set up, a study made, a report written, the problem is expected to have been "wiped out" or "mopped up." . . . Our approach to social problems is to decrease their visibility: out of sight, out of mind. (P. Slater, The Pursuit of Loneliness 13, 15 (1970).)

b. Why indeed is social neglect, as measured by such basic needs as housing, poverty, public health and prison reform, greater in the world's wealthiest nation than in countries like Norway, Sweden, Denmark, England, Canada? One cause is racial heterogeneity, which intensifies the problem of neglect in other societies where it exists.

> But there is no parallel to the corrosive and pervasive role played by race in the problem of social neglect in the United States. It is the obvious fact that the persons who suffer most from the kinds of neglect [mentioned above] are disproportionately

Negro. This merging of the racial issue with that of neglect serves as a rationalization for the policies of inaction that have characterized so much of the American response to need. Programs to improve slums are seen by many as programs to "subsidize" Negroes; proposals to improve conditions of prisons are seen as measures to coddle black criminals; and so on. In such cases, the fear and resentment of the Negro takes precedence over the social problem itself. The result, unfortunately, is that the entire society suffers from the results of a failure to correct social evils whose ill effects refuse to obey the rules of segregation. (Heilbroner, The Roots of Social Neglect in the United States, in Is Law Dead? 288, 296 (E. Rostow, ed. 1971).)

c. Perhaps as a consequence of all the above factors, there appears to be a pattern of predictable but hard-to-discern components which operate whenever the society or its courts are called on to solve a racial problem. They are:

1. An abiding, albeit seldom expressed and often unconscious, belief that blacks as a group are inferior to whites.
2. A predisposition to resolve conflicts involving black injustices and the needs of the white majority in a manner that protects and promotes the latter, even if it perpetuates the former.
3. Realization (in varying degrees) of the basic inconsistency between American ideals and the status to which blacks have been relegated on the basis of race.
4. An inability to recognize that actions seemingly taken to correct racial injustices are often in fact based on the promotion or preservation of white interests. (Bell, School Litigation Strategies for the 1970's: New Phases in the Continuing Quest for Quality Schools, 1970 Wis. L. Rev. 257, 270.)

See also Clark, Lawyer in the Civil Rights Movement — Catalytic Agent or Counter-Revolutionary? 19 Kan. L. Rev. 459 (1971).

QUESTIONS

1. In studying the problems of discrimination in voting, education, employment, etc., is it possible to discern these issues at work, albeit on a subliminal level, in judicial and legislative decisions that affect racial relationships?

2. Can the components listed above be reduced to a useful (if somewhat simplistic and sardonic) legal formula for predicting the resolution of social issues in the racial field?

White Racism v. Justice = White Racism
White Racism v. White Self-Interest = Justice

Self-interest has been described as

> *the most basic and important force underlying white policy and action vis-à-vis blacks. Such action more often than not serves the interests of the actors or is accounted for by incorrect perception of objective interest. Values and morals (i.e., the American creed) do under certain conditions prompt and guide the action, but they appear to be powerless to motivate any large segment of whites to action in*

unison against their perceived interests. (Glenn, The Role of White Resistance and Facilitation in the Negro Struggle for Equality, in Power and the Black Community 414 (S. Fisher, ed. 1970).)

3. An example of Mr. Glenn's point is the nation's shift in attitude toward blacks during wartime crisis, as described in Chapter Eight infra page 397. Note also the changed attitudes of store, restaurant and hotel owners when it became apparent, in those areas where major sit-in campaigns were waged, that it would be economically better to serve than to segregate blacks. (See, generally, Chapter Seven.) Is this a further example of the self-interest phenomenon at work? Can a sense of fair play or guilt be a component of self-interest?

4. Can other contemporary examples of similar occurrences be cited? Is it either helpful or accurate to conclude that the law tends to perceive and respond to racial issues so that relief is provided for racial injustices less because it is deserved than because such relief will either affirmatively benefit, or not seriously harm, white interests seen as important?

NOTE

The interplay of racism and self-interest is definitively illustrated in a biography of Paul Cuffe, the eighteenth-century shipowner who became the first wealthy black man in this country. The author, Sheldon H. Harris, relates an experience that illustrates the point. Cuffe, who was largely self-educated, was distressed that there were no school facilities in Westport, Massachusetts. Determined that his seven children should receive formal education, he called his neighbors together, and urged that they pool resources to provide a school. But his fellow townsmen refused to go along with the plan.

Some expressed reservations about the necessity for a school, and others declared their firm opposition to the proposed undertaking because of the potential costs involved. The real reason for their opposition was never expressed, but no doubt everyone was cognizant of its presence. In the 1790's the barriers of racial prejudice in the United States were too great to overcome even for the simple farmers of Westport, Massachusetts. They were as yet unprepared for a black man to take the lead in pointing out the need for civic improvements. And they were equally unprepared, no doubt, to offer the children of the community a nonsegregated educational experience.

Undeterred by this rebuff Cuffe resolutely and courageously decided to go ahead on his own. Setting aside some land on his own farm, and using his own funds, he proceeded to have a schoolhouse constructed. He then offered the people of Westport the free use of the school. Their Yankee penury overcoming their racism, and recognizing a good bargain when it came along, Westporters accepted the black man's generous proposal with alacrity. Paul Cuffe's school, erected in 1797, remained the town's sole educational institution for many years. It was, of course, one of the first integrated schools established in the United States. (S. Harris, Paul Cuffe: Black American and the African Return 30-31 (1972).)

C. CIVIL DISOBEDIENCE: AN ALTERNATIVE TO OR CATALYST FOR LEGAL CHANGE?

A discussion of the efficacy of law in eradicating manifest racism in the society leads inevitably to a discussion of civil disobedience. To what extent may it be resorted to? Some people sincerely believe that only through the intentional violation of an existing law or laws can they satisfy the demands of conscience to resist basic injustice, and at the same time dramatize the wrongfulness of existing law so as to attract public attention and enlist others to support change.

FRIED, MORAL CAUSATION
77 Harv. L. Rev. 1258, 1268-1269 (1964)

Take the case of those civil rights demonstrations which involve civil disobedience. In such cases the demonstrator — unlike the tax evader — does not depend for any benefits on the continued observance by others of the precise law he is violating. On the contrary, the demonstrator would count it a success if all alike disregarded the law of which he complains. But at another level of generality he must face the same charge as confronts the tax evader: that he seeks to benefit from an institution which depends on the sacrifices of others without contributing a like sacrifice. Only here the institution and the sacrifice are, respectively, the legal system as a whole and the readiness of individuals within that system to abide by the principle of "institutional settlement," that is, the readiness of each to forgo pressing his claim — even when he considers his claims justified — when by some fair procedure the issue has been determined against him. The demonstrators in violating this principle run the risk that if they are successful in procuring a change in the law those persons who believe that the old situation was justified and that the new unjustifiably prejudices their interests will feel entitled to resist the "remedial" legislation. And this feeling would not be wholly unwarranted, as the demonstrators' unwillingness to abide by the principle of institutional settlement does weaken their moral claim on the fidelity of others to that principle. The demonstrator's predicament is a very practical one. He recognizes the value of accepting the principle of institutional settlement and wishes to preserve the existing level of acceptance for the laws, which he hopes will soon include his proposed reforms. And yet without resorting to civil disobedience he believes that he can never accomplish these reforms.

In this quandary he may well see the good sense of a solution as old as Socrates' refusal to flee Athens in the Crito: to do what he believes necessary but stand ready to pay the penalty prescribed for that course of conduct. This gambit succeeds in making the most of the demonstrator's position: in showing his readiness to suffer the penalty for disobedience he is affirming the value of law in general, while at the same time disobeying it. His fidelity to law is, to be sure, not unqualified, as it would be if he obeyed the primary duty imposed, so that to a like extent he loses his claim on his opponents to obey his arrangements if he succeeds. But his willingness to pay the penalty calls attention to another aspect of his position which the demonstrator wishes to emphasize: that his complaint against the state of the law is based not simply on the ground that it is disadvantageous but that it is wrong. The demonstrator's willingness to pay the penalty shows that his protest does not arise from a mere calculation of advantages. Thus he can afford the implication that others may disobey his laws if they like him are willing to pay, for it is part of his position that his opponents' position has less (or no) moral force behind it, so that his opponents would be unwilling to support that position at the same cost that he, the demonstrator, gladly pays. This is a gamble, to be sure, but civil disobedience is a risky, maybe a desperate course.

KING, LETTER FROM BIRMINGHAM CITY JAIL
*Why We Can't Wait 84-86 (1963)**

You express a great deal of anxiety over our willingness to break laws. This is certainly a legitimate concern. Since we so diligently urge people to obey the Supreme Court's decision of 1954 outlawing segregation in the public schools, it is rather strange and paradoxical to find us consciously breaking laws. One may well ask, "How can you advocate breaking some laws and obeying others?" The answer is found in the fact that there are two types of laws: There are *just* laws and there are *unjust* laws. I would be the first to advocate obeying just laws. One has not only a legal but moral responsibility to obey just laws. Conversely, one has a moral responsibility to disobey unjust laws. I would agree with Saint Augustine that "An unjust law is no law at all."

Now what is the difference between the two? How does one determine when a law is just or unjust? A just law is a man-made code that squares with the moral law or the law of God. An unjust law is a code that is out of harmony with the moral law. To put it in the terms of Saint Thomas Aquinas, an unjust law is a human law that is not rooted in eternal and natural laws. Any law that uplifts human personality is just. Any law that degrades human personality is unjust. All segregation statutes are unjust because segregation distorts the soul and damages the personality. It gives the segregator a false sense of superiority and the segregated a false sense of inferiority. To use the words of Martin Buber, the great Jewish philosopher, segregation substitutes an "I-it" relationship for the "I-thou" relationship, and ends up relegating persons to the status of things. So segregation is not only politically, economically, and sociologically unsound, but it is morally wrong and sinful. Paul Tillich has said that sin is separation. Isn't segregation an existential expression of man's tragic separation, an expression of his awful estrangement, his terrible sinfulness? So I can urge men to obey the 1954 decision of the Supreme Court because it is morally right, and I can urge them to disobey segregation ordinances because they are morally wrong.

Let us turn to a more concrete example of just and unjust laws. An unjust law is a code that a majority inflicts on a minority that is not binding on itself. This is *difference* made legal. On the other hand a just law is a code that a majority compels a minority to follow that it is willing to follow itself. This is *sameness* made legal.

Let me give another explanation. An unjust law is a code inflicted upon a minority which that minority had no part in enacting or creating because they did not have the unhampered right to vote. Who can say the legislature of Alabama which set up the segregation laws was democratically elected? Throughout the state of Alabama all types of conniving methods are used to prevent Negroes from becoming registered voters and there are some counties without a single Negro registered to vote despite the fact that the Negro constitutes a majority of the population. Can any law set up in such a state be considered democratically structured?

These are just a few examples of unjust and just laws. There are some instances when a law is just on its face but unjust in its application. For instance, I was arrested Friday on a charge of parading without a permit. Now there is nothing wrong with an ordinance which requires a permit for a parade, but when the ordinance is used to preserve segregation and to deny citizens the First Amendment privilege of peaceful assembly and peaceful protest, then it becomes unjust.

I hope you can see the distinction I am trying to point out. In no sense do I advocate evading or defying the law as the rabid segregationist would do. This would lead to anarchy. One who breaks an unjust law must do it *openly, lovingly* (not hatefully as the white mothers did in New Orleans when they were seen on television screaming "nigger, nigger, nigger") and with a willingness to accept the penalty. I submit that an individual who breaks a law that conscience tells him is unjust, and willingly accepts the penalty by staying in jail to arouse the conscience of the community over its injustice, is in reality expressing the very highest respect for law.

NOTES

1. Neither excerpt raises the issue of armed violence as a direct action tactic, and of course resort to shooting, bombing and even threats of serious harm to persons or property presents very different moral and political issues than either disobedience or disruption. Some blacks do advocate armed violence and some few have used it as a planned strategy against those who, they argue, have not hesitated to use force and violence against blacks. Others raise moral and legal barriers in opposition to armed violence. But considering the magnitude of the provocations, such abstinence raises the question whether an excess of morality or a deficiency of courage better explains the failure of blacks to resort to armed force more frequently. The prestigious

black leader James Weldon Johnson added another dimension to the debate by urging blacks to refrain from armed violence on pragmatic grounds. Writing in 1934, he said that, while violence in self-defense is almost an obligation, in other situations:

> We must condemn physical force and banish it from our minds. But I do not condemn it on any moral or pacific grounds. The resort to force remains and will doubtless always remain the rightful recourse of oppressed peoples. Our own country was established upon that right. I condemn physical force because I know that in our case it would be futile. . . . We would be justified in taking up arms or anything we could lay hands on and fighting for the common rights we are entitled to and denied, if we had a chance to win. But I know and we all know there is not a chance. (J. Johnson, Negro Americans — What Now? 6-7 (1934).)

2. While civil disobedience and disruptive demonstrations are far less serious than violence, it is doubtful that the society and the courts are willing even to acknowledge a difference between the two, much less a justification for either. Former Justice Abe Fortas has expressed his view that violence or a breach of the public order prohibited by law can never be condoned, though the demonstrator be motivated by the highest moral principles, passionately inspired, and proven right in the eyes of history, morality or philosophy. Fortas concedes that:

> The Negroes in Detroit and Newark and Washington and Chicago who rioted, pillaged, and burned may have generations of provocation. They may have incontestable justification. They may have been pushed beyond endurance. In the riots following the assassination of Martin Luther King, Jr., the Negroes may have been understandably inflamed by the murder of their leading advocate of non-violence. But that provides no escape from the consequences of their conduct. (A. Fortas, Concerning Dissent and Civil Disobedience 32-33 (1968).)

3. Long before Justice Fortas published his views, blacks who urged violence against whites for any reason faced strong condemnation. In 1829, David Walker, a proprietor of a Boston secondhand clothing store, published his famous "Appeal" to American blacks, detailing the prejudices of whites in very plain terms and urging slaves to kill their masters. The book created great consternation throughout the South. Walker died the following year, the victim, many believed, of foul play. B. Brawley, A Social History of the American Negro 155-159 (1921).

In the early 1960s an NAACP leader in Monroe, North Carolina, Robert Williams, was removed as president of the local NAACP branch after national criticism of a statement in which he urged blacks to use force to protect themselves. Williams subsequently left the country to avoid a kidnapping charge arising out of a local racial disturbance. R. Williams, Negroes With Guns (1962). The Black Panthers and other revolutionary black groups who have appeared to advocate violence also charge continuing harassment and persecution at the hands of law enforcement officials.

QUESTIONS

1. Justice Fortas would apply stern standards to policemen who use unjustified violence as well as to rioters, but he concedes, before going on to reemphasize the importance of adherence to the law, "It is a deplorable truth that because they are officers of the state they frequently escape the penalty for their lawlessness." Fortas, id. at 33. Is it understandable that black victims of police violence are unable to gloss over the law's defects as facilely as Justice Fortas?

2. From a moral standpoint, is it fair to apply the limitations on justifiable civil disobedience suggested by Professor Fried to blacks, most of whom are literally the victims of the social system rather than either beneficiaries of or participants in it? If, of course, under Fried's notions, based on concern for the fidelity of the legal order, one sees the willingness to accept punishment as a tactical symbolic act rather than an obligation (which must be fulfilled regardless), then there are no limits, only a balancing of respected values as a standard of behavior. Should it make any difference in the obligation of the black victim that he sees the legal order as otherwise just?

3. Assuming that Steel is correct in his assessment of the benefits to white society that resulted from the Brown decision, the question remains: What factors led the Court to side with the minority "anti-segregation" view (if only in a symbolic way), when the hostile majority response was so predictable? Are there, as suggested in J. Peltason, Federal Courts in the Political Process (1965), "legal interests" consisting of special values, principles, ways of thinking and patterns of behavior evidenced in the judicial role, and articulated in the concept that some laws and principles (particularly free speech and equal protection, which can't always thrive in majoritarian settings) are beyond the manipulation of interest groups?

4. While not entirely effective, does the judiciary's efforts to maintain isolation, independence and professionalism provide a margin for response — even in the face of popular hostility — to those urging that they or their cause are protected by basic legal concepts or principles? In reading the balance of this book, consider to what extent it is this potential which makes the courts an attractive forum for blacks who, lacking political and economic power, place their hopes on judicial relief, even though relief is uncertain, often denied, when granted is usually inadequate, and when adequate may prove unenforceable.

D. SEPARATION AS AN ALTERNATIVE TO SOCIAL CHANGE

LESTER, THE NECESSITY FOR SEPARATION
*Ebony 166-169 (Aug. 1970)**

An ethnic or religious minority lives at the mercy of the majority which defines and governs the entire society. The minority is even dependent upon

* Reprinted by permission of Ebony and Johnson Publications.

the majority for its physical existence, because, at any juncture in history, the majority can make the minority the scapegoat for whatever problems the society may be confronting and attempt to eradicate it. This happened to the Jews and Gypsies of Europe for many centuries and it is happening today to the Vietnamese minority in Cambodia.

Having absolutely no power and being totally dependent on the goodwill of the majority, the minority can seek its survival in one of three ways: 1) try to assimilate by adopting the customs, mores, culture, values, etc., of the majority, as the European immigrant groups to America did successfully, and as blacks have tried to do; 2) try to be as unobtrusive and separate as possible, while remaining a part of and being governed by the political and economic apparatus of the majority, as the Chinese have done in America and Southeast Asia, and as the Indians have done in Africa; or, 3) separate geographically from the majority and become an independent political and economic unit, as in the case of Pakistan, a Moslem state, and Israel, a Jewish one.

Of these three courses, blacks in America have put the most effort into the first — assimilation or integration. Having been brought to America as slaves, having deliberately and consciously been cut off from their historical roots in Africa, the descendants of these Africans had no nation on earth which they could call their own. Though aware that they had come from Africa, African identity was (and to a great degree still is) based on tribe, not race or nation. The blacks of America had been successfully cut off from knowledge of their tribal origins. In fact, they came to constitute a new tribe — the Afro-American — but it was a tribe without land of its own. When the legal status of blacks was changed from slave to "free" people, they had little choice but to try and make America their country. Too, many of them, like Frederick Douglass, felt that this was the proper political course, because they had been indispensable in building America; they had defended it in every war; they had paid taxes. They had fulfilled all of the responsibilities of citizenship, but had not been accorded any of the concomitant privileges. However, to receive those privileges to which they were entitled, they had to convince the white majority that they were "worthy" of being accepted on the terms and conditions laid down by the white majority. Therefore, they adopted the cultural standards of the white majority and straight hair became "good" hair; a light complexion became the standard for beauty; Western literature, music and art became representative of "culture"; and, kinky hair, dark skin, black speech and jazz were to be avoided and eschewed as attributes which would prevent the race from being accepted by the white majority.

The acceptance of the cultural standards of the white majority, however, meant a denial of selfhood for the black minority. Perhaps this would not have mattered if the white majority had assimilated the black minority. It did not, however. No matter how much blacks emulated whites, their persecution as members of a racial minority continued. . . .

Blacks, however, persisted, and a significant number did become "acceptable." Though not accepted by the majority of whites, their existence became tolerable as a class of whites called "liberals" began to wield some power and influence in American political affairs. (The role of white liberals in the founding and successes of the NAACP was quite profound.) By the second decade of the 20th century, a black middle class became evident and it slowly flourished. Organizations like the NAACP and the Urban League were organized to fight the legal barriers of economic and political equality. Their efforts were primarily for the benefit of the new black middle class and these efforts were increasingly successful. More education and economic opportunities became available to blacks, opportunities of which the black middle class could take advantage and to which the lower class could aspire. The acquisition of a better job, a college education, a beautiful home and a Cadillac, however, did not significantly change the quality of relations between blacks and whites. The NAACP and the Urban League made one important miscalculation: they assumed that legislation insuring political and economic equality would also insure basic human respect. But for any law to be effective, it must be adhered to by the majority. And that is particularly true of any law passed for the benefit of a persecuted minority. That law can only work if the majority wants it to, or if the penalties for breaking the law are so severe that it is wiser to observe it than break it. But the penalties for breaking laws designed to insure the rights of the black minority were never severe and the enforcement of the law was never rigorous. The white landlord or real estate agent refusing to rent or sell to blacks; the white employer refusing to hire a black; the white employer who refuses to promote a black employee could not be affected by the law unless they believed in obedience to the law, no matter its content. Whatever benefit blacks derived from the law was due to this more than it was to any basic changes in the attitude of the white majority toward the black minority. It is possible to legislate behavior; however, behavior is determined by attitude and it is not possible to legislate attitudes. It was the attitude of the white majority toward the black minority which needed to be changed, an attitude which suffocated blacks even when whites thought their behavior toward blacks was unimpeachable, even when whites obeyed the law. The laws and the judicial decisions did not begin to deal with the reality of the every minute, every day persecution of the black minority by the white majority.

That attitude of the white majority toward the black minority came to be known as racism, an attitude which conferred the status of nonexistence on the black minority, of being "niggers." It is an attitude which is as much a part of America's beginning as the rhetoric of democracy, for it was racism-in-action which made the European settlers think that they had the right to appropriate for themselves an entire country which was occupied by a people — the Indian. It was racism-in-action which made Europeans think that they had the right to perform the largest human transplant in history taking tens of millions of people from the continent of Africa and distributing them throughout the Western hemisphere. And, it is racism-in-action which later led the United States to expropriate the natural resources of Asia, Africa and Latin America. It was this racism which blacks of all economic classes confronted each and every day of their lives. And, it was this racism which would have to be eradicated if blacks were ever to live and look upon themselves as human beings.

In the mid-60s, when blacks defined for themselves what the problem was, integration as a solution to that problem was shown to be unrealistic. . . .

The black consciousness movement of today is an effort toward the regaining of self. Many words and phrases are now being used to articulate this struggle to reclaim the black identity: black pride, black manhood, dignity, self-respect. The basic ingredient in the life of humanity is the need for every human being to respect himself and be respected by others. (This assumes, of course, that the basic physical necessities are being provided.) Blacks have made the Cadillac division of General Motors famous in their efforts "to be somebody." But a Cadillac can only give the illusion of being a complete human being and no matter how many Cadillacs a black person may have sitting in the garage, it is not possible for him to be a human being in white America. The social, political, cutural and economic institutions of white America are designed to tell whites that they are superior and to tell blacks that they are inferior. Either those institutions (and the attitudes which created them) must be changed or blacks must remove themselves from them and create their own social, political, cultural and economic institutions which will give them the opportunity to live their lives feeling that they are, indeed, "somebody."

There are those who contend that the institutions of America can be significantly changed. And, if they can be, it is maintained that integration then becomes a viable solution for blacks. That is debatable on both counts. For there to be a revolution in America, there has to be an effective white revolutionary force. At present, there is none, though there is much revolutionary rhetoric coming from some white youth. Unfortunately, white youth cannot make a revolution by themselves and the rest of white America is moving toward fascism as fast as Nixon and Agnew can get it there. If blacks wait for radical whites to get themselves together so that there can be a revolution, we may just end up as nothing more than a memory in world history. . . . Also, even if there were a successful revolution, blacks have no assurance that racism will not be as much a part of the new society as it was of the old one. . . .

[T]he only viable alternative is for blacks to separate themselves from this insanity called the United States of America. The very thought, however, frightens many blacks and simply makes others laugh. Separatism sounds totally unrealistic and unworkable. If the government would not give blacks equality, then why would it give them land for a separate nation? There is one reason: America will not survive otherwise. Racial antagonisms are higher now than they have ever been in American history. Blacks are arming themselves; whites are arming themselves. Racial war seems inevitable. (There is always the possibility that white America is so crazy that it would rather let itself be destroyed than to cede blacks land for a nation.) However, if it became clear that the desire for a separate nation was the will of a majority of blacks, whites would support it, simply because the white majority has never desired integration and would prefer to be rid of all blacks, one way or the other. If the white majority knew that it could be rid of "niggers" once and for all, we would have a nation almost before we'd know what to do with it.

There are precedents within contemporary history for such a nation. The nation of Pakistan was formed when the persecution of the Moslem minority of India by the Hindu majority became so severe that it was doubtful if the country would be able to function. The nation of Israel was organized by the persecuted Jewish minority of Europe. We should not, however, take either Pakistan or Israel as a model. Much injustice and suffering went into the formation of those nations; however, their existence gives a precedent in international law for the partitioning of the United States. Too, the United States has never shown a reluctance to support partitioning of other countries when it has been in its interest. Korea, Vietnam and Germany have all been partitioned in the past 25 years with the support and effort of the United States.

The other factor which makes black separatism much more than a fantasy at this time is that the separatist movement here is part of a world-wide separatist movement. There are strong separatist movements in Canada, Belgium and Spain, where ethnic and national minorities are fighting, politically and sometimes, militarily, to become autonomous political units. In Africa, there is a separatist movement in Chad, where the Arab minority is fighting the black majority which governs, and there is a separatist movement in Somalia, where the black minority is fighting the ruling Arab majority. Separatism is merely the logical and rational response of a minority to the death-in-life status conferred on it by a majority. Why should black people allow themselves to be subjected to white America any longer? We have never been regarded as human beings by the white majority. . . . There is no evidence that we ever will be. Therefore, it is impossible for us to live as human beings as long as we are a part of white America. . . .

It is indeed time for that "national dialogue" to begin. And, it is past time that we rid ourselves of our illusions. Yet, it would be nice if brotherhood were something more than a word in the dictionary. But it isn't. Yes, it would be nice if blacks and whites could live together in peace and harmony. But they can't (and how many more blacks have to be murdered for us to realize that?). For too long, black people have been high off the American dream. The American dream is a bad trip of infinitely terrifying proportions for anybody, black or white, who looks at it with undistorted vision. The only assurance which black people have of ever living on this earth and being regarded as human beings is in a nation of their own. If you must get high, then, it's time to get high on some black dreams.

However, it must not be thought that a black nation will automatically solve all problems. Quite the contrary. It will create its own new ones. There will be those blacks who will come to the new nation for the sole purpose of becoming the millionaires they couldn't become in America. Thus, the exact nature of the political and economic institutions of the black nation have to be determined and that will not be easy. The nature of the relations between the black nation and America will also have to be determined, for all blacks will not want to go to the black nation and all whites will not want to leave the territory taken for the black nation. There will be whites who will want to emigrate to the black nation. Will they be allowed? If so, what will be their status? And, there are those blacks, like this writer, who are married to whites and yet are committed to the liberation of their people. Whether or not this is a contradiction is, of course, a matter on which everyone has the strongest of feelings. However, it is a situation which has existed throughout black history and in the formation of the new nation, it will have to be decided if those blacks and their white wives, husbands and mixed children, will be allowed to be citizens of the nation with all the rights and privileges thereunto. Could Richard Wright, Frantz Fanon and the older Frederick Douglass have been citizens of the new nation? It is, on one level, a small question: however, it is a highly emotional issue for blacks and it will have to be confronted and dealt with. Implicit in this, however, is a much larger question: Can a nation in any way abridge the right of an individual to choose whom he or she will call friend, will love, or will marry? Can personal relationships be legislated?

Other tasks confronting the black nation would be the making of international alliances which could ensure the defense of the nation against possible (and likely) aggression from America. With whom and on what basis will those alliances be made? America, of course, will have to pay indemnities to the black nation, just as Germany still pays indemnities to Israel for the genocide of the Jews. The terms of this agreement with the U.S. will have to be worked out together.

Yes, the idea of a black nation seems so far-fetched as to be ludicrous, but if you entertain it for a minute, even as an impossible dream, it should give you a feeling of wholeness and belonging you've never had and can never have as long as blacks have to live in a country where they are despised. If we recognize the realities of what our lives are and will be in America, then, it is clear that a place on earth where we can put our weary feet and call ours is a matter of the highest priority. If we can recognize the life-giving power which this nation will give us, then we must turn our energies and our will to bringing it into existence. The only other course available to us is to stay where we are and continue to be denied our humanity and to continue to hope that white America will change and give us our humanity. White America can't give us our humanity. It has none itself. Our destiny is in our hands. It is not possible to sing the Lord's song in a strange land. That's why we've sung the blues for so long.

We were brought to this land more than three centuries ago. Our homeland was cut off from us and we tried to replace it with the only thing that was available — the United States of America. Let's admit what we already know. The white majority does not have any use for us if we try to be anything other than what it thinks we should be. America is not our home and never will be. We have no country. Only each other. Among ourselves, we have created a sense of nationhood, but without land a nation does not exist. The historical time has come to begin the long and difficult process of getting that land and the even longer and more difficult process of conceiving and building a nation. Yes, it will be difficult, but no more difficult (and perhaps a lot less) than existing at the whims of white America.

For more than 300 years, we tried the impossible — integration. Now, let's be rational.

NOTE ON BLACK EMIGRATION

Mr. Lester's pessimism about the future of blacks in America may come as a shock for some, but his views are neither unique nor new. Not unexpectedly, the initial movement to get blacks out of America and (so it was hoped) back to Africa came from whites. By 1816, the American Colonization Society had become the best known of several movements to colonize blacks. To win support for their goals, these groups generally painted a dreary picture of black degradation and wretchedness. They opposed equal rights for blacks and preached the inherent inferiority of the race.

White abolitionists divided on the issue, but blacks repudiated the Colonization Society and the idea of African colonization, maintaining that America was their country too. There were exceptions. Paul Cuffe, a black shipowner from Massachusetts, was, despite business success, the constant victim of discrimination. He was jailed as a result of his refusal to pay taxes, which he withheld in protest over the denial of the vote and other privileges of citizenship denied blacks. Finally, determining to "emancipate" Africa and provide a haven for those American blacks who wanted to go there, Cuffe led voyages of Blacks to Sierra Leone from 1811 to 1816, at his own expense. (The British had established a colony in Sierra Leone, where they hoped to resettle several hundred destitute and friendless blacks who had come to England after having fought for Great Britain during the Revolutionary War in return for their freedom. See infra page 397.) Cuffe's movement ended with his death in 1817. S. Harris, Paul Cuffe: Black America and the African Return (1972).

By the 1830s, the white colonization movement had placed some 1400 blacks in Liberia. Then it declined. It gained some support during the 1850s, when it was endorsed by the Republican party. Abraham Lincoln included a provision of $100,000 for the voluntary emigration of freedmen to Haiti and Liberia, in an 1862 bill later enacted, emancipating slaves in the District of Columbia. In the same year, he called a group of black leaders to the White House and urged them to support colonization, stating: "Your race suffer greatly, many of them, by living among us, while ours suffer from your presence. In a word we suffer on each side. If this is admitted, it affords a reason why we should be separated." J. Franklin, From Slavery to Freedom 281 (3d ed. 1969).

By the 1850s several black leaders had also become so discouraged with discrimination, exclusion and hostility that they supported the emigration idea, although some favored Central America or Haiti over Africa. The black leader, physician and journalist Martin R. Delany favored emigration. Considerable effort was expended in support of these plans, and early in 1861 a ship with 2000 black emigrants aboard sailed from Philadelphia to Haiti. W. Foster, The Negro People in American History 173 (1954).

Frederick Douglass, who represented the majority of the black leadership, opposed emigration, asserting: "We are Americans. We are not aliens. We are a component part of the nation. . . . We have no disposition to renounce our nationality." L. Litwack, North of Slavery 259 (1961). Those favoring emigration held a convention in 1854, but it won little black support, and even that lessened when the Civil War raised hope in blacks that slavery and inequality might be ended.

Emigration plans were revived around the turn of the century, during the period when blacks were lynched, burned, tortured and disenfranchised in record numbers. Bishop Henry M. Turner, a leader of the movement who looked longingly to Africa as the only possible place of Negro freedom, wrote, "We were born here, raised here, fought, bled and died here, and have a thousand times more right here than hundreds of thousands of those who help to snub, proscribe and persecute us, and that is one of the reasons I almost despise the land of my birth." E. Redkey, Black Exodus 32 (1969). Some blacks did go to Africa during these years. See authorities collected in E. Osofsky, Come Out From Among Them: Negro Migration and Settlement, 1890-1914 (1966).

Then, in the period following World War I, blacks again turned to emigration, this time forming what John Hope Franklin has called the largest black mass movement in American history. Once more despair was the chief motivation, as lynching, antiblack rioting and racial discrimination of every form took their toll of even the most optimistic blacks. In the 1920s Marcus Garvey, a charismatic Jamaican immigrant, founded the Universal Negro Improvement Association, which in a few years raised ten million dollars and attracted at least one half million members. Garvey told blacks that racial prejudice was so much a part of the white man's civilization that it was futile to appeal to his sense of justice and his high-sounding democratic principles. Garvey bought and equipped ships, but in 1925 entered federal prison for two years, following a conviction for mail fraud. He was pardoned in 1927 and deported as an undesirable alien. He tried to revive his movement, but failed. J. Franklin, supra at 489-493. See also E. Fax, Garvey (1972); E. Cronon, Black Moses: The Story of Marcus Garvey and the Universal Negro Improvement Association (1969); M. Garvey, Philosophy and Opinions of Marcus Garvey (A. Garvey ed., 2d ed. 1968).

Of course, while emigration efforts have not met with broad success, blacks have constantly migrated from one portion of the country to another, seeking opportunity and acceptance. The escapes from slavery via the Underground Railroad brought countless blacks to the North, and took many to Canada. After the Civil War, scores of blacks headed west to Kansas, Texas and California. There were major movements from South to North during both world wars — all seeking employment, a better life and racial equality. See A. Bontemps and J. Conroy, Anyplace But Here (1945); G. Groh, The Black Migration (1972).

Black nationalist groups traditionally have made emigration or separation a major goal. Paradoxically, the black-led emigration efforts, including contemporary efforts by Black Muslims and other militant nationalists to establish black communities in this country, have met with the most severe opposition and harassment from whites, particularly law enforcement officials. For example, in November 1969 white residents of St. Clair County, Alabama learned that Black Muslims had purchased two large farms in the area. They organized a "Stop the Muslims" movement, and almost immediately Muslim members were subjected to criminal prosecutions brought on various charges of trespass, "failure to register as a Muslim," acting as agent for an unlicensed foreign corporation and permitting livestock to run at large. A civil suit for $500,000 was also instituted against the Muslims, charging aggravated trespass and infringement upon use of land. The Muslims challenged these actions in a federal suit, and obtained partial relief from a three-judge federal court. Wallace v. Brewer, 315 F. Supp. 431 (M.D. Ala. 1970). The court rejected defendants' contention that plaintiffs were not entitled to equitable relief, because the Black Muslims are members of an organization whose purpose is to establish a separate nation, and are not citizens of the United States. The court then invalidated the Alabama statute requiring registration of "communists, nazis, Muslims, and members of communist front organizations," but did not void other statutes which plaintiffs claim were being used to harass them. The court enjoined all the criminal prosecutions brought against plaintiffs except the charge of "permitting livestock to run at large," finding that plaintiffs had failed to show that this charge was used to discourage assertion of their First Amendment rights. The court also refused to enjoin the $500,000 damages action. It acknowledged that the suit had a chilling effect on the plaintiffs' freedom of association rights, but held that the suit was not based on any statute alleged to be unconstitutional on its face.

The Black Muslims later decided to sell their farm, after almost one third of their 300 head of cattle had been poisoned or shot. The white man who had originally sold the land to the Muslims also suffered retaliatory violence. His business was burned, acid was poured on his car and his life was threatened. The Ku Klux Klan bought land surrounding the Muslim farm to "keep an eye on things." Thoroughly discouraged, the Muslims said they would sell their farm even to the Klan. N.Y. Times, May 17, 1970, at 32, c. 2.

Another nationalist group, the Republic of New Africa (RNA), has experienced similar difficulties in Mississippi. In 1971, the group purchased a twenty-acre farm near Bolton, Mississippi and declared that its action was the first step in an eventual take-over of Mississippi, Louisiana, Alabama, Georgia and South Carolina, as reparations for the crimes committed against black people. Following the purchase, the leaders issued a declaration of independence to the Mississippi Attorney General, who, in turn, sought clarification from the Department of Justice as to the federal government's position in case open hostility should break out between the separatists and the State of Mississippi. N.Y. Times, April 10, 1971, at 21, c. 1. The RNA later reported harassment by whites posing as FBI agents, a civil action by the former owner of the land purchased by the group, and arrest warrants and a court injunction to prevent the establishment of RNA, obtained by the Mississippi Attorney General. N.Y. Times, May 9, 1971, at 32, c. 1.

In August 1971, fifteen policemen and fourteen FBI agents sought to serve fugitive warrants on three members of RNA at 6:00 A.M. at their Jackson headquarters. The seven occupants were flushed out with tear gas after a "reasonable period of no reply." There was a gun battle in which two policemen and an FBI agent were seriously wounded. None of the RNA members were injured, since all had found shelter in a Viet Cong–type bunker constructed in the house. N.Y. Times, Aug. 19, 1971 at 27, c. 1. Charges of murder (one police officer died) and treason were brought against eleven RNA members, (including some not present at the shootout). A "prisoner of war" fund was started to help finance trial expenses. N.Y. Times, Aug. 24, 1971, at 24, c. 3.

Another group of black Americans, who sought to join a "Black Israelite" community in Israel, were deported by that government because they were the cause of tension. N.Y. Times, Oct. 8, 1971, at 2, c. 4, and N.Y. Times, Dec. 20, 1971, at 4, c. 4.

QUESTIONS

1. Consider the basically historical material covered in this book thus far. How accurate are separatists like Lester in concluding that American whites will never cease their racist behavior toward blacks? Does the absence of realistic alternatives necessitate a continuing struggle by blacks for equality in this country, even if such efforts can never be more than spasmodically successful?

2. The recent efforts by black parents to organize black schools and by black students to set up black studies programs and facilities in predominantly white colleges (see generally Chapter Ten), and the hostile opposition to those efforts by most whites, provide an interesting parallel to the opposition experienced by blacks attempting to build emigration movements. Is there a common motivation to this opposition? Do whites see it as in their self-interest both to maintain the mass of black people in a subcitizen status, and to discourage them from organizing emigration and separatist movements?

3. Most serious black emigration efforts have come in periods of severe racial repression, and those blacks who leave the country are motivated as much by fear as by ideology. For example, the stringent provisions of the 1850 Fugitive Slave Act created chaos among the 100,000 fugitive slaves, as well as among free blacks then living in the North. An exodus to Canada began at once, and several hundred blacks departed within days after the new measure became law. W. Foster, The Negro People in American History 171-172 (1954). Some writers see a contemporary danger for American blacks. Can such fear be justified? See, e.g., S. Willhelm, Who Needs the Negro? (Anchor ed. 1971); S. Yette, The Choice: The Issue of Black Survival in America (1971). They assert that blacks were imported for their labor and that racism served to justify the exploitation. With automation, black labor is no longer necessary, but racism remains, and like the Indian the black may be headed for extermination.

Assume that, fearing extermination, large numbers of blacks emigrated. What effect would their departure have on white society? Would the mass exodus present a serious ideological crisis for the country? Would the societal scapegoat role, filled by blacks for 300 years, be transferred to another group?

4. These questions are not entirely theoretical, particularly if in the next several years the presently emerging nonwhite nations in Africa, Asia and South America reach a stage of development and stability sufficient to encourage Afro-Americans to emigrate and become citizens. Assume that white opposition to black progress, apparent during the 1972 presidential campaign, continues. You are general counsel of a major black group which contains a large faction urging acceptance of foreign emigration invitations. Those opposing this move seek your advice as to whether there is a reasonable likelihood that during the next decade racial discrimination in those areas critical to black equality can be controlled through laws and court decisions. How would you respond?

Part II
THE RIGHTS OF CITIZENSHIP

Freedom without rights, the newly freed slaves learned — as those blacks who were never slaves had long known — is almost no freedom at all, and citizenship as conferred by Civil War Amendments was definable by those rights blacks did not enjoy. The effort to obtain the more basic rights of citizenship is, of course, the subject of this book.

But, in fact, the catalog of these rights is endless, for they represent the totality of benefits of political membership in a society which other members recognize and governments protect. Thus, the rights to vote meaningfully, to share public facilities, to exercise a choice of marriage partners not limited by race, and to effectively protest the denial of these rights, are only representative of definable activities where participation has been circumscribed by racial barriers.

4. THE RIGHT TO VOTE

A. GAINING ACCESS TO THE BALLOT

L. LITWACK, NORTH OF SLAVERY
*74, 75, 79 (1961)**

Negroes did not share in the expansion of political democracy in the first half of the nineteenth century; indeed, such expansion frequently came at the expense of their rights and privileges. By 1840, some 93 per cent of the northern free Negro population lived in states which completely or practically excluded them from the right to vote. Only in Massachusetts, New Hampshire, Vermont, and Maine could Negroes vote on an equal basis with whites.

In New York, they could vote if they first met certain property and residence requirements. In New Jersey, Pennsylvania, and Connecticut, they were completely disfranchised, after having once enjoyed the ballot.

In several states the adoption of white manhood suffrage led directly to the political disfranchisement of the Negro. Those who opposed an expanded electorate — for both whites and Negroes — warned that it would, among other things, grant the Negro political power. Adopt universal manhood suffrage, a Pennsylvania constitutional convention delegate declared in 1837, and "every negro in the State, worthy and worthless — degraded and debased, as nine tenths of them are, will rush to the polls in senseless and unmeaning triumph." Would this not constitute, he asked, "a highly *coloured* illustration of the beauty and perfectability of *universal suffrage*?" In New York, a Federalist opponent of universal manhood suffrage warned that "the whole host of Africans that now deluge our City (already too impertinent to be borne), would be placed upon an equal with the citizens." In the face of increasing demands for a liberalized suffrage, a Rhode Island legislative committee advised against extending the vote in 1829, citing as one of its reasons the addition of Negroes and Indians to the electorate. "We ought to recollect," the committee warned, "that all the evils which may result from the extension of suffrage will be evils beyond our reach. We shall entail them upon our latest posterity without remedy."

. . . But even the friends of equal suffrage had their reservations. One Pennsylvanian, for example, opposed disfranchisement but conceded that Negroes "in their present depressed and uncultivated condition" were not "a desirable species of population," and he "should not prefer them as a matter of choice." Such admissions as these hardly added to the popular acceptance of Negro suffrage, and the advocates of such a dangerous doctrine found themselves labeled as either radical amalgamationists or hypocrites. There could be no middle ground. "Has any gentleman on this floor, the boldest and the warmest advocate for negro equality and suffrage," a Pennsylvania constitutional convention delegate asked, "gone so far as to say — to insinuate that he is willing to extend to the blacks his social equality and rights; to receive him in his family or at his table, on the same footing and terms with his white friends and acquaintances; allow them to marry with his children, male and female? — not a word of the kind. They will give him the rights of the people — of the commonwealth — but not of their own houses and homes."

Utilizing various political, social, economic, and pseudoanthropological arguments, white suffragists moved to deny the vote to the Negro. From the admission of Maine in 1819 until the end of the Civil War, every new state restricted the suffrage to whites in its constitution. In New Jersey and Connecticut, where no racial distinctions had appeared in the original constitutions, the legislatures limited the suffrage to whites, and subsequent constitutions incorporated the restrictions. The changes occasioned little public debate or opposition.

NOTE: THE FIFTEENTH AMENDMENT — RIGHT OF CITIZENS TO VOTE

Section 1. The right of citizens of the United States to vote shall not be denied or abridged by the United States or by any State on account of race, color, or previous condition of servitude.

Section 2. The Congress shall have power to enforce this article by appropriate legislation.

The third and last of the Civil War Amendments, designed to grant Negroes the right of suffrage, was enacted only with the greatest difficulty. Those favoring the measure argued that the right to vote was essential if blacks were to participate sufficiently in government to protect their lives against the continuing violence they suffered. News accounts of the time are filled with atrocity stories of blacks who were killed by whites. For example, in June 1868, a Congressional Committee on Lawlessness and Violence reported that 373 freedmen between 1866 and 1868 had been killed by whites.

But black suffrage was far from a popular idea. According to P. Bergman,

> The Republicans did not include in their [1868] Presidential platform a demand for free negro suffrage in Northern states, since several Northern states had recently rejected the idea. Instead, their platform read: "The guarantee by Congress of equal suffrage to all loyal men in the South was demanded by every consideration of public safety, of gratitude and of justice, and must be maintained; while the questions of suffrage in all the loyal states properly belongs to the people of those states." (Bergman, The Chronological History of the Negro in America 258 (1969).)

After lengthy debate, the Fifteenth Amendment was enacted by Congress in December 1868. Its purpose was "to safeguard Negroes against a future white supremacy, by guaranteeing that their right to vote could not be 'denied or abridged by the U.S. or any state.'" (See Bergman, supra, at 258.) Ratification of the Fifteenth Amendment was demanded as a condition of readmittance for those few Southern states still out of the Union, and it was only with their votes that the amendment was passed. New York rescinded her adoption of the amendment, and it was rejected by California, Delaware, Kentucky, Maryland, Oregon and Tennessee. See A. Blaustein and R. Zangrando, Civil Rights and the American Negro at 423 (1968).

The mobilization of law by the Southerners, while the major focus of the discussion here, should be seen as a supplement to the violence, intimidation and economic pressure which were the major weapons used to disenfranchise blacks after the Civil War. If the altruism of all too many radical Republicans who advocated black suffrage was motivated by considerations of political expediency and strategy, Southerners, determined to rebuild the Democratic party, were convinced that the achievement of this goal required that blacks be kept from the polls by any means possible.

To this end, secret bands of whites with exotic names — "Regulators," "Jayhawkers," "Knights of the White Camelia," and of course the "Ku Klux Klan" — were organized as early as 1866; and, as the head of the Freedman's Bureau in Georgia reported, they committed the "most fiendish and diabolical outrages on the freedmen," generally with the sympathy of both the populace and the reconstructed governments.

In describing the era, John Hope Franklin writes:

> The Camelias and the Klan were the most powerful of the secret orders. Armed with guns, swords, or other weapons, their members patrolled some parts of the South day and night. Scattered Union troops proved wholly ineffectual in coping with them, for they were sworn to secrecy, disguised themselves and their deeds in many ways, and had the respect and support of the white community. They used intimidation, force, ostracism in business and society, bribery at the polls, arson, and even murder to accomplish their deeds. Depriving the Negro of political equality became, to them, a holy crusade in which a noble end justified any means. Negroes were run out of communities if they disobeyed orders to desist from voting; and the more resolute and therefore insubordinate blacks were whipped, maimed, and hanged. In 1871 several Negro officials in South Carolina were given fifteen days to resign and they were warned that if they failed, "then retributive justice will as surely be used as night follows day." (From Slavery to Freedom 326-328 (Vintage ed. 1969).)

1. Post–Civil War Voting Statutes

CHRISTOPHER, THE CONSTITUTIONALITY OF THE VOTING RIGHTS ACT OF 1965
*18 Stan. L. Rev. 1-8 (1965)**

Immediately after ratification of the fifteenth amendment in 1870, Congress enacted legislation to enforce the amendment's prohibition against denial of the right to vote on account of race or color. The Enforcement Act of 1870[3] required election officials to give all citizens the same opportunity to perform any act prerequisite to voting.[4] In addition, the Enforcement Act made it a federal crime to violate state laws governing the election of federal officers,[5] to interfere privately or officially with a citizen's right to vote,[6] or to commit fraudulent acts in connection with registering voters or counting ballots.[7]

3. Act of May 31, 1870, ch. 114, 16 Stat. 140.

4. Act of May 31, 1870, ch. 114, §2, 16 Stat. 140.

5. Act of May 31, 1870, ch. 114, §22, 16 Stat. 145-46.

6. Act of May 31, 1870, ch. 114, §§4-6, 19, 16 Stat. 141, 144. Compare Voting Rights Act §12(a).

7. Act of May 31, 1870, ch. 114, §§20, 22, 16 Stat. 145. Compare Voting Rights Act, §§11(a), 12(b).

In 1871 the act was amended to establish a system of federal supervisors of elections.[8]

But these protections were neither adequately enforced nor of long duration. In 1894 Congress repealed most of the provisions of the Enforcement Act, including those dealing with federal supervision of state elections.[9] However, five general voting rights provisions survived: a statutory declaration of each citizen's right to vote without regard to race or color;[10] two sections creating civil liability on the part of persons who interfere with a citizen's right to vote;[11] and two sections imposing criminal sanctions on persons who hinder a citizen in his attempt to exercise his right to vote.[12]

Although Negro suffrage gained widespread currency throughout the South in the years immediately following the Civil War, white political dominance was reestablished by 1885. Thereafter, the states of the Old Confederacy undertook systematic programs which resulted in the disfranchisement of the Negroes. Between 1890 and 1910 twelve states enacted measures calculated to make the franchise exclusively white, the most common devices being literacy tests and poll taxes.[13] In Louisiana, for example, Negroes had constituted as much as 44 per cent of the electorate prior to this movement to restrict suffrage; by 1920 Negro voting had been reduced to less than 1 per cent.[14]

Literacy tests had a tremendous impact in restricting Negro voting in the seven southern states that adopted them: over 70 per cent of the adult Negroes were illiterate as compared to a figure of less than 20 per cent for the adult whites. At the same time, alternate provisions for qualifying to vote were enacted to insure that illiterate whites were not totally disfranchised. Some of these measures were the "voting grandfather" clauses,[16] the "fighting grandfather" clauses,[17] exemptions from the literacy test for those holding

8. Act of Feb. 28, 1871, ch. 99, 16 Stat. 433. Compare Voting Rights Act §§6, 11(b).

9. Act of Feb. 8, 1894, ch. 25, 28 Stat. 36.

10. Rev. Stat. §2004 (1875), 42 U.S.C. §1971(a)(1) (1964). Compare Voting Rights Act §2.

11. Rev. Stat. §§1979-81 (1875), 42 U.S.C. §§1983, 1985 (1964). Compare Voting Rights Act §§11(a), 12(d).

12. Act of May 31, 1870, ch. 110, §§6, 17, 16 Stat. 141, 144 (now 18 U.S.C. §§241-42 (1964)).

13. 1959 Civil Rights Comm'n Rep. 31-32.

14. Louisiana v. United States, 380 U.S. 145, 147-48 (1965).

16. La. Const. art. 197, §5 (1898); Okla. Const. art. III, §4a (1910). The Oklahoma clause was typical: "[N]o person who was, on January 1st, 1866 [before passage of the fifteenth amendment], or any time prior thereto, entitled to vote . . . , and no lineal descendent of such person, shall be denied the right to register and vote because of his inability to read and write . . . ."

17. Ala. Const. §180 (1901); Ga. Const. art. II, §1, ¶IV(1-2) (1908); Va. Const. §19 (1902). Like the voting grandfather clause, the fighting grandfather clause provided exemptions for the descendents of persons who, as for example under §19 of the Virginia constitution, served in time of war in the army or navy of the United States, of the Confederate States, or of any state of the United States or Confederate States.

property,[18] exemptions for those of good moral character who understood the obligations of citizenship under a republican form of government,[19] and exemption for those who could understand and interpret a section of the state or federal constitution when it was read to them.[20] Although the United States Supreme Court struck down the grandfather clauses,[21] the other devices remained and discrimination continued.

From 1871 to 1957, however, Congress did not enact any further legislation to enforce the fifteenth amendment.[22] The only federal statutory remedies which could be invoked to redress discriminatory administration of elections were the provisions which had survived the 1894 repeal of the Enforcement Act,[23] and they were extremely limited in application and rarely used.[24] Section 242, which provides *criminal* penalties for deprivation of constitutional rights under color of state law, was used but once prior to 1941 to protect the right to vote.[25] Section 241 was used to protect against election frauds, but was infrequently invoked to punish deprivations of the right to vote on account of race.

The *civil* remedies that survived from the Reconstruction acts were invoked in a number of cases which declared the white primaries unconstitutional,[27] but, as with the criminal provisions, they were seldom used to challenge discriminatory administration of election laws. The major stumbling block here was the dependence upon private initiation of litigation under the sections; as a practical matter, Negro complainants did not want to risk the intimidation likely to occur if they individually initiated proceedings against local election officials. Even if they had been willing and financially able to institute litigation they would have faced almost insurmountable difficulties in adducing evidence and securing a jury verdict in communities with deeply-rooted segregationist attitudes. In effect, the Reconstruction legislation "was clear as to rights, but inadequate as to remedies."

18. Ala. Const. §181 (1901); Ga. Const. art. II, §1, ¶IV(5) (1877); La. Const. art. 197, §4 (1898); Va. Const. §19 (1902).

19. Ala. Const. §180 (1901); Ga. Const. art. II, §1, ¶IV(3) (1908).

20. La. Const. art. VIII, §1(d) (1921); Miss. Const. §244 (1890); S.C. Const. art. II, §4(c) (1895); Va. Const. §19 (1902).

21. Guinn v. United States, 238 U.S. 347 (1915).

22. In 1939 Congress did include as part of the Hatch Act a provision making it a crime to intimidate any person in the exercise of his voting rights in an election of federal officials. 53 Stat. 1147 (1939), 18 U.S.C. §594 (1964). This provision, however, has apparently never been used to combat racially motivated voter discrimination. See 1961 Civil Rights Comm'n Rep. 74.

23. See notes 9-12 supra.

24. See, *e.g.*, United States v. Cruikshank, 92 U.S. 542 (1875); United States v. Reese, 92 U.S. 214 (1875); 1961 Civil Rights Comm'n Rep. 75 n. 18.

25. See United States v. Stone, 188 Fed. 836 (D. Md. 1911).

27. See, *e.g.*, Smith v. Allwright, 321 U.S. 649 (1944), and Nixon v. Herndon, 273 U.S. 536 (1927), invoking 42 U.S.C. §1983.

NOTE: THE WHITE PRIMARY

In Nixon v. Herndon, 273 U.S. 536, 47 S. Ct. 446, 71 L. Ed. 759 (1924), the Supreme Court held that a Texas statute forbidding the participation of blacks in primary elections violated the petitioners' constitutional rights under the Fourteenth Amendment. Texas then changed the statute, delegating to the State Executive Committee of the Democratic Party the right to fix qualifications for voting in the primary. The committee promptly adopted a resolution designed to effect the same result as the voided statute. The Court rejected this arrangement in Nixon v. Condon, 286 U.S. 73, 52 S. Ct. 484, 76 L. Ed. 984 (1932), holding that the committee operated as the state's representative in the discharge of the state's authority. But in 1932, the State Convention of the Democratic Party passed a resolution limiting membership in the state party and thus qualification for voting in the primary; and in Grovey v. Townsend, 295 U.S. 45, 55 S. Ct. 662, 79 L. Ed. 1292 (1935), the Supreme Court held that the determination by the state convention of the membership of the Democratic party made a significant change from a determination by the Executive Committee, because the convention action was not state action but party action, "voluntary in character" and protected as an exercise of private associational rights by the Texas Bill of Rights. Later, in United States v. Classic, 313 U.S. 299, 61 S. Ct. 1031, 85 L. Ed. 1368 (1941), the Court held that corrupt acts of election officials in a Louisiana primary were subject to congressional sanctions "where the primary is by law made an integral part of the election machinery."

In Smith v. Allwright, 321 U.S. 649, 64 S. Ct. 757, 88 L. Ed. 987 (1944), the Court reopened the question of whether discrimination effected by the state convention, which denied to blacks the right to participate in primaries, was private or state action when in conducting the primary the party was fulfilling duties delegated to it by a statutory electoral scheme. The Texas statutes regulating primaries were substantially similar to the Louisiana statutes considered in Classic; and the Court said, "Such a variation in the result from so slight a change in form influences us to consider anew the legal validity of the distinction which has resulted in barring Negroes from participating in the nominations of candidates of the Democratic party in Texas." 321 U.S. at 661. Then, after reviewing the importance of the primary to the election process, the Court concluded: "We think that this statutory system for the selection of party nominees for inclusion on the general election ballot makes the party which is required to follow these legislative directions an agency of the state in so far as it determines the participants in a primary election." 321 U.S. at 663. There was thus the state action requisite to a finding of a violation of Fourteenth and Fifteenth Amendment rights.

The decision in Smith v. Allwright did not discourage Texas officials. In Terry v. Adams, 345 U.S. 461, 73 S. Ct. 809, 97 L. Ed. 2d 1152 (1953), the Supreme Court reviewed still another scheme designed to divorce the effective election process from the nondiscrimination standards of the Fourteenth and Fifteenth Amendments. The Jaybird Association, a private organization whose membership included all the white members of the Democratic party appearing on the voting rolls of Fort Bend County, Texas, followed a "three-step" electoral process to select county officials. There was first a Jaybird primary; next, the Jaybird selections appeared on the ballot in the Democratic party primary, and finally the Democratic nominees appeared as such on the general election ballot. The Jaybirds claimed that their exclusion of Negroes from their primaries did not violate the Fifteenth Amendment, because it did not involve any action on the part of the state, inasmuch as their primary was not provided for or regulated by any state statutes. The candidates victorious in the Jaybird primaries, with few exceptions, proceeded to success in the general elections. Justice Black, for the Court, held that the scheme violated the Fifteenth Amendment, reversed the court of appeals, and reinstated the decree granted by the district court declaring that the plaintiffs and others similarly situated had the right to vote in the Jaybird Association's primaries.

The Court relied upon recently decided cases, voiding the South Carolina white primary: Rice v. Elmore, 165 F.2d 387, (4th Cir. 1947), *cert. denied,* 333 U.S. 875 (1948), and Baskin v. Brown, 174 F.2d 391 (4th Cir. 1949), in which South Carolina's Democratic primaries were held to violate the Fifteenth Amendment, even though South Carolina had repealed all statutory control of the primaries, and left them ostensibly in private hands.* The Court quoted Allwright for the principle that "the constitutional right to be free from racial discrimination in voting . . . is not to be nullified by a state through casting its electoral process in a form which permits a private organization to practice racial discrimination in the election." The Court gave short shrift to the "state action" requirement:

> For a state to permit such a duplication of its election processes is to permit a flagrant abuse of those processes to defeat the purposes of the Fifteenth Amendment. The use of the county-operated primary to ratify the result of the prohibited election merely compounds the offense. It violates the Fifteenth Amendment for a state, by such circumvention, to permit within its borders the use of any device that produces an equivalent of the prohibited election.
>
> The only election that has counted in this Texas county for more than fifty years has been that held by the Jaybirds from which Negroes were excluded. It is immaterial that the state does not control that part of this elective process which it

* The federal district judge in both South Carolina cases was J. Waties Waring. In Brown v. Baskin, 80 F. Supp. 1017 (E.D.S.C. 1948), he told the voting officials, "It is time to realize that the people of the United States expect [you] to follow the American way of elections." These decisions won Judge Waring national fame and local notoriety, and when in 1951 he dissented from the ruling of a three-judge court that South Carolina's segregation laws were constitutional, he became the target of intense local abuse, his life was threatened, his wife slandered, and he soon retired from the bench and moved to New York. J. Peltason, Fifty-Eight Lonely Men 10 (1961).

leaves for the Jaybirds to manage. The Jaybird primary has become an integral part, indeed the only effective part, of the elective process that determines who shall rule and govern in the county. (345 U.S. at 469.)

NOTE: THE POLL TAX

For the eleven Southern states that enacted poll taxes, the tax served less as a financial deterrent to the prospective black voter than as a grant of administrative discretion to registration officials, who used the device in myriad ways, all designed to bar the ballot to blacks. The tax, usually $1 to $2 and payable annually, had little revenue-raising value. Indeed, blacks in one Mississippi county alleged in a suit that the sheriff and tax collector had simply refused to accept their poll tax payments. United States v. Dogan, 314 F.2d 767 (5th Cir. 1963). But since presentation of poll tax receipts (often for a few years back) was required, and deadlines for payment of the tax were set on dates far from election time and at times and places inconvenient for the black voter, the tax was worth its weight in gold for whites who wished to discourage the black (and a goodly part of the white) electorate from voting. At the least, payment of the poll tax alerted registration officials (and others) as to which blacks might actually be contemplating registration and voting.

Over the years, efforts to end the poll tax through national legislation and judicial action failed. See Emerson, Haber, Dorsen, Political and Civil Rights in the United States 1120-1122 (Student ed. 1967). The Supreme Court in 1937 found that poll taxes did not violate any rights protected by the Constitution. Breedlove v. Shuttles, 302 U.S. 277, 58 S. Ct. 205, 82 L. Ed. 252 (1937). But almost three decades later, the Court acknowledged the barriers to voting posed by such taxes. In Harman v. Forssenius, 380 U.S. 528, 85 S. Ct. 1177, 14 L. Ed. 20 (1965), Virginia, seeking to avoid the effect of the Twenty-fourth Amendment (barring use of taxes to deny or abridge the exercise of voting rights in federal elections), enacted a provision enabling citizens either to pay the tax or to file a notarized or witnessed certificate of residence six months before election. The Court voided the measure, concluding that the certificate requirement posed an obstacle to voting more onerous than the poll tax.

Then in 1966 the Court overruled Breedlove v. Shuttles, and declared that to the extent that it required payment as a condition for voting, Virginia's poll tax provision violated the Fourteenth Amendment's equal protection clause. Harper v. Virginia Board of Elections, 383 U.S. 663, 86 S. Ct. 1079, 16 L. Ed. 2d 169 (1966). Observing that the right to vote in federal elections is conferred by Art. 1, §2 of the federal Constitution, the Court conceded that the right to vote in state elections is nowhere expressly mentioned. But once the franchise is granted, the Equal Protection Clause of the Fourteenth Amendment prohibits the states from drawing artificial and discriminatory lines among the voters. "We conclude that a State violates the Equal Protection Clause of the Fourteenth Amendment whenever it makes the affluence of the voter or payment of any fee an electoral standard." 383 U.S. at 666. Voter qualifications are for the state to determine, but the state may not draw arbitrary lines, and affluence or the payment of the poll tax bears no reasonable relationship to qualification for voting. In justifying its action the Court pointed to its overruling of Plessy v. Ferguson, 163 U.S. 537, in Brown v. Board of Education, 347 U.S. 483, stating: "In determining what lines are unconstitutionally discriminatory, we have never been confined to historic notions of equality. . . ."

Poll taxes in Texas and Alabama were invalidated in, respectively, United States v. Texas, 252 F. Supp. 234 (W.D. Tex. 1966), *aff'd mem.*, 384 U.S. 155 (1966), and United States v. Alabama, 252 F. Supp. 95 (M.D. Ala. 1966). Both courts found that the poll taxes were instituted as a means of subverting the Fifteenth Amendment.

Anderson v. Martin illustrates that blatant as well as statutory schemes have been used in recent years to dilute the effects of increased voting by blacks. As the Court in Anderson indicates, racial labels are bad whether or not they help blacks. Could it be aspects of this thinking that influenced the decision in Whitcomb v. Chavis? (403 U.S. 124, 91 S. Ct. 1858, 29 L. Ed. 363 (1971), printed infra at page 179.)

ANDERSON v. MARTIN, 375 U.S. 399, 84 S. Ct. 454, 11 L. Ed. 2d 430 (1964). Two Negro candidates for the school board in East Baton Rouge Parish, Louisiana, brought suit in the United States District Court for the District of Louisiana to enjoin the Louisiana secretary of state from effectuating a state statute requiring that, in all primary, general or special elections, the nomination papers and ballots designate the race of candidates for elective office. A three-judge federal district court denied injunctive relief on the ground that the statute was constitutional.

Justice Clark, per curiam, held that the statute operated as a discrimination against the Negro candidates and was therefore violative of the Equal Protection Clause of the Fourteenth Amendment. The right of the voters to vote for whomever they chose for whatever reason they chose was not involved; what was involved was the right of the state to "require or encourage" voters to discriminate on the basis of race. The statute placed a "racial label" on the candidates "at the most crucial stage in the electoral process — the instant before the vote is cast"; this encouraged voters to pick out a single issue or consideration on which to make their choice. The results for the Negro plaintiffs would differ, depending upon whether the electoral unit was predominantly white or predominantly black; but "The vice lies not in the resulting injury but in the placing of the power of the state behind a racial classification that induces racial prejudice at the polls."

The provision in the statute was added in 1960, at a time when pressure on Negroes was great and hence could not help but have a "repressive effect" which was "brought to bear only after the exercise of government power."

Nor can the provision be deemed to be reasonably designed to meet legitimate governmental interest in informing the electorate. The state's contention that the provision was nondiscriminatory because it applied both to whites and blacks was rejected as superficial. "Race is the factor upon which the statute operates and its involvement promotes the ultimate discrimination which is sufficient to make it invalid."

HAMM v. VIRGINIA STATE BOARD OF ELECTIONS, 230 F. Supp. 156 (E.D. 1964). Action by several Negro and white citizens of Virginia was brought to attack the validity of Virginia statutes requiring designation of persons by races. A three-judge district court held that Virginia constitutional and statutory provisions requiring separation of white and colored persons on poll tax, residence-certificate and registration lists, and on assessment rolls were invalid under the Equal Protection Clause of the Fourteenth Amendment, but that the Virginia statute requiring inclusion in divorce decrees of recitation showing race of husband and wife is not constitutionally objectionable. Citing Anderson v. Martin, the court said, "To be within the condemnation, the governmental action need not effectuate segregation of facilities directly. . . . The result of the statute or policy must not tend to separate individuals by reason of difference in race or color." But designation of race may serve some useful purposes in areas where it will not operate discriminatorily: "Vital statistics, obviously, are aided by denotation in the divorce decrees of the race of the parties," so the divorce provisions were sustained. *Aff'd per curiam,* Tancil v. Woolls, 379 U.S. 19, 85 S. Ct. 157, 13 L. Ed. 91 (1964).

2. Twentieth-Century Voting Rights Acts

NOTE: VOTING RIGHTS ACTS OF 1957, 1960 AND 1964

The effort by blacks to remedy voting discrimination through legal attacks on barriers such as the poll tax and the white primary had little effect on the overall problem of voter discrimination, which remained widespread throughout many parts of the country. In 1947, President Truman's Committee on Civil Rights recommended new federal legislation to protect voting rights. There was little response from a Congress that, session after session, refused to enact even an antilynching law. Nevertheless, both Presidents Truman and Eisenhower recommended new civil rights legislation to protect voting rights; and Congress, shocked by the flouting of federal law by the states in the wake of the school desegregation cases, overcame determined filibusters by Southern members and enacted the Civil Rights Act of 1957. 71 Stat. 634 (1957), 43 U.S.C. §§1971, 1975(d) (1964). This was the first modern legislation designed to enforce the right secured by the Fifteenth Amendment.

Under the 1957 Act the Attorney General of the United States was authorized to institute civil actions on behalf of one or more named individuals for injunctive relief against proscribed deprivations of the right to vote in federal elections. 71 Stat. 637 (1957), 42 U.S.C. §1971(c)-(d) (1964). Penalties were provided for interference with federal voting rights (71 Stat. 637 (1957), 42 U.S.C. §1971(b) (1964)), and criminal contempt cases arising under the act could be tried without a jury where the sentence was less than a $300 fine or 45 days imprisonment. 71 Stat. 638 (1957), 42 U.S.C. §1995(c) (1964). Finally, a six-member bipartisan Civil Rights Commission was created to investigate deprivations of voting rights on account of race, religion or national origin. 71 Stat. 635 (1957), 42 U.S.C. §1975(c) (1964).

The 1960 Civil Rights Act, 74 Stat. 86 (1960), 42 U.S.C. §§1971(c),(e), 1974(e), 1975(h) (1964), provided that if injunctive relief was granted in a suit brought by the Attorney General under the provisions of the 1957 Act, to which the state could now be made a party defendant (74 Stat. 92 (1960), 42 U.S.C. §1971(c) (1964)), the Attorney General could ask the court to find a "pattern or practice" of discrimination. Upon such a finding, any individual within the jurisdiction of the defendant could apply to the court for an order that he was qualified to vote in any election. The applicant was required to prove that he was qualified to vote under state election laws, and that he had been denied the opportunity to register or vote by persons acting under color of law subsequent to the court's finding of "pattern or practice." The court was authorized to appoint referees to hear the evidence on such applications ex parte. 74 Stat. 90 (1960), 42 U.S.C. §1971(e) (1964). The act also contained provisions for the preservation, production and inspection of voting records. 74 Stat. 88 (1960), 42 U.S.C. §§1974-1974(e) (1964).

The voting rights provisions of the 1964 Civil Rights Act, 78 Stat. 241 (1968), 42 U.S.C. §§1971, 1975(a)-(d), 2000(a) to 2000(h)-(4) (1964), were directed largely at the standards applied by state election officials in the voter registration process. The act required that registration standards, practices and procedures for federal elections be uniformly applied. The right to vote could not be denied because of immaterial errors or omissions in registration forms, and literacy tests were to be conducted in writing, with a certified copy made available to the applicant. The use of literacy tests was further limited: in any action brought by the Attorney General in a jurisdiction where literacy tests were used, a sixth-grade education would create a rebuttable presumption of sufficient literacy to vote in federal elections. To expedite review of voting rights cases, the Attorney General could request hearing by a three-judge district court.

As the cases that follow indicate, none of these legislative efforts to remedy voting discrimination through use of the judicial process proved successful.

UNITED STATES v. DUKE
332 F.2d 759 (5th Cir. 1964)

Before TUTTLE, Chief Judge, and RIVES and WISDOM, Circuit Judges.

TUTTLE, Chief Judge: When this suit was filed by the United States on

October 16, 1961, Panola County, Mississippi, had 7,639 white persons, and 7,250 Negroes of voting age. At least 5,343 white persons were then registered to vote. The only Negro registered to vote in Panola County was R. H. Hightower, 92 years old, who had registered in 1892. This does not tell the whole story, because another Negro, E. H. Holloway, was registered on January 5, 1952, but he is now deceased. Also, after this suit was filed, and before the trial in the court below, one Houston Potts, Jr., was registered in April, 1962.

Proceeding on the theory that such a situation could exist only because of state action which unconstitutionally interfered with the exercise of the voting franchise by the Negro citizens of Panola County, the United States brought this suit against Duke, Circuit Court Clerk and Registrar of Panola County, and the state of Mississippi.

The complaint alleged that the defendants, in conducting registration for voting, have engaged in certain racially discriminatory acts and practices which deprived Negro citizens of Panola County of the right to register to vote without distinction of race and color; that these deprivations were pursuant to a pattern and practice; and that, unless restrained, appellees will continue to engage in such acts and practices. The prayer was that the trial court make a finding of the existence of a pattern and practice of discrimination and issue an injunction enjoining appellees, their agent, employees and successors from engaging in certain acts and practices.

Considering the registration requirements in Mississippi, there are three periods of substantial significance touching on the issues of this case. The Mississippi Constitution of 1890 requires registration as a prerequisite to voting. Prior to 1955, Section 244 required that an applicant, otherwise qualified, be able to read any section of the Mississippi Constitution, *or* understand it when read to him, *or* give a reasonable interpretation thereof.

To be otherwise qualified, an applicant must (1) have fulfilled the residence qualification; (2) be a citizen not less than 21 years of age (or reach the age 21 before the next election); (3) not have been convicted of any disqualifying crimes enumerated in the Constitution or laws of Mississippi; and not be insane. Payment of poll taxes, while required for voting, is not a prerequisite to registration.

After April 4, 1955, when the State legislature implemented the amendment of Section 244 of the Mississippi Constitution, the following additional requirements for registration became effective: applicants must be able to read and write any Section of the Mississippi Constitution *and* give a reasonable interpretation thereof; they must demonstrate a reasonable understanding of the duties and obligations of citizenship under a constitutional form of government; and they must make sworn written application of registration on a form prescribed by the State Election Commission. These additional requirements applied only to persons registered to vote after January 1, 1954.

In 1960, shortly before the passage of the Civil Rights Act of 1960, the state legislature authorized the destruction of the application forms. Mississippi Code, Section 3209.6, as amended. In addition, a new section (241-A) of the

Mississippi Constitution added the requirement that an elector be of good moral character. In 1962, implementing legislation was enacted (Section 3235, Mississippi Code). The legislature also amended Section 3209.6 to require the State Election Commission to include in any application forms which they prepare for the use of the registrars spaces for information showing good moral character (in order that the applicant might demonstrate his good moral character to the registrar). Finally, two additional statutes were passed and became effective in May 1962. One (H.B. 882, Reg. Sess. 1962) provides for the publication of the names of all applicants for two successive weeks following which a two-week waiting period is required before an applicant may become registered. The second (H.B. 904 Reg. Sess. 1962) provides for a procedure by which qualified electors may challenge the good moral character of an applicant.

Although we have given the requirements down through the enactment of the laws in 1932, the three periods of importance here are the period before 1955, the period between 1955 and 1960, and the period from 1960 until this suit was filed on October 16, 1961. It must be borne in mind that registration is permanent in the state of Mississippi, and, once a citizen's name is on the registration books, he is not required to reregister.

The record before the trial court fully substantiates the contention of the United States that at least until the date of the filing of this suit voting was, for white persons in Panola County, Mississippi, a simple corollary of citizenship. It is equally clear that the exercise of this basic right of citizenship was exclusively enjoyed by the white people of this county. The question presented to the trial court, and preserved for our attention, is whether this condition existed without a course of conduct by the state or local officials which amounted to an illegal interference with the Fifteenth Amendment rights of Negro citizens of Panola County.

The trial court, after requiring the United States to file a more definite statement to charge specifically the alleged discriminations with the degree of specificity required under Rule 9(b), Federal Rules of Civil Procedure, dealing with allegations of fraud,[1] proceeded to a hearing of the case on oral testimony. Although in its findings of fact the trial court did not resolve all of the conflicting testimony, it found that between 1932 and 1959 not more than five or six Negroes had applied to register in Panola County, and that one of these had been registered. It found that there was no evidence showing that any particular Negro who had been otherwise qualified had been denied the right to register because of race or color and further that there was no evi-

1. This Court had previously criticized such a requirement at the pleading stage of a similar injunction suit in the United States v. Lynd, 5 Cir., 301 F.2d 812, 822, where we said: "Likewise it is clear that there was no justification for the Court's requiring the government to amend its complaint in this civil rights action to allege specific details of voter discrimination as if this were an action for fraud or mistake under Rule 9, Federal Rules of Civil Procedure." This ruling was confirmed by this Court when the Lynd case came on for final hearing on appeal on the merits at 321 F.2d 26, 27.

dence that any Negro had been denied such right because of race or color. It found that there "was no evidence"[2] that Duke or the state of Mississippi or *anyone else* in Panola County had done anything to intimidate or discourage Negroes from attempting to register. The court doubtless intended to say that it found against such evidence rather than that there was "no evidence."[3] The court found that Duke and his deputies helped white applicants but it found that there was evidence showing that he refused to help Negroes. The court found that the registration of white people who should not have been registered apparently occurred "largely by inadvertence because of the lack of training of the sometimes inept deputies and without the knowledge or discretion of the defendant Duke." The court found that women deputies always referred Negroes to Duke "as a matter of personal preference by the women." It is undisputed that on each occasion when Negro applicants sought to register, they had to wait for Duke's arrival from some other place if he was not in the office. He was usually at Sardis.[4] The court found that no denial of the rights of Negroes was shown from the fact that whites had been registered who did not meet the standards for registration set by the Mississippi laws. It also found that it was not shown with respect to any of the Negroes who testified that the "lesser and mistaken standards applied to some white people could be met or surpassed by them."

Statistical evidence agreed to by the parties showed that there were more than 2,000 Negro residents of Panola County who had received seven or more years of schooling. Although no figures were introduced, we can doubtless take judicial notice of the fact that with approximately 750 Negro residents having had some high school training, there must have been a significant number of high school as well as grade school teachers, principals and other school professional personnel among the Negro race to conduct the public schools of Panola County, under the "separate but equal" school operation that is required under the Mississippi laws.

This Court has said, "In the problem of racial discrimination, statistics often tell much, and courts listen." State of Alabama v. United States, 304 F.2d 583, 586. In United States v. Harpole 5 Cir., 263 F.2d 71, at page 78, we said:

2. This finding is clearly erroneous because, over the objection of defendants, the court permitted the Negro witness, Kuykendall, to testify that when he went to the courthouse to register he was told by Deputy Mrs. Draper to wait and that he then heard a conversation described by him as: "Well I could hear them talking in there, the door was partly open and I heard Mrs. Draper ask Mr. Travis [the Sheriff] was he going to bother me in there or wait until I went out," to which Kuykendall testified that Travis replied, "No, wait until he comes out." And further that Mr. Travis said, "If we let them get by with this some of them will be running for Sheriff."

3. Another Negro witness testified that he was hurried and flustered by Duke by the manner in which Duke handled the books and papers while he was attempting to complete the application form.

4. Panola County had two courthouses, one at Batesville and one at Sardis. Mr. Duke resided in Sardis. A permanent woman deputy was regularly present at Batesville.

> We cannot assume that Negroes, the majority class in Carroll County, had en masse, or in any substantial numbers, voluntarily abstained from registering as electors and, by such action, had rendered themselves ineligible for jury duty. If the registration officials freely and fairly registered qualified Negroes as electors, that fact rested more in the knowledge of the State. The burden was on appellee, as the State's representative, to refute the strong prima facie case developed by the appellant. The only Negroes ever proved registered as electors in Carroll County were two who had died before 1954.

Here, the trial court assumed precisely what we said could not be assumed. The court particularly alluded to the fact that only a small number of Negroes had made an effort to register prior to 1959.

Prior to 1955, according to the record before us, white citizens "merely had to sign the book," to be registered voters. However, there was always lurking in the background the constitutional requirements that the registrant be able to interpret a provision of the Constitution. Any Negro citizen optimistic enough to seek the right to participate in governmental affairs would also be smart enough to know that this requirement could be placed as a stumbling block in his path since it would be a subjective test by the registrar upon which his success or failure would be measured. After 1955, the test became even more subjective, in that "the understanding" clause was placed into the questionnaire as a requirement. The form also stated that the applicant must complete it "in his own handwriting . . . and without assistance or suggestion of any other person."

Several years after this law was passed some local interest was aroused by the creation of a Negro Voters League. The first three persons to try to get some information on the subject went to Sardis, the site of one of the courthouses, and asked Mr. Duke what the requirements were for voting. He replied that he couldn't say because he hadn't got the questionnaires yet from Jackson, the state capital.[5] Duke then told them that they should apply at Batesville, the site of the other courthouse, and the proper place according to their residence. Several weeks later they tried again and went to the courthouse in Batesville, where the woman deputy told them they would have to wait for Mr. Duke to handle the matter personally. They waited some 25 or 30 minutes and he came over and told them he would take them one at a time, although there was no personal examination involved, only the filling out of a questionnaire. When these and other applicants at about the same time reached that part of the application requiring them to interpret a provision of the Constitution, they were given sections that, so far as this record discloses, were never given to any white applicant. Some of these are Section

5. The trial court did not resolve any issue as to whether this actually occurred. However, since in his answer Duke admitted that these persons called on him in Sardis in 1959, we accept as undisputed their version of the affair, even though Duke, when later examined, testified that he "believed" that they came in 1955, at which time he had no questionnaires under the new law. This is entirely inconsistent with the testimony of everyone that the Voters League was not organized until 1959.

212, dealing with the interest rate on the Chickasaw School Fund, Section 228, dealing with alluvial land; Section 226, dealing with restrictions on state office holding, and Section 282, dealing with the validity of recognizances and other obligations entered into before the adoption of the 1890 Constitution.

Although none of the applicants received word from Mr. Duke as to their success or failure, and although the application forms had been destroyed by Duke prior to the trial, he testified that none of them passed. So, also, did some of the witnesses themselves say they either were not satisfied with the answers or they did not complete the answers.

During the time that these efforts were being made, some ten Negroes applied and none was registered. One testified that he was within a few days of his 21st birthday, and he was told that he could not register until he was 21 years of age; this was denied by Mr. Duke. The court's findings on this matter are inconsistent with both the testimony of the Negro witness and of Mr. Duke. Another Negro would-be registrant testified that he was rejected as a registrant by Mr. Duke because he did not have two poll tax receipts. Duke testified that he had not refused to register him but had suggested to him that he wait until he had paid two years of poll taxes because he would not be permitted to vote in the election unless he had such receipts. Many white persons were registered who had not paid their two years poll taxes.

However that may be, testimony by the Negro witnesses was that they then "became discouraged" and that was the end of the Voters League. During the same time, white applicants were still being registered without the necessity either of waiting for Mr. Duke personally to come to register them, to be taken up one at a time, to answer any questions as to the meaning of a constitutional section more than three lines long. In fact, a number of white witnesses were produced to testify that they did not know the answers to these simple questions or that they were assisted by the registrar or one of his assistants in answering them. It was also demonstrated by application blanks of some white registrants that they were illiterate. Nevertheless they had been registered on the day they applied. It is small wonder that the Voters League members got discouraged and quit trying. . . .

The state made no effort to "refute the strong prima facie case" that the registration officials had not "freely and fairly registered qualified Negroes," United States v. Harpole, supra. The trial court should therefore have determined that until 1955, and for an undetermined later period, Negroes in most rural communities in Mississippi simply were not expected to, and they did not, offer themselves as voters, and they did not seek to register because of this accepted pattern of life in rural Mississippi. As this Court said in the Harpole case, supra, this is not to select Mississippi as being unique in this regard among the states. We there stated, "We have called the figures startling, but we do not feign surprise because we have long known that there are counties not only in Mississippi, but in the writer's own home State of Alabama, in which Negroes constitute the majority of the residents but take no part in government either as voters or as jurors. Familiarity with such a condition thus prevents shock, but it all the more increases our concern over its existence."

The Court then stated what must be done when such a case arises, by saying, "When, in a proper case such as this, there is added to our common knowledge proof that some of the Negro citizens are qualified educationally and by other legal standards but are excluded from serving as jurors solely because of their race or color, the courts must declare the maintenance of such a condition violative of the Constitution and must not tolerate its longer continued existence." 263 F.2d 71, 78.

Commencing, then, with 1955, at which time white people were permitted to register by "merely signing the book" in Panola County, and thousands had registered by that simple process, we arrive at a time when Negroes' interest became aroused in the rights of citizenship, and we find that this awakened interest met with what might be called polite but effective discouragement. For the first time technical provisions of the Mississippi Constitution having little to do in general with the true obligations of the citizen to his state or nation, are put to a Negro applicant who knows from the very nature of the question that he simply can't answer it to the satisfaction of the registrar. He is also met with the subtle but typical rebuff in the response that the white lady can't wait on him but he must wait for the registrar. The officials and the trial court completely overlooked the fact that the deputies were public officials elected and paid by the county to serve the public and all of its citizens. The trial court here, as did the trial court in the Lynd case supra, erred in dismissing this fact by a finding that the women deputies referred Negroes to Duke "as a matter of personal preference."

This official conduct was a double discouragement to registration. The first, a subtle one, an expression of distaste or distrust of the public official for the citizen based solely on race and without reference to the personal qualities of the individual concerned, and second by requiring a delay awaiting Mr. Duke's arrival from the other county seat.

When following by the other undisputed course of conduct in making all but the first one of several Negro applicants await their turn, and thus requiring a delay of up to two or three hours, this record, without more and without reference to the findings of fact made by the trial court demonstrates clearly that there was a pattern and practice in Panola County, which, existing in full vigor in 1955, denied the Negro citizen an opportunity to register, and was carried forward by the different treatment accorded him subsequent to that time.

As efforts were subsequently made to overcome these barriers, and indications were that more Negroes would make the effort, the barriers grew successively higher, so that in 1960 the understanding clause was inserted, and in 1962 the good character requirement was added. The United States does not, in this action, attack the constitutionality of any of the requirements for registration per se. This attack has been made in another suit. . . .

Evidence adduced on the trial below shows that even after the latest of the enactments, the terms of the statute were being disregarded in the registration of white voters. . . . The fact is there were no standards applied to some white people. It is perfectly apparent from the testimony given by the Negro witnesses, including their reading without error from the witness stand somewhat involved sections of the Constitution, they could more than meet the "lesser and mistaken standards applied to some white people." They clearly demonstrated they were better qualified than some of the persons registered. A holding or finding to the contrary is clearly erroneous.

If, upon the enactment of the implementing statute in 1955, the registration officials of Panola County had immediately begun treating Negro applicants in precisely the same manner which they accorded to white citizens of the county, by either treating the application form as merely an information blank from which the necessary statistical information could be obtained to ascertain age and residence and precinct of the applicant, or as a literacy test (although this was not even applied to all white applicants), and if the processing of Negro applications had been as prompt and as routine as those of white citizens, and, to the extent that any attention at all was paid to the interpretation requirement, the same simple sections of the Constitution were presented to Negro applicants, the defendants would be in better case here supporting the action of the trial court in denying a permanent injunction. This is not what happened. The Negro citizens were not treated in the same manner as the white citizen. The application was treated largely as an information form when submitted by a white person. It was a test of skill for the Negro. It was not even a test of literacy for the white, whereas any Negro applicant demonstrated his literacy in filling out the form. Much more difficult sections of the Constitution were given to the Negroes to write and construe than those given to the white applicants. Delay and refusal of deputies to serve the Negroes was uniform, whereas speed and dispatch, to the extent of permitting the applicant to sign immediately, was the lot of the white.

By extending the discriminatory treatment of the Negro applicants and thus discouraging further applications, a higher and higher percentage of the white residents of the county have become registered under the lax procedures, some of which were followed up until the very date of the trial. It doesn't help to say, as did the registrar on the trial, that he would see to it that all of the persons illegally registered would be stricken from the rolls because there is no possible way to know how many thousands of white citizens of Panola County were registered by "just signing the book." Many of them may well be thoroughly qualified even under the most stringent requirements as they appear in today's statute. On the other hand, relatively few of them will ever have to face this hurdle. As it now stands every Negro citizen in Panola County, except two, who wish to become registered voters must satisfy the stricter requirements of today's law.

What, then, is the court's duty in such a situation? Ordinary principles of fairness and justice seem to indicate the correct answer. Would anyone doubt the utter unfairness of permitting the unrestricted application by the state of higher and stricter standards of eligibility to all of the Negroes of the county where 70% of the white voters of the county have qualified under simple standards or no standards at all, and where the Negro citizens were prevented from qualifying under the simpler standards by reason of a practice or pattern of discrimination?

While theoretically applicable to all, these new requirements primarily affect those who bore the brunt of previous discriminations and tend to maintain the position of advantage which one class has already obtained over the other. See United States v. Louisiana, E.D. La. 1963, 225 F. Supp. 353, at pp. 391-398 (three-judge court); [other citation omitted].

The obvious way to avoid such unfair and inequitable result is by applying the principle of "freezing." The term "freezing" is used in two senses. It may be said that when illegal discrimination or other practices have worked inequality on a class of citizens and the court puts an end to such a practice but a new and more onerous standard is adopted before the disadvantaged class may enjoy their rights, already fully enjoyed by the rest of the citizens, this amounts to "freezing" the privileged status for those who acquired it during the period of discrimination, and "freezing out" the group discriminated against. "Freezing results when there have been past discriminatory practices in the registration process, these discriminatory practices are discontinued, but new and more onerous requirements are imposed." United States v. Ramsey, [331 F.2d 824, 837 (5th Cir. 1964)].

"The cessation of prior discriminatory practices cannot justify the imposition of new and onerous requirements, theoretically applicable to all, but practically affecting primarily those who bore the brunt of previous discrimination. An appropriate remedy therefore should undo the results of past discrimination as well as prevent future inequality of treatment. A court of equity is not powerless to eradicate the effects of former discrimination. If it were, the State could seal into permanent existence the injustices of the past." United States v. State of Louisiana (E.D. La.) three-judge court, 225 Fed. Supp. 353, 393. See also Lane v. Wilson, 307 U.S. 276, where the Supreme Court said,

> Exemption from this onerous provision was enjoyed by all who had registered in 1941. But this registration was held under the statute which was condemned in the Guinn case. Unfair discrimination was thus retained by automatically granting voting privileges for life to the white citizens whom the unconstitutional "grandfather clause" had sheltered while subjecting colored citizens to a new burden. 307 U.S. 276.

This Court has also construed the term "freezing" as keeping in effect, at least temporarily, those requirements for qualifications to vote, which were in effect, to the benefit of others, at the time the Negroes were being discriminated against.

In United States v. Dogan, this Court clearly approved the application of the principle of "freezing" where the record indicates that later and more burdensome requirements will maintain in effect a prior policy of discrimination. The District Court for the Middle District of Alabama in United States v. Penton, 212 Fed. Supp. 193, applied the principle by enjoining the defendants "from using . . . different and more stringent qualification requirements for registration . . . than . . . [those] used by the Board . . . since at least January 1, 1956." This Court has further recognized the principle, although not applying it in that particular case, in United States v. Atkins, 5 Cir., 323 F.2d 733. The Court said there, "We do not dispute the power of the federal courts to invoke the freezing principle to give relief when necessary. It has been used before in voting cases . . . ."

We have here an appeal from a final judgment and a denial of a permanent injunction. The case has been pending two and a half years. Effective relief is long overdue. The only effective relief here is by applying the principle of freezing the registration standards that were in effect when the great majority of the white citizens were registered. We conclude that the principle should be applied in this case without further delay.

We have considered the appellees' contention that the Court does not have the power under the Civil Rights Act to direct the registration of any person who is not otherwise qualified under the laws of the state of Mississippi. The argument goes that since it must be assumed that the Mississippi statutes are constitutional, the Court may not by its action require a suspension of the present statutes even though it appears that to do so is the only way to achieve real equality. We think that a provision of the 1957 Civil Rights Act, as amended in 1960, strongly supports the proposition that the relief sought is authorized by the statute. Subsection (e) of this Act, 42 U.S.C.A. 1971(e), dealing with the authority of a court-appointed referee in the event of the failure of the state registrar to act as required by the statute, defines "qualified under the state law" as follows: "qualified according to the laws, customs, or usages of the State, and shall not, in any event, imply qualifications more stringent than those used by the persons found in the proceeding to have violated subsection (a) of this section in qualifying persons other than those of the race or color against which the pattern or practice of discrimination was found to exist."

Obviously, when the court has found that a pattern of discrimination has denied an opportunity to Negroes to register, although it has permitted the registration of substantially all of the willing eligible white voters of a county, a non-discriminatory reregistration of all voters would be the only completely fair and effective means of clearing away the effect of the discrimination. That path, of course, lies open to the state if it sees fit to pursue it. Thus, any remedial injunction freezing the earlier standards to permit the qualification of the Negroes discriminated against, must in the alternative, authorize the state to require a reregistration of all citizens using such standards of eligibility as meet constitutional requirements.

Unless, and until, such reregistration is had, the disenfranchised class must be given a reasonable opportunity to get their names on the registration rolls on the same basis as was applied to the 5300 white voters who are now registered in Panola County. . . .

We conclude that the trial court erred in not finding a pattern and practice of discrimination. We also find that the trial court erred in not issuing an injunction to guarantee that the effects of the discrimination should be eliminated and a repetition for the future be prohibited.

This Court has not the power, if it had the desire, which it has not, to prescribe the qualifications that will ultimately apply to the registration of voters in the state of Mississippi. The Court will therefore not undertake to deal with registrations as to persons who first became eligible to register following the date on which the present Registrar, Mr. Shankle, assured the Court that he would apply all of the present Mississippi statutes with an even hand and completely without regard to race. This, of course, assumes that Mr. Shankle will assure himself that such tests as are required of proposed registrants shall be fairly and uniformly given, including the selection in some completely fair and objective way of the sections of the Mississippi Constitution that may be required to be answered.

However, with respect to all Negro residents of Panola County who were otherwise qualified by residence and not disqualified by any of the statutory grounds of disqualification, they must be given an opportunity to register upon their subjecting themselves to the same requirements as were actually administered by defendant Duke and his deputies up until the date of the trial of this case in the district court.

Provided that reasonable opportunities to register are given to the Negro citizens of Panola County, there should be a limitation upon the time during which they may take advantage of this special registration. This Court will not attempt to frame the terms of the order to be issued by the trial court, but it is strongly suggested that a period of a year after the date of the trial court's order should be adequate for those Negroes who desire to do so to undertake to complete their registration upon the terms here outlined, provided, however, that the trial court shall satisfy itself that reasonable opportunities will be given during such period for all who desire to do so to offer themselves for registration. . . .

The judgment of the trial court is reversed and the case is remanded for further proceedings not inconsistent with this opinion. . . .

NOTE: WHITE RESISTANCE AND THE NEW VOTING RIGHTS ACT

In forbidding for five years the application of voter qualifications, tests, or devices other than requirements of age, residency, and lack of felony conviction, the 1965 Voting Rights Act (79 Stat. 437, 42 U.S.C. §§1973 et seq. (1965), printed in Appendix), adopted and expanded the "freezing" principle evolved by the Fifth Circuit in United States v. Duke, 332 F.2d 759 (5th Cir.

1964). The suspension provision of the 1965 Act was applied to cases pending at the time of its enactment. United States v. Ward, 352 F.2d 329 (5th Cir. 1965); United States v. Clement, 358 F.2d 89 (5th Cir. 1966); United States v. Ramsey, 353 F.2d 650 (5th Cir. 1965); United States v. Palmer, 356 F.2d 951 (5th Cir. 1966). But enforcing the act was not simply a matter of judicial pronouncement followed by willing — or even grudging — compliance. Protracted and repeated litigation was usually required in order to obtain meaningful relief, and even then, some forms of discriminatory behavior were not controlled.

The difficulties experienced by black residents of Sunflower County, Mississippi are illustrative. A federal district court had, on April 8, 1965, ordered a one-year "freeze" period during which blacks would be allowed to "catch up" in registering to vote. Under state law, however, an otherwise qualified elector could not vote in municipal general elections unless he had registered at least four months before the date of the election, and unless he had paid the poll tax for the preceding two years.

In Hamer v. Campbell, 358 F.2d 215 (5th Cir. 1966), plaintiffs brought a class action seeking relief from these requirements, and an injunction delaying the primary elections scheduled for May 11 and 18 and the June 8 general election. The district court denied relief on the grounds that the plaintiffs lacked standing to bring a class action in behalf of black residents of Sunflower County.

The court of appeals approved the district court ruling as to five of the six municipalities in the county, because no plaintiff was a citizen of any of four of these towns, and because the plaintiff who was a resident of the fifth city was not qualified to vote under state law. However, with respect to the sixth, Sunflower itself, the plaintiffs were held to have standing to sue. The court ruled that the challenged state registration requirements were invalid, and set aside the election results. The district court was instructed to set aside the results in the other five municipalities as well if the plaintiffs could cure the defects in representation. The court made clear that election results should be set aside only in cases where plaintiffs had unsuccessfully sought relief prior to the date of the challenged election.

In 1967, Sunflower County was designated for inspection by federal examiners, but only after scores of complaints had been filed with the Justice Department. See Note, 3 Civ. Rights–Civ. Lib. L. Rev. 383-384. Just before an election in May 1967, black residents of Sunflower received two circulars. The first was signed by the Mayor and Chief of Police: "No one, including the United States Government can make you vote in any election." The second, distributed on the morning of election day, read, "Your homes and property are at stake. You have a chance to vote for a good town or a bad town in this election. The choice is yours. If you are smart, you will not be misled by paid racial agitators." Note, supra at 391.

In Hamer v. Ely, 410 F.2d 152 (5th Cir. 1969), *cert. denied,* 390 U.S. 942 (1969), black voters in Sunflower contested the results of a 1968 court-ordered election on the grounds that it had been conducted discriminatorily. The voting list had included 160 white registrants and 190 black registrants; one third of the latter were known to need assistance in marking their ballots. Plaintiffs' attorney and an assistant state attorney had informally agreed that two blacks would be appointed as election clerks, authorized to assist illiterate voters who asked for help. The Board of Election Commissioners refused to implement that "understanding" on the ground that, by law, only members of the commission were permitted to assist illiterates. The two black election officials were allowed to perform only ministerial duties. No black candidates were elected.

The district court held that the election had been properly and fairly conducted. The court of appeals affirmed the decision, against plaintiffs' claim that the use of only white assistants did not meet the 1965 Voting Rights Act requirement of adequate assistance to illiterate voters. The court held that the standard had been met, because each voter had been informed of his right to assistance and to the presence of a federal observer to oversee the quality of the assistance given. Although the attitude of the Board of Election Commissioners "may have been shoddy," it did not, the court felt, justify overturning the election results.

Litigation intended to ensure black voting rights was also thwarted in Greene County, Alabama. In Gilmore v. Greene County Democratic Executive Committee, 368 F.2d 328 (5th Cir. 1966), the district court had ruled that candidates of the National Freedom Democratic party did not have valid certificates of nomination, on the ground that the meetings at which they were nominated did not meet the statutory requirements of a party convention. The court of appeals reversed and stayed the election in order to provide enough time for the district court to determine whether the plaintiffs wanted to be recognized as Democratic or Independent nominees. Subsequently an individual not party to the federal suit obtained a state court injunction prohibiting state election officials from placing appellants' names on the ballot. The federal court refused to intervene, considering that the question was one of state law, and that the state court interpretation would be binding on the federal court. Other cases in Greene County declared the right to the presence of a federal observer while voting, United States v. Executive Committee of Democratic Party of Greene County, 254 F. Supp. 543 (D. Ala. 1966), and the right of illiterate black voters to sample ballots, Gilmore v. Greene City Democratic Executive Committee, 433 F.2d 487 (5th Cir. 1970). And see Hadnott v. Amos, 394 U.S. 358, 89 S. Ct. 1101, 22 L. Ed. 2d 336 (1969), referred to infra page 152.

R. LOGAN AND M. WINSTON, II THE NEGRO IN THE UNITED STATES
27-29 (1971)

While protection of registering and voting by Negroes were part of the Civil Rights Act of 1957, 1960, and 1964, the 1965 Act dealt exclusively with voting. Attention was focused on the issue — as well as others — by President Johnson's support of the Civil Rights Act of 1964 and the opposition to it by the Republican candidate for president, Senator Barry Goldwater, who declared the Act unconstitutional. Despite opposition and violence in the South, the number of Negro voters increased, but not in a significant measure. So many were still denied the right to register and vote, however, that in January, 1965, the Reverend Martin Luther King, Jr., and several civil rights organizations began demonstrations to support a registration drive in Selma, Alabama, where only two per cent of voting-age Negroes had been permitted to register. Photographs and television documentaries of the vicious attack by state troopers who broke up a planned march from Selma to Montgomery aroused almost nationwide shock and condemnation. The marchers were kicked by horses, lashed with whips, beaten with clubs, and subjected to tear gas. A second attempt, two days later, was likewise turned back. Two white civil rights activists, the Reverend James J. Reeb, a Unitarian minister from Boston and Mrs. Viola Liuzzo, a housewife from Michigan, were killed by local whites.

On March 15, President Johnson in an address to Congress urged a new civil rights bill, which he concluded with the words of one of the Negro crusading songs, "We shall overcome." The next week, thousands of demonstrators, a few of them white, made a memorable march from Selma to Montgomery under the protection of federal troops. On August 6, President Johnson signed the 1965 Civil Rights Law.

. . . Despite . . . somewhat less than rigid enforcement of the Act, in the November, 1968, election there was an increase of nearly one million in Negro registration in the South over that in the 1964 election. Most of the increase since August, 1965 — 740,000 — occurred in the six states fully covered by the Act. This was double that of the registration prior to that time; in addition, the number of elected Negro officials in the region rose from about 70 in 1965 to 400 in 1969. On the other hand, in early 1969, nearly 2,000,000 or 38 per cent of Negroes of voting age in the South remained unregistered. Moreover, in the six states fully covered by the law, 43 per cent of Negroes and only 21 per cent of whites of voting age were unregistered.

. . . Investigations in 1966 by the United States Commission on Civil Rights led to renewed efforts to strengthen the 1965 Voting Rights Act. The more widely used new devices involved the dilution of the Negro vote through such state measures as conversion from elections by district to elections-at-large, state laws permitting the legislature to consolidate predominantly Negro counties with predominantly white counties, and reapportionment and redistricting statutes. Some states also adopted measures to prevent Negroes from becoming candidates or obtaining office. . . . During 1966 and 1967, in some areas of Louisiana, South Carolina, Mississippi, Alabama, Georgia, and Virginia, Negro candidates and their campaign workers and poll watchers, as well as Negro voters and persons active in urging and aiding Negroes to register and vote, were subjected to various forms of harassment and intimidation, including arrests by law enforcement officials and economic and physical reprisals.

The Voting Rights Act of 1965 is fully set out in the Appendix, and its crucial provisions are reviewed here in South Carolina v. Katzenbach.

SOUTH CAROLINA v. KATZENBACH
383 U.S. 301, 86 S. Ct. 803, 15 L. Ed. 2d 769 (1966)

Chief Justice WARREN.

I

The constitutional propriety of the Voting Rights Act of 1965 must be judged with reference to the historical experience which it reflects. Before enacting the measure, Congress explored with great care the problem of racial discrimination in voting.

Two points emerge vividly from the voluminous legislative history of the Act contained in the committee hearings and floor debates. First: Congress felt itself confronted by an insidious and pervasive evil which had been perpetuated in certain parts of our country through unremitting and ingenious defiance of the Constitution. Second: Congress concluded that the unsuccessful remedies which it had prescribed in the past would have to be replaced by sterner and more elaborate measures in order to satisfy the clear commands of the Fifteenth Amendment. We pause here to summarize the majority reports of the House and Senate Committees, which document in considerable detail the factual basis for these reactions by Congress.[5] See H.R. Rep. No. 439, 89th Cong., 1st Sess., 8-16 (hereinafter cited as House Report); S. Rep. No. 162, pt. 3, 89th Cong., 1st Sess., 3-16 (hereinafter cited as Senate Report).

The Fifteenth Amendment to the Constitution was ratified in 1870. Promptly thereafter Congress passed the first Enforcement Act,[6] which made it a crime for public officers and private persons to obstruct exercise of the right to vote. The statute was amended in the following year,[7] to provide for detailed federal supervision of the electoral process, from registration to the certification of returns. As the years passed and fervor for racial equality waned, enforcement of the laws became spotty and ineffective, and most of

5. The facts contained in these reports are confirmed, among others, by United States v. Louisiana, 225 F. Supp. 353, 363-385 (Wisdom, J.), *aff'd,* 380 U.S. 145; United States v. Mississippi, 229 F. Supp. 925, 983-997 (dissenting opinion of Brown, J.), *rev'd and rem'd,* 380 U.S. 128; United States v. Alabama, 192 F. Supp. 677 (Johnson, J.), *aff'd,* 304 F.2d 583, *aff'd,* 371 U.S. 37; Comm'n on Civil Rights, Voting in Mississippi; 1963 Comm'n on Civil Rights Rep., Voting, pt. 2; 1959 Comm'n on Civil Rights Rep., pt. 2. See generally Christopher, The Constitutionality of the Voting Rights Act of 1965, 18 Stan. L. Rev. 1; Note, Federal Protection of Negro Voting Rights, 51 Va. L. Rev. 1051.

6. 16 Stat. 140.

7. 16 Stat. 433.

their provisions were repealed in 1894.[8] The remnants have had little significance in the recently renewed battle against voting discrimination.

Meanwhile, beginning in 1890, the States of Alabama, Georgia, Louisiana, Mississippi, North Carolina, South Carolina, and Virginia enacted tests still in use which were specifically designed to prevent Negroes from voting.[9] Typically, they made the ability to read and write a registration qualification and also required completion of a registration form. These laws were based on the fact that as of 1890 in each of the named States, more than two-thirds of the adult Negroes were illiterate while less than one-quarter of the adult whites were unable to read or write.[10] At the same time, alternate tests were prescribed in all of the named States to assure that white illiterates would not be deprived of the franchise. These included grandfather clauses, property qualifications, "good character" tests, and the requirement that registrants "understand" or "interpret" certain matter.

The course of subsequent Fifteenth Amendment litigation in this Court demonstrates the variety and persistence of these and similar institutions designed to deprive Negroes of the right to vote. Grandfather clauses were invalidated in Guinn v. United States, 238 U.S. 347, and Myers v. Anderson, 238 U.S. 368. Procedural hurdles were struck down in Lane v. Wilson, 307 U.S. 268. The white primary was outlawed in Smith v. Allwright, 321 U.S. 649, and Terry v. Adams, 345 U.S. 461. Improper challenges were nullified in United States v. Thomas, 362 U.S. 58. Racial gerrymandering was forbidden by Gomillion v. Lightfoot, 364 U.S. 339. . . . discriminatory application of voting tests was condemned in Schnell v. Davis, 336 U.S. 933; Alabama v. United States, 371 U.S. 37; and Louisiana v. United States, 380 U.S. 145.

According to the evidence in recent Justice Department voting suits, the latter strategem is now the principal method used to bar Negroes from the polls. Discriminatory administration of voting qualifications has been found

8. 28 Stat. 36.

9. The South Carolina Constitutional Convention of 1895 was a leader in the widespread movement to disenfranchise Negroes. Key, Southern Politics, 537-539. Senator Ben Tillman frankly explained to the state delegates the aim of the new literacy test: "[T]he only thing we can do as patriots and as statesmen is to take from [the 'ignorant blacks'] every ballot that we can under the laws of our national government." He was equally candid about the exemption from the literacy test for persons who could "understand" and "explain" a section of the state constitution: "There is no particle of fraud or illegality in it. It is just simply showing partiality, perhaps [laughter], or discriminating." He described the alternative exemption for persons paying state property taxes in the same vein: "By means of the $300 clause you simply reach out and take in some more white men and a few more colored men." Journal of the (1895) Constitutional Convention of the State of South Carolina 464, 469, 471. Senator Tillman was the dominant political figure in the state convention, and his entire address merits examination.

10. Prior to the Civil War, most of the slave States made it a crime to teach Negroes how to read or write. Following the war, these States rapidly instituted racial segregation in their public schools. Throughout the period, free public education in the South had barely begun to develop. See Brown v. Board of Education, 347 U.S. 483, 489-90, n. 4; 1959 Comm'n on Civil Rights Rep. 147-151.

in all eight Alabama cases, in all nine Louisiana cases, and in all nine Mississippi cases which have gone to final judgment.[11] Moreover, in almost all of these cases, the courts have held that the discrimination was pursuant to a widespread "pattern or practice." White applicants for registration have often been excused altogether from the literacy and understanding tests or have been given easy versions, have received extensive help from voting officials, and have been registered despite serious errors in their answers.[12] Negroes, on the other hand, have typically been required to pass difficult versions of all the tests, without any outside assistance and without the slightest error.[13] The good morals requirement is so vague and subjective that it has constituted an open invitation to abuse at the hands of voting officials.[14] Negroes obliged to obtain vouchers from registered voters have found it virtually impossible to comply in areas where almost no Negroes are on the rolls.[15]

In recent years, Congress has repeatedly tried to cope with the problem by facilitating case-by-case litigation against voting discrimination. The Civil Rights Act of 1957[16] authorized the Attorney General to seek injunctions against public and private interference with the right to vote on racial grounds. Perfecting amendments in the Civil Rights Act of 1960[17] permitted the joinder of States as party defendants, gave the Attorney General access to local voting records, and authorized courts to register voters in areas of systematic discrimination. Title I of the Civil Rights Act of 1964[18] expedited the hearing of voting cases before three-judge courts and outlawed some of the tactics used to disqualify Negroes from voting in federal elections.

Despite the earnest efforts of the Justice Department and of many federal judges, these new laws have done little to cure the problem of voting discrimination. According to estimates by the Attorney General during hearing on the Act, registration of voting age Negroes in Alabama rose only from

11. For example, see three voting suits brought against the States themselves: United States v. Alabama, 192 F. Supp. 677, *aff'd*, 304 F.2d 583, *aff'd* 371 U.S. 37; United States v. Louisiana, 225 F. Supp. 353, *aff'd*, 380 U.S. 145; United States v. Mississippi, 339 F.2d 679.

12. A white applicant in Louisiana satisfied the registrar of his ability to interpret the state constitution by writing, "FRDUM FOOF SPETGH." United States v. Louisiana, 225 F. Supp. 353, 384. A white applicant in Alabama who had never completed the first grade of school was enrolled after the registrar filled out the entire form for him. United States v. Penton, 212 F. Supp. 193, 210-211.

13. In Panola County, Mississippi, the registrar required Negroes to interpret the provision of the state constitution concerning "the rate of interest on the fund known as the 'Chickasaw School Fund.'" United States v. Duke, 332 F.2d 759, 765. In Forrest County, Mississippi, the registrar rejected six Negroes with baccalaureate degrees, three of whom were also Masters of Arts. United States v. Lund, 301 F.2d 818, 821.

14. For example, see United States v. Atkins, 323 F.2d 733, 743.

15. For example, see United States v. Logue, 344 F.2d 290, 292.

16. 71 Stat. 634.

17. 74 Stat. 86.

18. 78 Stat. 241.

10.2% to 19.4% between 1958 and 1964; in Louisiana it barely inched ahead from 31.7% to 31.8% between 1956 and 1965; and in Mississippi it increased only from 4.4% to 6.4% between 1954 and 1964. In each instance, registration of voting age whites ran roughly 50 percentage points or more ahead of Negro registration.

The previous legislation has proved ineffective for a number of reasons. Voting suits are unusually onerous to prepare, sometimes requiring as many as 6,000 man-hours spent combing through registration records in preparation for trial. Litigation has been exceedingly slow, in part because of the ample opportunities for delay afforded voting officials and others involved in the proceedings. Even when favorable decisions have finally been obtained, some of the States affected have merely switched to discriminatory devices not covered by the federal decrees or have enacted difficult new tests designed to prolong the existing disparity between white and Negro registration.[19] Alternatively, certain local officials have defied and evaded court orders or have simply closed their registration offices to freeze the voting rolls.[20] The provision of the 1960 law authorizing registration by federal officers has had little impact on local maladministration because of its procedural complexities.

During the hearings and debates on the Act, Selma, Alabama, was repeatedly referred to as the pre-eminent example of the ineffectiveness of existing legislation. In Dallas County, of which Selma is the seat, there were four years of litigation by the Justice Department and two findings by the federal courts of widespread voting discrimination. Yet in those four years, Negro registration rose only from 16 to 383, although there are approximately 15,000 Negroes of voting age in the county. Any possibility that these figures were attributable to political apathy was dispelled by the protest demonstrations in Selma in the early months of 1965. The House Committee on the Judiciary summed up the reaction of Congress to these developments in the following words:

> The litigation in Dallas County took more than four years to open the door to the exercise of constitutional rights conferred almost a century ago. The problem on a national scale is that the difficulties experienced in suits in Dallas County have been encountered over and over again under existing voting laws. Four years is too long. The burden is too heavy — the wrong to our citizens is too serious — the damage to our national conscience is too great not to adopt more effective measures than exist today. Such is the essential justification for the pending bill. House Report 11.

19. The Court of Appeals for the Fifth Circuit ordered the registrars of Forrest County, Mississippi, to give future Negro applicants the same assistance which white applicants had enjoyed in the past, and to register future Negro applicants despite errors which were not serious enough to disqualify white applicants in the past. The Mississippi Legislature promptly responded by requiring applicants to complete their registration forms without assistance or error, and by adding a good-morals and public-challenge provision to the registration laws. United States v. Mississippi, 229 F. Supp. 925, 996-997 (dissenting opinion).

20. For example, see United States v. Parker, 236 F. Supp. 511; United States v. Palmer, 230 F. Supp. 716.

II

The Voting Rights Act of 1965 reflects Congress' firm intention to rid the country of racial discrimination in voting.[21] The heart of the Act is a complex scheme of stringent remedies aimed at areas where voting discrimination has been most flagrant. Section 4(a)(d) lays down a formula defining the States and political subdivisions to which these new remedies apply. The first of the remedies, contained in §4(a), is the suspension of literacy tests and similar voting qualifications for a period of five years from the last occurrence of substantial voting discrimination. Section 5 prescribes a second remedy, the suspension of all new voting regulations pending review by federal authorities to determine whether their use would perpetuate voting discrimination. The third remedy, covered in §§6(b), 7, 9, and 13(a), is the assignment of federal examiners by the Attorney General to list qualified applicants who are thereafter entitled to vote in all elections.

Other provisions of the Act prescribe subsidiary cures for persistent voting discrimination. Section 8 authorizes the appointment of federal poll-watchers in places to which federal examiners have already been assigned. Section 10(d) excuses those made eligible to vote in sections of the country covered by §4(b) of the Act from paying accumulated past poll taxes for state and local elections. Section 12(e) provides for balloting by persons denied access to the polls in areas where federal examiners have been appointed.

The remaining remedial portions of the Act are aimed at voting discrimination in any area of the country where it may occur. Section 2 broadly prohibits the use of voting rules to abridge exercise of the franchise on racial grounds. Sections 3, 6(a), and 13(b) strengthen existing procedures for attacking voting discrimination by means of litigation. Section 4(e) excuses citizens educated in American schools conducted in a foreign language from passing English-language literacy tests. Section 10(a)-(c) facilitates constitutional litigation challenging the imposition of all poll taxes for state and local elections. Sections 11 and 12(a)-(d) authorize civil and criminal sanctions against interference with the exercise of rights guaranteed by the Act. . . .

. . . [T]he only sections of the Act to be reviewed at this time are §§4(a)-(d), 5, 6(b), 7, 9, 13(a), and certain procedural portions of §14, all of which are presently in actual operation in South Carolina. . . .

III

These provisions of the Voting Rights Act of 1965 are challenged on the fundamental ground that they exceed the powers of Congress and encroach on an area reserved to the States by the Constitution. South Carolina and certain of the amici curiae also attack specific sections of the Act for more particular reasons. They argue that the coverage formula prescribed in §4(a)-

21. For convenient reference, the entire Act is reprinted in an Appendix to this opinion. (Omitted here. See 10 Race Rel. L. Rep. 1326.)

(d) violates the principle of the equality of States, denies due process by employing an invalid presumption and by barring judicial review of administrative findings, constitutes a forbidden bill of attainder, and impairs the separation of powers by adjudicating guilt through legislation. They claim that the review of new voting rules required in §5 infringes Article III by directing the District Court to issue advisory opinions. They contend that the assignment of federal examiners authorized in §6(b) abridges due process by precluding judicial review of administrative findings and impairs the separation of powers by giving the Attorney General judicial functions; also that the challenge procedure prescribed in §9 denies due process on account of its speed. Finally, South Carolina and certain of the amici curiae maintain that §§4(a) and 5, buttressed by §14(b) of the Act, abridge due process by limiting litigation to a distant forum. . . .

The ground rules for resolving this question are clear. The language and purpose of the Fifteenth Amendment, the prior decisions construing its several provisions, and the general doctrines of constitutional interpretation, all point to one fundamental principle. As against the reserved powers of the States, Congress may use any rational means to effectuate the constitutional prohibition of racial discrimination in voting. Cf. our rulings last Term, sustaining Title II of the Civil Rights Act of 1964, in Heart of Atlanta Motel v. United States, 379 U.S. 241, 258-259, 261-262; and Katzenbach v. McClung, 379 U.S. 294, 303-304. We turn now to a more detailed description of the standards which govern our review of the Act.

Section 1 of the Fifteenth Amendment declares that "the right of citizens of the United States to vote shall not be denied or abridged by the United States or by any State on account of race, color, or previous condition of servitude." This declaration has always been treated as self-executing and has repeatedly been construed, without further legislative specification, to invalidate state voting qualifications or procedures which are discriminatory on their face, or in practice . . . . These decisions have been rendered with full respect for the general rule, reiterated last Term in Carrington v. Rash, 380 U.S. 89, 91, that States "have broad powers to determine the conditions under which the right of suffrage may be exercised." The gist of the matter is that the Fifteenth Amendment supersedes contrary exertions of state power. "When a State exercises power wholly within the domain of state interest, it is insulated from federal judicial review. But such insulation is not carried over when state power is used as an instrument for circumventing a federally protected right." Gomillion v. Lightfoot, 364 U.S., at 347.

South Carolina contends that the cases cited above are precedents only for the authority of the judiciary to strike down state statutes and procedures — that to allow an exercise of this authority by Congress would be to rob the courts of their rightful constitutional role. On the contrary, §2 of the Fifteenth Amendment expressly declares that "Congress shall have the power to enforce this article by appropriate legislation." By adding this authorization, the Framers indicated that Congress was to be chiefly responsible for implementing the rights created in §1. "It is the power of Congress which has been enlarged. Congress is authorized to *enforce* the prohibitions by appropriate legislation. Some legislation is contemplated to make the [Civil War] amendments fully effective." Ex parte Virginia, 100 U.S. 339, 345. Accordingly, in addition to the courts, Congress has full remedial powers to effectuate the constitutional prohibition against racial discrimination in voting.

Congress has repeatedly exercised these powers in the past, and its enactments have repeatedly been upheld. For recent examples, see the Civil Rights Act of 1957, which was sustained in United States v. Raines, 362 U.S. 17; United States v. Thomas, supra; and Hannah v. Larche, 363 U.S. 420; and the Civil Rights Act of 1960, which was upheld in Alabama v. United States, supra; Louisiana v. United States, supra; and United States v. Mississippi, 380 U.S. 128. On the rare occasions when the Court has found an unconstitutional exercise of these powers, in its opinion Congress had attacked evils not comprehended by the Fifteenth Amendment. See United States v. Reese, 92 U.S. 214; James v. Bowman, 190 U.S. 127.

The basic test to be applied in a case involving §2 of the Fifteenth Amendment is the same as in all cases concerning the express powers of Congress with relation to the reserved powers of the States. Chief Justice Marshall laid down the classic formulation, 50 years before the Fifteenth Amendment was ratified:

> Let the end be legitimate, let it be within the scope of the constitution, and all means which are appropriate, which are plainly adapted to that end, which are not prohibited, but consist with the letter and spirit of the constitution, are constitutional. McCulloch v. Maryland, 4 Wheat. 316, 421.

The Court has subsequently echoed his language in describing each of the Civil War Amendments:

> Whatever legislation is appropriate, that is, adapted to carry out the objects the amendments have in view, whatever tends to enforce submission to the prohibitions they contain, and to secure to all persons the enjoyment of perfect equality of civil rights and the equal protection of the laws against State denial or invasion, if not prohibited, is brought within the domain of congressional power. Ex parte Virginia, 100 U.S., at 345-346. . . .

We therefore reject South Carolina's argument that Congress may appropriately do no more than to forbid violations of the Fifteenth Amendment in general terms — that the task of fashioning specific remedies or of applying them to particular localities must necessarily be left entirely to the courts. Congress is not circumscribed by any such artificial rules under §2 of the Fifteenth Amendment. In the oft-repeated words of Chief Justice Marshall, referring to another specific legislative authorization in the Constitution, "This power, like all others vested in Congress, is complete in itself, may be exercised to its utmost extent, and acknowledges no limitations, other than are prescribed in the constitution." Gibbons v. Ogden, 9 Wheat. 1, 196.

IV

Congress exercised its authority under the Fifteenth Amendment in an inventive manner when it enacted the Voting Rights Act of 1965. First: The measure prescribes remedies for voting discrimination which go into effect without any need for prior adjudication. This was clearly a legitimate response to the problem, for which there is ample precedent under other constitutional provisions. See Katzenbach v. McClung, 379 U.S. 294, 302-304; United States v. Darby, 312 U.S. 100, 120-121. Congress had found that case-by-case litigation was inadequate to combat widespread and persistent discrimination in voting, because of the inordinate amount of time and energy required to overcome the obstructionist tactics invariably encountered in these lawsuits. After enduring nearly a century of systematic resistance to the Fifteenth Amendment, Congress might well decide to shift the advantage of time and inertia from the perpetrators of the evil to its victims. The question remains, of course, whether the specific remedies prescribed in the Act were an appropriate means of combatting the evil, and to this question we shall presently address ourselves.

Second: The Act intentionally confines these remedies to a small number of States and political subdivisions which in most instances were familiar to Congress by name. This, too, was a permissible method of dealing with the problem. Congress had learned that substantial voting discrimination presently occurs in certain sections of the country, and it knew no way of accurately forecasting whether the evil might spread elsewhere in the future. In acceptable legislative fashion, Congress chose to limit its attention to the geographic areas where immediate action seemed necessary. See McGowan v. Maryland, 366 U.S. 420, 427; Salsburg v. Maryland, 346 U.S. 545, 550-554. The doctrine of the equality of States, invoked by South Carolina, does not bar this approach, for that doctrine applies only to the terms upon which States are admitted to the Union, and not to the remedies for local evils which have subsequently appeared. See Coyle v. Smith, 221 U.S. 559, and cases cited therein.

[In the balance of the opinion, Chief Justice Warren reviewed and approved the coverage formula, the use of examiners, and the necessity of obtaining approval of changes in election laws from the Attorney General or the federal court in the District of Columbia.

Justice Black concurred with most of the majority opinion, but dissented from the holding that every part of §5 is constitutional. In his view, the provision of §5 that a state covered by §4(b) can in no way amend its constitution or laws relating to voting without first trying to persuade the Attorney General that the new laws do not have the purpose or effect of denying the right to vote, violates the Constitution on two grounds. First, he found it hard to believe that a justiciable controversy can arise giving jurisdiction in the federal courts under such a scheme as §5 proposes. Second, he believed that such a scheme distorts the separation of federal and state powers. For him, "the states have power to pass laws and amend their constitutions without first sending their officials hundreds of miles away to beg federal authorities to amend them." He believed that §5 undermines this power of the states.]

NOTE: SECTION 5 OF THE 1965 CIVIL RIGHTS ACT

Section 5 (see Appendix infra) prohibits those jurisdictions covered by §4(a) from denying the right to vote because of changes in election procedures made after November 1, 1964, unless approval is obtained from the courts or the Attorney General. It has proved a major deterrent to state efforts to frustrate black voters. Thus, in Allen v. State Board of Elections, 393 U.S. 544, 89 S. Ct. 817, 22 L. Ed. 2d 1 (1969), the Court held each of the following measures a voting matter within the meaning of §5: permitting county boards of supervisors to have board members elected at large rather than by district; requiring that county superintendents of education be appointed by the Board of Education rather than having the option of election or appointment; altering requirements for qualification as an independent candidate so as to make such qualification more difficult; and empowering election judges to provide illiterate voters with assistance in marking their ballots.

In Perkins v. Matthews, 400 U.S. 379, 91 S. Ct. 431, 27 L. Ed. 2d 476 (1971), the Court concluded that §5 required prior submission by a Mississippi municipality of even seemingly minor changes in election procedures. Such changes, the Court felt, could significantly affect election results. Thus, changed locations of polling places may affect one's ability to vote, and may have a racially discriminatory purpose or effect; changes in boundary lines through annexations determine who may vote in city elections through inclusion of certain voters, and therefore dilute the weight of the votes of those who had the franchise prior to annexation; a change from ward to at-large election of aldermen also reflects a great potential for racial discrimination.

In Hadnott v. Amos, 394 U.S. 358, 89 S. Ct. 1101, 22 L. Ed. 336 (1969), the Court ruled that a statute requiring every candidate for state office to file an official declaration of candidacy before March 1st, constituted a change in voting procedures that required approval in accordance with the provisions of §5. Black candidates of the National Democratic Party of Alabama (NDPA) had been denied a place on the ballot for their failure to comply with this and other statutory requirements. A three-judge district court held that the "official declaration" statute did not come within §5 and was a reasonable exercise of the state's interest in supervising election campaigns. The Supreme Court restored the district court's original temporary restraining order; some NDPA nominees were elected in some counties, but in Greene County their names were not even on the ballot. The plaintiffs filed a motion to show cause why the Greene County probate judge, who was responsible for placing the names of candidates on the ballot, should not be held in contempt. The Supreme Court reversed the judgment of the three-judge court, holding, inter alia, that the statute had been discriminatorily applied, and could not be enforced without prior approval, as required by §5. The Court remanded the case to the district court for entry of an order requiring that new elections be held. Determination of the contempt issue was left to the district court.

In the following cases, various state enactments or proposals were held to come within the terms of §5: United States v. Garner, 349 F. Supp. 1054 (N.D. Ga. 1972) (new election required where city failed to secure approval of proposal to change standards for election of candidates for city council); Evers v. State Board of Election Commissioners, 327 F. Supp. 640 (S.D. Miss. 1971), *appeal dismissed,* 405 U.S. 1001 (1972) (changes in state election laws regarding qualifications of candidates, conduct of primaries and election procedures); Moore v. LeFlore County Board of Election Commissioners, 3 Race Rel. L. Sur. 183 (N.D. Miss., Oct. 18, 1971) (change from single-member districts to at-large elections); Clayton v. North Carolina State Board of Elections, 317 F. Supp. 915 (E.D.N.C. 1970) (statutory amendment prohibiting electioneering within 500 feet of polling places in 6 of 100 counties, where previous limit for all counties was 50 feet); Wilson v. North Carolina State Board of Elections, 317 F. Supp. 1299 (M.D.N.C. 1970) (Democratic party agreement, made pursuant to state statute, providing for rotation of state senatorship among counties in electoral district); Dyer v. Love, 307 F. Supp. 974 (N.D. Miss. 1969) (proposed change from single-member districts to at-large election in order to correct malapportionment; court-ordered redistricting into equal population districts); Mississippi Freedom Democratic Party v. Johnson, 299 F. Supp. 93 (S.D. Miss. 1969) (amendment to state constitution providing for consolidation of counties); Sellers v. Trussell, 253 F. Supp. 915 (M.D. Ala. 1966) (statute changing term of office of incumbent county commissioners from four years to six).

But see Oden v. Brittain, 396 U.S. 1210, 90 S. Ct. 4, 24 L. Ed. 2d 32 (1969) (denial by Justice Black of application for injunction to prohibit holding city elections to elect five members of city council established under new state law authorizing city to change from commission to council-manager form of government, on the ground that the change was merely from a three-member council elected at large to a five-member council elected at large); and Fowler v. Adams, 315 F. Supp. 592 (M.D. Fla. 1970), *appeal dismissed,* 400 U.S. 986, 91 S. Ct. 477, 27 L. Ed. 2d 436 (1971) (approving a requirement that candidates for office pay a fee of 5 percent of the salary of that office as a condition to being placed on the ballot, and holding that the 1965 Voting Rights Act was not applicable, because Florida is not a "covered" state). In Jenness v. Little, 306 F. Supp. 925 (N.D. Ga. 1969), *appeal dismissed sub nom.* Matthews v. Little, 397 U.S. 94, 90 S. Ct. 820, 25 L. Ed. 2d (1970), an identical requirement was held not to come within §5 because the statute authorizing enactment of the challenged ordinance had been approved by the

Attorney General, but was declared to be an unconstitutional denial of equal protection of the laws. In Holt v. City of Richmond, 334 F. Supp. 228 (E.D. Va. 1971), the court upheld an annexation agreement between city and county that would have the effect of diluting black voting power, on grounds that the court would not inquire into legislative motive when the agreement was not suspect on its face. Citing 42 U.S.C. §1973(c) (1970), the court found it had no jurisdiction to consider questions arising under the 1965 Voting Rights Act.

NOTES

1. While designed to eliminate racial barriers to black voting in the South, the 1965 Civil Rights Act also aided non–English-speaking Americans. In Katzenbach v. Morgan, 384 U.S. 641, 86 S. Ct. 1717, 16 L. Ed. 2d 828 (1966), the Court sustained the constitutionality of §4(e) of the act, which provides that states may not prohibit registration because of the inability of persons to read, write or understand English, if they were educated in "American-flag" schools in which the dominant classroom language was other than English. New York constitutional and statutory provisions requiring literacy tests in English were invalidated, the Court ruling that §4(e) could be viewed as a measure to secure nondiscriminatory treatment by the government for the Puerto Rican community in New York. It ruled that Congress could reasonably have found that prejudice played a prominent role in the enactment of the New York English literacy tests, and that denial of the franchise is not a justifiable means of encouraging persons to learn the English language. Justice Douglas concurred in the opinion, and Justices Harlan and Stewart dissented, on the premise that it is the Court's responsibility to determine the scope of the Fourteenth Amendment and that the amendment does not reach state laws which are not so arbitrary or irrational as to offend the command of the Equal Protection Clause. See also Cardona v. Power, 384 U.S. 672, 86 S. Ct. 1728, 16 L. Ed. 2d 848 (1966); United States v. County Bd. of Elections, 248 F. Supp. 316 (W.D. N.Y. 1965), *appeal dismissed,* 383 U.S. 575, 86 S. Ct. 1077, 16 L. Ed. 2d 107 (1966). While the Civil Rights Act of 1965 was not controlling, the California Supreme Court cited decisions under that act in Castro v. California, 2 Cal. 3d 223, 466 P.2d 244, 85 Cal. Rptr. 20 (1970). There, provisions of the state constitution and election code conditioning the right to vote on the ability to read the state constitution in English were held to violate the Equal Protection Clause for citizens literate in the Spanish language. The English literacy requirement could not be justified, the court held, as a means of avoiding the cost of printing and distributing bilingual ballots and voting instructions. The court noted that there are twenty-eight Spanish language newspapers or magazines available in California and that Spanish-speaking citizens could adequately inform themselves of election issues from such publications. The court refused to order the state to establish a complete bilingual apparatus, but assumed that such persons could

adequately prepare themselves to vote through advanced study of sample ballots with the assistance of others capable of reading and translating them.

2. When it became clear in the years immediately following passage of the 1965 Voting Rights Act that the courts would not tolerate outright defiance of their commands (see In re Herndon, 325 F. Supp. 779 (N.D. Ala. 1971); United States v. Palmer, 356 F.2d 951 (5th Cir. 1966); United States v. Leflore County, 371 F.2d 368 (5th Cir. 1967); and Reynolds v. Katzenbach, 248 F. Supp. 593 (S.D. Ala. 1965)), the states resorted to more subtle techniques of evasion in a continuing effort to prevent blacks from voting or, failing that, to emasculate their votes. Where such attempts involved changes in election laws, they were usually dealt with under §5 of the 1965 Act. Other forms of discrimination or coercion took place at less visible levels. Consequently, plaintiffs in actions to enjoin such practices experienced difficulty in gathering sufficient unequivocal evidence to support their claims, and hostile district court judges were inclined to resolve uncertainties in favor of the defendants.

This was particularly true where the plaintiffs alleged economic coercion only, such as termination of credit or sharecropping arrangements. In United States v. Harvey, 250 F. Supp. 219 (E.D. La. 1966), the court held that the 1965 Act was unconstitutional insofar as it purported to reach individual acts, and that even assuming constitutionality, the evidence was insufficient to show that the defendants had acted with the purpose of depriving the plaintiffs of their voting rights. See also Miles v. Dickson, 40 F.R.D. 386 (M.D. Ala. 1966), *aff'd with modification,* 387 F.2d 716 (5th Cir. 1967).

Similar failure of proof was found in cases more directly related to the election process. See Davis v. Gallinghouse, 246 F. Supp. 208 (E.D. La. 1965); Gremillion v. Rinaudo, 325 F. Supp. (E.D. La. 1971) (held, inter alia, that since here a uniformed police chief assisted both black and white illiterate voters, there was no coercion, and hence no violation of the 1965 Act).

Even where courts granted relief from ad hoc discriminatory practices, they were reluctant to find discriminatory intent on the part of the defendants or to issue injunctions. In Gray v. Main, 291 F. Supp. 998 (M.D. Ala. 1966), the court refused to set aside election results on the ground that the proof of irregularities was not sufficient to justify such drastic action. Such irregularities included the use of different standards for blacks and whites in purging the voting lists of unqualified voters, assigning new polling places to black voters without notice, and filling out absentee ballots for white voters. The court held that the evidence raised a "suspicion" of discrimination, and issued a declaratory judgment setting out procedures to be followed by the defendants. See also Gilmore v. Greene County Democratic Party Executive Committee, 435 F.2d 487 (5th Cir. 1970) (denial of use of sample ballots to illiterate black voters was a denial of equal protection, but injunctive relief was held not appropriate). Cf. Jenness v. Little, 306 F. Supp. 925 (N.D. Ga. 1963), *appeal dismissed sub nom.* Matthews v. Little, 397 U.S. 94, 70 S. Ct. 820, 25 L. Ed. 2d 81 (1970) (ordinance requiring payment of fee as prerequisite to qualifying as candidate was denial of equal protection, but injunctive relief was deemed inappropriate where election was only a month away). Cf. Brown v. Post, 279 F. Supp 60 (W.D. La. 1968) (new election was ordered where defendants actively solicited absentee ballots from whites, but it was held also that there was no intentional plan to deprive blacks of voting rights); United States v. Post, 297 F. Supp. 46 (W.D. La. 1969) (new election was ordered where defendants altered voting machine without notice, so that pulling master level did not result in a vote for black candidate, but it was held also that the change was made in good faith).

In a few cases courts actively intervened in the ongoing election process to grant "preventive" relief as authorized by §12 of the 1965 Act. See, e.g., United States v. Executive Committee of Democratic Party of Dallas County, 254 F. Supp. 537 (S.D. Ala. 1966) (enjoining election officials from refusing to tabulate ballots alleged to be invalid because of failure to meet certain technical requirements). See also Thompson v. Brown, 434 F.2d 1092 (5th Cir. 1970) (defendants entitled to removal to federal court where unsuccessful white candidate brought action in state court contesting primary election results). Contrast Gilmore v. Greene County Democratic Executive Committee, 368 F.2d 328 (5th Cir. 1966), where the district court held that candidates were not entitled to have their names on ballot, and the court of appeals reversed and issued a preliminary injunction staying the election until ballots containing their names were prepared. But on appellants' motion to recall the mandate and grant further relief enjoining state court litigation on the validity of appellants' candidacy, initiated by third parties, the court refused, stating that the state court decision interpreting state law would be binding on the federal court absent constitutional questions. 370 F.2d at 919 (5th Cir. 1966).

3. Some courts refused to set aside election results as a means of prospectively enforcing the 1965 Act. See Mississippi Freedom Democratic Party v. Democratic Party of Mississippi, 362 F.2d 60 (5th Cir. 1966) (setting aside election results was held not proper to redress a century of discrimination, where there had been no serious impediment to black registration for more than a year). Cf. McGill v. Ryals, 253 F. Supp. 372 (M.D. Ala. 1966) (courts would not declare newly elected county officials illegally elected, where plaintiffs had failed to avail themselves of alternative remedies under earlier civil rights statutes prior to the election).

4. In Gaston County v. United States, 395 U.S. 285, 89 S. Ct. 1720, 23 L. Ed. 2d 309 (1969), the Court affirmed a trial court's refusal to permit plaintiff county to reinstate its literacy tests for voter registration, which tests had been suspended as required by the Voting Rights Act of 1965. Justice Harlan, speaking for the Court, concluded from a study of its legislative history that one of the principal reasons for adoption of the test suspension provisions of the 1965 Voting Rights Act was "the potential effect of unequal educational opportunities upon the exercise of the franchise." 395 U.S. at 289. Here the Court found that a segregated dual system had been maintained, and that substantial evidence had been introduced showing that, in fact, the county

had "deprived its black residents of equal educational opportunities, which in turn deprived them of an equal chance to pass the literacy test." 395 U.S. at 297. Evidence of progress in school desegregation and the removal of inequalities was held irrelevant because such recent improvements could not remove the educational disadvantages of the adult Negro population, and impartial administration of the literacy tests would serve only to perpetuate inequities. Justice Black dissented.

5. In the Civil Rights Act of 1968, 82 Stat. 73, 18 U.S.C. §245 (1969), printed in the Appendix, Congress sought to increase sanctions against forceful interference with an array of federally protected activities, including the right to vote. The act provides criminal penalties for intimidation of persons engaged in voting or qualifying to vote, of persons qualifying or acting as a poll watcher, or of any legally authorized election official, in any primary, special or general election. The act does not cover campaign workers and extends only to intimidation by "force, or threat of force." It thus will be more difficult to extend its coverage to economic intimidation, which, according to many reports (see Note 8 infra), is the most frequently used means of discouraging economically dependent black voters from exercising their franchise rights.

6. In the Voting Rights Act Amendment of 1970, 84 Stat. 314, Congress extended to the whole country its ban on the use of literacy tests. This provision, together with other sections of the 1970 Amendment lowering the minimum age of voters in both state and federal elections from twenty-one to eighteen, and abolishing state durational residency requirements with respect to voting for president and vice-president, except for a thirty-day period for advanced registration, were considered by the Court in Oregon v. Mitchell, 400 U.S. 112, 91 S. Ct. 260, 27 L. Ed. 2d 272 (1970). In several opinions, the justices all concurred that the provision abolishing literacy tests was an appropriate exercise of congressional power to enforce the Fifteenth Amendment by eliminating a device that served to discriminate against voters on the basis of race or color. With the exception of Justice Harlan, the justices agreed that the provision abolishing state durational residence requirements was an appropriate exercise of congressional power to protect freedom of travel and freedom to establish new residences as privileges of national citizenship. The members of the Court differed sharply on the provision reducing the voting age. Four members of the Court agreed with Justice Black that the provision was valid as to federal elections, and four agreed with his view that the provision was invalid with respect to voting in state and local elections. Constitutional authority for state and local voting by eighteen-year-olds was provided by the Twenty-sixth Amendment, adopted in 1971, §1 of which reads: "The right of citizens of the United States, who are eighteen years of age or older, to vote shall not be denied or abridged by the United States or by any State on account of age."

7. Residence barriers to voting were further lowered in Dunn v. Blumstein, 405 U.S. 330, 92 S. Ct. 995, 31 L. Ed. 2d 274 (1972). Tennessee laws requiring one year's residence in the state and three months' residence in the county as

prerequisites for registration were found to violate the Equal Protection Clause and unnecessary to further any compelling state interests. Noting the serious penalty that the statutes imposed on bona fide residents who have recently traveled from one jurisdiction to another, the Court concluded that a period of thirty days is ample to complete whatever administrative tasks are needed to prevent fraud and ensure the purity of the ballot box.

8. Despite emphasis on "legal tactics" to limit black voting potential, there is, particularly in the deep South, a continued reliance on economic pressure, intimidation and outright violence. For example, reports from Mississippi following the November 1971 election indicate that many black candidates and their racially mixed out-of-state supporters were kept from counting votes cast in the general election by such tactics — "incidents of widespread violence, harassment by local white officials and citizens." N.Y. Times, Nov. 7, 1971, 42, c. 1.

9. In 1972, civil rights groups planned litigation attacking the validity of a lengthy new "application for registration" form approved by the Mississippi legislature. The application asks sixteen questions, some having to do with religion, property ownership and income tax returns. Civil rights lawyers considered the new form an invasion of privacy and an obvious effort to deter voter registration, particularly among the estimated 277,000 newly eligible young voters, comprising 19.7 percent of Mississippi's potential electorate in that year. The Attorney General approved the form. N.Y. Times, Aug. 7, 1972, 21, c. 1.

B. EFFECTING BLACK VOTING POWER

In 1960, the Supreme Court, spurred to action by a blatant gerrymander designed to negate the growing strength of black voters in the college town of Tuskegee, Alabama, breached its long-standing policy not to involve itself in the "political thicket" of reapportionment issues. See Colegrove v. Green, 328 U.S. 549, 66 S. Ct. 1198, 90 L. Ed. 1432 (1946). In the very next term following its decision in Gomillion v. Lightfoot, infra, the Court decided Baker v. Carr, 369 U.S. 186, 82 S. Ct. 691, 7 L. Ed. 2d 663 (1962), and the reapportionment era was born. Thus, as frequently happens, litigation intended to eliminate racist practices resulted in new legal principles intended to broaden the rights of all Americans. The cases in this section, however, question the extent to which standards of proof required in reapportionment cases asserting dilution of black votes have frustrated efforts by blacks and other minorities to share in the benefits of the "one man, one vote" rule.

GOMILLION v. LIGHTFOOT

364 U.S. 339, 81 S. Ct. 125, 5 L. Ed. 2d 110 (1960)

Mr. Justice Frankfurter delivered the opinion of the Court.

This litigation challenges the validity, under the United States Constitution, of Local Act No. 140, passed by the Legislature of Alabama in 1957, redefining the boundaries of the City of Tuskegee. Petitioners, Negro citizens of Alabama who were, at the time of this redistricting measure, residents of the City of Tuskegee, brought an action in the United States District Court for the Middle District of Alabama for a declaratory judgment that Act 140 is unconstitutional, and for an injunction to restrain the Mayor and officers of Tuskegee and the officials of Macon County, Alabama, from enforcing the Act against them and other Negroes similarly situated. Petitioners' claim is that enforcement of the statute, which alters the shape of Tuskegee from a square to an uncouth twenty-eight-sided figure, will constitute a discrimination against them in violation of the Due Process and Equal Protection Clauses of the Fourteenth Amendment to the Constitution and will deny them the right to vote in defiance of the Fifteenth Amendment. . . .

At this stage of the litigation we are not concerned with the truth of the allegations, that is, the ability of petitioners to sustain their allegations by proof. The sole question is whether the allegations entitle them to make good on their claim that they are being denied rights under the United States Constitution. The complaint, charging that Act 140 is a device to disenfranchise Negro citizens, allege the following facts: Prior to Act 140 the City of Tuskegee was square in shape; the Act transformed it into a strangely irregular twenty-eight-sided figure as indicated in the diagram appended to this opinion. The essential inevitable effect of this redefinition of Tuskegee's boundaries is to remove from the city all save only four or five of its 400 Negro voters while not removing a single white voter or resident. The result of the Act is to deprive the Negro petitioners discriminatorily of the benefits of residence in Tuskegee, including, inter alia, the right to vote in municipal elections.

These allegations, if proven, would abundantly establish that Act 140 was not an ordinary geographic redistricting measure even within familiar abuses of gerrymandering. If these allegations upon a trial remained uncontradicted or unqualified, the conclusion would be irresistible, tantamount for all practical purposes to a mathematical demonstration, that the legislation is solely concerned with segregating white and colored voters by fencing Negro citizens out of town so as to deprive them of their pre-existing municipal vote.

It is difficult to appreciate what stands in the way of adjudging a statute having this inevitable effect invalid in light of the principles by which this Court must judge, and uniformly has judged, statutes that, howsoever speciously defined, obviously discriminate against colored citizens. "The [Fifteenth] Amendment nullifies sophisticated as well as simple-minded modes of discrimination." Lane v Wilson, 307 US 268.

The complaint amply alleges a claim of racial discrimination. Against this claim the respondents have never suggested, either in their brief or in oral argument, any countervailing municipal function which Act 140 is designed to serve. The respondents invoke generalities expressing the State's unrestricted power — unlimited, that is, by the United States Constitution — to establish, destroy, or reorganize by contraction or expansion its political subdivisions, to wit, cities, counties, and other local units. We freely recognize the breadth and importance of this aspect of the State's political power. To exalt this power into an absolute is to misconceive the reach and rule of this Court's decisions in the leading case of Hunter v Pittsburgh, 207 US 161, and related cases relied upon by respondents. . . .

If all this is so in regard to the constitutional protection of contracts, it should be equally true that, to paraphrase, such power, extensive though it is, is met and overcome by the Fifteenth Amendment to the Constitution of the United States, which forbids a State from passing any law which deprives a citizen of his vote because of his race. The opposite conclusion, urged upon us by respondents, would sanction the achievement by a State of any impairment of voting rights whatever so long as it was cloaked in the garb of the realignment of political subdivisions. . . . [The Court here distinguished Hunter v. Pittsburgh, supra, and Colegrove v. Green, 328 U.S. 549 (1949).]

In sum, as Mr. Justice Holmes remarked, when dealing with a related situation, in Nixon v Herndon, 273 US 536: "Of course the petition concerns political action," but "The objection that the subject matter of the suit is political is little more than a play upon words." A statute which is alleged to have worked unconstitutional deprivations of petitioners' rights is not immune to attack simply because the mechanism employed by the legislature is a redefinition of municipal boundaries. According to the allegations here made, the Alabama Legislature has not merely redrawn the Tuskegee city limits with incidental inconvenience to the petitioners; it is more accurate to say that it has deprived the petitioners of the municipal franchise and consequent rights and to that end it has incidentally changed the city's boundaries. While in form this is merely an act redefining metes and bounds, if the allegations are established, the inescapable human effect of this essay in geometry and geography is to despoil colored citizens, and only colored citizens, of their theretofore enjoyed voting rights. That was not Colegrove v Green.

When a State exercises power wholly within the domain of state interest, it is insulated from federal judicial review. But such insulation is not carried over when state power is used as an instrument for circumventing a federally protected right. This principle has had many applications. It has long been recognized in cases which have prohibited a State from exploiting a power acknowledged to be absolute in an isolated context to justify the imposition of an "unconstitutional condition." What the Court has said in those cases is equally applicable here, viz., that "Acts generally lawful may become unlawful when done to accomplish an unlawful end, United States v Reading Co. 226 US 324, 357, 57 L ed 243, 254, 33 S Ct 90, and a constitutional power cannot be used by way of condition to attain an unconstitutional result." Western U. Tel. Co. v Foster, 247 US 105. The petitioners are entitled to prove their allegations at trial.

For these reasons, the principal conclusions of the District Court and the Court of Appeals are clearly erroneous and the decision below must be

Reversed.

Mr. Justice DOUGLAS, while joining the opinion of the Court, adheres to the dissents in Colegrove v Green, 328 US 549, and South v Peters, 339 US 276. [Justice Whittaker, concurring, expressed the view that the decision should be rested not on the Fifteenth Amendment, but on the Equal Protection Clause of the Fourteenth Amendment, in that the redistricting was an unlawful segregation based on race. Subsequently, the Court has come to treat Gomillion like a Fourteenth Amendment case, and in Whitcomb v. Chavis, 403 U.S. 124, 149, 91 S. Ct. 1858, 1872, 29 L. Ed. 2d 363 (1971), actually cited Gomillion as though it had been decided on Fourteenth Amendment grounds.]

WRIGHT v. ROCKEFELLER

376 U.S. 52, 84 S. Ct. 603, 11 L. Ed. 2d 512 (1964)

Mr. Justice BLACK delivered the opinion of the Court.

Appellants, citizens and registered voters of New York's Seventeenth, Eighteenth, Nineteenth, and Twentieth Congressional Districts, all in New York County (the Island of Manhattan), brought this action in the United States District Court for the Southern District of New York challenging the constitutionality of that part of Chapter 980 of New York's 1961 congressional apportionment statute which defined these four districts. The Governor and several other New York state officials were named as defendants. Congressman Adam Clayton Powell, who represents the Eighteenth Congressional District, and several other New York County political leaders were permitted to intervene as defendants supporting the constitutionality of the apportionment act. Appellants charged that the part of the New York Act in question deprived them of rights guaranteed by the Due Process and Equal Protection Clauses of the Fourteenth Amendment and by the Fifteenth Amendment, which provides that "The right of citizens of the United States to vote shall not be denied or abridged by the United States or by any State on account of race, color, or previous condition of servitude." Their complaint alleged that:

> Chapter 980 establishes irrational, discriminatory and unequal Congressional Districts in the County of New York and segregates eligible voters by race and place of origin. It is contrived to create one district, the 17th Congressional District, which excludes non-white citizens and citizens of Puerto Rican origin and which is over-represented in comparison to the other three districts in the County of New York. The 18th, 19th and 20th Congressional Districts have been drawn so as to include the overwhelming number of non-white citizens and citizens of Puerto Rican origin in the County of New York and to be under-represented in relation to the 17th Congressional District.

The case was heard by a District Court of three judges. During these hearings, counsel for appellants made it clear that their case did not depend on "under-representation because of the variation in the size of the Congressional districts"; it was rather, he said, "a case of ghettoizing the Island of Manhattan" so as "to create a white Congressional district and a non-white

Congressional district." "I think," counsel said, "the only province of the Court in this area is to determine whether or not these districts have been created with racial considerations in mind, and, if they have, or if the results of this districting, the effect of the statute is to create racially segregated areas, we maintain that it violates the Fourteenth and Fifteenth Amendments." Appellants offered maps, statistics, and some oral evidence designed to prove their charge that it was impossible to have districts such as these were unless they "were drawn with regard to race." The statistics showed that the Eighteenth District contained 86.3% Negroes and Puerto Ricans; the Nineteenth, 28.5%; the Twentieth, 27.5%; and the Seventeenth, 5.1%. The evidence also showed irregularities in the boundaries of the districts and some variation in population among the four. Appellees presented no oral testimony but did offer historical maps, a table from the Bureau of the Census, and a message from the President to the Congress on the subject of congressional apportionment.

A majority of the District Court found that appellants had not made out their case on the crucial factual issues. Judge Moore broadly found that "[n]o proof was offered by any party that the specific boundaries created by Chapter 980 were drawn on racial lines or that the Legislature was motivated by considerations of race, creed or country of origin in creating the districts." He concluded, "Plaintiffs having failed upon the facts and the law to establish any violation of their constitutional rights as a result of the action of the New York Legislature in enacting Chapter 980 of the Laws of 1961, the complaint must be dismissed." Judge Feinberg concurred in Judge Moore's result because he, too, believed that appellants had

> not met their burden of proving that the boundaries of the new 17th, 18th, 19th, and 20th Congressional Districts were drawn along racial lines, as they allege. . . .
>
> . . . Plaintiffs did introduce evidence which might justify an inference that racial considerations motivated the 1961 reapportionment of congressional districts in Manhattan. However, other inferences, as set forth below, are equally or more justifiable. Plaintiffs have a difficult burden to meet in attacking the constitutionality of this state statute. . . . Upon analysis, I do not think that burden has been met.
>
> . . . In short, based upon the entire record, I do not feel that plaintiffs have proved their case.

Judge Murphy dissented. He viewed the evidence as "tantamount for all practical purposes, to a mathematical demonstration" that the legislation was "solely concerned with segregating" white voters from colored and Puerto Rican voters "by fencing colored and Puerto Rican citizens out of the 17th District and into a district of their own (the 18th)" and as establishing "per se a prima facie case of a legislative intent to draw congressional district lines in the 17th and 18th Districts on the basis of race and national origin." . . .

We accept the findings of the majority of the District Court that appellants failed to prove that the New York Legislature was either motivated by racial considerations or in fact drew the districts on racial lines. Compare Gomillion v Lightfoot, 364 US 339. It may be true, as Judge Feinberg thought, that there was evidence which could have supported inferences that racial considerations might have moved the state legislature, but, even if so, we agree that there also was evidence to support his finding that the contrary inference was "equally, or more, persuasive." Where there are such conflicting inferences one group of them cannot, because labeled as "prima facie proof," be treated as conclusive on the fact finder so as to deprive him of his responsibility to choose among disputed inferences. And this is true whether the conflicting inferences are drawn from evidence offered by the plaintiff or by the defendant or by both. Hernandez v Texas, 347 US 475, does not support the dissenting view of Judge Murphy that appellants' evidence here established a prima facie case compelling the District Court, despite conflicting inferences which could be drawn from that evidence, to find that New York created these districts on the basis of race and place of origin. Hernandez followed the rule laid down in Norris v Alabama, 294 US 587, and other cases, that proof of a long-continued state practice of not calling Negroes as jurors made out a prima facie case sufficient to justify but not necessarily to compel, a finding of discrimination on account of race. The conclusion of racial discrimination in those cases was reached only after an appraisal of this practice along with all the circumstances. It is plain to us that the District Court was not compelled to find that these districts were the product of a state contrivance to discriminate against colored or Puerto Rican voters. As the majority below pointed out, the concentration of colored and Puerto Rican voters in one area in the county made it difficult, even assuming it to be permissible, to fix districts so as to have anything like an equal division of these voters among the districts. Undoubtedly some of these voters, as shown by this lawsuit, would prefer a more even distribution of minority groups among the four congressional districts, but others, like the intervenors in this case, would argue strenuously that the kind of districts for which appellants contended would be undesirable and, because based on race or place of origin, would themselves be unconstitutional.

We accept the District Court's finding that appellants have not shown that the challenged part of the New York Act was the product of a state contrivance to segregate on the basis of race or place of origin. . . .

The judgment dismissing the complaint is

Affirmed.

Mr. Justice Douglas, with whom Mr. Justice Goldberg concurs, dissenting.

This case raises a question kin to that in Gomillion v Lightfoot, 364 US 339, where racial gerrymandering was used to deprive Negroes of the right to vote. Here no Negroes are deprived of the franchise. Rather, zigzag, tortuous lines are drawn to concentrate Negroes and Puerto Ricans in Manhattan's Eighteenth Congressional District and practically to exclude them from the Seventeenth Congressional District. Neighborhoods in our larger cities often contain members of only one race; and those who draw the lines of Congressional Districts cannot be expected to disregard neighborhoods in an effort to make each district a multiracial one. But where, as here, the line that is drawn can be explained only in racial terms, a different problem is presented.

I

Manhattan is divided into four districts and as a result of the serpentine path that the lines follow, those districts reflect substantial, though not complete, segregation by races:

District	*White % of district*	*Negro and Puerto Rican % of district*
17th	94.9	5.1
18th	13.7	86.3
19th	71.5	28.5
20th	72.5	27.5

In 1961 the legislature expanded the Seventeenth District by altering its boundaries in three respects: (1) it added an area on the upper East Side between 59th Street and 89th Street *of whose population Negroes and Puerto Ricans make up 2.7% of the total;* (2) it added an area on the lower East Side called Stuyvesant Town *of whose population Negroes and Puerto Ricans make up 0.5% of the total;* and (3) it dropped from the Seventeenth District and added to the Eighteenth District a two-block area from 98th Street to 100th Street between Fifth Avenue and Madison Avenue *of whose population Negroes and Puerto Ricans make up 44.5% of the total.*

To achieve this racial gerrymandering, careful manipulation of the boundaries of the Eighteenth District was necessary. . . .

The record strongly suggests that these twists and turns producing an 11-sided, step-shaped boundary between the Seventeenth and Eighteenth Districts were made to bring into the Eighteenth District and keep out of the Seventeenth as many Negroes and Puerto Ricans as possible. There is to be sure no finding to this effect by the three-judge District Court. One of the three judges thought, as I do, that the uncontradicted facts establish per se a prima facie case of a legislative purpose to design the Seventeenth and Eighteenth Districts on racial lines (211 F Supp 460, 472-473), saying that: "[In Gomillion] . . . it was a glaring exclusion of Negroes from a municipal district. Here it is a subtle exclusion from a 'silk stocking district' (as the 17th is so frequently referred to) and a jamming in of colored and Puerto Ricans into the 18th or the kind of segregation that appeals to the intervenors."

A second judge concluded that petitioners "have not met their burden of proving" that the boundaries in question were "drawn along racial lines." Id., at 468. The third judge expressed no view on the precise issue.

The evidence which I have summarized was not rebutted or challenged, the State introducing no evidence. We have not only inferences from conceded facts but also New York's frank concession that it is not possible to say "that race is irrelevant to districting."

Racial segregation that is state-sponsored should be nullified whatever may have been intended. In Johnson v Virginia, 373 US 61, we held segregation of a courtroom audience by race to be unconstitutional, without stopping to inquire what the motive may have been. A well-settled proposition applicable to many rights in the constitutional spectrum is that there may be an abridgment "even though unintended." See NAACP v Alabama, 357 US 449, 461, and cases cited. What the State has done is often conclusive irrespective of motive. Eubanks v Louisiana, 356 US 584, 587-588.

I had assumed that since Brown v Board of Education, 347 US 483, no State may segregate people by race *in the public areas.* The design of voting districts involves one important *public area* — as important as schools, parks, and courtrooms. We should uproot all vestiges of Plessy v Ferguson, 163 US 537, from *the public area.*

The intervenors are persons who apparently have a vested interest in control of the segregated Eighteenth District. They and the State seem to support this segregation not on the "separate but equal" theory of Plessy v Ferguson, supra, but on another theory. Their theory might be called the theory of "separate but better off" — a theory that has been used before. A like argument was made in Buchanan v Warley, 245 US 60, 81, in support of municipal segregation of residential areas; in District of Columbia v Thompson, 346 US 100, in support of segregation in restaurants; in Watson v Memphis, 373 US 526, in support of delayed integration of municipal parks. Indeed, the final argument of John W. Davis for South Carolina in Brown v Board of Education, supra, ended with the words, "The good is sometimes better than the best."

The fact that Negro political leaders find advantage in this nearly solid Negro and Puerto Rican district is irrelevant to our problem. Rotten boroughs were long a curse of democratic processes. Racial boroughs are also at war with democratic standards.

II

What we have in the Seventeenth and Eighteenth Districts in Manhattan is comparable to the Electoral Register System which Britain introduced into India. That system gave a separate constituency to Sikhs, Muslims, Anglo-Indians, Europeans, and Indian Christians. Religious minorities found comfort and safety in such an arrangement. A Muslim deputation made the following demand:

(1) That in the whole of India the Muslims number over 62 millions or between one-fifth and one-fourth of the total population;

(2) that as their numbers exceed the entire population of any first-class European Power, except Russia, Muslims might justly claim adequate recognition as an important factor in the State;

(3) that the representation hitherto accorded to them, almost entirely by nomination, had been inadequate to their requirements and had not always carried with it the approval of those whom the nominees were selected to represent; and

(4) that while Muslims are a distinct community with additional interests of their own, which are not shared by other communities, no Muslim would ever be returned by the existing electoral bodies, unless he worked in sympathy with the Hindu majority in all matters of importance.

Lord Morley made the following reply:

The Muslims demand three things. I had the pleasure of receiving a deputation from them and I know very well what is in their minds. They demand an election of their own representatives to these councils in all the stages just as in Cyprus, where, I think, Muslims vote by themselves; they have nine votes and the non-Muslims have three or the other way about; so in Bohemia where the Germans vote alone and have their own register; therefore we are not without a precedent and a parallel for the idea of a separate register. Secondly, they want a number of seats in excess of their numerical strength. These two demands we are quite ready and intend to meet in full.

Hindus responded favorably. The Joint Report of 1918 stated:

Some persons hold that for a people, such as they deem those of India to be, so divided by race, religion and caste as to be unable to consider the interests of any but their own section, a system of communal electorates and class representation is not merely inevitable but is actually best. They maintain that it evokes and applies the principle of democracy over the widest range over which it is actually alive at all, by appealing to the instincts which are strongest; and that we must hope to develop the finer, which are also at present the weaker instincts by using the forces that really count. According to this theory communal representation is an inevitable and even a healthy stage in the development of a nonpolitical people.

As already noted, the Electoral Register System was not peculiar to British India. Other nations used it. Lebanon today has a modified version: each of eight religious groups has electoral districts from which only a member of that faith can be chosen for the legislature.

Racial electoral registers, like religious ones, have no place in a society that honors the Lincoln tradition — "of the people, by the people, for the people." Here the individual is important, not his race, his creed, or his color. The principle of equality is at war with the notion that District A must be represented by a Negro, as it is with the notion that District B must be represented by a Caucasian, District C by a Jew, District D by a Catholic, and so on. Cf. Gray v Sanders, 372 US 368, 379. The racial electoral register system weights votes along one racial line more heavily than it does other votes. That system, by whatever name it is called, is a divisive force in a community, emphasizing differences between candidates and voters that are irrelevant in the constitutional sense. Of course race, like religion, plays an important role in the choices which individual voters make from among various candidates. But government has no business designing electoral districts along racial or religious lines. . . .

When racial or religious lines are drawn by the State, the multiracial, multireligious communities that our Constitution seeks to weld together as one become separatist; antagonisms that relate to race or to religion rather than to political issues are generated; communities seek not the best representative but the best racial or religious partisan. Since that system is at war with the democratic ideal, it should find no footing here. . . .

NOTE

In Gomillion v. Lightfoot the Supreme Court rejected the lower court's conclusion that the discriminatory gerrymandering should be upheld, on the ground that no improper legislative intent had been shown. Justice Frankfurter, writing for the Court, ignored the question of intent and focused instead upon the obvious effect of the plan. He stated that where members of a readily isolated segment of a racial minority are discriminatorily deprived of their right to vote in municipal elections, such plans violate the Fifteenth Amendment's prohibition against state deprivation of a citizen's right to vote because of race. The effort to apply this standard in Wright v. Rockefeller resulted in serious divisions at both the court of appeals and the Supreme Court level. The majority, apparently discarding the test formulated in Gomillion, affirmed the lower court's decision on the ground that plaintiffs had not shown an improper legislative intent — to segregate blacks — in creating the districts. Justice Goldberg felt that sufficient evidence had been shown to prove prima facie that the legislature acted discriminatorily, and Justice Douglas implied that an adverse effect was sufficient demonstration for a finding of discrimination. The standard set by the majority in Wright can be met in blatant efforts to frustrate black voting power, such as Gomillion, but it imposes an almost insuperable barrier to judicial relief in less obvious situations, such as Ince v. Rockefeller and Whitcomb v. Chavis (infra page 179). See Note, Chavis v. Whitcomb: Apportionment, Gerrymandering, and Black Voting Rights, 24 Rutgers L. Rev. 521, 527, 529 (1970).

INCE v. ROCKEFELLER, 290 F. Supp. 878 (S.D.N.Y. 1968). In 1966, under a federal court order, the New York State legislature was reapportioned. The predominately black community of East Elmhurst, in Queens, was divided between the Twenty-third and the Thirty-first Assembly District, five largely black election districts being included in the Twenty-third District, the rest of East Elmhurst being included in the Thirty-first. The five districts included in the Twenty-third District were not contiguous with the rest of that district. The plaintiffs brought a class action to have the apportionment plan declared to be racially motivated, irrational, invidiously discriminatory; they claimed it violated their Fourteenth and Fifteenth Amendment rights, in that the Negro citizens of East Elmhurst are deprived of the right to cast effective votes for their representatives.

The trial court dismissed the complaint on the basis of the abstention doctrine because it raised serious questions of state law, but expressed the view that the plaintiffs' claim of racial motivation was "barren of allegations of facts to support it" and therefore "devoid of legal significance." The New York Court of Appeals had appointed a blue-ribbon commission, which had drawn up the 1966 plan. Under the plan, nearly every district lacked "geometric symmetry and rectangular proportions"; East Elmhurst was not the only Queens community divided by the plan, since forty-four recognized "communities" in Queens were included in the sixteen equal assembly districts given the borough by the plan. Blacks are not denied their voting rights by the plan; in fact, for the first time, they are given voting strength equal to that of an upstate voter. The court observed:

> Framers of voting districts are required to be color blind. Neither the concept of "one person, one vote" nor the provisions of the Fourteenth or Fifteenth Amendments guarantee to Negroes or to any other racial or national group the right to concentrated voting power. . . . Any purposeful attempt to maintain a majority of persons of one race within a given district would, in fact, raise grave constitutional questions. (290 F. Supp. at 884.)

NOTES

1. The litigation in Wright v. Rockefeller and Ince v. Rockefeller reflects the continuing debate over how the black community can most effectively exert political influence. In both cases, it appears that election districts were drawn so as to minimize the influence of the totality of black voters. In Wright, this result was achieved by congressional district lines that guaranteed the election of one black representative, but minimized the political effectiveness of minority voters in the three adjoining districts. In Ince, the East Elmhurst black community was divided between two predominantly white districts, even though the black areas attached to one district were not contiguous to it. Here, theoretically, the black population, though a minority, was sufficiently large to exert some influence in election results. Obviously, though, the black plaintiffs in Ince agree with Congressman Powell's position in Wright: that one certain black seat was to be preferred over the uncertain potential of political influence. The distribution of a black population center among several adjoining predominantly white districts, while a frequently utilized method of racial or political gerrymandering, has proved difficult to defeat in the courts. Even when the gerrymandering is blatant, a rational, nonracial explanation can usually be provided. In Ince, that explanation seems to have been that all the district lines were gerrymandered, or, as the court observed, they lacked "geometric symmetry and rectangular propor-

tions." But New York holds no monopoly on gerrymandering practices designed to distribute black population areas among adjoining predominantly white districts.

2. In Jones v. Falcey, 48 N.J. 25, 222 A.2d 101 (1966), the state court upheld the redistricting of New Jersey so as to divide the predominantly black city of Newark between two congressional districts, each containing one inner city black ward and several suburban municipalities. The court dismissed allegations that the division would dilute the black vote, and accepted nonracial explanations as to the benefit of including urban and suburban areas in each district.

3. In Connor v. Johnson, 279 F. Supp. 619 (S.D. Miss. 1966), *aff'd per curiam,* 386 U.S. 483 (1967), the predominantly black Mississippi Freedom Democratic party challenged a congressional districting plan, charging that its intent and effect was to deny the black population (particularly in eighteen predominantly black counties) an opportunity to elect a representative sensitive to their special problems. The Court rejected the challenge, pointing out both that there was population equality between the districts, and that the plaintiffs' request for a predominantly black district violated concepts contained in both the majority and dissenting opinions in Wright v. Rockefeller.

4. In Cousins v. City Council of the City of Chicago, 466 F.2d 830 (7th Cir. 1972), the court found that ethnic (Puerto Rican) as well as racial groups are constitutionally protected from having councilmanic ward lines drawn for the purpose of diluting or minimizing their voting power. Plaintiffs introduced impressive evidence showing that ward lines were drawn both to protect incumbent councilmen and to minimize the number of wards with black or Puerto Rican majorities. This evidence included testimony by persons who had worked on the rezoning map as to the gerrymandering of certain wards, statistics showing serious racial disparities in these wards, and testimony by statistical experts as to the unlikelihood that such disparities were the result of chance. Nevertheless, the majority was unable to conclude "that the ward boundaries were the product of purposeful discrimination" and returned the case to the district court for a new trial. A dissenting judge would have affirmed the district judge's judgment for the city on the ground that the evidence that the lines were drawn to dilute the vote of minority groups was no stronger than that deemed insufficient in Wright v. Rockefeller and Whitcomb v. Chavis, infra.

5. In Cooper v. Power, 260 F. Supp. 207 (E.D.N.Y. 1966), *vacated as moot,* 282 F. Supp. 548 (E.D.N.Y. 1968), blacks in the Bedford-Stuyvesant section of Brooklyn charged that a congressional districting plan divided the black community among five districts. Evidence was introduced to demonstrate that the plan's effect reduced the residents' "political effectiveness in securing Congressional representation concerned with the interests and needs of the Bedford-Stuyvesant population, which is below average in income, jobs, housing and education, and is above average in dependence on public welfare, public medical and social services, and anti-poverty programs." 260

F. Supp. at 208. Before the trial was concluded, the legislature reapportioned Brooklyn, making the Bedford-Stuyvesant community a separate district, and the issue became moot. Two black candidates competed in the election that followed. Shirley Chisholm defeated James Farmer, former head of the Congress of Racial Equality, for the congressional seat. See Note, Chavis v. Whitcomb: Apportionment, Gerrymandering, and Black Voting Rights, 24 Rutgers L. Rev. 521, 544-545 (1970).

6. But Cooper v. Power is an exception to most litigation challenging the validity of district lines. Generally blacks have been hampered both by the difficulty in proving "hostile legislative intent" (assumed in Gomillion v. Lightfoot), and by the preoccupation of courts with population equality among the districts. When there is relative equality of population among the districts in a challenged apportionment plan, courts have been reluctant to accept evidence that election schemes such as the use of at-large rather than single-member districts serve to dilute the voting strength of racial minorities.

VAN LOON, REPRESENTATIVE GOVERNMENT AND EQUAL PROTECTION
5 Harv. Civ. Rights–Civ. Lib. L. Rev. 472 (1970)

[Dilution of Votes By At-Large Elections]

Implicit in the idea of representation in the decision-making process for racial and political groups is a de-emphasis on representation based primarily on geographic location. Through the accident of history, American thinking on representation has been tied to the concept of delegates representing geographic constituencies rather than political groups. This thinking was forged at a time when real property was the basis of power, and governmental councils, for that reason, had to be responsive to landed interests. In Representative Government, however, John Stuart Mill voiced the complaint that:

> I cannot see why the feelings and interests which arrange mankind according to localities should be the only ones thought worthy of being represented; or why people who have other feelings and interests, which they value more than they do their geographical ones, should be restricted to these as the sole principle of their political classification.[30]

Localities and cities do not vote any more than "land or trees or pastures" do.[31] When people vote, they express political, more than geographic, preferences. Only part of the essence of the suffrage right, therefore, is encompassed in the one man-one vote standard. The essence of the right is embodied in a

30. J. S. Mill, Representative Government 373 (1861) (World's Classics ed.).

31. Reynolds v. Sims, 377 U.S. 533, 580 (1964). *See Developments in the Law — Equal Protection,* 82 Harv. L. Rev. 1065, 1183 (1969).

pluralistic decision-making body in which racial and political minorities are represented despite their geographic dispersal.

. . .

At-large election systems have a long history of use as a means of diluting the votes of minority groups or political parties.[32] After allowing their use for more than half a century as a system for electing a state's Congressional delegation, Congress in 1842

> . . . conceiv[ed] that the system of electing all the members of the House of Representatives from a State by general ticket, . . . every elector voting for as many names as the State was entitled to representatives in that house, worked injustice . . . and gave an undue preponderance of power to the political party which had a majority of votes in the State, however small. . . .[33]

Accordingly, it outlawed at-large elections for Congress by requiring that each member be elected by a separate district of contiguous territory.

The 1842 decision was little more than a policy preference executed by Congress. Today, the unfair operation of at-large electoral systems is coming under increasing judicial attack as an unconstitutional denial of the substance of the right to vote. . . .

[A] line of constitutional attack on multi-member districts has been that they "operate to minimize or cancel out the voting strength of racial or political elements of the voting population."[41] The Supreme Court's thinking on this aspect of multi-member districting has been evolving since 1964. In Reynolds [v. Sims], the Court voiced support for multi-member districts by suggesting that one house of a state legislature might be apportioned on that basis.[42] In the companion case, Lucas v. Colorado General Assembly,[43] however, the Court articulated "certain [undesirable] aspects" of multi-member districts, while accepting their constitutionality in dicta. In Fortson v. Dorsey[44] and Burns v. Richardson,[45] two cases which reached the Court shortly after Reynolds, the Court stated that a multi-member district would be found unconstitutional as an invidious discrimination "if it [could] be shown that" it operated "designedly or otherwise . . . under the circumstances of a particular case . . . to minimize or cancel out the voting strength of racial or political elements of the voting population."[46] Recalling its own suggestion in Rey-

32. The arithmetic of the dilution in an at-large election is easily understood: if 51% of a group are of one persuasion and vote as a bloc, they can always elect 100% of the representatives; the "minority" 49% elects no representative at all.

33. *Ex parte* Yarbrough, 110 U.S. 651, 660-61 (1884).

41. Dusch v. Davis, 387 U.S. 112, 117 (1967).

42. 377 U.S. at 577, 579.

43. 377 U.S. 713, 731 n. 21 (1964).

44. 379 U.S. 433 (1965).

45. 384 U.S. 73 (1966).

46. *Id.* at 88.

nolds,[47] however, the Court again stated that multi-member districts were not unconstitutional per se and found that "the demonstration that a particular multi-member scheme effects an invidious result"[48] had not been made in the evidence on the record in either case. In one, appellees merely "asserted in one short paragraph of their belief" that the districting scheme was racially motivated,[49] while in the other, the appellant "concede[d] in his brief that . . . 'extensive proofs were not put in' as to the details of the submergence of minorities."[50]

The passage of the Voting Rights Act of 1965,[51] however, resulted in a new series of cases involving at-large elections. As growing numbers of blacks became registered to vote for the first time under the protections of the Act, Southern whites turned to at-large elections to dilute the strength of the new black vote.[52] In March 1966, for example, the Barbour County (Alabama) Democratic Party Executive Committee suddenly replaced its thirty-year-old system of electing members on a neighborhood-district basis with an at-large election sixteen days after six blacks qualified to run for office for the first time.[53] In Smith v. Paris, the United States District Court for the Middle District of Alabama held on constitutional grounds that the at-large system violated rights protected by the fourteenth and fifteenth amendments, for "the clear effect" of the change was "to turn Negro majorities into minorities in certain political areas, thus, as a practical matter, eliminating the possibility of a Negro candidate winning a place on the Executive Committee."[54] Similarly, in a case brought under the Voting Rights Act of 1965,[55] the Supreme

47. 377 U.S. at 577.
48. 384 U.S. at 88.
49. 379 U.S. at 439.
50. 384 U.S. at 88 n. 14.
[The Fortson court upheld the validity of a Georgia plan which divided rural areas into single-member districts, but urban areas into multimember districts, thus minimizing the effectiveness of black votes concentrated in the urban areas.]
51. 43 U.S.C. §1973 (Supp. II, 1967).
52. "Where Negroes are heavily concentrated in particular election districts their votes can be diluted effectively by converting to at-large elections, in which their votes are outweighted by white votes in adjoining districts. This technique has been used in Mississippi and Alabama." U.S. Comm'n on Civil Rights, Political Participation 21 (1968).
53. *Id.* at 24. [The Court found that the change was racially motivated and set aside the May 1968 election, United States v. Democratic Executive Committee of Barbour County, 288 F. Supp. 943 (M.D. Ala. 1968).
54. 257 F. Supp. 901, 904 (M.D. Ala. 1966), *modified & aff'd per curiam,* 386 F.2d 979 (5th Cir. 1967). The court also cited, however, "the long history of racial discrimination in Alabama," and its "firm . . . conviction that [the change] was racially motivated. . . ." 257 F. Supp. at 905. See also Sims v. Baggett, 247 F. Supp. 96 (M.D. Ala. 1965).
55. The Act applies only to six Southern states and to forty counties in North Carolina, where it suspends literacy tests and other discriminatory voter registration tests and requirements. U.S. Comm'n on Civil Rights, Political Participation 11 (1968). §5 of the Act requires approval by the D.C. District Court or the U.S. Attorney General before any changes in election procedures in these states become effective. 42 U.S.C. §1973c (Supp. I, 1964).

Court enjoined an amendment to the Mississippi Code[56] which allowed a change from district to at-large election of county supervisors. Although the decision rested on statutory[57] rather than constitutional grounds, the Court used this language in summary:

> The right to vote can be affected by a dilution of voting power as well as by an absolute prohibition in casting a ballot. . . . Voters who are members of a racial minority might well be in the majority in one district, but in a decided minority in the county as a whole. This type of change could therefore nullify their ability to elect the candidate of their choice just as would prohibiting some of them from voting.[58]

For the most part, the holdings in Southern voting rights cases have relied heavily on the clear discriminatory intent of the framers of the schemes, their history of racial discrimination, and the timing of the electoral change.[59] . . . In Sellers v. Trussel,[61] . . . [though] an Alabama district court held that even though an election change was made for legitimate purposes "and was not enacted because of a racially discriminating motive," that finding did "not dispose of these cases in view of the readily apparent discriminatory effect. . . ." Similarly, in Dusch v. Davis,[62] the Supreme Court expressed this reservation before approving an at-large city council election scheme: "As the plan becomes effective, if it then *operates* to minimize or cancel out the voting strength of racial or political elements of the voting population, it will be time enough to consider whether the system still passes constitutional muster."*

In summary, the Supreme Court has expressed ambivalence about at-large electoral schemes. While it has criticized certain aspects of their operation, voided one Mississippi system on statutory grounds where discriminatory intent was present, and opened the door to a decision upon a convincing showing of discriminatory effect,[63] it has nonetheless upheld their operation until such proof is brought forward by petitioners. . . .†

56. §2870, Miss. Code of 1942. Fairley v. Patterson, *consolidated on appeal in* Allen v. State Board of Elections, 393 U.S. 544 (1969).

57. §5, Voting Rights Act of 1965; 42 U.S.C. §1973c (Supp. I, 1964).

58. Allen v. State Board of Elections, 393 U.S. 544, 569 (1969).

59. Supra note 54.

61. 253 F. Supp. 915, 917 (M.D. Ala. 1966).

62. 387 U.S. 112, 117 (1967) (emphasis added). See also Kilgarlin v. Hill, 386 U.S. 120, 125 n. 3, 126 (1967).

* See also Nixon v. Brewer, 49 F.R.D. 122 (M.D. Ala. 1970); LeBlanc v. Rapides Parish Police Jury, 315 F. Supp. 783 (W.D. La. 1969), *remanded for reconsideration in light of 1970 census,* 431 F.2d 502 (5th Cir. 1970).

63. Dusch v. Davis, 387 U.S. 112, 117 (1967); Fortson v. Dorsey, 379 U.S. 433, 439 (1965).

† In Connor v. Johnson, 402 U.S. 690, 91 S. Ct. 1760, 29 L. Ed. 2d 268 (1971), the Supreme Court granted a stay of a three-judge district court's redistricting plan for the Mississippi legislature. The court had justified the use of multimember districts because

The most widely used electoral system, however, and the one requested by the plaintiffs in Owens [Owens v. School Committee of Boston, 304 F. Supp. 1307 (D. Mass. 1969), printed infra at 175] is the single-member district method of electing representatives. Single-member districts are alleged to have two advantages that are absent in at-large elections. For one, the cost and magnitude of campaigning is reduced. Campaigns are less of a burden on aspiring office-holders, and more candidates are presumably encouraged to seek office. The second advantage of election by districts is that candidates are answerable to a specific constituency, and electors who wish to communicate with their representative have one specific person to whom they can turn.

The disadvantages of single-member districts, on the other hand, are many. Most importantly, they also operate to diminish the voting strength of most minorities, although to a somewhat lesser degree than at-large elections. In most situations, the probability that a single-member district system would result in the election of a minority group member is less than under proportional representation or a cumulative voting system.[87] Where a black minority is geographically concentrated and the white majority has been enjoined to district them together, a single-member district is usually an advantage to the minority;[88] if it is united politically, it is able to elect its candidate without white votes. Very often, however, blacks are geographically dispersed in pockets throughout an area.

There are other drawbacks to a system of districts. When districts are drawn with discriminatory intent, they are readily adaptable to the dilution of votes through gerrymandering. Even when they are drawn in good faith to foster minority representation, they achieve their purpose only when the minority is large and geographically concentrated. Where the minority is substantial, however, the districtor is forced to decide whether minorities are treated more fairly (i.e., afforded greater political leverage) by being concentrated in one district or dispersed among several. This is a policy question on which there is likely to be disagreement even among members of the minority group. For a court to decide such matters in order to direct a districting

---

time and data were deemed inadequate to permit formulation of single-member districts. The Supreme Court expressed a preference for single-member districts, but when on remand the lower court concluded that there were insurmountable difficulties precluding immediate redistricting, 330 F. Supp. 521 (S.D. Miss. 1971), an application for a further stay was denied. 403 U.S. 928 (1971), *vacated and remanded sub nom.* Connor v. Williams, 404 U.S. 549 (1972).

87. "Geographic representation, the standard basis for at least one house in the legislatures of most Western democratic countries, falls somewhere between . . . purely randomized representation and purely functional representation." J. Buchanan & G. Tullock, The Calculus of Consent 219 (1962).

88. But cf. Wright v. Rockefeller, 376 U.S. 52 (1964). "[S]ome would argue that it is better for Negroes to constitute 40 percent of the voters of two districts — almost half the constituencies of two representatives — than 80 percent of the voters of one district." U.S. Comm'n on Civil Rights, Political Participation 21 n. 6 (1968).

remedy is virtually an impossible task.[89] The decision to maximize the effectiveness of any one group often minimizes other groups automatically. In the single-member district there can be only one winner; there is no way to apportion the spoils.

[The author discusses two alternative voting methods: (1) cumulative voting — in which an elector for five vacancies may cast all five votes for one candidate or divide them among the different candidates in any proportion, with the five candidates receiving the largest number of votes elected; (2) proportional representation — in which voters follow the cumulative voting principle, but a "spillover" mechanism automatically transfers any votes received by a candidate in excess of those needed for election to the second choice of the voters who elected him, or to the third choice, if the voters' second choice has already been elected, and so on.]

OWENS v. SCHOOL COMMITTEE OF BOSTON
304 F. Supp. 1327 (D. Mass. 1969)

Ford, J., District Judge.

Plaintiffs in this action, who include black voters, black pupils in Boston public schools and their parents and former black candidates for the Boston School Committee, allege in their complaint that the present method of electing the Boston School Committee deprives them of their rights under the Fourteenth and Fifteenth Amendments to the Constitution of the United States. . . .

Under the provisions of §18 of the Boston City Charter the School Committee is composed of five members elected at large for a term of two years. A preliminary election is held at which ten candidates are chosen to appear on the ballot at the final election at which five are chosen who will constitute the School Committee for the succeeding two years from the January following the election. Each voter is entitled to vote for five candidates both in the preliminary and final elections. The preliminary election was held on September 23, 1969 and the final election is to be held on November 4, 1969.

The at-large system of electing the School Committee has been used in Boston continuously since 1875 and the number of members has been fixed at five since 1905.

Plaintiffs purport to sue on behalf of themselves and of all black citizens of Boston, who are alleged to constitute at the present time about 13% of the total population of the city, most of whom are concentrated in one geographic area of the city. Plaintiffs' contention is that they constitute a definite racial minority group within the city who in an at-large election cannot elect by their own votes alone a member of their race or a candidate of any race favorable to their interests, while in an election by districts they might in one or more districts have enough votes to elect a candidate to represent them who would be favorable to their interests. . . .

89. See, e.g., Wright v. Rockefeller, 376 U.S. 52 (1964).

The system of electing members of a governmental board in an at-large election is, of course, a device quite commonly used. There are advantages and disadvantages to the use of either the at-large or the district system of election. One supposedly ensures the election of the type of official who can command a wide support throughout the whole community and will be representative of and responsive to the needs of the community as a whole. The other is designed to ensure representation of the particular interests of the separate geographical segments of the community, perhaps at the expense of the general interest. It is true that the same persons who would be elected under one system would not necessarily be able to win election under the other system. There are many justifiable considerations which may lead a city to adopt one method of election rather than the other.

The essential question here is whether a city which has for a long time and for sound reasons used the at-large system is under a constitutional compulsion to adopt a district system in order to better the chances of a minority group to secure representation of their own particular interests. There is no case that clearly holds that there is such a requirement in the situation presented here. It has been clearly held that the at-large system is not per se unconstitutional. Dusch v. Davis, 387 U.S. 112. Fortson v. Dorsey, 379 U.S. 433. It is true that dicta in those cases indicate that in some circumstances an at-large system might be invalid. Clearly this might be so if it were deliberately adopted for the purpose of minimizing the voting influence of some group within the electorate. But plaintiffs do not argue, and hardly could argue that a system adopted in 1875 was intentionally aimed at them. And it is rather fanciful to contend that because the change to an at-large system in 1875 was, conjecturally, aimed at some other then minority group, the system should be banned as having been infected ab initio with an unconstitutional taint. . . .

. . . Plaintiffs are rather vague in their definition of when, in their view, a minority group would be constitutionally entitled to have a district rather than an at-large system put into effect. They apparently concede that not every minority group is entitled to a district in which it might control an election, and that the group should be at least of some minimum size — a size which they only define as "cognizable". Moreover the district system would be helpful to a minority only when it is geographically concentrated and would do no good to a minority uniformly spread throughout the whole area. Indeed, even when a minority group is of a certain minimal size and geographically concentrated, a district system is not necessarily to its best advantage. A minority constituting 13% of the electorate in some circumstances might do better if located in a district where it would effectively control the election of one of the five members to be elected. But in other circumstances such a group of voters might in fact hold a balance of power position where it could effectively influence the election of all five members. It simply cannot be held a priori that a district system is constitutionally required to protect the effective voting rights of a minority group.

Of course, in a particular case, it may be possible to prove as a matter of fact that a district system is the only way to protect a group's voting effectiveness. At this state of the present case it is not clear that that fact can be shown here. Plaintiffs argue that in recent School Committee elections in Boston no black candidate has been elected, and that certain white candidates whom plaintiffs classify as responsive to their interests have also been defeated. . . .

The nine-member Boston City Council is also chosen at the same time as the School Committee and by the same at-large system of election. In the 1967 election one black candidate was elected at-large to the City Council and this year as a candidate for reelection is one of the eighteen from whom the final choice is to be made in November. . . .

. . . Without in any way anticipating what its final decision after a full trial on the merits may be, the court must find that at the present stage of the case, plaintiffs have not shown a sufficiently reasonable possibility of finally prevailing on the merits to justify the issuance of a preliminary injunction. . . .

NOTE

The "one-man, one-vote" principle has been applied to local units of government (Avery v. Midland County, Texas, 390 U.S. 474, 88 S. Ct. 1114, 20 L. Ed. 2d 45 (1968)), and specifically to elected school boards, in Hadley v. Junior College District, 397 U.S. 50, 90 S. Ct. 791, 25 L. Ed. 2d 45 (1970), in which the Court stated as a general rule that whenever a state or local government decides to select persons by popular election to perform governmental functions, the Equal Protection Clause of the Fourteenth Amendment requires that each qualified voter must be given an equal opportunity to participate in that election.

QUESTIONS

1. If the Owens plaintiffs' requested relief of a single-member district plan had been granted, and the reapportionment was accomplished in a manner that effectively divided the predominantly black population into five predominantly white districts, would the plaintiffs be able to obtain further relief? Assuming that plaintiffs had to show that the lines were racially motivated and reflected hostile legislative intent, what proof would they likely be able to offer? How would they prevail if defendants presented a rational, nonracial explanation for the lines?

2. Suppose the plaintiffs in Owens at the trial of their case were able to make a strong showing that they constitute a readily identifiable "racial element of the voting population" whose voting strength has been minimized by a particular districting scheme. Suppose further that they had shown the adverse effect of their voting impotence through the hostile or apathetic reactions of school board members to their problems. At some point, would not plaintiffs be able to argue that they had made out a prima facie case, so that the burden would be shifted to the school committee to establish that the scheme has a rational, nonracial justification, and does not dilute black voting power?

3. Having shown an adverse effect, i.e., the dilution of black voting power, why should blacks have to prove a hostile intent when such was not required in either Gomillion v. Lightfoot or in the reapportionment cases that followed?

4. In McLaughlin v. Florida, 379 U.S. 184, 85 S. Ct. 283, 13 L. Ed. 2d 222 (1964), printed infra page 275, the Supreme Court noted that the standard traditionally applied in equal protection cases, which prohibits only arbitrary or invidious discrimination and grants the legislature the widest discretion in making classifications, is not applicable to racial classifications because the strong policy embodied in the Fourteenth Amendment of eliminating racial classification renders racial discrimination constitutionally suspect. Therefore, necessity, and not mere rationality, is the controlling test in cases involving racial classifications. 379 U.S. at 196. At what point does this standard come into play in reapportionment cases containing allegations of racial discrimination?

Racism Hypo 1
UNREPRESENTED BLACK PARENTS v. MASSPORT SCHOOL COMMITTEE

This federal suit was filed at about the same time as Owens v. School Committee of Boston, supra, and contains facts similar to those set forth in the Owens opinion. Blacks, who constitute 20 percent of the town's population, live mostly in the southwest section of Massport, where they represent 85 percent of the area. There are few blacks in the other sections of the city. Plaintiffs sought the restructuring of the school board election districts on a single-member basis, which, experts agree, would guarantee the election of one black and enable blacks to strongly influence election of a second member of the school committee.

During the trial, plaintiffs introduced evidence that no black has ever been elected to the school committee. In support of allegations that whites elected to the board are generally hostile or apathetic to the educational concerns of the black community, plaintiffs' witnesses testified that: the committee has resisted all efforts to eliminate severe racial isolation in Massport's schools, and has successfully bogged down litigation initiated for this purpose; although community dissatisfaction with conditions in the black schools has resulted in several boycotts and other disruptions by parents and students, not one member of the Massport School Committee responded to invitations to attend meetings held in southwest schools on these problems.

The school committee has turned down all requests from the black community for active recruitment of black teachers, newer schools, a revised curriculum designed to meet the special problems of ghetto children, and more community participation in school policy decisions.

The district court denied plaintiffs' requested relief and granted the committee's motion to dismiss the suit. Judge Elite based his decision on the absence of any showing that the at-large method of selecting school board members was motivated by racial discrimination or that the black parents had shown that eligible black voters were being discriminated against at the polls. In his opinion, the district judge suggested that plaintiffs would do well to spend less of their energies and resources in litigation and more in organizing the lethargic black community. He pointed out further that redistricting the school board into a single-member plan as requested by plaintiffs would enable the black community to elect no more than one representative to the five-member school board. He suggested that such a "victory" would be simply one more instance of the tokenism against which many black spokesmen are bitter. Finally, the judge reported that he had voted for the one black member of the Massport City Council (also elected on an at-large basis), and was certain that white people would vote for qualified black candidates when such blacks appeared on the ballots.

Despite the Supreme Court's opinion in Whitcomb v. Chavis, printed infra, some of the parents wish to appeal. Others have concluded that Judge Elite's remarks, while insulting and racist, may contain good advice in view of the Whitcomb decision. To resolve the question, a community meeting has been scheduled.

Law Firm A will prepare and present arguments for going ahead with the appeal.

Law Firm B will prepare and present arguments supporting the conclusion that the present status of the law virtually guarantees that the dismissal will be affirmed on the appeal, with the added possibility that the case will become another adverse precedent like Whitcomb.

WHITCOMB v. CHAVIS
403 U.S. 124, 91 S. Ct. 1858, 29 L. Ed. 2d 363 (1971)

Mr. Justice WHITE. . . .

I

Indiana has a bicameral general assembly consisting of a house of representatives of 100 members and a senate of 50 members. Eight of the 31 senatorial districts and 25 of the 39 house districts are multi-member districts, that is, districts which are represented by two or more legislators elected at large by the voters of the district. Under the statutes here challenged, Marion County is a multi-member district electing eight senators and 15 members of the house.

On January 9, 1969, six residents of Indiana, five of whom were residents of Marion County, filed a suit described by them as "attacking the constitutionality of two statutes of the State of Indiana which provide for multi-member districting at large of General Assembly seats in Marion County, Indiana . . . ." Plaintiffs Chavis, Ramsey, and Bryant alleged that the two statutes invidiously diluted the force and effect of the vote of Negroes and poor persons living within certain Marion County census tracts constituting what was termed "the ghetto area." Residents of the area were alleged to have particular demographic characteristics rendering them cognizable as a minority interest group with distinctive interests in specific areas of the substantive law. With single-member districting, it was said, the ghetto area would elect three members of the house and one senator, whereas under the present districting voters in the area "have almost no political force or control over legislators because the effect of their vote is cancelled out by other contrary interest groups" in Marion County. The mechanism of political party organization and the influence of party chairmen in nominating candidates were additional factors alleged to frustrate the exercise of power by residents of the ghetto area.

Plaintiff Walker, a Negro resident of Lake County, also a multi-member district but a smaller one, alleged an invidious discrimination against Lake County Negroes because Marion County Negroes, although no greater in number than Lake County Negroes, had the opportunity to influence the election of more legislators than Lake County Negroes. The claim was that Marion County was one-third larger in population and thus had approximately one-third more assembly seats than Lake County, but that voter influence does not vary inversely with population and that permitting Marion County voters to elect 23 assemblymen at large gave them a disproportionate advantage over voters in Lake County. . . .

The three-judge court filed its opinion containing its findings and conclusions on July 28, 1969, holding for plaintiffs. Chavis v. Whitcomb, 305 F. Supp. 1364 (SD Ind. 1969). See also 305 F. Supp. 1359 (1969) (pre-trial orders) and 307 F. Supp. 1362 (1969) (statewide reapportionment plan and implementing order). In sum, it concluded that Marion County's multi-member district must be disestablished and, because of population disparities not directly related to the phenomena alleged in the complaint, the entire State must be redistricted.

The court's conclusions of law on the merits may be summarized as follows:

1. There exists within Marion County an identifiable racial element, "the Negro residents of the Center Township ghetto," with special interests in various areas of substantive law, diverging significantly from interests of nonresidents of the ghetto.[12]

12. "The first requirement implicit in Fortson v. Dorsey and Burns v. Richardson, that of an indentifiable racial or political element within that multi-member district, is met by the Negro residents of the Center Township Ghetto. These Negro residents have interests in areas of substantive law such as housing regulations, sanitation, welfare programs (aid to families with dependent children, medical care, etc.), garnishment statutes, and unemployment compensation, among others, which diverge significantly from the interests of nonresidents of the Ghetto." 305 F. Supp., at 1386.

2. The voting strength of this racial group has been minimized by Marion County's multi-member senate and house district because of the strong control exercised by political parties over the selection of candidates, the inability of the Negro voters to assure themselves the opportunity to vote for prospective legislators of their choice and the absence of any particular legislators who were accountable for their legislative record to Negro voters.

3. Party control of nominations, the inability of voters to know the candidate and the responsibility of legislators to their party and the county at large make it difficult for any legislator to diverge from the majority of his delegation and to be an effective representative of minority ghetto interests.

4. Although each legislator in Marion County is arguably responsible to all the voters, including those in the ghetto, "[p]artial responsiveness of all legislators is [not] . . . equal [to] total responsiveness and the informed concern of a few specific legislators."

5. The apportionment statutes of Indiana as they relate to Marion County operate to minimize and cancel out the voting strength of a minority racial group, namely Negroes residing in the Center Township ghetto, and to deprive them of the equal protection of the laws.

6. As a legislative district, Marion County is large as compared with the total number of legislators, it is not subdistricted to insure distribution of the legislators over the county and comprises a multi-member district for both the house and the senate. (See Burns v. Richardson, 384 U.S. 73, 88 (1966).)

7. To redistrict Marion County alone would leave impermissible variations between Marion County districts and other districts in the State. Statewide redistricting was required, and it could not await the 1970 census figures estimated to be available within a year.

8. It may not be possible for the Indiana general assembly to comply with the state constitutional requirement prohibiting crossing or dividing counties for senatorial apportionment and still meet the requirements of the Equal Protection Clause adumbrated in recent cases.

9. Plaintiff Walker's claim as a Negro voter resident of Lake County that he was discriminated against because Lake County Negroes could vote for only 16 assemblymen while Marion County Negroes could vote for 23 was deemed untenable. In his second capacity, as a general voter in Lake County, Walker "probably has received less effective representation" than Marion County voters because "he votes for fewer legislators and, therefore, has fewer legislators to speak for him," and, since in theory voting power in multi-member districts does not vary inversely to the number of voters. Marion County voters had greater opportunity to cast tie-breaking or "critical" votes. But the court declined to hold that the latter ground had been proven, absent more evidence concerning Lake County. In this respect consideration of Walker's claim was limited to that to be given the uniform districting principle in reapportioning the Indiana general assembly.

. . . Following further hearings and examination of various plans submitted by the parties, the court drafted and adopted a plan based on the 1960 census figures. With respect to Marion County, the court followed plaintiff's suggested scheme, which was said to protect "the legally cognizable racial minority group against dilution of its voting strength." Chavis v. Whitcomb, 307 F. Supp. 1362, 1365 (SD Ind. 1969). Single-member districts were employed throughout the State, county lines were crossed where necessary, judicial notice was taken of the location of the nonwhite population in establishing district lines in metropolitan areas of the State and the court's plan expressly aimed at giving "recognition to the cognizable racial minority group whose grievance lead [*sic*] to this litigation." Id., at 1366. . . .

Appeal was taken following the final judgment by the 3 judge court, we noted jurisdiction, 397 U.S. 984 (1970), and the State's motion for stay of judgment was granted pending our final action on this case, 396 U.S. 1055 (1970), thus permitting the 1970 elections to be held under the existing apportionment statutes declared unconstitutional by the District Court. On June 1, 1971, we were advised by the parties that the Indiana Legislature had passed, and the governor had signed, new apportionment legislation soon to become effective for the 1972 elections and that the new legislation provides for single-member house and senate districts throughout the State, including Marion County.

II

With the 1970 elections long past and the appearance of new legislation abolishing multi-member districts in Indiana, the issue of mootness emerges. Neither party deems the case mooted by recent events. . . .

We agree that the case is not moot and that the central issues before us must be decided. We do not, however, pass upon the details of the plan adopted by the District Court, since that plan in any event would have required revision in light of the 1970 census figures.

III

The line of cases from Gray v. Sanders, 372 U.S. 368 (1963), and Reynolds v. Sims, 377 U.S. 533 (1964), to Kirkpatrick v. Preisler, 394 U.S. 526 (1969), and Wells v. Rockefeller, 394 U.S. 542 (1969), recognize that "representative government is in essence self-government through the medium of elected representatives of the people, and each and every citizen has an inalienable right to full and effective participation in the political processes of his State's legislative bodies." Reynolds v. Sims, 377 U.S., at 565. Since most citizens find it possible to participate only as qualified voters in electing their representatives, "[f]ull and effective participation by all citizens in state government requires, therefore, that each citizen have an equally effective voice in the election of members of his state legislature." Ibid. Hence, apportionment schemes "which give the same number of representatives to unequal numbers of constituents," 377 U.S., at 563, unconstitutionally dilute the value of the votes in the larger districts. And hence the requirement that "the seats in both houses of a bicameral state legislature must be apportioned on a population basis." 377 U.S., at 568.

The question of the constitutional validity of multi-member districts has been pressed in this Court since the first of the modern reapportionment cases. These questions have focused not on population-based apportionment but on the quality of representation afforded by the multi-member district as compared with single-member districts. In Lucas v. General Assembly, 377 U.S. 713 (1964), decided with Reynolds v. Sims, we noted certain undesirable features of the multi-member district but expressly withheld any intimation "that apportionment schemes which provide for the at-large election of a number of legislators from a county, or any political subdivision, are constitutionally defective." 377 U.S., at 731, n.21. Subsequently, when the validity of the multi-member district, as such, was squarely presented, we held that such a district is not per se illegal under the Equal Protection Clause. Fortson v. Dorsey, 379 U.S. 433 (1965); Burns v. Richardson, 384 U.S. 73 (1966); Kilgarlin v. Hill, 386 U.S. 120 (1967). See also Burnette v. Davis, 382 U.S. 42 (1965); Harrison v. Schaefer, 383 U.S. 269 (1966). That voters in multi-member districts vote for and are represented by more legislators than voters in single-member districts has so far not demonstrated an invidious discrimination against the latter. But we have deemed the validity of multi-member district systems justiciable, recognizing also that they may be subject to challenge where the circumstances of a particular case may "operate to minimize or cancel out the voting strength of racial or political elements of the voting population." Fortson, 379 U.S., at 439, and Burns, 384 U.S., at 88. Such a tendency, we have said, is enhanced when the district is large and elects a substantial proportion of the seats in either house of a bicameral legislature, if it is multi-membered for both houses of the legislature or if it lacks provision for at-large candidates running from particular geographical subdistricts, as in Fortson. Burns, 384 U.S., at 88. But we have insisted that the challenger carry the burden of proving that multi-member districts unconstitutionally operate to dilute or cancel the voting strength of racial or political elements. We have not yet sustained such an attack.

IV

Plaintiffs level two quite distinct challenges to the Marion County district. The first charge is that any multi-member district bestows on its voters several unconstitutional advantages over voters in single-member districts or smaller multi-member districts. The other allegation is that the Marion County district, on the record of this case, illegally minimizes and cancels out the voting power of a cognizable racial minority in Marion County. The District Court sustained the latter claim and considered the former sufficiently persuasive to be a substantial factor in prescribing uniform, single-member districts as the basic scheme of the court's own plan. . . .

The District Court was [also] . . . impressed with the other branch of the claim that multi-member districts inherently discriminate against other districts. This was the assertion that whatever the individual voting power of Marion County voters in choosing legislators may be, they nevertheless have more effective representation in the Indiana general assembly for two reasons. First, each voter is represented by more legislators and therefore, in theory at least, has more chances to influence critical legislative votes. Second, since multi-member delegations are elected at large and represent the voters of the entire district, they tend to vote as a bloc, which is tantamount to the district having one representative with several votes. The District Court did not squarely sustain this position, but it appears to have found it sufficiently persuasive to have suggested uniform districting to the Indiana Legislature and to have eliminated multi-member districts in the court's own plan redistricting the State. See 307 F. Supp., at 1368-1383.

We are not ready, however, to agree that multi-member districts, wherever they exist, overrepresent their voters as compared with voters in single-member districts, even if the multi-member delegation tends to bloc-voting. The theory that plural representation itself unduly enhances a district's power and the influence of its voters remains to be demonstrated in practice and in the day-to-day operation of the legislature. Neither the findings of the trial court nor the record before us sustains it, even where bloc voting is posited. . . .

Rather than squarely finding unacceptable discrimination against out-state voters in favor of Marion County voters, the trial court struck down Marion County's multi-member district because it found the scheme worked invidiously against a specific segment of the county's voters as compared with others. The court identified an area of the city as a ghetto, found it predominantly inhabited by poor Negroes with distinctive substantive-law interests and thought this group unconstitutionally underrepresented because the proportion of legislators with residences in the ghetto elected from 1960 to 1968 was less than the ghetto's proportion of the population, less than the proportion of legislators elected from Washington Township, a less populous district, and less than the ghetto would likely have elected had the county consisted of single-member districts. We find major deficiencies in this approach.

First, it needs no emphasis here that the Civil War Amendments were designed to protect the civil rights of Negroes and that the courts have been vigilant in scrutinizing schemes allegedly conceived or operated as purposeful devices to further racial discrimination. There has been no hesitation in striking down those contrivances that can fairly be said to infringe on Fourteenth Amendment rights. Gomillion v. Lightfoot, 364 U.S. 339 (1960); Sims v. Baggett, 247 F. Supp. 96 (MD Ala. 1965); Smith v. Paris, 257 F. Supp. 901 (MD Ala. 1966), aff'd, 386 F.2d 979 (CA5 1967). See also Allen v. Board of Elections, 393 U.S. 544 (1969). But there is no suggestion here that Marion County's multi-member district, or similar districts throughout the State, were conceived or operated as purposeful devices to further racial or economic discrimination. As plaintiffs concede, "there was no basis for asserting that the legislative districts in Indiana were designed to dilute the vote of minorities." Brief of Appellees, pp. 28-29. Accordingly, the circumstances here lie outside the reach of decisions such as Sims v. Baggett, supra.

Nor does the fact that the number of ghetto residents who were legislators was not in proportion to ghetto population satisfactorily prove invidious discrimination absent evidence and findings that ghetto residents had less opportunity than did other Marion County residents to participate in the political processes and to elect legislators of their choice. We have discovered nothing in the record or in the court's findings indicating that poor Negroes were not allowed to register or vote, to choose the political party they desired to support, to participate in its affairs or to be equally represented on those occasions when legislative candidates were chosen. Nor did the evidence purport to show or the court to find that inhabitants of the ghetto were regularly excluded from the slates of both major parties, thus denying them the chance of occupying legislative seats. It appears reasonably clear that the Republican Party won four of the five elections from 1960 to 1968, that Center Township ghetto voted heavily Democratic and that ghetto votes were critical to Democratic Party success. Although we cannot be sure of the facts since the court ignored the question, it seems unlikely that the Democratic Party could afford to overlook the ghetto in slating its candidates. Clearly, in 1964 — the one election which the Democrats won — the party slated and elected one senator and one representative from Center Township ghetto as well as one senator and four representatives from other parts of Center Township and two representatives from census tract 220, which was within the ghetto area described by plaintiff. Nor is there any indication that the party failed to slate candidates satisfactory to the ghetto in other years. Absent evidence or findings we are not sure, but it seems reasonable to infer that had the Democrats won all of the elections or even most of them, the ghetto would have had no justifiable complaints about representation. The fact is, however, that four of the five elections were won by Republicans, which was not the party of the ghetto and which would not always slate ghetto candidates — although in 1962 it nominated and elected one representative and in 1968 two representatives from that area. If this is the proper view of this case, the failure of the ghetto to have legislative seats in proportion to its population emerges more as a function of losing elections than of built-in bias against poor Negroes. The voting power of ghetto residents may have been "cancelled out" as the District Court held, but this seems a mere euphemism for political defeat at the polls. . . .

Plainly, the District Court saw nothing unlawful about the impact of typical single-member district elections. The court's own plan created districts giving both Republicans and Democrats several predictably safe general assembly seats, with political, racial or economic minorities in those districts being "unrepresented" year after year. But similar consequences flowing from Marion County multi-member district elections were viewed differently. Conceding that all Marion County voters could fairly be said to be represented by the entire delegation, just as each voter in a single-member district by the winning candidate, the District Court thought ghetto voters' claims to the partial allegiance of eight senators and 15 representatives was not equivalent to the undivided allegiance of one senator and two representatives; nor was the ghetto voters' chance of influencing the election of an entire slate as significant as the guarantee of one ghetto senator and two ghetto representatives. As the trial court saw it, ghetto voters could not be adequately and equally represented unless some of Marion County's general assembly seats were reserved for ghetto residents serving the interests of the ghetto majority. But are poor Negroes of the ghetto any more underrepresented than poor ghetto whites who also voted Democratic and lost, or any more discriminated against than other interest groups or voters in Marion County with allegiance to the Democratic Party, or, conversely, any less represented than Republican areas or voters in years of Republican defeat? We think not. The mere fact that one interest group or another concerned with the outcome of Marion County elections have found themselves outvoted and without legislative seats of its own provides no basis for invoking constitutional remedies where, as here, there is no indication that this segment of the population is being denied access to the political system.

There is another gap in the trial court's reasoning. As noted by the court, the interest of ghetto residents in certain issues did not measurably differ from that of other voters. Presumably in these respects Marion County's assemblymen were satisfactorily representative of the ghetto. As to other matters, ghetto residents had unique interests not necessarily shared by others in the community and on these issues the ghetto was invidiously underrepresented absent their own legislative voice to further their own policy views.

Part of the difficulty with this conclusion is that the findings failed to support it. Plaintiffs' evidence purported to show disregard for the ghetto's distinctive interests; defendants claimed quite the contrary. We see nothing in the findings of the District Court indicating recurring poor performance by Marion County's delegation with respect to Center Township ghetto, nothing to show what the ghetto's interests were in particular legislative situations and nothing to indicate that the outcome would have been any different if the 23 assemblymen had been chosen from single-member districts. Moreover, even assuming bloc voting by the delegation contrary to the wishes of the ghetto majority, it would not follow that the Fourteenth Amendment had been violated unless it is invidiously discriminatory for a county to elect its delegation by majority vote based on party or candidate platforms and so to some extent predetermine legislative votes on particular issues. Such tendencies are inherent in government by elected representatives; and surely elections in single-member districts visit precisely the same consequences on the supporters of losing candidates whose views are rejected at the polls.

V

The District Court's holding, although on the facts of this case limited to guaranteeing one racial group representation, is not easily contained. It is expressive of the more general proposition that any group with distinctive interests must be represented in legislative halls if it is numerous enough to command at least one seat and represents a majority living in an area sufficiently compact to constitute a single-member district.[34] This approach would make it difficult to reject claims of Democrats, Republicans, or members of any political organization in Marion County who live in what would be safe districts in a single-member district system but who in one year or another, or year after year, are submerged in a one-sided multi-member district vote. There are also union oriented workers, the university community, religious or ethnic groups occupying identifiable areas of our heterogeneous cities and urban areas. Indeed, it would be difficult for a great many, if not most, multi-member districts to survive analysis under the District Court's view unless combined with some voting arrangement such as proportional representation or cumulative voting aimed at providing representation for minority parties or interests. At the very least, affirmance of the District Court would spawn endless litigation concerning the multi-member district systems now widely employed in this country.

We are not insensitive to the objections long voiced to multi-member district plans. Although not as prevalent as they were in our early history, they have been with us since colonial times and were much in evidence both before and after the adoption of the Fourteenth Amendment. Criticism is rooted in their winner-take-all aspects, their tendency to submerge minorities and to overrepresent the winning party as compared with the party's statewide electoral position, a general preference for legislatures reflecting community interests as closely as possible and disenchantment with political parties and elections as devices to settle policy differences between contending interests. The chance of winning or significantly influencing intraparty fights and issue-oriented elections has seemed to some inadequate protection to minorities, political, racial, or economic; rather, their voice, it is said, should also be heard in the legislative forum where public policy is finally fashioned. In our view, however, experience and insight have not yet demonstrated that multi-member districts are inherently invidious and violative of the Fourteenth Amendment. Surely the findings of the District Court do not demonstrate it. Moreover, if the problems of multi-member districts are unbearable or even unconstitutional it is not at all clear that the remedy is a single-member district system with its lines carefully drawn to ensure representation to sizable racial, ethnic, economic or religious groups and with its own capacity for over- and underrepresenting parties and interests

34. Interestingly enough, in Wright v. Rockefeller, 376 U.S. 52 (1964), challenge was to a single-member district plan with districts allegedly drawn on racial lines and designed to limit Negroes to voting for their own candidates in safe Negro districts. We rejected the challenge for failure of proof, but noted in passing that ". . . some of these voters . . . would prefer a more even distribution of minority groups among the four congressional districts, but others, like the intervenors in this case, would argue strenuously that the kind of districts for which appellants contended would be undesirable and, because based on race or place of origin, would themselves be unconstitutional." 376 U.S., at 57-58.

and even for permitting a minority of the voters to control the legislature and government of a State. The short of it is that we are unprepared to hold that district-based elections decided by plurality vote are unconstitutional in either single- or multi-member districts simply because the supporters of losing candidates have no legislative seats assigned to them. As presently advised we hold that the District Court misconceived the Equal Protection Clause in applying it to invalidate the Marion County multi-member district.

VI

Even if the District Court was correct in finding unconstitutional discrimination against poor inhabitants of the ghetto, it did not explain why it was constitutionally compelled to disestablish the entire county district and to intrude upon state policy any more than necessary to ensure representation of ghetto interests. The court entered judgment without expressly putting aside on supportable grounds the alternative of creating single-member districts in the ghetto and leaving the district otherwise intact, as well as the possibility that the Fourteenth Amendment could be satisfied by simple requirement that some of the at-large candidates each year must reside in the ghetto. Cf. Fortson v. Dorsey, supra.

We are likewise at a loss to understand how on the court's own findings of fact and conclusions of law it was justified in eliminating every multi-member district in the State of Indiana. It did not forthrightly sustain the theory that multi-member districts always overrepresent their voters to the invidious detriment of single-member residents. Nor did it examine any multi-member district aside from Marion County for possible intradistrict discrimination. . . .

VII

[The Court agreed that statewide reapportionment was required because disparities among legislative districts violated principles enunciated in cases since Reynolds v. Sims, 377 U.S. 533, 84 S. Ct. 1362, 12 L. Ed. 2d 506 (1964).]

We therefore reverse the judgment of the District Court and remand the case to that court for further proceedings consistent with this opinion. It is so ordered.

Mr. Justice Stewart joins in Part I through VI of the Court's opinion, holding that the multi-member districting scheme here in issue did not violate the Equal Protection Clause of the Fourteenth Amendment. He dissents from Part VII of the Court's opinion. . . .

[Mr. Justice Harlan in a separate dissent reiterated his opposition to the reapportionment cases.]

Mr. Justice Douglas, with whom Mr. Justice Brennan and Mr. Justice Marshall concur, dissenting. . . .

In Gomillion v. Lightfoot, 364 U.S. 339, we dealt with the problem of a State intentionally making a district smaller to exclude black voters. Here we have almost the converse problem. The State's districts surround the black voting area with white voters.

Gomillion, involving the turning of the City of Tuskegee from a geographical square "to an uncouth twenty-eight-sided figure," 364 U.S., at 340, was only one of our cases which dealt with elevating the political interests of one identifiable group over those of another. Georgia's county unit system was similar, although race was not a factor. Under the Georgia system a farmer in a rural county could have up to 99 times the voting power of his urban-dwelling brother. See Gray v. Sanders, 372 U.S. 368. Here the districting plan operates to favor "upper-middle class and wealthy" suburbanites.

A showing of racial motivation is not necessary when dealing with multi-member districts. Burns v. Richardson, 384 U.S. 73, 88; Fortson v. Dorsey, 379 U.S. 433, 439. Although the old apportionment plan which is in full harmony with the State's 1851 constitution, may not be racially motivated, the test for multi-member districts is whether there are invidious effects.

That rule is but an application of a basic principle applied in Hunter v. Erickson, 393 U.S. 385. There a city passed a housing law which provided that before an ordinance regulating the sale or lease of realty on the basis of race could become effective it must be approved by a majority vote. Thus the protection of minority interests became much more difficult. We held that a State or a state agency could not in its voting scheme so disadvantage black interests. . . .

In Burns v. Richardson, supra, we again considered the problems of multi-member districts. The doubts noted in Fortson v. Dorsey were resolved and we stated that assuming the requirements of Reynolds v. Sims, 377 U.S. 533 were satisfied, multi-member districts are unconstitutional "only if it can be shown that 'designedly or otherwise' . . . [such a district would operate] to minimize or cancel out the voting strength of racial or political elements of the voting population." 384 U.S., at 88. We went on to suggest how the burden of proof could be met.

> It may be that this invidious effect can more easily be shown if, in contrast to the facts in Fortson, districts are large in relation to the total numbers of legislators, if districts are not appropriately subdistricted to assure distribution of legislators that are resident over the entire district, or if such districts characterize both houses of a bicameral legislature rather than one. Ibid.

These factors are all present in this case. Between the largest (Marion) and second largest (Lake) counties in the State, 26% of each house of the legislature is controlled. There is no subdistricting under the Indiana plan. Cf. Dusch v. Davis, 387 U.S. 112. And multi-member districts are used in both houses of the legislature.

In both Fortson and Burns we demanded that the invidious effects of multi-member districts appear from evidence in the record. Here that demand is satisfied by (1) the showing of an identifiable voting group living in Center Township, (2) the severe discrepancies of residency of elected members of the general assembly between Center and Washington Townships, . . . (3) the finding of pervasive influence of the county organizations of the political parties, and (4) the finding that legislators from the county maintain "common, undifferentiated" positions on political issues.[4] . . .

It is said that if we prevent racial gerrymandering today, we must prevent gerrymandering of any special interest group tomorrow, whether it be social, economic, or ideological. I do not agree. Our Constitution has a special thrust when it comes to voting; the Fifteenth Amendment says the right of citizens to vote shall not be "abridged" on account of "race, color, or previous condition of servitude."

Our cases since Baker v. Carr have never intimated that "one man, one vote" meant "one white man, one vote." Since "race" may not be gerrymandered, I think the Court emphasizes the irrelevant when it says that the effect on "the actual voting power" of the blacks should first be known. They may be all Democratic or all Republican; but once their identity is purposefully washed out of the system, the system, as I see it, has a constitutional defect. It is asking the impossible for us to demand that the blacks first show that the effect of the scheme was to discourage or prevent poor blacks from voting or joining such party as they chose. On this record, the voting rights of the blacks have been "abridged," as I read the Constitution. . . .

QUESTIONS

1. In view of (a) the rather complicated intermixture of political and racial motivation for the alleged dilution of minority group voting power in Whitcomb, (b) the fact that the state legislature had reapportioned all districts on a single-member basis in accordance with the three-judge court's order while the case was pending before the Supreme Court, and finally (c) what the Court did, as opposed to what it said, in Fortson v. Dorsey, 379 U.S. 433, 85 S. Ct. 498, 13 L. Ed. 2d 401 (1965), and Burns v. Richardson, 384 U.S. 73, 86 S. Ct. 1286, 6 L. Ed. 2d 376 (1966): were plaintiffs' counsel well advised to argue in the Supreme Court that the reapportionment action by the Indiana legislature did not moot the case? Was there any serious likelihood that, in the absence of an affirmative statement by the Supreme Court, the

4. The three-judge court "emphasized that the black plaintiffs were members of an identifiable interest group whose voting strength had been minimized by the multi-member districting scheme. They were not only unable to elect a legislator who was attuned to their interests, but were also saddled with lawmakers who reflected white suburban ideology and were controlled by political leaders." Solomon, Chavis v. Whitcomb, 24 Rutgers L. Rev. 521, 533 (1970).

Indiana legislature would revive the apportionment scheme voided by the lower court?

2. In litigation raising controversial racial issues, are lawyers ever justified in jeopardizing a positive lower court decision in the hope of obtaining a landmark precedent from an appellate court?

NOTES

1. In Whitcomb v. Chavis, the plaintiff conceded that there was no legislative purpose to dilute black political effectiveness. 403 U.S. at 157-159, supra. It has been suggested that this concession was not necessary and that plaintiff might have argued that when the Indiana legislature re-enacted legislation preserving the Marion County District, it knew, or should have known, of the resultant effect on black voting strength, and therefore could be said to have the purpose of discriminating against the ghetto minority. See Note, Whitcomb v. Chavis, the Supreme Court, 1970 Term, 85 Harv. L. Rev. 135, 140, note 30 (1971).

2. Illustrative of the priority generally accorded "one man, one vote" cases intended to correct population disparities in voting districts, even when such correction seriously dilutes votes cast by blacks, is Conner v. Board of Supervisors of Oktibbeha County, 334 F. Supp. 280 (N.D. Miss. 1971). There black voters sought relief in a three-judge federal district court against redistricting of the county's five supervisor districts so that the majority of the population in each district was white. Prior to the reapportionment, two of the districts were predominantly black. Relief was sought on the basis that the changes were made without complying with the requirements of §5 of the Voting Rights Act of 1965 requiring approval by the United States Attorney General or the Federal District Court for the District of Columbia. The court dismissed the suit, however, accepting defendants' contention that the 1965 Voting Rights Act was inapplicable, in that the contested districting changes had been made pursuant to an order of a single judge in a 1966 reapportionment suit initiated to gain compliance with Reynolds v. Sims, 377 U.S. 533, 84 S. Ct. 1362, 12 L. Ed. 2d 506 (1964). In fact, the county defendants in the earlier reapportionment suit had adopted the current districting plan and advised the court; the court then approved the new plan. Nevertheless, the three-judge court asserted:

> It is extremely difficult for us to envision that Congress intended, by the enactment of Section 5 of the Voting Rights Act, to give the Executive Department of the Government, through the Attorney General, the right to veto a decree of a district court, when such court is sitting as a court of equity, and possessed of broad powers to protect the constitutional rights of litigants seeking its protection.

The dismissal was made without prejudice to the rights of plaintiffs to institute another action in a single-judge district court to test the constitutionality of existing reapportionment arrangements. Based on the standards in Whitcomb v. Chavis, to succeed in such a suit plaintiffs would have to show hostile racial intent, a perhaps not impossible standard, but one certainly more difficult than that provided in §5 of the Voting Rights Act of 1965. See also Howell v. Mahan, 330 F. Supp. 1138 (E.D. Va. 1971), *affirmed in part and reversed in part sub nom.* Mahan v. Howell, 41 U.S.L.W. 4277 (1973).

3. But in Bussie v. Governor of Louisiana, 333 F. Supp. 452 (E.D. La. 1971), *aff'd,* 457 F.2d 796 (5th Cir. 1971), the court, noting the almost total exclusion of blacks from the Louisiana legislature in this century as proof that black votes had been diluted, rejected the state's multimember plan in favor of a single-member plan prepared by a special master. The court of appeals reversed the district court findings that certain single-member districts had been gerrymandered to dilute black votes, but the Supreme Court vacated the Fifth Circuit's action and remanded for further consideration. Taylor v. McKeithen, 407 U.S. 191, 92 S. Ct. 1980, 32 L. Ed. 2d 648 (1972). Expressing bewilderment as to the basis for the Fifth Circuit's summary reversal, the Court's per curiam opinion observes:

> An examination of the record in this case suggests that the Court of Appeals may have believed that benign districting by federal judges is itself unconstitutional gerrymandering even where (a) it is employed to overcome the residual effects of past state dilution of Negro voting strength and (b) the only alternative is to leave intact the traditional "safe" white districts. If that were in fact the reasoning of the lower court, then this petition would present an important federal question of the extent to which the broad equitable powers of a federal court, Swann v. Charlotte-Mecklenburg Board of Educ., 402 U.S. 1, 15, 91 S. Ct. 1267, 28 L. Ed. 2d 554, are limited by the color-blind concept of Gomillion v. Lightfoot . . . .[3] In reapportionment cases, as Justice Stewart has observed "the federal courts are often going to be faced with hard remedial problems" in minimizing friction between their remedies and legitimate state policies. (407 U.S. at 193-194.)

4. As a further indication that at-large districting in Southern states may face increasingly close judicial scrutiny, a three-judge court adopted a single-member districting plan for the Alabama legislature after that body ignored earlier warnings that multimember districts in the large cities probably discriminated against blacks. The court referred to the Supreme Court's stated preference for single-member districts, Connor v. Johnson, 402 U.S. 690, 692,

3. Although similar in some respects, this case is not controlled by Whitcomb v. Chavis, 403 U.S. 124, 91 S. Ct. 1858, 29 L. Ed. 2d 363. To be sure, in both cases the District Courts were writing on clean slates in the sense that they were fashioning court-imposed reapportionment plans. And, in each case the equitable remedy of the court conflicted with a state policy. (There the state policy favored multi-member districts whereas here the policy favors maintenance of traditional boundaries.) The important difference, however, is that in Whitcomb it was conceded that the State's preference for multi-member districts was not rooted in racial discrimination, 403 U.S. at 149. Here, however, there has been no such concession, and, indeed, the District Court found a long "history" of bias and franchise dilution in the State's traditional drawing of district lines.

91 S. Ct. 1760, 1762, 29 L. Ed. 2d 268 (1971). It also acknowledged the finding in Whitcomb v. Chavis that multimember districts were not inherently discriminatory, but noted that "Whitcomb arose in Indiana, a State without the long history of racial discrimination evident in Alabama. Thus we feel justified in pointing out that in Alabama it is reasonable to conclude that multimember districts tend to discriminate against the black population." Sims v. Amos, 336 F. Supp. 924, 936 (N.D. Ala. 1972). See also Lipscomb v. Jonsson, 459 F.2d 335 (5th Cir. 1972) (dismissal of suit challenging the at-large composition of the Dallas City Council reversed).

5. Graves v. Barnes, 343 F. Supp. 704 (W.D. Tex. 1972), involved consolidated litigation brought by blacks, whites and Chicanos who charged that the Texas legislative plan, containing both single-member and multimember legislative districts, favored the rich and was disadvantageous to racial, ethnic, religious and political minorities.

After finding that throughout the state unjustified deviations in population size existed from district to district, the court noted the equal protection question resulting from the fact that it costs far more money for a candidate to run and to communicate with his or her electorate in any multimember district than it does in any single-member district, given roughly similar geographic and demographic circumstances, particularly in a metropolitan area.

In addition to this serious disadvantage, the court concluded that the multimember districts were inherently discriminating against blacks in Dallas County and Chicanos in Bexar County. Citing the "rather colorful history of racial segregation" in Texas, and various discriminatory election devices superimposed on the multimember system, the court found that minorities have little chance to elect persons who reflect their interests, and that representatives from those counties exhibit a record of recurring poor performance in serving minority interests. This proof was deemed by the court sufficient to meet the standards set in Whitcomb v. Chavis, supra, and immediate relief was granted.

The court rejected the argument that Chicanos in Bexar County cannot be a politically deprived ethnic minority because they constitute about half the population:

"Such a suggestion misconceives the meaning of the word 'minority'. In the context of the Constitution's guarantee of equal protection, 'minority' does not have a merely numerical denotation; rather it refers to an identifiable and specially disadvantaged group. That Mexican-Americans in Texas are such a group is well-established." 343 F. Supp. at 730.

The court acknowledged Supreme Court statements that minorities are not automatically entitled to representation and that no interest group has a constitutional right to be successful. But, the court said, "a state may not design a system that deprives such groups of a reasonable chance to be successful." 343 F. Supp. at 734. See Derfner, Multi-Member Districts and Black Voters, 2 Black L.J. 120 (1972).

6. Less than two weeks after the three-judge court's decision in Graves v. Barnes, Justice Powell refused to stay the creation of single-member districts in Dallas and Bexar counties. He observed that the district court had found the two multimember districts unconstitutional under the standard prescribed in Fortson, Burns and Whitcomb, and the "opinions attest to a conscientious application of principles enunciated by this Court." Graves v. Barnes, 405 U.S. 1201, 1204, 92 S. Ct. 752, 754, — L. Ed. 2d — (1972).

7. Several months after the Graves v. Barnes decision and Justice Powell's denial of a stay, the Fifth Circuit approved at-large elections for school board and police jury members in a sparsely populated rural Louisiana parish, basing its decision in part on the fact that blacks constitute a "commanding majority" of 58.7 percent of the parish. In dissent, Judge Gewin pointed out that, while a majority of the population, blacks constitute a minority (46 percent) of the registered voters. He also noted that no blacks voted before 1961, that 2122 of 2899 black voters were federally registered, and that prior to the court-ordered change to at-large elections in 1968, black representatives were elected to both the school board and police jury.

5. RIGHT OF ACCESS TO PUBLIC FACILITIES

A. THE HISTORIC DIMENSION

J. FRANKLIN, HISTORY OF RACIAL SEGREGATION IN THE UNITED STATES

Annals of the American Academy of Political and Social Science
34 (March 1956) 1-5

The enactment of state segregation statutes is a relatively recent phenomenon in the history of race relations in the United States. Of course there had been numerous segregation practices and some segregation statutes for many years, even before the nineteenth century. But it was not until the final quarter of the nineteenth century that states began to evolve a systematic program of legally separating whites and Negroes in every possible area of activity. And it was not until the twentieth century that these laws became a major apparatus for keeping the Negro "in his place." They were both comprehensive and generally acceptable, because they received their inspiration from a persistent and tenacious assumption of the innate inferiority of the Negro and because they had their roots deep in the ante-bellum period. . . .

The slaveholder's task of keeping the Negro slave in his place was complicated by the presence of several hundred thousand Negroes who were not slaves, although they can hardly be described as wholly free. So that they would not constitute a threat to the slave regime, free Negroes were denied the full rights and privileges of citizens. They enjoyed no equality in the courts, their right to assemble was denied, their movements were circumscribed, and education was withheld. Their miserable plight caused them to be unfavorably compared with slaves and confirmed the views of many that Negroes could not profit by freedom. They were regarded as the "very drones and pests of society," pariahs of the land, and an incubus on the body politic.

Outside the South free Negroes fared only slightly better. White Christians began to segregate them in the churches in the first decade of the national period, and Negroes in Philadelphia and New York City withdrew rather than accept this humiliation. As early as 1787 a white philanthropic organization opened a separate school for Negroes in New York City. In 1820 the city of Boston established a Negro elementary school. Separate schools became the practice throughout the North. When Charles Sumner challenged the constitutionality of segregated schools in Massachusetts in 1849, [see Roberts v. City of Boston, 59 Mass. 198 (5 Cush.) (1850), printed infra page 438] his position was bitterly opposed; and it was not until 1855 that the legislature of that state abolished them. Meanwhile numerous acts of violence in urban communities underscored Northern hostility to free Negroes. Between 1830 and 1840 anti-Negro riots occurred in Utica, Palmyra, New York City, and Philadelphia.

These ante-bellum experiences with free Negroes proved invaluable in the period following the close of the Civil War. In 1865 white Southerners were not "caught short" in facing the problem of the freedmen. From their point of view the former slaves simply augmented the group of free Negroes that they already regarded as "the most ignorant . . . vicious, impoverished, and degraded population of this country." Thus, the whites merely applied to the former slaves the principles and practices that had guided them in their relations with ante-bellum free Negroes. The latter had subsisted somewhere in the hazy zone between slavery and freedom. To concede the freedmen this "place" was regarded by white Southerners as generous, the Emancipation Proclamation and the Reconstruction amendments to the contrary notwithstanding.

New Laws, Old Relationships

When the economic and social structure of the Old South toppled at the end of the Civil War, the ex-Confederates immediately began to erect a new structure based on the old philosophy. As a distinguished Southern writer put it not many years ago, "If the war had smashed the Southern world, it had left the Southern mind and will — the mind and will arising from, corresponding to, and requiring this world — entirely unshaken." The smoke of battle had hardly cleared when the vanquished leaders, enjoying a remarkable amount of autonomy, began to fashion their new world upon the model of the old. With characteristic directness of action they went straight to the heart of their problem and worked out ways and means of holding on to the way of life that had meant so much to them.

As the ex-Confederates proceeded to restore order in their war-torn communities, they took little cognizance of the implications of the Emancipation Proclamation and the proposed Thirteenth Amendment. The major assumptions of the slave regime, the cornerstone of which was the permanent inferiority of the Negro, were still so powerful as to be controlling in most matters involving Negroes. While making some concessions, such as the competency of Negroes to testify in the courts, they nullified almost every semblance of freedom with numerous proscriptive laws. Mississippi legislators passed laws forbidding Negroes to rent or lease lands except in incorporated towns. They also enacted a law requiring every Negro, after January 1, 1866, to carry on his person written evidence that he had a home and an occupation. Louisiana forbade Negroes to move about in certain parishes or to be out at night without special permits. North Carolina extended to the freedmen the same privileges, burdens, and disabilities that had previously applied to free persons of color.

That the races should be kept apart, except where the whites were clearly in a superior role, was an important feature of most codes. Louisiana required that every Negro be in the regular service of some white person who was held responsible for his conduct. Mississippi forbade employees of railroads to permit Negroes to ride in first-class cars with white persons, except in the case of Negroes or mulattoes, "traveling with their mistress, in the capacity of maids." Many states provided that if Negro offenders could not pay their fines they were to be hired out to "any white person" who would pay the fines and costs and take the convicts for the shortest period of time.

Negroes were not indifferent to the process by which their former masters and their associates were nullifying the gains of the war. While they displayed no spirit of vindictiveness against those who had held them in slavery, they manifested a firm determination to secure the rights to which they, as free men, were entitled. The better educated and the more articulate among them assumed the leadership in expressing apprehension regarding the developments that were pushing them back toward slavery. They were especially concerned about the numerous acts of violence perpetrated against the freedmen, the burning of their schools and churches, and the economic proscriptions to which they were subjected. In Harrisburg, Pittsburgh, Indianapolis, and Cleveland they met in conventions and solicited the support of their Northern fellows in the effort to attain first-class citizenship. In Alexandria, Norfolk, Raleigh, Charleston, and other Southern communities they met, exchanged views, and addressed appeals to Southerners, Northerners, and federal officials. These supplications fell on deaf ears in the South, but they contributed to the increasing awareness elsewhere that the victory at Appomattox was empty.

Federal Intervention

The ex-Confederates looked upon the lenient Reconstruction policies of Lincoln and Johnson, which gave them virtual autonomy in every phase of life, as a normal concession to a section which was right on all the basic points in the dispute that led to the war. In the North, however, many people viewed the policy of leniency with skepticism from the outset; and congressional leaders made no secret of the fact that they regarded the resultant Presidential actions as unwise and improper, if not actually illegal. The first significant assertion of their own prerogatives was the passage of the Freedmen's Bureau Bill in March 1865, which called for an extensive program of relief and rehabilitation in the South.

The Bureau's establishment of schools for the former slaves and its attempt to protect them in their relations with white employers were especially obnoxious to the white Southerners. They were loud in their condemnation of both these features of the Bureau's program, calling them incendiary, radical, and political. They realized all too well the adverse effect that a successful prosecution of the program would have on the continued subordination of Negroes. The attempts of whites to drive out teachers of Negroes and to assert their authority over their employees were well calculated to subvert the program of complete emancipation and to preserve the old relationships between Negroes and whites.

The findings of the Joint Committee on Reconstruction, established by Congress in 1865, convinced a majority of congressional members that federal intervention was necessary to salvage the victory over the South. The committee was of the opinion that there was in the South "no general disposition to place the colored race . . . upon terms even of civil equality" and that no semblance of order could be maintained without the interposition of federal authority. In accordance with the recommendation of the Joint Committee, Congress proceeded to enact a civil rights measure, to submit the Fourteenth Amendment to the states, and to pass a series of laws placing the reconstruction of the former Confederate states under congressional control.

Civil Rights Act of 1866

The Civil Rights Act that became law on April 9, 1866, defined citizenship so as to include Negroes. Senator Lyman Trumbull of Illinois said that the purpose of the bill was to destroy the discrimination against the Negro in the laws of Southern states and to make effective the Thirteenth Amendment. White Southerners were, of course, outraged that Congress should undertake to guarantee the equality of Negroes, especially since the law had been enacted in the absence of representatives from the former Confederate states. As a matter of fact, fear that at some later date a majority of Congress or a federal court would strike down the Civil Rights Act was an important motivation for writing the provisions of the act into the Fourteenth Amendment.

Fourteenth Amendment

During the debates on the resolution that was to become the Fourteenth Amendment the question arose as to whether the proposed amendment protected Negroes against discrimination and segregation. There was no agreement, but proponents of the amendment were optimistic regarding its effect. In supporting the amendment, Senator Jacob M. Howard of Michigan said that the equal protection clause "abolishes all class legislation in the states and does away with the injustice of subjecting one caste of persons to a code not applicable to another." Representative John Bingham of Ohio declared that the amendment would protect "by national law the privileges and immunities of all the citizens of the Republic and the inborn rights of every person within its jurisdiction whenever the same shall be abridged or denied by the unconstitutional acts of any state."

Southern resistance

Neither the Fourteenth Amendment nor the radical legislation embodied in congressional Reconstruction was sufficient to protect the Negro in his political and civil rights. Southern resistance was stiff and effective, while efforts at enforcement left much to be desired. Once they recovered from the initial staggering blow of Radical Reconstruction legislation the ex-Confederates grimly went about the task of nullifying it in every possible way. By violence, intimidation, and ingenious schemes of economic pressure, by increased participation in political affairs, they began to "redeem" their state governments. Neither the Fifteenth Amendment nor the Ku Klux Klan Acts could stem the tide. In one state after another, between 1870 and 1877, they were successful; and as they took over the Southern state governments, they began to enact laws to separate Negroes and whites.

Civil Rights Act of 1875

Congress, against the bitter opposition of the ex-Confederates who were taking over the seats the Radicals had occupied, made one final effort to prevent the destruction of the rights of Negroes. Between 1871 and 1875 it devoted much attention to various proposals for a comprehensive national civil rights bill. While the act that was passed in 1875 omitted the provision of earlier drafts requiring the admission of persons regardless of race to all public schools, it declared that all persons, regardless of race or color, should be entitled to the full and equal enjoyment of the accommodations, advantages, facilities, and privileges of inns, public conveyances, theaters, and other places of public amusement. In its scope and in its provisions for enforcement it far surpassed anything that had ever been done in the area of protecting the civil rights of Negroes.

Although the Southern whites viewed the Act of 1875 with utter contempt and violated it with impunity, they were not entirely comfortable so long as it was on the statute books. They found it impossible, therefore, to restrain their elation when the Supreme Court declared the act unconstitutional in 1883. When the decision was announced during a performance at the Atlanta Opera House, the audience broke into "such a thunder of applause . . . as was never before heard within the walls of the opera house." An Arkansas newspaper expressed hearty agreement with the majority of the Court when it said, "Society is a law unto itself, which in matters in their nature overrides the statutes. Against its decrees the written law is powerless."

QUESTIONS

1. In considering the opinions in the Civil Rights Cases, keep in mind the country's political situation at the time. The Hayes-Tilden compromise in 1876 had averted a major crisis (albeit at the expense of blacks) that threatened to split the nation for the second time in less than a generation. As a part of that compromise, federal troops had been withdrawn from the South, and the settlement of racial problems was left to the states. The belief that blacks were inferior was almost universal. In view of these facts, was Justice Bradley's decision a reasonable interpretation of the Fourteenth Amendment at the time it was written? If Justice Harlan's views had been adopted by a majority of the Court, could the decision have been enforced?

2. *The requirement in the Civil Rights Cases that the state must be involved in discriminatory behavior to evoke the Fourteenth Amendment has been expanded but never overturned. Was this interpretation merely the result of the pragmatic pressures of the era, or is it defensible on the basis of an objective analysis of the Fourteenth Amendment?*

CIVIL RIGHTS CASES, 109 U.S. 3, 3 S. Ct. 18, 27 L. Ed. 835 (1883). These cases arose under the provisions of the Civil Rights Act of March 1, 1875, which provided that all persons within the jurisdiction of the United States "shall be entitled to the full and equal enjoyment of the accommodations, advantages, facilities, and privileges of inns, public conveyances on land or water, theatres, and other places of public amusement; subject only to the conditions and limitations established by law, and applicable alike to citizens of every race and color, regardless of any previous condition of servitude."

Justice Bradley saw the "essence of the law" as declaring not that all should be entitled to full and equal enjoyment, but that such enjoyment should not be subject to any conditions applicable only to persons of a particular race. Congress, he concluded, did not have power under the Fourteenth Amendment to enact such a law. The Fourteenth Amendment effected a "prohibition" of "state action" of particular character; the fifth section of the amendment, the enabling provisions, empowered Congress to effect the prohibitions, nothing more. Thus, the power it gives Congress is negative: especially, "It does not authorize Congress to create a code of municipal law for the regulation of private rights. . . ." Otherwise, the power granted Congress by the amendment might be limitless. The Fourteenth Amendment does not guard against private wrongs; the redress for such wrongs must be provided by state laws, not federal law, except where Congress is otherwise clothed with direct and plenary power over the matter involved. Nor does the Thirteenth Amendment grant Congress the power to enact such legislation. Justice Bradley conceded that the amendment grants Congress power to enact all laws necessary to obliterate slavery "with all its badges and incidents," but concluded that full and equal access to public accommodations was not implied by the elimination of "badges of slavery":

> When a man has emerged from slavery, and by the aid of beneficent legislation has shaken off the inseparable concomitants of that state, there must be some stage in the progress of his elevation when he takes the rank of a mere citizen, and ceases to be the special favorite of the laws, and when his rights, as a citizen or a man, are to be protected in the ordinary modes by which other men's rights are protected. There were thousands of free colored people in this country before the abolition of slavery, enjoying all the essential rights of life, liberty and property the same as white citizens; yet no one, at that time, thought that it was any invasion of their personal status as freemen because they were not admitted to all the privileges enjoyed by white citizens, or because they were subjected to discriminations in the enjoyment of accommodations in inns, public conveyances and places of amuse-

ment. Mere discriminations on account of race or color were not regarded as badges of slavery. (109 U.S. at 25.)

Justice Harlan dissented, unable "to resist the conclusion that the substance and spirit of the recent Amendments of the Constitution have been sacrificed by a subtle and ingenious verbal criticism":

> Were the States against whose protest the institution [of slavery] was destroyed, to be left free, so far as national interference was concerned, to make or allow discriminations against that race, as such, in the enjoyment of those fundamental rights which by universal concession, inhere in a state of freedom? . . .
>
> I do not contend that the Thirteenth Amendment invests Congress with authority, by legislation, to define and regulate the entire body of the civil rights which citizens enjoy, or may enjoy, in the several States. But I hold that since slavery, as the court has repeatedly declared, [citations omitted] was the moving or principal cause of the adoption of that amendment, and since that institution rested wholly upon the inferiority, as a race, of those held in bondage, their freedom necessarily involved immunity from, and protection against, all discrimination against them, because of their race, in respect of such civil rights as belong to freemen of other races. Congress, therefore, under its express power to enforce that amendment, by appropriate legislation, may enact laws to protect that people against the deprivation, because of their race, of any civil rights granted to other freemen in the same State; and such legislation may be of a direct and primary character, operating upon States, their officers and agents, and, also, upon, at least, such individuals and corporations as exercise public functions and wield power and authority under the State. . . . (109 U.S. at 34, 36.)

With respect to the Fourteenth Amendment, Justice Harlan laid stress upon the provision in §1 that all persons are citizens of the United States and of the states wherein they reside, as being "of a distinctly affirmative character," and thus construed the enabling provisions in §5 as granting Congress the power to protect the citizens by legislation "of a primary direct character." Corporations running railroads or public inns are regulated by the state and operate as the state's agents, and may be subjected to the federal government's newly granted power to protect the privileges and immunities of the citizens of the various states.

NOTES

1. One historian — Scott, Justice Bradley's Evolving Concept of the Fourteenth Amendment from the Slaughterhouse Cases to the Civil Rights Cases, 25 Rutgers L. Rev. 552 (1971) — has pointed out that Justice Bradley's highly restrictive interpretation of the Fourteenth Amendment in the Civil Rights Cases represented a total change from the very broad reading he gave that amendment in the Slaughterhouse Cases, 83 U.S. (16 Wall.) 36, 21 L. Ed. 394 (1873). In 1870, when Justice Bradley was "riding circuit" in New

Orleans, he heard the first of several challenges to an 1869 Louisiana statute which chartered a private corporation and granted it exclusive rights for twenty-five years to conduct all slaughtering operations in three parishes, including the city of New Orleans. The legislation, justified as a health measure, prohibited the slaughter of cattle except in facilities operated by the new corporation. Litigation challenging the statute was initiated by a group of New Orleans butchers who sought to invalidate the measure on grounds, inter alia, that it violated the Thirteenth and Fourteenth Amendments. Justice Bradley agreed, in effect, holding that white citizens enjoyed rights, including the right to pursue a trade under the direct protection of the Fourteenth Amendment and congressional legislation enacted to effectuate it. Bradley found that the Fourteenth Amendment "prohibits any state from abridging the privileges and immunities of citizens of the United States. . . . It not merely requires equality of privileges, but it demands that the privileges and immunities of all citizens be absolutely unabridged, unimpaired." While he acknowledged that a state was entitled to make police regulations to protect public health, Justice Bradley held that local authorities cannot abridge the fundamental rights of citizens under pretense of police regulations. He concluded that the federal government had a duty "to prevent the invasion of any clear and undoubted individual rights of the citizen which are secured to him by the constitution." As to congressional authorization for federal courts to assume jurisdiction in such cases, Justice Bradley ruled that the Civil Rights Act of 1866, even though passed before the Fourteenth Amendment, provided direct protection to white citizens in the enjoyment of their rights. Live-Stock Dealers' and Butchers' Ass'n v. Crescent City Live-Stock Landing and Slaughter-House Co., 15 F. Cas. 649, 652-653 (No. 8,408) (C.C.D. La. 1870).

Justice Bradley's decision was overruled, and he dissented when the Slaughterhouse Cases reached the Supreme Court. The majority, rejecting the Bradley position, ruled that the principal purpose of the Fourteenth Amendment was to admit black people to citizenship. Even so, the Court held that the clear distinction that had existed before the war between federal and state citizenship remained in force. The primary authority for the protection of civil rights was state authority. 83 U.S. at 75. The federal role was a secondary or corrective one and would only arise in the event that states failed to provide equal protection. The majority concluded, "We doubt very much whether any action of a State not directed by way of discrimination against the negroes as a class, or on account of their race, will ever be held to come within the purview of this provision." 109 U.S. at 81. In his dissent, Justice Bradley said that United States citizenship was now primary; state citizenship was secondary. He felt that a citizen could claim citizenship in any state, and the whole power of the nation was pledged to sustain him in an equality of rights with every other citizen.

In explaining why Justice Bradley's ruling in the Civil Rights Cases was precisely the opposite of the position taken thirteen years before, Professor

Scott suggests that both positions represent the philosophy of the Republican party during the two periods. He points out that the turmoil created in 1877 by the Hayes v. Tilden crisis had been settled by a special electoral commission, including five members of the Supreme Court with Justice Bradley one of the members. The Republican, Hayes, was awarded the disputed returns and was immediately inaugurated. In the years that followed, the Republicans sought to put aside their differences with the South by granting the latter "home rule" with respect to the freed slaves. The decisions in the Civil Rights Cases fit that policy to perfection.

2. Professor John Hope Franklin, in his article History of Racial Segregation in the United States, in Annals of the American Academy of Political and Social Science 34 (March 1956) 5-6, describes the impact on the country of the Civil Rights Cases.

Before the momentous decision in the Civil Rights Cases in 1883 segregation by statutes was confined to a relatively few but highly important areas. In many states, for example, the laws against intermarriage preceded the Civil War by many years. Although they were omitted from some state codes during Reconstruction, there was no wholesale repeal of them, and they remained in effect in many parts of the North as well as in the South. The practice of maintaining separate schools for white and Negro children was well established in the North before the Civil War; and in the South if ex-Confederates provided schools for Negro children at all they were of course separate. Although the Radicals made some attempts to break down segregated schools during their brief period of control, they met with little success. In the military services Negroes had almost always been segregated, and the Civil War did much to strengthen the practice.

The decision in the Civil Rights Cases was an important stimulus to the enactment of segregation statutes. It gave the assurance the South wanted that the federal government would not intervene to protect the civil rights of Negroes. The decision coincided, moreover, with a series of political and intellectual developments that greatly accelerated the program of segregation. In the eighties several Southern governments were embarrassed by financial scandals, and some of them outstripped the Reconstruction governments in defalcations and pilfering. Meanwhile, the agrarian unrest induced by widespread economic distress frightened the conservatives and forced them to adopt extreme measures in order to regain the leadership which in some states they had temporarily lost to white and Negro Populists. Distressed by the possibility of a strong new party composed of white and Negro farmers and workers, they dominated the Negro vote where they could and expressed grave fears of "Negro domination" where they could not. Thus, the magical formula of white supremacy, "applied without stint and without any of the old reservations of paternalism, without deference to any lingering resistance of Northern liberalism, or any fear of further check from a defunct Southern Populism," gained ascendancy in the final decade of the nineteenth century.

These were the years that witnessed the effective constitutional disfranchisement of Negroes by such devices as understanding clauses, grandfather clauses, and good conduct clauses. They also saw the launching of an intensive propaganda campaign of white supremacy, negrophobia, and race chauvinism, supported by a sensational and irresponsible press that carried lurid stories of alleged Negro bestiality. New waves of violence broke out, with increased lynchings of Negroes, unspeakable atrocities against them, and race riots. Concurrently, and at a "higher level," the literary and scientific leaders of the South wrote numerous tracts and books designed to "prove" the inhumanity of the Negro. In this climate segregation took a giant step toward a fully developed white supremacy apparatus.

PLESSY v. FERGUSON, 163 U.S. 537, 16 S. Ct. 1138, 41 L. Ed. 256 (1896). Plessy brought suit for a writ of prohibition against the judge who was to try him for the violation of a Louisiana statute, adopted in 1890, which provided for separate facilities for white and black passengers on trains, and which prescribed criminal penalties for violators.

For the Court, Justice Brown affirmed the Supreme Court of Louisiana's denial of the writ, upholding the statute as not violative of the Fourteenth Amendment's prohibition of unequal protection of the laws. The object of the Fourteenth Amendment "was undoubtedly to enforce the absolute equality of the two races before the law, but in the nature of things it could not have been intended to abolish distinctions based upon color, or to enforce social, as distinguished from political, equality, or a commingling of the two races upon terms unsatisfactory to either."

It is, said the Court, a generally recognized power of the state legislatures to enforce racial segregation, especially in schools. The Court supported its statement by citing Roberts v. City of Boston, 59 Mass. (5 Cush.) 198 (1850), an early Massachusetts case upholding the right of the Boston School Committee to make separate provision for the "instruction of colored children." To the plaintiff's claim that the right to be treated as a white man was a property right and that the Fourteenth Amendment prohibited the states from unlawfully depriving him of this right, the Court responded circularly that "If he be a colored man and be so assigned [to a colored coach], he has been deprived of no property, since he is not lawfully entitled to the reputation of being a white man." To the plaintiff's argument that the logic of racial segregation could be used to enforce segregation on the basis of hair color or some other such arbitrary circumstance, the Court responded "that every exercise of the police power must be reasonable. . . . So far, then, as a conflict with the Fourteenth Amendment is concerned, the case reduces itself to the question whether the statute of Louisiana is a reasonable regulation. . . ." In determining reasonableness, the state could

> act with reference to the established usages, customs and traditions of the people, and with a view to the promotion of their comfort, and the preservation of the public peace and good order. Gauged by this standard, we cannot say that a law which authorizes or even requires the separation of the two races in public conveyances is unreasonable, or more obnoxious to the Fourteenth Amendment than the acts of congress requiring separate schools for colored children in the District of Columbia, the constitutionality of which does not seem to have been questioned, or the corresponding acts of state legislatures.

Justice Harlan dissented strongly, saying that the legislation was inconsistent not only with the equality of rights of citizenship guaranteed by the Fourteenth Amendment, but with the personal liberty enjoyed by "everyone in the United States." He foresaw great social evils resulting from the decisions:

The present decision, it may well be apprehended, will not only stimulate aggressions, more or less brutal and irritating, upon the admitted rights of colored citizens, but will encourage the belief that it is possible, by means of state enactments, to defeat the beneficent purposes which the people of the United States had in view when they adopted the recent amendments of the Constitution, by one of which the blacks of this country were made citizens of the United States and of the States in which they respectively reside, and whose privileges and immunities, as citizens, the States are forbidden to abridge. Sixty millions of whites are in no danger from the presence here of eight millions of blacks. The destinies of the two races, in this country, are indissolubly linked together, and the interests of both require that the common government of all shall not permit the seeds of race hate to be planted under the sanction of law. What can more certainly arouse race hate, what more certainly create and perpetuate a feeling of distrust between these races, than state enactments, which, in fact, proceed on the ground that colored citizens are so inferior and degraded that they cannot be allowed to sit in public coaches occupied by white citizens? That, as all will admit, is the real meaning of such legislation as was enacted in Louisiana.

J. FRANKLIN, HISTORY OF RACIAL SEGREGATION IN THE UNITED STATES

Annals of the American Academy of Political and Social Science 34 (March 1956) 6-8

[The accuracy of Justice Harlan's prediction in his Plessy v. Ferguson dissent was proven during the ensuing years.]

In the decade after the Civil War few laws were enacted demanding segregation. The first state segregation statutes were those of Mississippi and Florida in 1865, requiring segregation on public carriers. Texas followed in 1866, but five years later repealed the act. The Tennessee law of 1881, sometimes referred to as the first Jim Crow law, directed railroad companies to provide separate cars or portions of cars for first-class Negro passengers, instead of relegating them to second-class accommodations as had been the custom. There were only two votes against the measure in the House and one in the Senate.

In the ensuing twenty years separation of Negroes and whites on public carriers became a favorite preoccupation of Southern legislators. By 1892 six other Southern states had joined the ranks — Texas, Louisiana, Alabama, Arkansas, Georgia, and Kentucky. In some states, however, opposition had been bitter. In Louisiana, for example, a Negro representative declared that the law would humiliate Negroes and "make them appear before the world as a treacherous and a dangerous class of people." In Arkansas, a Negro member of the House sought to ridicule the bill's supporters by insisting that if whites did not want to associate with Negroes there should be laws to divide the streets and sidewalks so that Negroes could go on one side and white people on the other. "He would like to see an end put to all intercourse between white and colored people by day, and especially by night."

With the pattern firmly established in a number of Southern states and the pressure for segregation growing, the other Southern states followed before the end of the century. South Carolina passed its laws segregating Negroes and whites on railroads in 1898; North Carolina, Virginia, and Maryland soon after. When Oklahoma entered the Union in 1907 segregation had already been provided for.

By this time laws were being extended to cover all activities related to transportation. In 1888 the railroad commission of Mississippi was authorized to designate separate waiting rooms for Negroes and whites. By 1893 the railroad companies, on their own initiative, were doing the same thing in South Carolina, and in 1906 the state required separation of the races in all station restaurants and eating houses. Ultimately, legislation covered steamboats, buses, and other forms of transportation.

Twentieth-century varieties

The first decade of the twentieth century witnessed the enactment of a wide variety of segregation statutes. Georgia had required separation of the races on streetcars as early as 1891. It was between 1901 and 1907, however, that North Carolina, Virginia, Louisiana, Arkansas, South Carolina, Tennessee, Mississippi, Maryland, Florida, and Oklahoma followed suit. Ordinances in Southern cities were even more specific than state laws. In 1906, for example, the city of Montgomery, Alabama, went so far as to insist that Negroes and whites use separate streetcars.

Wards of society — still separated

As the states assumed greater responsibility for the various wards of society they were careful to provide separate facilities for whites and Negroes. In 1875 Alabama made it unlawful for any jailer or sheriff to imprison white and Negro prisoners before conviction in the same apartments of the jail, if there were sufficient apartments, and ten years later prohibited the chaining of white and Negro convicts together or housing them together. In 1903 Arkansas directed that in the state penitentiary and in county jails, stockades, convict camps, and all other places where prisoners were confined, separate apartments should be provided and maintained for white and Negro prisoners. Within the next ten years most of the other Southern states had similar legislation. During the same period segregation of white and Negro insane, feeble-minded, blind and deaf, paupers, tubercular patients, and juvenile delinquents was provided for.

No detail too small

In rounding out the system of legal segregation some states provided for the separation of whites and Negroes at work, at play, and at home. In 1915 South Carolina forbade textile factories to permit employees of different races to work together in the same room, or to use the same entrances, pay windows, exits, doorways, stairways, or windows at the same time, or the same lavatories, toilets, drinking-water buckets, pails, cups, dippers, or glasses at any time. In 1905 Georgia passed a law making illegal the use by Negroes and whites of the same park facilities; individuals were permitted to donate land for playground use only if they specified which race alone was to make use of it. Until 1940 Negroes and whites in Atlanta, Georgia, were not permitted to visit the municipal zoo at the same time. In 1929 Oklahoma authorized the Conservation Commission to segregate the races in the use of fishing, boating, and bathing facilities on lakes and streams under the supervision of the state. Arkansas enacted a law in 1935 requiring the separation of Negroes and whites at all race tracks and gaming establishments. Beginning in 1910 several cities, among them Baltimore, Atlanta, and Louisville, passed ordinances designating certain blocks, territories, and districts as Negro or white and forbidding members of one race to live in the area assigned to the other. Such zoning laws, however, were declared unconstitutional in 1917.

The supply of ideas for new ways to segregate whites and Negroes seemed inexhaustible. In 1915 Oklahoma authorized the Corporation Commission to order telephone companies to maintain separate booths for white and Negro patrons. North Carolina and Florida provided that textbooks used by the children of one race be kept separate from those used by children of the other race, despite the fact that both states have stringent rules covering fumigation of textbooks. In 1922 Mississippi forbade members of both races to ride in taxicabs at the same time unless the vehicle held more than seven passengers and was traveling from one city to another. New Orleans deemed it in the interest of the public welfare to enact an ordinance separating Negro and white prostitutes.

Two worlds — roads closed

The law had created two worlds, so separate that communication between them was almost impossible. Separation bred suspicion and hatred, fostered rumors and misunderstanding, and created conditions that made extremely difficult any steps toward its reduction. Legal segregation was so complete that a Southern white minister was moved to remark that it "made of our eating and drinking, our buying and selling, our labor and housing, our rents, our railroads, our orphanages and prisons, our recreations, our very institutions of religion, a problem of race as well as a problem of maintenance."

QUESTIONS

1. Justice Harlan's dissent in Plessy v. Ferguson has been justly praised for its foresight. But, by the standards used to measure the reasonableness of racial classifications in public facilities, was the majority wrong, in the context of race relations at the turn of the century?

2. Given the economic, social and probable psychological commitment to white superiority at that time, would a decision invalidating segregation laws have been correct? Would it have been enforceable?

3. Consider the history of the next fifty years. Was it the needs of whites or the plight of blacks that rendered decisions voiding "separate but equal" laws both correct and enforceable?

NOTE: THE IMPACT OF BROWN v. BOARD OF EDUCATION ON NON-SCHOOL SEGREGATION

The 1954 decision in Brown v. Board of Education, 347 U.S. 483, 74 S. Ct. 686, 98 L. Ed. 873 (1954), printed infra page 431, did not expressly overrule Plessy v. Ferguson. The Court simply concluded "that in the field of public education the doctrine of 'separate but equal' has no place." In the years that followed, the Supreme Court delayed its implementation of public school desegregation, but experienced no difficulty in ordering the immediate end of state-sponsored racial segregation in a wide variety of facilities. Many of these decisions were summary per curiam orders in which the only authority cited by the Court was Brown v. Board of Education.

The Court voided "Jim Crow" policies in streetcars and buses (see discussion infra page 296), public parks, beaches and bathhouses, municipal golf courses, cafeterias, auditoriums, and courtroom seating. Lower courts followed suit, with the result that in the first half dozen years after Brown, civil rights lawyers experienced far more success with Brown in desegregating recreational facilities, such as golf courses and swimming pools, than in litigation involving public schools, where the Court had found separate facilities "inherently unequal."

But, of course, most of the public facilities which excluded or segregated blacks were privately owned, and not subject to constitutional constraints under the Supreme Court interpretations of the Reconstruction Amendments and the early civil rights acts in the Civil Rights Cases and Plessy v. Ferguson.

B. TITLE II — ITS DEVELOPMENT AND POTENTIAL

A full decade after the Brown decision, and following three years of civil rights protests against the continued maintenance of segregated facilities (see the discussion in Chapter Seven), Congress enacted the Civil Rights Act of 1964, which rendered illegal racial discrimination in a number of areas, including public accommodations, employment, voting, education and other federally financed activities. The prohibition against racial bias in public facilities, included as Title II of the 1964 Act, 78 Stat. 241, 42 U.S.C. §2000a, is set forth in the Appendix. By the time of its enactment, many of the larger public facilities in the South had desegregated in order to halt the disruptive sit-in protests that had captured the interest and the support of peoples all over the world and had (perhaps more importantly) resulted in serious economic loss to many business interests.

There has been a great deal of litigation interpreting the scope of Title II. The validity of the act was established in Heart of Atlanta Motel, Inc. v. United States and Katzenbach v. McClung.

HEART OF ATLANTA MOTEL, INC. v. UNITED STATES
379 U.S. 241, 85 S. Ct. 348, 13 L. Ed. 2d 258 (1964)

Mr. Justice Clark delivered the opinion of the Court.

This is a declaratory judgment action, . . . attacking the constitutionality of Title II of the Civil Rights Act of 1964, 78 Stat. 241, 243. In addition to declaratory relief the complaint sought an injunction restraining the enforcement of the Act and damages against appellees based on allegedly resulting injury in the event compliance was required. Appellees counterclaimed for enforcement under §206(a) of the Act and asked for a three-judge district court under §206(b). A three-judge court, empaneled under §206(b) as well as 28 U.S.C. §2282 (1958 ed.) sustained the validity of the Act and issued a permanent injunction on appellees' counterclaim restraining appellant from continuing to violate the Act. . . . We affirm the judgment.

1. *The Factual Background and Contentions of the Parties.* The case comes here on admissions and stipulated facts. Appellant owns and operates the Heart of Atlanta Motel which has 216 rooms available to transient guests. The motel is located on Courtland Street, two blocks from downtown Peachtree Street. It is readily accessible to interstate highways 75 and 85 and state highways 23 and 41. Appellant solicits patronage from outside the State of Georgia through various national advertising media, including magazines of national circulation; it maintains over 50 billboards and highway signs within the State, soliciting patronage for the motel; it accepts convention trade from outside Georgia and approximately 75% of its registered guests are from out of State. Prior to passage of the Act the motel had followed a practice of refusing to rent rooms to Negroes, and it alleged that it intended to continue to do so. In an effort to perpetuate that policy this suit was filed.

The appellant contends that Congress in passing this Act exceeded its power to regulate commerce under Art. I, §8, cl. 3, of the Constitution of the United States; that the Act violates the Fifth Amendment because appellant is deprived of the right to choose its customers and operate its business as it wishes, resulting in a taking of its liberty and property without due process of law and a taking of its property without just compensation; and, finally, that by requiring appellant to rent available rooms to Negroes against its will, Congress is subjecting it to involuntary servitude in contravention of the Thirteenth Amendment.

The appellees counter that the unavailability to Negroes of adequate accommodations interferes significantly with interstate travel, and that Congress, under the Commerce Clause, has power to remove such obstructions and restraints; that the Fifth Amendment does not forbid reasonable regulation and that consequential damage does not constitute a "taking" within the meaning of that amendment; that the Thirteenth Amendment claim fails because it is entirely frivolous to say that an amendment directed to the abolition of human bondage and the removal of widespread disabilities associated with slavery places discrimination in public accommodations, beyond the reach of both federal and state law. . . .

[The History of the Act is omitted.]

3. *Title II of the Act.* This Title is divided into seven sections beginning with §201(a) which provides that:

> All persons shall be entitled to the full and equal enjoyment of the goods, services, facilities, privileges, advantages, and accommodations of any place of public accommodation, as defined in this section, without discrimination or segregation on the ground of race, color, religion, or national origin.

There are listed in §201(b) four classes of business establishments, each of which "serves the public" and "is a place of public accommodation" within the meaning of §201(a) "if its operations affect commerce, or if discrimination or segregation by it is supported by State action." The covered establishments are:

> (1) any inn, hotel, motel, or other establishment which provides lodging to transient guests, other than an establishment located within a building which contains not more than five rooms for rent or hire and which is actually occupied by the proprietor of such establishment as his residence;
> (2) any restaurant, cafeteria . . . [not here involved];
> (3) any motion picture house . . . [not here involved];
> (4) any establishment . . . which is physically located within the premises of any establishment otherwise covered by this subsection, or . . . within the premises of which is physically located any such covered establishment . . . [not here involved].

Section 201(c) defines the phrase "affect commerce" as applied to the above establishments. It first declares that "any inn, hotel, motel, or other establishment which provides lodging to transient guests" affects commerce per se. Restaurants, cafeterias, etc., in class two affect commerce only if they serve or offer to serve interstate travelers or if a substantial portion of the food which they serve or products which they sell have "moved in commerce." Motion picture houses and other places listed in class three affect commerce if they customarily present films, performances, etc., "which move in commerce." And the establishments listed in class four affect commerce if they are within, or include within their own premises, an establishment "the operations of which affect commerce." Private clubs are excepted under certain conditions. See §201(e).

Section 201(d) declares that "discrimination or segregation" is supported by state action when carried on under color of any law, statute, ordinance, regulation or any custom or usage required or enforced by officials of the State or any of its subdivisions.

In addition, §202 affirmatively declares that all persons "shall be entitled to be free, at any establishment or place, from discrimination or segregation of any kind on the ground of race, color, religion, or national origin, if such discrimination or segregation is or purports to be required by any law, statute, ordinance, regulation, rule, or order of a State or any agency or political subdivision thereof."

Finally, §203 prohibits the withholding or denial, etc., of any right or privilege secured by §201 and §202 or the intimidation, threatening or coercion of any person with the purpose of interfering with any such right or the punishing, etc., of any person for exercising or attempting to exercise any such right.

The remaining sections of the Title are remedial ones for violations of any of the previous sections. Remedies are limited to civil actions for preventive relief. The Attorney General may bring suit where he has "reasonable cause to believe that any person or group of persons is engaged in a pattern or practice of resistance to the full enjoyment of any of the rights secured by this title, and that the pattern or practice is of such a nature and is intended to deny the full exercise of the rights herein described. . . ." §206(a).

A person aggrieved may bring suit, in which the Attorney General may be permitted to intervene. Thirty days' written notice before filing any such action must be given to the appropriate authorities of a State or subdivision the law of which prohibits the act complained of and which has established an authority which may grant relief therefrom. §204(c). In States where such condition does not exist the court after a case is filed may refer it to the Community Relations Service which is established under Title X of the Act. §204(d). This Title establishes such service in the Department of Commerce, provides for a Director to be appointed by the President with the advice and consent of the Senate and grants it certain powers, including the power to hold hearings, with reference to matters coming to its attention by reference from the court or between communities and persons involved in disputes arising under the Act.

4. *Application of Title II to Heart of Atlanta Motel.* It is admitted that the operation of the motel brings it within the provisions of §201(a) of the Act and that appellant refused to provide lodging for transient Negroes because of their race or color and that it intends to continue that policy unless restrained.

The sole question posed is, therefore, the constitutionality of the Civil Rights Act of 1964 as applied to these facts. The legislative history of the

Act indicates that Congress based the Act on §5 and the Equal Protection Clause of the Fourteenth Amendment as well as its power to regulate interstate commerce under Art. I, §8, cl. 3, of the Constitution.

The Senate Commerce Committee made it quite clear that the fundamental object of Title II was to vindicate "the deprivation of personal dignity that surely accompanies denials of equal access to public establishments." At the same time, however, it noted that such an objective has been and could be readily achieved "by congressional action based on the commerce power of the Constitution." S. Rep. No. 872, supra, at 16-17. Our study of the legislative record, made in the light of prior cases, has brought us to the conclusion that Congress possessed ample power in this regard, and we have therefore not considered the other grounds relied upon. This is not to say that the remaining authority upon which it acted was not adequate, a question upon which we do not pass, but merely that since the commerce power is sufficient for our decision here we have considered it alone. Nor is §201(d) or §202, having to do with state action, involved here and we do not pass upon either of those sections.

5. *The Civil Rights Cases, 109 U.S. 3, 3 S. Ct. 18 (1883), and their Application.* In light of our ground for decision, it might be well at the outset to discuss the Civil Rights Cases, supra, which declared provisions of the Civil Rights Act of 1875 unconstitutional. 18 Stat. 335, 336. We think that decision inapposite, and without precedential value in determining the constitutionality of the present Act. Unlike Title II of the present legislation, the 1875 Act broadly proscribed discrimination in "inns, public conveyances on land or water, theaters, and other places of public amusement," without limiting the categories of affected businesses to those impinging upon interstate commerce. In contrast, the applicability of Title II is carefully limited to enterprises having a direct and substantial relation to the interstate flow of goods and people, except where state action is involved. Further, the fact that certain kinds of businesses may not in 1875 have been sufficiently involved in interstate commerce to warrant bringing them within the ambit of the commerce power is not necessarily dispositive of the same question today. Our populace had not reached its present mobility, nor were facilities, goods and services circulating as readily in interstate commerce as they are today. Although the principles which we apply today are those first formulated by Chief Justice Marshall in Gibbons v. Ogden, 9 Wheat. 1, 6 L. Ed. 23 (1824), the conditions of transportation and commerce have changed dramatically, and we must apply those principles to the present state of commerce. The sheer increase in volume of interstate traffic alone would give discriminatory practices which inhibit travel a far larger impact upon the Nation's commerce than such practices had on the economy of another day. Finally, there is language in the Civil Rights Cases which indicates that the Court did not fully consider whether the 1875 Act could be sustained as an exercise of the commerce power. Though the Court observed that "no one will contend that the power to pass it was contained in the constitution before the adoption of

the last three amendments [Thirteenth, Fourteenth, and Fifteenth]," the Court went on specifically to note that the Act was not "conceived" in terms of the commerce power and expressly pointed out:

> Of course, these remarks [as to lack of congressional power] do not apply to those cases in which congress is clothed with direct and plenary powers of legislation over the whole subject, accompanied with an express or implied denial of such power to the states, as in the regulation of commerce with foreign nations, among the several states, and with the Indian tribes . . . . In these cases congress has power to pass laws for regulating the subjects specified, in every detail, and the conduct and transactions of individuals in respect thereof. 109 U.S. at 18, 3 S. Ct. at 26. . . .

6. *The Basis of Congressional Action.* While the Act as adopted carried no congressional findings the record of its passage through each house is replete with evidence of the burdens that discrimination by race or color places upon interstate commerce. [Citations omitted.] This testimony included the fact that our people have become increasingly mobile with millions of people of all races traveling from State to State; that Negroes in particular have been the subject of discrimination in transient accommodations, having to travel great distances to secure the same; that often they have been unable to obtain accommodations and have had to call upon friends to put them up overnight, . . . and that these conditions had become so acute as to require the listing of available lodging for Negroes in a special guidebook which was itself "dramatic testimony to the difficulties" Negroes encounter in travel. . . . These exclusionary practices were found to be nationwide, the Under Secretary of Commerce testifying that there is "no question that this discrimination in the North still exists to a large degree" and in the West and Midwest as well. . . . This testimony indicated a qualitative as well as quantitative effect on interstate travel by Negroes. The former was the obvious impairment of the Negro traveler's pleasure and convenience that resulted when he continually was uncertain of finding lodging. As for the latter, there was evidence that this uncertainty stemming from racial discrimination had the effect of discouraging travel on the part of a substantial portion of the Negro community. . . . We shall not burden this opinion with further details since the voluminous testimony presents overwhelming evidence that discrimination by hotels and motels impedes interstate travel.

7. *The Power of Congress Over Interstate Travel.* [The Court sustained Congress's power under the Commerce Clause to prohibit travel obstructions traceable to discrimination by hotels and motels. Relying heavily on Gibbons v. Ogden, 22 U.S. (9 Wheat.) 1, 6 L. Ed. 23 (1824), and the wide variety of regulations that had been sustained on the basis of the Commerce Clause, the Court found that the means Congress had used to relieve this obstruction was reasonable and appropriate. In doing so the Court rejected the argument that the act deprived restaurant owners of liberty or property under the Fifth Amendment. The Court pointed to the thirty-two states that prohibit

racial discrimination in public accommodations through statutes or executive orders that had repeatedly been upheld when attacked as violative of the Due Process Clause. Moreover, the Court refused to accept the "involuntary servitude" argument, indicating that it could not believe that the Thirteenth Amendment had abolished the common-law innkeeper rule, which was in effect long before this amendment and which the Court found was codified by the laws of the thirty-two states that prohibit racial discrimination in public accommodations.]

. . . We, therefore, conclude that the action of the Congress in the adoption of the Act as applied here to a motel which concededly serves interstate travelers is within the power granted it by the Commerce Clause of the Constitution, as interpreted by this Court for 140 years. It may be argued that Congress could have pursued other methods to eliminate the obstructions it found in interstate commerce caused by racial discrimination. But this is a matter of policy that rests entirely with the Congress not with the courts. How obstructions in commerce may be removed — what means are to be employed — is within the sound and exclusive discretion of the Congress. It is subject only to one caveat — that the means chosen by it must be reasonably adapted to the end permitted by the Constitution. We cannot say that its choice here was not so adapted. The Constitution requires no more. Affirmed.

[Justices Black, Douglas and Goldberg wrote separate concurring opinions applicable to both the Heart of Atlanta Motel case and Katzenbach v. McClung. Justice Black felt that Title II was appropriately applied to the facilities involved in this litigation. He recognized, however, that some isolated and remote lunchrooms that sell only to local people, and buy almost all their supplies in the locality, may be beyond the reach of Congress's power to regulate commerce. Both Justice Douglas and Justice Goldberg expressed the view that, in addition to the Commerce Clause, Congress had authority under the Fourteenth Amendment to protect blacks from racial discrimination, as provided for in Title II.]

KATZENBACH v. McCLUNG, 379 U.S. 294, 85 S. Ct. 377, 13 L. Ed. 2d 290 (1964). The plaintiff sued to enjoin enforcement of the 1964 Civil Rights Act, urging that racial discrimination in restaurants did not have an effect on interstate commerce substantial enough to enable Congress to enact legislation regulating the matter. The government appealed from an adverse judgment by a three-judge federal court.

Plaintiff was the owner of Ollie's Barbecue, a restaurant in Birmingham located on a state highway eleven blocks from an interstate highway. In the twelve months preceding enactment of the act, the restaurant purchased $150,000 worth of food, 46 percent or almost $70,000 of which was meat obtained from a local supplier who had procured it from outside the state.

Justice Clark, in reversing the decision of the district court and rejecting the plaintiff's arguments, held that there was a substantial relation between racial discrimination in restaurants and interstate commerce, and that the act was thus a valid exercise of congressional power. Referring consistently to the Heart of Atlanta case, the Court noted that the power to regulate interstate commerce, under Art. 1, §8, Clause 3, has been held in a long line of cases to extend to the regulation of intrastate activities which have a substantial impact upon interstate commerce or upon Congress's power to regulate it. The Court referred extensively to and quoted from hearings before the Senate and House Committees on Commerce, in which were documented, statistically and authoritatively, the aggregate impact upon interstate commerce of racial discrimination in restaurants.

Moreover, the fact that the individual plaintiff's contribution was trivial did not remove him from the scope of federal regulation, since the success of that regulation depended upon the regulation of all who contributed to the problem, in however minor a way; nor did Congress have to await the "total dislocation of commerce": it was free to act preventively, as it often had done in the past.

NOTES

1. Title II does not represent the first effort to utilize the Interstate Commerce Clause to attack racial segregation in public facilities. In fact, the provision of the Interstate Commerce Act prohibiting common carriers from giving "undue or unreasonable preference or advantage to any particular person . . . in any respect whatsoever, or [subjecting] any particular person . . . to any unreasonable or undue prejudice or disadvantage" became the basis of a complaint filed by a black minister before the commission in 1887, the same year the act took effect. Interstate Commerce Act, Part I, 24 Stat. 380 (1887), 49 U.S.C. §3(1) (1958). In this proceeding, the commission found that racial segregation on terms of equality is permissible, but that the act barred provision of second-class accommodations to blacks who paid a first-class fare. Council v. Western and A.R.R., 1 I.C.C. 339 (1887). Earlier, state courts had reached conflicting results as to whether state laws requiring segregation in travel facilities violated the Commerce Clause. Some of these cases were influenced by the Supreme Court's decision in Hall v. DeCuir, 95 U.S. 485, 24 L. Ed. 547 (1878), which held invalid a state law forbidding racial segregation on an interstate steamboat plying the Mississippi River and serving states where the law might vary between requiring and forbidding segregation.

In a series of cases in the 1930s and 1940s, the Court struck down segregation practices of interstate carriers as a direct burden on commerce or because they violated antidiscrimination provisions of the Interstate Commerce Act. See Mitchell v. United States, 313 U.S. 80, 61 S. Ct. 873, 85 L. Ed. 1201 (1941) (failure to provide blacks with first-class accommodations equal to those furnished whites violated the Interstate Commerce Act notwithstanding the carrier's contention that racial segregation was required by state law and that there were insufficient black passengers to justify providing a separate car for them); Morgan v. Virginia, 328 U.S. 373, 66 S. Ct. 1050, 90 L. Ed. 1317 (1946) (a state statute requiring segregation on interstate buses was held an unconstitutional burden on commerce, despite arguments that state police power justified segregation to "keep down racial frictions"); Henderson v. United States, 339 U.S. 816, 70 S. Ct. 843, 94 L. Ed. 1302 (1950) (a railroad's practice of providing segregated dining facilities on its cars was held invalid under the Interstate Commerce Act in situations where blacks were delayed in receiving dining service because of limited accommodations for them, while seats were vacant in the section of the dining car reserved for whites); Boynton v. Virginia, 364 U.S. 454, 81 S. Ct. 182, 5 L. Ed. 2d 206 (1960) (the trespass conviction of a black bus passenger who had refused to leave the premises of a restaurant located in the bus terminal was held invalid as a violation of the nondiscrimination provision of the Interstate Commerce Act; the Court found that the restaurant, while privately owned, was part of the facility devoted to interstate transportation as defined by the act).

2. In Daniel v. Paul, 395 U.S. 298, 89 S. Ct. 1697, 23 L. Ed. 2d 318 (1969), the Court held that since a snack bar located in a privately owned recreational facility (the Lake Nixon Club, a 232-acre amusement area with swimming, boating, miniature golf and dancing facilities, located twelve miles from Little Rock, Arkansas) was principally engaged in selling food for consumption on the premises, and since it served interstate travelers with food that moved in commerce, there was sufficient reason to find the club a covered "public accommodation" within Title II of the Civil Rights Act of 1964. The Court also found the club a "place of entertainment" under the act. Efforts to transform the facility into a private club were deemed a subterfuge.

3. In Newman v. Piggie Park Enterprises, Inc., 390 U.S. 400, 88 S. Ct. 964, 19 L. Ed. 2d 1263 (1968), the Court in a per curiam decision held Title II applicable to drive-in restaurants. More importantly, it read §204(b), 78 Stat. 244, 42 U.S.C. §2000a-3(b), of Title II as entitling the "prevailing party" to "a reasonable attorney's fee" unless special circumstances would render such an award unjust. The court below had awarded counsel fees only to the extent that defendants' defenses had been advanced "for purposes of delay and not in good faith." Enforcement of Title II, the Court explained, is dependent in part on private litigation, and thus such suits are private in form only.

> When a plaintiff brings an action under that Title, he cannot recover damages. If he obtains an injunction, he does so not for himself alone, but also as a "private attorney general" vindicating a policy that Congress considered of the highest priority. If successful plaintiffs were routinely forced to bear their own attorneys' fees, few aggrieved parties would be in a position to advance the public interest by invoking the injunctive powers of the federal courts. Congress therefore enacted the provision for counsel fees — not simply to penalize litigants who deliberately advance arguments they know to be untenable but, more broadly, to encourage individuals injured by racial discrimination to seek judicial relief under Title II. (390 U.S. at 402.)

4. The Supreme Court further encouraged blacks to exercise their rights under Title II by holding in United States v. Johnson, 390 U.S. 563, 88 S. Ct. 1231, 20 L. Ed. 2d 132 (1968), that §207(b) of the act, 42 U.S.C. §2000a-6(b), does not preclude a criminal conspiracy indictment under 18 U.S.C. §241 against hoodlums who assaulted blacks for exercising their rights to equality in public accommodation. Justice Douglas interpreted the language of §207(b), providing that injunctive remedies are the exclusive means of enforcing the rights under Title II, as referring to those charged with refusing service to blacks, and not as preventing criminal prosecutions for outsiders who interfere with the exercise of rights protected by the act.

5. Under the provisions of Title II, and with the encouragement of the Supreme Court decisions reviewed above, discriminatory policies have been attacked in a wide range of activities:

Restaurants. A policy of seating the whites in a front dining area and blacks in a separate rear dining room, allegedly on a "freedom of choice" basis, was held violative of Title II in United States v. Gramer, 418 F.2d 692 (5th Cir. 1969). In a similar case, a barbecue resturant's policy of serving blacks in a rear room and whites in the front was enjoined. Subsequently, the government sought further relief because the two areas were still being used on a racially segregated basis, albeit voluntarily by the customers and without direction from defendants. The court then filed a supplemental order requiring either that the back room be used for carry-out service and the front dining room be used for seated trade, both without regard to race, or that the dividing wall be removed to create a single racially integrated dining room. The court also ordered the posting of appropriate signs advising customers of the nondiscriminatory policy. United States v. Boyd, 327 F. Supp. 998 (S.D. Ga. 1971). A number of cases have held that bars and cocktail lounges not serving food are not covered by Title II. United States v. De Rosier, 332 F. Supp. 316 (S.D. Fla. 1971) (maintenance of a jukebox, a coin-operated shuffleboard and a coin-operated pool table, all manufactured outside the state, did not enable consideration of the bar as a "place of exhibition or entertainment" under §201(b)(3) of Title II). See also Selden v. Topaz 1-2-3 Lounge, Inc., 447 F.2d 165 (5th Cir. 1971). But bars in Plaquemines Parish, Louisiana, were covered under §202 where policies of racial discrimination were mandated by a local ordinance which prohibited serving persons in military uniform. The law was intended to frustrate efforts of nearby military bases to integrate. United States *v.* Cantrell, 307 F. Supp. 259 (S.D. La. 1969).

YMCA facilities. In addition to hotels and motels, Title II has been applied frequently to YMCA facilities. See Smith v. YMCA of Montgomery, 462 F.2d 634 (5th Cir. 1972); Stout v. YMCA of Bessemer, 404 F.2d 687 (5th Cir. 1968); Nesmith v. YMCA of Raleigh, 397 F.2d 96 (4th Cir. 1968); United States v. YMCA of Columbia, 310 F. Supp. 79 (D.S.C. 1970); Alexander v. YMCA of Birmingham, 1 Race Rel. L. Sur. 87 (N.D. Ala. 1969). The courts have generally rejected the "Y" contentions that their facilities were "private clubs" and that they did not provide rooms for "transients." Frequently, the recreational activities of the YMCAs are so intertwined with those of the municipality in which a facility is located that courts have found the requisite state action to enjoin racial discrimination under 42 U.S.C. §1983. See Smith v. YMCA of Montgomery, supra at 637-639, 647.

Trailer parks. They have been held covered by Title II. Dean v. Ashling, 409 F.2d 754 (5th Cir. 1969).

Recreational facilities. Section 201(b)(3) provides specifically that "any motion picture house, theater, concert hall, sports arena, stadium or other place of exhibition or entertainment" is covered; but the act has been given a broad reading to include a remote fishing camp, United States v. Skidmore, 1 Race Rel. L. Sur. 267 (M.D. Fla. 1969), and an amusement park, Miller v. Amusement Enterprises, Inc., 394 F.2d 342 (5th Cir. 1968). (The word "entertainment" in the act was defined to include participatory as well as spectator recreation.) The Fourth Circuit reached a similar conclusion about a recreational facility containing swimming and boating facilities in Scott v. Young, 421 F.2d 143 (4th Cir. 1970). Other successful challenges included skating rinks, Evans v. Seamen, 452 F.2d 749 (5th Cir. 1971), and United States v. All Weather Roller Drome, 1 Race Rel. L. Sur. 190 (M.D. Tenn. 1969); a golf course, United States v. Central Carolina Bank and Trust Co., 431 F.2d 972 (4th Cir. 1970); a golf tournament, Wesley v. City of Savannah, 294 F. Supp. 698 (S.D. Ga. 1969) (tournament held on municipal golf course that excluded black golfers held covered by Title II); a beach club, United States v. Beach Associates, 286 F. Supp. 801 (D. Md. 1968); and bowling alleys, Fazzio Real Estate v. Adams, 396 F.2d 146 (5th Cir. 1968), and United States v. All Star Triangle Bowling, 283 F. Supp. 300 (D.S.C. 1968). Occasionally, where it is uncertain whether the challenged facility is an "exhibition or entertainment" facility as defined by the act, Title II coverage will be based on the presence of a lunch counter or other food service functions. This often results in two-stage litigation. For example, in United States v. William and Kate B. Reynolds Memorial Park, 2 Race Rel. L. Sur. 37 (M.D.N.C. 1970), after an injunction prohibiting the operation of an 1100-acre recreational facility on a segregated basis, defendants closed the dining facilities and discontinued the offering of lodging to transients. The court then found that the park continued to offer a wide variety of exhibitive, as well as participatory, entertainment and was thus a place of exhibition and entertainment under the act. Movie theaters were held covered by Title II in Twitty v. Vogue Theater Corporation, 242 F. Supp. 281 (M.D. Fla. 1965); Thomas v. Orangeburg Theatres, Inc., 241 F. Supp. 317 (E.D.S.C. 1964); Bryant v. Guillory, 11 Race Rel. L. Rep. 426 (W.D. La. 1965).

Private clubs. Section 201(e) excludes from coverage "a private club or other establishment not in fact open to the public." As could have been expected, this provision has encouraged proprietors of hitherto open facilities to form "private clubs" which, in many instances, have only one membership criterion — race. In the obvious instances, the courts have branded such schemes as "shams" and have enjoined the discriminatory policies. See United

States v. Richberg, 398 F.2d 523 (5th Cir. 1968) (restaurant transformed into the "Dixie Dinner Club"); United States v. Johnson Lake, Inc., 312 F. Supp. 1376 (S.D. Ala. 1970) (previous patronage was the only qualification for membership to formerly all-white recreational facility); United States v. Northwest Louisiana Restaurant Club, 256 F. Supp. 151 (W.D. La. 1966) (club consisted of ninety white-owned restaurants formerly operated on a segregated basis). For a thorough analysis of the public-private accommodation dichotomy, see Note, Public Accommodations: What Is a Private Club?, 30 Mont. L. Rev. 47 (1968). Of course, organizations that are legitimate private clubs may nevertheless find that their racially discriminatory policies are under attack, based on state public accommodation statutes or "state action" arguments. See Moose Lodge No. 107 v. Irvis, 407 U.S. 163, 92 S. Ct. 1965, 32 L. Ed. 2d 627 (1972), printed infra page 227.

6. Based on the decision in Jones v. Alfred H. Mayer Co., 392 U.S. 409, 88 S. Ct. 2186, 20 L. Ed. 2d 1189 (1968), printed infra page 626, litigation to desegregate private facilities often cites 42 U.S.C. §1981 or §1982, in addition to Title II, as the basis for jurisdiction. The advantages and limitations of these sections are discussed infra in Chapters Eleven and Thirteen.

C. STATE ACTION AND PUBLIC FACILITIES

Title II does not, of course, prohibit all private activity that is discriminatory. In addition to the litigation developing the scope of Title II's coverage, courts have been asked to find significant "state action" in the contacts with the government processes that are inevitable for every group or activity in modern society. The increasingly subtle issues of discrimination have led to divided courts and unpredictable results. Thus, the Supreme Court has held that the leasing of government-owned facilities to private operators is sufficient state involvement to require the operation of the restaurant on a desegregated basis. Burton v. Wilmington Parking Authority, 365 U.S. 715, 81 S. Ct. 856, 6 L. Ed. 2d 45 (1961). But in other situations seemingly involving government connections as clear and critical as those in Burton, the Court has refused to find that the discriminatory activity was "state action" under the equal protection guarantee of the Fourteenth Amendment.

EVANS v. ABNEY, 396 U.S. 435, 90 S. Ct. 628, 24 L. Ed. 634 (1970). Under a 1911 will, the city of Macon, Georgia received a tract of land for use as a park for white people only. The will provided that the park be operated by a board of seven managers, all of whom were to be white. After maintaining the park on a segregated basis for some years, the city admitted blacks, citing Supreme Court decisions forbidding its operation on a segregated basis. A suit was filed in state court by individual members of the Board of Managers and residual beneficiaries under the will, asking that the city be removed as trustee, and the title to the park transferred to new trustees who could enforce racial segregation. On an appeal by black intervenors, the Georgia Supreme Court affirmed the trial court's granting of this request, holding that the transfer was necessary to carry out the purpose of the trust.

The Supreme Court reversed. Evans v. Newton, 382 U.S. 296, 86 S. Ct. 486, 15 L. Ed. 2d 373 (1966). Justice Douglas held that the Georgia court's action violated the Equal Protection Clause in that, while a testator may leave property to one race without raising constitutional issues, here the park had been an integral part of the city of Macon's activities for years, receiving city care, maintenance and tax exemptions. He found that the generally public nature of the park had not changed because the city no longer served as trustee, and that it thus remained subject to the Fourteenth Amendment. Since the Georgia court gave effect to the purpose of maintaining the park on a segregated basis, reversal of its order was justified. Justices Black, Harlan and Stewart dissented.

After remand, the Georgia Supreme Court affirmed a decision of the trial court that since the trust established by the will had failed because the city could not limit use of the park to whites, the trust property reverted to the heirs of the testator. The Supreme Court affirmed in a 5 to 2 decision. Speaking for the majority, Justice Black pointed out that charitable trusts for the exclusive benefit of members of one race were authorized under Georgia statutes, but that the particular purpose of the Macon park trust failed when segregated operation of the park was declared unconstitutional. The cy pres doctrine was found not to be available to carry out a general charitable intent of the donor, because his will specified that "under no circumstances" was the property to be devoted to any other purpose than as a park for white persons, and he thereby indicated that he had no "general charitable intent" apart from the racial restriction. Further, under the law of the state, when the express purpose of a trust fails, the property reverts to the donor or his heirs. Justice Black concluded that "in ruling as they did the Georgia courts did no more than apply well-settled general principles of Georgia law to determine the meaning and effect of a Georgia will."

In response to the contentions of black petitioners, he found that the action of the Georgia courts did not violate the Constitution by imposing a forfeiture of the park merely because of the city's compliance with constitutional mandates, since the decision was based on "relevant trust laws, which are long standing and neutral with regard to race"; and that no state action sanctioning private racial discrimination was involved because the inclusion of the racial restrictions in the trust was the personal action of the donor, and because, in effect, the Georgia court decisions "eliminated all discrimination against Negroes in the park by eliminating the park itself, and the termination of the park was a loss shared equally by the white and Negro citizens of Macon. . . ." Chief Justice Burger and Justices Harlan, Stewart and White joined in the opinion of Justice Black.

Justice Brennan dissented, on the ground that in this case the Equal Protection Clause was violated because a public facility was closed with involvement of state action, in order to avoid the duty to desegregate the facility.

Justice Douglas dissented, in a separate opinion, on the ground that, since the donor's will left "all remainders and reversions" in the property to the city of Macon rather than to the donor's heirs, giving the property back to the heirs frustrates the donor's general intention that it be devoted to some municipal use, which is still possible.

PALMER v. THOMPSON
403 U.S. 217, 91 S. Ct. 1940, 29 L. Ed. 2d 438 (1971)

Mr. Justice BLACK delivered the opinion of the Court.

In 1962 the city of Jackson, Mississippi, was maintaining five public parks along with swimming pools, golf links, and other facilities for use by the public on a racially segregated basis. Four of the swimming pools were used by whites only and one by Negroes only. Plaintiffs brought an action in the United States District Court seeking a declaratory judgment that this state-enforced segregation of the races was a violation of the Thirteenth and Fourteenth Amendments, and asking an injunction to forbid such practices. After hearings the District Court entered a judgment declaring that enforced segregation denied equal protection of the laws but it declined to issue an injunction. The Court of Appeals affirmed, and we denied certiorari. The city proceeded to desegregate its public parks, auditoriums, golf courses, and the city zoo. However, the city council decided not to try to operate the public swimming pools on a desegregated basis. Acting in its legislative capacity, the council surrendered its lease on one pool and closed four which the city owned. A number of Negro citizens of Jackson then filed this suit to force the city to reopen the pools and operate them on a desegregated basis. The District Court found that the closing was justified to preserve peace and order and because the pools could not be operated economically on an integrated basis. It held the city's action did not deny black citizens equal protection of the laws. The Court of Appeals sitting en banc affirmed, six out of 13 judges dissenting. That court rejected the contention that since the pools had been closed either in whole or in part to avoid desegregation the city council's action was a denial of equal protection of the laws. We granted certiorari to decide that question. We affirm.

I

Petitioners rely chiefly on the first section of the Fourteenth Amendment which forbids any State to "deny to any person within its jurisdiction the equal protection of the laws." There can be no doubt that a major purpose of this amendment was to safeguard Negroes against discriminatory state laws — state laws that fail to give Negroes protection equal to that afforded white people. History shows that the achievement of equality for Negroes was the urgent purpose not only for passage of the Fourteenth Amendment but for the Thirteenth and Fifteenth Amendments as well. See, e.g., Slaughter-House Cases, 16 Wall. 36, 71-72 (1873). Thus the Equal Protection Clause was principally designed to protect Negroes against discriminatory action by the States. Here there has unquestionably been "state action" because the official local government legislature, the city council, has closed the public swimming pools of Jackson. The question, however, is whether this closing of the pools is state action that denies "the equal protection of the laws" to Negroes. It should be noted first that neither the Fourteenth Amendment nor any Act of Congress purports to impose an affirmative duty on a State to begin to operate or to continue to operate swimming pools. Furthermore, this is not a case where whites are permitted to use public facilities while blacks are denied access. It is not a case where a city is maintaining different sets of facilities for blacks and whites and forcing the races to remain separate in recreational or educational activities. See, e.g., Watson v. City of Memphis, 373 U.S. 526 (1963); Brown v. Board of Education, 347 U.S. 483 (1954).

Unless, therefore, as petitioners urge, certain past cases require use to hold that closing the pools to all denied equal protection to Negroes, we must agree with the courts below and affirm.

II

Although petitioners cite a number of our previous cases, the only two which even plausibly support their argument are Griffin v. County School Board of Prince Edward County, 377 U.S. 218 (1964), and Reitman v. Mulkey, 387 U.S. 369 (1967). For the reasons that follow, however, neither case leads us to reverse the judgment here.

[Here the Court distinguished Griffin, which involved a state plan that closed the public schools in one county, and replaced them with private schools that received substantial state support, while at the same time public schools remained open in other sections of the state. As to Reitman v. Mulkey, the Court found that the state constitutional amendment served as an official authorization of racial discrimination, significantly involving the state in the discriminatory acts of private parties. On the other hand, the Court said that merely closing the pools did not constitute state encouragement of discrimination. This, the Court found, was true even though two of the pools had been turned over to private groups which operated them on a segregated basis. The Court found that the city was neither directly nor indirectly involved in the continued operation or funding of either pool.]

III

Petitioners have also argued that respondents' action violates the Equal Protection Clause because the decision to close the pools was motivated by a desire to avoid integration of the races. But no case in this Court has held that a legislative act may violate equal protection solely because of the motivations of the men who voted for it. The pitfalls of such analysis were set forth clearly in the landmark opinion of Mr. Chief Justice Marshall in Fletcher v. Peck, 6 Cranch 87, 130 (1810), where the Court declined to set aside the Georgia Legislature's sale of lands on the theory that its members were corruptly motivated in passing the bill.

A similar contention that illicit motivation should lead to a finding of unconstitutionality was advanced in United States v. O'Brien, 391 U.S. 367, 383 (1968), where this Court rejected the argument that a defendant could not be punished for burning his draft card because Congress had allegedly passed the statute to stifle dissent. That opinion explained well the hazards of declaring a law unconstitutional because of the motivations of its sponsors. First, it is extremely difficult for a court to ascertain the motivation, or collection of different motivations, that lie behind a legislative enactment. Id., at 383, 384. Here, for example, petitioners have argued that the Jackson pools were closed because of ideological opposition to racial integration in swimming pools. Some evidence in the record appears to support this argument. On the other hand the courts below found that the pools were closed because the city council felt they could not be operated safely and economically on an integrated basis. There is substantial evidence in the record to support this conclusion. It is difficult or impossible for any court to determine the "sole" or "dominant" motivation behind the choices of a group of legislators. Furthermore, there is an element of futility in a judicial attempt to invalidate a law because of the bad motives of its supporters. If the law is struck down for this reason, rather than because of its facial content or effect, it would presumably be valid as soon as the legislature or relevant governing body repassed it for different reasons.

It is true there is language in some of our cases interpreting the Fourteenth and Fifteenth Amendments which may suggest that the motive or purpose behind a law is relevant to its constitutionality. Griffin v. County School Board, supra; Gomillion v. Lightfoot, 364 U.S. 339, 347 (1960). But the focus in those cases was on the actual effect of the enactments, not upon the motivation which led the States to behave as they did. In Griffin, as discussed supra, the State was in fact perpetuating a segregated public school system by financing segregated "private" academies. And in Gomillion the Alabama Legislature's gerrymander of the boundaries of Tuskegee excluded virtually all Negroes from voting in town elections. Here the record indicates only that Jackson once ran segregated public swimming pools and that no public pools are now maintained by the city. Moreover, there is no evidence in this record to show that the city is now covertly aiding the maintenance and operation of pools which are private in name only. It shows no state action affecting blacks differently from whites.

Petitioners have argued strenuously that a city's possible motivations to ensure safety and save money cannot validate an otherwise impermissible state action. This proposition is, of course, true. Citizens may not be compelled to forgo their constitutional rights because officials fear public hostility or desire to save money. Buchanan v. Warley, 245 U.S. 60 (1917); Cooper v. Aaron, 358 U.S. 1 (1958); Watson v. City of Memphis, 373 U.S. 526 (1963). But the issue here is whether black citizens in Jackson *are* being denied their constitutional rights when the city has closed the public pools to black and white alike. Nothing in the history or the language of the Fourteenth Amendment nor in any of our prior cases persuades us that the closing of the Jackson swimming pools to all its citizens constitutes a denial of "the equal protection of the laws."

IV

Finally, some faint and unpersuasive argument has been made by petitioners that the closing of the pools violated the Thirteenth Amendment which freed the Negroes from slavery. The argument runs this way: The first Mr. Justice Harlan's dissent in Plessy v. Ferguson, 163 U.S. 537, 552 (1896), argued strongly that the purpose of the Thirteenth Amendment was not only to outlaw slavery but also all of its "badges and incidents." This broad reading of the amendment was affirmed in Jones v. Alfred H. Mayer Co., 392 U.S. 409 (1968). The denial of the right of Negroes to swim in pools with white people is said to be a "badge or incident" of slavery. Consequently, the argument seems to run, this Court should declare that the city's closing of the pools to keep the two races from swimming together violates the Thirteenth Amendment. To reach that result from the Thirteenth Amendment would severely stretch its short simple words and do violence to its history. Establishing this Court's authority under the Thirteenth Amendment to declare new laws to govern the thousands of towns and cities of the country would grant it a law-making power far beyond the imagination of the amendment's authors. Finally, although the Thirteenth Amendment is a skimpy collection of words to allow this Court to legislate new laws to control the operation of swimming pools throughout the length and breadth of this Nation, the Amendment does contain other words that we held in Jones v. Alfred H. Mayer Co. could empower Congress to outlaw "badges of slavery." The last sentence of the Amendment reads: "Congress shall have power to enforce this article by appropriate legislation." But Congress has passed no law under this power to regulate a city's opening or closing of swimming pools or other recreational facilities.

It has not been so many years since it was first deemed proper and lawful for cities to tax their citizens to build and operate swimming pools for the public. Probably few persons, prior to this case, would have imagined that cities could be forced by five lifetime judges to construct or refurbish swimming pools which they choose not to operate for any reason, sound or unsound. Should citizens of Jackson or any other city be able to establish in court that public, tax-supported swimming pools are being denied to one group because of color and supplied to another, they will be entitled to relief. But that is not the case here.

The judgment is affirmed.

Mr. Chief Justice Burger, concurring. . . .

We are, of course, not dealing with the wisdom or desirability of public swimming pools; we are asked to hold on a very meagre record that the Contitution *requires* that public swimming pools, once opened, may not be closed. But all that is good is not commanded by the Constitution and all that is bad is not forbidden by it. We would do a grave disservice, both to elected officials and to the public, were we to require that every decision of local governments to terminate a desirable service be subjected to a microscopic scrutiny for forbidden motives rendering the decision unconstitutional. . . .

Mr. Justice DOUGLAS, dissenting. . . .

May a State in order to avoid integration of the races abolish all of its public schools? That would dedicate the State to backwardness, ignorance, and existence in a new Dark Age. Yet is there anything in the Constitution that says that a State must have a public school system? Could a federal court enjoin the dismantling of a public school system? Could a federal court order a city to levy the taxes necessary to construct a public school system? Such supervision over municipal affairs by federal courts would be a vast undertaking, conceivably encompassing schools, parks, playgrounds, civic auditoriums, tennis courts, athletic fields, as well as swimming pools.

My conclusion is that the Ninth Amendment has a bearing on the present problem. It provides: "The enumeration in the Constitution, of certain rights, shall not be construed to deny or disparage others retained by the people."

Rights, not explicitly mentioned in the Constitution, have at times been deemed so elementary to our way of life that they have been labeled as basic rights. Such is the right to travel from State to State. United States v. Guest, 383 U.S. 745, 758. Such is also the right to marry. Loving v. Virginia, 388 U.S. 1, 12. The "rights" retained by the people within the meaning of the Ninth Amendment may be related to those "rights" which are enumerated in the Constitution. Thus the Fourth Amendment speaks of the "right of the people to be secure in their persons, houses, papers, and effects" and protects it by well-known procedural devices. But we have held that that enumerated "right" also has other facets commonly summarized in the concept of privacy. Griswold v. Connecticut, 381 U.S. 479.

There is, of course, not a word in the Constitution, unlike many modern constitutions, concerning the right of the people to education or to work or to recreation by swimming or otherwise. Those rights, like the right to pure air and pure water, may well be rights "retained by the people" under the Ninth Amendment. May the people vote them down as well as up? . . .

In determining what municipal services may not be abolished the Court of Appeals drew the line between "an essential public function" and other public functions. Whether state constitutions draw that line is not our concern. Certainly there are no federal constitutional provisions which make that distinction.

Closing of the pools probably works a greater hardship on the poor than on the rich; and it may work greater hardship on poor Negroes than on poor whites, a matter on which we have no light. Closing of the pools was at least in part racially motivated. And, as stated by the dissenters in the Court of Appeals:

> The closing of the City's pools has done more than deprive a few thousand Negroes of the pleasures of swimming. It has taught Jackson's Negroes a lesson:

In Jackson the price of protest is high. Negroes there now know that they risk losing even segregated public facilities if they dare to protest segregation. Negroes will now think twice before protesting segregated public parks, segregated public libraries, or other segregated facilities. They must first decide whether they wish to risk living without the facility altogether, and at the same time engendering further animosity from a white community which has lost its public facilities also through the Negroes' attempts to desegregate these facilities. . . .

While Chief Justice Marshall intimated in Fletcher v. Peck, 6 Cranch 87, 130, that the motives which dominate or influence legislators in enacting laws are not fit for judicial inquiry, we do look closely at the thrust of a law to determine whether in purpose or effect there was an invasion of constitutional rights. See Epperson v. Arkansas, 393 U.S. 97, 109; Griffin v. County School Board, 377 U.S. 218, 231. A candidate may be defeated because the voters are bigots. A racial issue may inflame a community causing it to vote a humane measure down. The federal judiciary cannot become involved in those kinds of controversies. The question for the federal judiciary is not what the motive was, but what the consequences are.

In Reitman an active housing program had been racially dominated and then controlled by a state law ending discrimination. But in time the State reversed its policy and lifted the anti-discrimination controls. Thus it launched or at least tolerated a regime of racially discriminatory housing.

It is earnestly argued that the same result obtains here because the regime of desegregated swimming decreed by the District Court is ended and is supplanted by state-inspired, state-favored private swimming pools by clubs and others which perpetuate segregation.

We are told that the history of this episode shows the "steel-hard, inflexible, undeviating official policy of segregation" in Mississippi. United States v. City of Jackson, 318 F.2d 1, 5.

I believe that freedom from discrimination based on race, creed, or color has become by reason of the Thirteenth, Fourteenth, and Fifteenth Amendments one of the "enumerated rights" under the Ninth Amendment that may not be voted up or voted down. . . .

"The Fourteenth Amendment and the two escorting amendments establish a principle of absolute equality, an equality which is denied by racial separation or segregation because the separation in truth consecrates a hierarchy of racial relations, and hence permits inequality."

The Solicitor General says:

[T]o the extent that the municipality had voluntarily undertaken to provide swimming facilities for its citizens, making it unnecessary for the private sector to develop equally adequate facilities, the closing of the pools has insured that racial segregation will be perpetuated. . . .

I conclude that though a State may discontinue any of its municipal services — such as schools, parks, pools, athletic fields, and the like — it may not do so for the purpose of perpetuating or installing *apartheid* or because it finds life in a multi-racial community difficult or unpleasant. If that is its reason, then abolition of a designated public service becomes a device for perpetuating a segregated way of life. That a State may not do. . . .

Mr. Justice WHITE, with whom Mr. Justice BRENNAN and Mr. Justice MARSHALL join, dissenting.

[In a lengthy opinion, Mr. Justice White suggested that closing pools to prevent interracial swimming is little different from laws or customs forbidding blacks and whites to eat together, cohabit or intermarry. The basis, he felt, for enjoining the state's action is that it was predicated solely on opposition to a lawful Court order to desegregate. As such, it is denial of equal protection of the laws. "The city has only opposition to desegregation to offer as a justification for closing the pool, and this opposition operates both to demean the Negroes of Jackson and to deter them from exercising their constitutional and statutory rights. The record is clear that these public facilities had been maintained and would have been maintained but for one event: a court order to open them to all citizens without regard to race." 403 U.S. at 271.]

NOTES

1. Legal commentators have been severely critical of the decision in Palmer v. Thompson. See, e.g., Brest, Palmer v. Thompson: An Approach to the Problem of Unconstitutional Legislative Motive, 1971 Sup. Ct. Rev. 95; Note, Closing Public Pools to Avoid Desegregation: Treading Water, 58 Geo. L.J. 1220 (1970); Note, 16 Wayne U.L. Rev. 1434 (1970); Note, 85 Harv. L. Rev. 86 (1971). The critics generally support the positions taken by the dissenters in Palmer. They assert that Justice Black seriously misread earlier decisions in the civil rights field, where the court had clearly considered the racial motivation in striking down discriminatory statutes and government actions. Reviewing the problem of legislative motive, Professor Brest said, "Palmer v. Thompson is but the latest addition to one of the most muddled areas of our constitutional jurisprudence. The Court's opinion is typical of the current state of the art." Brest at 99.

2. In what is certainly the most exhaustive analysis of the motivation issue, Ely, Legislative and Administrative Motivation in Constitutional Law, 79 Yale L.J. 1205 (1970), the author states, "The Supreme Court's traditional confusion about the relevance of legislative and administrative motivation in determining the constitutionality of governmental actions, has, over the past few terms, achieved disaster proportions." Id. at 1207.

MOOSE LODGE NO. 107 v. IRVIS
407 U.S. 163, 92 S. Ct. 1965, 32 L. Ed. 2d 627 (1972)

Mr. Justice REHNQUIST delivered the opinion of the Court.

Appellee Irvis, a Negro, was refused service by appellant Moose Lodge, a local branch of the national fraternal organization located in Harrisburg, Pennsylvania. Appellee then brought this action under 42 U.S.C. §1983 for injunctive relief in the United States District Court for the Middle District of Pennsylvania. He claimed that because the Pennsylvania liquor board had issued appellant Moose Lodge a private club license that authorized the sale of alcoholic beverages on its premises, the refusal of service to him was "state action" for the purposes of the Equal Protection Clause of the Fourteenth Amendment. He named both Moose Lodge and the Pennsylvania Liquor Authority as defendants, seeking injunctive relief that would have required the defendant liquor board to revoke Moose Lodge's license so long as it continued its discriminatory practices. Appellee sought no damages.

A three-judge district court, 318 F. Supp. 1246, convened at appellee's request, upheld his contention on the merits, and entered a decree declaring invalid the liquor license issued to Moose Lodge "as long as it follows a policy of racial discrimination in its membership or operating policies or practices." . . .

II

Moose Lodge is a private club in the ordinary meaning of that term. It is a local chapter of a national fraternal organization having well defined requirements for membership. It conducts all of its activities in a building that is owned by it. It is not publicly funded. Only members and guests are permitted in any lodge of the order; one may become a guest only by invitation of a member or upon invitation of the house committee.

Appellee, while conceding the right of private clubs to choose members upon a discriminatory basis, asserts that the licensing of Moose Lodge to serve liquor by the Pennsylvania Liquor Control Board amounts to such State involvement with the club's activities as to make its discriminatory practices forbidden by the Equal Protection Clause of the Fourteenth Amendment. The relief sought and obtained by appellee in the District Court was an injunction forbidding the licensing by the liquor authority of Moose Lodge until it ceased its discriminatory practices. We conclude that Moose Lodge's refusal to serve food and beverages to a guest by reason of the fact that he was a Negro does not, under the circumstances here presented, violate the Fourteenth Amendment.

In 1883, this Court in The Civil Rights Cases, 109 U.S. 3, 3 S. Ct. 18, 27 L. Ed. 835, set forth the essential dichotomy between discriminary action by the State, which is prohibited by the Equal Protection Clause, and private conduct, "however discriminatory or wrongful," against which that clause "erects no shield," Shelley v. Kraemer, 334 U.S. 1, 13, 68 S. Ct. 836, 842, 92 L. Ed. 1161 (1948). That dichotomy has been subsequently reaffirmed in Shelley v. Kraemer, supra, and in Burton v. Wilmington Parking Authority, 365 U.S. 715, 81 S. Ct. 856, 6 L. Ed. 2d 45 (1961).

While the principle is easily stated, the question of whether particular discriminatory conduct is private, on the one hand, or amounts to "State action," on the other hand, frequently admits of no easy answer. "Only by sifting facts and weighing circumstances can the nonobvious involvement of the State in private conduct be attributed its true significance." Burton v. Wilmington Parking Authority, supra, at 722, 81 S. Ct., at 860.

Our cases make clear that the impetus for the forbidden discrimination need not originate with the State if it is state action that enforces privately originated discrimination. Shelley v. Kraemer, supra. The Court held in Burton v. Wilmington Parking Authority, supra, that a private restaurant owner who refused service because of a customer's race violated the Fourteenth Amendment, where the restaurant was located in a building owned by a state created parking authority and leased from the authority. The Court, after a comprehensive review of the relationship between the lessee and the parking authority concluded that the latter had "so far insinuated itself into a position of interdependence with Eagle [the restaurant owner] that it must be recognized as a joint participant in the challenged activity, which, on that account, cannot be considered to have been so 'purely private' as to fall without the scope of the Fourteenth Amendment." 365 U.S., at 725, 81 S. Ct., at 862.

The Court has never held, of course, that discrimination by an otherwise private entity would be violative of the Equal Protection Clause if the private entity receives any sort of benefit or service at all from the State, or if it is subject to state regulation in any degree whatever. Since state-furnished services include such necessities of life as electricity, water, and police and fire protection, such a holding would utterly emasculate the distinction between private as distinguished from State conduct set forth in The Civil Rights Cases, supra, and adhered to in subsequent decisions. Our holdings indicate that where the impetus for the discrimination is private, the State must have "significantly involved itself with invidious discriminations," Reitman v. Mulkey, 387 U.S. 369, 380, 87 S. Ct. 1627, 1634, 18 L. Ed. 2d 830 (1967), in order for the discriminatory action to fall within the ambit of the constitutional prohibition. . . .

Here there is nothing approaching the symbiotic relationship between lessor and lessee that was present in Burton, where the private lessee obtained the benefit of locating in a building owned by the State created parking authority, and the parking authority was enabled to carry out its primary public purpose of furnishing parking space by advantageously leasing portions of the building constructed for that purpose to commercial lessees such as the owner of the Eagle Restaurant. Unlike Burton, the Moose Lodge building is located on land owned by it, not by any public authority. Far from apparently holding itself out as a place of public accommodation, Moose Lodge quite ostentatiously proclaims the fact that it is not open to the public at large. Nor is it located and operated in such surroundings that although private in name, it discharges a function or performs a service that would otherwise in all likelihood be performed by the State. In short, while Eagle was a public restaurant in a public building, Moose Lodge is a private social club in a private building. . . .

[T]he Pennsylvania Liquor Control Board plays absolutely no part in establishing or enforcing the membership or guest policies of the club which it licenses to serve liquor. There is no suggestion in this record that the Pennsylvania Act, either as written or as applied, discriminates against minority groups either in their right to apply for club licenses themselves or in their right to purchase and be served liquor in places of public accommodation. The only effect that the state licensing of Moose Lodge to serve liquor can be said to have on the right of any other Pennsylvanian to buy or be served liquor on premises other than those of Moose Lodge is that for some purposes club licenses are counted in the maximum number of licenses which may be issued in a given municipality. Basically each municipality has a quota of one retail license for each 1,500 inhabitants. Licenses issued to hotels, municipal golf courses and airport restaurants are not counted in this quota, nor are club licenses until the maximum number of retail licenses is reached. Beyond that point, neither additional retail licenses nor additional club licenses may be issued so long as the number of issued and outstanding retail licenses remains above the statutory maximum.

The District Court was at pains to point out in its opinion what it considered to be the "pervasive" nature of the regulation of private clubs by the Pennsylvania Liquor Control Board. As that court noted, an applicant for a club license must make such physical alterations in its premises as the board may require, must file a list of the names and addresses of its members and employees, and must keep extensive financial records. The board is granted the right to inspect the licensed premises at any time when patrons, guests or members are present.

However detailed this type of regulation may be in some particulars, it cannot be said to in any way foster or encourage racial discrimination. Nor can it be said to make the State in any realistic sense a partner or even a joint venturer in the club's enterprise. The limited effect of the prohibition against obtaining additional club licenses when the maximum number of retail licenses allotted to a municipality has been issued, when considered together with the availability of liquor from hotel, restaurant, and retail licensees falls far short of conferring upon club licensees a monopoly in the dispensing of liquor in any given municipality or in the State as a whole. We therefore hold that, with the exception hereafter noted, the operation of the regulatory scheme enforced by the Pennsylvania Liquor Control Board does not sufficiently implicate the State in the discriminatory guest policies of Moose Lodge so as to make the latter "State action" within the ambit of the Equal Protection Clause of the Fourteenth Amendment.

The District Court found that the regulations of the Liquor Control Board adopted pursuant to statute affirmatively require that "every club licensee shall adhere to all the provisions of its constitution and by-laws." Appellant argues that the purpose of this provision "is purely and simply and plainly the prevention of subterfuge," pointing out that the bona fides of a private club, as opposed to a place of public accommodation masquerading as a private club, is a matter with which the State Liquor Control Board may legitimately concern itself. Appellee concedes this to be the case, and expresses disagreement with the District Court on this point. . . .

Even though the Liquor Control Board regulation in question is neutral in its terms, the result of its application in a case where the constitution and by-laws of a club required racial discrimination would be to invoke the sanctions of the State to enforce a concededly discriminatory private rule. . . .

Appellee was entitled to a decree enjoining the enforcement of §113.09 of the regulations promulgated by the Pennsylvania Liquor Control Board insofar as that regulation requires compliance by Moose Lodge with provisions of its constitution and by-laws containing racially discriminatory provisions. He was entitled to no more. The judgment of the District Court is reversed, and the cause remanded with instructions to enter a decree in conformity with this opinion.

Reversed and remanded.

Mr. Justice DOUGLAS, with whom Mr. Justice MARSHALL joins, dissenting.

My view of the First Amendment and the related guarantees of the Bill of Rights is that they create a zone of privacy which precludes government from interfering with private clubs or groups. The associational rights which our system honors permits all white, all black, all brown, and all yellow clubs to be formed. They also permit all Catholic, all Jewish, or all agnostic cubs to be established. Government may not tell a man or woman who his or her associates must be. The individual can be as selective as he desires. So the fact that the Moose Lodge allows only Caucasians to join or come as guests is constitutionally irrelevant, as is the decision of the Black Muslims to admit to their services only members of their race.

The problem is different, however, where the public domain is concerned. I have indicated in Garner v. Louisiana, 368 U.S. 157, 82 S. Ct. 248, 7 L. Ed. 2d 207, and Lombard v. Louisiana, 373 U.S. 267, 83 S. Ct. 1122, 10 L. Ed. 2d 338, that where restaurants or other facilities serving the public are concerned and licenses are obtained from the State for operating the business, the "public" may not be defined by the proprietor to include only people of his choice; nor may a State or municipal service be granted only to some. Evans v. Newton, 382 U.S. 296, 298-299, 86 S. Ct. 486, 487-488, 15 L. Ed. 2d 373.

Those cases are not precisely apposite, however, for a private club, by definition, is not in the public domain. And the fact that a private club gets some kind of permit from the State or municipality does not make it ipso facto a public enterprise or undertaking, any more than the grant to a householder of a permit to operate an incinerator puts the householder in the public domain. We must therefore examine whether there are special circumstances involved in the Pennsylvania scheme which differentiate the liquor license possessed by Moose Lodge from the incinerator permit.

Pennsylvania has a state store system of alcohol distribution. Resale is permitted by hotels, restaurants, and private clubs which all must obtain licenses from the Liquor Control Board. The scheme of regulation is complete and pervasive; and the state courts have sustained many restrictions on the licensees. See Tahiti Bar Inc. Liquor License Case, 395 Pa. 355, 150 A.2d 112. Once a license is issued the licensee must comply with many detailed requirements or risk suspension or revocation of the license. Among these requirements is Regulation No. 113.09 which says "Every club licensee shall adhere to all the provisions of its Constitution and By-laws." This regulation means, as applied to Moose Lodge, that it must adhere to the racially discriminatory provision of the Constitution of its Supreme Lodge that "The membership of the lodge shall be composed of male persons of the Caucasian or White race above the age of twenty-one years, and not married to someone other than the Caucasian or White race, who are of good moral character, physically and mentally normal, who shall profess a belief in a Supreme Being."

It is argued that this regulation only aims at the prevention of subterfuge and at enforcing Pennsylvania's differentiation between places of public accommodation and bona fide private clubs. It is also argued that the regulation only gives effect to the constitutionally protected rights of privacy and of association. But I cannot so read the regulation. While those other purposes are embraced in it, so is the restrictive membership clause. And we have held that "a State is responsible for the discriminatory act of a private party when the State, by its law, has compelled the act." Adickes v. S. H. Kress & Co., 398 U.S. 114, 170, 90 S. Ct. 1598, 1615, 26 L. Ed. 2d 142. See Peterson v. City of Greenville, 373 U.S. 244, 248, 83 S. Ct. 1119, 1121, 10 L. Ed. 2d 323. It is irrelevant whether the law is statutory, or an administrative regulation. Robinson v. Florida, 378 U.S. 153, 156, 84 S. Ct. 1693, 1695, 12 L. Ed. 2d 771. And it is irrelevant whether the discriminatory act was instigated by the regulation, or was independent of it. Peterson v. City of Greenville, supra. The result, as I see it, is the same as though Pennsylvania had put into its liquor licenses a provision that the license may not be used to dispense liquor to Blacks, Browns, Yellows — or atheists or agnostics. Regulation No. 113.09 is thus an invidious form of state action.

Were this regulation the only infirmity in Pennsylvania's licensing scheme, I would perhaps agree with the majority that the appropriate relief would be a decree enjoining its enforcement. But there is another flaw in the scheme not so easily cured. Liquor licenses in Pennsylvania, unlike driver's licenses, or marriage licenses, are not freely available to those who meet racially neutral qualifications. There is a complex quota system, which the majority accurately describes. Ante, at —. What the majority neglects to say is that the Harrisburg quota, where Moose Lodge No. 107 is located, has been full for many years.[2] No more club licenses may be issued in that city.

2. Indeed, the quota is more than full, as a result of a grandfather clause in the law limiting licenses to one per 1,500 inhabitants. Act 702 of December 17, 1959, §2. There

This state-enforced scarcity of licenses restricts the ability of blacks to obtain liquor, for liquor is commercially available *only* at private clubs for a significant portion of each week.[3] Access by blacks to places that serve liquor is further limited by the fact that the state quota is filled. A group desiring to form a nondiscriminatory club which would serve blacks must purchase a license held by an existing club, which can exact a monopoly price for the transfer. The availability of such a license is speculative at best, however, for, as Moose Lodge itself concedes, without a liquor license a fraternal organization would be hard-pressed to survive.

Thus, the State of Pennsylvania is putting the weight of its liquor license, concededly a valued and important adjunct to a private club, behind racial discrimination. . . .

I would affirm the judgment below.

Mr. Justice BRENNAN, with whom Mr. Justice MARSHALL joins, dissenting.

When Moose Lodge obtained its liquor license, the State of Pennsylvania became an active participant in the operation of the Lodge bar. Liquor licensing laws are only incidentally revenue measures; they are primarily pervasive regulatory schemes under which the State dictates and continually supervises virtually every detail of the operation of the licensee's business. Very few, if any, other licensed businesses experience such complete state involvement. Yet the Court holds that that involvement does not constitute "state action" making the Lodge's refusal to serve a guest liquor solely because of his race a violation of the Fourteenth Amendment. The vital flaw in the Court's reasoning is its complete disregard of the fundamental value underlying the "state action" concept. That value is discussed in my separate opinion in Adickes v. S. H. Kress & Co., 398 U.S. 144, 190-191, 90 S. Ct. 1598, 1620, 26 L. Ed. 2d 142 (1970):

> The state-action doctrine reflects the profound judgment that denials of equal treatment, and particularly denials on account of race or color, are singularly grave when government has or shares responsibility for them. Government is the social organ to which all in our society look for the promotion of liberty, justice, fair and equal treatment, and the setting of worthy norms and goals for social conduct. Therefore something is uniquely amiss in a society where the government, the authoritative oracle of community values, involves itself in racial discrimination. Accordingly, . . . the cases that have come before us [in which] this Court has

---

are presently 115 licenses in effect in Harrisburg, and based on 1970 census figures, the quota would be 45.

3. Hotels and restaurants may serve liquor between 7:00 a.m. and 2:00 a.m. the next day, Monday through Saturday. On Sunday, such licensees are restricted to sales between 12:00 a.m. and 2:00 am., and between 1:00 p.m. and 10:00 p.m. Pennsylvania Liquor Code, §406(a). Thus, such licensees may serve a total of 123 hours per week. Club licensees, however, are permitted to sell liquor to members and guests from 7:00 a.m. to 3:00 a.m. the next day, seven-days-a-week. Ibid. The total hours of sale permitted club licensees is 140, 17 more than is permitted hotels and restaurants. (There is an additional restriction on election day sales as to which only club licensees are exempt. Ibid.)

condemned significant state involvement in racial discrimination, however subtle and indirect it may have been and whatever form it may have taken[,] . . . represent vigilant fidelity to the constitutional principle that no State shall in any significant way lend its authority to the sordid business of racial discrimination.

Plainly, the State of Pennsylvania's liquor regulations intertwine the State with the operation of the Lodge bar in a "significant way [and] lend [the State's] authority to the sordid business of racial discrimination." The opinion of the late Circuit Judge Freedman, for the three-judge District Court, most persuasively demonstrates the "state action" present in this case: . . .

The issuance or refusal of a license to a club is in the discretion of the Liquor Control Board. In order to secure one of the limited number of licenses which are available in each municipality an applicant must comply with extensive requirements, which in general are applicable to commercial and club licenses equally. The applicant must make such physical alterations in his premises as the Board may require and, if a club, must file a list of the names and addresses of its members and employees, together with such other information as the Board may require. He must conform his over-all financial arrangements to the statute's exacting requirements and keep extensive records. He may not permit "persons of ill repute" to frequent his premises nor allow thereon at any time any "lewd, immoral or improper entertainment." He must grant the Board and its agents the right to inspect the licensed premises at any time when patrons, guests or members are present. It is only on compliance with these and numerous other requirements and if the Board is satisfied that the applicant is "a person of good repute" and that the license will not be "detrimental to the welfare, health, peace and morals of the inhabitants of the neighborhood," that the license may issue.

Once a license has been issued the licensee must comply with many detailed requirements or risk its suspension or revocation. He must in any event have it renewed periodically. Liquor licenses have been employed in Pennsylvania to regulate a wide variety of moral conduct, such as the presence and activities of homosexuals, performance by a topless dancer, lewd dancing, swearing, being noisy or disorderly. So broad is the state's power that the courts of Pennsylvania have upheld its restriction of freedom of expression of a licensee on the ground that in doing so it merely exercises its plenary power to attach conditions to the privilege of dispensing liquor which a licensee holds at the sufferance of the state.

These are but some of the many reported illustrations of the use which the state has made of its unrestricted power to regulate and even to deny the right to sell, transport or possess intoxicating liquor. It would be difficult to find a more pervasive interaction of state authority with personal conduct. The holder of a liquor license from the Commonwealth of Pennsylvania therefore is not like other licensees who conduct their enterprises at arms-length from the state, even though they may have been required to comply with certain conditions, such as zoning or building requirements, in order to obtain or continue to enjoy the license which authorizes them to engage in their business. The state's concern in such cases is minimal and once the conditions it has exacted are met the customary operations of the enterprise are free from further encroachment. Here by contrast beyond the act of licensing is the continuing and pervasive regulation of the licensees by the state to an unparalleled extent. The unique power which the state enjoys in this area, which has put it in the business of operating state liquor stores and in the role of licensing clubs, has been exercised in a manner which reaches intimately and deeply into the operation of the licensees. . . .

This is thus a case requiring application of the principle that until today has governed our determinations of the existence of "state action": "Our prior decisions leave no doubt that the mere existence of efforts by the State, through legislation or otherwise, to authorize, encourage, or otherwise support racial discrimination in a particular facet of life constitutes illegal state involvement in those pertinent private acts of discrimination that subsequently occur." . . .

I therefore dissent and would affirm the final decree entered by the District Court.

NOTES

1. In addition to a federal suit, K. Leroy Irvis filed a complaint with the Pennsylvania Human Relations Commission after being refused service in the Moose Lodge Dining Room and Bar. The commission, which administers Pennsylvania's human relations law, filed a complaint against the lodge, which responded that it was not a place of public accommodation and that the commission had no authority over it. Following a hearing, the commission found the lodge in violation of the Human Relations Act — a finding which was reversed on appeal to the common pleas court and affirmed by a divided superior court. The Pennsylvania Supreme Court accepted an appeal. Several weeks after the United States Supreme Court's decision reviewed above, the Pennsylvania Court held that the lodge was a place of public accommodation for guests and was therefore subject to the antidiscrimination provisions of the Human Relations Act. Commonwealth v. Loyal Order of Moose Lodge 107, 448 Pa. 451, 294 A.2d 594 (1972). In a concurring opinion, Chief Justice Jones emphasized that the issue before the Pennsylvania court is entirely different from the issue decided by the United States Supreme Court in Moose Lodge No. 107 v. Irvis. He said that the Pennsylvania law permits a purely private club to limit its membership or guest privileges solely to whites, but that the lodge for years had opened its dining room and bar facilities to public organizations for banquets and dinners on a nondiscriminatory basis. Thus, the lodge had diminished its status as a purely private club and had become a "place of public accommodation" within the meaning of the Human Relations Act. Chief Justice Jones concluded: "By opening its dining room and bar facilities to organizations and non-guest members, without discrimination, Moose Lodge 107 has become to that extent a center of community activity and, as such, legislatively mandated by . . . the Human Relations Act . . . not to engage in discriminatory practices." An appeal to the Supreme Court was dismissed for lack of a substantial federal question.

Loyal Order of Moose Lodge No. 107 v. Pennsylvania Human Relations Commission, 409 U.S. 1052, 93 S. Ct. 557, 34 L. Ed. 2d 506 (1972).

2. The problem of "private clubs" whose membership is based on residence in a certain area was the subject of litigation in Sullivan v. Little Hunting Park, Inc., 396 U.S. 229, 90 S. Ct. 400, 24 L. Ed. 2d 386 (1969), printed in part infra page 644. There, the Court held that under 42 U.S.C. §1982, which guarantees the property rights of all citizens against racial discrimination, a community recreational corporation open to all whites within the geographic area can be enjoined from barring a black resident of the area and from expelling a white member for advocating the black applicant's cause, and can be required to pay damages to both.

3. In a somewhat similar case, the Supreme Court held that a swimming pool association that was made up of a voluntarily associated group of neighborhood residents who built the pool, and that had set up a residential preference for persons living within a three-quarter-mile radius of the facility, was not an exempt "private club" under §2000a(e), and could not deny membership to a black who purchased a home within the area without violating rights protected under both Title II and 42 U.S.C. §1982. Tillman v. Wheaton-Haven Recreation Association, Inc., 410 U.S. 431, 93 S. Ct. 1190 (1973), summarized infra page 646. As in the Sullivan case, supra, the Court found "no plan or purpose of exclusiveness" in that a person residing within the geographical preference area, unlike one living outside, needs no endorsement for membership from a current member, and receives a priority on the waiting list if the membership is full.

QUESTIONS

1. In his opinion in Moose Lodge No. 107 v. Irvis, Justice Rehnquist carefully classified the lodge as a purely private organization. Does the decision of the Pennsylvania Supreme Court that the lodge's use of its facilities for public banquets and dinners had diminished its status as a private club and transformed those facilities into a "public accommodation," as defined by the state's Human Relations Act, provide the basis for a new Fourteenth Amendment argument?

2. Justice Rehnquist in Moose Lodge stated that the Equal Protection Clause would be utterly emasculated if it were to be read to reach a private entity receiving any sort of benefit or service at all from the state, such as electricity, water, or fire and police protection. However, in doing so, the justice ignored the argument posed by counsel for respondent that distinguished between those forms of government aid merely providing a private benefit to the recipient, e.g., a liquor license, and those government services aimed at protecting the public welfare, such as restaurant licenses requiring certain sanitary and safety conditions to be met, and police and fire protection. Is such a private benefit test versus a public welfare test sound?

NOTES

1. A review of thirty-seven states with public accommodations laws indicated that seventeen of them contained exemptions for bona fide private clubs. See generally Note, Discrimination in Private Social Clubs: Freedom of Association and the Right of Privacy, 1970 Duke L.J. 1181; Note, Public Accommodations and Private Clubs, 54 Geo. L.J. (1966); Note, Private Club Discrimination, 1970 Wis. L. Rev. 525. Fraternal groups mounted massive lobbying campaigns during the congressional debate leading to the enactment of Title II of the Civil Rights Act of 1964. It is unlikely that any legislation would have been passed without an exemption for private clubs.

2. Proponents of open membership have adopted new tactics to circumvent the barrier immunizing private clubs and fraternal orders. Rather than directly attacking discriminatory membership policies, recent litigation seeks to eliminate tax benefits conferred upon these organizations by state and federal governments. The apparent rationale of such tactics is that, by eliminating governmental involvement in private discrimination, the constitutional prohibition against state encouragement or support of private discrimination will be vindicated. Burton v. Wilmington Parking Authority, 365 U.S. 715, 81 S. Ct. 856, 6 L. Ed. 2d 45 (1961). Also, financial pressure will presumably be exerted on the organizations to eliminate discriminatory policies.

McGLOTTEN v. CONNALLY, 338 F. Supp. 448 (D.C. Cir. 1972). A black who had been denied membership in Local Lodge 142 of the Benevolent and Protective Order of the Elks (BPOE) of Portland, Oregon, asked a three-judge court to permanently enjoin the Secretary of Treasury and the Commissioner of the Internal Revenue Service from granting or continuing to grant federal tax benefits under the Internal Revenue Code to the BPOE, its subordinate lodges, and other fraternal orders and social clubs which discriminate against nonwhites in their membership policies. Under Internal Revenue Service rulings, the Elks are exempt from the payment of federal income taxes, and contributions made to the lodges for charitable purposes are deductible from gross incomes of individual and corporate tax returns.

The suit alleges that the conferral of such benefits violates the Fifth Amendment of the Constitution, the Internal Revenue Code, and Title VI of the Civil Rights Act of 1964.

As to the constitutional question, the plaintiff contends that the tax benefits are the functional equivalent of providing the Elks with a direct disbursement of funds and, therefore, that the benefits are unconstitutional under the principle enunciated in the state tuition grant case, Green v. Connally, 330 F. Supp. 1150 (D.D.C. 1971), *aff'd sub nom.* Coit v. Green, 404 U.S. 997, 92 S. Ct. 564, 30 L. Ed. 2d 550 (1971). See discussion infra page 496. Moreover, the plaintiff maintains that the government is giving credence to the general activities of the Elks by allowing them to solicit funds for worthy causes, and holding the Elks out as social benefactors, when, in fact, their racially discriminatory policies represent a serious detriment to society.

In ruling on the defendant's motion to dismiss, the primary issue was stated by the court through Chief Judge Bazelon as follows: "[W]e must determine whether by granting tax benefits to private organizations which discriminate on the basis of race in membership, the federal government has supported or encouraged private discrimination so as to have itself violated plaintiff's right to the equal protection of the laws."

The court held that both the exemption and deduction provisions of the code as applied to the Elks served as governmental approval of private discrimination, thereby impermissibly involving the government in such discrimination. Moreover, the three-judge panel also determined that the tax benefit circumvented the 1964 Civil Rights Act and the Internal Revenue Code itself. Title VI of the 1964 Act, forbidding federal financial assistance to programs or activities offered on a discriminatory basis, was held by the court to prohibit the conferring of tax benefits on segregated fraternal orders. The court, in addition, concluded that the Internal Revenue Code could not be construed to allow a charitable deduction for racially discriminatory fraternal organizations, in light of the strong national policy against providing federal financial support to those practicing discrimination.

In conclusion, the McGlotten court stated:

> We have no illusion that our holding today will put an end to racial discrimination or significantly dismantle the social and economic barriers that may be more subtle but are surely no less destructive. Individuals may retain their own beliefs however odious or offensive. But the Supreme Court has declared that the Constitution forbids the Government from supporting and encouraging such beliefs. By eliminating one more nonobvious involvement of the State in private conduct, we obey the court's claim to quarantine racism. (338 F. Supp. at 462.)

FALKENSTEIN v. DEPARTMENT OF REVENUE, 350 F. Supp. 887 (D. Ore. 1972). McGlotten also challenged the constitutionality of tax exemptions for fraternal organizations conferred upon the Elks under the Oregon property and corporate exise tax laws. In rejecting the state's claim that the Moose Lodge case, supra, required a finding against the plaintiff, the court distinguished the governmental involvement in private discrimination inherent in the granting of a liquor license from that present in the conferring of lucrative tax exemptions. The court reasoned:

> The state contends that the tax exemptions do not encourage or foster racial discrimination. They assert that the exemptions, like the liquor license in Moose Lodge No. 107 v. Irvis, 407 U.S. 163, 40 LW 4715 (1972), do not constitute state action within the meaning of the Fourteenth Amendment. We disagree.
>
> Unlike the liquor license in Moose Lodge, tax exemptions for fraternal organizations benefit both the state and the organizations. Oregon relieves fraternal organizations from the burden of property and corporate excise taxes and, in return, the

public benefits from the charitable and benevolent activities of these organizations. This is the kind of "symbiotic relationship" that was lacking in Moose Lodge, supra, at 175.

The state grants tax exemptions to encourage private support of activities in which the state has a vital interest . . . and to support "a service that would otherwise in all likelihood be performed by the state." Moose Lodge, supra, at 175. The public receives services that would require the expenditure of state funds. These mutual benefits constitute a degree of state involvement in discriminatory activity that the Fourteenth Amendment prohibits. Burton v. Wilmington Parking Authority, 365 U.S. 715 (1961).

These exemptions are important in the operation of the Lodge because they give the Lodge a fiscal freedom it would otherwise not enjoy. By accepting the state's generosity, the Elks Lodge is obligated to comply with the Equal Protection Clause of the Fourteenth Amendment. And the state, as in Burton, is under a duty to ensure that the Lodge meets this obligation. Oregon may not "effectively abdicate its responsibilities by either ignoring them or by merely failing to discharge them whatever the motive may be."

Moreover . . . before granting an exemption, the state is required to find that the fraternal organization engages in benevolent and charitable activities. With this finding, the state places its stamp of approval on the club as an organization that furthers legislative policy. Here, as in Burton, the state "has not only made itself a party to the [discrimination] but has elected to place its power . . . and prestige behind the admitted discrimination." 350 F. Supp. at 888-889.

PITTS v. WISCONSIN DEPARTMENT OF REVENUE, 333 F. Supp. 662 (E.D. Wis. 1971). A three-judge federal court held that a property tax exemption provided a segregated fraternal order in the state of Wisconsin was significant state action, since the effect of the exemption was to encourage discrimination, in violation of the Fourteenth Amendment. The court declared that "whatever its nature in other contexts, the tax exemption constitutes affirmative significant state action in an equal protection context where racial discrimination fostered by the State is claimed." Pitts at 668.

In reaching its decision, the Pitts court stated that its holding was motivated by the peculiar historical background of the Fourteenth Amendment, which indicated a desire by its authors to eliminate all examples of state-sponsored discrimination. The court also indicated that its decision might well be different if the plaintiffs had not raised racial discrimination claims.

NOTES

1. It is not certain how the Supreme Court's decision in Moose Lodge No. 107 v. Irvis will affect the outcome of this series of challenges to discriminatory policies of private organizations. It is likely that if these cases reach the Supreme Court, the defendants will present arguments similar to that relied upon by the counsel for Moose Lodge before the Supreme Court. He contended:

The right of individuals to choose their social intimates so as to express their own preferences and dislikes and to fashion their private lives by forming or joining a club is an aspect of the constitutional right of privacy and private association that is protected by the First Amendment against governmental intrusion or limitation. (Brief for appellant, Moose Lodge, No. 107, Docket No. 70-75.)

Paradoxically, the precedents pointed to by the Moose Lodge as supporting their position included: NAACP v. Alabama, 357 U.S. 449, 78 S. Ct. 1163, 2 L. Ed. 2d 1488 (1958); Shelton v. Tucker, 364 U.S. 479, 81 S. Ct. 247, 5 L. Ed. 2d 231 (1960); Gibson v. Florida Legislative Investigating Comm., 372 U.S. 539, 83 S. Ct. 889, 9 L. Ed. 2d 929 (1963); NAACP v. Button, 371 U.S. 415, 83 S. Ct. 328, 9 L. Ed. 2d 405 (1963). More specifically, counsel for Moose Lodge argued that the removal of the tax benefits would be an unconstitutional penalty placed upon lodge members for exercising their First Amendment right of private association.

2. An alternate means of attacking discrimination in private organizations is suggested in Hawthorne v. Kenbridge Recreation Association Inc., 341 F. Supp. 1382 (E.D. Va. 1972). There, blacks sought an injunction requiring a rural recreational association to consider membership applications without regard to race, creed or national origin. It was plaintiffs' contention that the defendant organization had received a direct loan from the Federal Farmers Home Association of funds which were used to improve old facilities and construct new ones. The court held that both Title VI of the Civil Rights Act of 1964, 42 U.S.C. §2000d, and 7 U.S.C. §1926, permitting loans to nonprofit corporations for recreational development by rural residents, reflects a congressional intent that such loans would be made to public, not private, groups for uses that would not further racial segregation.

3. For a highly critical analysis of the McGlotten decision, see Bittker and Kaufman, Taxes and Civil Rights: "Constitutionalizing" the Internal Revenue Code, 82 Yale L.J. 51 (1972). Basically, the authors, while sympathetic to the goal of eliminating governmental involvement in private discrimination, feel that the court failed to fully comprehend the complexities of the tax structure. In addition to serious technical failings, the authors fear that the McGlotten decision represents poor policy. They concede that the objectives and membership qualifications of many groups and clubs are invidious but warn that:

. . . a governmental program to discover and eradicate them necessarily imposes social costs; a society that tries to punish every instance of man's inhumanity to man may lose its humanity while crusading against the enemy. The "right of free association" and "the right of privacy" . . . are labels recognizing the social value of membership organizations and the dangers inherent in governmental controls. Like free speech and the privilege against self-incrimination, however, the rights of free association and privacy cannot be reserved for the noblest among us.

If full sway is given to the McGlotten theory the tax allowances are equivalent to direct grants of public funds and hence impose constitutional obligations on the recipient, no one will be immune. As we have pointed out, the Internal Revenue Code is a pudding with plums for everyone. In theory, the "tax subsidy" theory does not constrict the right of free association or the right to privacy, because the tax allowances can be renounced by the recipient or eliminated by Congress. But the former remedy, by distinguishing among associations by reference to their ideologies, would make some pay a high price for their enjoyment of the rights in question. On the other hand, the congressional remedy of repeal, resting on the dubious premise that there is a "constitutionally neutral" definition of taxable income, would be costly to all associations.

The McGlotten court sought to minimize these consequences by picking and choosing among tax subsidies. But its distinctions, in our opinion, are unworkable and, as adumbrated by the court, impose or withhold constitutional obligations in a puzzling fashion.

Unlike the state action standards under the Equal Protection Clause, application of which depends upon a review of appropriate facts, the article concludes that the tax subsidy theory — even "as watered down" by McGlotten —

. . . turns on technical niceties of tax law that are unrelated to the impact of the organization's behavior on the persons excluded by its membership rules or other restrictive practices. It would, therefore, be a mistake to use this theory to "constitutionalize" the Internal Revenue Code. (82 Yale L. Rev. at 86-87.)

QUESTION

What have black people actually lost as a result of the adverse decisions in Evans v. Abney, Palmer v. Thompson, and Moose Lodge No. 107 v. Irvis? Obviously the Court's decisions validated their exclusion from a park in Macon, Georgia, from Jackson, Mississippi's swimming pools, and from a Harrisburg, Pennsylvania fraternal lodge. In addition, there is the factor noted by Justice White, dissenting in Palmer, supra page 227, that decisions affirming racial discrimination are demeaning to blacks and discourage them from using the courts to vindicate their rights as citizens. Finally, there are the adverse precedents that will be emulated by others, and that could pose barriers to obtaining relief against discrimination in other areas. Without diminishing these losses, is it possible that, during any given period, there is some real if unascertainable limit to the gains blacks can wrest from white society? Do courts recognize and tend to remain within these limits, where the subject matter of each case involves areas of activity — i.e., testamentary disposition of property, swimming, and private association — that are important to whites and of marginal interest to blacks? Are there indications in the opinions that these considerations affected the outcome? Should they have?

Racism Hypo 2
BLACK FILM FANS v. THE JAYBIRD CLUB THEATER

The Jaybird Club Movie Theater is located in the downtown section of a small Southern town. The theater is owned and operated by the Jaybird Club, a hundred-year-old fraternal association, all of whose members are descendants of Confederate soldiers or of Confederate sympathizers. Proof of descent and the payment of a twenty-five-dollar annual membership fee are the only prerequisites for membership. A majority of the town's white population are members. None of the members are known to be black.

Traditionally, the Jaybird Theater, the only one in town, has been open to the public, and run on a "whites only" basis. This policy was adhered to for more than five years after enactment of the Civil Rights Act of 1964. Finally, in 1970, a federal district court, acting pursuant to litigation initiated by a local group calling themselves the Black Film Fans, issued an injunction under Title II enjoining the Jaybird Theater from continuing its racially exclusionary policy. This decision was affirmed per curiam by the court of appeals in 1972. The Supreme Court denied certiorari. Even so, the Jaybird management continued to exclude blacks until contempt proceedings were initiated, after which it promised to admit customers under a new policy not based on race.

A few weeks later, the Jaybird announced its new "Club" policy for its theater:

> *1. Acting on an evaluation of appropriate legal precedent, the Jaybird Club will, effective immediately, limit admissions to its theater to members, their families, and their white guests.*
>
> *2. If policy number one is invalidated by the courts, and the Jaybird Club is required to admit patrons on a nonracial basis, the Jaybird Club, not wishing to contribute to the growing racial unrest which threatens violence, destruction, and bloodshed in our town, will no longer accept for viewing the so-called "black films," many of which portray interracial violence, sex, and other similar provocative themes.*

The plaintiffs immediately seek further relief to void both sections of the new theater policy. Law Firm A will represent the plaintiffs. Law Firm B will represent the Jaybird Club Theater.

HAWKINS v. TOWN OF SHAW, MISSISSIPPI
437 F.2d 1286 (5th Cir. 1971)

Before TUTTLE, BELL and GOLDBERG, Circuit Judges.

TUTTLE, Circuit Judge:

Referring to a portion of town or a segment of society as being "on the other side of the tracks" has for too long been a familiar expression to most Americans. Such a phrase immediately conjures up an area characterized by poor housing, overcrowded conditions and, in short, overall deterioration. While there may be many reasons why such areas exist in nearly all of our cities, one reason that cannot be accepted is the discriminatory provision of municipal services based on race. It is such a reason that is alleged as the basis of this action.

Appellants are Negro citizens of the Town of Shaw, Mississippi. They alleged that the town has provided various municipal services including street paving and street lighting, sanitary sewers, surface water drainage as well as water mains and fire hydrants in a discriminatory manner based on race. Appellants brought a class action seeking injunctive relief under 42 U.S.C. §1983 against the town, the town's mayor, clerk and five aldermen. After a three-day trial, the trial court applied the traditional equal protection standard despite the presence of appellants' undisputed statistical evidence which we feel clearly showed a substantial qualitative and quantitative inequity in the level and nature of services accorded "white" and "black" neighborhoods in Shaw. The court stated:

> If actions of public officials are shown to have rested upon rational considerations, irrespective of race or poverty, they are not within the condemnation of the Fourteenth Amendment, and may not be properly condemned upon judicial review. Persons or groups who are treated differently must be shown to be similarly situated and their unequal treatment demonstrated to be *without any rational basis* or based upon an invidious factor such as race. 303 F. Supp. 1162, 1168 (N.D. Miss. 1969). (Emphasis added.)

Because this court has long adhered to the theory that "figures speak and when they do, Courts listen," Brooks v. Beto, 366 F.2d 1, 9 (1969), [printed infra at page 978] we feel that appellants clearly made out a prima facie case of racial discrimination. The trial court thus erred in applying the traditional equal protection standard, for as this Court and the Supreme Court have held: "Where racial classifications are involved, the Equal Protection and Due Process Clauses of the Fourteenth Amendment 'command a more stringent standard' in reviewing discretionary acts of state or local officers. Jackson v. Godwin, 400 F.2d 529, 537 (5th Cir., 1968)." In applying this test, defendants' actions may be justified only if they show a compelling state interest. Loving v. Virginia, 388 U.S. 1, 87 S. Ct. 1817, 18 L. Ed. 2d 1010 (1967). We have thoroughly examined the evidence and conclude that no such compelling interests could possibly justify the gross disparities in services between black and white areas of town that this record reveals.

Facts

The Town of Shaw, Mississippi, was incorporated in 1886 and is located in the Mississippi Delta. Its population, which has undergone little change since 1930, consists of about 2,500 people — 1,500 black and 1,000 white residents.

Residential racial segregation is almost total. There are 451 dwelling units occupied by blacks in town, and, of these, 97% (439) are located in neighborhoods in which no whites reside. That the town's policies in administering various municipal services have led to substantially less attention being paid to the black portion of town is clear.

Nearly 98% of all homes that front on unpaved streets in Shaw are occupied by blacks. Ninety-seven percent of the homes not served by sanitary sewers are in black neighborhoods. Further, while the town has acquired a significant number of medium and high intensity mercury vapor street lighting fixtures, every one of them has been installed in white neighborhoods. The record further discloses that similar statistical evidence of grave disparities in both the level and kinds of services offered regarding surface water drainage, water mains, fire hydrants, and traffic control apparatus was also brought forth and not disputed. Finally, it was alleged that this disparity was the result of a long history of racial discrimination.

Surely, this was enough evidence to establish a prima facie case of racial discrimination. The only question that remains to be examined is whether or not these disparities can possibly be justified by any compelling state interests. . . .

In short, even if we assume that such criteria as traffic usage, need and width constitute compelling state interests, they were not applied equally to both black and white neighborhoods. We are led to the inevitable conclusion that Shaw's policies, which have resulted in such significant disparities between the black and white portions of town, are, in no way, justifiable.

Street Lights

The record clearly shows that absolutely no high power mercury vapor street lights have been installed in black residential areas. Only the much weaker bare bulb fixtures are to be found. . .

The fact that there was no specific showing that lighting was not adequate is not significant. What is significant is that it is clear that all of the *better* lighting that exists in Shaw can be found *only* in the white parts of town. Surely, this cannot be justified merely on the ground that the bare bulb fixtures are not shown to be inadequate. One might readily assume, it seems, that the modern high intensity lights are *more* adequate from the fact of their use by the city. *Improvements* to existing facilities provided in a discriminatory manner may also constitute a violation of equal protection. . . .

Sanitary Sewers

While 99% of white residents are served by a sanitary sewer system, nearly 20% of the black population is not so served. . . . We find that since over one-third of the black population was not served when the original sewer system was constructed and nearly twenty percent of this population remains unserved, a policy of serving only new areas would freeze in the results of past discrimination.

The trial court, however, also stated that:

> While the complaint about less than 100% sanitary sewage for all residences is certainly a real one, that condition arises basically from the fact that local law does not yet require indoor plumbing. The lack of sanitary sewers in certain areas of the town is not the result of racial discrimination in withholding a vital service; rather it is a consequence of not requiring through a proper housing code, certain minimal conditions for inhabited housing.

While we recognize that a proper housing code would help this situation, it is circular reasoning to argue that because indoor plumbing is not required, sewers are not provided. If sewers were provided, indoor plumbing could be more easily installed. Indeed, without it, black residents desiring such facilities are forced to incur the extra expense of installing individual sewage disposal apparatus. In short, the justifications offered for the disparities that exist in the town's sewerage system are not valid.

Surface Water Drainage

We do not doubt that as the trial court notes: "Having flat nonporous soil with slow run-off conditions, Shaw suffers from drainage problems common to the Delta area." Indeed, there are serious drainage problems in both the black and white sections of town. However, the record reveals that the problems of the black community are far more serious. Whereas, the white community has been provided with either underground storm sewers or a continuous system of drainage ditches, the black neighborhoods have been provided with a poorly maintained system of drainage ditches and, on many streets, none at all. . . .

Appellees point to various impediments to justify this disparity including haphazard subdividing, the absence of zoning regulations and rights of way of insufficient width. We have already dealt with the claim that roads in the black area are of insufficient width. Regarding the other impediments, we only note that they have been substantially overcome in white neighborhoods. We see no acceptable reason why they should not have been overcome in the black community as well.

Water Mains, Fire Hydrants and Traffic Control Signs

Although water is supplied to all residents of the town, the trial court found that "at all times water pressure is inadequate in certain localities, irrespective of their racial character." We agree that the record discloses inadequate water pressure, but disagree that it is not related to the racial make-up of the locality.

The record reveals that the two areas where water pressure is most inadequate are black and constitute 63% of the town's black population. As appellants note, in the Gale street area, 211 homes are served by 4″ water mains while in the Promised Land, most of the 74 homes are served by 2″ or 1¼″

mains. Most of the white community is served by 6″ mains. The 4″ mains that do exist in the white portion of town serve, however, far fewer homes than the 4″ mains in the black section. In short, as with the previously examined municipal services, the town's policies have again created a situation in which the black portion of town is severely disadvantaged. An examination of the record regarding the placement of fire hydrants as well as the placement of any traffic control signs in black neighborhoods leads us to the same conclusion.

Intent

Yet, despite the fact that we conclude that no compelling state interests can justify the disparities that exist in the black and white portions of town, it may be argued that this result was not intended. That is to say, the record contains no direct evidence aimed at establishing bad faith, ill will or an evil motive on the part of the Town of Shaw and its public officials. We feel, however, that the law on this point is clear. In a civil rights suit alleging racial discrimination in contravention of the Fourteenth Amendment, actual intent or motive need not be directly proved, for:

> "equal protection of the laws" means more than merely the absence of governmental action designed to discriminate; . . . we now firmly recognize that the arbitrary quality of thoughtlessness can be as disastrous and unfair to private rights and the public interest as the perversity of a willful scheme. Norwalk CORE v. Norwalk Redevelopment Agency, 395 F.2d 920, 931 (2d Cir., 1968). See also, United States ex rel. Seals v. Wiman, 304 F.2d 53 at 65 (5 Cir. 1962); Jackson v. Godwin, 400 F.2d 529 (1968).

Having determined that no compelling state interests can possibly justify the discriminatory *results* of Shaw's administration of municipal services, we conclude that a violation of equal protection has occurred.

Relief

[The court's review of its authority and precedent for providing relief is omitted.]

We feel that issuing a specific order outlining exactly how the equalization of municipal services should occur is neither necessary nor proper in the context of this case. We do require, however, that the Town of Shaw, itself, submit a plan for the court's approval detailing how it proposes to cure the results of the long history of discrimination which the record reveals. We are confident that the municipal authorities can, particularly because they so staunchly deny any racial motivation, propose a program of improvements that will, within a reasonable time, remove the disparities that bear so heavily on the black citizens of Shaw.

The case is reversed and remanded for further proceedings not inconsistent with the above opinion.

BELL, Circuit Judge (specially concurring): . . . All in all, . . . the record tells a story of a strengthening of the political system through the guarantee of the right to vote. There was no paved street in the Town of Shaw until the mid 1930's when the highway through the town was paved. Over the years other streets and highways have been paved. It was not until 1956 that any of the streets in the Negro residential areas were paved and this paving was in an insubstantial amount. The situation has changed rapidly since 1966. The present situation is that the city has 231 white residences and 437 Negro residences. Of these, 97 per cent of the white residences are located on paved streets and highways while only 43 per cent of the Negro residences are so located.

Since the Negro citizens obtained the right to vote some four years ago under the Voting Rights Act of 1965 and under the present government which took office in 1965, there has been a considerable improvement in most of the services rendered them by the city. They have approximately 50 per cent of the vote and we were told at oral argument and in brief that a Negro now has been elected to the city council. In addition, we find that a bi-racial committee has been appointed to advise with the mayor and council regarding services. A federal grant has been approved to resolve the problems with regard to water pressure and fire hydrants. The principal areas to be resolved in an equalization of services will be the street paving, sanitary sewers, storm drainage, street lights, and traffic control. The total cost of replacing all of the existing street lights in Negro neighborhoods is indicated as $3,100. A substantial start has been made in the other areas of service. . . .

Given the remedy and the facts of this case, appellants are entitled to relief. Judge Tuttle has wisely provided for a remedy with respect to such relief as may be due in the form of defendants presenting a plan to the district court whereunder the disparities based on race are to be ended. This will afford the governing authorities, as assisted by the bi-racial planning committee, an opportunity to resolve the problem. This approach is in the highest tradition of Federalism whereunder local governments are to carry out their function and responsibilities in a system where every level of government, federal, state and local, is subject to the federal Constitution.

HAWKINS v. TOWN OF SHAW, MISSISSIPPI
461 F.2d 1171 (5th Cir. 1972)

[Following publication of the opinion printed supra, Hawkins v. Shaw was heard by the Fifth Circuit en banc. The court, per curiam, agreed that the order directing defendants to submit to the district court a plan for eliminating the disparities was a sound approach under the facts. The court held that plaintiffs had standing to initiate this action, but declined to articulate a general principle of "finality" for such cases. The court commented at some length on the standard by which liability was imposed.]

In judging human conduct, intent, motive and purpose are elusive subjective concepts, and their existence usually can be inferred only from proven facts. As stated in the original opinion, the record before us does not contain direct evidence which establishes bad faith, ill will or any evil motive on the part of the town of Shaw and its public officials. However, the record proof does clearly establish conduct which cannot be judicially approved.

In order to prevail in a case of this type it is not necessary to prove intent, motive or purpose to discriminate on the part of city officials. We feel that the law on this point is clear, for " 'equal protection of the laws' means more than merely the absence of governmental action designed to discriminate . . . 'we now firmly recognize that the *arbitrary quality of thoughtlessness* can be as disastrous and unfair to private rights and to public interest as the perversity of a willful scheme'." (Emphasis supplied.) Norwalk CORE v. Norwalk Redevelopment Agency, 2 Cir. 1968, 395 F.2d 920, 931. See also Kennedy Park Homes Association, Inc. v. City of Lackawanna, New York (2 Cir. 1970) 436 F.2d 108, 114, *cert. den.* 401 U.S. 1010, 91 S. Ct. 1256, 28 L. Ed. 2d 546 (1971) and United States ex rel. Seals v. Wiman, 5 Cir. 1962, 304 F.2d 53 at 65.

Moreover, in our judgment the facts before us squarely and certainly support the reasonable and logical inference that there was here neglect involving clear overtones of racial discrimination in the administration of governmental affairs of the town of Shaw resulting in the same evils which characterize an intentional and purposeful disregard of the principle of equal protection of the laws. See Yick Wo v. Hopkins, 118 U.S. 356, 6 S. Ct. 1064, 30 L. Ed. 220 (1886); Loving v. Virginia, 388 U.S. 1, 10, 87 S. Ct. 1817, 18 L. Ed. 2d 1010 (1966); Snowden v. Hughes, 321 U.S. 1, 8, 64 S. Ct. 397, 88 L. Ed. 497; Kennedy Park Homes Association, Inc. v. City of Lackawanna, supra; Rodriguez v. Brown, 5 Cir. 1970, 429 F.2d 269, 273; Norwalk CORE v. Norwalk Redevelopment Agency, supra 395 F.2d at page 931.

Federal Courts are reluctant to enter the field of local government operations. The conduct of municipal affairs is "an extremely awkward vehicle to manage." It is apparent from our original opinion, and we repeat here, that we do not imply or suggest that every disparity of services between citizens of a town or city creates a right of access to the federal courts for redress. We deal only with the town of Shaw, Mississippi, and the facts as developed in this record.

[Judge Wisdom concurred, expressing the view that the decision recognizes the right of every citizen, regardless of race, to equal municipal services. Judge Brown concurred with Judge Wisdom, but emphasized that §1983 suits should follow the rejection by city officials of requests to correct inequalities in facilities.

Judge Gewin, joined by Judges Coleman and Dyer, concurred in the decision, except for that portion directing the district court to submit a plan, which it characterized as appellate court meddling.

Judges Roney, Simpson and Clark dissented. Judge Roney complained that, after permitting plaintiffs to establish a prima facie case of racial discrimination with statistical evidence, the court foreclosed defendants' opportunity to disprove the prima facie case by a preponderance of the evidence and, instead, required justification for the racial discrimination by a compelling state interest, thereby "converting the compelling interest doctrine into a standard of evidence and procedure that has despoiled the processes of law. . . ."

Judge Clark, joined by Judge Simpson, expressed his further concerns with the substantive aspects of the majority decision.]

The en banc court's reaffirmance of the original panel opinion embarks this circuit on what must surely become another weary journey to an inefficient and insufficient remedy for a problem that cannot find a solution in the courts. Judge Wisdom is right when he observes in concurring that the Town of Shaw does not present a unique case. Rather, Shaw is typical of thousands of towns and hundreds of cities in this nation. An examination of any urban gathering of people will highlight the inequalities among the places where they live. The degree of affluence or poverty of each family in the community is almost uniformly reflected in its home. Whether one counts it good or bad, such variance in living standards is a hallmark of our American liberty. It inheres in every free society. Only in some egalitarian Utopia do all families live in equal surroundings. A failure to recognize this fact is at the heart of the mistake the court makes in choosing the course it launches today. . . .

An overview of this case shows that the trier of fact looked at the physical characteristics of the municipal services provided to the inhabitants of the Town of Shaw and concluded that the actions of its public officials in providing governmental services to the various property owners within its corporate limits rested upon rational considerations of the varying physical factors involved — irrespective of race; on appeal this court saw only that these disparities *could* be grouped by race to show more Negroes than whites received lesser municipal services. From this statistical *possibility* this court concluded that the trial court was in error. Yet, in reaching its determination, the district court expressly acknowledged its study and consideration of the very same racially compartmented statistical information which the en banc court finds decisive. The difference is that the lower court refused to ignore the dissimilar situations of geography, housing patterns, antiquated streets, limited finances and the existence of a conservative, unprogressive municipal policy in resolving the basic issue of whether plaintiffs proved unconstitutional discrimination by the defendants.

The district court's determination that racial discrimination was not a basis for the lack of equality in municipal services throughout the Town of Shaw is supported in this record by substantial rational considerations which explain the quality and quantity of present municipal functions. It is plain error on our part to upset this factual support for the district court's decision solely because of the plaintiffs' ability to cast these disparities into a racial mold. The economic and sociological problems that under-lie why the preponderant number of black citizens of Shaw, Mississippi are poorer than the whites who live there are facts of life, albeit uncomfortable ones for a nation concerned with social justice. However, these statistics alone no more demonstrate constitutionally impermissible racial discrimination in providing civic support by Shaw, Mississippi than would the same readily made showing in Chicago, Illinois or Los Angeles, California or Houston, Texas or Newark, New Jersey. They cannot be combined with the ever-present fact that the less well-developed areas of every urban community receive a lower level of many municipal functions to make out a case for racial discrimination where there is none.

What's worse, this travel toward a false hope starts on the wrong foot. The district court is incorrectly faulted for applying an erroneous legal standard. This holding simply will not withstand impartial analysis as Judge Bell demonstrated in the second paragraph of his original concurring opinion at 437 F.2d 1293, 1294. See also Judge Roney's dissent. The opinion of the district court is expressly based on correct legal precedent. Any reversal should necessarily have been based upon our demonstration of a clearly erroneous resolution of the facts. That this is the correct approach may be at least tacitly conceded by the panel opinion which the en banc court adopts, since that opinion spent far more than a majority of its length in attempting to rationalize factual inferences different from those reached by the trial court. . . .

In remitting Mr. Hawkins and the members of his class to a solution at the ballot box, rather than dangling the carrot of reform by judicial injunction before them, the district court followed the course of wisdom and practicality. Hard reality fore-ordains that no plan can be devised which will solve the complex variables of "equalizing" municipal services. This court's broad-brush approach to this case guarantees such a fruitless result. By generally describing the service areas the court uses to justify overturning the district court's fact finding, this court has multiplied the problems for the planning function it requires, if it has not rendered it impossible. Shaw's resources are finite. Its daily needs must be met by public servants who must anticipate long-range requirements both for the handful of classes of projects specifically dealt with and also for that wide spectrum of services and facilities that aren't even mentioned. Our opinion leaves too many areas in these classes too wide-open to permit intelligent planning. While requiring city officials to devise and the district court to approve a program to "eliminate the disparities," we not only give no real guidance as to what is expected but create impediments to the development of effective programs in the areas we discuss.

For example: As to paving — Does the court intend for the city to pave enough of the streets of inadequate width in the areas inhabited by Negro citizens to equal the length of similar narrow streets which were paved in white neighborhoods in the 1930s, or should Shaw now plan to condemn sufficient property in Negro neighborhoods to construct a modern street system in those areas?

As to sanitary sewers — Can the city comply with our wishes by constructing sanitary sewerage collection lines to houses having no indoor plumbing, or must the city adopt a "proper housing code"?

As to surface drainage — Is it sufficient for the city to construct surface water drainage structures in lowlying areas which will be equal to the drainage structures in other areas of the city; or must some new legal route be found to empower the city to engage in the major channel improvement and dredging outside its city limits which the district court found was the real key to elimination of flooding in these areas of this essentially flat town; or will the city be required to undertake land fills in the lower areas to correct these deficient elevations?

As to water mains — Must water supply mains be sized on a present house count basis to reach equality, or may they be sized on the basis of anticipated demand for water? Here again, we ought to be explicit as to whether a new housing code is required that would mandate more residential water using facilities, i.e. sinks, tubs and toilets. Now is also the time the city should be advised of the place in any plan's list of priorities for the proposed construction of the new water storage tank and large water well which this litigation has already delayed by two years.

On a broader basis as to all required plan ingredients, the court should certainly now make explicit whether our criterion is to be proportionately adequate service to the town's individual parcels of property as they are now developed; or equal service based upon the race of the property occupants; or something yet different from these. . . .

In our haste to mandate that all things in Shaw become equal, we ought to pause to realize that we require changes in living patterns and property utilization that the individual property owners cannot afford to use. At the same time, under the generalized approach adopted, the plan could wind up failing to bring meaningful improvements to the very parties who brought this action. These observations are meant only to highlight the need for approaching and finding solutions for such property problems on a specific rather than a wholesale basis. We err in adopting the analogy that equalization of municipal services is akin to school desegregation or to jury discrimination and holding that the simple way to perfect a remedy is to require the town to develop a program to "eliminate the disparities." . . .

NOTES

1. In Hadnott v. City of Prattville, 309 F. Supp. 967 (M.D. Ala. 1970), black residents of Prattville (population 12,200) alleged that city officials were discriminating against them in such municipal facilities and services as garbage collection, paved streets, streetlights, fire hydrants, recreational facilities, and the employment of blacks as policemen and firemen. After a full hearing, the court found discrimination only in the operation of recreational facilities. The city was ordered to cease limiting use of the facilities on the basis of race and to make parks in the black community equal to those

patronized mainly by whites. The court also found a city policy against hiring black policemen and firemen, but found that the plaintiffs lacked standing to obtain injunctive relief because none of them had ever applied for one of the positions.

2. Selmont Improvement Association v. Dallas County Commission, 339 F. Supp. 477 (S.D. Ala. 1972), involved allegations by black residents of an unincorporated area of the county that, as a result of racial discrimination, their streets had not been paved. The court ordered the county to pave the streets, an order based on a finding of discrimination prior to 1954, and notwithstanding the absence of any showing of discrimination in recent times.

3. In Beal v. Lindsay, 468 F.2d 287 (2d Cir. 1972), while accepting the principle in Hawkins v. Shaw, Chief Judge Friendly, speaking for the court, found that the City of New York was not constitutionally obliged to maintain a park located in a black and Puerto Rican neighborhood at the level of other city parks, since the city provided equal or greater services to the park but was unable to achieve the same results because of continued vandalism.

4. The Hawkins v. Town of Shaw decision attracted attention in both the popular media and scholarly journals. See, e.g., Fessler and Haar, Beyond the Wrong Side of the Tracks: Municipal Services in the Interstices of Procedure, 6 Harv. Civ. Rights–Civ. Lib. L. Rev. 441 (1971); Note, Equal Protection: Is There a Constitutional Right to a Sewer?, 32 Md. L. Rev. 70 (1972). Much of the discussion has focused on whether the Hawkins precedent can be extended to disparities based on classification criteria other than race. The decision in Serrano v. Priest, 5 Cal. 3d 597, 487 P.2d 1242 (1971), printed infra page 602, raises hopes that relative wealth may be such a classification, but the Serrano court placed great emphasis on the fact that the disparities in funding affected public education, a crucial state service. See Note, The Evolution of Equal Protection — Education, Municipal Services and Wealth, 7 Harv. Civ. Rights–Civ. Lib. L. Rev. 103 (1972).

5. "[I]t is plain that where the burden of proof lies may be decisive of the outcome." Speiser v. Randall, 357 U.S. 513, 525, 78 S. Ct. 1332, 1342, 2 L. Ed. 2d 1460, 1472 (1958). This statement is particularly true in racial cases. Permitting plaintiffs in Hawkins to establish a prima facie case of forbidden discrimination by statistical proof of segregated residential patterns, and of the corresponding inequality of municipal services between those sectors, is critical to the successful prosecution of service equalization suits. Fessler and Haar, supra at 446-447. A requirement of discriminatory intent would likely prove fatal to plaintiffs in such cases, as it has in all but the more blatant reapportionment cases. See Wright v. Rockefeller, 376 U.S. 52, 84 S. Ct. 603, 11 L. Ed. 2d 512 (1964), printed supra at page 161.

6. Jury discrimination cases (see Chapter Sixteen) are the best example of how statistical evidence of exclusion of blacks from jury service is used to create a prima facie case, which the state must then rebut by showing through positive proof that the exclusion was not caused by racial discrimination. See, e.g., Whitus v. Georgia, 385 U.S. 545, 87 S. Ct. 643, 17 L. Ed. 2d

599 (1967). The difficulty in the jury cases — one which poses a threat to relief in service equalization suits — is the tendency of courts to accept as rational and nonracial the explanations offered by state officials in cases where the statistical evidence is less than absolutely obvious proof of discrimination. See, e.g., Swain v. Alabama, 380 U.S. 202, 85 S. Ct. 824, 13 L. Ed. 2d 759 (1965).

NOTE: RIGHT OF ACCESS TO MEDICAL CARE

Segregation of blacks in hotels, restaurants and other places of public accommodation was usually inconvenient and always the source of deep humiliation. Exclusion from or segregation in hospitals and other health services, however, was all too frequently a matter of life or death. The four areas of voluntary hospital activity in which discriminatory practices were likely to arise were education and training programs, employment, patient administration and treatment, and medical and professional staff appointments. Public attention to the problem of discrimination in the medical area was largely focused on the South.* But discrimination in health facilities and services — like other forms of discrimination — was demonstrably present in many Northern communities.† Agitation during the civil rights era of the 1960s brought the problem and the underlying issues into sharp focus.‡ Con-

* Note, Working Rules for Assuring Nondiscrimination in Hospital Administration, 74 Yale L.J. 151 (1964). See also Meltsner, Equality and Health, 115 U. Pa. L. Rev. 22, 24-25 (1966), describing conditions that prevailed until the late 1960s:

"When Southern hospitals construct or modernize health facilities the old building or portion of building conventionally becomes a restricted area [for Negroes]. Where a building or floor is shared, a hospital may maintain separate wards, private or semi-private rooms, lavatories, eating facilities, entrance ways, emergency rooms, maternity wards or nurseries. Some hospitals provide one ambulance service for whites, another for Negroes; others schedule out-patient clinics on 'Negro' and 'white' days or rigidly segregate thermometers. A Florida hospital developed the practice of placing Negroes in the basement unless they were 'prominent' and one Mississippi facility has refused to permit Negroes to visit 'white' wards. At many hospitals, when a Negro seeks admission he is required to show greater financial security than a white and is turned away if he does not demonstrate ability to pay. Although refusal to admit Negro emergency patients is said to be a thing of the past, an alarming number of seriously ill Negroes are refused hospital admission until a guarantor of their fees can be found. Segregation also means a gross disparity in physical conditions and professional services: a surprising number of southern hospitals force Negro patients — male and female — to use a single lavatory, and a common method of obtaining rooms for whites is to move Negro beds into hallways when the white section of the hospital has been filled. Negro patients complain of antiquated facilities, poor service and outright discourtesy from hospital personnel."

† See Morris v. Chicago Hosp. Council, 9 Race Rel. L. Rep. 1838 (1964); New York State Advisory Comm. to the U.S. Comm'n on Civil Rights, Report on New York City: Hospital Facilities (1964); New York State Advisory Comm. to the U.S. Comm'n on Civil Rights, Report on Buffalo: Health Facilities (1964); National Urban League, Health Care and the Negro Population (1965).

‡ The Report of the Council to the White House Conference, To Fulfill These Rights

stitutional and statutory obligations of the federal government to eliminate racial discrimination in the provision of medical facilities and services were established by federal courts and Congress. In a landmark decision, the Fourth Circuit found racial discrimination by governmentally owned, operated or subsidized hospitals to violate the Due Process Clause of the Fifth Amendment and the Equal Protection Clause of the Fourteenth Amendment. Simkins v. Moses H. Cone Hospital, 323 F.2d 959 (4th Cir. 1963), *cert. denied*, 376 U.S. 938 (1964). Denial of certiorari in this landmark case is significant in that the Court's action left undisturbed a declaration of the unconstitutionality of an act of Congress. See also Flagler Hospital, Inc. v. Hayling, 344 F.2d 950 (5th Cir. 1965); Smith v. Holiday Inns of America, Inc. 336 F.2d 630 (6th Cir. 1963).

Title VI of the Civil Rights Act of 1964 prohibited racial exclusion, denial of benefits or discrimination "under any program or activity receiving federal financial assistance" and provided federal administrators with ample power to enforce racial equality by refusal, withdrawal or termination of funds, or by litigation. 78 Stat. 252 (1964), 42 U.S.C. §§2000d to 2000d-4 (1964); 45 C.F.R. §§80.1 to 80.13 (Supp. 1966). In addition to Title VI, Title III of the 1964 Civil Rights Act empowered the Attorney General to bring suit to enjoin discrimination at public facilities owned or operated by state governments. 78 Stat. 246 (1964), 42 U.S.C. §2000b (1964). Title IX of the same act authorized him to intervene in suits seeking relief from denial of equal protection of the laws. 78 Stat. 266 (1964), 42 U.S.C. §2000h-2 (1964). See, e.g., United States v. Medical Society of South Carolina, 298 F. Supp. 145 (D.S.C. 1969), where the court acted under Title III, Title II, and Title VII of the Civil Rights Act of 1964, to enjoin all racial segregation and discriminatory policies in a Charleston hospital which had discontinued its participation in all federal programs rather than comply with Title VI.

(June 1 and 2, 1966), contained a recommendation that "in the near future a national conference on the special health problems confronted by Negroes and other minorities be specifically and urgently considered." The council suggested that the issues to be considered include:

"1. There must be better understanding of the specific causes of the high infant mortality rate and the lower life expectancy among low income Negroes, and there should be developed a comprehensive program for attacking these problems.

"2. There must be an improvement in the health services available to Negroes, both in quality and in the method of distribution. In this connection, a study of the efficacy of neighborhood health centers is urged, and there should be a vast expansion of this type of health service which is made available on a coordinated basis to all members of the family, in a single location, and under flexible time schedules.

"3. Attention should be paid to greater involvement of Negroes in the delivery of health services, on both the professional and sub-professional levels.

"4. There should be developed more thorough methods of discovering the medical problems of Negro children at an early stage.

"5. Although Medicare and Title XIX, providing health care for indigent families, are promising starts, there is an urgent need for expanded medical care for those who cannot afford it." 99-100.

Under Title VI, medical facilities are required to execute agreements with federal officers in which they pledge to eliminate racial discrimination as a condition to receipt of federal funds, agreements which may be enforced by the United States in its courts. 45 C.F.R. §80.4 (Supp. 1966). The required assurances may be found at 9 Race Rel. L. Rep. 1960 (1964).

Prior to 1964, federal law sanctioned racial discrimination in hospitals. The Public Health Service took the view that the nondiscrimination clause of the Hill-Burton Act, §622, 60 Stat. 1041 (1946), as amended, 42 U.S.C. §291(c) (1964), applied only to admission of Negro patients, and the act itself expressly permitted waiver of the clause, even as applied to admissions in cases of "separate facilities" approved for "separate population groups."

Discrimination in medical facilities generated only a small volume of litigation and little public attention. Those cases filed were not very successful.* The difficulties of bringing about change through individual cases were great.

> Private litigation in the best circumstances is costly and time consuming and a difficult means of changing the behavior of large numbers of persons playing a variety of roles. A privately initiated federal court suit for injunctive relief against a medical facility raises particular difficulties. The primary object of discrimination — the Negro patient — has but transient personal interest in or knowledge of the terms and conditions of treatment in local hospitals. At the time his interest is greatest — when he is ill — he is least likely to express interest in litigation. Negro physicians, dentists and nurses have litigated the legality of hospital practices, such as restrictive admission of professionals, but many are so successful within the confines of the segregated systems that they have little incentive to change it. Others lag behind the skills of better educated whites and hesitate to challenge racial barriers for fear their ability will be questioned. Others are unable to overcome the imposing evidentiary hurdle of proving they have been rejected for racial and not professional reasons. Indeed, it is so difficult for private litigants and a district court to police anything other than a nondiscriminatory admission policy that some hospitals have continued to discriminate notwithstanding decrees ordering desegregation. (Meltsner, Equality and Health, 115 U. Pa. L. Rev. 22, 29 n.38 (1966).)

Despite the obstacles, civil rights lawyers persevered, and in 1963 their efforts were rewarded with the Fourth Circuit's decision in Simkins v. Moses H. Cone Memorial Hospital, 323 F.2d 959 (1963).

From 1954 to 1962, two Greensboro, North Carolina hospitals received approximately $3.2 million from the United States in order to defray construction costs of facilities for new patient care and nurses' training. Both

* Rackley v. Board of Trustees, 310 F.2d 141 (4th Cir. 1962) (preliminary injunction inappropriate; remanded for trial); Eaton v. Board of Managers, 261 F.2d 521 (4th Cir. 1958), *cert. den.*, 359 U.S. 984 (1959) (insufficient "state action"; Fourteenth Amendment inapplicable); Wood v. Hogan, 215 F. Supp. 53 (W.D. Va. 1963) (Hill-Burton hospital not subject to Fourteenth Amendment); Wood v. Vaughn, 209 F. Supp. 106 (W.D. Va. 1962), *aff'd sub nom.* 321 F.2d 474 (4th Cir. 1963) (citizen-taxpayer has no standing to desegregate home for senile and aged).

refused treatment of blacks desiring hospitalization and excluded black physicians and dentists from staff affiliation (a prerequisite to placement of their patients in the hospital). Although the racial policies of both hospitals antedated receipt of federal funds, exclusion of blacks was sanctioned under the Hill-Burton Act provision permitting "separate facilities" in grantee hospitals for "separate population groups." Hill-Burton Act §622, 60 Stat. 1041 (1946), as amended, 42 U.S.C. §291(c) (1964); 21 Fed. Reg. 9841 (1956).

In a suit brought by black "patients," physicians, and dentists for injunctive and declaratory relief, the United States intervened† in support of the alleged unconstitutionality of the statute permitting racial exclusion.‡ The district court found that the hospitals had not been "shown to be so impressed with a public interest as to render them instrumentalities of government" and dismissed the complaint. Simkins v. Moses H. Cone Memorial Hospital, 211 F. Supp. 628, 634 (M.D.N.C. 1962). The Fourth Circuit, sitting en banc, reversed, holding both hospitals subject to the restraints against racial discrimination of the Due Process Clause of the Fifth Amendment and the Equal Protection Clause of the Fourteenth.

Chief Judge Sobeloff, speaking for the court, rested the constitutional responsibility of the hospitals on the receipt of public funds pursuant to joint federal-state area plans for health facility construction, and emphasized that each grantee hospital implemented the Hill-Burton goal of "adequate" hospital service for all the people of a state.* The court also found "state" and "federal" action in the Hill-Burton provision, which enabled the Greensboro hospitals to avoid giving an assurance not to discriminate, and declared that the language which sanctioned segregation was unconstitutional. 323 F.2d at 969. As a result, the Surgeon General amended implementing regulations

† The motion, under 28 U.S.C. §2403 (1964) and Fed. R. Civ. P. 24(a), asserted the government's right to intervene since "the constitutionality of an Act of Congress . . . affecting the public interest . . . [was] drawn in question. . . ."

‡ The Hill-Burton Act, prior to Amendment 1965, prohibited racial discrimination by providing that state hospital construction plans "shall provide for adequate hospital facilities for the people residing in a state without discrimination on account of race, creed or color. . . ." Section 622, 60 Stat. 1043 (1946), as amended 42 U.S.C. §291(d) (1964). However, the act authorized the Surgeon General to make regulations permitting state plans to provide an exception to the nondiscrimination rule, by establishing separate hospital facilities for separate population groups if there is "equitable provision" for each group. Section 622, 60 Stat. 1043 (1946), as amended, 42 U.S.C. §291(c) (1964). The Surgeon General promulgated such a regulation, 21 Fed. Reg. 9841 (1956).

* 323 F.2d 959, 964, 968-969 (1963). In the first fifteen years of the program (1947-1961), approximately $1.55 billion of federal funds were approved for new or additional facilities for governmentally owned and voluntary nonprofit hospitals and other health facilities. Slightly more than half of the total went to voluntary nonprofit hospital projects. In the same period state and local funds (governmental and nongovernmental) totaled about $3.38 billion; thus, the federal share of Hill-Burton projects was slightly more than 30 percent of their total cost. About 238,946 additional hospital beds were made available by the program.

to require nondiscriminatory admission and treatment of Negro patients and professionals in all Hill-Burton hospitals. 42 C.F.R. §53.112 (1964).

The Simkins case has not been restricted to hospitals authorized by Hill-Burton to totally exclude blacks. Federal courts enjoined discriminatory policies in publicly owned and nongovernmental medical facilities, as well as the exclusion of black patients and professionals. Although Negro physicians have obtained full staff membership under the Simkins theory, the extent to which Negro professionals are protected when a hospital denies that exclusion has been racial presents troublesome questions which remain unresolved. See Note, Working Rules for Assuring Nondiscrimination in Hospital Administration, 74 Yale L.J. 151 (1964). The Fourth Circuit also extended the rule to a North Carolina hospital which was not a Hill-Burton grantee but which, among other interrelations with government, had been forced to obtain a license because of the state's Hill-Burton participation. Eaton v. Gubbs, 329 F.2d 710 (4th Cir. 1964). With the enactment of the Medicare program, few medical facilities are beyond the reach of the federal equity power. Social Security Amendments of 1965, 79 Stat. 286 (1965) (codified in scattered sections of 26, 42, 45 U.S.C.).

Simkins and subsequent decisions had a significant and valuable impact in eliminating individual instances of discrimination, and most medical facilities have partially complied with Title VI through their desire to participate in federal programs, particularly Medicare. Federal enforcement, however, has been spasmodic in nature, and thus has not always been equal to the deep-rooted aspects of the problem.

6. RIGHT TO INTERRACIAL SEX AND MARRIAGE

On its face, the title of this chapter appears misleading. The law provides no right to pre- or extramarital sex, whether intra- or interracial, although the courts now clearly, if belatedly, recognize the right to interracial marriage. And yet society's attraction-repulsion ambivalence to interracial sex not only preceded the array of prohibitions on such unions, but survives their repeal. This chapter examines the origins of the hostility to interracial unions, its development and incorporation into law, and the residue of racial problems that have accompanied the new sexual freedom, whether in or outside the bounds of matrimony.

A. MISCEGENATION LAWS AND THE SOCIAL SCIENCES

W. JORDAN, WHITE OVER BLACK
136-140 (*1968*)

When Europeans met Africans in America the result was slavery, revolt, the sociability of daily life, and, inevitably, sexual union. The blending of black and white began almost with the first contact of the two peoples and has far outlasted the institution of chattel slavery. It became, in some English colonies, almost an institution in itself. It rivaled the slave revolt as a source of tension. It may even have equaled the pressure of daily contact as a mechanism of cultural fusion. Most important, however, was the reticular complex of tensions which arose concerning interracial mixture. . . .

Miscegenation was extensive in all the English colonies, a fact made evident to contemporaries by the presence of large numbers of mulattoes. It is impossible to ascertain how much intermixture there actually was, though it seems likely there was more during the eighteenth century than at any time since. Although miscegenation was probably most common among the lower orders, white men of every social rank slept with Negro women. The colonists, as well as European travelers in the colonies, frequently pointed to this facet of American life.

No one thought intermixture was a good thing. Rather, English colonials were caught in the push and pull of an irreconcilable conflict between desire and aversion for interracial sexual union. The perceptual prerequisite for this conflict is so obvious as to be too easily overlooked: desire and aversion rested on the bedrock fact that white men perceived Negroes as being *both alike and different* from themselves. Without perception of similarity, no desire and no widespread gratification was possible. Without perception of difference, on the other hand, no aversion to miscegenation nor tension concerning it could have arisen. Without perception of difference, of course, the term *miscegenation* had no meaning. Given the simultaneous feelings of desire and aversion, it seems probable that of the two the latter is more demanding of explanation. The sexual drive of human beings has always, in the long run, overridden even the strongest sense of difference between two groups of human beings and, in some individuals, has even overridden the far stronger sense which men have of the difference between themselves and animals. What demands explanation, in short, is why there was any aversion among the white colonists to sexual union with Negroes. More than desire, aversion was a manifestation of cultural rather than biological patterns, so that the answers may be looked for in the qualities of the various cultural settings which were emerging in English America and to the prevailing patterns of miscegenation which constituted important elements in New World cultural styles.

In most colonies virtually all the offspring of these unions were illegitimate, but legally sanctified interracial marriages did occur, especially though not exclusively in New England. Miscegenation in colonial America, as has been true since, typically involved fornication between white men and Negro women, though the inverse combination was common, far more common than is generally supposed. Probably a majority of interracial marriages in New England involved Negro men and white women of "the meaner sort." In the plantation colonies, though there were occasional instances of white women marrying Negroes, legitimization of this relationship was unusual. Yet white men were sometimes left to ponder indignities such as that suffered (and in return imposed) by a Maryland man who advertised in 1759 that he would no longer be responsible for his wife's debts because "*Mary Skinner,* my Wife, has, after all the Love and Tenderness which could possibly be shown by Man to a Woman, polluted my Bed, by taking to her in my Stead, her own Negro Slave, by whom she hath a Child, which hath occasioned so much Disgrace to me and my Family, that I have thought proper to forbid her my Sight any more."

Public feeling about miscegenation was strong enough to force itself over the hurdles of the legislative process into the statute books of many English continental colonies. As early as the 1660's the Maryland and Virginia assemblies had begun to lash out at miscegenation in language dripping with distaste and indignation. By the turn of the century it was clear in many continental colonies that the English settlers felt genuine revulsion for interracial sexual union, at least in principle. About 1700 the Chester County Court in Pennsylvania ordered a Negro "never more to meddle with any white woman more uppon paine of his life." Statutory prohibitions roughly similar to those of the tobacco colonies and Bermuda were adopted by Massachusetts in 1705, North Carolina in 1715, South Carolina in 1717, Pennsylvania in 1726, and by Georgia when Negroes were admitted to the colony in 1750.

Delaware enacted no outright prohibition but prescribed heavier fines for interracial bastardy cases than for such cases involving two white persons. Thus two northern and all the plantation colonies legally prohibited miscegenation. Community feeling was of course not monolithically arrayed against interracial union: in 1699 several citizens petitioned the Virginia Council for repeal of the intermarriage prohibition, and as late as 1755 the North Carolina Assembly responded favorably to a petition by inhabitants from several counties asking repeal of the laws in which "free Negroes and Mulatto's Intermarrying with white women are obliged to pay taxes for their wives and families." In general, though, the weight of community opinion was set heavily against the sexual union of white and black, as the long-standing statutory prohibitions indicated. Even in South Carolina, where interracial liaisons were less carefully concealed than elsewhere on the continent, a grand jury in 1743 publicly condemned "THE TOO COMMON PRACTICE of CRIMINAL CONVERSATION with NEGRO and other SLAVE WENCHES IN THIS PROVINCE, as an Enormity and Evil of general Ill-Consequence." In significant contrast, none of the West Indian assemblies prohibited extramarital miscegenation and only one took the probably unnecessary step of banning racial intermarriage.

ALPERT, THE ORIGIN OF SLAVERY IN THE UNITED STATES — THE MARYLAND PRECEDENT

14 Am. J. Legal Hist. 189, 194-195, 209-211 (*1970*)

[The author writes that, while legislation in Maryland recognizing the existence of slavery can be found as early as 1639, it was not until 1664 that the first legislation which unquestionably attests to the existence of Negro slavery was enacted. Much of the act is devoted to establishing prohibitions against interracial marriages.]

Entitled "An Act Concerning Negroes & other Slaves," it provided:

> Bee it Enacted by the Right Honorable the Lord Proprietary by the advice and Consent of the upper and lower house of this present General Assembly That all Negroes or other slaves already within the Province And all Negroes and other slaves to bee hereafter imported into the Province shall serve Durante Vita [for life] And all Children born of any Negro or other slave shall be Slaves as their ffathers were for the terme of their lives And forasmuch as divers freeborne English women forgettful of their free Condition and to the disgrace of our Nation doe intermarry with Negro Slaves by which also divers suites may arise touching the Issue of such woemen and a great damage doth befall the Masters of such Negros for prevention whereof for deterring such freeborne women from such shameful Matches Bee it further enacted by the Authority advice and Consent aforesaid That whatsoever free borne woman shall inter marry with any slave from and after the Last day of this present Assembly shall serve the master of such slave dureing the life of her husband And that all the Issue of such freeborne woemen soe marryed shall be slaves as their fathers were And Bee it further Enacted that all the Issues

of English or other freeborne woemen that have already marryed Negroes shall serve the Masters of their Parents till they be Thirty years of age and noe longer[34]. . . .

In . . . [1681], the 1664 slave statute was repealed and replaced with new legislation. The new law continued the 1664 provision that Negroes and other slaves already imported or "hereafter to be imported" were to be held durante vita. The anti-miscegenation section of the earlier statute, however, was revised. The act recites the reason:

And for as much a[s] diverse ffreeborne Englishe or Whitewoman *sometimes* by the Instigation Procurement or Conievance of theire Masters Mistres or dames, & *always* to the Satisfaction of their Lascivious & Lustfull desires, & to the disgrace not only of the English butt allso of many other Christian Nations, doe Intermarry with Negroes & Slaves by which means diverse Inconveniencys Controversys & suits may arise . . .

The legislation provides that if a master, "by any Instigation procurement knowledge permission or Contriveance whatsoever . . ." permits any woman servant to marry a slave, then she is ". . . absolutely discharged manymitted & made free Instantly upon her Intermarriage . . . And all Children borne . . . shall bee ffree. . . ." The statute also levies fines of ten thousand pounds of tobacco on masters who permit such marriages and on ministers who perform them.

The 1681 anti-miscegenation provision, as the earlier 1664 law, is more concerned with the possible legal consequences of interracial marriage than with the interracial marriage itself. The earlier statute on its face does not prohibit all interracial matches, only those between servants and slaves. The plain meaning of the 1681 statute is the same, although by 1681 the legislators are clearly thinking in terms of marriages with "Negroes & Slaves," not just marriages with "Negro Slaves."

The law was passed for two reasons. First, Lord Baltimore had returned to the colony in 1681. He had brought with him a servant girl by the name of Irish Nell, who had almost immediately married a slave. Rather than lose her to the slave's master, Lord Baltimore wished to have the earlier statute repealed. Second, the General Assembly suspected that some masters would purchase or had purchased Negro slaves and white female indentured servants with the hope of enticing the servants into marrying the slaves. Under the earlier act, the girls would then become servants for the lives of their black husbands and their children would have to serve for thirty years, perhaps sufficient reason for masters to encourage miscegenation, contrary to the policy of the law. . . .

. . . By that time the General Assembly realized that the 1681 statute, although it discouraged masters from promoting miscegenation, emboldened

34. "An Act Concerning Negroes & other Slaves," 1 Md. Archives 533-34.

female servants to miscegenate because by so doing their terms of service would conclude. The 1692 statute forbids all interracial marriages and sexual relations:

> . . . any free born English or white woman be shee free or Servant and shall hereafter intermarry with any Negro or other Slave or to any Negro made free, shall immediately upon such marriage forfeit her freedome and become a Servant during the Terme of seven years to the use and benefitt of the Ministry of the Poor. . . and if he be a free Negro or Slave to whom she intermarried, he shall thereby also forfeit his freedom and become a Servant to the use aforesaid during his natural life [.] But . . . if the Marriage be without the Connivance or procurement of her Master . . . she shall finish her time of Servitude together with what damage shall accrew to her Master . . . by occasion of any Children that may happen to be begott . . . and the issues of such women shall likewise be Servants to the use aforesaid till they arrive at the Age of one and twenty years . . . .

The statute also provides that any free woman who had a bastard by a Negro shall serve for seven years and, if the Negro is free, he shall serve for seven years "to the use aforesaid . . . and all such Bastard Children to be Servants . . . until they arrive at the age of thirty one years . . ." If a master instigates an interracial marriage, the woman servant is to be freed. In addition, the same penalties which white women incur are made applicable to white men who "inter marry with or begett with Child any negro woman. . . ."

This legislation is replete with examples of the differences between servant and slave status. A servant can be required to serve for an additional seven years. A slave cannot. The problems of servant-slave marriages seem to be resolved by the statute. Both the servants and the masters are discouraged from promoting them. The discouragement takes the form of extra service for the servant and no additional service for the master if he promoted the match. Neither the fear of additional servitude for the slave nor the hope of additional servitude for the slave's master would be inducements in their case. Consequently this statute, as the earlier ones, is not phrased in these terms.

What would particularly disturb the free black, however, who must have been daily confronted with the spectacle of the slave status of his race, was the fear of being reduced to such a status himself. Therefore the act provides that any "free Negro or Slave" who intermarries shall "become a Servant . . . during his naturall life . . . ." In the context of the statute this does not mean that a slave shall become a servant for life. "Free Negro or Slave" means free Negro or *freed* slave because the fornication provision, quoted above, only penalizes free Negroes and not slaves. If this exegesis of the statute is incorrect and the intermarriage penalty does apply to slaves, its purpose was undoubtedly to discourage slaves' masters from permitting such matches and to encourage them to keep a watchful eye on the possible marital complications of their chattels. This was the first statute to reduce free Negroes to life servitude for certain acts.

APPLEBAUM, MISCEGENATION STATUTES: A CONSTITUTIONAL AND SOCIAL PROBLEM

53 Geo. L.J. 49, 50, 56-57, 62-64 (1964)

[T]he idea of a prohibition of interracial marriage originated in this country; there was no ban on miscegenation at common law or by statute in England at the time of the establishment of the American Colonies . . . .* Pioneers from the Atlantic seaboard venturing westward enacted similar [miscegenation] statutes where they settled.[8] The popularity of the statutes continued so that during the nineteenth century thirty-eigh states had miscegenation statutes at one time or another.[9] The period surrounding the Civil War found nine of these states repealing their statutes.[10] There appear to have been no further repeals until 1951, at which time twenty-nine statutes were still standing. Ten states have repealed their statutes since 1951[12] as a result of the publicity and attention occasioned by the 1948 decision of the Callifornia Supreme Court which struck down the California miscegenation statute,[13] coupled with the momentum of the legal and political battle for Negro equality in the past decade. . . .

* Despite the absence of legal recognition, there is substantial evidence that seventeenth-century Englishmen viewed Africans as inferior beings and sexual contact with them as odious. W. Jordan, White Over Black 32-40 (1968). Indeed, the idea of a prohibition on interracial marriage may not have existed only because it was so unthinkable that no legislation was necessary. It is clear that a society over long periods of time will deem the same conduct as warranting penalties of varying degrees, and at some point in time will not punish it at all. See P. Sorokin, II Social and Cultural Dynamics 591-593 (1962). Thus, Brazil has never prohibited and even officially encourages mixed marriages, although public opposition to such unions is widespread. C. Degler, Neither Black Nor White 185-195 (1971).

8. Nebraska is illustrative of how these statutes were carried to frontier states. Although the Iowa statute had been repealed, Iowans who had migrated to Nebraska controlled the Nebraska legislature in 1855 and passed a miscegenation statute. See Note, 28 Neb. L. Rev. 475, 477 (1949). The statute was repealed in 1963. Neb. Laws 1963, ch. 243, §1.

9. It appears that forty-one states have at one time or another enacted miscegenation statutes. In addition to the thirty-eight statutes existing during the nineteenth century, Pennsylvania appears to have repealed its statute before the nineteenth century, and Arizona and Wyoming did not pass their statutes until the twentieth century. Cummins & Kane, Miscegenation, The Constitution, and Science, 38 Dicta 24, 28 (1961).

10. The states which repealed their statutes during this period were Iowa (1851), Kansas (1857), Maine (1883), Massachusetts (1840), Michigan (1883), New Mexico (1886), Ohio (1887), Rhode Island (1881) and Washington (1867). Note, 10 Wyo. L.J. 131 n. 2 (1956).

12. Ariz. Laws 1962, ch. 14, §1; Colo. Laws 1957, ch. 124, §1; Idaho Laws 1959, ch. 44, §1; Mont. Laws 1953, ch. 4, §1; Neb. Laws 1963, ch. 234, §1; Nev. Laws 1959, ch. 193, §1; N.D. Laws 1955, ch. 126, §1; Ore. Laws 1959, ch. 531, §1; Ore. Laws 1955, ch. 694, §1; S.D. Laws 1957, ch. 38; Utah Laws 1963, ch. 43, §1.

13. Perez v. Sharp, 32 Cal. 2d 711, 198 P.2d 17 (1948).

[This review covers the period prior to the Supreme Court's decision in McLaughlin v. Florida, infra page 275.]

. . . Miscegenation statutes . . . [were] attacked on constitutional grounds. The courts of last resort of fifteen states . . . reached the question of their constitutionality and all but one . . . upheld them.[66] In addition, the federal circuit courts[67] and the one federal court of appeals[68] . . . confronted with the statutes . . . sustained their constitutional validity. The Alabama Supreme Court invalidated its statute in 1872,[69] but this decision was promptly overruled.[70] There is only one state supreme court decision standing which has struck down a miscegenation statute; that is the 1948 California decision of Perez v. Sharp.[71]

The statutes have been sustained in the face of arguments that they violated the impairments of contracts clause,[72] the Civil Rights Act of 1866,[73] the privileges and immunities clause,[74] the equal protection clause[75] and the

66. The fourteen state supreme court decisions upholding miscegenation statutes are Green v. State, 58 Ala. 190 (1877); State v. Pass, 59 Ariz. 16, 121 P.2d 882 (1942); Dodson v. State, 61 Ark. 57, 31 S.W. 977 (1895); Jackson v. City & County of Denver, 109 Colo. 196, 124 P.2d 240 (1942); McLaughlin v. State, 153 So.2d 1 (Fla. 1963), *prob. juris. noted,* 377 U.S. 914 (1964); Scott v. State, 39 Ga. 321 (1869); State v. Gibson, 36 Ind. 389 (1871); State v. Brown, 236 La. 562, 108 So.2d 233 (1959); Miller v. Lucks, 203 Miss. 824, 36 So.2d 140 (1948); State v. Jackson, 80 Mo. 175 (1883); State v. Kennedy, 76 N.C. 251 (1877); Eggers v. Olson, 104 Okla. 297, 231 Pac. 483 (1924); Lonas v. State, 50 Tenn. 287 (1871); Naim v. Naim, 197 Va. 80, 87 S.E.2d 749, *remanded,* 350 U.S. 891 (1955), *aff'd,* 197 Va. 734, 90 S.E.2d 849, *appeal dismissed,* 350 U.S. 985 (1956).

67. State v. Tutty, 41 Fed. 753 (C.C.S.D. Ga. 1890); Ex parte Kinney, 14 Fed. Cas. 602 (No. 7825) (C.C.E.D. Va. 1879); Ex parte Francois, 9 Fed. Cas. 699 (No. 5047) (C.C.W.D. Tex. 1879); In re Hobbs, 12 Fed. Cas. 262 (No. 6550) (C.C.N.D. Ga. 1871).

68. Stevens v. United States, 146 F.2d 120 (10th Cir. 1944).

69. Burns v. State, 48 Ala. 195 (1872).

70. Green v. State, 58 Ala. 190 (1877).

71. 32 Cal. 2d 711, 198 P.2d 17 (Perez v. Lippold) (1948). The Criminal Court of Baltimore declared the Maryland statute unconstitutional in an unreported case. State v. Howard, Daily Record, April 22, 1957.

72. U.S. Const. art. I, §10, State v. Tutty, 41 Fed. 753 (C.C.S.D. Ga. 1890); Ex parte Kinney, 14 Fed. Cas. 602 (No. 7825) (C.C.E.D. Va. 1879); In re Hobbs, 12 Fed. Cas. 262 (No. 6550) (C.C.N.D. Ga. 1871); Green v. State, 58 Ala. 190 (1877); Dodson v. State, 61 Ark. 57, 31 S.W. 977 (1895); State v. Gibson, 36 Ind. 389 (1871); Lonas v. State, 50 Tenn. 287 (1871).

73. Civil Rights Bill of April 9, 1866, ch. 31, §1, 14 Stat. 27, 42 U.S.C. §1981 (1958), Stevens v. United States, 146 F.2d 120 (10th Cir. 1944); Ex parte Francois, 9 Fed. Cas. 699 (No. 5047) (C.C.W.D. Tex. 1879); In re Hobbs, supra note 72; Green v. State, supra note 72; Dodson v. State, supra note 72; State v. Gibson, supra note 72; Lonas v. State, supra note 72.

74. U.S. Const. amend. XIV, §1, Ex parte Kinney, 14 Fed. Cas. 602 (No. 7825) (C.C. E.D. Va. 1879); In re Hobbs, 12 Fed. Cas. 262 (No. 6550) (C.C.N.D. Ga. 1871); Dodson v. State, 61 Ark. 57, 31 S.W. 977 (1895); State v. Gibson, 36 Ind. 389 (1871); State v. Jackson, 80 Mo. 175 (1883); Lonas v. State, 50 Tenn. 287 (1871).

75. U.S. Const. amend. XIV, §1, Ex parte Francois, 9 Fed. Cas. 699 (No. 5047) (C.C.

due process clause.[76] In Perez, the California statute was attacked on the novel ground that it violated the constitutional guarantee of freedom of religion. Commentators have also argued that the statutes are bills of attainder and violate the full faith and credit clause. One brief has argued that the statutes interfered with equitable administration of the immigration laws, and another that the statute was unconstitutionally vague in its definition of "Negro."

The Supreme Court of the United States . . . [prior to 1964] never ruled on the constitutionality of miscegenation legislation. Pace v. Alabama[81] is often cited by courts and proponents of the statutes as support. In Pace, a Negro man and white woman had been convicted of fornication. The Alabama statute punished interracial adultery or fornication much more severely than when these offenses occurred between members of the same race. The Court upheld the statute against a claim that it discriminated on the basis of race, answering that there was no discrimination because both races were punished equally. . . .*

In Naim v. Naim,[88] the Supreme Court of Appeals of Virginia upheld the statute challenged there on the basis that the legislature had complete power to control the vital institution of marriage. The parties, a white woman and a Chinese man, had been married in North Carolina, which permits such a marriage. The record was clear that prior to the marriage the woman was a resident of Virginia, and the man was not. It was also clear that both returned to Virginia shortly after the marriage and were residing there. Virginia does not recognize such a marriage if between Virginia residents or if Virginia residents go elsewhere to evade the statute. In addition to citing the long line of cases upholding similar statutes, the court relied on recent United States Supreme Court decisions for support. Shelley v. Kraemer[89] was cited for language distinguishing social legislation from other legislation affecting fourteenth amendment rights; the court found that marriage was in the former category. The court also sought support in the language of Brown v. Board of Educ.,[90] where the Supreme Court referred to education as a "foundation

---

W.D. Tex. 1879); In re Hobbs, supra note 74; Jackson v. City & County of Denver, 109 Colo. 196, 124 P.2d 240 (1942); McLaughlin v. State, 153 So.2d 1 (Fla. 1963), *prob. juris. noted,* 377 U.S. 914 (1964); State v. Gibson, 36 Ind. 389 (1871); State v. Brown, 236 La. 562, 108 So.2d 233 (1959); Naim v. Naim, 197 Va. 80, 87 S.E.2d 749 (1955).

76. U.S. Const. amend. XIV, §1, Jackson v. City & County of Denver, supra note 75; State v. Gibson, supra note 75; Naim v. Naim, supra note 75.

81. 106 U.S. 583 [1 S. Ct. 637, 27 L. Ed. 207] (1883).

* The Alabama Court of Appeals affirmed the miscegenation conviction of a black man who married a white woman. Jackson v. State, 37 Ala. App. 519, 72 So.2d 114 (1954). Although the case presented constitutional issues under the Fifth and Fourteenth amendments, the Supreme Court denied certiorari, 348 U.S. 888, 75 S. Ct. 210, 99 L. Ed. 698 (1954), only a few months after the decision in Brown v. Board of Education.

88. 197 Va. 80, 87 S.E.2d 749, *remanded,* 350 U.S. 891 (1955), *aff'd,* 197 Va. 734, 90 S.E.2d 819, *appeal dismissed,* 350 U.S. 985 (1956).

89. 334 U.S. 1 (1918).

90. 347 U.S. 483 (1954).

of good citizenship;" the Virginia court stressed that interracial marriage could hardly be considered necessary for good citizenship.

Upon appeal, Naim afforded the United States Supreme Court an opportunity to rule on the constitutionality of miscegenation laws. After hearing oral argument, the Court found the record incomplete with respect to the domicile of the parties and remanded to the Virginia Court of Appeals so that the case could be remanded to the trial court.[91] The Court of Appeals refused to comply with the mandate, stating there was no Virginia procedure available to reopen a cause of action.[92] On application to recall the remand the Court dismissed the appeal on the ground that the second Virginia decision left the case devoid of a substantial federal question.[93] . . .

In Perez v. Sharp,[104] the California Supreme Court struck down that state's miscegenation statute by a 4-3 decision. The case arose when a white woman and a Negro man sued for a writ of mandamus compelling the Los Angeles County Clerk to issue them a marriage license after he had refused, relying on the miscegenation statute. Justice Traynor, announcing the decision of the court, found that the statute violated the equal protection clause of the United States Constitution. Under the equal protection clause, he said, the legislation could be sustained only if there was a clear and present danger established, or alternatively, if there was a reasonable classification by the legislature. The burden was placed upon the legislature to overcome a presumption that the statute was invalid since a racial classification was involved. It was held that the statute survived neither test and was, in addition, unconstitutionally vague. Jusice Carter concurred[105] on the ground that there was a denial of due process, reasoning that marriage was a fourteenth amendment liberty, and that the policy evinced in the statute was clearly weak, since California recognized "carfare" marriage whereby local residents went to another state to avoid the California statute. The California statute also imposed no criminal sanctions. Also concurring, Justice Edmonds found that the statute was an infringement of religious freedom,[106] since the parties, Roman Catholics, were denied reception of a Church sacrament, Matrimony. In his dissent, Justice Shenk,[107] relying upon a presumption that the legislation was constitutional, argued that the statute should be sustained since it had a rational basis and a legitimate legislative purpose. He also concluded that since all races were treated equally, it was not proper for the court to go behind the legislative findings of fact.

Perez was the first case to inquire into the evidence and support for the

91. 350 U.S. 891 (1955).

92. 197 Va. 734, 90 S.E.2d 849 (1956).

93. 350 U.S. 985 (1956). Professor Wechsler remarked that this dismissal was "wholly without basis in law." Wechsler, Toward Neutral Principles of Constitutional Law, 73 Harv. L. Rev. 1, 34 (1959).

104. 32 Cal. 2d 711, 198 P.2d 17 (Perez v. Lippold) (1948).

105. Id. at 732, 198 P.2d at 29.

106. Id. at 740-42, 198 P.2d at 34-35.

107. Id. at 742, 198 P.2d at 35.

statute; previous decisions had all rested on "well authenticated facts" with very little reference to authority.[108] The cases since Perez, have again returned to the older pattern of upholding the statute without any real inquiry into the facts supporting the statute.[109]

Experts in the field have concluded that fear of miscegenation and interracial intercourse is at the heart of the white man's desire to keep the Negro permanently segregated. Myrdal lists six items in the "white man's rank order of discriminations" and "highest in this order stands the bar against intermarriage and sexual intercourse involving white women."[111] Miscegenation is followed on this list respectively by social conventions, public facilities, political franchise, legal equality and employment. . . . With miscegenation at the crux of racial prejudice in the United States, it is then not surprising that state legislatures have expressed social policy by legally condemning miscegenous marriages and making them subject to criminal sanctions. The geographical distribution of the statutes has followed the lines of racial feeling against Negroes in the South and Orientals in the western states. The inclusion or exclusion of other so-called racial groups in different statutes appears due to fortuitous historical circumstances and local prejudices within particular states.

The Negro does not concur in the white man's emphasis of miscegenation as the crucial problem; Myrdal found that the rank of grievances for the Negro is exactly reversed, with miscegenation being the least significant among the barriers of segregation.[114] Negro writers have often claimed that there is no desire among their people to intermarry with whites,[115] and this claim was borne out by a recent Ford Foundation survey of 721 Chicago Negro families which concluded: "there is no evidence of a desire for miscegenation, or even interest in promoting it, except among a very tiny minority."[116] Reflecting both this minimal significance of miscegenation for the Negro and a recognition of the highly inflammatory nature of the issue, the NAACP and other civil rights groups have until very recently refrained from

108. Note, 58 Yale L.J. 472 (1949); Note, 41 Va. L. Rev. 860 (1955). In State v. Jackson, 80 Mo. 175, 179 (1883) the court said: "It is stated as a well authenticated fact that if the issue of a black man and a white woman and a white man and a black woman, intermarry, they cannot possibly have any progeny, and such a fact sufficiently justifies those laws which forbid the intermarriage of blacks and whites . . . ." In Scott v. State, 39 Ga. 321, 323 (1869), the court said: "Our daily observation shows us, that the offspring of these unnatural connections are generally sickly and effeminate, and that they are inferior in physical development and strength to the full blood of either race."

109. State v. Brown, 236 La. 562, 108 So.2d 233 (1959); Naim v. Naim, 197 Va. 80, 87 S.E.2d 749 (1955).

111. 1 Myrdal, An American Dilemma 60 (1944).

114. 1 Myrdal, op. cit. supra note 111, at 61.

115. E.g., Logan, A Negro's Faith in America 27 (1946).

116. Bogue & Dizard, Race, Ethnic Prejudice and Discrimination as Viewed by Subordinate and Superordinate Groups, Paper Read at Midwest Sociological Society Meetings, Kansas City, Mo., April 17, 1964, quoted in Time, June 5, 1964, p. 24.

attempting to have miscegenation statutes struck down.[117] But Negroes do object to the statutes in theory if not in practice. There is a general contention that freedom of the individual is curtailed, but it is also argued that the statutes encourage illicit intercourse and exploitation of Negro women since there is no imposition of the normal marital consequences of such intercourse upon the white male.[118] There also exists a feeling that such statutes are a stigma upon the Negro race to the extent that they imply Negroes are not fit to marry white people; one writer has said the proposition "that all colored folk shall write themselves down as limited by a general assertion of their unfitness to marry other decent folk is a nightmare."[119] Some commentators argue that miscegenation statutes serve only to offer legal support for the popular concept that one race is inferior.[120]

The possibility that the statutes may do no more than create a stamp of inferiority upon certain races is born out by the fact that they do not accomplish their ultimate purpose of preventing mixed breed offspring. From one-third to three-fourths of all Negroes have some mixed blood in them, and it has been primarily illicit intercourse rather than actual intermarriage that has produced this high ratio. The ban on marriage has thus not had much of an effect in preventing mixed breeds. Indeed, as noted above, the statutes may actually have promoted illicit relations since the white male will bear no marital consequences.

O. COX, CASTE, CLASS, AND RACE, 386-387, 526-527 (1948). Professor Oliver Cox, a black sociologist, rejects the conclusions of experts like Gunnar Myrdal (cited in the Applebaum article, supra page 267) that fear of miscegenation and sexual intercourse between the two races is at the heart of white society's desire to permanently segregate blacks, and that employment discrimination comes last in the "white man's rank order of discriminations." Cox also thinks Dr. Myrdal is wrong in his conclusion that blacks reverse this list in ranking their racial grievances, i.e., placing employment at the top of the list and interest in interracial sex at the bottom.

Cox maintains that:

> In reality both the Negroes and their white exploiters know that economic opportunity comes first and that the white woman comes second; indeed, she is merely a significant instrument in limiting the first. Moreover, these selected ele-

117. Weinberger, A Reappraisal of the Constitutionality of Miscegenation Statutes, 42 Cornell L.Q. 208, 210-11 (1957); Greenberg, op. cit. supra note 112, at 344. But the appellants in McLaughlin are represented by attorneys of the NAACP Legal Defense and Education Fund.

118. 1 Myrdal, op. cit. supra note 111, at 63.

119. DuBois, The Crisis 106 (1920) as quoted in 1 Myrdal, op. cit. supra note 11, at 64.

120. See Weinberger, supra note 117, at 222. See generally Riley, Miscegenation Statutes — A Re-Evaluation of Their Constitutionality in Light of Changing Social and Political Conditions, 32 So. Cal. L. Rev. 28 (1958).

ments of social discrimination should not be thought of as discrete social phenomena; they are rather intermeshed in a definite pattern supporting a dominant purpose. If the white ruling class intends to keep the colored people in their place — that is to say, freely exploitable — this class cannot permit them to marry white women; neither can it let white men marry Negro women. If this were allowed to happen Negroes would soon become so whitened that the profit makers would be unable to direct mass hatred against them and would thus lose their principal weapon in facilitating their primary business of exploiting the white and the black workers of the South. If a Negro could become governor of Georgia it would be of no particular social significance whether his wife is white or colored; or, at any rate, there would be no political power presuming to limit the color of his wife. But if, in a "democracy", you could insist that his wife must be black, you could also make him do most of your dirty and menial work at your wages. Sexual obsession, then, functions in the fundamental interest of economic exploitation. (Caste, Class, and Race 526-527.)

At another point in his book, Cox reiterates his thesis that economic exploitation rather than an abhorrence of interracial sex is the real basis for miscegenation prohibitions:

it is not intermarriage, per se, which is determining, but rather the cultural advantage which restriction secures to the white group. Protecting the "honor and sanctity of white womanhood" constitutes a most convincing war cry and an excellent covering for the basic purpose that colored people must never be given the opportunity to become the cultural peers of whites. (Id. at 387.)

Cox seeks to bolster his point further by dismissing any thought that opposition to interracial marriage is intended to preserve white women for white men,

. . . for the hostility is not diminished when Negroes come into the area with white women from abroad. The size of the white sex ratio is not ordinarily a factor. Neither are white Southerners, for example, particularly disturbed over the fact that in other countries there is considerable interracial marriage. We should miss the point entirely if we take as literally describing the situation the defense that white men must protect their sisters and daughters from the lust of black men. The status quo would be as effectively damaged if colored men went to Mars, married Martian white women, and brought them into the South as wives. (Id. at 387.)

Finally, in supporting his contention that black leaders were merely being politic when they told Myrdal that black men are not interested in white women, he argues that whenever whites are in a ruling-class situation,

. . . there is a social urge among colored men to marry white women. This urge, of course, is not an "ungovernable sexual craving" for white flesh, as some rationalists would have us believe, for women of any color are totally sufficient for the satisfaction of any such simple desire. In fact, under such passion, white men have found colored women of every race fully adequate. Thus it must not be supposed that it is the white woman as a mere sexual object which is the preoccupation of colored men, it is rather her importance to him as a vehicle in his struggle for economic and cultural position. (Id. at 386.)

NOTE

Cox's theory of economic exploitation as the moving force behind the opposition to intermarriage is probably a minority view. But many people, notably Marxists, subscribe to this "economic" explanation for the deep resistance by whites to interracial unions. While rejecting the theory as "too mechanical," Calvin Hernton, in his book Sex and Racism in America 32-33 (1965), points out that both white women and black men are in a "semi-oppressed" class in terms of jobs, political power, money, property and access to opportunities for higher status. He contends that the economic and social pressures they face tend to serve as "magnets" drawing together white women and black men.

Most scholars favor Myrdal's position that a basic fear and abhorrence of interracial relationships motivated the sanctions, legal and extralegal, imposed on them for 300 years. Generally, it seems reasonable to assume that attitudes about sex are embedded in a given cultural and historical context, and that even if sexuality is basically biological, its form of expression is influenced by social variables, including economics, status, and access to power. See F. Fanon, The Wretched of the Earth 39 (1963).

Psychiatrists have offered a third basis for society's centuries-long fixation on interracial sex, which takes cognizance of both the "exploitation" and "racial purity" themes. The following excerpts are intended to illustrate the clinical theories.

A. KARDINER AND L. OVESEY, THE MARK OF OPPRESSION: EXPLORATIONS IN THE PERSONALITY OF THE AMERICAN NEGRO *44-45 (1951)*

[In their discussion of the psychology of slavery, the authors state that the slaves' needs were usually met in a manner that harmonized with maximum utility. There was little "reciprocity of feeling" between master and slave, and virtually no possibility for emotional interchange. Sick slaves were treated — like sick horses — to restore their utility. The rage or protest of slaves could be ignored or countered with violence. This factor distinguished the relationship from that existing between equals, which is characterized by complete emotional reciprocity. Differences between equals are generally resolved by the establishment of certain "conventions," e.g., property rights are largely a convention among equals. The conditions of slavery not only destroyed the possibility of reciprocal interaction between master and slave, but in large measure seriously impaired free emotional interaction among the slaves themselves.]

The fate of the Negro family under slavery is a case in point. Marriage was not recognized; paternity was not recognized. Offspring became the property of whoever owned the *mother*. The child-mother relationship had to be respected, at least until the utility potential of the child was realized, i.e. until the child was able to work, and, therefore, had a sale value. The biological father had no social significance, whether he was white or colored. There were, however, exceptions to this. White fathers occasionally did recognize and care for offspring from Negro mistresses. On the whole, marriage between Negroes was a loose arrangement without mutual obligations. However, slaveowners did recognize the fact that the cohesion of the slave group was greater where the family was allowed to remain intact, and that flight was commonest where the families were broken up.

This takes us to a feature of slavery, which altered the relations between white and Negro, and that is the relation of the white male to the Negro female. This could not be confined to the domain of pure utility, as it was with the male. The Negro female did have the opportunity for more emotional interaction with white masters by virtue of her sexual attractiveness. This can never be confined within the limits of *utility*. A white master (or his son) could become attached emotionally to his Negro mistress. He could care for his Negro offspring and could discriminate in their favor, or free them.

A second function of the Negro female, commonly underestimated, is the role of the Negro nursemaid. Here the attachment of the growing child to the Negro mammy could become very strong indeed, and even predispose the white male to a predilection for the Negro woman as a sexual object. There is little question that the Negro female was attractive to the white male for mating purposes. The universality of laws prohibiting marriage of whites and Negroes is an eloquent testimonal to this fact. These two features, the sexual usefulness of the female and her role as a mammy, could only have the effect of increasing the white man's fear of the Negro male, her rightful mate and legitimate possessor. This could not help but lead to the fantastic exaggeration in the white man's mind of the Negro male's sexual prowess. And this, in turn, would necessitate more repressive measures against the Negro male — all caused by the white man's guilt and anxiety. The necessity to "protect" the white female against this fancied prowess of the male Negro thus became a fixed constellation in the ethos of the South.

J. KOVEL, WHITE RACISM: A PSYCHOHISTORY *67-71 (1970)**

. . . A mountain of evidence has accumulated to document the basically sexualized nature of racist psychology. Yet it is doubtful whether the ma-

* From White Racism: A Psychohistory, by Joel Kovel. Copyright © 1970 by Joel Kovel. Reprinted by permission of Pantheon Books / A Division of Random House, Inc.

jority of educated people have any idea of the extent, organization, or intensity of such fantasies. Allegations as to the Negro's sexual prowess, or the heroic proportions of his genitalia are a widely known legend. And it need scarcely be emphasized that discussions and speculations about Negro sexuality are neither casual and dispassionate, nor uncharged. The utmost passion has been devoted to the topic throughout our history. We know that the archetypal lynching in the old South was for the archetypal crime of having a black man rape (= touch, approach, look at, be imagined to have looked at, talk back to, etc.) a white lady. Moreover, the archetypal lynching often included a castration of the black malefactor; and even when it didn't, the idea of castration was immanent in the entire procedure. Before there were lynchings in the South, there were laws to do what mobs took upon themselves to perform after the Civil War, and these same laws often punished Negro infractions of all kinds with castration.

Throughout our history, even in these progressive days when the wish to actually punish sexual crimes by castration has been repressed out of the consciousness of all but a few psychotics,† sexuality remains a widely acknowledged core of the race problem. Miscegenation is indeed the most forbidden of inter-racial practices — a taboo only now cracking as the media seek to remake the American mentality — and so sexuality and racism must be indeed intertwined.

Even from the few facts presented above, however, it is clear that sexuality in racism is not an isolated phenomenon but is most intimately connected with issues of power and dominance. The fullest versions of the sexual fantasies have sprung forth from the American South, the land of direct domination. Northerners, right from the start, were more secretive and guilty about all aspects of their sexual behavior toward blacks, and locked within the darktowns of their minds what was openly acted upon in the South.

In the classic South — and, as the fantasies generated there were diffused, throughout America — the sex fantasy has been incorporated into the white assumption of superiority and the demand for black submission. Whenever a black man bowed and scraped, whenever a white man called a black man "boy," or in other ways infantilized him, just below the surface of the white man's consciousness, a sexual fantasy would be found yoked to the symbol of power and status. These sex fantasies erupted whenever the power relationships were threatened. In the colonies, the slightest rumor of a slave re-

† In several countries, sexual offenders seek to avoid long prison sentences by "volunteering" for castration. In Denmark, for example, about ten sexual offenders apply for this operation each year. Stürup, Will This Man Be Dangerous? in The Mentally Abnormal Offender 10 (A. deRouck and R. Porter eds. 1968).

The procedure has been discussed in this country, and a Denver, Colorado district court judge authorized the castration of a forty-three-year-old man who admitted molesting several hundred young girls in his lifetime. The defendant chose the operation rather than serving a life sentence. Olsen, D.A. Firm in Opinion on Castration Case, Denver Post, July 30, 1972.

volt was accompanied by wild stories of blacks wreaking their ultimate revenge in wholesale rape of white women. Nor should anyone think that, below the surface of reasonable concern, the fears aroused in whites by the current black rebellion are different. The specter of omnipotent black sexuality has obsessed whites from their first glimpse of an African until this very day. And, as will all such fantasies, the truth it represents is of secondary importance, and may itself be caused by belief and wish, rather than the converse. The key to this is not in the content of the fantasy so much as in the fascination it has held for white minds.

In classical Southern society, alongside the white man's obsessive fear of black male sexuality was his preoccupation with the bodies of black females. Black women were supposed to be more passionate than white women; and they doubtless were, since the whole of Southern culture converged to force the white woman into being the most worshipped, the purest, the least vital, and certainly the least sexual of females. The evidence for this is perhaps too well known to need documentation. . . .

Now consider the complications this dual maternity implied for the white Southern male: to forever split his affection between a warm impure black "mammy" among whose kind he would later seek free sexual pleasure, and a cold, "pure" white mother whom he would idealize and for whose virtue he could later, as a man with power in a patriarchal society, kill and castrate any black who could be imagined to entertain sexual wishes toward white women. Consider further that these same black men, so debased and humiliated in actual life, should be invested in white men's fantasy life with the most prurient of wishes and the most prodigious of sexual capacities, and should be in fact the subject of profound envy by those who dominated them. These despised men also became the object of a desire so secret that it could be admitted only by way of projection or from the underside of culture: whatever black men may have wished of white women, the true source of the desire was often those "pure," repressed white bodies who were held as an asexual ideal by the men in power. If we bear these remarkable contradictions in mind, we will be able to realize, as John Dollard wrote in his classical study, Caste and Class in a Southern Town, "What a peculiar state of affairs is to be explained and how bizarre the white attitude toward the rape problem seems; and we grant that some potent, but not very obvious explanation is required." The reader will have no doubt surmised from the context of this work the kind of explanation to be offered. Only the theory of the Oedipus complex — enlarged into a cultural apparatus that defines and binds real roles even as it apportions fantasies amongst the players of these roles — will account for this variety of phenomena. And in these cultural fantasies, the symbolic freedom of the human mind is allowed full sway. Black man, white man, black woman, white woman — each realizes some aspect of the oedipal situation; and in this realization, the infantile impossibilities of the oedipal conflicts attain their perverted resolution by being projected onto split elements — elements split into black and white — of culture.

We have seen the pattern: blackness is bad, what goes on in the dark comes from the dark: therefore, make the black man represent *both* father and son in their destructive aspects. There is evidence for this in the structure of his social role: he is the bad father who possesses the black mammy (who is herself impure), and he has the genital power which forever excites the child's envy; he is also the bad child who lusts after the pure and utterly forbidden white mother (made sexless, in reality). By making the rape fantasy the cornerstone of his culture, the white male only repeats in adulthood the central incest taboo of his childhood. And here Southern culture makes its unique contribution to an ageless human problem: the Southern white male simultaneously resolves both sides of the conflict by keeping the black man submissive, and by castrating him when submission fails. In both these situations — in the one symbolically, in the other directly — he is castrating the father, as he once wished to do, and also identifying with the father by castrating the son, as he once feared for himself. All that he has to do to maintain this delectable situation is to structure his society so that he directly dominates black men.

NOTES

1. The parent-child relationship described by Dr. Kovel is particularly intense in the authoritarian home where parental rule is rigid and harsh, and where the child's impulses of sexual feeling and hostility toward the parents are projected onto others. Thus, as one writer explains:

> The boy who has been held in check by a stern father and deprived of freedom to develop his own masculinity, who is inhibited by the antisexual morality and exaggerated respect for womanhood of his authoritarian home, displays a tenderness toward his mother and "respectable" white women in general that conflicts with his anger and his desire for sexual expression. He may always find it difficult to have both sexual and tender, loving impulses toward the same woman. In a roundabout way, his thwarted urges in childhood and adulthood lead to total acceptance of prevailing stereotypes of asexual whites and hypersexual blacks. In accepting the taboo and teaching black men to avoid white women, the white man tells himself not to harbor a lust for good white women and, au fond, for his good mother. It is no wonder that "motherfucker" is America's most potent projective malediction. (R. Sickels, Race, Marriage, and the Law 23 (1972).)

2. The tremendous impact of these pressures on the personalities of blacks as manifested in their sexual functioning are extensively examined in W. Grier and P. Cobbs, Black Rage (1968), an excerpt from which is printed infra page 285. See also E. Cleaver, Soul On Ice 6-17, 158-159 (1968).

3. In reading, below, two Supreme Court opinions that voided penalties for interracial sex and marriage, note the failure to discuss the historical and deep-seated aversion to such conduct represented by the antimiscegenation statutes.

McLAUGHLIN v. FLORIDA
379 U.S. 184, 13 L. Ed. 2d 222, 85 S. Ct. 283 (1964)

Mr. Justice White delivered the opinion of the Court.

At issue in this case is the validity of a conviction under §798.05 of the Florida statutes providing that:

> Any negro man and white woman, or any white man and negro woman, who are not married to each other, who shall habitually live in and occupy in the nighttime the same room shall each be punished by imprisonment not exceeding twelve months, or by fine not exceeding five hundred dollars. . . .

The challenged statute is a part of chapter 798 entitled "Adultery and Fornication." Section 798.01 forbids living in adultery and §798.02 proscribes lewd cohabitation. Both sections are of general application, both require proof of intercourse to sustain a conviction, and both authorize imprisonment up to two years. Section 798.03, also of general application, proscribes fornication and authorizes a three-month jail sentence. . . . 798.04 makes criminal a white person and a Negro living together in adultery or fornication. A one-year prison sentence is authorized. The conduct it reaches appears to be the same as is proscribed under the first two sections of the chapter. Section 798.05 . . . is distinguishable from the other sections of the chapter in that it is the only one which does not require proof of intercourse along with the other elements of the crime.

Appellants were charged with a violation of §798.05 . . . and the jury returned a verdict of guilty. Solely on the authority of Pace v. Alabama, 106 U.S. 583, 1 S. Ct. 637, 27 L. Ed. 207, the Florida Supreme Court affirmed and sustained the validity of §798.05 as against appellants' claims that the section denied them equal protection . . . .

It is readily apparent that §798.05 treats the interracial couple . . . differently than it does any other couple. No couple other than a Negro and a white person can be convicted under §798.05 and no other section proscribes the precise conduct banned by §798.05. . . .

In this situation, Pace v. Alabama is relied upon as controlling authority. . . . In that case, the Court let stand a conviction under an Alabama statute forbidding adultery or fornication between a white person and a Negro and imposing a greater penalty than allowed under another Alabama statute of general application and proscribing the same conduct whatever the race of the participants. The opinion acknowledged that . . . equality of protection under the laws implies that any person, "whatever his race . . . shall not be subjected, for the same offense, to any greater or different punishment." But taking quite literally its own words, "for the same *offense*" (emphasis supplied), the Court pointed out that Alabama had designated as a separate offense the commission by a white person and a Negro of the identical acts forbidden by the general provisions. There was, therefore, no impermissible discrimination because the difference in punishment was "directed against the offence designated" and because in the case of each offense all who committed it, white and Negro, were treated alike. [This was] without regard to the fact that the statute did not reach other types of couples performing the identical conduct and without any necessity to justify the difference in penalty established for the two offenses. Because each of the Alabama laws applied equally to those to whom it was applicable, the different treatment accorded interracial and intraracial couples was irrelevant.

This narrow view of the Equal Protection Clause was soon swept away. . . . Classification "must always rest upon some difference which bears a reasonable and just relation to the act in respect to which classification is proposed . . . . This approach was confirmed in . . . numerous other cases. . . ."

Normally, the widest discretion is allowed the legislative judgment in determining whether to attack some rather than all of the manifestations of the evil aimed at; and normally that judgment is given the benefit of every conceivable circumstance which might suffice to characterize the classification as reasonable rather than arbitrary and invidious. . . . But we deal here with a classification based upon the race of the participants, which must be viewed in light of the historical fact that the central purpose of the Fourteenth Amendment was to eliminate racial discrimination emanating from official sources in the States. This strong policy renders racial classifications "constitutionally suspect," . . . and subject to the "most rigid scrutiny," . . . and "in most circumstances irrelevant" to any constitutionally acceptable legislative purpose. . . .

We deal here with a racial classification embodied in a criminal statute. In this context, where the power of the State weighs most heavily upon the individual or the group, we must be especially sensitive to the policies of the Equal Protection Clause . . . .

Our inquiry, therefore, is whether there clearly appears in the relevant materials some overriding statutory purpose requiring the proscription of the specified conduct when engaged in by a white person and a Negro, but not otherwise. Without such justification the racial classification contained in §798.05 is reduced to an invidious discrimination forbidden by the Equal Protection Clause.

. . . The State [argues] that the legislative purpose of §798.05, like the other sections of chapter 798, was to prevent breaches of the basic concepts of sexual decency . . . .

We find nothing in this suggested legislative purpose, however, which makes it essential to punish promiscuity by one racial group and not that of another. There is no suggestion that a white person and a Negro are any more likely habitually to occupy the same room together than the white or the Negro couple or to engage in illicit intercourse if they do. Sections 798.01-798.05 indicate no legislative conviction that promiscuity by the interracial couple presents any particular problems requiring separate or different treatment if the suggested over-all policy of the chapter is to be adequately served. . . . This is not, therefore, a case where the class defined in the law is that from which "the evil mainly is to be feared," . . . or where the "[e]vils in the same field may be of different dimensions and proportions, requiring different remedies," . . . or even one where the State has done as much as it can as fast as it can. . . . That a general evil will be partially corrected may at times, and without more, serve to justify the limited application of a criminal law; but legislative discretion to employ the piecemeal approach stops short of permitting a State to narrow statutory coverage to focus on a racial group. Such classifications bear a far heavier burden of justification. . . .

Florida's remaining argument is related to its law against interracial marriage, §741.11, which, in the light of certain legislative history of the Fourteenth Amendment, is said to be immune from attack under the Equal Protection Clause. Its interracial cohabitation law, §798.05, is likewise valid, it is argued, because it is ancillary to and serves the same purpose as the miscegenation law itself.

We reject this argument, without reaching the question of the validity of the State's prohibition against interracial marriage or the soundness of the arguments rooted in the history of the Amendment. For even if we posit the constitutionality of the ban against the marriage of a Negro and a white, it does not follow that the cohabitation law is not to be subjected to independent examination under the Fourteenth Amendment. . . .

There is involved here an exercise of the state police power which trenches upon the constitutionally protected freedom from invidious official discrimination based on race. Such a law . . . will be upheld only if it is necessary, and not merely rationally related to, the accomplishment of a permissible state policy. . . . Those provisions of Chapter 798 which are neutral as to race . . . would reach illicit relations of any kind and in this way protect the integrity of the marriage laws of the State, including what is claimed to be a valid ban on interracial marriage. These same provisions, moreover, punish premarital sexual relations as severely or more severely in some instances than do those provisions which focus on the interracial couple. Florida has offered no argument that the State's policy against interracial marriage cannot be as adequately served by the general, neutral, and existing ban on illicit behavior . . . . In short, it has not been shown that §798.05 is a necessary adjunct to the State's ban on interracial marriage. We accordingly invalidate §798.05 without expressing any views about the State's prohibition of interracial marriage, and reverse these convictions.

Mr. Justice Harlan, concurring.

I join the Court's opinion with the following comments.

I agree with the Court that the cohabitation statute has not been shown to be necessary to the integrity of the antimarriage law, assumed arguendo to be valid, and that necessity, not mere reasonable relationship, is the proper test . . . . The necessity test which developed to protect free speech against state infringement should be equally applicable in a case involving state racial discrimination — prohibition of which lies at the very heart of the

Fourteenth Amendment. . . . If the legitimacy of the cohabitation statute is considered to depend upon its being ancillary to the marriage statute, the former must be deemed "unnecessary" . . . in light of the nondiscriminatory extra-marital relations statutes. If, however, the interracial cohabitation statute is considered to rest upon a discrete state interest, existing independently of the antimarriage law, it falls of its own weight.

Mr. Justice STEWART, with whom Mr. Justice DOUGLAS joins, concurring.

I concur in the judgment and agree with most of what is said in the Court's opinion. But the Court implies that a criminal law of the kind here involved might be constitutionally valid if a State could show "some overriding statutory purpose." This is an implication in which I cannot join, because I cannot conceive of a valid legislative purpose under our Constitution for a state law which makes the color of a person's skin the test of whether his conduct is a criminal offense. . . . There might be limited room under the Equal Protection Clause for a civil law requiring the keeping of racially segregated public records for statistical or other valid public purposes. Cf. Tancil v. Wools, 379 U.S. 19, 85 S. Ct. 157. . . . I think it is simply not possible for a state law to be valid under our Constitution which makes the criminality of an act depend upon the race of the actor. Discrimination of that kind is invidious per se.

NOTE

Upon remand of the McLaughlin case, the Florida Supreme Court said that, since the Constitution had not been amended in the interim, it had assumed that the 1883 decision in Pace v. Alabama settled the issue of the validity of statutes prohibiting interracial cohabitation. "In the light of this new and contrary construction of the Constitution we are required, perforce, to recede from our affirmance of the conviction appealed from and remand the cause for disposition in accordance with the new Law of the Land." 172 So.2d 460 (1965).

LOVING v. VIRGINIA
388 U.S. 1, 18 L. Ed. 2d 1010, 87 S. Ct. 1817 (1967)

Mr. Chief Justice WARREN delivered the opinion of the Court.

This case presents a constitutional question never addressed by this Court: whether a statutory scheme adopted by the State of Virginia to prevent marriages between persons solely on the basis of racial classifications violates the Equal Protection and Due Process Clauses of the Fourteenth Amendment. For reasons which seem to us to reflect the central meaning of those constitutional commands, we conclude that these statutes cannot stand consistently with the Fourteenth Amendment.

In June 1958, two residents of Virginia, Mildred Jeter, a Negro woman, and Richard Loving, a white man, were married in the District of Columbia pursuant to its laws. Shortly after their marriage, the Lovings returned to Virginia and established their marital abode in Caroline County. At the October Term, 1958, the Circuit Court of Caroline County, a grand jury issued an indictment charging the Lovings with violating Virginia's ban on interracial marriages. On January 6, 1959, the Lovings pleaded guilty to the charge and were sentenced to one year in jail; however, the trial judge suspended the sentence for a period of 25 years on the condition that the Lovings leave the State and not return to Virginia together for 25 years. He stated in an opinion that:

> Almighty God created the races white, black, yellow, malay and red, and he placed them on separate continents. And but for the interference with his arrangement there would be no cause for such marriages. The fact that he separated the races shows that he did not intend for the races to mix.

After their convictions, the Lovings took up residence in the District of Columbia. On November 6, 1963, they filed a motion in the state trial court to vacate the judgment and set aside the sentence on the ground that the statutes which they had violated were repugnant to the Fourteenth Amendment. The motion not having been decided by October 28, 1964, the Lovings instituted a class action in the United States District Court for the Eastern District of Virginia requesting that a three-judge court be convened to declare the Virginia antimiscegenation statutes unconstitutional and to enjoin state officials from enforcing their convictions. On January 22, 1965, the state trial judge denied the motion to vacate the sentences, and the Lovings perfected an appeal to the Supreme Court of Appeals of Virginia. On February 11, 1965, the three-judge District Court continued the case to allow the Lovings to present their constitutional claims to the highest state court.

The Supreme Court of Appeals upheld the constitutionality of the antimiscegenation statutes and, after modifying the sentence, affirmed the convictions.[2] The Lovings appealed this decision, and we noted probable jurisdiction on December 12, 1966, 385 US 986.

The two statutes under which appellants were convicted and sentenced are part of a comprehensive statutory scheme aimed at prohibiting and punishing interracial marriages. The Lovings were convicted of violating §20-58 of the Virginia Code:

> *Leaving State to evade law.* — If any white person and colored person shall go out of this State, for the purpose of being married, and with the intention of returning, and be married out of it, and afterwards return to and reside in it, cohabiting as man and wife, they shall be punished as provided in §20-59, and the marriage shall be governed by the same law as if it had been solemnized in this State. The fact of their cohabitation here as man and wife shall be evidence of their marriage.

2. 206 Va. 924, 147 S.E.2d 78 (1966).

Section 20-59, which defines the penalty for miscegenation, provides:

Punishment for marriage. — If any white person intermarry with a colored person, or any colored person intermarry with a white person, he shall be guilty of a felony and shall be punished by confinement in the penitentiary for not less than one nor more than five years.

Other central provisions in the Virginia statutory scheme are §20-57, which automatically voids all marriages between "a white person and a colored person" without any judicial proceeding, and §§20-54 and 1-14 which, respectively, define "white persons" and "colored persons and Indians" for purposes of the statutory prohibitions.[4] The Lovings have never disputed in the course of this litigation that Mrs. Loving is a "colored person" or that Mr. Loving is a "white person" within the meanings given those terms by the Virginia statutes.

Virginia is now one of 16 States which prohibit and punish marriages on the basis of racial classifications. Penalties for miscegenation arose as an incident to slavery and have been common in Virginia since the colonial period. The present statutory scheme dates from the adoption of the Racial Integrity Act of 1924, passed during the period of extreme nativism which followed the end of the First World War. The central features of this Act, and current Virginia law, are the absolute prohibition of a "white person" marrying other than another "white person" . . . .

In upholding the constitutionality of these provisions in the decision below, the Supreme Court of Appeals of Virginia referred to its 1955 decision in Naim v Naim, 197 Va 80, 87 SE2d 749, as stating the reasons supporting the validitly of these laws. In Naim, the state court concluded that the State's legitimate purposes were "to preserve the racial integrity of its citizens," and to prevent "the corruption of blood," "a mongrel breed of citizens," and "the obliteration of racial pride," obviously an endorsement of the doctrine

4. Section 20-54 of the Virginia Code provides:

"*Intermarriage prohibited; meaning of term 'white persons.'* — It shall hereafter be unlawful for any white person in this State to marry any save a white person, or a person with no other admixture of blood than white and American Indian. For the purpose of this chapter, the term 'white person' shall apply only to such person as has no trace whatever of any blood other than Caucasian; but persons who have one-sixteenth or less of the blood of the American Indian and have no other non-Caucasic blood shall be deemed to be white persons. All laws heretofore passed and now in effect regarding the intermarriage of white and colored persons shall apply to marriages prohibited by this chapter." Va. Code Ann. §20-54 (1960 Repl. Vol.).

The exception for persons with less than one-sixteenth "of the blood of the American Indian" is apparently accounted for, in the words of a tract issued by the Registrar of the State Bureau of Vital Statistics, by "the desire of all to recognize as an integral and honored part of the white race the descendants of John Rolfe and Pocahontas . . . ." Plecker, The New Family and Race Improvement, 17 Va Health Bull, Extra No. 12, at 25-26 (New Family Series No. 5, 1925), cited in Wadlington, The Loving Case: Virginia's Anti-Miscegenation Statute in Historical Perspective, 52 Va L Rev 1189, 1202, n. 93 (1966). . . .

of White Supremacy. Id, at 90, 87 SE2d, at 756. The court also reasoned that marriage has traditionally been subject to state regulation without federal intervention, and, consequently, the regulation of marriage should be left to exclusive state control by the Tenth Amendment.

While the state court is no doubt correct is asserting that marriage is a social relation subject to the State's police power, Maynard v Hill, 125 US 190 (1888), the State does not contend in its argument before this Court that its powers to regulate marriage are unlimited notwithstanding the commands of the Fourteenth Amendment. Nor could it do so in light of Meyer v Nebraska, 262 US 390 (1923), and Skinner v Oklahoma, 316 US 535 (1942). Instead, the State argues that the meaning of the Equal Protection Clause, as illuminated by the statements of the Framers, is only that state penal laws containing an interracial element as part of the definition of the offense must apply equally to whites and Negroes in the sense that members of each race are punished to the same degree. Thus, the State contends that, because its miscegenation statutes punish equally both the white and the Negro participants in an interracial marriage, these statutes, despite their reliance on racial classifications, do not constitute an invidious discrimination based upon race. The second argument advanced by the State assumes the validity of its equal application theory. The argument is that, if the Equal Protection Clause does not outlaw miscegenation statutes because of their reliance on racial classifications, the question of constitutionality would thus become whether there was any rational basis for a State to treat interracial marriages differently from other marriages. On this question, the States argues, the scientific evidence is substantially in doubt and, consequently, this Court should defer to the wisdom of the state legislature in adopting its policy of discouraging interracial marriages.*

Because we reject the notion that the mere "equal application" of a statute containing racial classifications is enough to remove the classifications from the Fourteenth Amendment's proscription of all invidious racial discriminations, we do not accept the State's contention that these statutes should be upheld if there is any possible basis for concluding that they serve a rational purpose. . . . In the case at bar, however, we deal with statutes containing racial classifications, and the fact of equal application does not immunize the statute from the very heavy burden of justification which the Fourteenth

* In its brief, the state cited a host of authorities — few of them modern and many of them published in the early decades of the century — presenting arguments in opposition to interracial marriage on genetic, anthropological, cultural, psychological and sociological grounds. Brief and Appendix for Appellant at 42-50, App. 4-28. Virtually none of this material is based on statistical data, and much of it implicitly restates a view of race relied on by the trial court in denying a motion to vacate judgment in the Loving case:

"This unmistakable policy of the legislature [is] founded, I think, on wisdom and the moral development of both races. . . . Almighty God created the races white, yellow, malay and red, and he placed them on separate continents. And but for the interference with his arrangement there would be no cause for such marriages. The fact that he separated the races shows that he did not intend for the races to mix." Transcript of Record at 16.

Amendment has traditionally required of state statutes drawn according to race.

The State argues that statements in the Thirty-ninth Congress about the time of the passage of the Fourteenth Amendment indicate that the Framers did not intend the Amendment to make unconstitutional state miscegenation laws. Many of the statements alluded to by the State concern the debates over the Freedman's Bureau Bill, which President Johnson vetoed, and the Civil Rights Act of 1866, 14 Stat 27, enacted over his veto. While these statements have some relevance to the intention of Congress in submitting the Fourteenth Amendment, it must be understood that they pertained to the passage of specific statutes and not to the broader, organic purpose of a constitutional amendment. As for the various statements directly concerning the Fourteenth Amendment, we have said in connection with a related problem, that although these historical sources "cast some light" they are not sufficient to resolve the problem; "[a]t best, they are inconclusive. The most avid proponents of the post-War Amendments undoubtedly intended them to remove all legal distinctions among 'all persons born or naturalized in the United States.' Their opponents, just as certainly, were antagonistic to both the letter and the spirit of the Amendments and wished them to have the most limited effect." . . .

There can be no question but that Virginia's miscegenation statutes rest solely upon distinctions drawn according to race. The statutes proscribe generally accepted conduct if engaged in by members of different races. Over the years, this Court has consistently repudiated "[d]istinctions between citizens solely because of their ancestry" as being "odious to a free people whose institutions are founded upon the doctrine of equality." Hirabayashi v United States, 320 US 81, 100 (1943). At the very least, the Equal Protection Clause demands that racial classifications, especially suspect in criminal statutes, be subjected to the "most rigid scrutiny," Korematsu v United States, 323 US 214, 216 (1944), and, if they are ever to be upheld, they must be shown to be necessary to the accomplishment of some permissible state objective, independent of the racial discrimination which it was the object of the Fourteenth Amendment to eliminate. Indeed, two members of this Court have already stated that they "cannot conceive of a valid legislative purpose . . . which makes the color of a person's skin the test of whether his conduct is a criminal offense." McLaughlin v Florida, . . . 379 US 184, 198 . . . (1964) (Stewart, J., joined by Douglas, J., concurring).

There is patently no legitimate overriding purpose independent of invidious racial discrimination which justifies this classification. The fact that Virginia prohibits only interracial marriages involving white persons demonstrates that the racial classifications must stand on their own justification, as measures designed to maintain White Supremacy. We have consistently denied the constitutionality of measures which restrict the rights of citizens on account of race. There can be no doubt that restricting the freedom to marry solely because of racial classifications violates the central meaning of the Equal Protection Clause. . . .

These statutes also deprive the Lovings of liberty without due process of law in violation of the Due Process Clause of the Fourteenth Amendment. The freedom to marry has long been recognized as one of the vital personal rights essential to the orderly pursuit of happiness by free men.

Marriage is one of the "basic civil rights of man," fundamental to our very existence and survival. Skinner v Oklahoma, 316 US 535, 541 (1942). See also Maynard v Hill, 125 US 190 (1888). To deny this fundamental freedom on so unsupportable a basis as the racial classifications embodied in these statutes, classifications so directly subversive of the principle of equality at the heart of the Fourteenth Amendment, is surely to deprive all the State's citizens of liberty without due process of law. The Fourteenth Amendment requires that the freedom of choice to marry not be restricted by invidious racial discriminations. Under our Constitution, the freedom to marry, or not marry, a person of another race resides with the individual and cannot be infringed by the State.

These convictions must be reversed.

Mr. Justice STEWART, concurring.

I have previously expressed the belief that "it is simply not possible for a state law to be valid under our Constitution which makes the criminality of an act depend upon the race of the actor." McLaughlin v Florida, 379 US 184 (concurring opinion). Because I adhere to that belief, I concur in the judgment of the Court.

NOTES

1. While there was no massive resistance to Loving v. Virginia, legislatures did not rush to repeal miscegenation measures, and from time to time a lower court vainly attempted to enforce them. See United States v. Brittain, 319 F. Supp. 1058 (N.D. Ala. 1970) (the court voided Alabama statutes relied on by a probate judge who refused a white army sergeant a license to marry a black woman); Davis v. Ashford, 2 Race Rel. L. Sur. 152 (S.D. Miss. 1970) (after some prodding by the court of appeals, a district court voided Mississippi miscegenation statutes barring the marriage of two interracial couples; a state court had promised a hearing, but the district court said "any delay in granting the licenses . . . would be unwarranted and indefensible . . ."); Davis v. Gately, 269 F. Supp. 996 (D. Del. 1967) (a three-judge federal court refused to apply the abstention doctrine and invalidated the Delaware miscegenation statute); Hook v. Blanton, 12 Race Rel. L. Rep. 2079 (Fla. 1967) (the Florida Supreme Court ordered a local court to grant a marriage license to a black man seeking to marry a white woman).

2. In Dick v. Reaves, 434 P.2d 295 (Okla. 1967), the court gave retroactive effect to Loving v. Virginia in settling entitlement to the estate of the surviving spouse of an interracial couple.

3. The voiding of miscegenation laws has undermined the validity of statutes and regulations barring interracial adoptions. See, e.g., In re Gomez, 424 S.W.2d 656 (Tex., 1967); Grossman, A Child of a Different Color: Race

as a Factor in Adoption and Custody Proceedings, 17 Buffalo L. Rev. 303 (1968).

QUESTIONS

1. In the Loving case the Supreme Court repeated its oft stated standard that classifications based on race are suspect, but not absolutely void, thereby keeping open the possibility that, under certain circumstances, a statute might be upheld as a "necessary" exercise of the state's police power, even though it had a discriminatory effect on a racial group. Marriages between close blood relatives are barred both because they are deemed abhorrent by society and because offspring of such unions may be defective. If the state, in defending its antimiscegenation statute, offered proof that offspring of mixed marriages are somehow deficient, would such evidence — perhaps combined with a showing of society's deep psychological aversion to interracial unions — meet the heavy burden for such racial classifications set by the Court? Would it be possible to develop legally cognizable arguments, based on clinical grounds, to sustain the validity of such a statute?

2. Critics of the psychological theories of Kardiner-Ovesey and Kovel think it overstates the case to suggest that sexual issues constitute the basic motive for racist attitudes and practices. While conceding that sexual conflict influences the racial attitudes of some people, the critics believe that it is far from the core of society's racial problem. Two writers point out:

> *If sexual conflicts originating in early infancy are at the root of racial attitudes, then eradication of racism must await the development of a new kind of human being that is somehow free of "Oedipal conflict." With such a perspective, the struggle against political and economic oppression may have some limited usefulness but cannot hope to achieve a fundamental change. Black liberation becomes contingent on emancipation from the id. (A. Thomas and S. Sillen, Racism and Psychiatry 106 (1972).)*

Can Cox's "economic status" thesis, supra page 268, be used to support critics of the psychological theories?

B. SEX AND RACE ISSUES SINCE LOVING V. VIRGINIA

NOTE: RACIAL PROBLEMS IN THE NEW SEXUAL FREEDOM

The Supreme Court decisions invalidating miscegenation laws removed the legal support from societal sanctions on mixed marriages and interracial romance. The decisions did not eliminate the continuing, though less rabid, opposition to such relationships.* Nor did the Court's decisions resolve the

* A 1970 Gallup Poll found that 56 percent of those surveyed nationwide disapproved of laws prohibiting marriage between whites and blacks. An earlier survey in 1965 showed

problems that blacks may experience in sexual relationships, both interracial and intraracial, which reflect the hangover harm caused by the miscegenation laws and by the economic, sociological and psychological pressures that led to the early enactment and centuries-long enforcement of these state laws. As the readings in this section will show, many writers believe that the societal scars inflicted on blacks and whites by miscegenation laws are permanent. Even assuming an obligation to undo the damage done, many will conclude that efforts to legislate interpersonal relations — marriage, divorce, abortion, birth control and adoption — create more problems than they solve. Others will respond that, at the least, courts must be cognizant of the residual difficulties of interracial marriage.

W. GRIER and P. COBBS, BLACK RAGE *91-100 (1968)*

[Two black psychiatrists provide a picture of the range of emotions, many of them unconscious, that may accompany interracial sexual unions in a society where such conduct has been subject to the strongest sanctions.]

When a black man and a white woman unite, one can assume that unnumbered racially connected issues will arise. For the black man, the white woman represents the *socially identified* female ideal and thus an intensely exciting object for his sexual possession. She has been identified as precisely the individual to whom access is barred by every social institution. The forbiddenness and desirableness of the white woman make her a natural recipient of his projected oedipal fantasies. He sees himself as finally possessing the maternal object under circumstances which reproduce the dangerous, defiant quality of oedipal interest as experienced by the child. He feels a sense of power at having acquired this highly valuable woman and a sense

---

national opinion closely divided on the issue. N.Y. Times, Sept. 10, 1970, at 22, c. 3. But a Harris Poll taken in 1970 revealed that 72 percent of white Americans would be opposed to marriage between a close friend or a relative and a black.

Are the 72 percent simply concerned about the social ostracism their friends and relatives might suffer? Or does their position accord with that taken a century ago by radical Republicans who, in the congressional debates on the Fourteenth Amendment, responded to Democratic fears that civil rights for blacks would lead to miscegenation? In the words of Illinois Congressman John F. Farnsworth:

"[The Democrat] refers to another bugbear with which to scare ignorant people, that of amalgamation. He recites the statutes of various States against the intermarriage of blacks and whites. Well, sir, while I regard that as altogether a matter of taste, and neither myself nor my friends require any restraining laws to prevent us from committing any error in that direction, still, if my friend from New Jersey and his friends are fearful that they will be betrayed into forming any connection of that sort, I will very cheerfully join with him in voting the restraining influence of a penal statute. I will vote to punish it by confinement in the State prison, or, if he pleases, by hanging — anything rather than they should be betrayed into or induced to form any such unnatural relations." Avins, Anti-Miscegenation Laws and the Fourteenth Amendment: The Original Intent, 52 Va. L. Rev. 1224, 1231 (1966).

of power that she finds him desirable and indeed that she finds him *more* desirable than a white lover. But at the same time he perceives her as white and as a representative of all the white oppressors who have made his life so wretched. In a sense then, she becomes the target for a hatred which far transcends the encounter between this man and this woman.

The sexual act itself carries aggressive overtones, and in the fantasy of all men there is a likening of male aggression in the sexual act to murderous aggression and a likening of the female partner to the victim of murder. The black man then has an opportunity to live out murderous fantasies of revenge. In possessing the white woman he sees himself as degrading her (a function of his own feelings of degradation), in this instance sharing the community's feeling that a white woman who submits to a black lover becomes as debased as he. In this way he may feel the gratification of turning the tables on his white oppressor and thus becoming the instrument through which a white person is degraded.

Finally, and perhaps most importantly, he sees himself as having vanquished the white man in the field of love and of having rendered him impotent and castrated, for the white woman, in fantasy at least, has embraced a white lover and then chosen a black one. While in every other area of life the black man may feel emasculated and humiliated by the white man, here he can reverse the roles and, because of the central importance of the sexual function in human affairs, may feel that the scales are almost balanced.

His fantasies find reinforcement in the keen delight his partner takes in his embrace. Her delight may rest on her own set of fantasies, but they both know that, whatever the causes may be, she finds more intense gratification from her black lover than she does from her white one.

Should the relationship progress to marriage, the problems increase exponentially, since in this culture marriage progressively downgrades the importance of the sexual act and lays increasing emphasis on the economic and social functioning of the partners. The black man married to a white woman is hounded by the knowledge that outside the bedroom his manhood is compromised. In fact, both the initial delight of his partner and his own intense satisfaction may pall under the certain knowledge that in the outside world he is an emasculated half-man. This places a grave strain on the relationship. The greatest stress seems to come, however, from the perception by the partners of the nature of the world in which they live, a perception which is sufficiently tied to reality to change in response to a change in that external world. The evidence for this is seen in the happy marriages between blacks and whites which flourish outside this country and which emphasize that the love relationship, given half a chance by society, can flourish between people of disparate origins.

The white woman who seeks a black lover finds him to be an intensely exciting partner because of his forbiddenness and because of the ease with which she can project onto him her own oedipal fantasies. Since black people are a minority, representing less than one-tenth of the population, they may not find the physical appearance of the Caucasian so exotic. This is not true for the Caucasian. A white woman finds her black lover sufficiently strange, and she is able to experience the excitement of having a forbidden sexual object as well as a lover who is so different-looking as to allow her to see him as a different kind of human being or even a subhuman animal. She is thus able to experience herself as different or subhuman along with her partner and in that way to participate in sexuality of an intensity and quality forbidden her as "herself," with all of the strictures and inhibitions that go along with that self-perception. Though she may view her black lover as a degraded object, she also views him as a sexual master.

As she submits to him, her own masochistic strivings feed her excitement at being possessed by such a being. These feelings contribute in a major way to her gratification. In his arms she merges with him and abandons her previous identity. In so doing she finds it easy to isolate the experience as a unique, intensely gratifying moment which has no relationship to the rest of her life. The emasculation of her black lover in the outside world makes it easier for her to feel separated and different from him and, in fact, safe from the invasion of her own forbidden fantasies into everyday life.

In fact, her attraction to him may rest in large measure specifically on these grounds. The relationship allows her uninhibited enjoyment of otherwise forbidden sexual impulses without experiencing any threat to her life generally. Should such a union eventuate in marriage, she would likely be concerned primarily with his ability to bring home the bacon, and if she found him lacking in this respect, her resulting bitterness might well cause her latent hostility toward all black people to emerge.

If, on the other hand, she experienced no disadvantages economically, her primary concern would surely focus on the social problems they met as a couple. The contempt she would encounter from the majority of white people would be a constant burden and the contempt she would feel when they saw her with her brown children would cause even greater pain. . . .

The relationship which has the longest history and the most complex psychological structure is the relationship between the white man and the black woman. From the very first introduction of black slaves into America, black women have been used sexually by their white owners. In contrast to the male slaves they had a threefold use — their labor was economically valuable, their bodies had a marketable value as sexual objects, and their potential as breeders of additional slaves was also a source of wealth to their owners.

Even now in many areas a black woman has no protection from the sexual appetites of white men. In the raw circumstance of power and the imposition of the will of the powerful on the weak, the most significant aspect of the woman's position is her helplessness against sexual assault. She cannot protect herself against sexual use by a powerful male. Her only protection lies in binding herself sexually to a powerful man who can in turn protect her from other men. It would seem that both the erotic component of a woman's masochism and her tendency to gain narcissistic gratification from being chosen by a powerful man make it easy for her to yield herself to a powerful man and to gain special gratification out of such submission. In addition, a woman need feel no qualms of conscience if she is taken sexually against her will and must submit to the sexual act under pain of violence. Under such circumstances her own conscience, moral code, and inhibitions stand in suspension.

All these factors are important in the manner in which a black woman relates herself to a white lover. However weak in fact he may be, however ineffective and poor, he is potentially more powerful than any black lover. He is a part of and a representative of the powerful white majority — a representative of the wealth and prestige accrued in the United States and throughout the Western world over the past two thousand years.

In a historical sense, she, on the other hand, stands in the position of all the black people who have been exploited and dominated by white men since the beginning of recorded time. In a historical sense and in a very real contemporary sense, she faces a powerful lover. The prospect of sexually submitting to him evokes excitement in her. In addition to the explicit pleasure involved in masochistic submission, she gains some of the strength and power of the white man. . . .

This type of passive submission, strongly colored by eroticism, historically characterized the relationship between black women and white men. It is the converse of the relationship between black men and white women. The black man is highly excited by possessing the valuable ideal female and the black woman is intensely aroused at being subdued and possessed by the powerful white man. His power, desirability, and forbiddenness evoke her own oedipal fantasies and she finds herself particularly gratified that this powerful man chooses her in preference to a white woman.

In her relationship with a white man, the black woman can partake of his power and masculinity and can for once free herself of her degraded self-perception. In his embrace she is whole again and can experience the sexual act as simply a woman submitting to a desirable man. Her own thwarted narcissistic strivings can for once find embodiment in a lover whose possibilities for living them out are apparently limitless — an experience she cannot have with a black lover.

To the extent that she sees her own blackness as ugly and repellent, her possession of a white lover and her identification with him allow her to view herself as white and therefore beautiful. The problem arises, however, when she must leave his bed and face the real world again. However much her white lover protests his devotion to her, she is beset with feelings of self-depreciation, depression, and futility. She sees herself as having been used and debased for the satisfaction of a powerful man who only took advantage of her weakness and susceptibility. She perceives herself as having striven for something beyond her, and her remorse is her "punishment" for "reaching above her station." Should she return to a black lover, she might well feel herself all the more degraded and oppressed.

If her relationship with the white man leads to marriage, the prospect is that as the bloom of romance fades she will find herself dreading that he will abandon her. Past experiences make her feel truly worthless and undesirable. It is only in his arms that she feels a whole woman, sexually desirable to men. Away from him she is again potentially the ugly, despised black woman. She is convinced that he has a false perception of her which makes her seem beautiful and desirable to him, and she dreads the moment when he sees her as she sees herself and, in revulsion, thrusts her away from him. Her position is a wretched one.

On the other side of the coin, the white man, by taking to himself a black woman, acts in defiance of all socially accepted norms. Our society allows a white man to surreptitiously experiment with black women sexually but never to take one into a love relationship. As a prostitute or as a casual mistress, a black woman can be a meaningless sexual toy and involvement with her need have no profound effect on his life. Psychologically, he can look upon her as a debased human animal who finds pleasure in a sexual life no decent woman would tolerate. The uninhibited pleasures he shares with her might serve to further dichotomize his emotional life, and his relationship with his white wife might suffer. But beyond this there need be no grave disruption of his functioning.

If, on the other hand, the black woman assumes some emotional importance for him, his problems are compounded. It is likely that he would enter into a relationship only in response to feelings of defiance toward the social order generally, and perhaps his family or parents specifically. Under these circumstances the black woman serves a *specific* psychological purpose for him because of her general unacceptability as a mate.

Whatever gratification the two of them might share in their union, her role as evidence of his defiance and her functioning as a social curiosity will clearly limit the richness of their relationship and dull their satisfaction. In any event, in the United States, the psychological truth is that when a white man chooses a black woman, both in his own eyes and in the eyes of his confreres, he has chosen a depreciated sexual object rather than a highly valued one. This factor is obviously of greater social importance than the desirability of the black woman as an exotic and forbidden representative of his inner desires. Such fantasies and strivings allow him to act out unconscious wishes which intensify his pleasure. The social value set on each of the partners reverses their roles, making him the highly valued object whom the woman has been fortunate enough to obtain.

His own narcissism is enhanced thereby and he finds a special gratification in their relationship. He feels constantly inferior to black men, however, feeling that sexually he is less satisfying as a partner than *any* black man. He is the victim of the stereotype which played such an important part in his choosing a black woman in the first place. . . .

NOTE: BLACK OPPOSITION TO INTERRACIAL LOVE AND MARRIAGE

In recent years, periodicals and books aimed at black readers have published a number of articles reflecting the contemporary debate in the black community as to whether interracial romance and marriage, now that it is legal, will further or retard the development of their ethnic pride and solidarity. Will such marriages destroy the militance of the black partners and render them "suspect" on racial issues? Can normal romantic interest between blacks and whites exist in a racist society, or are interracial relationships a reflection of societally induced neurosis, as described in the Grier-Cobbs Black Rage excerpt?

While generalizations are difficult, black men tend to be more tolerant than black women of a mixed couple (particularly when a black male and white female). They see the availability of white women as a civil rights gain, and discount the argument that such romances or marriages will lessen black militancy by pointing to militant black leaders such as Frederick Douglass, Walter White and James Farmer, who married white women. They view as a suppression of their manhood such demands as those made by black women that they voluntarily place white women off limits. Finally, some black men feel that interracial romance and marriage represent one hope for lessening the racial separation and conflicts in this society, which are based on ignorance and the adherence to racial myth.

These arguments cover a broad range of thinking, and only a minority of black men subscribe to all of these views. Black women, on the other hand, are much more uniform in their opposition to interracial relationships, particularly interracial marriage. Their arguments are both pragmatic and philosophical. On the practical side, they point to statistics which show that there are almost a million more black females than black males in the United States, and that the statistical chances for black women to form strong black relationships should not be further decreased by black males' choosing white mates.* Indeed, because racial discrimination is more of a burden to males

* This argument is supported by a study of population tables indicating that "[If] no adjustment is made for age, at least 1,069,694 of the 11,885,595 black females in the population of the United States would have been without available, monogamous mates." In the twenty-five to thirty-four-year-old age group, there are only 84.3 black men for every 100 black women. The study suggests that these statistics contribute to the bitterness of black women, who fear that the shortage of black men will prevent them from conforming to traditional patterns of sex, marriage and family living. Jackson, But Where Are the Men? in 3 Black Scholar 30 (1971).

The concern of black women that the most eligible black men are increasingly marrying white women is borne out by census figures. In 1960 there were, according to a 1966 Census Bureau bulletin on marital status, 25,496 black males married to white females, and 25,913 white males married to black females. See Carter, Racial-Caste Hypogamy: A Sociological Myth? 29 Phylon 347 (1968). But the 1970 census showed a marked in-than to females, the educated and accomplished black woman finds that she has even less chance of finding black men at her socioeconomic level than does her less talented sister. The situation, which is changing now, was for years most noticeable at predominantly black colleges, where a majority of students were women, outnumbering the men by two- or three-to-one ratios at many schools.

When black women are reminded that the decision in Loving v. Virginia also applies to them, and that black women should consider partnerships with white men, they respond that most white males think of black women as sexual objects, and that even when attracted to them as individuals, few white men are willing to jeopardize their social and professional position by marrying a woman who does not have status in the general society. Black women add that when a white man marries a black woman she is usually a highly educated and accomplished individual. As an example, they point out the number of successful black women movie stars and entertainers who have white husbands. Moreover, they say, honest feeling for a white man is difficult because they can't forget the centuries of white exploitation of black women. Meriwether, Black Man, Do You Love Me? Essence 15, 64 (May 1970).

On the philosophical side, one black woman, a free-lance writer, summed up the position in a debate on the subject published in a national magazine:

> I . . . think that people who discuss the question of a black nation, of black people getting themselves together, can't even begin . . . if black men can't get along with black women and black women can't get along with black men. The whole black outlook is a fallacy if the reality is that black men are increasingly turning to white women. In that case, we should stop all these abstract discussions about black identity. If we can't deal with each other as individuals, then it's ridiculous for us to try dealing with each other collectively. (Mehlinger, Grant, Davis, A Sister Debates Brother on that Black Man–White Woman Thing, Ebony 130-133 (Aug. 1970).)

For Miss Gant and thousands of black women who share her views, practical and philosophical opposition to interracial romance and marriage merge. She says:

> I would find it impossible to fight for my rights as a black person and at the same time integrate into white society. To me, it would be schizophrenic to be talking

---

crease — to 41,233 — in black man–white woman marriages, and a decrease — to 23,566 — in the number of white man–black woman marriages.

During the decade of the 1960s, there were more than twice as many marriages of black men and white women as those of white men and black women. As with previous surveys, the new census data reveals that the black man who marries a white woman tends to have a higher level of income than the average black male. Chapman, Marriage and Race, Washington Post, Feb. 14, 1973 at F1, col. 8.

about black power, black control of our resources and then turn around and go to my white home in the suburbs because I've married this white doctor. I don't see how I could continue to work for black people. But maybe we aren't serious about what we are saying. Maybe most black people want to remain a part of white society. If this is true, then we need to reassess our entire position.

There is a strong emotional undercurrent to much of the opposition by black women to interracial relationships. They see the black man's choice of a white woman as a rejection of them. They resent the charges hurled at them by some black men that they are threatening, castrating, too independent, impatient, contemptuous, sexually inhibited and unimaginative, and lacking in the subtle art of getting and keeping a man. Reena, a black woman character in a recent story, repeated the above list of reasons that black men put forward for rejecting black women.

"They condemn us," Reena said softly but with anger, "without taking history into account. We are still, most of us, the Black women who had to be almost frighteningly strong in order for us all to survive. For, after all, she [the black woman] was the one whom they left (and I don't hold this against them; I understand) with the children to raise, who had to make it somehow or other. And we are still, so many of us, living that history.

"You would think that they would understand this, but few do. So it's up to us. We have got to understand them and save them for ourselves. How? By being, on one hand, persons in our own right and, on the other, the woman and the wife. . . ." (P. Marshall, "Reena," 32-33 in The Black Woman (T. Cade ed., 1970).)

Achieving this dual status will be difficult enough, but, as one interviewee is reported to have stated:

Probably the most painful part of being a black woman . . . is the rape of the short male supply by white women. Black women already sense a shortage of black men, and it hurts to have to share them with white women (who get a whack at men from both races and whose motives are generally not thought to be trustworthy or commendable). What is worse, black women take it as a personal insult, a denunciation of their own black beauty. . . . Invariably, black women feel, the union is rooted in pathology and/or white subterfuge. Either the white woman is relieving guilt or the black man is compensating for his historical rejection ("lynched for touching white women") and chasing after forbidden fruit. (Nathan and Julia Hare, Black Women 1970, Trans-Action 65, 67 (Nov.-Dec. 1970).)

Even this cursory summary should make it clear that the complex and emotionally charged problem of interracial romance or marriage is one that black people view quite seriously. Blacks with militant images to protect go to all lengths to avoid the charge often made by bitter black women that they "blow black by day, and sleep white at night." Thus, aspirants for leadership positions in the black community often do not bring white spouses or girlfriends to black public meetings or social gatherings. In short, credibility as a black leader can be seriously compromised by an open — albeit legal — mixed relationship, because of any one of the concerns discussed here. The origin of these concerns dates back to the first miscegenation statute; the stress of these concerns is so severe that, at least in the short run, the invalidation of miscegenation laws, while a clear indication of individual rights, serves to exacerbate rather than relieve racial antipathy and distrust in the black community.

QUESTIONS

1. Assuming the validity of the Grier-Cobbs thesis regarding the psychological attractions and problems of interracial sex, is it likely that militant black women will accept the Cox view that interracial romance and marriage should be welcomed by blacks, as a means of gaining status and power?

2. Is it possible that a court might take sufficient notice of the conflict in the black community on this issue to create exceptions to the principle of Loving v. Virginia, if a class representative of the community asserted that such a result would contribute to the community's efforts to strengthen black pride and unity?

3. Would the possibility of a decision favoring the black group be aided or hindered because such an outcome would accord with the continuing opposition of a majority of whites to interracial marriage and romance for relatives and close friends?

Racism Hypo 3
JONES *v.* ALL SOUL COMMUNITY CENTER

After experiencing years of frustration in efforts to obtain a recreation and cultural center for teenagers in the black community, black parents, working under the sponsorship of the All Soul Interdenominational Church, obtained funds from government agencies to establish the All Soul Community Center.

The center is directed by a board elected in the black community, and is intended to provide black youth with a place to play, meet and enjoy sports and entertainment. In addition, the center seeks to instill pride in race and self through specialized programs in black history and culture. The "black pride" theme is present in all aspects of the center's program. Indeed, a major center goal is to neutralize the "brainwashing" effect on black youth of themes — constantly reinforced by the media — that Caucasians are the standard for physical attractiveness, desirability, etc. To this end, the center's motto, "Black Is Beautiful," is inculcated in all center activities. The center is not limited to blacks, but its location in the heart of an all-black area results in whites' attending only occasionally for special events.

The All Soul Center operated smoothly until the board unanimously decided to discharge the center's director, W. P. Jones, who, despite repeated warnings from the board, regularly escorted a young white woman to center social functions. The board acted after receiving several complaints from parents concerning Jones's conduct. There were no allegations that Jones's relationship with the woman was in itself immoral, but parents felt that it presented the wrong image to young impressionable black people. Thus, while Jones was an otherwise satisfactory director, the board concluded that his behavior was detrimental to the center's effort to counteract society's immemorial brainwashing of blacks about sex and white women.

Jones sought and was given an open hearing before the center's board and the All Soul Community Church. In addition to asserting that the center's action violated his constitutional rights, as set forth in Supreme Court decisions voiding antimiscegenation statutes, Jones maintained that his social life did not subvert but rather reinforced center goals, by illustrating that black men need no longer fear to choose female companions without regard to race. A minority of the All Soul Community Church membership supported Jones in this position, but the great majority voted with the board to affirm his dismissal.

In dismissing Jones, the board states: "Jones has an absolute right to choose white women as social companions, but when he does, he surrenders any right to a leadership position in a black institution devoted to developing pride in blackness. Interracial dating and marriage are incompatible with the concept of black identity."

Jones has filed suit in federal court for reinstatement, or in the alternative, full payment on his two-year contract. He asserts that his dismissal constituted illegal state action in that the center is operated with government funds.

Law Firm A will represent W. P. Jones in the federal court action.

Law Firm B will represent the Community Center.

At a pretrial conference, the following stipulations have been agreed to by the parties:

— The All Soul Community Center is a public facility for state action purposes.

— The hearing provided by the All Soul Community Center Board met all due process requirements.

Attorneys for Jones conceded that cases in several civil rights areas (preferential hiring, correcting racial imbalance in public schools, "freezing" voter registration rules, etc.) have approved distinctions based on race even though such distinctions benefit blacks at the expense of whites, but they refused to agree that these cases are applicable to this litigation.

7. THE RIGHT TO PROTEST

A. BACKGROUND OF BLACK PROTEST

ADDITIONAL STATEMENT OF JUDGE HIGGINBOTHAM

Commission Statement on Civil Disobedience, Natl. Comm'n on the Causes and Prevention of Violence 16 (Dec. 1969)

Recent advances in the field of civil rights have not come about and could never have come about solely through judicial tests made "by one individual" while all others in the silent black majority waited for the ultimate constitutional determination.

Rather, the major impetus for the Civil Rights Acts of 1957, 1960, 1964 and 1965, which promised more equal access to the opportunities of our society, resulted from the determination, the spirit and the nonviolent commitment of the many who continually challenge the constitutionality of racial discrimination and awakened the national conscience.

Federal District Judge A. Leon Higginbotham served as a member of the National Commission on the Causes and Prevention of Violence. In this quotation he is speaking as one of the minority in a 7-6 decision by the commission to condemn even nonviolent massive civil disobedience because it could lead to anarchy. The majority suggest that the constitutionality of a law can be effectively challenged in a test case brought by one individual or a small group. "While the judicial test is in progress," the majority urged, "all other dissenters should abide by the law involved until it is declared unconstitutional."

NOTES

1. While the majority of the President's Commission on the Causes and Prevention of Violence was not ready, even in 1969, to accept Judge Higginbotham's assessment of the limitations of litigation as an effective challenge to racial discrimination, thousands of blacks had reached Higginbotham's conclusion that the long awaited promise of Brown v. Board of Education would not be self-executing.

2. The famous Montgomery bus boycott, which brought Dr. Martin Luther King, Jr. to national prominence, provided a definitive model for combining

a committed community with effective litigation. According to Dr. King, the months of walking and the constant harassment of local officials had taken their toll and the boycott was about to collapse. M. King, Stride Toward Freedom 151-153, 157-160 (1958). But then the Supreme Court affirmed a three-judge court order that voided the state and local laws requiring segregation on Montgomery's motor buses. Browder v. Gayle, 142 F. Supp. 707 (N.D. Ala. 1956), *aff'd per curiam,* 352 U.S. 903 (1956).

3. The Montgomery saga was actually presaged by efforts from 1870 to 1902 in Savannah, Georgia, where blacks used economic pressure to forestall segregation on streetcars for thirty years. A. Meier and E. Rudwick, II, The Making of Black America 14 (1969). In 1872, after several complaints and threats of lawsuits by blacks, the streetcar company abandoned its three-year-old policy of providing separate horsecars for blacks. The desegregation policy was rescinded, however, when whites reacted violently. On one night in July 1872, eleven whites and twenty blacks were injured when shooting broke out along the railway lines. Blacks then refused to patronize the line, and according to one writer, "a Negro was a curiosity in a street car." Two months later, the company again dropped its segregation policy, citing the "pecuniary loss" that segregation entailed, and not admitting to its white public the effectiveness of the boycott instituted by Savannah's black people. The streetcars remained integrated until 1906.

In 1899 a Savannah suburb voted to segregate a line running to a summer resort area favored by Negroes. The blacks responded with a boycott of the line, and the Jim Crow rule was rescinded within two months. Id. at 16-17. By 1902, a new wave of Jim Crow laws was being passed throughout the South. However, an attempt to enact a new streetcar segregation ordinance in Savannah was not only defeated, but was opposed by much of the white community, anxious to maintain racial peace and avoid the disruptions of a boycott. A similar law was enacted four years later, nonetheless, and while the blacks mounted an impressive boycott, it was to no avail. There were no courts to turn to in 1906. Id. at 17-18. Black protests and demonstrations led to the elimination of streetcar segregation in New Orleans, Richmond and Charleston in 1867, and in Louisville in 1870-1871.

BOYNTON v. VIRGINIA, 364 U.S. 454, 81 S. Ct. 182, 5 L. Ed. 2d 206 (1960). The Supreme Court reversed a black law student's trespass conviction for refusing to leave the white section of a restaurant operated by a leasee in the Richmond, Virginia Trailways Bus Terminal.

The case had seemed a hard one to win for the NAACP lawyers who handled it. The record was slim; Boynton had been arrested under the state's trespass statute, not a segregation measure; and whatever his right to ride an interstate bus on a desegregated basis, he was arrested in a privately operated restaurant which merely leased the premises from Trailways. Indeed, as two justices pointed out in dissent, Boynton's attorneys had at no point challenged the trespass conviction as in violation of the Interstate Commerce Act.

But the majority, evidencing the sympathy for blacks convicted in nonviolent efforts to use public facilities on a nonsegregated basis that was to prevail for five years, found little difficulty in deciding the case under §316 (d), the nondiscrimination clause of Part II of the Interstate Commerce Act, dealing with motor carriers. Justice Black, speaking for the majority, wrote:

. . . we have no doubt that the reasoning underlying the Mitchell and Henderson cases would compel the same decision as to the unlawfulness of discrimination in transportation services against interstate passengers in terminals and terminal restaurants owned or operated or controlled by interstate carriers.

Respondent correctly points out, however, that, whatever may be the facts, the evidence in this record does not show that the bus company owns or actively operates or directly controls the bus terminal or the restaurant in it. But the fact that §203(a)(19) says that the protections of the motor carrier provisions of the Act extend to "include" facilities so operated or controlled by no means should be interpreted to exempt motor carriers from their statutory duty under §216(d) not to discriminate should they choose to provide their interstate passengers with services that are an integral part of transportation through the use of facilities they neither own, control nor operate. The protections afforded by the Act against discriminatory transportation services are not so narrowly limited. We have held that a railroad cannot escape its statutory duty to treat its shippers alike either by use of facilities it does not own or by contractual arrangement with the owner of those facilities. And so here, without regard to contracts, if the bus carrier has volunteered to make terminal and restaurant facilities and services available to its interstate passengers as a regular part of their transportation, and the terminal restaurant have acquiesced and cooperated in this undertaking, the terminal and restaurant must perform these services without discriminations prohibited by the Act. In the performance of these services under such conditions the terminal and restaurant stand in the place of the bus company in the performance of its transportation obligations. Although the courts below made no findings of fact, we think the evidence in this case shows such a relationship and situation here. (364 U.S. at 459-461.)†

Finally, in an effort to narrow the scope of the decision, Justice Black concluded the majority opinion with the caveat:

Because of some of the arguments made here it is necessary to say a word about what we are not deciding. We are not holding that every time a bus stops at a wholly independent roadside restaurant the Interstate Commerce Act requires that restaurant services be supplied in harmony with the provisions of that Act. We decide only this case, on its facts, where circumstances show that the terminal

† The Boynton decision marked the end of a long series of efforts to utilize the Interstate Commerce Commission to specifically prohibit all racial segregation on interstate carriers. Later that year, the ICC issued an order (49 C.F.R. §180(a)) that specifically prohibited motor carriers from in any way utilizing terminal facilities that segregate on the basis of race, color, creed or national origin. The cases and readings are found in T. Emerson, D. Haber, N. Dorsen, II Political and Civil Rights in the United States 1708-1715 (student ed. 1967). See also discussion supra pages 215-216.

and restaurant operate as an integral part of the bus carrier's transportation service for interstate passengers. Under such circumstances, an interstate passenger need not inquire into documents of title or contractual arrangements in order to determine whether he has a right to be served without discrimination. (364 U.S. at 463-464.)

QUESTIONS

Was it necessary to exclude the wholly independent roadside restaurant from the provisions of the Interstate Commerce Act, at least at that point when the proprietor opened his doors to a whole busload of passengers? Is Justice Black implying that Congress lacked the power to extend coverage under the Interstate Commerce Act to the roadside restaurant, or stating that Congress had not done so? What rights of the private proprietor was the Court seeking to protect? Did the caveat expose blacks to discrimination at just those isolated stops where it would not be possible for blacks to find unsegregated food service?

NOTE: THE BOYNTON CASE AND THE "FREEDOM RIDES"

The Boynton decision served as a painful reminder to blacks that long before the 1954 Brown decision, the Interstate Commerce Act had been used to invalidate racial segregation in interstate carriers and facilities, in rulings that were simply ignored throughout the South. Civil rights groups determined that the combined enforcement of segregation in interstate travel must be exposed. Organized first by the Congress of Racial Equality (CORE), and continued later by the Student Nonviolent Coordinating Committee (SNCC), racially mixed groups rode interstate buses into the South. In a repetition of the violence that blacks had experienced when they integrated streetcars in Savannah eighty-nine years before, the freedom riders were attacked and beaten. Police harassed and arrested the protesters instead of providing them protection. Then, as later, white protesters were singled out for violent attacks by police and spectators. Finally, the federal government took action to end violence over the issue in United States v. United States Klans, Knights of the Ku Klux Klan, Inc., 194 F. Supp. 897 (N.D. Ala. 1961).

B. THE SIT-INS AND MARCHES

As has been shown, neither is it a compliment to blacks nor is it accurate to suggest that the black protest movement began in the 1960s. The slave revolts and the later willingness of blacks to defend their communities against invading whites, as well as to initiate boycotts and demonstrations, provide sufficient testimony on this score. But a number of factors, certainly including the rising expectations resulting from the Brown decision and the Montgomery boycott, provided prideful young black college students with the impetus to begin a movement that greatly altered the law of race in America.

WASKOW, FROM RACE RIOT TO SIT-IN, 1919 AND THE 1960's *226-228 (1967)*

[The author traces the beginnings of what he calls "creative disorder" to 1919 and a speech by NAACP Field Secretary James Weldon Johnson, in which he suggested that "the negroes in a city like Jacksonville, Florida, could send a committee representing 10,000 negroes to the city government and tell them that if they did not receive protection [against white violence] they would not cook or work in any way. . . . Such a course," Johnson emphasized, "would be a method more effective than the shotgun." Waskow at 203.]

The new techniques of the sit-in generation brought to fruition James Weldon Johnson's bare hint of "creative disorder" . . . .

The first act of that generation was the invention of the sit-in on February 1, 1960, in Greensboro, North Carolina. Four Negro college freshmen sat down at a lunch counter where Negroes had never been served, refused to leave, although they were denied service, and attracted both shouted curses and whispered support from increasing numbers of white bystanders. Their act at once reverberated in their own college, and within six weeks across the South. . . .

Within months the original sit-in notion had been generalized to wade-ins at segregated beaches, read-ins at segregated libraries, kneel-ins at segregated churches, walk-ins at segregated theaters and amusement parks. In a number of cases, the initial shock and anger of the white community was translated into mob attacks, police brutality, and jail sentences. . . .

As the sit-in movement developed, many of its members rejected any moral or religious commitment to nonviolence in the Gandhian sense, and adopted instead a stance in which the choice not to use violence was based on tactical political considerations. Even on this basis, the decision to reject violence was almost universally followed.

But even in the absence of violence, the sit-in and all its permutations were in many places taken to be clear cases of criminal trespass. Not everywhere: for by September 1961, restaurants in 108 southern or border cities had ended racial segregation as a result of the sit-ins. But there were pockets of resistance (especially, though not exclusively, in the Deep South) where the sit-ins were regarded as a major challenge to what might be called the "territorial" sense of private property, the sense that along with ownership goes a defensible "boundary."

GREENBERG, THE SUPREME COURT, CIVIL RIGHTS, AND CIVIL DISSONANCE, 77 Yale L.J. 1520, 1528 (1968).

Between 1961 and 1965 the Court passed on the merits of more than 30 sit-in prosecutions. . . . The protestors won virtually all of their cases in the Supreme Court. . . . [T]he Court's constant involvement can be understood as reflecting concern that a nonviolent movement, struggling toward the same goals that the

Court itself had urged more or less abstractly on the nation in the early school desegregation cases, should not be worn down by petty prosecutions.

Compare Jack Greenberg's comments with those of Lewis Steel supra page 94. Read the summaries of judicial actions that follow and consider which view seems more accurate. If Greenberg's, what happened to the Court's support after 1965? (See Steel comment infra page 394.) If Steel's, why did the Court become involved at all? Recall the discussion on this subject in Chapter Three, page 108.

C. "CREATIVE DISORDER" AND THE COURTS

1. The Supreme Court

Most of the sit-in cases were decided on narrow Fourteenth Amendment grounds, while the Court avoided questions as to both the scope of First Amendment rights, and the potential applicability of Shelley v. Kraemer, at page 609, infra. Indeed, the parameters of the "state action" concept were not significantly broadened during the sit-in period. In Burton v. Wilmington Parking Authority, 365 U.S. 715, 81 S. Ct. 856, 6 L. Ed. 2d 45 (1961), a restaurant's refusal to serve a black person was held to be state action in violation of the Fourteenth Amendment, because of the intertwined property and financial interests of the state authority and its lessee, the privately owned restaurant. But the Court warned that its decision was not to be construed as a formula for finding "state action" in every situation involving a state leasing agreement. Each case would have to be determined on its peculiar facts or circumstances.

The narrow grounds of decision in these cases provided a basis for withdrawing the judicial support extended to the protesters. Warnings that such a withdrawal would occur were easily apparent in the opinions — and finally in the decisions themselves, as the following chronological summary should make clear.

1961-1962

GARNER v. LOUISIANA, BRISCOE v. LOUISIANA, HOSTON v. LOUISIANA, 368 U.S. 157, 82 S. Ct. 248, 7 L. Ed. 2d 207 (1961). Sixteen blacks were convicted of disturbing the peace after refusing requests by lunch counter proprietors to move from seats reserved for whites. The Supreme Court reversed their \$100 fines and thirty-day jail terms on the ground that there was no evidence to sustain their breach of peace convictions. The Court emphasized that the protesters' conduct was orderly and that their mere presence could not constitute a valid disturbance. 368 U.S. at 174.

Moreover, the Court held that the record was devoid of any indication that the trial judge had taken judicial notice that the protesters' presence might lead to a disturbance which would justify police action. The decision was unanimous, but Justice Harlan expressed the view that the protesters were obviously engaged in a protest with all the rights and limitations that pertain generally to free speech. He expressed doubts that the demonstrations, as such, could be conducted on private property over the objections of the owner, and stated that reversal was justified only by the uncertainty of the record as to whether the protesters had, in fact, been asked to leave, and by the vagueness and uncertainty of the "breach of peace" provision as applied in the cases. 368 U.S. at 199.

Only Justice Douglas, in a separate concurrence, tried to reach the racial issue by asserting that the arrests were unconstitutional state action in that they were in response to the coercive state custom of segregation. Douglas contended that the restaurants licensed by the state had become property affected with a public interest and hence could not segregate.

Douglas's effort to establish that defendants had a constitutional right to be where they were, and to avoid the limits on state action created in the Civil Rights Cases, 109 U.S. 3, 3 S. Ct. 18, 27 L. Ed. 835 (1883), failed to win any support from the other justices.

TAYLOR v. LOUISIANA, 370 U.S. 154, 82 S. Ct. 1188, 8 L. Ed. 2d 395 (1962). Again using the "utter absence of evidence" rationale of Garner v. Louisiana, the Court reversed breach of peace convictions of blacks arrested for a sit-in in a bus terminal waiting room.

1963

PETERSON v. CITY OF GREENVILLE, 373 U.S. 244, 83 S. Ct. 1119, 10 L. Ed. 2d 323 (1963); LOMBARD v. LOUISIANA, 373 U.S. 267, 83 S. Ct. 1122, 10 L. Ed. 2d 338 (1963); GOBER v. CITY OF BIRMINGHAM, 373 U.S. 374, 83 S. Ct. 1311, 10 L. Ed. 2d 419 (1963); AVENT v. NORTH CAROLINA, 373 U.S. 375, 83 S. Ct. 1311, 10 L. Ed. 2d 420 (1963). In another set of sit-in cases, the Court again reversed all convictions. Ignoring petitioners' arguments that they were engaged in constitutionally protected free speech, and that the Fourteenth Amendment prohibited their prosecution for violating segregation rules of even managers of public facilities, the Supreme Court reversed the trespass convictions on the ground that the segregation complained of was not "private discrimination," but was mandated by local ordinances. Actually, while there were such ordinances in Peterson and Gober, in the Durham Case (Avent) the ordinance was not in the record. The case, however, was sent back to the Supreme Court in North Carolina for reconsideration in light of the Peterson and Gober decisions. In Lombard, there was no statute or ordinance mandating segregation, but the Court held that the rule in Peterson governed because of highly publicized statements of local officials that desegregation and sit-ins would not be permitted. The Court found that "state action" may include action by the executive branch.

Referring to the Peterson case, the Court subsequently vacated judgments of conviction in five demonstration cases.*

During the same year, the Court reversed cases involving hundreds of convictions growing out of marches and similar demonstrations against segregation. The principal one of these was Edwards v. South Carolina, 372 U.S. 229, 83 S. Ct. 680, 9 L. Ed. 2d 697 (1963). College students were arrested for breach of the peace after a peaceful assembly and parade on statehouse grounds. The Court found the statute so general and vague that it permitted invalid interference with First Amendment rights. Similar results were reached in Fields v. South Carolina, 375 U.S. 44, 84 S. Ct. 149, 11 L. Ed. 2d 107 (1963), and Henry v. Rock Hill, 376 U.S. 776, 84 S. Ct. 1042, 11 L. Ed. 2d 38. See also Wright v. Georgia, 373 U.S. 284, 83 S. Ct. 1240, 10 L. Ed. 2d 349 (1963).

1964

GRIFFIN v. MARYLAND, 378 U.S. 130, 84 S. Ct. 1770, 12 L. Ed. 2d 754 (1964); BARR v. CITY OF COLUMBIA, 378 U.S. 146, 84 S. Ct. 1734, 12 L. Ed. 2d 766 (1964); BOUIE v. CITY OF COLUMBIA, 378 U.S. 347, 84 S. Ct. 1697, 12 L. Ed. 2d 894 (1964); ROBINSON v. FLORIDA, 378 U.S. 153, 84 S. Ct. 1693, 12 L. Ed. 2d 771 (1964). In Griffin, involving the arrest for trespass of Negroes who had entered a private amusement park, convictions were reversed because the arrests were effected by a park employee, who was also a deputy sheriff. The Court held that participation in the attempted exclusion, by an individual vested with state authority, constituted sufficient state action to invalidate the conviction.

In Barr, the Court found no evidence to sustain convictions for breach of the peace; the record showed that the demonstrators had been peaceful, and thus conviction denied them due process of law.

In Bouie, it was held that a South Carolina trespass statute had been applied to the demonstrators in violation of the Fourteenth Amendment, because under prior South Carolina decisions the law covered only initial entry

* Randolph v. Virginia, 374 U.S. 97, 83 S. Ct. 1685, 10 L. Ed. 1025 (1963); Henry v. Virginia, 374 U.S. 98, 83 S. Ct. 1685, 10 L. Ed. 1025 (1963); Thompson v. Virginia, 374 U.S. 99, 83 S. Ct. 1686, 10 L. Ed. 1025 (1963); Wood v. Virginia, 374 U.S. 100, 83 S. Ct. 1686, 10 L. Ed. 1025 (1963); Daniels v. Virginia, 374 U.S. 500, 83 S. Ct. 1877, 10 L. Ed. 2d 1045 (1963).

Paradoxically, many very serious protesters — including those in Garner v. Louisiana, supra, Taylor v. Louisiana, supra, Barr v. Columbia, infra, and Shuttlesworth v. Birmingham, 382 U.S. 87, 86 S. Ct. 211, 15 L. Ed. 2d 176 (1965) — had their convictions reversed in partial reliance on what civil rights lawyers often referred to as the "Shufflin' Sam Thompson" case. Thompson had been convicted of loitering and disorderly conduct for "patting and shuffling his feet" to the music from a cafe jukebox, while he was waiting for a bus. The Court reversed for lack of evidence to support the conviction. Thompson v. City of Louisville, 362 U.S. 199, 80 S. Ct. 624, 4 L. Ed. 2d 654 (1960). See 80 A.L.R.2d 1355 (1961).

on premises after notice to stay off, and did not cover a refusal to leave after having come on with permission. The convictions were thus deemed unconstitutional because they were based on grounds which differed from prior interpretations of the law, and thus had provided the defendants with no fair warning of what conduct was prohibited.

Finally, in Robinson the Court construed state board of health regulations requiring segregated toilets as sufficient coercion to permit the conclusion, as in Peterson, Gober and Lombard, that the owner's segregation policy resulted from a state policy encouraging segregation. Several other cases were vacated for reconsideration in the light of these decisions. Green v. Virginia, 378 U.S. 550, 84 S. Ct. 1910, 12 L. Ed. 2d 1035 (1960); Harris v. Virginia, 378 U.S. 552, 84 S. Ct. 1923, 12 L. Ed. 2d 1038 (1964); Williams v. North Carolina, 378 U.S. 548, 84 S. Ct. 1900, 12 L. Ed. 2d 1032 (1964); Fox v. North Carolina, 378 U.S. 587, 84 S. Ct. 1901, 12 L. Ed. 2d 1032 (1964); Mitchell v. City of Charleston, 378 U.S. 551, 84 S. Ct. 1901, 12 L. Ed. 2d 1033 (1964); Drews v. Maryland, 378 U.S. 547, 84 S. Ct. 1900, 12 L. Ed. 2d 1032 (1964), *judgment reinstated and reaffirmed,* 236 Md. 349, 204 A.2d 64 (1964), *cert. denied,* 381 U.S. 421 (1965).

HAMM v. CITY OF ROCK HILL and LUPPER v. ARKANSAS, 379 U.S. 306, 85 S. Ct. 384, 13 L. Ed. 2d 300 (1964) (companion cases). There seems little doubt that the Court was aware, in handing down the group decisions on June 22, 1964, that the Civil Rights Act of 1964, including a National Public Accommodations Act, Title II, would be enacted within two weeks. Based on the Court's decisions in Griffin v. Maryland and Bell v. Maryland, one could expect that defendants in future sit-in cases would argue strongly that their convictions were abated by the 1964 Civil Rights Act. The Supreme Court late in 1964 accepted such arguments in the Hamm and Lupper cases.

BELL v. MARYLAND, 378 U.S. 226, 84 S. Ct. 1814, 12 L. Ed. 2d 822 (1964). In Bell, for the first time, the Court was able to reverse and remand (albeit after two rearguments) sit-in cases utilizing changes in state law quite likely initiated as a result of the sit-in demonstrations. In the period since the 1960 trespass convictions, the city of Baltimore had adopted a public accommodations ordinance, and the Maryland legislature had enacted a public accommodations statute, under which law it appeared that defendants' conduct would no longer be criminal. The Supreme Court concluded that the Maryland courts followed the common-law rule: when a legislature legalizes conduct formerly deemed criminal, a criminal prosecution which charges that conduct and which is not yet final should be dismissed. Because of an arguable issue under Maryland law as to whether a general savings clause statute saved the convictions from the effect of supervening enactments, the Court remanded the case for further consideration by the Maryland Court of Appeals. *Judgment reaffirmed,* 236 Md. 356, 204 A.2d 54 (1964).

In concurring and dissenting opinions, members of the Court expressed the growing divergence of views as to the extent of constitutional protection for demonstrators who refused to leave private property.

Justice Douglas urged the outright reversal of the convictions, on the basis that the right to be served at places of public accommodations is a privilege of national citizenship protected from state interference by the Fourteenth Amendment. Under the Shelley v. Kraemer doctrine, Douglas asserted that state judicial action, in the form of prosecution of demonstrators, served to enforce the private property owners' racially discriminatory policies and thus denied the affected Negroes the equal protection of the laws.

Justice Goldberg expressed the view that the Fourteenth Amendment was intended to obligate a state, either by statutory law or by common law, to guarantee all citizens access to places of public accommodation. Civil Rights Cases, 109 U.S. 3, 3 S. Ct. 18, 27 L. Ed. 835 (1833). The failure of a state to protect the constitutional right of Negroes is no justification, in Justice Goldberg's view, for its judiciary's participation in prosecutions of citizens for exercising such rights. Further, according to Justice Goldberg, this right of access to public accommodations could not be frustrated by permitting a proprietor to exercise a right of self-help to exclude black citizens from his premises. Lunch counters and soda fountains should be viewed, he concluded, as serving essentially the same needs today as those served by the innkeeper and common carrier in common law, and thus any interest of the proprietor in discriminatorily refusing service must be subordinated to a citizen's right to use public accommodations.

Justice Black, joined by Justices Harlan and White, dissented, in an opinion concluding that the convictions should have been affirmed, and the effect of intervening changes in state law left for independent consideration by the Maryland courts. Justice Black asserted that the rights of property include the right to select business associates or patrons, subject to regulation by proper state or federal legislation. The Fourteenth Amendment was not intended to assure access to privately owned accommodations, and a license to do business by the state should not be considered to convert private activity into state action for Fourteenth Amendment purposes, so long as there is no official state action or policy coercing or encouraging discrimination by private parties. As to arguments based on rights of free speech and protest, Justice Black contended that such rights do not include a right to force a private owner to furnish his property as a platform for criticism of his use of that property. The use of judicial proceedings to enforce trespass laws was therefore justified on the ground that the Fourteenth Amendment permits a state to prosecute crime committed against a person or his property, regardless of the prejudice or bigotry of the victim of the crime.

Justice Black made clear what he viewed as the dangers inherent in group demonstrations. The purpose of freedom of speech and press, he believed, was to provide a forum for the peaceful settlement of disputes without resort to "intimidation, force or violence." Justice Black warned:

The experience of ages points to the inexorable fact that people are frequently stirred to violence when property which the law recognizes as theirs is forcibly invaded or occupied by others. Trespass laws are born of this experience. They have been, and doubtless still are, important features of any government dedicated, as this country is, to a rule of law. Whatever power it may allow the States or grant to the Congress to regulate the use of private property, the Constitution does not confer upon any group the right to substitute rule by force for rule by law. (378 U.S. at 346.)

1965

COX v. LOUISIANA (No. 24), 379 U.S. 536, 85 S. Ct. 453, 13 L. Ed. 2d 471 (1965). In Cox v. Louisiana, there were further indications that the Supreme Court had about exhausted its sympathy for sit-ins and street demonstrations, which, however peaceful, carried with them a strong potential for disruption and violence.* The Reverend B. Elton Cox, a civil rights leader, was convicted of disturbing the peace, obstructing public passages and picketing before a courthouse, and received a total of twenty-one months in jail and $5700 in fines. The Court found that the Louisiana Breach of Peace Statute was unnecessarily broad, that the defendant was well behaved and that the police fear of a violent reaction from white onlookers was not justified by the record. The Obstructing Public Passages Statute was invalidated, as lodging too broad discretion in public officials and therefore infringing on First Amendment rights.

But in the majority opinion reversing Cox's conviction for obstructing public passages, Justice Goldberg stated:

We emphatically reject the notion urged by appellant that the First and the Fourteenth Amendments afford the same kind of freedom to those who would communicate ideas by conduct such as patrolling, marching, and picketing on streets and highways, as these amendments afford to those who communicate ideas by pure speech. (379 U.S. at 555.)

COX v. LOUISIANA (No. 49), 379 U.S. 559, 85 S. Ct. 476, 13 L. Ed. 2d 487 (1965). In reversing Cox's third conviction, the Court (379 U.S. 559)

* The signals were not uniform. The Court continued to reverse convictions in peaceful sit-ins. Abernathy v. Alabama, 380 U.S. 447, 85 S. Ct. 1101, 14 L. Ed. 2d 151 (1965) ("freedom riders" arrested at a lunch counter in a Montgomery, Alabama bus station). Even a group of blacks who congregated in a small vestibule of a Nashville cafeteria after being refused service, thus effectively blocking the entrance and exit of other patrons, had their convictions reversed on the authority of Hamm and Lupper, supra. McKennie v. Tennessee, 380 U.S. 449, 85 S. Ct. 1191, 14 L. Ed. 2d 151 (1965). See also Callendar v. Florida, 380 U.S. 519, 85 S. Ct. 1325, 14 L. Ed. 2d 265 (1965); Parrot v. City of Tallahassee, 381 U.S. 129, 85 S. Ct. 1322, 14 L. Ed. 2d 263 (1965); Thomas v. Mississippi, 380 U.S. 524, 85 S. Ct. 1327, 14 L. Ed. 2d 265 (1965); Walker v. Georgia, 381 U.S. 355, 85 S. Ct. 1557, 14 L. Ed. 2d 681 (1965).

conceded that the state's statute prohibiting interference with the administration of justice by picketing or parading in or near a courthouse was sufficiently narrow and precisely drawn, but concluded that its application to the facts in this case was not justified by the record, which, the Court felt, did not indicate that courtroom proceedings were interfered with by the demonstration.

Justice Goldberg emphasized that Cox was 125 feet from the courthouse at a point where officials had given him permission to demonstrate, that it was not suggested that he move, and that the order to disperse resulted from what Cox said, not from where he said it. Goldberg felt that "to sustain appellant's later conviction for demonstrating where they told him he could would be to sanction an indefensible sort of entrapment by the State — convicting a citizen for exercising a privilege which the state had clearly told him was available to him." 379 U.S. at 571.*

Justice Black concurred in the majority's reversal of Cox's conviction for violation of a Louisiana statute prohibiting breach of the peace and obstructing public passages, but he dissented from the Court's reversal of the courthouse picketing conviction. He stated that it was his belief that the evidence showed without dispute that appellant violated the statute, adding:

> . . . I have no doubt that the State has power to protect judges, jurors, witnesses, and court officers from intimidation by crowds which seek to influence them by picketing, patrolling, or parading in or near the courthouse in which they do their business or the homes in which they live, and I therefore believe that the Louisiana statute which protects the administration of justice by forbidding such influence is constitutional, both as written and as applied. (379 U.S. at 575.)

Justice Black also delivered a stern warning to minority groups that irresponsible protest did harm to their cause as well as to their country. See Chapter Three at page 93.

Justice Clark also dissented from the Court's reversal of the conviction for picketing near a courthouse, agreeing with Justice Black that the evidence supported the conviction and adding:

> I have always been taught that this Nation was dedicated to freedom under law not under mobs, whether they be integrationists or white supremacists. Our concept of equal justice under law encompasses no such protection as the Court gives Cox today. The contemporary drive for personal liberty can only be successful when conducted within the framework of due process of law. Goals, no matter how laudable, pursued by mobocracy in the end must always lead to further restraints of free expression. To permit, and even condone, the use of such anarchistic devices to influence the administration of justice can but lead us to disaster. For the Court

* Two years later, the Court was to deny certiorari in a Mississippi protest case in which civil rights workers who made speeches on the courthouse steps were prosecuted under a statute identical to the one struck down in Cox. McLaurin v. Greenville, 385 U.S. 1011, 87 S. Ct. 704, 17 L. Ed. 2d 548 (1967).

to place its imprimatur upon it is a misfortune that those who love the law will always regret. (379 U.S. at 589).†

COX v. LOUISIANA, 348 F.2d 750 (5th Cir. 1965). Following the Supreme Court's reversal of Cox's convictions, the district attorney for East Baton Rouge Parish initiated a new prosecution against Cox, charging him with "attempting" to obstruct justice. A removal petition was remanded by the federal district court, but on appeal the remand order was stayed. Speaking for the court, Judge Wisdom asserted that the district attorney was renewing the charges against Cox "in the teeth" of the Supreme Court's holding. "The second prosecution is without any hope of success. The district attorney's transparent purpose is to harass and punish the petitioner for his leadership in the civil rights movement, and to deter him and others from exercising rights of free speech and assembly in Louisiana — in this instance, by advocating integration of public accommodations." 348 F.2d at 752.

NOTE: WITHHOLDING REVIEW IN DISRUPTION CASES

The Court's concern over the potential for violence in civil rights demonstrations, and the threat posed thereby to the traditional concepts of private property, was observable not only in judicial warnings, but also in its unwillingness to grant review in a number of cases involving disorder. In such cases, convictions were permitted to stand by the procedural techniques of denying certiorari, dismissal of appeal, or summary affirmance. This was the fate of Ford v. Tennessee, 377 U.S. 994, 84 S. Ct. 1901, 12 L. Ed. 2d 1046 (1964), where defendants were reported to have run down the aisles and seated themselves during a segregated outdoor religious service, despite requests to stay in the rear. In Jones v. Georgia, 379 U.S. 935, 85 S. Ct. 330, 13 L. Ed. 2d 345 (1964), defendants were reported to have acted raucously in and about a church. In Diamond v. Louisiana, a nonstudent had been convicted of disturbing the peace by speeches on a black university campus, urging demonstrations on campus and a boycott of classes in protest against racial segregation in the community. The Court had first granted certiorari, 373 U.S. 931, 83 S. Ct. 1537, 10 L. Ed. 2d 689 (1963), then dismissed certiorari as improvidently granted. See also the action taken in Wells v. Reynolds, 382 U.S. 39, 86 S. Ct. 160, 15 L. Ed. 2d 32 (1965), *aff'd,* Wells v. Hand, 283 F. Supp. 779 (M.D. Ga. 1965).

Is there another rationale that better explains the Court's refusal to review

† In comparing the Court's decision in Cox v. Louisiana with its earlier decision in Edwards v. South Carolina, Professor Kalven commented on "the extraordinary ambivalence of the Court's reaction. As the parade leaves the State House grounds and moves down toward the Courthouse," Kalven observes, "it changes from an attractive group of concerned citizens using democratic avenues of protest on public issues to a mob, heavy with the promise of anarchy, seeking to dominate." Kalven, The Concept of the Public Forum: Cox v. Louisiana, 1965 Sup. Ct. Rev. 1.

some convictions resulting from protest activity? Was the disruptive behavior contained in the cases reviewed above merely accidental to other considerations? Consider whether the Court's actions in later protest cases support or weaken the "antidisruption" theory of Supreme Court review expressed in this Note.

1966-1968

During this period, the nonviolent, prayer-oriented Southern protests of the early 1960s were becoming more militant, and the North was experiencing a succession of urban race riots. The views expressed earlier by a minority of the Court now became those of a new majority. Not only was there a continuance of the earlier practice of denying review to convictions, and adverse judgments where protests had been accompanied by violence or where they posed serious threats of disorder (McLaurin v. Greenville, 385 U.S. 1011, 87 S. Ct. 704, 17 L. Ed. 2d 548 (1967), and NAACP v. Overstreet, 21 Ga. 16, 142 S.E.2d 816 (1965), *cert. denied,* 384 U.S. 118 (1966)), but for the first time a majority affirmed the conviction of civil rights demonstrators in two cases.

BROWN v. LOUISIANA, 383 U.S. 131, 86 S. Ct. 719, 15 L. Ed. 2d 637 (1966). The Court again reversed convictions, under Louisiana's Breach of the Peace Statute, of protesters who sat in a public library that barred blacks. (See Garner v. Louisiana, Taylor v. Louisiana and Cox v. Louisiana, supra.) As in the earlier cases, the Court found no support in the records for the state's charges of disorderly conduct and concluded that it was the defendants' race and not their behavior that led to their arrest. Nevertheless, Justice Fortas, writing for the majority, felt constrained to admonish:

> It is an unhappy circumstance that the locus of these events was a public library — a place dedicated to quiet, to knowledge, and to beauty. It is a sad commentary that this hallowed place in the Parish of East Feliciana bore the ugly stamp of racism. It is sad, too, that it was a public library which, reasonably enough in the circumstances, was the stage for a confrontation between those discriminated against and the representatives of the offending parish. Fortunately, the circumstances here were such that no claim can be made that use of the library by others was disturbed by the demonstration. Perhaps the time and method were carefully chosen with this in mind. Were it otherwise, a factor not present in this case would have to be considered. Here, there was no disturbance of others, no disruption of library activities, and no violation of any library regulations. (383 U.S. at 142.)

Four justices dissented. Speaking for them, Justice Black refused to concede "that a state must measure disturbances in its libraries and on the streets with identical standards. . . ." He felt that the state's use of its breach of peace statute was appropriate, warning that, if one group can take over libraries for one cause, other groups will assert the right to do so for other less appealing causes. He predicted that the rights to paralyze libraries would lead to assertion of the right to paralyze schools, adding that efforts to this effect had already been made all over the country. Justice Black concluded:

> I am deeply troubled with the fear that powerful private groups throughout the Nation will read the Court's action, as I do — that is, as granting them a license to invade the tranquillity and beauty of our libraries whenever they have quarrel with some state policy which may or may not exist. It is an unhappy circumstance in my judgement that the group, which more than any other has needed a government of equal laws and equal justice, is now encouraged to believe that the best way for it to advance its cause, which is a worthy one, is by taking the law into its own hands from place to place and from time to time. (383 U.S. at 167-168.)

Significantly, those protest cases in which the Court reversed convictions during this period were generally peaceful in nature. See Klopfer v. North Carolina, 386 U.S. 213, 87 S. Ct. 988, 18 L. Ed. 2d 1 (1967), a classic lunch counter sit-in case in which the Court reversed a ruling that after a nolle prosequi the prosecutor can reinstitute suit. In Mason v. Biloxi, 385 U.S. 370, 87 S. Ct. 533, 17 L. Ed. 2d 427 (1966), the Court reversed a conviction for trespass on a beach that had been constructed with federal funds.

ADDERLEY v. FLORIDA, 385 U.S. 39, 87 S. Ct. 242, 17 L. Ed. 2d 149 (1966). The facts in Adderley were quite similar to those in Edwards v. South Carolina, 372 U.S. 229, 83 S. Ct. 680, 9 L. Ed. 2d 697 (1963), except that the protest took place on jail property rather than on statehouse grounds, and the protesters were charged with trespass rather than with common-law breach of the peace. Thirty-two students from Florida A. & M. University were convicted of "trespass with a malicious and mischievous intent" on the premises of the Tallahassee County Jail. They had gone there from the campus, about a mile away, to demonstrate in protest of the arrest of other students the day before, and perhaps to protest more generally against state and local policies of racial segregation, including segregation of the jail. The county sheriff, legal custodian of the jail and jail grounds, failed in his efforts to persuade the students to leave; after warning that he would arrest them for trespassing, he arrested those who remained.

Justice Black, speaking for the majority, rejected the petitioners' contention that their cases must be reversed because of Edwards v. South Carolina and Cox v. Louisiana. He distinguished jails "built for security purposes" from state capitol grounds that are open to the public. Dismissing contentions that the Florida trespass statute was unconstitutionally vague, he found that there were adequate facts in the record to support the jury's guilty verdict. Finding that the sheriff had power to direct the large crowd to depart, Justice Black said that the record contained "not a shred of evidence" that this power was exercised because the sheriff objected to what the demonstrators were doing or disagreed with the objective of their protest.

Speaking for the dissenters in the 5 to 4 opinion, Justice Douglas viewed the jailhouse, like the statehouse, as a seat of government, which "when it houses political prisoners or those whom many think are unjustly held . . . is an obvious center for protest." Thus, the dissenters would distinguish this case from those involving private trespass actions. The Court, they felt, should not so easily close off access to effective protest for petitioners who cannot afford to advertise in newspapers or circulate elaborate pamphlets. Conceding that there are some public places, like the Senate gallery, which are improper sites for a protest rally, the dissenters maintained that this recognition is quite different from placing all public places off limits to people with grievances.

WALKER v. CITY OF BIRMINGHAM, 388 U.S. 307, 87 S. Ct. 1824, 18 L. Ed. 2d 1210 (1967). In Walker, the majority upheld the contempt conviction of Dr. Martin Luther King, Jr. and others for having violated an injunction forbidding the celebrated Good Friday and Easter Sunday Birmingham marches, which many believe were crucial to the demonstrations that led to passage of the 1964 Civil Rights Act. Greenberg, The Supreme Court, Civil Rights, and Civil Dissonance, 77 Yale L. Rev. at 1538. The Court did not rule on the validity of the injunction or the statute under which the request for parade permits had been denied. (In fact, the statute was later invalidated in Shuttleworth v. City of Birmingham, 394 U.S. 147, 89 S. Ct. 935, 22 L. Ed. 2d 162 (1969).) Rather, the majority emphasized the critical importance of order and orderly judicial procedure, holding, in effect, that such procedure takes precedence even over freedom of speech. The majority concluded: "One may sympathize with the petitioners' impatient commitment to their cause. But respect for judicial process is a small price to pay for the civilizing hand of law, which alone can give abiding meaning to constitutional freedom." 388 U.S. at 321.

In dissent, Justice Brennan criticized the majority's overriding concern with public order:

> We cannot permit fears of "riots" and "civil disobedience" generated by slogans like "Black Power" to divert our attention from what is here at stake — not violence or the right of the State to control its streets and sidewalks, but the insulation from attack of ex parte orders and legislation upon which they are based even when patently impermissible prior restraints on the exercise of the First Amendment rights. . . . (388 U.S. at 349.)

CAMERON v. JOHNSON, 390 U.S. 611, 88 S. Ct. 1335, 20 L. Ed. 2d 182 (1968). On January 22, 1964, appellants began picketing voter registration facilities located in the Forrest County Courthouse in Hattiesburg, Mississippi in a demonstration that was part of a drive to register blacks as voters in Hattiesburg. They maintained the pickets thereafter every day of the week except Sunday. To facilitate access to the courthouse, the sheriff mapped out a "march route" along which the picketers regularly paraded.

On April 8, 1964, the Mississippi legislature enacted a statute which prescribed criminal punishment for anyone "to engage in picketing . . . in such a manner as to obstruct or unreasonably interfere with free ingress or egress to and from any . . . county or municipal courthouses. . . ." On April 9, the sheriff read the new law to the picketers; on April 10, thirty-five to forty persons were arrested under it, and the following day nine more persons were arrested. On April 13, appellants filed the complaint in this action: they asked the federal district court to declare the Mississippi statute unconstitutionally vague and overbroad, and sought an injunction against the state's prosecution of the appellants, on the grounds that the prosecutions were instituted in bad faith, without any hope of conviction, purely for the purpose of disrupting the demonstration. The demonstrations ended on May 18, when nine more persons were arrested.

The district court dismissed the complaint, citing the abstention doctrine. On appeal, the Supreme Court, in Cameron v. Johnson, 381 U.S. 741, 85 S. Ct. 1751, 14 L. Ed. 2d 715 (1965), vacated the judgment and remanded the case for consideration in the light of Dombrowski v. Pfister, 380 U.S. 479, 85 S. Ct. 1116, 14 L. Ed. 2d 22 (1965). On remand, the district court refused both declaratory and injunctive relief. 262 F. Supp. 873. The Supreme Court, per Justice Brennan, affirmed. The statute was held neither too vague nor overbroad; the words "obstruct" or "interfere" were plain and understandable; taken in connection with them, the word "unreasonably" had a clearly understandable meaning. The statute recognized the regulation of picketing and parading, and, as First Amendment rights were not unlimited, the specific form of regulation involved here was permissible. The injunctive relief sought by plaintiffs depends upon a showing that the police were, in enforcing the statute, acting in bad faith, with no hope of convicting the plaintiffs. Here, though it was doubtful that the appellants' acts had amounted to an unreasonable obstruction of the courthouse, it could not be said that the state was acting in bad faith. Even though the evidence presented at the hearing on the injunction was insufficient to obtain a criminal conviction, it did not prove that the state had no expectation of securing valid convictions, and had only intended to discourage exercise of protected rights. Thus there was no showing of the "special circumstances" required in Dombrowski before interference by a federal court with a state court criminal prosecution could be justified.

Justice Fortas, joined by Justice Douglas, dissented, finding but a "few unimpressive shreds" of evidence that the appellants had in fact violated the statute, and thinking it was clear that the Mississippi legislature had enacted the statute merely for the purpose of disrupting the Hattiesburg demonstrations. He therefore would apply the "strong medicine" of Dombrowski v. Pfister, and use the federal court to enjoin the state from using its criminal process.

NOTE: ABSTENTION AND CIVIL RIGHTS PROTESTS

The Supreme Court's decision in Cameron v. Johnson greatly diminished the hopes raised by Dombrowski v. Pfister that criminal prosecutions initiated against civil rights protesters in a state court could be enjoined where, as was frequently the case, it was obvious that the prosecution was intended to punish the expression of antisegregation views. To enjoin such pending state court criminal prosecutions after Cameron, civil rights attorneys had to show that: (1) the statute under which prosecution is threatened is unconstitutional on its face; (2) the threatened prosecution has been undertaken in bad faith; and (3) there is irreparable harm to the plaintiff — i.e., more than the injury ordinarily incident to a criminal prosecution.

In Younger v. Harris, 401 U.S. 37, 91 S. Ct. 746, 27 L. Ed. 2d 669 (1971), the Cameron v. Johnson standard was further refined so as to preclude (1) injunctive relief unless the threat to plaintiff's federal rights cannot be eliminated by a single criminal prosecution, and (2) declaratory relief where injunctive relief is not appropriate. In a case decided the same day as Younger, the Court in Boyle v. Landry, 401 U.S. 37, 91 S. Ct. 746, 27 L. Ed. 2d 696 (1971), reversed injunctive relief granted as to two of seven statutes challenged by a group of blacks who alleged that they were threatened with prosecution under the provision. The Supreme Court reversed, noting that none of the plaintiffs had been prosecuted under the statutes and that "The normal course of state criminal prosecutions cannot be disrupted or blocked on the basis of charges which in the last analysis amount to nothing more than speculation about the future."

Federal injunctions against criminal prosecutions of civil rights protesters have been more difficult to obtain since Cameron v. Johnson, and in the wake of Younger v. Harris, there has been a series of decisions vacating federal injunctions and declaratory judgments granted by lower courts. See, e.g., Hunter v. Allen, 286 F. Supp. 830 (N.D. Ga.), 422 F.2d 1158 (5th Cir. 1970), *reversed and remanded sub nom.* Embry v. Allen, 401 U.S. 989, 91 S. Ct. 1237, 28 L. Ed. 2d 528 (1971) (vacating judgment upholding a statute forbidding violent interference with another's occupation); Wright v. Montgomery, 282 F. Supp. 291 (M.D. Ala.), 406 F.2d 867 (5th Cir. 1969), *reversed and remanded,* 401 U.S. 989 (1971) (vacating judgment upholding disorderly conduct, loitering, and failure to obey statutes under which voting rights demonstrators were arrested); Jackson v. Dobbs, 442 F.2d 928 (5th Cir. 1971) (remanding for dismissal of district court's declaratory judgment upholding parade permit ordinance); Fuller v. Scott, 328 F. Supp. 842 (M.D. N.C. 1971) (vacating prior judgment declaring part of a riot control act invalid, where plaintiffs were charged as a result of their participation in a food service strike at a state university).

Neither Cameron nor Younger settled the question whether §1983 creates an express exception to 28 U.S.C. §2283, which forbids federal courts to stay state proceedings except when expressly authorized by Congress, or when necessary in aid of their jurisdiction or to effectuate their judgments. But this long debated issue was settled in Mitchum v. Foster, 407 U.S. 225, 92 S. Ct. 2151, 32 L. Ed. 2d 705 (1972), in which the Court concluded that §1983 was a statute with the "expressly authorized" exception of §2283. Justice Stewart made clear that the Court's decision was not intended to "question or qualify in any way the principles of equity, comity, and federalism that must restrain a federal court when asked to enjoin a state court proceeding." Thus the Mitchum v. Foster holding that §2283 does not absolutely bar federal injunctions of state court prosecutions under §1983, does not affect the understanding that federal courts may not grant injunctive or declaratory relief where a state criminal proceeding is pending, unless the stringent Cameron-Younger requirements are satisfied. See, e.g., Brooks v. Peters, 322 F. Supp. 1273 (E.D. Wis. 1971) (holding abstention proper where state proceedings were pending in a §1983 action brought by Indians seeking injunction against interference with their demonstration in a private parking lot, but also declaring that a private parking lot is not a public place for First Amendment purposes); Hunter v. Allen, supra; Fuller v. Scott, supra. See also Henry v. First National Bank of Clarksdale, 50 F.R.D. 251, 444 F.2d 1300 (5th Cir. 1971) (dismissing §1983 action for lack of jurisdiction, on the ground that state antitrust action against plaintiff's boycott was not "state action").

Courts may be able to find a way to circumvent the stringent requirements for injunctive action in cases they consider compelling. See Montgomery Court Board of Education v. Shelton, 327 F. Supp. 811 (N.D. Miss. 1961) (enjoining enforcement of a state court order restricting protest activities in contravention of a prior federal court order, on the ground that the federal court had injunctive power "in aid of its jurisdiction" under §2283, but also holding that the danger to plaintiff's constitutional rights was so great and immediate as to justify intervention). Nevertheless, the net effect of Cameron and Younger will probably be to ensure that the moment for effective protest is lost, as the demonstrators wend their way through the state court system.

2. The Lower Courts

Even during the period when the Supreme Court was reversing convictions in peaceful sit-in cases, few lower courts followed their lead. State courts routinely convicted protesters on a wide variety of misdemeanor and sometimes felony charges, only a small percentage of which cases reached and were reversed by the Supreme Court.* In addition, although peaceful

* While most arrested protesters were charged with misdemeanors, civil rights adherents have been subjected to a variety of felony charges, including: "criminal syndicalism," Ware v. Nichols, 266 F. Supp. 564 (N.D. Miss. 1967); "criminal anarchy," People v.

protest campaigns were protected by a few federal district court judges, they were more frequently enjoined. If the civil rights demonstrations were thought to involve actual or threatened violence, the lower courts almost uniformly responded in a negative and even hostile fashion.

These cases were marked by several almost predictable components: the responsibility for disturbances or disruption was generally placed on the protesters, even though disorder was frequently the result of action by police or hostile spectators; there was a presumption that police and city officials were enforcing the laws impartially and with fairness, although this was seldom the case; federal courts in suits filed by city officials often assumed jurisdiction and granted injunctive relief, even though there was clearly no basis for federal jurisdiction; there was a markedly greater concern for property than for personal rights; extraordinary restrictions were placed on picketers; and even when the protesters were clearly entitled to injunctive relief, it was delayed (often by refusal of district courts to grant it, and the unwillingness of courts of appeal to provide injunctions pending appeal) until arrests and harassment had seriously damaged the protest movement.

The pattern is clearly discernible in a series of cases reviewing efforts by NAACP and CORE to enjoin arrests and harassment by local law enforcement officials. Consider whether the results in these cases can be equated with the traditional view that the courts aided civil rights protests. Were there only procedural barriers preventing the appellate courts from issuing effective orders, before the protest movements lost momentum because of harassment and arrests?

CONGRESS OF RACIAL EQUALITY v. CLEMMONS, 323 F.2d 54 (5th Cir. 1963). In December 1961, civil rights activists in Baton Rouge, Louisiana had undertaken a boycott of white merchants that was accompanied by picketing. Following the arrest of some of the picketers, there was a mass demonstration, during which traffic was blocked and the demonstrators were harassed by spectators. Ultimately, the police used tear gas against the pro-

---

Epton, 281 N.Y.S.2d 9, 227 N.E.2d 829 (1967), and State v. Cade, 153 So.2d 382 (1963); "insurrection," Harris v. Chappell, 219 Ga. 522, 133 S.E.2d 855 (1963); "inciting to riot," South Carolina v. Sellers, 3 Race Rel. L. Sur. 47 (Cir. Ct. 1971).

In addition, courts often imposed tight restrictions on minors who took part in protests, using for this purpose the more flexible juvenile court process. Thus in Florence v. Myers, 9 Race Rel. L. Rep. 144 (M.D. Fla. 1964), a federal district judge voided an order of a juvenile court judge which barred civil rights picketing or demonstrations by persons under seventeen without court authorization. See also, e.g., Griffin v. Hay, 10 Race Rel. L. Rep. 111 (E.D. Va. 1965); State ex rel. Singleton v. Walters, 158 So.2d 513 (Fla. 1963).

School boards also tried to impose sanctions on student protest participants. Birmingham school officials suspended and expelled students who had participated in the spring 1963 demonstrations. An immediate order by the Fifth Circuit restored them to school, which action was affirmed on appeal of the case. Woods v. Wright, 334 F.2d (5th Cir. 1964). And see Jackson v. Ellington, 316 F. Supp. 1071 (W.D. Tenn. 1970) (upholding a statute that prohibits urging children to be absent from school for the purpose of participating in demonstrations).

testers, justifying this action on the basis that, in their belief, violence was imminent. City authorities and police then obtained an injunction in federal court, based on allegations that the protesters were interfering with the performance of their duties. The district court permanently enjoined the protesters from sponsoring demonstrations in which state statutes would be violated or in which violation of state statutes would be advocated. 201 F. Supp. 737 (E.D. La. 1962).

The Fifth Circuit reversed the district court without reaching the issues of freedom of speech and assembly raised by CORE on appeal. The court found that the suit had failed to state a federal cause of action. Judge Wisdom observed:

> The thrust of the holding below is that the State action here was action of the Congress of Racial Equality and Negro demonstrators. The State invoked the Fourteenth Amendment against private individuals, although the Fourteenth Amendment established the constitutional rights in favor of private individuals and against the State. Moreover, this unusual federal action is in an area that is essentially one of State responsibility — the preservation of public order; and there is no lack of breach of peace statutes in Louisiana. (323 F.2d at 55.)

The court also determined that there was neither diversity nor "federal question" jurisdiction in the suit, and that the action could not be justified under 42 U.S.C. §1985(3). The decision notes that a similar "injunctive order" was obtained against civil rights leaders in Albany, Georgia, and that on motion of the defendants, Chief Judge Elbert P. Tuttle had set aside the order as "null and void." Kelly v. Page, 335 F.2d 114 (5th Cir. 1964).

In Congress of Racial Equality v. Douglas, 318 F.2d 95 (5th Cir. 1963), the district court at the request of the city of McComb, Mississippi enjoined CORE and certain private persons. There the appellate court ignored the jurisdictional problem, and the district court's injunction was reversed on findings that there was no "clear and present" danger of violence, and that the protest had been conducted in an "appropriate manner." As the Fifth Circuit so frequently held when protest matters finally reached it on appeal, "the fundamental rights to speak, assemble, seek redress and demonstrate peacefully in pursuance thereto cannot be abridged merely because a riot might be threatened to be staged or [because] the police officers are afraid that breaches of the peace will occur if these rights are exercised." 318 F.2d at 102.

NAACP v. WEBB'S CITY INC., 152 So. 2d 179 (Fla. D. Ct. App. 1963). The NAACP, picketing in protest of plaintiff's lunch counter segregation and Negro employment policy, was enjoined on the grounds that, while the picketing was peaceful, it had resulted in one demonstration inside the store leading to a trespass arrest and conviction, and "had created an atmosphere of apprehension and potential violence." A Florida appellate court upheld the injunction, pointing out that "the primary purpose of the picketing was to interfere with Webb's right to an unhampered market for the sale of its commodities and services by coercing customers . . . into withholding patronage." Such action was found by the court to be enjoinable as an unlawful interference with plaintiff's property. The Supreme Court granted review, 375 U.S. 939, 84 S. Ct. 346, 11 L. Ed. 2d 270 (1963), and later vacated the judgment of the Florida court, 376 U.S. 190, 84 S. Ct. 635, 11 L. Ed. 2d 602 (1964). Explaining its decision in a brief per curiam statement, the Court based its action on "respondent's suggestion of mootness . . . ." The case was remanded to the Florida court "for appropriate proceedings to effectuate respondent's representation that the injunction below will be set aside, without prejudice to the right of petitioner to move to vacate today's order in the event the injunction is not promptly vacated by the trial court." 376 U.S. at 190.

NAACP v. THOMPSON, 321 F.2d 199 (5th Cir. 1963), *cert. denied sub nom.* Johnson v. NAACP, 385 U.S. 820, 87 S. Ct. 45, 17 L. Ed. 2d 58 (1966). In the spring of 1963, the NAACP, having attempted without success to establish a biracial committee to deal with grievances of blacks in the community, began a series of protests, including picketing, boycotts, sit-ins and marches. All were peaceful and nonobstructive, but many demonstrators were arrested nevertheless, including one youth who was wearing an NAACP T-shirt while walking along a main street. To halt these arrests, the NAACP and others sought injunctive relief in federal district court. After a hearing in June 1963, at which conflicting evidence was introduced as to the nature of the conduct in question, the district court entered an order taking the motion for injunction under advisement, and expressly declining either to grant or to deny the motion. The plaintiffs immediately appealed, treating the court's order as a "refusal" of injunctive relief, and sought an injunction pending appeal from the Fifth Circuit. Somewhat reluctantly, Chief Judge Tuttle dismissed the appeal, holding that because this is "an area of constitutional law which has been recognized by the Supreme Court to be extremely difficult of application," 321 F.2d at 202, it could not be said that the trial court had abused its discretion in taking the motion under advisement, or that this amounted to a refusal of injunctive relief. The order was thus deemed not appealable.* When the case returned to the Fifth Circuit, almost two years later, and after the district court had dismissed the complaint, the court

* When the NAACP filed its federal court action, its protest movement had already been seriously threatened by a state court injunction suit brought by the City of Jackson, charging civil rights forces with a conspiracy to illegally boycott, picket and demonstrate so as to force businesses into hiring blacks, to paralyze the city and to storm the police force. The Mississippi Supreme Court refused to dissolve a temporary injunction broadly preventing parades, sit-ins, unlawful picketing and acts calculated to cause breaches of the peace. City of Jackson v. Salter, 8 Race Rel. L. Rep. 433 (1963). A petition to the Supreme Court to dissolve or stay the order was denied. 374 U.S. 818, 83 S. Ct. 1714 (1963).

of appeals reversed, holding that the plaintiffs had no adequate remedy at law for the "chilling effect" intentionally created by the local officials who had abused their authority. The defendants were enjoined from interfering with protests so long as they were peaceful and nonobstructive.

NOTES

1. The Jackson scenario of protests, leading to involved and prolonged litigation in both state and federal courts, was repeated in virtually every large civil rights effort. See, e.g., the 1963 Birmingham protests in 8 Race Rel. L. Rep. 435-448 (1963); Plaquemine, Louisiana, 8 Race Rel. L. Rep. 862-874 (1963); the 1965 Selma voter registration marches, 10 Race Rel. L. Rep. 209-244, 1472-73 (1965); the night marches of St. Augustine, Florida in 1964, 9 Race Rel. L. Rep. 590-597, 1515-1521 (1964); Americus, Georgia, 247 F. Supp. 794 (N.D. Ga. 1965).

2. Not infrequently, courts were confronted by injunction requests from both protesters and city officials in the same or in companion litigation. Sometimes the court sought to enjoin excesses by either side. See, e.g., Kelly v. Page, 335 F.2d 114 (5th Cir. 1964); Cottonreader v. Johnson, 252 F. Supp. 492 (N.D. Ala. 1966); Young v. Munn, 1 Race Rel. L. Sur. 54 (N.D. Miss. 1969); Houser v. Hill, 278 F. Supp. 920 (M.D. Ala. 1968); Bluefield YMCA-YWCA, Inc. v. Nettles, 9 Race Rel. L. Rep. 1733 (1964).

But any incidents of violence, intimidation or coercion attributable to the protesters generally led to prompt injunctions against the civil rights groups. Gannon v. Action, 303 F. Supp. 1240 (E.D. Mo. 1969), *aff'd,* 450 F.2d 1227 (8th Cir. 1971); Central Presbyterian Church v. Black Liberation Front, 303 F. Supp. 894 (E.D. Mo. 1969). See also Wright v. Alabama, 282 F. Supp. 291, *aff'd,* 406 F.2d 867 (5th Cir. 1965) (declaratory judgment); Evers v. Birdsong, 287 F. Supp. 900 (S.D. Miss. 1968); City of Danville v. Campbell, 8 Race Rel. L. Rep. 434 (1965).

Picketing (in furtherance of boycotts) was enjoined in the following cases on grounds that it was intimidating or coercive or tended to create a violent atmosphere: City of Jackson v. Salter, 8 Race Rel. L. Rep. 433 (1965); Fair Share Organization v. Nagdeman & Sons, Inc., 9 Race Rel. L. Rep. 1079, 1375 (1963); NAACP v. Webb's City Inc., 152 So. 2d 179 (1963); Orlando v. Stearnes, 6 Race Rel. L. Rep. 821 (1961).

QUESTIONS

1. Whatever the value of the Supreme Court's decisions in the early 1960s supporting the sit-in protests, it is clear that most communities experiencing antisegregation protests, as well as the courts that served them, did not feel bound to conform their decisions in protest cases within the standards set by the high court. The civil rights forces actually lost many, if not a majority, of these suits. Do these lower court decisions reflect a breakdown of stare decisis, or were the Supreme Court decisions so narrow that lower courts were able to distinguish them easily?

2. Militants today might condemn the utilization of litigation as worse than a waste of time and resources, since protest leaders put more emphasis in their planning on the likely legality, rather than the potential effectiveness, of their tactics. Civil rights lawyers, though, would contend that legal action was essential to defend against criminal charges and civil actions brought to frustrate protest activities, and that affirmative litigation — whether or not successful, as to relief — served to publicize the protests, and, more important, involved the courts as monitors of counterprotest activities. With varying degrees of reluctance, even state tribunals and unsympathetic federal courts could be expected to enjoin the most flagrant denials of constitutional rights. Which position is more accurate? Are civil rights lawyers more effective in defensive roles or in initiating litigation?

NOTE: PRIVATE "SELF-HELP" EFFORTS BY WHITES

The legality of the actions of law enforcement officers during the sit-in period varied widely, but in many demonstrations they harassed, arrested and prosecuted civil rights adherents, and in some instances they virtually joined those onlookers who opposed the protests. It was not difficult to conclude that officials generally served the interests of whites and the status quo, rather than the blacks who sought change. But for some white people, official efforts were not enough, and acting in private groups (sometimes with the help of public officials), they sought to maintain by force racial policies that the courts had determined could no longer be justified by law.

In the main, white "self-help" resistance took the form of economic coercion. A black employee might have the constitutional right to vote, send his child to a white school, or protest peacefully, but he had no right to his job, credit or lease. At least, so those whites who were employers, bankers and landlords believed. The difficulties in proving racial discrimination gave actual, if not legal, validity to their beliefs in most cases.

Not infrequently, of course, whites supplemented economic coercion with physical threats, harassment and violence.* It is impossible to ascertain the amount of loss, suffering and sacrifice resulting from the extralegal actions of whites willing to demonstrate their opposition to equality for blacks.

In Haywood County, Tennessee, a well organized group of white landowners, merchants, bankers and public officials — including the mayor of Brownsville, the sheriff and school superintendent — sought to interfere with voting rights of blacks by exerting economic pressures and evicting black sharecroppers. Relief was sought by the United States under the 1957 Voting Rights Act. The district court with some reluctance enjoined defendants from

* Cases dealing with murder and other serious physical violence are discussed in more detail in Chapter Fifteen.

interfering with efforts by blacks to register and vote, but found the Civil Rights Act did not "vest the courts with authority to adjudge contracts and property rights." The Sixth Circuit reversed and granted relief against the threatened evictions and economic pressures. United States v. Beaty, 288 F.2d 653 (6th Cir. 1961). The various orders in the case are set out in 6 Race Rel. L. Rep. 200-206 (1961-1962), 7 Race Rel. L. Rep. 484-487 (1962).

The government was less successful in a suit under the 1965 Voting Rights Act to prevent the eviction of sharecroppers and tenant farmers in West Feliciana Parish, Louisiana, Judge West ruling that the evidence failed to show any intimidation or coercion. United States v. Harvey, 250 F. Supp. 219 (E.D. La. 1966). Blacks failed to obtain relief against alleged evictions in Lowndes County, Alabama, and Judge Johnson not only granted summary judgment for the defendants, but even taxed the attorneys for the blacks with court costs, asserting that the evidence indicated that few, if any, of the plaintiffs had specifically authorized the suit, and finding that it was instigated by certain "civil rights organizations," from whom he suggested plaintiffs' attorneys could secure reimbursement. Miles v. Dickson, 40 F.R.D. 386 (M.D. Ala. 1966). On appeal, the assessment of costs was reversed, but the summary judgment was affirmed. Miles v. Dickson, 387 F.2d 716 (5th Cir. 1967).

The federal government was instrumental in obtaining relief against similar efforts mounted against school integration in Bullock v. United States, 265 F.2d 683 (6th Cir. 1959); United States v. Farrar, 414 F.2d 936 (5th Cir. 1969); and United States v. Crenshaw Co. Unit United Klans, 290 F. Supp. 181 (M.D. Ala. 1968). A school board, seeking to comply with school desegregation decisions, also obtained relief against outside interference in Brewer v. Hoxie School District, 238 F.2d 91 (8th Cir. 1956).

More recently, a Maryland court affirmed the breach of peace convictions of whites who participated in a riotous demonstration against a black family which had moved into a white neighborhood. Luthardt v. Maryland, 6 Md. App. 251, 251 A.2d 40 (1969). In Jennings v. Patterson, 460 F.2d 1021 (5th Cir. 1972), the court reversed a district court's dismissal of a suit by blacks against white residents of Dadeville, Alabama, who, acting with the acquiescence of city councilmen, erected a fence across a public street so as to deny blacks public access to their homes.

D. CIVIL RIGHTS BOYCOTTS

Many of the civil rights protest demonstrations reviewed earlier in this chapter were staged to gain support for consumer boycotts of segregated facilities. The earlier discussion centered on litigation initiated either to protect or to enjoin picketing and other protest activity. The cases in this section examine direct counterattacks that were mounted against civil rights boycotts through private litigation, and were prosecuted, often with devastating effect, through sympathetic state courts.

NAACP v. OVERSTREET

384 U.S. 118, 86 S. Ct. 1306, 16 L. Ed. 2d 409 (1966)

PER CURIAM.

The writ of certiorari is dismissed as improvidently granted. [221 Ga. 16, 142 S.E.2d 816.]

Mr. Justice DOUGLAS, with whom The Chief Justice, Mr. Justice BRENNAN and Mr. Justice FORTAS concur, dissenting.

In May 1962, a 14-year-old Negro boy complained to his school principal and to his mother that he had been mistreated by respondent. The boy claimed that respondent, the owner of a market at which the boy was employed, had accused him of stealing merchandise and had thereafter slapped and kicked him. The truth of this charge remains disputed. The boy's mother, dissatisfied with the response of the local police, contacted the Savannah Branch of the National Association for the Advancement of Colored People. The Branch responded by organizing a campaign to withhold patronage from respondent. Pickets were established, and customers were asked to refrain from shopping in the market. Although the record does not contain any evidence of misconduct on the part of the Branch's members or officers, the picketing apparently attracted substantial crowds. There were incidents involving the intimidation of customers, blocking of sidewalks, and scattered incidents of violence. The trial judge instructed the jury that it might hold the Branch responsible for the respondent's damages if it found that the picketing was the "proximate cause" of the misconduct of others.[1] The judge further instructed the jury that should it hold the Branch liable, it might also hold petitioner — the national NAACP — if the Branch were found to be its "agent." The jury held both the Branch and petitioner liable. Damages totaling $85,793 were assessed: this figure includes $50,000 in punitive damages. The Georgia Supreme Court affirmed, 221 Ga. 16, 142 S.E.2d 816, and we granted certiorari, limited to the question of whether holding petitioner, the national organization, liable "for acts performed without its knowledge and by persons beyond its control" denied it rights secured by the Fourteenth Amendment. 382 U.S. 937.

Respondent has suffered economic loss as a result of the conduct of those who blocked his sidewalk and threatened his customers. I assume that nothing in the Constitution bars recovery for his injuries from those individuals. See Giboney v. Empire Storage Co., 336 U.S. 490. The courts below found that the Branch was responsible for these injuries, and no questions as to that aspect of the case are now before us. We have only the question whether, given the liability of the Branch, petitioner, the national NAACP, may be

1. "I charge you that in this case you can consider the effect of the picket[ing]. Did . . . the fact that the pickets were there incite activity upon people who were not at all connected with the organization[?]; and if that was incited by the pickets, *by their mere presence,* you could consider the pickets and the placing of the pickets as the proximate cause of what resulted." (Emphasis added.)

held responsible for respondent's loss — and for the punitive damages imposed.

The amended complaint alleged that W. W. Law, an officer of the Branch, "in using such tactics, was acting in and for the services" of petitioner "as its agents, employee, and servant, within the scope of said agency, employment and service." That allegation was denied by petitioner and the record does not contain one iota of proof that petitioner controlled, authorized, or even knew of these activities.

Petitioner is a nonprofit corporation organized in New York for the purpose of promoting equality of treatment for Negro citizens.[2] The Branch is concededly an affiliate of that national organization. A portion of the dues it collects is forwarded to the national, and members of the local branch are automatically members of the national organization. Members of the local association can and do attend the annual national convention at which they participate in workshops and discussions relating to NAACP activities. The Branch makes an annual report of its activities to the national NAACP.

That, for all the record shows, is the full extent of the relations between petitioner and the Branch. There is no evidence of any power on the part of petitioner to control the conduct of the Branch. There is no evidence of any effort in past years by petitioner to exercise such control. The Branch officers were not, for all the record shows, national officers. The petitioner did not order the demonstrations nor did it authorize them. The record affirmatively shows that petitioner had no knowledge of the demonstrations against respondent and did not learn of them until it was sent the restraining order that was served upon the Branch president. And nothing in the record suggests "ratification" — even by inaction over a sustained period — of the local's activities against respondent or of similar activities.

The standards by which the trial court allowed this "agency" to be measured were, to say the least, unclear. The trial judge instructed the jury that the petitioner was a New York corporation which could "only be represented in Georgia by agents, and the agents must conduct themselves in a manner that is compatible with the purposes of that organization." He then instructed as follows:

> Now did the National Association for the Advancement of Colored People have an agent in Savannah? Who was that agent? Was it W. W. Law [the Branch's president]? . . . Is the National Association responsible for what this affiliate does? . . . Are they so connected that one is responsible for the act of the other by reason of the agency; by reason of their concerted activities as expressed in this conspiracy?

2. See N.A.A.C.P. v. Alabama, 357 U.S. 449, 451-452. Its certificate of incorporation states that its principal objectives are "voluntarily to promote equality of rights and eradicate caste or race prejudice among the citizens of the United States; to advance the interest of colored citizens; to secure for them impartial suffrage; and to increase their opportunities for securing justice in the courts, education for their children, employment according to their ability, and complete equality before the law." Ibid.

> *As the Court sees it, you can't get agency and conspiracy separated in this case.* A corporation may be a member of a conspiracy if its officers and agents take part in it and it furthers the conspiracy. You look to the evidence and see if it preponderates as to these organizations. Was there an agency that bound the National Association . . . ? Did they participate through their agents and members and people who had a right to bind them in this conspiracy? (Emphasis added.)

These instructions, to which the defendants excepted and assigned as error on appeal, gave the jury little guidance as to the circumstances in which it would be appropriate to hold liable the national NAACP. The remarks of the trial judge in considering petitioner's motion for a nonsuit are, in this respect, revealing: "[S]o far as the evidence is concerned, there [is] no evidence to the effect that any member [of the Branch] was the agent of the national corporation. *In other words, they were just affiliated.*" (Emphasis added.)

To equate the liability of the national organization with that of the Branch in the absence of any proof that the national authorized or ratified the misconduct in question could ultimately destroy it. The rights of political association are fragile enough without adding the additional threat of destruction by lawsuit. We have not been slow to recognize that the protection of the First Amendment bars subtle as well as obvious devices by which political association might be stifled. See Bates v. Little Rock, 361 U.S. 516, 523. Thus we have held that forced disclosure of one's political associations is, at least in the absence of a compelling state interest, inconsistent with the First Amendment's guaranty of associational privacy. E.g., DeGregory v. New Hampshire, 383 U.S. 825; Gibson v. Florida Legislative Comm., 372 U.S. 539, 543-546; Shelton v. Tucker, 364 U.S. 479; N.A.A.C.P. v. Alabama, 357 U.S. 449, 462-463. Recognizing that guilt by association is a philosophy alien to the traditions of a free society (see Schware v. Board of Bar Examiners, 353 U.S. 232, 245-246) and the First Amendment itself, we have held that civil or criminal disabilities may not be imposed on one who joins an organization which has among its purposes the violent overthrow of the Government, unless the individual joins knowing of the organization's illegal purposes (Wieman v. Updegraff, 344 U.S. 183) and with the specific intention to further those purposes. . . .

The present case contains no less a threat to political association. That the threat comes in the form of civil suits for damages rather than that of direct governmental restraints is of no consequence as we noted in New York Times v. Sullivan, 376 U.S. 254, 265. Today a judgment of more than $80,000 is fastened on the national NAACP. Juries hostile to the aims of an organization in the educational or political field, unless carefully confined by meticulous instructions and judicial supervision, can deliver crushing verdicts that may stifle organized dissent from the views and policies accepted by the majority.

This case thus carries us into territory in which principles of state law must be accommodated with overriding federal precepts. The law of agency which a State chooses to follow functions, for the most part, free of constitutional restraint; in our federal system, each State may regulate the relations between principal, agent, and third parties according to its own standards of fairness and sound policy. But when a state policy thwarts interests which the Federal Constitution affords special protection, that state policy must yield. For example, though state law customarily determines whether a particular contract is enforceable, notwithstanding the applicable commercial law a state court may not enforce covenants restricting sale of real property to non-whites. Shelley v. Kraemer, 334 U.S. 1. While the States may preserve order on the public streets and punish conduct constituting a "breach of the peace" as defined by local law, peaceful expression may not, regardless of the label put upon it, be punished. Cantwell v. Connecticut, 310 U.S. 296. And see Edwards v. South Carolina, 372 U.S. 229. Questions of legislative apportionment, though primarily matters of state law, must be resolved in compliance with the Federal Equal Protection Clause. Reynolds v. Sims, 377 U.S. 533. The same is true of voter registration, Harper v. Virginia State Board of Elections, 383 U.S. 663. State regulation of the practice of law — more specifically, the rules regarding solicitation of legal business — must yield in favor of the First Amendment right to join together in a common effort to assert legal rights. N.A.A.C.P. v. Button, 371 U.S. 415; Railroad Trainmen v. Virginia Bar, 377 U.S. 1.

In N.A.A.C.P. v. Button, supra, we rejected the State's claim that "solicitation" of legal business is outside the area of freedoms protected by the First Amendment. We said that "a State cannot foreclose the exercise of constitutional rights by mere labels." 371 U.S., at 429. So it should be in this case. Terms such as "agency" and "affiliation" have no talismanic significance. In the context of this case, they obscure rather than promote sound analysis. The question we must answer is whether a national political association can be held responsible for wrongs committed by those beyond its control in a constitutional system where freedom of expression and association is treasured.

The threats which political organizations of this kind today face were once a great burden on labor unions. Congress acted to relieve that burden by enacting §6 of the Norris-LaGuardia Act:

> No officer or member of any association or organization, and no association or organization participating or interested in a labor dispute, shall be held responsible or liable in any court of the United States for the unlawful acts of individual officers, members, or agents, except upon clear proof of actual participation in, or actual authorization of, such acts, or of ratification of such acts after actual knowledge thereof. 47 Stat. 71.

See Brotherhood of Carpenters v. United States, 330 U.S. 395. We recently held in United Mine Workers v. Gibbs, 383 U.S. 715, that an international union could not be held liable for the tortious conduct of a local in the absence of "clear proof" of "participation, authorization, or ratification" by the international union.

We have of course no like statute here. But the First Amendment, which commands vigilance lest the rights it assures be denied the "breathing space" (N.A.A.C.P. v. Button, supra, 433) necessary for survival, provides guidance. In my view, it forbids the imposition of liability on a national political association on account of the misconduct of a local branch without proof that the national organization specifically authorized or ratified the conduct for which liability is sought to be imposed. A *general* finding of "agency" or "affiliation" is not enough. In the present case, the record discloses at most a loose relationship between petitioner and this independently controlled Branch. This record discloses no specific authorization or ratification by petitioner of the acts which the Georgia courts found tortious. Nor is there any evidence of any participation by petitioner in such conduct. The trial judge himself stated that there was no "agency" shown, but only an "affiliation" between petitioner and the local Branch. So weak a link cannot, for the reasons I have stated, warrant holding the national NAACP responsible for the damages sustained.

I would reverse this judgment.

NOTES

1. Justice Douglas in the course of his dissent in Overstreet, supra page 320, refers to several efforts by Southern states to suppress the activities of civil rights organizations, principally the NAACP, through their authority to regulate corporations. Most of these efforts were ultimately defeated in the courts, but not without doing great harm to the organizational structure of the civil rights groups. For example, in the wake of the Supreme Court's "freedom of association" decision in NAACP v. Alabama, 357 U.S. 449, 78 S. Ct. 1163, 2 L. Ed. 2d 1488 (1958), which dissolved a $100,000 civil contempt fine levied against the association for its refusal to disclose its membership lists to state authorities, the NAACP was banned from doing business in Alabama by a state court from 1961 until the Supreme Court's final vindication of the group's activity on First Amendment grounds in 1964. NAACP v. Alabama, 377 U.S. 288, 84 S. Ct. 1302, 12 L. Ed. 2d 325 (1964). See also NAACP v. Thompson, 357 F.2d 831 (5th Cir. 1966), *cert. denied sub nom.* Johnson v. NAACP, 385 U.S. 820 (1966), ending a three-year effort by state officials in Mississippi to bar the group.

2. In Virginia, in addition to NAACP v. Button, cited by Justice Douglas, there was a long history of litigation in which the state legislative committees sought to hamstring NAACP legal programs. The cases are reviewed in Jordan v. Hutchinson, 323 F.2d 597 (4th Cir. 1963). Louisiana statutes requiring annual filing of names and addresses of members, and requiring certain "non-trading" associations to file annual affidavits that none of its officers were Communists or members of subversive organizations, were voided in

Louisiana ex rel. Gremillion v. NAACP, 181 F. Supp. 37, *aff'd,* 366 U.S. 293 (1961).

3. In the wake of the Brown decision, eleven Southern states acted separately through legislation or litigation to restrict NAACP efforts to end segregation through court cases. See 2 Race Rel. L. Rep. 892 (1957). Other groups espousing civil rights causes were also attacked. Dombrowski v. Pfister, 380 U.S. 479, 85 S. Ct. 1116, 14 L. Ed. 2d 22 (1965), was an unsuccessful effort by Louisiana to use its Subversive Activities and Communist Control law as a basis for harassing and prosecuting the Southern Conference Educational Fund (SCEF), a group active in fostering civil rights for blacks in Louisiana and other Southern states. Legislative harassment of civil rights groups was not limited to the states. In Braden v. United States, 365 U.S. 431, 81 S. Ct. 584, 5 L. Ed. 2d 653 (1961), the Supreme Court affirmed a contempt conviction obtained by the House Committee on Un-American Activities against an official of a pro-integration organization who refused to answer questions concerning his alleged Communist connections.

4. The history and significance of anti-NAACP litigation is far greater than this limited mention indicates. Imagine the proof problems in defending against the charges leveled against the NAACP; consider the constitutional and statutory interpretation questions presented. In this area, the judgments made by civil rights lawyers involved great risks and were central to the organization's survival. Should membership lists be disclosed to avoid a ruinous fine? Should litigation efforts be circumscribed to avoid proceedings for barratry and maintenance? How do you defend against such state proceeding, when there is the strongest basis for belief that the real intent is to harass and eventually force a cessation of the group's civil rights activity?

These cases and their final outcomes illustrate important aspects about the issues discussed in Chapter Three. One notes immediately the willingness of the legal structure (courts and legislative committees) closest to the threat (civil rights activity) to manipulate legal norms to remove or at least neutralize that threat. But legal norms that have deep historical antecedents develop a life of their own, which cannot be totally ignored when they conflict with the desire of lawmakers to manipulate them in order to retain control over what is deemed a dangerous situation. The inevitable erosion of the legal norms is couched in objective, neutral, legal language or well recognized legal procedures. Note the ultimate reliance that such a political process places on the lawyer. Of course, it falls to higher (more removed) courts and legislative bodies to uphold the legal norms and thereby protect the rights of those under attack. Compare the cases just summarized and those to follow, and note the differences in the protection provided when the civil rights groups have taken affirmative rather than negative action — when they have initiated a boycott rather than been ordered to disclose their membership lists. Note also how difficult it is to determine the real winners in this litigation. Even when the rights of the organization are eventually upheld, their losses — stemming from the initial arrests, injunction against boycott activity, impounding of bank accounts and demand for membership lists — have diluted their programs, frightened their followers and turned energies from attack to a defensive posture. Are there more effective alternative means to defend against such attacks?

5. Despite the uncertainty of judicial support, civil rights groups have obtained impressive changes in discriminatory policies through the use of boycotts. The activity is surveyed below.

Since 1955 when the black citizens of Montgomery, Alabama crippled the city bus system by refusing to ride, black leaders have continued to use the boycott as a most effective weapon in their fight for civil rights. Any doubt that the boycott can be a successful weapon is quickly erased by a few examples. In 1963 the Birmingham, Alabama, retailers estimated that they were losing about $750,000 per week because of the boycott of black customers and the added loss of business of whites who were afraid to come downtown. The blacks of Macon, Georgia, discontinued riding buses in 1962 to protest segregated seating. The bus company, suffering a 50 percent fare loss, gave in to the demands. The Evening Bulletin, a Philadelphia newspaper, estimated that it lost 25,000 to 50,000 subscriptions between April 15 and June 10, 1962, due to a boycott protesting certain policies regarding news about the black community.

Boycotts are not necessarily confined to a single area or a single object. Operation Breadbasket, led by the Reverend Jesse Jackson, is a national boycott based in Chicago. For sixteen weeks in the spring of 1969 blacks boycotted all of the A&P Company stores of Chicago. The objective was to secure more jobs for blacks and a market for twenty-five products manufactured by black-owned firms. The boycott ended when A&P promised 286 more jobs for blacks and placed all the products on their shelves. Nationally, Operation Breadbasket has created 5,000 jobs and acquired $40 million in annual salaries for blacks. . . .

Before Easter of 1960 approximately 98 percent of Nashville, Tennessee's black population stopped buying downtown. Formerly they had spent about seven million dollars per year in Nashville stores. The results, as reported for the National Community Relations Conference, were that the local transit company found business dwindling seriously; the approximate 20 percent of department store customers who were black stayed home; another 20 percent from within a seventy-five mile radius of Nashville stayed home because of the racial tension; hundreds of white moderates in the city sympathized with the boycotters and also decided to wear old clothes on Easter. By early May white merchants had met with black leaders and subsequently opened formerly segregated eating facilities to blacks.

The 1963 Birmingham boycott listed earlier, in which merchants estimated a loss of $750,000 per week, is another example of a boycott with an extensive effect on trade. More serious boycotts have been threatened. In 1964 black leaders publicly asked banking houses to refuse loans to the state of Mississippi. After the Selma violence in 1965, Martin Luther King asked for a nationwide boycott of Alabama products. This received some response; the 308 delegates to the convention of the International Longshoremen and Warehouse Union voted unanimously not to handle Alabama products. There is no evidence that any widespread boycotts materialized, but in view of past success, the threats were not empty ones. . . . (Note, The Consumer Boycott, 42 Miss. L.J. 226-227, 239-242 (1971).)

6. The Mississippi Law Journal reviews the legal means by which the targets of consumer boycotts might halt such protests. The Sherman Antitrust Act, 15 U.S.C. §§1-7 (1964), the writers conclude, is theoretically available, particularly in boycotts of large dimensions, but enforcement is generally focused on those acting with commercial rather than consumer purposes. Of course, state antitrust laws may be applied, as in the Montgomery bus boycott, where Dr. King and 114 others were convicted. The appeal was dismissed on procedural grounds. Common-law tort actions are also likely to fail where the boycotters are persons with a special interest to protect and when they seek legitimate objectives in a peaceful manner.

7. An effort by the Alabama legislature to meet the boycott problem head-on failed. In Kirkland v. Wallace, 403 F.2d 413 (5th Cir. 1968), the Fifth Circuit declared invalid on its face a statute prohibiting the circulation of notices that a boycott exists or is contemplated. The ruling came despite a district attorney's claim that a prosecution under the statute had been a "slip-up," and that he always "avoided this boycott statute." Business targets of civil rights boycotts have had more success, though, especially in state courts.

SCLC v. A.G. CORPORATION
241 So.2d 619 (Miss. 1970)

Robertson, Justice:

Appellee, A. G. Corporation, brought suit in the Chancery Court of Grenada County, Mississippi, against the Southern Christian Leadership Conference, Inc., a non-resident corporation, (hereafter SCLC), the B. and P. Enterprises, Inc., a corporation, and a large number of individual non-resident and resident defendants.

The appellee charged all the defendants with an illegal and unlawful conspiracy and with a secondary boycott "the malicious and unlawful object of which was to ruin and cause injury to the business of the complainant and others."

The appellee prayed for an attachment, temporary injunction, and damages for causing injuries to appellee's business.

A temporary injunction was authorized and issued and the case was tried on its merits by the Chancery Court of Grenada County . . . .

The chancellor found the Southern Christian Leadership Conference, Inc., a Georgia Corporation, the B. and P. Enterprises, Inc., a Mississippi Corporation, and thirty-nine individual defendants jointly and severally liable to the appellee for $114,572.95 damages.

Appellee had gone out of business so, the need for an injunction no longer existed, the temporary injunction was dissolved. . . .

We affirm as to liability, but reverse and remand as to damages. . . .

The bill of complaint was filed on September 28, 1966, and the appellee went out of business on December 24, 1966.

The events immediately preceding the acts and actions of the defendants complained of were chronicled by the chancellor in his opinion, thusly:

> The "Meredith March," publicized by Negro James F. Meredith as his march from Memphis to Jackson, for the purpose of emphasizing the importance of Negro voter registration, is a matter of common knowledge. It began in early June, 1966, and a matter of common knowledge, though not clearly reflected in the record, Meredith was fired upon and wounded in southern DeSoto County, when his march was very young. Defendants, in their Brief, saw that "In June, 1966 James Meredith, in cooperation with the SCLC, led a civil rights march through Grenada." The Court accepts as accurate this statement that it was in cooperation with the SCLC. Nevertheless, the late Dr. Martin Luther King, otherwise identified in the record as President at all times of SCLC, arrived in Grenada with the march and made certain demands upon Grenada County officials, including extended and expanded opportunities to the Colored people of the County to be registered to vote. The march continued onward, but SCLC remained interested that agreements by Grenada County officials would be kept, would not be "reneged on," as termed by one witness.
>
> For some time prior to the Meredith march, there existed a Ministerial Alliance in Grenada, whose membership included ministers of both races. The Colored members of it, about the end of June or early in July, 1966, resolved to organize what is called in the record the Grenada County Freedom Movement. It was and is an unincorporated, apparently loosely organized group of Negroes with kindred thoughts and ambitions for their betterment. It will be referred to usually herein as "GCFM." Defendant the Reverend C. C. Coleman, then pastor of First New Hope Baptist Church and President of the Ministerial Alliance, presided over the organizational meeting which was held in Defendant Vincent Chapel Church, and attended by other ministers and by certain SCLC employes or workers, as hereinafter to be shown. In the organization, the organizers defined its purpose as being the improvement of conditions in the Negro community, particularly in areas of voter registration, political education, and in use of public accommodations covered by the 1964 Civil Rights Act. . . .
>
> GCFM was described as having as its members all Negro citizens of Grenada County who were interested and participated and wish to be identified with it, but it was more boldly described as having for members all the Negroes of Grenada County. There are no dues, but its expenses are borne by contributions at meetings, and from throughout the country. Some of the defendants denied that they were members of GCFM.
>
> After its organization, there were mass meetings almost every night, and these were held in various Churches, including those named defendants in the Bill of Complaint. The responsible officers of the several Churches either affirmatively voted for their Church buildings to be so used, or acquiesced in such use. Bell Flowers Baptist Church, by affirmative approval of its responsible officers, became

the headquarters for both SCLC and GCFM, and they maintained offices there, and picketing and marching generally emanated from there, until the Church edifice was damaged by fire.

Following the departure of the Meredith march from Grenada, SCLC representatives and workers either stayed behind in Grenada, or immediately returned thereto, to press for compliance with understandings had by SCLC with Grenada County officials and to test public accommodations. . . .

The record overwhelmingly established that SCLC closely cooperated with GCFM in the activities complained of in the Bill of Complaint, and actively assisted in carrying out these activities. In the boycott complained of, the record reflects that the strategic decisions were made by GCFM and the tactical decisions to be employed in carrying out the strategic decisions were usually made by SCLC, and the decisions were carried out by SCLC. The SCLC staff assisted in whatever GCFM was doing.

The services of SCLC were made available to GCFM, which, in mass meeting, accepted the offer by vote. In the language of Defendant Cunningham, GCFM President, "Well, they were to be at our disposal and to assist us in accomplishing our objectives."

Continuing to lay the background, the chancellor said:

On the 10th day of July, 1966, Colored people marched to the Grenada County jail to protest the jailing of certain people of the Colored community, and Defendants' position is that Highway Patrolmen, the Sheriff and his Deputies, and City Police beset them and beat some of their number, dispersing them. Complainant, asserting and proving by a preponderance of the evidence that no officer, stockholder, or employe of it participated in any way in the occurrence, did not seriously controvert Defendants' testimony as to the occurrence.

The demonstrators retreated into a mass meeting held on that night, and a boycott of white merchants was launched, set off largely, apparently, by the jail experience. The launching of it was variously described by Defendants who testified. The mass meeting seems definitely to have been a GCFM meeting. It was described as being a spontaneous decision of Grenada people in a mass meeting attended by several hundred people, and as a result of initiative from the people in Grenada. Some witnesses present at the meeting testified that SCLC Official Hosea Williams was speaking on the incident and asked the question, "What shall we do?" and everybody cheered and said, "Boycott!" and the boycott was on. Another account has it that Project Director Leon Hall was present and stated, "Since they beat us on Sunday, we will put on a boycott on Monday."

The record establishes that SCLC operatives Hosea Williams, Leon Hall, and J. T. Johnson, and perhaps Alphonzo Harris, urged the boycott, and that GCFM President Cunningham and Mrs. Beulah Washington and Defendant Robert Edward Johnson urged the boycott.

Regardless of whether the people at the GCFM mass meeting or the GCFM or SCLC actually set off the boycott, it was launched and the record clearly supports the conclusion that SCLC and GCFM were in complete agreement on it and worked together for the achievement of complete success in it, and the record reveals that SCLC considered itself here to assist in what the Colored community wanted.

The Court considers that SCLC's direct action program here reveals itself. SCLC furnished a man, Defendant R. B. Cottonreader, Jr., who would largely be in overall charge of picketing activities in connection with the boycott, and it furnished a man, Henry Brownlee, who was adept at making picket signs for the group. Defendant Major Wright helped from time to time with the picketing, as did others of SCLC.

The chancellor in stating what he believed to be the basic issue said:

Complainant asserts and argues that Defendants entered into a conspiracy to hurt, damage, and put it out of business. The Court believes that existence or not of conspiracy is a basic, threshold issue, and should be resolved.

In Mississippi Power and Light Company v. Town of Coldwater, 234 Miss., 615, 636, 106 So.2d, 375, 1958, the Supreme Court defined conspiracy:

"A sufficient definition of conspiracy is 'a combination of persons to accomplish an unlawful purpose or a lawful purpose unlawfully.' 15 C.J.S. Conspiracy, Sec. 1, page 996. . . .

And it added:

". . . of course, it is not a fraud or unlawful to do what one has a legal right to do. State v. Wilde [Wilbe] Lumber Co., 217 Miss. 346, 64 So.2d 327."

The chancellor noted in his opinion that Federal District Judge Clayton had issued a temporary injunction on July 22, 1966, in Cunningham, individually and on behalf of all those similarly situated, et al. v. Suggs Ingram, individually and in his capacity as Sheriff of Grenada County, Mississippi, et al., enjoining Sheriff Ingram and city officials from arresting, jailing, prosecuting or punishing "the plaintiffs or members of the class they represent while they are engaged in exercising rights guaranteed and protected by the First and Fourteenth Amendments to the United States Constitution in accordance with the terms of this temporary injunction."

District Judge Clayton defined and delineated in rather great detail the manner in which plaintiffs and the class they represented could parade, demonstrate, march, picket and otherwise assert their rights. In his order, Judge Clayton not only provided for the protection of the plaintiffs in the exercise of their rights, but also provided for the protection of the public and other citizens in the exercise of their personal and property rights.

The chancellor recognized the rights of these defendants to peacefully picket and march and demonstrate as long as they stayed within the limits and bounds so carefully and fairly outlined by Judge Clayton. Every member of this Court agrees with the chancellor and Judge Clayton that the defendants had the right to peacefully meet, picket, march and boycott to secure redress of their grievances and complaints specifically made against particular employers or businesses.

The defendants argued that they were only exercising rights vouchsafed to them by the First and Fourteenth Amendments to the United States Constitution and that they did abide by the order of the district judge.

The whole trouble in this case was that these defendants had no complaint or grievance or even gripe against the appellee. One of their assignments of error was:

> The court erred in holding that defendants had acted in concert against complainant for an unlawful purpose because:
> a) Defendants' right *to boycott complainant* for the purpose of protesting *its racially discriminatory employment practices and other discriminatory treatment of Negroes* is protected by the First and Fourteenth Amendments to the United States Constitution; (Emphasis added).

But the truth of the matter was that no complaint of any kind, oral or written, was ever made by any of these defendants or by any employee or any customer to the appellee, its officers or agents.

The appellee was, in effect, an innocent bystander who ultimately became the innocent victim of this struggle for political and economic power. Appellee was especially vulnerable because two-thirds of its trade was with black customers. The defendants were very aware of this fact.

The chancellor found that the defendants had entered into an illegal and unlawful conspiracy for the illegal and unlawful purpose of ruining the business of appellee, that the means employed, namely, a secondary boycott, threats, intimidation, duress and force, were unlawful and illegal and were clearly outside the constitutional guaranties, and the bounds set by District Judge Clayton. . . .

> Peaceful picketing is a lawful act. Mass picketing, which is the use of a large number of pickets, is not peaceable picketing, is illegal, and entitles the one being picketed to resort to equity and obtain an injunction. [Citations omitted.]
> *When any individual or organization under whatsoever name attempts to use force to gain his or her ends, they are attempting to usurp a governmental function. When a picket line becomes a picket fence, it is time for the government to act.* Carnegie-Illinois Steel Corporation v. United Steelworkers of America, 353 Pa. 420, 45 A.2d 857, 205 Miss. at 374 and 376, 38 So.2d at 768 and 769. (Emphasis added).

The Fourteenth Amendment to the United States Constitution, among other things, specifically provides: ". . . nor shall *any State deprive any person of* life, liberty, or *property, without due process of law* . . ." (Emphasis added).

Surely this prohibition should apply with equal or greater force to private persons or organizations.

In condemning a conspiracy of private persons to destroy the business and livelihood of another, we said, in Southern Bus Lines, Inc. [38 So.2d 765 (1949):]

> *Private persons cannot conspire to illegally destroy the business of another, and where two or more persons conspire together, the conspiracy makes the wrongful*

acts of each the joint acts of all of them. Globe & Rutgers Fire Ins. Co. v. Firemen's Fund Ins. Co. et al., 97 Miss. 148, 52 So. 454, 29 L.R.A., N.S., 869; State ex rel. Rice v. Hasson Grocery Co., 177 Miss. 204, 170 So. 234, 107 A.L.R. 663, 205 Miss. at 375, 38 So.2d at 769. (Emphasis added).

Although this is not a res ipsa loquitur case, we can not avoid noting, as the chancellor probably did, that even though the appellee's business had been a profitable one for ten years before the boycott began, six months later the business had been destroyed. Surely this is strong circumstantial evidence of the effectiveness of the secondary boycott which was promoted, encouraged, guided, directed and executed by these forty-one defendants-appellants.

In proving conspiracy, this Court in Wagley v. Colonial Baking Company, et al., 208 Miss. 815, 45 So.2d 717 (1950), said:

The law permits great latitude in the admission of circumstantial evidence tending to establish a conspiracy, and to connect those advising, encouraging, aiding, abetting, and ratifying the overt acts committed for the purpose of carrying into effect the objects of the conspiracy, as the jury should have before them and are entitled to consider every fact which has a bearing on and a tendency to prove the ultimate fact in issue and which will enable them to come to a satisfactory conclusion. 208 Miss. at 856, 45 So.2d at 725.

The Chancellor, in specifically finding that illegal means were used, said:

The Court returns to a review of the evidence and the application of these legal principles above. The pickets, operating all days some days, parts of days at other times, led by a leader, Defendant Cottonreader or another, sang, "hollered," made loud noises in the square, Defendant Cottonreader voiced hatred of whites as he led the pickets in the Square, then walked back and forth in front of AG, and when a customer would vacate the store, he would have a conversation with him; mass picketing, they blocked the store entrance and customers could not go in and out; once when entreated to move on and not block the way, they sat down in the sidewalk, making their obstacle even worse; they carried signs conveying the message to AG, "Pak 'N Sak, pack up and sack out," and other signs warning of danger downtown, and "Your days are numbered"; Cottonreader intercepted and led away a young lady about to pay a bill in the store. Soon after the school incident, a large mob of pickets, with newsmen accompanying them, stretched out over a half block, blocking entrance into AG's store for fifteen or twenty minutes, as they passed, and this occurred two or three times. These are some of the activities of the pickets, and the picketing was augmented by, and punctuated with, speeches in the public square, with boasts, threats, in which AG was the principal target, and condemnation of "Uncle Toms." Then there were J. D. Willis, uncontradicted, and Defendant Wonzo Bowdry, contradicted, and the car with the CB radio, Willis, in particular, standing often at AG's front door talking to, and succeeding in getting Colored customers to turn away from AG. There was the contradictory testimony about Defendant Ward and the Colored girl with the turnip greens.

The chancellor also found that for a short time pictures were taken of black customers of the appellee, that the name of the customer was added to each picture, and the pictures were then posted at the Bell Flowers Church where the mass meetings were being held nightly, so that pressure could be brought to bear on those guilty of shopping with the appellee.

After extensive and detailed findings of fact, the trial court stated its conclusions of law:

> The Court concludes that the boycott was not conducted within peaceful and legal limits, that the picketing and other admissible incidents exceeded free speech rights of the Constitution, and that, what the Court has hereinbefore found to be the agreement, the means to the end, of the boycotter Defendants, does in fact amount to a conspiracy, and that one of the conspiracy's goals was to injure AG in its business or to force it out of business. The record, almost without contradiction, demonstrates that the activity of the Defendants caused terror and fright among the Colored community, and the Court cannot from the testimony conclude that that was unintended on the part of the conspirators. Thus, returning to the Southern Bus Lines case, there was coercion or intimidation (both are not necessary to be present) to prevent, and prevented, shoppers from patronizing AG. . . .

We cannot say that the chancellor's findings of fact as to liability are manifestly wrong. In fact, we are of the opinion that his findings of fact are supported by substantial evidence and that he was correct in finding and concluding that the forty-one defendants named in the trial court's final decree are jointly and severally liable in damages to the appellee.

The only other point that the defendants-appellants seriously argue is that chancellor's award of damages was greatly excessive on this record. We agree. . . .

[W]e feel that the figure of $114,572.95 is clearly excessive and is too conjectural and speculative. . . .

Affirmed as to liability, but reversed and remanded as to damages.*

HENRY v. FIRST NATIONAL BANK OF CLARKSDALE, 444 F.2d 1300 (5th Cir. 1971). In 1966, a group of black citizens in Fort Gibson, Mississippi initiated a boycott against local officials and white merchants. It was designed to achieve fair employment practices and fair treatment of black customers, and to otherwise eliminate discrimination. The boycott was effectuated by picketing, leafleting and public meetings. After it had been in effect for several years, twenty-three white merchants of Fort Gibson who

* A Mississippi civil rights attorney, Melvyn Leventhal, reports that no further action was taken in the case because all the assets of SCLC and B. and P. (Black and Proud) Enterprises were seized upon the chancellor's decision, and then sold when B. and P. could not post an appeal bond. The $17,000 to $18,000 gained from the sale of B. and P. assets was paid to attorneys for A.G. Corporation. Letter from Melvyn Leventhal to author, June 14, 1972.

were subject to the boycott filed suit in a state court against the national NAACP, a local civil rights group, and 150 named individuals. They also joined fifty banks located in Mississippi which allegedly contained funds and property of the nonresident defendant NAACP. The suit alleged that the civil rights groups had entered into a conspiracy in restraint of trade and had engaged in secondary boycotts and other malicious and wrongful interference with their businesses, all in violation of the Mississippi antitrust laws. The suit also alleged that the boycotters had abused customers of the businesses with threats, obscene and insulting language, destruction of property, and physical assault. For relief, the white merchants sought the attachment (presumably for damages) of all NAACP funds in the defendant banks, injunctions against picketing, boycotting, etc., and damages in excess of $3.5 million.

Shortly after this suit was filed, the state court clerk served writs of attachment, as provided by state law, ordering various banks around Mississippi to hold NAACP funds until further notice. As it turned out, the banks had not frozen the assets of the nonresident NAACP, which was named the defendant, but rather the assets of the Mississippi State Conference of the NAACP, and of the local NAACP branches in the state of Mississippi, and all of the organizations which claimed not to have been named as defendants. The state NAACP branches asserted this claim in a federal suit against the banks which had frozen their funds pursuant to the writ of attachment. Following a hearing, the federal court agreed that the attachments had infringed on the branches' due process rights, and ordered the banks to release the funds upon posting by plaintiffs of a bond in the amount of 110 percent of these funds.

Following this order, the NAACP filed an amended complaint that sought to restrain the white merchants from continuing to prosecute their state court suit, on the ground that the antitrust statutes upon which they relied were either patently unconstitutional or were invalidly applied. The white merchants contended that the federal court lacked jurisdiction because there was no "state action," and that the Federal Anti-Injunction Statute, 28 U.S.C.A. §2283 (1965), barred enjoining their pending state civil suit. The merchants appealed from an adverse ruling, and the Fifth Circuit reversed, holding that the mere filing of an action in state court does not constitute "state action" for purposes of litigation under the Civil Rights Statutes. Asserting that the NAACP's reliance on Shelley v. Kraemer, 334 U.S. 1, 68 S. Ct. 836, 92 L. Ed. 1161 (1948), printed infra at 609, was misplaced, the court asserted that in Shelley,

> . . . it is judicial *enforcement* of a private discriminatory contract that brings the otherwise "private action" within the ambit of the Fourteenth Amendment. . . . To say that an open courthouse door constitutes "state action" is to assume that the party whose private suit is challenged as "state action" already has the court on his side before the adjudicatory process even commences. (444 F.2d at 1309.)

The court designated the attachment process as "ministerial acts" that did not serve to clothe the underlying suit in the garb of "state action." The court also pointed out that there was no indication that the plaintiffs in the state suit would be able to support their allegations of violence and damage in the amount of $3.5 million, and that no Mississippi court had ever applied its antitrust statutes to a noncommercial situation.

MACHESKY v. BIZZELL
414 F.2d 283 (5th Cir. 1969)

Before BELL and THORNBERRY, Circuit Judges, and CHOATE, District Judge.
1, 28 U.S.C.A. §2283:

BELL, Circuit Judge.

This appeal involves First Amendment rights. Suit was filed in the state court to enjoin the picketing and boycotting activities of appellants. They, in turn, sought declaratory and injunctive relief in the federal court. The federal district court denied relief and dismissed the complaint. . . . This appeal followed. We reverse for further proceedings for the reasons to be set out and within stated limits.

Appellants are members of the "Greenwood Movement," a civil rights group active in Greenwood, Mississippi. Two of the appellees are class representatives of some sixty merchants and bankers in Greenwood who appeared as plaintiffs in the state court suit, some appearing in an individual capacity, some in a corporate capacity. The third appellee is Honorable William H. Bizzel, Chancellor of the Chancery Court of Leflore County, Mississippi, who issued the injunction in the state court suit. . . .

The Greenwood Movement was organized in November of 1967. Its activities greatly increased after the murder of Dr. Martin Luther King, Jr. in April of 1968. A boycott of white merchants began on April 10, 1968. The Movement stated its objectives to be, inter alia, "To eliminate segregation and discrimination; to make all men free; to create fair employment practices." The state court found the specific goals to be equal employment by the city, equal job opportunities in business, use of courtesy titles, improved city services in Negro areas, fair treatment by police, representation on various public boards and agencies, and dialogue with elected officials. The picketing which supported the boycott was very intensive, being carried on every day except Sunday. The state court found that ". . . In a few instances the size of groups has been sufficient to interfere with vehicles and pedestrians, but this has not been a major problem."

The state court found that the Movement did, however, involve activities of a more questionable nature. There was testimony to indicate that members of the Movement had harassed and used abusive language toward Negroes who continued to patronize the white merchants. There were instances of violence. The most serious was a firebomb thrown into the house of a Negro family who had continued to shop at stores of the white merchants. There were several instances of windows having been broken, in one case by a bottle containing a note saying, "Don't shop downtown or fire next time — The Spirit."

The state court order enjoined:

> 1. Picketing or marching, or persuading or inducing any other person or persons to picket or march, in any organized form whatsoever, with or without signs or placards, upon Howard Street or upon Carrollton Avenue or in the Highland Park Shopping Center in the City of Greenwood, or within 300 feet of the place of business in the City of Greenwood of any of the Complainants in this cause. . . .
>
> 2. Loitering or congregating, or inducing or persuading any person or persons to loiter or congregate, upon any sidewalk or street or other public area in the City of Greenwood for the purpose of doing anything whatsoever, directly or indirectly, to induce, persuade, or coerce any person or persons not to trade or do other business with the business establishments of any of the said Complainants in the City of Greenwood, Mississippi.
>
> 3. Stationing themselves or anyone else as a lookout or lookouts for the purpose of observing customers entering, leaving, or shopping or doing other business in the business establishments of any of the said Complainants in the City of Greenwood, Mississippi.
>
> 4. Making or preparing or causing to be made or prepared a record of the names, automobile license numbers or other identification of person or persons entering or trading in the business establishments of any of the said Complainants in the City of Greenwood, Mississippi.
>
> 5. Publishing, distributing, or announcing in any manner the name or names of persons who have entered or traded in or shall hereafter enter or trade in the business establishments of any of said Complainants in the said City of Greenwood or causing such names to be published, distributed or announced; and
>
> 6. Threatening, intimidating, coercing, or using force or violence upon any person or persons so as to dissuade such person or persons from entering or trading in the business establishments of any of said Complainants in the said City of Greenwood.[2]

The prayer of appellants in the federal court was for a declaration of their federal rights and an order vacating the state court injunction, or in the alternative, that the bounds of the state court injunction be limited. On August 13, 1968, the district court dismissed the complaint. Machesky v. Bizzell, N.D. Miss., 1968, 288 F. Supp. 295. . . .

[The court's full discussion justifying a federal court injunction despite the restrictions of the anti-injunction statute, 28 U.S.C.A. §2283 (1965) is omitted.]

The right to picket is not absolute. It must be "asserted within the limits of not unreasonably interfering with the rights of others to use the sidewalks and streets, to have access to store entrances, and where conducted in such

2. The boycott itself was not enjoined. On July 20, 1968 the state court denied a request to modify the injunction except to the extent that the proscription against loitering and congregating was limited to the main business area.

manner as not to deprive the public of police and fire protection." Kelly v. Page, 5 Cir., 1964, 335 F.2d 114, 119. These interests can, of course, be protected by state injunctions narrowly drawn. The injunction here, however, has not struck such a balance. It prohibits all picketing in the designated business areas of Greenwood, for whatever purpose and in whatever manner carried out. This overshoots the mark and the situation cannot be saved by Milk Wagon Drivers Union v. Meadowmoor Dairies, 1941, 312 U.S. 287, 61 S. Ct. 552, 85 L. Ed. 836, a case premised on violence of an intensity and duration in no way present here, or at least on the record before the district court.

The injunction here in question goes even further than prohibiting protected picketing. It enjoins "loitering or congregating . . . to induce, persuade, or coerce any person or persons not to trade or to do other business with . . . Complainants. . . ." This, for aught else appearing, prohibits the distribution of leaflets or even speech directed toward the boycott effort.

We hold that the state court injunction here is unconstitutionally overbroad in that it lumps the protected with the unprotected in such a way as to abridge important public interests in the full dissemination of public expression on public issues. We hold also that where important public rights to full dissemination of expression on public issues are abridged by state court proceedings, the principles of comity embodied in §2283 must yield, and that the district court is empowered to enjoin the state court proceedings to the extent that they violate these First Amendment rights. . . .

NOTE: CIVIL RIGHTS PROTESTS AND LABOR LAW RULES

As indicated in Machesky v. Bizzell, picketing undertaken to promote an economic boycott that is part of a general protest movement against segregation and discrimination has been held lawful on First Amendment grounds, without reference to the question of applicability of labor laws. See also Smith v. Grady, 411 F.2d 181 (5th Cir. 1965); NAACP v. Thompson, 357 F.2d 831 (5th Cir. 1966); Kelley v. Page, 335 F.2d 114 (5th Cir. 1964); Young v. Munn, 1 Race Rel. L. Sur. (N.D. Miss. 1969); Cottonreader v. Johnson, 252 F. Supp. 492 (M.D. Ala. 1966). The cited cases, all of which involved boycotts of white merchants, upheld the right to picket in a peaceful and nonobstructive manner. Usually these cases were brought to enjoin alleged illegal harassment by either police and local officials or the protesters.

Actions by business proprietors to enjoin alleged interference with and damage to their property have often brought labor law concepts into play and yielded less consistent results. The statutory provisions arguably applicable to boycotts for equal employment opportunities include the Norris-La Guardia Act, which, inter alia, deprived federal courts of jurisdiction to issue injunctions against nonviolent picketing and other forms of publicity in "labor disputes," 29 U.S.C.A. §104 (1965), and defined "labor dispute" as "any controversy concerning terms or conditions of employment, or concerning the association of persons in negotiating . . . changing, or seeking to arrange terms or conditions of employment regardless of whether or not the disputants stand in the proximate relation of employer and employee." 29 U.S.C. §113. (The National Labor Relations Act contains the same definition of labor dispute, 29 U.S.C. §152.) Such an injunction may be issued only after a full hearing where it is found that unlawful acts have been threatened or committed, substantial irreparable injury to the plaintiff's property will result, greater injury will occur to the plaintiff if the injunction is not issued than to the defendant if it is granted, plaintiff has no adequate remedy at law, and all reasonable efforts have been made to settle the dispute. 29 U.S.C.A. §§107-108 (1965).

NEW NEGRO ALLIANCE v. SANITARY GROCERY COMPANY, 303 U.S. 552, 58 S. Ct. 703, 82 L. Ed. 1012 (1938). A black "mutual improvement" group requested plaintiff grocery company to adopt a policy of employing Negro clerks, in the course of personnel changes, in stores which were patronized largely by blacks but in which no black clerks were employed. When the request was ignored, the organization picketed with a placard reading: "Do your part! Buy where you can work! No Negroes employed here!" The picketing was for only one day, but the group threatened to place similar pickets at two other stores. The grocery company obtained an injunction from a federal district court, which was affirmed by the court of appeals, but reversed by the Supreme Court on a finding that the controversy constituted a "labor dispute" under the "Norris-LaGuardia Act." The fact that the dispute was "racial" in that it grew out of racial discrimination did not, the Court found, remove the case from the scope of the act.

NOTES

1. A few years before New Negro Alliance was decided, the Maryland Court of Appeals ruled that no labor dispute was involved where a black group in Baltimore had been enjoined from conducting its boycott of stores in a black area. The blacks were demanding "one hundred per cent colored help," and turned down an offer of 50 percent black personnel as not satisfactory. Holding the case "a racial or social question," which thus had no application to the rules of labor disputes, the court nevertheless reversed in part to amend the injunction so as to permit publicizing the boycott in a noncoercive fashion. Green v. Samuelson, 168 Md. 421, 178 A. 109 (1935).

An injunction of boycott picketing was also obtained in Beck Shoe Corporation v. Johnson, 153 Misc. 363, 274 N.Y.S. 946 (Sup. Ct. 1934), in which the court refused to extend the policy in labor disputes to racial controversies.

2. Despite the holding of New Negro Alliance, courts have usually taken the view either that boycotts and similar activities to promote nondiscriminatory employment policies are not labor disputes within the meaning of federal labor laws, or that such activities have an unlawful purpose or are carried

out in an unlawful manner, and thus are prohibited whether or not they involve or grow out of a labor dispute.

HUGHES v. SUPERIOR COURT, 339 U.S. 460, 70 S. Ct. 718, 94 L. Ed. 985 (1950). A grocery chain, Lucky Stores, Inc., refused a demand by a group, the Progressive Citizens of America, that at a particular store near a housing project, when white employees quit or were transferred, blacks be hired in proportion to the percentage of black customers — estimated to be 50 percent. The blacks then picketed the store and ignored a state court order obtained by the store chain enjoining the protest. The blacks were found guilty of contempt. This decision was affirmed by the Supreme Court, which held that the picketing had an unlawful purpose in that it was contrary to the judicially stated California public policy of nondiscrimination in employment, and thus could be prohibited.

Justice Frankfurter, speaking for the Court, accepted the California court's assumption that picketing to protest racial discrimination would not be unlawful. In affirming the state court's conclusion that "it would encourage discriminatory hiring to give constitutional protection to petitioner's efforts to subject the opportunity of getting a job to a quota system," Frankfurter asserted:

> To deny to California the right to ban picketing in the circumstances of this case would mean that there could be no prohibition of the pressure of picketing to secure proportional employment on ancestral grounds of Hungarians in Cleveland, of Poles in Buffalo, of Germans in Milwaukee, of Portuguese in New Bedford, of Mexicans in San Antonio, of the numerous minority groups in New York, and so on through the whole gamut of racial and religious concentrations in various cities. States may well believe that such constitutional sheltering would inevitably encourage use of picketing to compel employment on the basis of racial discrimination. In disallowing such picketing States may act under the belief that otherwise community tensions and conflicts would be exacerbated. The differences in cultural traditions instead of adding flavor and variety to our common citizenry might well be hardened into hostilities by leave of law. The Constitution does not demand that the element of communication in picketing prevail over the mischief furthered by its use in these situations. (339 U.S. at 464.)

NOTES

1. Justice Frankfurter used a line of argument quite familiar to those blacks whose requests for correction of inequality have been met with the response that the system could not withstand similar requests from redheads and other identifiable groups, most of whom have not been and are not likely to be victims of racial discrimination. Such responses ignore past discrimination actually suffered by blacks, condemn requests for remedial action as "reverse discrimination," and are so frequently repeated that they represent a phenomenon worthy of study by social psychologists.

2. Justice Traynor dissented from the California court's decision in Hughes, stating:

Those racial groups against whom discrimination is practiced may seek economic equality either by demanding that hiring be done without reference to race or color or by demanding a certain number of jobs for members of their group. The majority opinion holds that economic equality cannot be sought by the second method if picketing is adopted as the means of attaining that objective. In the absence of a statute protecting them from discrimination it is not unreasonable for Negroes to seek economic equality by asking those in sympathy with their aims to help them secure jobs that may be opened to them by the enlistment of such aid. In their struggle for equality the only effective economic weapon Negroes have is the purchasing power they are able to mobilize to induce employers to open jobs to them. . . . There are so few neighborhoods where Negroes can make effective appeals against discrimination that they may reasonably regard the seeking of jobs in neighborhoods where their appeal may be effective the only practical means of combating discrimination against them. In arbitrating the conflicting interests of different groups in society courts should not impose ideal standards on one side when they are powerless to impose similar standards upon the other. Only a clear danger to the community would justify judicial rules that restrict the peaceful mobilization of a group's economic power to secure economic equality. . . . There is no reality in the reasoning that those who seek to secure jobs where they have an opportunity to enlist public support on their behalf are thereby seeking illegal discrimination in their favor, for the fact remains that everywhere they turn for jobs they are likely to encounter the barrier of discrimination.

The picketing in this case is directed at persuading Lucky to take action that it may lawfully take on its own initiative. No law prohibits Lucky from discriminating in favor of or against Negroes. It may legally adopt a policy of proportionate hiring. The picketing confronts Lucky with the choice of adopting a policy that is not illegal in itself or risking the loss of patronage that may result from the picketing. Had California adopted a fair employment practices act that prohibited consideration of the race of applicants for jobs, it might be said that the demand for proportional hiring would be a demand that Lucky violate the law. Neither the Legislature nor the people have adopted such a statute, and I find no implication in the majority opinion that its equivalent exists under the common law of this state. (198 P.2d at 896.)

3. In recent years, the need to establish standards by which to measure progress in the elimination of discrimination has been recognized in school and employment discrimination cases. (See Chapters Nine and Thirteen.) But the Hughes v. Superior Court doctrine has been used to enjoin efforts by several civil rights groups. An Indiana civil rights group, Fair Share Organization, Inc. (FSO), lost several injunction cases because of its demands for selective hiring of black employees based on the proportion of black customers patronizing the particular stores. See FSO v. Nagdeman, 135 Ind. App. 610, 193 N.E.2d 257 (1963) (picketing of clothing store enjoined and damages of $10,000 awarded against leaders of group), *cert. denied,* 379 U.S. 818 (1964); FSO v. Mitnick, 134 Ind. App. 675, 188 N.E.2d 840 (1963) (court

found that picketing of drugstore was designed to replace white clerk with black), *aff'd,* 245 Ind. 324, 198 N.E.2d 765 (1964), *cert. denied,* 379 U.S. 843 (1964); FSO v. Kroger Co., 240 Ind. 461, 165 N.E.2d 606 (1960) (court enjoined picketing requiring employment policy change even if whites had to be discharged or reassigned). See also Young Adults for Progressive Action, Inc. v. B & B Cash Grocery Store, Inc., 151 So.2d 877 (Fla. 1963); Orlando v. Stearnes, 6 Race Rel. L. Rep. 821 (1961).

BRANDENBURG v. METROPOLITAN PACKAGE STORE ASSOCIATION, 29 Misc. 2d 817, 211 N.Y.S.2d 621 (1961). When Harlem retail liquor stores refused to purchase from black wholesale liquor salesmen, a black group urging such purchases began, in July 1959, to picket and boycott the stores. Suffering serious economic losses as a result of the boycott, the Harlem stores, members of the Metropolitan Package Store Association, switched their liquor purchases from white to black salesmen. Sixty-two white salesmen and their union sued the association to enjoin the switches, which, they asserted, were based solely on race. An injunction was granted prohibiting "all other persons . . . having notice" of the order from engaging in any conduct or otherwise inducing transfer of accounts on account of race. The black group continued picketing, and contempt proceedings were subsequently brought against their coordinator, John Young. The court found that, although Young was not a party to the injunction proceeding, he was bound because of willful disobedience to a known mandate. The court, citing Hughes v. Superior Court, held that the black group's boycott was in violation of the state policy against employment discrimination. The opinion berated the black group's practices.

> There smoulders among us an unlawful condition both distressing and disgraceful. In Harlem, Negro leaders, civic, political and clerical, and the local branch of an association dedicated to promoting the lot of their fellows, including elimination of racial discrimination, are fomenting racial discrimination, against white men. To [respondent and other blacks] its implications, the sting and degradation, are meaningful. . . . They have been its victims . . . as Negroes they know fully what racial discrimination is. And yet as men of dark skin they agitate by word and action — speech, print, boycott and picketing — to deprive white men of their livelihoods solely because they are white skinned, so as to replace these victims with their selected Negroes. . . . (211 N.Y.S.2d at 623.)

The court urged blacks to

> . . . reappraise their position, for themselves and even more of their community. Their active or even tacit approval of this anathematized intolerance, racial discrimination in connection with employment is beyond understanding. Insistence upon compliance with the policy of the law bespeaks consistency in application to all. It is not a one way proposition for Negroes alone, it is rather for equal application to all. There can be no two ways, one liberal policy for a single race, and for

all others, to limbo. This accepted policy of the State cannot be circumscribed so as to restrict its application only to those who invoke it. It applies universally to all races and creeds. In the latter respect, rightfully, no racial group may be characterized as a minority. No Constitution, no law, makes such a distinction. (211 N.Y.S.2d at 632-633.)

NOTES

1. Compare the admonitions to the black community made in Brandenburg v. Metropolitan Package Store Association with the conclusions in the Report of the National Advisory Commission on Civil Disorders 1 (1968): "What white Americans have never fully understood — but what the Negro can never forget — is that white society is deeply implicated in the ghetto, white institutions created it, white institutions maintain it, and white society condones it."

2. Black groups have also been enjoined from picketing in cases where a store refused to provide them with information regarding employment practices, Williams v. Maloof, 223 Ga. 640, 157 S.E.2d 479 (1967); and where the asserted purpose of picketing, deemed "unlawful by the court, was to drive white merchants out of the black community," Weisman v. Moore, 12 Race Rel. L. Rep. 1183 (1967). But an injunction against boycott-picketing was held to have been erroneously issued where it appeared that black demands for a racial quota had been changed to demands for nondiscriminatory hiring three weeks before the company filed suit. Centennial Laundry Co. v. West Side Organization, 34 Ill. 2d 257, 215 N.E.2d 443 (1966).

3. Lack of judicial support has not prevented black consumer boycotts from attaining their goals in many efforts, including some in which picketing and other boycott activity were enjoined. As in defamation cases, the plaintiff's business may obtain the requested relief, but the litigation serves to publish the message (i.e., that the business is racially biased) far more effectively than did the protesters whose efforts were enjoined. Moreover, a lawsuit aligning white firms against black protesters conveys a clear message to the black community, which may take many years to erase. Some black shoppers never returned to the "five-and-dime" stores.

POTOMAC ELECTRIC POWER COMPANY v. CORE, 210 F. Supp. 418 (D.D.C. 1962). Defendants distributed to plaintiff's customers stickers reading "We Believe in Merit Hiring," to be pasted on computer cards that were returned with payments. The consequence of this novel form of boycott was that the company's billing machines were put out of commission. The court ruled that it had the power to grant injunctive relief because no labor dispute was involved, but went on to hold that even if there were a labor dispute, defendants' activities were unlawful because they constituted interference with plaintiff's business in the nature of a continuous trespass. Cases where the purpose of a boycott has been "quota hiring" of blacks have held that such a purpose is unlawful because it is against public policy. The court concluded that the sticker program was "mischief for mischief's sake," and had no connection with the desire of defendants to induce the power company to employ Negroes.

MEIER, CIVIL RIGHTS STRATEGIES FOR NEGRO EMPLOYMENT

Employment, Race and Poverty 193-198, 200
(A. Ross and H. Hill, eds. 1967) *

. . . Following the victories in the 1960 lunch-counter sit-ins, in which many NAACP youth councils and college chapters participated, local NAACP units, such as those at Durham, North Carolina and at Savannah, Georgia, employed similar direct action to obtain from dozens to hundreds of jobs in drug stores, variety stores, and other retail outlets. In 1963 the NAACP demonstrated against building trades unions in New York, Philadelphia, Cleveland, Pittsburgh, and other cities, but the "less-than-token" accomplishments of these demonstrations did not break the general pattern of discrimination. On the other hand, in 1964, as a result of demonstrations in forty-one cities from Buffalo, New York, to San Francisco, the NAACP compelled General Motors to employ Negroes in secretarial, managerial, professional, and supervisory capacities for the first time. . . .

SCLC affiliates and CORE chapters have become very active in campaigns against job bias, and their work has been supplemented by local ad hoc groups, often led by ministers. One of the outstanding cases involved Philadelphia clergymen, under whose leadership selective buying campaigns opened 3,000 jobs for Negroes in consumer-goods industries between 1960 and 1963. Less successful were the Brooklyn ministers who in 1963 demonstrated against discrimination in the building trades; like the NAACP and CORE they foundered on the rock of union intransigence. In the South, one can point to a number of efforts, including the highly successful "Operation Breadbasket," sponsored in Atlanta by SCLC and local ministers, which opened up many white-collar clerical and sales positions in 1963. . . .

The power of the boycott became very evident during the sit-in campaigns against variety and drug stores in 1960-1961, and once the lunch counters were open, it was natural that there would be efforts in many Southern cities to secure employment in such stores, and later in other downtown businesses that had a significant proportion of Negro customers. It is important to point out that these selective buying campaigns differed from the "Don't Buy Where You Can't Work" campaigns of the 1930's in that they were directed at downtown stores also patronized by whites. This development was in part

* Excerpted from "Civil Rights Strategies for Negro Employment" by August Meier in Employment, Race and Poverty edited by Arthur Ross and Herbert Hill, copyright © 1967 by Harcourt Brace Jovanovich, Inc. and reprinted with their permission.

made possible by the growing purchasing power of Negroes and by the rising proportion of Negroes in the central core of urban centers, both trends leading to greater dependence on the Negro market by downtown businesses. A further change in tactics occurred in 1963, especially in the South, with the appearance of the tendency to package all sorts of demands, economic and otherwise, into one thrust for "Freedom Now." Generally this approach did not prove especially successful as a technique for improving job opportunities, and it was soon dropped.

The first type of business to receive the attention of the activists of the sixties was the retail establishment — the variety store, the downtown specialty and department store, and the chain food store. Once these had changed their policies, civil rights groups moved on to other types of firms. Generally they picked as targets those businesses that are most sensitive to pressures from direct actionists because they manufacture consumer goods, because they are regulated by public commissions, or because, for other reasons, they are seriously concerned with their public image. These categories include telephone companies, gas and electric companies, milk and bread companies, and banks. CORE has been pre-eminent in dealing with these types of companies. It has, moreover, specialized in obtaining semiskilled jobs, requiring a minimum of training — jobs for which high school graduates can easily qualify. It has been unusually successful with banks in many parts of the country. For example, in Boston one bank alone agreed to hire over two hundred Negroes in a wide variety of job categories. And the agreement CORE made in the summer of 1964 with the Bank of America, in California, was a major victory that provided for the hiring of 8,000 Negroes in a twelve-month period. . . .

By late 1963 and 1964, the lessons derived from direct action were evident to business as well as to civil rights groups. Consequently the very threat of a demonstration was often sufficient to bring about a settlement. . . .

Since 1962 the direct action movement, particularly CORE's, has stressed not token representation, but rather the theory that special consideration is required to compensate for past discrimination. Agreements now often carry definite stipulations that among new personnel hired a disproportionate number will be nonwhite until a fair representation of Negroes is achieved. For example, CORE's agreement with the A & P food stores in New York City in 1964 provided that during the next year ninety percent of new employees would be nonwhite. This figure is unusually high, but it is representative of the insistence of direct actionists that there must be compensatory or preferential treatment of Negroes until a reasonable balance of white and nonwhite employment is achieved. . . .

The varied approaches of the different organizations, particularly the direct action strategy, have in the years 1961-1964 created substantial increases in job opportunities for Negroes. Yet clearly the continuing high rate of Negro unemployment suggests that all of the techniques and organizations put together have not been able to solve the problem of mass Negro unemployment. There is, in fact, some evidence that civil rights organizations have come to believe that direct action has its limitations; that it cannot by itself end the economic problems of the masses. This is true even of CORE, the pioneer in nonviolent direct action. Civil rights groups have become increasingly convinced that only changes in Federal economic policies can get to the heart of the problem of structural unemployment. Consequently there has been increasing discussion, especially in CORE and SCLC, of the thesis that the civil rights organizations should get directly involved in partisan politics in order to secure government intervention in solving the enormous economic and social problems that Negro poverty and deprivation present.

QUESTIONS

1. Based on court rulings growing out of boycott-type protests, what guidelines would you be able to draw up, if any, for a group planning a consumer boycott? Is it possible to devise boycott-picketing, leafleting, etc. that will be effective and not subject the protesting group to serious danger of injunction or damage suits?

2. Why should it be necessary for civil rights groups to organize boycotts, with all their potential for liability, in order to convince blacks not to buy from businesses which discriminate against blacks? Why did black people in Grenada, Mississippi (see SCLC v. A.G. Corporation, supra) need the James Meredith march and officials of the Southern Christian Leadership Conference to combat racist practices which had burdened them from birth?

NOTE: DISRUPTIVE DEMONSTRATIONS AND DEFAMATORY STATEMENTS

Since the early 1960s, when the Supreme Court's sensitivity to state action, equal protection and free speech issues was heightened by the nonviolent protests of that time, courts have generally held that sit-ins, lie-ins and similar conduct on private or public premises may be prohibited. Thus sit-ins and lie-ins by CORE members that obstructed entry and exit from a bank have been barred. Curtis v. Tozer, 374 S.W.2d 557 (Ct. App. Mo. 1964), *habeas corpus denied sub nom.* Ford v. Bueger, 236 F. Supp. 831 (E.D. Mo. 1964). A black woman who protested limited job opportunities at a factory by lying down in front of the gate, blocking the entrance, and encouraging two minor companions to follow her example, was convicted of trespass, illegal picketing and unlawfully inducing juveniles to commit misdemeanors. Hubbard v. Commonwealth, 207 Va. 673, 152 S.E.2d 250 (1967).

See also Evers v. Birdsong, 287 F. Supp. 900 (S.D. Miss. 1968) (enjoining students from inciting, leading or participating in marches and demonstrations on Alcorn A & M campus, where a peaceful protest march had been followed by riotous demonstrations that involved damage to college property); People v. Deutsch, 172 N.W.2d 392 (Mich. Ct. App. 1969) (reversing conviction for loitering, on the ground that directed verdict was in derogation of presumption of innocence; but upholding the statute and rejecting First Amendment arguments, where appellant, demonstrating for passage of a fair housing ordinance, sat down with others in the street and completely blocked traffic); Houser v. Hill, 278 F. Supp. 920 (M.D. Ala. 1968), which was a class action seeking to enjoin law enforcement officers from interfering with lawful protests and failing to provide protection to defendants. Part of the court's order enjoined defendants from arranging meetings to be addressed by persons advocating violence, and from using violent means of protest. Stokely Carmichael had spoken at a meeting of a black citizens' group, gunfire had erupted, and tension was high.

Threatening words as well as disruptive protests by militant blacks have resulted in injunctions, judgments for money damages, and even criminal convictions. In United States v. Mitchel, 463 F.2d 187 (8th Cir. 1972), the court affirmed the conviction of a CORE job developer who had threatened the white proprietor of a business. The business was engaged in the rental and sale of television and phonograph sets, primarily in the black community. The CORE agent had demanded the rehiring of a former black employee and a $1000 contribution to the CORE Educational Fund. He threatened picketing, boycotts, adverse advertising and physical violence. In affirming the conviction obtained under the Hobbs Act, 18 U.S.C.A. §1951 (1970),* the court found that the statute was applicable in that the proprietor of the store purchased much of its inventory from an out-of-state manufacturer, and that the store is part of a chain operated in more than one state. The court denied appellant's argument that his statements were merely "strong negotiations" and that they were protected speech under the First Amendment. The Mitchell case illustrates that the law is likely to move swiftly when black militants resort to threats of physical violence in their efforts to end what they perceive as racially discriminatory policies.

But even when they do not contain threats, militant statements against whites may subject blacks to legal liability where such statements can be interpreted as defamatory. This danger is real despite the tremendous extension given freedom of expression in New York Times v. Sullivan, 376 U.S. 254, 84 S. Ct. 710, 11 L. Ed. 2d 686 (1964). There, the Supreme Court reversed damages of $500,000 awarded by Alabama courts to the elected police commissioner of Montgomery, who charged that a full-page advertisement soliciting funds for various civil rights groups constituted libel, in that it imputed improper conduct to him and contained statements that were untrue in a

* The statute provides: "(a) Whoever in any way or degree obstructs, delays, or affects commerce or the movement of any article or commodity in commerce, by robbery or extortion or attempts or conspires so to do, or commits or threatens physical violence to any personal property in furtherance of a plan or purpose to do anything in violation of this section, shall be fined not more than $10,000 or imprisoned not more than twenty years or both."

number of respects. He alleged that the statements damaged his reputation, and tended to bring him into public contempt. The Supreme Court determined that the list of racial abuses contained in the advertisement was not "commercial," but was an expression protected by the First and Fourteenth Amendments, the suppression of which would discourage newspapers from providing an important outlet for the promulgation of information and ideas by persons who do not themselves have access to publishing facilities. Speaking through Justice Brennan, the Court concluded, "The constitutional guarantees require, we think, a federal rule that prohibits a public official from recovering damages for a defamatory falsehood relating to his official conduct unless he proves that the statement was made with 'actual malice' — that is, with knowledge that it was false, or with reckless disregard of whether it was false or not. . . ."

As happened in Gomillion v. Lightfoot, 364 U.S. 339, 81 S. Ct. 125, 5 L. Ed. 2d 110 (1960), printed supra page 158, the New York Times case, while protecting the rights of blacks, established a precedent which substantially increased the First Amendment rights of all citizens. Thus, the New York Times rule has been extended (1) to prohibit punishment under a state criminal defamation statute based on charges respecting district court judges, Garrison v. Louisiana, 379 U.S. 364, 85 S. Ct. 209, 13 L. Ed. 2d 125 (1964); (2) to bar a suit for seditious libel based on impersonal criticism of the government's operations, Rosenblatt v. Baer, 383 U.S. 75, 86 S. Ct. 669, 15 L. Ed. 2d 597 (1966); and (3) to hold that an invasion of privacy action would not lie against a publication which erroneously stated that a play was based upon a true incident involving the plaintiff's family, Time, Inc. v. Hill, 385 U.S. 374, 87 S. Ct. 534, 17 L. Ed. 2d 456 (1967). In Rosenbloom v. Metromedia, Inc., 403 U.S. 29, 91 S. Ct. 1811, 29 L. Ed. 2d 296 (1971), the Court held that the New York Times rule of knowing or reckless falsity applied in a state civil libel action, which was brought by a private individual for a defamatory falsehood that had been uttered in a radio news broadcast about his involvement in an event of public or general interest. There, the defendant radio station had broadcast news stories about the plaintiff's arrest on a charge of possession of obscene literature and about a police seizure on his premises of what were described as "obscene" books. Justice Brennan explained that the New York Times case did not turn on the question of whether the person allegedly libeled was a "public official" or a "public figure," but that it was enough that the comment referred to matters of public interest. If a matter is of such interest, the Court explained, it cannot suddenly become less so merely because a private individual is involved, or because in some sense the individual did not "voluntarily" choose to become involved. The public's primary interest is in the event.

The following cases raise a substantial question as to whether courts are willing to apply the New York Times precedent in a manner helpful to militant black spokesmen. Note that frustration born of group powerlessness rather than malice served to trigger the alleged defamatory remarks. Are judges likely to be sensitive to what must appear a subtle distinction to many of them? Is there a distinction which the law can or should recognize?

AFRO-AMERICAN PUBLISHING COMPANY v. JAFFE
366 F.2d 649 (D.C. Cir. 1966)

Before BAZELON, Chief Judge, and FAHY, WASHINGTON, DANAHER, BURGER, WRIGHT, MCGOWAN and LEVENTHAL, Circuit Judges, sitting en banc.

LEVENTHAL, Circuit Judge.

This is an appeal from a judgment in favor of appellee (plaintiff) in an action for libel and for invasion of privacy, based on an article and a photograph in the October 14, 1961 issue of the Washington Afro-American ("Afro"), published by appellant (defendant) corporation. It was stipulated that plaintiff sustained no economic loss as a result of the publication. The court, which tried the case without a jury, found injury to the plaintiff consisting of his disturbance and concern as a result of the publication and awarded $500 as compensatory damages. The court also ruled that the publication was made with malice, said malice being presumed from the nature of the published words and the lack of justification therefor, and awarded punitive damages in the amount of $2000. The court stated that its awards were based on both counts of the complaint, i.e., libel, and invasion of privacy. As to compensatory damages, we affirm. As to punitive damages, we reverse and remand.

The material facts are not complicated and for the most part require no resolution of dispute. Plaintiff, a pharmacist, operates a local drugstore. About eighty percent of his customers are Negroes. He and his wife are white, but his employees are all Negroes. His store is a retail outlet for publications of interest to Negro readers. From 1954 until June 1961, it was one of some 400 retail outlets in the Washington area selling the Afro, a newspaper of some 11,000-12,000 circulation, published twice weekly.

In June 1961 plaintiff telephoned Mr. C. Sumner Stone, editor and manager of the Afro, to discuss headlines he considered inflammatory, and to voice his view that the newspaper was not contributing to a better understanding between the races. The two men had a general conversation, and there was no talk of any cancelation.

In September 1961 plaintiff telephoned the circulation department in order to cancel his handling of the Afro. His call was routed to Mr. Stone, who was responsible for maintaining circulation in addition to news and editorial policy. When Mr. Stone asked why plaintiff wanted to cancel, plaintiff responded that the paper's headlines and policies were causing racial mistrust and ill feeling and directing animosity against himself. A week or two later Mr. Stone went to the store and asked again why plaintiff wanted to cancel, and was told again that plaintiff thought the paper was spreading racial hatred and distrust. Apparently at this time plaintiff also raised the point that the newspaper had carried a paid advertisement of the Communist Party, and seemed uninterested when Mr. Stone noted that the same ad had been carried by prominent New York and Washington newspapers. Mr. Stone became angry and walked out.

In the October 14, 1961 edition of the Afro, Mr. Stone's column, "A Stone's Throw," was captioned: "One Man's War in SE Against the Afro." The subject-matter was the refusal of the proprietor of the named drugstore to continue to handle Afro. Mr. Stone reiterated in his column, what he said he had told plaintiff in conversation, that plaintiff's action, along with plaintiff's accusation that Afro was spreading racial hatred and distrust, made plaintiff appear to be a bigot. The column further stated that plaintiff had told Mr. Stone a story illustrating the ignorance of his customers and the low level of intelligence of the people in the neighborhood. Plaintiff's trial testimony denying this assertion was obviously given credit over Mr. Stone's testimony. Plaintiff's witnesses testified that he was not bigoted and enjoyed a good reputation for racial relations; these assertions were given credit and indeed were not disputed. [After reviewing the authorities, the court reversed the trial judge's finding that the published statements involved an actionable invasion of privacy.] When a proprietor of a news vending outlet in a predominantly Negro neighborhood discontinues the handling of a newspaper oriented to Negro readers, the matter is appropriate for newspaper discussion, with pictorial accompaniment, without fear of an overhanging action for invasion of privacy.

II

Although his interest in privacy for his actions and racial sentiments did not give plaintiff an immunity from public discussion, he had, we think, a right to responsible newspaper discussion, which does not descend to the level of false, defamatory statements. We now discuss the reasons why we reject appellant's prayer for dismissal of plaintiff's libel action.

A

The District Court characterized the charges as "tending to bring the plaintiff into contempt, ridicule and disgrace in the community in which he operated his business." The facts support this finding. The finding if anything applied a stricter standard of defamation than defendant was entitled to. Under the ultimate and broader standard a publication is defamatory if it tends to injure plaintiff in his trade, profession or community standing, or lower him in the estimation of the community. Moreover, defamation turns on whether the communication or publication tends, or is reasonably calculated, to cause harm to another's reputation, and it is not necessary for plaintiff to prove that this was its actual result.

Appellant's publication must be taken as a whole, and in the sense in which it would be understood by the readers to whom it was addressed. The article, captioned One Man's War in SE Against the Afro, stated that plaintiff, by canceling his subscription, "would appear to be a bigot," and that he told a story about a customer's ignorance which he said illustrated the low level of intelligence of the people in the neighborhood near his drugstore. These false statements were critical in the total impact of the article. The article contained other items that were true, but in the setting already described these only reinforced the defamatory impression.[13] Partial truths are not necessarily even mitigating in this branch of the law, for the defamer may be the more successful when he baits the hook with truth. What counts is not the painstaking parsing of a scholar in his study, but how the newspaper article is viewed through the eye of a reader of average interest.

It suffices, in support of the judgment, that the column under discussion would be reasonably understood by the average reader in the community concerned to signify that plaintiff is a bigot, racially prejudiced, and scornful of the Negro race.

Appellant contends that as a matter of law the article is not libelous, since Mr. Stone did not flatly state that plaintiff was prejudiced, and because it is not a statement of fact about plaintiff's conduct but a statement of opinion about his attitude. Where readers would understand a defamatory meaning liability cannot be avoided merely because the publication is cast in the form of an opinion, belief, insinuation or even question. A statement about one's attitude is defamatory if it tends to lower him in the esteem of the community. See Christopher v. American News Co., 171 F.2d 275 (7th Cir. 1948), where it was held actionable to charge that one is pro-Nazi.

B

Appellant's arguments that as a matter of law the article is not libelous shade into a contention that the statements are within the scope of a privilege provided by law, and hence are not actionable.

There are two analytically distinct claims of privilege. Although the "public interest" privilege, discussed below, is stressed by appellant's counsel, what Mr. Stone's testimony highlights is a defense of privilege based on appellant's own interest in Afro's circulation. Following the June 1961 discussion Mr. Stone wrote an article taking philosophical issue with the position then expressed to him by plaintiff. That article did not mention plaintiff's

13. Thus the article stressed that plaintiff "like a good many white people" refused to live in the colored neighborhood where his business is located. Plaintiff testified that he lived in that colored neighborhood for five years, and that he moved to Virginia four years ago to get a larger house and not for racial reasons.

The article stated that plaintiff is "attempting to tell colored people just how fast and hard they should run in their race toward racial equality" and "he wants to decide just what kind of colored people we should be."

The testimony of both sides agrees that plaintiff's concern expressed to Mr. Stone was that the headlines were spreading racial hatred and distrust, and stirring up ill feeling between Negroes and white people in the community. Mr. Stone testified that he considered his headlines militant, crusading, forthright, and sociologically oriented, urging faster action in the area of racial equality.

name or otherwise identify him. The identification and attack came in the fall after the newspaper had been canceled. An effort was made to give this private pecuniary interest of appellant a gloss of public concern with the claim that plaintiff was seeking to interpose himself as a censor and black-out of news. This was barren ground, since the record makes plain that the Afro was available in numerous drugstores within a few blocks of appellant's premises. There is no claim that plaintiff tried to induce others to drop the distribution of Afro.

Historically a privilege has been marked out for the person who publishes an alleged libel in the bona fide prosecution of his own interests. The interests protected by this privilege include the protection of one's business. But this is a conditional privilege and the defendant is not protected without regard to the reasonableness of his expression. The privilege is applicable only if the publisher believes the statements to be true, has reasonable grounds for this belief and says no more than reasonably appears to be necessary to protect the interest.

Afro's business interest justified putting to its readers the fairness of withdrawal of a newspaper oriented to Negro readership by a dealer doing business in a Negro neighborhood. But that interest did not justify calling him a bigot with a low opinion of the intelligence of his clientele, so as to absolve the defamation even if false.

Appellant's loftier claim of privilege invokes the doctrine of privileged criticism, or fair comment, which permits the publication of comment, although defamatory, on the activities and views of another which are matters of "public concern" or "public interest." Definition of the range of matters of public concern or interest is a never-ending task of the law. Certain distinctive subcategories have evolved: e.g., the public acts and qualifications of public officials and candidates; the management of educational, charitable and religious institutions; public offerings of a literary, artistic and scientific nature; public offerings of products for use and consumption. The principle underlying these categories, but extending beyond them, proclaims a general privilege of criticism or comment concerning another's appeal for public support or his participation in public activities.

If the person allegedly defamed has made an appeal to the public, the law allows a wide range of comment and expression. We need not concern ourselves here with the question whether, and to what extent, permissible latitude is governed by the "fair comment" doctrine, which embraces statements of opinion or comment, but not false statements of fact, or by the broader doctrine announced by the Supreme Court as to public officials, who cannot recover even for misstatements of fact in the absence of actual malice. One who enters the public arena must expect latitude in the give-and-take of public debate, extending to sharp and coarse comment, and to excessive and perhaps unwarranted characterization. However, the public interest privilege applicable against one who invites public judgment is no defense to the action brought by plaintiff. He made a personal telephone call to the editor.

But he in no sense mounted a public rostrum, not even by a letter expressly or implicitly intended for publication.

The touchstone is not whether the public is interested in plaintiff's views or conduct, for presumptively that applies to everything in a newspaper. "In some sense each person's prejudices involve a matter of importance to the whole community. But so to hold would radically alter the law of libel and too severely limit the class of libels for which redress would lie." . . .

The privilege of comment on a product offered to the public is not lost because it incidentally affects the reputation of the producer or distributor. Here, however, there is not an offering by plaintiff to the public, but rather a non-offering of a service. Certainly there could be no merit in a general approach conferring a "public" attribute on situations because of a supposed public interest in the mere fact that an offering or invitation is not extended to the public. Such an approach would violate general understanding and cause the exception to swallow the rule, since non-offerings obviously far exceed offerings. It would obliterate any reasoned effort to achieve working principles accommodating diverse interests in this field of law.

In limited instances, like a group boycott, non-offerings may take on a public quality giving rise to privileged criticism. Here the plaintiff did not offer to the public his views or reasons for failing to offer the product or service. There is nothing in the record to show that the discontinuance of the paper was presented or appeared to the public as other than a conventional business decision.

The discontinuance by this small retailer was visible to the public in a limited sense, and hence his actions could be depicted without violating his privacy. But his views were not presented to the public, and appellant's defamatory comment concerning those views is not justified either by appellant's private interest, as we have already noted, or by a broader public-interest privilege.

It has been suggested that an expansion of the common law of the public interest privilege is required in the light of New York Times v. Sullivan, and that it protects discussion of all items of public interest, and not merely items concerning public officials. See Note, First Amendment Protection for Good-Faith Defamatory Error, 75 Yale L.J. 642 (1966). If New York Times has application, it would be our duty to do what the Supreme Court did in Rosenblatt v. Baer, 383 U.S. 75, 86 S. Ct. 669, 15 L. Ed. 2d 597 (1966), and accompany the remand with appropriate indication of the proper principles to govern the new trial, and any reassessment of the facts.

Undoubtedly New York Times is a seminal decision. [The court then discussed what it felt were the foreseeable extensions of the New York Times case.] We conclude that New York Times, as written and likely to be extended, does not and will not preclude recovery, even in the absence of malice, by a man whose role is as non-public as plaintiff's, by a man who has not mounted a public rostrum, made an appeal to the public, sought or received public funds, offered a service or product for public use or comment, or organized a boycott or other group activity by members of the public. . . .

C

We turn now to the suggestion that even though this case does not permit invocation of the public interest privilege as a complete defense, the public interest in broad discussion of the subject-matter of race relations is significant enough to warrant a protective rule precluding recovery except at the instance of a plaintiff who can show special, pecuniary damage. . . .

In the common law of defamation the pecuniary damage requirement was imposed only in the case of oral slander, save for certain exceptions. In the common law of libel damage was said to be "presumed" from the defamation, so that no pecuniary damage need be shown. . . .

In the case before us the bigotry libel is apt to cause pecuniary damage because the Afro is addressed to Negroes, who are the plaintiff's clientele. But plaintiff need not show any pecuniary damage in order to establish the libel and recover nominal damages, or compensation for nonpecuniary damage supported by the proof. In Peck v. Tribune Co., 214 U.S. 185, 29 S. Ct. 554, 53 L. Ed. 960 (1909), Justice Holmes rejected incorporation of a special damage requirement into the law of libel. We adhere to the rule that no special, i.e. pecuniary damage is necessary. Nor do we consider that a special damage requirement is interposed even assuming facts extrinsic to the publication are required to establish the libel. The allowance of nominal damages performs a vindicatory function by enabling the plaintiff to brand the defamatory publication as false. The rule that permits satisfaction of the deep-seated need for vindication of honor is not a mere historic relic, but promotes the law's civilizing function of providing an acceptable substitute for violence in the settlement of disputes. The judgment also partakes of the nature of relief in equity by subduing, or at least minimizing, the spread of harm to reputation.

Moreover, a special damage requirement would thwart the function of the law in providing compensation for damage that does not take a demonstrable pecuniary form. It is common knowledge that persons who are defamed tend to lose opportunities in fact that they cannot prove at law. The law of libel provides redress in general damages for the impact of the libel on reputation, with mental suffering a recognized element of damage recoverable.

We turn now to Sweeney v. Patterson [128 F.2d 457 (D.C. Cir. 1942)], where this court held that "It is not actionable to publish erroneous and injurious statements of fact . . . regarding the political conduct and views of public officials, so long as no charge of crime, corruption, gross immorality or gross incompetence is made and no special damage results."

The additional substantive requirement of special damage in Patterson was in furtherance of freedom of speech and criticism concerning *public officials*. Judge Edgerton's notable opinion was quoted approvingly by the Supreme

Court in New York Times v. Sullivan, a decision which precluded liability in the absence of malice. We need not here consider whether the Sweeney requirement of special damage should be treated as a half-way house that may now be razed in view of the subsequent Times shelter requiring a showing of malice.

The pecuniary damage requirement of Sweeney has not been extended in a case of a charge of gross misconduct. . . . And we do not believe it should be extended beyond the case of statements concerning public officials. While society's concern in preventing and redressing attacks upon reputation may be offset "when interests in public discussion are particularly strong," those interests should be protected within the doctrine of public interest privilege. On balance we do not think the public interest privilege should be expanded by permitting libel of a private individual, on the ground of alleged public interest in the news item that defames him, because he is unable to establish pecuniary damage.

III

Punitive damages were granted by the District Court, which ruled that malice is implied from the fact of publication of a falsehood. At one stage in the evolution of the common law of defamation, the action was not maintainable except upon a showing of wrong motive, i.e., malice. Later, liability was extended even in the absence of intention to defame the plaintiff. A legal fiction was employed; the requirement that malice be pleaded was retained, but malice was said to be presumed from the fact of publication. This language is misleading; what is really meant is that malice is not required for the basic defamation action. Due to a misunderstanding of the fiction of implied malice some courts have ruled it sufficient as a basis for award of exemplary or punitive damages. We do not agree.

The proper award of punitive damages in certain common law torts, including libel, is dependent on a determination of actual malice or wanton conduct. Day v. Woodworth, 54 U.S. (13 How.) 363, 371, 14 L. Ed. 181 (1851). Since that standard was not here followed — and there was no determination of either actual malice or wanton conduct — we are bound to remand. Should appropriate findings sustain an application of the proper standard, the trial judge will take into account the elements upon which his award must be based. . . .

We need not pursue this subject in the present case, for even assuming, without suggesting, that the District Court will conclude on remand that an award for exemplary damages is proper, the award of $2,000 previously made in this case is not so large as to require us to grapple with the problem of outer limits. We could not in this case find such an award excessive, or larger than should be condoned in simple justice, in view of the probable cost of litigation and even a modest provision for deterrence. We say this, however, not in derogation but in contemplation of the authority and duty of courts to reduce verdicts when they are excessive. Our express reiteration of that authority should help assure that the protection of individual reputation maintained by our decision does not carry overhanging punitive prospects excessively restrictive of freedom of press and comment.

The award of $500 compensatory damages is affirmed. The award of $2,000 punitive damages is reversed and remanded to the District Court for further proceedings not inconsistent with this opinion.

It is so ordered.

Bazelon, Chief Judge (dissenting).

The court is called upon to reconcile two interests of critical importance, freedom of discussion and protection against defamation. In my view, this end is best served here by applying the rule that "erroneous and injurious statements of fact and injurious comment or opinion" regarding a matter of public interest are not actionable libel unless "special damage results." Sweeney v. Patterson, 76 U.S. App. D.C. 23, 24, 128 F.2d 457, 458, cert. denied, 317 U.S. 678, 63 S. Ct. 160, 87 L. Ed. 544 (1942).[1] Without such damage, the existence of "malice" whether presumed or "actual" or a finding that the article was libel "per se" should not establish liability. Moreover, "in view of the propensity of juries to award excessive damages for defamation," special damage should be not only a prerequisite to actionable libel, but also a limitation on the amount recoverable.

In addition to the facts described in the court's opinion, I rely on the testimony of the article's author, Mr. Stone, as to how the subject matter appeared to him:

> The subject of that article is the total relationship of white and Negroes in America. . . . this is a specific instance in which a white man . . . holding a business in a Negro community, deriving a major share of his income from Negroes, is he himself determining how fast or how militant Negroes should be. He is making this determination by his expression of our headlines and refusing to take the paper based upon his dislike of our headlines, which he regarded as too militant or too aggressive or not to his taste. That is the subject of that article and I thought [it] was of very vital concern to Negroes and whites everywhere.

1. This court stated in Sweeney: "Errors of fact, particularly in regard to a man's mental states and processes, are inevitable. Information and discussion will be discouraged, and the public interest in public knowledge of important facts will be poorly defended, if error subjects its author to a libel suit without even a showing of economic loss. Whatever is added to the field of libel is taken from the field of free debate." 76 U.S. App. D.C. at 24, 128 F.2d at 458. That Sweeney is not restricted to criticism of public officials appears from its reliance on the earlier case of Sullivan v. Meyer, 67 U.S. App. D.C. 228, 91 F.2d 301 (1937) involving newspaper criticism of a private citizen relating "exclusively to [his] attitude towards a question of public interest." Sullivan was read to require special damage for liability for such criticism. 76 U.S. App. D.C. at 25, 128 F.2d at 459.

In some cases an exception to this rule allows recovery for a false imputation of *gross* misconduct without special damage, . . . Such charges are not, however, involved in this case. Moreover, this exception should be narrowly restricted to those cases where the extreme character of the alleged libel indicates that some damage must have resulted even though the plaintiff is not able directly to prove it. . . .

Appellee denies that his refusal to sell appellant's newspaper involves a question of public interest. He says that "the general public [had no] legitimate interest whatsoever in the matter of Eli Jaffe, the proprietor of a small neighborhood drug store, cancelling his subscription to a newspaper" and that his action was a "private matter." But the existence of a public interest question depends "upon the facts as they *reasonably* appear to the person whose liability is in question." Personal and narrow commercial interests may in part have motivated Stone's criticism of Jaffe. But the dispute between Jaffe and the newspaper is so overladen with questions of pressing contemporary importance that I am unwilling to say Stone could not reasonably believe, as he testified, that Jaffe's actions raised an issue of public interest.

In New York Times Co. v. Sullivan, 376 U.S. 254, 84 S. Ct. 710, 11 L. Ed. 2d 686 (1964), the Court held that criticism of public officials, containing misstatements of fact, was not actionable libel unless "the statement was made with 'actual malice' — that is, with knowledge that it was false or with reckless disregard of whether it was false or not." 376 U.S. at 279-280, 84 S. Ct. at 726. If this rule were to be extended to the present case, appellee would be required to show not only special damage, under Sweeney v. Patterson, supra, but also "actual malice." I would not apply the New York Times rule here. Although the same policies which support free criticism of public officials also support free discussion of publicly significant issues, private citizens, who like Mr. Jaffe, become embroiled in public controversy may, in some circumstances, warrant greater protection from injurious and false defamation than public officials. I find this protection in requiring such individuals to show only special damage.

The requirement of special damage is not satisfied by the emotional distress alleged here. Otherwise freedom of public discussion would be unduly impaired. I would therefore direct judgment in appellee's favor.

Wright, Circuit Judge, with whom Fahy, Circuit Judge, concurs (dissenting).

Since this case was tried and decided before the Supreme Court's decision in New York Times Co. v. Sullivan, 376 U.S. 254, 84 S. Ct. 710, 11 L. Ed. 2d 686 (1964), I would remand it for retrial and reconsideration in the light of that case, compare Pauling v. National Review, Inc., 49 Misc. 2d 975, 269 N.Y.S.2d 11 (1966), and its possible effect on the traditional fair comment rule. See Note, The Scope of First Amendment Protection for Good-Faith Defamatory Error, 75 Yale L.J. 642 (1966).

NOTES

1. We now know that the majority in the Jaffe case missed the mark in predicting that the rule in New York Times v. Sullivan would not be extended to preclude recovery by nonpublic plaintiffs, but the publisher of the Afro-American, Dr. Carl Murphy, decided to settle the case rather than spend more money in legal fees seeking Supreme Court review. Letter from Chuck

Stone to author, Oct. 20, 1972. The Jaffe case did not represent the first instance in which the Afro-American Publishing Company was held liable for statements critical of whites. In Afro-American Publishing v. Rudbeck, 248 F.2d 655 (D.C. Cir. 1957), the defense of privileged communication was held inapplicable to an account of an alleged brutal beating of a black person by two white plainclothesmen, who initiated the action for libel and slander.

2. In Naimaster v. NAACP, 296 F. Supp. 1277 (D. Md. 1969), *aff'd,* 423 F.2d 1227 (4th Cir. 1970), the defendant NAACP was unsuccessful in its efforts to remove to a federal court a state action for damages brought by a bus driver because of published statements that he was acting Grand Dragon for the Ku Klux Klan in Maryland. In seeking $200,000 in damages, the plaintiff did not deny the charge, but asserted that its publication by defendants, who had urged his dismissal in communications to the transit authorities, was defamatory and constituted an invasion of privacy.

3. A civil rights group in Marks, Mississippi had published a circular charging a local police officer with brutally beating blacks, and with many other acts of brutality inflicted upon the black community, by what it called "untrained, uneducated, inhuman law enforcement officers of Quitman County, namely L. C. Pride, J. W. Jenkins, and others." One of the officers filed suit, charging that the statement was libelous and defamatory. He appealed from the trial court's sustaining of defendant's demurrer, and the Mississippi Supreme Court reversed and remanded. It mentioned the New York Times test, but determined that the circular was not conditionally privileged as "fair comment" about public officials under state precedence.

4. In August 1972, the Atlanta, Georgia branch NAACP requested the Federal Communications Commission to prohibit the further broadcasting of advertisements by a segregationist candidate, because such broadcasts posed an imminent threat to safety. The NAACP asserted that earlier telecasts of the candidate's statement had resulted in threats of bombing and violence, and had served to incite racial hatred, exacerbate fears, and reverse the tide of understanding and progress between the races. The statement read:

> I am J. B. Stoner. I am the only candidate for U.S. Senator who is for the white people. I am the only candidate who is against integration. All of the other candidates are race mixers to one degree or another. I say we must repeal Gambrell's civil rights law. Gambrell's law takes jobs from us whites and gives those jobs to the niggers. The main reason why niggers want integration is because the niggers want our white women. I am for law and order with the knowledge that you cannot have law and order and niggers too. Vote white. This time vote your convictions by voting white racist J. B. Stoner into the run-off election for U.S. Senator. Thank you. (FCC News Report No. 10844, Aug. 3, 1972.)

The commission refused to prohibit further broadcast of the statement, saying it "would amount to an advance approval by the Commission of licensee censorship of a candidate's remarks." The commission concluded that such action would constitute a prior restraint that could not be justified unless the advocacy is directed to inciting or producing imminent lawless action. The commission determined that "the public interest is best served by permitting the expression of any views that do not involve 'a clear and present danger of serious substantive evil that rises far above the public inconvenience, annoyance, or unrest.' " It concluded: "If there is to be free speech, it must be free for speech that we abhor and hate as well as for speech that we find tolerable or congenial." Id.

E. RACIAL DEMONSTRATIONS SINCE THE SIT-IN PERIOD

It is important to remember that by 1965-1966, when the Supreme Court was reflecting its unwillingness to provide further support of civil rights protests by affirming some convictions and denying review in others, most of the "sat-in" facilities had long since been desegregated, either by "voluntary" action or as a result of the Civil Rights Act of 1964. In a sense, the protesters' ends had been attained despite the Court's subsequent condemnation of some of their means.

It is doubtful whether the mass of blacks locked in Northern urban ghettos were aware of the Court's hardened position on civil rights protests, but it is certain that they had little reason to believe they would share in the progress made in the South. The urban riots, unlike the sit-ins and marches in the South, were generally unplanned (if not unprovoked), violent, destructive and costly in both human and financial terms. Neither the rioting itself nor the often totally arbitrary and vindictive response of the courts to the rioters can be evaluated in traditional legal terms.*

Many of the protests after the sit-in period were not prayerfully nonviolent, but neither were they riots. Rather, they fell somewhere between these two extremes. The courts, though, generally condemned all but those close to the classical nonviolent model; where the demonstrators resorted to violence, questions of provocation and even of self-defense did not serve as restraints to prompt judicial condemnation.

1. The Judicial "Hard Line" on Militant Black Protests

STREET v. NEW YORK
394 U.S. 576, 89 S. Ct. 1354, 22 L. Ed. 2d 572 (1969)

[A state statute made it a misdemeanor to "publicly mutilate, deface, defile, or defy, trample upon, or cast contempt upon either by words or act [any flag of the United States]." In this case, according to the Court:]

* The major racial confrontations, from East St. Louis in 1917 to the killings at Jackson State University in 1970, as seen by the official commissions appointed to investigate them, are summarized together with critical analyses of those reports in A. Platt, The Politics of Riot Commissions, 1917-1970 (1971).

Appellant testified that during the afternoon of June 6, 1966, he was listening to the radio in his Brooklyn apartment. He heard a news report that civil rights leader James Meredith had been shot by a sniper in Mississippi. Saying to himself, "They didn't protect him," appellant, himself a Negro, took from his drawer a neatly folded, 48-star American flag which he formerly had displayed on national holidays. Appellant left his apartment and carried the still-folded flag to the nearby intersection of St. James Place and Lafayette Avenue. Appellant stood on the northeast corner of the intersection, lit the flag with a match, and dropped the flag on the pavement when it began to burn.

Soon thereafter, a police officer halted his patrol car and found the burning flag. The officer testified that he then crossed to the northwest corner of the intersection, where he found appellant "talking out loud" to a small group of persons. The officer estimated that there were some 30 persons on the corner near the flag and five to 10 on the corner with appellant. The officer testified that as he approached within 10 or 15 feet of appellant, he heard appellant say, "We don't need no damn flag," and that when he asked appellant whether he had burned the flag appellant replied: "Yes; that is my flag; I burned it. If they let that happen to Meredith we don't need an American flag." Appellant admitted making the latter response, but he denied that he said anything else and asserted that he always had remained on the corner with the flag.

[In a 5 to 4 decision, the Court reversed a conviction by the New York Supreme Court because it was unclear whether conviction was based on the act of burning or on the spoken words. If based on the latter, or on a combination of act and words, it was violative of rights of free expression. At the conclusion of his majority opinion, Justice Harlan added, "disrespect for our flag is to be deplored no less in these vexed times than in calmer periods of our history."

Chief Justice Warren and Justices Black, White and Fortas each wrote dissenting opinions, totaling twenty-three pages in the official reports. Each believed that the issue of whether appellant could be convicted of burning the flag was properly before the Court, and that the conviction should be affirmed.

On remand, the New York Court of Appeals, while asserting its opinion that defendant had been tried and convicted solely for the act of burning the flag, conceded that the conviction must be reversed under the Supreme Court's mandate. A new trial was ordered at which defendant was "to be tried solely for his act of burning the flag." 24 N.Y.2d 1026, 250 N.E.2d 250 (1969).]

NOTES

1. In Street, the Court's opposition to flag burning, even when done with great provocation, was shown more by the opinion than the result. None of the opinions expressed any sympathy for Street, who, the record shows, was

clearly patriotic, but who, upon hearing of the Meredith shooting, had simply lost control. The New York Court of Appeals had recognized the situation, but, concerned about the threat to public order posed by Street's act, said:

> The violation of the statute may not be condoned simply because the defendant's agitation resulted from the distressing news he had heard on the radio or because no violence actually did occur as a result of the flag burning. These were mitigating circumstances that were properly taken into account by the trial court when it suspended sentence for the conviction. (People v. Street, 20 N.Y.2d 231, 237, 282 N.Y.2d 491, 497, 229 N.E.2d 187, 191 (1967).)

2. Upon remand of the case, Street was retried and convicted in Criminal Court, Kings County of burning the flag. During the pendency of his appeal to the appellate term, Street died and the prosecution was abated. Letter to author dated Sep. 21, 1972, from Burt Neuborne, N.Y. Civil Liberties Union, 84 Fifth Ave., New York, N.Y. 10011.

QUESTIONS

1. In view of the obvious distress Street suffered when he learned of the shooting, and the sense of powerlessness to do anything about it which motivated his action, what factors likely prompted the District Attorney to prosecute this case? Would Street's distress have been more comprehensible if he had been a close relative of Meredith? What if Street had been a white construction worker, angered by a federal court order requiring the placement of a given percentage of black workers on his job and requiring their admission to his union? Would the white worker's case have been prosecuted? Would the policeman have sent the white worker home rather than arrest him?

2. Is it possible to argue that the Supreme Court after Street v. New York might not sustain a conviction for flag burning? Does such an argument gain validity from the fact that most public flag burnings are intended as protest statements, as speech, whether or not anything is said during the act?

NOTE: THE END OF THE NONVIOLENT ERA

As open resistance to black demands spread from the South to the rest of the nation, blacks became increasingly unwilling to play a deserving, nonviolent, supplicant role. James Meredith, whose courage had thrilled the nation in 1962, was shot on a protest walk through his home state in June 1966; and in the demonstrations that followed, Stokely Carmichael coined the phrase "Black Power," which in one fell swoop cost blacks millions of dollars in white contributions and other support, while providing them with a new sense of racial pride not measurable in financial terms.

On April 4, 1968, Martin Luther King was killed by a white assassin, precipitating racial violence in scores of cities. Although the revolution that some blacks called for did not come, clearly the era of prayerful nonviolence was at an end. The protests that followed were intended to end racial injustices no less serious than those which had been opposed with much of the nation's support in the early 1960s. Indeed, the injustices were frequently more serious, but the protests were also more threatening.

GANNON v. ACTION, 303 F. Supp. 1240 (E.D. Mo. 1969). In a suit brought by the pastor of a St. Louis Catholic church, a federal district court was requested to enjoin black activists, who during a period of several weeks had interrupted church services with demands based on asserted racism in the church. The demands included the removal of all church investments from firms that refused to hire or upgrade black employees, and the relinquishment to the defendants of 75 percent of the church's income "for the purpose of financing energetic community based programs that are actively combating white racism in other areas, regardless of creed." On one Sunday, twenty-nine members of the group entered the church during a service, marched down the center aisle, and, after forming a line in front of the communion rail, read a notice that included their demands and threatened further disruptions. On another Sunday, a member of the group interrupted the service and requested permission to speak for five minutes. When permission was denied, she read aloud from a paper containing the group's demands, until it was taken from her by ushers. She then sat in the vestibule of the church and refused to move, necessitating her forcible removal by police officers. During another demonstration on a subsequent Sunday, a member of the group who was dressed to resemble the bishop walked to the front of church with a sign indicating that the archbishop was making a mockery of the church, and then walked toward the rear, chanting "Racist, racist — white Christian racist." An altercation followed, and members of the St. Louis police force removed the demonstrators.

Although the defendants were private individuals, the district court found that it had jurisdiction to grant the requested relief under the Civil Rights Statutes, 42 U.S.C. §§1981, 1982, 1983, and 1985(3) (1970). Ignoring questions of "state action," the court granted broad injunctive relief. In a similar suit brought by another church, the court granted similar relief on similar jurisdictional grounds. Central Presbyterian Church v. Black Liberation Front, 303 F. Supp. 894 (E.D. Mo. 1969).

The Gannon case was appealed. The Eighth Circuit did not decide the case until 1971. It affirmed, but narrowed the injunction so as not to deprive the defendants of their First Amendment rights which, the court held, included reasonable picketing and pamphleting. In the period between the district court's order and the appeal, the Supreme Court had decided Griffin v. Breckenridge, 403 U.S. 88, 91 S. Ct. 1790, 29 L. Ed. 338 (1971), reversing an earlier decision that §1985(3) could not be used to reach private conspiracies. The appellate court found that the injunction was properly based on §1985(3), avoiding discussion of whether there was jurisdiction under the other civil rights statutes. Action v. Gannon, 450 F.2d 1227 (8th Cir. 1971).

NOTE: BLACK DISRUPTION OF WHITE CHURCHES

The Missouri church demonstrations were modeled on the well publicized interruption by former Student Nonviolent Coordinating Committee (SNCC) president James Forman of New York's Riverside Church on Sunday, May 4, 1969, at which he read his "Black Manifesto." The statement, which condemned racism in the church and in the country, and stated the failure of antidiscrimination programs, demanded $500,000,000 from the "Christian white churches and the Jewish synagogues." The money was to be used, inter alia, to establish a Southern Land Bank that would assist blacks in organizing cooperative farms; to set up publishing firms, television networks and other audiovisual agencies to provide blacks with an alternative to racist propaganda; and to start a skills center for research on the problems of blacks, training centers to teach marketable skills, and a "National Black Labor Strike and Defense Fund" to protect black workers and their families. To justify his demands, Forman claimed, "We are not unaware that the exploitation of colored peoples around the world is aided and abetted by the white Christian churches and synagogues."

The subject is thoroughly reviewed in A. Schuchter, Reparations: The Black Manifesto and Its Challenge to White America (1970). See also Black Manifesto (R. Lecky, H. Wright eds. 1969). Schuchter writes, "Forman's violation of the most 'sacred' hour of the week and his violent anti-American rhetoric against America, capitalism and the church touched millions of nerve ends like a multi-pronged cattle prod." Schuchter, supra, at 5. Some churchmen were extremely critical, but during the next year various churches and denominational groups gave several million dollars to black church programs, generally specifying that the money not go to Forman or the group he represented.

Despite some vocal opposition, it is evident that many churchmen shared the view of Dr. Ernest Campbell, the minister of Riverside Church, whose service was interrupted by James Forman. According to Schuchter, Dr. Campbell commented on the incident:

> . . . the shame of it all was not that a service of worship was interrupted, indefensible as that action was. The shame centers in the fact that in the population of this most prosperous nation there are people who feel, rightly or wrongly, that they have to use such tactics to draw attention to their grievances. . . . Let's be done with rationalizing. Wherever you go in this country the white man rides higher than the black. He lives in better parts of town, sends his children to more desirable schools, borrows books from finer libraries, holds down higher paying jobs. . . . And where has the church been in all of this? By its silence it has blessed these arrangements and given them an extra aura of divine approval. It has conveniently exalted the virtue of obedience and order — getting fat in the process. . . . Reparations,

restitution, redress, call it what you will. We subscribe to the conviction that given the demeaning and heinous mistreatment that black people suffered in this country at the hands of white people in the slave economy, and given the lingering handicaps of that system that still works to keep the black man at a disadvantage in our society, it is just and reasonable that amends be made by many institutions in society — including, and perhaps especially the church. . . . (Schuchter, supra, at 6.)

Is there a basis in the statements of James Forman and Dr. Campbell for a legal argument that would convince a court to recognize a "right to reparation" for blacks in America? Is there a basis for a legal argument that might be used to defend against criminal charges, assuming these were filed against the participants in the Missouri church protest? The legal issues are discussed in B. Bittker, The Case For Black Reparations (1973).

2. Balancing Protest Rights with Peace and Order

GRAYNED v. CITY OF ROCKFORD
408 U.S. 104, 92 S. Ct. 2294, 33 L. Ed. 2d 222 (1972)

Mr. Justice MARSHALL delivered the opinion of the Court.

Appellant Richard Grayned was convicted for his part in a demonstration in front of West Senior High School in Rockford, Illinois. Negro students at the school had first presented their grievances to school administrators. When the principal took no action on crucial complaints, a more public demonstration of protest was planned. On April 25, 1969, approximately 200 people — students, their family members, and friends — gathered next to the school grounds. Appellant, whose brother and twin sisters were attending the school, was part of this group. The demonstrators marched around on a sidewalk about 100 feet from the school building, which was set back from the street. Many carried signs which summarized the grievances: "Black cheerleaders to cheer too"; "Black history with black teachers"; "Equal rights, Negro counselors." Others, without placards, made the "power to the people" sign with their upraised and clenched fists.

In other respects, the evidence at appellant's trial was sharply contradictory. Government witnesses reported that the demonstrators repeatedly cheered, chanted, baited policemen, and made other noise that was audible in the school; that hundreds of students were distracted from their school activities and lined the classroom windows to watch the demonstration; that some demonstrators successfully yelled to their friends to leave the school building and join the demonstration; that uncontrolled latenesses after period changes in the school were far greater than usual, with late students admitting that they had been watching the demonstration; and that, in general, orderly school procedure was disrupted. Defense witnesses claimed that the demonstrators were at all times quiet and orderly; that they did not seek to violate the law, but only to "make a point"; that the only noise was made by policemen using loudspeakers; that almost no students were noticeable at the schoolhouse windows; and that orderly school procedure was not disrupted.

After warning the demonstrators, the police arrested 40 of them, including appellant. For participating in the demonstration, Grayned was tried and convicted of violating two Rockford ordinances, hereinafter referred to as the "anti-picketing" ordinance and the "anti-noise" ordinance. A $25 fine was imposed for each violation. . . . We conclude that the anti-picketing ordinance is unconstitutional, but affirm the court below with respect to the anti-noise ordinance.

I

At the time of appellant's arrest and conviction, Rockford's anti-picketing ordinance provided that

> A person commits disorderly conduct when he knowingly: . . .
>
> (i) Pickets or demonstrates on a public way within 150 feet of any primary or secondary school building while the school is in session and one-half hour before the school is in session and one-half hour after the school session has been concluded, provided that this subsection does not prohibit the peaceful picketing of any school involved in a labor dispute . . . . Code of Ordinances, c. 28, §18.1(i).

With the exception of two unimportant words, this ordinance is identical to the Chicago disorderly conduct ordinance we have today considered in Police Department of Chicago v. Mosley.* . . .

II

The anti-noise ordinance reads, in pertinent part, as follows:

> [N]o person, while on public or private grounds adjacent to any building in which a school or any class thereof is in session, shall willfully make or assist in the making of any noise or diversion which disturbs or tends to disturb the peace or good order of such school session or class thereof . . . . Code of Ordinances, c. 28, §19.2(a).

Appellant claims that, on its face, this ordinance is both vague and overbroad, and therefore unconstitutional. We conclude, however, that the ordinance suffers from neither of these related infirmities.

* 408 U.S. 92, 92 S. Ct. 2286, 33 L. Ed. 2d 212 (1972). In Mosley, Justice Marshall, speaking for the Court, held the Chicago ordinance unconstitutional because it makes an impermissible distinction between picketing over a labor dispute and other peaceful picketing. The challenge was brought by a black who, for seven months prior to the passage of the ordinance, had been peacefully picketing a high school with a sign that read: "Jones High School practices black discrimination. Jones High School has a black quota." There had been no incidents.

A. *Vagueness*

It is a basic principle of due process that an enactment is void for vagueness if its prohibitions are not clearly defined. Vague laws offend several important values. First, because we assume that man is free to steer between lawful and unlawful conduct, we insist that laws give the person of ordinary intelligence a reasonable opportunity to know what is prohibited, so that he may act accordingly. Vague laws may trap the innocent by not providing fair warning. Second, if arbitrary and discriminatory enforcement is to be prevented, laws must provide explicit standards for those who apply them. A vague law impermissibly delegates basic policy matters to policemen, judges, and juries for resolution on an ad hoc and subjective basis, with the attendant dangers of arbitrary and discriminatory application. Third, but related, where a vague statute "abut[s] upon sensitive areas of basic First Amendment freedoms," it "operates to inhibit the exercise of [those] freedoms." Uncertain meanings inevitably lead citizens to " 'steer far wider of the unlawful zone' . . . than if the boundaries of the forbidden areas were clearly marked." [Citations omitted.]

Although the question is close, we conclude that the anti-noise ordinance is not impermissibly vague. The court below rejected appellant's arguments "that proscribed conduct was not sufficiently specified and that police were given too broad a discretion in determining whether conduct was proscribed." 46 Ill. 2d 492, 494, 263 N.E.2d 866, 867 (1970). Although it referred to other, similar statutes it had recently construed and upheld, the court below did not elaborate on the meaning of the anti-noise ordinance. In this situation, as Justice Frankfurter put it, we must "extrapolate its allowable meaning." Here, we are "relegated, at best, to the words of the ordinance itself," to the interpretations the court below has given to analogous statutes, and, perhaps to some degree, to the interpretation of the statute given by those charged with enforcing it. "Extrapolation," of course, is a delicate task, for it is not within our power to construe and narrow state laws. [Citations omitted.]

With that warning, we find no unconstitutional vagueness in the anti-noise ordinance. Condemned to the use of words, we can never expect mathematical certainty from our language. The words of the Rockford ordinance are marked by "flexibility and reasonable breadth, rather than meticulous specificity," Esteban v. Central Missouri State College, 415 F.2d 1077, 1088 (CA8 1969) (Blackmun, J.), *cert. denied,* 398 U.S. 965, 90 S. Ct. 2169, 26 L. Ed. 2d 548 (1970), but we think it is clear what the ordinance as a whole prohibits. Designed, according to its preamble, "for the protection of Schools," the ordinance forbids deliberately noisy or diversionary[16] activity which dis-

16. "Diversion" is defined by Webster's Third New International Dictionary as "the act or an instance of diverting from one course [or use] to another . . . : the act or an instance of diverting (as the mind or attention) from some activity or concern . . . : a turning aside . . . : something that turns the mind from serious concerns or ordinary matters and relaxes or amuses."

rupts or is about to disrupt normal school activities. It forbids this willful activity at fixed times — when school is in session — and at a sufficiently fixed place — "adjacent" to the school. Were we left with just the words of the ordinance, we might be troubled by the imprecision of the phrase "tends to disturb." However, in Chicago v. Meyer, 44 Ill. 2d 1, 4, 253 N.E.2d 400 (1969), and Chicago v. Gregory, 39 Ill. 2d 47, 233 N.E.2d 422 (1968), *reversed on other grounds,* 394 U.S. 111, 89 S. Ct. 946, 22 L. Ed. 2d 134 (1969), the Supreme Court of Illinois construed a Chicago ordinance prohibiting, inter alia, a "diversion tending to disturb the peace," and held that it permitted conviction only where there was "*imminent* threat of violence." (Emphasis supplied.) See Gregory v. Chicago, 394 U.S. 111, 116-117, 121-122, 89 S. Ct. 946, 947, 951-952 (1969) (Black, J., concurring). Since Meyer was specifically cited in the opinion below, and it in turn drew heavily on Gregory, we think it proper to conclude that the Supreme Court of Illinois would interpret the Rockford ordinance to prohibit only actual or imminent interference with the "peace or good order" of the school.

Although the prohibited quantum of disturbance is not specified in the ordinance, it is apparent from the statute's announced purpose that the measure is whether normal school activity has been or is about to be disrupted. We do not have here a vague, general "breach of the peace" ordinance, but a specific statute for the school context, where the prohibited disturbances are easily measured by their impact on the normal activities of the school. Given this "particular context," the ordinance gives "fair notice to whom [it] is directed." . . .

Cox v. Louisiana, 379 U.S. 536, 85 S. Ct. 453, 13 L. Ed. 2d 471 (1965), and Coates v. Cincinnati, 402 U.S. 611, 91 S. Ct. 1686, 29 L. Ed. 2d 214 (1971), on which appellant particularly relies, presented completely different situations. In Cox, a general breach of the peace ordinance had been construed by state courts to mean "to agitate, to arouse from a state of repose, to molest, to interrupt, to hinder, to disquiet." The Court correctly concluded that, as construed, the ordinance permitted persons to be punished for merely expressing unpopular views. In Coates, the ordinance punished the sidewalk assembly of three or more persons who "conduct themselves in a manner annoying to persons passing by . . . ." We held, in part, that the ordinance was impermissibly vague because enforcement depended on the completely subjective standard of "annoyance."

In contrast, Rockford's anti-noise ordinance does not permit punishment for the expression of an unpopular point of view, and it contains no broad invitation to subjective or discriminatory enforcement. Rockford does not claim the broad power to punish all "noises" and "diversions." The vagueness of these terms, by themselves, is dispelled by the ordinance's requirements that (1) the "noise or diversion" be actually incompatible with normal school activity; (2) there be a demonstrated causality between the disruption which occurs and the "noise or diversion"; and (3) the acts be "willfully" done. "Undesirables" or their "annoying" conduct may not be punished. The ordinance does not permit people to "stand on a public sidewalk . . . only at the whim of any police officer." Rather, there must be demonstrated interference with school activities. As always, enforcement requires the exercise of some degree of police judgment, but, as confined, that degree of judgment here is permissible. The Rockford City Council has made the basic policy choices, and has given fair warning as to what is prohibited. "[T]he ordinance defines boundaries sufficiently distinct" for citizens, policemen, juries, and appellate judges. It is not impermissibly vague.

B. Overbreadth

A clear and precise enactment may nevertheless be "overbroad" if in its reach it prohibits constitutionally protected conduct. Although appellant does not claim that, as applied to him, the anti-noise ordinance has punished protected expressive activity, he claims that the ordinance is overbroad on its face. Because overbroad laws, like vague ones, deter privileged activity, our cases firmly establish appellant's standing to raise an overbreadth challenge. The crucial question, then, is whether the ordinance sweeps within its prohibitions what may not be punished under the First and Fourteenth Amendments. Specifically, appellant contends that the Rockford ordinance unduly interferes with First and Fourteenth Amendment rights to picket on a public sidewalk near a school. We disagree.

"In considering the right of a municipality to control the use of public streets for the expression of religious [or political] views, we start with the words of Mr. Justice Roberts that 'Wherever the title of streets and parks may rest, they have immemorially been held in trust for the use of the public and, time out of mind, have been used for purposes of assembly, communicating thoughts between citizens, and discussing public questions.' Hague v. C. I. O., 1939, 307 U.S. 496, 515, 59 S. Ct. 954, 964, 83 L. Ed. 1423."

Clearly, government has no power to restrict such activity because of its message. Our cases make equally clear, however, that reasonable "time, place and manner" regulations may be necessary to further significant governmental interests, and are permitted. For example, two parades cannot march on the same street simultaneously, and government may allow only one. Cox v. New Hampshire, 312 U.S. 569, 576, 61 S. Ct. 762, 765, 85 L. Ed. 1049 (1941). A demonstration or parade on a large street during rush hour might put an intolerable burden on the essential flow of traffic, and for that reason could be prohibited. Cox v. Louisiana, 379 U.S. 536, 554, 85 S. Ct. 453, 464, 13 L. Ed. 2d 471 (1965). If overamplified loudspeakers assault the citizenry, government may turn them down. Kovacs v. Cooper, 336 U.S. 77, 69 S. Ct. 448, 93 L. Ed. 513 (1949); Saia v. New York, 334 U.S. 558, 562, 68 S. Ct. 1148, 1150, 92 L. Ed. 1574 (1948). Subject to such reasonable regulation, however, peaceful demonstrations in public places are protected by the First Amendment. Of course, where demonstrations turn violent, they lose their protected quality as expression under the First Amendment.

The nature of a place, "the pattern of its normal activities, dictates the kinds of regulations of time, place, and manner that are reasonable." Although a silent vigil may not unduly interfere with a public library, Brown v. Louisiana, 383 U.S. 131, 86 S. Ct. 719, 15 L. Ed. 2d 637 (1966), making a speech in the reading room almost certainly would. That same speech should be perfectly appropriate in a park. The crucial question is whether the manner of expression is basically incompatible with the normal activity of a particular place at a particular time. Our cases make clear that in assessing the reasonableness of regulation, we must weigh heavily the fact that communication is involved; the regulation must be narrowly tailored to further the State's legitimate interest. "Access to [the streets, sidewalks, parks, and other similar public places] for the purpose of exercising [First Amendment rights] cannot constitutionally be denied broadly . . . ." Free expression "must not, in the guise of regulation, be abridged or denied."

In light of these general principles, we do not think that Rockford's ordinance is an unconstitutional regulation of activity around a school. Our touchstone is Tinker v. Des Moines Independent Community School District, 393 U.S. 503, 89 S. Ct. 733, 21 L. Ed. 2d 731 (1969), in which we considered the question of how to accommodate First Amendment rights with the "special characteristics of the school environment." Id., at 506, 89 S. Ct. at 736. Tinker held that the Des Moines School District could not punish students for wearing black armbands to school in protest of the Vietnam War. Recognizing that "wide exposure to . . . robust exchange of ideas" is an "important part of the educational process" and should be nurtured, id., at 512, 89 S. Ct., at 739, we concluded that free expression could not be barred from the school campus. We made clear that "undifferentiated fear or apprehension of disturbance is not enough to overcome the right to freedom of expression," id., at 508, 89 S. Ct., at 737, and that particular expressive activity could not be prohibited because of a "mere desire to avoid the discomfort and unpleasantness that always accompany an unpopular viewpoint," id., at 509, 89 S. Ct., at 738. But we nowhere suggested that students, teachers, or anyone else has an absolute constitutional right to use all parts of a school building or its immediate environs for his unlimited expressive purposes. Expressive activity could certainly be restricted, but only if the forbidden conduct "materially disrupts classwork or involves substantial disorder or invasion of the rights of others." Id., at 513, 89 S. Ct., at 740. The wearing of armbands was protected in Tinker because the students "neither interrupted school activities nor sought to intrude in the school affairs or the lives of others. They caused discussion outside of the classrooms, but no interference with work and no disorder." Id., at 514, 89 S. Ct., at 740. Compare Burnside v. Byars, 363 F.2d 744 (CA5 1966), and Butts v. Dallas Ind. School District, 436 F.2d 728 (CA5 1971), with Blackwell v. Issaquena County Board of Education, 363 F.2d 749 (CA5 1966).

Just as Tinker made clear that school property may not be declared off-limits for expressive activity by students, we think it clear that the public sidewalk adjacent to school grounds may not be declared off-limits for expressive activity by members of the public. But in each case, expressive activity may be prohibited if it "materially disrupts classwork or involves substantial disorder or invasion of the rights of others." Tinker v. Des Moines School District, supra, 393 U.S., at 513, 89 S. Ct., at 740.

We would be ignoring reality if we did not recognize that the public schools in a community are important institutions, and are often the focus of significant grievances. Without interfering with normal school activities, daytime picketing and handbilling on public grounds near a school can effectively publicize those grievances to pedestrians, school visitors, and deliverymen, as well as to teachers, administrators, and students. Some picketing to that end will be quiet and peaceful, and will in no way disturb the normal functioning of the school. For example, it would be highly unusual if the classic expressive gesture of the solitary picketer disrupts anything related to the school, at least on a public sidewalk open to pedestrians. On the other hand, schools could hardly tolerate boisterous demonstrators who drown out classroom conversation, make studying impossible, block entrances, or incite children to leave the schoolhouse. . . .

We recognize that the ordinance prohibits some picketing which is neither violent nor physically obstructive. Noisy demonstrations which disrupt or are incompatible with normal school activities are obviously within the ordinance's reach. Such expressive conduct may be constitutionally protected at other places or other times, . . . but next to a school, while classes are in session, it may be prohibited.[45] The anti-noise ordinance imposes no such restriction on expressive activity before or after the school session, while the student/faculty "audience" enters and leaves the school. . . .

The anti-noise ordinance is not invalid on its face.

The judgment is affirmed in part and reversed in part.

Affirmed in part and reversed in part.

Mr. Justice Blackmun joins in the judgment and in Part I of the opinion of the Court. He concurs in the result as to Part II of the opinion.

Mr. Justice Douglas, dissenting in part.

While I join Part I of the Court's opinion, I would also reverse the appellant's conviction under the antinoise ordinance. . . .

Appellant was one of 200 people picketing a school and carrying signs promoting a Black cause — "Black cheerleaders to cheer too," "Black history with black teachers," "We want our rights" and the like. Appellant, however, did not himself carry a picket sign. There was no evidence that he yelled or made any noise whatsoever. Indeed, the evidence reveals that appellant simply marched quietly and on one occasion raised his arm in the "power to the people" salute.

The picketers were mostly students; but they included former students,

45. Different considerations, of course, apply in different circumstances. For example, restrictions appropriate to a single building high school during class hours would be inappropriate in many open areas on a college campus, just as an assembly which is permitted outside a dormitory would be inappropriate in the middle of a mathematics class.

parents of students, and concerned citizens. They had made proposals to the school board on their demands and were turned down. Hence the picketing. The picketing was mostly by black students who were counselled and advised by a faculty member of the school. The school contained 1,800 students. Those counselling the students advised they must be quiet, walk hand in hand, no whispering, no talking.

Twenty-five policemen were stationed nearby. There was noise but most of it was produced by the police who used loudspeakers to explain the local ordinance and to announce that arrests might be made. The picketing did not stop and some 40 demonstrators, including appellant, were arrested.

The picketing lasted 20 to 30 minutes and some students went to the windows of the classrooms to observe it. It is not clear how many there were. The picketing was, however, orderly or as one officer testified "very orderly." There was no violence. And appellant made no noise whatever. . . .

We held in Cox v. Louisiana, 379 U.S. 536, 544-545, 85 S. Ct. 453, 458-459, 13 L. Ed. 2d 471, that a State could not infringe a person's right of free speech and free assembly by convicting him under a "disturbing the peace" ordinance where all that the students in that case did was to protest segregation and discrimination against Blacks by peaceably assembling and marching to the courthouse where they sang, prayed, and listened to a speech, but where there was no violence, no rioting, no boisterous conduct.

The school where the present picketing occurred was the center of a racial conflict. Most of the picketers were indeed students in the school. The dispute doubtless disturbed the school; and the blaring of the loudspeakers of the police was certainly a "noise or diversion" in the meaning of the ordinance. But there was no evidence that appellant was noisy or boisterous or rowdy. He walked quietly and in an orderly manner. As I read this record the disruptive force loosened at this school was an issue dealing with race — an issue that is preeminently one for solution by First Amendment means. That is all that was done here; and the entire picketing, including appellant's part in it, was done in the best First Amendment tradition.

NOTES

1. The strong emotional component in racial issues almost guarantees that any protest involving this area will lead to noisy confrontations. Under the standards in the Grayned case, it is difficult to imagine how a meaningful protest can be mounted around a school protected by an ordinance of the type involved there. See Street v. New York, printed supra page 358.

2. Even before the Supreme Court's decision in Grayned, black school protests received only limited protection from the courts. In Jackson v. Ellington, 316 F. Supp. 1071 (W.D. Tenn. 1970), the court conceded that statutes prohibiting absenting of children from school and contributing to the delinquency of a minor should not be applied to suppress First Amendment activity, but refused to enjoin use of such statutes against parents who kept

their children home to protest racial policies of the board of education. And in New York, parents who protested school segregation by sitting-in following an evening school board meeting in the Malverne Junior High School, Long Island had their disorderly conduct convictions affirmed by the state's high court, albeit with three judges dissenting. People v. Martin, 43 Misc. 2d 355, 251 N.Y.S.2d 66 (App. Term 1964), *aff'd,* 15 N.Y.2d 933, 259 N.Y.S.2d 152, 207 N.E.2d 197 (1965), *cert. denied,* 382 U.S. 828 (1965).

3. School protests by black students involving violence and the destruction of property have been uniformly condemned by the courts. See, e.g., Locke v. Vance, 307 F. Supp. 439 (S.D. Tex. 1969). In the wake of disruptive school protests, courts seem willing to ignore procedural difficulties to uphold disciplinary penalties. There are exceptions. In Marzette v. McPhee, 294 F. Supp. 562 (W.D. Wisc. 1968), black students at Wisconsin State University at Oshkosh were suspended after a highly destructive protest, which included taking over a building, harassment and imprisonment of the university president, breaking windows and typewriters, rifling files, tearing down drapes and blinds, slashing furniture and pictures, and overturning equipment.

Judge Doyle, in holding that the students were entitled to a prompt hearing, said:

> The events described in these affidavits cannot be recounted without evoking deep sadness; sadness in the memory of decades, even centuries, of injustice, the fruits of which are now so insistently with us; sadness that this legacy seems now to be producing a profound sickness in some of our people, including some of our younger black people; and sadness that some of them appear so unaware that there is a sickness there.
>
> This is the reality with which we all struggle. The court appreciates the nature of the instinct which prompted the disturbance. The court appreciates the anxiety and shock induced in others by such bizarre behavior. The court appreciates that those who bear the heavy burden of governing our universities are solemnly obliged to take the necessary measures to preserve them against irrational assault.
>
> Conduct by students of the kind described in the affidavits of the president and the other administrators is obviously constitutionally subject to severe sanctions, including suspension or expulsion. So long as the rules allegedly violated are themselves valid, those charged with governance of the university are not only free to proceed to discipline the offenders; they are duty bound to do so. But most particularly in complex and difficult situations, it is essential that those entrusted with the awful force of governmental power — regents, administrators, and courts — apply it carefully, precisely, justly. Faced with problems of such gravity, it would not be irrational to doubt the efficacy of some of the restrictions we have imposed by our constitution upon the exercise of governmental power. But we are committed as a people to exist as a constitutional community and we must persevere in the convictions which prompted that commitment. (294 F. Supp. at 569.)

NOTE: BLACK ATHLETES AND RACIAL PROTESTS

Traditionally, black athletes have been able to translate their sports abilities into a measure of acceptance denied less physically gifted members of their race. Thus, colleges with no noticeable drive to educate black students have avidly recruited blacks with skills that would help bring them a "winning team." But at the collegiate as well as the professional level, the lives of even "star" black athletes are far less prejudice-free than appearances indicate. Olsen, The Black Athlete, Sports Illustrated, July 1, 8, 15, 22, 29 (1968). Alcindor, with Olsen, My Story, Sports Illustrated, Oct. 3, Nov. 3, 10 (1969). See also H. Edwards, The Sociology of Sports (1973).

Statistical studies of racial bias in sports are reviewed in Yetman and Eitzen, Black Americans in Sports: Unequal Opportunity for Equal Ability, 5 Civ. Rights Digest 20, U.S. Comm. on Civ. Rights (Aug. 1972). These studies indicate that to make the team at all, blacks have to be superior players or stars. In competition between black and white journeymen players, the white player will generally get the job. As a result, blacks are overrepresented in starting positions, but are not randomly distributed throughout the team. Second-string or substitute players are usually white. In addition, the authors detail the use of quotas to limit the number of blacks on a team, and the "stacking" phenomenon, in which blacks are relegated to specific team roles (running backs in football, the outfield in baseball), but excluded or discouraged from others (quarterbacks in football). Thus, what is commonly seen as the superior athletic ability of blacks is in reality a discriminatory policy that requires black players to excel, in order to both make and retain a team position. For example, the batting averages of black players in the major leagues for the period from 1953 to 1970 averaged twenty points higher than the averages for white players.

When black athletes began to join the protest movement in the mid-1960s, they found that such activity adversely affected the acceptance won by their superior athletic abilities, and when they sought to bring their protests to the playing field, white society was appalled. In H. Edwards, The Revolt of the Black Athlete (1969), the author traces the inequities surrounding black athletes as background for the 1968 Olympic boycott, which he directed. During the 1972 Olympics, two American black athletes, Vince Matthews and Wayne Collett, who had finished first and second in the final of the 400-meter dash, were expelled by the International Olympic Committee for fidgeting and chatting, instead of standing at attention, during the playing of "The Star-Spangled Banner" after they received their medals. They denied that they were protesting, but were refused a hearing. Two U.S. Athletes Barred from Future Games, N.Y. Times, Sep. 9, 1972, p. 1, c. 2.

In January 1973, officials at the Knights of Columbus track meet held at the Nassau Colliseum in Uniondale, Long Island disqualified an Eastern Michigan track team after observing that three black members of the team were doing stretching exercises during the playing of the national anthem. Anthem "Incident" Stirs Fans, N.Y. Times, Jan. 15, 1973, p. 39, c. 4.

Efforts to litigate protest rights of black athletes have met with little success. In Evans v. State Board of Agriculture, 325 F. Supp. 1353 (D. Colo. 1971), after some Colorado State students had protested the racist tenets of

Mormonism during a basketball game with Brigham Young University in the Colorado State gymnasium, the court approved as "manifestly reasonable" a policy issued by Colorado State University banning all protests in a building where an athletic event was being held.

Fourteen black athletes at the University of Wyoming fared no better. They were dropped from the team because of their plan to wear black armbands during a game with Brigham Young University, as a protest against the teachings of the Mormon Church. A federal district court rejected their claims for damages, on the ground that school officials, as state agents, were immune under the Eleventh Amendment. Injunctive relief was denied because the court found that plaintiffs' conduct, if permitted by the school, would violate both state and federal constitutional restrictions concerning the separation of church and state and the free exercise of religion. Williams v. Eaton, 310 F. Supp. 1342 (D. Wyo. 1970). The court of appeals affirmed as to damages, but reversed as to the request for injunctive relief, holding that the district court should not have summarily disposed of First Amendment issues and the likelihood of disturbances. 443 F.2d 422 (10th Cir. 1971). On remand, the district court affirmed its earlier ruling on similar grounds. The case of Tinker v. Des Moines Independent School District, 393 U.S. 503, 89 S. Ct. 733, 21 L. Ed. 2d 731 (1969), was distinguished in that the wearing of black armbands in that case was for the purpose of opposing the Vietnam war, a governmental activity within the "prime zone of protected areas of free speech," whereas in the instant case, the wearing of the armbands clashed with fundamental principles of religious freedom. Regarding plaintiffs' own reliance on First Amendment rights, the court declared:

> The rights of the Plaintiffs to freedom of speech as guaranteed by the First Amendment cannot be held paramount to the rights of others to practice their religion free from state-supported protest since "individual liberties cannot be left completely uncontrolled to clash with similarly asserted liberties of several thousand others." The complaint was again dismissed as "insubstantial and without merit." (333 F. Supp. 107 (D. Wyo. 1972), *aff'd*, 468 F.2d 1079 (10th Cir. 1972).)

GREGORY v. CITY OF CHICAGO
394 U.S. 111, 89 S. Ct. 946, 22 L. Ed. 2d 134 (*1969*)

[Chief Justice Warren reversed the disorderly conduct convictions of petitioners who had been arrested and convicted for refusing police orders to disperse, after their protest march had attracted a large number of unruly bystanders. Justice Warren said it was a "simple case" in that the record was entirely without evidence that petitioners had been disorderly. Without questioning police motives, the Court held that the convictions violated due process in that they were "totally devoid of evidentiary support." The Court also found that the trial judge's charge permitted the jury to convict for acts clearly entitled to First Amendment protection, and that this independently required reversal.

Justice Black, with whom Justice Douglas joined, wrote a concurring opinion.]

Mr. Justice Black, with whom Mr. Justice Douglas joins, concurring.

This I think is a highly important case which requires more detailed consideration than the Court's opinion gives it. It in a way tests the ability of the United States to keep the promises its Constitution makes to the people of the Nation. . . . Shortly after the original Constitution was adopted, . . . the Bill of Rights was added to the Constitution, in which the First Amendment, later made applicable to the States by the Fourteenth Amendment, provides that: "Congress shall make no law . . . abridging the freedom of speech, or of the press; or the right of the people peaceably to assemble, and to petition the Government for a redress of grievances."

In 1954 our Court held that laws segregating people on the basis of race or color in the public schools unconstitutionally denied Negroes equal protection of the laws. Negroes, and many others who sympathized with them, cooperatively undertook to speed up desegregation. These groups adopted plans under which they marched on the streets carrying placards, chanting, and singing songs, all designed to publicize their grievances and to petition the various units of government, state and national, for a redress of these grievances. Their activities along these lines quite obviously aroused highly emotional feelings both on their part and on the part of others who opposed the changes in local laws and customs which the "picketers" and "demonstrators" advocated. Agitation between groups brought about sharp conflicts and clashes, threats, fights, riots, and near-riots. This Court, to be sure, has had its difficulties and sharp differences of opinion in deciding the precise boundaries dividing what is constitutionally permissible and impermissible in this field.[2] There have also been sharp disputes over whether the Court can hold laws unconstitutional because the Court deems them to be "unreasonable," "arbitrary," or contrary to fundamental standards of ethics, morals, or conscience. Fortunately, however, these differences need not concern us here. For while we have pointed out in many cases that the States and their subordinate units do have constitutional power to regulate picketing, demonstrating, and parading by statutes and ordinances narrowly drawn so as not to abridge the rights of speech, press, assembly, or petition, neither Chicago nor Illinois at the time these petitioners were demonstrating had passed any such narrowly drawn laws.

The facts upon which these arrests and convictions for disorderly conduct occurred were these.

Petitioner Gregory and his group had become dissatisfied because Benjamin Willis, Superintendent of Chicago's public school system, was not moving speedily enough to desegregate the public schools. While Mayor Daley did not appear to have legal authority to remove Dr. Willis, the group evidently

2. See, e.g., Cox v. Louisiana, 379 U.S. 536, 85 S. Ct. 453, 13 L. Ed. 2d 471 (1965); Adderley v. Florida, 385 U.S. 39, 87 S. Ct. 242, 17 L. Ed. 2d 149 (1966).

believed the Mayor could cause him to be removed if he wanted to do so, and their prodding was therefore directed at the Mayor as well as against Willis. The group march began near the Chicago Loop District at 4:30 p.m. and ended five miles away in the neighborhood of Daley's home. A lieutenant of police, four police sergeants, and about forty policemen met Gregory at the gathering place in Grant Park. There Gregory addressed the marchers, saying:

> First we will go over to the snake pit [city hall]. When we leave there, we will go out to the snake's house [the mayor's home]. Then, we will continue to go out to Mayor Daley's home until he fires Ben Willis [Superintendent of Schools].

The demonstrators marched to the city hall, and then they marched to the Mayor's home about five miles away, arriving at about 8 p.m. The demonstrators were accompanied by the police and by the Assistant City Attorney from the park to the Mayor's home. When they reached this neighborhood, the demonstrators began marching around and around near the Mayor's home. Meanwhile the crowd of spectators from the neighborhood kept increasing, and its language and conduct became rougher and tougher. The events leading up to the arrest of the demonstrators are set out in detail in the opinion of the Illinois Supreme Court, and I agree fully with that court's description of these events, which I have reprinted as an appendix to this opinion. This episode finally came to a conclusion at about 9:30 p.m. Fearful that the threatening crowd of onlookers could no longer be contained, the police asked Gregory and his marchers to leave the area. When they refused, they were arrested and charged with violation of Chicago's disorderly conduct ordinance, which provides as follows:

> All persons who shall make, aid, countenance, or assist in making any improper noise, riot, disturbance, breach of the peace, or diversion tending to a breach of the peace, within the limits of the city; all persons who shall collect in bodies or crowds for unlawful purposes, or for any purpose, to the annoyance or disturbance of other persons; . . . shall be deemed guilty of disorderly conduct, and upon conviction thereof, shall be severally fined not less than one dollar nor more than two hundred dollars for each offense. Municipal Code of Chicago, §193-1.

I agree with the Illinois Supreme Court that the "record shows a determined effort by the police to allow the marchers to peacefully demonstrate and at the same time maintain order." I also think the record shows that outside of the marching and propagandizing of their views and protests, Gregory and his group while marching did all in their power to maintain order. Indeed, in the face of jeers, insults, and assaults with rocks and eggs, Gregory and his group maintained a decorum that speaks well for their determination simply to tell their side of their grievances and complaints. Even the "snake" and "snake pit" invectives used by Gregory and his demonstrators, unlike some used by their hecklers, remained within the general give-

and-take of heated political argument. Thus both police and demonstrators made their best efforts faithfully to discharge their responsibilities as officers and citizens, but they were nevertheless unable to restrain the hostile hecklers within decent and orderly bounds. These facts disclosed by the record point unerringly to one conclusion, namely, that when groups with diametrically opposed, deep-seated views are permitted to air their emotional grievances, side by side, on city streets, tranquility and order cannot be maintained even by the joint efforts of the finest and best officers and of those who desire to be the most law-abiding protestors of their grievances.

It is because of this truth, and a desire both to promote order and to safeguard First Amendment freedoms, that this Court has repeatedly warned States and governmental units that they cannot regulate conduct connected with these freedoms through use of sweeping, dragnet statutes that may, because of vagueness, jeopardize these freedoms. In those cases, however, we have been careful to point out that the Constitution does not bar enactment of laws regulating conduct, even though connected with speech, press, assembly, and petition, if such laws specifically bar only the conduct deemed obnoxious and are carefully and narrowly aimed at that forbidden conduct. The dilemma revealed by this record is a crying example of a need for some such narrowly drawn law. It is not our duty and indeed not within our power to set out and define with precision just what statutes can be lawfully enacted to deal with situations like the one confronted here by police and protestors, both of whom appear to us to have been conscientiously trying to do their duties as they understood them. Plainly, however, no mandate in our Constitution leaves States and governmental units powerless to pass laws to protect the public from the kind of boisterous and threatening conduct that disturbs the tranquility of spots selected by the people either for homes, wherein they can escape the hurly-burly of the outside business and political world, or for public and other buildings that require peace and quiet to carry out their functions, such as courts, libraries, schools, and hospitals.

The disorderly conduct ordinance under which these petitioners were charged and convicted is not, however, a narrowly drawn law, particularly designed to regulate certain kinds of conduct such as marching or picketing or demonstrating along the streets or highways. Nor does it regulate the times or places or manner of carrying on such activities. To the contrary, it might better be described as a meat-ax ordinance, gathering in one comprehensive definition of an offense a number of words which have a multiplicity of meanings, some of which would cover activity specifically protected by the First Amendment. The average person charged with its violation is necessarily left uncertain as to what conduct and attitudes of mind would be enough to convict under it. . . . And it must be remembered that only the tiniest bit of petitioners' conduct could possibly be thought illegal here — that is, what they did after the policeman's order to leave the area. The right "peaceably to assemble, and to petition the Government for a redress of grievances" is specifically protected by the First Amendment. For the entire five-mile march, the walking by petitioners in a group, the language, and the chants and songs were all treated by the city's assistant attorney and its specially detailed policemen as lawful, not lawless, conduct.

The so-called "diversion tending to a breach of the peace" here was limited entirely and exclusively to the fact that when the policeman in charge of the special police detail concluded that the hecklers observing the march were dangerously close to rioting and that the demonstrators and others were likely to be engulfed in that riot, he ordered Gregory and his demonstrators to leave, and Gregory — standing on what he deemed to be his constitutional rights — refused to do so. The "diversion" complained of on the part of Gregory and the other marchers was not any noise they made or annoyance or disturbance of "other persons" they had inflicted. Their guilt of "disorderly conduct" therefore turns out to be their refusal to obey instanter an individual policeman's command to leave the area of the Mayor's home. Since neither the city council nor the state legislature had enacted a narrowly drawn statute forbidding disruptive picketing or demonstrating in a residential neighborhood, the conduct involved here could become "disorderly" only if the policeman's command was a law which the petitioners were bound to obey at their peril. But under our democratic system of government, lawmaking is not entrusted to the moment-to-moment judgment of the policeman on his beat. Laws, that is valid laws, are to be made by representatives chosen to make laws for the future, not by police officers whose duty is to enforce laws already enacted and to make arrests only for conduct already made criminal. . . . There are ample ways to protect the domestic tranquility without subjecting First Amendment freedoms to such a clumsy and unwieldy weapon.

[The Court acknowledged that it was bound by a state court interpretation that limited liability of the ordinance to situations where there is an "imminent threat of violence" and where demonstrators refuse police requests to stop, but the Court found that the trial judge had merely read the ordinance to the jury.]

In agreeing to the reversal of these convictions, however, I wish once more to say that I think our Federal Constitution does not render the States powerless to regulate the conduct of demonstrators and picketers, conduct which is more than "speech," more than "press," more than "assembly," and more than "petition," as those terms are used . . . . Were the authority of government so trifling as to permit anyone with a complaint to have the vast power to do anything he pleased, wherever he pleased, and whenever he pleased, our customs and our habits of conduct, social, political, economic, ethical, and religious, would all be wiped out, and become no more than relics of a gone but not forgotten past. Churches would be compelled to welcome into their buildings invaders who came but to scoff and jeer; streets and highways and public buildings would cease to be available for the purposes for which they were constructed and dedicated whenever demonstrators and picketers wanted to use them for their own purposes. And perhaps worse than all other changes, homes, the sacred retreat to which families repair for their privacy and their daily way of living, would have to have their doors thrown open to all who desired to convert the occupants to new views, new morals, and a new way of life. Men and women who hold public office would be compelled, simply because they did hold public office, to lose the comforts and privacy of an unpicketed home. I believe that our Constitution, written for the ages, to endure except as changed in the manner it provides, did not create a government with such monumental weaknesses. Speech and press are, of course, to be free, so that public matters can be discussed with impunity. But picketing and demonstrating can be regulated like other conduct of men. I believe that the homes of men, sometimes the last citadel of the tired, the weary and the sick, can be protected by government from noisy, marching, tramping, threatening picketers and demonstrators bent on filling the minds of men, women, and children with fears of the unknown.

For these reasons I concur in the reversal.

QUESTIONS

1. Had there been evidence that some of Gregory's followers were unable — despite his admonitions — to resist responding to the physical and verbal assaults from the crowd, would such evidence justify affirmance of their convictions? Would the plea of self-defense be available to these protesters? If not, are they, in fact, being convicted for having failed to "turn the other cheek"?

2. Assume a carefully drawn law requiring the dispersal of protesters when there is "imminent threat of violence." Given the "aroused highly emotional feelings" which Justice Black found generally accompany racial demonstrations, of what value would First Amendment rights be to blacks? Would not such a law have permitted the valid arrest and conviction of even the most determinedly nonviolent sit-ins?

PEOPLE ACTING THROUGH COMMUNITY EFFORT (PACE) v. DOORLEY, 338 F. Supp. 574 (D.R.I. 1972). In Providence, R.I., the plaintiff, the Reverend James Ford, together with seven members of his group, picketed the residence of Abraham Konoff, carrying signs which read, "Mr. Konoff fix your property on Dudley Street." Other signs contained pictures of the Dudley Street property, showing what were termed violations of the housing code. The group was advised that their action was in violation of an anti-residential-picketing ordinance, and they were ordered to disperse. Fearing arrest and prosecution, the plaintiffs departed.

Then, in a suit against Mayor Joseph A. Doorley, plaintiffs challenged the validity of the ordinance in federal court. The ordinance prohibited picketing "before or about the residence or dwelling of any individual," but not "lawful picketing during a labor dispute at the place of employment" involved, or assembly on any premises "commonly used for the discussion of subjects of general interest." The district court declared the ordinance constitutional and not in violation of either First or Fourteenth Amendments. Rather, the court concluded that the ordinance reflects a legislative judgment that residential picketing is meant to harass and cause emotional stress, destroying tranquillity and the privacy of the home. The court conceded that judicial protection has traditionally been given to the use of public places for purposes of assembly in exchange of thought and opinion. However, quoting from Kamin, Residential Picketing and the First Amendment, 61 Nw. U.L. Rev. 177, 226 (1966), the court added: "But it is also true that time out of mind the home has been man's sanctuary, the shelter of his family, the repositories of his memories, and the center of his hopes. . . ." The state's power to protect its citizenry against the invasion of privacy is indisputable, the court held, adding:

> It is my opinion there is no significant resultant difference between picketing and raucous loudspeaker noises. In both situations, the privacy of the trapped homeowner is invaded and both may be regulated. More important than protection against nuisances is the "right to be left alone" encompassed in the right of privacy. This right to be left alone is crucial where the individual is helpless to respond, a captive of those invading his privacy. (338 F. Supp. at 579.)

The court concluded that residential picketing is not a conventional means for the exercise of First Amendment rights. "On the contrary, it is an instrument of harassment and oppression, pregnant with 'physical intimidation and coercion.' . . . I find this undemocratic and violative of constitutional protection belonging to all citizens — innocent or otherwise." 338 F. Supp. at 580. Concerning the plaintiffs' equal protection argument, growing out of the ordinance's exemption of picketing during labor disputes, the court stated that "such exemption is necessary so as not to deny an employee the right of picketing at the subject matter of his dispute." 338 F. Supp. at 580. The court found that the home is protected unless it is a place of employment.

QUESTIONS

Is there any doubt as to how Justice Black would vote on the Doorley case were it presented to him on review? Can the Doorley court's handling of the equal protection problem (growing out of the ordinance's exception for labor picketing where the employee works at his employer's home) be squared with the result in Grayned v. City of Rockford?

VIRGINIA STATE UNIT, SCLC v. CITY OF PETERSBURG, 2 Race Rel. L. Sur. 83 (E.D. Va. 1970). An injunction was issued against enforcement of an ordinance under which the city council had prohibited plaintiffs from selling lapel tags as a fund-raising device in residential and shopping areas. The ordinance was deemed void for vagueness and violative of First and Fourteenth Amendment rights.

ORGANIZATION FOR A BETTER AUSTIN v. KEEFE, 402 U.S. 415, 91 S. Ct. 1575, 29 L. Ed. 2d — (1971). The Court reversed, on the ground of unjustified prior restraint, a state court injunction obtained by a real estate broker to halt a racially integrated community organization's distribution of leaflets charging the broker with "blockbusting" and "panic peddling." The state court had found that the leaflets invaded the realtor's right of privacy and were coercive and intimidating rather than informative. The Supreme Court disagreed, finding the leafleting within the organization's First Amendment right to freedom of expression. They were engaged openly and vigorously in making the public aware of Keefe's real estate practices, and although their tactics were offensive to him, they were peaceful and need not meet standards of acceptability. The Court found that no prior decisions support the claim that the interest of an individual in being free from public criticism of his business practices in pamphlets or leaflets warrants use of the injunctive power.

LLOYD CORPORATION LTD. v. TANNER
407 U.S. 551, 92 S. Ct. 2219, 33 L. Ed. 2d 131 (1972)

Mr. Justice POWELL delivered the opinion of the Court. . . .

Lloyd Corporation, Ltd. (Lloyd), owns a large, modern retail shopping center in Portland, Oregon. Lloyd Center embraces altogether about 50 acres, including some 20 acres of open and covered parking facilities which accommodate more than 1,000 automobiles. It has a perimeter of almost one and one-half miles, bounded by four public streets. It is crossed in varying degrees by several other public streets, all of which have adjacent public sidewalks. Lloyd owns all land and buildings within the Center, except these public streets and sidewalks. There are some 60 commercial tenants, including small shops and several major department stores.

The Center embodies a relatively new concept in shopping center design. The stores are all located within a single large, multi-level building complex sometimes referred to as the "Mall." Within this complex, in addition to the stores, there are parking facilities, malls, private sidewalks, stairways, escalators, gardens, and an auditorium and a skating rink. Some of the stores open directly on the outside public sidewalks, but most open on the interior privately owned malls. Some stores open on both. There are no public streets or public sidewalks within the building complex, which is enclosed and entirely covered except for the landscaped portions of some of the interior malls.

The distribution of the handbills occurred in the malls. They are a distinctive feature of the Center, serving both utilitarian and esthetic functions. Essentially, they are private, interior promenades with 10-foot sidewalks serving the stores, and with a center strip 30 feet wide in which flowers and shrubs are planted, and statuary, fountains, benches and other amenities are located. There is no vehicular traffic on the malls. An architectural expert described the purpose of the malls as follows:

In order to make shopping easier and pleasant, and to help realize the goal of maximum sales [for the Center], the shops are grouped about special pedestrian ways or malls. Here the shopper is isolated from the noise, fumes, confusion and distraction which he normally finds along city streets, and a controlled, carefree environment is provided . . . .

Although the stores close at customary hours, the malls are not physically closed, as pedestrian window shopping is encouraged within reasonable hours. Lloyd employs 12 security guards who are commissioned as such by the city of Portland. The guards have police authority within the Center, wear uniforms similar to those worn by city police, and are licensed to carry handguns. They are employed by and subject to the control of Lloyd. Their duties are the customary ones, including shoplifting surveillance and general security.

At a few places within the Center small signs are embedded in the sidewalk which state:

NOTICE — Areas In Lloyd Center Used By The Public Are Not Public Ways But Are For The Use Of Lloyd Center Tenants And The Public Transacting Business With Them. Permission To Use Said Areas May Be Revoked At Any Time. Lloyd Corporation, Ltd.

The Center is open generally to the public, with a considerable effort being made to attract shoppers and prospective shoppers, and to create "customer motivation" as well as customer good will in the community. In this respect the Center pursues policies comparable to those of major stores and shopping centers across the country, although the Center affords superior facilities for these purposes. Groups and organizations are permitted, by invitation and advance arrangement, to use the auditorium and other facilities. Rent is charged for use of the auditorium except with respect to certain civic and charitable organizations, such as the Cancer Society, Boy and Girl Scouts. The Center also allows limited use of the malls by the American Legion to sell "Buddy Poppies" for disabled veterans, and by the Salvation Army and Volunteers of America to solicit Christmas contributions. It has denied similar use to other civic and charitable organizations. Political use is also forbidden, except that presidential candidates of both parties have been allowed to speak in the auditorium.[3]

The Center had been in operation for some eight years when this litigation commenced. Throughout this period it had a policy, strictly enforced, against the distribution of handbills within the building complex and its malls. No exceptions were made with respect to handbilling, which was considered likely to annoy customers, to create litter, potentially to create disorders, and

3. The manager of the Center, explaining why presidential candidates were allowed to speak, said: "We do that for one reason and that is great public interest. It . . . brings a great many people to Lloyd Center who may shop before they leave." App. 51.

generally to be incompatible with the purpose of the Center and the atmosphere sought to be preserved.

On November 14, 1968, the respondents in this case distributed within the Center handbill invitations to a meeting of the "Resistance Community" to protest the draft and the Vietnam War. The distribution, made in several different places on the mall walkways by five young people, was quiet and orderly, and there was no littering. There was a complaint from one customer. Security guards informed the respondents that they were trespassing and would be arrested unless they stopped distributing the handbills within the Center. The guards suggested that respondents distribute their literature on the public streets and sidewalks adjacent to but outside of the Center complex. Respondents left the premises as requested "to avoid arrest" and continued the handbilling outside. Subsequently this suit was instituted in the District Court seeking declaratory and injunctive relief.

I

The District Court, emphasizing that the Center "is open to the general public," found that it is "the functional equivalent of a public business district." 308 F. Supp., at 130. That court then held that Lloyd's "rule prohibiting the distribution of handbills within the Mall violates . . . First Amendment rights." 308 F. Supp., at 131. In a per curiam opinion, the Court of Appeals held that it was bound by the "factual determination" as to the character of the Center, and concluded that the decisions of this Court in Marsh v. Alabama, 326 U.S. 501, 66 S. Ct. 276, 90 L. Ed. 265 (1946), and Amalgamated Food Employees Union Local 590 v. Logan Valley Plaza, Inc., 391 U.S. 308, 88 S. Ct. 1601, 20 L. Ed. 2d 603 (1968), compelled affirmance.

Marsh involved Chickasaw, Alabama, a company town wholly owned by the Gulf Shipbuilding Corporation. The opinion of the Court, by Mr. Justice Black, described Chickasaw as follows:

> Except for [ownership by a private corporation] it has all the characteristics of any other American town. The property consists of residential buildings, streets, a system of sewers, a sewage disposal plant and a "business block" on which business places are situated. A deputy of the Mobile County Sheriff, paid by the company, serves as the town's policeman. Merchants and service establishments have rented the stores and business places on the business block and the United States uses one of the places as a post office from which six carriers deliver mail to the people of Chickasaw and the adjacent area. The town and the surrounding neighborhood, which can not be distinguished from the Gulf property by anyone not familiar with the property lines, are thickly settled, and according to all indications the residents use the business block as their regular shopping center. To do so, they now, as they have for many years, make use of a company-owned paved street and sidewalk located alongside the store fronts in order to enter and leave the stores and the post office. Intersecting company-owned roads at each end of the business block lead into a four-lane public highway which runs parallel to the business block at a distance of thirty feet. There is nothing to stop highway traffic from coming into

the business block and upon arrival a traveler may make free use of the facilities available there. In short the town and its shopping district are accessible to and freely used by the public in general and there is nothing to distinguish them from any other town and shopping center except the fact that the title to the property belongs to a private corporation. 326 U.S., at 502-503, 66 S. Ct., at 277.

A Jehovah's Witness undertook to distribute religious literature on a sidewalk near the post office and was arrested on a trespassing charge. In holding that First and Fourteenth Amendment rights were infringed, the Court emphasized that the business district was within a company-owned town, an anachronism long prevalent in some southern States and now rarely found.[6]

In Logan Valley the Court extended the rationale of Marsh to peaceful picketing of a store located in a large shopping center, known as Logan Valley Mall, near Altoona, Pennsylvania. Weis Markets, Inc. (Weis), an original tenant, had opened a supermarket in one of the larger stores and was employing a wholly nonunion staff. Within 10 days after Weis opened, members of Amalgamated Food Employees Union Local 590 (Union) began picketing Weis, carrying signs stating that it was a nonunion market and that its employees were not receiving union wages or other union benefits. The picketing, conducted by nonemployees, was carried out almost entirely in the parcel pickup area immediately adjacent to the store and on portions of the adjoining parking lot. The picketing was peaceful, with the number of pickets varying from four to 13.

Weis and Logan Valley Plaza, Inc., sought and obtained an injunction against this picketing. The injunction required that all picketing be confined to public areas outside the shopping center. On appeal the Pennsylvania Supreme Court affirmed the issuance of the injunction, and this Court granted certiorari. In framing the question, this Court stated:

The case squarely presents . . . the question whether Pennsylvania's generally valid rules against trespass to private property can be applied in these circumstances to bar petitioners from the Weis and Logan premises. 391 U.S., at 315, 88 S. Ct., at 1606.

The Court noted that the answer would be clear "if the shopping center premises were not privately owned but instead constituted the business area of a municipality." 391 U.S., at 315, 88 S. Ct., at 1607. In the latter situation, it has often been held that publicly owned streets, sidewalks and parks are so historically associated with the exercise of First Amendment rights that

6. In commenting on the necessity of citizens who reside in company towns having access to information, the Court said: "Many people in the United States live in company-owned towns. These people, just as residents of municipalities, are free citizens of their State and country. Just as all other citizens they must make decisions which affect the welfare of community and nation. To act as good citizens they must be informed." 326 U.S., at 508, 66 S. Ct., at 280.

access to them for purposes of exercising such rights cannot be denied absolutely. [Citations omitted.]

The Court then considered Marsh v. Alabama, *supra,* and concluded that:

> The shopping center here is clearly the functional equivalent of the business district of Chickasaw involved in Marsh. 391 U.S., at 318, 88 S. Ct., at 1608.

But the Court was careful not to go further and say that for all purposes and uses the privately owned streets, sidewalks and other areas of a shopping center are analogous to publicly owned facilities:

> All we decide here is that because the shopping center serves as the community business block "and is freely accessible and open to the people in the area and those passing through," Marsh v. State of Alabama, 326 U.S., at 508, 66 S. Ct., at 279, the State may not delegate the power, through the use of its trespass laws, wholly to exclude those members of the public wishing to exercise their First Amendment rights on the premises in a manner and for a purpose generally consonant with the use to which the property is actually put. 391 U.S., at 319-320, 88 S. Ct., at 1609.

The Court noted that the scope of its holding was limited, and expressly reserved judgment on the type of issue presented in this case:

> The picketing carried on by petitioners was directed specifically at patrons of the Weis Market located within the shopping center and the message sought to be conveyed to the public concerned the manner in which that particular market was being operated. We are, therefore, not called upon to consider whether respondents' property rights could, consistently with the First Amendment, justify a bar on picketing which was not thus directly related in its purpose to the use to which the shopping center property was being put." 391 U.S., at 320 n. 9, 88 S. Ct., at 1609.

The Court also took specific note of the facts that the Union's picketing was "directed solely at one establishment within the shopping center," 391 U.S., at 321, 88 S. Ct., at 1610, and that the public berms and sidewalks were "from 350 to 500 feet away from the Weis store." 391 U.S., at 322, 88 S. Ct., at 1610. This distance made it difficult "to communicate [with] patrons of Weis" and "to limit [the] effect [of the picketing] to Weis only." 391 U.S., at 322, 323, 88 S. Ct. at 1611.[7] Logan Valley was decided on the basis of this factual situation, and the facts in this case are significantly different.

7. The Court also commented on the increasing role of shopping centers and on the problem which they would present with respect to union activities if picketing were totally proscribed within shopping center areas: "Business enterprises located in downtown areas [on public streets and sidewalks] would be subject to on-the-spot public criticism for their [labor] practices, but businesses situated in the suburbs could largely immunize themselves from similar criticism by creating a cordon sanitaire of parking lots around their stores." 391 U.S., at 324-325, 88 S. Ct. at 1612. The concurring opinion

II

The courts below considered the critical inquiry to be whether Lloyd Center was "the functional equivalent of a public business district." This phrase was first used in Logan Valley, but its genesis was in Marsh. It is well to consider what Marsh actually decided. As noted above, it involved an economic anomaly of the past, "the company town." One must have seen such towns to understand that "functionally" they were no different from municipalities of comparable size. They developed primarily in the deep south to meet economic conditions, especially those which existed following the Civil War. Impoverished States, and especially backward areas thereof, needed an influx of industry and capital. Corporations attracted to the area by natural resources and abundant labor were willing to assume the role of local government. Quite literally, towns were built and operated by private capital with all of the customary services and utilities normally afforded by a municipal or state government: there were streets, sidewalks, sewers, public lighting, police and fire protection, business and residential areas, churches, postal facilities, and sometimes schools. In short, as Mr. Justice Black said, Chickasaw, Alabama, had "all the characteristics of any other American town." 326 U.S., at 502, 66 S. Ct., at 277. The Court simply held that where private interests were substituting for and performing the customary functions of government, First Amendment freedoms could not be denied where exercised in the customary manner on the town's sidewalks and streets. Indeed, as title to the entire town was held privately, there were no publicly owned streets, sidewalks or parks where such rights could be exercised.

Logan Valley extended Marsh to a shopping center situation in a different context from the company town setting, but it did so only in a context where the First Amendment activity was related to the shopping center's operations. There is some language in Logan Valley, unnecessary to the decision, suggesting that the key focus of Marsh was upon the "business district," and that whenever a privately owned business district serves the public generally its sidewalks and streets become the functional equivalents of similar public facilities. . . .

The holding in Logan Valley was not dependent upon the suggestion that the privately owned streets and sidewalks of a business district or a shopping center are the equivalent, for First Amendment purposes, of municipally owned streets and sidewalks. No such expansive reading of the opinion for the Court is necessary or appropriate. The opinion was carefully phrased to limit its holding to the picketing involved, where the picketing was "directly related in its purpose to the use to which the shopping center property was being put," 391 U.S., at 320 n. 9, 88 S. Ct., at 1609, and where the store was located in the center of a large private enclave with the consequence that no

---

of Mr. Justice Douglas also emphasized the related purpose of the picketing in Logan Valley: "Picketing in regard to labor conditions the Weis Supermarket is directly related to that shopping center business." 391 U.S. at 326, 88 S. Ct., at 1612.

other reasonable opportunities for the pickets to convey their message to their intended audience were available.

Neither of these elements is present in the case now before the Court.

A

The handbilling by respondents in the malls of Lloyd Center had no relation to any purpose for which the center was built and being used. It is nevertheless argued by respondents that since the Center is open to the public the private owner cannot enforce a restriction against handbilling on the premises. The thrust of this argument is considerably broader than the rationale of Logan Valley. It requires no relationship, direct or indirect, between the purpose of the expressive activity and the business of the shopping center. The message sought to be conveyed by respondents was directed to all members of the public, not solely to patrons of Lloyd Center or of any of its operations. Respondents could have distributed these handbills on any public street, on any public sidewalk, in any public park, or in any public building in the city of Portland.

Respondents' argument, even if otherwise meritorious, misapprehends the scope of the invitation extended to the public. The invitation is to come to the Center to do business with the tenants. It is true that facilities at the Center are used for certain meetings and for various promotional activities. The obvious purpose, recognized widely as legitimate and responsible business activity, is to bring potential shoppers to the Center, to create a favorable impression, and to generate goodwill. There is no open-ended invitation to the public to use the Center for any and all purposes, however incompatible with the interests of both the stores and the shoppers whom they serve. . . .

It is noteworthy that respondent's argument based on the Center being "open to the public" would apply in varying degrees to most retail stores and service establishments across the country. They are all open to the public in the sense that customers and potential customers are invited and encouraged to enter. In terms of being open to the public, there are differences only of degree — not of principle — between a free standing store and one located in a shopping center, between a small store and a large one, between a single store with some malls and open areas designed to attract customers and Lloyd Center with its elaborate malls and interior landscaping.

B

A further fact, distinguishing the present case from Logan Valley, is that the Union picketers in that case would have been deprived of all reasonable opportunity to convey their message to patrons of the Weis store had they been denied access to the shopping center. The situation at Lloyd Center was notably different. The central building complex was surrounded by public sidewalks, totaling 66 linear blocks. All persons who enter or leave the private areas within the complex must cross public streets and sidewalks, either on foot or in automobiles. When moving to and from the privately owned parking lots, automobiles are required by law to come to a complete stop. Handbills may be distributed conveniently to pedestrians, and also to occupants of automobiles, from these public sidewalks and streets. Indeed, respondents moved to these public areas and continued distribution of their handbills after being requested to leave the interior malls. It would be an unwarranted infringement of property rights to require them to yield to the exercise of First Amendment rights under circumstances where adequate alternative avenues of communication exist. Such an accommodation would diminish property rights without significantly enhancing the asserted right of free speech. In ordering this accommodation the courts below erred in their interpretation of this Court's decisions in Marsh and Logan Valley.

III

The basic issue in this case is whether respondents, in the exercise of asserted First Amendment rights, may distribute handbills on Lloyd's private property contrary to its wishes and contrary to a policy enforced against *all* handbilling. In addressing this issue, it must be remembered that the First and Fourteenth Amendments safeguard the rights of free speech and assembly by limitations on *state* action, not on action by the owner of private property used nondiscriminatorily for private purposes only. . . .

Respondents contend, however, that the property of a large shopping center is "open to the public," serves the same purposes as a "business district" of a municipality, and therefore has been dedicated to certain types of public use. The argument is that such a center has sidewalks, streets, and parking areas which are functionally similar to facilities customarily provided by municipalities. It is then asserted that all members of the public, whether invited as customers or not, have the same right of free speech as they would have on the similar public facilities in the streets of a city or town.

The argument reaches too far. The Constitution by no means requires such an attenuated doctrine of dedication of private property to public use. The closest decision in theory, Marsh v. Alabama, supra, involved the assumption by a private enterprise of all of the attributes of a state-created municipality and the exercise by that enterprise of semiofficial municipal functions as a delegate of the State. In effect, the owner of the company town was performing the full spectrum of municipal powers and stood in the shoes of the State. In the instant case there is no comparable assumption or exercise of municipal functions or power.

Nor does property lose its private character merely because the public is generally invited to use it for designated purposes. . . .

We hold that there has been no such dedication of Lloyd's privately owned and operated shopping center to public use as to entitle respondents to exercise therein the asserted First Amendment rights. Accordingly, we reverse the judgment and remand the case to the Court of Appeals with directions to vacate the injunction.

It is so ordered.

Judgment reversed and case remanded.

Mr. Justice MARSHALL, with whom Mr. Justice DOUGLAS, Mr. Justice BRENNAN, and Mr. Justice STEWART join, dissenting. . . .

A. The question presented by this case is whether one of the incidents of petitioner's private ownership of the Lloyd Center is the power to exclude certain forms of speech from its property. In other words, we must decide whether ownership of the Center gives petitioner unfettered discretion to determine whether or not it will be used as a public forum.

This Court held in Marsh v. Alabama, supra, that even though property is privately owned, under some circumstances it may be treated as though it were publicly held, at least for purposes of the First Amendment. . . . Finding that the shopping center was the functional equivalent of the business district involved in Marsh, we could see "no reason why access to a business district in a company town for the purpose of exercising First Amendment rights should be constitutionally required, while access for the same purpose to property functioning as a business district should be limited simply because the property surrounding the 'business district' is not under the same ownership." Id., at 319, 88 S. Ct., at 1608. Thus, we held that the union activity was constitutionally protected. . . .

The Lloyd Center is similar to Logan Valley Plaza in several respects: both are bordered by public roads, and the entrances of both lead directly into the public roads; both contain large parking areas and privately owned walkways leading from store to store; and the general public has unrestricted access to both. The principal differences between the two centers are that the Lloyd Center is larger than Logan Valley, that Lloyd Center contains more commercial facilities, the Lloyd Center contains a range of professional and nonprofessional services that were not found in Logan Valley, and the Lloyd Center is much more intertwined with public streets than Logan Valley. Also, as in Marsh, supra, Lloyd's private police are given full police power by the city of Portland, even though they are hired, fired, controlled, and paid by the owners of the Center. This was not true in Logan Valley. . . .

In sum, the Lloyd Center is an integral part of the Portland community. From its inception, the city viewed it as a "business district" of the city and depended on it to supply much needed employment opportunities. To insure the success of the Center, the city carefully integrated it into the pattern of streets already established and planned future development of streets around the Center. It is plain, therefore, that Lloyd Center is the equivalent of a public "business district" within the meaning of Marsh and Logan Valley. In fact, the Lloyd Center is much more analogous to the company town in Marsh than was the Logan Valley Plaza. . . .

III

As I have pointed out above, Lloyd Center is even more clearly the equivalent of a public business district than was Logan Valley Plaza. The First Amendment activity in both Logan Valley and the instant case was peaceful and nondisruptive; and both cases involve traditionally acceptable modes of speech. Why then should there be a different result here? The Court's answer is that the speech in this case was directed at topics of general interest — the Vietnam war and the draft — whereas the speech in Logan Valley was directed to the activities of a store in the shopping center, and that this factual difference is of constitutional dimensions. I cannot agree.

A. It is true that in Logan Valley we explicitly left open the question whether "property rights could, consistently with the First Amendment, justify a bar on picketing [or handbilling] which was not . . . directly related in its purpose to the use to which the shopping center property was being put." 391 U.S., at 320 n. 9, 88 S. Ct., at 1609. But, I believe that the Court errs in concluding that this issue must be faced in the instant case.

The District Court observed that Lloyd Center invites schools to hold football rallies, presidential candidates to give speeches, and service organizations to hold Veteran's Day ceremonies on its premises. The court also observed that the Center permits the Salvation Army, the Volunteers of America, and the American Legion to solicit funds in the Mall. Thus, the court concluded that the Center was already open to First Amendment activities, and that respondents could not constitutionally be excluded from leafletting solely because Lloyd Center was not enamored of the form or substance of their speech. The Court of Appeals affirmed, taking the position that it was not extending either Logan Valley or Marsh. In other words, the District Court found that Lloyd Center had deliberately chosen to open its private property to a broad range of expression and that having done so it could not constitutionally exclude respondents, and the Court of Appeals affirmed this finding.

Petitioner apparently concedes that if the lower courts are correct, respondents should prevail. Brief for Petitioner, p. 19. This concession is, in fact, mandated by our decision in Logan Valley, in which we specifically held that members of the public may exercise their First Amendment rights on the premises of a shopping center that is the functional equivalent of a business district if their activity is "generally consonant with the use to which the property is actually put." 391 U.S., at 320, 88 S. Ct., at 1609. If the property of Lloyd Center is generally open to First Amendment activity, respondents cannot be excluded.

On Veteran's Day, Lloyd Center allows organizations to parade through the Center with flags, drummers, and color guard units and to have a speaker deliver an address on the meaning of Veteran's Day and the valor of American soldiers. Presidential candidates have been permitted to speak without restriction on the issues of the day, which presumably include war and peace. The American Legion is annually given permission to sell poppies in the Mall because Lloyd Center believes that "veterans . . . deserves [*sic*] some comfort and support by the people of the United States."[3] In light of these facts, I

3. App., 62 (Testimony of R. Horn, Manager of Lloyd Center). It is widely known

perceive no basis for depriving respondents of the opportunity to distribute leaflets inviting patrons of the Center to attend a meeting in which different points of view would be expressed than those held by the organizations and persons privileged to use Lloyd Center as a forum for parading their ideas and symbols.

I believe that the lower courts correctly held that respondents' activities were directly related in purpose to the use to which the shopping center was being put. In my view, therefore, this case presents no occasion to consider whether or not Logan Valley should be extended. But, the Court takes a different view and concludes that Lloyd Center was never open to First Amendment activity. Even if I could agree with the Court on this point, I would not reach a different result in this case.

B. If respondents had distributed handbills complaining about one or more stores in Lloyd Center or about the Center itself, petitioner concedes that our decision in Logan Valley would insulate that conduct from proscription by the Center.[4] I cannot see any logical reason to treat differently speech that is related to subjects other than the Center and its member stores.

We must remember that it is a balance that we are striking — a balance between the freedom to speak, a freedom that is given a preferred place in our hierarchy of values, and the freedom of a private property-owner to control his property. When the completing interests are fairly weighted, the balance can only be struck in favor of speech.

Members of the Portland community are able to see doctors, dentists, lawyers, bankers, travel agents, and persons offering countless other services in Lloyd Center. They can buy almost anything that they want or need there. For many Portland citizens, Lloyd Center will so completely satisfy their wants that they will have no reason to go elsewhere for goods or services. If speech is to reach these people, it must reach them in Lloyd Center. The Center itself recognizes this. For example, in 1964 its director of public relations offered candidates for President and Vice-President the use of the center for political speeches, boasting "that our convenient location and setting would provide the largest audience [the candidates] could attract in Oregon." App., 187.

For many persons who do not have easy access to television, radio, the major newspapers, and the other forms of mass media, the only way they can

---

that the American Legion is a Veteran's organization. See Encyclopedia of Associations, Vol. I p. 963 (6th Ed. 1970). It is also common knowledge that the poppy is the symbol sold by the Legion to finance various of its activities. At times the proceeds from selling poppies were used to finance lobbying and other activities directed at increasing the military capacity of the United States. Jones, A History of the American Legion 330-332 (1946).

4. The record indicates that when unions have picketed inside the Mall, Lloyd Center has voiced no objections. App., 108 (testimony of R. Horn, Manager of Lloyd Center). It is apparent that petitioner has no difficulty in accepting our decision in Logan Valley and in complying with it.

express themselves to a broad range of citizens on issues of general public concern is to picket, or to handbill, or to utilize other free or relatively inexpensive means of communication. The only hope that these people have to be able to communicate effectively is to be permitted to speak in those areas in which most of their fellow citizens can be found. One such area is the business district of a city or town or its functional equivalent. And this is why respondents have a tremendous need to express themselves within Lloyd Center.

Petitioner's interests, on the other hand, pale in comparison. For example, petitioner urges that respondents' First Amendment activity would disturb the Center's customers. It is undisputed that some patrons will be disturbed by any First Amendment activity that goes on, regardless of its object. But, there is no evidence to indicate that speech directed to topics unrelated to the shopping center would be more likely to impair the motivation of customers to buy than speech directed to the uses to which the Center is put, which petitioner concedes is constitutionally protected under Logan Valley. On the contrary, common sense would indicate that speech that is critical of a shopping center or one or more of its stores is more likely to deter consumers from purchasing goods or services than speech on any other subject. Moreover, petitioner acknowledges that respondents have a constitutional right to leaflet on any subject on public streets and sidewalks within Lloyd Center. It is difficult for me to understand why leafletting in the Mall would be so much more disturbing to the Center's customers.

I also find patently frivolous petitioner's argument that if handbilling in the Mall is permitted, Lloyd Center would face inordinate difficulties in removing litter from its premises. The District Court found that respondents' activities were litter-free. . . . But, even assuming that the litter might have increased, that is not a sufficient reason for barring First Amendment activity. See, e.g., Schneider v. State of New Jersey, 308 U.S. 147, 60 S. Ct. 146, 84 L. Ed. 155 (1939). If petitioner is truly concerned about litter, it should accept a previous suggestion by this Court and prosecute those who throw handbills away, not those who use them for communicative purposes. Id., at 162, 60 S. Ct., at 151.

In sum, the balance plainly must be struck in favor of speech.

C. Petitioner's other grounds for denying respondents access to the Mall can be dealt with quickly. The assertion is made that petitioner had the right to regulate the manner in which First Amendment activity took place on its property, and that because the public streets and sidewalks inside the Center offered sufficient access to the public, it was permissible to deny respondents use of the Mall. The District Court found that certain stores in the Center could only be reached by using the private walkways of the Mall. Those persons who drove into the Center, parked in the privately owned parking lots, and who entered the stores accessible only through the Mall could not be safely reached from the public streets and sidewalks. Hence, the District

Court properly found that the Mall was the only place where respondents had reasonable access to all of Lloyd Center's patrons.[7] 308 F. Supp., at 131. At one point in this litigation, petitioner also attempted to assert that it was entitled to bar respondents' distribution of leaflets on the ground that the leaflets violated the Selective Service laws. The District Court found that this contention was without merit. 308 F. Supp., at 132-133. It seems that petitioner has abandoned the contention in this Court. In any event, it is meritless for the reasons given by the District Court. . . .

IV

. . . The vote in Logan Valley was 6-3, and that decision is only four years old. But, I am aware that the composition of this Court has radically changed in four years. The fact remains that Logan Valley is binding unless and until it is overruled. There is no valid distinction between that case and this one, and, therefore, the results in both cases should be the same.

We noted in Logan Valley that the large scale movement of this country's population from the cities to the suburbs has been accompanied by the growth of suburban shopping centers. In response to this phenomenon, sites like Portland are providing for large-scale shopping areas within the city. It is obvious that privately owned shopping areas could prove to be greatly advantageous to cities. They are totally self-sufficient, needing no financial support from local government; and if, as here, they truly are the functional equivalent of a public business area, the city reaps the advantages of having such an area without paying for them. Some of the advantages are an increased tax base, a drawing attraction for residents, and a stimulus to further growth.

It would not be surprising in the future to see cities rely more and more on private businesses to perform functions once performed by governmental agencies. The advantage of reduced expenses and an increased tax base cannot be overstated. As governments rely on private enterprise, public property decreases in favor of privately owned property. It becomes harder and harder

7. The Court implies that it is willing to reverse both lower courts and hold that their findings that alternative forums for leafleting in Lloyd Center were either not as effective as the Mall or dangerous are clearly erroneous. I too have read the record in this case and I find no warrant for such a holding. The record plainly shows that it was impossible to reach many of the shoppers in the Center without using the Mall unless respondents were willing to approach cars as they were leaving the center. The District Court and the Court of Appeals took the view that requiring respondents to run from the sidewalk, to knock on car windows, to ask that the windows be rolled down so that a handbill could be distributed, to offer the handbill, run back to the sidewalk, and to repeat this gesture for every automobile leaving Lloyd Center involved hazards not only to respondents but also to other pedestrians and automobile passengers. Having never seen Lloyd Center, except in photographs contained in the record, and having absolutely no idea of the amount of traffic entering or leaving the Center, the Court cavalierly overturns the careful findings of facts below. This in my opinion, exceeds even the most expansive view of the proper appellate function of this Court.

for citizens to find means to communicate with other citizens. Only the wealthy may find effective communication possible unless we adhere to Marsh v. Alabama and continue to hold that "[t]he more an owner, for his advantage, opens up his property for use by the public in general, the more do his rights become circumscribed by the statutory and constitutional rights of those who use it," 326 U.S. 276, at 506, 66 S. Ct. 276, at 278.

When there are no effective means of communication, free speech is a mere shibboleth. I believe that the First Amendment requires it to be a reality. Accordingly, I would affirm the decision of the Court of Appeals.

QUESTIONS

1. After a rather tentative departure during the emotion-charged period of the nonviolent civil rights protests of the early 1960s, the majority of the Supreme Court settled securely into Justice Black's view that only peaceful, nondisruptive civil rights protests should receive constitutional protection. There remains the question whether protests that meet the standards of Justice Black are politically effective. To cite one example, is there any substantial evidence indicating that the 1964 Civil Rights Act would have been enacted in the absence of the protests, most of which Justice Black condemned?

2. Is it significant that many of the facilities that were subjects of sit-ins and other protests were desegregated long before the cases of those arrested for such protests were resolved in the courts?

3. How relevant to this discussion is the following statement by the famous theologian Reinhold Niebuhr?

> *It is hopeless for the Negro to expect complete emancipation from the menial social and economic position into which the white man has forced him, merely by trusting in the moral sense of the white race. . . . However large the number of individual white men who do and who will identify themselves completely with the Negro cause, the white race in America will not admit the Negro to equal rights if it is not forced to do so. Upon that point one may speak with a dogmatism which all history justifies. (R. Niebuhr, Moral Man and Immoral Society 252-253 (1932).)*

4. Assuming that Justice Black is wrong and Dr. Niebuhr right about the necessity of forceful protests to effect improvement in the status of blacks in America, are courts ever likely to take a position condoning disruptive demonstrations, even those conducted to protest serious racial injustices? A negative answer, of course, raises the issues of civil disobedience discussed in Chapter Three.

5. Courts implicitly and sometimes expressly measure the disruption of the protest by the seriousness of the wrongs protested. Thus, after reciting the brutal treatment of the protesters at Selma, Judge Johnson said: "it seems basic to our constitutional principles that the extent of the right to assemble, demonstrate and march peaceably along the highways and streets in an orderly manner should be commensurate with the enormity of the wrongs that are being protested and petitioned against. In this case the wrongs are enormous." William v. Watson, 240 F. Supp. 100 (M.D. Ala. 1965).

All but the hardest heart would be moved by the events at Selma. But using Judge Johnson's standard, what must blacks or other disadvantaged minorities do, when those against whom they protest peacefully are not so obligingly vicious in their response, or when the cause is less symbolic and more practical than voting (if more threatening), such as employment rights or a guaranteed minimum income? What if the protest is over an issue of great importance to American blacks, such as the plight of white-dominated African societies, involving wrongs for which no Americans are directly responsible?

STEEL, NINE MEN IN BLACK WHO THINK WHITE, N.Y. Times Magazine, Oct. 13, 1968, p. 56. Lewis Steel suggested, in his controversial magazine article, that the Supreme Court's decisions in the protest cases were intended to harmonize with the views of the white community rather than the needs of blacks. Steel wrote:

> When Negroes and their white supporters began demonstrating, they were considered to be humble supplicants seeking succor from white America. Toward the middle of the 1960's, civil rights demonstrators, rather than playing a humble role, proclaimed that they would not be moved. Negroes had become assertive in a society which considered such behavior anathema, and repression became the order of the day. White America, without any basis in fact, decided that demonstrations and riots were synonymous. . . .
>
> The new approach [after Cox v. Louisiana] was not based on a fundamental difference between recent demonstrations and earlier ones; nothing had occurred which would indicate that civil rights advocates had abandoned their philosophy of peaceful protest. The new restrictions against demonstration were first applied in Adderley v. Florida in 1966. The Court held that, although there was no violence, a peaceful protest outside a police station could be curtailed. The inconsistency between this and earlier cases can be explained only in terms of a judicial concession to white anxieties. (Id. at 115.)

QUESTIONS

1. Based on your review of the cases discussed above, how accurate is Steel's analysis? Assuming Steel is correct, is it reasonable to expect leaders of black and other minorities to mount effective protests that accord with majority interests and concerns?

2. Can we assume that, if the leafleteers in Lloyd Corporation v. Tanner, supra, were black and nonviolent, the majority's decision (a) would have ruled for the protesters if they were protesting the refusal of stores to serve or employ blacks, but (b) would have ruled against them if they were pro-

testing de facto segregation in the public schools or the exclusion of blacks from suburban housing?

3. What if the protests at Lloyd Center were aimed at foreign activities or policies of a company with a store located in the Center? Assuming that Justice Marshall's fears that Tanner will undercut Marsh v. Alabama are valid, does this not also indicate restrictions on picketing of private residences for reasons similar to those cited by the majority in Tanner? Both issues are presented in the Racism Hypo that follows.

Racism Hypo 4
MASSIVE MANUFACTURING & MINISCULE MODELS v. POWER, INC. and D. WARBUCKS v. POWER, INC.

I

Massive Manufacturing Company is a large office machine and computer firm. Its products are marketed on a worldwide basis, generally through retail outlets, one of which is located in the Eden Garden Shopping Center. Massive has been generally acclaimed for its exemplary record of hiring minorities, but it has been attacked because it has a plant and extensive investments in Massaland, a South African nation with a worldwide reputation for exploiting and subjugating blacks.

POWER, Inc. (People on the Way to Eradicating Racism), a militant black organization, has publicly advocated a consumer boycott of Massive products as a means of pressuring Massive to withdraw from South Africa. To achieve this end, POWER members for weeks had picketed Massive's retail outlet in the Eden Garden Shopping Center, a privately owned development quite similar in scope and business philosophy to Lloyd Center in Lloyd Corporation v. Tanner, supra. Because the shopping center is surrounded by high brick walls, outside of which there is a high-speed freeway on one side and the Eden River on the other, the pickets have paraded on center property in front of the entrance to that section of the shopping mall where Massive's retail outlet is located. The picket signs read: "Massive Invests in Apartheid" and "Massive's Computers Murder Massaland's Millions."

The pickets were orderly and were not disturbed by the shopping center security guards, but the picketing had no effect on Massive. POWER then altered its tactics and for several days staged small "guerrilla theater" skits portraying atrocities perpetrated by the white leadership of Massaland against its black natives. The portrayals showed men working in mines while being whipped, political prisoners being executed by firing squads, and native women being humiliated by white overseers. The portrayals, while performed without sound, were graphic and gripping. Leaflets distributed during the events asserted that the exploitation of Massaland natives was furthered by the computerized equipment provided by Massive.

The effect of the new protest strategy was immediate. It is estimated that within one week business at the Massive store dropped 50 percent, and other stores in the shopping center also reported decreased sales. Shopping center guards' requests that the POWER people desist were politely refused. Arrests were threatened, but local police were not called in.

Massive initiated litigation in state court, seeking injunctive relief on allegations that POWER, Inc. is interfering with its business and thereby causing it irreparable harm.

Miniscule Models, a small hobby shop located next door to Massive, intervened in the suit, asserting that it has no sales in Massaland, but that the loss of customers due to the POWER protests has brought its business to the brink of bankruptcy. It sought relief similar to that requested by Massive.

II

To increase the effectiveness of their protest, POWER leaders stationed pickets outside the home of Massive's president, D. Warbucks, whose family lives in Eden Towers, a high-rise cooperative apartment building located in an exclusive area. There is a local ordinance prohibiting residential picketing, identical to the measure in PACE v. Doorley, supra; but rather than call police, Warbucks filed suit in state court for injunctive relief to halt the picketing. He asserted that the protest was an invasion of his family's privacy. Several of his neighbors joined in the action, asserting that the protest was an unjustified annoyance. Other residents of the area have threatened to use "self-help" if the POWER group doesn't halt its illegal picketing, but there has been no violence. The protest has attracted extensive media coverage, including, on several days, the deployment of a television camera crew to Eden Towers.

The state court issued temporary restraining orders halting the protests in both suits, and then indicated its readiness to consider a motion to consolidate the cases for an early hearing on plaintiffs' motions for preliminary injunctions.

Law Firm A will represent Massive Manufacturing and Miniscule Models in Suit I, and D. Warbucks and his neighbors in Suit II.

Law Firm B will represent POWER, Inc. in both suits I and II.

(Classes may wish to present arguments on the two cases separately because of their length.)

8. RIGHT TO MILITARY SERVICE AND CONSCIENTIOUS OBJECTOR STATUS

INTRODUCTORY NOTE

There is a pattern of racial conduct discernible throughout the nation's history that was dramatically in evidence at its birth. By an almost predictable process, whites will permit blacks to perform hitherto forbidden activities whenever the potential benefit of such performance outweighs racially oriented preferences and fears. Service of blacks with the military forces is a clear example of this behavior pattern.

At the start of the Revolutionary War, despite the heroic model of Crispus Attucks (the first man to die at the Boston Massacre) and other black men who fought at Lexington, Concord, Ticonderoga and Bunker Hill, George Washington, upon taking command of the American troops in July 1775, issued an order that no Negroes should be enlisted.

Several factors influenced Washington's decision. Many officers felt that blacks would make poor soldiers; others feared that they would become too skilled with their weapons and might turn against their masters. Still others argued that it would be shameful to ask blacks to die for white men.

Subsequently, the British, through John Murray, Earl of Dunmore, governor of Virginia, offered freedom to slaves who joined their side. This tactic, combined with the unenthusiastic response from most whites to his urgent recruitment pleas, caused Washington to change his mind and accept Negroes. They fought in several major battles during the Revolution. See L. Bennett, Before the Mayflower 56-59 (1961).

Despite the record of Negroes in the military service in the Revolution, the secretaries of war and navy in 1798 issued separate directives forbidding Negro enlistments in the Marine Corps and on naval warships. But again, military necessity negated this policy. Negro soldiers and sailors served prominently, and often courageously, during the naval war with France (1798-1800) and the War of 1812. See L. Litwack, North of Slavery 32-33 (1961).

Efforts by blacks to serve in the Civil War were initially rejected, and the same pattern prevailed at the outset of both the First and Second World Wars. But Lincoln in the Civil War and military leaders in the Spanish-American War and both world wars underwent changes of attitude similar to those experienced by Washington, when faced with shortages of men willing to fight.

President Harry S. Truman officially brought integration to the military services in 1948. In Executive Order 9981, he declared it to be the policy of the President that "there shall be equality of treatment and opportunity for all persons in the armed services without regard to race, color, religion or national origin." The Korean War served to reduce opposition to the order's implementation, and, as the high percentage of blacks in Vietnam attests, much progress has been made.* Unfortunately, integration did not eliminate discrimination.

Serious problems of discrimination remain, as periodic reports and studies made by civil rights groups show. The National Association for the Advancement of Colored People has received complaints of discrimination from black servicemen, as a result of which it has launched investigations and issued a number of reports. See, e.g., The Search for Military Justice, April 1971, and White On — A Report of the Relationship Between the Marine Corps and Black Marines in Hawaii, Oct. 1971. The NAACP studies found that racial discrimination becomes a serious problem when blacks (or their wives) adopt ethnic symbols, such as hair and dress styles or handshakes. There are reported charges that court-martials and discharges other than honorable are used to rid the service of activist blacks.

Concerned by these reports and further prompted by scores of letters from black servicemen, the Congressional Black Caucus (composed of thirteen black congressmen) initiated an investigation in 1971, which included on-site visits to ten military bases and three days of open hearings in Washington. They found widespread racial discrimination in job assignments, promotions, complaint processing procedures, military justice and discharges. The caucus's report and recommendations are printed in 118 Cong. Rec. 8674 (daily ed. Oct. 14, 1972).

On December 20, 1971, the Department of Defense responded to the NAACP's "White On" report with a detailed statistical summary of the participation of blacks in the military service. The NAACP prepared an analysis of these statistics, and on the basis of the analysis charged that "one in every three blacks received a less than honorable discharge from the Navy or Ma-

* The black experience in the nation's military service has been amply documented. See, e.g., J. Marszalek, Jr., Court-Martial: A Black Man in America (1973); J. Carroll, The Black Military Experience in the American West (1971); J. Carroll, Buffalo Soldiers West (1971); A. Fowler, The Black Infantry in the West, 1869-1891 (1971); W. Gatewood, Smoked Yankees and the Struggle for Empire: Letters from Negro Soldiers, 1898-1902 (1971); J. Johnson, A Pictorial History of Black Soldiers in the United States: 1619-1969 (1970); R. Wallcut, The Negro Soldier (1970); P. Drotning, Black Heroes in Our Nation's History (1969); I. Lee, Negro Medal of Honor Men (1969); J. Margolis and A. Wildavsky, Social Research and the Desegregation of the U.S. Army (1969); J. Johnson, Ebony Brass (1967); J. McPherson, The Negro's Civil War (1965); S. Dakota Adv. Comm. to the U.S. Commission on Civil Rights, Negro Airmen in a Northern Community (1963); T. Higginson, Army Life in a Black Regiment (1962); B. Quarles, The Negro in the American Revolution (1961); L. Nichols, Breakthrough on the Color Front (1954); D. Mandelbaum, Soldier Groups and Negro Soldiers (1952); S. Schoenfeld, The Negro in the Armed Forces (1945).

rine Corps in 1970." In addition, the analysis concluded that throughout the military service blacks are more than three times as likely to be imprisoned as whites, and more than three times as likely to be dishonorably discharged. Moreover, the statistics show that whites are six times as likely to be officers as blacks and almost fifty times as likely to be high-ranking officers, and that it is twice as hard for blacks to reach the top enlisted ranks. Memorandum dated Dec. 27, 1971, for Leonard Carter, Western Regional Director, NAACP.

A special handshake is apparently an example of ethnic activity that can lead to a court-martial. A black army private was convicted and sentenced to six weeks of solitary confinement for dapping (the military term for special handshakes denoting black unity and pride), after his battalion commander had banned all such gestures from the post "in order to promote harmony." Three black marines on Okinawa were threatened with court-martials for dapping in a mess hall. IV Newsletter on Military Law and Counseling (NOMLAC) 17, No. 3 (June-July 1972).

Toward the end of 1972, an increasing amount of racial hostility in the military service erupted into violence, some of which assumed mutinous proportions. The navy underwent several incidents, including serious fighting between black and white sailors on board an aircraft carrier. See, e.g., Kitty Hawk Officer Traces Riot to Marine Dispersal of Blacks, N.Y. Times, Jan. 26, 1973, at 6, c. 1.

A. BLACKS AND CONSCIENTIOUS OBJECTOR STATUS

> They asked me if I knew what Conscientious Objector meant. I told them that when the white man asked me to go off somewhere and fight and maybe to die to preserve the way the white man treated the Black man in America, then my conscience made me object. (A. Haley, The Autobiography of Malcolm X 205 (1964).)

It should be made clear that while most blacks have been willing to participate in America's wars, there have always been those whose faith in America was overcome by their experience. Many of them decided to cast their lots with the other side. During the American Revolution, thousands of black slaves responded to Governor Dunmore's promise of freedom for those who assisted England (see B. Quarles, The Negro in the American Revolution (1961)); and both before and after the Revolution there was continual apprehension of slave uprisings. See H. Aptheker, American Negro Slave Revolts, at 18-33 (1943).

There is no doubt that the black people have made major gains during wartime. Often enough, much of this progress is lost when peace returns. Nevertheless, black Americans have not resisted military service and, in fact, have pressured for front line service.

But arguments can be made against requiring blacks to serve in America's wars. During the Vietnam conflict, a number of blacks who faced prosecution for refusal to comply with induction orders or other draft offenses presented such arguments. But even with efforts far advanced to achieve an all-volunteer military service, the judicial response to those blacks who sought exemption because of their assertion of religious or moral objection to fighting for this country merits study.

UNITED STATES v. LEWIS
275 F. Supp. 1013 (E.D. Wisc. 1967)

REYNOLDS, District Judge.

Marc Anthony Lewis was indicted on September 29, 1966, for violating the Universal Military Training and Service Act in that he refused to submit to induction on June 22, 1966, after having been classified 1-A.

On October 10, 1966, on motion of the United States Government, this court entered an order giving Lewis permission to return "to Eutaw, Alabama, . . . for the purpose of working as a staff member of the Student Nonviolent Coordinating Committee subject to the call of this Court for any further proceedings." On November 14, 1966, an attorney was appointed to represent him under the Criminal Justice Act. He entered a plea of "not guilty" on May 31, 1967.

This case is presently before this court on Lewis' motion to remand this matter to the Selective Service System for further consideration of his claim that he is entitled to a conscientious objector classification. This court held an evidentiary hearing on July 28, 1967, which, together with stipulations of counsel, revealed the facts set forth below.

Lewis is an intelligent, idealistic twenty-two year old Negro who was born in Milwaukee, Wisconsin, on July 8, 1945. He graduated from Milwaukee's Riverside High School and completed two years at Howard University. In recent years he has been active in the civil rights movement. He has participated in demonstrations in Milwaukee as well as registering Negroes to vote in Alabama. He has worked with the Milwaukee United School Integration Committee, Southern Christian Leadership Conference, and the Student Non-violent Coordinating Committee.

On May 17, 1965, Lewis registered for the draft and completed his Classification Questionnaire (SSS Form 100) wherein he did not claim to be a conscientious objector.

On May 24, 1965, he was classified 1-A by Local Board #44 and was sent notice of his classification which included a notice of his right to appeal. He testified that when he received this notice, he "looked at it" but at that time gave no thought to appealing his 1-A classification. Shortly after May 1965, he left Milwaukee for Eutaw, Alabama.

On July 23, 1965, he was ordered, by mail, to report for a physical examination on August 13, 1965, and he failed to report; on August 27, 1965, he was ordered, by mail, to report for a physical examination on September 17, 1965, and he failed to report; on September 23, 1965, he was ordered, by mail, to report for a physical examination on October 6, 1965, and he failed to report; and on November 9, 1965, for the fourth time, he was ordered, by mail, to report for a physical examination on November 29, 1965. On November 29, 1965, he did report for his physical examination.

Defendant stated that he received "several" notices to report for a physical examination while he was living in Eutaw but ignored them all until November 29, 1965, when he complied by coming to Milwaukee for the examination. He indicated that on December 16, 1965, since the problem of military service had become "more pressing," he picked up a form for conscientious objectors. At that time he felt he could not in good conscience join the Armed Forces because he was "black and American."[1] But he did not fill out the conscientious objector form at that time and thinks that he lost it in January of 1966.

On January 31, 1966, a statement of acceptability was mailed to Lewis. On March 1, 1966, he was ordered to report for induction on March 18, 1966, but he failed to do so. Instead, he filed a conscientious objector form with his Board on March 21, 1966.

Although defendant had failed to report for induction on March 18, 1966, his Board proceeded to consider his conscientious objector claim. On May 16, 1966, the Board denied his application and on May 17, 1966, mailed to him in Eutaw a Notice of Classification as 1-A along with a notice of his right to appeal and to a personal appearance. Lewis admits living at this address during the month of May but denies receiving this notice.

On June 3, 1966, an order to report for induction in Milwaukee on June 22, 1966, was sent to Lewis in Alabama. He admits receiving this order "early in June." He made no effort to contact his local board until the afternoon of June 21, 1966. On that day he made two phone calls from Milwaukee to his Board and to the State headquarters in Madison. The Draft Board personnel told defendant that he no longer had a right to pursue his claim to a different draft status. On June 22, 1966, he reported to the induction center but refused to submit to induction.[2]

1. During the hearing, the defendant described himself as a "conscientious objector" for the reason that he was "black and American." This remark nicely illustrates the distinction between the term "conscientious objector" as it is used in everyday laymen's language and the same term as it is used in the law, a distinction which cures much current misunderstanding and confusion. Laymen, like defendant, use this term to describe anyone who "conscientiously," i.e., in good conscience, refuses for moral reasons to join the armed services. In contrast, the law uses the same term to characterize a class among those morally opposed to war who have been singled out by Congress for exemption from certain obligations under the Selective Service laws. The former use of the terms is far broader and more comprehensive than the latter. In particular, an individual may in perfect sincerity feel that he cannot morally support the Armed Forces of this country; but this does not necessarily mean that he is a "conscientious objector" as a matter of law and as such exempt from certain types of military service. Only certain types of "conscientious objectors," as the layman understands the term — types spelled out in statute and regulation — are "conscientious objectors" in the contemplation of the law.

2. On April 17, 1967, after the indictment in this case issued, defendant was accorded a "courtesy hearing" at which he appeared before the Board on his claim to conscientious

The above-stated facts indicate neither excusable neglect on the part of the defendant nor unfairness on the part of the Draft Board. The course of conduct of the defendant can only lead to the conclusion that the defendant completely ignored the administrative machinery available to him.

In the first place, the defendant ignored Draft Board communications including several orders to report for a physical examination.

In the second place, defendant's pursuance of his claim to conscientious objector status has been so haphazard as to lead to the conclusion that he intentionally ignored the administrative remedies available to him. The record indicates that the views which he presently has matured at least by December of 1965, but that it was not until March 1966, *after* he had received an order to report for induction, that he filed the conscientious objector form with his Board. He did not inquire about the disposition of his claim until the day before he was scheduled to be inducted on June 21, 1966, although he had received the June 3, 1966, order to report for induction.

In the third place, the gist of defendant's claim to a conscientious objector status is that as a Negro he cannot "conscientiously" serve in the Armed Forces of a nation whose laws and customs do not afford him the same opportunities and protection afforded to white citizens.[3] One need not be unsym-

---

objector status. Both parties to this proceeding agree that the courtesy hearing neither cured nor entailed any procedural infirmities. Thus, neither question is considered.

3. The defendant submitted the following written statement to the Local Board on April 17, 1967, after he was indicted, which reflects in essence the views that he has had since December 1965:

"Milwaukee Co. Local Bd. 44
Selective Service System
135 West Wells Street
Milwaukee, Wis.

"For me to be a member of the United States Army means that I, a black man, would have to defend and perpetuate the political, social, and economic system of this country. It means that I, a black man, would have to defend and perpetuate the 'American way of life.' This is an atrocious paradox.

"Why should I defend a country that kidnapped my people from their homeland, brought them to this country, enslaved and oppressed them, raped them, beat them, and tried to rob them of their basic humanity? Would you if you were black? Why should I, a black man, defend a country that continues to oppress black people, rape black people, beat black people, and tries to make black people belive [*sic*] that they are inferior? Would you?

"Why should I defend a system that on one hand says that all men are created equal and that all citizens have the same rights, and on the other hand allows a red neck sheriff and his deputies to put you in jail and beat you when you try to exercise these rights? Why should I defend a system that allows the white population of a town to stomp your picket line into the ground while men from the Justice Department and the F.B.I. stand around and watch and say that all they can do is take notes? Why should I defend a system that teaches black people that everything black is bad and worthless, and everything white is good and virtuous?

"Realizing all along that some of these acts could be interpreted as individual acts by individual people the mere fact that these individuals are allowed to commit these acts

pathetic with his convictions nor oblivious to the depth and sincerity of his feelings to find that his asserted grounds for conscientious objector status have no basis whatsoever.

Under prevailing legal standard in law, defendant's claim is patently frivolous. This court may not consider the merits of his claim or give the defendant a trial de novo. United States v. Kurki, (E.D. Wis. 1966) 255 F. Supp. 161 (1966) (affirmed 384 F.2d 905, July 12, 1967, 7th Cir.). But when an intelligent, educated, articulate, and politically active young man asserts a claim which we believe he knows to be frivolous under the law, we can only conclude that he is not acting in good faith.

The sum total of the defendant's conduct constitutes a willful disregard for the Selective Service System and its administrative procedures. His conduct cannot be classified as even "neglectful," to say nothing of "excusable neglect."

Lewis claims, and this court accepts as a fact, that since he did not receive the notice of classification as 1-A, which was mailed to him on May 17, 1966, his case should now be remanded to the Selective Service System so that he can appeal this classification. If this fact were standing alone, this court would remand the case. But the record here is clear that Lewis has had ample opportunity to pursue his claim and has failed to do so. Based on the record before this court, to remand this case would make a mockery of the whole Selective Service System.

For the foregoing reasons,

It is ordered that the defendant's motion to remand must be and it hereby is denied.*

QUESTIONS

Is it arguable that the court might have reviewed Lewis's claim more sympathetically had he more faithfully exhausted his administrative remedies?

---

against black people and get away with them means that they have the sanction of the system.

"Would you defend a system that talked about freedom, justice, and equality for all men and then waited two hundred years before it said that people could sit at the same lunch counter or ride anywhere on a bus, and then acted as if full equality had been acheived [*sic*]? Would you defend a system where people had to be beat, killed, and put in jail before it could be prodded into making even these token gestures?

"What would you do if you lived in a system that had been crushing you, warping you, and lying to you for over three hundred years and then this system said that you had to put yourself in a position to kill another human being, or possibly [*sic*] be killed yourself, in order for that system to continue to prosper and grow? Because I am a black man in America I very conscientiously object, in fact I absolutely refuse, to defend this very racist society and system of government."

* For similar cases with similar results, see United States v. Brooks, 415 F.2d 502 (6th Cir. 1969); Richmond and Key v. Commanding Officer, 12 Race Rel. L. Rep. 19 (C.D. Cal. 1966).

See Joseph v. United States, infra. Might a different result have been possible had Welsh v. United States, infra, been decided prior to the Lewis case?

JOSEPH v. UNITED STATES
405 U.S. 1006, 92 S. Ct. 1274, 31 L. Ed. 2d 473 (1972)

. . . After this Court granted the writ of certiorari in this case, the Solicitor General, in his Memorandum for the United States on the merits, took a position different from that previously asserted by the United States in the United States Court of Appeals for the Third Circuit and in his opposition to the petition for a writ of certiorari. We, therefore, vacate the judgment of the Court of Appeals and remand the case to that court for consideration in light of the position now asserted by the Solicitor General.

Mr. Justice DOUGLAS, with whom Mr. Justice MARSHALL concurs, dissenting.

While I think the judgment should be vacated and the case remanded, I would not do so on the Solicitor General's confession of error, but rather for the reason that meaningful administrative and judicial review of selective service classification decisions is impossible where the service does not state reasons for its actions.

Joseph, then classified I-A, applied for a conscientious objector exemption in April, 1967. He stated in his conscientious objector form (SSS Form 150) that he believed in a Supreme Being, that he was a member of the Nation of Islam (Black Muslims), and that he had joined Muhammed's Mosque No. 12, in Philadelphia in April 1965, at the age of 17. He represented the views of the Black Muslims regarding participation in war as follows:

> We believe that we who declared ourselves to be Rightous [*sic*] Muslims Should not Participate in wars which take the lives of humans. We do not believe this nation should force us to take part in such wars, for we have nothing to gain from it unless America agrees to give us the necessary territory wherein we may have something to fight for.

Joseph's board met on June 8, 1967. Based on the information in the SSS Form 150 and in the rest of Joseph's file, but without the benefit of a meeting with Joseph, the board voted unanimously to retain him in Class I-A, and sent him a notice of classification (SSS Form 110) to this effect. No reasons were given for the classification decision.

The Solicitor General argues from the premise that when the board acted, it effectively "re-opened" Joseph's classification. According to the Solicitor General, the applicable regulations then in force prohibited a board from reopening a classification without first determining that a prima facie case had been made out. See 32 CFR §§1625.2, 1625.4. "[N]ot prepared to assume" that the board violated the reopening regulations, the Solicitor General reasons that the fact of reopening must therefore mean that the board had concluded (albeit erroneously) that Joseph had made out a prima facie case, and denied the claim because it questioned his sincerity.

The first difficulty with this argument is that a local board may well have the power to reopen a classification on a lesser showing than a prima facie case. See, e.g., United States v. Stephens, 445 F.2d 192, 196 (CA3 1971). Second, the Solicitor General's argument rests on the intent of the board. If the board did not think that it was reopening, there would have been no reason for it to worry about the prima facie case requirements allegedly contained in the reopening regulations. And the Solicitor General concedes that "some confusion" as to whether the June 8 action was a "reopening" developed at trial. Memorandum for the United States, pp. 18-19.

Assuming, however, that there was a reopening, the Solicitor General's argument still fails, for the board's subsequent handling of Joseph's claim rebuts any "presumption of regularity" that might otherwise be appropriate. Joseph's letter requesting an appeal from the June 8, 1967, decision was received by the board July 6, 1967. The request was thus timely under 32 CFR §1626.2(c)(1). No action was taken, however, until August 1, 1967, when Joseph was notified that his "statutory rights have expired," but that he was requested to appear August 10, 1967, for an interview. Joseph appeared as requested, and on August 14, 1967, the board forwarded his file to the appeal board. There is no indication in Joseph's file that the board took any action as a result of the August 10 "interview."

The above course of action embodied several violations of the selective service regulations. First, Joseph's statutory rights had not expired on August 1, 1967. His appeal was timely, and was required to be processed in accordance with 32 CFR §1626.14, which stipulates that "in no event shall [a registrant's] file be forwarded [to the appeal board] later than five days after the period for taking the appeal has elapsed." The board violated this regulation by keeping Joseph's file past July 13, 1967.

Had Joseph requested a personal appearance in his July 6, 1967, letter, the board would have been authorized to retain his file. But he did not. The interview which the board granted him was a mere courtesy. As such, it was unauthorized by statute, United States v. Hayden, 445 F.2d 1365, 1374 (CA9 1971), and could not operate to relieve the board of its statutory obligation to forward Joseph's file pursuant to the mandate of 32 CFR §1626.14.

It can also be argued, from the fact that Joseph was given an interview after the board received his letter on July 6, 1967, that the letter was deemed a request to reopen, as well as an appeal. There was testimony at Joseph's trial that the board's failure to indicate any action following the interview meant that it had refused to reopen Joseph's classification. (Testimony of Mr. Plaskow, App. 14.) But where a board refuses a registrant's written request to reopen his classification, it must so advise him, by letter, and it must place a copy of the letter in his file. 32 CFR §1625.4. Joseph's board did not do so.

Whatever force the "presumption of regularity" might have in the ordinary case, it is a weak reed on which to rest under these circumstances. But the "presumption" is the lynch-pin of the Solicitor General's analysis; without it, a number of alternate hypotheses become equally, if not more, plausible than that offered by the Solicitor General.

For example, it was the Government's consistent position, until the Solicitor General's confession in Clay v. United States, 403 U.S. 698, 91 S. Ct. 2068, 29 L. Ed. 2d 810, that conscientious objector claims based on Black Muslim teachings did not satisfy the statutory requirement that they be based on "religious training and belief." The Justice Department letter quoted in Clay, supra, is representative of the Government's views at the time that Joseph's claim was under consideration:

> It seems clear that the teachings of the Nation of Islam precludes fighting for the United States not because of objections to participation in war in any form but rather because of political and racial objections to policies of the United States as interpreted by Elijah Muhammad. . . . It is therefore our conclusion that registrant's claimed objections to participation in war insofar as they are based upon the teachings of the Nation of Islam, rest on grounds which primarily are political and racial. 403 U.S., at 702, 91 S. Ct., at 2071.

If one is to decide this case by speculation and assumption, a likely analysis is that Joseph's local board knew of, and followed, the Justice Department's articulated policy with respect to Black Muslim conscientious objector claims. Joseph stated in his SSS Form 150, "I receive my training from the honorable Elijah Muhammad Last Messenger of Allah Leader and Teacher of the Nation of Islam herein. The Wilderous [*sic*] of North America." Given the Government's oft-articulated views as to the insufficiency of such teachings to support a conscientious objector claim, Joseph's local board may well have denied his exemption for failure to demonstrate it was based on "religious training and belief." The Solicitor General concedes that such a ground would have been clear error. Memorandum for the United States, p. 14, n. 13. See Clay, 91 S. Ct. at 2071.

There is also the possibility that Joseph's board thought him to be a selective objector, because his statement of belief left open the possibility that he might fight if "America agrees to give us the necessary territory wherein we may have something to fight for." The Solicitor General strenuously insists that this is indeed the correct analysis of Joseph's claim.[1]

Finally, there is the difficulty inherent in accepting the Solicitor General's assumption that Joseph's claim was not denied for failure to meet any of the statutory criteria, but for insincerity. It is well-settled that mere disbeliefs in the sincerity of a registrant, based on no objective evidence of insincerity, will not suffice to deny a conscientious objector claim once a prima facie case

1. Joseph argues persuasively, however, that this statement is nothing more than the Muslim equivalent of a Jehovah's Witness' declaration that he will fight in defense of "Kingdom Interests." Sicurella v. United States, 348 U.S. 385, 75 S. Ct. 403, 99 L. Ed. 436. See Brief for Petitioner, pp. 23-25.

is made out. Dickinson v. United States, 346 U.S. 389, 74 S. Ct. 152, 98 L. Ed. 132; United States v. Hayden, supra, 445 F.2d at 1373. The "evidence of insincerity" pointed to by the Solicitor is ambiguous at best. He notes Joseph joined the Muslims a year before he first registered for the draft, and two years before filing for his conscientious objector exemption, but that he made no claim to conscientious objector status in his Classification Questionnaire, and no subsequent claim of late crystallization. By themselves, these facts seem insufficient. Joseph was a 17-year-old high school dropout when he became a Muslim. His lack of sophistication and minimal writing skills are apparent from his communications with the board. If we are to assume with the Solicitor General that Joseph's board found he made out a prima facie case, I should think it also follows that the board, having gone thus far, would have made further inquiries into Joseph's sincerity rather than rely on such an ambiguous and inartful record.[2]

These speculations should not be taken to mean that I think the Solicitor General's analysis should be rejected. It is perhaps no less probable than the alternatives that I have suggested. The point is that it is no *more* probable.

Joseph's local and appeal boards might have denied his claim because he was thought to be insincere, because his Black Muslim beliefs were not thought to be religious, because he was thought to be a selective objector, or perhaps for some other reason not apparent from the record. Viewing this bare record from our perspective, there is simply no way to decide why it was that Joseph's claim was denied.

The conviction must be reversed, therefore, not because Joseph made out a prima facie case and is thereby entitled to reasons, but because without a statement of reasons, it is impossible even to tell if Joseph's prima facie showing was a relevant factor in the administrative process. I would require the Selective Service to provide a concise statement of reasons whenever a requested classification is denied, and whatever the administrative level at which the denial takes place.

WELSH v. UNITED STATES

398 U.S. 333, 90 S. Ct. 1792, 26 L. Ed. 2d 308 (1970)

Mr. Justice Black announced the judgment of the Court and delivered an opinion in which Mr. Justice Douglas, Mr. Justice Brennan, and Mr. Justice Marshall join.

2. Other alleged indicia of insincerity need little comment. Many smokers would take issue with the Solicitor's attempt to demean Joseph's statement that his ability to give up smoking was a demonstration of his faith. And, the statement by an unknown Army official that a psychological interview of petitioner revealed him to have "a mature attitude and interest in the Armed Forces" is simply meaningless without more information as to the nature of the interview in question and particular responses on which the Army's conclusory remark was based. Moreover, the interview took place over five months before petitioner first filed his conscientious objector clam, and thus certainly cannot be taken as representing his views at the time his conscientious objector claim was denied.

The petitioner, Elliott Ashton Welsh, II, was convicted by a United States district judge of refusing to submit to induction into the Armed Forces. . . . One of petitioner's defenses to the prosecution was that §6(j) of the Universal Military Training and Service Act exempted him from combat and noncombat service because he was "by reason of religious training and belief . . . conscientiously opposed to participation in war in any form."[1] After finding that there was no religious basis for petitioner's conscientious objector claim, the Court of Appeals, Judge Hamley dissenting, affirmed the conviction. 404 F2d 1078 (1968). We granted certiorari chiefly to review the contention that Welsh's conviction should be set aside on the basis of this Court's decision in United States v Seeger, 380 US 163, 13 L Ed 2d 733, 85 S Ct 850 (1965). . . . For the reasons to be stated, and without passing upon the constitutional arguments which have been raised, we reverse the conviction because of its fundamental inconsistency with United States v Seeger, supra.

The controlling facts in this case are strikingly similar to those in Seeger. Both Seeger and Welsh were brought up in religious homes and attended church in their childhood, but in neither case was this church one which taught its members not to engage in war at any time for any reason. Neither Seeger nor Welsh continued his childhood religious ties into his young manhood, and neither belonged to any religious group or adhered to the teachings of any organized religion during the period of his involvement with the Selective Service System. At the time of their registration for the draft, neither had yet come to accept pacifist principles. Their views on war developed only in subsequent years, but when their ideas did fully mature both made application with their local draft boards for conscientious objector exemptions from military service under §6(j) of the Universal Military Training and Service Act. That section then provided, in part:[2]

> Nothing contained in this title shall be construed to require any person to be subject to combatant training and service in the armed forces of the United States who, by reason of religious training and belief, is conscientiously opposed to participation in war in any form. Religious training and belief in this connection means an individual's belief in a relation to a Supreme Being involving duties superior to those arising from any human relation, but does not include essentially political, sociological, or philosophical views or a merely personal moral code.

In filling out their exemption applications both Seeger and Welsh were unable to sign the statement which, as printed in the Selective Service form, stated "I am, by reason of my religious training and belief, conscientiously opposed to participation in war in any form." Seeger could sign only after

1. 62 Stat 612. See also 50 USC App §456(j).

2. 62 Stat 612. An amendment to the Act in 1967, subsequent to the Courts decision in the Seeger case, deleted the reference to a "Suprme Being" but continued to provide that "religious training and belief" does not include "essentially political, sociological, or philosophical views, or a merely personal moral code." 81 Stat 104, 50 USC App §456(j).

striking the words "training and" and putting quotation marks around the word "religious." Welsh could sign only after striking the words "religious training and." On those same applications, neither could definitely affirm or deny that he believed in a "Supreme Being," both stating that they preferred to leave the question open.[3] But both Seeger and Welsh affirmed on those applications that they held deep conscientious scruples against taking part in wars where people were killed. Both strongly believed that killing in war was wrong, unethical, and immoral, and their consciences forbade them to take part in such an evil practice. Their objection to participating in war in any form could not be said to come from a "still, soft voice of conscience"; rather, for them that voice was so loud and insistent that both men preferred to go to jail rather than serve in the Armed Forces. There was never any question about the sincerity and depth of Seeger's convictions as a conscientious objector, and the same is true of Welsh. In this regard the Court of Appeals noted, "[t]he government concedes that (Welsh's) beliefs are held with the strength of more traditional religious convictions." 404 F2d, at 1081. But in both cases the Selective Service System concluded that the beliefs of these men were in some sense insufficiently "religious" to qualify them for conscientious objector exemptions under the terms of §6(j). Seeger's conscientious objector claim was denied "solely because it was not based upon a 'belief in a relation to a Supreme Being' as required by §6(j) of the Act." United States v Seeger, 380 US 163, 167, 13 L Ed 2d 733, 737, 85 S Ct 850 (1965), while Welsh was denied the exemption because his Appeal Board and the Department of Justice hearing officer "could find no religious basis for the registrant's belief, opinions, and convictions." . . . Both Seeger and Welsh subsequently refused to submit to induction into the military and both were convicted of that offense.

In Seeger the Court was confronted, first, with the problem that §6(j) defined "religious training and belief" in terms of a "belief in a relation to a Supreme Being . . . ," a definition which arguably gave a preference to those who believed in a conventional God as opposed to those who did not. Noting the "vast panoply of beliefs" prevalent in our country, the Court construed the congressional intent as being in "keeping with its long-established policy of not picking and choosing among religious beliefs," id., at 175, 13 L Ed 2d at 742, and accordingly interpreted "the meaning of religious training and belief so as to embrace *all* religions . . . ." Id., at 165, 13 L Ed 2d at 737. (Emphasis added.) But, having decided that all religious conscientious objectors were entitled to the exemption, we faced the more serious problem of determining which beliefs were "religious" within the meaning of the statute. This question was particularly difficult in the case of Seeger himself. Seeger stated that his was a "belief in and devotion to goodness and virtue for their

3. In this original application in April 1964, Welsh stated that he did not believe in a Supreme Being, but in a letter to his local board in March 1965, he requested that his original answer be stricken and the question left open. App., at 29.

own sakes, and a religious faith in a purely ethical creed." 380 US, at 166, 13 L Ed 2d at 737. In a letter to his draft board, he wrote:

> My decision arises from what I believe to be considerations of validity from the standpoint of the welfare of humanity and the preservation of the democratic values which we in the United States are struggling to maintain. I have concluded that war, from the practical standpoint, is futile and self-defeating, and that from the more important moral standpoint, it is unethical. 326 F.2d 846, 848 (1964).

On the basis of these and similar assertions, the Government argued that Seeger's conscientious objection to war was not "religious" but stemmed from "essentially political, sociological, or philosophical views or a merely personal moral code."

In resolving the question whether Seeger and the other registrants in that case qualified for the exemption, the Court stated that "(the) task is to decide whether the beliefs professed by a registrant are sincerely held and whether they are, *in his own scheme of things,* religious." 380 US, at 185, 13 L Ed 2d at 747. (Emphasis added.) The reference to the registrant's "own scheme of things" was intended to indicate that the central consideration in determining whether the registrant's beliefs are religious is whether these beliefs play the role of a religion and function as a religion in the registrant's life. The Court's principal statement of its test for determining whether a conscientious objector's beliefs are religious within the meaning of §6(j) was as follows:

> The test might be stated in these words: A sincere and meaningful belief which occupies in the life of its possessor a place parallel to that filled by the God of those admittedly qualifying for the exemption comes within the statutory definition. 380 US, at 176, 13 L Ed 2d at 743.

The Court made it clear that these sincere and meaningful beliefs which prompt the registrant's objection to all wars need not be confined in either source or content to traditional or parochial concepts of religion. It held that §6(j) "does not distinguish between externally and internally derived beliefs," id., at 186, 13 L Ed 2d at 748, and also held that "intensely personal" convictions which some might find "incomprehensible" or "incorrect" come within the meaning of "religious belief" in the Act. Id., at 184-185, 13 L Ed 2d at 747. What is necessary under Seeger for a registrant's conscientious objection to all war to be "religious" within the meaning of §6(j) is that this opposition to war stem from the registrant's moral, ethical, or religious beliefs about what is right and wrong and that these beliefs be held with the strength of traditional religious convictions. Most of the great religions of today and of the past have embodied the idea of a Supreme Being or a Supreme Reality — a God — who communicates to man in some way a consciousness of what is right and should be done, of what is wrong and therefore should be shunned. If an individual deeply and sincerely holds beliefs which are purely ethical or moral in source and content but which nevertheless impose upon him a duty of conscience to refrain from participating in any war at any time, those beliefs certainly occupy in the life of that individual "a place parallel to that filled by . . . God" in traditionally religious persons. Because his beliefs function as a religion in his life, such an individual is as much entitled to a "religious" conscientious objector exemption under §6(j) as is someone who derives his conscientious opposition to war from traditional religious convictions.

Applying this standard to Seeger himself, the Court noted the "compulsion to 'goodness'" which informed his total opposition to war, the undisputed sincerity with which he held his views, and the fact that Seeger had "decried the tremendous 'spiritual' price man must pay for his willingness to destroy human life." 380 US, at 186-187, 13 L Ed 2d at 748. The Court concluded:

> We think it clear that the beliefs which prompted his objection occupy the same place in his life as the belief in a traditional deity holds in the lives of his friends, the Quakers. 380 US, at 187, 13 L Ed 2d at 748.

Accordingly, the Court found that Seeger should be granted conscientious objector status. . . .

The Government also seeks to distinguish Seeger on the ground that Welsh's views, unlike Seeger's, were "essentially political, sociological, or philosophical or a merely personal moral code." As previously noted, the Government made the same argument about Seeger, and not without reason, for Seeger's views had a substantial political dimension. Supra, at —, 26 L Ed 2d at 318. In this case, Welsh's conscientious objection to war was undeniably based in part on his perception of world politics. In a letter to his local board, he wrote:

> I can only act according to what I am and what I see. And I see that the military complex wastes both human and material resources, that it fosters disregard for (what I consider a paramount concern) human needs and ends; I see that the means we employ to 'defend' our 'way of life' profoundly change that way of life. I see that in our failure to recognize the political, social, and economic realities of the world, we *as a nation,* fail our responsibility *as a nation.* App. at 30.

We certainly do not think that §6(j)'s exclusion of those persons with "essentially political, sociological, or philosophical views or a merely personal moral code" should be read to exclude those who hold strong beliefs about our domestic and foreign affairs or even those whose conscientious objection to participation in all wars is founded to a substantial extent upon considerations of public policy. The two groups of registrants which obviously do fall within these exclusions from the exemption are those whose beliefs are not deeply held and those whose objection to war does not rest at all upon moral, ethical, or religious principle but instead rests solely upon considerations of policy, pragmatism, or expediency. In applying §6(j)'s exclusion of those whose views are "essentially political, etc.," it should be remembered that these exclusions are definitional and do not therefore restrict the category of persons who are conscientious objectors "by religious training and belief." Once the Selective Service System has taken the first step and determined under the standards set out here and in Seeger that the registrant is a "religious" conscientious objector, it follows that his views cannot be "essentially political, sociological, or philosophical." Nor can they be a "merely personal moral code." See United States v Seeger, 380 US, at 186, 13 L Ed 2d at 748.

Welsh stated that he "believe[d] the taking of life — anyone's life — to be morally wrong." App, at 44. In his original conscientious objector application he wrote the following:

> I believe that human life is valuable in and of itself; in its living; therefore I will not injure or kill another human being. This belief (and the corresponding 'duty' to abstain from violence toward another person) is not 'superior to those arising from any human relation.' On the contrary: *it is essential to every human relation.* I cannot, therefore, conscientiously comply with the Government's insistence that I assume duties which I feel are immoral and totally repugnant. . . .

On the basis of these beliefs and the conclusion of the Court of Appeals that he held them "with the strength of more traditional religious convictions," 404 F2d, at 1081, we think Welsh was clearly entitled to a conscientious objector exemption. Section 6(j) requires no more. That section exempts from military service all those whose consciences, spurred by deeply held moral, ethical, or religious beliefs, would give them no rest or peace if they allowed themselves to become a part of an instrument of war.

The judgment is reversed.

[Justice Harlan concurred in the result, but took the occasion to confess that he considered the Seeger case an improper exercise in statutory construction, in which he should not have joined. He felt that the Court, in Welsh was compounding that error in order to avoid the constitutional issue which presented itself when the exemption clause was given a natural reading. He asserted that the Congress had clearly intended to distinguish between theistic and nontheistic religions, intending not to grant exemption to those who claimed it on ethical grounds only. The removal of the theistic requirement in Seeger, he felt, was a "feat of judicial surgery," and in Welsh he charged the Court with performing "a lobotomy" that completely transformed the statute "by reading out of it any distinction between religiously acquired beliefs and those deriving from 'essentially political, sociological, or philosophical views, or a merely personal moral code.'" Justice Harlan asserted that the statute, by limiting exemptions to those whose objections are based on religious training and belief, violates the Establishment Clause of the First Amendment, since a preference based on religious training and belief violates the neutrality principle. Such distinctions, he charged, have been condemned in prior opinions of the Court under the Establishment

Clause. It is his position that legislation with respect to conscientious objectors can be neutral only if it grants exemptions to all those whose beliefs emanate from a purely moral, ethical or philosophical source and that the intensity of moral conviction with which the belief is held should be the standard for granting exemption. Justice Harlan concluded, somewhat reluctantly, that it was more in accord with the policy of Congress to accept the judicial patchwork involved in preserving the constitutionality of §6(j) by extending exemptions to persons like Welsh than to invalidate the statute and so deny the exemption to all.

Justice White, joined by Chief Justice Burger and Justice Stewart, dissented. In their view, the majority opinion represented an unwarranted extension of §6(j) that violated rather than enforced the will of Congress. They would affirm Welsh's conviction even if the statute is unconstitutional, since Congress clearly did not intend to exempt individuals with his belief. Justice White asserted that he would affirm Welsh's conviction even if he is wrong in thinking that Welsh cannot benefit from invalidation of §6(j) on Establishment Clause grounds.

In exempting religious conscientious objectors, Congress was making one of two judgements, perhaps both. First §6(j) may represent a purely practical judgment that religious objectors, however admirable, would be of no more use in combat than many others unqualified for military service. Exemption was not extended to them to further religious belief or practice but to limit military service to those who were prepared to undertake the fighting which the armed services have to do. On this basis, the exemption has neither the primary purpose nor the effect of furthering religion.

NOTES

1. In the period after the decisions in United States v. Seeger and Welsh v. United States, two courts interpreted the law as permitting selective conscientious objection. In United States v. Sisson, 297 F. Supp. 902 (D. Mass. 1969), *cert. granted and hearing postponed,* 396 U.S. 812, 90 S. Ct. 92, 24 L. Ed. 2d 65 (1969), *appeal dismissed,* 399 U.S. 267, 90 S. Ct. 2117, 26 L. Ed. 2d 608 (1970), the court granted a motion to arrest judgment of conviction for refusing to submit to induction. The motion was based on petitioner's claim of entitlement to exemption as a conscientious objector based on his opposition solely to the Vietnam War. The Court found on due process and First Amendment grounds that §6(j) could not be used to require combat service in Vietnam. In United States v. MacFadden, 309 F. Supp. 502 (N.D. Cal. 1970), *vacated* 401 U.S. 1006, 91 S. Ct. 1248, 28 L. Ed. 2d 541 (1971) (remanded for reconsideration in light of Gillette), defendant's motion to dismiss his indictment for refusal to submit to induction was granted on a finding that §6(j) is unconstitutional on due process and First Amendment grounds.

2. It has been suggested that, as a result of Gillette v. United States, the

selective conscientious objector must either conceal the selective nature of his views, or find some constitutional basis other than the First Amendment to support the compulsion of exemption for his specialized exemption request. Note, Gillette v. United States: The End of Selective Conscientious Objection, 39 Tenn. L. Rev. 157, 175-177 (1971).

CLAY [Muhammad Ali] v. UNITED STATES
403 U.S. 698, 91 S. Ct. 2068, 29 L. Ed. 2d 810 (1971)

PER CURIAM.

The petitioner was convicted for willful refusal to submit to induction into the Armed Forces. 62 Stat. 622, as amended, 50 U.S.C. App. §462(a). (1964 ed., Supp. V). The judgment of conviction was affirmed by the Court of Appeals for the Fifth Circuit. We granted certiorari, 400 U.S. 990, 91 S. Ct. 457, 27 L. Ed. 2d 438 to consider whether the induction notice was invalid because grounded upon an erroneous denial of the petitioner's claim to be classified as a conscientious objector.

I

The petitioner's application for classification as a conscientious objector was turned down by his local draft board, and he took an administrative appeal. The State Appeal Board tentatively classified him I-A (eligible for unrestricted military service) and referred his file to the Department of Justice for an advisory recommendation, in accordance with then-applicable procedures. 50 U.S.C.A. App. §456(j) (1964 ed., Supp. V). The FBI then conducted an "inquiry" as required by the statute, interviewing some 35 persons, including members of the petitioner's family and many of his friends, neighbors, and business and religious associates.

There followed a hearing on "the character and good faith of the [petitioner's] objections" before a hearing officer appointed by the Department. The hearing officer, a retired judge of many years' experience, heard testimony from the petitioner's mother and father, from one of his attorneys, from a minister of his religion, and from the petitioner himself. He also had the benefit of a full report from the FBI. On the basis of this record the hearing officer concluded that the registrant was sincere in his objection on religious grounds to participation in war in any form, and he recommended that the conscientious objector claim be sustained.

Notwithstanding this recommendation, the Department of Justice wrote a letter to the Appeal Board, advising it that the petitioner's conscientious objector claim should be denied. Upon receipt of this letter of advice, the Board denied the petitioner's claim without a statement of reasons. After various further proceedings which it is not necessary to recount here, the petitioner was ordered to report for induction. He refused to take the traditional step forward, and this prosecution and conviction followed. . . .

The petitioner's criminal conviction stemmed from the Selective Service

System's denial of his appeal seeking conscientious objector status. That denial, for which no reasons were ever given, was, as we have said, based on a recommendation of the Department of Justice, overruling its hearing officer and advising the Appeal Board that it "finds that the registrant's conscientious-objector claim is not sustained and recommends to your Board that he be not [so] classified." This finding was contained in a long letter of explanation, from which it is evident that Selective Service officials were led to believe that the Department had found that the petitioner had failed to satisfy each of the three basic tests for qualification as a conscientious objector.

As to the requirement that a registrant must be opposed to war in any form, the Department letter said that the petitioner's expressed beliefs "do not appear to preclude military service in any form, but rather are limited to military service in the Armed Forces of the United States. . . . These constitute only objections to certain types of war in certain circumstances, rather than a general scruple against participation in war in any form. However, only a general scruple against participation in war in any form can support an exemption as a conscientious objector under the Act. United States v. Kauten, 2 Cir., 133 F.2d 703."

As to the requirement that a registrant's opposition must be based upon religious training and belief, the Department letter said: "It seems clear that the teachings of the Nation of Islam preclude fighting for the United States not because of objections to participation in war in any form but rather because of political and racial objections to policies of the United States as interpreted by Elijah Muhammad. . . . It is therefore our conclusion that registrant's claimed objections to participation in war insofar as they are based upon the teachings of the Nation of Islam, rest on grounds which primarily are political and racial."

As to the requirement that a registrant's opposition to war must be sincere, that part of the letter began by stating that "the registrant has not consistently manifested his conscientious-objector claim. Such a course of overt manifestations is requisite to establishing a subjective state of mind and belief." There followed several paragraphs reciting the timing and circumstances of the petitioner's conscientious objector claim, and a concluding paragraph seeming to state a rule of law — that "a registrant has not shown overt manifestations sufficient to establish his subjective belief where, as here, his conscientious-objector claim was not asserted until military service became imminent. Campbell v. United States, 4 Cir., 221 F.2d 454. United States v. Corliss, 280 F.2d 808, *cert. denied,* 364 U.S. 884, 81 S. Ct. 167, 5 L. Ed. 2d 105."

In this Court the Government has now fully conceded that the petitioner's beliefs *are* based upon "religious training and belief," as defined in United States v. Seeger, supra: "There is no dispute that petitioner's professed beliefs were founded on basic tenets of the Muslim religion, as he understood them, and derived in substantial part from his devotion to Allah as the Supreme Being. Thus, under this Court's decision in United States v. Seeger,

380 U.S. 163, 85 S. Ct. 850, 13 L. Ed. 2d 733, his claim unquestionably was within the 'religious training and belief' clause of the exemption provision." This concession is clearly correct. For the record shows that the petitioner's beliefs are founded on tenets of the Muslim religion as he understands them. They are surely no less religiously based than those of the three registrants before this Court in Seeger. See also Welsh v. United States, 398 U.S. 333, 90 S. Ct. 1792, 26 L. Ed. 2d 308.

The Government in this Court has also made clear that it no longer questions the sincerity of the petitioner's beliefs. This concession is also correct. The Department hearing officer — the only person at the administrative appeal level who carefully examined the petitioner and other witnesses in person and who had the benefit of the full FBI file — found "that the registrant is sincere in his objection." The Department of Justice was wrong in advising the Board in terms of a purported rule of law that it should disregard this finding simply because of the circumstances and timing of the petitioner's claim. See Ehlert v. United States, 402 U.S. 99, 103-104, 91 S. Ct. 1319, 1322-1323, 28 L. Ed. 625; United States ex rel. Lehman v. Laird, 4 Cir., 430 F.2d 96, 99; United States v. Abbott, 8 Cir., 425 F.2d 910, 915; United States ex rel. Tobias v. Laird, 4 Cir., 413 F.2d 936, 939-940; Cohen v. Laird, D.C., 315 F. Supp. 1265, 1277-1278.

Since the Appeal Board gave no reasons for its denial of the petitioner's claim, there is absolutely no way of knowing upon which of the three grounds offered in the Department's letter it relied. Yet the Government now acknowledges that two of those grounds were not valid. And, the Government's concession aside, it is indisputably clear, for the reasons stated, that the Department was simply wrong as a matter of law in advising that the petitioner's beliefs were not religiously based and were not sincerely held.

This case, therefore, falls squarely within the four corners of this Court's decision in Sicurella v. United States, 348 U.S. 385, 75 S. Ct. 403, 99 L. Ed. 436. There as here the Court was asked to hold that an error in an advice letter prepared by the Department of Justice did not require reversal of a criminal conviction because there was a ground on which the Appeal Board might properly have denied a conscientious objector classification. This Court refused to consider the proffered alternative ground:

> [W]e feel that this error of law by the Department, to which the Appeal Board might naturally look for guidance on such questions, must vitiate the entire proceedings at least where it is not clear that the Board relied on some legitimate ground. Here, where it is impossible to determine on exactly which grounds the Appeal Board decided, the integrity of the Selective Service System demands, at least, that the Government not recommend illegal grounds. There is an impressive body of lower court cases taking this position and we believe that they state the correct rule. Id., at 392, 75 S. Ct., at 406.

The doctrine thus articulated 16 years ago in Sicurella was hardly new. It was long ago established as essential to the administration of criminal justice.

Stromberg v. California, 283 U.S. 359, 51 S. Ct. 532, 75 L. Ed. 1117. In Stromberg the Court reversed a conviction for violation of a California statute containing three separate clauses, finding one of the three clauses constitutionally invalid. As Chief Justice Hughes put the matter, "[I]t is impossible to say under which clause of the statute the conviction was obtained." Thus, "if any of the clauses in question is invalid under the Federal Constitution, the conviction cannot be upheld." Id., at 368, 51 S. Ct., at 535. . . .

The long established rule of law embodied in these settled precedents thus clearly requires that the judgment before us be reversed.

It is so ordered[:] Judgment reversed.

GILLETTE v. UNITED STATES
401 U.S. 437, 91 S. Ct. 828, 28 L. Ed. 2d 168 (1971)

Mr. Justice Marshall delivered the opinion of the Court.

These cases present the question whether conscientious objection to a particular war, rather than objection to war as such, relieves the objector from responsibilities of military training and service. Specifically, we are called upon to decide whether conscientious scruples relating to a particular conflict are within the purview of established provisions relieving conscientious objectors to war from military service. . . .

For purposes of determining the statutory status of conscientious objection to a particular war, the focal language of §6(j) is the phrase, "conscientiously opposed to participation in war in any form." This language, on a straightforward reading, can bear but one meaning; that conscientious scruples relating to war and military service must amount to conscientious opposition to participating personally in any war and all war. . . . It matters little for present purposes whether the words, "in any form," are read to modify "war" or "participation." On the first reading, conscientious scruples must implicate "war in any form," and an objection involving a particular war rather than all war would plainly not be covered by §6(j). On the other reading, an objector must oppose "participation in war." It would strain good sense to read this phrase otherwise than to mean, "participation in all war." For the word "war" would still be used in an unqualified, generic sense, meaning war as such. Thus, however the statutory clause be parsed, it remains that conscientious objection must run to war in any form.

A different result cannot be supported by reliance on the materials of legislative history. Petitioners and amici point to no episode or pronouncement in the legislative history of §6(j), or of predecessor provisions, that tends to overthrow the obvious interpretation of the words themselves. . . .

Sicurella v. United States, 348 U.S. 385, 75 S. Ct. 403, 99 L. Ed. 436 (1955), presented the only previous occasion for this Court to focus on the "participation in war in any form" language of §6(j). In Sicurella a Jehovah's Witness who opposed participation in secular wars was held to possess the requisite conscientious scruples concerning war, although he was not opposed to participation in a "theocratic war" commanded by Jehovah. The Court noted that the "theocratic war" reservation was highly abstract — no such war had occurred since biblical times, and none was contemplated. Congress, on the other hand, had in mind "real shooting wars," id., at 391, 75 S. Ct., at 406, and Sicurella's abstract reservations did not undercut his conscientious opposition to participating in such wars. Plainly Sicurella cannot be read to support the claims of those, like petitioners, who for a variety of reasons consider one particular "real shooting war" to be unjust, and therefore oppose participation in that war.

It should be emphasized that our cases explicating the "religious training and belief" clause of §6(j), or cognate clauses of predecessor provisions, are not relevant to the present issue. The question here is not whether these petitioners' beliefs concerning war are "religious" in nature. Thus petitioners' reliance on United States v. Seegar, 380 U.S. 163, 85 S. Ct. 850, 13 L. Ed. 2d 733 (1965), and Welsh v. United States, 398 U.S. 333, 90 S. Ct. 1792, 26 L. Ed. 2d 308 (1970), is misplaced. Nor do we decide that conscientious objection to a particular war necessarily falls within §6(j)'s expressly excluded class of "essentially political, sociological, or philosophical views, or a merely personal moral code." Rather we hold that Congress intended to exempt persons who oppose participation in all war — "participation in war in any form" — and that persons who object solely to participation in a particular war are not within the purview of the exempting section, even though the latter objection may have such roots in a claimant's conscience and personality that it is "religious" in character.

A further word may be said to clarify our statutory holding. Apart from abstract theological reservations, two other sorts of reservations concerning use of force have been thought by lower courts not to defeat a conscientious objector claim. Willingness to use force in self-defense, in defense of home and family, or in defense against immediate acts of aggressive violence toward other persons in the community, has not been regarded as inconsistent with a claim of conscientious objection to war as such. . . . But surely willingness to use force defensively in the personal situations mentioned is quite different from willingness to fight in some wars but not in others. Cf. Sicurella v. United States, 348 U.S., at 389, 75 S. Ct., at 405. Somewhat more apposite to the instant situation are cases dealing with persons who oppose participating in all wars, but cannot say with complete certainty that their present convictions and existing state of mind are unalterable. See, e.g., United States v. Owen, 415 F.2d 383, 390 (CA8 1969). Unwillingness to deny the possibility of a change of mind, in some hypothetical future circumstances, may be no more than humble good sense, casting no doubt on the claimant's present sincerity of belief. At any rate there is an obvious difference between present sincere objection to all war, and present opposition to participation in a particular conflict only. . . .

[The Court considered and rejected petitioners' contentions that §6(j) violates the Establishment and Free Exercise Clauses of the First Amendment. As a pragmatic matter, the Court examined and found merit in the government's position: granting exemption to service, based on an objection to a particular war, was intrinsically so difficult that it could lead to erratic or discriminatory decision making in administrative practice. The Court also took note of the fear that exemptions to selective conscientious objectors, even on grounds of conscience and religion, would "open the doors to a general theory of selective disobedience to law" and jeopardize the binding quality of democratic decisions. Justice Douglas dissented. Expressing the view that First Amendment requirements control the cases, he wrote, "I had assumed that the welfare of the individal human soul was the ultimate test of the vitality of the First Amendment."]

NOTES

1. The criteria for conscientious objector status are religion, sincerity and pacifism. The Supreme Court's decisions in Seegar and Welsh appear to have defined the religion requirement to mean sincerity, but its decision in Gillette holds firm the requirement of total pacifism, excepting only the Jehovah's Witnesses' willingness to fight only in a "theocratic" war commanded by God.

2. The Muhammad Ali and Joseph convictions were reversed on procedural grounds, and thus the Court in those cases did not reach the question of whether Muslim beliefs qualify for conscientious objector exemption. But note that in the Joseph case, supra, Justice Douglas termed as "persuasive" the argument that the Muslim willingness to fight, if America provides land for which to fight, is equivalent to the readiness of Jehovah's Witnesses to fight for "Kingdom Interests."

3. Even if the exemption were extended to Black Muslims, there is a serious question whether a black militant like Marc Anthony Lewis could gain exemption, because of his apparently selective objections to war. The challenge in such a case is to distinguish the beliefs of a black militant from those held by men like Gillette, who oppose the Vietnam War but perhaps would have fought in World War Two.

4. Standards for the conscientious objector exemption require the registrant to demonstrate that his ethical or moral convictions were gained through training, study, contemplation or other activity, comparable in rigor and dedication to the processes by which traditional religious convictions are formulated. Statistics would seem to indicate that a greater percentage of blacks than whites would be adversely affected by standards which put a premium on education and on a decidedly middle-class outlook. Indeed, it might be argued that the historical experience of most blacks, as well as their religious and philosophical views, would incline them to some form of selective objection, rather than to the absolute pacifism required by Gillette v. United States.

5. The Gillette opinion recognizes that there may be pragmatic reasons

for limiting exemptions to those opposed to all wars, but it is fairly clear from history that there have been strong reasons for keeping out of the service those so opposed to fighting that their presence would be more hindrance than help. The stance of some black militants clearly places them in this category. See A. Haley, Autobiography of Malcolm X, at 106-108 (1964).

B. BLACK REPRESENTATION ON SELECTIVE BOARDS

Black defendants in selective service cases have frequently sought to forestall conviction by alleging systematic exclusion of blacks from the local, appeal or national selective service boards which passed on their claims. Such efforts not only have failed, but have usually been dismissed on reasoning that reflects a firm unwillingness to apply the jury exclusion cases to the selective service issues.

CLAY v. UNITED STATES
397 F.2d 901 (5th Cir. 1968)

[In the decision that was reversed on other grounds in Clay v. United States, 403 U.S. 698, 91 S. Ct. 2068, 29 L. Ed. 2d 810 (1971), printed supra at 414, the court of appeals reviewed appellants' claim that blacks had been systematically excluded from selective service boards.]

AINSWORTH, J.

The Selective Service System is based on the constitutional provision which grants to Congress the power "To raise and support Armies. . . ." U.S. Const. art. I, §8(12). The Universal Military Training and Service Act provides (50 U.S.C. App. §460(b) (3)) that the President is authorized to create civilian local boards and appeal boards. Each local board shall consist of three or more members to be appointed by the President from recommendations made by the respective governors of each of the states. No member of any board shall be a member of the armed forces but each member shall be a citizen residing in the local board jurisdiction. Appeal boards shall also be composed of citizens who are not members of the armed forces and consist normally of five members appointed by the President upon recommendation of the governor. The appeal board shall be a composite board representative of the activities of its areas and shall include one member from labor, one member from industry, one physician, one lawyer and, where applicable, one member from agriculture. (32 C.F.R. §1604.22.)

Thus the racial composition of the local and appeal boards about which appellant complains, because of the absence of a proportion of Negroes in accordance with their ratio to the population, results from appointment by the President upon recommendation of the governor of each state. The appointments are therefore federal, not state.

There is also a National Selective Service Appeal Board (sometimes called the Presidential Appeal Board) composed of three members who are appointed by the President from citizens who are not members of the armed forces. This board acts for the President himself, being vested with the functions and duties of the President provided by the Act (50 U.S.C. App. §460 (b) (3)), which reads in pertinent part as follows:

> The President, upon appeal or upon his own motion, shall have power to determine all claims or questions with respect to inclusion for, or exemption or deferment from training and service under this title, and the determination of the President shall be final.

This board shall be in all respects independent of the Director of Selective Service. (32 C.F.R. §1604.6(a), (b), (c).) It was stipulated in the present record that one of the three members of the President Appeal Board was a Negro. However, there was no Negro member on any of the local or appeal boards which considered appellant's draft case.

According to the report of the National Advisory Commission on Selective Service (the Marshall Commission), in Kentucky, only 0.2% of 641 local board members is Negro, though 7.1% of the total population is Negro. In Texas, only 1.1% of local board members is Negro, though 12.4% of the total population is Negro. In the City of Louisiville, the total population (1964) is 389,044, of which the white population is 310,717 and the Negro population 78,245, or 21% of the total population.[4] The Jefferson County, Kentucky, total population (1960) number 610,947, of which there are 532,057 whites and 78,350 Negroes, or 12.8% of the total population. In Harris County, Texas, of a total population of 1,243,158, 19.81%, or 246,351, is Negro.[5]

According to the Marshall Commission Report, the unequal percentage of Negroes on draft boards was not peculiar to Kentucky, Texas or the South, but the imbalance was nationwide. Only in the District of Columbia and in Delaware were there substantial percentages of Negroes on the boards. In twenty-three states, there were no Negroes on draft boards, the Report stated.[6]

Nevertheless the Marshall Commission said significantly in its report, "There is no evidence that the variability of the Selective Service System leads to any systematic biases against poor people, or Negroes, insofar as the final proportion of men serving in the Armed Forces is a measure of this."

As a direct result of the Marshall Commission Report, the President in his

4. Appellant's brief asserts the Negro population of Louisville (1964) to be 78,327 and the percentage of Negroes to be 20.1% — a slight error. The difference is, of course, not significant. See Special Censuses, Series P-28, No. 1377, Louisville, Kentucky (United States Department of Commerce).

5. Appellant in brief supplies other calculations from the record as follows: 9.60% of the total population of the Western District of Kentucky is Negro; 14.25% of the total population of the Southern District of Texas is Negro.

6. For example, there were no Negroes on draft boards in such states as Indiana, Iowa, Kansas, Maine, Minnesota, New Jersey and Rhode Island.

message to the Congress on Selective Service dated March 6, 1967, instructed the Director of the Selective Service System to work with the governors "to assure that all local boards are truly representative of the communities they serve and to submit periodic reports on the progress in this area."

The Universal Military Training and Service Act in its congressional declaration of policy declares that the obligations and privileges of serving in the armed forces should be shared generally in accordance with a system of selection which is "fair and just" (50 U.S.C. App. §451(c)). The Act further provides (50 U.S.C. App. §455(a)) that "The selection of persons for training and service . . . shall be made in an impartial manner, under such rules and regulations as the President may prescribe, from the persons who are liable for such training and service and who at the time of selection are registered and classified, but not deferred or exempted: *Provided,* That in the selection of persons for training and service under this title . . . , and in the interpretation and execution of the provisions of this title . . . , there shall be no discrimination against any person on account of race or color. . . ."

The Selective Service Regulations (32 C.F.R. §1622.1(d)) provide, "In classifying a registrant there shall be no discrimination for or against him because of his race, creed, or color, or because of his membership or activity in any labor, political, religious, or other organization. Each such registrant shall receive equal justice."

Appellant argues that the quoted statistics evidence racial exclusion in the composition of draft boards, in violation of the Fifth Amendment. He cites United States v. Jefferson County Board of Education, 5 Cir., 1966, 372 F.2d 836, 837, *aff'd on rehearing,* en banc, 380 F.2d 385 (1967), *cert. denied, sub nom.* Board of Education of the City of Bessemer v. United States, 389 U.S. 840, 88 S. Ct. 77, 19 L. Ed. 2d 104 (1967), where this Court said that it has frequently relied on percentages in jury exclusion cases and in other civil rights cases for evidence of deliberate discrimination against Negroes. He concludes that if systematic exclusion of Negroes is constitutionally barred in the composition of juries, their exclusion in the Selective Service System likewise infringes his rights and requires a holding that draft boards, such as those in Kentucky and Texas which considered appellant's case, have no jurisdiction over appellant or in fact over any Negro. Thus he argues that the local boards have acted beyond their jurisdiction and may not act as to that class of registrants (including appellant) against whom it is claimed the appointing process has discriminated. Appellant concedes that considerable progress in rectifying this disparity in the several states has been made since the President's March 6, 1967, message to Congress on Selective Service, but contends that Negroes should not be selected in the future until the alleged systematic exclusion of members of that race from draft boards has ceased.

Appellant likens his classification and induction into the armed forces to a criminal prosecution because, as in a criminal prosecution, the Government restrains a registrant of his liberty and may even cause his death by sending him into combat.

No court has held, so far as we can determine, nor do we here, that a Negro registrant for selective service is entitled to be classified and inducted by a selective service board composed of a percentage of Negro members which the Negro population bears to the total population, or that a board lacks jurisdiction of a registrant unless so constituted. No question is raised that the boards which considered appellant's classification were not regularly and properly constituted under appointment by the President, recommended by the governor. We do not justify the failure to include substantial numbers of Negroes on such boards. The Selective Service System must not only be fair, it must likewise have the appearance of fairness. Negro draftees should be selected for military service by a system which gives Negro citizens a full participation in the selection process. The Marshall Commission affirmed the necessity of greater participation by Negroes who are underepresented as a class on local draft boards. The Commission said that the Negro's position in the military manpower situation is in many ways disproportionate, even though he does not serve in the armed forces out of proportion to his percentage to the population. The President in his March 6, 1967, message to Congress said in this regard: "The Nation's requirement that men must serve, however, imposes this obligation: that in this land of equals, men are selected as equals to serve. A just nation must have the fairest system that can be devised for making that selection." We concur with these remarks to the fullest. But nothing we have said justifies exemption from service in the armed forces for Negro registrants.

It is undeniable, as appellant contends, that conscription deprives an individual of his liberty and may even take his life. But we cannot properly compare the military draft to a criminal prosecution. There is no stigma attached to wearing the military uniform of the United States. To the contrary, it is a badge of the highest honor. Service under the flag of our country cannot properly be likened to imprisonment in a penitentiary. A proud nation with a long tradition of valor and bravery on the battlefield, with vivid memories in modern times of distant places some with unusual names, such as Chateau-Thierry, Normandy, Iwo Jima and Khe Sanh, where Americans have fought and died to preserve freedom, would never permit a comparison so odious. It is the same willingness of Americans to sacrifice their lives in the military service of the country which has made it possible to establish the United States as a free nation, and which has successfully warded off the encroachments of its enemies. "The knowledge that military service must sometimes be borne by — and imposed on — free men so their freedom may be preserved is woven deeply into the fabric of the American experience." President Johnson, Message on Selective Service to the Congress, March 6, 1967.

The Government argues — and we agree — that a draft board system which does not have a sufficiently representative number of Negro members is comparable to a malapportioned legislature. The acts of such a legislature are not invalid and the laws which it passes are not null and void. The acts of a malapportioned legislature or local or county commission or board are acts of a de facto political authority and valid despite their failure to be apportioned in accordance with Baker v. Carr, 369 U.S. 186, 82 S. Ct. 691, 7 L. Ed. 2d 663 (1962), and Avery v. Midland County, Texas, 390 U.S. 474, 88 S. Ct. 1114, 20 L. Ed. 2d 45 (1968).

Nor is appellant's argument meritorious that composition of draft boards is similar to that of grand and petit juries. The right to trial by jury has specific constitutional authority. However, nothing in the Constitution or the Universal Military Training and Service Act requires racially proportionate selective service boards. It is not difficult to understand the reasons which support the prior rulings of the Supreme Court and this Court in the jury selection cases where convictions have been set aside for failure to have representative numbers of Negroes on jury venires. See Whitus v. State of Georgia, 385 U.S. 545, 87 S. Ct. 643, 17 L. Ed. 2d 599 (1967); Rabinowitz v. United States, 5 Cir., 1966, 366 F.2d 34; Mobley v. United States, 5 Cir., 1967, 379 F.2d 768. The boards are administrative agencies with specific duties, many of them purely ministerial, which are provided for by the Act and Selective Service Regulations. A jury's verdict arrived at by secret deliberation has a finality which is not at all applicable to selective service classification and induction. As we shall see, draft board appeals are considered de novo and are not judicial proceedings. . . .

It will be recalled that there were seven different occasions on which appellant was classified 1-A: four by his local board, twice by two different appeal boards in Kentucky and Texas, and once by the Presidential Appeal Board. The appeals in each instance were considered de novo. "It is universally held that the Appeal Board considers matters of classification de novo and its classification is one of first instance, not a mere affirmance or reversal of the Local Board, and that any . . . prejudice on the local level is cured by a fair consideration on the appeal." . . .

The appeal to the Presidential Appeal Board was also de novo. Any error or invalidity in the selective service procedures up to and including the Presidential Appeal Board was cured by de novo consideration by that board which acted in the place and stead of the President himself. One third of the membership of the Presidential Appeal Board (one of three) was a Negro, which is obviously a greater proportion than Negroes bear to the total population. The decision of the board was unanimous that appellant should be classified 1-A, which action thereby cleared the way for his induction into the armed forces. Nowhere in the record in this care or in appellant's brief do we find any specific charge or evidence of discrimination against appellant because he is a Negro. There are conclusory allegations that the absence of Negroes from local and appeal boards (other than the Presidential Appeal Board) in and of itself establishes discrimination. But we have been unable to find any evidence which shows in the slightest particular that the treatment acocrded Clay (Ali) by any board or member thereof was different from that given to any other registrant. Afforded every procedure known to the Act and the regulations, and an appeal to the Presidential Appeal Board to which he was not specifically entitled, appellant's refusal of induction and subsequent trial and conviction by a jury are the result of his own voluntary choice to violate the law of the land. . . .

QUESTIONS

Is there any inconsistency between the Marshall Commission's finding that the absence of blacks from selective service boards had not resulted in any discrimination, and that commission's affirmation of the need for greater participation on boards by blacks? Is proof of harm required as a prerequisite for relief in either jury discrimination cases or reapportionment cases? Is the promise of due process in the future sufficient response to Ali's allegations of denial of due process in a criminal case?

NOTES

1. Judge Ainsworth not only refused to hold selective service boards to the jury discrimination standards, but indicated that the defendant must show that prejudice resulted from the all-white boards. Such a showing, however, might be difficult.

In DuVernay v. United States, 394 F.2d 279 (5th Cir. 1968), a black youth sought reversal of his conviction for refusing induction, on the grounds that no Negroes had served on his local draft board for the last five years, and also that the trial judge committed reversible error when he refused to permit questions concerning the Ku Klux Klan affiliation of the chairman of the board which had classified the youth as 1-A. The court avoided both issues and affirmed the conviction and a five-year sentence on procedural grounds.

2. A majority of the Supreme Court refused to review the applicability of the jury discrimination standard to selective service boards. In Sellers v. McNamara, 398 F.2d 893 (1968), the Fifth Circuit adhered to its decision in Clay; notwithstanding allegations that in South Carolina, where the population is nearly 35 percent Negro, only one of 161 board members was a Negro, and in Georgia (where appellant moved) only one of 509 board members was a Negro. The Supreme Court denied appellant's application for a writ of certiorari, 395 U.S. 950, 89 S. Ct. 2022, 23 L. Ed. 2d 470 (1969). Justice Douglas, joined by Chief Justice Warren and Justice Marshall, dissented, arguing that the Court should hear the case on the issue of whether racial discrimination was involved in the decision of the local board to reclassify the plaintiff. While conceding that the present record did not contain the necessary facts, Justice Douglas said:

> The system of using an all-white Board may well result in black registrants being sent to Viet Nam to do service for white registrants. . . . It is common talk that in some areas where all-white Boards sit, the white registrant as distinguished from

the black, need not even ask for deferments in order to obtain them. The presence of an all-white Board may, however, not be the basis of any lawful complaint. For on the facts of a particular case, a 1-A classification may be wholly warranted, irrespective of the racial context of the Board. On the other hand, the presence of an all-white Board in a racially prejudiced community may well result in the blacks carrying more than their fair share of the Viet Nam burden.

The dissenters were also critical of the process by which Sellers' conviction was obtained. Justice Douglas noted that Sellers had challenged the composition of the selective service board in a civil suit prior to receiving his orders to report for induction. After denial of his injunction request by the district court, he appealed. In the meantime, he was ordered to report for induction and refused. His conviction and sentence to five years in prison came after several unsuccessful attempts to stay prosecution pending resolution of his civil appeal. While a registrant's classification is not ordinarily subject to judicial review, Justice Douglas pointed out that there have been exceptions, such as Oestereich v. Selective Service System Local Board, 393 U.S. 233, 89 S. Ct. 414, 21 L. Ed. 2d 402 (1968), where the action of the board was "lawless." In the Oestereich case, the board had used delinquency proceedings to deprive a divinity student of his statutory exemption, in retaliation for his having returned his registration ticket as a protest against the Vietnam policy. The dissenters felt that petitioner Sellers was entitled to make a similar claim, and that if the claim were valid, "a Board compounds the injury by bulldozing the man into the army. I cannot believe we would ever hold that lawless Board action can render a case moot."*

3. In United States v. Prince, 398 F.2d 686 (1968), the Second Circuit followed the Clay decision, observing that "even the acts of a 'malapportioned' draft board are the acts of a de facto political authority." The Sixth Circuit

* The dissenting opinion noted that Judge Tuttle had expressed serious reservations about the Sellers case, and concurred in it only because he felt that the circuit had stated its position on the issue in Clay v. United States, 397 F.2d 901 (5th Cir. 1968). The dissenters also pointed out that "In filling out his 'Current Information Questionnaire,' petitioner [Sellers] noted that his job with the Student Nonviolent Coordinating Committee (SNCC) consisted of coordinating 'organizational program to develop a political and economical awareness in the black community,' for an organization whose admitted purpose was to develop 'Black Power.' His conviction in federal court for 'trespassing,' an offense arising out of a civil rights demonstration, is also in the record. Finally, a member of the local Board admitted to the State Director of the Selective Service that she had allowed an FBI agent to review petitioner's file, even though such access was in violation of Selective Service regulations.

"A psychiatrist filed, as part of petitioner's Armed Forces physical, the following: '[Petitioner] states he has animosities toward the Armed Forces Services. The Negroes are "10% of the U.S. population, yet 30% of the casualties in Vietnam are Negroes." They are "the front line foot soldiers." He feels that the country "will not give the Negroes any room." He states that the Vietnamese are basically colored people and the Negro soldiers have no business there fighting other colored people. . . . He is considered to be a semi-professional race agitator.' "

also adopted the reasoning of Clay, in United States v. Brooks, 415 F.2d 502, 504-505 (1969).

4. Predictably, the courts have not been any more willing to find a denial of rights based on the fact that members of defendant's religion were absent from his draft board. In Haven v. United States, 403 F.2d 384 (9th Cir. 1969), the court rejected appellant's contention that no members of his religious sect (Jehovah's Witnesses) had ever served on the local board, stating:

> We find no support in administrative law or in constitutional law for the contention that the composition of the membership of an administrative board, comprised under laws which are not themselves void for constitutional infringement, may be attacked by showing that certain groups or classes of persons, racial, religious or otherwise, have never been privileged to serve on such a board. We see no fair analogy between the composition of a jury, required by the Sixth Amendment to be fair and impartial, where systematic and deliberate exclusion of classes of persons will destroy the constitutional qualification of the tribunal, and the composition of an administrative board in the executive department of the Government. (403 F.2d at 386.)

QUESTIONS

1. In 1971, the Selective Service Act was amended to provide, inter alia:

> *Each local board shall consist of three or more members to be appointed by the President from recommendations made by the respective Governors of comparable executive officials. In making such appointments after the date of the enactment of the Act enacting this sentence [September 28, 1971], the President is requested to appoint the membership of each local board so that to the maximum extent practicable it is proportionately representative of the race and national origin of those registrants within its jurisdiction, but no action by any local board shall be declared invalid on the ground that any board failed to conform to any particular quota as to race or national origin. (50 U.S.C.A. App. §460(b)(3) (Supp. 1973).)*

Does this provision bar a court from finding that a registrant's constitutional rights were violated by the systematic exclusion of minorities from the selective service board which classified him? Does the congressional action constitute an implied acknowledgement of past racial discrimination by local boards? Is its failure to address past injustices justified by the direction that selection of future boards will be more representative of the race and national origin of registrants?

2. In future cases raising the issue of discrimination by local boards, how should the courts determine whether the membership of the board is proportionately representative "to the maximum extent practicable," as required by §460(b)(3)?

Racism Hypo 5
NATIONALIST v. UNITED STATES

John B. Nationalist is a twenty-year-old black youth who is appealing his conviction and five-year sentence for failing to report for induction. Nationalist, who was raised in a home that stressed "black power" in all its aspects, applied for exemption as a conscientious objector to military service, citing in support of his claim beliefs identical to those asserted by the defendant in the Lewis case, supra page 400.

Nationalist asserts that for all those reasons he will not fight for the United States, and maintains also that he would not fight against the United States, for reasons identical to those cited by James Weldon Johnson, supra page 107. He adds that he cannot imagine any war in which he would participate, with the possible exception of a God-inspired revolution by the blacks in South Africa. Nationalist gave notice that he would seek exemption from the service at the time of his registration at eighteen, and he has renewed his claim at every appropriate opportunity. At his hearing before the local selective service board, he provided evidence of activity with militant black groups. He told the board that he favors emigration of all black Americans as the only lasting political solution of the racial problem. He reported that he believes in God, but has no church affiliation.

After lengthy quotations from the works of DuBois, Fanon, Malcolm X and Ameer Baraka, Nationalist charged the board with racism, in that no blacks have ever served on it even though the population of the area over which the board has jurisdiction is almost 50 percent black. He charged further that a higher percentage of blacks was drafted than whites, adding that the board seemed to promptly draft all young blacks who were identified with black power groups or activities.

At this point, the board chairman, obviously irritated, interrupted Nationalist. He denied that the board was "racist" and explained that all registrants were treated alike, but that fewer blacks than whites were eligible for exemptions and deferrals. At the conclusion of the hearing, the board found that Nationalist was sincere, but denied his conscientious objector claim because he did not appear to oppose participation in war in any form.

After Nationalist had exhausted his appeals from the board's 1-A classification, he received a notice of induction, which he ignored. Arrest and prosecution followed.

At the trial, the board members denied that they were racist and that they discriminated against blacks. The chairman testified that he had approached a number of black people about serving on the board, but that all had refused, one stating that "no right-thinking black would serve on a draft board during these times." The chairman explained that the board denied Nationalist's conscientious objector claim because of the interpretation given §6(j) by the courts, and because of the necessity to give conscientious objector status to any black who requested it, should Nationalist's claim be recognized.

On appeal, Law Firm A will represent Nationalist. Law Firm B will represent the United States.

Part III
RIGHT TO EDUCATION

As the materials that follow will show, efforts to obtain quality schooling for black children, integrated or separate, did not begin in the 1950s, but more than 150 years earlier. In 1787, the Massachusetts legislature, which was then establishing the first public schools for the poor, ignored a petition from black parents seeking schools for their children. See L. Litwack, North of Slavery. Throughout the nineteenth century, black people repeatedly sought judicial help in their efforts to enter white schools or to upgrade the usually inferior facilities provided for them. Thus, controversies over "neighborhood schools," "bussing," and "de facto" segregation represent only a late phase of what has been perhaps the most important aspect of the black struggle for equality: important both because a quality education is essential to personal success, and because, since Brown v. Board of Education, the right to an integrated education is the foundation upon which all legal claims to full citizenship for blacks have been built.

9. DISCRIMINATION IN EDUCATION

A. BROWN AND ITS PREDECESSORS

BROWN v. BOARD OF EDUCATION (No. 1)
347 U.S. 483, 74 S. Ct. 686, 98 L. Ed. 873 (1954)

Mr. Chief Justice Warren delivered the opinion of the Court.

These cases come to us from the States of Kansas, South Carolina, Virginia, and Delaware. They are premised on different facts and different local conditions, but a common legal question justifies their consideration together in this consolidated opinion.[1]

1. In the Kansas case, Brown v. Board of Education, the plaintiffs are Negro children of elementary school age residing in Topeka. They brought this action in the United States District Court for the District of Kansas to enjoin enforcement of a Kansas statute which permits, but does not require, cities of more than 15,000 population to maintain

In each of the cases, minors of the Negro race, through their legal representatives, seek the aid of the courts in obtaining admission to the public

---

separate school facilities for Negro and white students. Kan. Gen. Stat. §72-1724 (1949). Pursuant to that authority, the Topeka Board of Education elected to establish segregated elementary schools. Other public schools in the community, however, are operated on a nonsegregated basis. The three-judge District Court, convened under 28 U.S.C. §§2281 and 2284, found that segregation in public education has a detrimental effect upon Negro children, but denied relief on the ground that the Negro and white schools were substantially equal with respect to buildings, transportation, curricula, and educational qualifications of teachers. 98 F. Supp. 797. The case is here on direct appeal under 28 U.S.C. §1253. [The Topeka, Kansas case would be analogous to a Northern school case inasmuch as the school segregation that existed in Topeka was not mandated by state law, and some of the system was integrated. It would be eighteen years before the Court would accept another such case for review. Keyes v. School District No. 1, Denver, 445 F.2d 990 (10th Cir. 1971), *cert. granted,* 404 U.S. 1036 (1972). See page 544 infra.]

In the South Carolina case, Briggs v. Elliott, the plaintiffs are Negro children of both elementary and high school age residing in Clarendon County. They brought this action in the United States District Court for the Eastern District of South Carolina to enjoin enforcement of provisions in the state constitution and statutory code which require the segregation of Negroes and whites in public schools. S.C. Const., Art. XI, §7; S.C. Code §5377 (1942). The three-judge District Court, convened under 28 U.S.C. §§2281 and 2284, denied the requested relief. The court found that the Negro schools were inferior to the white schools and ordered the defendants to begin immediately to equalize the facilities. But the court sustained the validity of the contested provisions and denied the plaintiffs admission to the white schools during the equalization program. 98 F. Supp. 529. This Court vacated the District Court's judgment and remanded the case for the purpose of obtaining the court's views on a report filed by the defendants concerning the progress made in the equalization program. 342 U.S. 350. On remand, the District Court found that substantial equality had been achieved except for buildings and that the defendants were proceeding to rectify this inequality as well. 103 F. Supp. 920. The case is again here on direct appeal under 28 U.S.C. §1253.

In the Virginia case, Davis v. County School Board, the plaintiffs are Negro children of high school age residing in Prince Edward County. They brought this action in the United States District Court for the Eastern District of Virginia to enjoin enforcement of provisions in the state constitution and statutory code which require the segregation of Negroes and whites in public schools. Va. Const., §140; Va. Code §22-221 (1950). The three-judge District Court, convened under 28 U.S.C. §§2281 and 2284, denied the requested relief. The court found the Negro school inferior in physical plant, curricula, and transportation, and ordered the defendants forthwith to provide substantially equal curricula and transportation and to "proceed with all reasonable diligence and dispatch to remove" the inequality in physical plant. But, as in the South Carolina case, the court sustained the validity of the contested provisions and denied the plaintiffs admission to the white schools during the equalization program. 103 F. Supp. 337. The case is here on direct appeal under 28 U.S.C. §1253.

In the Delaware case, Gebhart v. Belton, the plaintiffs are Negro children of both elementary and high school age residing in New Castle County. They brought this action in the Delaware Court of Chancery to enjoin enforcement of provisions in the state constitution and statutory code which require the segregation of Negroes and whites in public schools. Del. Const., Art. X, §2; Del. Rev. Code §2631 (1935). The Chancellor gave judgment for the plaintiffs and ordered their immediate admission to schools previously attended only by white children, on the ground that the Negro schools were inferior with respect to teacher training, pupil-teacher ratio, extracurricular activities, physical plant, and time and distance involved in travel. 87 A.2d 862. The Chancellor also found that segregation itself results in an inferior education for Negro children (see note 10,

schools of their community on a nonsegregated basis. In each instance, they had been denied admission to schools attended by white children under laws requiring or permitting segregation according to race. This segregation was alleged to deprive the plaintiffs of the equal protection of the laws under the Fourteenth Amendment. In each of the cases other than the Delaware case, a three-judge federal district court denied relief to the plaintiffs on the so-called "separate but equal" doctrine announced by this Court in Plessy v. Ferguson, 163 U.S. 537. Under that doctrine, equality of treatment is accorded when the races are provided substantially equal facilities, even though these facilities be separate. In the Delaware case, the Supreme Court of Delaware adhered to that doctrine, but ordered that the plaintiffs be admitted to the white schools because of their superiority to the Negro schools.

The plaintiffs contend that segregated public schools are not "equal" and cannot be made "equal," and that hence they are deprived of the equal protection of the laws. Because of the obvious importance of the question presented, the Court took jurisdiction.[2] Argument was heard in the 1952 Term, and reargument was heard this Term on certain questions propounded by the Court.[3]

Reargument was largely devoted to the circumstances surrounding the adoption of the Fourteenth Amendment in 1868. It covered exhaustively consideration of the Amendment in Congress, ratification by the states, then existing practices in racial segregation, and the views of proponents and opponents of the Amendment. This discussion and our own investigation convince us that, although these sources cast some light, it is not enough to resolve the problem with which we are faced. At best, they are inconclusive. The most avid proponents of the post–War Amendments undoubtedly intended them to remove all legal distinctions among "all persons born or naturalized in the United States." Their opponents, just as certainly, were antagonistic to both the letter and the spirit of the Amendments and wished them to have the most limited effect. What others in Congress and the state legislatures had in mind cannot be determined with any degree of certainty.

An additional reason for the inconclusive nature of the Amendment's history, with respect to segregated schools, is the status of public education at that time.[4] In the South, the movement toward free common schools, sup-

---

infra), but did not rest his decision on that ground. Id., at 865. The Chancellor's decree was affirmed by the Supreme Court of Delaware, which intimated, however, that the defendants might be able to obtain a modification of the decree after equalization of the Negro and white schools had been accomplished. 91 A.2d 137, 152. The defendants, contending only that the Delaware courts had erred in ordering the immediate admission of the Negro plaintiffs to the white schools, applied to this Court for certiorari. The writ was granted, 344 U.S. 891. The plaintiffs, who were successful below, did not submit a cross-petition.

2. 344 U.S. 1, 141, 891.

3. 345 U.S. 972. The Attorney General of the United States participated both Terms as amicus curiae.

4. For a general study of the development of public education prior to the Amendment, see Butts and Cremin, A History of Education in American Culture (1953), Pts. I, II;

ported by general taxation, had not yet taken hold. Education of white children was largely in the hands of private groups. Education of Negroes was almost nonexistent, and practically all of the race were illiterate. In fact, any education of Negroes was forbidden by law in some states. Today, in contrast, many Negroes have achieved outstanding success in the arts and sciences as well as in the business and professional world. It is true that public school education at the time of the Amendment had advanced further in the North, but the effect of the Amendment on Northern States was generally ignored in the congressional debates. Even in the North, the conditions of public education did not approximate those existing today. The curriculum was usually rudimentary; ungraded schools were common in rural areas; the school term was but three months a year in many states; and compulsory school attendance was virtually unknown. As a consequence, it is not surprising that there should be so little in the history of the Fourteenth Amendment relating to its intended effect on public education.

In the first cases in this Court construing the Fourteenth Amendment, decided shortly after its adoption, the Court interpreted it as proscribing all state-imposed discriminations against the Negro race.[5] The doctrine of "sep-

Cubberley, Public Education in the United States (1934 ed.), cc. II-XII. School practices current at the time of the adoption of the Fourteenth Amendment are described in Butts and Cremin, supra, at 269-275; Cubberley, supra, at 288-339, 408-431; Knight, Public Education in the South (1922), cc. VIII, IX. See also H. Ex. Doc. No. 315, 41st Cong., 2d Sess. (1871). Although the demand for free public schools followed substantially the same pattern in both the North and the South, the development in the South did not begin to gain momentum until about 1850, some twenty years after that in the North. The reasons for the somewhat slower development in the South (e.g., the rural character of the South and the different regional attitudes toward state assistance) are well explained in Cubberley, supra, at 408-423. In the country as a whole, but particularly in the South, the War virtually stopped all progress in public education. Id., at 427-428. The low status of Negro education in all sections of the country, both before and immediately after the War, is described in Beale, A History of Freedom of Teaching in American Schools (1941), 112-132, 175-195. Compulsory school attendance laws were not generally adopted until after the ratification of the Fourteenth Amendment, and it was not until 1918 that such laws were in force in all the states. Cubberley, supra, at 563-565.

5. Slaughter-House Cases, 16 Wall. 36, 67-72 (1873); Strauder v. West Virginia, 100 U.S. 303, 307-308 (1880): "It ordains that no State shall deprive any person of life, liberty, or property, without due process of law, or deny any person within its jurisdiction the equal protection of the laws. What is this but declaring that the law in the States shall be the same for the black as for the white; that all persons, whether colored or white, shall stand equal before the laws of the States, and, in regard to the colored race, for whose protection the amendment was primarily designed, that no discrimination shall be made against them by law because of their color? The words of the amendment, it is true, are prohibitory, but they contain a necessary implication of a positive immunity, or right, most valuable to the colored race, — the right to exemption from unfriendly legislation against them distinctively as colored, — exemption from legal discriminations, implying inferiority in civil society, lessening the security of their enjoyment of the rights which others enjoy, and discriminations whch are steps towards reducing them to the condition of a subject race." See also Virginia v. Rives, 100 U.S. 313, 318 (1880); Ex parte Virginia, 100 U.S. 339, 344-345 (1880).

arate but equal" did not make its appearance in this Court until 1896 in the case of Plessy v. Ferguson, supra, involving not education but transportation.[6] American courts have since labored with the doctrine for over half a century. In this Court, there have been six cases involving the "separate but equal" doctrine in the field of public education.[7] In Cumming v. County Board of Education, 175 U.S. 528, and Gong Lum v. Rice, 275 U.S. 78, the validity of the doctrine itself was not challenged.[8] In more recent cases, all on the graduate school level, inequality was found in that specific benefits enjoyed by white students were denied to Negro students of the same educational qualifications. Missouri ex rel. Gaines v. Canada, 305 U.S. 337; Sipuel v. Oklahoma, 332 U.S. 631; Sweatt v. Painter, 339 U.S. 629; McLaurin v. Oklahoma State Regents, 339 U.S. 637. In none of these cases was it necessary to re-examine the doctrine to grant relief to the Negro plaintiff. And in Sweatt v. Painter, supra, the Court expressly reserved decision on the question whether Plessy v. Ferguson should be held inapplicable to public education.

In the instant cases, that question is directly presented. Here, unlike Sweatt v. Painter, there are findings below that the Negro and white schools involved have been equalized, or are being equalized, with respect to buildings, curricula, qualifications and salaries of teachers, and other "tangible" factors.[9] Our decision, therefore, cannot turn on merely a comparison of these tangible factors in the Negro and white schools involved in each of the cases. We must look instead to the effect of segregation itself on public education.

In approaching this problem, we cannot turn the clock back to 1868 when the Amendment was adopted, or even to 1896 when Plessy v. Ferguson was written. We must consider public education in the light of its full develop-

6. The doctrine apparently originated in Roberts v. City of Boston, 59 Mass. 198, 206 (1850), upholding school segregation against attack as being violative of a state constitutional guarantee of equality. Segregation in Boston public schools was eliminated in 1855. Mass. Acts 1855, c. 256. But elsewhere in the North segregation in public education has persisted in some communities until recent years. It is apparent that such segregation has long been a nationwide problem, not merely one of sectional concern. [See Note 1 infra, page 438.]

7. See also Berea College v. Kentucky, 211 U.S. 45 (1908).

8. In the Cumming case, Negro taxpayers sought an injunction requiring the defendant school board to discontinue the operation of a high school for white children until the board resumed operation of a high school for Negro children. Similarly, in the Gong Lum case, the plaintiff, a child of Chinese descent, contended only that state authorities had misapplied the doctrine by classifying him with Negro children and requiring him to attend a Negro school.

9. In the Kansas case, the court below found substantial equality as to all such factors. 98 F. Supp. 797, 798. In the South Carolina case, the court below found that the defendants were proceeding "promptly and in good faith to comply with the court's decree." 103 F. Supp. 920, 921. In the Virginia case, the court below noted that the equalization program was already "afoot and progressing" (103 F. Supp. 337, 341); since then, we have been advised, in the Virginia Attorney General's brief on reargument, that the program has now been completed. In the Delaware case, the court below similarly noted that the state's equalization program was well under way. 91 A.2d 137, 149.

ment and its present place in American life throughout the Nation. Only in this way can it be determined if segregation in public schools deprives these plaintiffs of the equal protection of the laws.

Today, education is perhaps the most important function of state and local governments. Compulsory school attendance laws and the great expenditures for education both demonstrate our recognition of the importance of education to our democratic society. It is required in the performance of our most basic public responsibilities, even service in the armed forces. It is the very foundation of good citizenship. Today it is a principal instrument in awakening the child to cultural values, in preparing him for later professional training, and in helping him to adjust normally to his environment. In these days, it is doubtful that any child may reasonably be expected to succeed in life if he is denied the opportunity of an education. Such an opportunity, where the state has undertaken to provide it, is a right which must be made available to all on equal terms.

We come then to the question presented: Does segregation of children in public schools solely on the basis of race, even though the physical facilities and other "tangible" factors may be equal, deprive the children of the minority group of equal educational opportunities? We believe that it does.

In Sweatt v. Painter, supra, in finding that a segregated law school for Negroes could not provide them equal educational opportunities, this Court relied in large part on "those qualities which are incapable of objective measurement but which make for greatness in a law school." In McLaurin v. Oklahoma State Regents, supra, the Court, in requiring that a Negro admitted to a white graduate school be treated like all other students, again resorted to intangible considerations: ". . . his ability to study, to engage in discussions and exchange views with other students, and, in general, to learn his profession." Such considerations apply with added force to children in grade and high schools. To separate them from others of similar age and qualifications solely because of their race generates a feeling of inferiority as to their status in the community that may affect their hearts and minds in a way unlikely ever to be undone. The effect of this separation on their educational opportunities was well stated by a finding in the Kansas case by a court which nevertheless felt compelled to rule against the Negro plaintiffs:

> Segregation of white and colored children in public schools has a detrimental effect upon the colored children. The impact is greater when it has the sanction of the law; for the policy of separating the races is usually interpreted as denoting the inferiority of the negro group. A sense of inferiority affects the motivation of a child to learn. Segregation with the sanction of law, therefore, has a tendency to [retard] the educational and mental development of negro children and to deprive them of some of the benefits they would receive in a racial[ly] integrated school system.[10]

10. A similar finding was made in the Delaware case: "I conclude from the testimony that in our Delaware society, State-imposed segregation in education itself results in the Negro children, as a class, receiving educational opportunities which are substantially inferior to those available to white children otherwise similarly situated." 87 A.2d 862, 865.

Whatever may have been the extent of psychological knowledge at the time of Plessy v. Ferguson, this finding is amply supported by modern authority.[11] Any language in Plessy v. Ferguson contrary to this finding is rejected.

We conclude that in the field of public education the doctrine of "separate but equal" has no place. Separate educational facilities are inherently unequal. Therefore, we hold that the plaintiffs and others similarly situated for whom the actions have been brought are, by reason of the segregation complained of, deprived of the equal protection of the laws guaranteed by the Fourteenth Amendment. This disposition makes unnecessary any discussion whether such segregation also violates the Due Process Clause of the Fourteenth Amendment.[12]

Because these are class actions, because of the wide applicability of this decision, and because of the great variety of local conditions, the formulation of decrees in these cases presents problems of considerable complexity. On reargument, the consideration of appropriate relief was necessarily subordinated to the primary question — the constitutionality of segregation in public education. We have now announced that such segregation is a denial of the equal protection of the laws. In order that we may have the full assistance of the parties in formulating decrees, the cases will be restored to the docket, and the parties are requested to present further argument on Questions 4 and 5 previously propounded by the Court for the reargument this Term.[13]

11. K. B. Clark, Effect of Prejudice and Discrimination on Personality Development (Midcentury White House Conference on Children and Youth, 1950); Witmer and Kotinsky, Personality in the Making (1952), c. VI; Deutscher and Chein, The Psychological Effects of Enforced Segregation: A Survey of Social Science Opinion, 26 J. Psychol. 259 (1948); Chein, What are the Psychological Effects of Segregation Under Conditions of Equal Facilities?, 3 Int. J. Opinion and Attitude Res. 229 (1949); Brameld, Educational Costs, in Discrimination and National Welfare (MacIver, ed., 1949), 44-48; Frazier, The Negro in the United States (1949), 674-681. And see generally Myrdal, An American Dilemma (1944).

12. See Bolling v. Sharpe. . . . [347 U.S. 483, 497, 74 S. Ct. 686, 693, 98 L. Ed. 873, 884 (1954). In this companion case to Brown, involving segregation in the District of Columbia schools, the Court held that the Due Process Clause of the Fifth Amendment barred the district from discriminating on the basis of race.]

13. "4. Assuming it is decided that segregation in public schools violates the Fourteenth Amendment

"(a) would a decree necessarily follow providing that, within the limits set by normal geographic school districting, Negro children should forthwith be admitted to schools of their choice, or

"(b) may this Court, in the exercise of its equity powers, permit an effective gradual adjustment to be brought about from existing segregated systems to a system not based on color distinctions?

"5. On the assumption on which questions 4(a) and (b) are based, and assuming further that this Court will exercise its equity powers to the end described in question 4(b),

"(a) should this Court formulate detailed decrees in these cases;

"(b) if so, what specific issues should the decrees reach;

"(c) should this Court appoint a special master to hear evidence with a view to recommending specific terms for such decrees;

The Attorney General of the United States is again invited to participate. The Attorneys General of the states requiring or permitting segregation in public education will also be permitted to appear as amici curiae upon request to do so by September 15, 1954, and submission of briefs by October 1, 1954.

It is so ordered.

NOTES

1. In Roberts v. City of Boston, 59 Mass. (5 Cush.) 198 (1850), referred to by the Court in Brown No. 1 (footnote 6 supra, page 435), counsel for petitioners was the famous abolitionist Charles Sumner. His associate was Robert Morris, one of the first black lawyers admitted to practice in this country. See J. Daniels, In Freedom's Birthplace 448 (Johnson Reprint ed. 1968). Sumner and Morris had urged the Massachusetts court to end segregated public schools, for reasons quite similar to those that finally prevailed a century later:

> 1. According to the spirit of American institutions, and especially of the constitution of Massachusetts, (Part First, Articles I. and VI.,) all men, without distinction of color or race, are equal before the law.
>
> 2. The legislation of Massachusetts has made no discrimination of color or race in the establishment of the public schools. The laws establishing public schools speak of "schools for the instruction of children," generally, and "for the benefit of *all* the inhabitants of the town," not specifying any particular class, color, or race. . . . The provisions . . . , appropriating small sums out of the school fund, for the support of common schools among the Indians, do not interfere with this system. They partake of the anomalous character of all our legislation with regard to the Indians. And it does not appear, that any separate schools are established by law among the Indians, or that they are in any way excluded from the public schools in their neighborhood.
>
> 3. The courts of Massachusetts have never admitted any discrimination, founded on color or race, in the administration of the common schools, but have recognized the equal rights of all the inhabitants. . . .
>
> 4. The exclusion of colored children from the public schools, which are open to white children, is a source of practical inconvenience to them and their parents, to which white persons are not exposed, and is, therefore, a violation of equality.
>
> 5. The separation of children in the public schools of Boston, on account of color or race, is in the nature of caste, and is a violation of equality. . . .
>
> 6. The school committee have no power, under the constitution and laws of Massachusetts, to make any discrimination on account of color or race, among children in the public schools. . . .
>
> The regulations and by-laws of municipal corporations must be reasonable, or

---

"(d) should this Court remand to the courts of first instance with directions to frame decrees in these cases, and if so what general directions should the decrees of this Court include and what procedures should the courts of first instance follow in arriving at the specific terms of more detailed decrees?"

they are inoperative and void. . . . It is clear, that the committee may classify scholars, according to age and sex, for these distinctions are inoffensive, and recognized as legal . . . ; or according to their moral and intellectual qualifications, because such a power is necessary to the government of schools. But the committee cannot assume, without individual examination, that an entire race possess certain moral or intellectual qualities, which render it proper to place them all in a class by themselves.

But it is said, that the committee, in thus classifying the children, have not violated any principle of equality, inasmuch as they have provided a school with competent instructors for the colored children, where they enjoy equal advantages of instruction with those enjoyed by the white children. To this there are several answers: . . . 2d. It is not in fact an equivalent. It is the occasion of inconveniences to the colored children, to which they would not be exposed if they had access to the nearest public schools; it inflicts upon them the stigma of caste; and although the matters taught in the two schools may be precisely the same, a school exclusively devoted to one class must differ essentially, in its spirit and character, from that public school known to the law, where all classes meet together in equality. 3d. Admitting that it is an equivalent, still the colored children cannot be compelled to take it. They have an equal right with the white children to the general public schools.

7. The court will declare the by-law of the school committee, making a discrimination of color among children entitled to the benefit of the public schools, to be unconstitutional and illegal, although there are no express words of prohibition in the constitution and laws. Slavery was abolished in Massachusetts, by virtue of the declaration of rights in our constitution, without any specific words of abolition in that instrument, or in any subsequent legislation. Commonwealth v. Aves, 18 Pick. 193, 210. The same words, which are potent to destroy slavery, must be equally potent against any institution founded on caste. . . . If there should be any doubt in this case, the court should incline in favor of equality; as every interpretation is always made in favor of life and liberty. Rousseau says that "it is precisely because the force of things tends always to destroy equality, that the force of legislation ought always to tend to maintain it." In a similar spirit the court should tend to maintain it.

The fact, that the separation of the schools was originally made at the request of the colored parents, cannot affect the rights of the colored people, or the powers of the school committee. The separation of the schools, so far from being for the benefit of both races, is an injury to both. It tends to create a feeling of degradation in the blacks, and of prejudice and uncharitableness in the whites. (59 Mass. at 201-204.)

2. The litigation in Roberts was only one phase of a campaign that also utilized petitions, picketing and school boycotts, before the legislature ended school segregation in 1855. J. Daniels, supra at 448-49. The Roberts case was one of countless efforts made by blacks in the antebellum North to obtain access to the developing public school system. As can be seen in Leon Litwack's summary of this educational crusade, the opposition relied on arguments similar to those raised to evade or delay school desegregation in the post-Brown era.

L. LITWACK, NORTH OF SLAVERY
113-117, 120-121 (1961) *

EDUCATION: SEPARATE AND UNEQUAL

Education was one of the foremost aspirations of the northern Negro. "If we ever expect to see the influence of prejudice decrease and ourselves respected," a Negro national convention resolved in 1832, "it must be by the blessings of an enlightened education." This sentiment was repeated throughout the antebellum period. Through education, the Negro hoped to improve his economic status, produce his own literary and scientific figures, and break down the barriers of discrimination. However, the Negro's quest for educational opportunities, partly because he hoped to accomplish such goals, prompted some strong and frequently violent protests in the North. The possibility that Negro children would be mixed with white children in the same classroom aroused even greater fears and prejudices than those which consigned the Negro to an inferior place in the church, the theater, and the railroad car. This, indeed, constituted virtual amalgamation.

Although some white schools admitted Negroes, especially before 1820, most northern states either excluded them altogether or established separate schools for them. As early as 1787, Boston Negroes petitioned the legislature to grant them educational facilities, since they "now receive no benefit from the free schools." Forty years later, the first Negro newspaper repeated this complaint. "While the benevolence of the age has founded and endowed seminaries of Learning for all other classes and nations," it declared, "we have to lament, that as yet, no door is open to receive the degraded children of Africa. Alone they have stood — alone they remain stationary; while charity extends the hands to all others."

The means employed to exclude Negroes from the public schools varied only slightly from state to state. In New England, local school committees usually assigned Negro children to separate institutions, regardless of the district in which they resided. Pennsylvania and Ohio, although extending their public school privileges to all children, required district school directors to establish separate facilities for Negro students whenever twenty or more could be accommodated. The New York legislature authorized any school district, upon the approval of a town's school commissioners, to provide for segregation. The newer states frequently excluded Negroes from all public education, but by 1850, most of them had consented to separate instruction. In the absence of legal restrictions, custom and popular prejudice often excluded Negro children from the schools. For example, an Indianan noted in 1850 that the laws provided no racial distinctions in the state school system, but "the whites rose *en-masse*, and said your children shall not go to schools with our children, and they were consequently expelled. Thus, then, we see that in this respect, there is a higher law than the Constitutional law." By the 1830's, statute or custom placed Negro children in separate schools in nearly every northern community.

Proposals to educate Negroes invariably aroused bitter controversy, particularly in the new western states. The admission of Negroes to white schools, opponents maintained, would result in violence and prove fatal to public education. Moreover, some contended that Negroes, "after a certain age, did not correspondingly advance in learning — their intellect being apparently incapable of being cultured beyond a particular point." When an Ohio legislative committee rejected a petition to grant Negroes a share of the education fund, it conceded that this might "at first appear unnatural, and unbecoming a charitable, high-minded, and intelligent community," but the security of the government depended upon "the morality, virtue, and wisdom" of its white citizens and the school fund should thus not be confused with charity. Opponents also warned that equal educational privileges would encourage Negro immigration and antagonize southern-born residents. On the basis of such a pretext, a California mayor vetoed appropriations for Negro schools as "particularly obnoxious to those of our citizens who have immigrated from Southern States." The city aldermen defended his action with a warning against placing the two races on an equal basis, "not withstanding the distinction stamped by Divinity between them."

Delegates to the state constitutional conventions debated various proposals to exclude Negroes from the schools. Westerners, fearing an increase in Negro immigration, voiced some especially vehement objections. "They are not by nature equal to the whites," an Iowan declared, "and their children cannot be made equal to my children, or those of my constituents." In 1850, an Ohio convention delegate opposed any measure, including education, which would tend to encourage Negro immigration or impede colonization. Nine years later, a Kansas Republican warned that he would immediately object to any Negro's attending school with white children. However, he opposed any legal bars, claiming that the "neighborhood could protect itself." Other Kansas convention delegates predicted that voters would reject the proposed constitution unless it explicity prohibited racial mixing in the schools. As late as 1860, an Iowa congressman warned that no northwestern state would countenance biracial education. Antebellum constitutional provisions and legislation confirmed his prediction.

Southern representatives denounced congressional efforts to provide for Negro education in Washington, D.C. White parents would allow their children to remain in ignorance, opponents contended, rather than send them to school with Negroes. Moreover, integrated schools would conflict with the established policy of the southern and many northern states. Senator Jefferson Davis of Mississippi opposed any appropriations for Negro schools and charged that, aside from some men "led away by a sickly sentimentality," northern whites rejected any racial mixing.

The objections to classroom integration extended beyond the public schools to private academies and colleges. . . .

Excluded from white schools, Negroes moved to establish their own educational institutions and enlisted the support of abolitionists, some white philanthropists, and several state legislatures. By 1860, a number of private ventures had been attempted, with varying success, and nearly every northern state had provided for a Negro public school system.*

NOTE ON POSTBELLUM SCHOOL LITIGATION

Despite their defeat in Roberts v. City of Boston, 59 Mass. 198 (1850), blacks initiated a number of other legal actions across the North, in what usually proved vain efforts to invalidate laws and policies relegating blacks to segregated and highly inferior schools. Adverse decisions were often founded on the premise that, because race was a reasonable basis for classification, a state law requiring segregation was a simple "regulation" and not an "abridgement of rights protected by the Thirteenth and Fourteenth Amendments." Ward v. Flood, 48 Cal. 36, 17 Am. Rep. 405 (1874) (San Francisco). The court in Ward followed what became a pattern: (1) It relied on Roberts v. City of Boston in rejecting petitioner's argument that segregation was based on "an odious distinction of caste, founded on a deep-rooted prejudice in public opinion." (2) It found of no moment the fact that the petitioner lived closer to the white than the black school. (3) It limited its decision to cases where separate schools were actually available. Where only one public school was maintained in a district, blacks could not be excluded. See State ex rel. Pierce v. Union District School Trustees, 46 N.J. 76 (1884) (Burlington); Commonwealth ex rel. Brown v. Williamson, 30 Leg. Int. 406 (1873) (Wilkes-Barre, Pa.); State ex rel. Stoutmeyer v. Duffy, 7 Nevada 342, 8 Am. Rep. 713 (1872); People ex rel. Workman v. Board of Education, 18 Mich. 400 (1869) (Detroit).

Courts not only upheld the refusal of school boards to admit black children to white schools located closer to their homes, Ward v. Flood, supra; People ex rel. Dietz v. Easton, 13 Abb. Pr. (n.s.) 159 (S. Ct. Albany, N.Y. 1872), but upheld assignments to segregated schools even when these were located three to five miles away. People ex rel. King v. Gallagher, 93 N.Y. 438, 45 Am. Rep. 232 (1883) (Brooklyn); Cory v. Carter, 48 Ind. 327, 17 Am. Rep. 738 (1874) (Marion County); United States v. Buntin, 10 F. 730 (C.C.S.D. Ohio 1882) (Washington township). After reviewing a black father's request for admission of his three children to a nearby white school, based on the fact that they were forced to walk four miles to school, passing

* See also A. Meier and E. Rudwick, From Plantation to Ghetto 84-88 (Am. Cent. ed. 1966). Early school efforts for blacks in the South are summarized by Meier and Rudwick, supra at 141-148; and the subject is covered in great detail in both C. Woodson, The Education of the Negro Prior to 1861 (1919), and H. Bullock, A History of Negro Education in the South (Praeger ed. 1970).

white schools en route, while no white child had to walk more than two miles, the court in Ohio ex rel. Lewis v. Board of Education, 7 Ohio Dec. Reprint 129 (Dist. Ct. 1876) (Cincinnati), denied relief, ruling: "somebody must walk further than the rest. It is not possible for all the children to live in one spot, so as to place them all equally distant from the school."

In Lehew v. Brummell, 103 Mo. 546 (1890), white parents obtained an injunction against the school board to prevent the only four black children in their district from attending its only school. This order necessitated the black children's attendance at a separate school in a town three and one half miles away. A state law was approved providing that, where a school district contained fewer than twenty black students, it might form a joint district with a contiguous district if the result would enable the establishment of a separate school for more than twenty blacks. State ex rel. Garnes v. McCann, 21 Ohio St. 198 (1871) (Norwich township, Ohio).

The court in Garnes followed its earlier decision in Van Camp v. Board of Education, 9 Ohio St. 406 (1859), which upheld the exclusion of black children from white schools in a district where their number was insufficient to justify organizing a separate school. In Van Camp, petitioners argued that they were five-eighths white and three-eighths colored, and were indistinguishable from whites. Therefore, they argued that they were white in the legal sense. The court ruled against their construing the statutory words "white" and "colored" in their popular and ordinary sense. Moreover, the court found that petitioners were regarded as "colored" by the community and should not be forced upon white pupils even though they were more white than colored. The Ohio court's rather broad reading of the state statute took no more liberty with the principles of statutory construction than did the Supreme Court nearly seventy years later. In Gong Lum v. Rice, 275 U.S. 78, 48 S. Ct. 91, 72 L. Ed. 172 (1927), the Court upheld the exclusion of a Chinese child from a white school on the ground that Mississippi law required separate schools for the "white" and "colored" races, and the word "colored" could be interpreted to include all but the "white race."

Sometimes the disparities became too much even for nineteenth-century courts. Thus, a federal court used the Equal Protection Clause to void a Kentucky statute which directed that school taxes collected from whites be used to maintain white schools, and taxes from blacks to operate black schools. In operation, the scheme required duplication of facilities and resulted in a greatly inferior education for black children. Claybrook v. City of Owensboro, 16 F. 297 (D. Ky. 1883). Other courts reached similar conclusions where the law limited the taxing power to whites, who could raise funds to be used exclusively for white schools. Davenport v. Cloverport, 72 F. 689 (D. Ky. 1896). See also McFarland v. Goins, 96 Miss. 67, 50 So. 493 (1909); Williams v. Board of Education of Fairfax District, 45 W. Va. 199, 31 S.E. 985 (1898). But see Chrisman v. City of Brookhaven, 70 Miss. 477 (1892), which approved a bond issue for $15,000, of which $3,000 was for building a school for blacks, and $12,000 was for a white school.

Several courts refused to follow Roberts v. City of Boston, supra, and held that where local officials segregated their schools without legislative authority, mandamus would lie ordering the admission of black children to white schools. Clark v. Board of Directors, 24 Iowa 266 (1868); People ex rel. Workman v. Board of Education of Detroit, supra page 442. But the Kansas Supreme Court, in a radical departure from most authority, not only granted a writ of mandamus requiring a school board to admit a black child to a white school, because in the absence of a state statute expressly requiring segregated schools, the school board lacked authority to exclude children on the basis of race or color; but also expressed a preference for integrated schools. Board of Education of Ottawa v. Tinnon, 26 Kan. 1 (1881). The court saw no good reason for separating children on the basis of race, and asked, "Is it not better for the grand aggregate of human society, as well as for individuals, that all children should mingle together and learn to know each other?" Answering its question in a fashion foreshadowing decisions in the mid-twentieth century, the Kansas court stated:

> At the common schools, where both sexes and all kinds of children mingle together, we have the great world in miniature; there they may learn human nature in all its phases, with all its emotions, passions and feelings, its loves and hates, its hopes and fears, its impulses and sensibilities; there they may learn the secret springs of human actions, and the attractions and repulsions, which lend with irresistible force to particular lines of conduct. But on the other hand, persons by isolation may become strangers even in their own country; and by being strangers, will be of but little benefit either to themselves or to society. As a rule, people cannot afford to be ignorant of the society which surrounds them; and as all kinds of people must live together in the same society, it would seem to be better that all should be taught in the same schools. (26 Kan. at 19.)

QUESTIONS

1. In the antebellum South, the fear that literacy would expose the slaves to abolitionist literature and ideas led to legal restrictions on any education for blacks not deemed necessary to their work. In the post–Civil War period, the general belief in black inferiority, the desire to maintain blacks at the bottom of the societal scale, and the unwillingness to devote scarce educational resources to black schools, all probably contributed to the continuing opposition to education for blacks. But do these factors explain why most courts rejected the arguments advanced in 1850 by counsel in Roberts v. City of Boston, supra, and adopted in 1881 by the Kansas Supreme Court in Board of Education of Ottawa v. Tinnon, supra? Why did these courts so readily uphold community decisions to bar black children from public schools or approve their attendance at segregated facilities that by distance and condition were usually inferior to white schools?

2. Does Professor Harlan's study of New Orleans school desegregation in the 1870s, infra, suggest that blacks generally were denied decent schools for their children because they lacked the political or economic power needed to obtain them?

HARLAN, DESEGREGATION IN NEW ORLEANS PUBLIC SCHOOLS DURING RECONSTRUCTION, 67 Am. Hist. Rev. 663-75 (April 1962). Professor Louis Harlan's essay on this hard-to-believe occurrence is summarized here, in order to facilitate comparison with other school districts in which, during both the nineteenth and twentieth centuries, public schools have been successfully integrated.

It is a fact little known even among historians that the city of New Orleans in the 1870s experienced a six-year period of school desegregation, unparalleled in any other Southern community before 1954. Historians of the Louisiana Reconstruction and of Southern education have been quick to pronounce the New Orleans experiment a total failure; but these historians have been swayed too much by newspaper headlines and stories about violence and white resistance to the experiment, while ignoring the less dramatic evidence of the return to quiet that usually followed. Harlan quotes the radical Republican State Superintendent of Education, Thomas Conway, who, in an 1874 interview with the editor of the Washington National Republican, spoke somewhat hyperbolically about color-blind "dancing on the green." Harlan concludes that the truth of the Louisiana experiment lies "somewhere in between" Conway's half-rhapsodic description and historians' evidence of evasion and resistance.

The story begins at the Louisiana Constitutional Convention of 1867, at which the state's constitution was adopted with a clause requiring desegregation of the schools. After the convention, New Orleans whites, who outnumbered the city's blacks by a ratio of three to one, united behind white Republican officials and the white members of the school board in an effort to block desegregation; white newspapers urged whites to place their children in segregated private schools and to refuse to pay the school tax, and they predicted violence and race war if desegregation were effected. Pupil placement laws and other devices that would become familiar after 1954 were employed. But finally a court order in December 1870 was acknowledged by all parties to be binding, and desegregation went into effect.

There are difficulties in measuring the extent to which the New Orleans schools were actually desegregated, largely because of the peculiar nature of New Orleans' racially mixed population, which included many light-skinned persons of mixed black and Latin origins. But it is possible, from records of examinations and the closing exercises of the school, to recognize at least twenty-one desegregated schools — one third of the schools in the city. Desegregation was never required or imposed; the school children simply made application to the schools of their choice, and the applications were approved without regard to the race of the applicant. First- and eighth-graders were all required to choose their schools; other school children could either make a choice or be assigned to a school on the basis of previous attendance. The most thoroughly desegregated schools were those wherein resided most of the old French and Spanish residents of the city, as well as the newer German, Italian and Irish immigrants; each of five schools in this area had at least seventy-five blacks throughout the period. More surprising, perhaps, was the fact that there was considerable desegregation even in the so-called "American" districts. Two of three high schools there were desegregated. The total enrollment in the New Orleans schools declined immediately after desegregation, from 24,892 in 1870 to 19,901 in 1871, but by 1875 the enrollment had risen to 26,251, the highest number registered for the city at any time in the nineteenth century. Of this enrollment, about 21,000 were white students and 5000 colored. The elementary schools which had the highest percentages of students qualifying for high schools, the Fillmore Boys' School and the Bienville School, remained overcrowded despite desegregation, as the quality of the education they offered remained attractive to black and white alike.

Private school attendance increased in New Orleans at the outset of desegregation, only to fall back later. Figures for such attendance rose from about 10,000 in 1870 to about 17,000 in 1873, but declined to about 14,000 two years later. The violence and tax resistance predicted in the late 1860s never materialized. Harlan suggests two reasons for this: first, the skill with which desegregation was administered; and second (and more important), the fact that New Orleans whites were at the time seeking an alliance with Negro voters, offering to exchange guarantees of black civil rights for black assistance in ridding the state of the carpetbaggers. From 1871 to 1874, white interest lay essentially in ousting the carpetbaggers and reducing taxes. White political leaders made overtures to the blacks in 1871 and 1872, vaguely promising protection of black civil rights — office holding, suffrage and desegregation in schools and public accommodations — in exchange for black assistance in ousting carpetbaggers. When these efforts failed in the elections of 1872, the whites made even more explicit commitments to black rights in the 1873 Unification Movement. Among those promises was one to support the school desegregation policies. Former Confederate General P. G. T. Beauregard, the merchant Isaac Marks and a thousand other citizens of both races signed a manifesto endorsing the New Orleans desegregation program; it was read to wildly cheering rallies.

But the unification movement failed and its failure signaled to New Orleans whites a change in policy and leadership: if the blacks could not be persuaded to vote with the whites, then enough blacks must be kept from the polls to ensure a white majority. The White League was forming throughout 1874. In September the league staged a three-day coup d'état in New Orleans, and took over the city government until ousted by federal troups. The league's activities led to the well-known school riots of December 1874, in which gangs of white youths, who came to be called the "boy regulators," went into the New Orleans schools and bodily threw out black pupils. Although some were students, these gangs were probably organized and manned by White League outsiders; in any event, after a few days of rioting the league was persuaded to call off the "regulators." The rise of the White League signaled the end of the Louisiana Reconstruction. Even so, there was no immediate rush to resegregate the schools. But when the city school board voted to segregate the schools for the next term, neither the governor nor the courts, in spite of the 1867 constitution, came to the aid of the blacks. The constitution itself was rewritten in 1879 to permit segregation, and again in 1898 to require it.

The author concludes that a major reason for what brief success the New Orleans desegregation experiment enjoyed was universal Negro suffrage, backed by strong federal sanctions. Black votes secured the passage of the 1867 constitution and elected school board officials to carry out desegregation. For black votes, the whites were willing to use acquiescence to desegregation as a tool for bargaining. In 1877, the federal sanctions backing black suffrage were removed, and desegregation was an early casualty.

Black suffrage, however, does not wholly explain the situation, because the black majorities were in rural Louisiana — where desegregation was never accomplished — rather than in New Orleans, and because other states with black voting majorities in this period never undertook a comparable experiment. Nor does the urban setting explain what happened: the city of Charleston, for example, never desegregated its schools, even though the 1868 South Carolina constitution, like Louisiana's 1867 document, required it. There were certain unique factors in the New Orleans experience. New Orleans was the South's most cosmopolitan city: not only was its population derived from diverse and unusual, largely Latin, sources, but its frequent travelers and clients must have reminded the residents that Southern racial attitudes and practices were not widely accepted. Also, the city's merchants were anxious for federal subsidies, harbor and river projects and the like; indeed, the whole spirit of the unification movement, which had great support in New Orleans, suggested that many whites were more interested in economic development than social control.

Although New Orleans did not initially support secession and was in the Confederacy for less than two years, it underwent Reconstruction for fifteen. The colored population was residentially dispersed throughout the city, and comprised only one fourth of the population, which must have reduced the white fears of engulfment and subjugation. In addition, the black community in New Orleans was unique; many of the blacks had been educated in the North or in France; many served with the Union occupation forces; there were many doctors, lawyers, caterers, merchants, cotton manufacturers, and even newspaper editors and poets. The blacks maintained an efficient political organization, and they achieved an impressive degree of unity, since light-skinned Negroes abandoned early efforts to be classed as whites, and the black bourgeoisie showed none of the isolation which E. Franklin Frazier has discerned in the black bourgeoisie of the twentieth century. Thus, the short-lived successful desegregation in New Orleans was a function of a unique set of circumstances — the existence of a black elite, the cosmopolitan nature of the city, the economic concern of the mercantile community, and the political alliance of the rural black majority, the urban black minority, and the Northern Republicans in control of federal and state governments. "Such a fortuitous convergence, however, depended too heavily on one sine qua non, the temporary sojourn of federal power in the South. Not until the whole region came more closely to resemble New Orleans, not until an urban South and a more strongly based Negro community emerged, could the experiment be renewed auspiciously." 67 Am. Hist. Rev. at 75.

QUESTIONS

1. Perhaps unconsciously, Harlan refers to school desegregation in New Orleans as an "experiment" even though the state's constitution required it. What is the significance of his explanation of the brief success of desegregated schools for contemporary black leaders and civil rights lawyers?

2. Are the factors Harlan saw as critical to the New Orleans "experiment" in the 1870s prerequisites for successful school desegregation in the 1970s?

CUMMING v. RICHMOND COUNTY BOARD of EDUCATION, 175 U.S. 528, 20 S. Ct. 197, 44 L. Ed. 262 (1899). The Supreme Court's adoption of the "separate but equal" doctrine in Plessy v. Ferguson, 163 U.S. 537, 16 S. Ct. 1138, 41 L. Ed. 256 (1896), page 204 supra, extinguished any hope either that the New Orleans experiment might soon be repeated, or that the pro-integration rationale expressed in Board of Education of Ottawa v. Tinnon, page 444 supra, might spread. Three years after Plessy, the Court also dashed expectations that it would seriously enforce the "equal" part of its "separate but equal" standard.

In Cumming, three black parents and taxpayers sought, in 1897, to enjoin a Georgia school board from collecting school tax levies from them for a high school for black children which the board had closed. The board had been maintaining two high schools: one for black children, charging $10 per year tuition, and one for white girls, charging an annual tuition of $15. (There were in the county a private high school for white boys, also charging a tuition of $15 per year, and three private sectarian high schools that accepted black students.) The school board had subsidized both public high schools out of tax funds to which the plaintiffs had contributed. When a serious shortage of educational facilities for black children in the primary grades developed, the board decided, for what it called "purely economic reasons," to discontinue the black high school and open four primary schools in the same building. In the absence of other funds to provide for the needed primary school facilities, said the board in its answer to the plaintiffs' petition, "it would be unwise and unconscionable to keep up a high school for sixty pupils and turn away three hundred little negroes who are asking to be taught their alphabet and to read and write. No part of the funds of this

Board accrued or accruing and no property appropriated to the education of the negro race has been taken from them." 175 U.S. at 533. The lower court granted an injunction restraining the board from operating any high school for white children until it also provided equal high school facilities for blacks. The Georgia Supreme Court, however, reversed the lower court's decision, and ordered the case dismissed. On appeal to the United States Supreme Court, the plaintiffs argued that they had been denied the equal protection of the laws, but once again they lost. Not only did the Court fail to repudiate the doctrine of "separate but equal"; it also refused to establish standards as to the degree of equality that would satisfy that formula. Justice Harlan, who had dissented in Plessy v. Ferguson, wrote for a unanimous Court:

It was said at the argument that the vice in the common-school system of Georgia was the requirement that the white and colored children of the state be educated in separate schools. But we need not consider that question in this case. No such issue was made in the pleadings. Indeed, the plaintiffs distinctly state that they have no objection to the tax in question so far as levied for the support of primary, intermediate, and grammar schools, in the management of which the rule as to the separation of races is enforced. We must dispose of the case as it is presented by the record.

The plaintiffs in error complain that the board of education used the funds in its hands to assist in maintaining a high school for white children without providing a similar school for colored children. The substantial relief asked is an injunction that would either impair the efficiency of the high school provided for white children or compel the board to close it. But if that were done, the result would only be to take from white children educational privileges enjoyed by them, without giving to colored children additional opportunities for the education furnished in high schools. The colored school children of the county would not be advanced in the matter of their education by a decree compelling the defendant board to cease giving support to a high school for white children. The board had before it the question whether it should maintain, under its control, a high school for about 60 colored children or withhold the benefits of education in primary schools from 300 children of the same race. It was impossible, the board believed, to give educational facilities to the 300 colored children who were unprovided for if it maintained a separate school for the 60 children who wished to have a high-school education. Its decision was in the interest of the greater number of colored children, leaving the smaller number to obtain a high-school education in existing private institutions at an expense not beyond that incurred in the high school discontinued by the board.

We are not permitted by the evidence in the record to regard that decision as having been made with any desire or purpose on the part of the board to discriminate against any of the colored school children of the county on account of their race. But if it be assumed that the board erred in supposing that its duty was to provide educational facilities for the 300 colored children who were without an opportunity in primary schools to learn the alphabet and to read and write, rather than to maintain a school for the benefit of the 60 colored children who wished to attend a high school, that was not an error which a court of equity should attempt to remedy by an injunction that would compel the board to withhold all assistance from the high school maintained for white children. If, in some appropriate proceeding instituted directly for that purpose, the plaintiffs had sought to compel the board of education, out of the funds in its hands or under its control, to establish and maintain a high school for colored children, and if it appeared that the board's refusal to maintain such a school was in fact an abuse of its discretion and in hostility to the colored population because of their race, different questions might have arisen in the state court.

The state court did not deem the action of the board of education in suspending temporarily and for economic reasons the high school for colored children a sufficient reason why the defendant should be restrained by injunction from maintaining an existing high school for white children. It rejected the suggestion that the board proceeded in bad faith or had abused the discretion with which it was invested by the statute under which it proceeded or had acted in hostility to the colored race. Under the circumstances disclosed, we cannot say that this action of the state court was, within the meaning of the Fourteenth Amendment, a denial by the state to the plaintiffs and to those associated with them of the equal protection of the laws or of any privileges belonging to them as citizens of the United States. We may add that while all admit that the benefits and burdens of public taxation must be shared by citizens without discrimination against any class on account of their race, the education of the people in schools maintained by state taxation is a matter belonging to the respective states, and any interference on the part of Federal authority with the management of such schools cannot be justified except in the case of a clear and unmistakable disregard of rights secured by the supreme law of the land. We have here no such case to be determined; and as this view disposes of the only question which this court has jurisdiction to review and decide, the judgment is affirmed. (175 U.S. at 543-545.)

QUESTIONS

1. What did Justice Harlan mean when he wrote "we need not consider that question [the validity of Georgia school segregation laws] in this case. No such issue was made in the pleadings"? Didn't plaintiffs' request that the white high school be closed until the black school was reopened raise this issue sufficiently to permit review? Was it possible to support the school board's action without, in effect, approving the state's segregation laws?

2. Did counsel for the black high school children in Cumming v. Board of Education make a tactical error in not placing greater emphasis on the Equal Protection Clause, and seeking admission of the black students to the white school during the "temporary" suspension of the black school? Would the "separate but equal" rule of Plessy v. Ferguson support or bar such relief?

3. Does the result in Cumming reveal the "separate but equal" doctrine as a rule based on reason or convenience? Assuming that, given the state of knowledge about race at the turn of the century, it is possible to conclude that state laws requiring separation of the races had a rational basis, what deficiencies in the courts permitted condoning such flagrant breaches of the equal portion of the separate but equal doctrine?

4. Can it be that once the law validates the enforced separation of a majority and minority group, the pressures to exploit the minority become overwhelming, and requirements of equality for the minority — even though the condition upon which the law's acquiescence to the separation was based — become impossible to enforce?

NOTES

1. Following its decision in Cumming v. Board of Education, it was an apparently easy step for the Court to uphold a Kentucky statute that subjected to heavy fine a private college that admitted both white and black students. The Court reasoned that, since the state which chartered the college could revoke that charter, it could also amend it to prohibit instruction of the two races at the same time and in the same place without defeating or impairing the object of the original charter. Berea College v. Kentucky, 211 U.S. 45, 29 S. Ct. 33, 53 L. Ed. 81 (1908). Justice Harlan, after his surprising lapse in Cumming, returned to his dissenting role in the Berea College case. He warned that, if the state could limit the association of white and colored persons in private schools, it could also bar minority religious and nationality groups, not only from schools, but from churches, the marketplace and other public places — a warning that by 1908 had become fact in many jurisdictions. See C. Woodward, The Strange Career of Jim Crow (2d rev. ed. 1966).

2. Predictably, after the decisions in the Plessy, Cumming, and Berea College cases, blacks encountered even more difficulty in obtaining from the lower courts relief from serious racial inequities. A Maryland court upheld the exclusion of a black pupil who had been nominated by a city council member to an educational institution which was not a part of the public school system, but which received aid from the municipality, under a contract in which the school agreed to provide instruction for a number of pupils nominated by the city council. State ex rel. Clark v. Maryland Institute for Promotion of Mechanic Arts, 87 Md. 643, 41 A. 126 (1898).

3. In a Kansas case, black children had been assigned to a school near a noisy railroad yard. The children had to travel long distances and cross several busy railroad tracks, with unavoidable, lengthy delays at the crossings, where they had to wait in all kinds of weather. The court acknowledged that they were in effect excluded from school unless they risked life and limb. Nevertheless, the court refused to order their admission to white schools, but held them entitled to attend some school where these difficulties did not exist. Williams v. Board of Education, 79 Kan. 202, 99 P. 216 (1908).

4. But despite these setbacks, blacks continued to challenge applications of the separate but equal doctrine. Professor Arthur Larson has compiled cases in which at least sixty objective factors of disparity have been litigated, involving, for example, physical facilities and equipment, the number and qualification of teachers, the richness of the curriculum, and teachers' salaries. Larson, The New Law of Race Relations, 1969 Wis. L. Rev. 470, 482-483.

5. But litigation could not bring equality for blacks under the easily evaded "separate but equal" standard, in a society whose attitude toward the education of blacks ranged from apathy to outright hostility. In 1915, South Carolina was spending an average of $23.76 on the education of each white child and $2.91 on that of each black child. As late as 1931, six Southern states (Alabama, Arkansas, Florida, Georgia, and North and South Carolina) spent less than one third as much for black children as for whites, and ten years later this figure had risen to only 44 percent. At the time of the 1954 decision in Brown v. Board of Education, the South as a whole was spending on the average $165 a year for a white pupil, and $115 for a black. A. Lewis, The School Desegregation Cases, Portrait of a Decade 17 (1965). See also L. Harlan, Separate and Unequal (Atheneum ed. 1968).

6. In the late 1940s, the Supreme Court, in the series of graduate school cases cited in Brown v. Board of Education, supra page 435, finally began recognizing both the physical and inherent inequality of segregated schools. While the Court in each case was able to strike down the segregation policy without re-examining the separate but equal doctrine, it became apparent that this issue would be raised in the context of public school segregation. The fact that society had greatly changed raised the possibility that the Court might finally adopt an interpretation of the Constitution that had been urged on behalf of blacks for over a century.

NOTE: RIGHTS UNDER BROWN AND THE ASSOCIATIONAL DILEMMA

Many believe that the essence of Brown I is the associational right of black children to attend the same schools as whites. And the Supreme Court did find that "To separate [black children] from others of similar age and qualifications solely because of their race generates a feeling of inferiority as to their status in the community that may affect their hearts and minds in a way unlikely ever to be undone." 347 U.S. at 494. But it is the associational aspects of school desegregation that appear to cause much of the resistance to compliance. Professor Herbert Wechsler criticized the Court's failure to base the Brown opinion on grounds of "adequate neutrality and generality." He felt that the real issue in state-enforced segregation is "the denial by the state of freedom to associate, a denial that impinges in the same way on any groups or races that may be involved. . . .

"But if the freedom of association is denied by segregation, integration forces an association upon those for whom it is unpleasant or repugnant. . . ." If the state must choose between denying the association to those who wish it, or imposing it on those who would avoid it, Wechsler wondered whether there is a basis in neutral principles for holding that the Constitution demands that the claims for association should prevail. He concludes, "I should like to think there is, but I confess I have not written the opinion. To write it is for me the challenge of the school-segregation cases." Wechsler, Toward Neutral Principles of Constitutional Law, 73 Harv. L. Rev. 1, 15, 31-34 (1959).

Several writers accepted Wechsler's challenge. See Pollak, Racial Discrimination and Judicial Integrity: A Reply to Professor Wechsler, 108 U. Pa. L. Rev. 1 (1959); Black, The Lawfulness of the Segregation Decisions, 69 Yale L.J. 421 (1960); Heyman, The Chief Justice, Racial Segregation and the Friendly Critics, 49 Calif. L. Rev. 104 (1961). But the suggested rationales have not altered public resistance, which delayed measurable compliance with Brown for more than a decade and which, if anything, has stiffened in recent years as courts have required assignments of students to other than their neighborhood schools to effect desegregation of the system.

Although Judge Weick was a dissenter in Northcross v. Board of Education of Memphis, 466 F.2d 890 (6th Cir. 1972), in which the court ordered the bussing of thousands of students to eliminate one-race schools, he probably spoke for a large number of citizens when he wrote:

> But what about the black and white children who do not want to be bused away from their neighborhood schools? Do they have no constitutional rights? It would appear that this issue has been given scant consideration by the Courts. Yet, merely because a child's skin is white or black, he is on that account, and without his consent or that of his parents, assigned to a particular school, and bused away from his neighborhood school in order to achieve a mixture of the races in each school in the city. I submit that the Constitution requires no such thing.
>
> It is not claimed that these unfortunate children, who are the victims of induced busing, have committed any offense. And we are living in a free society in which one of the privileges is the right of association.
>
> The average American couple who are raising their children, scrape and save money to buy a home in a nice residential neighborhood, near a public school. One can imagine their frustration when they find their plans have been destroyed by the judgment of a federal court.
>
> The elimination of neighborhood schools necessarily interferes with the interest in and participation by parents in the operation of the schools through parent-teachers' associations, interferes with activities of children out of school, and interferes with their privilege of association, and it deprives them of walk in schools. It can even lower the quality of education. (466 F.2d at 898.)

As the following excerpt from the transcript of a 1965 hearing in a Mobile school case shows,* there is educational value growing out of black-white contact in an integrated school setting. But how many black children can be expected to share the courage and faith by which Miss Davis transformed hostility into a learning experience?

* Record at 128-133, Davis v. Board of School Comm'n of Mobile Co., 364 F.2d 896 (5th Cir. 1966).

Birdie Mae Davis — for Plaintiff's — Direct

Q. You indicated that at first it was very bad, tell us how it has been since the early days? A. Well, now, it has gotten a little better, but it is still pretty bad. Some of the boys will gang around and get in gangs and mock us and call us names and try to do things to make us feel bad, but that is all; most of the girls are pretty nice. It is just the boys.

Q. How do you feel when they do this? Do they succeed in making you feel badly or do they make you cry? A. At first, it used to worry me, but now it does not, because after I have made a distinction between the two races, I find that at least, in my opinion, that they don't want us there, because they are afraid that we could do better, because I had an incident in class where we were debating, and I think I was getting the best of the debate.

Q. Do you recall the nature of the debate at all? A. Yes, it was involving Martin Luther King. There was an editorial in the paper, and he made a statement which was not true, he said that Martin Luther King was a communist, and I asked him on what he based his statement, what facts, and he didn't have any, and so the debate continued from that, and our teacher had to stop us, because there was getting to be a lot of fussing and turmoil in the class. . . .

Q. How about the teachers? A. The teachers are very nice. At first, about one or two were pretty prejudiced, but they became much better.

Q. How did you determine they were pretty prejudiced? A. Because our government teacher, whenever she would call on someone in class and no one would know and I would raise my hand, she would disregard my hand and she would go on and answer the question herself, or when we would give our current events — we would be talking about politics and extremists, and she would take the side of the class and we would be the only ones not for extremism. . . .

Q. How about the situation in your classes, in your courses, do you find there is any difference in the way you are taught at Murphy as opposed to Negro schools? A. I think that at Murphy, due to the fact that they have more equipment, I think we learn much more. . . .

Q. In your opinion, are you learning more or less? A. I think more. . . .

Q. After you consider all of the good things that happened and the bad things that happened, would you recommend to other Negro children that they try to go to desegregated schools and get a desegregated education? A. Yes, sir.

QUESTIONS

1. While the associational issue was a critical feature of Brown for Wechsler, is there anything in the history of black efforts to obtain quality public schooling which suggests that the desegregation cases were brought to enable black children to associate with whites in public schools? Was there a stronger and more pragmatic reason, based on the bitter experience of black parents and their lawyers with "separate but equal" schools, that black children could hope to obtain the same quality education as white children only by attending white schools? Is it possible to satisfy the constitutional rights of blacks, under Brown, to a desegregated education, as long as whites are determined to resist the associational aspects of those rights?

2. How important was the associational feature of Brown to the decision? Was it the racial classification that the Court decided was invalid? Such a conclusion is supported by the per curiam reversal of other public facilities on the authority of Brown, see supra page 208, but what of the Court's refusal to expressly reverse Plessy v. Ferguson?

3. Did Wechsler miss the mark by defining the issue as the right of association or nonassociation? Is it rather the right of whites to maintain a higher societal status than blacks which motivates resistance to Brown? After all, blacks and whites, particularly in the South, have long experienced a close association in many areas, but with the enforced or easily enforceable qualification that whites were dominant and blacks subordinant in any given relationship. This being so, does phrasing the question in terms of a "right to association" provide it with a constitutional legitimacy that is perhaps not deserved?

4. But if the issue for whites is really class status, isn't the resistance to Brown likely to prove far stronger than if the concern were a mere constitutional right of association?

B. POST-BROWN SOUTHERN SCHOOL LITIGATION

1. Defining "All Deliberate Speed"

BROWN v. BOARD OF EDUCATION (No. 2), 349 U.S. 294, 75 S. Ct. 753, 99 L. Ed. 1083 (1955). Following reargument on the question of relief, at which argument the Attorney General and those states requiring or permitting segregated public schools were invited to present their views, the Court rejected petitioners' requests for immediate relief in favor of remand of the cases to the district courts for the formulation of individual decrees. The United States, as did the states and the school boards, had urged this disposition, pointing out in great detail the administrative and academic problems involved in compliance. While acknowledging that community hostility might be experienced, the federal government's brief predicted: "We do not believe that there is a warrant for presuming that responsible officials and citizens will tolerate violations of the Constitution." Brief for the United States at 18.

Speaking for the Court, Chief Justice Warren adopted the position of the states and the federal government:

> Full implementation of these constitutional principles may require solution of varied local school problems. School authorities have the primary responsibility for elucidating, assessing, and solving these problems: courts will have to consider whether the action of school authorities constitutes good faith implementation of the governing constitutional principles. Because of their proximity to local conditions and the possible need for further hearings, the courts which originally heard these cases can best perform this judicial appraisal. Accordingly, we believe it appropriate to remand the cases to those courts.

In fashioning and effectuating the decrees, the courts will be guided by equitable principles. Traditionally, equity has been characterized by a practical flexibility in shaping its remedies and by a facility for adjusting and reconciling public and private needs. These cases call for the exercise of these traditional attributes of equity power. At stake is the personal interest of the plaintiffs in admission to public schools as soon as practicable on a nondiscriminatory basis. To effectuate this interest may call for elimination of a variety of obstacles in making the transition to school systems operated in accordance with the constitutional principles set forth in our May 17, 1954, decision. Courts of equity may properly take into account the public interest in the elimination of such obstacles in a systematic and effective manner. But it should go without saying that the vitality of these constitutional principles cannot be allowed to yield simply because of disagreement with them.

While giving weight to these public and private considerations, the courts will require that the defendants make a prompt and reasonable start toward full compliance with our May 17, 1954, ruling. Once such a start has been made, the courts may find that additional time is necessary to carry out the ruling in an effective manner. The burden rests upon the defendants to establish that such time is necessary in the public interest and is consistent with good faith compliance at the earliest practicable date. To that end, the courts may consider problems related to administration, arising from the physical condition of the school plant, the school transportation system, personnel, revision of school districts and attendance areas into compact units to achieve a system of determining admission to the public schools on a nonracial basis, and revision of local laws and regulations which may be necessary in solving the foregoing problems. They will also consider the adequacy of any plans the defendants may propose to meet these problems and to effectuate a transition to a racially nondiscriminatory school system. During this period of transition, the courts will retain jurisdiction of these cases.

The judgments below, except that in the Delaware case, are accordingly reversed and the cases are remanded to the District Courts to take such proceedings and enter such orders and decrees consistent with this opinion as are necessary and proper to admit to public schools on a racially nondiscriminatory basis with all deliberate speed the parties to these cases. The judgment in the Delaware case — ordering the immediate admission of the plaintiffs to schools previously attended only by white children — is affirmed on the basis of the principles stated in our May 17, 1954, opinion, but the case is remanded to the Supreme Court of Delaware for such further proceedings as that Court may deem necessary in light of this opinion.

It is so ordered.

CARTER, THE WARREN COURT AND DESEGREGATION
The Warren Court: A Critical Analysis, 46, 52-57
(R. Sayler, B. Boyer, R. Gooding, eds. 1969)

After declaring in Brown I that segregated education denied the constitutional guaranty of equal protection, a year later in Brown II the Warren Court addressed itself to the question of what remedy should be granted. The formula adopted by the Court — requiring a "good faith" start in the transformation from a dual to a unitary school system, with compliance being accomplished with "all deliberate speed" — was a grave mistake. . . .

Although the Court denied that this formula was intended to do more than allow time for necessary administrative changes which transformation to a desegregated school system required, it is clear that what the formula required was movement toward compliance on terms that the white South could accept. Until Brown II, constitutional rights had been defined as personal and present. In the exercise of that ephemeral quality called judicial statesmanship, the Warren Court sacrificed individual and immediate vindication of the newly discovered right to desegregated education in favor of a mass solution. This was frequently reflected by the Court's tendency to avoid individual solutions in favor of approving long-range desegregation plans that would presumably benefit large groups of students in the future.[45]

The Court undoubtedly failed to realize the depth or nature of the problem. It undertook to oversee the pace of desegregation and apparently believed that its show of compassion and understanding of the problem facing the white South would help develop a willingness to comply. Instead, the "all deliberate speed" formula aroused the hope that resistance to the constitutional imperative would succeed. . . . [T]he Court did condemn open resistance with firm resolve;* but since its concern was to secure "an initial

45. In Hawkins v. Board of Control of Florida, 350 U.S. 413 (1956), the Court made clear that its "all deliberate speed" formula was applicable only to grade and secondary school desegregation. The personal and present nature of the right to equal education remained unimpaired at all other educational levels and thus required immediate vindication. More recently, in Watson v. Memphis, 373 U.S. 526 (1963), involving segregation in a public park, it made the same point.

* Cooper v. Aaron, 358 U.S. 1, 78 S. Ct. 1401, 3 L. Ed. 2d 5 (1958). In its first school decision after Brown, the Court convened specially to review a petition by the Little Rock, Arkansas School Board, requesting a stay of its 1958 integration plan because of the widespread public hostility. The governor's dispatching of National Guard units to keep black students from entering the high school had received nationwide attention. The school board argued that normal educational activities could not be conducted in the hostile atmosphere caused by the presence of the black students. In an unprecedented opinion signed by all nine justices, the Court unanimously affirmed the Brown holding and, notwithstanding its recognition of the chaotic, tense and violent conditions that had existed during the 1957-1958 school year, denied the requested delay. It found that the adverse conditions were directly traceable to the behavior of state officials and stated that such conditions could be brought under control by state action. Citing Buchanan v. Warley, 245 U.S. 60 (1917), the Court said, "the constitutional rights of [the black children] are not to be sacrificed or yielded to the violence and disorder which have followed upon the actions of the Governor and Legislature. Thus, law and order are not here to be preserved by depriving the Negro children of their constitutional rights." 358 U.S. at 16. Rejecting contentions of the governor and legislature that they were not bound by the holding in the Brown case, the Court cited Article 6 of the Constitution, which makes the Constitution the supreme law of the land, and stated that under Marbury v. Madison, 1 Cranch 137 (1803), "The federal judiciary is supreme in the exposition of the law of the Constitution. . . . No state legislator or executive or judicial officer can war against the Constitution without violating his undertaking to support it. . . ." 358 U.S. at 18.

Courts gave short shrift to "interposition acts" passed by Southern legislatures in their attempts to negate the effect of the Brown decision. In Bush v. New Orleans Parish School Board, 188 F. Supp. 916 (E.D. La.), *aff'd,* 365 U.S. 569 (1961), the court found the

break in the long established pattern of excluding Negro children from schools attended by white children, the principal focus was in obtaining for these Negro children courageous enough to break with tradition a place in the white school." [Green v. County School Board, 391 U.S. 430, 435 (1968), infra page 462.]

In its anxiety to get the desegregation process moving at all costs, the Court condoned the application of procedural requirements and pupil placement laws which it knew were designed to delay or evade substantial compliance with the principles enunciated in Brown I. For eight years after its implementation decision, the Court refused to review any case in which questions were raised concerning the validity of pupil placement regulations or the appropriateness of applying the doctrine of exhaustion of administrative remedies to frustrate suits seeking to vindicate the right to a desegregated education.[47]† Plans which called for the desegregation of only one grade per year were left standing.[48]

As time passed and no appreciable progress was made, the Warren Court began to manifest impatience. In 1962, it announced in Bailey v. Patterson [369 U.S. 31 (1962)], that no substantial question was involved as to the

---

Louisiana interposition statute unconstitutional, relying on the language in Cooper v. Aaron. But the clearly invalid measures served to delay desegregation while school boards devised more sophisticated evasion programs.

47. Covington v. Edwards, 264 F.2d 780 (4th Cir. 1959), *cert. denied,* 361 U.S. 840 (1959) (pupil placement law validated and procedures established required to be followed); Carson v. Warlick, 238 F.2d 724 (4th Cir. 1956), *cert. denied,* 353 U.S. 910 (1956) (exhaustion of administrative remedies); Hood v. Board of Trustees, 232 F.2d 626 (4th Cir. 1956), *cert. denied,* 352 U.S. 870 (1956) (exhaustion of administrative remedies required); Shuttlesworth v. Birmingham Bd. of Educ., 162 F. Supp. 372 (N.D. Ala. 1958), *aff'd* (on the limited ground on which the district court rested its decision), 358 U.S. 101 (1958); accord, Holt v. Raleigh City Bd. of Educ., 265 F.2d 95 (4th Cir.), *cert. denied,* 361 U.S. 818 (1959) (requirement that parent and child follow procedures established by pupil placement board sustained); DeFebio v. County Bd., 199 Va. 511, 100 S.E.2d 760 (1957), *appeal dismissed and cert. denied,* 357 U.S. 218 (1958).

† In the Shuttlesworth case, supra, the district court had held that the Alabama pupil placement statute was not unconstitutional on is face. There, the standards under the act included: (1) psychological qualification of the pupils; (2) possibility or threat of friction or disorder among the pupils or others; and (3) maintenance or severance of established social or psychological relationships with the pupils and teachers. For a general discussion of the pupil placement laws, and the years of delay they provided school systems, see 1961 U.S. Commission on Civil Rights Report, Education at 15-31. See also Bickel, The Decade of School Desegregation: Progress and Prospects, 64 Colum. L. Rev. 33 (1964).

48. Kelley v. Board of Educ., 270 F.2d 209 (6th Cir. 1959), *cert. denied,* 361 U.S. 924 (1959); Slade v. Board of Educ., 252 F.2d 291 (4th Cir. 1958), *cert. denied,* 357 U.S. 906 (1958) (a plan of desegregation spread over a shorter space of time). But see Ennis v. Evans, 281 F.2d 385 (3d Cir. 1960), *cert. denied,* 364 U.S. 933 (1961) (state plan calling for desegregation grade-by-grade over twelve-year span, disapproved and total integration ordered by fall 1961); Evans v. Buchanan, 256 F.2d 688 (3d Cir. 1958), *cert. denied,* 358 U.S. 836 (1958) (state superintendent and state board of education under orders to formulate a plan of desegregation for entire state).

invalidity of state laws requiring segregation; the issue, the Court stated, had been resolved. The following year the Court ruled that the doctrine requiring exhaustion of administrative remedies before relief could be sought in federal court had no application to questions of school desegregation.[50]‡ In Griffin v. Prince Edward County Board of Education, which was decided in 1964, the Court stated that the time for mere deliberate speed had run out.[51]** And a year later, in Bradley v. School Board of Richmond,[52]* it stated that "[d]elays in desegregating school systems are no longer tolerable."[53]

In spite of these belated efforts, the Warren Court's formula . . . accom-

50. McNeese v. Board of Educ., 373 U.S. 668, [83 S. Ct. 1433, 10 L. Ed. 2d 622] (1963).

‡ In the same year the Court invalidated a transfer procedure which allowed students who had been initially assigned on the basis of school zone boundaries to transfer from a school where their race was in the minority to a school where their race was a majority. In voiding the plan, the Court stated, "It is readily apparent that the transfer system proposed lends itself to perpetuation of segregation. Indeed, the provisions can work only toward that end." Goss v. Board of Education, 373 U.S. 683, 83 S. Ct. 1405, 10 L. Ed. 2d 632 (1963).

51. 377 U.S. 216, 234, [84 S. Ct. 1226, 12 L. Ed. 2d 256 (1967)].

** Litigation to desegregate Prince Edward schools began in 1951; the case was one of those consolidated in the Brown decision. Rather than comply with this decision, the county closed its public schools although it continued to contribute to the support of private schools. For some time, black children had no schooling until a temporary arrangement was financed by a private foundation. Public schools remained open in all other counties of the state. In Griffin, the Court held that the action of the county school board in closing the public schools and meanwhile contributing to the support of private, segregated schools, resulted in denying equal protection of the laws to black school children. The Court found that the only reason for closing the county schools in one county was to permit a continued system of segregated education. If necessary, the Court held, the lower courts could require the county supervisors to exercise the power to levy taxes for school funds adequate to operate and maintain the public school system without racial discrimination. Justice Clark, joined by Justice Harlan, disagreed with the holding that the federal courts were empowered to order the reopening of the public schools in Prince Edward County, but otherwise joined in the Court's opinion.

Notwithstanding the decision in Griffin, courts subsequently were required to strike down several schemes by which states sought to finance so-called private schools with state funds. In a principal "tuition grant" case, Poindexter v. Louisiana Financial Commission, 275 F. Supp. 833 (E.D. La. 1967), *aff'd per curiam,* 389 U.S. 215 (1968), Judge Wisdom formulated the issue: Has the state, by providing tution grants to racially discriminatory academies, significantly involved itself in private discrimination in violation of the Equal Protection Clause of the Fourteenth Amendment?

52. 382 U.S. 103 (1965).

* During the same year, the Court, by per curiam opinion and without argument, held that an Arkansas school district, whose grade-a-year desegregation plan had not yet reached the high school grades, must honor the requests of black high school students for admission to desegregated grades so that they could take courses not offered at the all-black schools to which they were initially assigned. The Court also held that faculty desegregation was a part of the relief required by the Brown decision. Rogers v. Paul, 382 U.S. 198, 86 S. Ct. 358, 15 L. Ed. 2d 265 (1965).

53. 382 U.S. at 105.

plished very little school desegregation. By the 1963-1964 school year, for example, the eleven states of the old Confederacy had a mere 1.17 per cent of their black students attending schools with white students. In 1964-1965, the percentage had risen to 2.25 per cent because of the effect of the Civil Rights Act of 1964.[54] For the 1965-1966 school year — as a result of guidelines devised by the United States Department of Health, Education, and Welfare — the percentage reached 6.01 per cent.[55] Fear of losing federal funds had become a motivating factor inducing school authorities to effectuate some small measure of desegregation.[56]† . . .

Brown v. Board of Education fathered a social upheaval the extent and consequences of which cannot even now be measured with certainty. It marks a divide in American life. The holding that the segregation of blacks in the nation's public schools is a denial of the Constitution's command implies that all racial segregation in American public life is invalid — that all racial discrimination sponsored, supported, or encouraged by government is unconstitutional. As a result of this seminal decision, blacks had the right to use the main, not the separate, waiting room; to choose any seat in the bus; to relax in the public parks on the same terms as any other member of the community. This and more became their birthright under the Constitution.

Equal rights legislation could no longer be regarded as a gift benignly bestowed by an enlightened and liberal-minded electorate. Antidiscrimination laws were no longer great milestones; rather, they served merely as ad-

54. See United States v. Jefferson County Bd. of Educ., 372 F.2d 836, 903 (5th Cir. 1966); Southern Educ. Rep. Serv. Statistical Summary (15th ed. 1965). See also Kurland, Equal Educational Opportunity: The Limits of Constitutional Jurisprudence Undefined, 35 U. Chi. L. Rev. 583, 594 (1968).

55. For discussion of effectiveness of the Department of Health, Education, and Welfare guidelines in increasing the pace of desegregation, see Dunn, Title VI, The Guidelines in School Desegregation in the South, 53 Va. L. Rev. 42 (1967).

56. See, e.g., Green v. County School Bd., 391 U.S. 430 (1968).

† The Fifth Circuit's opinion, by Judge Wisdom in United States v. Jefferson County Board of Education, supra, reviews in some detail the frustration experienced by courts as they sought to obtain compliance with Brown on a case-by-case basis. They welcomed the assistance provided by Congress and the Executive in Title VI of the Civil Rights Act of 1964. 78 Stat. 252, 42 U.S.C. §2000d to 2000d-4 (1964). The enforcement leverage of Title VI was increased greatly by the passage in 1965 of the Elementary and Secondary Education Act, authorizing the direct payment of billions of dollars in federal money to local school districts. In addition, the Fifth Circuit indicated that it would attach great weight to the guidelines in determining whether school districts had made suitable progress in complying with the Brown decision.

In administering Title VI, HEW established uniform standards for all school districts (guidelines) in 1965 and revised them in 1966. Under the revised guidelines, plans giving freedom of choice were held appropriate only if they served to disestablish the former dual school system. To measure progress, percentages for desegregation were established in 1968, and the guidelines were again rewritten, requiring the adoption of an "effective plan" for the elimination of all vestiges of the dual school system by a certain date.

But the school desegregation progress made in the South during this period had to be weighed against the fact that it was fourteen years since the Brown decision.

ministrative machinery useful for accomplishing what the fundamental law required. While such machinery was, of course, vital and important, these statutes could now be critically assessed not in respect to the "good intentions" which led to their enactment, but rather in terms of the results achieved in alleviating the particular forms of discrimination they were supposed to regulate.

Thus, the psychological dimensions of America's race relations problem were completely recast. Blacks were no longer supplicants seeking, pleading, begging to be treated as full-fledged members of the human race; no longer were they appealing to morality, to conscience, to white America's better instincts. They were entitled to equal treatment as a right under the law; when such treatment was denied, they were being deprived — in fact robbed — of what was legally theirs. As a result, the Negro was propelled into a stance of insistent militancy. Now he was demanding — fighting to secure and possess what was rightfully his. The appeal to morality and to conscience still was valid, of course, but in a nation that was wont to describe itself as a society ruled by law, blacks had now perhaps the country's most formidable claim to fulfillment of their age-old dream of equal status — fulfillment of their desire to become full and equal participants in the mainstream of American life.

Brown's indirect consequences, therefore, have been awesome. It has completely altered the style, the spirit, and the stance of race relations. Yet the pre-existing pattern of white superiority and black subordination remains unchanged; indeed, it is now revealed as a national rather than a regional phenomenon. Thus, Brown has promised more than it could give, and therefore has contributed to black alienation and bitterness, to a loss of confidence in white institutions, and to the growing racial polarization of our society. This cannot in any true sense be said to be the responsibility of the Warren Court. Few in the country, black or white, understood in 1954 that racial segregation was merely a symptom, not the disease; that the real sickness is that our society in all of its manifestations is geared to the maintenance of white superiority. . . .

QUESTIONS

1. Carter observes that for blacks, the major value of the Brown decision was that it placed the Constitution squarely on the side of their struggle for equality. He then concludes that the opposition to Brown revealed that segregation was merely a symptom and that the real disease in our society is its commitment to the maintenance of white superiority. Is this an optimistic or deeply pessimistic comment about the ultimate utility of Brown as a legal vehicle for blacks and other nonwhite minorities?

2. Carter reports, supra page 458, that in 1962, by which time no appreciable progress in school desegregation had been made, "the Warren Court began to manifest impatience." But didn't the "all deliberate speed" doctrine literally invite precisely the evasion and delay that occurred? Bickel argued that, while the Court in Brown II specified the administrative problems that might take time to solve, and specifically excluded opposition to the decision as a permissible basis for delay, "It went without saying also that while the vitality of constitutional principles as reflected in specific court orders ought, to be sure, not be allowed to yield simply because of disagreement with them, disagreement is legitimate and relevant and will, in our system, legitimately and inevitably cause delay in compliance with law laid down by the Supreme Court, and will indeed, if it persists and is widely enough shared, overturn such law." Bickel, The Decade of School Desegregation: Progress and Prospects, 64 Colum. L. Rev. 193, 196 (1964). Is Bickel correct? Are Americans (and law professors) as sympathetic with law violators in other areas? Whether the answer is yes or no, is there any reason for optimism among blacks?

GREEN v. COUNTY SCHOOL BOARD OF NEW KENT COUNTY

391 U.S. 430, 88 S. Ct. 1689, 20 L. Ed. 2d 716 (1968)

Mr. Justice BRENNAN delivered the opinion of the Court.

The question for decision is whether, under all the circumstances here, respondent School Board's adoption of a "freedom-of-choice" plan which allows a pupil to choose his own public school constitutes adequate compliance with the Board's responsibility "to achieve a system of determining admission to the public schools on a nonracial basis . . . ." Brown v. Board of Education, 349 U.S. 294, 300-301 (Brown II).

Petitioners brought this action in March 1965 seeking injunctive relief against respondent's continued maintenance of an alleged racially segregated school system. New Kent County is a rural county in Eastern Virginia. About one-half of its population of some 4,500 are Negroes. There is no residential segregation in the county; persons of both races reside throughout. The school system has only two schools, the New Kent school on the east side of the county and the George W. Watkins school on the west side. In a memorandum filed May 17, 1966, the District Court found that the "school system serves approximately 1,300 pupils, of which 740 are Negro and 550 are White. The School Board operates one white combined elementary and high school [New Kent], and one Negro combined elementary and high school [George W. Watkins]. There are no attendance zones. Each school serves the entire county." The record indicates that 21 school buses — 11 serving the Watkins school and 10 serving the New Kent school — travel overlapping routes throughout the county to transport pupils to and from the two schools.

The segregated system was initially established and maintained under the compulsion of Virginia constitutional and statutory provisions mandating racial segregation in public education . . . . The respondent School Board continued the segregated operation of the system after the Brown decisions, presumably on the authority of several statutes enacted by Virginia in resistance to those decisions. Some of these statutes were held to be unconstitutional on their face or as applied. One statute, the Pupil Placement Act . . . divested local boards of authority to assign children to particular schools and placed that authority in a State Pupil Placement Board. Under that Act children were each year automatically reassigned to the school previously attended unless upon their application the State Board assigned them to another school; students seeking enrollment for the first time were also assigned at the discretion of the State Board. To September 1964, no Negro pupil had applied for admission to the New Kent school under this statute and no white pupil had applied for admission to the Watkins school.

The School Board initially sought dismissal of this suit on the ground that petitioners had failed to apply to the State Board for assignment to New Kent school. However on August 2, 1965, five months after the suit was brought, respondent School Board, in order to remain eligible for federal financial aid, adopted a "freedom-of-choice" plan for desegregating the schools. Under that plan, each pupil, except those entering the first and eighth grades, may annually choose between the New Kent and Watkins schools and pupils not making a choice are assigned to the school previously attended; first and eighth grade pupils must affirmatively choose a school. After the plan was filed the District Court denied petitioners' prayer for an injunction and granted respondent leave to submit an amendment to the plan with respect to employment and assignment of teachers and staff on a racially nondiscriminatory basis.

[The lower courts approved the freedom of choice plans, although remanding for a more specific plan for faculty desegregation. The Supreme Court granted certiorari, and found the totally segregated dual system of "white" and "Negro" schools in New Kent County precisely the pattern invalidated in the Brown cases.]

It is against this background that 13 years after Brown II commanded the abolition of dual systems we must measure the effectiveness of respondent School Board's "freedom-of-choice" plan to achieve that end. The School Board contends that it has fully discharged its obligation by adopting a plan by which every student, regardless of race, may "freely" choose the school he will attend. The Board attempts to cast the issue in its broadest form by arguing that its "freedom-of-choice" plan may be faulted only by reading the Fourteenth Amendment as universally requiring "compulsory integration," a reading it insists the wording of the Amendment will not support. But that argument ignores the thrust of Brown II. In the light of the command of that case, what is involved here is the question whether the Board has achieved the "racially nondiscriminatory school system" Brown II held must be effectuated in order to remedy the established unconstitutional deficiencies of its segregated system. In the context of the state-imposed segregated pattern of long standing, the fact that in 1965 the Board opened the doors of the former "white" school to Negro children and of the "Negro" school to white children merely begins, not ends, our inquiry whether the Board has taken steps adequate to abolish its dual, segregated system. Brown II was a call for the dismantling of well-entrenched dual systems tempered by an awareness that complex and multifaceted problems would arise which would require time and flexibility for a successful resolution. School boards such as the respondent then operating state-compelled dual systems were nevertheless clearly charged with the affirmative duty to take whatever steps might be necessary to convert to a unitary system in which racial discrimination would be eliminated root and branch. See Cooper v. Aaron . . . ; Bradley v. School Board, 382 U.S. 103; cf. Watson v. City of Memphis, 373 U.S. 526. The constitutional rights of Negro school children articulated in Brown I permit no less than this; and it was to this end that Brown II commanded school boards to bend their efforts.

In determining whether respondent School Board met that command by adopting its "freedom-of-choice" plan, it is relevant that this first step did not come until some 11 years after Brown I was decided and 10 years after Brown II directed the making of a "prompt and reasonable start." This deliberate perpetuation of the unconstitutional dual system can only have compounded the harm of such a system. Such delays are no longer tolerable, for "the governing constitutional principles no longer bear the imprint of newly enunciated doctrine." Watson v. City of Memphis, supra, at 529; see Bradley v. School Board, supra; Rogers v. Paul, 382 U.S. 198. Moreover, a plan that at this late date fails to provide meaningful assurance of prompt and effective disestablishment of a dual system is also intolerable. "The time for mere 'deliberate speed' has run out," Griffin v. County School Board, 377 U.S. 218, 234; "the context in which we must interpret and apply this language [of Brown II] to plans for desegregation has been significantly altered." Goss v. Board of Education, 373 U.S. 683, 689. See Calhoun v. Latimer, 377 U.S. 263. The burden on a school board today is to come forward with a plan that promises realistically to work, and promises realistically to work *now*.

The obligation of the district courts, as it always has been, is to assess the effectiveness of a proposed plan in achieving desegregation. There is no universal answer to complex problems of desegregation; there is obviously no one plan that will do the job in every case. The matter must be assessed in light of the circumstances present and the options available in each instance. It is incumbent upon the school board to establish that its proposed plan promises meaningful and immediate progress toward disestablishing state-imposed segregation. It is incumbent upon the district court to weigh that claim in light of the facts at hand and in light of any alternatives which may be shown as feasible and more promising in their effectiveness. Where the court finds the board to be acting in good faith and the proposed plan to have real prospects for dismantling the state-imposed dual system "at the earliest practicable date," then the plan may be said to provide effective relief. Of course, the availability to the board of other more promising courses of action may indicate a lack of good faith; and at the least it places a heavy burden upon the board to explain its preference for an apparently less effective method. Moreover, whatever plan is adopted will require evaluation in practice, and the court should retain jurisdiction until it is clear that state-imposed segregation has been completely removed. See No. 805, Raney v. Board of Education . . . .

We do not hold that "freedom of choice" can have no place in such a plan. We do not hold that a "freedom-of-choice" plan might of itself be unconstitutional, although that argument has been urged upon us. Rather, all we decide today is that in desegregating a dual system a plan utilizing "freedom of choice" is not an end in itself. . . .

Although the general experience under "freedom of choice" to date has been such as to indicate its ineffectiveness as a tool of desegregation,[5] there may well be instances in which it can serve as an effective device. Where it offers real promise of aiding a desegregation program to effectuate conversion of a state-imposed dual system to unitary, nonracial system there might be no objection to allowing such a device to prove itself in operation. On the other hand, if there are reasonably available other ways, such for illustration as zoning, promising speedier and more effective conversion to a unitary, nonracial school system, "freedom of choice" must be held unacceptable.

The New Kent School Board's "freedom-of-choice" plan cannot be accepted as a sufficient step to "effectuate a transition" to a unitary system.

5. The views of the United States Commission on Civil Rights, which we neither adopt nor refuse to adopt, are as follows:

"Freedom of choice plans, which have tended to perpetuate racially identifiable schools in the Southern and border States, require affirmative action by both Negro and white parents and pupils before such disestablishment can be achieved. There are a number of factors which have prevented such affirmative action by substantial numbers of parents and pupils of both races:

"(a) Fear of retaliation and hostility from the white community continue to deter many Negro families from choosing formerly all-white schools;

"(b) During the past school year [1966-1967], as in the previous year, in some areas of the South, Negro families with children attending previously all-white schools under free choice plans were targets of violence, threats of violence and economic reprisal by white persons, and Negro children were subjected to harassment by white classmates notwithstanding conscientious efforts by many teachers and principals to prevent such misconduct;

"(c) During the past school year, in some areas of the South public officials improperly influenced Negro families to keep their children in Negro schools and excluded Negro children attending formerly all-white schools from official functions.

"(d) Poverty deters many Negro families in the South from choosing formerly all-white schools. Some Negro parents are embarrassed to permit their children to attend such schools without suitable clothing. In some districts, special fees are assessed for courses which are available only in the white schools;

"(e) Improvements in facilities and equipment . . . have been instituted in all-Negro schools in some school districts in a manner that tends to discourage Negroes from selecting white schools." Southern School Desegregation, 1966-1967, at 88 (1967). See id. at 45-69; Survey of School Desegregation in the Southern and Border States, 1965-1966, at 30-44, 51-52 (U.S. Commission on Civil Rights 1966).

In three years of operation not a single white child has chosen to attend Watkins school and although 115 Negro children enrolled in New Kent school in 1967 (up from 35 in 1965 and 111 in 1966) 85% of the Negro children in the system still attend the all-Negro Watkins school. In other words, the school system remains a dual system. Rather than further the dismantling of the dual system, the plan has operated simply to burden children and their parents with a responsibility which Brown II placed squarely on the School Board. The Board must be required to formulate a new plan and, in light of other courses which appear open to the Board, such as zoning,[6] fashion steps which promise realistically to convert promptly to a system without a "white" school and a "Negro" school, but just schools.

The judgment of the Court of Appeals is vacated insofar as it affirmed the District Court and the case is remanded to the District Court for further proceedings consistent with this opinion.

It is so ordered.*

NOTES

1. The Green v. New Kent decision is considered by many the most important Supreme Court statement on school desegregation since the Brown decisions. In effect, it supported the HEW guideline standards, which required not merely the cessation of discriminatory activities (a frequently cited decision, Briggs v. Elliott, 132 F. Supp. 776 (E.D.S.C. 1955), had held that Brown required no more), but the prompt adoption and effectuation of a plan that actually disestablished the dual school system. The Fifth Circuit had reached the same decision in an appeal consolidating a number of tests of the HEW guidelines. United States v. Jefferson County Board of Education, 372 F.2d 836 (5th Cir. 1966), *aff'd en banc,* 380 F.2d 385 (5th Cir. 1967), *cert. denied,* 389 U.S. 840 (1967). There, Judge Wisdom had concluded: "The only school desegregation plan that meets constitutional

6. "In view of the situation found in New Kent County, where there is no residential segregation, the elimination of the dual school system and the establishment of a 'unitary, non-racial system' could be readily achieved with a minimum of administrative difficulty by means of geographc zoning — simply by assigning students living in the eastern half of the county to the New Kent School and those living in the western half of the county to the Watkins School. Although a geographical formula is not universally appropriate, it is evident that here the Board, by separately busing Negro children across the entire county to the 'Negro' school, and the white children to the 'white' school, is deliberately maintaining a segregated system which would vanish with non-racial geographic zoning. The conditions in this county present a classical case for this expedient." Bowman v. County School Board . . . (concurring opinion).

* In two companion cases to Green, the Court held freedom of choice plans and free transfer plans inadequate to convert previously segregated school systems to the unitary, non-discriminatory standard required by Brown. Monroe v. Board of Commissioners of the City of Jackson, Tenn., 391 U.S. 450, 88 S. Ct. 1700, 20 L. Ed. 2d 733 (1968); Raney v. Board of Education of Gould School District, 391 U.S. 443, 88 S. Ct. 1697, 20 L. Ed. 2d 727 (1968).

standards is one that works." 372 F.2d at 847. He reviewed the long history of school desegregation efforts, said that the courts acting alone on a case-by-case basis had failed, and welcomed the help of Congress and the Executive under Title VI of the 1964 Civil Rights Act. He found the guidelines adopted by HEW pursuant to Title VI a valid and effective means of desegregating the schools, repeating findings of earlier Fifth Circuit cases that they were "minimum standards" to which the Court would "attach great weight."

2. As the Civil Rights Commission reports show, "freedom of choice" was never more than a theoretical concept for most blacks, who feared, frequently with justification, that the exercise of their constitutional right to send their children to a formerly all-white school would cost them their jobs. Frequently, the price was much higher. In a typical case, Chief Judge Haynsworth of the Fourth Circuit reviewed events in a school district which, after ignoring the Brown decision for a decade, adopted a freedom of choice plan in 1965.

> There followed . . . numerous acts of violence and threats directed against Negro members of the community, particularly those requesting transfers of their children into formerly all-white schools. Shots were fired into houses, oil was poured into wells, and some of the Negro leaders were subjected to a barrage of threatening telephone calls. Violence was widely reported in the local press, and an implicit threat was carried home to everyone by publication of the names of Negro applicants for transfer. (Coppedge v. Franklin County Board of Education, 394 F.2d 410 (4th Cir. 1968).)

3. The potential effectiveness of Title VI was greatly enhanced by passage of the 1965 Elementary and Secondary Education Act, which made the nation's school districts eligible for billions of dollars in federal aid. This incentive, combined with enforcement procedures that from stumbling beginnings became quite efficient by 1967, led to substantial increases in the percentage of black students attending formerly all-white schools. As seen above, the courts were generally supportive of HEW efforts; the Justice Department increased its participation in school litigation, having been granted authority in Title IV to initiate such litigation; and, while resistance remained, the combination of these factors enabled reports that more school systems in the South than in the North were integrated by 1971. N.Y. Times, Jan. 21, 1971, at 1, col. 6.

4. But the advances were met with increasing white opposition to school desegregation in 1968, and following the presidential election of that year, the new administration adopted policies that had the effect of slowing the federal government's participation in the school desegregation process. Although setting forth an unequivocal commitment to ending racial discrimination in the schools, a joint statement made on July 3, 1969 by the Secretary of HEW and the Attorney General stated that too much emphasis had been placed on deadlines, coercion and punishment. At that point, 121 school dis-

tricts had lost federal funds for failing to comply with Title VI requirements. The new administration indicated that it would try to work more closely with these districts and that generally some limited delay in completing the desegregation process might be justified. The statement also announced that, in the future, litigation by the Justice Department would be the government's favored tool for bringing schools into compliance, while HEW administrative enforcement proceedings (fund cut-offs) were to be de-emphasized.

5. Reaction to the new policies was mixed. Civil rights adherents felt that the government was cutting back its program and "scuttling" the guidelines. The United States Civil Rights Commission saw the abandonment of uniform standards, in favor of negotiating individually with school districts, as "repeat[ing] an experiment that had previously failed," and believed that the emphasis upon judicial rather than administrative proceedings "can be expected to slow the pace of school desegregation." See C.R.C. Federal Enforcement at 50 (1969). The government denied such charges. However, the slowdown in federal enforcement is detailed in a book published by the director of HEW's Office for Civil Rights, Leon Panetta, who was fired in the spring of 1970, purportedly because of his efforts to continue administrative enforcement of Title VI. L. Panetta and P. Gall, Bring Us Together, The Nixon Team and the Civil Rights Retreat (1971).

The new policy was also protested by Justice Department personnel. Sixty-five of the seventy-four nonsupervisory attorneys in the Civil Rights Division signed a statement to the Attorney General and the Assistant Attorney General for Civil Rights, expressing concern that "clear legal mandates" were being sacrificed to "other" considerations. During the first six months of 1970, nineteen Civil Rights Division attorneys resigned, and others, experienced in school cases, sought positions outside the education section. See Greenburg, Revolt at Justice, 1 The Washington Monthly 32 (Dec. 1969); 2 National Journal 1188-1190 (June 6, 1970).

The specific cause for the revolt within the Civil Rights Division was a motion filed by the Department of Justice seeking a delay in the implementation of desegregation plans in several Mississippi cases which the department itself had supported months before. The Fifth Circuit granted the delay, but lawyers for the black children took the case to the Supreme Court. On October 29, 1969, the Court rejected the Government's arguments in Alexander v. Holmes County Board of Education.

ALEXANDER v. HOLMES COUNTY BOARD OF EDUCATION, 396 U.S. 19, 90 S. Ct. 29, 24 L. Ed. 2d 19 (1969). The Fifth Circuit had entered an order requiring the submission by thirty-three Mississippi school districts of desegregation plans which would be put into effect during the forthcoming school year. Upon a motion of the Department of Justice and the recommendation of the Secretary of Health, Education and Welfare, the court suspended its order and postponed the date for submission of the plans. The government's position (which, for the first time since the Brown decision, opposed that of counsel for the black plaintiffs) was that the time was too short to accomplish a complete and orderly implementation of the segregation plan for the coming school year. Justice Black, as Circuit Justice, denied an application by plaintiffs to vacate the court of appeals suspension of its earlier order. In doing so, however, he expressed his personal view that there could be no justification for postponing the enforcement of the constitutional rights of the Negro students. 396 U.S. 1218, 90 S. Ct. 14, 24 L. Ed. 2d 41 (1969).

The Supreme Court granted review, set the case down for early argument, and in a per curiam decision stated:

> The question presented is one of paramount importance, involving as it does the denial of fundamental rights to many thousands of school children, who are presently attending Mississippi schools under segregated conditions contrary to the applicable decisions of this Court. Against this background the Court of Appeals should have denied all motions for additional time because continued operation of segregated schools under a standard of allowing "all deliberate speed" for desegregation is no longer constitutionally permissible. Under explicit holdings of this Court the obligation of every school district is to terminate dual school systems at once and to operate now and hereafter only unitary schools. (396 U.S. at 20.)

The Court cited Green v. New Kent County, supra, and Griffin v. School Board, 377 U.S. 218, 234 (1964), in support of its action.

NOTES

1. Later in the same term, the Court issued similar rulings in school cases appealed to it from other circuits. See Dowell v. Board of Education of the Oklahoma City Public Schools, 396 U.S. 269, 90 S. Ct. 415, 24 L. Ed. 2d 414 (1969); Northcross v. Memphis City Schools Board of Education, 397 U.S. 232, 90 S. Ct. 891, 25 L. Ed. 2d 246 (1970).

2. Less than three months after the "at once" edict of Alexander, the Supreme Court again ruled on school board requests supported by the federal government for further delay in school desegregation. Carter v. West Feliciana, 396 U.S. 290, 90 S. Ct. 608, 24 L. Ed. 2d 477 (1970). The Court in a brief per curiam opinion reversed the lower court's order requiring prompt faculty desegregation, but delaying pupil desegregation until the next school year.

Chief Justice Burger and Justice Stewart deemed the lower court order sufficiently prompt under the Alexander standard, and would not have reversed without argument and a review of the individual school problems. Justice Harlan, joined by Justice White, wrote a concurring opinion to explain "the intended effect of the Alexander decision." He suggested that a maximum timetable of eight weeks was permissible in implementing desegregation plans, a position which Justices Black, Douglas, Brennan and Marshall viewed as a "retreat from our holding in Alexander. . . ."

But a doubt that Alexander really meant "at once" had taken hold. A few months later, the Fifth Circuit reversed a lower court's order delaying pupil desegregation until fall 1971, but itself refused to order immediate desegregation in the spring because "Nothing could be accomplished by requiring an upheaval and shift of students from one school to another this late in the school year." To supports its decision, the court quoted extensively from Justice Harlan's concurring opinion in the Carter case.

Moreover, the Justice Department, which after the Green decision had filed sixty-eight motions for further relief, covering 143 school systems, took no such action after Alexander and Carter, and failed to initiate contempt actions in districts in which there were apparent violations of orders contained in those two decisions. See Lawyers Review Committee to Study the Department of Justice 20-33 (Aug. 6, 1972).

3. Disenchantment with the federal government's civil rights policies continued to grow. A federal suit alleged that HEW was failing to obtain compliance with Title VI of the Civil Rights Act of 1964, with the result that institutions were receiving federal funds in violation of the provisions of that act. After lengthy discovery proceedings, the court found that segregated school systems on the elementary, secondary, vocational, and higher educational levels were receiving federal assistance in violation of Title VI. It found, moreover, that while HEW had initiated approximately 100 enforcement proceedings in both 1968 and 1969, no enforcement proceedings had been initiated from March 1970 until February 1971, and only a token number had been commenced since February 1971. No termination of funds had occurred since the summer of 1970.

HEW justified its administrative inaction on the ground that it was seeking voluntary compliance through negotiation and conciliation. The court conceded that HEW has discretion in this area, but asserted that this discretion is not unlimited. After a substantial period of time has elapsed and voluntary compliance is not achieved, the limited discretion is ended, and HEW must proceed with enforcement proceedings as provided in the statute. Adams v. Richardson, 480 F.2d 1159 (D.C. Cir. 1973).

QUESTIONS

1. In the wake of the Green and Alexander decisions, even the most diehard opponents of Brown could not expect to sustain further delay by repeating the decade-old argument gleaned from the dictum attributed to Fourth Circuit Judge John Parker that "The Constitution . . . does not require integration. It merely forbids discrimination." Briggs v. Elliott, 132 F. Supp. at 776 (E.D.S.C. 1955). Was it the logic of Judge Parker's language or its harmony with the views of those who opposed Brown that gave the Briggs dictum so long and active a life? If the former, wasn't there a simple answer in the language of Brown I that should have stifled this oft quoted phrase in its infancy? If the latter, is there any cause for cheer (for clients as opposed to their lawyers) in the decisions which buried Briggs if in fact resistance to Brown — that gave life to Briggs — remains strong?

2. If, as suggested earlier, the resistance to Brown is based on the desire of whites to protect their superior status in the society, then isn't Wechsler seeking an opinion that would vindicate black rights without offending white sensibilities or threatening white interests? Is it possible to write such an opinion?

3. Assuming an affirmative answer, should the decree in Brown II have been more firm? Should it have provided more guidance for the district courts? In short, should the directions in Green and Alexander have been incorporated into Brown II? Brown I? Is this what the Supreme Court decided to do in the abortion cases, Roe v. Wade, 410 U.S. 113, 93 S. Ct. 705 (1973); Doe v. Bolton, 410 U.S. 179, 93 S. Ct. 739 (1973)?

2. Tactics for Diluting Compliance

The difficult task of weighing the speed and effectiveness of school desegregation plans did not relieve federal courts of the obligation to review a continuing stream of increasingly innovative policies, the effect of which was to provide the appearance of compliance while avoiding the actual practise of desegregation. The cases which follow provide illustrations of how these techniques — unnecessary closing of black schools, maintenance of segregated classes within "integrated" schools, student "ability groupings," use of I.Q. and achievement tests, dismissal and downgrading of black administrators and faculty, and "secessions" by pupils and systems — have all been used to dilute the impact of school desegregation orders.

ALLEN v. ASHEVILLE CITY BOARD OF EDUCATION
434 F.2d 902 (4th Cir. 1970)

Before BOREMAN, BRYAN and CRAVEN, Circuit Judges.

CRAVEN, Circuit Judge: This is another school case, but a distinctive one. In Asheville, North Carolina, there are neither black schools nor white schools, just schools. Green v. County School Board of New Kent County, Virginia, 391 U.S. 430 . . . (1968). The Asheville City Board of Education operates 12 schools . . . . According to the Chairman of the Board, the purpose of the school board's plan, approved by the district court, was to "eliminate the all-white school" and to "eliminate all segregated schools and to balance the racial mix as nearly as possible." That the purpose has been fully achieved is obvious from an examination of the racial characteristics of each school set out below. The population ratio throughout the school system is 30 percent black and 70 percent white.

In Chambers v. Iredell County Board of Education, 9 Cir., 423 F.2d 613

(1970), we expressed doubt "that many school systems have achieved a higher degree of integration than presently prevails in Iredell County." Asheville tops Iredell. Doubtless Asheville is at or near the pinnacle of arithmetical desegregation in America.

II

Able counsel for plaintiffs are unable to fault the Board's plan other than a complaint with respect to the closing of two previously all-black schools and the impact of their closing, in the context of the rest of the plan, upon black students. For purposes of analysis plaintiffs formulate this complaint as presenting two questions to the Court, the first of which is whether the district court erred in approving the invidious selection of two all-black schools for closing.

We reject plaintiffs' contention that the school board has unfairly discriminated against black children in the selection of schools to be closed and that the district court should have compelled the closing of different schools in order to achieve the principle of Brown II.

In the first place, we think the mechanics of integration, where the purpose is obviously to implement the Brown II principle and effectively achieves that end, is ordinarily a matter within the discretion of school administrators. The question is not whether we might have selected different schools for extinction, nor even whether substantial evidence supports the Board's decision, but is instead whether the Board's decision is so plainly unfair that it clearly amounts to invidious discrimination in violation of the equal protection clause.

We are unable to perceive any invidious discrimination in the Board's plan. All students, black and white, attend one high school. All students, black and white, attend one 9th grade school. All students, black and white, attend two 7th and 8th grade schools, located on each side of the French Broad River, and without significant difference in racial balance. All students, black and white, attend one sixth grade school, with the insignificant exception of Newton School which continues to embrace the 6th grade and is itself in substantial racial balance.

South French Broad High School and Hill Street School were formerly all-black schools and are now being attended by all students, black and white, in the 9th and 6th grades respectively, except for the Newton School students previously noted. The white students coming to these formerly all-black schools have as far to travel as do the black pupils who now attend formerly all-white schools.

In order to accomplish racial balance the school board decided that it was necessary to close three schools, Livingston Street and Herring, formerly all-black, and Newton Elementary School, formerly all-white. After plaintiffs objected to the proposed plan on the basis of the closing of the two all-black schools . . . , the Board modified the plan on December 29, 1969, to provide for the continued operation of the Newton Elementary School with the two black schools remaining closed.

The Board says that the criteria used by it for determining which schools to use and which to close were (a) achievement of racial balance; (b) elimination of excess classrooms; (c) the size and accessibility of the schools involved; and (d) the amount of surrounding acreage. Plaintiffs insist, however, that the school board's true reason for selection is undisclosed and is simply its "reluctance to send primary grade white children into traditionally all-black schools located in all-black neighborhoods."

The motivation of individual members of a governing entity is not the same as administrative intent. Members may vote a good measure for bad reasons and vice versa. Plaintiffs' contention is pure speculation. We find nothing in the record to support it. The district judge did not so find nor was he requested to do so. Areas of any city, black or white in complexion, may be undesirable places for congregating children for reasons having nothing to do with race. Regardless of motivation, the school board's overriding intent was to achieve a unitary school system. It should not be thwarted by mere conjecture that some or even a majority of its members may have entertained unpleasant thoughts about placing white children in a black neighborhood.

It is true that more black *elementary* pupils than white will be required to ride reasonable distances in free public school buses in order to enter and become integrated in formerly white schools, but it is equally true that more white pupils than black in the higher grades will be required to ride to schools generally located close to the areas of black residents and away from the white residential pattern. Moreover, the situation of which plaintiffs complain cannot possibly be changed except at the cost of increasing the transportation of pupils approximately 40 percent. This is so because if the two black schools that have been closed were reopened, 70 percent of the black students formerly in each school would have to be moved out into other schools and this 70 percent replaced by white students.

We reiterate that there is nothing in the record that substantiates the charge of invidious discrimination against Negroes. Under the Board's plan that is now effectively operating, 60 percent of the students in the entire system are attending schools located in areas of the city that are 80 to 85 percent black in housing pattern. Six of the 12 schools operated by the Board are located in or very close to predominately black residential areas. Relatively more blacks are located in close proximity to the schools they attend than whites.

It is urged upon us that even so, both schools that were closed are newer and physically better than most of the other schools retained. We agree that this is a relevant factor. But neither alone nor in context does it establish invidious discrimination. Such a factor is only one of many that enter into a school closing decision. We repeat that we do not sit to review state administrative decisions beyond the very limited reach of the Constitution.

We find the decisions relied upon by plaintiffs to be distinguishable or inapplicable. In Felder v. Harnett County Board of Education, 4 Cir., 409 F.2d 1070, 1074, we affirmed the district court's rejection of the school board's plan in part because "there was no explanation offered as to how the school board determined upon particular schools for extinction, nor did the closing plan disclose criteria for the assignment of students from the closed schools except for cryptic reference to bus routes." But our primary concern and the basis of decision was the complete failure of the school board to disestablish an entrenched dual school system in which only 4.3 percent of the black children were attending previously all-white schools. In short, in Felder there was not the slightest assurance of achieving a unitary plan and the selection of schools for closing was therefore suspect. . . .

More in point, we think, is Chambers v. Iredell County Board of Education, 423 F.2d 613 (4th Cir. 1970), in which we sustained a decision of the district judge approving the closing of an all-black school and refusing to find that doing so amounted to invidious discrimination.

III

Plaintiffs' second question is but a broader and more dramatic variation of the first one. We are asked to decide whether the district court, in approving the plan, unconstitutionally placed "the burden of desegregation" upon black pupils in the school system. It is urged upon us that the plan approved by the district court "places an unfair, racially discriminatory burden upon black children" in that black children in grades 1 through 5 who previously attended all-black Livingston and Herring Elementary Schools will be required to travel as much as five or six miles in order to attend previously all-white schools. This is said to be an unfair allocation of the "burden" of integration, and it is suggested that the Constitution requires that an equivalent number or proportion of white children in the same grades be required to travel an equivalent distance to enter schools outside their previous attendance zones.

We hold that such a pattern of assignment implemented by free school bus transportation does not violate the equal protection clause of the Fourteenth Amendment.

If achieving integration by free bus transportation for reasonable distances must now be characterized as a "burden" and if we also assume, without deciding, that this burden must be equally shared between the races, the school board's plan is nevertheless valid. The worst that can be said of the plan is that in grades 1 through 5 the burden falls disproportionately on black children, whereas in grades 6 through 12 it falls disproportionately upon white children. We have previously noted that proportionately more white children than black travel away from their residential areas to attend school and that six out of 12 schools are maintained in or in close proximity to the black residential areas of the city.

Affirmed.

NOTES

1. The thrust of opposition by blacks in these cases is not that desegregation or bussing are objectionable per se, but that, as argued in Allen, the whole burden of being transported to school should not be placed on them. The impetus for "two-way bussing" also emanates from the desire to retain black schools, which — despite segregation — are often sources of pride and achievement, and serve as resources for the black community. Paradoxically, the efforts to defend such schools are often undermined by the age of the buildings and their poor condition and location, often near railroad tracks or polluted streams — facts of no concern to school boards until they faced the long-delayed necessity of complying with Brown.

2. The Eighth Circuit approved a desegregation plan under which an all-black school district was annexed by a white district. The court stated that, while there was possible merit in the black contention that a unitary school system could have been achieved by a consolidation of the two districts, "we do not find constitutional error in ordering the larger more populous former white school district to annex the smaller less populous former black school district if that annexation does in fact accomplish a unitary non-racial school system." Haney v. County Board of Education of Sevier County, 429 F.2d 364 (8th Cir. 1970). See also Robinson v. Shelby County Board of Education, 467 F.2d 1187 (6th Cir. 1972) (dissenting opinion).

3. In Bell v. West Point Municipal Separate School District, 446 F.2d 1362 (5th Cir. 1971), the Fifth Circuit found that school authorities could not constitutionally close two formerly all-black schools, located in black neighborhoods, for fear that whites would not attend them. Circuit Judge Morgan, speaking for the court, held:

> The closing of schools for purely racial reasons is impermissible under Brown . . . which commands that public schools must be free from racial discrimination. While it is undisputed that a particular school may be terminated for sound educational reasons, an otherwise useful building may not be closed merely because the school board speculates that whites will refuse to attend the location. (446 F.2d at 1365. See also Gordon v. Jefferson Davis Parish School Board, 446 F.2d 266 (5th Cir. 1971).)

But in Mims v. Duval County School Board, 447 F.2d 1330 (1971), the Fifth Circuit determined that the closing of black schools for sound educational reasons was justified. Distinguishing the case from its Bell v. West Point School case, the court found that in each of the five formerly black schools the closings were motivated by nonracial considerations, such as deterioration, close proximity to polluted creeks, and vandalism.

4. The two-way bussing issue has been raised in Northern school desegregation suits, with the issue usually settled as it is in the South. Thus the

Second Circuit, in a case with facts similar to Allen, also concluded that the school board was justified in closing a black school located in a ghetto area. Norwalk CORE v. Norwalk Board of Education, 423 F.2d 121 (1970). Accord, Parris v. School Comm. of Medford, Mass., 305 F. Supp. 356 (D. Mass. 1969). But see Moss v. Stanford Board of Education, 350 F. Supp. 879 (D. Conn. 1972), denying a motion to dismiss a suit protesting one-way bussing.

5. In granting a preliminary injunction prohibiting closing of a black school, the federal court in Brice v. Landis, 314 F. Supp. 974 (W.D. Cal. 1969), recognized that

> As a practical matter some transfer of bussing of negro children will obviously be involved in most integration plans. . . .
>
> Where, however, the closing of an apparently suitable negro school and transfer of its pupils back and forth to white schools without similar arrangements for white pupils, is not absolutely or reasonably necessary under the particular circumstances, consideration must be given to the fairly obvious fact that such a plan places the burden of desegregation entirely upon one racial group.
>
> The minority children are placed in the position of what may be described as second-class pupils. White pupils, realizing that they are permitted to attend their own neighborhood schools as usual, may come to regard themselves as "natives" and to resent the negro children bussed into the white schools every school day as intruding "foreigners." It is in this respect that such a plan, when not reasonably required under the circumstances, becomes substantially discriminating in itself. This undesirable result will not be nearly so likely if the white children themselves realize that some of their number are also required to play the same role at negro neighborhood schools. (314 F. Supp. at 974.)

6. Despite the broad language of the opinion, the preliminary injunction actually entered in Brice was quite narrow, the court simply enjoining the school board from disposing of the school or leasing it on terms which would prevent the board from reoccupying on short notice. While the litigation proceeded, the children who formerly attended the black school (named for Martin Luther King) were bussed to three white schools. Following the trial, the district judge ruled that plaintiffs had not met their burden of proving that closing the King school was an invidious attempt to discriminate against the black community. Letters to author dated Feb. 26, 1971 and July 8, 1971, from William B. Turner, attorney for plaintiffs.

7. Not all of the burden of school desegregation has been borne by blacks. One of the effects of desegregation efforts in the Southwest has been to relieve racial imbalance between blacks and whites at the expense of Mexican-American students. In United States v. Texas Education Agency, 467 F.2d 848 (5th Cir. 1972), the court, after finding that the Mexican-Americans are a racially identifiable group for purposes of the Fourteenth Amendment's Equal Protection Clause and that they had previously been segregated by the state, added:

> The present case presents the special problem of dismantling a dual system based on race within the context of a tri-ethnic school system. No remedy for the dual system can be acceptable if it operates to deprive members of a third ethnic group of the benefits of equal educational opportunity. To dismantle the black-white segregation system without including the third ethnic group in the desegregation process would be to deny to that group all the benefits of integrated schooling. . . . To exclude Mexican-Americans from the benefits of tri-partite integration in the very act of effecting a unitary system would be to provide blacks with the benefit of integration while denying it to another (and larger) group on the basis of ethnic origin. This in itself is a denial of equal protection of the laws. (467 F.2d at 869.)

In a footnote, the court stated:

> The district court said that it would "consider the effect upon [Mexican-Americans] . . . of any plan submitted by the parties." This was not sufficient. The Mexican-American students must be specifically included in the plan and its operation. The district court apparently chose to include Mexican-American students in the elementary school plan despite the finding of no "de jure" segregation of Mexican-Americans. (467 F.2d at 870.)

See also Cisneros v. Corpus Christi Independent School District, 467 F.2d 142 (5th Cir. 1972); Rangel and Alcala, De Jure Segregation of Chicanos in Texas Schools, 7 Harv. Civ. Rights–Civ. Lib. L. Rev. 370 (1972).

8. Not only are Mexican-American children entitled to a desegregated education, but one court has ruled that an educational program tailored to the middle-class child from an English-speaking family denies an equal educational opportunity to children from Spanish-speaking homes. Noting the lower achievement levels in a predominantly Mexican-American school, the court ordered the school board to reassess and enlarge its program directed to the specialized needs of its Spanish-surnamed students at this school and to establish bilingual-bicultural programs at the other schools. The board contended that the special educational needs of Spanish-surnamed children are not the result of state action and that defendant did not create these problems through classification or racially motivated discrimination, but the court found that "it would be a deprivation of equal protection for a school district to effectuate a curriculum which is not tailored to the educational needs of minority students. Serna v. Portales Municipal Schools, 351 F. Supp. 1279, 1283 (D. N.Mex. 1972).

9. Note how the two-way bussing and school closing issues reflect school boards' efforts to handle the clearly present but seldom mentioned problem of association or status, i.e., the unwillingness of white parents to send their children to schools with substantial numbers of nonwhites. In the "two-way bussing" cases, blacks are manifesting a long-felt resistance to paying any price for the sake of school integration. Could their arguments on this point have been better presented? Are such arguments inherently antagonistic to the principles of Brown? The two cases that follow reflect less the attempts

of school boards to resolve this difficult question than their adding insult to injury. The boards had not only closed black schools but sought to maintain segregated classes in the white schools.

JACKSON v. MARVELL SCHOOL DISTRICT NO. 22
425 F.2d 211 (8th Cir. 1970)

Before MATTHES, LAY and HEANEY, Circuit Judges.

Per Curiam.

This is the third time we are required to determine whether the appellee school district has adopted and placed into effect a plan for fully desegregating its schools.

In Jackson II, decided on October 2, 1969, reported at 416 F.2d 380, 8 Cir., we reversed the judgment of the district court and directed it "to require the Marvell School District to file . . . a plan which will convert the present organization of the public schools of Marvell to a unitary, nonracial system. The plan shall eliminate all vestiges of the freedom-of-choice provisions and shall be fully implemented and become effective no later than January 19, 1970." . . .

On remand, the district court entered an order on October 16, 1969, directing the district to submit a plan not later than December 1, 1969, and granting plaintiffs 20 days thereafter to respond. In compliance with that order, the district filed a report in which it proposed to restructure the schools beginning January 19, 1970, as follows: (a) all students in grades 1 through 3 were to be assigned to the site now known as Marvell Elementary School; (b) all students in grades 4 through 9 were to be assigned to the site now known as Tate Elementary School and Tate High School; (c) all students in grades 10 through 12 were to be assigned to the site now known as Marvell High School; (d) all faculty members willing to remain were to be retained and will be so assigned as to realize the maximum utilization of their training and experience without regard to their race.

Under date of December 15, counsel for plaintiffs informed counsel for the school district that in light of the plan proposed by the school district "to which plaintiffs have no objections at this time" there was no need for a hearing to be held.

In the meantime, however, and apparently without knowledge by plaintiffs' counsel at the time the aforesaid letter was written, the superintendent of the district notified all parents in writing of the restructuring of the schools as shown above and further informed them that "insofar as possible students will stay with their same teachers."

The notice from the superintendent precipitated the filing by plaintiffs on January 12, 1970, of a motion to cite the defendants for contempt of court. The motion was premised upon the proposal of the defendants to continue segregation of the classes.

Evidence was not heard on the motion for citation for contempt. However, the district court did hold a hearing on January 14, 1970, at which time the judge ruled from the bench that the plan submitted would be approved with the exception of Subsection (d) relating to the faculty. On January 19, the court's formal order, dated January 16, approving the plan as modified with respect to Subsection (d), was filed. In due time, plaintiffs appealed from that order.

The effect of the approval of the order as demonstrated by correspondence attached to appellees' brief between counsel for appellees and the district judge is to approve the segregation of the races among classes within the several facilities for the remainder of the 1969-70 school year.

Plaintiffs challenge the propriety of the court's failure to require the district to desegregate not only the school facilities but the classes beginning January 19, 1970. They insist that we should reverse and require immediate desegregation of the classes.

We hold the court fell into error in sanctioning the district's ingenious effort to circumvent the plain meaning of our decision. It is settled doctrine that segregation of the races in classrooms constitutes invidious discrimination in violation of the Fourteenth Amendment to the Constitution. . . .

Accordingly, we reverse and remand to the district court. Upon due consideration and with particular reference to the brief time remaining in the school year, we refrain from interfering with the assignment of students in the Marvell School District for the 1969-70 school year. However, we direct the district court to enter an order requiring the district to fully and effectively desegregate not only all facilities but the faculty and classes effective at the beginning of the 1970-71 school year. . . .

MOSES v. WASHINGTON PARISH SCHOOL BOARD, 330 F. Supp. 1340 (E.D. La. 1971). Following an order requiring complete unification of the system, the school board closed the black elementary school, which had been operated on a normal graded structure with heterogeneously grouped students — i.e., students of varying abilities — and reassigned them to the formerly all-white school, which was run on a system of "level structure" division and "homogeneously grouped" students — i.e., students of roughly similar abilities. In the integrated school, the students were assigned to eleven levels, instead of six grades, on the basis of scores made on standardized tests. Within each level, they were grouped homogeneously into sections. The school board justified this policy as intended to put students of more or less equal ability and achievement into small groups which could progress at a similar pace through the various levels of materials to be learned.

In enjoining the policy, the district court found "that testing, as presently used . . . denies plaintiffs equal educational opportunity and impedes establishing of a truly unitary school . . . and has the effect of tending to preserve the dual system of education prohibited under Brown v. Board of Education." The court also found that the closing of the black school was unjustified and violated the principle that formerly all-black schools should be integrated, rather than closed, wherever possible. The court noted that the construction of fifteen temporary classrooms at the white school was a misuse of funds, granted under Title I of the Elementary and Secondary Education Act.

NOTES

1. The Fifth Circuit in 1969 reviewed plans in which school assignments were based on achievement scores, and expressly declared that "testing cannot be employed in any event until unitary school systems have been established." Singleton v. Jackson Municipal Separate School District, 419 F.2d 1211 (5th Cir. 1969). Six years earlier, the court had granted an injunction pending appeal, where a federal district judge had refused to order desegregation because of evidence offered by white intervenors that the children of each race have "distinguishable educability capabilities" and that desegregation would cause psychological harm to the children of both races and adversely affect the educational standards of the school system. Stell v. Savannah-Chatham County Board of Education, 318 F.2d 425 (5th Cir. 1963).

2. With or without the use of I.Q. or achievement tests, civil rights groups report widespread in-school segregation in the wake of implementation of school desegregation plans based on Green and Alexander. These reports indicate that black and white students are assigned to different classrooms, or that segregated racial seating assignments are made within classrooms, on school buses and in extracurricular activities. Investigators have uncovered segregated cafeterias, lunchrooms, dressing rooms and recreation areas. Social activities have been canceled or segregated; black students have been excluded from participation in student government and honor societies; and they have suffered discrimination in athletics, cheerleading and school bands. Black students are also subject to arbitrary suspensions and expulsions. See, e.g., Dunn v. Tyler Independent School District, 327 F. Supp. 528 (E.D. Tex. 1971).

As indicated above, school boards tend wherever possible to close formerly all-black schools. When such schools are made a part of an integration plan, their names are frequently changed, and the colors, songs and symbols of the black students' former schools are abandoned. High school trophies and school pictures are destroyed or consigned to storage. Often, long-sought repairs to formerly black schools are made when white students are assigned to them, and sometimes needless maintenance, such as fumigation, is also carried out. On the other hand, black students assigned to formerly white schools frequently protest the continued use of symbols deemed synonymous with segregation and white supremacy. See, e.g., Smith v. St. Tammany Parish School Board, 448 F.2d 414 (5th Cir. 1971), where the court affirmed an order banning the display by the school board or its employees of symbols or indicia expressing their desire to maintain segregated schools; and Melton v. Young, 465 F.2d 1332 (6th Cir. 1972), affirming suspension of a student who insisted on wearing a Confederate flag (the former school flag) on his jacket, after this symbol had been discontinued because it caused disruptions that interfered materially with the functioning of the school. See, generally, Lawyers Review Committee to Study the Department of Justice 41-44 (Aug. 6, 1972).

3. Perhaps the chief victims of school integration have been black teachers and principals. Despite Supreme Court rulings that students are entitled to challenge faculty segregation (Rogers v. Paul, 382 U.S. 198, 86 S. Ct. 358, 15 L. Ed. 2d 265 (1965)), and the imposition of formulas setting specific quotas for teacher assignments in order to ensure that the racial composition of each school's teaching staff equals the racial composition of all teachers in the entire system (United States v. Montgomery County Board of Education, 395 U.S. 225, 89 S. Ct. 1670, 23 L. Ed. 2d 263 (1969)), literally thousands of black educators have been discharged or demoted in recent years. Investigations conducted by the National Education Association (NEA) indicate that during the three school years 1968-1970, in the Deep South states of Alabama, Florida, Georgia, Louisiana and Mississippi, (1) the number of black teachers decreased by 5 percent or more in 216 school districts, and by 15 percent or more in 128 of these. (2) Among these 216 districts, where the number of black teachers diminished substantially, were 141 that increased the number of white teachers. In those districts where white teachers decreased, the rate of decrease was usually lower than that of blacks, and where the decline in the number of white teachers was greater than that of blacks, it reflected a sharp decline in the number of white students who had left the public school system. (3) In the four states of Florida, Georgia, Louisiana and Mississippi, one out of every five black principalships was eliminated during this period, while white principalships increased by 4 percent. Often, black principals were demoted and became assistants to less qualified whites. See amicus curiae brief for the National Educational Association, United States v. Georgia, No. 30,338 (5th Cir. 1971) at 920-921, 34, 42.

4. In the main, demoted black educators, fearing for their jobs, and dismissed teachers, unwilling to jeopardize future job possibilities, do not challenge the actions taken against them. But literally dozens of suits have been filed on behalf of black teaching professionals who lost their jobs during the desegregation process. Many of these suits have resulted in reinstatement and back pay. See, e.g., Chambers v. Hendersonville City Board of Education, 364 F.2d 189 (4th Cir. 1966); Sparks v. Griffin, 460 F.2d 433 (5th Cir. 1972); Lee v. Roanoke City Board of Education, 466 F.2d 1378 (5th Cir. 1972); Lee v. Macon County Board of Education (Muscle Shoals School System), 453 F.2d 1104 (5th Cir. 1971); McFerren v. County Board of Education of Fayette County, Tenn., 455 F.2d 199 (6th Cir. 1972); Moore v. Board of Education of Chidester School District No. 59, 448 F.2d 709 (8th Cir. 1971); Smith v. Board of Education of Morrilton School District No. 32, 365 F.2d 770 (8th Cir. 1966).

In determining whether personnel reductions necessitated by desegregation were conducted on a discriminatory basis, courts have followed standards similar to those established by the Fifth Circuit in Singleton v. Jackson Municipal Separate School District, 419 F.2d 1211 (1970), where the court directed:

> If there is to be a reduction in the number of principals, teachers, teacher-aides, or other professional staff employed by the school district which will result in a dismissal or demotion of any such staff members, the staff member to be dismissed or demoted must be selected on the basis of objective and reasonable non-discriminatory standards from among all the staff of the school district. In addition if there is any such dismissal or demotion, no staff vacancy may be filled through recruitment of a person of a race, color, or national origin different from that of the individual dismissed or demoted, until each displaced staff member who is qualified has had an opportunity to fill the vacancy and has failed to accept an offer to do so.
>
> Prior to such a reduction, the school board will develop or require the development of nonracial objective criteria to be used in selecting the staff member who is to be dismissed or demoted. These criteria shall be available for public inspection and shall be retained by the school district. The school district also shall record and preserve the evaluation of staff members under the criteria. Such evaluation shall be made available upon request to the dismissed or demoted employee. (419 F.2d at 1218.)

Courts have also had to determine whether school districts in the desegregation process could utilize standardized test results as a basis for teacher retention and hiring.

BAKER v. COLUMBUS MUNICIPAL SEPARATE SCHOOL DISTRICT

462 F.2d 1112 (5th Cir. 1972)

Before Rives, Coleman and Dyer, Circuit Judges.

Dyer, Circuit Judge:

In January, 1970, Columbus Municipal Separate School District initiated a policy that required teachers hired for the first time during the 1969-1970 school year, and all future teacher applicants, to achieve a combined score of 1000 on the National Teachers Examination (NTE) as a condition of employment. The score requirement excluded proportionally more incumbent black than white teachers. Of the 133 black teachers, 18 were required to take the test. Only one achieved the minimum score of 1000. Of the 243 white teachers, 73 were required to take the test and 64 either met or surpassed the minimum score requirement. The district court held that the use of the NTE was unlawful under the equal protection clause of the Fourteenth Amendment because it created a racial classification, and it was not shown to have a manifest relation to job performance. The court also found that Columbus had purposely discriminated against blacks by the use of the NTE score requirement.

The purposeful discrimination finding of the district court was based upon three factors in addition to the racially disproportionate effect produced by the NTE score requirement. First, Columbus knew that the use of the NTE would produce racially disproportionate results because the test had been used in the three preceding years as an element of a merit pay program. During the first year of its use in that program 20 percent of the black teachers who took the test achieved the minimum score while 96 percent of the white teachers tested met the minimum score. In the second and third years of its use 14 percent and 53 percent respectively of the black teachers tested and 87 percent and 95 percent respectively of the white teachers tested achieved a minimum score.

Another indicia of discrimination was found by the court when Columbus required two black teachers hired during the spring term of the 1968-1969 school year to take the test while other teachers employed during that year did not have to take the test. Finally, Columbus hired only one black out of 44 new teachers hired when 9 NTE qualified blacks had applied.

In matters concerning faculty standards and other internal administrative and professional procedures we prefer, if possible, to defer to the judgment of the school administrators. However, the percentage of blacks who failed to meet the 1000 cut-off score compared to the percentage of whites who failed is a circumstance that cannot be dealt with lightly.[3] Whenever the effect of a law or policy produces such a racial distortion it is subject to strict scrutiny. See Korematsu v. United States, 1944, 323 U.S. 214, 216. . . . Even though this policy does not on its face purport to classify along racial lines as in Korematsu and in McLaughlin v. Florida, 1964, 379 U.S. 184, . . . its effects can be just as devastating. See Hawkins v. Shaw, 5 Cir. 1972, 461 F.2d 1171, 1172 (en banc). In order to withstand an equal protection attack it must be justified by an overriding purpose independent of its racial effects.

A school district's desire to improve its faculty may be such an overriding purpose, provided the policies and procedures employed to implement this goal are clearly related to it. See Armstrong v. Starkville Municipal Separate School District, 5 Cir. 1972, 461 F.2d 276; Chance v. Board of Examiners, 2d Cir. 1972, 458 F.2d 1167. But this is not such a case.

It is uncontradicted that the NTE cut-off score requirement was set by

3. In addition to the racial discrepancies evidenced by the use of the NTE in the merit pay program, an Educational Testing Service survey showed that the national average of students taking the NTE Commons examinations from predominantly white institutions is 600 while those students taking the test from predominantly black institutions average 460. The average scores for Mississippi students are lower in both categories. The averages from predominantly white institutions varied from 507-622 while the averages from the predominantly black institutions ranged from 392-438.

appellants without any investigation or study of the validity and reliability of the examination or the cut-off score as a means of selecting teachers for hiring or re-employment, and without consultation with the Educational Testing Service. The superintendent disavowed any expertise in the matter, albeit he was aware of the disparate results that would ensue. It was established that the NTE measures only a fraction of the characteristics required for effective classroom performance. It does not measure manual skills, teaching aptitude, attitudes, personal characteristics or classroom teaching performance. In short, the evidence supports the finding below that the appellants' purpose in using the NTE was not in fact independent of invidious racial discrimination, but was, on the contrary, used for the purpose of discrimination.

The district court found, and the record amply supports the finding, that Columbus acted with the purpose of barring proportionately more black teachers than white teachers from employment and re-employment. We cannot overlook the long history of racial discrimination coupled with the disproportionate reduction of black teachers when desegregation was ordered, the school district's knowledge from prior actual experience that the NTE cut-off score would eliminate relatively more black than white in service teachers and new applicants, and the uneven manner in which appellants applied the NTE cut-off score which eliminated two black teachers who were not subject to the requirement. Finally, stark evidence of a discriminatory hiring policy was shown by the hiring of 43 new white teachers and only 1 black teacher while 9 other black applicants with satisfactory NTE scores were rejected although there were 36 vacancies the day before school was open.

Columbus also appeals that portion of the district court's judgment that requires it to hire as many black teachers for the 1972-1973 school year as may be necessary to attain the racial ratio that existed during the 1969-1970 school year. It maintains that because the judgment does not refer to qualification, it requires Columbus to hire on the basis of race, not qualification, in violation of Carter v. West Feliciana Parish School Board, 5 Cir. 1970, 432 F.2d 875. We disagree. Of course any new teacher, black or white, must be qualified. The district court has properly required Columbus to turn back the faculty clock to the time when the NTE scores did not disqualify teachers for re-employment. See Smith v. Concordia Parish School Board, 5 Cir. 1971, 445 F.2d 285.

Finally, we attach a caveat to what has been said. We look with disfavor upon a test or policy which obviously disadvantages the black teachers, especially when this is due to the past inferior educational opportunities suffered by them. On the other hand, we fully recognize that a school district has the responsibility of providing the best possible education for its pupils, including efforts to constantly improve its faculty. When a test has a valid function in such a process and is fairly applied to all teachers, it outweighs the fact that it may result in excluding proportionally more blacks than whites.

The judgment of the district court is affirmed.

NOTES

1. The Fifth Circuit in Armstead v. Starkville Municipal Separate School District, 461 F.2d 276 (1972), affirmed a district court's finding that neither the National Teachers Examination (NTE) nor the Graduate Record Examination had been designed and could be used to measure teaching competency or future teaching effectiveness, and for this reason, the tests could be invalidated even without a showing that the policy requiring their use created a racial classification. However, the court refused to uphold a similar finding as to the school system's policy providing that a master's degree or an "AA Teaching Certificate" could be substituted for the requisite grade on the Graduate Record Examination. (Judge Rives dissented.) The same circuit in Lee v. Macon County Board of Education (Sumter County School System), 463 F.2d 1174 (5th Cir. 1972), held that the use of the National Teacher's Examination, as one of several nonracial objective criteria for employing, dismissing, transferring, promoting and demoting teachers and staff members, was not improper. See also United States v. Texas Education Agency, 459 F.2d 600, 604 (5th Cir. 1972).

2. In Chance v. Board of Examiners, 458 F.2d 1167 (2d Cir. 1972), the court upheld a preliminary injunction granted against the New York City Board of Examiners. It prohibited the use of tests which discriminate against blacks and Puerto Ricans and are not job related, as prerequisites for supervisory positions in the city's school system. The lower court had found that the examinations were not valid as to content or predictiveness, and that white candidates passed the examinations "at almost one and one-half times the rate of Black and Puerto Rican candidates." The court's finding that the tests were discriminatory was based not only on the small number of minority candidates who passed, but also on the small number of principals and assistant principals employed in the city's system, as compared to the number of such personnel in other large cities not utilizing similar tests.

3. But in United States v. Nansemond County School Board, 351 F. Supp. 196 (E.D. Va. 1972), a district court has approved as "reasonable" the limited use of portions of the NTE by a school board as one criterion for measuring new teacher applicants. The court acknowledged that the NTE is lacking in content validity, i.e., a correlation between a score and ultimate effectiveness on the job. But referring to expert testimony, the court found that an accurate test was impossible, particularly when no one could define the qualities of an "effective teacher," and that the NTE's content does have some job-relatedness, particularly in the section used by the board. In reaching its conclusions about the test, the court relied heavily on testimony of

fered by officials of the Educational Testing Service who administer the NTE.

4. In the next two cases, the Supreme Court reviewed an issue of potentially major value to school systems hoping to escape — or at least limit — the impact of Brown by totally restructuring school district lines. Their efforts posed this question for the Court: Under what circumstances may a federal court enjoin local officials from carving out a new school district from an existing district that has not yet completed the process of dismantling a system of enforced racial segregation?

WRIGHT v. COUNCIL OF CITY OF EMPORIA
407 U.S. 451, 92 S. Ct. 2196, 33 L. Ed. 2d 51 (1972)

[In this case and its companion, United States v. Scotland Neck City Board of Education, 407 U.S. 484, 92 S. Ct. 2214, 33 L. Ed. 2d 75 (1972), the Court reviewed reversal by the Fourth Circuit of orders enjoining the creation of new school districts. The district court deemed the new districts a subterfuge to evade effectuation of earlier school desegregation orders. In Wright, the Court, by a 5 to 4 vote, ruled that the district court had properly enjoined the city of Emporia from withdrawing from the Greensville County School District, which had not yet completed disestablishment of its former dual school system, because evidence indicated that the effect of the proposed withdrawal would be to impede school desegregation.

The city of Emporia had been an integral part of the county school system until 1967, when, by state law, it was given the duty to provide resident children with free public education. To satisfy this obligation, Emporia had contracted to purchase educational services from the county, determining that such action was in the educational interest of its citizens, their children, and the citizens and children of Greensville County. At this time, a school desegregation suit initiated by the Wright petitioners in 1966 had resulted in a "freedom of choice" plan, which plan produced only minimal integration. In 1969, however, compliance with the Supreme Court's decision in Green v. County School Board, supra page 462, resulted in the district court's ordering a "pairing" plan that required the school board to match a formerly all-white school with a nearby formerly all-black school. Two weeks after the district court entered its decree, Emporia advised Greensville County that it was terminating the contract for purchase of educational services, and was assuming control of the schools within its boundaries so as to operate a separate school system beginning in September 1969. At that time 66 percent of the students in the entire county system were black. Emporia's withdrawal would have increased the figure in the county to 72 percent, while in the new city district, 52 percent of the students would have been black. At the request of petitioners, the district court granted a preliminary injunction, which it subsequently made permanent. In concluding that the proposed secession would have adverse effects on the court-sanctioned desegregation plan, the district judge pointed out the disparity in racial makeup between the proposed city school system and the resulting county system, and the possibility that the city's withdrawal would leave the county without the financial means or leadership ability necessary to make a successful transition to a unitary system. In reversing, the Fourth Circuit discounted the district court's findings on the likely practical effect of secession, and held that unless the "primary" or "dominant" purpose of the city was "to retain as much separation of the races as possible," the district court lacked authority to enjoin. 442 F.2d 570, 572 (1971).]

Mr. Justice Stewart delivered the opinion of the court.

II

Emporia takes the position that since it is a separate political jurisdiction entitled under state law to establish a school system independent of the county, its action may be enjoined only upon a finding either that the state law under which it acted is invalid, that the boundaries of the city are drawn so as to exclude Negroes, or that the disparity of the racial balance of the city and county schools of itself violates the Constitution. As we read its opinion, the District Court made no such findings, nor do we.

The constitutional violation that formed the predicate for the District Court's action was the enforcement until 1969 of racial segregation in a public school system of which Emporia had always been a part. That finding has not been challenged, nor has Emporia questioned the propriety of the "pairing" order of June 25, 1969, which was designed to remedy the condition that offended the Constitution. Both before and after it became a city, Emporia educated its children in the county schools. Only when it became clear — 15 years after our decision in Brown v. Board of Education, 347 U.S. 483 . . . — that segregation in the county system was finally to be abolished, did Emporia attempt to take its children out of the county system. Under these circumstances, the power of the District Court to enjoin Emporia's withdrawal from that system need not rest upon an independent constitutional violation. The court's remedial power was invoked on the basis of a finding that the dual school system violated the Constitution, and since the city and the county constituted but one unit for the purpose of student assignments during the entire time that the dual system was maintained, they were properly treated as a single unit for the purpose of dismantling that system. . . .

The effect of Emporia's proposal was to erect new boundary lines for the purpose of school attendance in a district where no such lines had previously existed, and where a dual school system had long flourished. Under the principles of Green and Monroe, such a proposal must be judged according to whether it hinders or furthers the process of school desegregation. If the proposal would impede the dismantling of the dual system, then a district court, in the exercise of its remedial discretion, may enjoin it from being carried out.

The Court of Appeals apparently did not believe this case to be governed by the principles of Green and Monroe. It held that the question whether new school district boundaries should be permitted in areas with a history of state-enforced racial segregation is to be resolved in terms of the "dominant purpose of [the] boundary realignment." . . .

This "dominant purpose" test finds no precedent in our decisions. It is true that where an action by school authorities is motivated by a demonstrated discriminatory purpose, the existence of that purpose may add to the discriminatory effect of the action by intensifying the stigma of implied racial inferiority. And where a school board offers non-racial justifications for a plan that is less effective than other alternatives for dismantling a dual school system, a demonstrated racial purpose may be taken into consideration in determining the weight to be given to the proffered justification. . . . But as we said in Palmer v. Thompson, 403 U.S. 217, 225, . . . it "is difficult or impossible for any court to determine the 'sole' or 'dominant' motivation behind the choices of a group of legislators," and the same may be said of the choices of a school board. In addition, an inquiry into the "dominant" motivation of school authorities is as irrelevant as it is fruitless. The mandate of Brown II was to desegregate schools, and we have said that "[t]he measure of any desegregation plan is its effectiveness." Davis v. Board of School Commissioners, 402 U.S. 33, 37. . . . Thus, we have focused upon the effect — not the purpose or motivation — of a school board's action in determining whether it is a permissible method of dismantling a dual system. The existence of a permissible purpose cannot sustain an action that has an impermissible effect.

The reasoning of the Court of Appeals in this case is at odds with that of other federal courts which have held that splinter school districts may not be created "where the effect — to say nothing of the purpose — of the secession has a substantial adverse effect on desegregation of the county school district." Lee v. Macon County Bd. of Education, 5 Cir. 448 F.2d 746, 752. See also Stout v. United States (Jefferson County Bd. of Education v. Board of Education for City of Pleasant Grove), 5 Cir., 448 F.2d 403, 404; Haney v. County Bd. of Education, 8 Cir., 410 F.2d 920, 924; Burleson v. County Bd. of Election Commissioners, D.C., 308 F. Supp. 352, 356, *aff'd,* 8 Cir., 432 F.2d 1356; Aytch v. Mitchell, D.C., 320 F. Supp. 1372, 1377. Though the *purpose* of the new school districts was found to be discriminatory in many of these cases, the courts' holdings rested not on motivation or purpose, but on the *effect* of the action upon the dismantling of the dual school systems involved. That was the focus of the District Court in this case, and we hold that its approach was proper.

III

The basis for the District Court's ruling was its conclusion that if Emporia were allowed to establish an independent system, Negroes remaining in the county schools would be deprived of what Brown II promised them: a school system in which all vestiges of enforced racial segregation have been eliminated. The District Court noted that the effect of Emporia's withdrawal would be a "substantial increase in the proportion of whites in the schools attended by city residents, and a concomitant decrease in the county schools." 309 F. Supp., at 680. In addition, the court found that the departure of the city's students, its leadership, and its financial support, together with the possible loss of teachers to the new system, would diminish the chances that transition to unitary schools in the county would prove "successful."

Certainly, desegregation is not achieved by splitting a single school system operating "white schools" and "Negro schools" into two new systems, each operating unitary schools within its borders, where one of the two new systems is, in fact, "white" and the other is, in fact, "Negro." Nor does a court supervising the process of desegregation exercise its remedial discretion responsibly where it approves a plan that, in the hope of providing better "quality education" to some children, has a substantial adverse effect upon the quality of education available to others. In some cases, it may be readily perceived that a proposed subdivision of a school district will produce one or both of these results. In other cases, the likelihood of such results may be less apparent. This case is of the latter kind, but an examination of the record shows that the District Court's conclusions were adequately supported by the evidence.

Data submitted to the District Court at its December hearing showed that the school system in operation under the "pairing" plan, including both Emporia and the county, had a racial composition of 34% white and 66% Negro. If Emporia had established its own system, and had total enrollment remained the same, the city's schools would have been 48% white and 52% Negro, while the county's schools would have been 28% white and 72% Negro.

We need not and do not hold that this disparity in the racial composition of the two systems would be a sufficient reason, standing alone, to enjoin the creation of the separate school district. The fact that a school board's desegregation plan leaves some disparity in racial balance among various schools in the system does not alone make that plan unacceptable. We observed in Swann, supra, that "the constitutional command to desegregate schools does not mean that every school in every community must always reflect the racial composition of the school system as a whole." 402 U.S., at 24. . . .

But there is more to this case than the disparity in racial percentages reflected by the figures supplied by the school board. In the first place, the District Court found that if Emporia were allowed to withdraw from the existing system, it "may be anticipated that the proportion of whites in county schools may drop as those who can register in private academies," 309 F. Supp., at 680, while some whites might return to the city schools from the private schools in which they had previously enrolled. Thus, in the judgment of the District Court, the statistical breakdown of the 1969-1970 enrollment figures between city residents and county residents did not reflect what the situation would have been had Emporia established its own school system.

Second, the significance of any racial disparity in this case is enhanced by the fact that the two formerly all-white schools are located within Emporia, while all the schools located in the surrounding county were formerly all-Negro. The record further reflects that the school buildings in Emporia are better equipped and are located on better sites than are those in the county. We noted in Swann that factors such as these may in themselves indicate that enforced racial segregation has been perpetuated. . . .

Just as racial balance is not required in remedying a dual system, neither are racial ratios the sole consideration to be taken into account in devising a workable remedy.

The timing of Emporia's action is a third factor that was properly taken into account by the District Court in assessing the effect of the action upon children remaining in the county schools. While Emporia had long had the right under state law to establish a separate school system, its decision to do so came only upon the basis of — and, as the city officials conceded, in reaction to — a court order that prevented the county system from maintaining any longer the segregated system that had lingered for 15 years after Brown I. In the words of Judge Winter, dissenting in the Court of Appeals, "[i]f the establishment of an Emporia school district is not enjoined, the black students in the county will watch as nearly one-half the total number of white students in the county abandon the county schools for a substantially whiter system." 442 F.2d 588, at 590. The message of this action, coming when it did, cannot have escaped the Negro children in the county. As we noted in Brown I: "To separate [Negro school children] from others of similar age and qualifications solely because of their race generates a feeling of inferiority as to their status in the community that may affect their hearts and minds in a way unlikely ever to be undone." 347 U.S., at 494 . . . . We think that, under the circumstances, the District Court could rationally have concluded that the same adverse psychological effect was likely to result from Emporia's withdrawal of its children from the Greensville County system.

The weighing of these factors to determine their effect upon the process of desegregation is a delicate task that is aided by a sensitivity to local conditions, and the judgment is primarily the responsibility of the district judge. See Brown II, supra, 349 U.S. at 299 . . . . Given the totality of the circumstances, we hold that the District Court was justified in its conclusion that Emporia's establishment of a separate system would actually impede the process of dismantling the existing dual system.

IV

Against these considerations, Emporia advances arguments that a separate system is necessary to achieve "quality education" for city residents, and that it is unfair in any event to force the city to continue to send its children to schools over which the city, because of the character of its arrangement with the county, has very little control. These arguments are entitled to consideration by a court exercising its equitable discretion where they are directed to the feasibility or practicality of the proposed remedy. See Swann v. Charlotte-Mecklenburg Board of Education, supra, 402 U.S., at 31 . . . . But as we said in Green v. County School Board, etc., supra, the availability of "more promising courses of action" to dismantle a dual system "at the least . . . places a heavy burden upon the board to explain its preference for an apparently less effective method." 391 U.S., at 439 . . . .

In evaluating Emporia's claims, it must be remembered that the city represents the interests of less than one-third of the students in the system being desegregated. Only the city officials argue that their plan is preferable to the "pairing" plan encompassing the whole of the city-county system. Although the county school board took no position in the District Court either for or against Emporia's action, it had previously adopted a resolution stating its belief that the city's action was not in the best interests of the county children. In terms of Green, it was only the respondents — not the county school board — who expressed a "preference for an apparently less effective method" of desegregation.

At the final hearing in the District Court, the respondents presented detailed budgetary proposals and other evidence demonstrating that they contemplated a more diverse and more expensive educational program than that to which the city children had been accustomed in the Greensville County schools. These plans for the city system were developed after the preliminary injunction was issued in this case. In August, 1969, one month before classes were scheduled to open, the city officials were intent upon operating a separate system despite the fact that the city had no buildings under lease, no teachers under contract, and no specific plans for the operation of the schools. Thus, the persuasiveness of the "quality education" rationale was open to question. More important, however, any increased quality of education provided to city students would, under the circumstances found by the District Court, have been purchased only at the price of a substantial adverse effect upon the viability of the county system. The District Court, with its responsibility to provide an effective remedy for segregation in the entire city-county system, could not properly allow the city to make its part of that system more attractive where such a result would be accomplished at the expense of the children remaining in the county.

A more weighty consideration put forth by Emporia is its lack of formal control over the school system under the terms of its contract with the county. This argument is properly addressed to the practicality of the District Court's action. . . .

We do not underestimate the deficiencies, from Emporia's standpoint, in the arrangement by which it undertook in 1968 to provide for the education of its children. Direct control over decisions vitally affecting the education of one's children is a need that is strongly felt in our society, and since 1967 the citizens of Emporia have had little of that control. But Emporia did find its arrangement with the county both feasible and practical up until the time of the desegregation decree issued in the summer of 1969. While city officials testified that they were dissatisfied with the terms of the contract prior to that time, they did not attempt to change it. They argued that the arrangement became intolerable when the "pairing" decree was entered, because the county officials who would control the budget of the unitary system lacked the desire to make the unitary system work. The District Court did not accept the contention that a lack of enthusiasm on the part of county leaders would, if Emporia children remained in the system, block a successful transition to unitary schools. The court felt that the "desire of the city leaders, coupled with their obvious leadership ability," would make itself felt despite the absence of any formal control by the city over the system's budget and operation, and that the city's leadership would be "an important facet in the successful operation of any court-ordered plan." 309 F. Supp., at 679. Under these circumstances, we cannot say that the enforced continuation of the single city-county system was not "reasonable, feasible, and workable."

The District Court explicitly noted in its opinion that its injunction does not have the effect of locking Emporia into its present circumstances for all time. As already noted, our holding today does not rest upon a conclusion that the disparity in racial balance between the city and county schools resulting from separate systems would, absent any other considerations, be unacceptable. The city's creation of a separate school system was enjoined because of the effect it would have had at the time upon the effectiveness of the remedy ordered to dismantle the dual system that had long existed in the area. Once the unitary system has been established and accepted, it may be that Emporia, if it still desires to do so, may establish an independent system without such an adverse effect upon the students remaining in the county, or it may be able to work out a more satisfactory arrangement with the county for joint operation of the existing system. We hold only that a new school district may not be created where its effect would be to impede the process of dismantling a dual system. And in making that essentially factual determination in any particular case, "we must of necessity rely to a large extent, as this Court has for more than 16 years, on the informed judgment of the district courts in the first instance and on courts of appeals." Swann, supra, 402 U.S., at 28 . . . . In this case, we believe that the District Court did not abuse its discretion. For these reasons, the judgment of the Court of Appeals is reversed.

Reversed.

Mr. Chief Justice BURGER, with whom Mr. Justice BLACKMUN, Mr. Justice POWELL, and Mr. Justice REHNQUIST join, dissenting.

[Based on their review of the record, the dissenters found that severance of the two systems would not result in school assignments based on race, and would not affect the unitary nature of the two school systems. While the racial ratios of the two school systems would differ, both would remain majority blacks systems, and the elimination of such disparities is not the mission of desegregation. Chief Justice Burger observed that the facts of this case indicate the pointlessness of a "racial balancing" approach, since normal population shifts could change such a balance within a short period of time. The dissent noted: "The Court disavows a 'racial balancing' approach, and seeks to justify the District Court's ruling by relying on several additional factors thought to aggravate the effect of the racial disparity. The real significance of these additional factors is so negligible as to suggest that the racial imbalance itself may be what the Court finds most acceptable."

Reviewing these three factors, Chief Justice Burger concluded that the likelihood of white flight was "highly speculative." He could find no support in the record or the lower court opinions for the proposition that the facilities of the county schools were inferior. Finally, he did not believe that the psychological impact on black children of dividing the county school district could be equated with the feelings of inferiority considered in Brown I. He argued, rather, that neither "common experience nor . . . scientific authority" supports the Court's conclusion that an "adverse psychological effect" would result from the city's secession.

The dissent was also critical of the short shrift given by the majority to Emporia's express desire to create a high quality separate system. It found no basis in the record for the fear that the quality of education in the county schools would suffer, and suggested that, if desegregation in the county was destined should Emporia establish its own school system, it is difficult to understand why there would not be an undue risk in allowing separation in the future, as promised by the district court.

Finally, while acknowledging that a school desegregation plan must be effective, the dissenters suggested that, even after a dual school system is dismantled (as they felt it plainly had been in Emporia), courts must be alert to make sure that ostensibly nondiscriminatory actions are not designed to discriminate against children on the basis of race. But, the dissent concluded:]

There is no basis for concluding, on this record, that Emporia's decision to operate a separate school system was the manifestation of a discriminatory purpose. The strongest finding made by the District Court was that race was "in a sense" a factor in the city's decision; read in context, this ambiguous finding does not relate to any invidious consideration of race. The District Court relied solely on the following testimony of the chairman of the city school board:

> Race, of course, affected the operation of the schools by the county, and I again say, I do not think, or we felt that the county was not capable of putting the monies in and the effort and the leadership into a system that would effectively make a unitary system work. . . . 309 F. Supp. at 680.

I cannot view this kind of consideration of race as discriminatory or even objectionable. The same doubts about the county's commitment to the operation of a high-quality unitary system would have come into play even if the racial composition of Emporia were precisely the same as that of the entire county area, including Emporia.

Nor is this a case where we can presume a discriminatory purpose from an obviously discriminatory effect. Cf. Gomillion v. Lightfoot, 364 U.S. 339 . . . . We are not confronted with an awkward gerrymander or striking shift in racial proportions. The modest difference between the racial composition of Emporia's proposed separate school system and that of the county as a whole affords no basis for an inference of racial motivation. And while it seems that the more cumbersome features of the District Court's plan hastened the city's inevitable decision to operate a separate unitary school system, this was not because of any desire to manipulate the racial balance of its schools.

Read as a whole this record suggests that the District Court, acting before our decision in Swann was reaching for some hypothetical perfection in racial balance, rather than the elimination of a dual school system. To put it in the simplest terms the Court, in adopting the District Court's approach, goes too far.

NOTES

1. In the companion case, United States v. Scotland Neck City Board of Education, Justice Stewart, speaking for the Court, found that implementation of a North Carolina statute that authorized creation of a new school district for a city which at the time was part of a county school district undergoing the school desegregation process, would have the effect of carving out of the existing district a new unit in which 57 percent of the students would be white and 43 percent black. Schools remaining in the existing county district would be 89 percent black, a factor which would impede disestablishment of the dual school system in the county. In the Scotland Neck case, the Court relied primarily on a substantial disparity in the racial composition of the two proposed school systems, in finding that division of the existing school system would delay ending the racial identification of the schools. In addition to noting the statistical results, by race, of the proposed separation, the Court added that enthusiastic response to the plan by whites in one of the proposed divisions confirmed that the process of removal of racial identification would be impeded. The four dissenters in Wright joined in the Scotland Neck case in a concurring opinion, written by Chief Justice Burger. They agreed that the effect of that city's proposed secession from a larger school district would be to impede desegregation. The Chief Justice stressed the facts that the Scotland Neck City schools would be predominantly white, that special legislation had to be passed by the North Carolina legislature to enable the city to secede, and that the action was "substantially motivated by the desire to create a predominantly white school system." 407 U.S. at 491-492.

2. Despite the efforts by the Wright majority to distinguish Palmer v. Thompson, 403 U.S. 217, 91 S. Ct. 1940, 29 L. Ed. 438 (1971), printed supra

page 221, its rejection of the Fourth Circuit's "dominant purpose" test, close scrutiny of discriminatory purpose (as measured by the student racial ratios, the disparity in school quality, and the timing of the secession effort), and the summary rejection of the city's justifying arguments, all reflect a willingness to review motive or purpose and conclude that the effect is discriminatory. See also Whitcomb v. Chavis, 403 U.S. 124, 91 S. Ct. 1858, 29 L. Ed. 2d 363 (1971), printed supra page 179.

3. One comment, 86 Harv. L. Rev. 62 (1972), has suggested that the majority in Wright v. Council of City of Emporia may have decided to cast its consideration of the city's decision to secede in terms of effect, rather than purpose, in a desire to avoid confrontation with the principles enunciated the previous term in Palmer, in which the Court affirmed lower court decisions upholding the city of Jackson's decision to close its municipal swimming pools after a federal court had ordered them desegregated. It distinguished earlier cases which had indicated that the purpose behind official action was relevant in determining the action's constitutionality, on the ground that legislative motivation has never been "solely" the reason for finding a denial of equal protection. The Court then ruled that constitution inquiry should focus, rather, on the "effects" of the action. See 86 Harv. L. Rev. 62 (1972). But in school desegregation cases like Wright, a court must predict the effects of a proposed plan, and, as the dissent indicates, those predictions need not prove accurate. In Palmer, on the other hand, the effects of the action were known immediately.

4. The Fifth Circuit has read the Supreme Court's rule on purpose in Wright v. City of Emporia as conforming the law of the land with a rule it has long followed. Citing a long list of its decisions, the Fifth Circuit wrote, "this Court has never tempered its prohibition of school board actions that create, maintain, or foster segregation by the requirement that the discriminatory intent be shown. The underpinning of our decisions is a determination of the unlawful effect of state action upon the existence of unitary school systems." Cisneros v. Corpus Christi Independent School District, 467 F.2d 142, 150 (5th Cir. 1972). See also United States v. Texas Education Agency, 467 F.2d 848 (5th Cir. 1972).

5. But in Bullock v. Washington, 468 F.2d 1096 (D.C. Cir. 1972), the District of Columbia Circuit refused to consider congressional motive or purpose in a measure which prohibited the District of Columbia schools from funding a school integration program involving the bussing of black children from the district to a predominantly white suburban school. While the majority conceded that the inevitable effect of the measure is removal of the possibility of the district's providing financial support for the integration plan, virtually the only one in a predominantly (97.7 percent) black inner-city school, such facts, in its view, did not make out a case of racial discrimination that raised a substantial constitutional question.

In dissent, Judge Robinson said that the congressional action must be measured by the control Congress exercises over the district and its schools, the history of segregation in the district's schools, and a federal court's direction to the district board (Hobson v. Hansen, 269 F. Supp. 401, 510-511 (D.D.C. 1967)) to explore cooperative programs with suburban school systems. The measure serves as an "antibussing" law that burdens the implementation of educational policies designed to deal with race on the local level. Judge Robinson felt that for these reasons the measure should have been submitted to a three-judge court for a determination of its validity.

NOTE ON PRIVATE SCHOOLS AND ACADEMIES

While school systems have had little success in avoiding desegregation by secession, white children have left public schools by the thousands to enroll in private schools and academies. The Southern Regional Council in Atlanta, Georgia estimated that 300,000 Southern white children were attending such establishments by the start of the 1969-1970 school year, and that during that year (with the decisions in Alexander and Carter) another 100,000 white children left the public schools. As happened during the early 1960s (see Griffin v. County School Board of Prince Edward County, 377 U.S. 218, 84 S. Ct. 1226, 12 L. Ed. 2d 256 (1964), and discussion supra page 459, states have attempted to aid these private schools in a variety of forms that have been challenged in the courts. In Mississippi, state tuition grants were held unconstitutional because they "encouraged, facilitated and supported the establishment of" a system of segregated schools. Coffey v. State Educational Finance Committee, 296 F. Supp. 1389 (S.D. Miss. 1969). And black Mississippians, contesting the federal government's policy of granting tax exemptions to such schools and allowing contributions to them to be deductible, obtained a ruling that the granting of tax benefits to racially discriminatory private schools was invalid under the Internal Revenue Code, as being contrary to the federal public policy of providing unitary and desegregated schools. Green v. Connolly, 330 F. Supp. 1150 (D.D.C. 1971), *aff'd sub nom.* Coit v. Green, 404 U.S. 997.

But the value of Green was seriously diminished by IRS policies permitting a private school to obtain or retain exempt status, merely by submitting a signed statement that its admissions policy is nondiscriminatory, and that it has so informed its community or will do so. No more stringent policy was required because of IRS "hopes" that those who signed assurances of nondiscrimination would abide by them. Lawyers' Review Committee to Study the Department of Justice, 35-37 (Aug. 6, 1972).

Federal courts have been less sympathetic with efforts by private schools to lease or purchase public school buildings — see, e.g., McNeal v. Tate County School District, 460 F.2d 568 (5th Cir. 1972); Wright v. City of Brighton, Ala., 441 F.2d 447 (5th Cir. 1971) — or to use city-owned recreational facilities, Gilmore v. City of Montgomery, 337 F. Supp. 22 (M.D. Ala. 1972). But a three-judge court in Mississippi refused to invalidate a state law that authorized the provision of textbooks to all school children —

including those attending private segregated schools. The court held the procedure constitutional on the basis that the textbook policy preceded school desegregation, and that the provision of textbooks did not constitute direct or indirect aid to the private academies. The court also distinguished cases such as Poindexter v. Louisiana Financial Commission, 275 F. Supp. 833 (E.D. La. 1967), *aff'd* 389 U.S. 571 (1968), and Green v. Connolly, supra, on the basis that the Mississippi statute was not limited to students attending segregated academies, but ensured that all Mississippi students received textbooks, thus making the program "racially neutral." Norwood v. Harrison, 340 F. Supp. 1003 (N.D. Miss. 1972). The Supreme Court reversed, 413 U.S. 455, 93 S. Ct. 2804, 37 L. Ed. 2d 723 (1973).

C. ESTABLISHING THE LIMITS OF BROWN

In the aftermath of the Green and Alexander decisions in 1968 and 1969, there remained the question of what techniques could be employed by federal courts to effectuate the new "at once" requirement. Noting the confusion, Chief Justice Burger observed in 1970 that the Court

> . . . as soon as possible . . . ought to resolve some of the basic practical problems when they are appropriately presented, including whether, as a constitutional matter, any particular racial balance must be achieved in the schools; to what extent school districts and zones may or must be altered is a constitutional matter; to what extent transportation may or must be provided to achieve the ends sought by prior holdings of the Court. (Northcross v. Board of Education of Memphis, Tenn., 397 U.S. 232, 237, 90 S. Ct. 891, 893, 25 L. Ed. 2d 246, 251 (1970).)

In Swann v. Charlotte-Mecklenburg Board of Education the Supreme Court attempted to deal comprehensively with the permissibility of certain school desegregation procedures.

SWANN v. CHARLOTTE-MECKLENBURG BOARD OF EDUCATION
402 U.S. 1, 91 S. Ct. 1267, 28 L. Ed. 2d 554 (1971)

Mr. Chief Justice BURGER delivered the opinion of the Court. We granted certiorari in this case to review important issues as to the duties of school authorities and the scope of powers of federal courts under this Court's mandates to eliminate racially separate public schools established and maintained by state action. Brown v. Board of Education, 347 U.S. 483 . . . (1954).

This case and those argued with it arose in states having a long history of maintaining two sets of schools in a single school system deliberately operated to carry out a governmental policy to separate pupils in schools solely on the basis of race. That was what Brown v. Board of Education was all about. These cases present us with the problem of defining in more precise terms than heretofore the scope of the duty of school authorities and district courts in implementing Brown I and the mandate to eliminate dual systems and establish unitary systems at once. Meanwhile district courts and courts of appeals have struggled in hundreds of cases with a multitude and variety of problems under this Court's general directive. Understandably, in an area of evolving remedies, those courts had to improvise and experiment without detailed or specific guidelines. This Court, in Brown I, appropriately dealt with the large constitutional principles; other federal courts had to grapple with the flinty, intractable realities of day-to-day implementation of those constitutional commands. Their efforts, of necessity, embraced a process of "trial and error," and our effort to formulate guidelines must take into account their experience.

I

The Charlotte-Mecklenburg school system, the 43d largest in the Nation, encompasses the city of Charlotte and surrounding Mecklenburg County, North Carolina. The area is large — 550 square miles — spanning roughly 22 miles east-west and 36 miles north-south. During the 1968-1969 school year the system served more than 84,000 pupils in 107 schools. Approximately 71% of the pupils were found to be white and 29% Negro. As of June 1969 there were approximately 24,000 Negro students in the system, of whom 21,000 attended schools within the city of Charlotte. Two-thirds of those 21,000 — approximately 14,000 Negro students — attended 21 schools which were either totally Negro or more than 99% Negro.

This situation came about under a desegregation plan approved by the District Court at the commencement of the present litigation in 1965, 243 F. Supp. 667 (W.D.N.C.), *aff'd,* 369 F.2d 29 (CA4 1966), based upon geographic zoning with a free transfer provision. The present proceedings were initiated in September 1968 by Petitioner Swann's motion for further relief based on Green v. County School Board, 391 U.S. 430 . . . (1968), and its companion cases. All parties now agree that in 1969 the system fell short of achieving the unitary school system that those cases require.

[Here the opinion reviews a series of plans submitted by the school board and by a court-appointed educational expert, Dr. John Finger. His plan, in addition to redrawing school zone lines to promote desegregation, assigned inner-city black children to outlying predominantly white schools and vice versa, and used various other zoning, pairing and grouping techniques, with the result that student bodies throughout the system ranged from 9 to 38 percent black. After various appeals, the district court in August 1970 approved the Finger plan.]

II

Nearly 17 years ago this Court held, in explicit terms, that state-imposed segregation by race in public schools denies equal protection of the laws. At no time has the Court deviated in the slightest degree from that holding or its constitutional underpinnings. . . .

Over the 15 years since Brown II, many difficulties were encountered in implementation of the basic constitutional requirement that the State not discriminate between public school children on the basis of their race. Nothing in our national experience prior to 1955 prepared anyone for dealing with changes and adjustments of the magnitude and complexity encountered since then. Deliberate resistance of some to the Court's mandates has impeded the good-faith efforts of others to bring school systems into compliance. The detail and nature of these dilatory tactics have been noted frequently by this Court and other courts.

By the time the Court considered Green v. County School Board, 391 U.S. 430 . . . in 1968, very little progress had been made in many areas where dual school systems had historically been maintained by operation of state laws. In Green, the Court was confronted with a record of a freedom-of-choice program that the District Court had found to operate in fact to preserve a dual system more than a decade after Brown II. While acknowledging that a freedom-of-choice concept could be a valid remedial measure in some circumstances, its failure to be effective in Green required that "The burden on a school board today is to come forward with a plan that promises realistically to work *now* . . . until it is clear that state-imposed segregation has been completely removed." Green, at 439.

The problems encountered by the district courts and courts of appeals make plain that we should now try to amplify guidelines, however incomplete and imperfect, for the assistance of school authorities and courts.[5] The failure of local authorities to meet their constitutional obligations aggravated the massive problem of converting from the state-enforced discrimination of racially separate school systems. This process has been rendered more difficult by changes since 1954 in the structure and patterns of communities, the growth of student population,[6] movement of families, and other changes, some of which had marked impact on school planning, sometimes neutralizing or negating remedial action before it was fully implemented. Rural areas accustomed for half a century to the consolidated school systems implemented by bus transportation could make adjustments more readily than metropolitan areas with dense and shifting population, numerous schools, congested and complex traffic patterns.

III

The objective today remains to eliminate from the public schools all vestiges of state-imposed segregation. . . .

5. The necessity for this is suggested by the situation in the Fifth Circuit where 166 appeals in school desegregation cases were heard between December 2, 1969, and September 24, 1970.

6. Elementary public school population (grades 1-6) grew from 17,447,000 in 1954 to 23,103,000 in 1969; secondary school population grew from 11,183,000 in 1954 to 20,-775,000 in 1969. Digest of Educational Statistics, 1964 ed. 1, 6, Office of Education Publication No. 10024-64; Digest of Educational Statistics, 1970 ed. Table 28, Office of Education Publication No. 10024-70.

If school authorities fail in their affirmative obligations under these holdings, judicial authority may be invoked. Once a right and a violation have been shown, the scope of a district court's equitable powers to remedy past wrongs is broad, for breadth and flexibility are inherent in equitable remedies. . . .

This allocation of responsibility once made, the Court attempted from time to time to provide some guidelines for the exercise of the district judge's discretion and for the reviewing function of the courts of appeals. However, a school desegregation case does not differ fundamentally from other cases involving the framing of equitable remedies to repair the denial of a constitutional right. The task is to be correct, by a balancing of the individual and collective interests, the condition that offends the Constitution.

In seeking to define even in broad and general terms how far this remedial power extends it is important to remember that judicial powers may be exercised only on the basis of a constitutional violation. Remedial judicial authority does not put judges automatically in the shoes of school authorities whose powers are plenary. Judicial authority enters only when local authority defaults.

School authorities are traditionally charged with broad power to formulate and implement educational policy and might well conclude, for example, that in order to prepare students to live in a pluralistic society each school should have a prescribed ratio of Negro to white students reflecting the proportion for the district as a whole. To do this as an educational policy is within the broad discretionary powers of school authorities; absent a finding of a constitutional violation, however, that would not be within the authority of a federal court. As with any equity case, the nature of the violation determines the scope of the remedy. In default by the school authorities of their obligation to proffer acceptable remedies, a district court has broad power to fashion a remedy that will assure a unitary school system.

The school authorities argue that the equity powers of federal district courts have been limited by Title IV of the Civil Rights Act of 1964, 42 U.S.C. §2000c et seq. The language and the history of Title IV shows that it was not enacted to limit but to define the role of the Federal Government in the implementation of the Brown I decision. It authorizes the Commissioner of Education to provide technical assistance to local boards in the preparation of desegregation plans, to arrange "training institutes" for school personnel involved in desegregation efforts, and to make grants directly to schools to ease the transition to unitary systems. It also authorizes the Attorney General, in specified circumstances, to initiate federal desegregation suits. Section 2000c(b) defines "desegregation" as it is used in Title IV:

> "Desegregation" means the assignment of students to public schools and within such schools without regard to their race, color, religion, or national origin, but "desegregation" shall not mean the assignment of students to public schools in order to overcome racial imbalance.

Section 2000c-6, authorizing the Attorney General to institute federal suits, contains the following proviso:

> nothing herein shall empower any official or court of the United States to issue any order seeking to achieve a racial balance in any school by requiring the transportation of pupils or students from one school to another or one school district to another in order to achieve such racial balance, or otherwise enlarge the existing power of the court to insure compliance with constitutional standards.

On their face, the sections quoted support only to insure that the provisions of Title IV of the Civil Rights Act of 1964 will not be read as granting new powers. The proviso in §2000c-6 is in terms designed to foreclose any interpretation of the Act as expanding the *existing* powers of federal courts to enforce the Equal Protection Clause. There is no suggestion of an intention to restrict those powers or withdraw from courts their historic equitable remedial powers. The legislative history of Title IV indicates that Congress was concerned that the Act might be read as creating a right of action under the Fourteenth Amendment in the situation of so-called "de facto segregation," where racial imbalance exists in the schools but with no showing that this was brought about by discriminatory action of state authorities. In short, there is nothing in the Act which provides us material assistance in answering the question of remedy for state-imposed segregation in violation of Brown I. The basis of our decision must be the prohibition of the Fourteenth Amendment that no State shall "deny to any person within its jurisdiction the equal protection of the laws."

IV

We turn now to the problem of defining with more particularity the responsibilities of school authorities in desegregating a state-enforced dual school system in light of the Equal Protection Clause. Although the several related cases before us are primarily concerned with problems of student assignment, it may be helpful to begin with a brief discussion of other aspects of the process.

In Green, we pointed out that existing policy and practice with regard to faculty, staff, transportation, extracurricular activities, and facilities were among the most important indicia of a segregated system. 391 U.S., at 435. . . . Independent of student assignment, where it is possible to identify a "white school" or a "Negro school" simply by reference to the racial composition of teachers and staff, the quality of school buildings and equipment, or the organization of sports activities, a prima facie case of violation of substantive constitutional rights under the Equal Protection Clause is shown.

When a system has been dual in these respects, the first remedial responsibility of school authorities is to eliminate invidious racial distinctions. With respect to such matters as transportation, supporting personnel, and extracurricular activities, no more than this may be necessary. Similar corrective action must be taken with regard to the maintenance of buildings and the distribution of equipment. In these areas, normal administrative practice should produce schools of like quality, facilities, and staffs. . . .

[Concerning faculty desegregation, the Court, citing United States v. Montgomery County Board of Education, 395 U.S. 225 (1969), approved the setting of ratios designed to result in roughly the same ratio of black to white teachers in each school throughout the system.]

The construction of new schools and the closing of old ones is one of the most important functions of local school authorities and also one of the most complex. They must decide questions of location and capacity in light of population growth, finances, land values, site availability, through an almost endless list of factors to be considered. The result of this will be a decision which, when combined with one technique or another of student assignment, will determine the racial composition of the student body in each school in the system. Over the long run, the consequences of the choices will be far reaching. People gravitate toward school facilities, just as schools are located in response to the needs of people. The location of schools may thus influence the patterns of residential development of a metropolitan area and have important impact on composition of inner city neighborhoods.

In the past, choices in this respect have been used at a potent weapon for creating or maintaining a state-segregated school system. In addition to the classic pattern of building schools specifically intended for Negro or white students, school authorities have sometimes, since Brown, closed schools which appeared likely to become racially mixed through changes in neighborhood residential patterns. This was sometimes accompanied by building new schools in the areas of white suburban expansion farthest from Negro population centers in order to maintain the separation of the races with a minimum departure from the formal principles of "neighborhood zoning." Such a policy does more than simply influence the short-run composition of the student body of a new school. It may well promote segregated residential patterns which, when combined with "neighborhood zoning," further lock the school system into the mold of separation of the races. Upon a proper showing a district court may consider this in fashioning a remedy.

In ascertaining the existence of legally imposed school segregation, the existence of a pattern of school construction and abandonment is thus a factor of great weight. In devising remedies where legally imposed segregation has been established, it is the responsibility of local authorities and district courts to see to it that future school construction and abandonment is not used and does not serve to perpetuate or re-establish the dual system. When necessary, district courts should retain jurisdiction to assure that these responsibilities are carried out. Cf. United States v. Board of Public Instruction, 395 F.2d 66 (CA5 1968); Brewer v. School Board, 397 F.2d 37 (CA4 1968).

V

The central issue in this case is that of student assignment, and there are essentially four problem areas:

(1) to what extent racial balance or racial quotas may be used as an implement in a remedial order to correct a previously segregated system;

(2) whether every all-Negro and all-white school must be eliminated as an indispensable part of a remedial process of desegregation;

(3) what are the limits, if any, on the rearrangement of school districts and attendance zones, as a remedial measure; and

(4) what are the limits, if any, on the use of transportation facilities to correct state-enforced racial school segregation.

(1) *Racial Balances or Racial Quotas*

The constant theme and thrust of every holding from Brown I to date is that state-enforced separation of races in public schools is discrimination that violates the Equal Protection Clause. The remedy commanded was to dismantle dual school systems.

We are concerned in these cases with the elimination of the discrimination inherent in the dual school systems, not with myriad factors of human existence which can cause discrimination in a multitude of ways on racial, religious, or ethnic grounds. The target of the cases from Brown I to the present was the dual school system. The elimination of racial discrimination in public schools is a large task and one that should not be retarded by efforts to achieve broader purposes lying beyond the jurisdiction of school authorities. One vehicle can carry only a limited amount of baggage. It would not serve the important objective of Brown I to seek to use school desegregation cases for purposes beyond their scope, although desegregation of schools ultimately will have impact on other forms of discrimination. We do not reach in this case the question whether a showing that school segregation is a consequence of other types of state action, without any discriminatory action by the school authorities, is a constitutional violation requiring remedial action by a school desegregation decree. This case does not present that question and we therefore do not decide it.

Our objective in dealing with the issues presented by these cases is to see that school authorities exclude no pupil of a racial minority from any school, directly or indirectly, on account of race; it does not and cannot embrace all the problems of racial prejudice, even when those problems contribute to disproportionate racial concentrations in some schools.

In this case it is urged that the District Court has imposed a racial balance requirement of 71%-29% on individual schools. The fact that no such objective was actually achieved — and would appear to be impossible — tends to blunt that claim, yet in the opinion and order of the District Court of December 1, 1969, we find that court directing:

> that efforts should be made to reach a 71-29 ratio in the various schools so that there will be no basis for contending that one school is racially different from the others . . . , that no school [should] be operated with an all-black or predominantly black student body, [and] that pupils of all grades [should] be assigned in such a way that as nearly as practicable the various schools at various grade levels have about the same proportion of black and white students.

The District Judge went on to acknowledge that variation "from that norm may be unavoidable." This contains intimations that the "norm" is a fixed mathematical racial balance reflecting the pupil constituency of the system. If we were to read the holding of the District Court to require, as a matter of substantive constitutional right, any particular degree of racial balance or mixing, that approach would be disapproved and we would be obliged to reverse. The constitutional command to desegregate schools does not mean that every school in every community must always reflect the racial composition of the school system as a whole.

As the voluminous record in this case shows, the predicate for the District Court's use of the 71%-29% ratio was twofold: first, its express finding, approved by the Court of Appeals and not challenged here, that a dual school system had been maintained by the school authorities at least until 1969; second, its finding, also approved by the Court of Appeals, that the school board had totally defaulted in its acknowledged duty to come forward with an acceptable plan of its own, notwithstanding the patient efforts of the District Judge who, on at least three occasions, urged the board to submit plans. As the statement of facts shows, these findings are abundantly supported by the record. It was because of this total failure of the school board that the District Court was obliged to turn to other qualified sources, and Dr. Finger was designated to assist the District Court to do what the board should have done.

We see therefore that the use made of mathematical ratios was no more than a starting point in the process of shaping a remedy, rather than an inflexible requirement. From that starting point the District Court proceeded to frame a decree that was within its discretionary powers, an equitable remedy for the particular circumstances. As we said in Green, a school authority's remedial plan or a district court's remedial decree is to be judged by its effectiveness. Awareness of the racial composition of the whole school system is likely to be a useful starting point in shaping a remedy to correct past constitutional violations. In sum, the very limited use made of mathematical ratios was within the equitable remedial discretion of the District Court.*

* In companion cases, the Court reversed a holding by the Supreme Court of Georgia that a desegregation plan violated equal protection standards because race was considered in fixing attendance lines, McDaniel v. Barrosi, 402 U.S. 39, 91 S. Ct. 1287, 28 L. Ed. 2d 582 (1971). The Court also approved the use of racial ratios to effect faculty and staff desegregation, and required pupil desegregation based on percentages of black pupils attending white schools throughout the district. Davis v. Board of School Commission of Mobile County, 402 U.S. 33, 91 S. Ct. 1289, 28 L. Ed. 2d 577 (1970).

The Supreme Court's approval of the use of racial criteria in Swann is consistent with the procedures of several lower federal courts in de jure situations. See, e.g., Georgia v. Mitchell, 450 F.2d 1317 (5th Cir. 1971), discussed infra page 545. The technique has been used by state and federal courts where no de jure findings were made and desegregation was voluntarily embarked upon.

Thus, voluntary programs to alleviate racial imbalance where there was no evidence

(2) *One-Race Schools*

The record in this case reveals the familiar phenomenon that in metropolitan areas minority groups are often found concentrated in one part of the city. In some circumstances certain schools may remain all or largely of one race until new schools can be provided or neighborhood patterns change. Schools all or predominantly of one race in a district of mixed population will require close scrutiny to determine that school assignments are not part of state-enforced segregation.

In light of the above, it should be clear that the existence of some small number of one-race, or virtually one-race, schools within a district is not and of itself the mark of a system which still practices segregation by law. The district judge or school authorities should make every effort to achieve the greatest possible degree of actual desegregation and will thus necessarily be concerned with the elimination of one-race schools. No per se rule can adequately embrace all the difficulties of reconciling the competing interests involved; but in a system with a history of segregation the need for remedial criteria of sufficient specificity to assure a school authority's compliance with its constitutional duty warrants a presumption against schools that are substantially disproportionate in their racial composition. Where the school authority's proposed plan for conversion from a dual to a unitary system contemplates the continued existence of some schools that are all or predominately of one race, they have the burden of showing that such school assignments are genuinely nondiscriminatory. The court should scrutinize such schools, and the burden upon the school authorities will be to satisfy the court that their racial composition is not the result of present or past discriminatory action on their part.

An optional majority-to-minority transfer provision has long been recognized as a useful part of every desegregation plan. Provision for optional transfer of those in the majority racial group of a particular school to other schools where they will be in the minority is an indispensable remedy for those students willing to transfer to other schools in order to lessen the impact on them of the state-imposed stigma of segregation. In order to be effective, such a transfer arrangement must grant the transferring student free transportation and space must be made available in the school to which he desires to move. Cf. Ellis v. Board of Public Instruction, 423 F.2d 203, 206 (CA5 1970). The court orders in this and the companion Davis case now provide such an option.

---

of de jure segregation have been upheld where transfer policies applied only to blacks, Offerman v. Nitowski, 378 F.2d 22 (2d Cir. 1967), and where gerrymandering was voluntarily employed by school authorities, Balaban v. Rubin, 14 N.Y.2d 281, 199 N.E.2d 375 (1964). See also Tometz v. Board of Education, Waukegan City School District No. 61, 39 Ill. 2d 593, 237 N.E.2d 498 (1968), printed infra page 535, upholding the validity of a state statute that required revision of school attendance zones to eliminate racial imbalance, despite the lack of standards for defining imbalance.

(3) *Remedial Altering of Attendance Zones*

The maps submitted in these cases graphically demonstrate that one of the principal tools employed by school planners and by courts to break up the dual school system has been a frank — and sometimes drastic — gerrymandering of school districts and attendance zones. An additional step was pairing, "clustering," or "grouping" of schools with attendance assignments made deliberately to accomplish the transfer of Negro students out of formerly segregated Negro schools and transfer of white students to formerly all-Negro schools. More often than not, these zones are neither compact nor contiguous; indeed they may be on opposite ends of the city. As an interim corrective measure, this cannot be said to be beyond the broad remedial powers of a court.

Absent a constitutional violation there would be no basis for judicially ordering assignment of students on a racial basis. All things being equal, with no history of discrimination, it might well be desirable to assign pupils to schools nearest their homes. But all things are not equal in a system that has been deliberately constructed and maintained to enforce racial segregation. The remedy for such segregation may be administratively awkward, inconvenient and even bizarre in some situations and may impose burdens on some; but all awkwardness and inconvenience cannot be avoided in the interim period when remedial adjustments are being made to eliminate the dual school systems.

No fixed or even substantially fixed guidelines can be established as to how far a court can go, but it must be recognized that there are limits. The objective is to dismantle the dual school system. "Racially neutral" assignment plans proposed by school authorities to a district court may be inadequate; such plans may fail to counteract the continuing effects of past school segregation resulting from discriminatory location of school sites or distortion of school size in order to achieve or maintain an artificial racial separation. When school authorities present a district court with a "loaded game board," affirmative action in the form of remedial altering of attendance zones is proper to achieve truly nondiscriminatory assignments. In short, an assignment plan is not acceptable simply because it appears to be neutral.

In this area, we must of necessity rely to a large extent, as this Court has for more than 16 years, on the informed judgment of the district courts in the first instance and on courts of appeals.

We hold that the pairing and grouping of non-contiguous school zones is a permissible tool and such action is to be considered in light of the objectives sought. Judicial steps in shaping such zones going beyond combinations of contiguous areas should be examined in light of what is said in subdivisions (1), (2), and (3) of this opinion concerning the objectives to be sought. Maps do not tell the whole story since non-contiguous school zones may be more accessible to each other in terms of the critical travel time, because of traffic patterns and good highways, than schools geographically closer together. Conditions in different localities will vary so widely that no rigid rules can be laid down to govern all situations.

(4) Transportation of Students

The scope of permissible transportation of students as an implement of a remedial decree has never been defined by this Court and by the very nature of the problem it cannot be defined with precision. No rigid guidelines as to student transportation can be given for application to the infinite variety of problems presented in thousands of situations. Bus transportation has been an integral part of the public education system for years, and was perhaps the single most important factor in the transition from the one-room schoolhouse to the consolidated school. Eighteen million of the nation's public school children, appoximately 39% were transported to their schools by bus in 1969-1970 in all parts of the country. . . .

The Charlotte school authorities did not purport to assign students on the basis of geographically drawn zones until 1965 and then they allowed almost unlimited transfer privileges. The District Court's conclusion that assignment of children to the school nearest their home serving their grade would not produce an effective dismantling of the dual system is supported by the record.

Thus the remedial techniques used in the District Court's order were within that court's power to provide equitable relief; implementation of the decree is well within the capacity of the school authority.

The decree provided that the buses used to implement the plan would operate on direct routes. Students would be picked up at schools near their homes and transported to the schools they were to attend. The trips for elementary school pupils average about seven miles and the District Court found that they would take "not over 35 minutes at the most."[12] This system compares favorably with the transportation plan previously operated in Charlotte under which each day 23,600 students on all grade levels were transported an average of 15 miles one way for an average trip requiring over an hour. In these circumstances, we find no basis for holding that the local school authorities may not be required to employ bus transportation as one tool of school desegregation. Desegregation plans cannot be limited to the walk-in school.

An objection to transportation of students may have validity when the time or distance of travel is so great as to risk either the health of the children or significantly impinge on the educational process. District courts must weigh the soundness of any transportation plan in light of what is said in

12. The District Court found that the school system would have to employ 138 more buses than it had previously operated. But 105 of those buses were already available and the others could easily be obtained. Additionally, it should be noted that North Carolina requires provision of transportation for all students who are assigned to schools more than one and one-half miles from their homes. N.C. Stat. §115-186(b).

subdivisions (1), (2), and (3) above. It hardly needs stating that the limits on time of travel will vary with many factors, but probably with none more than the age of the students. The reconciliation of competing values in a desegregation case is, of course, a difficult task with many sensitive facets but fundamentally no more so than remedial measures courts of equity have traditionally employed. . . .

VI

The Court of Appeals, searching for a term to define the equitable remedial power of the district courts, used the term "reasonableness." In Green, supra, this Court used the term "feasible" and by implication, "workable," "effective," and "realistic" in the mandate to develop "a plan that promises realistically to work, and . . . to work *now*." On the facts of this case, we are unable to conclude that the order of the District Court is not reasonable, feasible and workable. However, in seeking to define the scope of remedial power or the limits on remedial power of courts in an area as sensitive as we deal with here, words are poor instruments to convey the sense of basic fairness inherent in equity. Substance, not semantics, must govern, and we have sought to suggest the nature of limitations without frustrating the appropriate scope of equity.

At some point, these school authorities and others like them should have achieved full compliance with this Court's decision in Brown I. The systems will then be "unitary" in the sense required by our decisions in Green and Alexander.

It does not follow that the communities served by such systems will remain demographically stable, for in a growing, mobile society, few will do so. Neither school authorities nor district courts are constitutionally required to make year-by-year adjustments of the racial composition of student bodies once the affirmative duty to desegregate has been accomplished and racial discrimination through official action is eliminated from the system. This does not mean that federal courts are without power to deal with future problems; but in the absence of a showing that either the school authorities or some other agency of the State has deliberately attempted to fix or alter demographic patterns to affect the racial composition of the schools, further intervention by a district court should not be necessary.

NOTES

1. The Swann v. Charlotte-Mecklenburg case received a mixed reaction from legal commentators. Professor Owen Fiss found four doctrinal advances in the opinion: (1) the rejection of geographic proximity (neighborhood schools) as a criterion for school assignments where such policy fails to bring about a "unitary nonracial school system"; (2) the creation of an evidentiary presumption that segregated school patterns are the result of past discriminatory conduct; (3) the requirement that school boards take all feasible

steps to eliminate segregation, including massive, long-distance transportation programs; (4) the validation of using race in student assignments to achieve school desegregation. Fiss, The Charlotte-Mecklenburg Case, 38 U. Chi. L. Rev. 697, 699-703 (1971).

2. While the standards announced in Swann were explicitly limited to districts where "dual school systems" based on race had been maintained as a deliberate government policy, some commentators criticized the opinion's failure to consider situations. In addition, one comment complained:

> . . . the Court seemed unwilling to take a vigorous anti-segregation stand. It stressed it would not condone the strict use of mathematical ratios by courts to ensure racial balance throughout a school system since "[t]he constitutional command to desegregate schools does not mean every school in every community must always reflect the racial composition of the school system as a whole." Furthermore the Court indicated that the continuation of an indefinite but small number of one race schools within a district would be viewed as evidence of continued de jure segregation. . . . Finally although Swann ruled that the busing of students to achieve racial balance was permissible within the confines of the case, there was a strong implication that at some point busing might become violative of the Constitution. (Note, School Busing and Desegregation: The Post-Swann Era, 46 N.Y.U.L. Rev. 1079, 1094-1095 (1971).)

3. What is a unitary school system? Predictably, Swann's lack of clarity in answering this question has led to differing approaches by the lower courts. For example, in Bivins v. Bibb County Board of Education, 331 F. Supp. 9 (M.D. Ga. 1971), the plaintiffs, after obtaining a desegregation order, applied for supplemental relief following the Swann decision. They argued that, in the light of the continued imbalance in the local school system, a unitary system had yet to be achieved. The district court denied the relief, stating:

> . . . this school system is a unitary system, legally desegregated. . . . All vices [of state imposed segregation] have been removed in Bibb County . . . root and branch and no vestige remains. All racial barriers have been removed from the Bibb County system and from every school in it. The schoolhouse doors are open to all completely without discrimination. Housing patterns are not vestiges of state imposed school segregation. Similar housing patterns exist throughout the nation where school segregation is said to be de facto rather than de jure. (331 F. Supp. at 14.)

On appeal, the Fifth Circuit reversed with instructions that the district court consider plans that would eliminate the one-race schools; and, citing Lee v. Macon County Board of Education, 448 F.2d 746, 753-754 (5th Cir. 1971), urged the district court to "bear in mind that the burdens of closed schools and being bussed should not fall unequally on the minority race." Bivins v. Bibb County Board of Education, 460 F.2d 430 (5th Cir. 1972). See also Flax v. Potts, 450 F.2d 1118 (5th Cir. 1972), remanding a case in which the plan left intact "16 unjustified virtually all-black, one-race schools, relegating almost 12,000 of the approximately 21,000 black public school students in Fort Worth to a constitutionally proscribed segregated education."

A similar approach has been followed by several federal courts which have held that the mere implementation of a desegregation plan, nondiscriminatory on its face, did not end the school board's affirmative duty to eliminate all vestiges of state-imposed segregation. Rather, the duty required the school authorities to undertake a careful vigilance to ensure that the plan proved effective. See, e.g., Judge McMillan's opinion in Swann, remanded 334 F. Supp. 623 (W.D. N.C. 1971) and 29 U. Chi. L. Rev. at 421.

4. When is a plan "reasonable, feasible, and workable" as required by Swann? Chief Justice Burger's conception of reasonableness was set forth in Winston Salem Board of Education v. Scott, no. 71-274 (Burger, Circuit Justice, *stay den.* 404 U.S. 1221, 92 S. Ct. 1236 (1971)). There, a desegregation plan which had been remanded to the district court for reconsideration, in the light of Swann's approval of bus transportation and split zoning, was appealed by the board, following the district court's approval of a plan submitted by an educational expert calling for the use of those techniques. Although refusing to stay the lower court's desegregation order, Chief Justice Burger found it "disturbing" that the circuit court had read Swann as requiring that the racial balance in individual schools be close to that of the school system as a whole. He viewed the district court's approval of extensive bussing as suggesting an acceptance of strict racial apportionment, and reiterated the fact that Swann had proscribed the setting of any mathematical ratios.

Other courts, even in the same circuit, rendered different decisions regarding the term "reasonableness." Thus, in United States v. Texas, 447 F.2d 441 (1971), the Fifth Circuit approved a detailed and demanding district court order, less than two weeks after it had remanded a desegregation case to a Mississippi district court directing it merely to "implement at the elementary level a plan which will accomplish a greater degree of desegregation than that achieved by the present elementary attendance zone plan." Russell v. Greenwood School District, 445 F.2d 388, 389 (5th Cir. 1971). The Sixth Circuit has given a similarly restrictive reading to Swann. See Goss v. Board of Education, 444 F.2d 632, 636 (1971), in which the court interpreted Swann as "primarily a command to all school authorities in states in which de jure segregation was once the rule to do a better job of mixing the races and teaching staffs, than they have heretofore done." District courts have appeared similarly confused, with some of them ordering bussing to further integration, and others refusing to order bussing for fear it would promote "white flight." Compare Mannings v. Board of Public Instruction, 3 Race Rel. L. Sur. 91 (M.D. Fla. 1971), with Calhoon v. Cook, 332 F. Supp. 804 (N.D. Ga. 1971). See, generally, Note, 46 N.Y.U.L. Rev. 1079, 1098-1100 (1971).

5. What is the permissible number of one-race schools in a unitary school

system? Federal courts have also differed about the limit imposed by the Swann case upon one-race schools in unitary school systems. In Northcross v. Memphis School District, 466 F.2d 890 (6th Cir. 1972), Swann was interpreted to require rejection of a school plan which left 87 percent of the city's black students in one-race schools. The court stated:

> Even were we to assume that the existence of the large number of one-race schools in this case is not a per se indication that the Memphis Board has failed to eliminate its dual system, there is still a presumption that such is the case under Swann. . . . To overcome this presumption according to the Supreme Court, the School Board would have to demonstrate that at the very least its remaining one-race schools are not in any way the product of its past or present discriminatory conduct. It is clear that the School Board has not met that burden in this case. (466 F.2d at 893.)

Other courts have given a much more restrictive reading to the one-race school language. See Bivins v. Bibb County, supra, page 509.

NOTE: BUSSING AND SCHOOL DESEGREGATION

The most controversial aspect of the Swann decision concerns its approval of bussing school children to effectuate school desegregation plans, without specifically outlining the limits of permissible bussing. In the absence of guidelines, the lower federal courts have struggled with determining the outer limits of bussing school children.*

In Acree v. County Board of Education, 458 F.2d 486 (1972), the Fifth Circuit approved a desegregation order requiring "forced bussing" of school children to help eliminate a dual school system. After citing Swann's approval of bussing, the court in Acree found that the proposed transportation would not adversely affect the health of the children involved or impinge upon the educational process. See also Dandridge v. Jefferson Parish School Board, 456 F.2d 552 (5th Cir. 1972), which approved a plan that required the bussing of 6000 school children an average of seven miles each, in order to eliminate nineteen one-race schools in the school district. The court found the order within the outer limits of Swann, where the corresponding figures were 23,000 students and fifteen miles.

In Brewer v. School Board of City of Norfolk, 456 F.2d 943 (1972), the Fourth Circuit sanctioned a lower court order requiring bussing of school

* In denying the requested stay in Winston Salem/Forsyth County Board of Educ. v. Scott, 404 U.S. 1221, 92 S. Ct. 1236 (1971), Chief Justice Burger provided an example of what he would consider excessive:

"By way of illustration, if the record showed — to take an extreme example of a patent violation of Swann — that the average time was three hours daily or that some were compelled to travel three hours daily when school facilities were available at a lesser distance, I would not hesitate to stay such an order forthwith until the Court could act, at least as to the students imposed upon. The burdens and hardships of travel do not relate to race. . . ." 404 U.S. at 1227, n.1.

children an average of one hour's round trip. The court rejected in the process the school board's allegation that the plan was too costly to be financed by the school system, and that the bussed students must pay for their own transportation. The court agreed with plaintiffs that: (1) the providing of free transportation was a necessary corollary of the bussing order, and (2) the failure to so provide would make any desegregation plan a futile gesture. The court found that the annual cost of $600,000 to finance the bussing was reasonable and did not justify abandoning the transportation edict. Applying the standards of Swann, the court found that the $600,000 transportation amount, out of a budget of $35,000,000, was within the limits set by Swann, where the figures were $1,000,000 out of a total budget of $66,000,000. See also Brown v. Board of Education of City of Bessemer, Ala., 464 F.2d 382 (5th Cir. 1972), where the court rejected a board contention that a system which had never operated a transportation system, and did not promote a dual system by use of buses, cannot be required to furnish transportation to meet the constitutional requirement of a unitary school system. The same circuit, in Dandridge v. Jefferson Parish School Board, 456 F.2d 552 (5th Cir. 1972), approved bussing for 3000 of 63,000 students over an average daily round trip of seven miles.

But if the courts see bussing as an appropriate school desegregation tool, the public does not. Two thirds of those queried in a 1972 survey approve of desegregated public schools, but 69 percent oppose bussing as a means of achieving that goal. Newsweek, Mar. 13, 1972 at p. 24. Almost 45 percent of the country's 18,975,000 pupils are transported to school daily, according to HEW statistics, with 256,000 buses traveling 2.2 billion miles, and the numbers increase every year. Although bussing permits better school utilization, is safer than walking, and does no harm to the bussed students, the opposition has been immense when it is utilized to take black children into white schools or white children into black schools. Politicians are elected or defeated solely on this issue by whites who, having invested in a home in an area where the schools are seen as "good," feel that their investments will be threatened if blacks are brought to those schools, or entirely wasted if their children are bussed back to inner-city schools where blacks predominate. Increasingly, blacks discouraged by the hostility of whites on the subject have announced their opposition to bussing. Given the growing segregation of housing patterns (see Chapters 11 and 12), this amounts to giving up on school desegregation as well.

Legislatures have responded to the antibussing pressures by passing laws which, to date, have been uniformly struck down by the courts. In North Carolina State Board of Education v. Swann, 402 U.S. 43, 91 St. Ct. 1284, 28 L. Ed. 2d 586 (1971), a companion case to Swann v. Charlotte-Mecklenburg, the Supreme Court affirmed a lower court which struck down a North Carolina statute that prohibited assignment or involuntary bussing of students on account of race in order to create a racial balance.

> The legislation before us flatly forbids assignment of any student on account of race or for the purpose of creating a racial balance or ratio in the schools. The prohibition is absolute. . . . But more important the statute exploits an apparently neutral form to control school assignment plans by directing that they be "color blind;" that requirement, against the background of segregation, would render illusory the promise of [Brown I]: "Just as the race of students must be considered in determining whether a constitutional violation occurred, so also must race be considered in formulating a remedy. To forbid, at this stage, all assignments made on the basis of race would deprive school authorities of the one tool absolutely essential to fulfillment of their constitutional obligation to eliminate existing dual school systems."
>
> Similarly, the flat prohibition against assignment of students for purposes of creating a racial imbalance must inevitably conflict with the duty of school authorities to disestablish dual school systems. (402 U.S. at 45-46.)

A three-judge court in Lee v. Nyquist, 318 F. Supp. 710 (W.D. N.Y.), declared unconstitutional a New York statute prohibiting assignment of students on a racial basis. The court found that the statute constituted an invidious classification of minority students and, in the absence of a compelling justification for the classification, was constitutionally infirm.

But political pressures against bussing have not been limited to state legislatures. Following the Swann decision, numerous congressional proposals to limit court-ordered bussing were offered. After the narrow defeat in the Senate of two similar proposals that would have deprived federal courts of jurisdiction to order bussing on the basis of race, religion, color or national origin, President Nixon, in a lengthy address to Congress, described his plan to curtail court-imposed bussing. N.Y. Times, Mar. 18, 1972, at 1, col. 18. The proposed legislation consisted of two parts. First, the statute would place an immediate moratorium on all court-ordered bussing, pending an investigation by Congress to devise standards for the guidance of federal courts in determining the extent of student reassignment and transportation that would satisfy the commands of the Fourteenth Amendment. Second, the legislation would (1) provide federal funds to improve the quality of inadequate educational facilities, and (2) outline permissible remedial techniques available for the elimination of dual school systems. Under the remedial provisions, bussing would be prohibited for children below seventh grade, and would be allowable for higher grades only if all other listed remedies (transfer plans, construction of new schools, etc.) were found to be inadequate.

The Nixon proposal was not adopted by the Ninety-second Congress. But Congress did include, in the 1972 Amendments to the Higher Education Act, provisions designed to slow the school desegregation process (see Appendix). In the course of denying a stay, sought under §803 of the Amendments, in Drummond v. Acree, 409 U.S. 1228, 93 S. Ct. 18, 34 L. Ed. 2d 33 (1972), Justice Powell discussed those provisions and their inapplicability to orders intended to eliminate segregation mandated by law.

By its terms, the statute requires that the effectiveness of a district court order be postponed pending appeal only if the order requires the "transfer or transportation" of students "for the purpose of achieving a balance among students with respect to race." It does not purport to block all desegregation orders which require the transportation of students. If Congress had desired to stay all such orders, it could have used clear and explicit language appropriate to that result.

In §802(a), Congress prohibited the use of federal funds to aid in any program for the transportation of students if the design of the program is to "overcome racial imbalance" or to "carry out a plan of racial desegregation." . . . It is clear from the juxtaposition and the language of these two sections that Congress intended to proscribe the use of federal funds for the transportation of students under any desegregation plan but limited the stay provisions of §803 to desegregation plans that seek to achieve racial balance.

In light of the holding in Swann v. Charlotte-Mecklenburg Board of Education, 402 U.S. 1 (1971), it could hardly be contended that Congress was unaware of the legal significance of its "racial balance" language. In that case school authorities argued that §407(a) of the Civil Rights Act of 1964 . . . restricted the power of federal courts in prescribing a method for correcting state-imposed segregation. The Chief Justice's interpretation of §407(a), which applies only to orders "seeking to achieve racial balance," is controlling here: "The proviso . . . is in terms designed to foreclose any interpretation of the Act as expanding the existing powers of federal courts to enforce the Equal Protection Clause. . . ." [A]s employed in §407(a), the phrase "achieve a racial balance" was used in the context of eliminating "de facto segregation. . . ." Nothing in the instant statute or in the legislative history suggests that Congress used these words in a new and broader sense. At most, Congress may have intended to postpone the effectiveness of transportation orders in "de facto" cases and in cases in which district court judges have misused their remedial powers. (93 S. Ct. at 20.)

While Justice Powell seized upon the "racial balance" language of §803, to save from the statutory ban on bussing orders those orders that were necessary to desegregate school systems formerly operated on a dual basis, a district court in Medley v. Danville School Board, 41 U.S.L.W. 2236 (Nov. 7, 1972), granted a stay relying on what it held the "completely unambiguous" language of §803. The court reasoned that the whole purpose of the suit was to achieve a balance among students with respect to race, which is exactly within the precise wording of the statute. "The purpose of achieving racial balance, of course, is to eliminate the last vestiges of a state imposed system of segregated schools." The court also ruled that the statute is not an unwarranted intrusion by Congress into the affairs of the judiciary. Since Congress may impose limitations on the jurisdiction of the federal courts, the district judge saw no reason why it should not have the power to require a stay. Citing Wright, Federal Courts 23 (1970 ed.) the court said, "It can take away from the court the power to grant a particular remedy or to enforce a particular kind of contract."

In another case dealing with the applicability of the Education Amendments of 1972, the Ninth Circuit held that the amendments do not operate to suspend implemented bussing orders. In denying the retroactivity of the statute, the court ruled the provisions inapplicable to a bussing decree issued one year before the effective date of the Education Amendments of 1972. Soria v. Oxnard School District Board of Trustees, 467 F.2d 59 (9th Cir. 1972). See also Darville v. Dade County School Board, 351 F. Supp. 1249 (S.D. Fla. 1972), rejecting the contention of white children that §806 of the Education Amendments prevented their assignment to a school other than the one closest to their home, to overcome racial imbalance by a board that had achieved a unitary system. The court found that the provision (barring court-ordered bussing) was not applicable where the purpose is to end state-imposed segregation or its vestiges, and does not restrict action voluntarily undertaken by the school board.

Former Supreme Court Justice Goldberg finds the congressional antibussing provisions unconstitutional on a number of grounds, in an article, The Administration's Anti-Busing Proposals, 67 Nw. U.L. Rev. 319 (1972).

But legal arguments have not reduced public opposition to bussing, and there are likely to be more legislative efforts to curb it, if not ban it entirely, as a desegregation tool. California voters approved overwhelmingly an amendment to the state constitution prohibiting school transfers on a racial basis, and efforts to enact an amendment to the federal Constitution for this purpose will likely intensify. One such proposal, H.R. Joint Resolution 620, 92nd Cong., 1st Sess. (1971), provided: "§1. No public school student shall, because of his race, creed, or color, be assigned to or required to attend a particular school." Similar amendments have been proposed in the Senate. The legislative efforts to curtail so explicitly the scope of federal courts' authority have little precedent in our history. Currie, Three Judge District Court, 32 U. Chi. L. Rev. 1, 5, 9-10 nn. 49-52 (1964). The Eighteenth Amendment, which forbade the manufacture and sale of liquor in the United States and was repealed after fourteen years, is the only amendment that rivals the antibussing proposals in specificity. The operation of such an amendment would seemingly result in conflicts with rights guaranteed by the Fourteenth and other amendments. See Note, School Desegregation, 60 Geo. L.J. 1279, 1286-1289 (1972).

QUESTIONS

1. "One day during the [1972] campaign Michigan's Democratic candidate for Senator, Frank Kelley, saw a line of people waiting for unemployment compensation. He went up and asked a man what was on his mind in this election. The man answered: 'Busing.'" Lewis, What is the Question? N.Y. Times, Nov. 11, 1972 at 31, c.1. Does the growing opposition of the early 1970s to meaningful school desegregation, which developed in the wake of effective implementation of Brown, moot the long debate over whether the Supreme Court should have required immediate desegregation in 1954?

2. Despite its statements in Brown II and Cooper v. Aaron, supra page 457, that opposition was not a valid ground for failing to implement school de-

segregation orders, should the Court now acknowledge the barrier posed by widespread opposition to desegregation plans, particularly those involving substantial amounts of bussing? If so, what should the Court do about the problem? Recall Justice Holmes' observation in Giles v. Harris, 189 U.S. 475, 23 S. Ct. 639, 47 L. Ed. 909 (1903), printed supra page 94, as he denied judicial relief to disenfranchised blacks: "The bill imparts that the great mass of the white population intends to keep the blacks from voting." In the face of such intent, Holmes felt that an order which the Court could not enforce would be useless, and that relief "from a great political wrong" committed by the people and the state can come only from them. Has the Court reached a similar point in its generation-long effort to enforce Brown?

3. Whatever the wisdom of Justice Holmes' philosophy in refusing to grant judicial relief to a minority whose rights have been infringed by a hostile majority, modern courts — with few exceptions — simply haven't followed it. Despite public opposition to school desegregation, which has increased since Swann, a Congress that is no longer supportive, and a federal administration whose intentions, on the subject are widely questioned, many federal courts have continued to approve sweeping school desegregation plans. Is there a distinction between white opposition to blacks voting in 1903 and the resistance to school desegregation sixty years later that justifies rejection of the Holmes philosophy by modern courts? Are there other factors which increase the likelihood that contemporary court orders will be enforced?

4. Federal Judge Merhige received national attention in 1972 when he ordered the school board of increasingly black Richmond to merge with two neighboring suburban, and predominantly white, county school systems. Bradley v. School Board of City of Richmond, Va., 338 F. Supp. 67 (E.D. Va. 1972). The Fourth Circuit stayed the order, accelerated the appeal, 456 F.2d 6 (1972), and sitting en banc, reversed. 462 F.2d 1058 (1972). The Supreme Court granted certiorari, — U.S. —, 35 L. Ed. 2d 255 (1973). In reading the summary of the Fourth Circuit's opinion in the Richmond case, which follows, consider whether there are limits to the remedies that courts can apply (or hope to enforce), even when the proof of de jure segregation is clear. Are there legally viable and less disruptive alternatives to balancing students by race in each school, which will meet both constitutional and educational standards?

BRADLEY v. SCHOOL BOARD OF CITY OF RICHMOND, VIRGINIA
462 F.2d 1058 (4th Cir. 1972)

Before HAYNSWORTH, Chief Judge, and BRYAN, WINTER, CRAVEN, RUSSELL and FIELD, Circuit Judges, sitting en banc.

CRAVEN, Circuit Judge: . . .

This is a new aspect of an old school case begun in 1961 . . .[1] [I]t is virtually

1. The history of this litigation unfolds in Bradley v. School Board of the City of Rich-

conceded and established beyond question that, albeit belatedly, Richmond has at this juncture done all it can do to disestablish to the maximum extent possible the formerly state-imposed dual school system within its municipal boundary.

What is presented on appeal is whether the district court may compel joinder with Richmond's unitary school system two other school districts (also unitary) in order to achieve a greater degree of integration and racial balance. The district judge felt compelled to order consolidation of the three school units partly because of his concern with what seemed to him an unfortunate racial balance in the three separate systems and partly because he felt this racial balance was the result of invidious state action. In his concern for effective implementation of the Fourteenth Amendment he failed to sufficiently consider, we think, a fundamental principle of federalism incorporated in the Tenth Amendment and failed to consider that Swann v. Charlotte-Mecklenburg Board of Education, 402 U.S. 1 . . . (1971), established limitations on his power to fashion remedies in school cases.

[The court then reviewed the history of the Richmond school litigation, including the decision of the Richmond Board to seek relief against the boards in adjoining Chesterfield and Henrico Counties so as to make possible an order requiring the consolidation of the three school systems. This consolidation, given the heavily white school population in the adjoining counties, would provide a "better" racial mix when combined with the largely black school population of Richmond. The court then noted that, if it were to sustain the consolidation subsequently ordered by the lower court, the result would create a district containing over 750 square miles and in excess of 100,000 students. The district would be the twenty-eighth largest in the country and the second largest in Virginia. Whether children would be assigned to schools within their normal attendance zones or would be transported elsewhere would depend on a lottery program. The basis for this far-reaching order, the court found, was the desirability of achieving a "viable racial mix," noting that the district court placed such importance on the achievement of this goal that it did not rule out the possibility of joining additional counties to the Richmond consolidation program.

In attempting to ascertain the weight that the district court had given to the "racial mix" concept, the court of appeals referred to portions of the district court opinion, quoting witnesses who testified on the subject.]

It is not clear from the district court's decision the weight given to the

---

mond, 317 F.2d 429 (4th Cir. 1963); 345 F.2d 310 (4th Cir. 1965), *rev'd and remanded,* 382 U.S. 103, 86 S. Ct. 224, 15 L. Ed. 2d 187 (1965). After four years under a consent decree, the subsequent litigation in the district court is found in Bradley v. School Board of the City of Richmond, 51 F.R.D. 139 (E.D. Va. 1970); 317 F. Supp. 555 (E.D. Va. 1970); 324 F. Supp. 396 (E.D. Va. 1971); 324 F. Supp. 439 (E.D. Va. 1971); 324 F. Supp. 456 (E.D. Va. 1971); and 325 F. Supp. 828 (E.D. Va. 1971). The opinion of the district court which is the subject of this appeal is Bradley v. School Board of the City of Richmond, D.C., 338 F. Supp. 67 (E.D. Va. 1972), hereinafter referred to as Bradley.

testimony of various witnesses. Some importance, however, undoubtedly attaches to the testimony of Dr. Pettigrew adopted in part by the court below.[4]

> To achieve "integration," in Dr. Pettigrew's terms one must have the "mix plus positive inter-action, as we would want to say, between whites and blacks." Current research indicates that in order to achieve these benefits there is an optimum racial composition which should be sought in each school. Dr. Pettigrew placed this at from 20 to 40% black occupancy. These figures are not at all hard and fast barriers, but merely indicate to the racial composition range in which inter-action of a positive sort is the more likely to occur. Social science is not such an exact science that the success or failure of integration depends upon a few percentage points. The low level of 20% fixes the general area below which the black component takes on the character of a token presence. Where only a few black students are in the particular school, there simply are insufficient numbers for them to be represented in most areas of school activities. Such participation would be crucial to the success of integration. The high level of 40% is linked not to the likely behavior of the students so much as it is to the behavior of their parents. When the black population in a school rises substantially above 40%, it has been Dr. Pettigrew's experience that white students tend to disappear from the school entirely at a rapid rate, and the Court so finds. This is only possible, of course, when alternative facilities exist with a lesser black proportion where the white pupils can be enrolled. The upper limit, then, relates to stability.
>
> Bradley, at 194.

The district court concluded (Bradley, at 185) that "taking the three jurisdictions together," (Chesterfield, Henrico, Richmond) over the past ten years "the racial proportions have remained quite constant, at about 67% white and 33% black." The court stated that he rejected the notion that a goal of placing 20 to 40 percent black students in each school could be characterized as the imposition of a fixed racial quota, but did note that "if the goal were achieved, Negroes would be in a minority in each school." Bradley, at 186. He emphasized that this corresponded to the demographic pattern of the units combined, and, indeed, corresponded to the racial balance of the nation as a whole. However, in discussing the Richmond Metropolitan School Plan, the district court also emphasized the fact that without consolidation, very few pupils in the city or the counties would attend schools whose racial mix corresponded to that considered "viable" by Dr. Pettigrew, while with consolidation under the proposed plan,

4. In apparently adopting Dr. Pettigrew's viable racial mix theory, the district court rejected the testimony of another expert that the idea of a viable racial mix in which blacks must be in the minority in order to have a good education is a racist proposal. Dr. Hooker thought that the consolidation of schools in the Richmond area would "disenfranchise" black residents by preventing them from achieving control of the school system and would in time be resented by black citizens as paternalistic and patronizing. The position of one of the amici, the Congress of Racial Equality, is similar to that expressed by Dr. Hooker.

97% of the black students in the area would attend schools in the range of 20-40% black; the remainder would be in 15-20% black schools. Under that plan 92.5% of the white students in the area would be in schools of the optimum mix determined by Dr. Pettigrew, and 7.5% would be in schools with a 15-20% black enrollment.
Bradley, at 195.

The desire of the district judge to achieve such a racial mix is quite understandable since the evidence seemed to indicate its workability in practice. But we think the adoption of the Richmond Metropolitan Plan in toto by the district court, viewed in the light of the stated reasons for its adoption, is the equivalent, despite disclaimer, of the imposition of a fixed racial quota. The Constitution imposes no such requirement, and imposition as a matter of substantive constitutional right of any particular degree of racial balance is beyond the power of a district court. Swann v. Charlotte-Mecklenburg Board of Education, 402 U.S., at 24 . . . ; Spencer v. Kugler, 326 F. Supp. 1235 (D.N.J.1971), *aff'd mem.* 404 U.S. 1027 . . . (1972).

III

The boundaries of the three school districts, Richmond, Chesterfield and Henrico, have always been (for more than 100 years) coterminous with the political subdivision of the City of Richmond, the County of Chesterfield and the County of Henrico. The boundaries have never been changed except as occasioned by annexation of land within the two counties caused by the expansion and growth of the City of Richmond. The most recent annexation has resulted in adding to the school population of Richmond 10,240 pupils, of which approximately 9,867 are white. It is not contended by any of the parties or by amici that the establishment of the school district lines more than 100 years ago was invidiously motivated. We have searched the 325-page opinion of the district court in vain for the slightest scintilla of evidence that the boundary lines of the three local governmental units have been maintained either long ago or recently for the purpose of perpetuating racial discrimination in the public schools. As the brief of the United States points out, to the extent, if at all, there are district court findings of inter-district discrimination, they are delineated with such a "broad brush" as to make "it difficult on review to say precisely what the violation, if any, was." We agree with the position of the United States that "this is not primarily a case about segregation required by law, because state law has never required segregation as between Richmond and the neighboring school systems." . . .

It is thus established that in each of the three school districts the formerly dual system of schools has been disestablished and effectively replaced with a unitary school system within which no child is excluded from any school by reason of his race. The issue, also as urged by the United States, is whether the maintenance of three separate unitary school divisions constitutes invidious racial discrimination in violation of the Fourteenth Amendment.

It is urged upon us that within the City of Richmond there has been state (also federal) action tending to perpetuate apartheid of the races in ghetto patterns throughout the city, and that there has been state action within the adjoining counties also tending to restrict and control the housing location of black resident. We think such findings are not clearly erroneous, and accept them. Just as all three units formerly operated dual school systems, so likewise all three are found by the district court to have in the past discriminated against blacks with respect to places and opportunity for residence. But neither the record nor the opinion of the district court even suggests that there was ever joint interaction between any two of the units involved (or by higher state officers) for the purpose of keeping one unit relatively white by confining blacks to another. What the district court seems to have found, though this is not clear, is that there has been in the past action by the counties which had a tendency to keep blacks within the boundaries of the City of Richmond and excluded them from the counties. In arriving at this conclusion, the district court seemed to place great reliance on the selection of new school construction sites over the years, racially restrictive covenants in deeds, the nonparticipation of the counties in federally assisted low income housing, and testimony concerning private acts of discrimination in the sale of housing. If the district court's theory was that the counties were thus keeping blacks in Richmond schools while allowing whites to flee to relatively white sanctuaries, the facts do not support this theory.

[Examining student transfers between the three school districts, the court of appeals found little statistical support for the district court's fear that white students were increasingly moving to the county systems, with the result that Richmond was becoming increasingly black. Indeed, the court found that the percentage of black students in the two county systems was growing, despite the nonparticipation by the county in low-income housing and other real estate policies that might have given blacks access to residences in the counties. The court was unable to determine whether discrimination in the housing area had had any impact upon movement by blacks out of the city.]

We think that the root causes of the concentration of blacks in the inner cities of America are simply not known and that the district court could not realistically place on the counties the responsibility for the effect that inner city decay has had on the public schools of Richmond. We are convinced that what little action, if any, the counties may seem to have taken to keep blacks out is slight indeed compared to the myriad reasons, economic, political and social, for the concentration of blacks in Richmond and does not support the conclusion that it has been invidious state action which has resulted in the racial composition of the three school districts. Indeed this record warrants no other conclusion than that the forces influencing demographic patterns in New York, Chicago, Detroit, Los Angeles, Atlanta and other metropolitan areas have operated in the same way in the Richmond metropolitan area to produce the same result. Typical of all of these cities is a growing black population in the central city and a growing white population in the surrounding suburban and rural areas. Whatever the basic causes, it has not been school assignments, and school assignments cannot reverse the trend. That there has been housing discrimination in all three units is deplorable, but a school case, like a vehicle, can carry only a limited amount of baggage. Swann v. Charlotte-Mecklenburg Board of Education, 402 U.S. at 24 . . . .

IV

To approve the consolidation of these three school districts would require us to ignore the tradition and history of the Commonwealth of Virginia with respect to its establishment and operation of schools, as well as hold invalid various enactments of the Legislature of Virginia structuring Virginia's system of free public schools. In addition, there are some practical problems involving money and finance and taxes.

The power to operate, maintain and supervise public schools in Virginia is, and has always been, within the exclusive jurisdiction of the local school boards and not within the jurisdiction of the State Board of Education. County School Board of Prince Edward County v. Griffin, 204 Va. 650, 133 S.E.2d 565 (1963). Indeed, the operation of public schools has been a matter of local option. See Griffin v. School Board of Prince Edward County, 377 U.S. 218 . . . .

But even if we were to ignore Virginia law, as we are urged to do, there are practicalities of budgeting and finance that boggle the mind. Each of the three political subdivisions involved here has a separate tax base and a separate and distinct electorate. The school board of the consolidated district would have to look to three separate governing bodies for approval and support of school budgets. The Turner Commission in its 1967 report on raising the level of public education in Virginia concluded that consolidation of school districts in Virginia could not work under Virginia's fiscal structure: "It would appear that the *compulsory* consolidation of School Boards, not accompanied by a consolidation of all functions of local government, would need to have a degree of fiscal independence not available under present statutes." Apparently none of the numerous witnesses examined in the district court was aware of any instance in American education in which any expert in the field had ever recommended the consolidation of three separate school divisions into a single consolidated school division having three separate tax bases.

We think it fair to say that the only "educational" reason offered by the numerous school experts in support of consolidation was the egalitarian concept that it is good for children of diverse economic, racial and social background to associate together more than would be possible within the Richmond school district. The experts thought that the optimum size school district was one having a school population of from 20,000 to 50,000 pupils. When a district is too small, specialized programs tend to be eliminated, and when a school district is too large, it tends to become unwieldy and cumbersome and to lose parent participation. Thus the consensus was that the three separate school districts were about the right size, and the consolidated district much larger than desirable for educational and administrative purposes.

V

By the Tenth Amendment to the Constitution of the United States it is provided that: "The powers not delegated to the United States by the Constitution, nor prohibited by it to the States, are reserved to the States respectively, or to the people."

One of the powers thus reserved to the states is the power to structure their internal government. . . .

"When a state exercises power wholly within the domain of state interest, it is insulated from federal judicial review." Gomillion v. Lightfoot, 364 U.S. 339, 347 . . . (1960). The Supreme Court has always recognized "the breadth and importance of this aspect of the State's political power," Gomillion, supra at 342 . . . , but "has never acknowledged that the States have power to do as they will with municipal corporations regardless of consequences." Gomillion, supra at 344 . . . . If the states' near plenary power over its political subdivisions "is used as an instrument for circumventing," Gomillion, supra at 347 . . . , the Fourteenth Amendment equal protection right of blacks to attend a unitary school system, then the Tenth Amendment is brought into conflict with the Fourteenth, and it settled that the latter will prevail. Gomillion, supra. The facts of this case do not establish, however, that state establishment and maintenance of school districts coterminous with the political subdivisions of the City of Richmond and the Counties of Chesterfield and Henrico have been intended to circumvent any federally protected right. Nor is there any evidence that the consequences of such state action impairs any federally protected right, for there is no right to racial balance within even a single school district, Swann v. Charlotte-Mecklenburg Board of Education, 402 U.S. at 24 . . . , but only a right to attend a unitary school system.

In seeking to define the extent of a district judge's remedial power in a school case,

> it is important to remember that judicial powers may be exercised only on the basis of a constitutional violation. Remedial judicial authority does not put judges automatically in the shoes of school authorities whose powers are plenary. Judicial authority enters when local authority defaults. . . . Swann v. Charlotte-Mecklenburg Board of Education, 402 U.S. 1, 16 . . . (1971).

Because we are unable to discern any constitutional violation in the establishment and maintenance of these three school districts, nor any unconstitutional consequence of such maintenance, we hold that it was not within the district judge's authority to order the consolidation of these three separate political subdivisions of the Commonwealth of Virginia. When it became "clear that state-imposed segregation . . . [had] been completely removed," Green, 391 U.S. 430, at 439 . . . , within the school district of the City of Richmond, as adjudged by the district court, further intervention by the district court was neither necessary nor justifiable. . . .

In devising remedies in school cases it is difficult to know "how far a court can go, but it must be recognized that there are limits. Swann, 402 U.S. at 28 . . . . In Spencer v. Kugler, 326 F. Supp. 1235 (D.N.J. 1971), *aff'd mem.* 404 U.S. 1027 . . . (1972), black plaintiffs sought to compel the joinder of separate school districts within the State of New Jersey for the purpose of achieving racial balance and preventing de facto segregation. The three-judge court held de facto segregation, defined as racial imbalance that exists through no discriminatory action of state authorities, to be beyond the ambit of the Fourteenth Amendment. On appeal the decision was affirmed without opinion by a nearly unanimous United States Supreme Court. We think Spencer v. Kugler, supra, is indistinguishable and controls decision in this case.

Because we think the last vestiges of state-imposed segregation have been wiped out in the public schools of the City of Richmond and the Counties of Henrico and Chesterfield and unitary school systems achieved, and because it is not established that the racial composition of the schools in the City of Richmond and the counties is the result of invidious state action, we conclude there is no constitutional violation and that, therefore, the district judge exceeded his power of intervention.

Reversed.

WINTER, Circuit Judge (dissenting):

It was unfortunately predictable that a court which approved the dismantling of existing school districts so as to create smaller whiter enclaves,[1] now rejects the consolidation of school districts to make effective the mandate of Brown I and its progeny. My view of this case is that the district court formulated appropriate relief and, indeed, that it decreed the only relief permissible under the fourteenth amendment. Nothing in the controlling decisions of the Supreme Court points to the contrary. I would affirm.

[Reviewing in detail the plan condemned by the majority, Judge Winter explained that the single consolidated district would be subdivided into six geographical subdivisions, five of which would have a student population of 17,000 to 20,000. One subdivision in a sparsely populated area would contain approximately 9,000 students. Each subdivision would have its own board, to exercise close supervision over instruction and to maintain close contact with parents. He reviewed how racial balance would be maintained in each subdivision at two thirds white and one third black, and expressed the view that the method of assignment and transportation was reasonable.

The dissent then traced the long history of evasion of Brown both by the state and by officials in the three school districts. He also examined the record

1. United States v. Scotland Neck City Board of Education, 442 F.2d 575 (4 Cir. 1971), *cert. granted* 404 U.S. 821 . . . (1971); Wright v. Council of the City of Emporia, 442 F.2d 570 (4 Cir. 1971), *cert. granted* 404 U.S. 820 . . . (1971). . . .

of discrimination at every level in the housing industry, disagreeing with the majority's conclusion that the responsibility for such discrimination could not realistically be placed on the school system. To the contrary, Judge Winter expressed the view that requiring consolidation of the three school districts was an appropriate means of bringing them into compliance with the Fourteenth Amendment. Compliance should not be circumvented by existing boundaries of political subdivisions, particularly when a substantial percentage of the residents in one area work in another. The dissent also pointed out the many facilities, including hospitals, libraries and shopping areas, which the communities share.

Judge Winter agreed that the Equal Protection Clause does not require that there be a homogeneous racial mixture in every school throughout the state, but he denied that this was the purpose of the consolidated school district. He also distinguished Spencer v. Kugler, supra, which was relied on by the majority. He pointed out that this action was intended to require elimination of racial imbalance between school districts where there was no history of a state-imposed dual system of education, where there was no allegation that the school district boundaries had been invidiously drawn, and where there was no allegation that state action caused or contributed to the racial imbalance.]

QUESTIONS

1. Assume that the Supreme Court reverses the Fourth Circuit's decision in the Bradley case and approves the district court's order for a metropolitan school desegregation plan in Richmond. Assume further that plaintiffs' counsel then decides to settle the case by agreeing to give up plaintiffs' right to have the three districts merged, in return for a commitment by the Richmond School Board to hire a black school superintendent and to integrate fully all administrative positions in the system. Can the Court approve such a settlement? If some black parents in the class covered by the Bradley suit object to the settlement, what should the Court do? For a somewhat similar development in the Atlanta school litigation, see N.Y. Times, Feb. 25, 1973, at 39, c.1, and Mar. 2, 1973, at 34, c.1.

2. Assume that the Supreme Court affirms the Fourth Circuit's Bradley decision, and plaintiffs' counsel then asks the district court to order the school board to take action identical to that contained in the settlement offer discussed above. What would result under the doctrine of Brown?

3. Is it either legally possible or prudent for black parents and their attorneys to attempt to transform rights to student desegregation into increased participation in school policy-making? Is it possible to structure such compromises so as to avoid obtaining no more than a new serving of "separate but equal" education?

4. If such negotiations seem impractical at the public school level, how about using this approach with public black colleges which, while technically covered by the Brown mandate, have not in most instances been integrated? As the cases that follow indicate, most blacks want to see black colleges survive and grow as basically black institutions at which whites are free to enroll. Can such a role for these institutions be justified under Brown?

ALABAMA STATE TEACHERS ASSOCIATION v. ALABAMA PUBLIC SCHOOL AND COLLEGE AUTHORITY
289 F. Supp. 784 (M.D. Ala. 1968)

Before GEWIN, Circuit Judge, and JOHNSON and PITTMAN, District Judges.

Frank M. JOHNSON, Jr., District Judge:

[The plaintiffs, black teachers and college students, in a class action challenged the constitutionality of Alabama statutes under which defendants were continuing to operate a dual racial college system. The focus of their attack was an act which authorized the issuance and sale of $5 billion in bonds to build a four-year college at the Montgomery branch of Auburn University. After dismissing various procedural claims, Judge Johnson addressed himself to the major issue.]

Plaintiffs' primary attack on Act No. 403 may be stated as a syllogism: Alabama historically has had a dual system of higher education by law; although no longer supported by law, the dual system in fact remains largely intact; this Court and the Fifth Circuit recognize in the elementary and secondary education area an affirmative duty to dismantle the dual system [citations omitted]; that duty is equally applicable to higher education; that duty requires officials to utilize new construction or expansion of facilities as an opportunity to dismantle the dual system; the history and operation of Acts Nos. 243 and 403 indicate that in planning the construction of the Auburn branch at Montgomery defendants did not maximize desegregation; therefore, their action is unconstitutional and should be enjoined.

At the outset it should be noted that this argument presents a case of first impression. To our knowledge, no court in dealing with desegregation of institutions in the higher education area has gone farther than ordering nondiscriminatory admissions. That is also as far as Congress went in the 1964 Civil Rights Act.[2] The Department of Health, Education and Welfare has also largely limited its concern to admissions policies in administering Title 6 of the 1964 Civil Rights Act.[3]

We too are reluctant at this time to go much beyond preventing discriminatory admissions. Although much of plaintiffs' argument is valid, several faulty premises lead us to reject the conclusion they urge upon us. We would judi-

2. 42 U.S.C. §2000c-4(a) (2). Compare subsection (2) with subsection (1), which seems to authorize a wider range of civil action by the Attorney General in the elementary and secondary school area.

3. 45 C.F.R. §80.4(d). Compare subsection (d) with subsection (c) which for elementary and secondary schools requires a plan for desegregation. Pursuant to this, H.E.W. has compiled an elaborate set of guidelines. See 45 C.F.R. §181 (1967).

cially notice that Alabama has traditionally had a dual system of higher education. Furthermore, we find as a fact that the dual system in higher education has not been fully dismantled. The law is clear also that the State is under an affirmative duty to dismantle the dual system. Indeed, in Lee v. Macon County Board of Education, supra, we required the state colleges and junior colleges to refrain from discrimination in admissions and to begin faculty desegregation. We do not agree, however, with the characterization of the college authorities' conduct, nor do we agree that the *scope* of the duty should be extended as far in higher education as it has been in the elementary and secondary public schools area.

Plaintiffs fail to take account of some significant differences between the elementary and secondary public schools and institutions of higher education and of some related differences concerning the role the courts should play in dismantling the dual systems. Public elementary and secondary schools are traditionally free and compulsory. Prior to "freedom of choice," children were assigned to their respective schools. This could be done with equanimity because, in principle at least, one school for a given grade level is substantially similar to another in terms of goals, facilities, course offerings, teacher training and salaries, and so forth. In this context, although reluctant to intervene, when the Constitution and mandates from the higher courts demanded it, we felt that desegregation could be accomplished, and that the requirements of the law would be met, without our being involved in a wide range of purely educational policy decisions. Accordingly, we felt, in dealing with the problem of desegregating the elementary and secondary public schools, that we could and should review decisions concerning the impact of site selection for new construction or expansion without overreaching our area of competence.

Higher education is neither free nor compulsory. Students choose which, if any, institution they will attend. In making that choice they face the full range of diversity in goals, facilities, equipment, course offerings, teacher training and salaries, and living arrangements, perhaps only to mention a few. From where legislators sit, of course, the system must be viewed on a statewide basis. In deciding to open a new institution or build a branch or expand an existing institution, and in deciding where to locate it, the legislature must consider a very complicated pattern of demand for and availability of the above-listed variables, including, also, impact on the dual system. We conclude that in reviewing such a decision to determine whether it maximized desegregation we would necessarily be involved, consciously or by default, in a wide range of educational policy decisions in which courts should not become involved. A brief review of the background of this case will, we think, reveal the wisdom of this conclusion.

[The court pointed out that there were two public colleges in Montgomery: Alabama State, a public, predominantly Negro four-year liberal arts college which emphasized teacher education; and a non–degree-granting Extension Center of the University of Alabama. It was decided that Auburn University would undertake to expand the Extension Center into a degree-granting college, calling for a projected long-range enrollment of 15,000 students. Plaintiffs maintain that Auburn was chosen in order to provide for white students in the Montgomery area. The court noted, however, that black students would not be excluded, and added that the selection of Auburn did not therefore represent perpetuation of an identifiably "white" institution, any more than the selection of Alabama State would have reflected the maintenance of a dual school system by enlarging an identifiably "black" institution. Rather, the court said, the Auburn branch would be a "new institution," neither a white nor a Negro school, but just a school. The court noted that Auburn University was under court order to admit all qualified blacks, and that the school was also recruiting more black faculty members.]

We conclude, therefore, that as long as the State and a particular institution are dealing with admissions, faculty and staff in good faith the basic requirement of the affirmative duty to dismantle the dual school system on the college level, to the extent that the system may be based upon racial considerations, is satisfied.

This is not to suggest that we view the problem as merely personal rather than systematic. As plaintiffs indicated, nondiscriminatory admissions in higher education are analogous to a freedom-of-choice plan in the elementary and secondary public schools. We are also cognizant that recent Supreme Court decisions have cast doubt on the continued viability of freedom of choice in the public schools. But we do not interpret those decisions as applying to the operation of an educational system on a college level. Freedom to choose where one will attend college, unlike choosing one's elementary or secondary public school, has a long tradition and helps to perform an important function, viz., fitting the right school to the right student.

We believe that an effective beginning has been made at Auburn to dismantle the racial characteristics of that school system and that, as effective desegregation plans are developed in the elementary and secondary public schools, the problem will probably resolve itself in the case of higher education. If the Auburn branch at Montgomery is administered as "just a school," as we are assured it will be and as we are confident it will be, our conclusions as herein outlined will receive significant confirmation. . . .

NOTES

1. On appeal, the Supreme Court granted motions to affirm the district court's judgment. Alabama State Teacher's Association v. Alabama Public School and College Authority, 393 U.S. 400, 89 S. Ct. 581, 21 L. Ed. 2d 631 (1969). Justice Douglas dissented, on the basis that the distinction drawn by the district court between elementary and secondary schools on the one hand, and colleges and universities on the other, constitutes an element of "freedom of choice" on which probable jurisdiction should have been noted and the case set for argument. 393 U.S. at 401.

2. In a similar factual situation, a district court refused to enjoin construction of a new educational center at an existing white school in Nashville, Tennessee, which plaintiffs maintained would perpetuate the dual school system because of an existing black college in that city. Sanders v. Ellington, 288 F. Supp. 937 (M.D. Tenn. 1968). The court in Sanders did interpret Green v. County School Board, supra, to require the state to take affirmative action to dismantle the dual system of higher education which, it found, presently existed in Tennessee. But the court found that the state had made efforts in good faith toward this end, even though it had not fulfilled the obligation. Therefore, the court ordered the submission of a plan that would fully dismantle the dual system. The court provided a substantial amount of time for submission of the plan, but noted that the state's failure to make Tennessee Agricultural and Industrial (the black school) a viable desegregated institution could lead to its continued deterioration as an institution of higher learning. As to Tennessee State, the court said: "It is clearly apparent on the record that something must be done for that school and that the one thing that is absolutely essential is a substantial desegregation of that institution by whatever means can be devised by the best minds that the State of Tennessee can bring to it." 288 F. Supp. at 943.

Following a subsequent hearing in the Tennessee State case, the court reviewed the seeming conflict between this decision and that in Alabama State Teacher's Association, supra, concluded that there was no conflict, and reaffirmed its earlier holding that there is an affirmative duty on the state to dismantle a dual system of education at the college level. The court found that little progress had been made in desegregating the formerly all-black Tennessee State, and concluding that little progress could be expected from an "open door" policy until there was a "white presence" on the campus that would attract substantial numbers of white students, it ordered defendants to provide a plan that would substantially desegregate the Tennessee State faculty. The court also pointed out duplicate programs at Tennessee State and the predominantly white University of Tennessee-Nashville, suggesting that such programs might be merged, and ordered defendants to study the feasibility of merging or consolidating Tennessee State and the University of Tennessee-Nashville into a single institution. Geier v. Dunn, 337 F. Supp. 573 (M.D. Tenn. 1972).

3. Many black educators have been concerned with the tendency of states to build new white colleges or develop existing ones, while ignoring predominantly black institutions located nearby. On the other hand, they fear that desegregation such as called for in the Sanders opinion, supra, would transform a black institution into a predominantly white college that will basically serve the needs of whites. They urge that black schools should be permitted to retain their identity, although allowing admissions on a nondiscriminatory basis, and that such institutions be given both adequate budgets and the primary responsibility for those aspects of education of particular interest to the black community, such as social welfare, community planning

and community health. They maintain that to measure a black school's eligibility for new programs or new extensions by comparing it with the nearest white college, which traditionally has received more attention and funding under the separate but equal policy, is to perpetuate the discrimination of the pre-Brown era. They urge in addition that black schools can play an important role in the development of the black community, that effective functioning was impossible under the "separate but equal" doctrine, and that the black colleges should not be consigned to oblivion through abandonment or consolidation just at the period when their services are most needed. See The Future of the Black Colleges, Daedalus (Summer 1971).

4. Another three-judge court in Alabama did require a specific desegregation plan for the state's trade schools and junior colleges, after finding (1) that the institutions were operating on a segregated basis, with only a token few blacks attending the white schools; (2) that some of the schools were operated so as to serve only pupils of one race within overlapping dual attendance zones; and (3) that the white schools received more funds and offered a wider variety of courses than the black schools. The court ordered the State Board of Education to eliminate duplicate programs in the trade schools (which were paired in five cities), desegregate the faculties of the junior colleges and twelve trade schools by exchanging faculty members, desegregate transportation facilities, establish definite attendance areas on a nonracial basis, and implement a recruiting program designed to integrate the student bodies at both the junior colleges and trade schools. On appeal, the Fifth Circuit expressed "some reluctance to require school attendance zones for college age level institutions," but approved this phase of the district court's plan, although staying its effective date until the 1972-1973 school year. The court noted that the physical facilities and curriculum of the predominantly black schools and junior colleges were being equalized, a fact which, it suggested, might provide a "reasonable basis for hope and optimism that substantial integration will be achieved. . . ." Lee v. Macon County Board of Education, 453 F.2d 525, 527 (5th Cir. 1971).

5. A federal court in Virginia, refusing to follow the Alabama State Teachers Association, supra, granted an injunction prohibiting the state from enlarging a two-year white college to four-year status, because such action would frustrate the efforts of a neighboring predominantly black college to desegregate. The court distinguished the Auburn University decision on the basis that there the new institution had had no prior racial identification. Moreover, the court said that the mandate of Green v. County School Board requires the conversion of racially identifiable colleges to "just colleges," even though the "means of eliminating discrimination" may differ between public schools and colleges. Norris v. State Council of Higher Education for Virginia, 327 F. Supp. 1368 (E.D. Va. 1971), *aff'd sub nom.* Board of Visitors of the College of William and Mary in Va., 404 U.S. 907, 92 S. Ct. 227, 30 L. Ed. 2d 180 (1971).

6. In the North, many colleges which for years had been admitting "quali-

fied" blacks began broadening their admissions policies so as to increase the number of black students. These students then pressured the colleges and universities to admit more black students, hire black faculty, establish black studies programs, and, in some instances, set up dormitories and eating and recreational areas strictly for blacks. The last-mentioned actions were very controversial, and when officially approved by a college they were cited by HEW as racial discrimination in violation of Title VI of the 1964 Civil Rights Act. See Federal Agency Backs Antioch on All-Negro Black Studies Unit, N.Y. Times, May 3, 1969, at 1, cols. 7-8. There has been little litigation on this issue, mainly because if no official policy is published as to a facility set up at the request of blacks, very few whites will attempt to use it without invitation.

QUESTIONS

1. Could black colleges defend their predominantly black status, at least for a period, by arguing that to best serve the needs of many black students burdened by inadequate prior education in segregated, inferior schools, the colleges must provide a black identification, including black leadership and a curriculum structured to meet the special needs of the students? Could the schools point to the time provided public school systems under the "all deliberate speed" standard to support their argument?

2. There is little legal precedent to explain the broad gains in minority student admissions, hiring of minority faculty, and setting up of special black studies programs, courses and facilities, which were achieved by black students in Northern colleges effective during the late 1960s. If you were requested to represent a college that had established special admissions policies for blacks, and was now being sued by white students whose "traditional qualifications" were higher than those of the blacks who were admitted, how would you defend the school's policy? See DeFunis v. Odegaard, 3 Race Rel. L. Sur. 164 (Wash. Super. Ct. 1971). In the DeFunis case, a white applicant who had been refused admission to the University of Washington Law School filed suit, asserting that the defendant's minority recruitment program denied him equal protection of the law, since less qualified minority group individuals were given preferential treatment in admission to the school. Testimony showed that only one minority student out of the thirty-one admitted had a predicted first-year average higher than plaintiff's. Finding the defendant's admissions system discriminatory for its failure to treat members of all races alike, the court ordered that plaintiff be admitted to the law school. The law school appealed. What arguments can be made in defense of the law school's admissions policy?

D. POST-BROWN NORTHERN SCHOOL LITIGATION

Beginning in the early 1960s, efforts were made in litigation initiated on behalf of black children living in the North to have the Brown decision made applicable to school systems which had no recent history of official segregation, but whose schools were in fact predominantly either black or white. Where there was proof that school board policies had caused the racially imbalanced schools, the principles of Brown were applied. Where the school board had acted voluntarily or at the behest of state law to integrate its schools, courts almost always found such actions a reasonable exercise of discretion which did not infringe on the rights of white parents and children. See, e.g., Tometz v. Board of Education, infra. But early efforts to get federal courts to order relief based solely on the harmfulness of racial segregation, without proof of school board responsibility, were almost uniformly unsuccessful. See, e.g., Bell v. School City of Gary, Ind., infra. The district court opinion in Barksdale v. Springfield is one of the exceptions.

BARKSDALE v. SPRINGFIELD SCHOOL COMMITTEE

237 F. Supp. 543 (D. Mass. 1965)

Sweeney, Chief Justice. . . .

The Springfield school system is composed of fifty schools, including four high schools, grades 9-12 (which are not involved in this action); eight junior high schools, grades 7-9; thirty-seven elementary schools, K-6; and one elementary school, K-2. The elementary and junior high schools are organized on the neighborhood plan. Some of them, as will be shown, have a heavy concentration of negro children, while others are attended by only white children. It is the contention of the plaintiffs that the racial imbalance in some of the schools is segregation in the constitutional sense, and within the decision of the Supreme Court in Brown v. Board of Education, 347 U.S. 483 . . . (1954); and that continued adherence to the neighborhood policy is tantamount to a law compelling segregation. The plaintiffs claim also that the defendants have deliberately drawn district lines and assigned pupils so as to segregate them by race.

I find that there is no deliberate intent on the part of the school authorities to segregate the races. If segregation exists, it results from a rigid adherence to the neighborhood plan of school attendance. . . .

Since the latter part of the nineteenth century, attendance at elementary and junior high schools in Springfield has been organized on the neighborhood plan. District lines are drawn with reference to the location and capacity of the various schools and take into account the safety and convenience of the children in going to and from school. In general, children are required to attend the school within the district in which they live. While there are exceptions to this rule in a few optional areas, and where transfers are permitted when schools are overcrowded, I find that these exceptions are not designed or used to segregate the children by race. I find further that district lines have been drawn in conformity with the criteria mentioned above and not in order to segregate children by race.

However, segregation in the sense of racial imbalance, exists in the Springfield school system. While the experts did not agree on what constitutes racial imbalance in general, or in Springfield in particular, it is unnecessary to define the term. In the light of the ratio of white to non-white in the total population in the City of Springfield, I do find, however, that a non-white attendance of appreciably more than fifty per cent in any one school is tantamount to segregation. Although several members of the School Committee denied any knowledge of racial patterns and racial concentration in housing and, consequently, in the schools, census data and statistics compiled by employees of the school department at the request of the School Committee indicate that at least seven elementary schools and one junior high school have a majority of negro or negro and Puerto Rican students, while other schools are one hundred per cent white.

The total elementary school enrollment for the 1963-64 school year was 19,417, of which 15,588 or 80.3% were white; 3,386 or 17.4% were negroes and 443, or 2.3% Puerto Rican. This latter group is not involved in this action and will be disregarded for the purposes of this opinion. Of the 3,386 negroes in all of the thirty-eight elementary schools, all but 595 are enrolled in eight of them; i.e., the Homer, Hooker, Brookings, Deberry, Eastern Avenue, Ells, Tapley and Carew Schools.

Of the 6,546 students enrolled in the eight junior high schools, 946 are negroes. 702 of that number are enrolled in the Buckingham Junior High School and 117 in the Chestnut Junior High School, making a total of 819. The remaining 127 pupils of the junior high schools are distributed through the other six junior high schools. Incidentally, of 52 Puerto Rican junior high school students, all are enrolled in the Chestnut Street Junior High School.

From the evidence, I find that those schools in which the vast majority of negro students are enrolled consistently rank lowest in achievement ratings based on the Iowa Test of Basic Skills. Those students, when transferred to other schools, had difficulty keeping abreast with their contemporaries. Special programs in science and French for gifted children who have attained a high achievement level have had few, and sometimes no, negro participants.

While it is not possible to determine how much of this is the result of home environment and how much is attributable to schools and teachers, these facts, nonetheless, bear out the testimony of the plaintiffs' expert, Dr. Thomas F. Pettigrew, that racially imbalanced schools are not conducive to learning, that is, to retention, performance, and the development of creativity. Racial concentration in his school communicates to the negro child that he is different and is expected to be different from white children. Therefore, even if all schools are equal in physical plant, facilities, and ability and number of teachers, and even if academic achievement were at the same level at all schools, the opportunity of negro children in racially concentrated schools to obtain equal educational opportunities is impaired, and I so find.

The defendants argue, nevertheless, that there is no constitutional mandate to remedy racial imbalance. Bell v. School City of Gary, Indiana, 324 F.2d 209 (7th Cir. 1963). But that is not the question. The question is whether there is a constitutional duty to provide equal educational opportunities for all children within the system. While Brown answered that question affirmatively in the context of coerced segregation, the constitutional fact — the inadequacy of segregated education — is the same in this case, and I so find. It is neither just nor sensible to proscribe segregation having its basis in affirmative state action while at the same time failing to provide a remedy for segregation which grows out of discrimination in housing, or other economic or social factors. Education is tax supported and compulsory, and public school educators, therefore, must deal with inadequacies within the educational system as they arise, and it matters not that the inadequacies are not of their making. This is not to imply that the neighborhood school policy per se is unconstitutional, but that it must be abandoned or modified when it results in segregation in fact. Blocker v. Board of Education of Manhasset, New York, 226 F. Supp. 208 (E.D.N.Y. 1964) Branche v. Board of Education, 204 F. Supp. 150 (E.D.N.Y. 1962), Jackson v. Pasadena City School District, 59 Cal. 2d 876, 31 Cal. Rptr. 606, 382 P.2d 878 (1963), Taylor v. Board of Education, 191 F. Supp. 181, 187 (S.D.N.Y.) (dictum) *aff'd* 294 F.2d 36 (2d Cir.) *cert. den.* 368 U.S. 940, 942 . . . (1961). I cannot accept the view in Bell that only forced segregation is incompatible with the requirements of the Fourteenth Amendment, nor do I find meaningful the statement that "[t]he Constitution . . . does not require integration. It merely forbids discrimination." 324 F.2d at 213. In view of the disparity in population and school attendance, there cannot be equal representation of white and negro students in each school, but there must be no segregated schools. . . .

BELL v. SCHOOL CITY OF GARY, INDIANA, 324 F.2d 209 (7th Cir. 1963). When litigation was initiated in the 1961-1962 school year, there were 43,090 students in the public school system, and 23,055 or approximately 53 percent were black. At that time, 16,242 students attended twelve schools which were 99 to 100 percent black, and 6981 students attended five schools which were 77 to 95 percent black. Black students constituted 13 to 37 percent of the student bodies in four schools, and in five schools the school population was from 95 to 99 percent white. Based mainly on these facts, the black plaintiffs contended that the rule in Brown v. Board of Education was applicable and the school system should be desegregated.

The Gary School Board through its president, who was black, testified that there was no policy of racial segregation in the system, that students were transferred to maximize efficient use of school facilities on a nonracial basis, and that blacks served as teachers and administrators at every level of the system. The board also pointed out that all the schools were overcrowded as a result of the tremendous population growth the area had experienced.

The district court ruled against the plaintiffs and the court of appeals affirmed. In its opinion by Judge Duffy, the court stated:

> Plaintiffs' position is grounded on their fundamental theory that their right to be integrated in school is such an over-riding purpose that little, if any, consideration

need to be given to the safety of the children, convenience of pupils and their parents, and costs of the operation of the school system. There was testimony that under plaintiffs' plan, at least six thousand pupils would have to be transported on each school day, presumably by bus, and that the cost of operating one bus was $20 per day.

The District Judge pointed out "The safety factors are difficult to solve in this school system. Three U. S. Highways and the Indiana Toll Road traverse Gary from East to West. At least nine railroads cross the city, mostly at grade, as they converge on Chicago from the east or southeast. Some of these railroads have multiple tracks through the city and the streets crossing them are several blocks apart in some areas. The Little Calumet River crosses the city from east to west and is infrequently bridged. These are all safety factors that have to be considered in locating schools and fixing attendance districts."

Let us consider Tolleston School in Gary. In the school year 1951-1952, this school was in a predominantly white neighborhood, only 4.3% of its school-age children were colored. But, in the following ten years, colored people, on their own volition, moved in large numbers into this school district area. There was no change in the school district boundary lines. At the end of this period, the percentage of colored pupils was 76.65%. The plaintiffs claim that the voluntary Negro influx into this area has caused imbalance which defendants have the affirmative duty to change. In effect, plaintiffs say that defendants must somehow transplant from Tolleston enough Negro pupils to reduce their number to 50% of capacity, or some other arbitrary figure, and then, by some means, go out into the forty-two square miles of the City of Gary into the so-called white districts, and bring into the Tolleston School a sufficient number of white students to correct the imbalance.

Plaintiffs are unable to point to any court decision which has laid down the principle which justifies their claim that there is an affirmative duty on the Gary School System to recast or realign school districts or areas for the purpose of mixing or blending Negroes and whites in a particular school.

Plaintiffs argue that Brown v. Board of Education, 347 U.S. 483, proclaims that segregated public education is incompatible with the requirements of the Fourteenth Amendment in a school system maintained pursuant to state law. However, the holding in Brown was that the forced segregation of children in public schools solely on the basis of race, denied the children of the minority group the equal protection of the laws granted by the Fourteenth Amendment.

The situation in Brown is a far cry from the situation existing in Gary, Indiana. The School District boundaries in Gary were determined without any consideration of race or color. We agree with the argument of the defendants stated as "there is no affirmative U. S. Constitutional duty to change innocently arrived at school attendance districts by the mere fact that shifts in population either increase or decrease the percentage of either Negro or white pupils." . . .

We agree with and the record fully sustains the District Court's finding, "An examination of the school boundary lines in the light of the various factors involved such as density of population, distances that the students have to travel and the safety of the children, particularly in the lower grades, indicates that the areas have been reasonably arrived at and that the lines have not been drawn for the purpose of including or excluding children of certain races."

We approve also of the statement in the District Court's opinion, "Nevertheless, I have seen nothing in the many cases dealing with the segregation problem which leads me to believe that the law requires that a school system developed on the neighborhood school plan, honestly and conscientiously constructed with no intention or purpose to segregate the races, must be destroyed or abandoned because the resulting effect is to have a racial imbalance in certain schools where the district is populated almost entirely by Negroes or whites. . . ."

We hold that the constitutional rights of the plaintiffs and others similarly situated, were not violated by the manner in which the defendant School District of Gary, Indiana maintained and operated its schools, and that the District Court was correct in dismissing the complaint herein.

Affirmed. (324 F.2d at 212-213.)

TOMETZ v. BOARD OF EDUCATION, WAUKEGAN CITY
39 Ill. 2d 593, 237 N.E.2d 498 (1968)

WARD, Justice.

[On June 13, 1963, the legislature approved an amendment to §10-21.3 of the Illinois School Code relating to the duties of school boards. (Ill. Rev. Stat. 1967, chap. 122, par. 10-21.3.) This amendment, commonly called the Armstrong Act, provides in part: "As soon as practicable, and from time to time thereafter, the board shall change or revise existing [attendance] units or create new units in a manner which will take into consideration the prevention of segregation and the elimination of separation of children in public schools because of color, race or nationality."

On August 4, 1965, the plaintiffs, seven children, by their respective parents, instituted a suit in the circuit court of Lake County claiming that the Waukegan City School District had violated the Armstrong Act and seeking a mandatory injunction requiring the district to revise the boundaries of its school attendance units. The district and the local board of education were named as defendants.

Trial was had on the plaintiffs' complaint, and at its conclusion, on July 20, 1966, the court found inter alia that the racial imbalance in the Whittier School area had not been created by any deliberate conduct on the part of the defendants and that the defendants had not been guilty of any intentional racial discrimination. Also, the trial court held that the Armstrong Act was constitutional and applicable to "so-called de facto segregation in schools, i.e., racial imbalance in schools not created by the deliberate intent of a school board." The trial court judged that the defendants' failure to make any change in the boundaries of the district's attendance units was unreasonable under the circumstances and in violation of the Armstrong Act. The court therefore ordered the defendants to submit a plan making reasonable boundary revisions so as to "in some measure ameliorate the racial imbalance" in the attendance units concerned. August 4, 1966, was set for a hearing to consider the plan to be proposed.]

In this direct appeal the defendants challenge the constitutionality of the Armstrong Act, alleging that the Act's requirement that race be considered as a factor in changing or forming school attendance unit boundaries, constitutes a racial classification condemned by the equal protection clause and due process clause of the fourteenth amendment to the United States constitution and the due process clause of the Illinois constitution.

To support this claim, the defendants heavily rely on three Federal cases, each of which held, no State law being involved, that a local school board does not have an affirmative constitutional duty to act to alleviate racial imbalance in the schools that it did not cause. (Deal v. Cincinnati Board of Education (6th Cir. 1966) 369 F.2d 55, *cert. denied* 389 U.S. 847 . . . ; Downs v. Board of Education of Kansas City (10th Cir. 1964) 336 F.2d 988, *cert. denied* 380 U.S. 914 . . . ; Bell v. School City of Gary, Indiana (7th Cir. 1963) 324 F.2d 209, *cert. denied* 377 U.S. 924 . . . .) However, the question as to whether the constitution requires a local school board, or a State, to act to undo de facto school segregation is simply not here concerned. The issue here is whether the constitution permits, rather than prohibits, voluntary State action aimed toward reducing and eventually eliminating de facto school segregation.

State laws or administrative policies, directed toward the reduction and eventual elimination of de facto segregation of children in the schools and racial imbalance, have been approved by every high State court which has considered the issue. (Pennsylvania — Pennsylvania Human Relations Commission v. Chester School District (Sept. 1967) 427 Pa. 157, 233 A.2d 290; Massachusetts — School Committee of Boston v. Board of Education (June, 1967) Mass., 227 N.E.2d 729, *appeal dismissed* (Jan. 15, 1968) 389 U.S. 572 . . . ; New Jersey — Booker v. Board of Education of Plainfield, Union County (1965) 45 N.J. 161, 212 A.2d 1, 11 A.L.R.3d 754; Morean v. Board of Education of Town of Montclair (1964) 42 N.J. 237, 200 A.2d 97; California — Jackson v. Pasadena City School District (1963) 59 Cal. 2d 876, 31 Cal. Rptr. 606, 382 P.2d 878; New York — Addabbo v. Donovan (1965) 16 N.Y.2d 619, 261 N.Y.S.2d 68, 209 N.E.2d 112, *cert. denied* 382 U.S. 905 . . . ; Vetere v. Allen (1965) 15 N.Y.2d 259, 258 N.Y.S.2d 77, 206 N.E.2d 174; see also Guida v. Board of Education of City of New Haven (1965) 26 Conn. Sup. 121, 213 A.2d 843.) Similarly, the Federal courts which have considered the issue, including Deal v. Cincinnati Board of Education (6th Cir.) 369 F.2d 55, *cert. denied* 389 U.S. 847 . . . , relied on by the defendants, have recognized that voluntary programs of local school authorities designed to alleviate de facto segregation and racial imbalance in the schools are not constitutionally forbidden. E.g., Offermann v. Nitkowski (2d Cir. 1967) 378 F.2d 22; Deal v. Cincinnati Board of Education (6th Cir. 1966) 369 F.2d 55, 61 *cert. denied* 389 U.S. 847 . . . ; Wanner v. County School Board of Arlington County (4th Cir. 1966) 357 F.2d 452, 455; Springfield School Committee v. Barksdale (1st Cir. 1965) 348 F.2d 261; Hobson v. Hansen (D.D.C. 1967) 269 F. Supp. 401, 509, 510.

In Springfield School Committee v. Barksdale (1st Cir. 1965) 348 F.2d 261, the school authorities of Springfield, Massachusetts, had passed a resolution to take appropriate action "to eliminate to the fullest extent possible, [de facto] racial concentration in the schools within the framework of effective educational procedures." Addressing itself to the resolution, the Court of Appeals for the First Circuit stated at page 266 that: "It has been suggested that classification by race is unlawful regardless of the worthiness of the objective. We do not agree. The defendants' proposed action does not concern race except insofar as race correlates with proven deprivation of educational opportunity. This evil satisfies whatever 'heavier burden of justification' there may be. Cf. McLaughlin v. State of Florida, 1964, 379 U.S. 184 . . . .' It would seem no more unconstitutional to take into account plaintiffs' special characteristics and circumstances that have been found to be occasioned by their color than it would be to give special attention to physiological, psychological or sociological variances from the norm occasioned by other factors. That these differences happen to be associated with a particular race is no reason for ignoring them. Booker v. Board of Education etc., 1965, 45 N.J. 161, 212 A.2d 1, 11 A.L.R.3d 754 . . . ."

In Morean v. Board of Education of Town of Montclair (1964) 42 N.J. 237, 200 A.2d 97, the Supreme Court of New Jersey sustained the constitutionality of a school board's plan to assign students from a predominantly Negro junior high school to the town's three remaining junior high schools, even though race had been a consideration. The court stated there that: "The motivation was, to avoid creating a situation at Hillside [school] which would deprive the pupils there of equal educational opportunities and subject them to the harmful consequences of practical segregation. Constitutional color blindness may be wholly apt when the frame of reference is an attack on official efforts toward segregation; it is not generally apt when the attack is on official efforts toward the avoidance of segregation." 200 A.2d at 99; *accord,* Offermann v. Nitkowski (2d Cir. 1967) 378 F.2d 22, 24.

Also pertinent is the observation of the Supreme Court of Pennsylvania in Pennsylvania Human Relations Commission v. Chester School District (Sept. 1967) 427 Pa. 157, 233 A.2d 290. In this case, which involved de facto segregation in public schools, the court said: "The School District does not suggest that it would be unconstitutional for the Legislature to command them to consider race in their redistricting proposals in order to achieve a semblance of racial balance in its schools, nor do we believe there would be any merit in such a contention." 233 A.2d at 294.

Too, the United States Supreme Court on January 15, 1968, dismissed an appeal in School Committee of Boston v. Board of Education (Mass. 1967) 227 N.E.2d 729, which challenged the statute providing for elimination of racial imbalance in public schools "for want of a substantial federal question." 389 U.S. 572 . . . .

The test of any legislative classification essentially is one of reasonableness. This court stated in City of Chicago v. Vokes, 28 Ill. 2d 475, 193 N.E.2d 40, that neither the fourteenth amendment nor any provision of the Illinois constitution forbids legislative classifications reasonably calculated to promote or serve a proper police-power purpose. "Rather, they invalidate only enactments that are arbitrary, unreasonable and unrelated to the public purpose sought to be attained, or those which, although reasonably designed to promote the public interest, effect classifications which have no reasonable basis and are therefore arbitrary." (28 Ill. 2d at 479, 193 N.E.2d at 44; see Chicago Real Estate Board v. City of Chicago, 36 Ill. 2d 530, 542, 543, 224 N.E.2d 793.) And, of course, the burden rests upon one assailing a statute or a classification in a law, to show that it does not rest upon any reasonable basis but is essentially arbitrary. Thillens, Inc. v. Morey, 11 Ill. 2d 579, 591, 144 N.E.2d 735; Stewart v. Brady, 300 Ill. 425, 436, 133 N.E. 310.

Here, the legislature has directed school boards "as soon as practicable" to fix or revise the boundaries of school attendance units in a manner that "takes into consideration" the prevention and elimination of segregation. We cannot say that the legislature acted arbitrarily and without a reasonable basis in so directing the school boards of this State.

The legislature is necessarily vested with broad discretion to determine not only what the public interest and welfare require, but what measures are necessary to secure such interests. (Thillens, Inc. v. Morey, 11 Ill. 2d 579, 593, 144 N.E.2d 735; People v. City of Chicago, 413 Ill. 83, 91, 108 N.E.2d 16, 21.) We have said: "With the growth and development of the state, the police power necessarily develops, within reasonable bounds, to meet the changing conditions. The power is not circumscribed by precedent arising out of past conditions but is elastic and capable of expansion to keep up with human progress. It extends to the great public needs, that which is sanctioned by usage or held by prevailing morality or strong and preponderant opinion to be greatly and immediately necessary to the public welfare. . . . Too, not to be disregarded is article VIII of the constitution which directs the general assembly to "provide a thorough and efficient system of free schools, whereby all children of this state may receive a good common school education."

When, in Brown v. Board of Education of Topeka (1954) 347 U.S. 483 . . . the Supreme Court declared unconstitutional de jure segregation in public schools, it made clear its position that all segregation of children solely on the basis of race deprives children of the minority group of equal educational opportunities. Though Brown directly concerned de jure segregation, segregation caused by official governmental action, courts since Brown have recognized that de facto segregation has a seriously limiting influence on educational opportunity. Booker v. Board of Education of City of Plainfield, Union County (1965) 45 N.J. 161, 212 A.2d 1, 4, 5, 7, 11 A.L.R.3d 754; Jackson v. Pasadena City School District (1963) 59 Cal. 2d 876, 31 Cal. Rptr. 606, 382 P.2d 878, 881, 882; Pennsylvania Human Relations Commission v. Chester School District (1967) 427 Pa. 157, 233 A.2d 290; Barksdale v. Springfield School Committee (D.C. Mass.) 237 F. Supp. 543, vacated on other grounds (1st Cir. 1965) 348 F.2d 261.

The fact that children other than Negro children may be deprived of equal educational opportunities does not form a constitutional impediment to the Act concerned. The legislature is not required to choose between legislating against all evils of the same genus or not legislating at all. It may recognize degrees of harm confining itself to where the need seems most acute. . . . Too, the Armstrong Act would apply to the offensive segregation of school children of any "color, race or nationality."

We deem that neither the fourteenth amendment nor any provision of the Illinois constitution deprives the legislature of the authority to require school boards "as soon as practicable" to fix or change the boundaries of school attendance units "in a manner which will take into consideration" the prevention and eventual elimination of segregation. . . . [Dissenting opinion of Judges House, Klingbiel and Klucsynaki omitted.]

NOTES

1. The First Circuit reversed Chief Judge Sweeney's Barksdale decision even though it accepted his findings of fact. 348 F.2d 261 (1965). While conceding that the Springfield Board must consider the entitlement of black students to equal educational opportunity, the court stated that this was only one of several factors pertinent to the administration of the school system, and did not vest in the blacks an absolute constitutional right to have "de facto segregation" removed at all costs. The court relied in part for this conclusion on Bell v. School City of Gary, Ind., supra. It then directed that the suit be dismissed without prejudice because the board, prior to litigation, had evidenced willingness to "take whatever action is necessary to eliminate to the fullest extent possible, racial concentration in the schools within the framework of effective educational procedures."

2. Tometz v. Board of Education, supra, cites Deal v. Cincinnati Board of Education, 369 F.2d 55 (6th Cir. 1966), and Downs v. Board of Education of Kansas City, 336 F.2d 988 (10th Cir. 1964), which, with Bell v. School City of Gary, supra, are the principal circuit court decisions refusing to find a constitutional obligation on school boards to correct racial-imbalance for which they are not responsible. The Tometz court also reviews state court cases approving state policies and voluntary actions by boards to eliminate de facto segregation.

3. Examples of early Northern cases in which Brown was held applicable, based on findings that racially imbalanced schools were the result of school board policies, include Taylor v. Board of Education of New Rochelle, 191 F. Supp. 181 (S.D.N.Y. 1961), and United States v. School District 151 of Cook County, 404 F.2d 1125 (7th Cir. 1968). In the New Rochelle case, a court reviewed school records revealing that for more than thirty years the school board had drawn and redrawn district lines so as to ensure confinement of blacks within the Lincoln School. After the Brown decision, a small number of whites were enrolled in that school, reducing the total of blacks to 94 percent. The presence of these whites was used to support defendants' arguments that the school was not segregated. The district judge saw Brown

as imposing a legal and moral duty on all school officials who had created or maintained segregated schools to undo the damage they had fostered.

> I see no basis to draw a distinction, legal or moral, between segregation established by the formality of a dual system of education, as in Brown, and that created by gerrymandering of school district lines and transferring of white children as in the instant case. . . . The result is the same in each case: the conduct of responsible school officials has operated to deny to Negro children the opportunities for a full and meaningful educational experience guaranteed to them by the Fourteenth Amendment. . . . In a community such as New Rochelle, the presence of some 29 white children certainly does not afford the 454 Negro children in the school the educational and social contacts and interaction envisioned by Brown. (191 F. Supp. at 193.)

In the Cook County case, the court rejected the school board's arguments that it had no obligation to correct de facto school segregation, finding that a long series of policies based on race — including formal drawing of attendance zones, bussing of pupils, assignment of teachers, location and construction of schools, and rejection of a plan for restructuring the school district — had all contributed to the racial isolation about which the plaintiffs complained.

4. Perhaps the most important of the early Northern school segregation cases was Hobson v. Hansen, 269 F. Supp. 401 (D.D.C. 1967), *aff'd sub nom.* Smuck v. Hobson, 408 F.2d 175 (D.C. Cir. 1969). The summary portion of Judge Wright's opinion, printed below, provides a pattern of discriminatory school policies which have been repeated in non-Southern school systems across the country.

HOBSON v. HANSEN
269 F. Supp. 401 (D.D.C. 1967)

J. SKELLY WRIGHT, Circuit Judge:

SUMMARY

In Bolling v. Sharpe, 347 U.S. 497 . . . (1954), the Supreme Court held that the District of Columbia's racially segregated public school system violated the due process clause of the Fifth Amendment. The present litigation, brought in behalf of Negro as well as poor children generally in the District's public schools, tests the current compliance of those schools with the principles announced in Bolling, its companion case, Brown v. Board of Education of Topeka, 347 U.S. 483 . . . (1954), and their progeny. The basic question presented is whether the defendants, the Superintendent of Schools and the members of the Board of Education, in the operation of the public school system here, unconstitutionally deprive the District's Negro and poor public school children of their right to equal educational opportunity with the District's white and more affluent public school children. This court concludes that they do.

In support of this conclusion the court makes the following principal findings of fact:

1. Racially and socially homogeneous schools damage the minds and spirit of all children who attend them — the Negro, the white, the poor and the affluent — and block the attainment of the broader goals of democratic education, whether the segregation occurs by law or by fact.

2. The scholastic achievement of the disadvantaged child, Negro and white, is strongly related to the racial and socio-economic composition of the student body of his school. A racially and socially integrated school environment increases the scholastic achievement of the disadvantaged child of whatever race.

3. The Board of Education, which is the statutory head of the public schools in the District, is appointed pursuant to a quota system which, until 1962, for over half a century had limited the Negro membership of the nine-man Board to three. Since 1962 the Negro quota on the Board has been four, one less than a majority. The city of Washington, which is the District of Columbia, presently has a population over 60% Negro and a public school population over 90% Negro.

4. Adherence to the neighborhood school policy by the School Board effectively segregates the Negro and the poor children from the white and the more affluent children in most of the District's public schools. This neighborhood school policy is relaxed by the Board through the use of optional zones for the purpose of allowing white children, usually affluent white children, "trapped" in a Negro school district, to "escape" to a "white" or more nearly white school, thus making the economic and racial segregation of the public school children more complete than it would otherwise be under a strict neighborhood school assignment plan.

5. The teachers and principals in the public schools are assigned so that generally the race of the faculty is the same as the race of the children. Thus most of the schools can be identified as "Negro" or "white," not only by reference to the predominant race of the children attending, but by the predominant race of the faculty as well. The heaviest concentration of Negro faculty, usually 100%, is in the Negro ghetto schools.

6. The median annual per pupil expenditure ($292) in the predominantly (85-100%) Negro elementary schools in the District of Columbia has been a flat $100 below the median annual per pupil expenditure for its predominantly (85-100%) white schools ($392).

7. Generally the "white" schools are underpopulated while the "Negro" schools generally are overcrowded. Moreover, all of the white elementary schools have kindergartens. Some Negro schools are without kindergartens entirely while other Negro schools operate kindergartens in shifts or consecutive sessions. In addition to being overcrowded and short on kindergarten space, the school buildings in the Negro slums are ancient and run down. Only recently, through the use of impact aid and other federal funds, have the Negro slum schools had sufficient textbooks for the children's use.

8. As they proceed through the Washington school system, the reading

scores primarily of the Negro and poor children, but not the white and middle class, fall increasingly behind the national norm. By senior high school the discrepancy reaches several grades.

9. The track system as used in the District's public schools is a form of ability grouping in which students are divided in separate, self-contained curricula or tracks ranging from "Basic" for the slow student to "Honors" for the gifted.

10. The aptitude tests used to assign children to the various tracks are standardized primarily on white middle class children. Since these tests do not relate to the Negro and disadvantaged child, track assignment based on such tests relegates Negro and disadvantaged children to the lower tracks from which, because of the reduced curricula and the absence of adequate remedial and compensatory education, as well as continued inappropriate testing, the chance of escape is remote.

11. Education in the lower tracks is geared to what Dr. Hansen, the creator of the track system, calls the "blue collar" student. Thus such children, so stigmatized by inappropriate aptitude testing procedures, are denied equal opportunity to obtain the white collar education available to the white and more affluent children.

Other incidental, but highly indicative, findings are as follows: a. The June 1964 — December 1965 study by the Office of the Surgeon General, Army, shows that 55.3% of the 18-year-olds from the District of Columbia failed the Armed Services mental test, a higher percentage than any of the 50 states. b. The average per pupil expenditure in the District's public schools is only slightly below the national average. The 1964-65 Bureau of the Census Report on Governmental Finances shows, however, that the District of Columbia spends less per capita on education generally than all states except Arkansas and Tennessee. c. The same report shows that the District of Columbia spends more per capita on police protection than all states without exception. In fact, the District of Columbia spends more than double any state other than Nevada, New York, New Jersey and California. The inferences, including those bearing on the relationship of the quality of education to crime, which arise from these findings are obvious. Indeed, the National Crime Commission's Task Force Report: Juvenile Delinquency and Youth Crime indicates that the very deficiencies in the District's public school system noted by the record in this case — prejudging, through inappropriate testing, the learning abilities of the disadvantaged child as inferior to the white middle class child; placing the child in lower tracks for reduced education based on such tests, thus implementing the self-fulfilling prophecy phenomenon inherent in such misjudgments; placing inferior teachers in slum schools; continuing racial and economic segregation of pupils; providing textbooks unrelated to the lives of disadvantaged children; inadequate remedial programs for offsetting initial psychological and social difficulties of the disadvantaged child — all have contributed to the increase in crime, particularly juvenile crime.

In sum, all of the evidence in this case tends to show that the Washington school system is a monument to the cynicism of the power structure which governs the voteless capital of the greatest country on earth.

Remedy

To correct the racial and economic discrimination found in the operation of the District of Columbia public school system, the court has issued a decree attached to its opinion ordering: 1. An injunction against racial and economic discrimination in the public school system here. 2. Abolition of the track system. 3. Abolition of the optional zones. 4. Transportation for volunteering children in overcrowded school districts east of Rock Creek Park to underpopulated schools west of the Park. 5. The defendants, by October 2, 1967, to file for approval by the court a plan for pupil assignment eliminating the racial and economic discrimination found to exist in the operation of the Washington public school system. 6. Substantial integration of the faculty of each school beginning with the school year 1967-68. 7. The defendants, by October 2, 1967, to file for approval by the court a teacher assignment plan fully integrating the faculty of each school.

NOTES

1. In a 1965 article, Judge Wright had argued that compulsory education laws constitute sufficient state action for application of the Equal Protection Clause to racial imbalance. In his view, school boards should be required to act affirmatively against racial imbalance, in order to provide equal educational opportunity for all. Public School Desegregation: Legal Remedies for De Facto Segregation, 40 N.Y.U.L. Rev. 285 (1965). But Hobson v. Hansen provided a dramatic illustration that reliance on compulsory school laws would not be necessary to prove de jure segregation in many Northern school districts. Setting a standard followed in later cases, Judge Wright based his decision on both the ample evidence that the board's policies had discriminated against black students, and the findings of educational and psychological damage suffered by blacks in segregated schools. This evidence had not sufficed to convince the Sixth, Seventh and Tenth Circuits that Brown was applicable to racially imbalanced schools, in the cases where plaintiffs sought to obtain relief without undertaking the major evidentiary burden of proving overt discriminatory policies. Once such evidence had been uncovered, however, the sociological proof could be added to good effect. And the increasing number of desegregation orders in Northern school litigation have generally followed the Hobson v. Hansen model. See Los Angeles — Crawford v. Board of Education, Civ. No. 822854 (Super. Ct. L.A. City, Feb. 11, 1970); Pasadena — Spangler v. Pasadena Board of Education, 311 F. Supp. 501 (C.D. Cal. 1970); San Francisco — Johnson v. San Francisco Unified School District, 339 F. Supp. 1315 (N.D. Cal. 1971); Oxnard, Calif. — Soria v. Oxnard School District Board of Trustees, 328 F. Supp. 155 (C.D. Cal. 1971);

Las Vegas — Kelly v. Brown, Civ. No. LV-1146 (D. Nev. 1970); Indianapolis — United States v. Board of School Commissioners, 332 F. Supp. 655 (S.D. Ind. 1971); Minneapolis — Booker v. Special School District No. 1, 351 F. Supp. 799 (D. Minn. 1972); Pontiac, Mich. — Davis v. School District, 443 F.2d 573 (6th Cir. 1971), *cert. denied,* 404 U.S. 913 (1971); Detroit — Bradley v. Milliken, 338 F. Supp. 582 (E.D. Mich. 1971), *aff'd* — F.2d — (6th Cir. 1972), *rehearing en banc granted,* — F.2d —; South Hollard, Ill. — United States v. School District 151, 404 F.2d 125 (7th Cir. 1968), *modified,* 432 F.2d 1147 (7th Cir. 1970), *cert. denied,* 402 U.S. 943 (1971).

2. Despite the Hobson v. Hansen model, suits are filed — and lost — attempting to attain desegregation orders based solely on the existence of racially imbalanced schools. Thus, in Spencer v. Kugler, 326 F. Supp. 1235 (D.N.J. 1971), *aff'd,* 404 U.S. 1027 (1972), an action to desegregate all of the school systems in New Jersey, the court found that a complaint alleging only de facto segregation did not state a claim upon which relief could be granted. As a practical matter, the court concluded that the "continuing trend toward racial imbalance caused by housing patterns . . . is not susceptible to federal judicial intervention." 326 F. Supp. at 1243. As a legal matter, the court relied on Swann, which, it found, drew a "critical distinction between those states which have a history of dual school systems . . . and those wherein so-called 'de-facto' segregation results from housing patterns and conventional drawing of school district zones." 326 F. Supp. at 1242.

3. In Lawlor v. Board of Education of the City of Chicago, 458 F.2d 660 (7th Cir. 1972), a group of white plaintiffs precipitated a de facto–de jure confrontation by a complaint alleging that certain "practices and policies" of the board had caused the number of black students in the area schools to increase to well over 10 to 25 percent. As a result of this rapid influx of blacks, whites were being "forced" and "driven" out of their schools, homes and businesses, and the area schools had become or were becoming segregated. Plaintiffs sought a halt to school board policies, including reclassifying schools, construction of temporary facilities, and permissive transfer and school zone boundary changes, so that the percentage of blacks in the area schools would be limited to a range of 10 to 25 percent. The court, in affirming dismissal of the suit, said that the requested percentage limit would deny equal protection to black people desiring to move into the area. If the school board policies were motivated by unlawful discrimination, the board would have an affirmative duty to remedy the situation. "However, the mere fact of imbalance of races is not alone a deprivation of equality of educational opportunity in the absence of purposeful invidious discrimination." 458 F.2d at 662.

4. One Northern school case raised elements of both de jure and de facto segregation within the same system. In Keyes v. School District No. 1, Denver, Colo., 445 F.2d 990, 1004, 1005 (10th Cir. 1971), *cert. granted,* 404 U.S. 1036 (1972), the district court ordered the desegregation of several schools in the "core" area of Denver, the population of which was historically pre-

dominantly black and Mexican. Ruling that board policies had not caused the racial isolation, although some board policies had unintentionally operated to exacerbate the degree of imbalance, the court found nevertheless that these schools were segregated in fact, producing an inferior educational opportunity, contrary to the mandate of Brown. The lower court concluded that this segregation was as violative of the Constitution as that in the schools of the Park Hill area of Denver, which were segregated as a result of board policies. On appeal, the Tenth Circuit affirmed as to the Park Hill schools, but refused to enforce the order to desegregate the core area schools, finding that a constitutional deprivation did not exist in the absence of proof that they were segregated as a result of intentional state action.

5. Regarding this holding, the Fifth Circuit predicted: "We have no doubt that the [Tenth Circuit] view that racially or ethnically motivated state action is a necessary prerequisite to the establishment of a constitutional violation in the field of public education is overruled by the decision in Wright [Wright v. Council of City of Emporia, 407 U.S. 451 (1972)]." Cisneros v. Corpus Christi Indiana School District, 467 F.2d 142, note 7 (1972). The implications of the "effect" standards on Northern school litigation are obvious. They were not lost on the Fifth Circuit, which found it clear

> . . . beyond peradventure that the contour of unlawful segregation extends beyond statutorily mandated segregation to include the actions and policies of school authorities which deny to students equal protection of the laws by separating them ethnically and racially in public schools. . . . Such actions are "state action" for the purposes of the Fourteenth Amendment, and result in dual school systems that cannot be somehow less odious because they do not flow from a statutory source. The imprimatur of the state is no less visible. The continuing attempt to cast segregation that results from such action as de facto and beyond the power of the court to rectify is no longer entitled to serious consideration. (467 F.2d at 148.)

6. The Fifth Circuit, of course, hears no Northern school cases, but the South has long noted the similarity of Northern school segregation to Southern and at every opportunity has complained about the lack of federal enforcement action in the North. The governor of Georgia, top school officials, and several parents filed suit in the District of Columbia, charging that the Attorney General and Secretary of HEW had selectively discriminated against them "by ignoring certain blatant conditions of school segregation in other geographical areas while pressing for compliance in the southern states." Plaintiffs claimed that they were denied Fourteenth Amendment rights by the "lopsided imposition of racial exclusions and quotas upon Southern children, parents, teachers and school districts alone. . . ." In affirming dismissal of the suit, the court of appeals found the government's enforcement policy valid as to the South, and not discriminatory in the absence of allegations that de facto segregation in the North was caused by "state action." Georgia v. Mitchell, 450 F.2d 1317, 1318 (D.C. Cir. 1971).

QUESTIONS

1. Assuming that Northern school districts whose policies are shown to have contributed to racial isolation in their schools have an obligation to take corrective action, could that responsibility be of a different nature and scope without confirming the charge of critics that the courts have "one rule for the South and another for the North"?

2. Consider as you read the note that follows: If racism is as fundamental a force in our society as the Kerner Commission suggested, is it either rational or prudent to place on school boards the obligation to correct in schools racial imbalances attributable to realtors, bankers and urban planners?

NOTE: SCHOOL BOARD LIABILITY FOR NON-SCHOOL STATE ACTION

Efforts have been made to expand the concept of de jure segregation to include racial imbalance attributable to the actions not only of school authorities, but also of other state agencies. This approach recognizes that the various arms of government are not autonomous units, and that the cumulative impact of all state involvement resulting in racial imbalance must be considered for purposes of ascertaining whether a violation of the Equal Protection Clause exists. The courts and commentators who have discussed this approach have focused upon the interrelationship between residential segregation and school imbalance. Professor Owen Fiss, one of the earliest advocates of this position, believes that

> . . . local governments need not be considered as a mere collection of autonomous or unrelated units. In many communities the power connection and links are multifarious. Moreover, even if another unit is responsible, it would not be unreasonable to think in terms of cumulative impact. . . . In many communities a deeper governmental involvement in the creation of ghettoized residential patterns exists, and this serves to reinforce the ascription of responsibility to government for the creation and maintenance of racially imbalanced schools. . . . In some instances this involvement will consist of statutes and regulations that openly require residential racial segregation. . . .
>
> Furthermore, the government may be responsible for the residential pattern through past rather than present private choice. Residential patterns have a tendency to become fixed and remain stable, and it is unrealistic to assume that those who in the past have been segregated by government will or can move out of the ghetto and into a white neighborhood immediately after the racial restrictions have been removed. (Fiss, Racial Imbalance in the Public Schools: The Constitutional Concepts, 78 Harv. L. Rev. 564, 584-586 (1965).)

All too often, school boards, by superimposing neighborhood school policies upon government-supported residential segregation, have determined the imbalanced racial makeup of public schools. See United States Commission on Civil Rights, Racial Imbalance in the Public Schools 71 (1967).

Justice Douglas, in his denial of a stay pending appeal in Gomperts v. Chase, 329 F. Supp. 1142 (N.D. Cal.), *injunction denied pending appeal,* 404 U.S. 1237 (1971), discussed the "expanded de jure" argument. After admitting that the "precise contours of de jure segregation have not been drawn by the Court," Justice Douglas outlined the following sources, alleged by plaintiffs to be the governmental agencies responsible for racial imbalance:

(1) California's Bayshore Freeway effectively isolated Blacks and resulted in a separate and predominantly Black High School.
(2) State planning groups fashioned and built the Black community around that school.
(3) Realtors — licensed by the State — have kept "White property" White and "Black property" Black.
(4) Banks chartered by the State shaped the policies that handicapped Blacks in financing homes other than Black ghettoes.
(5) Residential segregation, fostered by state enforced restrictive covenants, resulted in segregated schools. (404 U.S. at 1239.)

Even if the above did not amount to de jure segregation, Justice Douglas said that the problem is not resolved unless the school facilities provided blacks and whites are equal. He suggested that Plessy v. Ferguson, 163 U.S. 537 (1896), had not been overruled on its mandate that separate facilities be equal, and that this doctrine might require a plan under which white as well as black students use the inferior high school. He deemed such a plan "an acceptable alternative to removing the inequalities through an upgrading of the subnormal school." 404 U.S. at 1241.

A variation of the cumulative impact theory, urged by a few courts and commentators, would look to the actions of other state agencies in determining whether a constitutional violation existed, even in the absence of a showing of active school board involvement in creating the racial imbalance. This approach generally focuses upon the strict adherence of a school board to a neighborhood school policy in the face of residential segregation attributable to state action. A federal district court in Branche v. Town of Hempstead, 204 F. Supp. 150 (E.D. N.Y. 1962), ordered elimination of racial imbalance in a school system resulting from the school board's strict adherence to a neighborhood school policy superimposed upon residential segregation.

While it might be possible to apply the state action doctrine to eliminate racial imbalance even in the absence of overt acts of a school board contributing to such imbalance, most factual situations will likely contain state action elements attributable to both school and other state officials. For a discussion of the variations of the state action concept, see Goodman, De Facto School Segregation: A Constitutional and Empirical Analysis, 60 Calif. L. Rev. 275, 292 (1972).

A most detailed judicial discussion of the cumulative impact theory is contained in Bradley v. Milliken, 338 F. Supp. 582 (E.D. Mich. 1971), infra.

QUESTIONS

1. Most courts adopt the Fiss position in order to implement Brown effectively. If so, what is left of Wechsler's concern about the right of whites to nonassociation with blacks? Should poorer whites unable to afford private schools have access to a predominantly white education for their children? Is attending school with these whites really what Brown entitled blacks to do?

2. Justice Douglas raises old problems when he suggests in Gomperts v. Chase, supra, that even if it is decided that school boards have no obligation to correct "de facto" segregation, they may be required, under what he sees as the still viable "separate but equal" standard of Plessy v. Ferguson, to equalize school facilities. But wasn't it the experience of a century of litigation, from 1850 to 1950, that (a) the courts were virtually never successful in efforts to equalize physical facilities in segregated schools, and (b) the intangible factors of quality, noted both in Brown and in the pre-Brown college cases (see Sweatt v. Painter, supra page 435), simply could not be duplicated? Is it merely cynical to predict that Plessy's separate but equal standard will be "overruled" by school boards any time they are really required to comply with it?

BRADLEY v. MILLIKEN
338 F. Supp. 582 (E.D. Mich. 1971)

ROTH, District Judge

This action was commenced August 18, 1970, by plaintiffs, the Detroit Branch of the National Association for the Advancement of Colored People and individual parents and students, on behalf of a class later defined by order of the Court dated February 16, 1971, to include "all school children of the City of Detroit and all Detroit resident parents who have children of school age." Defendants are the Board of Education of the City of Detroit, its members and its former superintendent of schools, Dr. Norman A. Drachler, the Governor, Attorney General, State Board of Education and State Superintendent of Public Instruction of the State of Michigan. In their complaint, plaintiffs attacked a statute of the State of Michigan known as Act 48 of the 1970 Legislature on the ground that it put the State of Michigan in the position of unconstitutionally interfering with the execution and operation of a voluntary plan of partial high school desegregation (known as the April 7, 1970 Plan) which had been adopted by the Detroit Board of Education to be effective beginning with the fall 1970 semester. Plaintiffs also alleged that the Detroit Public School System was and is segregated on the basis of race as a result of the official policies and actions of the defendants and their predecessors in office.

Additional parties have intervened in the litigation since it was commenced. The Detroit Federation of Teachers (DFT) which represents a majority of Detroit Public school teachers in collective bargaining negotiations with the defendant Board of Education, has intervened as a defendant, and a group of parents has intervened as defendants. . . .

Trial, limited to the issue of segregation, began April 6, 1971 and concluded on July 22, 1971, consuming 41 trial days, interspersed by several brief recesses necessitated by other demands upon the time of Court and counsel. Plaintiffs introduced substantial evidence in support of their contentions, including expert and factual testimony, demonstrative exhibits and school board documents. At the close of plaintiffs' case, in chief, the Court ruled that they had presented a prima facie case of state imposed segregation in the Detroit Public Schools; accordingly, the Court enjoined (with certain exceptions) all further school construction in Detroit pending the outcome of the litigation.

The State defendants urged motions to dismiss as to them. These were denied by the Court.

At the close of proofs intervening parent defendants (Denise Magdowski, et al.) filed a motion to join, as parties 85 contiguous "suburban" school districts — all within the so-called Larger Detroit Metropolitan area. This motion was taken under advisement pending the determination of the issue of segregation. . . .

In considering the present racial complexion of the City of Detroit and its public school system we must first look to the past and view in perspective what has happened in the last half century. In 1920 Detroit was a predominantly white city — 91% — and its population younger than in more recent times. By the year 1960 the largest segment of the city's white population was in the age range of 35 to 50 years, while its black population was younger and of childbearing age. The population of 0-15 years of age constituted 30% of the total population of which 60% were white and 40% were black. In 1970 the white population was principally aging — 45 years — while the black population was younger and of childbearing age. Childbearing blacks equaled or exceeded the total white population. As older white families without children of school age leave the city they are replaced by younger black families with school age children, resulting in a doubling of enrollment in the local neighborhood school and a complete change in student population from white to black. As black inner city residents move out of the core city they "leap-frog" the residential areas nearest their former homes and move to areas recently occupied by whites.

The population of the City of Detroit reached its highest point in 1950 and has been declining by approximately 169,500 per decade since then. In 1950, the city population constituted 61% of the total population of the standard metropolitan area and in 1970 it was but 36% of the metropolitan area population. The suburban population has increased by 1,978,000 since 1940. There has been a steady out-migration of the Detroit population since 1940. Detroit today is principally a conglomerate of poor black and white plus the aged. Of the aged, 80% are white.

If the population trends evidenced in the federal decennial census for the years 1940 through 1970 continue, the total black population in the City of Detroit in 1980 will be approximately 840,000, or 53.6% of the total. The total population of the city in 1970 was 1,511,000 and, if past trends continue, will be 1,338,000 in 1980. In school year 1960-61, there were 285,512 students in the Detroit Public Schools of which 130,765 were black. In school year 1966-67, there were 297,035 students, of which 168,299 were black. In school year 1970-71 there were 289,743 students of which 184,194 were black. The percentage of black students in the Detroit Public Schools in 1975-76 will be 72.0%, in 1980-81 will be 80.7% and in 1992 it will be virtually 100% if the present trends continue. In 1960, the non-white population, ages 0 years to 19 years, was as follows:

0 — 4 years	42%
5 — 9 years	36%
10 — 14 years	28%
15 — 19 years	18%

In 1970 the non-white population, ages 0 years to 19 years, was as follows:

0 — 4 years	48%
5 — 9 years	50%
10 — 14 years	50%
15 — 19 years	40%

The black population as a percentage of the total population in the City of Detroit was:

(a)	1900	1.4%
(b)	1910	1.2%
(c)	1920	4.1%
(d)	1930	7.7%
(e)	1940	9.2%
(f)	1950	16.2%
(g)	1960	28.9%
(h)	1970	43.9%

The black population as a percentage of total student population of the Detroit Public Schools was as follows:

(a)	1961	45.8%
(b)	1963	51.3%
(c)	1964	53.0%
(d)	1965	54.8%
(e)	1966	56.7%
(f)	1967	58.2%
(g)	1968	59.4%
(h)	1969	61.5%
(i)	1970	63.8%

For the years indicated the housing characteristics in the City of Detroit were as follows:

(a) 1960 total supply of housing units was 553,000
(b) 1970 total supply of housing units was 530,770

The percentage decline in the white students in the Detroit Public Schools during the period 1961-1970 (53.6% in 1960; 34.8% in 1970) has been greater than the percentage decline in the white population in the City of Detroit during the same period (70.8% in 1960; 55.21% in 1970), and correlatively, the percentage increase in black students in the Detroit Public Schools during the nine-year period 1961-1970 (45.8% in 1961; 63.8% in 1970) has been greater than the percentage increase in the black population of the City of Detroit during the ten-year period 1960-1970 (28.9% in 1960; 43.9% in 1970). In 1961 there were eight schools in the system without white pupils and 73 schools with no Negro pupils. In 1970 there were 30 schools with no white pupils and 11 schools with no Negro pupils, an increase in the number of schools without white pupils of 22 and a decrease in the number of schools without Negro pupils of 62 in this ten-year period. Between 1968 and 1970 Detroit experienced the largest increase in percentage of black students in the student population of any major northern school district. The percentage increase in Detroit was 4.7% . . . .

In 1960, there were 266 schools in the Detroit School System. In 1970, there were 319 schools in the Detroit School System.

In the Western, Northwestern, Northern, Murray, Northeastern, Kettering, King and Southeastern high school service areas, the following conditions exist at a level significantly higher than the city average:

(a) Poverty in children
(b) Family income below poverty level
(c) Rate of homicides per population
(d) Number of households headed by females
(e) Infant mortality rate
(f) Surviving infants with neurological defects
(g) Tuberculosis cases per 1,000 population
(h) High pupil turnover in schools

The City of Detroit is a community generally divided by racial lines. Residential segregation within the city and throughout the larger metropolitan area is substantial, pervasive and of long standing. Black citizens are located in separate and distinct areas within the city and are not generally to be found in the suburbs. While the racially unrestricted choice of black persons and economic factors may have played some part in the development of this pattern of residential segregation, it is, in the main, the result of past and present practices and customs of racial discrimination, both public and private, which have and do restrict the housing opportunities of black people. On the record there can be no other finding.

Governmental actions and inaction at all levels, federal, state and local, have combined, with those of private organizations, such as loaning institutions and real estate associations and brokerage firms, to establish and to maintain the pattern of residential segregation throughout the Detroit metropolitan area. It is no answer to say that restricted practices grew gradually (as the black population in the area increased between 1920 and 1970), or that since 1948 racial restrictions on the ownership of real property have been removed. The policies pursued by both government and private persons and agencies have a continuing and present effect upon the complexion of the community — as we know, the choice of a residence is a relatively infrequent affair. For many years FHA and VA openly advised and advocated the maintenance of "harmonious" neighborhoods, i.e., racially and economically harmonious. The conditions created continue. While it would be unfair to charge the present defendants with what other governmental officers or agencies have done, it can be said that the actions or the failure to act by the responsible school authorities, both city and state, were linked to that of these other governmental units. When we speak of governmental action we should not view the different agencies as a collection of unrelated units. Perhaps the most that can be said is that all of them, including the school authorities, are, in part, responsible for the segregated condition which exists. And we note that just as there is an interaction between residential patterns and the racial composition of the schools, so there is a corresponding effect on the residential pattern by the racial composition of the schools.

Turning now to the specific and pertinent (for our purposes) history of the Detroit school system so far as it involves both the local school authorities and the state school authorities, we find the following:

During the decade beginning in 1950 the Board created and maintained optional attendance zones in neighborhoods undergoing racial transition and between high school attendance areas of opposite predominant racial compositions. In 1959 there were eight basic optional attendance areas affecting 21 schools. Optional attendance areas provided pupils living within certain elementary areas a choice of attendance at one of two high schools. In addition there was at least one optional area either created or existing in 1960 between two junior high schools of opposite predominant racial components. All of the high school optional areas, except two, were in neighborhoods undergoing racial transition (from white to black) during the 1950s. The two exceptions were: (1) the option between Southwestern (61.6% black in 1960) and Western (15.3% black); (2) the option between Denby (0% black) and Southeastern (30.9% black). With the exception of the Denby-Southeastern option (just noted) all of the options were between high schools of opposite predominant racial compositions. The Southwestern-Western and Denby-Southeastern optional areas are all white on the 1950, 1960 and 1970 census maps. Both Southwestern and Southeastern, however, had substantial white pupil populations, and the option allowed whites to escape integration. The natural, probable, foreseeable and actual effect of these optional zones was to allow white youngsters to escape identifiably "black" schools. There had also been an optional zone (eliminated between 1956 and 1959) created in "an attempt . . . to separate Jews and Gentiles within the system," the effect of which was that Jewish youngsters went to Mumford High School and Gentile youngsters went to Cooley. Although many of these optional areas had served their purpose by 1960 due to the fact that most of the areas had become predominantly black, one optional area (Southwestern-Western affecting Wilson Junior High graduates) continued until the present school year (and will continue to affect 11th and 12th grade white youngsters who elected to escape from predominantly black Southwestern to predominantly white Western High School). Mr. Hendrickson, the Board's general fact witness, who was employed in 1959 to, inter alia, eliminate optional areas, noted in 1967 that: "In operation Western appears to be still the school to which white students escape from predominantly Negro surrounding schools." The effect of eliminating this optional area (which affected only 10th graders for the 1970-71 school year) was to decrease Southwestern from 86.7% black in 1969 to 74.3% black in 1970.

The Board, in the operation of its transportation to relieve overcrowding policy, has admittedly bused black pupils past or away from closer white schools with available space to black schools. This practice has continued in several instances in recent years despite the Board's avowed policy, adopted in 1967, to utilize transportation to increase integration.

With one exception (necessitated by the burning of a white school), defendant Board has never bused white children to predominantly black schools. The Board has not bused white pupils to black schools despite the enormous amount of space available in inner-city schools. There were 22,961 vacant seats in schools 90% or more black.

The Board has created and altered attendance zones, maintained and altered grade structures and created and altered feeder school patterns in a manner which has had the natural, probable and actual effect of continuing black and white pupils in racially segregated schools. The Board admits at least one instance where it purposefully and intentionally built and maintained a school and its attendance zone to contain black students. Throughout the last decade (and presently) school attendance zones of opposite racial compositions have been separated by north-south boundary lines, despite the Board's awareness (since at least 1962) that drawing boundary lines in an east-west direction would result in significant integration. The natural and actual effect of these acts and failures to act has been the creation and perpetuation of school segregation. There has never been a feeder pattern or zoning change which placed a predominantly white residential area into a predominantly black school zone or feeder pattern. Every school which was 90% or more black in 1960, and which is still in use today, remains 90% or more black. Whereas 65.8% of Detroit's black students attended 90% or more black schools in 1960, 74.9% of the black students attended 90% or more black schools during the 1970-71 school year.

The public schools operated by defendant Board are thus segregated on a racial basis. This racial segregation is in part the result of the discriminatory acts and omissions of defendant Board.

In 1966 the defendant State Board of Education and Michigan Civil Rights Commission issued a Joint Policy Statement on Equality of Educational Opportunity, requiring that

> Local school boards must consider the factor of racial balance along with other educational considerations in making decisions about selection of new school sites, expansion of present facilities. . . . Each of these situations presents an opportunity for integration.

Defendant State Board's "School Plant Planning Handbook" requires that "Care in site locations must be taken if a serious transportation problem exists or if housing patterns in an area would result in a school largely segregated on racial, ethnic, or socio-economic lines." The defendant City Board has paid little heed to these statements and guidelines. The State defendants have similarly failed to take any action to effectuate these policies. Exhibit NN reflects construction (new or additional) at 14 schools which opened for use in 1970-71; of these 14 schools, 11 opened over 90% black and one opened less than 10% black. School construction costing $9,222,000 is opening at Northwestern High School which is 99.9% black, and new construction opens at Brooks Junior High, which is 1.5% black, at a cost of $2,500,000. The construction at Brooks Junior High plays a dual segregatory role: not only is the construction segregated, it will result in a feeder pattern change which will remove the last majority white school from the already almost all-black Mackenzie High School attendance area.

Since 1959 the Board has constructed at least 13 small primary schools with capacities of from 300 to 400 pupils. This practice negates opportunities to integrate, "contains" the black population and perpetuates and compounds school segregation.

The State and its agencies, in addition to their general responsibility for and supervision of public education, have acted directly to control and maintain the pattern of segregation in the Detroit schools. The State refused, until this session of the legislature, to provide authorization or funds for the transportation of pupils within Detroit regardless of their poverty or distance from the school to which they were assigned, while providing in many neighboring, mostly white, suburban districts the full range of state supported transportation. This and other financial limitations, such as those on bonding and the working of the state aid formula whereby suburban districts were able to make far larger per pupil expenditures despite less tax effort, have created and perpetuated systematic educational inequalities.

The State, exercising what Michigan courts have held to be its "plenary power" which includes power "to use a statutory scheme, to create, alter, reorganize or even dissolve a school district, despite any desire of the school district, its board, or the inhabitants thereof," acted to reorganize the school district of the City of Detroit.

The State acted through Act 48 to impede, delay and minimize racial integration in Detroit schools. The first sentence of Sec. 12 of the Act was directly related to the April 7, 1970 desegregation plan. The remainder of the section sought to prescribe for each school in the eight districts criterion of "free choice" (open enrollment) and "neighborhood schools" ("nearest school priority acceptance"), which had as their purpose and effect the maintenance of segregation.

In view of our findings of fact already noted we think it unnecessary to parse in detail the activities of the local board and the state authorities in the area of school construction and the furnishing of school facilities. It is our conclusion that these activities were in keeping, generally, with the discriminatory practices which advanced or perpetuated racial segregation in these schools.

It would be unfair for us not to recognize the many fine steps the Board has taken to advance the cause of quality education for all in terms of racial integration and human relations. The most obvious of these is in the field of faculty integration.

Plaintiffs urge the Court to consider allegedly discriminatory practices of the Board with respect to the hiring, assignment and transfer of teachers and school administrators during a period reaching back more than 15 years. The short answer to that must be that black teachers and school administrative personnel were not readily available in that period. The Board and the intervening defendant union have followed a most advanced and exemplary course in adopting and carrying out what is called the "balanced staff concept" — which seeks to balance faculties in each school with respect to race, sex and experience, with primary emphasis on race. . . .

The Detroit School Board has, in many other instances and in many other respects, undertaken to lessen the impact of the forces of segregation and attempted to advance the cause of integration. Perhaps the most obvious one was the adoption of the April 7 Plan. Among other things, it has denied the use of its facilities to groups which practice racial discrimination; it does not permit the use of its facilities for discriminatory apprentice training programs; it has opposed state legislation which would have the effect of segregating the district; it has worked to place black students in craft positions in industry and the building trades; it has brought about a substantial increase in the percentage of black students in manufacturing and construction trade apprenticeship classes; it became the first public agency in Michigan to adopt and implement a policy requiring affirmative act of contractors with which it deals to insure equal employment opportunities in their work forces; it has been a leader in pioneering the use of multi-ethnic instructional material, and in so doing has had an impact on publishers specializing in producing school texts and instructional materials; and it has taken other noteworthy pioneering steps to advance relations between the white and black races.

In conclusion, however, we find that both the State of Michigan and the Detroit Board of Education have committed acts which have been causal factors in the segregated condition of the public schools of the City of Detroit. As we assay the principles essential to a finding of de jure segregation, as outlined in rulings of the United States Supreme Court, they are:

1. The State, through its officers and agencies, and usually, the school administration, must have taken some action or actions with a purpose of segregation.

2. This action or these actions must have created or aggravated segregation in the schools in question.

3. A current condition of segregation exists.

We find these tests to have been met in this case. We recognize that causation in the case before us is both several and comparative. The principal causes undeniably have been population movement and housing patterns, but state and local governmental actions, including school board actions, have played a substantial role in promoting segregation. It is, the Court believes, unfortunate that we cannot deal with public school segregation on a no-fault basis, for if racial segregation in our public schools is an evil, then it should make no difference whether we classify it de jure or de facto. Our objective, logically, it seems to us, should be to remedy a condition which we believe needs correction. In the most realistic sense, if fault or blame must be found it is that of the community as a whole, including, of course, the black components. We need not minimize the effect of the actions of federal, state and local governmental officers and agencies, and the actions of loaning institutions and real estate firms, in the establishment and maintenance of segregated residential patterns — which lead to school segregation — to observe that blacks, like ethnic groups in the past, have tended to separate from the larger group and associate together. The ghetto is at once both a place of confinement and refuge. There is enough blame for everyone to share.

[Conclusions of law omitted.]

The foregoing constitutes our findings, of fact and conclusions of law on the issue of segregation in the public schools of the City of Detroit.

Having found a de jure segregated public school system in operation in the City of Detroit, our first step, in considering what judicial remedial steps must be taken, is the consideration of intervening parent defendants' motion to add as parties defendant a great number of Michigan school districts located out county in Wayne County, and in Macomb and Oakland Counties, on the principal premise or ground that effective relief cannot be achieved or ordered in their absence. Plaintiffs have opposed the motion to join the additional school districts, arguing that the presence of the State defendants is sufficient and all that is required, even if, in shaping a remedy, the affairs of these other districts will be affected.

In considering the motion to add the listed school districts we pause to note that the proposed action has to do with relief. Having determined that the circumstances of the case require judicial intervention and equitable relief, it would be improper for us to act on this motion until the other parties to the action have had an opportunity to submit their proposals for desegregation. Accordingly, we shall not rule on the motion to add parties at this time. Considered as a plan for desegregation the motion is lacking in specificity and is framed in the broadest general terms. The moving party may wish to amend its proposal and resubmit it as a comprehensive plan of desegregation.

NOTES

1. On the appeal of Bradley v. Milliken the Sixth Circuit found, "The record in this case amply supports the findings of the District Court of unconstitutional actions by public officials at both the local and state level." It agreed with Judge Roth's conclusion that desegregation plans submitted by both plaintiffs and defendants were incapable of effecting significant desegregation, and affirmed his order requiring defendants to prepare a multidistrict plan for cross-system assignment and transportation of school children throughout the Detroit metropolitan area. The Sixth Circuit found its legal justification for this order in a long list of state policies and actions which had contributed to segregation, deeming them "significant, pervasive and causally related to the substantial amount of segregation found in the Detroit school system by the District Judge." It then concluded that "the record establishes that the State has committed de jure acts of segregation and that the State controls the instrumentalities whose action is necessary to remedy the harmful effects of the State acts." Bradley v. Milliken, — F.2d — (6th Cir., Dec. 8, 1972). Subsequently, the Sixth Circuit agreed to rehear Bradley en banc, an action that had the effect of vacating its Dec. 8, 1972 decision.

2. The school litigation in Detroit evolved out of an effort by a liberal, integration-minded school board in the late 1960s to combine integration with school decentralization in a city with a steadily increasing black population. Black parents, disenchanted with integration, were more concerned with obtaining a larger voice in policy making at the schools their children attended. But the board, reluctant to draw decentralized school zone lines in a manner that would "lock in" segregation, opted for a decentralization plan that mapped out racially integrated local school districts. White opposition to the integration aspects of the plan developed immediately. Within less than a year, the liberal board members had been recalled from office after what has been described as "a vitriolic campaign with racist overtones." Subsequently, Detroit voters elected a new school board with the smallest proportion of black representatives in fifteen years. In the meantime, the Michigan legislature had approved a new decentralization plan that divided the system into four white-controlled and four black-controlled regions, and prohibited the board from carrying out further desegregation in the schools.

The latter provision was successfully attacked in litigation that later led to the decisions reviewed above. The Detroit controversy is reviewed in detail in Grant, Community Control vs. School Integration — The Case of Detroit, 24 The Public Interest 62 (Summer 1971).

3. Whatever the validity of the charge that judges decide civil rights cases with one eye on the public opinion polls, there is no doubt that judges who order the elimination of segregated schools in the North require as much courage as their Southern counterparts who issue similar orders. In fact, the assumption of most Northerners that their schools are not segregated by law can result in as much bitterness and hostility to desegregation orders in Pontiac, Michigan or Queens, New York, as was ever experienced in Mississippi or Alabama.

4. Judge Alfred Gitelson, who ordered desegregation of the massive Los Angeles school system, Crawford v. Board of Education, Cov. No. 822854 (Sup. Ct. for Los Angeles City, Feb. 11, 1970), was defeated in his bid for re-election to a second ten-year term. Local newspapers reported that Judge Gitelson reacted bitterly to his defeat, attributing his loss to "enough people who are truly racist" and oppose equal opportunity for all children. Gitelson said that the election "turned into a busing referendum. It could not be otherwise." He lost to an aerospace company lawyer, who had campaigned almost exclusively against the controversial school decision. Los Angeles Times, Nov. 5, 1970 at 1, 35. As with many Northern school decisions, the Los Angeles case was decided in the main on evidence that school board policies had resulted in de facto segregation, but Gitelson added his view that even de facto or adventitious school segregation would violate the Constitution, because of the harm and stigma imposed on minority students. In Gitelson's view, "In our present society, an equal educational opportunity . . . is indispensable to a meaningful life. . . . It is the duty of every school board to provide integrated education so that every student receives the same educational opportunity." Los Angeles Times, supra.

QUESTIONS

1. Why are Northern courts willing to "follow the law" in ordering school desegregation where white opposition is great, black support minimal, and the applicability of Brown unsettled? What motivates their willingness to pursue the integration remedy even in large urban centers like Washington, D.C., Detroit and Los Angeles, where meaningful integration will require consolidation of urban and suburban school districts, and transportation of large numbers of students over substantial distances?

2. Is it significant in political or economic terms that, if blacks fail in the effort to require metropolitan school desegregation plans, they will soon assume control of the school systems in many of the country's largest cities? Several cities already have predominantly black school populations, with blacks either in control or gaining control of school boards.

3. With new social studies raising questions as to the value of integration to the educational achievement of black children, is it possible to argue that the authority to determine appointments of school principals, as in Porcelli v. Titus, infra, is more important than the racial balancing of students in the schools?

PORCELLI v. TITUS
431 F.2d 1254 (3d Cir. 1970)

Before GANEY, VAN DUSEN and GIBBONS, Circuit Judges.

Opinion of the Court

Per Curiam:

The plaintiffs herein, Victor Porcelli et al., ten white teachers employed by the Newark Board of Education, brought suit under the Civil Rights Act alleging that as of May 28, 1968, the defendant, Superintendent of Schools in the City of Newark Franklyn Titus, acting under color of law for the Newark School System, subjected the plaintiffs to deprivation of their rights, privileges or immunities secured to them by the Constitution of the United States of America. This allegedly was accomplished by the abolition of a promotional list which had been in existence since 1953, which provided for oral and written examinations for anyone wishing to aspire to be principals or vice-principals in the System and which, it was contended by so doing, racially discriminated against whites whose names appeared on the promotional list for appointment. At the time of the abolition or suspension of the said promotional list, the first fifteen thereon had been appointed, but Porcelli, Bigley and Shapiro, plaintiffs herein, though eligible, had not yet been appointed.

The school population in the City of Newark in October, 1961, was 67,134 of which the Negro population was 55.1%. In September, 1968, the total school population was 75,876, with a Negro student population of 72.5% reflecting an increase in seven years of 8,742 students and a percentage increase of Negro students of 17.4%. During the school year 1967-1968, there were 249 administrative and supervisory positions (superintendents, principals and vice-principals, senior and junior high school principals, etc.), of which 27, or 10%, were held by Negroes. On August 22, 1968, only one Negro each for principal and vice-principal was eligible on the promotional list and of the 72 principals in the system none were Negro and of 67 vice-principals, 64 were white and 3 Negro.

On February 1, 1967, School Board of the City of Newark entered into a contract with the Teachers Association.

Under date of May 28, 1968, defendant Board of Education passed a resolution suspending and abolishing the making of appointments from this list and instead the defendant, Franklyn Titus, Superintendent of the School System in Newark, presented certain recommendations for the appointments of principals, vice-principals, senior and junior high school principals, which the Board adopted, representing a total of 35 white appointments and 20 Negro appointments. The appointments were designated as temporary appointments and the Board was to later review the appointments recommended, the criteria to be used by the Board having not as yet been finalized. In his recommendation to the Board the Superintendent candidly admitted that color was one of the criteria which he utilized, contending that the pattern by which principals, vice-principals and others were appointed reflected an era in 1953, when the promotional list was adopted, and as of 1968, conditions had so changed in the Newark School System that the promotional list had become outmoded by virtue of the changing population, community-wise and in the school system, which had occurred since its adoption.

This action was begun by a motion for summary judgment on the pleading, but the lower court denied it and ordered a full evidentiary hearing at which both sides were heard at great length. Superintendent Titus, one of the defendants, stated as one of his reasons for the abolition of the promotional list the fact that the Newark Public School System, especially in reading, was well below the national norm which obtained throughout the country; that there was such a great imbalance in the principal and vice-principal positions that, in his professional judgment, he felt that adding a Negro who was qualified to these important positions, thus making the faculty more integrated, would the more readily lend itself to an upgrading of the Public School System in Newark. Although, as has been indicated, color was frankly admitted by all the witnesses for the appellees as being one of the factors in the selection of the principals and vice-principals, and one Simeon Moss, who was the assistant superintendent for elementary education who made the recommendations to the Superintendent for the appointments, stated that color was a prime factor, it was not the only factor, as the procuring of qualified individuals was the real objective. Plaintiffs' position was that this use of color in the selection of principals and vice-principals and the device used to achieve that selection by abolition or suspension of the promotional list was a violation of their Constitutional rights under the Fourteenth Amendment.

With this contention we do not agree. State action based partly on considerations of color, when color is not used per se, and in furtherance of a proper governmental objective, is not necessarily a violation of the Fourteenth Amendment. Proper integration of faculties is as important as proper integration of schools themselves, as set forth in Brown v. Board of Education, 349 U.S. 294, 295 . . . (1955), the thrust of which extends to the selection of faculties. In Kemp v. Beasley, 389 F.2d 178, at 189 (8 Cir. 1968), the court held, where race was a consideration in the selection of teachers and faculties, "We reaffirm the principle that faculty selection must remain for the board and sensitive expertise of the School Board and its officials." And, at page 190, "The question thus becomes, when is there such faculty distribution as to provide equal opportunities to all students and to all teachers — whether white or Negro? Students in each school should have the same quality of instruction as in any other school. Every predominantly Negro school should have, wherever possible, substantially as integrated a faculty as the predominantly white school."

Again, in Springfield School Committee v. Barksdale, 348 F.2d 261, 266 (5 Cir. 1965), the court stated, "It has been suggested that classification by race is unlawful regardless of the worthiness of the objective. We do not agree. The defendants' proposed action does not concern race insofar as race correlates with proven deprivation of educational opportunity." Further, in United States v. Jefferson County Board of Education, 372 F.2d 836, 895 (5 Cir. 1966), it was stated, "As to faculty, we have found that school authorities have an affirmative duty to break up the historical pattern of segregated faculties, the hall-mark of the dual system."

It would therefore seem that the Boards of Education have a very definite affirmative duty to integrate school faculties and to permit a great imbalance in faculties — as obtained on August 22, 1968, when a new plan was proposed to the School Board in Newark for the increasing of qualified Negro administrators — would be in negation of the Fourteenth Amendment to the Constitution and the line of cases which have followed Brown v. Board of Education, supra. . . . The judgment of the lower court [dismissing the case] will be affirmed.

ANDERSON v. SAN FRANCISCO UNIFIED SCHOOL DISTRICT, 357 F. Supp. 248 (N.D. Cal. 1972), involved white school teachers and administrative personnel who requested an injunction against the school board's 1968 Affirmative Action Policy, designed to bring about "faculty racial and ethnic balance which more closely approximates the racial and ethnic distribution of the total school population so long as such efforts maintain or improve quality of education."

Under this policy, various regulations and procedures were adopted calling for the appointment and upgrading of more minority group personnel. Following an unsuccessful effort to eliminate fifty administrative positions held by whites, the board adopted a December 1971 resolution setting forth a series of percentage quotas for the employment of minority persons as administrators. Special training programs were instituted to prepare minority persons for administrative posts, and experience and academic requirements were reduced. As a result, the number of minority group administrators increased from eighteen in 1966 to sixty-nine (20.7 percent of the total) in 1971.

Because of budget restrictions and a general reduction in the number of administrative positions available in the school system, the court found that meeting the board's percentage quotas would require granting virtually all administrative assignments, appointments and promotions to minority personnel. The resulting exclusion of qualified whites from such jobs was found to constitute a denial of their right to equal employment opportunities.

Based on these findings, the court enjoined the board from enforcing its

December 1971 resolution. The court cited no authority for its action, but expressed the view that

> Preferential treatment under the guise of "affirmative action" is the imposition of one form of racial discrimination in place of another. . . . No one race or ethnic group should ever be accorded preferential treatment over another. No race or ethnic group should ever be granted privileges or prerogatives not given to every other race. There is no place for race or ethnic groupings in America. Only in individual accomplishment can equality be achieved.

NOTE: THE VALUE OF INTEGRATED EDUCATION — THE SOCIAL RESEARCH CONTROVERSY

The reference to social science studies in Brown v. Board of Education, 347 U.S. at 494-495, note 11, supra page 437, was apparently included to support the finding that segregated schools have an adverse psychological effect on black children. The finding seemed an added support for the decision, reflecting the concurrence of social science with the conclusions of legal analysis: that the basic concept of equal protection was incompatible with forced segregation in public schools. Subsequent data seemed to strengthen the findings cited by the Court. Thus, a major study undertaken in 1965 by the U.S. Commission on Civil Rights, at the request of President Lyndon Johnson, concluded:

> The central truth which emerges from this report and from all of the Commission's investigations is simply this: Negro children suffer serious harm when their education takes place in public schools which are racially segregated, whatever the source of such segregation may be.
>
> Negro children who attend predominantly Negro schools do not achieve as well as other children, Negro and white. Their aspirations are more restricted than those of other children and they do not have as much confidence that they can influence their own futures. When they become adults, they are less likely to participate in the mainstream of American society, and more likely to fear, dislike, and avoid white Americans. The conclusion drawn by the U.S. Supreme Court about the impact upon children of segregation compelled by law — that it "affects their hearts and minds in ways unlikely ever to be undone" — applies to segregation not compelled by law.
>
> The major source of the harm which racial isolation inflicts upon Negro children is not difficult to discover. It lies in the attitudes which such segregation generates in children and the effect these attitudes have upon motivation to learn and achievement. Negro children believe that their schools are stigmatized and regarded as inferior by the community as a whole. Their belief is shared by their parents and by their teachers. And their belief is founded in fact.
>
> Isolation of Negroes in the schools has a significance different from the meaning that religious or ethnic separation may have had for other minority groups because the history of Negroes in the United States has been different from the history of all other minority groups. Negroes in this country were first enslaved, later segregated by law, and now are segregated and discriminated against by a combination of

governmental and private action. They do not reside today in ghettos as the result of an exercise of free choice and the attendance of their children in racially isolated schools is not an accident of fate wholly unconnected with deliberate segregation and other forms of discrimination. In the light of this history, the feelings of stigma generated in Negro children by attendance at racially isolated schools are realistic and cannot easily be overcome. (Summary, Racial Isolation in the Public Schools, 11-12, U.S. Commission on Civil Rights (Mar. 1967).)

At that point, those who had evidenced concern about the Court's inclusion of social science data seemed far off the mark. But more recent studies, summarized by Pat Lines below, provide ample justification for an early warning by Professor Herman Cahn, who wrote:

> . . . I would not have the constitutional rights of Negroes — or of other Americans — rest on any such flimsy foundation as some of the scientific demonstrations in these records. . . . [S]ince the behavioral sciences are so very young, imprecise, and changeful, their findings have an uncertain expectancy of life. Today's sanguine asseveration may be cancelled by tomorrow's new revelation — or new technical fad. It is one thing to use the current scientific findings, however ephemeral they may be, in order to ascertain whether the legislature has acted reasonably in adopting some scheme of social or economic regulation; deference here is shown not so much to the findings as to the legislature. It would be quite another thing to have our fundamental rights rise, fall, or change along with the latest fashions of psychological literature. (Cahn, Jurisprudence, 30 N.Y.U. L. Rev. 150, 157-158, 167 (1955).)

LINES, RACE AND LEARNING: A PERSPECTIVE ON THE RESEARCH
11 Inequality in Education 26 (Mar. 1972)

Social scientists have forwarded a variety of theories to explain why racially balanced schools should aid or retard learning. Each has different implications. Most focus on school resources, arguing that predominantly white[1] schools are better endowed with some resource or another, and that equal educational opportunity would require giving minority pupils equal access to these superior resources. These may include pupil-teacher ratio, experienced teachers and diversified facilities (the conventional measures), or it may include the presence of advantaged children who "teach" their less advantaged peers (the "peer group learning" theory), or higher expectations and better morale among teachers in white schools.

The social science research now available fails to show a relationship between conventional resources and achievement. The teacher expectation theory is also tenuous since teachers are able to distinguish poor, minority kids (usually black) from middle-class, white ones, and hold different expecta-

1. "White," as used here, refers to the HEW census term "other whites;" it excludes, for example, Spanish-speaking whites.

tions for each. Thus, by process of elimination, the "peer group learning" theory is most popular among busing advocates while the "teacher morale" theory is supreme among white antibusing teachers. If any of these resources increase achievement, two-way busing schemes would, according to the theory, dilute resources available to whites while increasing those available to black children, with a consequent improvement in test scores of black pupils and a decline for whites.

Other theoretical explanations can also be postulated. If black pupils feel stigmatized by an all-black school, for example, removal of the stigma should boost their educational attainment without having an adverse effect on whites. If combining two or more cultures in a single school produces a lively and exciting atmosphere unattainable among homogeneous children, everyone might gain.

Although decisions seem to be made on the basis of these theories, none have been proven. No experiment has compared test scores of various racial groups, rich and poor, as classroom racial and socioeconomic composition was systematically varied. Analysis has had to rest instead on surveys, and studies of desegregation efforts. These have led to inconsistent conclusions — or none at all.

Coleman Report

The Coleman Report, based upon an examination of data collected in HEW's 1965 Equality of Educational Opportunity Survey, lends some support to the "peer group learning" theory. It noted a small relationship between pupils' achievement test scores and the percentage white in the school, and a stronger relationship between test scores and socioeconomic backgrounds.[2] Coleman concluded:

> The higher achievement of all racial and ethnic groups in schools with greater proportions of white students is largely, perhaps wholly, related to effects associated with the student body's educational background and aspirations. This means that the apparent beneficial effect of a student body with a high proportion of white students comes not from racial composition per se, but from the better educational background and higher education aspirations that are on the average found among white students.

Research results often depend, however, on how the data are handled. Christopher Jencks of Harvard's Center for Educational Policy Research, using the same data as Coleman, compared first and sixth grades in schools in the urban North which were 50 to 75 percent white. Black first graders in these schools scored below the national average for black children; black

2. U.S. Office of Education, Equality of Educational Opportunity, p. 29 (1965) [hereafter referred to as Coleman Report]. A summary and critique of the report and subsequent major reports on the EEOS data is found in R. O'Reilly, Racial and Social Class Isolation in the Schools, pp. 160-91 (Praeger, New York, 1970).

sixth graders scored above. White first graders scored below their peers elsewhere, while white sixth graders in the same school scored very close to the white national average. This analysis must be received with reservations: first grade children might have had different socioeconomic characteristics than sixth grade children in the same schools, the tests administered to the first and sixth grade children were different and the first grade test was not reliable.[3] Nonetheless, the analysis offers tentative support for maintaining that racial balance increases both black and white pupils' test scores. It also undermines the "peer group learning" theory since white pupils experienced no loss on attendance at schools 25 to 50 percent black.

Several other surveys of more limited populations have produced mixed results.[4]

Studies of Desegregation Programs

Studies of actual desegregation reveal more confusing results. Reviews of the research by Meyer Weinberg, Nancy St. John and Robert O'Reilly report mostly statistically insignificant results.[5] However, of the 30-odd studies reviewed, most report a few significant differences in minority pupils' test scores in predominantly white and predominantly minority schools, at some grade

3. C. Jencks, Memorandum to colleagues at the Center for Educational Policy Research, Harvard Graduate School of Education (Feb. 12, 1971).

4. A review of these studies appears in N. St. John, Desegregation and Minority Group Performance, 40 R. of Educ. Research 111, 116-19 (1970). She reviews 12 pre-Coleman surveys, some of which attempted to follow black students for a period of years, and concludes that integration does have a positive effect, and that this might be attributed to factors which co-vary with integration.

M. Weinberg, Desegregation Research: An Appraisal, 44-82 (Phi Delta Kappa, Bloomington, Ind., 1970) reports over 30 formal studies which attempt to assess the effect of integration on pupil achievement. Most of the studies failed to control for socioeconomic or other factors, although a possibility existed that the high scoring black pupils were a select group.

In the few studies where some attempt was made to control selectivity factors, results were very mixed. A study of 1388 black ninth graders in Pittsburgh, for example, revealed a positive relation between arithmetic achievement and percentage of whites in the schools, after controlling for sex, and for individual and neighborhood socioeconomic status. N. St. John and M. Smith, "School Racial Composition, Aspiration and Achievement" (mimeograph, 1969). The Dumbarton Research Council, in a survey sample from Oakland, included children with comparable parental income, educational and occupational status. The researchers found that the high scoring blacks had significantly higher status if family size, stability, and home ownership, were taken into consideration. Dumbarton Research Council, "Race and Education in the City of Oakland" (unpublished draft, 1966), reported in Weinberg, pp. 44-56. The results of another survey were not even this encouraging. The researcher reported no relation between attendance at an integrated school and black pupil achievement. R. Klein, "A Comparative Study of the Academic Achievement of Negro 10th Grade High Schools in Metropolitan Areas of the South" (doctoral dissertation, Univ. of So. Car., 1967), reported in Weinberg, pp. 70-71. See also D. Long, "Educational Performance in Integrated and Segregated Elementary Schools" (doctoral dissertation, Yeshiva Univ., 1968), reported in Weinberg, pp. 73-74.

5. These reviews are described in footnotes 4 and 2.

levels on some tests.[6] More often than not, the differences show higher scores for minorities attending majority white schools. White kids' scores are reported less frequently, and significant findings are scarcer.

More recent studies of cities implementing desegregation plans — i.e., Ann Arbor,[7] Riverside,[8] Chapel Hill,[9] Evanston,[10] Sacramento[11] and New Albany, Mississippi[12] — have produced similar results. Usually minority pupils in some grades posted small gains on some tests; in a few cases they regressed. Usually the results were statistically insignificant. Changes in white test scores were even more difficult to find. White Ann Arbor pupils improved slightly, but the change was statistically insignificant. White Chapel Hill fifth graders made significant gains in math courses. New Albany, Mississippi also reported a small improvement in white test scores; but statistical significance

6. Of the 14 studies reported in O'Reilly, for example, only one reported *no* significant differences between integrated and nonintegrated students at any grade level. This one imposed the strictest controls for socioeconomic status and school quality. Students in grades K-2 were matched for intelligence and social class and attendance at schools with comparable facilities, personnel and programs. D. Long, "Educational Performance in Integrated and Segregated Elementary Schools" (doctoral dissertation, Yeshiva Univ., 1968), reported in Dissertation Abstracts 412 (1968).

7. P. Carrigan, "School Desegregation via Compulsory Pupil Transfer: Early Effects on Elementary School Children" (Report for the U.S. Office of Education, Bureau of Research, Sept. 1969). The transfer group (all the children from a segregated school which was closed) included 132 blacks, 31 whites and two other minority pupils. At the end of the first year 34 pupils had been lost from the group [p. 22]. The non-transferring group attended a school which was 48 percent black, and therefore comparisons are not of highly segregated *versus* integrated pupils [p. 23]. Moreover, the non-transferring children may have received more supportive services than the transferring group.

Some significant gains were made for the following black pupils: fourth grade non-transferring boys, third grade transferring and non-transferring girls, and fifth grade transferring and non-transferring girls. However, significant gains were also made by non-transferring and receiving white pupils in these same grades [pp. 101-05].

8. I. Hendrick, "The Development of a School Integration Plan in Riverside, California: A History and Perspective," pp. 34-40 (published by the Riverside Unified School District and the Univ. of Calif., Riverside, 1969); H. Singer, "Effect of Integration on Achievement of Anglos, Blacks and Mexican-Americans," (University of California, Riverside, mimeograph, Mar. 1970); M. Purl, "The Achievement of Elementary Pupils in Integrated Schools, Riverside Unified School District," (Mimeographs, March 1970 and 1971, reading scores only); "Construction and Interpretation of the Achievement Study Baseline, Riverside School Study, A Progress Report," pp. 71, 106 (published by the Riverside Unified School District and the University of California, Riverside, Aug. 31, 1967).

9. P. Prichard, Effects of Desegregation on Student Success in the Chapel Hill City School, Integrated Education, Vol. 7, No. 6, p. 33 (Nov.-Dec. 1969).

10. Jayjia Hsia, "Integration in Evanston, 1967-71: A Longitudinal Evaluation," (Educational Testing Service, Evanston, Ill., Aug. 1970).

11. E. Morrison, "A Summary of the Assessments of the District's Integration Program," (Research Report No. 9, Sept. 28, 1971); Boston Globe, Sept. 23, 1971, p. 5, col. 4; National Observer, Oct. 2, 1971, p. 6, col. 1.

12. New York Times, Oct. 18, 1970, p. 1, col. 4.

was not reported. In Evanston both black and white eighth graders scored lower. Usually white test scores were virtually unaffected.

In sum, analysis of surveys and desegregation efforts fail to "prove" any of the theories outlined at the outset of this article. Since school desegregation takes place under a variety of radically different conditions, one school might do well, while another of the same coloration would fail. Breaking the research down more finely might explain the frequent lack of results, suggest a more likely theoretical base, and suggest better methods of achieving desegregation.

The Absence of Desegregation

In some studies, a closer analysis has revealed the absence of real desegregation, that is, classroom desegregation. The widespread use of ability grouping, or tracking, in perhaps 75 to 90 percent of all schools[13] sometimes results in studies of "desegregated" youngsters who were actually separated from middle-class whites and isolated in their classroom. After the two years of "desegregation" in Riverside, California, for example, someone noticed that most minority students had been grouped together or placed with low achievers; of course, this group continued to perform below norms. The most able minority-group children, however, were placed in majority-white classes and experienced increases in test scores.[14] The study, in effect, reveals nothing about the effects of desegregation on minority-group pupils generally.

Desegregation may also be too shortlived to be real. A few days in an integrated school are unlikely to produce a long lasting or measurable educational change, and even a full school year may be insufficient. One study of a city-to-suburb busing program, Hartford's Project Concern,[15] noted a cumulative effect after the program had been underway for three years. Children who had been in the suburban system all three years scored consistently higher than children who participated only one or two years. No statistical analysis was made of the data, however. Coleman also reported a

13. A 1962 survey of 3,418 school districts of over 2,500 in population reported that 77% of the elementary schools and 90.5% of the high schools were ability grouped to some degree. National Education Association, Research Division, Ability Grouping (Research Memo 1962-29, Washington, D.C., 1962). Most of those who reported no ability grouping were planning to institute grouping in the future. See also, Cohen, Pettigrew and Riley, "Race and Outcomes of Schooling," in Mosteller and Moynihan, eds., On Equality of Educational Opportunity, (Random House, 1971), p. 355. Based on EEOS data, they reported that among secondary schools surveyed 89.9% at Grade twelve and 91.3% at Grade nine practiced some form of ability grouping.

14. H. Gerard, "Factors Contributing to Adjustment and Achievement," (Progress Report 15-16, Dept. of Psychology, U. of C. at Los Angeles, mimeograph, May 1969).

15. T. Mahan, Jr., "Project Concern, 1966-69: A Report on the Effectiveness of Suburban School Placement for Inner City Youth," (Conn. Dept. of Educ., Aug. 1968); T. Crane, "A Three Year Summary of Hartford Project Concern," (Conn. Dept. of Education, Oct. 1970).

small positive relation between the number of years minority students spent in white schools and improvement in their achievement test scores.[16] This relation remained when the socioeconomic status of the school was held constant. Similarly, according to surveys in Boston[17] and Pittsburgh,[18] black children in whiter schools for two years scored higher on arithmetic tests than did their peers in such schools only one year. An Indiana study[19] reported black first graders were at roughly comparable levels in segregated and desegregated schools, but by the third grade, those in integrated schools moved ahead. Their advantage continued into the sixth grade. Similarly, a comparison of majority white and majority black schools in an upstate New York town[20] revealed no significant differences in achievement test scores, but a cumulative advantage appeared for black students experiencing at least two years in majority schools. The long-term effect on white test scores has not been adequately measured. Until there are more studies of long-term classroom desegregation, it will be impossible to attempt proof of any theory.

Age and Theory

A closer look at the research might also suggest another theory. Many integration studies suggest, for example, that integration in the early grades may be the decisive element in improving achievement scores of minority children. A Nashville study of 75 black children enrolled in desegregated schools found, for example, that those who entered the desegregated schools in the early grades scored higher on academic achievement tests than peers from the same neighborhoods who remained in segregated schools; in the fifth and sixth grades, however, the segregated children performed better than their black peers in the white schools.[21] A study of 87 low income blacks in a suburban New York town reported similarly that the youngest children showed the greatest test score improvement in achievement after transferring to upper income white schools.[22] In New Rochelle, only kindergarten children showed a significant gain when transferred from all-black to white

16. Coleman Report 29, 32 (Table 22), 331.

17. N. St. John and R. Lewis, "The Influence of School Integration on Academic Achievement," (mimeograph, Harvard Univ., Apr. 1971).

18. N. St. John and M. Smith, "School Racial Experience, Achievement and Aspiration," (draft mimeograph, 1970).

19. I. Samuels, "Desegregated Education and Differences in Academic Achievement," (Ph.D. thesis, Ind. Univ., 1968).

20. J. Lockwood, "An Examination of Scholastic Achievement, Attitudes and Home-Background Factors of Sixth-Grade Negro Students in Balanced and Unbalanced Schools," (Ph.D. thesis, Univ. of Mich., 1966) pp. 47, 50.

21. L. Anderson, "The Effects of Desegregation on the Achievement and Personality Patterns of Negro Children," (Ph.D. thesis, George Peabody College for Teachers, 1966), pp. 69, 85.

22. Denmark, Guttetag and Riley, "Communication Patterns in Integrated Classrooms and Pre-Integration Subject Variables as They Affect the Academic Achievement and Self-Concept of Previously Segregated Children," (Aug. 1967), reported in Weinberg, p. 75.

schools.[23] An Ann Arbor study also found that transferred kindergarten pupils (minority-to-majority) showed the greatest I.Q. gains, but because of the small number, the researcher was unable to conclude that the gain was statistically significant.[24] Hartford's Project Concern reported test score gains for participating children in grades K-3; the first grade children were above grade level, but by the fourth grade, the difference between the scores of children in the suburban schools and children remaining in Hartford schools (80% black) had become less noticeable. By the fifth grade scores evened up.[25] In Sacramento, desegregated children in grades 1-4 surpassed their peers in reading and arithmetic scores. Still segregated fifth graders, however, "beat" desegregated children on the reading test; desegregated fifth graders came out ahead in arithmetic scores, but the margin was slimmer than it was for the younger children.[26] In Evanston, elementary school pupils apparently made small gains following desegregation, while eighth grade pupils did not, although other factors may have caused backsliding among older students.[27] Less data are available for analyzing the effects of desegregation on white scores, since many of the desegregation programs studied placed only a few black children in white schools, leaving its racial composition virtually unchanged; or the differences were insignificant. . . . If racial isolation, for example, produces a sense of inferiority, children probably acquire it early and find it difficult to shake. Disparate responses of younger and older children are inexplicable within the other theoretical frameworks.

Procedural Defects

This discussion of the research findings demonstrates what little basis supports beliefs about educational gains or losses resulting from busing. The crudity of the techniques is yet another reason for rejecting arguments based on social science research. First, the research usually defines educational attainment by ability or intelligence tests, a wavering and uncertain measure which varies over time for an individual, and for whole groups of children. Moreover, because it is so unclear what it is society really wants schools to do, there is no guarantee that tests measure the right things. At best, test scores provide a somewhat reliable and objective measure of a child's acquisition of specific, limited skills.

But this is not the only defect in the techniques. Some of it, such as the

23. T. G. Wolman, Learning Effects of Integration in New Rochelle, Integrated Education, Vol. 2, No. 6, p. 31 (Dec.-Jan. 1965).

24. P. Carrigan, "School Desegregation via Compulsory Pupil Transfer: Early Effects on Elementary School Children," (Report to U.S. Office of Education, Bureau of Research, Sept. 1967) pp. 101-08.

25. T. Mahan, Jr., "Project Concern, 1966-69: A Report on the Effectiveness of Suburban School Placement for Inner City Youth," (Conn. Board of Education, Aug. 1968).

26. Boston Globe, Sept. 23, 1971, p. 5, col. 4; National Observer, Oct. 2, 1971, p. 6, col. 1.

27. Jayjia Hsia, "Integration in Evanston, 1967-71; A Longitudinal Evaluation," (Educational Testing Service, Evanston, Ill., Aug. 1970) pp. 38-40.

Coleman Report, is based on survey data. Yet, surveys do not "prove" causality. Moreover, where several factors are bound together in a statistical relationship, it is difficult to determine which relates to which. A variety of interpretations may also be extracted from the same data. The close associations of affluence, parental achievement, class status, good health, school quality, and higher test scores, for example, make it difficult to assess the impact of any isolated factor.

Both surveys and studies of actual integration efforts are further plagued by the absence of adequate comparison, or control groups. They are also extremely sensitive to the statistical procedures followed. Thus, in order to evaluate fully the conclusion made in the research, it would be necessary to re-examine data, procedures, statistical methods, and even arithmetic. The list of potential defects is long enough to obscure the results and make it foolhardy to put much faith in any single study or report.

Research as a Capricious Guide

Even if the research tools could be improved, and it would be possible to "prove" desegregation benefited one racial group at the expense of another (or benefited no one), it is nonetheless inappropriate to determine desegregation requirements on the basis of such proof. The fact is the Constitution requires desegregation as a remedy for past wrongful segregation.

Given the present state of the research, allowing it to guide basic desegregation decisions would require absurd results. The research suggests, for example, that it is most beneficial to desegregate younger children. To pursue this logically, without reference to moral standards, would lead governments to desegregate the early grades, but not the older children. The arbitrariness of this should be obvious. The research suggests even more absurd results. Some researchers believe they have detected a difference in male and female responses to integration. Based on her own, and a few other studies, Nancy St. John, for example, has observed a tendency for black boys to benefit more than black girls in recently desegregated schools.[28] If this analysis is followed, among blacks, boys, but not girls, would be assigned to schools with white pupils. (Since there is some evidence that white girls fare better than white boys following desegregation, one might also suggest placing them with black boys, while maintaining separate schools for the black girls and white boys.)

Pursuing the research as a guiding star leads into even thicker morasses. The EEOS data show a strong trend in southern metropolitan areas toward higher test scores for children in totally black schools; a similar, but weaker relationship exists in the rural South; in the North it is negligible.[29] If a rise

28. N. St. John, "The Effects of School Segregation and Desegregation on Children," (draft, 1971) p. B-15.

29. Coleman Report, p. 31 (Table 21), 331. See also D. Armor, "School and Family Effects on Black and White Achievement: A Re-examination of the USOE Data," (mimeograph, June 1969) p. 49.

in test scores were the only justification for desegregation, the metropolitan South should be exempted: black pupils would be placed in 100 percent black schools. Professor Armor, who examined a sample of black ninth graders, found upper ability males in the Northeast were more likely to plan for college if they attended desegregated schools, and the reverse in the Midwest.[30] This would suggest desegregation for black upper ability males in the Northeast, but not for lower ability peers, or male black students elsewhere in the country. Moreover, it is likely that the groups which benefit will change from time to time. Allowing the evidence of educational benefit to guide desegregation policy leads inevitably to capricious results.

NOTES

1. A Harvard research team announced in 1972, at the conclusion of a three-year study, that efforts to provide better schooling for poor children would have "surprisingly little effect" on their prospects for economic success as adults, even if such efforts were successful. In their report, based on an extensive computerized analysis of data gathered over a decade on family, schooling, jobs and income, the researchers found that neither racial desegregation, compensatory education, preschool programs, increased school spending, nor anything the schools have tried, has significantly affected inequalities in "cognitive skills" — i.e., the ability to manipulate words and numbers, assimilate information, and make logical inferences. Those skills, they found, depend mainly on the characteristics of children entering school. The report also asserted that even if cognitive skills could be equalized, there is little connection between them and earning power. The latter, the report asserted, depend mainly on personality, personal contacts, and luck. The report also concluded that improvements in the schools would do little to wipe out poverty or reduce the gap in income between the top 20 percent of the population, who in 1970 earned an average of $22,500 a year, and the bottom 20 percent, who averaged $2800. Erasing this disparity could only be accomplished by a government-established ceiling and floor on income.

The study findings have been published in a book: C. Jencks, M. Smith, H. Acland, M. Bane, D. Cohen, H. Gintis, B. Heyns, and S. Michelson, Inequality: A Reassessment of the Effect of Family and Schooling in America (1972). The report is summarized in Bane and Jencks, The Schools and Equal Opportunity, Saturday Review 37 (Sep. 16, 1972).

2. One educational expert, Dr. Ermon Hogan, National Urban League Educational Specialist, is critical of many of the social science studies used to measure the educational value of desegregated schools. He testified before the Senate Select Committee on Equal Educational Opportunity, 92nd Cong., 1st Sess., Vol. 13, 6115, 6124 (1971), that "The major barrier to im-

30. D. Armor, "The Racial Composition of Schools and College Aspirations of Negro Students," (U.S. Civil Rights Commission, 1967), p. 145.

proving the quality of the educational environment for black and poor children is covert and often unconscious racism in educational personnel." Hogan asserts that the barrier of racism is imposed in both segregated and integrated school settings, and that the failure of studies to adequately consider its presence and impact raises serious questions about the validity of such research findings.

QUESTIONS

While several recent studies indicate that school integration may be less beneficial for black children than was earlier thought, few conclude that it has no value. If studies showing the minimal educational value of integration are introduced in a Northern case where the evidence is strong that school board policies affected the complaint of racial imbalance, should the court order integration? Should integration be ordered if major bussing is required and massive white flight to the suburbs can be predicted? Should an order be issued if a plan is submitted which lessens the chance of white opposition and flight, by closing all ghetto black schools and bussing blacks to white schools? At what point, if any, should opposition of blacks to the one-way bussing plan be heeded?

Racism Hypo 6
BLACK PARENTS v. SCHOOL BOARD OF NORTHERN CITY

The Northern School Board has been under pressure to do something about racial imbalance in its public schools. After a thorough study of recent cases indicated that its policies on pupil and teacher assignment, transfer, and school construction might not withstand judicial review, the board adopted a plan for integration which would phase out the ten predominantly black schools, and bus the system's black students (25 percent) to schools in white areas. It stated that such action would accord with both the constitutional and educational rights of the black children.

The board asserts that its new plan is acceptable to some black parents, who believe that the disadvantages of being bussed to white schools are more than outweighed by the advantages of attending better schools in better neighborhoods.

The board reportedly considered a plan utilizing two-way bussing, but decided against it because six of the ten predominantly black schools are in such poor condition that it would cost too much money to bring them up to the standard met by the predominantly white schools. The four remaining black schools are relatively new and in good condition, but two are located in decaying ghetto areas where vandalism is a serious problem, and the other two are in unsafe areas near railroad tracks or polluted streams. The board admitted giving some consideration to white parents who would have op-

posed sending their children into ghetto areas to school. It fears that this opposition would have led to white boycotts, prolonged litigation and eventually a "white exodus."

A dissenting group of black parents filed suit in federal district court to enjoin the board from placing the plan in effect. They submit that the board's plan meets neither constitutional nor educational standards for black children, and that bussing black students to achieve racial balance, thereby perpetuating neighborhood schools only in white areas, constitutes a "badge of servitude" that violates plaintiffs' rights under the Thirteenth Amendment and the Equal Protection Clause of the Fourteenth Amendment. From an educational standpoint, plaintiffs contend that the board's plan condemned all black schools, regardless of condition, and is thus exposed as a policy based on concern for white interests no less than was their former policy of segregation. The one-way bussing is a signal that white interests will remain paramount and that there will be no school programs designed to meet the specific needs of black children. They assert that they are not opposed to integrated schools which would be predominantly black in ghetto areas. They charge that the board's plan is based on paternalism and will lead to continued black powerlessness.

Finally, the black parents seek a provision in the board's integration plan that will ensure the continuation for the next ten years of the present percentage of black school administrators and teachers in the school system. They point out the experience of other systems, where the number of black teachers has decreased and black principals have been eliminated when schools are integrated. About 25 percent of the principals and teachers are now black. Virtually all are assigned to the black schools scheduled for closing under the plan. The black parents believe that all of the black teachers and administrators are competent, although they concede that many of them might score lower than the average white teacher on the National Teachers Examinations. The board has made it known that the integration process will enable it to reduce the professional staff by almost 25 percent, and that it expects to retain those professionals who rank highest according to a series of standards: amount of education, seniority in the system, and NTE scores. The board has stated that use of the test is not racially motivated, since many of the black professionals are highly educated and will certainly pass the NTE with very high grades, while some white teachers with poor educational backgrounds will certainly do poorly.

Law Firm A will represent the black parents.

Law Firm B will represent the Northern School Board.

10. ALTERNATIVES TO INTEGRATED SCHOOLS

As white resistance to enforcement of Brown persisted, more and more black parents and leaders wearied of their long, frustrating effort to desegregate the public schools, and sought means by which black children might receive the long-promised equal educational opportunity — in predominantly black schools. In this effort, they repeated a decision reached for similar reasons by black people in the early years of the nineteenth century.

Community control, compensatory education, free schools and equalized school funding are all potential alternatives to integrated public schools, and for some black children they may prove quite functional. Whether any of them are attainable by the masses of blacks is a different and harder question to answer.

A. SCHOOLS CONTROLLED BY THE COMMUNITY

BELL, SCHOOL LITIGATION STRATEGIES FOR THE 1970'S: NEW PHASES IN THE CONTINUING QUEST FOR QUALITY SCHOOLS
1970 Wis. L. Rev. 257, 290-292

Increasingly, particularly in the North, black leaders . . . have begun to push hard for decentralization and local control of black schools. This push is accelerating despite mammoth administrative, legal, and political obstacles. In the South, while the effort to achieve compliance with Brown is in many areas unrealized, the memory of segregated schools is sufficiently vivid to discourage most black parents from seeking another round of "separate but equal." One might observe, unkindly, that in much of the South there is little need to demand more of what one already has in overabundance. Such an observation would also be inaccurate. Segregated schools and the all-black schools sought by militant black leaders may appear identical and, many critics think, may turn out the same inferior product, but at least the *potential* difference is substantial.

Simply stated, segregated schools are black institutions dominated and controlled by whites. As such, the crucial decisions concerning the administration, faculty, funding, and curriculum are made to harmonize with the white view. Blacks have no effective voice in the crucial decisions concerning the schools, and those making such decisions give little or no weight to the needs or desires of black parents and students. In former times, this system at its worst meant the Negro school received money, books, and equipment not needed in the white schools and was headed by an "Uncle Tom," who was acceptable to whites (even if resented by blacks), and who was free to do whatever he liked as long as he maintained order.[107] More frequently today it means Negro schools are staffed, supplied, and administered with the basic idea that black students, or most of them, can't learn very much because they are inferior (Southern theme), or because they come from culturally and economically deprived backgrounds (Northern theme). As studies have shown, when school administrators and faculty feel children can't learn, they don't.[108]

Even one of the pioneers of school integration, Dr. Kenneth Clark, has concluded on the basis of years of observation and research of ghetto education that there is a significant correlation between a pattern of *deprivation* and ghetto schools, and a pattern of *advantage* and white urban and suburban schools. He now asserts: "It is not the presence of the white child per se that leads to higher achievement for the Negro child who associates with him in class; it is the quality of the education provided because the white child is there that makes the difference . . . ."[109]

Those advocating schools under local control expect that black school boards, genuinely concerned about their responsibilities, will appoint administrators who will create atmospheres of mutual respect and pride in which learning can take place. More important, they insist that ability to teach and sensitivity to the special needs of black children will be the primary qualifications for a teaching position, and success in teaching the only guarantee of retention. Capable teachers will place major emphasis on black history, black art and culture. By using these ethnic vehicles to build pride and counteract the socially perpetuated propensities for low self-esteem that sap achievement potential, it is hoped that black students will improve in the traditional fare.

While demands for local control, especially when combined with "separatist" philosophies, are viewed as creating long-range problems by some writers and are regarded with abhorrence by some blacks who have worked

107. The divided allegiance of many Negro administrators of state schools is reflected in the report of a black law professor who recalls, "As late as the 1950's, when I was a teacher in the South, Negro presidents of more than one college vied with one another in seeing how much of the state's paltry appropriation they could return to the legislature." Groves, The Revolt of Black Students, 1969 Utah L. Rev. 13, 16. The genre is definitively drawn in the character of Dr. Bledsoe in R. Ellison, The Invisible Man 90-98, 122-32 (Signet ed. 1947).

The need for change is recognized by both black students, see Davenport, Farewell to the Old School Tie, Saturday Review, Oct. 19, 1968, at 66; Smith, I Am the New Black, Id. at 68; Stephens, The Black University in America Today: A Student Viewpoint, 7 Freedomways 131 (1967), and aware black educators, see Harding, Black Students and the "Impossible" Revolution, Ebony, Aug. 1969, at 141, 145-46.

108. R. Rosenthal & L. Jacobson, Pygmalion in the Classroom (1968).

109. Clark, Fifteen Years of Deliberate Speed, Saturday Review, Dec. 20, 1969, at 59, 61.

hard to achieve integrated schools,[112] there is little doubt that sentiment in black communities in favor of such plans is growing . . . .

HAMILTON, RACE AND EDUCATION: A SEARCH FOR LEGITIMACY
38 Harv. Ed. Rev. 671 (1968)

[While the vision of community-controlled schools appears an unfortunate mirage to those committed to integration, the attraction is real for an increasing number of black parents. Professor Charles Hamilton speaks for these parents and for some educators as well, as he first suggests why black parents have become disenchanted with school integration, and then explains how schools designed to fill the needs of their communities would function.]

A Crisis of Educational Legitimacy

It is absolutely crucial to understand that the society cannot continue to write reports accurately describing the failure of the educational institutions *vis-à-vis* black people without ultimately taking into account the impact those truths will have on black Americans. There comes a point when it is no longer possible to recognize institutional failure and then merely propose more stepped-up measures to overcome those failures — especially when the proposals come from the same kinds of people who administered for so long the present unacceptable and dysfunctional policies and systems. Professor Seymour Martin Lipset once wrote:

> Legitimacy involves the capacity of the system to engender and maintain the belief that the existing political institutions are the most appropriate ones for the society. The extent to which contemporary democratic political systems are legitimate depends in large measure upon the ways in which the key issues which have historically divided the society have been resolved.
>
> While effectiveness is primarily instrumental, legitimacy is evaluative. Groups regard a political system as legitimate or illegitimate according to the way in which its values fit with theirs.[1]

And in another place, he has written:

> All claims to a legitimate title to rule in new states must ultimately win acceptance through demonstrating effectiveness. The loyalty of the different groups to the sys-

112. Typical of the views:

Roy Wilkins: "We have suffered too many heartaches and shed too much blood in fighting the evil of racial segregation to return in 1969 to the lonely and dispiriting confines of its demeaning prison." Saturday Review, June 21, 1969, at 70. See also Wilkins, The Case Against Separatism: "Black Jim Crow," Newsweek, Feb. 10, 1969, at 57.

Bayard Rustin: "What in hell are soul courses worth in the real world? No one gives a damn if you've taken soul courses. They want to know if you can do math and write a sentence." Saturday Review, Jun. 21, 1969, at 70.

1. Seymour Martin Lipset, Political Man: The Social Bases of Politics (New York: Doubleday, 1963), p. 64.

tem must be won through developing *in them* the conviction that this system is the best — or at least an excellent — way to accomplish their objectives. And even claims to legitimacy of a supernatural sort, such as "the gift of grace," are subjected on the part of the populace to a highly pragmatic test — that is, what is the payoff.[2]

The United States gradually acquired legitimacy as a result of being *effective*.[3]

. . .

An Alternative Model

The rhetoric of race and education, as stated earlier, is prolific with dichotomies of segregation vs. integration, quality education vs. integrated education, compensatory programs vs. busing, and so forth. Too much is assumed by these simplistic terms, and a superficial use of these labels frequently restricts and predetermines discussion at the outset. While this is unfortunate, it is probably unavoidable, given the historical context and the highly emotional atmosphere. Those persons favoring "neighborhood" schools and opposing busing have traditionally been, in the North, white parents and taxpayer groups, usually identified as anti-Negro in their basic racial views. These groups would normally be found opposing open housing laws as well. Therefore their motivations are questioned when they argue that they are essentially concerned about "educational standards" and property values. When it is pointed out to them that white students do not suffer academically and (if panic selling is avoided) property values do not go down, they do not listen. And their intransigence leads their opponents to label them as racial bigots and segregationists.

Proponents of busing and integration see a positive academic and social value in racially heterogeneous classrooms. Integration to these people is virtually synonymous with quality. And black people who once worked for desegregated schools but who no longer do so are viewed as having given up the fight, as having joined the white racists, and, indeed, as having become black racists and advocates of "Black Power separatism."[18]

I state this simply to acknowledge an awareness of some of the positions taken before I proceed to suggest an alternative educational plan. The fact that my ideas would appear more closely akin to the views of some white segregationists whose ultimate goal is to deny educational opportunity to black people is an *appearance* I cannot avoid. It is important however to point out that a close examination of the ultimate goals of my suggestions will

2. Seymour Martin Lipset, The First New Nation: The United States in Historical and Comparative Perspective (New York: Basic Books, 1963), pp. 45-46. (Emphasis added.)

3. Ibid., p. 59. (Emphasis in original.)

18. An example of this attitude was contained in the report of the President's civil disorders commission (Kerner Commission). "The Black Power advocates of today consciously feel that they are the most militant group in the Negro protest movement. Yet they have retreated from a direct confrontation with American society on the issue of integration and, by preaching separatism, unconsciously function as an accommodation to white racism" (Report of the National Advisory Commission on Civil Disorders [New York: E. P. Dutton & Company, 1968], p. 235).

indicate a clear divergence from views held by the segregationists. In other words I am motivated by an attempt to find an educational approach which is relevant to black people, not one that perpetuates racism. The plan I am suggesting is not a universal panacea; it is not applicable in all black ghettos. Where it is feasible — particularly in the large urban communities — I strongly propose it for consideration.

This is a model which views the ghetto school as the focal point of community life. The educational system should be concerned with the entire family, not simply with the children. We should think in terms of a Comprehensive Family-Community-School Plan with black parents attending classes, taking an active, day-to-day part in the operation of the school. Parents could be students, teachers, and legitimate members of the local school governing board. A similar plan is already in operation in Chicago: the Family Education Center. There are two centers, the Westinghouse and Doolittle Centers, which provide basic adult education, prevocational and vocational training, and work experience programs.

Mr. William H. Robinson, Director of the Cook County Department of Public Aid, has stated:

> The Center's most unique feature is the Child Development Program for the students' (parents') pre-school children, who come to school with their mothers and spend the day in a well-equipped, professionally staffed nursery school. Mothers can attend classes with the assurance that their children are receiving proper care and mental stimulation. Thus, the program makes participation in an educational program possible for many recipients who were prevented previously because they could not obtain adequate child care services.

Since the inception of the program two years ago, 1,300 adults and 500 children have been involved in the centers.

This concept should be expanded to include fathers as well, those unemployed and willing to obtain skills. Many of these parents could serve as teachers, along with a professional staff. They could teach courses in a number of areas (child care, auto mechanics, art, music, home economics, sewing, etc.) for which they are obviously now trained. The Comprehensive Plan would extend the school program to grades through high school — for adults and children — and it would eliminate the traditional calendar year of September to June. (There is no reason why the educational system could not be revised to take vacations for one month, say in December of post-Christmas, and another month in August. The community educational program would be a year-round function, day and evening.)

The school would belong to the community. It would be a union of children, parents, teachers (specially trained to teach in such communities), social workers, psychologists, doctors, lawyers, and community planners. Parent and community participation and control would be crucial in the hiring and firing of personnel, the selection of instructional materials, and the determination of curriculum content. Absolutely everything must be done to make the system a functioning, relevant part of the lives of the local people. Given the present situation of existing and growing alienation, such involvement is essential.

If it can be demonstrated that such a comprehensive educational institution can gain the basic trust and participation of the black community, it should become the center of additional vital community functions. Welfare, credit unions, health services, law enforcement, and recreational programs — all working under the control of the community — could be built around it. Enlightened private industry would find it a place from which to recruit trained, qualified people and could donate equipment and technical assistance. The several advantages of such a plan are obvious. It deals with the important agencies which are in daily, intimate contact with black people; it reduces a vast, fragmented service bureaucracy which now descends on the black community from many different directions, with cumbersome rules and regulations, uncontrolled by and unaccountable to the community. It provides the black people with a meaningful chance for participation in the very important day-to-day processes affecting their lives; it gives them educational and vocational tools for the future. All these things reflect the yearnings and aspirations of masses of black people today.

The Comprehensive Plan envisions the local school as a central meeting place to discuss and organize around community issues, political and economic. All of the establishments functioning under the plan would provide relevant intermediary groups to which the people could relate. The size of the community involved would vary, with several factors to be considered: geography, number of participating agencies, available funds (from federal, state, and local governmental sources), and manageability. At all times, the primary concern would be about the active involvement of people and about their possession of real power to make decisions affecting the Comprehensive Plan. They would hire consultants and experts whose legitimacy would be determined by their relevance to the community, not by a predetermined set of criteria superimposed from outside.

The proposed Comprehensive Plan attempts to come to grips with the understandable alienation discussed in the first section and with the appropriateness of the agenda items described in the second section of the paper. This plan is better understood when one keeps in mind the premise presented earlier: black people are questioning, evaluating the *legitimacy* of existing educational institutions, not simply searching for ways to make those institutions more *effective*. I am suggesting that we are at a point in the process of modernization and social transformation when we must begin to think and act in wholly new normative and structural terms.

NOTES

1. The Ravenswood City School Board serves a predominantly black community of 26,000 people in northern California. During the period from 1957 to 1967, Ravenswood schools changed from predominantly white to black,

with what a school board member, Robert S. Hoover, describes as a corresponding decrease in the quality of education. At first, the community tried to retain integrated schools, but, according to Mr. Hoover,

> Stokely Carmichael came to town one day. He suggested community control as an alternative to the Black struggle to integrate the schools against the white struggle to keep them as they were. "Stokely said that what we need to be talking about is control of our institutions — our destinies," Hoover said. "And a group of people who had been working hard for integration began to turn around and take a second look and to ask themselves, 'why isn't it possible for *us* to educate our own children?' "

This question was extremely relevant, because the Black children of Ravenswood were not doing very well in the schools as run by the present system, and their parents and the other Black community people knew that there was nothing wrong with the children. The children's scores on reading ability as compared with the national norm looked like this:

First Grade:	50th percentile
Second Grade:	35th percentile
Third Grade:	25th percentile

Community control was approached through a school board election. In 1967, the school board was composed of three whites, one Black, and one Chicano. Two Blacks were nominated for the election that year, one of them being Hoover. Through a magnificent community effort, and much support from the local Black high school students, they won. "With a Black majority on the school board, things began to move," Hoover said. "The first thing we did was to establish a citizens' committee to look at the reading situation in our community. They spent eight months doing an in-depth study, and ended up with a report making 26 recommendations for changes in the Ravenswood School District's reading program. The school board implemented every one of them."

The two most critical recommendations of the citizens' committee concerned reading methods and teacher training. The committee found that teachers in California are free to use any of the 16 or so reading methods approved by the State Board of Education, and Ravenswood teachers seemed to be using all of them, Hoover reported. "They found students being taught by the ITA method in first grade, the Sullivan in second, the Ginn in third, and so on," he said. "The children were totally confused. And if one happened to transfer in the middle of the year, he wouldn't know where he was. There was no consistency or continuity in the program."

The committee also found that only 25 percent of the teachers in the district had ever had a course in teaching reading. "Not only were they using all the methods known to man," Hoover observed, "but they didn't even know how to use them."

The school board selected a single reading program using a phonics method and began its implementation. They also instituted a massive teacher training program that not only dealt with the teaching of basic skills, but also with attitudes. "We had to implement the reading program year by year because it would have been too expensive to change all the grades at once. This year we are into the fourth grade, and the results have been very good. In 1968, prior to the implementation of the new program, it was predicted from kindergarten test scores that roughly half of the children in our school district would fail in the first grade. In 1971, only 41 children out of a total of 562 kindergarten children were singled out as potential failures in first grade. The same positive pattern is repeated in the first, second, and third grades, where the children are reading above grade level," Hoover said. "The district is 90 percent Black, we haven't bused anybody anywhere, we've demanded that teachers teach, and we have been successful." (Summary of Speech, Hoover, Proceedings, National Policy Conference on Education for Blacks 135-137 (April 1, 1972).)

2. Based on the success of community control efforts such as Ravenswood City, this alternative to integrated schools is supported by an impressive list of educators. See Fantini, Participation, Decentralization, Community Control, and Quality Education, 71 The Teachers College Record 93 (Colum. Univ. 1969); Haskins, The Case for Local Control, Saturday Review 52, Jan. 11, 1969; Wilcox, Education for Black Liberation, New Generation 17 (Winter 1969). The subject is discussed from several points of view in A. Altshuler, Community Control (1970); Community Control of Schools (H. Levin, ed. 1970); L. Fein, The Ecology of the Public Schools (1971).

3. Most community control advocates are not hostile to school integration, but they point out that white resistance has prevented most black children from experiencing it, almost two decades after Brown. Moreover, one advocate, Dr. Mario Fantini, draws a distinction between desegregation and integration. He suggests:

> Desegregation refers to the physical mixing of black and white students; integration refers to humans connecting as equals. Agreeing on the goal of integration, one could argue that it is necessary for black and other minority groups to have a sense of cohesion and identity. This can in part be achieved through the control of their own institutions. Once blacks attain a status of potency, they will be in a better position to connect up with white society as equals rather than as "junior" members. Therefore, such participatory efforts as decentralization and community control can be viewed as necessary steps toward a further stage of integration. (Fantini, supra Note 2 at 95.)

4. Some black leaders are far less charitable to the concept of integrated schools. At the national black political convention held in Gary, Indiana in March 1972, Roy Innis, the director of CORE, succeeded in pushing through a resolution that condemned both bussing and racial integration of schools as a "bankrupt, suicidal method . . . based on the false notion that black children are unable to learn unless they are in the same setting as white children." The resolution, which demanded quality education in the black community, received major news coverage.

5. Most educators supporting community control are not opposed to integrated schools, but feel that the integration process consumes valuable resources and energies which at this point in history should be used in education. During 1971 and 1972, a Senate Select Committee on Equal Educational Opportunity held a series of hearings, some of which were

devoted to the community control issue. Testimony was given by Kenneth Haskins, who had served as principal for an integrated school in Greenburgh, New York and at the experimental Morgan Community School in Washington, D.C. Senator Walter Mondale, the Committee Chairman, then asked Mr. Haskins to comment on the differences in the two situations. His response is set forth below.

HASKINS, STATEMENT COMPARING INTEGRATED AND COMMUNITY CONTROL SCHOOLS

Hearings, U.S. Senate Select Committee on Equal Educational Opportunity, 5873-5874 (July 27, 1971)

Mr. Haskins . . . From my point of view, the problems were the same. The concept of integration very quickly seemed to be defined differently by the white community and the black community.

Greenburgh, was I guess one of the first communities that did a lot around desegregation. They had an arrangement — I think Berkeley has something like that now — in which every classroom reflected the makeup of the community.

The school population was about 35 percent black, and it was not all poor blacks, so that there were some middle-class black people too, which some people seemed to feel necessary.

The biggest problem was that the input in the decisionmaking on the part of the black people in no way came up to their representation in the community.

And it just was taken as a natural order of things. Little things, for instance, the first time that the student organization in the high school had more blacks on it than whites, there was a great deal of stir in the community, when for years before that it had been all white and no one raised the question, because this seemed to be the natural order of things.

Most people felt . . . that the purpose of integration was to benefit the black children, and really the white community was doing them a favor, by allowing this to happen.

And originally, to go back a little further, the reason for the distribution of children in the schools in that way had little to do with race. It had to do with saving money. Because physically, the situation had occurred in the community that was opposite to what usually occurs; the newest school that was underpopulated was in the black part of the community, and the old school was being overpopulated because of new families from New York moving in — the question was whether to build another school or to find some way so that the balance was a little different.

The solution came when they decided to use one school for the first three grades, and the other school for the second three grades.

Throughout, then, it became one of trying to help black people and trying to help the white community to — if you will, for want of a better term — allow black people to have those things to say about the school, the curriculum, and so forth, that would influence their children.

And everything was a struggle. Even a question of pictures on the wall — could we see that Ebony magazine was used to cut pictures out of as well as Life and Look, and being told by teachers that they didn't know where to find any black dolls to put in the doll corner of the kindergarten. These were the kinds of things that went on.

Now in a way, progress was made; not as much as you would have liked. And then, as usual, there are certain points at which you come up against a stone wall.

What happens to a social situation as the children become a bit older? What happens at the high school level when the athletic team ends up being all black and the cheer leaders are all white? And the kind of panic that the community goes through with that.

And when they changed the plays, for instance, so that they make sure there are no more love stories, once it is integrated. They make it an extravaganza where everybody can be a Roman soldier and not touch anybody.

These are the kinds of fears you run across, which in some way I think dilute the educational experiences that people can have, because you no longer go into things in depth. You keep them superficial.

Effects of Community Control

In community control, working with almost totally black community, those things didn't occur. You taught black history and in some ways those of us who talk about black history like to consider that black history is really only true history, and not the kind of propaganda you get otherwise.

And if children fought in school, you could deal with it as a fight between two kids, and not have to get involved in whether it was a racial incident.

You just had a completely different kind of thing, and I really feel, for the black children in this instance. I would say that the amount of progress that we were able to make, at least for the 2 years I was at Morgan, toward improving reading scores, improving math scores, helping the children feel better about themselves, was done much more easily than I was able to do in what was then called an integrated setting.

Now whether or not community control is the final point to which this country moves, that I don't know. All I know is that at this present time in our history, given the psychological set of both the white and the black community, of the things I would like to see done for black children, I found much more easily done not only when black children were together, but when the parents were in control also, than I found when I had to deal and struggle with many of the things in an integrated setting, although I felt an integrated setting, if it means anything, I was having some impact on the education of some of the white people there.

QUESTIONS

1. Will it be possible for community control advocates to resolve the dilemma resulting from the fact that their positions often elicit immediate praise and support from diehard segregationists? Professor Hamilton, for example, acknowledges that his ideas appear closely akin to the views of those who would deny educational opportunity to blacks, but states that the difference, apparent on "close examination," is that "I am motivated by an attempt to find an educational approach which is relevant to black people, not one that perpetuates racism." Hamilton, supra at 576. Is this response convincing? How should community control spokesmen handle the similarity problem, with its concomitant potential for support from segregationists and opposition from integrationists?

2. Spokesmen for community-controlled schools are far more articulate in describing their educational potential than in explaining how the concept can be harmonized with the Brown decisions and their progeny. As you read Oliver v. Donovan, infra, consider what evidence and arguments plaintiffs might have used to strengthen their position. Would the legal arguments be easier if the school board had decentralized the schools voluntarily, and the legality of this action was tested by litigation? Will judicial recognition of community control plans that serve to condone perpetuation of racially isolated schools result in erosion of the Brown principle?

OLIVER v. DONOVAN
293 F. Supp. 958 (E.D. N.Y. 1968)

[This case represents one of the first judicial tests of the community control concept. It arose when an experimental school district in the Ocean Hill–Brownsville section of New York City sought to discharge or have transferred teachers and administrators it deemed "unfit".]

TRAVIA, District Judge.

The plaintiffs bring on this matter by way of order to show cause seeking a temporary restraining order enjoining the defendants from continuing to:

1. take any action to compel the plaintiffs to retain within the School District of Ocean Hill–Brownsville teachers whom the Local Governing Board of the District has determined should be transferred out of the District . . .

3. enforce the suspension and/or removal of principals of the Ocean Hill–Brownsville schools and the unit administrator Rhody McCoy, who have been selected by the community and/or community representatives. . . .

In their complaint, the plaintiffs invoke the jurisdiction of this Court under Title 28 U.S.C. §§1331, 1343(3) and (4). In addition, they assert the action is authorized by Title 42, U.S.C. §§1981, 1983, 1985, 1986 and 1988. They claim the action arises under the 13th and 14th Amendments to the Constitution of the United States. . . .

[P]laintiffs assert that the dispute came to a head when the Governing Board and Administrator of the Ocean Hill–Brownsville Demonstration School District attempted to transfer 13 teachers and 6 administrators out of the district because of their actions in opposition to school decentralization. As a result of the attempted transfer of the 19 staff members, some 350 teachers in the district remained away from their jobs in sympathy during the last 6 weeks of school in the Spring of 1968. New teachers were recruited over the summer to replace most of those who left their positions in the Spring. By the opening of school in September, 1968 it appeared that approximately 100 of the original 350 wanted to return. The Governing Board, however, requested that these 100 teachers be assigned elsewhere.

Problems relating to these teachers led to a strike.

In paragraph "25" plaintiffs charge defendants Lindsay, Donovan and members of the Central Board of Education, with encouraging, aiding, and giving sanction to the illegal strike of the United Federation of Teachers, and that the teachers have not lost pay as a result of their illegal strike.

In paragraph "26" of the complaint it is alleged the specific demand of the defendant Shanker has been that notwithstanding the determination of the community to rid itself of teachers who took action contrary to the decentralization program and who illegally struck against their children, the Governing Board be compelled to place those teachers in teaching positions in the classrooms of the Ocean Hill–Brownsville District, and in order to compel adoption of his program the defendant Shanker is willing to prevent the functioning of the entire educational system of the City.

In paragraph "27" of the complaint the plaintiffs allege that notwithstanding that it must be acknowledged that any insistence that the said teachers be placed in teaching positions not only is contrary to the wishes of the community but is destructive of any possibility of successful development of the educational program of the Ocean Hill–Brownsville District, the defendants Central Board, Donovan, and Mayor Lindsay have yielded to continued threats of a third illegal strike by the defendant Shanker. Pursuant thereto, the defendants Central Board, Donovan, Mayor Lindsay and Chief of Police have sought to compel the placement of the replaced teachers in classrooms in the Ocean Hill–Brownsville District and, beginning October 7, 1968, have placed over 1,000 policemen in the said District. As a result of all the foregoing, education in the Ocean Hill–Brownsville District is at a standstill.

In paragraph "28" of the complaint the plaintiffs allege as follows:

The adoption of a plan of decentralization and the involvement of the community in the development of a new approach to education was designed to correct the denial of education for the Black and Puerto Rican children of the Ocean Hill–Brownsville District. The defendants have deprived these children of quality education as developed by the Ocean Hill–Brownsville District and have therefore deprived rights guaranteed under the Thirteenth and Fourteenth Amendments to the Constitution of the United States, to wit:

A. The defendants are attempting to impose the terms of an agreement negotiated by the New York Central Board of Education and the United Federation of Teachers, without the participation of the Ocean Hill–Brownsville Governing Board or any other representatives from the local communities of New York City having a stake in quality education through decentralized community control. The agreement itself and the attempt to enforce the agreement were not made to meet any lawful need or purpose, but expressly as a response to a strike declared illegal by the New York Supreme Court. This action was taken by the defendants knowing full well that the consequences thereof would be disruption of education in the Ocean Hill–Brownsville District, and the disruption of decentralization in the entire City of New York.

B. The attempt to impose and enforce the terms of the aforementioned agreement has in fact resulted in the disruption of the school system in Ocean Hill–Brownsville and in the education of the children who attend school in that District, to wit:

(1) Defendants have caused massive numbers of police to be stationed in and around the Ocean Hill–Brownsville schools to enforce the terms of the aforementioned agreement. The police have and are continuing to:

a. deny parents and other members of the community the right to enter the schools;

b. harass, intimidate, molest and arrest members of the community who wish to enter the schools;

(2) At least one school in the district has been closed;

(3) The Local Governing Board and the Unit Administrator, pursuant to a directive issued by the Central Board, have been suspended, thereby denying to plaintiffs the right to run and control schools through representatives of the community;

(4) Principals chosen by the community or its representatives have been suspended and removed from the District's schools pursuant to a directive issued by the Central Board.

C. Defendants' attempt to enforce the agreement, and the actions taken pursuant thereto, are designed to destroy and/or have the effect of destroying the rights of plaintiffs and the class they represent to achieve quality education through a system of decentralized community control of the schools in New York City.

In paragraph "29" plaintiffs assert their basic position, which is, that the 13th and 14th Amendments impose on defendants a duty not to interfere with the development of quality education for the Black and Spanish-speaking children of New York and equality of education with White children. And finally, the Amendments also impose an affirmative duty to develop, support and protect quality and equality of education for the Black and Spanish-speaking children of New York. . . .

An understanding of the legal status of the Ocean Hill Board is essential to an appraisal of the legal sufficiency of plaintiffs' attempts to state a cause of action predicated upon a denial of equal protection.

Until the Marchi Act (Laws 1968, Ch. 568, effective June 5, 1968) was enacted, there was nothing in the Education Law or any other statute authorizing (a) the establishment of any such local board as a body having official powers or (b) the exercise of any educational or other powers by such a local board or (c) the delegation of any of the powers of the Board of Education to such a local board.

During the entire period involved, therefore, and in the Spring of 1968 when the Ocean Hill Board first purported to "dismiss" and then "transfer" 19 teachers and supervisors, it had no legal or governmental powers and no status other than as an unofficial body of citizen advisors. The Ocean Hill demonstration project, as then existing, consisted of the operation of a special group of schools by and under the control of Board of Education personnel, with the Ocean Hill Board acting in an advisory capacity.

The Marchi Act authorizes the Board of Education, with the approval of the Regents, to delegate functions, powers and duties of that Board to local boards until June 30, 1969 and the Board of Education on September 4, 1968, adopted a resolution providing for delegation of certain of its functions, powers and duties to local boards (Exhibit C attached to Donovan affidavit). The Regents approved this delegation on October 17, 1968, effective October 18, 1968. . . .

The witnesses of the plaintiff testified in substance that the Ocean Hill–Brownsville area is a poor section of the City, having a large majority of Black and Puerto Rican inhabitants; that most of the children in the 8 schools in the district are Black and Puerto Rican; that some of the schools selected for inclusion in the district were among the worst in the area; that prior to the time the demonstration project began functioning in the Fall of 1967, there were high rates of pupil and teacher absenteeism, there were high rates of student dropouts, serious disciplinary problems existed, and the students' performance was frequently below grade level; that, in addition, the schools were over-crowded, run-down, and under-staffed; that during the course of this past year, however, most of these problems have been relieved or have disappeared altogether; that new I.S. 55 was opened in the district in February 1968; that a pupil-teacher ratio of about 19 to 1 has been achieved; that parents have taken a much greater interest in the operation of the schools; new programs and new methods of teaching have been devised to improve student performance; special classes have been introduced for the more gifted pupils; absenteeism, disciplinary problems and the drop-out rate have shown marked improvement. In general, the witnesses from the district testified that remarkable progress had been made during the past year in the schools in that area. . . .

It appears from the papers before this Court that in May, 1968, the Ocean Hill Board notified 13 teachers and 6 supervisors of the district that they were "dismissed". This action was taken without charges or a hearing on the basis of a claim by the Ocean Hill Board that these employees were unfit for service. Subsequently the Ocean Hill Board changed this action to a request for a transfer of these employees on the ground of claimed unfitness.

In accordance with the usual procedure of the Board of Education in cases where allegations of dereliction are made against teachers and supervisors, the Superintendent of Schools refused to transfer these employees without an investigation of the allegations and an opportunity for the employees to respond to the accusations.

The Ocean Hill Board filed charges of unfitness against 10 of the accused 19 employees, the other 9 employees having been eliminated from the attempted ouster by voluntary transfer or otherwise. The teachers were acquitted of these charges after a trial before Mr. Justice Rivers, acting as a Trial Examiner for the Board of Education. Judge Rivers recommended to the Board of Education that the demand of the Ocean Hill Board for the transfer of the teachers be rejected. (The report and recommendations of Judge Francis E. Rivers, dated August 26, 1968, is attached to the affidavit of Abraham Wilner, Assistant Superintendent of Schools, in charge of personnel, dated October 21, 1968.)

The Superintendent of Schools and the Board of Education accepted the recommendation of Judge Rivers.

Despite the acquittal, the Ocean Hill Board, prior to the opening of the Fall, 1968, term, declared that it would not permit the 10 teachers to return to their teaching positions and, in addition, that it would also oust approximately 100 teachers who absented themselves from their schools in the Spring of 1968 in protest against the attempted transfer.

The Ocean Hill Board did not have, at the time of these actions, and up to the time of the conclusion of this hearing did not possess, any legal power, jurisdiction or authority (a) to transfer teachers out of the schools of the Ocean Hill–Brownsville district or (b) to determine the fitness and competency of teachers, or (c) to refuse teaching assignments to any teacher duly assigned to the district or (d) to countermand orders of the Board of Education on any subject.

The Board of Education, after efforts to persuade the Ocean Hill Board and the Unit Administrator, Mr. McCoy, to allow these teachers to return to their rightful teaching positions, submitted the matter to the State Commissioner of Education. The Commissioner, after reviewing the facts and hearing the contentions of the Ocean Hill Board, the Board of Education and the United Federation of Teachers, issued a determination on September 14, 1968, ruling (a) that the efforts of the Ocean Hill Board to oust the teachers were illegal and contrary to sound educational principles, (b) that this Board should be suspended temporarily, and (c) that the 10 teachers be temporarily assigned outside the Ocean Hill District.

Under the broad jurisdiction to review educational matters conferred upon the Commissioner by the Education Law, including §§310 and 311 thereof

(See Matter of Vetere v. Allen, 15 N.Y.2d 259, at pp. 265-266 . . . (1965)), he had full authority to review and determine all aspects of the legality and propriety of the attempted transfer of the teachers. The Commissioner may set aside a transfer of a teacher if he finds that it was arbitrarily made. (55 St. Dept. 581). In effect, therefore, the Commissioner sustained the refusal of the Board of Education and the Superintendent of Schools to permit the ouster.

Under New York Law, the determination of the Commissioner rejecting the claims and demands of the Ocean Hill Board as to the teachers is conclusive upon the Board and will not be set aside by the New York courts unless purely arbitrary. Matter of Chapin v. Board of Education, 291 N.Y. 241 . . . (1943); Matter of Vetere v. Allen, supra.

On September 15, 1968, the Board of Education issued directives carrying out the determinations of the Commissioner of Education and notified the Ocean Hill Board members of this action.

On September 20, 1968, the Board of Education, with the approval of the Commissioner of Education, revoked the temporary suspension of the members of the Ocean Hill Board and directed that all 110 teachers sought to be excluded be reassigned to teaching duties in the Ocean Hill District.

Notwithstanding Board of Education orders issued on September 20, 1968 to the Ocean Hill Board and the Unit Administrator of the Ocean Hill District, Mr. McCoy, that the 10 acquitted teachers and the 100 other teachers be given teaching assignments in the schools of the area, the Ocean Hill Board and Mr. McCoy defied the Board of Education and during the week preceding October 6th, 1968 purported to order that these teachers be refused teaching assignments. The Ocean Hill Board was suspended by the Board of Education for 30 days on October 6, 1968, following the attempt of the Ocean Hill Board to countermand these orders of the Board of Education. . . .

The Plaintiffs seem to set out what is essentially a three-part theory.

(1) Their basic assertion is that the centralized school system existing before the decentralization experiment violated:

(a) The 13th Amendment in that "quality" education was not given the Black and Spanish-speaking children of New York and that this meant the imposition of "a badge or indicia" of slavery, contrary to the 13th Amendment mandate.

(b) The 14th Amendment in that "equality" of education was denied children because the present system of education did not respond to the particular educational needs of Black and Spanish-speaking children, resulting in high illiteracy rates;

(2) The Ocean Hill project was instituted to correct these constitutional deficiencies and is succeeding; and

(3) Any interference with the operating of the Ocean Hill project is unconstitutional, as it forces the children back to the unconstitutional system previously existing.

None of these allegations, considering all the papers, pleadings, exhibits and testimony adduced, give this Court jurisdiction.

There has been no allegation made, or proven, that would tend to show any act, overt or subtle, that would violate the 13th Amendment.

While it might be a violation of the 13th Amendment for the state — or individuals — to deny to Negroes the *right* to education, the complaint nowhere alleges that this is the case. Neither do we have the situation, as in Reitman v. Mulkey, 387 U.S. 369 . . . (1967), where the state is standing aside and permitting individuals to deny basic right to citizens. Nor is there indicated the extent to which the differences in education alleged are attributable to the centralized school system. Rather, we have the bald assertion that the New York school system violates the 13th Amendment because of the end product of the system.

There has been no allegation made, or proven, that could lead to the position that anyone either conspired or acted under color of state law to *deny* equal educational rights to anyone. There has been no allegation that less qualified teachers were forced, in a discriminatory manner, upon Negro schools, nor of any other arbitrary, discriminatory, or capricious action that could be deemed to violate the right of the inhabitants of the experimental district to equality of education. The mere showing that inequality exists, without more, does not make out a case of constitutional violations. . . .

The plaintiffs' claim that the nature of their Constitutional rights and the substantiality of their claims warrant that the Court assume jurisdiction. They rely on Jones v. Mayer Realty, 392 U.S. 409 . . . ; Brown v. Board of Education, 347 U.S. 483, 486, . . . ; United States v. Jefferson County Board of Education, 5 Cir., 372 F.2d 836; and Hobson v. Hansen, D.C., 269 F. Supp. 401.

This Court fails to see the similarity in any of these cases with the case at bar.

In the Brown case, supra, the Court declared school segregation to be against the equal protection of the laws guaranteed by the 14th Amendment, even if tangible factors are equal. The Court also stated:

> Today, education is perhaps the most important function of state and local governments. (347 U.S. p. 493 . . .) It is the very foundation of good citizenship. . . . In these days, it is doubtful that any child may reasonably be expected to succeed in life if he is denied the opportunity of an education. Such an opportunity, *where the state has undertaken to provide it,* is a right which must be made available to all on equal terms. (Emphasis added.)

With relation to the present case, education, it seems, is not a constitutional right in and of itself, but must be equally provided if provided at all.

Segregation obviously connotes inferiority. But no finding or general feeling is present stating that centralized school systems are *inherently* inferior.

Plaintiffs do not point to a federal statute that defines and protects the rights they claim in the context presented here. Basically they rely on the

13th and 14th Amendments themselves. This claims too much. These Amendments are self-executing in fundamental but limited areas only. Contrast the situation before the Court in Jones v. Alfred H. Mayer Co., 392 U.S. 409 . . . (1968) relied upon by plaintiffs, where Congress had passed a statute authorized by the 13th Amendment, 42 U.S.C. §1982, to give all citizens equal rights in the purchase, lease or sale of real property. There the statute was intended to relieve former slaves of one of the disabilities of their prior status and give them equal opportunity with white persons.

Unaided by the statute it would appear impossible for the Court to have based relief on the 13th Amendment alone.

By the same token, in the present case there is no statute to give plaintiffs the rights they claim. When viewed in light of the facts pleaded and presented at the trial neither the 13th nor 14th Amendment affords a basis for jurisdiction . . . .

It must be recognized that the results of the Ocean Hill experiment have been greatly encouraging. The concept of community involvement is one that appears to have great possibilities. But even admitting all of this, the complaint, the papers and the testimony adduced do not allege any facts that can lead this Court to the conclusion that the present situation is one involving the danger of destruction of the Ocean Hill experiment. There has been no showing that the presence of the police in any way stifles the experiment. And while the competence of Mr. McCoy as an Educator is apparent, neither his removal nor that of the principals of the schools has been shown to be part of an attempt to destroy the experiment. The concept and its operation can certainly continue even if certain individuals are no longer part of the experiment. Mr. McCoy has no constitutional right to his job.

The Ocean Hill experiment is just that, an experiment. It is an attempt to see how the effectiveness of the educational structure may be improved. But thc State should not be put into a constitutional straight-jacket, forbidding it from attempting other experiments. The alternative to segregation was some form of integration — that was the clear alternative. There is no such obvious solution to the education problems of the large cities. The State should not be prevented from ending one experiment and trying others, if the action is taken in good faith, without discriminatory intent or result.

The acts complained of by plaintiffs are not sufficient to establish the jurisdiction of this Court. . . .

On the basis of the foregoing, the motion of the defendants to dismiss for want of jurisdiction is granted and the proceeding dismissed.

NOTES

1. The Ocean Hill–Brownsville story is reported in detail in Confrontation at Ocean Hill–Brownsville (M. Berobe and M. Gittell eds. 1968). A selection of writings commenting on both sides of the New York school decen-

tralization struggle is contained in F. Michelman and T. Sandalow, Materials on Government in Urban Areas 446-490 (1970).

2. Oliver v. Donovan illustrates that, while a shift by black parents from school integration to community control may please some antibussing whites, it will incur stiff opposition from teachers, administrators, suppliers and others who have vested interests in school systems as they are presently structured.

3. The Oliver decision also reveals how difficult it will be to convince courts oriented toward the standard of Brown (equality of facilities, and integration) to extend constitutional protection to the community control concept. See, for example, the almost hostile response by the court to black parents' concern that no blacks had ever sat on the Boston School Committee. Owens v. School Committee, 304 F. Supp. 1327 (D. Mass. 1969), printed supra page 175. The dilemma is set forth in the following statement, delivered by Ron Edmonds, Assistant Superintendent of the Michigan State Department of Education, to the National Policy Conference on Education for Blacks in April 1972.

EDMONDS, JUDICIAL ASSUMPTIONS ON THE VALUE OF INTEGRATED EDUCATION FOR BLACKS

Proceedings, National Policy Conference on Education for Blacks 140-144 (1972)

It is a basic assumption of this discussion that the present judicial perception of the means by which Black Americans should obtain redress of educational grievance is not in the best interest of Black Americans.

The Federal Courts have inadvertently developed an educational ideology that consists of the assumptions that: (1) segregation in public instruction is illegal; (2) justice for Black children requires that those children attend schools where the majority of the students are white; and, (3) Black pupil performance need not be considered since 1 and 2 automatically improve performance.

By defining integration as an educational setting in which Black children are in the minority and are likely to remain so, court-ordered desegregation has often been as coercive for Black parents as for white. The coercion occurs because substantial portions of the Black community have developed considerable doubt about the positive relationship between court-ordered integration and Black pupil performance and thus, given a choice, might not send their children to judicially integrated schools.

The court's disinterest in Black pupil performance has its origin in the nature of the 1954 Brown decision. The most important assumptions in the Brown decision's description of the relationship between race and education can be summarized as follows:

A. The existence in the United States of state-imposed white schools is accompanied by the discriminatory treatment of those schools. That discrimination consists of inequitable distribution of educational resources such as to deny to Black children the minimal resources prerequisite to proper schooling.

B. Even if the distribution of educational resources is made equitable, justice will still be denied Black children, because state-imposed segregation persuades Black children that they are inferior and their belief in their inferiority interferes with their ability to acquire school skills.

C. Therefore, appropriate Black pupil performance must be preceded by Black pupils being mixed with white pupils.

The research literature since 1954 compels the following summary with respect to the basic premises in the Brown decision. Under court-ordered integration, some Black pupils do better, some Black pupils do about the same and some Black pupils do worse. Therefore, court-ordered desegregation, in and of itself, is an insufficient and sometimes inappropriate response to the present inequity that characterizes public instruction for Black children.

In 1954, Black advocates were nearly unanimous in their commitment to the belief that educational integration was synonymous with justice for Black children. That unanimity had its origin in the nature of American race relations between 1865 and 1965. In decisions like Cruikshank, Reese and Harris, the Supreme Court was instrumental in denying to Black Americans choices as to the means of their redress of grievance.

Black efforts at political, economic and social progress were thwarted by a national climate that was codified in these decisions. The NAACP led the legal assault on the Supreme Court's narrow and perverse perception of citizenship for Black Americans. The NAACP appropriately defined the Supreme Court as hostile to any activity that could be characterized as a Black attempt at self-improvement.

It is, therefore, understandable that the ideology of the NAACP should historically have spurned discussion of racial difference and espoused, as its goal, a society virtually unaware of the difference between being Black and white. Since the arena in which the NAACP carried on its principal struggle was the law, and since its adversary was most often the Supreme Court, integration seemed the most efficacious form of redress of Black grievance.

Such circumstances help to explain why American history does not identify effective and successful organizations devoted to political or economic redress of grievance for Blacks.

In summary, Black Americans were denied choices as to the means of their redress of grievance because Supreme Court decisions, in concert with other characteristics of American life, had the effect of making any organized Black activity that was not legalistic, impractical. We, therefore, find ourselves observing a historic dialogue between the federal judiciary and the NAACP with the inference that the NAACP ideology of integration represents the best interests of Black Americans in all circumstances.

Nothing in this discussion should be construed as critical of the NAACP. The NAACP is unchallenged in the consistency and sincerity of its commitment to the cause of Black Americans. What is suggested is that no single ideology, such as integration, should bear the burden of representing so extensive a portion of the population.

Since it has already been noted that integration improves performance for some Black pupils, then we must continue our interest in integrated education. However, if circumstances compel improved Black pupil performance in majority Black settings, then we must attend to that also, partly by challenging demonstrably ineffective educational ideologies like integration as presently pursued by the courts.

Judicial hostility to majority Black schools reinforces the national belief that majority black schools are bad schools. Such a belief insures that integration in education must continue to reflect preference for middle-class, white behavior and precludes the possibility of identifying or developing appropriate Black educational behavior in a majority Black setting. Since majority Black settings are, and will remain, a part of American life, it is a disservice to preclude attention to that fact.

Finally, redefining integration so as to make it more culturally democratic and thus more educationally effective may ultimately depend on developing effective instruction for majority Black schools.

What is, therefore, concluded is that Black Americans have not had choices of the means of their deliverance from societal disability. The Supreme Court, and other factors in American life inadvertently conspired to compel integration as a means of racial redress to the exclusion of all other means of redress.

This discussion recommends that the judicial basis for evaluating desegregation proposals be expanded to include pupil performance and other variables responsive to the needs of Black Americans. This discussion finally recommends that extraordinary means to achieve integration, such as metropolitan cross-district busing, be undertaken only after exhaustive inquiry compels the conclusion that no other means of redressing Black grievance would be effective. Exhaustive inquiry requires far more reliable data on the relationship between court-ordered integration and Black pupil performance than has thus far been available.

Since these remarks are intended to assist those who contribute to desegregation litigation, it would be inappropriate to conclude without some reference to the minimal prerequisites to educational equity in those instances where the courts are compelled to respond to segregation. To be just, as well as legal, court-ordered desegregation must be characterized by the following minimal characteristics:

1. Judicially assured open housing in the entire area within the court's jurisdiction.
2. Judicially assured equity in the distribution of educational resources.
3. Judicial assurance that the desegregated setting shall afford the aggrieved Black citizens access to educational decision-making in such manner as will make the school more appropriately responsive to the cultural characteristics of the Black community.

4. Judicial assurance that desegregation will be characterized by Black pupil acquisition of school skills at least equal to white pupil acquisition of school skills with the inference that all public schools can be held accountable for providing all public school children demonstrable acquisition of basic school skills.
5. Judicial assurance that the desegregation proposal shall eliminate all discriminatory pupil placement.

This discussion, taken as a whole, confirms premises A and B of the 1954 Brown decision as recited earlier.

This discussion recommends the following as a replacement for Brown's original premise C.

C. Opposition to segregation need not imply opposition to majority Black schools. Majority Black schools can be appropriate and effective education settings for all children when the majority Black school is characterized by:

1. Black residence that is a function of choice rather than discrimination.
2. Equity in the distribution of the community's educational resources.
3. Attendance area majority control of the uses to which the school is to be put.
4. Implementation of an accountability model whose goal is that all matriculating children be assured basic school skills in reading, writing and computation.
5. Pupil assignment that is a function of residence and is free from discrimination.

Justice requires providing citizens choices. Integration as presently perceived by the federal courts does not expand educational or cultural choices for Black citizens. Morality, logic and pragmatism compel the recommendation that this discussion become a part of the Black advocate's perspective on how best to achieve equity in the social order.

KIRP, COMMUNITY CONTROL, PUBLIC POLICY, AND THE LIMITS OF LAW

68 Mich. L. Rev. 1355, 1365-1367, 1369-1370 (1970)

Judicial insistence that Southern schools integrate "at once," coupled with the increasing willingness of Northern courts to identify racially motivated practices of city school boards as illegitimate, makes evident the potential conflict between community control in the North and the Brown rule. The conflict may be simply put: decentralization promotes racial isolation; Brown inveighs against it. If Brown is read to disallow all racial separation, community control will be found to be unconstitutional; and no expression favoring separateness, even if made by the majority of a black community, will be able to cure the constitutional defect.

Yet that reading of Brown seems overly mechanical and is peculiarly unresponsive to different factual contexts and to the educational consequences of alternative arrangements. It also fuses two elements of the decision that merit separate analysis: Brown's concern with *educational* consequences, and its concern with *associational* consequences.

In Brown the Court explicitly framed its ruling in terms of educational outcomes, citing the effect of segregated schooling on black children. This effect presumably would have existed whether segregation had come about adventitiously or through force of law. In the intervening fifteen years, the educational evidence has changed. [See Note, Race and Learning: A Perspective On the Research, printed supra page 563.]

The Brown Court apparently assumed that racial isolation causes racially different outcomes and that racial integration will yield racially identical results. Current social-science evidence drastically qualifies that assumption. It suggests that race has only a modest effect on schooling success and that social-class integration is more likely than is racial integration to lead to significant educational benefits for poor and black school children. Even more important, the limitations of the evidence from social science are also more plain today. The research commends no single strategy as likely to produce educational equality, no strategy likely to overcome the nonschool differentials that find their way into outcomes measured by reading and arithmetic comprehension tests. In short, equality of educational outcomes — the most significant measure of opportunity to the children primarily affected — appears unattainable by any single pattern of educational intervention. . . .

In the face of such an educational dilemma, the Court would be unwise to equate equality of educational opportunity — the constitutional standard — with equality of educational outcome; exhortations to do the impossible do not make good law. . . .

Does community control, insofar as it promotes racially identifiable communities, fall within the category of discriminatory association condemned by Brown and Green? The question is more sharply posed in the context of a hypothetical lawsuit, brought by a black parent, challenging a community control arrangement on the grounds that the effect of such an arrangement is to deny his children the opportunity to associate with white school children. If the community is indeed racially defined, and if the arrangement offers the parent no option but to send his child to the neighborhood (and black) school, the parent's argument is appealing: his children do not have the chance to go to school with white children; and the source of that denial is the official policy of the school board, not just the happenstance of residence.

Certainly, there are differences between the rationale that prompts community control and the rationale for other forms of segregated schooling. But the effect is the same — state-promoted racial isolation. The remedy in such a situation, however, is not necessarily that community control be struck down in its entirety. If unconstrained choice is the value to be conserved, the parent's concern extends only to his children and to the class of children in the community who are prevented by the community control plan from attending integrated schools. If the arrangement were structured in such a manner as to attend, at public expense, a school in which his race is a minority, this constraint on choice would be removed. The arrangement might then, and only then, be constitutionally acceptable. The constitutional question has not, however, been posed to the courts in this form. Decisions striking down freedom-of-choice plans in the South assumed, quite rightly, that freedom of choice in that context was but a subterfuge to avoid disestablishing the dual educational system. Yet where such a system has not previously existed (and Deal, Bell, and Downs all suggest that this is the conventional judicial understanding of many Northern school situations), freedom of choice for the integration-minded, predicated on the wishes of the black community, might well be permissible.

But discussions of constitutional possibility do not foreclose the educational problems. Coupling community control with a "majority-to-minority transfer" provision places the burden of choosing an integrated education on the parent, rather than on the state; in so doing it implies that communitarianism is to be regarded as the norm and integration as the exception. Furthermore, it subjects the parent who prefers an integrated education for his children to considerable community pressure. Whether the burden and the pressure ought to rest with the integration-minded parent is a dilemma not easily resolved.

QUESTIONS

1. Mr. Kirp's article outlines a possible argument supporting the adoption of community control policies by a school board, but, as Oliver v. Donovan teaches, school boards are not likely to transfer voluntarily the authority and resources necessary for meaningful community control. In the face of the traditional reading of Brown, can a lawyerlike argument be made that community control is constitutionally required? Is there a basis for such an argument in the foregoing statement by Assistant Superintendent Ron Edmonds?

2. Even assuming that a court was convinced of the educational advantages of community-controlled schools, would it not be extremely reluctant to commit itself to a continuing search for standards to determine which schools are entitled to local control? What are the necessary components of community control? What rights or protections should be provided for students, parents and teachers who don't wish to participate in the new plan? While the "majority to minority" transfer privilege for parents preferring an integrated to a community-controlled school places the burden for choosing integration on the parent, would the imposition of this burden pose an impossible constitutional barrier?

3. Would the constitutional problems of validating community control plans be lessened if courts were urged to approve them for a limited period of, say, five years as a "transitional measure," during which the stigma imposed on black schools and students during the century of segregation and inequality could be remedied?

Racism Hypo 7
INTEGRATED SCHOOLS, INC. v. SCHOOL BOARD AND MALCOLM X SCHOOL

A group of black parents, all of whom have children attending the Malcolm X Elementary School, located in the black ghetto section of a Southern town, have moved to intervene in a school desegregation suit initially filed in 1960 by Integrated School, Inc., a civil rights organization. After long delays and protracted litigation, the school board has been ordered to implement a plan requiring full integration. The motion seeks to have the Malcolm X School excluded from the plan. Because a substantial percentage of the town's black children are attending the Malcolm X School, the school board agreed to exclude the school from its desegregation plan, and is not opposing the motion. Plaintiffs, Integrated Schools, Inc., does oppose the motion.

The Malcolm X motion asserts, that, by reason of the generations of discrimination and segregation which black people have experienced, their children have special educational needs (including, but not limited to, black history, culture, psychology, awareness, etc.). Those needs would not be met in the integrated schools to which the students would be assigned under the board's integration plan. The plan calls for closing the Malcolm X School, even though the facility is only ten years old. The board even refused to rename one of the other schools for a legitimate black hero, and the intervenors contend that this is illustrative of how unresponsive the integrated schools will be to the needs of black children.

The Malcolm X parents contend that they organized what they call a "black curriculum" only after years of unsuccessful efforts to get the school board either to desegregate or to improve the quality of the black school. They point out that, as a result of the "black curriculum," discipline and dropout problems have decreased and student achievement levels have increased. A black principal, who was appointed by the board in response to demands by parents, has permitted parents to participate in key school policy decisions.

The Malcolm X parents concede that the integration plan may benefit black children in other schools in the system, where no community control program is in effect, but contend that desegregation of the Malcolm X School would be arbitrary and unnecessary: an evasion, not an enforcement, of Brown v. Board of Education. They assert that the applicable cases do not require desegregation where the victims of segregation, despairing of ever obtaining compliance with the law and disenchanted with the prospects that integrated schools will bring about equal educational opportunities, have evolved a remedy satisfactory to them. They claim that the board's plan will violate their rights to equal protection, and assert that Brown was intended to guarantee not integration, but an equal educational opportunity. Maintaining that they have the latter, and have no need for the former, they seek an injunction against the proposed board action.

Plaintiffs maintain that the suit must fail, by reason of Brown v. Board of

Education I and II and the long series of cases based on those decisions. They point out that the integration plan adopted by the court is designed to create the unitary, nonracial system required both by Brown and Title VI of the Civil Rights Act of 1964. A provision for schools to opt out of the plan, even for good faith reasons such as those offered by Malcolm X, would, they argue, return the constitutional standard for desegregation to "freedom of choice." Thus, while the parents of children attending the Malcolm X School may be sincere, judicial recognition of their plan would set a precedent that would undermine Brown and endanger the Title VI enforcement program, and could lead to resegregation of schools all over the South.

Law Firm A will represent the Malcolm X School parents in a hearing on their motion.

Law Firm B will represent the plaintiffs, Integrated Schools, Inc.

B. OTHER SCHOOL INTEGRATION ALTERNATIVES

The concept of community control deserves the most serious attention as an alternative to school integration, both because it has support in the black community, and because at heart it seeks to make the school administrators and faculty responsive and responsible to black children, in the same manner as the better suburban school systems. But there are other plans for improving the quality of education for inner-city black children that merit discussion, although their potential depends — even more than the community control alternative — on financial resources, political support, and other factors beyond the powers of litigation.

1. Free Schools

The most courageous advocates of community control have turned their backs on the public schools and established small private schools in poor areas. With exciting programming, less restrictive scheduling, and innovative teaching techniques, children — often those on whom the public schools have given up — are learning, and what is more important, liking it. See, generally, J. Kozol, Free Schools (1972); G. Dennison, Lives of Children (1969). But making such schools a reality requires great dedication. Sponsors must overcome myriad problems, including state and local educational requirements, health and safety standards, teacher certification and, of course, ongoing financial support. Many of these projects have nonetheless moved beyond the experimental stage and achieved impressive academic success. Perhaps significantly, many such schools, which began deep in black communities for black children, have waiting lists of white children whose parents are more than willing to pay to have their children share in the innovative, integrated educational programs that often characterize free schools.

The schools are "free" only for parents totally unable to pay; for others, tuition is on a sliding scale based on parental means. Subsidies come from foundation grants, fund-raising efforts, and sometimes public school systems.

One system of nonpublic schools that seeks no outside financial help and seems to need none is operated by the Black Muslims. Rigid discipline and strict segregation are the rule, but the children generally achieve at or above their grade levels; by the time they reach high school, they are several grade levels above most of the black teenagers attending the public schools. Pride, discipline and self-sufficiency are emphasized in the schools, as they are in the Black Muslim religion generally. "The Muslim Way," Newsweek 106 (Sep. 25, 1972). See also C. Lincoln, The Black Muslims in America, 32, 126-128, 250 (1961). Once open to all blacks, many Muslim schools have become so popular that only the children of Muslims are admitted.

While the religious fervor of a Black Muslim is not essential, free schools — almost by definition — require a degree of commitment, competence and courage difficult to mass-produce for those millions of black children whose schooling continues to reflect a separate and highly unequal character.

2. Compensatory Education

In the mid-1960s educators began effectively pressuring the federal government for more money for schools in poor areas. It was hoped then that compensatory education programs might serve as suitable substitutes to integration, particularly in large urban areas where meaningful integration would have been difficult even without the massive opposition that developed. The plans called for special programs in ghetto schools, extra teachers, the latest teaching aids, and the commitment of additional resources to target schools.

Some of these programs have been financed under Title I of the Elementary and Secondary Education Act of 1965,* but serious problems have occurred with the administration of this act. Civil rights groups have charged that Title I funds were incompetently and corruptly administered, resulting in the misuse, waste, and diversion of a substantial percentage of the billions of dollars appropriated under the act.† There is also evidence that school systems have not, as the act intended, supplemented the funding of target schools already receiving their fair share of state funds. Rather, they have used Title I money to reduce the disparity that existed between have and have-not schools. Money has often been spent to spruce up black schools in order to discourage integration, rather than to improve the education being provided. See 1969 Civil Rights Commission Report 32.

But even if the program were efficiently and honestly administered, there

* 79 Stat. 27-35, as amended, 20 U.S.C. §§236-244 (1965). Title I is the largest compensatory education plan ever attempted.

† Title I of ESEA — Is It Helping Poor Children?, a study prepared by civil rights groups, was reported in the New York Times, Nov. 9, 1969, at 1, col. 1. Reports of mismanagement have continued sporadically.

is serious doubt that enough money would be provided to ensure the sustained effectiveness of compensatory education programs.‡ A society willing to deny black children a decent education in order to preserve segregation is not likely to spend three or four times as much on black children's education as on whites', even if this expenditure kept black children out of white schools. And lacking the power to either desegregate or gain a measure of control over the schools, the black community is unlikely to make itself heard concerning how funds for compensatory education are to be used. It must count itself fortunate if the funds even reach the target schools at all.

3. Tuition Grants

A similar problem threatens the future of tuition grants, or family voucher plans. A few years ago educators were excited by the possibility that the quality of education provided the poor could be improved by stimulating competition between existing public schools and private schools.** Parents would receive "tuition vouchers" which could be cashed at the school where they enrolled their child. Parents would become education "buyers," and schools would theoretically become sensitive to satisfying the educational needs of the children enrolled.

For this plan to work, poor parents would have to receive a substantially larger grant than well-to-do parents to entice schools to undertake the more difficult educational challenge presented by the ghetto child, and to offset the more affluent parents' ability to supplement their grant. Such a program would be difficult to enact for political reasons. A program providing equal grants for all would invite middle-class parents to supplement their grants with private funds and set up superior schools that would perpetuate present inequalities. Moreover, early experiments with tuition grants, while highly publicized, have been disappointing in effectiveness.

Although pilot programs with tuition grants are underway, other experiments operating under a somewhat similar concept have met with mixed

‡ Cohen, Policies for the Public Schools: Compensation and Integration, 38 Harv. Ed. Rev. 114 (1968). Sen. Walter Mondale, Chairman of the Select Committee on Equal Educational Opportunity: "With few exceptions, an annual Federal investment of $1.5 billion in compensatory education has little perceptible impact on mounting educational disadvantages." New York Times, Feb. 27, 1972, at E 13, col. 8.

** See Sizer and Whitten, A Proposal for a Poor Children's Bill of Rights, Psychology Today 59 (Aug. 1968); Sizer, The Case for a Free Market, Saturday Review 34 (Jan. 11, 1969).

For a thorough discussion of the legal, political and educational issues, see Areen, Education Vouchers, 6 Harv. Civ. Rights-Civ. Lib. L. Rev. 466 (1971). A strategy for winning support for vouchers is set forth in Arons, Equity, Option, and Vouchers, 72 Teachers College Rec. 337 (1971). See also J. Coons, W. Clune, S. Sugarman, Private Wealth and Public Education 201-242 (1970). Serious constitutional questions are posed in King, Rebuilding the "Fallen House" — State Tuition Grants for Elementary and Secondary Education, 84 Harv. L. Rev. 1057 (1971).

results. In these cases, school systems contract out their educational responsibility for one or more schools to private firms, which guarantee that pupil achievement will reach certain levels. See Mecklenburger and Wilson, Learning C.O.D. — Can the Schools Buy Success? Saturday Review 62 (Sept. 18, 1971).

4. Equalized School Funding

For years, educators have been urging state legislatures to eliminate funding disparities between school districts by amending state statutes containing school funding formulas that discriminate against poor districts. Virtually all the states delegate the task of funding elementary and secondary education to local school districts, authorizing them to raise local property taxes as the primary means of financing this function. But the amount each district has available to spend on education varies widely, given the wide disparity in assessed property values and tax rates.

Legal writers took up the cause,* legal theories were evolved, and test cases were initiated. After a shaky start in the courts,† a number of decisions invalidated state funding plans and required legislatures to restructure funding laws to avoid discrimination based on district wealth.‡

Serrano v. Priest, 5 Cal. 3d 583, 487 P.2d 1241, 96 Cal. Rptr. 601 (1971),

* The theory was presented in Horowitz and Neitring, Equal Protection Aspects of Inequalities in Public Education and Public Assistance Programs from Place to Place Within a State, 15 U.C.L.A. L. Rev. 787 (1968). Workable alternatives to current financing schemes were analyzed in detail in Coons, Clune and Sugarman, Educational Opportunity: A Workable Constitutional Test for State Financial Structures, 57 Cal. L. Rev. 305 (1969). See also Silard and White, Intrastate Inequalities in Public Education: The Case for Judicial Relief Under the Equal Protection Clause, 1970 Wis. L. Rev. 1; Michelman, The Supreme Court 1968 Term, Foreword: On Protecting the Poor Through the Fourteenth Amendment, 83 Harv. L. Rev. 7 (1969).

† McInnis v. Shapiro, 293 F. Supp. 327 (N.D. Ill. 1968), *aff'd mem. sub nom.* McInnis v. Ogilvie, 394 U.S. 322 (1969). The district court found no constitutional requirement that public school expenditures must be made only on the basis of the pupils' educational need without regard to the financial strength of the local school district. Nor were rigid equal dollar expenditures per pupil required. See also Burruss v. Wilkerson, 310 F. Supp. 572 (W.D. Va. 1969), *aff'd,* 397 U.S. 44 (1970); Board of Educ. v. Michigan, Gen.-Civil No. 103342 (Wayne County, Mich. Civ. Ct., filed Feb. 2, 1968).

‡ Serrano v. Priest, 5 Cal. 3d 583, 487 P2d 1241, 96 Cal. Rptr. 601 (1971). Two federal courts reached conclusions similar to Serrano. Rodriguez v. San Antonio Ind. School Dist., 337 F. Supp. 280 (W.D. Tex. 1971), *prob. juris. noted,* 406 U.S. 966 (1972); Van Dusartz v. Hatfield, 334 F. Supp. 870 (D. Minn. 1971). Three state courts have declared their states' financing systems unconstitutional. Hollins v. Shofstall, No. C-253652 (Maricopa County Ariz. Super. Ct., Jan. 13, 1972); Robinson v. Cahill, 118 N.J. Super. 223, 287 A.2d 187 (1972); Sweetwater County Planning Comm. for the Organization of School Dists. v. Hinkle, 491 P.2d 1234 (Wyo. 1971). A New York trial court has held that state's system constitutional. Spano v. Board of Educ., 68 Misc. 2d 804, 328 N.Y.S.2d 229 (Sup. Ct. 1972). Similar suits are pending in perhaps twenty other states. See Note, The Evolution of Equal Protection — Education, Municipal Services and Wealth, 7 Harv. Civ. Rights-Civ. Lib. L. Rev. 103, 200-213 (1972).

was the first case to find that discrimination based on wealth results when public education is financed by means of local property taxes, inasmuch as revenues for educational purposes vary from district to district, depending on the tax base. The court found that education is a fundamental right ("the bright hope for entry of the poor and the oppressed into the mainstream of American society"), to which conditions dependent on wealth may not be applied. In the absence of an overriding, compelling state interest, disparity in funding between school districts violates the Equal Protection Clause and a similar provision in the California constitution.

The Serrano case, which reached the California Supreme Court on a demurrer, was sent back for trial. If this case and the cases following it survive their court tests, each affected state legislature will be required to alter its school funding apparatus. But there would be many options as to how this could be done, and an equal number of opportunities for the richer district (whose economic and political muscle enabled them to maintain the present system for so long) to build similar advantages into the new system. Therefore, even with the successes obtained thus far, litigation is expected to drag on for years.

While Serrano based its findings in substantial part on state law, a three-judge court in Rodriguez v. San Antonio Independent School District, 337 F. Supp. 280 (W.D. Tex. 1971), found that disparities in funding among Texas school districts constitute discrimination based on wealth that violates the Equal Protection Clause. The court distinguished the case from earlier litigation in which courts had expressed reluctance to grant requested relief requiring that educational expenditures be made solely on the basis of pupils' educational needs, a standard that "would have involved the court in the type of endless research and evaluation for which the judiciary is ill-suited." See, e.g., McInnis v. Shapiro, 293 F. Supp. 327 (N.D. Ill. 1968), *aff'd mem. sub nom.* McInnis v. Ogilvie, 394 U.S. 322 (1969). But in Rodriguez, the court pointed out:

> Plaintiffs have not advocated that educational expenditures be equal for each child. Rather, they have recommended the application of the principle of "fiscal neutrality." Briefly summarized, this standard requires that the quality of public education may not be a function of wealth, other than the wealth of the state as a whole. Unlike the measure offered in McInnis, this proposal does not involve the Court in the intricacies of affirmatively requiring that expenditures be made in a certain manner or amount. On the contrary, the state may adopt the financial scheme desired so long as the variations in wealth among the governmentally chosen units do not affect spending for the education of any child. (337 F. Supp. at 284.)

On March 21, 1973, the Supreme Court reversed in a 5 to 4 decision. The majority concluded that the Equal Protection Clause of the Constitution does not require "absolute equality or precisely equal advantages," and that the relative poverty of Mexican-American families living in the Edgewood district of San Antonio "has not occasioned an absolute deprivation of the desired [educational] benefit." Thus, the majority concluded, state laws for financing public services should not be declared unconstitutional "merely because the burdens or benefits thereof fall unevenly, depending upon the relative wealth of the political subdivisions in which citizens live." While stating that the Court's action "is not to be viewed as placing its judicial imprimatur on the status quo" in educational finance, Justice Powell, speaking for the majority, expressed the fear that the recommendations in the dissent would have produced "an unprecedented upheaval in public education." Citing the Court's lack of both the expertise and the familiarity with local problems necessary to the making of wise decisions regarding the raising and disposition of public revenues, Justice Powell wrote, "the judiciary is well advised to refrain from interposing on the states inflexible constitutional restraints that could circumscribe or handicap . . . continued research and experimentation."

But Justice Marshall, speaking for the four dissenters, expressed doubt that parents — like the plaintiff in this case — could persuade a legislature to rewrite the education spending formulas in their favor. Calling the decision "a retreat from our historic commitment to equality of educational opportunity," and an "unsupportable acquiescence in a system which deprives children in their earliest years of the chance to reach their full potential as citizens," Justice Marshall predicted that, while awaiting an ultimate political solution sometime in the indefinite future, "countless children unjustifiably receive inferior educations that 'may affect their hearts and minds in a way unlikely ever to be undone.'" San Antonio Independent School District v. Rodriguez, 411 U.S. 1, 93 S. Ct. 1278, 36 L. Ed. 2d 16 (1973).

Despite the decision in Rodriguez, some state courts may follow Serrano and invalidate school funding statutes on state grounds; but, as suggested above, implementation will require more years of legislative debate, manipulation, circumvention and delay. Ghetto schools are likely to need more than equal dollars even to approach the quality of suburban schools, but no court has yet recognized a legal right to such an entitlement. Indeed, since the Serrano decision has nothing to do with the special needs of either urban or rural schools, it may hurt some cities that are above average in assessed property value per pupil, such as New York, San Francisco, Los Angeles and Chicago. Other cities that are well below the average will be helped: Newark, Elizabeth, San Diego, Fresno, all the cities in Kansas and some in Illinois.*

* Coons, Fairness in the Distribution of Education, 1972 U. Ill. L.F. 215, 221. Professor Coons also cites other limitations on the scope of the decision.

The law review commentators have had a field day with Serrano. Predictably, the liberal activists have been supportive of the concepts embodied in the California court's decision (see, e.g., Karst, Serrano v. Priest: A State Court's Responsibilities and Opportunities in the Development of Federal Constitutional Law, 60 U. Cal. L. Rev. 720 (1972)), and those who decry every progressive social decision as an invalid court intrusion on the legislative perogative have now included Serrano in their condemnations. See, e.g., Kur-

Finally, there is little proof that school inputs (dollars) have much relation to school outputs (student achievement), nor are there clear standards for defining, much less measuring, "achievement."†

There is, of course, an entitlement to equality of state educational expenditures, even without proof that the reduction of the disparity will result in a measurable increase in student achievement. As Professor Coons stated, in J. Coons, W. Cline and S. Sugarman, Private Wealth and Public Education 30 (1970), "Whatever it is that money may be thought to contribute to the education of children, that commodity is something highly prized by those who enjoy the greatest measure of it. If money is inadequate to improve education, the residents of poor districts should at least have an equal opportunity to be disappointed by its failure."

---

land, Equal Educational Opportunity: The Limits of Constitutional Jurisprudence Undefined, 35 U. Chi. L. Rev. 583 (1968). But even those recognizing the need for reform in educational financing are concerned as to whether compliance with Serrano will further the aim of equal educational opportunity. Goldstein, Interdistrict Inequalities in School Financing: A Critical Analysis of Serrano v. Priest and Its Progeny, 120 U. Pa. L. Rev. 504 (1972); Dimond, Serrano: A Victory of Sorts for Ethics, Not Necessarily for Education, 2 Yale Rev. of Law and Social Action 133 (1971).

† The Coleman Report in 1966 contained data tending to show that there is little or no relationship between dollars spent in a school and the measurable cognitive skills of its graduates. Office of Education, U.S. Dept. HEW, Equality of Educational Opportunity (1966). More recent data has led some to assert the correctness of the Coleman Report conclusions. See, e.g., Jencks, The Coleman Report and the Conventional Wisdom, in On Equality of Educational Opportunity 69 (F. Mosteller and D. Moynihan, eds. 1972).

Part IV

RIGHTS TO HOUSING

In 1968, the Kerner Commission named segregated housing as among the ingredients of the explosive mixture accumulating in our cities since World War II. It is in the black ghettos, said the commission, that "segregation and poverty converge on the young to destroy opportunity and enforce failure. Crime, drug addiction, dependency on welfare, and bitterness and resentment against society in general and white society in particular are the result." National Advisory Commission on Civil Disorders 5 (1968).

But, as Litwack indicates below, black ghettos did not originate in the post-war period; and despite what has become a comparatively large array of remedies to combat individual discrimination in housing, little has been done to eliminate the ghettos. They remain today as they were when the nation's most physical manifestation of racial injustice began in the nineteenth century. Indeed, overt and institutional racial prejudice — in federal and local housing and redevelopment laws, financing policies, and realtor practices — have all served to increase the apartheidlike nature of the country's residential areas.

Litigation generally has provided only spasmodic relief, often of a temporary nature. Paradoxically, federal courts that grant broad relief in school desegregation cases lessen chances for meaningful implementation of school orders, by refusing to condemn urban development plans and suburban zoning schemes which maintain the confinement of all but the few successful blacks in ghetto areas, usually isolated from decent housing, schools and jobs.

11. HOUSING REMEDIES FOR INDIVIDUAL BLACKS

L. LITWACK, NORTH OF SLAVERY: THE NEGRO IN THE FREE STATES 1790-1860 *168-170 (1961)**

Economic exploitation and segregation produced the Negro ghetto. In Boston, Negroes congregated on "Nigger Hill" and along the wharves in

"New Guinea"; in Cincinnati, they crowded into wooden shacks and shanties in "Little Africa"; in New York, they concentrated in a few wards and mixed with poor whites in the notorious "Five Points," described by one visitor as "but a step into Hades" and "the worst hell of America"; and in Philadelphia, they settled in gloomy cellars and squalid houses located along narrow courts and alleys. Although some observers also pointed to the remarkable number of fine houses owned by Negroes in attractive neighborhoods, few could turn their eyes from the squalor of the Negro slums or deny their existence. To southern visitors in the North, such conditions demonstrated the folly of emancipation. "Thar they was," one southerner wrote, "covered with rags and dirt, livin in houses and cellars, without hardly any furniture; and sum of 'em without dores or winders. . . . This, thinks I, is nigger freedom; this is the condition to which the filanthropists of the North wants to bring the happy black people of the South!"

Such surroundings obviously had their impact on the general health of the Negro residents. In New York City, tuberculosis proved fatal to twice as many blacks as whites, a reflection of adverse living conditions. Philadelphia's coroner attributed the high mortality rate in Negro districts to intemperance, exposure, and malnutrition. After conducting an inspection in 1848, he reported that many Negroes had been "found dead in cold and exposed rooms and garrets, board shanties five and six feet high, and as many feet square, erected and rented for lodging purposes, mostly without any comforts, save the bare floor, with the cold penetrating between the boards, and through the holes and crevices on all sides." Some bodies had been recovered "in cold, wet, and damp cellars," while still others had been found lying in back yards and alleys. Most of these Negroes had sold rags and bones for a living. Not too far away, however, middle- and upper-class Negroes maintained some respectable living quarters.

The vigorous exclusion of Negroes from white residential neighborhoods made escape from the ghetto virtually impossible. The fear of depreciated property values overrode virtually every other consideration. As early as 1793, the attempt to locate "a Negro hut" in Salem, Massachusetts, prompted a white minister to protest that such buildings depreciated property, drove out decent residents, and generally injured the welfare of the neighborhood. Some years later, New Haven petitioners complained that the movement of Negroes into previously white neighborhoods deteriorated real estate values from 20 to 50 per cent; an Indianan asserted that the proposed establishment of a Negro tract would reduce the value of nearby white-owned lots by at least 50 per cent. Obviously, then, the Negro had to be contained in his own area. Thus when a Boston Negro schoolmistress considered moving to a better neighborhood, the inhabitants of the block where she proposed to settle resolved either to eject her or to destroy the house. By 1847, the residents of South Boston could boast that "not a single colored family" lived among them — only immigrants "of the better class who will not live in cellars."

Although whites frequently deprecated the Negro slums, some profited from them. In Cincinnati's Little Africa, for example, whites owned most of the wooden shacks and shanties and protested the attempt of municipal authorities to bar further construction of wooden buildings in the center of town. "Heaven preserve the shanties," a Cincinnati editor sarcastically remarked, "and supply the proprietors with tenants from whom the rent can be screwed, without respect to color or character." While white critics continued to deplore Negro housing conditions, white landlords made few, if any, improvements. Both conveniently concluded that Negroes naturally lived that way. . . .

Litwack's description of housing for Northern blacks in the middle of the nineteenth century — generally segregated and exploitative — improved but little during the next hundred years. The legal history is traced in Shelley v. Kraemer, set forth below.

SHELLEY v. KRAEMER
334 U.S. 1, 68 S. Ct. 836, 92 L. Ed. 1161 (1948)

Mr. Chief Justice Vinson delivered the opinion of the Court.

[Cases from Missouri and Michigan each attacked the validity of court enforcement of restrictive covenants that were intended to exclude persons of the designated race or color from owning or occupying real property covered by the agreements. In the Missouri case, a 1911 agreement signed by thirty of thirty-nine owners of property in a St. Louis community provided that for fifty years the land would not be "occupied by any person not of the Caucasian race, it being intended hereby to restrict the use of said property . . . against the occupancy . . . by people of the Negro or Mongolian Race." Some blacks lived in the district covered by the agreement. In 1945, Shelley, the black petitioner, without actual knowledge of the restrictive covenant purchased one of the covered parcels. Owners of other property subject to the agreement initiated suit to restrain Shelley from taking possession and to return title from him to the seller. The trial court refused relief on a technical ground, but the Missouri Supreme Court reversed and directed the trial court to grant the requested relief. The Michigan case presented similar circumstances, with the Michigan Supreme Court upholding the racially restrictive covenant in that case: ordering the black purchasers to move from the property and enjoining its future use or occupancy by them.

In both cases, the petitioners relied on contentions raised in the state courts that judicial enforcement of the restrictive agreements violated rights guaranteed by the Fourteenth Amendment.]

I

Whether the equal protection clause of the Fourteenth Amendment inhibits judicial enforcement by state courts of restrictive covenants based on race or color is a question which this Court has not heretofore been called upon to consider. Only two cases have been decided by this Court which in any way have involved the enforcement of such agreements. The first of these was the case of Corrigan v. Buckley, 1926, 271 U.S. 323 . . . . There, suit was brought in the courts of the District of Columbia to enjoin a threatened violation of certain restrictive covenants relating to lands situated in the city of Washington. Relief was granted, and the case was brought here on appeal. It is apparent that the case, which had originated in the federal courts and involved the enforcement of covenants on land located in the District of Columbia, could present no issues under the Fourteenth Amendment; for that Amendment by its terms applies only to the States. Nor was the question of the validity of court enforcement of the restrictive covenants under the Fifth Amendment properly before the Court, as the opinion of this Court specifically recognizes. The only constitutional issue which the appellants had raised in the lower courts, and hence the only constitutional issue before this Court on appeal, was the validity of the covenant agreements as such. This Court concluded that since the inhibitions of the constitutional provisions invoked, apply only to governmental action, as contrasted to action of private individuals, there was no showing that the covenants, which were simply agreements between private property owners, were invalid. Accordingly, the appeal was dismissed for want of a substantial question. Nothing in the opinion of this Court, therefore, may properly be regarded as an adjudication on the merits of the constitutional issues presented by these cases, which raise the question of the validity, not of the private agreements as such, but of the judicial enforcement of those agreements.

The second of the cases involving racial restrictive covenants was Hansberry v. Lee, 1940, 311 U.S. 32 . . . . In that case, petitioners, white property owners, were enjoined by the state courts from violating the terms of a restrictive agreement. The state Supreme Court had held petitioners bound by an earlier judicial determination, in litigation in which petitioners were not parties, upholding the validity of the restrictive agreement, although, in fact, the agreement had not been signed by the number of owners necessary to make it effective under state law. This Court reversed the judgment of the state Supreme Court upon the ground that petitioners had been denied due process of law in being held estopped to challenge the validity of the agreement on the theory, accepted by the state court, that the earlier litigation, in which petitioners did not participate, was in the nature of a class suit. In arriving at its result, this Court did not reach the issues presented by the cases now under consideration.

It is well, at the outset, to scrutinize the terms of the restrictive agreements involved in these cases. In the Missouri case, the covenant declares that no part of the affected property shall be . . . "occupied by any person not of the Caucasian race, it being intended hereby to restrict the use of said property . . . against the occupancy as owners or tenants of any portion of said property for resident or other purpose by people of the Negro or Mongolian Race." Not only does the restriction seek to proscribe use and occupancy of the affected properties by members of the excluded class, but as construed by the Missouri courts, the agreement requires that title of any person who uses his property in violation of the restriction shall be divested. The restriction of the covenant in the Michigan case seeks to bar occupancy by persons of the excluded class. It provides that . . . "This property shall not be used or occupied by any person or persons except those of the Caucasian race."

It should be observed that these covenants do not seek to proscribe any particular use of the affected properties. Use of the properties for residential occupancy, as such, is not forbidden. The restrictions of these agreements, rather, are directed toward a designated class of persons and seek to determine who may and who may not own or make use of the properties for residential purposes. The excluded class is defined wholly in terms of race or color; "simply that and nothing more."

It cannot be doubted that among the civil rights intended to be protected from discriminatory state action by the Fourteenth Amendment are the rights to acquire, enjoy, own and dispose of property. Equality in the enjoyment of property rights was regarded by the framers of that Amendment as an essential pre-condition to the realization of other basic civil rights and liberties which the Amendment was intended to guarantee. Thus, §1978 of the Revised Statutes, derived from §1 of the Civil Rights Act of 1866 which was enacted by Congress while the Fourteenth Amendment was also under consideration, provides: "All citizens of the United States shall have the same right in every State and Territory, as is enjoyed by white citizens thereof to inherit, purchase, lease, sell, hold, and convey real and personal property."

This Court has given specific recognition to the same principle. Buchanan v. Warley, 1917, 245 U.S. 60 . . . .

It is likewise clear that restrictions on the right of occupancy of the sort sought to be created by the private agreements in these cases could not be squared with the requirements of the Fourteenth Amendment if imposed by state statute or local ordinance. We do not understand respondents to urge the contrary. In the case of Buchanan v. Warley, supra, a unanimous Court declared unconstitutional the provisions of a city ordinance which denied to colored persons the right to occupy houses in blocks in which the greater number of houses were occupied by white persons, and imposed similar restrictions on white persons with respect to blocks in which the greater number of houses were occupied by colored persons. During the course of the opinion in that case, this Court stated: "The Fourteenth Amendment and these statutes enacted in furtherance of its purpose operate to qualify and entitle a colored man to acquire property without state legislation discriminating against him solely because of color."

In Harmon v. Tyler, 1927, 273 U.S. 668 . . . a unanimous court, on the authority of Buchanan v. Warley, supra, declared invalid an ordinance which forbade any Negro to establish a home on any property in a white community or any white person to establish a home in a Negro community, "except on the written consent of a majority of the persons of the opposite race inhabiting such community or portion of the City to be affected."

The precise question before this Court in both the Buchanan and Harmon cases, involved the rights of white sellers to dispose of their properties free from restrictions as to potential purchasers based on considerations of race or color. But that such legislation is also offensive to the rights of those desiring to acquire and occupy property and barred on grounds of race or color, is clear, not only from the language of the opinion in Buchanan v. Warley, supra, but from this Court's disposition of the case of City of Richmond v. Deans, 1930, 281 U.S. 704 . . . . There, a Negro, barred from the occupancy of certain property by the terms of an ordinance similar to that in the Buchanan case, sought injunctive relief in the federal courts to enjoin the enforcement of the ordinance on the grounds that its provisions violated the terms of the Fourteenth Amendment. Such relief was granted, and this Court affirmed, finding the citation of Buchanan v. Warley, supra, and Harmon v. Tyler, supra, sufficient to support its judgment.

But the present cases, unlike those just discussed, do not involve action by state legislatures or city councils. Here the particular patterns of discrimination and the areas in which the restrictions are to operate, are determined, in the first instance, by the terms of agreements among private individuals. Participation of the State consists in the enforcement of the restrictions so defined. The crucial issue with which we are here confronted is whether this distinction removes these cases from the operation of the prohibitory provisions of the Fourteenth Amendment.

Since the decision of this Court in the Civil Rights Cases, 1883, 109 U.S. 3, . . . the principle has become firmly embedded in our constitutional law that the action inhibited by the first section of the Fourteenth Amendment is only such action as may fairly be said to be that of the States. That Amendment erects no shield against merely private conduct, however discriminatory or wrongful.

We conclude, therefore, that the restrictive agreements standing alone cannot be regarded as a violation of any rights guaranteed to petitioners by the Fourteenth Amendment. So long as the purposes of those agreements are effectuated by voluntary adherence to their terms, it would appear clear that there has been no action by the State and the provisions of the Amendment have not been violated. Cf. Corrigan v. Buckley, supra.

But here there was more. These are cases in which the purposes of the agreements were secured only by judicial enforcement by state courts of the restrictive terms of the agreements. The respondents urge that judicial enforcement of private agreements does not amount to state action; or, in any event, the participation of the State is so attenuated in character as not to amount to state action within the meaning of the Fourteenth Amendment. Finally, it is suggested, even if the States in these cases may be deemed to have acted in the constitutional sense, their action did not deprive petitioners of rights guaranteed by the Fourteenth Amendment. We move to a consideration of these matters.

II

That the action of state courts and of judicial officers in their official capacities is to be regarded as action of the State within the meaning of the Fourteenth Amendment, is a proposition which has long been established by decisions of this Court. That principle was given expression in the earliest cases involving the construction of the terms of the Fourteenth Amendment. Thus, in Commonwealth of Virginia v. Rives, 1880, 100 U.S. 313, . . . this Court stated: "It is doubtless true that a State may act through different agencies, — either by its legislative, its executive, or its judicial authorities; and the prohibitions of the amendment extend to all action of the State denying equal protection of the laws, whether it be action by one of these agencies or by another." In Ex parte Commonwealth of Virginia, 1880, 100 U.S. 339, . . . the Court observed: "A State acts by its legislative, its executive, or its judicial authorities. It can act in no other way." . . .

The action of state courts in imposing penalties or depriving parties of other substantive rights without providing adequate notice and opportunity to defend, has, of course, long been regarded as a denial of the due process of law guaranteed by the Fourteenth Amendment. [Citations omitted.]

In numerous cases, this Court has reversed criminal convictions in state courts for failure of those courts to provide the essential ingredients of a fair hearing. Thus it has been held that convictions obtained in state courts under the domination of a mob are void. Moore v. Dempsey, 1923, 261 U.S. 86 . . . . And see Frank v. Mangum, 1915, 237 U.S. 309 . . . . Convictions obtained by coerced confessions, by the use of perjured testimony known by the prosecution to be such, or without the effective assistance of counsel, have also been held to be exertions of state authority in conflict with the fundamental rights protected by the Fourteenth Amendment.

But the examples of state judicial action which have been held by this Court to violate the Amendment's commands are not restricted to situations in which the judicial proceedings were found in some manner to be procedurally unfair. It has been recognized that the action of state courts in enforcing a substantive common-law rule formulated by those courts, may result in the denial of rights guaranteed by the Fourteenth Amendment, even though the judicial proceedings in such cases may have been in complete accord with the most rigorous conceptions of procedural due process. Thus, in American Federation of Labor v. Swing, 1941, 312 U.S. 321, . . . enforcement by state courts of the common-law policy of the State, which resulted in the restraining of peaceful picketing, was held to be state action of the sort prohibited by the Amendment's guaranties of freedom of discussion. In Cantwell v. Connecticut, 1940, 310 U.S. 296, . . . a conviction in a state court of the common-law crime of breach of the peace was, under the circumstances of the case, found to be a violation of the Amendment's commands relating to freedom of religion. In Bridges v. California, 1941, 314 U.S. 252, . . . enforcement of the state's common-law rule relating to contempts by publication was held to be state action inconsistent with the prohibitions of the Fourteenth Amendment. And cf. Chicago, B. & Q. Co. v. Chicago, 1897, 166 U.S. 226....

The short of the matter is that from the time of the adoption of the Fourteenth Amendment until the present, it has been the consistent ruling of this Court that the action of the States to which the Amendment has reference, includes action of state courts and state judicial officials. Although, in construing the terms of the Fourteenth Amendment, differences have from time to time been expressed as to whether particular types of state action may be said to offend the Amendment's prohibitory provisions, it has never been suggested that state court action is immunized from the operation of those provisions simply because the act is that of the judicial branch of the state government.

III

Against this background of judicial construction, extending over a period of some three-quarters of a century, we are called upon to consider whether enforcement by state courts of the restrictive agreements in these cases may be deemed to be the acts of those States; and, if so, whether that action has denied these petitioners the equal protection of the laws which the Amendment was intended to insure.

We have no doubt that there has been state action in these cases in the full and complete sense of the phrase. The undisputed facts disclose that petitioners were willing purchasers of properties upon which they desired to establish homes. The owners of the properties were willing sellers; and contracts of sale were accordingly consummated. It is clear that but for the active intervention of the state courts, supported by the full panoply of state power, petitioners would have been free to occupy the properties in question without restraint.

These are not cases, as has been suggested, in which the States have merely abstained from action, leaving private individuals free to impose such discriminations as they see fit. Rather, these are cases in which States have made available to such individuals the full coercive power of government to deny to petitioners, on the grounds of race or color, the enjoyment of property rights in premises which petitioners are willing and financially able to acquire and which the grantors are willing to sell. The difference between judicial enforcement and nonenforcement of the restrictive covenants is the difference to petitioners between being denied rights of property available to other members of the community and being accorded full enjoyment of those rights on an equal footing.

The enforcement of the restrictive agreements by the state courts in these cases was directed pursuant to the common-law policy of the States as formulated by those courts in earlier decisions. In the Missouri case, enforcement of the covenant was directed in the first instance by the highest court of the State after the trial court had determined the agreement to be invalid for want of the requisite number of signatures. In the Michigan case, the order of enforcement by the trial court was affirmed by the highest state court. The judicial action in each case bears the clear and unmistakable imprimatur of the State. We have noted that previous decisions of this Court have established the proposition that judicial action is not immunized from the operation of the Fourteenth Amendment simply because it is taken pursuant to the state's common-law policy. Nor is the Amendment ineffective simply because the particular pattern of discrimination, which the State has enforced, was defined initially by the terms of a private agreement. State action, as that phrase is understood for the purposes of the Fourteenth Amendment, refers to exertions of state power in all forms. And when the effect of that action is to deny rights subject to the protection of the Fourteenth Amendment, it is the obligation of this Court to enforce the constitutional commands.

We hold that in granting judicial enforcement of the restrictive agreements in these cases, the States have denied petitioners the equal protection of the laws and that, therefore, the action of the state courts cannot stand. We have noted that freedom from discrimination by the States in the enjoyment of property rights was among the basic objectives sought to be effectuated by the framers of the Fourteenth Amendment. That such discrimination has occurred in these cases is clear. Because of the race or color of these petitioners they have been denied rights of ownership or occupancy enjoyed as a matter of course by other citizens of different race or color. . . .

Respondents urge, however, that since the state courts stand ready to enforce restrictive covenants excluding white persons from the ownership or occupancy of property covered by such agreements, enforcement of covenants excluding colored persons may not be deemed a denial of equal protection of the laws to the colored persons who are thereby affected. This contention does not bear scrutiny. The parties have directed our attention to no case in which a court, state or federal, has been called upon to enforce a covenant excluding members of the white majority from ownership or occupancy of real property on grounds of race or color. But there are more fundamental considerations. The rights created by the first section of the Fourteenth Amendment are, by its terms, guaranteed to the individual. The rights established are personal rights. It is, therefore, no answer to these petitioners to say that the courts may also be induced to deny white persons rights of ownership and occupancy on grounds of race or color. Equal protection of the laws is not achieved through indiscriminate imposition of inequalities.

Nor do we find merit in the suggestion that property owners who are parties to these agreements are denied equal protection of the laws if denied access to the courts to enforce the terms of restrictive covenants and to assert property rights which the state courts have held to be created by such agreements. The Constitution confers upon no individual the right to demand action by the State which results in the denial of equal protection of the laws to other individuals. And it would appear beyond question that the power of the State to create and enforce property interests must be exercised within the boundaries defined by the Fourteenth Amendment. Cf. Marsh v. Alabama, 1946, 326 U.S. 501 . . . .

The historical context in which the Fourteenth Amendment became a part of the Constitution should not be forgotten. Whatever else the framers sought to achieve, it is clear that the matter of primary concern was the establishment of equality in the enjoyment of basic civil and political rights and the preservation of those rights from discriminatory action on the part of the States based on considerations of race or color. Seventy-five years ago this Court announced that the provisions of the Amendment are to be construed with this fundamental purpose in mind. Upon full consideration, we have concluded that in these cases the States have acted to deny petitioners the equal protection of the laws guaranteed by the Fourteenth Amendment. Having so decided, we find it unnecessary to consider whether petitioners have also been deprived of property without due process of law or denied privileges and immunities of citizens of the United States.

For the reasons stated, the judgment of the Supreme Court of Missouri and the judgment of the Supreme Court of Michigan must be reversed.

Reversed.

Mr. Justice REED, Mr. Justice JACKSON, and Mr. Justice RUTLEDGE took no part in the consideration or decision of these cases.

NOTES

1. Hurd v. Hodge, 334 U.S. 24, 68 S. Ct. 847, 92 L. Ed. 1187 (1948), was a companion case to Shelley, involving a restrictive covenant in the District of Columbia, where, of course, the Fourteenth Amendment had no application. Nevertheless, the Supreme Court held the covenant unenforceable, relying on 42 U.S.C. §1982. See Jones v. Alfred H. Mayer Company, 392 U.S. 409, 88 S. Ct. 2186, 20 L. Ed. 2d 1189 (1968), printed infra page 626. This statute was held to prohibit enforcement by the courts of racial covenants within the district. The Court did not reach the constitutional question of whether judicial implementation violated the Fifth Amendment's Due Process Clause, but determined that enforcement of the covenants would violate federal public policy.

2. In Barrows v. Jackson, 346 U.S. 249, 73 S. Ct. 1031, 97 L. Ed. 1586 (1953), the Court extended Shelley v. Kraemer by holding that damages could not be awarded by a state court for a breach of a racial restriction. The plaintiffs in the damage suit were white owners of property subject to the covenant, while the defendant, a former white owner, had violated the agreement by selling her land to a black. Thus, while blacks were not directly involved in the litigation, the Court concluded that an award of damages would effectively punish the defendant for failure to continue discriminating against non-Caucasians in the use of her property, which punishment would be the equivalent to state encouragement of restrictive covenants depriving blacks, "unidentified but identifiable," of equal protection of the laws, in

violation of the Fourteenth Amendment. To prevent such result, the Court permitted the white defendant to raise a defense resting on the assertion of another person's right, because "it would be difficult if not impossible for the persons whose rights are asserted to present their grievance before any court." 346 U.S. at 257. Chief Justice Vinson, who had written the majority opinion in Shelley, dissented in Barrows v. Jackson. He felt that defendant had no standing to raise the constitutional issue on behalf of persons not before the Court, and that there was no basis for finding that the rights of non-Caucasians would be impaired by requiring defendant to compensate plaintiffs for the injury which she had brought upon them.

3. The Court's action in the restrictive covenant cases held, in effect, that property owners had a right to enter into restrictive covenants, but no right to have them enforced. The cases precipitated a barrage of law review comment, both supportive and critical. Commentators noted the broad sweep of Shelley, and some expressed concern about the "freedoms" of property owners. See, e.g., Wechsler, Toward Neutral Principles of Constitutional Law, 73 Harv. L. Rev. 1 (1959). Other writers suggested means by which the scope of the opinion might be restricted. Henkin, Shelley v. Kraemer: Notes for a Revised Opinion, 110 U. Pa. L. Rev. 473 (1962); Pollak, Racial Discrimination and Judicial Integrity: A Reply to Professor Wechsler, 108 U. Pa. L. Rev. 1 (1959).

4. But while the commentators were concerned with the principle in Shelley, whites, determined to bar blacks from their neighborhoods, devised a seemingly inexhaustible list of restrictions, many of which took advantage of the Shelley holding that restrictions were valid between the parties. All manner of self-operating cooperatives, associations, and leasing arrangements were devised to protect the racial exclusiveness of white residential areas. Such arrangements were not foolproof, but they added to the barriers facing those few blacks in a position to take advantage of the Shelley decision. C. Abrams, Forbidden Neighbors, 224-225 (1955).

5. The issue of whether the Shelley analysis could be applied to a determinable fee, in which an owner's title would be forfeited upon breach of a racial covenant, brought contradictory results in lower courts. Compare Capitol Federal Savings and Loan Association v. Smith, 136 Colo. 265, 316 P. 2d 252 (1957) (where the court refused to enforce such an agreement) with Charlotte Park and Recreation Commission v. Barringer, 242 N.C. 311, 88 S.E.2d 114 (1955) (permitting such arrangements to have effect).

6. The Supreme Court has held that a will with a racial restriction cannot be administered by state trustees. Pennsylvania v. Board of Directors of City Trust, 353 U.S. 230, 77 S. Ct. 806, 1 L. Ed. 2d 792 (1957). But when city trustees are removed, the Supreme Court has permitted the substitution of private trustees to carry out the testator's discriminatory intent. In re Girard College Trusteeship, 391 Pa. 434, 138 A.2d 844 (1958), *cert. denied sub nom.* Pennsylvania v. Board of Directors of City Trust, 357 U.S. 570, 78 S. Ct. 1383, 2 L. Ed. 2d 1546 (1958).

In later litigation, blacks claimed in a federal court that the racial policy of Girard College violated the Pennsylvania Public Accommodations Act, 18 Pa. St. Ann. §4654, entitling nonracial admission to "all educational institutions under the supervision of this Commonwealth." The court of appeals reversed a district court decree granting relief, holding that federal courts are bound by state court determinations, implicit in early decisions on the subject that the act did not apply to Girard College. Commonwealth of Pennsylvania v. Brown, 373 F.2d 771 (3d Cir. 1967). But in Commonwealth of Pennsylvania v. Brown, 270 F. Supp. 782 (E.D. Pa. 1967), *aff'd* 392 F.2d 120 (3d Cir. 1968), the black litigants were successful, relying on the Supreme Court's decision in Evans v. Newton, 382 U.S. 296, 86 S. Ct. 486, 15 L. Ed. 2d 373 (1966), summarized supra page 220.

In Evans v. Newton, the Court found that while a testator can leave property to one race without raising constitutional issues, where the property had been operated by the city of Macon for many years as a public park, divestment of the city as trustee did not alter the park's generally public nature. It was deemed a public institution subject to the Fourteenth Amendment regardless of who held title under state law.

A subsequent state court decision in the Macon park case permitting the reversion of the property to the testator's heirs, because the purpose of the trust (to operate a segregated park) had failed, was held a matter of state law, not involving illegal "state action." Evans v. Abney, 396 U.S. 435, 90 S. Ct. 628, 24 L. Ed. 2d 634 (1970), summarized supra page 219.

7. Few expected that housing discrimination would be eliminated through use of the Shelley v. Kraemer principle. Efforts to enact fair housing laws at the state and local levels began in the 1940s, but few were enacted until the 1950s, and none without great resistance, particularly from real estate groups. The measures generally required the filing of individual complaints before commissions, which, when "probable cause" was found, had to exhaust efforts to secure voluntary compliance before imposing penalties or seeking judicial relief. See, e.g., Pearl and Terner, Fair Housing Laws: Halfway Mark, 54 Geo. L.J. 156 (1965). Although their effectiveness was never impressive, a number of efforts were made in the late 1960s to repeal these legislative attempts to curb discrimination in housing. The major litigation is reviewed below.

REITMAN v. MULKEY

387 U.S. 369, 87 S. Ct. 1627, 18 L. Ed. 2d 830 (1967)

Mr. Justice White delivered the opinion of the Court.

The question here is whether Art. I, §26, of the California Constitution denies "to any person . . . the equal protection of the laws" within the meaning of the Fourteenth Amendment of the Constitution of the United States. Section 26 of Art. I, an initiated measure submitted to the people as Proposiion 14 in a statewide ballot in 1964, provides in part as follows:

> Neither the State nor any subdivision or agency thereof shall deny, limit or abridge, directly or indirectly, the right of any person, who is willing or desires to sell, lease or rent any part or all of his real property, to decline to sell, lease or rent such property to such person or persons as he, in his absolute discretion, chooses.

The real property covered by §26 is limited to residential property and contains an exception for state-owned real estate.

The issue arose in two separate actions in the California courts, Mulkey v Reitman and Prendergast v Snyder. In Reitman, the Mulkeys, who are husband and wife and respondents here, sued under §51 and §52 of the California Civil Code alleging that petitioners had refused to rent them an apartment solely on account of their race. An injunction and damages were demanded. Petitioners moved for summary judgment on the ground that §§51 and 52, insofar as they were the basis for the Mulkeys' action, had been rendered null and void by the adoption of Proposition 14 after the filing of the complaint. The trial court granted the motion and respondents took the case to the California Supreme Court.

In the Prendergast case, respondents, husband and wife, filed suit in December 1964 seeking to enjoin eviction from their apartment; respondents alleged that the eviction was motivated by racial prejudice and therefore would violate §51 and §52 of the Civil Code. Petitioner Snyder cross-complained for a judicial declaration that he was entitled to terminate the month-to-month tenancy even if his action was based on racial considerations. In denying petitioner's motion for summary judgment, the trial court found it unnecessary to consider the validity of Proposition 14 because it concluded that judicial enforcement of an eviction based on racial grounds would in any event violate the Equal Protection Clause of the United States Constitution. The cross-complaint was dismissed with prejudice and petitioner Snyder appealed to the California Supreme Court which considered the case along with Mulkey v Reitman. That court, in reversing the Reitman case, held that Art. I, §26, was invalid as denying the equal protection of the laws guaranteed by the Fourteenth Amendment. 64 Cal 2d 529, 413 P2d 825. For similar reasons, the court affirmed the judgment in the Prendergast case. 64 Cal 2d 877, 413 P2d 847. We granted certiorari because the cases involve an important issue arising under the Fourteenth Amendment. 385 US 967 . . . .

We affirm the judgments of the California Supreme Court. We first turn to the opinion of that court in Reitman, which quite properly undertook to examine the constitutionality of §26 in terms of its "immediate objective," its "ultimate effect" and its "historical context and the conditions existing prior to its enactment." Judgments such as these we have frequently undertaken ourselves. . . . But here the California Supreme Court has addressed itself to these matters and we should give careful consideration to its views because they concern the purpose, scope, and operative effect of a provision of the California Constitution.

First, the court considered whether §26 was concerned at all with private discriminations in residential housing. This involved a review of past efforts by the California Legislature to regulate such discriminations. The Unruh Act, Civ. Code §§51-52, on which respondents based their cases, was passed in 1959. The Hawkins Act, formerly Health & Safety Code §§35700-35741, followed and prohibited discriminations in publicly assisted housing. In 1961, the legislature enacted proscriptions against restrictive covenants. Finally, in 1963, came the Rumford Fair Housing Act, Health & Safety Code §§35700-35744 superseding the Hawkins Act and prohibiting racial discriminations in the sale or rental of any private dwelling containing more than four units. That act was enforceable by the State Fair Employment Practice Commission.

It was against this background that Proposition 14 was enacted. Its immediate design and intent, the California court said, were "to overturn state laws that bore on the right of private sellers and lessors to discriminate," the Unruh and Rumford Acts, and "to forestall future state action that might circumscribe this right." This aim was successfully achieved: the adoption of Proposition 14 "generally nullifies both the Rumford and Unruh Acts as they apply to the housing market," and establishes "a purported constitutional right to *privately* discriminate on grounds which admittedly would be unavailable under the Fourteenth Amendment *should state action* be involved."

Second, the court conceded that the State was permitted a neutral position with respect to private racial discriminations and that the State was not bound by the Federal Constitution to forbid them. But, because a significant state involvement in private discriminations could amount to unconstitutional state action, Burton v Wilmington Parking Authority, 365 US 715, . . . the court deemed it necessary to determine whether Proposition 14 invalidly involved the State in racial discriminations in the housing market. Its conclusion was that it did.

To reach this result, the state court examined certain prior decisions in this Court in which discriminatory state action was identified. Based on these cases, Robinson v Florida, 378 US 153, 156 . . . ; Anderson v Martin, 375 US 399 . . . ; Barrows v Jackson, 346 US 249, 254 . . . ; McCabe v Atchison, Topeka & Santa Fe R. Co., 235 US 151, . . . it concluded that a prohibited state involvement could be found "even where the state can be charged with only encouraging", rather than commanding discrimination. Also of particular interest to the court was Mr. Justice Stewart's concurrence in Burton v Wilmington Parking Authority, 365 US 715, 726, . . . where it was said that the Delaware courts had construed an existing Delaware statute as "authorizing" racial discrimination in restaurants and that the statute was therefore invalid. To the California court "[t]he instant case presents an undeniably analogous situation" wherein the State had taken affirmative action designed to make private discriminations legally possible. Section 26 was said to have changed the situation from one in which discrimination was restricted "to one wherein it is encouraged, within the meaning of the cited decisions"; §26 was legislative action "which authorized private discrimination" and made the State "at least a partner in the instant act of discrimination . . . ." The court could "conceive of no other purpose for an application of section 26 aside from authorizing the perpetration of a purported private discrimination . . . ." The judgment of the California court was that §26 unconstitutionally involves the State in racial discriminations and is therefore invalid under the Fourteenth Amendment.

There is no sound reason for rejecting this judgment. Petitioners contend that the California court has misconstrued the Fourteenth Amendment since the repeal of any statute prohibiting racial discrimination, which is constitutionally permissible, may be said to "authorize" and "encourage" discrimination because it makes legally permissible that which was formerly proscribed. But, as we understand the California court, it did not posit a constitutional violation on the mere repeal of the Unruh and Rumford Acts. It did not read either our cases or the Fourteenth Amendment as establishing an automatic constitutional barrier to the repeal of an existing law prohibiting racial discriminations in housing; nor did the court rule that a State may never put in statutory form an existing policy of neutrality with respect to private discriminations. What the court below did was first to reject the notion that the State was required to have a statute prohibiting racial discriminations in housing. Second, it held the intent of §26 was to authorize private racial discriminations in the housing market, to repeal the Unruh and Rumford Acts and to create a constitutional right to discriminate on racial grounds in the sale and leasing of real property. Hence, the court dealt with §26 as though it expressly authorized and constitutionalized the private right to discriminate. Third, the court assessed the ultimate impact of §26 in the California environment and concluded that the section would encourage and significantly involve the State in private racial discrimination contrary to the Fourteenth Amendment.

The California court could very reasonably conclude that §26 would and did have wider impact than a mere repeal of existing statutes. Section 26 mentioned neither the Unruh nor Rumford Act in so many words. Instead, it announced the constitutional right of any person to decline to sell or lease his real property to anyone to whom he did not desire to sell or lease. Unruh and Rumford were thereby pro tanto repealed. But the section struck more deeply and more widely. Private discriminations in housing were now not only free from Rumford and Unruh but they also enjoyed a far different status than was true before the passage of those statutes. The right to discriminate, including the right to discriminate on racial grounds, was now embodied in the State's basic charter, immune from legislative, executive, or judicial regulation at any level of the state government. Those practicing racial discriminations need no longer rely solely on their personal choice. They could now invoke express constitutional authority, free from censure or interference of any kind from official sources. All individuals, partnerships, corporations and other legal entities, as well as their agents and representatives, could now discriminate with respect to their residential real property, which is defined as any interest in real property of any kind or quality, "irrespective of how obtained or financed," and seemingly irrespective of the relationship of the State to such interests in real property. Only the State is excluded with respect to property owned by it.

The Court has never attempted the "impossible task" of formulating an infallible test for determining whether the State "in any of its manifestations" has become significantly involved in private discriminations. "Only by sifting facts and weighing circumstances" on a case-by-case basis can a "non-obvious involvement of the State in private conduct be attributed its true significance." Burton v Wilmington Parking Authority, 365 US 715 . . . . Here the California court, armed as it was with the knowledge of the facts and circumstances concerning the passage and potential impact of §26, and familiar with the milieu in which that provision would operate, has determined that the provision would involve the State in private racial discriminations to an unconstitutional degree. We accept this holding of the California court.

The assessment of §26 by the California court is similar to what this Court has done in appraising state statutes or other official actions in other contexts. In McCabe v Atchison, Topeka & Santa Fe R. Co., 235 US 151, . . . the Court dealt with a statute which, as construed by the Court, authorized carriers to provide cars for white persons but not for Negroes. Though dismissal of the complaint on a procedural ground was affirmed, the Court made it clear that such a statute was invalid under the Fourteenth Amendment because a carrier refusing equal service to Negroes would be "acting in the matter under the authority of a state law." This was nothing less than considering a permissive state statute as an authorization to discriminate and as sufficient state action to violate the Fourteenth Amendment in the context of that case. Similarly, in Nixon v Condon, 286 US 73, . . . the Court was faced with a statute empowering the executive committee of a political party to prescribe the qualifications of its members for voting or for other participation, but containing no directions with respect to the exercise of that power. This was authority which the committee otherwise might not have had and which was used by the committee to bar Negroes from voting in primary elections. Reposing this power in the executive committee was said to insinuate the State into the self-regulatory, decision-making scheme of the voluntary association; the exercise of the power was viewed as an expression of state authority contrary to the Fourteenth Amendment.

In Burton v Wilmington Parking Authority, 365 US 715, . . . the operator-lessee of a restaurant located in a building owned by the State and otherwise operated for public purposes, refused service to Negroes. Although the State neither commanded nor expressly authorized or encouraged the discriminations, the State had "elected to place its power, property, and prestige behind the admitted discrimination" and by "its inaction . . . has . . . made itself a party to the refusal of service . . ." which therefore could not be considered the purely private choice of the restaurant operator.

In Peterson v City of Greenville, 373 US 244, . . . and in Robinson v Florida, 378 US 153, . . . the Court dealt with state statutes or regulations requiring, at least in some respects, segregation in facilities and services in restaurants. These official provisions, although obviously unconstitutional and unenforceable, were deemed in themselves sufficient to disentitle the State to punish, as trespassers, Negroes who had been refused service in the restaurants. In neither case was any proof required that the restaurant owner had actually been influenced by the state statute or regulation. Finally, in Lombard v Louisiana, 373 US 267, . . . the Court interpreted public statements by New Orleans city officials as announcing that the city would not permit Negroes to seek desegregated service in restaurants. Because the statements were deemed to have as much coercive potential as the ordinance in the Peterson case, the Court treated the city as though it had actually adopted an ordinance forbidding desegregated service in public restaurants.

None of these cases squarely controls the case we now have before us. But they do illustrate the range of situations in which discriminatory state action has been identified. They do exemplify the necessity for a court to assess the potential impact of official action in determining whether the State has significantly involved itself with invidious discriminations. Here we are dealing with a provision which does not just repeal an existing law forbidding private racial discriminations. Section 26 was intended to authorize, and does authorize, racial discrimination in the housing market. The right to discriminate is now one of the basic policies of the State. The California Supreme Court believes that the section will significantly encourage and involve the State in private discriminations. We have been presented with no persuasive considerations indicating that these judgments should be overturned.

Affirmed.

HUNTER v. ERICKSON, 393 U.S. 385, 89 S. Ct. 557, 21 L. Ed. 2d 616 (1969). In 1964, the Akron, Ohio City Council enacted a fair housing ordinance. It was premised on a recognition of the social and economic losses to society flowing from substandard ghetto housing, and it declared that the city's policy was to "Assure equal opportunity to all persons to live in decent housing facilities regardless of race, color, religion, ancestry or national origin." Subsequently, an amendment to the city charter was proposed requiring that any law dealing with the rental or sale of real property which pertained to race, color, religion, national origin or ancestry must first be approved by a majority of the electors at the next regular city election. Upon petition of more than 10 percent of Akron's voters, the charter amendment proposal was placed on the ballot and duly passed by a majority of voters at the next general election. Suit was filed on behalf of a black woman seeking to utilize the provisions of the fair housing ordinance.

The Supreme Court invalidated the charter amendment on the ground that it discriminated on racial or religious grounds, against groups seeking the law's protection, by setting up a new procedure of lawmaking which was more complex than the method used with regard to any other group. Although the law purported to apply to all races and religions, the Court held that its effect was to make it virtually impossible for certain minorities to secure protective legislation. The Court stated further that it was unimpressed with the state's justification of its action as simply a public decision to move slowly in the delicate area of race relations. The Court pointed out that the city already had a procedure which allowed a law passed by the city council to be passed upon by the electorate if 10 percent thereof filed a petition for a special election. Such a procedure would have been valid because of its neutrality in application, the Court asserted. In a concurring opinion, Justice Harlan, joined by Justice Stewart, said that a law which is neutral in its application is permissible even though it may sometimes make it more difficult for minorities to obtain legislation. The Akron charter amendment, however, was not neutral since it had the clear purpose of making it more difficult for religious and racial minorities to achieve legislation in their interest. Justice Black dissented on the grounds that the city had the right to repeal the fair housing law and that the Court's decision denied the city the power to do so. Black was shocked that in a government "of the people, for the people and by the people," Akron's conditioning the enactment of a law on a majority vote of the people condemns that law as unconstitutional.

NOTES

1. In a somewhat similar case, the city council of Toledo, Ohio enacted a fair housing ordinance. Local citizens subsequently utilized provisions within the city charter to subject the new law to a referendum election in which it was disapproved by a vote of more than two to one. The city charter provided that "After the people have legislated for themselves, either by initiating legislation or passing favorably or unfavorably upon legislation referred to them by any body, their action is final and shall not be subject to amendment or repeal, without a general vote of the people of Toledo on same." Thus, the effect of the referendum was to remove the question of fair housing practices from the jurisdiction of the city council and place it in the hands of the majority of the electorate. The Ohio Supreme Court affirmed the procedure, asserting that no substantial constitutional question existed. The Supreme Court denied certiorari. Holland v. The Lucas County Board of Elections, *cert. denied,* 393 U.S. 1080, 89 S. Ct. 849, 21 L. Ed. 2d 772 (1969).

2. Similarly, in Spaulding v. Blair, 403 F.2d 862 (4th Cir. 1968), the court refused to enjoin a referendum aimed at overturning an open-housing statute enacted the previous year. The referendum was to be held under Maryland's constitutional provision allowing the electorate to pass on any legislation upon petition of a sufficient number of citizens. When a referendum is called for, the statute does not take effect until after its approval by the voters. In affirming dismissal of the suit, the Fourth Circuit distin-

guished Reitman by finding that the Maryland referendum did not impermissibly involve the state in private racial discrimination by expressly protecting the right to discriminate and forbidding the legislature to interfere with its exercise. Here, the statute had not gone into effect, and its rejection by the voters could not diminish the rights of any individual or group. The court found the referendum neutral, and even rejection of the fair housing legislation would not constitute forbidden involvement.

3. But in Ofey v. Common Council, 281 F. Supp. 264 (E.D. Wis. 1968), the court enjoined a municipal referendum on a proposed resolution which would have barred the city council from enacting any law restricting the right of owners to sell, lease or rent private property. After a trial the court, citing Reitman v. Mulkey, supra, found that the purpose of the proposed resolution was to protect private racial discrimination from official interference.

4. The Supreme Court did affirm, without opinion, a state court holding that the principles in Reitman justified voiding a statute which prohibited the assignment of students or the establishment of school districts for the purpose of achieving racial equality in attendance, unless such action was taken with the express approval of a locally elected school board or with the consent of the parents. Lee v. Nyquist, 318 F. Supp. 710 (W.D.N.Y. 1970), *aff'd without opinion,* 402 U.S. 935, 91 S. Ct. 1618, 29 L. Ed 2d 105 (1971), summarized supra page 513.

5. Professor Charles Black asserts that an unjustified respect which courts continue to pay to the "state action" concept results in inconsistent and unfair results, unnecessarily prolonging the extinction of legally authorized racism in this country. Black, Foreword: "State Action," Equal Protection, and California's Proposition 14, 81 Harv. L. Rev. 69 (1967). The continuing problem of what is and what is not state action leads to the issues in the following questions.

QUESTIONS

1. Do decisions like Holland and Spaulding point the way for a "neutral" use of referenda to defeat legislation intended to protect minorities against racial or religious discrimination? Consider the extent to which communities have learned the lesson when reviewing, in Chapter 12, Section C, cases in which the referendum is used to defeat zoning measures permitting the construction of low-income housing.

2. Are the decisions in Reitman and Nyquist distinguishable from the results in Holland and Spaulding, in that the former cases concern efforts to overturn pre-existing rights and thus may have a racially discriminatory effect? If so, what of Justice Black's concern that the people should have an absolute right to repeal legislation deemed objectionable to them?

3. Is it possible to explain how state legislatures and city councils are convinced by civil rights groups to enact fair housing and other civil rights legislation, which, as the cases discussed above show, are opposed by the majority of the electorate? Are the public nature of lawmaking and the secrecy of the ballot influencing factors?

JONES v. ALFRED H. MAYER CO.

392 U.S. 409, 88 S. Ct. 2186, 20 L. Ed. 2d 1189 (1968)

Mr. Justice STEWART delivered the opinion of the Court.

In this case we are called upon to determine the scope and constitutionality of an Act of Congress, 42 U.S.C. §1982, which provides that:

> All citizens of the United States shall have the same right, in every State and Territory, as is enjoyed by white citizens thereof to inherit, purchase, lease, sell, hold, and convey real and personal property.

On September 2, 1965, the petitioners filed a complaint in the District Court for the Eastern District of Missouri, alleging that the respondents had refused to sell them a home in the Paddock Woods community of St. Louis County for the sole reason that petitioner Joseph Lee Jones is a Negro. Relying in part upon §1982, the petitioners sought injunctive and other relief. The District Court sustained the respondents' motion to dismiss the complaint, and the Court of Appeals for the Eighth Circuit affirmed, concluding that §1982 applies only to state action and does not reach private refusals to sell. We granted certiorari to consider the questions thus presented. For the reasons that follow, we reverse the judgment of the Court of Appeals. We hold that §1982 bars *all* racial discrimination, private as well as public, in the sale or rental of property, and that the statute, thus construed, is a valid exercise of the power of Congress to enforce the Thirteenth Amendment.

I

At the outset, it is important to make clear precisely what this case does *not* involve. Whatever else it may be, 42 U.S.C. §1982 is not a comprehensive open housing law.* In sharp contrast to the Fair Housing Title (Title VIII) of the Civil Rights Act of 1968, Pub. L. 90-284, 82 Stat. 81, the statute in this case deals only with racial discrimination and does not address itself to discrimination on grounds of religion or national origin. It does not deal specifically with discrimination in the provision of services or facilities in connection with the sale or rental of a dwelling. It does not prohibit adver-

* The text of Title VIII is printed in the Appendix infra. The value of §1982 as an alternative remedy for individual victims of housing discrimination is apparent from the far broader coverage of the older civil rights law. Unlike Title VIII, relief under §1982 does not depend on the bureaucratic uncertainties of a governmental agency that, as experience has shown, may lack adequate staff, suffer from political interference, and hinder its own effectiveness with overcautious procedures, unnecessary delays, protracted conciliation efforts and efficiency-killing jurisdictional wrangles with state and local commissions.

tising or other representations that indicate discriminatory preferences. It does not refer explicitly to discrimination in financing arrangements or in the provision of brokerage services. It does not empower a federal administrative agency to assist aggrieved parties. It makes no provision for intervention by the Attorney General. And, although it can be enforced by injunction, it contains no provision expressly authorizing a federal court to order the payment of damages.

Thus, although §1982 contains none of the exemptions that Congress included in the Civil Rights Act of 1968, it would be a serious mistake to suppose that §1982 in any way diminishes the significance of the law recently enacted by Congress. . . .

II

[Here, the Court reviews its earlier decisions in the restrictive covenant cases and applicable decisions by lower courts, and concludes that the question of whether §1982 applies to purely private racial discrimination has not been squarely raised in any prior cases.]

III

We begin with the language of the statute itself. In plain and unambiguous terms, §1982 grants to all citizens, without regard to race or color, "the same right" to purchase and lease property "as is enjoyed by white citizens." As the Court of Appeals in this case evidently recognized, that right can be impaired as effectively by "those who place property on the market" as by the State itself. For, even if the State and its agents lend no support to those who wish to exclude persons from their communities on racial grounds, the fact remains that, whenever property "is placed on the market for whites only, whites have a right denied to Negroes." So long as a Negro citizen who wants to buy or rent a home can be turned away simply because he is not white, he cannot be said to enjoy "the *same* right . . . as is enjoyed by white citizens . . . to . . . purchase [and] lease . . . real and personal property." 42 U.S.C. §1982. (Emphasis added.)

On its face, therefore, §1982 appears to prohibit *all* discrimination against Negroes in the sale or rental of property — discrimination by private owners as well as discrimination by public authorities. Indeed, even the respondents seem to concede that, if §1982 "means what it says" — to use the words of the respondents' brief — then it must encompass every racially motivated refusal to sell or rent and cannot be confined to officially sanctioned segregation in housing. Stressing what they consider to be the revolutionary implications of so literal a reading of §1982, the respondents argue that Congress cannot possibly have intended any such result. Our examination of the relevant history, however, persuades us that Congress meant exactly what it said.

IV

[In Section IV of its opinion (set forth below despite its length, which may justify first readers' skipping to Section V and returning to it after reading the balance of the opinion), the Court gives a detailed review of the congressional reports and debates preceding the enactment of the Civil Rights Act of 1866, which contained the provision presently found in 42 U.S.C. §1982. The Court concludes that Congress intended to do what the words of the act provide, namely prohibit private as well as public discrimination with respect to the rights covered therein, including the right to purchase or lease property. The section provides historical support for the Jones decision. It provides a worthwhile view of congressional concern for blacks in the first decade after the Civil War, and points up how effectively the statutes manifesting that concern were emasculated by the Court in the decades following Reconstruction.]

In its original form, 42 U.S.C. §1982 was part of §1 of the Civil Rights Act of 1866.[28] That section was cast in sweeping terms:

> *Be it enacted by the Senate and House of Representatives of the United States of America in Congress assembled,* That all persons born in the United States and not subject to any foreign power, . . . are hereby declared to be citizens of the United States; and such citizens, of every race and color, without regard to any previous condition of slavery or involuntary servitude, . . . shall have the same right, in every State and Territory in the United States, to make and enforce contracts, to sue, be parties, and give evidence, to inherit, purchase, lease, sell, hold, and convey real and personal property, and to full and equal benefit of all laws and proceedings for the security of person and property, as is enjoyed by white citizens, and shall be subject to like punishment, pains, and penalties, and to none other, any law, statute, ordinance, regulation, or custom, to the contrary notwithstanding.

The crucial language for our purposes was that which guaranteed all citizens "the same right, in every State and Territory in the United States, . . . to inherit, purchase, lease, sell, hold, and convey real and personal property . . . as is enjoyed by white citizens . . . ." To the Congress that passed the Civil Rights Act of 1866, it was clear that the right to do these things might be infringed not only by "State or local law" but also by "custom, or prejudice." Thus, when Congress provided in §1 of the Civil Rights Act that the right to purchase and lease property was to be enjoyed equally throughout the United States by Negro and white citizens alike, it plainly meant to secure that right against interference from any source whatever, whether governmental or private.[31]

28. Act of April 9, 1866, c. 31, §1, 14 Stat. 27, re-enacted by §18 of the Enforcement Act of 1870, Act of May 31, 1870, c. 114, §18, 16 Stat. 140, 144, and codified in §§1977 and 1978 of the Revised Statutes of 1874, now 42 U.S.C. §§1981 and 1982. For the text of §1981, see n. 78, infra.

31. When Congressman Bingham of Ohio spoke of the Civil Rights Act, he charged that it would duplicate the substantive scope of the bill recently vetoed by the President, see n. 30, supra, and that it would extend the territorial reach of that bill throughout the United States. Cong. Globe, 39th Cong., 1st Sess., 1292. Although the Civil Rights Act,

Indeed, if §1 had been intended to grant nothing more than an immunity from *governmental* interference, then much of §2 would have made no sense at all.[32] For that section, which provided fines and prison terms for certain individuals who deprived others of rights "secured or protected" by §1, was carefully drafted to exempt private violations of §1 from the criminal sanctions it imposed.[33] There would, of course, have been no private violations to

---

as the dissent notes, post, at 2212, 2214, made no explicit reference to "prejudice," cf. n. 30, supra, the fact remains that nobody who rose to answer the Congressman disputed his basic premise that the Civil Rights Act of 1866 would prohibit every form of racial discrimination encompassed by the earlier bill the President had vetoed. Even Senator Trumbull of Illinois, author of the vetoed measure as well as of the Civil Rights Act, had previously remarked that the latter was designed to "extend to all parts of the country," on a permanent basis, the "equal civil rights" which were to have been secured in rebel territory by the former, id., at 322, to the end that "*all* the badges of servitude . . . be abolished." Id., at 323. (Emphasis added.)

32. Section 2 provided: "That any person who, *under color of any law, statute, ordinance, regulation, or custom,* shall subject, or cause to be subjected, any inhabitant of any State or Territory to the deprivation of any right secured or protected by this act, or to different punishment, pains, or penalties on account of such person having at any time been held in a condition of slavery or involuntary servitude, except as a punishment for crime whereof the party shall have been duly convicted, or by reason of his color or race, than is prescribed for the punishment of white persons, shall be deemed guilty of a misdemeanor, and, on conviction, shall be punished by fine not exceeding one thousand dollars, or imprisonment not exceeding one year, or both, in the discretion of the court." (Emphasis added.)

For the evolution of this provision into 18 U.S.C. §242, see Screws v. United States, 325 U.S. 91, 98-99, 65 S. Ct. 1031, 1033-1034, 89 L. Ed. 1495; United States v. Price, 383 U.S. 787, 804, 86 S. Ct. 1152, 1162, 16 L. Ed. 2d 267.

33. When Congressman Loan of Missouri asked the Chairman of the House Judiciary Committee, Mr. Wilson of Iowa, "why [does] the committee limit the provisions of the second section to those who act under the color of law," Cong. Globe, 39th Cong., 1st Sess., 1120, he was obviously inquiring why the second section did not also punish those who violated the first *without* acting "under the color of law." Specifically, he asked: "Why not let them [the penalties of §2] apply to the whole community where the acts are committed?" Ibid.

Mr. Wilson's reply was particularly revealing. If, as floor manager of the bill, he had viewed acts not under color of law as not violative of §1 at all, that would of course have been the short answer to the Congressman's query. Instead, Mr. Wilson found it necessary to explain that the Judiciary Committee did not want to make "a general criminal code for the States." Ibid. Hence only those who discriminated "in reference to civil rights . . . under the color of . . . local laws" were made subject to the criminal sanctions of §2. Ibid.

Congress might have thought it appropriate to confine criminal punishment to state officials, oath-bound to support the supreme federal law, while allowing only civil remedies — or perhaps only preventive relief — against private violators. Or Congress might have thought that States which did not authorize abridgment of the rights declared in §1 would themselves punish all who interfered with those rights without official authority. See, e.g., Cong. Globe, 39th Cong., 1st Sess., 1758, 1785. Cf. Civil Rights Cases, 109 U.S. 3, 19, 24-25, 3 S. Ct. 18, 27, 30-31, 27 L. Ed. 835.

Whatever the reason, it was repeatedly stressed that the only violations "reached *and punished*" by the bill, see Cong. Globe, 39th Cong., 1st Sess., at 1294 (emphasis added), would be those "done under color of State authority." Ibid. It is observed in dissent, post, at 2213, that Senator Trumbull told Senator Cowan that §2 was directed not at "State

exempt if the only "right" granted by §1 had been a right to be free of discrimination by public officials. Hence the structure of the 1866 Act, as well as its language, points to the conclusion urged by the petitioners in this case — that §1 was meant to prohibit *all* racially motivated deprivations of the rights enumerated in the statute, although only those deprivations perpetrated "under color of law" were to be criminally punishable under §2.

In attempting to demonstrate the contrary, the respondents rely heavily upon the fact that the Congress which approved the 1866 statute wished to eradicate the recently enacted Black Codes — laws which had saddled Negroes with "onerous disabilities and burdens, and curtailed their rights . . . to such an extent that their freedom was of little value . . . ." Slaughter-House Cases, 16 Wall. 36, 70, 21 L. Ed. 394. The respondents suggest that the only evil Congress sought to eliminate was that of racially discriminatory laws in the former Confederate States. But the Civil Rights Act was drafted to apply throughout the country, and its language was far broader than would have been necessary to strike down discriminatory statutes.

That broad language, we are asked to believe, was a mere slip of the legislative pen. We disagree. For the same Congress that wanted to do away with the Black Codes *also* had before it an imposing body of evidence pointing to the mistreatment of Negroes by private individuals and unofficial groups, mistreatment unrelated to any hostile state legislation. "Accounts in newspapers North and South, Freedmen's Bureau and other official documents, private reports and correspondence were all adduced" to show that "private outrage and atrocity" were "daily inflicted on freedmen . . . ." The congressional debates are replete with references to private injustices against Negroes — references to white employers who refused to pay their Negro workers, white planters who agreed among themselves not to hire freed slaves without the permission of their former masters, white citizens who assaulted Negroes or who combined to drive them out of their communities.

Indeed, one of the most comprehensive studies then before Congress stressed the prevalence of private hostility toward Negroes and the need to protect them from the resulting persecution and discrimination. The report noted the existence of laws virtually prohibiting Negroes from owning or renting property in certain towns, but described such laws as "mere isolated cases," representing "the local outcroppings of a spirit . . . found to prevail everywhere" — a spirit expressed, for example, by lawless acts of brutality directed against Negroes who traveled to areas where they were not wanted. The report concluded that, even if anti-Negro legislation were "repealed in all the States lately in rebellion," equal treatment for the Negro would not yet be secured.

In this setting, it would have been strange indeed if Congress had viewed

officers especially, but [at] everybody who violates the law." That remark, however, was nothing more than a reply to Senator Cowan's charge that §2 was "exceedingly objectionable" in singling out state judicial officers for punishment for the first time "in the history of civilized legislation." Id., at 500.

its task as encompassing merely the nullification of racist laws in the former rebel States. That the Congress which assembled in the Nation's capital in December 1865 in fact had a broader vision of the task before it became clear early in the session, when three proposals to invalidate discriminatory state statutes were rejected as "too narrowly conceived." From the outset it seemed clear, at least to Senator Trumbull of Illinois, Chairman of the Judiciary Committee, that stronger legislation might prove necessary. After Senator Wilson of Massachusetts had introduced his bill to strike down all racially discriminatory laws in the South, Senator Trumbull said this:

> I reported from the Judiciary Committee the second section of the [Thirteenth Amendment] for the very purpose of conferring upon Congress authority to see that the first section was carried out in good faith . . . and I hold that under that second section Congress will have the authority, when the constitutional amendment is adopted, *not only to pass the bill of the Senator from Massachusetts, but a bill that will be much more efficient to protect the freedman in his rights*. . . . And, sir, when the constitutional amendment shall have been adopted, if the information from the South be that the men whose liberties are secured by it are deprived of the privilege to go and come when they please, *to buy and sell when they please,* to make contracts and enforce contracts, I give notice that, if no one else does, I shall introduce a bill and urge its passage through Congress that will secure to those men every one of these rights: they would not be freemen without them. *It is idle to say that a man is free who cannot go and come at pleasure, who cannot buy and sell, who cannot enforce his rights*. . . . [So] when the constitutional amendment is adopted I trust we may pass a bill, if the action of the people in the Southern States should make it necessary, that will be *much more sweeping and efficient than the bill under consideration.*

Five days later, on December 18, 1865, the Secretary of State officially certified the ratification of the Thirteenth Amendment. The next day Senator Trumbull again rose to speak. He had decided, he said, that the "more sweeping and efficient" bill of which he had spoken previously ought to be enacted

> at an early day for the purpose of quieting apprehensions in the minds of many friends of freedom lest by local legislation *or a prevailing public sentiment* in some of the States persons of the African race should continue to be oppressed and in fact deprived of their freedom . . . .

On January 5, 1866, Senator Trumbull introduced the bill he had in mind — the bill which later became the Civil Rights Act of 1866. He described its objectives in terms that belie any attempt to read it narrowly:

> Mr. President, I regard the bill to which the attention of the Senate is now called as the most important measure that has been under its consideration since the adoption of the constitutional amendment abolishing slavery. That amendment declared that all persons in the United States should be free. This measure is in-

tended to give effect to that declaration and secure to all persons within the United States practical freedom. There is very little importance in the general declaration of abstract truths and principles unless they can be carried into effect, unless the persons who are to be affected by them have some means of availing themselves of their benefits.

Of course, Senator Trumbull's bill would, as he pointed out, "destroy all [the] discriminations" embodied in the Black Codes, but it would do more: It would affirmatively secure for all men, whatever their race or color, what the Senator called the "great fundamental rights": "the right to acquire property, the right to go and come at pleasure, the right to enforce rights in the courts, to make contracts, and to inherit and dispose of property." As to those basic civil rights, the Senator said, the bill would "break down *all* discrimination between black men and white men."

That the bill would indeed have so sweeping an effect was seen as its great virtue by its friends and as its great danger by its enemies but was disputed by none. Opponents of the bill charged that it would not only regulate state laws but would directly "determine the persons who [would] enjoy . . . property within the States," threatening the ability of white citizens "to determine who [would] be members of [their] communit[ies] . . . ." The bill's advocates did not deny the accuracy of those characterizations. Instead, they defended the propriety of employing federal authority to deal with "the white man . . . [who] would invoke the power of local prejudice" against the Negro. Thus, when the Senate passed the Civil Rights Act on February 2, 1866, it did so fully aware of the breadth of the measure it had approved.

In the House, as in the Senate, much was said about eliminating the infamous Black Codes. But, like the Senate, the House was moved by a larger objective — that of giving real content to the freedom guaranteed by the Thirteenth Amendment. Representative Thayer of Pennsylvania put it this way:

> [W]hen I voted for the amendment to abolish slavery . . . I did not suppose that I was offering . . . a mere paper guarantee. And when I voted for the second section of the amendment, I felt . . . certain that I had . . . given to Congress ability to protect . . . the rights which the first section gave . . . .
>
> The bill which now engages the attention of the House has for its object to carry out and guaranty the reality of that great measure. It is to give to it practical effect and force. It is to prevent that great measure from remaining a dead letter upon the constitutional page of this country. . . . The events of the last four years . . . have changed [a] large class of people . . . from a condition of slavery to that of freedom. *The practical question now to be decided is whether they shall be in fact freemen. It is whether they shall have the benefit of this great charter of liberty* given to them by the American people.

Representative Cook of Illinois thought that, without appropriate federal legislation, any "combination of men in [a] neighborhood [could] prevent [a Negro] from having any chance" to enjoy those benefits. To Congressman

Cook and others like him, it seemed evident that, with respect to basic civil rights — including the "right to . . . purchase, lease, sell, hold, and convey . . . property," Congress must provide that "there . . . be *no* discrimination" on grounds of race or color.

It thus appears that, when the House passed the Civil Rights Act on March 13, 1866, it did so on the same assumption that had prevailed in the Senate: It too believed that it was approving a comprehensive statute forbidding *all* racial discrimination affecting the basic civil rights enumerated in the Act.

President Andrew Johnson vetoed the Act on March 27, and in the brief congressional debate that followed, his supporters characterized its reach in all-embracing terms. One stressed the fact that §1 would confer "the right . . . to purchase . . . real estate . . . without any qualification and without any restriction whatever . . . ." Another predicted, as a corollary, that the Act would preclude preferential treatment for white persons in the rental of hotel rooms and in the sale of church pews. Those observations elicited no reply. On April 6 the Senate, and on April 9 the House, overrode the President's veto by the requisite majorities, and the Civil Rights Act of 1866 became law.[70]

In light of the concerns that led Congress to adopt it and the contents of the debates that preceded its passage, it is clear that the Act was designed to do just what its terms suggest: to prohibit all racial discrimination, whether or not under color of law, with respect to the rights enumerated therein — including the right to purchase or lease property.

Nor was the scope of the 1866 Act altered when it was re-enacted in 1870, some two years after the ratification of the Fourteenth Amendment. It is quite true that some members of Congress supported the Fourteenth Amendment "in order to eliminate doubt as to the constitutional validity of the Civil Rights Act as applied to the States." Hurd v. Hodge, 334 U.S. 24 . . . . But it certainly does not follow that the adoption of the Fourteenth Amendment or the subsequent readoption of the Civil Rights Act were meant somehow to *limit* its application to state action. The legislative history furnishes not the slightest factual basis for any such speculation, and the conditions prevailing in 1870 make it highly implausible. For by that time, most if not all of the former Confederate States, then under the control of "reconstructed" legislatures, had formally repudiated racial discrimination, and the focus of congressional concern had clearly shifted from hostile statutes to the activities of groups like the Ku Klux Klan, operating wholly outside the law.

Against this background, it would obviously make no sense to assume, without any historical support whatever, that Congress made a silent decision in 1870 to exempt private discrimination from the operation of the Civil Rights Act of 1866. "The cardinal rule is that repeals by implication are not

70. "Never before had Congress over-ridden a President on a major political issue, and there was special gratification in feeling that this had not been done to carry some matter of material interest, such as a tariff, but in the cause of disinterested justice." W. Brock, [An American Crisis 115 (1963.]

favored." Posadas v. National City Bank, 296 U.S. 497, 503 . . . . All Congress said in 1870 was that the 1866 law "is hereby re-enacted." That is all Congress meant.

As we said in a somewhat different setting two Terms ago, "We think that history leaves no doubt that, if we are to give [the law] the scope that its origins dictate, we must accord it a sweep as broad as its language." United States v. Price, 383 U.S. 787, 801 . . . . "We are not at liberty to seek ingenious analytical instruments," ibid., to carve from §1982 an exception for private conduct — even though its application to such conduct in the present context is without established precedent. And, as the Attorney General of the United States said at the oral argument of this case, "The fact that the statute lay partially dormant for many years cannot be held to diminish its force today."

V

The remaining question is whether Congress has power under the Constitution to do what §1982 purports to do: to prohibit all racial discrimination, private and public, in the sale and rental of property. Our starting point is the Thirteenth Amendment, for it was pursuant to that constitutional provision that Congress originally enacted what is now §1982. The Amendment consists of two parts. Section 1 states: "Neither slavery nor involuntary servitude, except as a punishment for crime whereby the party shall have been duly convicted, shall exist within the United States, or any place subject to their jurisdiction."

Section 2 provides: "Congress shall have power to enforce this article by appropriate legislation."

As its text reveals, the Thirteenth Amendment "is not a mere prohibition of state laws establishing or upholding slavery, but an absolute declaration that slavery or involuntary servitude shall not exist in any part of the United States." Civil Rights Cases, 109 U.S. 3, 20 . . . . It has never been doubted, therefore, "that the power vested in Congress to enforce the article by appropriate legislation," ibid., includes the power to enact laws "direct and primary, operating upon the acts of individuals, whether sanctioned by state legislation or not." Id., at 23 . . . .

Thus, the fact that §1982 operates upon the unofficial acts of private individuals, whether or not sanctioned by state law, presents no constitutional problem. If Congress has power under the Thirteenth Amendment to eradicate conditions that prevent Negroes from buying and renting property because of their race or color, then no federal statute calculated to achieve that objective can be thought to exceed the constitutional power of Congress simply because it reaches beyond state action to regulate the conduct of private individuals. The constitutional question in this case, therefore, comes to this: Does the authority of Congress to enforce the Thirteenth Amendment "by appropriate legislation" include the power to eliminate all racial barriers to the acquisition of real and personal property? We think the answer to that question is plainly yes.

"By its own unaided force and effect," the Thirteenth Amendment "abolished slavery, and established universal freedom." Civil Rights Cases, 109 U.S. 3, 20 . . . . Whether or not the Amendment *itself* did any more than that — a question not involved in this case — it is at least clear that the Enabling Clause of that Amendment empowered Congress to do much more. For that clause clothed "Congress with power to pass *all laws necessary and proper for abolishing all badges and incidents of slavery in the United States.*" Ibid. (Emphasis added.)

Those who opposed passage of the Civil Rights Act of 1866 argued in effect that the Thirteenth Amendment merely authorized Congress to dissolve the legal bond by which the Negro slave was held to his master. Yet many had earlier opposed the Thirteenth Amendment on the very ground that it would give Congress virtually unlimited power to enact laws for the protection of Negroes in every State. And the majority leaders in Congress — who were, after all, the authors of the Thirteenth Amendment — had no doubt that its Enabling Clause contemplated the sort of positive legislation that was embodied in the 1866 Civil Rights Act. Their chief spokesman, Senator Trumbull of Illinois, the Chairman of the Judiciary Committee, had brought the Thirteenth Amendment to the floor of the Senate in 1864. In defending the constitutionality of the 1866 Act, he argued that, if the narrower construction of the Enabling Clause were correct, then

> the trumpet of freedom that we have been blowing throughout the land has given an "uncertain sound," and the promised freedom is a delusion. Such was not the intention of Congress, which proposed the constitutional amendment, nor is such the fair meaning of the amendment itself. . . . I have no doubt that under this provision . . . we may destroy all these discriminations in civil rights against the black man; and if we cannot, our constitutional amendment amounts to nothing. It was for that purpose that the second clause of that amendment was adopted, which says that Congress shall have authority, by appropriate legislation, to carry into effect the article prohibiting slavery. Who is to decide what that appropriate legislation is to be? The Congress of the United States; and it is for Congress to adopt such appropriate legislation as it may think proper, so that it be a means to accomplish the end.

Surely Senator Trumbull was right. Surely Congress has the power under the Thirteenth Amendment rationally to determine what are the badges and the incidents of slavery, and the authority to translate that determination into effective legislation. Nor can we say that the determination Congress has made is an irrational one. For this Court recognized long ago that, whatever else they may have encompassed, the badges and incidents of slavery — its "burdens and disabilities" — included restraints upon "those fundamental rights which are the essence of civil freedom, namely, the same right . . . to inherit, purchase, lease, sell and convey property, as is enjoyed by white citizens." Civil Rights Cases, 109 U.S. 3, 22 . . . .[78] Just as the Black Codes,

78. . . . In Hodges v. United States, 203 U.S. 1, . . . a group of white men had ter-

enacted after the Civil War to restrict the free exercise of those rights, were substitutes for the slave system, so the exclusion of Negroes from white communities became a substitute for the Black Codes. And when racial discrimination herds men into ghettos and makes their ability to buy property turn on the color of their skin, then it too is a relic of slavery.

Negro citizens, North and South, who saw in the Thirteenth Amendment a promise of freedom — freedom to "go and come at pleasure" and to "buy and sell when they please" — would be left with "a mere paper guarantee" if Congress were powerless to assure that a dollar in the hands of a Negro will purchase the same thing as a dollar in the hands of a white man. At the very least, the freedom that Congress is empowered to secure under the Thirteenth Amendment includes the freedom to buy whatever a white man can buy, the right to live wherever a white man can live. If Congress cannot say that being a free man means at least this much, then the Thirteenth Amendment made a promise the Nation cannot keep.

Representative Wilson of Iowa was the floor manager in the House for the Civil Rights Act of 1866. In urging that Congress had ample authority to pass

---

rorized several Negroes to prevent them from working in a sawmill. The terrorizers were convicted under 18 U.S.C. §241 (then Revised Statutes §5508) of conspiring to prevent the Negroes from exercising the right to contract for employment, a right secured by 42 U.S.C. §1981 (then Revised Statutes §1977, derived from §1 of the Civil Rights Act of 1866, see n. 28, supra). Section 1981 provides, in terms that closely parallel those of §1982 (then Revised Statutes §1978), that all persons in the United States "shall have *the same right . . . to make and enforce contracts,* to sue, be parties, give evidence, and to the full and equal benefit of all laws and proceedings for the security of persons and property as is enjoyed by white citizens . . . . (Emphasis added.)

This Court reversed the conviction. The majority recognized that "one of the disabilities of slavery, one of the indicia of its existence, was a lack of power to make or perform contracts." 203 U.S., at 17 . . . . And there was no doubt that the defendants had deprived their Negro victims, on racial grounds, of the opportunity to dispose of their labor by contract. Yet the majority said that "no mere personal assault or trespass or appropriation operates to reduce the individual to a condition of slavery," id., at 18, . . . and asserted that only conduct which actually enslaves someone can be subjected to punishment under legislation enacted to enforce the Thirteenth Amendment. Contra, United States v. Cruikshank, 25 Fed. Cas. No. 14,897, pp. 707, 712 (dictum of Mr. Justice Bradley, on circuit), *aff'd,* 92 U.S. 542 . . . ; United States v. Morris, D.C., 125 F. 322, 324, 330-331. Mr. Justice Harlan, joined by Mr. Justice Day, dissented. In their view, the interpretation the majority placed upon the Thirteenth Amendment was "entirely too narrow and . . . hostile to the freedom established by the Supreme Law of the land." 203 U.S. at 37 . . . . That interpretation went far, they thought, "towards neutralizing many declarations made as to the object of the recent Amendments of the Constitution, a common purpose of which, this court has said, was to secure to a people theretofore in servitude, the free enjoyment, without discrimination merely on account of their race, of the essential rights that appertain to American citizenship and to freedom." Ibid.

The conclusion of the majority in Hodges rested upon a concept of congressional power under the Thirteenth Amendment irreconcilable with the position taken by every member of this Court in the Civil Rights Cases and incompatible with the history and purpose of the Amendment itself. Insofar as Hodges is inconsistent with our holding today, it is hereby overruled.

the pending bill, he recalled the celebrated words of Chief Justice Marshall in McCulloch v. Maryland, 4 Wheat. 316, 421, 4 L. Ed. 579:

"Let the end be legitimate, let it be within the scope of the constitution, and all means which are appropriate, which are plainly adapted to that end, which are not prohibited, but consist with the letter and spirit of the constitution are constitutional."

"The end is legitimate," the Congressman said, "because it is defined by the Constitution itself. The end is the maintenance of freedom . . . . A man who enjoys the civil rights mentioned in this bill cannot be reduced to slavery. . . . This settles the appropriateness of this measure, and that settles its constitutionality."

We agree. The judgment is reversed.

Reversed.

[Justice Douglas wrote a concurring opinion in which he enumerated the badges of servitude imposed on blacks during slavery, and cited a long list of civil rights cases reflecting efforts by much of white society to retain blacks in a subservient status.

Justice Harlan, joined by Justice White, wrote a lengthy dissent to what he considered a "most ill-considered and ill-advised" decision. He reviewed at length the historical material, concluding that the legislative history of the 1866 Civil Rights Act does not support the majority's contention that Congress intended that it apply to purely private action. He suggested that, even if he were wrong on this, the enactment of a fair housing statute "so diminishes the public importance of this case that by far the wisest course would be for this Court to refrain from decision and to dismiss the writ as improvidently granted." 392 U.S. at 450. Justice Harlan viewed it as particularly unfortunate for the Court to persist in deciding this case on the basis of a highly questionable interpretation of a broad, century-old statute that contains none of the exemptions which the contemporary Congress found necessary to include in the new fair housing act. Although conceding that the coverage of the new law would not provide petitioner with relief, he reminded the Court that it sat to decide issues, the settlement of which would be of importance to the public as distinguished from the parties. He concluded, "The political process now having taken hold again in this very field, I am at a loss to understand why the Court should have deemed it appropriate or in the circumstances of this case, necessary to proceed with such precipitate and insecure strides." 392 U.S. at 478.]

NOTES

1. The Jones decision brought out in full force the legal commentators, many of them taking widely divergent views as to the decision's validity, wisdom and likely scope. One writer said, "It may well be that this decision, by infusing new vitality both into the early Reconstruction statutes and into the thirteenth amendment, will prove to be the most far-reaching race rela-

tions case since the Civil War." Larson, The New Law of Race Relations, 1969 Wis. L. Rev. 470, 486. Typically, concern was expressed that, without the "state action" qualification, congressional power to regulate private conduct under the Thirteenth Amendment would be unlimited. While conceding that the right to discriminate, taken alone, should not outweigh the right of blacks to fair treatment, commentators were concerned that discrimination often occurs in conjunction with interest in privacy, free association or free expression. For example, the proverbial Mrs. Murphy's boardinghouse, excluded from coverage under the 1968 Fair Housing Act, could, on the authority of Jones, be reached by a §1982 suit. One article suggests the possible resurrection of the "social rights" formula, developed by Justice Bradley in his Civil Rights Cases opinion, a formula which courts could use to encompass rights considered to be less than "fundamental" to blacks but denoting a sphere in which the discriminators' personal interests are especially strong. See Note, The "New" Thirteenth Amendment: A Preliminary Analysis, 82 Harv. L. Rev. 1294, 1313 (1969).

2. Justice Harlan's dissenting view, that the 1866 Civil Rights Act was not intended to reach private discriminatory conduct, has received strong support from Professor Charles Fairman's condemnation of the conclusions on the legislative history of the Civil Rights Act of 1866 reached by the majority in Jones v. Mayer Co. C. Fairman, History of the Supreme Court of the United States, Vol. VI: Reconstruction and Reunion 1864-1888, Part I (1971). In an analysis of the Civil Rights Act and the Fourteenth Amendment, encompassing almost one hundred pages, Fairman marshals, in adversarial fashion, the legislative history supporting his conclusion that the 1866 Act was not intended to reach discrimination practiced by private individuals. He charges that in Jones the Court intentionally ignored the fact that the phrase in the bill providing "there shall be no discrimination in civil rights or immunities . . . on account of race, color, or previous condition of slavery" was stricken. The Court then cited the statements of congressmen referring to this phrase in determining the scope of the clauses that remained. Fairman also criticized the Court's linking of the term "custom" as used in the act to "prejudice," when the former meant merely practices that had the force of law and were carried out by state officers. Finally, he rejects the Court's conclusion that the statutory language, "All citizens shall have the same right . . . as is enjoyed by white persons thereof to . . . purchase . . . real and personal property," was intended to end discrimination against blacks by private citizens as well as public authorities. There is, he says, a difference between guaranteeing to citizens the equal capacity to purchase property and creating in others an obligation to sell to them. Fairman believes that the statute created the capacity but not the obligation. He states that his "critique has been carried no further than was needed to disembarrass the field of history." Fairman supra at 1258. He recognizes the Court's desperate earnestness to rid the law of any tolerance of the discrimination which the Justice Department

characterized as pre-eminent among the causes of racial tensions besetting the nation, but he says, "In Jones v. Mayer the Court appears to have had no feeling for the truth of history, but only to have read it through the glass of the Court's own purpose. It allowed itself to believe impossible things — as though the dawning enlightenment of 1968 could be ascribed to the Congress of a century ago." Id. at 1258. In a final reproach to the Court, he says,

> If the 1860's are to be called to reprove the practices of the 1960's, let the lesson be restrained and truthful: that a Congress reflecting a wide range of opinion determined that the members of the emancipated race were now citizens of the national community, and secure to them the equal capacities and immunities that at the moment seemed appropriate. Measured from the situation six years earlier, this was a worthy achievement. (Fairman, supra at 1259.)

See also Casper, Jones v. Mayer: Clio, Bemused and Confused Muse, 1968 Sup. Ct. Rev. 89. Professor Casper criticized the Court's approach in Jones, calling it a combination of "creation by authoritative revelation and 'law-office' history." Id. at 100.

QUESTIONS

1. Is any contemporary effort by the Supreme Court to divine congressional intention as to the scope of a statute enacted more than a century before likely to attract attacks such as that made by Fairman? Should Fairman be surprised that his position — that the Civil Rights Act applied only to discrimination under color of state law — is also criticized for failing to adequately consider "that the word 'custom' must refer to private activities because Republicans were very much aware that, despite the apparent liberality of the new 'black codes' that southern states were framing in 1866, blacks in the South were subjected to systematic private oppression"? Benedict, Review of Fairman, History of the Supreme Court of the United States, Volume II: Reconstruction and Reunion, 39 U. Chi. L. Rev. 862, 869-870 (1972).

2. In construing statutes enacted almost contemporaneously with the constitutional provisions on which they are based, is a search for original intentions likely to be any more intellectually rewarding than a similar search as to the constitutional provision itself? Are courts more productively engaged when they consider the words and meanings of such statutes in the light of contemporary realities?

3. Does the interpretation given 42 U.S.C. §1982 in Jones v. Mayer Co. doom even good-faith schemes to establish integrated communities by setting "benign quotas" on the racial composition of families leasing or purchasing homes in the area? For a discussion of pre-Jones legal issues posed by such plans, see Bittker, The Case of the Checker-Board Ordinance: An Experiment in Race Relations, 71 Yale L.J. 1387 (1962).

NOTE ON TITLE VIII, CIVIL RIGHTS ACT OF 1968

Justice Harlan's dissent in Jones, criticizing what he viewed as a highly questionable interpretation of the 1866 Civil Rights Act when Congress had recently enacted new and far more detailed legislation on the subject, reflects his commitment to judicial restraint and the maintenance of continuity with earlier decisions. It assumes, however, that Title VIII is a viable remedy with which to relieve the plight of black victims of housing discrimination. But the history of this legislation, a reading of its provisions, and a review of its administration makes any such assumption difficult.

After years of unsuccessful efforts to pass a fair housing law, Congress enacted Title VIII exactly one week after Dr. Martin Luther King's death at the hands of a white assassin on April 4, 1968. The fair housing measure was attached to help win congressional approval for extremely broad legislation, enabling the federal government to prosecute persons involved in riots (18 U.S.C. §§2101-02 (1968)) and civil disorders (18 U.S.C. §§231-33 (1968)).

In the following month, after President Johnson requested $11.1 million to administer the new housing law (N.Y. Times, May 25, 1968, at 17, c. 1.), the same Congress refused to appropriate a single penny to enforce it. Subsequently, in October 1968, the Department of Housing and Urban Development (HUD) asked Congress for $8 million in a supplemental appropriation request. Congress approved $2 million, but a second supplemental request of $2 million, in January 1969, was turned down in July 1969. Samuel J. Simmons, Assistant Secretary for Equal Opportunity in HUD, reported that during 1969 only 94 of 927 housing complaints received had been successfully conciliated. N.Y. Times, Jan. 1, 1970 at 21, c. 1.

In 1970, HUD received 1025 Title VIII complaints. Conceding that the numbers represented only a small increase over the previous year, HUD believed the figure "significant in a year when the housing industry was depressed and fewer people sought housing changes." The department processed 169 cases through the conciliation process, but only half of these conciliation sessions were successful. One hundred and fifty-three complaints were dismissed without investigation and the remainder were in various stages of investigation. 1970 Annual Report of Dept. of Housing and Urban Development 110.

In 1971, the number of complaints rose to 1570, and the number dismissed to 213. From the backlog of pending cases, 351 cases were conciliated, 204 successfully. HUD Monthly Report on Complaint Activity, Jan. 26, 1972.

The relatively small number of complaints filed with HUD, and the less than impressive number of cases satisfactorily concluded, come as no surprise if one studies in detail the provisions of Title VIII (printed in full in the Appendix infra). While the law prohibits discrimination on the basis of race, color, religion or national origin in the sale, rental, and financing by private owners, real estate brokers, and financial institutions (42 U.S.C.

§§3604, 3605, 3607), the statute allows several exemptions, the most important of which excludes from coverage an owner who sells or rents his single-family house (§3603(b)(i)). This exemption effectively removes from protection the major source of most home sales. The impact of the exemption is lessened somewhat by other provisions, restricting it to owners who do not use brokerage services or discriminatory advertising §3604(c)) and who own no more than three single-family houses at any one time. Other exemptions include those for religious organizations selling or renting to members of their sect for community reasons, and for private clubs, not in fact open to the public, which provide housing for their members as an incident to their primary purpose (§3607).

Effective enforcement of Title VIII is further hampered by the fact that responsibility for administration was not placed in a new commission, but was added to the duties of the Secretary of Housing and Urban Development. Under the act he is empowered to receive complaints, although, unlike the Equal Employment Opportunity Commission (see Appendix infra), he is not given specific powers to initiate a complaint. Because most people searching for housing want shelter and not litigation, civil rights agencies have found that power to initiate complaints against widespread discriminatory policies is essential to an effective enforcement program. Once complaints are received, the secretary is empowered to investigate them and decide whether he will attempt to resolve the complaint, a decision evidently left to his discretion (§3610(a)). If he does decide to resolve it, he is limited to informal methods of persuasion. He must defer to state agencies that can provide relief. This deferral is not limited in time, but is virtually permanent unless the state or local agency does not proceed at all in the matter (§3610(c)).

Where the secretary attempts to conciliate and fails, the complaint may proceed to court. Title VIII, however, establishes a bar to federal court action where an available state court can provide a "judicial remedy . . . substantially equivalent to the rights and remedies provided" by Title VIII (§3610(d)). Where jurisdiction is established, the federal court will conduct a de novo hearing. There is, however, an alternative enforcement procedure (§3612). An aggrieved person apparently has the option of bypassing the secretary altogether and proceeding directly to federal court. Immediate access to the courts eliminates the thirty-day delay required when a complaint is filed with the secretary. In addition, §3614 provides that the hearing of a case brought directly to court should be "at the earliest practical date." Even the existence of a judicial remedy at the state level evidently does not prevent a plaintiff from choosing this alternative, since there is no jurisdictional bar to federal court action under §812, as there is when the complaint reaches federal court after first proceeding through the secretary under §810. The court, as it deems appropriate, is empowered to grant as relief an injunction, compensatory and punitive damages, and court costs, including attorneys' fees (§3612(c)). Punitive damages are limited to $1000.

The Seventh Circuit reversed a district court award of $250 for punitive damages granted under §3612(c), ruling in a lengthy opinion that:

(1) the constitutional right to trial by jury applies in at least some judicial proceedings to enforce rights created by statute; (2) this action for damages is "in the nature of a suit at common law;" (3) the nature of the claim is "legal" [rather than equitable]; (4) the right to a jury trial may not be denied on the ground that the damage claim is incidental to a claim for equitable relief; (5) cases involving an award of back pay pursuant to [Title VII of] the 1964 Act are inapplicable. . . . (Rogers v. Loether, 467 F.2d 1110, 1112-1113 (7th Cir. 1972).)

In addition to individual suits, the act authorizes the Attorney General to initiate actions in federal courts for preventive relief when he has "reasonable cause to believe that any person or group of persons is engaged in a pattern or practice of resistance to the full enjoyment of the rights granted by this subchapter . . ." (§3613). Utilizing this authority, the Attorney General has achieved some success. For example, in United States v. Mintzes, 304 F. Supp. 1305 (D. Md. 1969), the government utilized the "anti-blockbusting" section of the act, §3604(e), to obtain an injunction against a realty firm making representations to homeowners in order to convince them to sell. In sustaining the validity of the anti-blockbusting section, the court held in United States v. Bob Lawrence Realty, Inc., 313 F. Supp. 870 (N.D. Ga. 1970), that any inhibiting effect it may have on speech is justified by the government's interest in protecting its citizens from discriminatory housing practices. See also United States v. Mitchell, 327 F. Supp. 476 (N.D. Ga. 1971).

The Fifth Circuit found that the government had established a "pattern or practice" of discrimination where the evidence showed that the defendant realtor admitted to having had a discriminatory policy prior to the effective date of the 1968 Civil Rights Act, and where testimony as to his application procedures subsequent to passage of the act justified the conclusion that the discriminatory policy had not changed. United States v. West Peachtree Tenth Corporation, 437 F.2d 221 (5th Cir. 1971). See also United States v. Reddoch, 467 F.2d 897 (5th Cir. 1972), concluding that a "pattern and practice" are made out by a showing that the resident manager employed a "credit check" ruse to deny apartments to blacks, coupled with the fact that there were no black tenants in the complex during the three years of its operation, despite a 100 percent change in tenants during this time.

In United States v. Hunter, 459 F.2d 205 (4th Cir. 1972), the court held that 42 U.S.C. §3604(c) prohibited the publication of discriminatory housing advertisements, and that such prohibition does not violate First or Fifth Amendment righfts.

TRAFFICANTE v. METROPOLITAN LIFE INSURANCE COMPANY, 409 U.S. 205, 93 S. Ct. 364, 34 L. Ed. 2d 415 (1972). A group of white tenants, who charged that defendant owner's racially discriminatory policy "stigmatized" them in a white ghetto and denied them the benefits of being in an integrated community, were held to lack standing to sue under both §1982 and the Fair Housing Act of 1968. The Fourth Circuit affirmed on the basis that the acts were limited to the direct victims of discriminatory housing practices.

The Supreme Court reversed. Justice Douglas wrote that the definition of "persons aggrieved" in Title VIII, §810(a), is defined broadly as "any person who claims to have been injured by a discriminatory housing practice." Noting both that compliance with the act depends primarily on complaints by private persons, and that HUD has no enforcement powers and its Civil Rights division has less than two dozen lawyers, he concluded that Congress intended coverage to extend to tenants of the housing unit that is charged with discrimination. Again, the Court emphasized the important role of complainants as "private attorneys general." Justice White, with whom Justices Black and Powell joined, concurred on the basis that, because of the Civil Rights Acts of 1968, they agreed that petitioners' case presents a case or controversy within the jurisdiction of the federal courts.

NOTES

1. The Trafficante decision represents one of several instances in which courts have found that whites have standing to protect the rights of blacks to nondiscrimination. See Barrows v. Jackson, supra page 616, and Sullivan v. Little Hunting Park, Inc., printed supra. In Walker v. Pointer, 304 F. Supp. 56 (N.D. Tex. 1969), jurisdiction under §1982 was extended to whites who suffer racial discrimination because of their association with blacks. Two white college students, who had been evicted because they entertained blacks in their apartment, were able to obtain compensatory damages for loss and damage to personal property and exemplary damages for being evicted in a malicious manner. The court alternatively upheld its exercise of jurisdiction as protecting the freedom of blacks to come and go at the invitation of whites lawfully in control of their property. See also Pughsley v. 3750 Lake Shore Drive Cooperative Building, 463 F.2d 1055 (7th Cir. 1972), where the court reversed dismissal of a suit brought by a white couple who charged that defendant had denied them a cooperative apartment because they had a Negro child living with them.

2. Sullivan v. Little Hunting Park, Inc., represents, inter alia, another instance where whites were permitted to sue, this time under 42 U.S.C. §1982, to vindicate the rights of black victims of housing discrimination.

SULLIVAN v. LITTLE HUNTING PARK, INC.
396 U.S. 229, 90 S. Ct. 400, 24 L. Ed. 2d 386 (1969)

Mr. Justice DOUGLAS delivered the opinion of the Court. . . .

II

Little Hunting Park, Inc., is a Virginia nonstock corporation organized to operate a community park and playground facilities for the benefit of residents in an area of Fairfax County, Virginia. A membership share entitles all persons in the immediate family of the shareholder to use the corporation's recreation facilities. Under the bylaws a person owning a membership share is entitled when he rents his home to assign the share to his tenant, subject to approval of the board of directors. Paul E. Sullivan and his family owned a house in this area and lived in it. Later he bought another house in the area and leased the first one to T. R. Freeman, Jr., an employee of the U.S. Department of Agriculture; and assigned his membership share to Freeman. The board refused to approve the assignment because Freeman was a Negro. Sullivan protested that action and was notified that he would be expelled from the corporation by the board. A hearing was accorded him and he was expelled, the board tendering him cash for his two shares.

Sullivan and Freeman sued under 42 USC §§1981, 1982 for injunctions and monetary damages. Since Freeman no longer resides in the area served by Little Hunting Park, Inc., his claim is limited solely to damages.

The trial court denied relief to each petitioner. We reverse those judgments.

In Jones v Mayer Co. 392 US 409 . . . , we reviewed at length the legislative history of 42 USC §1982. We concluded that it reaches beyond state action and operates upon the unofficial acts of private individuals and that it is authorized by the Enabling Clause of the Thirteenth Amendment . . . .

The Virginia trial court rested on its conclusion that Little Hunting Park was a private social club. But we find nothing of the kind on this record. There was no plan or purpose of exclusiveness. It is open to every white person within the geographic area, there being no selective element other than race. See Daniel v Paul, 395 US 298, 301-302 . . . . What we have here is a device functionally comparable to a racially restrictive covenant, the judicial enforcement of which was struck down in Shelley v. Kraemer, 334 US 1 . . . , by reason of the Fourteenth Amendment.

In Jones v Mayer Co., the complaint charged a refusal to sell petitioner a home because he was black. In the instant cases the interest conveyed was a leasehold of realty coupled with a membership share in a nonprofit company organized to offer recreational facilities to owners and lessees of real property in that residential area. It is not material whether the membership share be considered realty or personal property, as §1982 covers both. Section 1982 covers the right "to inherit, purchase, lease, sell, hold and convey real and personal property." There is a suggestion that transfer on the books of the corporation of Freeman's share is not covered by any of those verbs. The suggestion is without merit. There has never been any doubt but that Freeman paid part of his $129 monthly rental for the assignment of the membership share in Little Hunting Park. The transaction clearly fell within the "lease." The right to "lease" is protected by §1982 against the actions of third parties, as well as against the actions of the immediate lessor. Respondent's actions in refusing to approve the assignment of the membership share in the case was clearly an interference with Freeman's right to "lease." A narrow construction of the language of §1982 would be quite inconsistent with the broad and sweeping nature of the protection meant to be afforded by §1 of the Civil Rights Act of 1866, from which §1982 was derived. See 392 US, at 422-437 . . . .

We turn to Sullivan's expulsion for the advocacy of Freeman's cause. If that sanction, backed by a state court judgment, can be imposed, then Sullivan is punished for trying to vindicate the rights of minorities protected by §1982. Such a sanction would give impetus to the perpetuation of racial restrictions on property. That is why we said in Barrows v Jackson, 346 US 249, 259, . . . that the white owner is at times "the only effective adversary" of the unlawful restrictive covenant. Under the terms of our decision in Barrows, there can be no question but that Sullivan has standing to maintain this action.

We noted in Jones v Mayer Co., that the Fair Housing Act of 1968, 82 Stat 81, in no way impaired the sanction of §1982. 392 US, at 413-417 . . . . What we said there is adequate to dispose of the suggestion that the Public Accommodations provision of the Civil Rights Act of 1964, 78 Stat 243, in some way supersedes the provisions of the 1866 Act. For the hierarchy of administrative machinery provided by the 1964 Act is not at war with survival of the principles embodied in §1982. There is, moreover, a saving clause in the 1964 Act as respects "any right based on any other Federal . . . law not inconsistent" with that Act.

Section 1982 of the 1866 Act is plainly "not inconsistent" with the 1964 Act, which has been construed as not "pre-empting every other mode of protecting a federal 'right' or as granting immunity" to those who had long been subject to federal law. United States v Johnson, 390 US 563, 566 . . . .

We held in Jones v Mayer Co. that although §1982 is couched in declaratory terms and provides no explicit method of enforcement, a federal court has power to fashion an effective equitable remedy. 392 US, at 414, n 13 . . . . That federal remedy for the protection of a federal right is available in the state court, if that court is empowered to grant injunctive relief generally, as is the Virginia court. . . .

Finally as to damages. Congress, by 28 USC §1343(4), created federal jurisdiction for "damages or . . . equitable or other relief under any Act of Congress providing for the protection of civil rights . . . ." We reserved in Jones v Mayer Co. 392 US, at 414-415, n 14 . . . , the question of what damages, if any, might be appropriately recovered for a violation of §1982. . . . [Citations omitted.]

Compensatory damages for deprivation of a federal right are governed by federal standards, as provided by Congress in 42 USC §1988, which states:

The jurisdiction in civil . . . matters conferred on the district courts by the provisions of this chapter and Title 18, for the protection of all persons in the United States in their civil rights, and for their vindication, shall be exercised and enforced in conformity with the laws of the United States, so far as such laws are suitable to carry the same into effect; but in all cases where they are not adapted to the object, or are deficient in the provisions necessary to furnish suitable remedies and punish offenses against law, the common law, as modified and changed by the constitution and statutes of the State wherein the court having jurisdiction of such civil or criminal cause is held, so far as the same is not inconsistent with the Constitution and laws of the United States, shall be extended to and govern the said courts in the trial and disposition of the cause . . . .

This means, as we read §1988, that both federal and state rules on damages may be utilized, whichever better serves the policies expressed in the federal statutes. Cf. Brazier v Cherry, 293 F2d 401. The rule of damages, whether drawn from federal or state sources, is a federal rule responsive to the need whenever a federal right is impaired. We do not explore the problem further, as the issue of damages was not litigated below.

It is suggested, not by any party but by the dissent, that any relief should await proceedings under the Fair Housing Act of 1968. 82 Stat 81, 42 USC (Supp IV) §3601 et seq. But these suits were commenced on March 16, 1966, two years before that Act was passed. It would be irresponsible judicial administration to dismiss a suit because of an intervening Act which has no possible application to events long preceding its enactment.

Reversed.

[Justice Harlan, joined by Chief Justice Burger and Justice White, dissented. As he had done in his Jones dissent, Justice Harlan argued that congressional enactment of the 1968 Fair Housing Act removed any necessity for the Court's reliance upon the 1866 antidiscrimination statute. He again pointed out that the new law contained specific provisions for relief and obviated the need for fashioning remedies, as the majority had done in this case. He particularly objected to the award of damages to the white owner since, he said, it was not clear from the record that the owner's expulsion was in retaliation for assigning his share to a Negro rather than because of the owner's conduct in dealing with the board.]

TILLMAN v. WHEATON-HAVEN RECREATIONAL ASSOCIATION, INC. 410 U.S. 431, 93 S. Ct. 1190, 35 L. Ed. 2d 403 (1973). Defendant is a nonprofit corporation organized for the purpose of operating a swimming facility in Silver Springs, Maryland. Funds for the pool were privately raised. Membership is largely keyed to the geographical area within a three-quarter-mile radius of the pool, and persons within that area may apply for membership without recommendation of existing members, as is required for persons living outside the preferential area. The record shows that the defendant discouraged membership by a black who had purchased a home within the preference area, and that after a white member had brought a black friend as a guest, the guest policy was limited to relatives of members. Suit was filed by the white member whose black guest was denied admission and by the black resident who was refused an application form. Jurisdiction for the case was based on Title II of the Civil Rights Act of 1964 and 42 U.S.C. §§1981 and 1982. The district court granted a summary judgment for the defendants, which was affirmed by the court of appeals, one judge dissenting.

Justice Blackmun, speaking for a unanimous court, found that the refusal to admit a black resident of the preference area to membership abridges and dilutes a property right on the basis of race. Justice Blackmun wrote "When an organization links membership benefits to residency in a narrow geographical area, that decision infuses those benefits into the bundle of rights for which an individual pays when buying or leasing within the area." At that point, the mandate of §1982 operates to ensure that the nonwhite resident is guaranteed the same rights as are enjoyed by a white resident.

To defendant's contention that even if §1982 applies, their facility is exempt as a private club under §2000a(e) of Title II, the court found it unnecessary to reach the issue as to whether that section could constitute a limitation on rights under §1982, because defendant's facility was not a truly private association and they found "no plan or purpose of exclusiveness," since membership, as in the Sullivan v. Little Hunting Park case, "is open to every white person within the geographic area, there being no selective elements other than race." Justice Blackmun also found that under the provisions of §§1981 and 1982, the defendant could not validly exclude black guests of white members.

LEE v. SOUTHERN HOME SITES CORPORATION, 444 F.2d 143 (5th Cir. 1971). The defendant was a realtor developing "Ocean Beach Estates" near Ocean Springs, Mississippi. The defendant offered by mail to sell the plaintiff a $600 lot for a down payment of $49.50; the same terms had been applied in the sale of 119 lots out of the 1206 lots sold by the time of the trial. The offer stipulated that the purchaser "must be a member of the white race," and the defendant refused to sell the lot, after the black plaintiff had traveled over 100 miles with $50 in cash, ready, willing and able to purchase the lot on the terms of the letter. On October 15, 1968, four months after the Supreme Court had resuscitated §1982 in Jones, the plaintiff brought suit; he prevailed both in the lower court and on appeal. On remand the district judge found that the defendant did not know of Jones v. Mayer at the time of refusing the plaintiff's offer; therefore the defendant's conduct was not so "'unreasonable and obdurately obstinate' to warrant an award for attorney's fees." On the second appeal, the court of appeals reversed the district court's denial of attorney's fees, holding that "attorney's fees are part of the effective remedy a court should fashion to carry out the congressional policy embodied in §1982." The court found as overriding considerations that private suits are necessary to effectuate congressional policy and that awards of attorney's fees are necessary to encourage private litigants to initiate such suits. While §1982 is not a statute providing detailed remedies, the award of attorney's fees is justified as effectuating congressional policy. Further, the actions of Congress in enacting the 1964 and 1968 Civil Rights Acts support the view that the award of attorney's fees is proper; both acts contained provisions allowing the "prevailing party" to recover reasonable attorney's fees. Moreover, both acts expressed an intention to retain older statutes directed at the same kind of social problems. Citing Newman v. Piggie Park, supra page 216, the court agreed that the nation must rely upon private individuals to enforce a strong congressional policy; in this situation, the award of attorney's fees should be freely available.

NOTES

1. As the Lee v. Southern Home Sites case indicates, a whole series of cases have tested the scope and effectiveness of relief under 42 U.S.C. §1982, since Jones v. Alfred Mayer Co. Though the Jones case itself involved only injunctive relief, cases such as Sullivan v. Little Hunting Park have held that damages are also available, citing 28 U.S.C. §1343(4) as creating federal jurisdiction for granting damages under §1982, as well as equitable relief.

2. The First Circuit has agreed with the Fifth regarding attorney's fees, stating:

> If a defendant may feel that the cost of litigation, and, particularly, that the financial circumstances of an injured party may mean that the chances of suit being brought, or continued in the face of opposition, will be small, there will be little brake upon deliberate wrongdoing. In such instances public policy may suggest an award of costs that will remove the burden from the shoulders of the plaintiff seeking to vindicate the public right. (Knight v. Auciello, 453 F.2d 852, 853 (1st Cir. 1972).)

See also Phillips v. Pinehurst Realty Company, 2 Race Rel. L. Sur. 33 (M.D. Tenn. 1970), granting a black Nashville couple $1500 as compensatory damages and attorney's fees, and an injunction to purchase a lot at a reduced price as set out in a mailed solicitation.

3. Not only do the reported cases show that effective relief has been obtained when individual victims of housing bias use §1982, but relief has often been quite prompt. For example, in Turner v. Lazurus, 1 Race Rel. L. Sur. 43 (1969), a black college student who had been denied rental of an apartment because of race was able to obtain a temporary restraining order the day after a discriminatory refusal occurred, and two weeks later was awarded $832.50 covering damages and attorney's fees.

In Harris v. Jones, 296 F. Supp. 1082 (D. Mass. 1969), a black couple, denied an apartment allegedly because the owner desired to rent to an older couple, proved discrimination by using a white "tester" of their age and ostensible intent, who was offered the apartment by the owner. The court ordered an injunction that made defendants execute a standard one-year lease to plaintiffs, but denied the damage claim as being negligible.

In Pina v. Homsi, 1 Race Rel. L. Sur. 183 (1969), an interracial couple, also denied rental of an apartment, were able to obtain a temporary restraining order the same day that the suit was filed, and two days later were awarded $200 each for emotional distress and $350 for counsel fees.

4. The fact that racial discrimination was not the sole basis for rejection of plaintiff's application is no bar for relief under a Seventh Circuit decision, which granted a young black mother an injunction requiring defendant to offer her the lease of an apartment, and a sum not to exceed $1000 to compensate her for loss of her civil rights and any mental anguish suffered by her. Smith v. Adler Realty Co., 436 F.2d 344 (7th Cir. 1971).

Damages for mental suffering awarded to a victim of housing discrimination under a state law were affirmed by the Massachusetts Supreme Judicial Court in Mass. Comm. Against Discrimination v. Franzaroli, 357 Mass. 112, 256 N.E. 2d 311 (1970).

5. In Wright v. Kaine Realty, 352 F. Supp. 222 (N.D. Ill. 1972), the court held that plaintiffs' request for $30,000 in punitive damages, as relief for alleged racial discrimination in failing to sell or show them homes available for sale, was not pre-empted by the specific damage limitation of $1000 provided in Title VIII, 42 U.S.C. §3612(c). If the Seventh Circuit's decision in Rogers v. Loether, supra page 642, requiring a jury trial for the award of punitive damages, is generally adopted, might its reasoning be applied to §1982? If so, what effect is it likely to have on the damages recovered in the cases reviewed above?

6. §1982 has had an impact on reducing the role of exemptions in state housing acts. In Richards v. Mangum, 303 N.Y.S. 2d 320 (1969), for example, plaintiffs argued that, in light of the Jones case, the provision of the state fair housing statute exempting from coverage rental units in owner-occupied two-family dwellings was unconstitutional. Although another New York court had previously rejected this argument, the court here agreed that, because of Jones, there were now serious doubts about the constitutionality of such exemptions in open housing laws. No final disposition was reached, however, as the case was set down for a hearing on certain procedural matters.

See also Barrick Realty, Inc. v. City of Gary, Ind., 354 F. Supp. 126 (N.D. Ind. 1973), upholding the validity of an ordinance banning the display of "For Sale," "Sold," or similar signs from premises in residential areas of the city. The ordinance, designed to combat segregated housing and rapid racial turnover of neighborhoods, was held a valid exercise of police power and not violative of due process, free speech or the right to travel.

7. §1982 has been used successfully by the survivors of a black serviceman killed in Vietnam against a cemetery that refused to sell them a lot because of their race. The court held that §1982 is not limited to housing, and found that cemetery lots are "property." Moreover, the racially restrictive covenants in the cemetery were held void and of no legal effect, not merely unenforceable under the doctrine of Shelley v. Kraemer. Terry v. Elmwood Cemetery, 307 F. Supp. 369 (N.D. Ala. 1969). See, to the same effect, Allen v. Hillcrest Memorial Cemetery, Inc., 3 Race Rel. L. Sur. 39 (Md. Cir. Ct. 1970).

8. In a further extension of §1982, which has implications for low-income blacks, a federal court has held that a group of black homeowners, suing as a class, stated a cause of action under §1982 against several real estate concerns and banks who, plaintiffs charged, had conspired to sell them used residential property at higher prices and under more burdensome conditions than would have been required had they been white. As the court interpreted the complaint,

> . . . the scheme of exploitation often included obtaining purchase money mortgages based on false and excessive appraisals of used residential property. The essence of the scheme is alleged to have been the purchase of residential properties from white homeowners, and the resale, often in the nature of quick "turn-around" transactions, at greatly inflated prices to negro purchasers, who were disadvantaged by the system of de facto segregation and the resulting shortage of housing for negroes in Chicago. The terms of the contracts, especially the price, are alleged to represent unlawful profit gained through this pattern of exploitation. (300 F. Supp. at 214.)

The complaint also alleged that some defendants were engaged in block-busting. The court stated that, assuming the plaintiffs' allegations were true, "violations of law resulted from defendants' concerted exploitation of de facto racial segregation." The court interpreted §1982 as establishing the rule that there cannot, in this country, be markets or profits based on the color of a man's skin. Contract Buyers League v. F & F Investment, 300 F. Supp. 210 (N.D. Ill. 1969). In an appeal on procedural issues, the Seventh Circuit held that the doctrine of laches was not applicable to the plaintiffs' suit, and that a five-year statute of limitations for civil state actions governed the civil rights claims of the plaintiffs, which period of limitations commenced when the contracts terminated. Baker v. F & F Investment, 420 F.2d 1191 (1970).

Racism Hypo 8
INTEGRATION v. RIGHT ON *FINANCING COMPANY*

A group of black realtors and savings and loan companies have organized a special home-financing plan called the Righteous In Getting Homes Together Organization for Negroes (RIGHT ON). The purpose of the organization, as explained by its founders, is to assist black families living in the ghetto to finance the purchases of homes. The persons eligible for financial assistance are generally stable individuals with good credit and steady jobs. Their incomes range from eight to eleven thousand dollars per year. They generally are unable to obtain mortgage loans through the usual channels, because of very high qualifying standards for such loans, and also because of obvious, but almost impossible to prove, racial discrimination, much of it of the "institutional" character.

The RIGHT ON Financing Company has been operating for about a year, during which time it has assisted dozens of black families to obtain mortgage loans at reasonable rates. It should be said that all the mortgage loans made are secured by guarantees from a major foundation, and there is, thus, little risk of serious loss to the participants in the mortgage operation. Officers of RIGHT ON have generally received the approbation of the community as well as the lasting appreciation of the black families they have helped.

Recently, the RIGHT ON Company became embroiled in a controversy as a result of a suit filed in federal district court by a black resident of the ghetto, John Integration. Integration alleges that he sought and was denied a mortgage loan by RIGHT ON, even though he has a credit rating and other qualifications at least equal to those possessed by successful applicants for RIGHT ON loans. He asserts further that his application was denied because he insisted on purchasing a home in an all-white area, and states that RIGHT ON will finance only homes located in the ghetto or in areas which are changing from white to black. Because he and similarly situated blacks are ineligible for other loans, Integration claims that RIGHT ON's refusal prevents his moving to an area where schools and other public facilities are better, the air is cleaner, and he can get a cheaper and much better house than is available in the ghetto or a "changing area." He asserts that limiting black homeowners to specified areas is a primary reason why neighborhoods become "changing areas," and that RIGHT ON is actually carrying out a form of blockbusting.

In a public statement made after the suit was filed, RIGHT ON officials acknowledged that, in fact, their loans are limited to homes outside predominantly white areas. They defend this policy on pragmatic, political and philosophical grounds, stating that the amount of mortgage money they have available is limited, and that it should go to those willing to remain in the ghetto and help in upgrading the housing there; that if they financed homes in predominantly white areas, they would be subject to "blockbusting" charges — perhaps litigation — and would incur the enmity of large real estate and banking interests, who might interfere and endanger the operation; and that they believe black people should remain together and develop political strength rather than dilute this potential by moving to all-white areas. They deny that their policy is in violation of any law or the constitutional rights of the plaintiff.

In his suit, John Integration asserts that RIGHT ON's policy is in violation of the 1866 Civil Rights Act (42 U.S.C. §1982), since it must be viewed in the light of the traditional housing segregation that has existed in this country. He seeks injunctive relief and appropriate money damages.

Law Firm A will represent John Integration in a motion for preliminary injunction to be heard by the district court.

Law Firm B will oppose the injunction on behalf of the RIGHT ON Financing Company.

12. HOUSING REMEDIES FOR BLACKS AS A CLASS

A. URBAN RENEWAL AND BLACK HOUSING

Clearly, slum clearance has not been for the benefit of slum residents, nor has slum rehabilitation benefited families of low and modest incomes. Instead, cities have substituted their own goals for national housing goals because solving the housing problem of the poor does not help solve the cities' financial problems; does not improve the tax rate; does not improve the cities' competitive position vis-à-vis the suburbs; and does not gain national recognition for leadership in creating symbols of civic grandeur.

Urban renewal has eliminated pockets of delapidated housing and blight in core cities and suburbs, reaped windfall profits for real estate investors, and paved the way for new public monuments. But urban renewal has hurt and scattered the poor and Negroes, while subsidizing the right of the more affluent to replace them, as the "highest and best use of the land." Except in private, the federal government refuses to admit this fact: slum clearance has failed to provide decent housing for slum-dwellers. Urban renewal and public housing programs have intensified segregation of Negroes in inner city ghettos. Today construction of public housing for families in major cities has come to a virtual standstill because of the fierce resistance of white neighborhoods to accept Negroes in general and low-income Negroes in particular. (A. Schuchter, White Power/Black Freedom 36-37 (1968).)

NORWALK CORE v. NORWALK REDEVELOPMENT AGENCY
395 F.2d 920 (2d Cir. 1968)

Before SMITH, KAUFMAN and HAYS, Circuit Judges.

J. JOSEPH SMITH, Circuit Judge:

This appeal raises timely and fundamental questions regarding the availability of the federal courts to persons who, displaced by urban renewal programs, claim that they have been deprived of the equal protection of the laws in connection with government efforts to assure their relocation, and that such relocation efforts have not been adequate under the mandate of a federal statute. The plaintiffs' complaint, which attempted to raise these two issues, was dismissed by the District Court for the District of Connecticut. Norwalk CORE v. Norwalk Redevelopment Agency, 42 F.R.D. 617 (1967). We hold that the District Court was in error, and remand for further proceedings not inconsistent with this opinion. . . .

Pursuant to section 105(c) of the Act, 42 U.S.C. §1455(c), the Contract required that the Agency provide, in the urban renewal area or in other areas not generally less desirable in regard to public utilities and public and commercial facilities, decent, safe and sanitary dwellings within the financial means of the families displaced by the project, equal in number to the number of displaced families, available to them, and reasonably accessible to their places of employment.

The plaintiffs are the Norwalk, Connecticut chapter of the Congress of Racial Equality, two nonprofit tenants' associations comprised of low-income Negroes and Puerto Ricans, and eight individuals representing four classes of low-income Negroes and Puerto Ricans who were allegedly subjected to discrimination in connection with the project.[2] They brought this class action in June 1967. . . .

Since the action was dismissed, the allegations of the complaint, summarized in the following paragraphs, must be accepted as true.

The Agency made its redevelopment plans without providing for the construction of low-rent housing on the ground that the existing low-rent public housing in the City, with its predicted turnover, would adequately meet the relocation needs of the low-income Negro and Puerto Rican families living within the project area. Prior to the time when it entered into the Contract, however, the Agency knew: (1) that its turnover figures were exaggerated, arrived at so as to present apparent facilities for relocation; (2) that there was a long waiting list for low-rent public housing in the City, substantially all Negro and Puerto Rican families and that any plan giving priority to families from the project area in the public housing would impair the housing opportunities of the Negroes and Puerto Ricans on the waiting list; and (3) that there was discrimination against Negroes and Puerto Ricans in the private housing market in the City. Thereafter, the Agency learned from reports by the Commission on Civil Rights of the State of Connecticut and by the Agency's "relocation experts," Urban Dynamics Consultants, that vacancies in housing projects in the City were running less than one-half of the predicted number, that the Housing Authority received an average of over 300 applications per year for public housing units, and that discrimination in rentals in the private or open market was rampant, rentals to Negro and Puerto Rican families averaging twice as much as that charged to white families for comparable housing. The annual report of the City's Department of Health for the year 1964 stated that families formerly living in the project area were being crowded into already overcrowded homes, and that multiple dwelling units were being created from homes which were barely adequate for one family. The Agency knew, plaintiffs allege, that Negro and Puerto

2. The four classes are: (1) those still occupying homes within the project area; (2) those whose homes in the project area have been demolished, and who now occupy "overcrowded" rental units outside of the project area but within the City of Norwalk; (3) those whose homes in the project area have been demolished, and who now occupy rental units "at excessive rentals" outside of the project area but within the City of Norwalk; and (4) those who formerly lived in Norwalk, but "by virtue of the acts of defendants" complained of, now occupy rental units outside of the City. . . .

Rican families were being subjected to such hardships and deprivations in connection with relocation (not experienced to any substantially equal degree by white families in the City) that many were being forced to leave the City entirely, but it continued, nonetheless, to demolish the homes of low-income Negro and Puerto Rican families in the project area and continued to make additions and revisions in its plans without making any provision for the construction of low-rent housing to be made available to the Negro and Puerto Rican families being relocated. The Agency also entered into a contract with defendant Towne House in May 1967 for the sale of a six-acre parcel of land in the project area to be used for 90 units of moderate-income housing at rentals beyond the financial means of the Negro and Puerto Rican families being displaced, and that parcel is the only plot of land owned by the City which is currently available for the construction of low-income housing.

Despite the requests of various groups and citizens of the City, including some of the plaintiffs, HUD has refused to require the construction of low-cost housing, and has approved the sale of the six-acre parcel. "Further recourse to HUD would be futile."

The complaint goes on to allege that the homes of various of the plaintiffs and other Negro and Puerto Rican families and individuals have been demolished, that some of them have been moved to rental units within the project area on a temporary basis, and that the City and Agency have "pursued a course of conduct to force the said Negro and Puerto Rican families out of the on-site housing structures by rendering such housing unsafe, unsanitary and indecent, by charging rents beyond the financial means of the families and individuals, by forcing excessive moving of families and individuals from one on-site location to another . . . and by carrying on heavy construction activities around the said on-site houses." Some of the displaced Negro and Puerto Rican families have been compelled to move into overcrowded housing, some into housing at rentals substantially in excess of their financial means, and some into housing outside of the City.

The plaintiffs make three claims based upon the foregoing allegations: (1) that they and those whom they represent have been denied the equal protection of the laws guaranteed by the Fourteenth Amendment and by the laws of the United States; (2) that the local defendants have intended to deprive low-income Negro and Puerto Rican families of the equal protection of the laws, and have intended to force such families out of the City; and (3) that the defendants have acted in violation of section 105(c) of the Act.

Plaintiffs' prayer for relief included requests that the Agency and City, and Towne House and Katz, be enjoined from transferring or encumbering the six-acre parcel, that the Agency be enjoined from demolishing any residential structure within the project area until the residents have been relocated into safe and decent housing at rentals they can afford, and that the District Court require the Agency, City and Authority to proceed "with all deliberate speed," under the supervision of the Court, to propose a plan for and to construct low-income housing units on the six-acre parcel.

The essential ground upon which the District Court dismissed the complaint was that both the association and individual plaintiffs "have no standing to challenge the official conduct here in question." 42 F.R.D. at 622. The District Court also held that the action was not a proper class action under Rule 23, F. R. Civ. P.

The court took into account that the relief asked for in the complaint was in its view inappropriate, but we are not sure of the extent to which this underlay its decision. The opinion concluded that "It is the use of [the] six acre tract for moderate-income housing rather than low-income rental units that forms the basis of the instant action." 42 F.R.D. at 619. This characterization of the action in terms of the prayer for relief was, in a sense, correct, for the complaint summarized the action as one for an injunction restraining the defendants from proceeding with the sale of the six-acre parcel and directing them to build low-rent housing on the parcel, and for an injunction restraining the defendants from evicting families living in the project area until all of the families were permanently relocated in housing within their financial means. Nevertheless, if the complaint was dismissed on the basis that the relief requested was inappropriate, or beyond the Court's power to grant, the Court moved too quickly. . . .

We hold that the allegations of this complaint state constitutional and statutory claims on which relief can be granted, that the individual plaintiffs have standing to make the claims, and that this action was appropriately brought as a class action. We turn first to the issues presented by plaintiffs' constitutional claim.

I

The plaintiffs contend that they were denied the equal protection of the laws when the defendants acted, knowingly and deliberately, so as to compound the problem of racial discrimination in the Norwalk housing market, with the inevitable and intended result that some Negroes and Puerto Ricans would be forced to leave the city altogether.

The District Court never reached the merits of this claim, for it concluded that

> Members of the public, whether living inside or outside a project area, ordinarily have no standing to challenge planning of an urban renewal project . . . nor, by alleging civil rights violations, do they gain standing they would otherwise not have [citing cases]. If residents of a project area cannot challenge a project while it is in the planning stages and before construction has begun, certainly they can have no standing to assert the same kind of challenge at a time when planning has been implemented, most of the land has been purchased and conveyed to developers, and construction of new buildings has been almost completed. 42 F.R.D. at 622.

It is true that courts have been reluctant to interfere with urban renewal planning. The fact that the reasons for this reluctance have been lumped together under the rubric of "lack of standing to sue" should not be allowed to obscure the distinction, necessary albeit not altogether clear, between the propriety of allowing particular plaintiffs to bring litigation (their standing to sue) and the propriety of judicial attempts to resolve the problem which the plaintiffs are attempting to bring before the court (the question of justiciability).

We consider first the issue of standing. [After reviewing the authorities, the court concluded that plaintiffs have standing because:] Their stake in the outcome of the case is immediate and personal, and the right which they allege has been violated — the right not to be subjected to racial discrimination in government programs — is one which the courts will protect. Their standing to sue is clear. . . .

The District Court opinion also raised, at least by implication, the question of justiciability. Holding that the plaintiffs could not "gain standing they would otherwise not have" by alleging "civil rights violations," the Court cited Green Street Association v. Daley, 373 F.2d 1 (7 Cir.), *cert. denied* 387 U.S. 932 . . . (1967).[11] The complaint in Green Street alleged, inter alia, that the urban renewal project which the plaintiffs were attempting to bring before the court was not undertaken in good faith, but was a "deliberate plan to create a no-Negro 'buffer zone' between [a] shopping area and [a] surrounding residential community so that the shopping area [would] be more attractive to white customers . . . ," and that the plan proposed "relocation of the residents in the cleared area in accordance with segregated housing patterns . . . ." 373 F.2d at 4.

The Seventh Circuit characterized the first count of the complaint, which attempted to raise constitutional issues as to the reasons for which the plan was undertaken, as "an attempt to obtain federal judicial review of a program of urban renewal prior to the exercise of the power of eminent domain." 373 F.2d at 6. It held that cases presenting such challenges are matters for condemnation proceedings in the state courts if the taking is ostensibly for a public purpose, and that only in exceptional cases such as Progress Dev. Corp. v. Mitchell, 286 F.2d 222 (7 Cir. 1961),[12] "where the facts alleged indicate to all outward appearances that the taking is designed solely to deny constitu-

11. The Court also cited Johnson v. Redevelopment Agency of the City of Oakland, California, 317 F.2d 872 (9 Cir.), cert. denied 375 U.S. 915 . . . (1963), on this issue. While violation of the Fifth and Fourteenth Amendments was alleged in that case, upon appeal the issues had narrowed to whether or not the defendant had formulated and was carrying out a feasible plan of relocation as required by section 105(c) of the Act.

12. In Progress, the plaintiffs were subdivision developers who had announced their intention to sell some of the houses they proposed to construct to Negroes. The complaint alleged, inter alia, that the defendants were abusing their power to condemn land and to enforce local building ordinances so as to discriminate against plaintiffs because of their announced intention to sell to Negroes. The Seventh Circuit, characterizing the case as one concerning "the corporate right to engage in business and make a profit," 286 F.2d at 234, held that the District Court had "erred in granting summary judgment [for defendants] on the complaint." Ibid.

tional rights, is the power of eminent domain subject to the prior scrutiny of the federal courts." 373 F.2d at 7.

The fourth count of the complaint in Green Street dealt with the alleged deficiencies in the relocation program. Claims were made under section 105 of the Housing Act of 1949, 42 U.S.C. §1455(c), section 601 of the Civil Rights Act of 1964, 42 U.S.C. §2000d, and the equal protection clause of the Fourteenth Amendment. The court discussed the issue of standing to sue under the two statutes, but not standing to raise the equal protection claim.

The Seventh Circuit thus did not say that the Green Street plaintiffs lacked standing to raise their constitutional claims. Much of what the court said about the first count of the complaint, however, implies that it harbored some doubt as to the justiciability of the issues which the plaintiffs were attempting to raise in that count. It was a concern for "the practical and efficient administration of urban renewal programs," 373 F.2d at 5, and a reluctance to inquire into the subjective reasons of the legislative authority seeking to acquire the land in question, id. at 6, which underlay the court's refusal to review the urban renewal program prior to the exercise of the power of eminent domain. The holding reached was narrow, however: that the issues should be raised, if at all, in state court condemnation proceedings.

It was contended at oral argument in this case that plaintiffs' constitutional claim is non-justiciable; in particular, that cases such as this one cannot be heard without involving the courts in over-all urban renewal planning, and thus in the resolution of questions which are ultimately political. We need not concern ourselves with the problem raised by the first count of the complaint in Green Street: the justiciability of a challenge to the basic validity of an urban renewal program, on the ground that the program as a whole, is intended to achieve or perpetuate racial segregation. Plaintiffs here complain that they were denied the equal protection of the laws in the planning and implementation of the relocation program, and this, at least, is a justiciable claim. (The Seventh Circuit agrees, for it reached the merits of the constitutional issues raised by the *fourth* count of the complaint in Green Street.)

We cannot doubt the necessity of discretionary decision making in urban renewal planning. This necessity would render unfit for judicial decision many questions concerning urban renewal. . . . This does not mean, however, that every case or controversy touching this area lies beyond judicial cognizance. Case-by-case inquiry is necessary, with due regard for the need for judicially discoverable and manageable standards for resolving problems to be undertaken, and with recognition of the role played by the coordinate branches of the Federal Government in the planning and implementation of urban renewal. . . .

The extent to which relocation of those displaced by urban renewal is required will necessarily affect the pace at which urban renewal can take place, and the priority of goals in urban renewal planning. Issues are at stake which are, in the truest sense of the word, political. For example, if public housing were required to be available for every displacee of urban renewal, then it would follow, at least in the present condition of the nation's cities, that the building of public housing would be assigned very high priority. The standard for relocation is thus appropriately set by the legislative and executive branches of government, and not by the courts. Congress has provided, in section 105(c) of the Act, that the standard for relocation is "decent, safe and sanitary dwellings" in the urban renewal area or in other areas not generally less desirable, within the financial means of the families displaced. The executive branch (HUD) is entrusted with the primary responsibility for enforcing this standard.

The basic constitutional claim raised by the allegations of the complaint, as we understand it, is that in Norwalk this standard was less sufficiently met in the relocation of Negroes and Puerto Ricans than in the relocation of whites. We need not consider the political question of the adequacy of the standard to conclude, as we have for reasons set out below, that proof of these allegations would make out a case of violation of the equal protection clause, and we see no reason to believe that the courts are incapable of fashioning remedies to insure that the standard is equally met for all citizens. With this case only at the pleadings stage, we do not think that we should speculate on what specific remedies might be appropriate if the plaintiffs' allegations are proved. As a general matter, the most appropriate form of judicial relief in cases such as this would be to require proof that the relocation standard is being met in general as adequately for non-whites as it is for whites before allowing the project to go forward. An affirmative form of relief, such as an order requiring the construction of low-income housing, would of course be much less appropriate, since it would necessarily involve the court in areas foreign to its experience and competence.

If the defendants' argument is that requiring that the relocation standard be met equally for all displacees, non-white as well as white, will result in delays in the implementation of some urban renewal programs, the answer is that such delays would be due to the standard, rather than its equal implementation for all. Whether or not such delays must be prevented is much more in the nature of a political question than is the constitutional issue which plaintiffs are attempting to raise.

Nothing we have said so far would require considering plaintiffs' constitutional claims, of course, if the complaint did not allege a deprivation of equal protection of the laws, in violation of the Fourteenth Amendment. . . .

. . . [T]he District Court in the case before us said that the defendants' relocation program "is designed to prevent displacees from suffering any consequences or change in circumstances, if and when they are relocated into the discriminatory housing market. They cannot owe a greater duty to end a situation which is merely 'accidental' to the plan." 42 F.R.D. at 623.

We do not understand plaintiffs' constitutional argument to be that defendants must end discrimination in the Norwalk open housing market through the relocation plan, or even that defendants must find integrated housing for those displaced by the Project. Those are arguments we need not consider until they are appropriately put to us.

What plaintiffs' complaint alleges, in substance, is that in planning and implementing the Project, the local defendants did not assure, or even attempt to assure, relocation for Negro and Puerto Rican displacees in compliance with the Contract to the same extent as they did for whites; indeed, they intended through the combination of the Project and the rampant discrimination in rentals in the Norwalk housing market to drive many Negroes and Puerto Ricans out of the City of Norwalk. The argument is that proof of these allegations would make out a case of violation of the equal protection clause. We agree.

Section 105(c) of the Act provides that contracts for loans or capital grants entered into under the Act shall require the availability or the provision of relocation housing for displacees which meets the standard set out in that section. That standard is designed, as the District Court recognized, to prevent displacees from suffering a change for the worse in their living conditions. It is no secret that in the present state of our society discrimination in the housing market means that a change for the worse is generally more likely for members of minority races than for other displacees.[17] This means that in many cases the relocation standard will be easier to meet for white than for non-white displacees.[18] But the fact that the discrimination is not inherent in the administration of the program, but is, in the words of the District Court, "accidental to the plan," surely does not excuse the planners from making sure that there is available relocation housing for all displacees. "Equal protection of the laws" means more than merely the absence of governmental action designed to discriminate; as Judge J. Skelly Wright has said, "we now firmly recognize that the arbitrary quality of thoughtlessness can be as disastrous and unfair to private rights and the public interest as the perversity of a willful scheme." Hobson v. Hansen, 269 F. Supp. 401, 497 (D.D.C. 1967).[19]

Since the plaintiffs are admittedly displaced as a result of the Project, there is no question of the presence of "state action" within the meaning of the Fourteenth Amendment. Where the relocation standard set by Congress is met

17. See, e.g., U.S. Advisory Commission on Intergovernmental Relations, Relocation: Unequal Treatment of People and Businesses Displaced by Governments (1965); and Hartman, The Housing of Relocated Families, 30 J. Am. Inst. Planners 266, 273-274 (1964).

18. We wish to stress that the specific problem is not that non-white displacees are, on the average, poorer than white displacees. That may be so, but it is a more general problem. What we are concerned with is that discrimination which forecloses much of the housing market to some racial groups, thereby driving up the price they must pay for housing. The situation is made worse by the fact that most people displaced by urban renewal are non-white. See Note, 77 Yale L.J. 966, 967 (1968).

19. See generally Black, Foreword: "State Action," Equal Protection, and California's Proposition 14, 81 Harv. L. Rev. 69 (1967).

for those who have access to any housing in the community which they can afford, but not for those who, by reason of their race, are denied free access to housing they can afford and must pay more for what they can get, the state action affirms the discrimination in the housing market. This is not "equal protection of the laws."

What we have said may require classification by race. That is something which the Constitution usually forbids, not because it is inevitably an impermissible classification, but because it is one which usually, to our national shame, has been drawn for the purpose of maintaining racial inequality. Where it is drawn for the purpose of achieving equality it will be allowed, and to the extent it is necessary to avoid unequal treatment by race, it will be required.

We hold that plaintiffs' complaint alleges a denial of the equal protection of the laws, and that the District Court should have proceeded to consider that claim on its merits.

II

The plaintiffs' statutory claim is that the federal and local defendants have violated section 105(c) of the Act, 42 U.S.C. §1455(c) (Supp. 1967). The District Court concluded that plaintiffs lacked standing to raise this issue. Since the section requires provision for the relocation of displaced families, it can hardly be thought that displaced families such as plaintiffs, do not have the required personal stake in the outcome of litigation where a violation of the section is claimed. If anybody can raise this claim, it is these plaintiffs. The question we must answer is whether actions taken by HUD and local public agencies under section 105(c) are ever subject to judicial review.

The proposition is now firmly established that "judicial review of a final agency action by an aggrieved person will not be cut off unless there is persuasive reason to believe that such was the purpose of Congress." . . .

III

The District Court held that this suit could not properly be brought as a class action under Rule 23 of the Federal Rules because there were no questions of law or fact common to the class or classes which the plaintiffs claim to represent. We think that the District Court erred in reading the complaint as requesting ultimately that the Court concern itself with the particular circumstances of each displacee's relocation. The complaint alleges both that Negroes and Puerto Ricans were discriminated against in connection with relocation and that the relocation standards of section 105(c) were generally not met for Negro and Puerto Rican displacees. These allegations clearly raise questions of fact common to the class which plaintiffs represent. The fact that some members of the class were personally satisfied with the defendants' relocation efforts is irrelevant. Cf. Potts v. Flax, 313 F.2d 284, 288-289 (5 Cir. 1963).

The association plaintiffs were denied standing below because they are "not themselves members of the classes whose rights they claim to be asserting." 42 F.R.D. at 622. We think that the reasons for requiring an individual plaintiff in a class action to be a member of the class do not necessarily preclude an association from representing a class where its *raison d'etre* is to represent the interests of that class. We do not decide, however, whether the association plaintiffs have standing. The answer to that question depends on whether there is a compelling need to grant them standing in order that the constitutional rights of persons not immediately before the court might be vindicated. See NAACP v. State of Alabama, ex rel. Patterson, 357 U.S. 449, 458-460. . . .[43] It appears to us that the individual plaintiffs can adequately represent the interests of all members of the relevant class, but we will not preclude the plaintiffs from trying to show to the District Court's satisfaction that it is only the association plaintiffs which can perform this function.

Judgment reversed. Remanded for further proceedings not inconsistent with this opinion.

HAYS, Circuit Judge (dissenting):

I would affirm the determination of the district court.

The issues which the plaintiffs offer are not justiciable and the remedies they seek are not within the power of the court to grant. See Perkins v. Lukens Steel Co., 310 U.S. 113, 131-132 . . . (1940) ("The interference of the courts with the performance of the ordinary duties of the executive departments of the Government, would be productive of nothing but mischief," quoting Decatur v. Paulding, 39 U.S. (14 Pet.) 497, 516 . . . (1840)); Berman v. Parker, 348 U.S. 26, 33 . . . (1954) ("We do not sit to determine whether a particular housing project is or is not desirable").

The holding that plaintiffs do not have standing to bring the action is another formulation of the same principles. See Green Street Association v. Daley, 373 F.2d 1 (7th Cir.), *cert. denied,* 387 U.S. 932 . . . (1967); Berry v. Housing and Home Finance Agency, 340 F.2d 939 (2d Cir. 1965) (per curiam); Johnson v. Redevelopment Agency, 317 F.2d 872 (9th Cir.), *cert. denied,* 375 U.S. 915 . . . (1963); Pittsburgh Hotels Association v. Urban Redevelopment Authority, 309 F.2d 186 (3d Cir. 1962), *cert. denied sub nom.* Hilton Hotels Corp. v. Urban Redevelopment Authority, 372 U.S. 916 . . . (1963); Taft Hotel Corp. v. Housing and Home Finance Agency, 262 F.2d 307 (2d Cir. 1958) (per curiam), *cert. denied,* 359 U.S. 967 . . . (1959); Allied-City Wide, Inc. v. Cole, 97 U.S. App. D.C. 277, 230 F.2d 827 (1956) (per curiam).

The Federal courts cannot administer the housing program.

43. We reject the local defendants' contention that an association cannot represent the rights of its members unless the interests of the association itself are involved. In NAACP v. State of Alabama, ex rel. Patterson, the Supreme Court specifically referred to the likelihood that the association itself would be adversely affected as a "further factor" pointing towards the holding of standing. 357 U.S. at 459-60. . . .

NOTES

1. Simply to find standing, the court in Norwalk CORE had to distinguish several contrary holdings reached by courts faced with greatly similar suits, brought by poor (and usually black) refugees of federally funded urban renewal programs, who were usually left with literally no place to go. For a long time, the courts provided no refuge, adopting the position that "urban renewal planning generally is not reviewable." Note, Family Relocation in Urban Renewal, 82 Harv. L. Rev. 864, 892 (1969). But this stance was relaxed somewhat when the courts and the public could no longer avoid the fact that urban renewal, while a boon to many, wreaked painful and often permanent financial and psychological damage on "[e]asily identified, relatively small numbers of people [who] are being handed a distinctly disproportionate and frequently excruciating share of the cost of whatever social gain is involved." Michelman, Property, Utility, and Fairness: Comments on the Ethical Foundations of "Just Compensation" Law, 80 Harv. L. Rev. 1165, 1255 (1967).

2. As the cases below show, even "successful" civil rights litigation in the urban renewal field — as with jury discrimination cases, see Chapter 16 — has served mainly to delay rather than remedy the asserted injustice. The whole dreary legal history is documented in considerable detail in McGee, Urban Renewal in the Crucible of Judicial Review, 56 Va. L. Rev. 826 (1970).

3. In Green Street Association v. Daley, 373 F.2d 1 (7th Cir. 1967), distinguished in Norwalk CORE, black plaintiffs claimed that the project was not a good-faith renewal plan but a Negro removal plan, under which they were being driven out to create a "no-Negro buffer zone" between a shopping area and the surrounding residential community on Chicago's South Side. The Seventh Circuit affirmed dismissal of the suit on the basis that plaintiffs lacked standing to sue, that their conspiracy claim should be considered in state court condemnation proceedings, and that only designated federal officials could employ the administrative procedure provided for enforcing Title VI of the 1964 Civil Rights Act. Finally, to the plaintiffs' allegation that defendant's action would force plaintiffs to relocate in segregated housing, the court replied that the plan does not, and could not, set up relocation machinery which compels displacees to move into segregated areas of the city, since the city has no power to require persons to relocate in any particular area. See also Kelly v. Romney, 316 F. Supp. 840 (S.D. Ohio 1970), where the court cited, inter alia, plaintiffs' laches in refusing to enjoin a federally funded park project which, they alleged, was displacing them without a feasible relocation plan.

4. The Green Street decision is said to illustrate "the extreme reluctance of courts, both state and federal courts, to touch an urban renewal case where an approved plan is under attack." Berger & Cogen, Responsive Urban Renewal: The Neighborhood Shapes the Plan, 1 Urban L. Annual 75 (1968). In discussing the underlying reasons for judicial self-restraint, Berger and Cogen explain that:

What lies at the root of the court's self-denial is reluctance to unravel a plan that has been many years in the making, that has built up community expectations, and that has presented several opportunities for discussion, persuasion and attack during its years of preparation. This unwillingness, in turn, is responsive to the widely shared opinion that the courtroom is the improper milieu for planning (or unplanning) the physical and human develoment of a community. Moreover, even the delay of such a plan for the course of a trial and inevitable appeals might set in motion a wave of repercussions that would be difficult to foresee and which few judges would risk unleashing on a community. During this interim, while condemnation is stayed, land values might rise, increasing project costs beyond the limits of local and federal funds committed or even available to the venture; demand conditions might change, so as to undo the reuse assumptions that underpin the renewal scheme; the terms and availability of construction financing or municipal borrowing might become less advantageous; existing community or political support for the program might despair and vanish; federal moneys might be diverted to citizens ready to proceed; urgently needed public improvements, such as schools and neighborhood centers, which depend upon the urban renewal scheme for their financing, might be indefinitely delayed; and assuming the neighborhood is indeed a "blighted" one, the deterioration might get far worse and even spread. (Id. at 78.)

But Professor Henry McGee suggests that judicial abdication occurs because "the political strength of the displacees is too diffused and lacks sufficient economic support to withstand the larger and more powerful forces that compel the adoption of the renewal scheme." He suggests that urban renewal cases are no more complex than reapportionment, school desegregation and welfare cases, but in the latter cases there is a "sufficiently powerful social and political consensus" for such action. McGee, supra Note 2, at 855-856.

5. But whatever the basis for judicial reticence, requests for judicial intervention that are deemed tardy have little chance. In Nashville I-40 Steering Committee v. Ellington, 387 F.2d 179 (6th Cir. 1967), an integrated group sought to enjoin construction of a highway which would destroy Nashville's black business community and erect a physical barrier between the predominantly black area and other parts of the city. In affirming dismissal, the court first found that procedural requirements had been met by defendants. Then, reflecting its concern about the delay that would attend granting relief requested by plaintiffs, it quoted approvingly another court:

"To enjoin defendants at this stage from carrying out the commitment of the federal government to provide 90 per cent of the necessary funds for this project would create a chaotic situation. Plaintiffs argue that the damage to the State could be mitigated, that the rights of way which the State has acquired could be sold or returned to their former owners, that the course of the road could be changed without undue hardship. These arguments do not seem to me to be realistic. Some loss, as for example, engineering expenses, would obviously be irretrievable. In all likelihood, the ultimate loss would amount to much more. Substantial delay, perhaps amounting to over two years, would be encountered before a new route could be surveyed and engineered." 270 F. Supp. at 664.

Under the standards of judicial review in this type of action we conclude that, despite the showing of heavy damage to the North Nashville area, we have no choice except to affirm the judgment of the District Court in refusing to grant a preliminary injunction. (387 F.2d at 185.)

Plaintiffs claimed that the harm done if defendants' routing was not changed was so serious as to require judicial relief to prevent violation of due process and equal protection rights. But the court replied:

> It would be virtually impossible to select a route for an interstate highway through a congested metropolitan area without working hardships upon many citizens. Appellants suggest possible alternative routes which they contend would avoid the unfortunate economic consequences which the proposed route will impose upon the North Nashville area. Alternative routes undoubtedly would impose hardships upon others. The minimizing of hardships and adverse economic effects is a problem addressing itself to engineers, not judges. The providing of just compensation to property owners falls within the purview of the laws of eminent domain. (387 F.2d at 185.)

6. Compare the Nashville I-40 result with Powelton Civic Homes Owners Association v. HUD, 284 F. Supp. 809 (E.D. Pa. 1968), where a project still in the condemnation stage was enjoined to enable plaintiffs to have a hearing on the adequacy of relocation shelter. See also Garrett v. Hamtramck, 335 F. Supp. 16 (E.D. Mich. 1971), in which the court took cognizance of housing segregation in the area, and said that defendants knew or should have known that renewal projects, combined with segregated housing patterns, had reduced the black population from 14.5 to 8.5 percent in six years. Defendants were ordered to submit a plan "designed to remedy the wrong suffered by virtue of defendants' conduct." The plan was to include provision for relocation of all displaced persons, construction of low- and moderate-income housing for blacks evicted by renewal projects, and a program to eliminate existing housing discrimination in the city.

WESTERN ADDITION COMMUNITY ORGANIZATION v. WEAVER
294 F. Supp. 433 (N.D. Cal. 1968)

SWEIGERT, District Judge.

This is a class action brought . . . by plaintiff, Western Addition Community Organization (WACO), an unincorporated association composed of individuals and organizations in the Western Addition area of San Francisco, on behalf of residents about to be displaced from their homes by construction of Western Addition Area II Urban Renewal Project.

The purpose of the suit is to obtain a declaratory judgment and an injunction prohibiting the Secretary of the United States Department of Housing and Urban Development and the Commissioner of the Federal Housing Administration, from continuing to approve and finance Western Addition Area II Urban Renewal Project.

The case is now before the court on plaintiff's application for a preliminary injunction and upon defendants' motion to dismiss. . . .

[The court reviewed the history of the Western Addition Project, its approval but with requirements for reappraisal of the relocation plans, none of which the secretary of HUD had approved. Nevertheless, financing for the project had been continued by HUD, and after an administrative protest to HUD, plaintiffs filed this suit charging that the Redevelopment Agency's relocation plans did not meet statutory requirements. The court found that plaintiffs had standing, and that statutory requirements for the relocation plan had not been met.]

Thus, the record shows that there has been no compliance by the local agency with the contractual provisions . . . that there be a feasible method for temporary relocation of individuals and families displaced from the urban renewal area and that there are, or are being provided, in the area, or in other areas — not less desirable in regard to public utilities and public and commercial facilities and at rents within the financial means of the individuals and families displaced from the area, decent, safe and sanitary dwellings, equal in number of and available to such displaced individuals and families and reasonably accessible to their places of employment.

Further, the record shows that there has been no determination in any legal sense that the purported assurances given by the local agency in its relocation plan of August 15, 1967, are "satisfactory" to the Regional Director within the meaning of Section 1455(c) (2) or his own regulation, which provides that the Secretary shall require within a reasonable time prior to actual displacement "satisfactory assurance" that decent, safe and sanitary dwellings . . . are available for the relocation of each displaced individual or family.

Nevertheless, the Secretary has continued to honor the local agency's requisitions for financing by advancing to the project $3 million for capital in June, 1967 and $3.7 million (for capital) and $159,000 (for relocation assistance) in September, 1967.

The court concludes, however, that it is not necessary for the protection of the plaintiffs' interests to now indicate any invalidation of these payments or to immediately and unconditionally restrain future similar financing of the project — although that power is reserved by the court to the extent hereinafter set forth. To completely restrain federal financing at this point might in the long run injuriously affect the whole project and all concerned — including plaintiffs themselves.

It is necessary, however, in order to protect the interests of plaintiffs and residents of the area faced with displacement, to restrain the defendant, San Francisco Redevelopment Agency, from proceeding with the enforced displacement of residents of the project area (individuals or families, owners, tenants or occupants of property in the area), by condemnation or eviction or threats of condemnation or eviction, pursuant to any powers granted to it by the State of California or the City and County of San Francisco for urban redevelopment of Western Addition Project, which has been thus far financed by federal funds under the provisions of the Federal Housing Act, unless and until the local agency has submitted to the Secretary a relocation plan, satisfactory to the Secretary and approved by this court, which will assure that decent, safe and sanitary housing is reasonably available to such persons within the meaning of the local agency's obligation assumed under its contracts with the Secretary under the provisions of the Federal Housing Act.

To the extent that relocation of families or individuals is dependent upon the accomplishment of the contingencies set forth in the Regional Director's letter of July 29, 1968, already set forth, and such contingencies have not been accomplished sufficiently to assure decent, safe and sanitary relocation housing meeting the standards of Section 1455(c) (1) to any individual or family threatened with displacement as above set forth, the local agency shall not proceed with the displacement.

This court recognizes that the "satisfactoriness" of the local agency's relocation plan can be and in practice will probably have to be determined, not once and for all, but under a plan for phased displacement and relocation according to the progress of demolition and according to availability of adequate relocation housing sufficient to reasonably accommodate such individuals and families as may be affected by each phase of dislocation.

At the present time, however, individuals and families in the area do not have any assurance of such protection and are left for all practical purposes to the pleasure of the local agency and of the federal financing agency as to when, how and under what conditions they can be involuntarily displaced or threatened with such displacement.

The interests of plaintiffs, individuals and families similarly situated, require injunctive protection because, absent such injunctive relief from this court, such individuals and families would remain uncertain and insecure in their residence within the project and, being under the impression that their displacement from their present residences can be legally enforced, such individuals and families may well conclude that they must leave the area notwithstanding the absence of reasonably available relocation housing. . . .

The interests of plaintiffs, individuals and families similarly situated, require the further protection of restraint upon the Secretary to the extent that he be enjoined from honoring future requisitions from the local agency for Western Addition II federal financing, until and unless, upon further application to this court, he can show that the relocation plan of the local agency is in fact satisfactory to him to the extent, at least, that it assures reasonable and present availability of decent, safe and sanitary housing . . . for any individuals or families about to be displaced by condemnation, eviction or threats of condemnation or eviction.

This injunctive relief does not mean that this court is presumptuously attempting to administer the complexities of urban redevelopment. That is not the function of the court nor is the court administratively equipped to do so.

Nor does it mean that this court is attempting to substitute its judgment for that of the Secretary concerning the "satisfactoriness" of the local agency's relocation plan.

Our decision simply means that the court can and should see to it that the Secretary complies with the requirements of the federal statute, and his own regulations, not merely in form but in substance, and that the administrative discretion vested in him by law is not arbitrarily abused, as in this case, but is reasonably exercised with some substantial basis in fact to support it. Such is the traditional function of the court upon review of administrative action of the kind here involved.

NOTES

1. "Characteristically, the area selected [for the San Francisco Redevelopment Agency's Western Addition II project] was the cultural, political and economic center of the black community." McGee, Urban Renewal in the Crucible of Judicial Review, 56 Va. L. Rev. 826, 874 (1970). The injunction granted against evictions and new funding for the program until an acceptable relocation plan was filed was generally hailed but short lived. It was dissolved on March 5, 1969, three months after it was issued, even though plaintiffs offered evidence that the relocation plan — found satisfactory to HUD — was still grossly inadequate. The court explained:

> Since the statute vests the function and responsibility squarely upon the secretary, the judicial function is narrowly limited to ascertaining whether the Secretary has made the determination required of him by law and if so, whether he has acted in apparent good faith, reasonably rather than arbitrarily, and with some factual basis for his decision. If so, judicial review can go no further. The Court may not, and should not, substitute its judgment for that of the Secretary — even if the court might believe that the Secretary could have made a different decision concerning the satisfactoriness of the local agency's relocation plan and assurances. (No. 45,053 (N.D. Cal. 1969). See also 56 Va. L. Rev. 826, 878 (1970).)

The second order placed plaintiffs back where they began, but their attorneys report that the first order caused the government agencies to be more "malleable" and "sensitive" to the needs of site residents. McGee, supra at 879.

2. The decision in the Norwalk CORE case also turned out to be a "paper victory" for plaintiffs. Returning to the district court, they were unable to obtain an injunction; the area was developed in basic conformance with the plan, and the process of dispersal was completed. McGee, supra at 866.

3. Arrington v. City of Fairfield, Alabama, a renewal project set in an area with a long history of racial discrimination, and with no federal participation, posed little difficulty for one federal court — although the plaintiffs were hardly in a worse situation than many of their Northern counterparts.

ARRINGTON v. CITY OF FAIRFIELD, ALABAMA
414 F.2d 687 (5th Cir. 1969)

Before COLEMAN and GODBOLD, Circuit Judges, and SCOTT, District Judge.

SCOTT, District Judge:

This is a class action in equity by Negro residents of the Englewood section of Fairfield, Alabama, seeking an injunction to prohibit the City of Fairfield and Engel Realty Company from displacing them from their residences and their consequent removal from the City of Fairfield in the absence of adequate relocation housing in the City of Fairfield. Plaintiffs' complaint was dismissed by the District Court for the Northern District of Alabama. We hold that the District Court was in error, and remand for further proceedings consistent with this opinion.

The complaint is founded upon Title 28, U.S.C. §1343(3) and (4), Title 42 U.S.C. §§1981, 1982, 1983, 1988 and the Thirteenth and Fourteenth Amendments to the United States Constitution. Plaintiffs-appellants also seek preliminary and permanent injunctions to "restrain defendants from continuing their present course of conduct, policies, practices, custom and usage of providing municipal facilities on a discriminatory basis and from pursuing an urban renewal program in such a way as will cause the involuntary relocation of plaintiffs and members of their class, without providing for suitable relocation within the City of Fairfield, and from making relocation outside the City inevitable by zone changes which foreclose adequate residential redevelopment."

The primary defendants in the action are the City of Fairfield and Engel Realty Company, a private company with which the City of Fairfield contracted to commercially develop the Englewood area. Other defendants named in the complaint are various city officials and agencies who have acted in the name of the City and the commissioner of the Fairfield Housing Authority. . . .

The plaintiffs live in Englewood, a predominantly Negro section of Fairfield. As found by the court below, most of the buildings are structurally defective and do not meet the health standards of the City of Fairfield. The streets are inadequate and unpaved and an open drainage ditch runs through the entire area. Furthermore, the majority of the plaintiffs are tenants.

In 1964 an interstate highway was proposed for building through portions of Englewood. To comply with state law, the City of Fairfield rezoned Englewood from predominantly residential to tourist and commercial.

During 1966 and 1967 the Fairfield Housing Authority and the regional office of the Department of Housing and Urban Development (HUD) discussed informal proposals for an urban renewal program in Englewood, which qualified as a "slum" area. The project was to displace 161 families of whom 150 were Negroes.

Before it was notified of the outcome of its request for federal urban renewal funds, the City of Fairfield decided to proceed with the commercial development of Englewood. The mayor met with owners of the property and Engel Realty Company, agent for the owners, to determine the feasibility of building a motel near the interstate highway in order to promote tourist business in the City. In furtherance of its plan, the City adopted the following resolution:

BE IT RESOLVED by the City Council of the City of Fairfield that the Mayor be and hereby is authorized to enter into a contract with Engel Realty Company in consideration of Engel Realty Company's completion of a commercial development in the Englewood area of the City of Fairfield, the City of Fairfield will install drainage pipe in and cover the drainage ditch in that area commonly known as 'tar ditch' and that the City of Fairfield will complete such work prior to the completion of the site preparation for the proposed development by the Engel Realty Company.
Adopted 4th day of December, 1967.
Approved 5th day of December, 1967.

In dismissing the plaintiffs' claim, the District Court made the following findings of fact:

1. That the plaintiffs were not property owners in Englewood; it concluded that, as such, they had no standing to invoke the jurisdiction of the court;
2. That there was no urban renewal program under submission, as provided by 42 U.S.C. Section 1451, and that the City had no intention of trying to renew the project;
3. That the property involved was "blighted" and 90% of the buildings were structurally defective and subject to being condemned for health reasons;
4. The property was not being condemned by the City or Housing Authority under the power of eminent domain;
5. That Engel Realty did attempt to purchase the property for the purpose of building a motel and other commercial enterprises, but that it was not acting as an agent for the City Housing Authority, or any other defendant in its attempt to purchase the property; and
6. That Engel Realty did not participate in the city's urban renewal program.

The trial court concluded that the plaintiffs as tenants had no interest in the property or in the contracts regarding the property and, therefore, had no right to invoke the jurisdiction of the federal court. The Court further stated that the director of the Housing Authority, clerk of the City, members of the City Council and planning committee and the mayor of the City were not proper party defendants. . . .

STANDING TO SUE

Appellants assert that as impoverished Negro tenants of the Englewood area of Fairfield they have standing to claim that displacement from their residences precipitated by state action and in the absence of relocation housing within the City, will deny them rights secured by the Thirteenth and Fourteenth Amendments and Acts of Congress which enforce these rights.

The District Court never reached the merits of the claim because it concluded that the "plaintiffs having no interest in the property or interest in contracts regarding the same, have no right to invoke the jurisdiction of this Court." In its findings of fact the District Court stated: "There is no evidence before the Court disclosing the true owners of said property described in the complaint and it does not appear that any party owning said property is now before the Court."

The District Court attached significance to the fact that appellants are tenants and are not property owners. What appellants seek to protect, however, is their right to reside in the City by owning or *renting* housing. The crux of their claim is not deprivation of property without due process [i.e., the "property right" of a lessee or tenant], but violation of equal protection. . . .

If the plaintiffs' allegations are correct, the adverse effects on them would be "immediate and personal." See Norwalk Core v. Norwalk Redevelopment Agency, 395 F.2d 920, 927 (2d Cir. 1968). . . .

Similarly, the concept of standing has been broadened to allow organizations and individuals representing "the community" to claim that the routing of a highway discriminates against Negroes by destroying a Negro business community, injuring Negro educational institutions and otherwise harming a Negro community. Nashville I–40 Steering Comm. v. Ellington, 387 F.2d 179 (6th Cir. 1967), *cert. denied* 390 U.S. 921 . . . (1968).

We hold that the Negro residents of the Englewood area of Fairfield have standing to bring this action. Since plaintiffs have standing, we must decide whether the District Court erred in granting defendants' motions to dismiss and for summary judgment.

EQUAL PROTECTION

. . . The trial court's disposal of the issues on summary judgment has resulted in an incomplete record. However, from that hearing, it is clear that the City of Fairfield was involved in the financing and promotion of the redevelopment project in Englewood. Although there is no evidence at this stage that Engle Realty has an agreement or contract to purchase the property from the property owners or that plaintiffs, if displaced, would have to move outside Fairfield, plaintiffs may be able to show that the City will knowingly and actively precipitate the dislocation of persons who, because of a city-wide practice of residential discrimination, will have no place to go. Exclusion by physical displacement resulting from public discrimination is no less objectionable than such exclusion by rezoning. . . . Where there is state involvement, the fact that the decision to discriminate may be made by private individual rather than a public official is not decisive. See Reitman v. Mulkey, 387 U.S. 369 . . . (1967); Shelley v. Kraemer, 334 U.S. 1 . . . (1948). Cf. Jones v. Alfred H. Mayer Co., supra. Under the unique circumstances of this case the City may involve itself in the discriminatory operation of the private housing market. The City acknowledges that installing storm sewers and covering the "tar ditch" is a substantial project.

There is little doubt that state action is present. . . . The issue for the trial court to determine is whether that state action is constitutional. The equal protection clause of the Fourteenth Amendment prohibits state discriminatory action of every kind, including state participation through any arrangement, management, funds or property. Cooper v. Aaron, 358 U.S. 1, 4 . . . (1958). Private conduct abridging individual rights does not violate the Amendment unless to some significant extent the state in any of its manifestations has become involved in it. Burton v. Wilmington Parking Authority, 365 U.S. 715, 722 . . . (1961). "Only by sifting facts and weighing circumstances can the nonobvious involvement of the state in private conduct be attributed its true significance." . . .

Appellants would have us incorporate the regulations and policy directives of the United States Department of Housing and Urban Development, Title VI, into the Thirteenth and Fourteenth Amendments as minimum standards in this housing problem. We need not cross this threshold of constitutional law. The District Court erred in granting defendants' motions to dismiss and for summary judgment. . . . We, therefore, remand this case to the District Court for proceedings consistent with this opinion.

Reversed and remanded.

QUESTIONS

1. What do the urban renewal cases indicate about the limitations of litigation in protecting minority interests, when major resources are committed to changes perceived to be of clear benefit to the majority community?

2. The value of early participation in urban renewal planning is clear, but even so, the difficulty in halting or altering such plans so as to prevent devastation of black communities is usually great. Are there additional equal protection arguments that might be used on behalf of politically weak minorities in these cases?

B. SEGREGATED PUBLIC HOUSING AND THE BROWN MANDATE

NOTE, RACIAL DISCRIMINATION IN PUBLIC HOUSING SITE SELECTION

*23 Stan. L. Rev. 63 (1970)**

The racial integration of public housing has been as slow a process as that of private housing. Public housing authorities have been content to preserve established living patterns when selecting the sites for their projects. If the tenants were to be poor blacks, then the project was located where poor blacks already lived. If the tenants were to be poor whites, then the projects were located where poor whites already lived. When public housing legislation was first enacted in 1937, the separate-but-equal doctrine of Plessy v. Ferguson still enjoyed judicial sanction. Laws against discrimination in public housing were passed later. New York forbade discrimination in public housing in 1939, Massachusetts in 1948, Connecticut and Wisconsin in 1949. Several other states followed in later years.[3] The United States Supreme Court struck down the separate-but-equal doctrine in 1954. Public housing authorities, however, continued to acquiesce in the perpetuation of segregated facilities.[5]

In 1962 an Executive Order declared that tenants in federally supported housing projects could not be selected on the basis of race.[6] The Public Housing Authority[7] (PHA) interpreted this order narrowly, limiting its effect to public housing completed after the date of the order[8] and applying it solely to tenant selection, leaving site selection unregulated.[9]

Title VI of the Civil Rights Act of 1964[10] required more positive measures to correct discrimination in public housing. All facilities, regardless of the date of completion, were to be integrated. In 1966 the Department of Housing and Urban Development (HUD) issued detailed regulations for the implementation of Title VI.[11] Title VI and the regulations thereunder apply to both site selection and tenant selection.[12]

Early judicial decisions in which public housing programs were considered involved tenant eviction and tenant selection exclusively. Pursuant to these decisions, public housing authorities had adopted a "free choice" policy in tenant selection, permitting tenants to go to any project they wished so long as a vacancy existed.[13] Although the selection of sites had never been challenged in the courts, site selection procedures had been strongly criticized. Public housing critics characterized site selection as the "most serious problem" in the public housing program,[14] and as "possibly insoluble."[15] Low

3. See Friedman, Government and Slum Housing: A Century of Frustration 123-124 (1968).

5. See generally Comment, The Public Housing Administration and Discrimination in Federally Assisted Low-Rent Housing, 64 Mich. L. Rev. 871 (1966).

6. Exec. Order No. 11,063, 3 C.F.R. 6562 (1964). See 42 U.S.C. §1982 (1964).

7. From 1942 to 1965 the public housing program was under the jurisdiction of the Public Housing Administration (PHA). In 1965 the PHA was put under the control of the newly created Department of Housing and Urban Development (HUD), and the agency's name was changed to the Housing Assistance Administration (HAA). See text accompanying note 28 infra.

8. Comment, supra note 5, at 879.

9. Id.

10. 42 U.S.C. §2000d (1964).

11. See 24 C.F.R. pt. 1 (1969).

12. See text accompanying note 65 infra.

13. Comment, supra note 5, at 881-882.

14. L. Friedman, supra note 3, at 122.

15. Ledbetter, Public Housing — A Social Experiment Seeks Acceptance, 32 Law & Contemp. Prob. 490, 524 (1967).

income housing projects have been most frequently located in predominantly nonwhite areas, and, since few white tenants are willing to move into such neighborhoods, the result has been further racial segregation. Recent judicial decisions on the site-selection issue make it clear that courts will no longer wait for federal and local authorities to work out answers to the site-selection problem; courts have begun to formulate independent solutions to this "insoluble" problem.

GAUTREAUX v. ROMNEY AND CHICAGO HOUSING AUTHORITY
457 F.2d 124 (7th Cir. 1972)

[This opinion is the third by the court of appeals in litigation involving two federal suits by blacks living in, or applying for, public housing in Chicago. One suit was against the Chicago Housing Authority, and the other against HUD. Both suits charged racial segregation in the defendants' policies on tenant assignment and site selection. Plaintiffs sought injunctive relief against the asserted discriminatory policies, and urged that federal funding used to support such policies be enjoined. Initially, district court Judge Austin had granted relief against the policies but refused to enjoin the federal funds. He subsequently ordered HUD to withhold $26,000,000 in Model Cities funds from Chicago, even though only six of fifty programs involved housing-related activities. In this appeal, reversing the district court's order, a majority of the Seventh Circuit found that Judge Austin had abused his discretion. Citing Board of Public Instruction of Taylor County, Florida v. Finch, 414 F.2d 1068 (5th Cir. 1969), the majority held that Congress had not intended social welfare funding to be held up because of some racial discrimination in some programs.

In dissenting, Judge Sprecher summarized the major events in the long litigation.]

I

Black tenants in and applicants for public housing brought suit in 1966 against the Chicago Housing Authority (CHA). Plaintiffs charged that CHA intentionally violated 42 U.S.C. §§1981 and 1983 in maintaining existing patterns of residential separation of races by its tenant-assignment and site-selection procedures, contrary to the Fourteenth Amendment.

In granting the plaintiffs a summary judgment upon "thousands of pages of depositions, affidavits and exhibits," the district court found: (1) Until 1954, CHA refused to permit black families to reside in four public housing projects located in white neighborhoods and built before 1944. (2) Since 1954, CHA had imposed a black quota on the four projects; as of December 31, 1967, black tenants occupied between 1 and 7 percent of the 1,654 units.[2] (3) As of

2. The non-white population of Chicago is 34.4 percent. Department of Commerce, General Population Characteristics — Illinois, Table 16.

July, 1968, CHA operated 64 public housing sites with 30,848 units; except for the four segregated white projects, the tenants were 99 percent black. (4) Exclusive of the four white projects, 99½ percent of the total units operated by CHA were located in areas which were or soon would be substantially all black.[3] (5) About 90 percent of the waiting list of 13,000 persons were black. (6) The City Council under Illinois law must approve all sites prior to acquisition by CHA. (7) A pre-clearance arrangement existed under which CHA informally submitted sites for family housing to the alderman in whose ward the site was located. The aldermen to whom sites in white neighborhoods were submitted vetoed these sites on racial grounds. Between 1954 and 1967 CHA selected sites for 18,784 family units, of which 7,883 were in white areas and 10,901 in black areas. The City Council rejected 99½ percent of the units proposed for white sites, but only 10 percent of the black units. (8) There were in the City of Chicago 188,000 white families and 76,000 black families eligible for public housing, but most white families did not choose to move into all-black projects in all-black neighborhoods. Gautreaux v. Chicago Housing Authority, 296 F. Supp. 907 (N.D. Ill. 1969).

No appeal was taken from these findings.

The district court denied the plaintiffs' request for "granting a narrow, drastic kind of relief — that of enjoining the use of federal funds" in favor of giving the parties time to attempt to formulate a comprehensive plan to prohibit the future use and remedy the past effects of CHA's unconstitutional site-selection and tenant-assignment procedures. This was done, however, without "precluding plaintiffs from showing on the basis of more facts that denial of federal funds is an appropriate form of relief." 296 F. Supp. at 915.

On July 1, 1969, the district court entered a judgment order which comprised a comprehensive plan under which 700 units were required to be built in predominantly white areas; thereafter, at least 75 percent of dwelling units built by CHA were required to be constructed in predominantly white areas.[4] In order to create small and widely dispersed housing units, family housing was to be built in structures of three stories or less. No more than 15 percent of a single census tract could be composed of public housing units. The judgment order was declared to bind not only CHA but also "those persons, including the members of the City Council of the City of Chicago, in active concert or participation with them who receive actual notice of this order by personal service or otherwise." Finally, the court required that "CHA shall affirmatively administer its public housing system . . . to the end of disestablishing the segregated public housing system which has resulted from

3. They were located in neighborhoods with between 50 and 100 percent black population.

4. The judgment order distinguished between "Limited Public Housing Area," meaning that part of Cook County lying within census tracts having 30 percent or more non-white population or within a distance of one mile from any point on the outer perimeter of any such census tract, and "General Public Housing Area," meaning the remaining part of Cook County.

CHA's unconstitutional site selection and tenant assignment procedures" and that "CHA shall use its best efforts to increase the supply of Dwelling Units as rapidly as possible. . . ." Gautreaux v. Chicago Housing Authority, 304 F. Supp. 736 (N.D. Ill. 1969).

No appeal was taken from this judgment order.

The district court retained jurisdiction. From the time of the entry of the judgment order of July 1, 1969 to December, 1970, CHA submitted no sites for family dwelling units to the City Council. Plaintiffs were advised that CHA had no intention to submit any sites prior to the Chicago mayoralty election scheduled for April, 1971.

On July 20, 1970, the district court modified the "best efforts" provision of the judgment order to require CHA to submit sites for no fewer than 1,500 dwelling units to the City Council on or prior to September 20, 1970. On appeal, the timetable order (revised to take into account appeal time) was affirmed by this court in Gautreaux v. Chicago Housing Authority, 436 F.2d 306 (7th Cir. 1970), *cert. denied,* 402 U.S. 922, 91 S. Ct. 1378, 28 L. Ed. 2d 661 (1971). Judge Duffy concluded (page 313):

> In view of the fact that HUD-approved sites for 1500 Dwelling Units were awaiting submission to the City Council and that the arguments put forward in favor of delaying submission were based on political considerations and community hostility, reasons which had been properly rejected by the lower court in the original litigation, we hold that it was no abuse of discretion for the District Judge to impose deadlines for submission one year after the entry of the original "best efforts" order.

The same plaintiffs who carried on the CHA litigation had, simultaneously with the filing of that complaint in 1966, filed another complaint against the Secretary of Housing and Urban Development (HUD). Plaintiffs sought a declaration that HUD had "assisted in the carrying on . . . of a racially discriminatory public housing system, within the City of Chicago" and an injunction against HUD's making available to CHA any federal funds to be used in connection with or in support of the racially discriminatory aspects of the Chicago public housing system.

In that case, the district court had dismissed all four counts of the complaint. On appeal, this court held that HUD had violated the due process clause of the Fifth Amendment and that summary judgment should be granted in plaintiffs' favor in Counts I (Fifth Amendment) and II (42 U.S.C. §2000d, which is section 601 of the Civil Rights Act of 1964). Gautreaux v. Romney, 448 F.2d 731 (7th Cir. 1971).

This court found and held: (1) Between 1950 and 1969 HUD approved and funded CHA-chosen family housing sites located in black areas of Chicago because of "HUD's decision . . . that it was better to fund a segregated housing system than to deny housing altogether to the thousands of needy Negro families of that city." (2) Between 1950 and 1966 alone HUD spent nearly $350 million on CHA projects. (3) HUD exercised its powers "in a manner which perpetuated a racially discriminatory housing system in Chicago;" HUD and its officials were aware of that fact. (4) ". . . [C]ommunity and local government resistance to . . . 'the only constitutionally permissible state policy' . . . has not yet been accepted as a viable excuse for a segregated result." (5) "[W]e are unable to avoid the conclusion that the Secretary's past actions constituted racially discriminatory conduct in their own right."

Judge Duffy, again writing for this court, said at pages 740-741:

> . . . [W]e state *only* that the Secretary must be adjudged liable on these particular facts and again point out that our holding should not be construed as granting a broad license for interference with the programs and actions of an already beleaguered federal agency. It may well be that the District Judge, in his wise discretion, will conclude that little equitable relief above the entry of a declaratory judgment and a simple "best efforts" clause will be necessary to remedy the wrongs which have been found to have been committed. . . . [W]e defer to the District Court for . . . resolution [of such considerations].

II

While the CHA and HUD cases were proceeding through the courts to determinations that both agencies were guilty of unconstitutional racial discrimination, HUD had approved a grant of some $38 million to the City of Chicago to be used during calendar year 1970 to administer its first-year activity under a contemplated five-year Comprehensive City Demonstration Program (Model Cities Program), established by the Demonstration Cities and Metropolitan Development Act of 1966 (42 U.S.C. §3301 et seq.). In approving the first-year grant, HUD advised the city:

> The Department . . . expects full compliance by the City and all its agencies . . . with the provisions of any decree finally entered by the U.S. District Court in the case of Gautreaux v. Chicago Housing Authority. . . .

An application for another $38 million for the second-year Model Cities Program during calendar year 1971 resulted in discussion between city and HUD officials regarding the Chicago housing supply. On November 19, 1970, a "team composed of city and HUD regional staff" had found that, to maintain the July 1, 1969 housing supply level for low-income families, 6,200 new units were required. However, HUD advised the city that, in view of the difficulty of accomplishing that task, it would accept the reduced figure of 4,300 units "if the plans to provide the lesser number of units are quite precise." HUD said it would not approve funds for the second year of the Model Cities Program nor funds for the second year of Chicago's Neighborhood Development Program under the Housing Act of 1949 (42 U.S.C. §§1469-1469c) until the city had provided "specific plans to overcome this deficit of 4300 units."

Thereafter a "letter of intention" was signed on May 12, 1971 by the mayor of Chicago, the chairman of CHA and the regional administrator of HUD, indicating in detail how the housing deficiency would be met. CHA was to acquire sites for 1,700 units under a time table of 500 units by June 15, 1971, 350 units by September 15, 1971, and 850 units by December 15, 1971. On June 21, 1971, HUD approved $26 million for the second year of the Model Cities Program (HUD had previously released $12 million) "on the condition that . . . Chicago Housing Authority will continue to show progress toward the housing goals set forth in the Letter of Intention."

By September 15, 1971, sites for only 288 low-income public housing units in predominantly white areas had been approved.

This court's opinion in Gautreaux v. Romney, 448 F.2d 731, was handed down September 10, 1971. On September 17, before the mandate issued, the plaintiffs moved the district court under Rule 62 (c) of the Federal Rules of Civil Procedure for an "injunction pending appeal." During a four-day hearing, the regional administrator of HUD testified that he had determined to release the Model Cities funds to Chicago. The court then enjoined HUD from paying Chicago any monies for the second year of the Model Cities Program unless and until 700 housing units had been given City Council approval. The order was appealed by CHA, the City of Chicago and the Central Advisory Council, an organization representing present tenants in CHA public housing, all of which had intervened in the HUD case prior to the entry of the order (Appeals Nos. 71-1732, 71-1733 and 71-1734).

The mandate issued on November 11, 1971 and, on plaintiff's motion for an order pending final judgment, the district court on the same day entered an order similar to the October 1 order. It enjoined HUD from paying Chicago any second-year Model Cities Program money unless at least 700 dwelling units in white areas had received City Council approval. HUD appealed the November 11 order (Appeal No. 71-1807).

[Judge Sprecher, citing the broad remedial discretion conferred by provisions in Civil Rights Statutes and used in school desegregation cases, argued that the district judge possessed sufficient equitable power to enjoin HUD's disbursement of Model Cities funds to Chicago until the city council approved sites for 700 units in predominantly white areas. He felt that injunctive relief in this case was appropriate, restrained, and not an abuse of discretion.]

Although the district court's remedy may appear to be harsh and drastic when viewed in isolation, the problem it seeks to alleviate is crucial and monumental. The failure of HUD and CHA to provide *any* low-cost housing for several years, in view of the city's huge housing deficit gauged as long ago as mid-1969, affects black and white alike. Lack of decent low-income housing is not only a major problem in itself,[13] but it is a prodigious spawner of prob-

13. In establishing a committee on urban housing in 1967, the President characterized the need to provide a decent home for every family "now imprisoned in the squalor of the slums" as "the most pressing unfulfilled need in our society." Report of the President's Committee on Urban Housing A Decent Home (1968) ("Kaiser Report") 1. The committee found that in 30 years of federal housing subsidies, only 800,000 subsidized units

lems for black and white equally: poverty, unemployment, illness, malnutrition, despair, family disunity, crime, violence and civil disorder.[14]

When there is added to the appalling problem of lack of low-income housing for everyone, the separate problem of racial discrimination, the amalgam requires priority status, emergency treatment and drastic if not "bizarre" remedies. The specific problem on which this appeal is focused is the increasing concentration of non-whites in the slums and ghettos of the inner city, where they are imprisoned by the "white suburban noose."[15] The prisoners of slums and ghettos endure not only substandard housing, but a higher incidence of death and disease, inferior schools, inferior job opportunities, inferior community services, inferior municipal services, "all amidst physical decay and psychological outrage."[16]

[In concluding his Gautreaux v. Romney dissent, Judge Sprecher reviewed the history of racial segregation in public housing:]

For many years the public housing program and its federal and local administrators have contributed to the increasing segregation of the black inner city from the white suburbs[17] through discriminatory site selection,[18] ghetto high-rise monstrosities,[19] and pervasive foot-dragging.

---

were built and that the then-current rate of building was about 50,000 a year. It found the future need to be from 600,000 to 800,000 subsidized units per year for the next ten years. Id. at 8, 23, 47. The Commission on Urban Problems found with "a sense of urgency and even alarm" that "we must put housing on the front burner" and must "focus our housing programs on housing for poor people." Report of the National Commission on Urban Problems, Building the American City (1968) ("Douglas Report") 30. It found a need for 500,000 units a year for poor- and moderate-income families. Id. at 180.

14. The Advisory Commission on Civil Disorders identified inadequate housing as one of the prime components of the "explosive mixture" leading to civil disorders and recommended that "the supply of housing suitable for low-income families should be expanded" on a massive basis. Report of the National Advisory Commission on Civil Disorders (1968). ("Kerner Report") 5,260. The Commission on the Causes and Prevention of Violence, in recommending more effective steps to realize "the 1968 Housing Act's goal of a decent home for every American within a decade" found that "the poverty and social isolation of minority groups in central cities is the single most serious problem of the American city today." Final Report of the National Commission on the Causes and Prevention of Violence, To Establish Justice, To Insure Domestic Tranquility (1969) ("Eisenhower Report") 49, 273.

15. Douglas Report, 1. "To date, housing programs serving low-income groups have been concentrated in the ghettos. Non-ghetto areas, particularly suburbs, have for the most part steadfastly opposed low-income, rent supplement, or below-market interest rate housing, and have successfully restricted use of these programs outside the ghetto." Kerner Report, 263.

16. Comment "Public Housing and Integration: A Neglected Opportunity," 6 Columbia Journal of Law and Social Problems 253, 270 (1970).

17. "Elected officials at all levels found it hard to stand up against the prevailing pressure for segregated neighborhoods. Those at the Federal level were no exception. For years they made little effort to resist the pressure. They closed their eyes to the massive federally supported building of largely white suburbia in the period following World War II." Douglas Report, 12.

18. Shannon v. United States Department of Housing and Urban Development, 436

The focal problem of racial polarization is not confined to Chicago by any means: it is a national crisis.[21] . . .

The idea of withholding federal funds from one program to enforce another is not entirely novel.[22]

NOTES

1. As the Gautreaux litigation and the cases discussed below show, new civil rights remedies such as Title VI have made only limited inroads on the continuing resistance to integrated public housing. Indeed, the majority opinion in Gautreaux expressed concern that a fund cut-off remedy would most hurt those poor blacks it was intended to help. One response to this concern appeared in an Amicus brief filed by the Chicago Chapter and Operation Breadbasket of the Southern Christian Leadership Conference. The group argued that:

> 4,000 jobs now held by, and which may become lost to model area residents may not be the most crucial issue in this case; certainly not against a background of more than twenty years of deliberate and covert racial discrimination in housing . . . and . . . an invidious, conscious and concerted refusal by the . . . City of Chicago and CHA to now provide additional housing (which would also mean increased employment opportunity) for this City's Black and White low income families. (457 F.2d at 138.)

2. But while the advantages of ending "deliberate and covert racial discrimination in housing" are obvious, there is no denying that the opposition of civil rights groups and middle-class blacks to further public housing projects in black areas, combined with the powerful political barrier to such projects that white communities are able to erect, results in harm to poor blacks — who, it may be presumed, would prefer apartments in a segregated project to no apartments at all.

F.2d 809 (3rd Cir. 1970). See also Comment, "Urban Housing," 46 New York University Law Review 560 (1971); Note, "Discriminatory Site Location and Tenant Allocation Procedures," 1970 Wisconsin Law Review 559 (1970); Note, "Discriminatory Site Selection in Public Housing and Federal Judicial Response," 64 Northwestern University Law Review 720 (1970).

19. Rockefeller Panel Reports, Prospect for America 303 (1961): "Our public housing programs have created many problems. They have crowded low income families, and especially minority groups, into high-density, many-storied apartments, thus intensifying economic segregation while breaking down constructive neighborhood relationships."

21. Note, "Racial Discrimination in Public Housing Site Selection," 23 Stanford Law Review 63 (1970); Comment, "Public Housing and Integration: A Neglected Opportunity," 6 Columbia Journal of Law and Social Problems 253, 256 (1970); Note, "Low-Income Housing and the Equal Protection Clause," 56 Cornell Law Review 343 (1971).

22. Note, "Segregation and the Suburbs: Low-Income Housing, Zoning and the Fourteenth Amendment," 56 Iowa Law Review 1298, 1318-19 (1971); Buchanan, "Federal Regulation of Private Racial Prejudice: A Study of Law in Search of Morality," 56 Iowa Law Review 473, 513-22 (1971).

A pre-Gautreaux survey, designed to ascertain the residential preferences of blacks in Chicago, revealed that 68 percent of blacks interviewed chose "mostly Negro" neighborhoods, given that all neighborhoods would be maintained equally well. Twenty-five percent preferred "mixed" areas or said there was no difference between black or integrated areas. Only 5 percent selected "mostly white" neighborhoods as their first choice. G. Marx, Protest and Prejudice: A Study of Belief in the Black Community 175 (1967). One writer reports that the Chicago City Council's refusal to approve any sites for public housing has cost an estimated $50,000,000 in public housing funds for that city. Lefcoe, From Capitol Hill: The Impact of Civil Rights Litigation on HUD Policy, 4 The Urban Law. 112, 115 (1972). See also Note, Public Housing and Urban Policy: Gautreaux v. Chicago Housing Authority, 79 Yale L.J. 712, 713 (1970), which states that the Gautreaux public housing order "represents a short-sighted and narrow response to the problem it attempts to remedy, and that such poor performance is a direct result of a court's failing to recognize its own limitations in making policy decisions."

The Yale note also points out that the late Senator Robert F. Kennedy, in testimony before the Senate Subcommittee on Housing and Urban Affairs in 1968, urged the selection of public housing sites by a racial formula that was almost the exact opposite of the one required by Judge Austin in Gautreaux:

> To seek a rebuilding of our urban slums is not to turn our backs on the goal of integration. It is only to say that open occupancy laws alone will not suffice and that sensitivity must be shown to the aspirations of Negroes and other non-whites who would build their own communities and occupy decent housing in neighborhoods where they now live. And, in the long run, this willingness to come to grips with blight of our center city will lead us toward an open society. For it is comparability of housing and full employment that are the keys to free movement and to the establishment of a society in which each man has a real opportunity to choose whom he will call neighbor. (Id. at 718.)

3. The dilemma for integration-oriented reformers was well stated by Frances Piven and Richard Cloward, who reviewed the cost of Gautreaux-type litigation:

> The myth that integrationist measures are bringing better housing to the Negro poor comforts liberals; it placates (and victimizes) the Negro masses; and it antagonizes and arouses the bulk of white Americans. The backlash is part of its legacy. White turmoil rages over integration, housing conditions worsen. They worsen partly because the solution continues to be defined in terms of desegregation, so that the energies and attention to reformers are diverted from attempts to ameliorate housing in the ghetto itself. (Piven and Cloward, Desegregated Housing: Who Pays for the Reformers' Ideal? New Republic, Dec. 17, 1966, at 14, 21.)

On the other hand, how can Judge Austin's opinion in Gautreaux be criticized from a legal standpoint, when it is based on Brown v. Board of Education? Judge Austin wrote: "It is also undenied that sites for the projects which have been constructed were chosen primarily to further the praiseworthy and urgent goals of low-cost public housing and urban renewal. Nevertheless, a deliberate policy to separate the races cannot be justified by the good intentions with which other laudable goals are pursued. [Citing Brown.]" 296 F. Supp. at 914.

The Seventh Circuit, in the second appeal of the Gautreaux case, also recognized the problem, noting that HUD had chosen to fund a segregated housing program rather than "to deny housing altogether to the thousands of needy Negro families of that city." 448 F.2d at 737. But even acknowledging the many efforts that HUD had made to get Chicago officials to locate new housing in white areas, the court concluded that such good-faith efforts were insufficient, even in the face of overwhelming opposition. It stated: "we do not feel free to carve out a wholly new exception to a firmly established general rule which, for at least the last sixteen years, has governed the standards of assessing liability for discrimination on the basis of race." 448 F.2d 738-739.

4. As in Gautreaux, blacks in Banks v. Perk, 341 F. Supp. 1175 (N.D. Ohio 1972), challenged the policies on site selection and tenant assignment of the Cuyahoga Metropolitan Housing Authority. Those policies had resulted in black projects and white projects. The court, while not questioning the authority's good faith, found that it had disregarded its statutory duty to act affirmatively to integrate existing projects and better disperse new ones. Citing Gautreaux, the court enjoined further projects in black neighborhoods, and ordered the city of Cleveland to issue building permits for two projects in predominantly white areas. See also Cuyahoga Metropolitan Housing Authority v. City of Cleveland, 342 F. Supp. 250 (N.D. Ohio 1972), where Cleveland was enjoined from canceling its cooperative agreement with CMHA. The court determined that the city's cancellation action would have a "racially discriminatory effect," since such agreements are a first step in obtaining federal resources for housing needed by blacks — who constitute the greater proportion of CMHA waiting lists.

Citing Gautreaux, the Arizona Court of Appeals imposed an affirmative duty to integrate in choosing public housing sites and tenants.

> We do not believe the Tucson Housing Authority can legitimately meet the mandate of the [HUD] regulations . . . and at the same time reject considering the racial character of the sites being selected. The duty imposed under the statute [Title VI of the 1964 Civil Rights Act] and the [HUD] regulation is not simply the negative duty not to discriminate. It is a mandate that prohibits housing authorities from acting in a manner that results in discrimination. (El Cortez Heights Residents and Property Owners Association v. Tucson Housing Authority, 10 Ariz. App. 132, 457 P.2d 294 (1969).)

5. Similarly, in Hicks v. Weaver, 302 F. Supp. 619 (E.D. La. 1969), the

court, faced with Gautreaux-type facts, concurred in the Gautreaux decision. It held that blacks are entitled to have sites for public housing projects selected without regard to the racial composition of either the surrounding neighborhood or the projects themselves. Cautioning that "this does not mean that the location of public housing in all-Negro neighborhoods is per se a violation of Title VI," the court declared: "it does create a strong inference which, if unexplained, may be sufficient to support that conclusion."

Thus, while courts have taken note of the massive opposition to integrated housing, they seem to resolve the issue as described in this comment: "Perhaps the existence of decent housing is more important to a man's dignity and well-being than its location. However, the court [in Gautreaux], soundly basing its decision on the Constitution, has found otherwise." Note, 44 Tul. L. Rev. 385, 392 (1970).

QUESTIONS

1. How important are the associational aspects of Brown in the public housing rights asserted by plaintiffs in these cases? The inability of blacks to obtain integrated public housing will often mean that their children will be confined to all-black schools. Should this consideration influence courts to follow Judge Austin's decision in Gautreaux, despite the predictable opposition?

2. Is there any indication that the failure under Plessy v. Ferguson to provide equal facilities to blacks will not be repeated when blacks opt for black housing rather than repeat the Gautreaux experience?

NOTE: THE REALITIES OF PUBLIC HOUSING FOR BLACKS

There is a fairly substantial literature on public housing in the United States. It contains a great deal of basic information that is relevant to, but seems not to have played a part in, the Gautreaux-type litigation. It is worth knowing, for example, that originally the public housing program was planned during the Depression for the benefit of the "submerged middle class," as a short-term solution for those deemed the innocent victims of the economic crisis. Most of the early projects were low-rise row houses, often suburban in location and design. Friedman, Public Housing and the Poor: An Overview, 54 Calif. L. Rev. 642-654 (1966).

Obviously, the beneficiaries of the program have changed. But there has been no new re-evaluation by Congress of how the public housing program will best aid today's poor, many of whom are nonwhite. In fact, the national perception that public housing is intended for the poor, and particularly poor blacks, has served to lessen interest in and decrease funding for public housing. Policy changes aimed at tailoring public housing for today's poor seem ad hoc and intuitive rather than carefully studied. For example, reflected in the Gautreaux order, which required scattered-site, low-rise buildings, is the popular notion that large high-rise projects can become unmanageable and often have to be abandoned. One example is the Pruitt-Igoe project in St. Louis, consisting of thirty-three eleven-story buildings. But while this project was being written off as a disaster, a single eleven-story building managed by a tenants' group, only a few blocks away, was functioning well. N.Y. Times, June 4, 1970 at 45, c. 4.

Public housing litigation has relied on Brown v. Board of Education, with the presumption that desegregation (because that is what Brown required) will result in quality housing (which, from available indications, is what most poor black families want). As the cases reviewed in this section show, federal and local agencies have traditionally taken the path of least resistance in meeting public housing needs: first, authorizing segregated housing when this was legally permissible; and then, after Brown and civil rights laws mandated desegregation, failing (as in Gautreaux and Shannon) to enforce the letter and spirit of their own nondiscriminatory regulations whenever opposition to integrated housing appeared — as it generally did.

In opting for more public housing in the ghetto rather than no new public housing at all, governmental agencies may have made the better choice for less than the best reasons. Academicians as well as black militants have argued the positive benefits of ghetto living for its inhabitants. Sociologist Lee Rainwater contends that a house, particularly for lower-class families, should be viewed as a haven from the threats which face them in the world.

> The house becomes the place of maximum exercise of individual autonomy, minimal conformity to the formal and complex rules of public demeanor. The house acquires a sacred character from its complex intertwining with the self and from the symbolic character it has as a representation of the family. These conceptions of the house are readily generalized to the area around it (the neighborhood). (Rainwater, Fear and the House-As-Haven in the Lower Class, 32 J. Am. Inst. Planners 23-24 (1966).)

Other studies indicate that, despite all the difficulties of slum living, social benefits are derived from the close association with people in the community and the sense of identity in the neighborhood. It is felt that these sources of residential satisfaction help provide a "framework for personal and social integration." Fried and Gleicher, Some Sources of Residential Satisfaction in an Urban Slum 27 J. Am. Inst. Planners 305 (Nov. 1961).

This view of "home" as an area or community rather than simply a place is so at variance with typical middle-class orientations that appreciation for the basic sense of identity involved, and particularly for the loss felt when an individual leaves the area, is very difficult. One writer, however, reports that "grieving for a lost home is evidently a wide-spread and serious phenomenon following in the wake of urban dislocation." Fried, Grieving for a Lost Home: Psychological Costs of Relocation in Urban Renewal, in The Record and the Controversy 359 (J. Wilson ed. 1966).

Not every observer of ghetto life would view the isolation of its residents as a blessing. It is assumed that those who see strengths in the sense of community would not condone decrepit housing, high rents, crime, poor health conditions and inadequate city services, all of which tend to be a part of life in the overcrowded black ghettos in this country. There can be little doubt that Dr. Kenneth Clark is correct when he says:

> Housing is no abstract social and political problem, but an extension of man's personality. If the Negro has to identify with a rat infested tenement, his sense of personal inadequacy and inferiority already aggravated by job discrimination and other forms of humiliation, is reinforced by the physical reality around him. If his home is clean and decent and even in some way beautiful, his sense of self is stronger. A house is a concrete symbol of what the person is worth. (K. Clark, Dark Ghetto 32-33 (1965).)

Most low-income blacks would prefer better housing close to their present neighborhoods. Public housing officials report that they frequently meet with resistance when they assign black families to outlying projects far removed from their accustomed living area. Certainly, concern about transportation to work, church and shopping, as well as fear of reactions from a white neighborhood, may spark some of this resistance, but identification with the familiar neighborhood may also be involved. To the extent that integration policies (whether or not prompted by court orders) require them to leave a black neighborhood in order to obtain public housing, blacks may be deprived of the liberty to decide where to live, just as they were under the former segregation policies. Comment, 5 Harv. Civ. Rights–Civ. Lib. L. Rev. 150, 156 (1970). Public housing quotas have not generally found favor with the courts in the past. See, e.g., Banks v. Housing Authority, 120 Cal. App. 2d 1, 260 P.2d 668 (1953); Taylor v. Leonard, 30 N.J. Super. 116, 103 A.2d 632 (1954); and Progress Development Corporation v. Mitchell, 182 F. Supp. 681 (N.D. Ill. 1960). But see Favors v. Randall, 40 F. Supp. 743 (E.D. Pa. 1941), which approved a public housing quota under which blacks received more than their share of units. Whether quotas such as those contained in Gautreaux, designed to remedy the effects of past discriminatory assignment policies, can survive judicial tests remains to be seen.

QUESTIONS

1. Despite the arguments of separatists and sociologists, such as Lee Rainwater, is the importance of home and community for poor families really different than for those in the middle class? Assuming a difference can be shown, what, if any, legal significance should be given to it in housing litigation?

2. Is one more likely to grieve for a lost home because it was in a lower-class area, or because he was forced to move from it by government requirements which seemed harsh and unfair?

SHANNON v. HUD
436 F.2d 809 (3d Cir. 1970)

[As one of several legal authorities barring HUD from condoning construction of public housing in segregated areas, the dissent in Gautreaux, supra, cited Shannon v. HUD. Shannon involved a renewal plan that was to be changed so that government-subsidized rental housing would be placed in a neighborhood of predominantly middle-class blacks, many of whom were themselves living in relatively new federally assisted or insured units. Residents strongly opposed the change, which would have brought a lower-income group into a middle-class island surrounded by a large area of low-income units. Noting that all federally assisted housing in Philadelphia was heavily concentrated in minority areas, the court ordered HUD to consider the racial impacts of the location of any HUD-assisted housing:]

The defendants assert that HUD has broad discretion to choose between alternative methods of achieving the national housing objectives set forth in the several applicable statutes. They argue that this broad discretion permitted HUD in this case to make an unreviewable choice between alternative types of housing. We agree that broad discretion may be exercised. But that discretion must be exercised within the framework of the national policy against discrimination in federally assisted housing, 42 U.S.C. §2000d, and in favor of fair housing. 42 U.S.C. §3601. When an administrative decision is made without consideration of relevant factors it must be set aside. . . . Here the agency concentrated on land use factors and made no investigation or determination of the social factors involved in the choice of type of housing which it approved. Whether such exclusive concentration on land use factors was originally permitted under the Housing Act of 1949, since 1964 such limited consideration has been prohibited.

Oddly enough, HUD in its Low Rent Housing Manual recognizes that concentration of low rent public housing can have adverse social, and hence planning, consequences. Paragraph 4(g) of that manual provides: "[a]ny proposal to locate housing only in areas of racial concentration will be prima facie unacceptable and will be returned to the Local Authority for further consideration." If there is a distinction between the effects of site selection of low rent public housing and of 221(d)(3) rent supplement housing, such distinction has not been developed in the record before us. No similar regulations applicable to 221(d)(3) projects or to the rent supplement program have been issued, though these programs, operating in conjunction, would seem to have the same potential for perpetuating racial segregation as the low rent public housing program has had. See Gautreaux v. Chicago Housing Authority, 296 F. Supp. 907 (N.D. Ill. 1969) . . . .

Defendants contend that the interests which plaintiffs seek to vindicate are adequately protected by the complaint and enforcement procedures of Title VIII of the Civil Rights Act of 1968, 42 U.S.C. §§3610-3613, and Title VI of the Civil Rights Act of 1964, 42 U.S.C. §2000d-1. They contend plaintiffs could have and did not exhaust enforcement remedies therein provided. We do not agree. Those sections of the 1968 Act establish a complaint and enforcement procedure for the redress of discriminatory housing practices prohibited by §§804, 805 and 806 of the Act, 42 U.S.C. §§3604, 3605, 3606. The complaint and enforcement procedures do not pertain to the Secretary's affirmative duties under §808(d)(5) of the 1968 Act, 42 U.S.C. §3608(d)(5), or under the 1964 Civil Rights Act, or under the Housing Act of 1949. As to these affirmative duties judicial review of his actions is available as outlined hereinabove. Similarly, the procedures afforded under the Civil Rights Act of 1964 are designed to provide redress against specific discriminatory acts, and do not pertain to the adequacy of HUD procedures.

Finally, defendants contend that there was no evidence in the record below of discriminatory site selection in the location of rent supplement projects. The district court found:

> What proof there is on this question shows without dispute that rent subsidy housing is evenly and well disbursed within the city as well as without, in both ghetto and non-ghetto areas. (305 F. Supp. at 225).

Leaving to one side the plaintiffs' contention that this finding goes beyond the proof and is in any event the result of the district court's circumscription of evidence on that point, we think the finding is irrelevant. Congress has since 1949 refined its view of the factors relevant to achieving national housing objectives. At least under the 1968 Civil Rights Act, and probably under the 1964 Civil Rights Act as well, more is required of HUD than a determination that some rent supplement housing is located outside ghetto areas. Even though previously located rent supplement projects were located in non-ghetto areas the choice of location of a given project could have the "effect of subjecting persons to discrimination because of their race . . . or have the effect of defeating or substantially impairing accomplishment of the objectives of the program or activity as respect persons of a particular race. . . ." 24 C.F.R. §1.4(b)(2)(i). That effect could arise by virtue of the undue concentration of persons of a given race, or socio-economic group, in a given neighborhood. That effect could be felt not only by occupants of rent supplement housing and low cost housing, but by occupants of owner occupied dwellings, merchants, and institutions in the neighborhood. Possibly before 1964 the administrators of the federal housing programs could, by concentrating on land use controls, building code enforcement, and physical conditions of buildings, remain blind to the very real effect that racial concentration has had in the development of urban blight. Today such color blindness is impermissible.

CROW v. BROWN, 332 F. Supp. 382 (N.D. Ga. 1971). Two cases in Atlanta, Georgia raising public housing issues similar to those in Gautreaux and

Shannon were consolidated for hearing. The court's opinion described the familiar circumstances that led to litigation:

> The City of Atlanta is a fair and progressive city which, despite its wealth, growth, and physical beauty, is beset by the same deep-seated and long-range problems that are found in most American cities today. Atlanta's slums are the root-cause of many of these problems. From these jugs of wrath emanate much of the city's crime, drug addiction, unemployment, and racial unrest.
>
> In an attempt to combat the slums, which are inhabited mostly by poor blacks, Atlanta has been engaged in a program of low-rent public housing administered by the Atlanta Housing Authority ("AHA"). This public housing has tended to attract large numbers of poor blacks, often illiterate and unskilled, from outlying areas and other sections of the city. At the present time over 80% of the tenants in public housing are black, and between 88% and 90% of the 30,000 people on the waiting list for such housing are black. Moreover, by design and chance, most of this public housing has been concentrated within eight of Atlanta's 132 square miles, in or near Atlanta's slums. Of the 14,000 units of public housing, 55.7% are located in areas which are 90% to 100% black, and another 19.4% in areas which are 70% to 90% black.
>
> Atlanta lies within Fulton County, and the AHA has entered into a Cooperation Agreement with both the city and the county which commits them to assist the AHA in its public housing program. Despite this agreement, and despite the fact that the jurisdiction of the AHA extends ten miles beyond the city limits of Atlanta into unincorporated Fulton County, not a single unit of low-rent public housing has ever been built in the unincorporated area.
>
> While poor blacks have been attracted to the low-rent public housing in Atlanta and the city's problems have rapidly mounted, whites have been fleeing in increasing numbers. In 1960 35% of the residents of Atlanta were black; today 51% are black. The public school population of Atlanta was 30% black; today it is 70% black. A fair percentage of the whites leaving Atlanta have moved to the unincorporated areas of Fulton County; a similar percentage of blacks from those areas have moved to the city.
>
> Within the immediate future, unless drastic changes occur, it is not merely possible but certain that Atlanta will become, in essence, a black city with a solid white perimeter. These two lawsuits, though analytically different, have been consolidated by this court because together they involve a plan to prevent this from happening to Atlanta by having some low-rent public housing built in unincorporated Fulton County. Some may say that this plan is unwise or that it may not succeed. It is not for this court to make such a determination. Unquestionably the design of the plan is to alleviate to some degree the crisis now at hand in Atlanta, and the goal of the plan is to preserve Atlanta's future as a city in which both whites and blacks may live.
>
> What this court must decide is whether certain actions of Fulton County officials, which have so far frustrated the initiation of this plan that may help save Atlanta, are unconstitutional and must be stopped. (332 F. Supp. at 383-384.)

The court then summarized the first action. It involved claims by plaintiffs who owned two tracts of land in Fulton County, both of which had been rezoned by the county for the construction of apartments before plaintiffs purchased the land.

It was plaintiffs' intention to construct apartments on the tracts and sell them to AHA. The authority would then lease them to qualified low-income tenants, but according to plaintiffs, when the defendant county officials learned that the plans were for public housing projects — which, they feared, would be black — they refused for racial reasons to grant the requested building permits. Defendants denied that the refusal of the permits was for racial reasons, citing as the basis for its action plaintiffs' failure to meet technical rezoning conditions. The district judge concluded, however, that the evidence indicated that the only reason for denying the permits was occupancy of the apartments by black tenants, and that such denial violated the Equal Protection Clause.

In the second suit, brought by black residents of Fulton County for themselves and all persons eligible for low-rent public housing, plaintiffs allege that their rights under the Fourteenth Amendment and the Civil Rights Act of 1964 and 1968 were violated by defendants' policies, which excluded them from public housing outside of racially concentrated areas. Again, the court ruled for plaintiffs, noting that the Atlanta Housing Program had made meaningful school desegregation virtually impossible, and had contributed to swelling unemployment roles. The court found the actions of the county in violation of the Fourteenth Amendment.

Decrees were entered for the plaintiffs in both cases. County officials were ordered to issue the building permits in the first case, and were further enjoined from interfering in any way with the completion of plaintiffs' project. In addition, county officials were ordered to take steps to provide for balanced and dispersed public housing.

In reaching this decision, the court cited most of the cases and statutory provisions reviewed in this section, and stated in regard to them, "For better or worse, both by legislative act and judicial decision, this nation is committed to a policy of balanced and dispersed public housing." The court took particular note of Kennedy Park Homes Association v. City of Lackawanna, 436 F.2d 108 (2d Cir. 1970), printed infra page 700, which held

> . . . that even though the deprivation of plaintiffs' equal housing rights had been caused to some extent by the sheer neglect and thoughtlessness of local officials, there was, nevertheless, a violation of the Equal Protection Clause. In so holding the court there cited Hobson v. Hansen, 269 F. Supp. 401 (D.D.C. 1967), *aff'd sub nom.*, Smuck v. Hobson, 408 F.2d 175 (D.C. Cir. 1969) (*en banc*) in which Judge J. Skelley Wright held:
>
> "The complaint that analytically no violation of equal protection vests unless the inequalities stem from a deliberately discriminatory plan is simply false. Whatever the law was once, it is a testament to our maturing concept of equality that, with the help of Supreme Court decisions in the last decade, we now firmly recognize that the arbitrary quality of thoughtlessness can be as disastrous to private rights and

the public interest as the perversity of a willful scheme." At 497. (332 F. Supp. at 390-91.)

Racism Hypo 9
BLACK MOTHERS ON WELFARE v. METROPOLIS HOUSING AUTHORITY

Metropolis is a large Northern city with racial population and housing problems quite similar to those in Atlanta, Chicago and other major urban areas. There is a growing black population (now 51 percent), mainly centered in substandard housing facilities in the inner city, while increasingly the white population has been moving to the suburbs. Public housing is inadequate and there is a long waiting list of applicants, 90 percent of whom are black. The four projects in black areas are virtually all black and tend to be poorly maintained, in comparison with the four projects in white areas, which are virtually all white. Opposition to new construction of public housing in white areas has been tremendous. The Metropolis Housing Authority (MHA) was petitioned by civil rights groups to conform its site selection and tenant assignment policies to the decisions in Gautreaux, El Cortez, Hicks, Shannon, and Crow. Fearing litigation on the problem, which its attorneys advised it could not win, MHA adopted new policies providing:

(1) 75 percent of apartments hereafter erected must be located at least one mile from the perimeter of those census tracts containing more than 30 percent nonwhite population, or from areas undergoing change from white to black. Every effort would be made to secure sites and construct new projects in areas with a population less than 15 percent nonwhite, with priority on outlying locations in Metropolis County recently rezoned from an agricultural to a residential classification.

(2) Public housing project buildings shall be designed for a maximum occupancy of 120 people, shall be built on "scattered sites" wherever possible, and shall not contain more than three floors — except those planned for elderly and families without children.

(3) All existing tenant waiting lists are voided. Persons on them (as well as the public generally) are advised that a new master list will be prepared, on which, upon application, eligible persons will be assigned a nonrecurring ordinal number for apartments with the appropriate number of bedrooms for a family of the applicant's size. Applicant preferences for particular projects will be observed when possible, but to prevent de facto segregation, no more than 50 percent of a project's apartments are to be available to eligible neighborhood residents, and the projects in predominantly white areas will be limited to 20 percent black families and 30 percent total "minority families" (including blacks, Indians, Chicanos, Spanish-Americans and Orientals).

Shortly after MHA announced its new policies, a group of present and prospective tenants called Black Mothers on Welfare filed suit in federal court against the MHA. The plaintiffs seek injunctive relief which will require modification of the site selection policy, in order to permit construction of high-rise public housing within existing ghetto areas, where space is not readily available to construct housing that meets the new standards. In addition, the suit seeks revision of the new tenant assignment system, so that black applicants will not be denied apartments for which they are otherwise eligible because of the racial quota.

Plaintiffs contend that the new housing regulations are arbitrary and in violation of their rights under the Equal Protection Clause in that: (1) their primary need is not integrated housing, but decent housing; (2) meaningful progress in desegregating housing patterns is prevented by the policies of the federal government and the continuing racist practices of white America, particularly the refusal through legal tactics — including zoning changes, manipulation of building permits, and referendum elections — to permit low-income housing developments in the suburbs; and (3) the effect of the defendant's new regulations will be to reduce the amount of public housing available for blacks.

Plaintiffs argue that the standard for housing eligibility should be based not on race, but on need. They contend that, because of widespread housing discrimination against blacks, their need for public housing exceeds that of almost all whites. The maintenance of eligibility standards established with integration as a goal is "arbitrary, altruistic, racist, and in violation of our constitutional rights." Those rights, the group maintains, entitle blacks to integration, but do not require it of them under circumstances involving great sacrifice and suffering.

This position is opposed by the housing authority, which contends that the new housing regulations are justified by the Gautreaux decision and other applicable cases. They argue further that adopting the revisions sought by the plaintiffs would violate new federal standards, would quickly bring about a completely segregated public housing system, and might jeopardize, because of Title VI of the 1964 Civil Rights Act, further federal financial assistance to the project.

Law Firm A will represent the Black Mothers on Welfare.

Law Firm B will represent the Metropolis Housing Authority.

C. THE REFERENDUM VERSUS THE BROWN MANDATE

The possibility that the almost hallowed right of referendum might be utilized by those whites who wished to elevate their preferences in neighbors to the status of a legal right, was posed and, many thought, deflected in Reitman v. Mulkey, printed supra page 618. But, as the decisions in this section will show, it is seldom easy to prove that the referendum or the community-backed zoning restriction has racial exclusion as its goal. The effort in James v. Valtierra, printed below, to extend the protection of the Equal Protection Clause to discrimination in the housing field based on poverty as well as race was not successful. The case, while ostensibly affecting only public housing, has ramifications because of its approval of the referendum to exclude low-income housing when no racial discrimination is proved, a decision which could affect the entire drive against suburban exclusionary practices.

JAMES v. VALTIERRA
402 U.S. 137, 91 S. Ct. 1331, 28 L. Ed. 2d 678 (*1971*)

Mr. Justice Black delivered the opinion of the Court.

These cases raise but a single issue. It grows out of the United States Housing Act of 1937, 42 U.S.C. §1401 et seq., which established a federal housing agency authorized to make loans and grants to state agencies for slum clearance and low-rent housing projects. In response, the California Legislature created in each county and city a public housing authority to take advantage of the financing made available by the Federal Housing Act. See California Health and Safety Code §34240. At the time the federal legislation was passed the California Constitution had for many years reserved to the State's people the power to initiate legislation and to reject or approve by referendum any Act passed by the state legislature. California Const. Art. IV, §1. The same section reserved to the electors of counties and cities the power of initiative and referendum over acts of local government bodies. In 1950, however, the State Supreme Court held that local authorities' decisions on seeking federal aid for public housing projects were "executive" and "administrative," not "legislative," and therefore the state constitution's referendum provisions did not apply to these actions. Within six months of that decision the California voters adopted Article XXXIV of the state constitution to bring public housing decisions under the State's referendum policy. The Article provided that no low-rent housing project should be developed, constructed or acquired in any manner by a state public body until the project was approved by a majority of those voting at a community election.

The present suits were brought by citizens of San Jose, California, and San Mateo County, localities where housing authorities could not apply for federal funds because low-cost housing proposals had been defeated in referendums. The plaintiffs, who are eligible for low-cost public housing, sought a declaration that Article XXXIV was unconstitutional because its referendum requirement violated: (1) the Supremacy Clause of the United States Constitution; (2) the Privileges and Immunities Clause; and (3) the Equal Protection Clause. A three-judge court held that Article XXXIV denied the plaintiffs equal protection of the laws and it enjoined its enforcement. 313 F. Supp. 1 (ND Cal. 1970). Two appeals were taken from the judgment, one by the San Jose City Council, and the other by a single member of the council. We noted probable jurisdiction of both appeals. . . . For the reasons that follow, we reverse. . . .

While the District Court cited several cases of this Court, its chief reliance plainly rested on Hunter v. Erickson, 393 U.S. 385, 89 S. Ct. 557, 21 L. Ed. 2d

616 (1969). The first paragraph in the District Court's decision stated simply: "We hold Article XXXIV to be unconstitutional. See Hunter v. Erickson . . . ." The court below erred in relying on Hunter to invalidate Article XXXIV. Unlike the case before us, Hunter rested on the conclusion that Akron's referendum law denied equal protection by placing "special burdens on racial minorities within the governmental process." Id., at 391 . . . . In Hunter the citizens of Akron had amended the city charter to require that any ordinance regulating real estate on the basis of race, color, religion, or national origin could not take effect without approval by a majority of those voting in a city election. The Court held that the amendment created a classification based upon race because it required that laws dealing with racial housing matters could take effect only if they survived a mandatory referendum while other housing ordinances took effect without any such special election. The opinion noted:

> Because the core of the Fourteenth Amendment is the prevention of meaningful and unjustified official distinctions based on race, [citing a group of racial discrimination cases] racial classifications are "constitutionally suspect" . . . and subject to the "most rigid scrutiny". . . . They "bear a far heavier burden of justification" than other classifications . . . . *Id.,* at 391-392 . . . .

The Court concluded that Akron had advanced no sufficient reasons to justify this racial classification and hence that it was unconstitutional under the Fourteenth Amendment.

Unlike the Akron referendum provision, it cannot be said that California's Article XXXIV rests on "distinctions based on race." Id., at 391, 89 S. Ct., at 561. The Article requires referendum approval for any low-rent public housing project, not only for projects which will be occupied by a racial minority. And the record here would not support any claim that a law seemingly neutral on its face is in fact aimed at a racial minority. Cf. Gomillion v. Lightfoot, 364 U.S. 339 . . . (1960). The present case could be affirmed only by extending Hunter, and this we decline to do.

California's entire history demonstrates the repeated use of referendums to give citizens a voice on questions of public policy. A referendum provision was included in the first state constitution, Calif. Const. of 1849, Art. VIII, and referendums have been a commonplace occurrence in the State's active political life. Provisions for referendums demonstrate devotion to democracy, not to bias, discrimination, or prejudice. Nonetheless, appellees contend that Article XXXIV denies them equal protection because it demands a mandatory referendum while many other referendums only take place upon citizen initiative. They suggest that the mandatory nature of the Article XXXIV referendum constitutes unconstitutional discrimination because it hampers persons desiring public housing from achieving their objective when no such roadblock faces other groups seeking to influence other public decisions to their advantage. But of course a lawmaking procedure that "disadvantages" a particular group does not always deny equal protection. Under any such holding, presumably a State would not be able to require referendums on any subject unless referendums were required on all, because they would always disadvantage some group. And this Court would be required to analyze governmental structures to determine whether a gubernatorial veto provision or a filibuster rule is likely to "disadvantage" any of the diverse and shifting groups that make up the American people.

Furthermore, an examination of California law reveals that persons advocating low-income housing have not been singled out for mandatory referendums while no other group must face that obstacle. Mandatory referendums are required for approval of state constitutional amendments, for the issuance of general obligation long-term bonds by local governments, and for certain municipal territorial annexations. See Calif. Const. Art. XVIII, Art. XIII, §40; Art. XI, §2(b). California statute books contain much legislation first enacted by voter initiative, and no such law can be repealed or amended except by referendum. Calif. Const. Art. IV, §24(c). Some California cities have wisely provided that their public parks may not be alienated without mandatory referendums, see, e.g., San Jose Charter, §1700.

The people of California have also decided by their own vote to require referendum approval of low-rent public housing projects. This procedure ensures that all the people of a community will have a voice in a decision which may lead to large expenditures of local governmental funds for increased public services and to lower tax revenues.[4] It gives them a voice in decisions that will affect the future development of their own community. This procedure for democratic decision-making does not violate the constitutional command that no State shall deny to any person "the equal protection of the laws."

The judgment of the three-judge court is reversed and the case is remanded for dismissal of the complaint.

Reversed.

Mr. Justice DOUGLAS took no part in the consideration or decision of this case.

Mr. Justice MARSHALL, whom Mr. Justice BRENNAN and Mr. Justice BLACKMUN join, dissenting.

By its very terms, the mandatory prior referendum provision of Article 34 applies solely to

4. Public low-rent housing projects are financed through bonds issued by the local housing authority. To be sure, the Federal Government contracts to make contributions sufficient to cover interest and principal, but the local government body must agree to provide all municipal services for the units and to waive all taxes on the property. The local services to be provided include schools, police, and fire protection, sewers, streets, drains, and lighting. Some of the cost is defrayed by the local governing body's receipt of 10% of the housing project rentals, but of course the rentals are set artificially low. Both appellants and appellees agree that the building of federally-financed low-cost housing entails costs to the local community. Appellant Shaffer's Brief, at 34-35. Appellee's Brief, at 47. See also 42 U.S.C. §§1401-1430.

any development composed of urban or rural dwellings, apartments or other living accommodations for persons of low income, financed in whole or in part by the Federal Government or a state public body or to which the Federal Government or a state public body extends assistance by supplying all or part of the labor, by guaranteeing the payment of liens, or otherwise.

Persons of low income are defined as

> persons or families who lack the amount of income which is necessary . . . to enable them, without financial assistance, to live in decent, safe and sanitary dwellings, without overcrowding.

The article explicitly singles out low-income persons to bear its burden. Publicly assisted housing developments designed to accommodate the aged, veterans, state employees, persons of moderate income, or any class of citizens other than the poor, need not be approved by prior referenda.[5]

In my view, Article 34 on its face constitutes invidious discrimination which the Equal Protection Clause of the Fourteenth Amendment plainly prohibits. "The States, of course, are prohibited by the Equal Protection Clause from discriminating between 'rich' and 'poor' *as such* in the formulation and application of their laws." Douglas v. California, 372 U.S. 353, 361 . . . (1963) (Mr. Justice Harlan, dissenting). Article 34 is neither "a law of general applicability that may affect the poor more harshly than it does the rich," ibid, nor an "effort to redress economic imbalances," ibid. It is rather an explicit classification on the basis of poverty — a suspect classification which demands exacting judicial scrutiny, see McDonald v. Board of Election Commissioners, 394 U.S. 802, 807 . . . (1969); Harper v. Virginia Board of Elections, 383 U.S. 663 . . . (1966); Douglas v. California, 372 U.S. 353 . . . (1963).

The Court, however, chooses to subject the article to no scrutiny whatsoever and treats the provision as if it contained a totally benign, technical economic classification. Both the appellees and the Solicitor General of the United States as amicus curiae have strenuously argued, and the court below found, that Article 34, by imposing a substantial burden solely on the poor, violates the Fourteenth Amendment. Yet after observing that the article does not discriminate on the basis of race, the Court's only response to the real question in this case is the unresponsive assertion that "referendums demonstrate devotion to democracy, not to bias, discrimination, or prejudice." It is far too late in the day to contend that the Fourteenth Amendment prohibits only racial discrimination; and to me, singling out the poor to bear a burden not placed on any other class of citizens tramples the values that the Fourteenth Amendment was designed to protect.

I respectfully dissent.

5. California law authorizes the formation of Renewal Area Agencies whose purposes include the construction of "low-income, middle-income and normal-market housing," California Health and Safety Code §33701 et seq. Only low income housing programs are subject to the mandatory referendum provision of Article 34 even though all of the agencies' programs may receive substantial governmental assistance.

NOTES

1. The Valtierra decision came as a shock to open-housing advocates, who were certain that the three-judge court's application of Hunter v. Erickson, printed supra page 623, was correct. They hoped that appeal of the three-judge court's decision, invalidating Article 34, would lead to a Supreme Court decision that extended equal protection rights in the housing area to the poor, without the often difficult task of proving racial discrimination. Just the opposite resulted. The majority refused to give close scrutiny to the statutory purpose which had been challenged as a suspect classification. Instead, the Court extolled the use of referenda as demonstrating "devotion to democracy, not to bias, discrimination, or prejudice." But, as one law review commented, "That referenda demonstrate a laudable devotion to principles of popular sovereignty is no justification for mandatory referenda in some instances but not in others." 85 Harv. L. Rev. 122, 126 (1971).

2. The rapid creation, incorporation and zoning of a new Missouri town in late 1970, all allegedly for the purpose of blocking plans to construct a subsidized housing project in the area, received nationwide attention. Suits challenging the action were filed by private attorneys and the Department of Justice. Park View Heights Corporation v. City of Black Jack, 467 F.2d 1208 (8th Cir. 1972), *rev'g* 335 F. Supp. 899 (E.D. Mo. 1971); United States v. City of Black Jack, Civ. Action No. 71 C372(1) (E.D. Mo. 1971).

In reversing dismissal of the Park View Heights Corporation challenge to the City of Black Jack scheme, the Eighth Circuit held that the sponsor and developer of the proposed housing has standing to question both whether the restrictive zoning ordinance resulted in a taking of property without due process, and whether the purpose and effect was to exclude low- and moderate-income persons, including blacks, from living in the locality. The issues are discussed in Note, Exclusionary Zoning and the Problem in Black Jack — A Denial of Housing To Whom? 16 St. Louis U.L.J. 294 (1971).

The Supreme Court's decision in James v. Valtierra may have encouraged schemes such as the new city of Black Jack, Missouri. But the growing number of court challenges to restrictive zoning plans and referendum procedures indicates that the Valtierra decision has dampened rather than destroyed hopes for judicial relief in this area.

Professor George Lefcoe believes that Valtierra may have benefits for low-income housing proponents. First, to the extent that Article 34 discourages public housing in California, it may serve to encourage other types of federally subsidized housing programs, which many experts believe can more effectively solve housing shortages for low-income people. Second, Valtierra won't provide protection to all referenda that affect exclusion of low-income housing projects. In his view, courts will examine more closely situations where, unlike California, there is no history of the referendum as an integral part of state and local practice, particularly when the establishment of a public housing referendum is accompanied by overtones of racial and class prejudice. Lefcoe, The Public Housing Referendum Case, Zoning, and the

Supreme Court, 59 Cal. L. Rev. 1384 (1971). But see English v. Town of Huntington, 448 F.2d 319 (2d Cir. 1971), involving efforts to bring code enforcement proceedings in residences occupied by minority group members who claim that the actions are intended to force them out of town. In affirming denial of relief, Judge Friendly read Valtierra as holding "that the mere fact that a requirement, otherwise proper, may have a greater impact on the poor, does not render it invalid under the Equal Protection Clause. . . ." 448 F.2d at 324.

3. One federal district court accepted an allegation that the city's refusal to rezone a parcel of land to accommodate federally assisted low- and moderate-income housing was sufficient to deny a motion to dismiss. A city cannot rely on existing zoning, absent a valid land use reason, where the effect is to further racial discrimination. The court said that the city need not rezone to accommodate minority groups if the subject land cannot carry a higher density, but that rezoning cannot be refused for black projects where variances would be granted for an all-white project. Sisters of Providence v. City of Evanston, 335 F. Supp. 396 (N.D. Ill. 1971).

4. It is clear that exclusionary housing practices greatly increase the difficulties of achieving full educational opportunities for black children. It may be less obvious that exclusionary patterns also severely limit job opportunities for their parents. In a 1970 report, the National Committee Against Discrimination in Housing found that, "Despite higher wage levels at suburban plants, employers continue to be plagued by job vacancies and high labor turnover," primarily because lower-income people, especially from minority groups, are prevented from living in the towns where the factories are situated. For example, during the period from 1959 to 1967 New York City lost 47,110 manufacturing jobs while its surrounding suburbs gained 138,440. N.Y. Times, Apr. 13, 1970 at 82 c. 1. Many minority group workers drive long distances into the suburbs for work, but travel expenses are high and the burden of commuting heavy for both employees and employers because of higher absentee rates. Litigation has been filed testing the legality of exclusionary zoning ordinances in suburban areas where large plants are located. See, e.g., United Automobile Workers v. Township of Mahwah, N.J. — N.J. Super. — (App. Div. 1972), petition for certification by New Jersey Supreme Court filed July 24, 1972. Suits have also been filed charging government agencies with racial discrimination when those agencies approve the relocation of major offices to suburban areas, where low-income and minority employees will experience great difficulty in finding housing. See, e.g., Brookhaven Housing Coalition v. Kunzig, 341 F. Supp. 1026 (E.D.N.Y. 1972), notice of appeal filed Sept. 15, 1972. See infra page 811 on the issue of whether private employers violate Title VII of the Civil Rights Act of 1964 when they move plants to areas where minority workers will experience serious discrimination in housing.

5. Prior to the Valtierra decision, there had been a number of cases involving building restrictions on low-income housing imposed by zoning agencies

or through referenda procedures. These restrictions were not specifically aimed at low-income housing, as in Valtierra, but had a "de facto effect" on most housing projects for which the poor and minority groups were eligible. Challenges to these restrictions were resolved according to whether proof supported the conclusion that the restrictions were intended to bar a minority group from a predominantly white residential area. Standards for determining intent varied widely.

RANJEL v. CITY OF LANSING, 417 F.2d 321 (6th Cir. 1969). Here, the court also expressed high regard for the citizens' right of referendum. It reversed a lower court's order enjoining a referendum required by a petition of whites, who opposed a city council zoning change that would have permitted construction of low-rent town houses and an apartment for the elderly in a white residential area. The court rejected findings that the referendum was motivated by racial factors. It felt that testimony on this point was unimpressive, and doubted whether the district court could reach such a conclusion "by searching the minds of 15 percent of the electorate who signed the referendum petition, and the remaining 85 percent who were enjoined from voting, none of whom were called as witnesses to testify in the case." The court noted that:

> A goodly portion of the opinion of the District Court was devoted to a vivid portrayal of the tragic conditions affecting the poor black and Mexican-Americans living in the slum areas in Lansing, and the need to alleviate these conditions by moving them out of the slums to more desirable neighborhoods. These conditions, however, concerning the plight of the poor, were not peculiar to Lansing nor indeed to the United States, but have existed for centuries in many places throughout the world.
>
> It would seem to us that there should be a better way to achieve this worthy goal without enjoining an election and thereby depriving the citizens of a community of their right of suffrage. (417 F.2d at 322.)

SOUTHERN ALAMEDA SPANISH SPEAKING ORGANIZATION v. CITY OF UNION CITY, 424 F.2d 291 (9th Cir. 1970). A city ordinance rezoning an area for a low-income project was nullified almost immediately by a citywide referendum. The record shows that in recent years the area had changed from an agricultural community inhabited almost exclusively by Mexican-Americans to a predominantly white suburban town, in which the old residents, due to limited incomes, had been unable to afford the new housing. But both trial and appeals courts rejected contentions that the referendum was racially motivated and that it was intended to perpetuate discrimination against Mexican-Americans with low incomes, stating:

> Under the facts of this case we do not believe that the question of motivation for the referendum (apart from a consideration of its effect) is an appropriate one

for judicial inquiry. In this respect, Reitman v. Mulkey, 387 U.S. 369 . . . (1967), is distinguishable.

There a constitutional amendment, adopted by the people of California through a statewide ballot, resulted in the repeal of existing fair housing laws and prohibited all legislative action abridging the rights of persons to sell, lease or rent property to whomsoever they chose. In examining the constitutionality of the amendment, its purpose was treated as a relevant consideration.

Purpose was judged, however, in terms of ultimate effect and historical context. The only existing restrictions on dealings in land (and thus the obvious target of the amendment) were those prohibiting private discrimination. The only "conceivable" purpose, judged by wholly objective standards, was to restore the right to discriminate and protect it against future legislative limitation. The amendment was held to constitute impermissible state involvement (in the nature of authorization or encouragement) with private racial discrimination. 387 U.S. at 381. . . .

The case before us is quite different. As we have noted, many environmental and social values are involved in determinations of land use. As the District Court noted, ". . . [T]here is no more reason to find that [rejection of rezoning] was done on the ground of invidious racial discrimination any more than on perfectly legitimate environmental grounds which are always and necessarily involved in zoning issues."

If the voters' purpose is to be found here, then, it would seem to require far more than a simple application of objective standards. If the true motive is to be ascertained not through speculation but through a probing of the private attitudes of the voters, the inquiry would entail an intolerable invasion of the privacy that must protect an exercise of the franchise. . . .

Appellants' equal protection contentions, however, reach beyond purpose. They assert that the effect of the referendum is to deny decent housing and an integrated environment to low-income residents of Union City. If, apart from voter motive, the result of this zoning by referendum is discriminatory in this fashion, in our view a substantial constitutional question is presented.

Surely, if the environmental benefits of land use planning are to be enjoyed by a city and the quality of life of its residents is accordingly to be improved, the poor cannot be excluded from enjoyment of the benefits. Given the recognized importance of equal opportunities in housing, it may well be, as matter of law, that it is the responsibility of a city and its planning officials to see that the city's plan as initiated or as it develops accommodates the needs of its low-income families, who usually — if not always — are members of minority groups. It may be, as matter of fact, that Union City's plan, as it has emerged from the referendum, fails in this respect. These issues remain to be resolved. (424 F.2d at 295-296.)

In addition to its equal protection claim, SASSO had challenged California's referendum procedures as applied to the zoning process, contending that they violated due process requirements by arbitrarily restricting the use by SASSO of its land. While the regulation of land use by zoning is valid because of procedural safeguards, the referendum process "destroys the necessary procedural safeguards upon which a municipality's power to zone is based and subjects zoning decisions to the bias, caprice and self-interest of the voter." The court disagreed:

A referendum . . . is far more than an expression of ambiguously founded neighborhood preference. It is the city itself legislating through its voters — an exercise by the voters of their traditional right through direct legislation to override the views of their elected representatives as to what serves the public interest. See Spaulding v. Blair, 403 F.2d 862 (4th Cir. 1968). This question lay at the heart of the proposition put to the voters. That some voters individually may have failed to meet their responsibilities as legislators to vote wisely and unselfishly cannot alter the result.

Nor can it be said that the resulting legislation on its face was so unrelated to acceptable public interest standards as to constitute an arbitrary or unreasonable exercise of the police power. . . . Many environmental and social values are involved in a determination of how land would best be used in the public interest. The choice of the voters of Union City is not lacking in support in this regard.

Thus in the present case neither the zoning process itself nor the result can be said to be such an arbitrary or unreasonable exercise of the zoning power as to be violative of appellants' right to due process of law. (424 F.2d at 294.)

DAILEY v. CITY OF LAWTON, OKLAHOMA, 425 F.2d 1037 (1970). The Tenth Circuit reached the opposite conclusion in a case with somewhat similar facts. There, the lower court enjoined the city from denying a zoning change and building permit requested by plaintiff: sponsors for a low-income housing project in a predominantly white residential section. Petitions opposing the zoning change and building permit were signed by 250 white residents of the area and submitted to the City Planning Commission, which denied the zoning change. In concluding that the lower court had properly found that actions of the planning commission and the city council were racially motivated, due to "the bias and prejudice" of the white property owners, the court noted:

Except for military personnel from Fort Sill, Lawton is in large measure a racially segregated city. The North Addition is predominately white. The housing project is designed to serve low-income groups which consist of Negroes, Spanish-Americans, and poor whites. The signers of the petitions in opposition were all white. The racial situation was discussed in connection with the circulation of the petitions. The project sponsors received numerous anonymous phone calls which opposed the project on a racial basis. The one dissenting member of the Planning Commission testified that the opposition was based on racial bias. The evidence is sufficient to show that the public bodies acted as they did because of the opposition to the project by the residents of the North Addition.

The appellants point out that the race issue was not discussed at any of the public meetings and that there was no evidence of racial prejudice on the part of any city official. If proof of a civil right violation depends on an open statement by an official of an intent to discriminate, the Fourteenth Amendment offers little solace to those seeking its protection. In our opinion it is enough for the complaining parties to show that the local officials are effectuating the discriminatory designs of private individuals. See e.g. Shelley v. Kraemer, 334 U.S. 1, . . . holding unconstitutional the judicial enforcement of restrictive covenants contained in deeds, and Reitman v. Mulkey, 387 U.S. 369, . . . holding unconstitutional an initiated amendment to the California constitution effectively permitting discriminatory practices in the housing market.

The appellants argue that a finding of discriminatory intent is barred because the project was opposed on the grounds of overcrowding of the neighborhood, the local schools, and the recreational facilities and the overburdening of the local fire fighting capabilities. The testimony in this regard was vague and general. No school, fire, recreational, traffic or other official testified in support of the appellants' claims. The racial prejudice alleged and established by the plaintiffs must be met by something more than bald, conclusory assertions that the action was taken for other than discriminatory reasons. (425 F.2d at 1039-1040.)

KENNEDY PARK HOMES ASSOCIATION v. CITY OF LACKAWANNA
436 F.2d 108 (2d Cir. 1970)

Clark, Justice, Retired:

This is an appeal from a judgment of the United States District Court for the Western District of New York, Cortin, J., requiring the City of Lackawanna to take all necessary steps to allow Kennedy Park Subdivision to proceed with its construction plans for the development of a low income housing project on a certain tract of land, together with the supporting orders necessary thereto. The suit was commenced by the Kennedy Park Homes Association, the Colored People's Civic and Political Organization (C.P.C.P.O.), a membership corporation interested in housing, the Diocese of Buffalo, New York, and individual home seekers. The defendants included the City of Lackawanna, its City Council and Mayor as well as other city officials. The United States of America was permitted to intervene. The complaint alleged that the defendants had deliberately rezoned the property that the plaintiffs had selected for its housing project as a park and recreation area, and had declared a moratorium on new subdivisions, in order to deny decent housing to low-income and minority families, in violation of the Equal Protection and Due Process Clauses of the Fourteenth Amendment to the Federal Constitution, the Civil Rights Act (42 U.S.C. §1983) and the Fair Housing Act of 1968 (42 U.S.C. §3601 et seq.). After an extended trial the Court entered its decision and order on August 13, 1970, 318 F. Supp. 669. . . .

We affirm the judgment. . . . [W]e find after careful study that . . . racial motivation resulting in invidious discrimination guided the actions of the City. The pattern is an old one and exists in many of our communities but appears to be somewhat more subtle in Lackawanna. However, when the chronology of events is considered, the discrimination is clear.

I

First, we have a three-ward city with 98.9 percent of all of its nonwhite citizens living in the First Ward. The Second Ward, with a population of 8,974, has only one nonwhite person, while only 29 nonwhites reside in the Third Ward. The Bethlehem Steel Company's plant, with its more than 20,000 employees, occupies at least half of the land area of the First Ward. This Ward also has the oldest, most dilapidated dwelling houses, and the highest residential density with the greatest percentage of persons per unit in the city. Health-wise it is classified as a "high risk area," having double the incidence of tuberculosis and the highest infant mortality rate of the entire city. Its juvenile crime rate is three times the city average, and its adult crime rate is double the average. The air pollution from the steel plant is at times unbearable because of the huge clouds of smoke, the dust and particles spewing from its furnaces and the open hearths that burn constantly. To add insult to injury, a series of parallel railroad tracks serves the steel mill, running along the east boundary of the First Ward and physically separating it from the rest of the City. Indeed the only traffic connection between the two is a single bridge that spans the railroad tracks at Ridge Road. This man made and City approved physical barrier actually segregates the black community of Lackawanna, located in the First Ward, from the rest of the City. The tracks are often tagged as the barrier "between the 'haves' and the 'have nots.'"

Second, the nonwhite residents of Lackawanna make up one-tenth of its population and 35.4 percent of the First Ward. The Planning and Development Board of Lackawanna has seven members, all of whom are white and none of whom reside in the First Ward. Each Ward has one councilman and two are elected at large but the First Ward has only one member of the Council. There are three low income housing projects in the City of Lackawanna. All of them are in the First Ward. The best housing in the First Ward, the Bethlehem Park project built by the Steel Company, was restricted to whites until recently.

Third, although many of the blacks residing in the First Ward wish to move out of it, building contractors generally will not build a house for a black citizen in the Third Ward. As the Planning Consultant to the City expressed it to the Planning and Development Board as late as February 1968:

> The Negro has indicated tremendous concern about his suspected confinement to the first ward. At almost every one of the Planning Board meetings, collectively they have stated they do not feel that any residential use should be allowed to remain in the first ward. In piercing through what they say, what they really mean is don't keep us in the first ward, let us live where our income or our desires allow us. You have a tremendous pressure building up in your community on the part of the non-whites to go across the bridge.

In fact, only the month before representatives of the C.P.C.P.O. had called on the Director of Development of the City to inquire about the availability of city-owned land for subdivision development. Subsequently one of the plaintiffs in this case offered to buy 74 contiguous lots in the Second Ward for a housing development but his offer was tabled by the City Council. Although a group of ministers urged the Mayor to permit the sale, he told them informally that any sale of city property might have to be by public bid but that he would look into it. He never replied to their inquiry. Neither the Mayor nor the Director of Development made further reply.

In March 1968 arrangements were made with the Diocese of Buffalo by plaintiff C.P.C.P.O. to purchase 30 acres of the Diocese land in the Third Ward to be used for a proposed Kennedy Park Subdivision, a low income housing project. The site was located south of Martin Road and east of the proposed route of the "McKinley Extension" highway. C.P.C.P.O. incorporated the Kennedy Park Homes Association as a housing or mortgagor company. This news was reported in the Buffalo and Lackawanna press. Petitions were circulated opposing the sale. One petition with 3,000 signatures was sent to Bishop McNulty of the Diocese opposing the sale for lack of sewer facilities and schools. It carried the name of both Mayor Balen and the President of the City Council. A meeting in the Third Ward also opposed the sale, and a group known as TICA (Taxpayers Interested in Civic Affairs) was a leader in opposition. In April 1968, at a meeting of the TICA group, concern was voiced over both the sewage problem and the schools as well as the damage that might result to property values if low income housing was constructed in the Third Ward. In addition some fears of increased unrest and misunderstanding were expressed if "a grand scale integration" rather than "the gradual way" resulted. At a later First Ward group meeting a report was made of this earlier meeting in the Third Ward. A spokesman for the First Ward group made reference to "rumored threats of violent action" if moves from the First to the Third Ward were made and indicated the Justice Department and Attorney General's Office had been alerted. A joint meeting was suggested but was never held. Both of these meetings in the Third and First Wards, respectively, were held under the auspices of the Commissioner of the New York State Human Rights Division and the Chairman of the Lackawanna Human Rights Commission.

Although plans were being studied for housing and sewerage improvements beginning in 1967, none had been adopted. On August 20, 1968, the Lackawanna Zoning Board of Appeals and the Planning and Development Board met in joint session and recommended to the City Council a moratorium on all new subdivisions until such time as the sewer problem was solved. It also recommended that parts of the Second and Third Wards be designated for open space and park area. This area included the land to be devoted to the proposed Kennedy Park Subdivision. Thereafter on October 7, 1968, the City Council adopted both a moratorium and zoning ordinance along the line recommended by the Zoning Board of Appeals and the Planning and Development Board, but the area encompassed by the zoning ordinance was more limited to the immediate area surrounding the Kennedy Park site.

This suit was filed soon thereafter. On February 26, 1969, after the United States had intervened, both ordinances were rescinded. Subsequently the subdivision requested permission to tie into the City sewer system. Before the Erie County Health Department will consider such requests, it must receive a "Sanitary Form 5," which is an application by the City on behalf of a subdivider to approve the sewer extension. The Mayor refused to sign this form. Without the sewer permit, the black citizens were unable to proceed with their project. . . .

[The court then reviewed the evidence supporting the trial judge's findings and found them substantial. Using standards applicable when the state action under inquiry is "insidious and subtle rather than direct and open," the court concluded that "The mosaic of Lackawanna's discrimination is a sad one." The panoply of events "indicates state action amounting to specific authorization and continuous encouragement of racial discrimination, if not almost complete racial segregation." 436 F.2d at 114.]

NOTE: EXCLUSIONARY ZONING LITIGATION IN STATE COURTS

In recent years, the Pennsylvania Supreme Court in a series of decisions has taken cognizance of the housing crisis and the impact of exclusionary zoning practices on the problem. Without specific mention of racial or economic discrimination, the Pennsylvania court has voided zoning schemes which seriously limit low-income housing construction, on the basis that such schemes are unreasonable and in excess of the state's police powers. These cases are summarized succinctly in the following excerpt:*

. . . One judicial technique that has been used to attack the problem of exclusionary zoning is the broadened application of due process requirements imposed by the Pennsylvania Supreme Court in recent decisions. As a result of this technique zoning ordinances adopted with an exclusionary intent have not fared well. In National Land & Investment Co. v. Easttown Township Board of Adjustment,[40] the Pennsylvania court considered a minimum lot size ordinance limiting home sites to four acres or more. Although it could be argued that this ordinance was reasonably calculated to promote in some measure the health and welfare of the current inhabitants of the township (enough to support its validity under traditional due process standards), the court closely examined the supposed foundations for the ordinance in relation to the needs of the township. The court found the township's reasons for large lot zoning insubstantial and concluded that the ordinance had been adopted more for exclusionary purposes than merely to prevent sewage disposal problems as the township contended. In applying the due process test, the court decided that retaining the character of the community by preventing population growth was not a reasonable exercise of the police power.[42]

Five years after the National Land decision, the Pennsylvania court again considered exclusionary practices in Appeal of Girsh.[43] There the court overturned a zoning ordinance because the township had failed to provide for apartments in its zoning scheme. In Girsh, the court hardly considered the purported rationale[44] for

* From Note, The Responsibility of Local Zoning Authorities to Nonresident Indigents, 23 Stan. L. Rev. 774 (1971). Copyright 1971 by the Board of Trustees of the Leland Stanford Junior University.

40. 419 Pa. 504, 215 A.2d 597 (1965).

42. "The question posed is whether the township can stand in the way of the natural forces which send our growing population into hitherto undeveloped areas in search of a comfortable place to live. We have concluded not." 419 Pa. at 532, 215 A.2d at 612.

43. 437 Pa. 237, 263 A.2d 395 (1970).

44. The township claimed that it did not expressly prohibit apartments and had allowed them in the past through variances. In addition, it claimed that "apartment uses would cause a significant population increase with a resulting strain on available municipal services and roads . . . ." Id. at 240, 243, 263 A.2d at 396, 398.

the township's ordinance. It dwelled instead on the effects and causes of exclusionary zoning, noting the origins of suburban antipathy to apartments and citing statistics to support the showing of need for more apartments in suburban areas. The emphasis of the opinion was upon the fact that the zoning ordinance in question significantly reduced the opportunities for outsiders to move into the community. This solicitude for the rights of an indefinite class of nonresidents, mere potential occupants of yet to be built apartments, hardly seems consistent with the application of the due process standard. The property rights of appellant Girsh, an apartment developer, seem lost in a contest between the township and potential residents; under the due process standard, the analysis should have focused on his rights. The same attitude determined, and was better explained by Appeal of Kit-Mar Builders, Inc.,[48] which closely followed Girsh. After invalidating a minimum lot size ordinance on facts very similar to National Land, the court acknowledged that, although the form of the litigation appeared to involve the due process rights of the landowner whose property had been zoned, the fundamental problem concerned the rights of nonresidents who desired to move into the area.[49] This suggests that the court is actually employing the "new" equal protection formula under which certain statutory classifications will be condemned unless the interests of the class discriminated against are outweighed by a compelling state interest.[50] It appears that the court balanced the interests of the township against the alleged rights of nonresidents and found the township's interests less than compelling.

It should be noted that the decisions of the Pennsylvania Supreme Court are not based on the type of suspect classification that ordinarily prompts the invocation of the equal protection clause. The court's analysis dodges the issues of economic and racial discrimination, indicating only that the common characteristic of those excluded by the township's plan is that they are "outsiders." The treatment of the problem in solely demographic terms fails to take into account or to rectify the economic consequences of the exclusionary ordinances. In order truly to overcome the pernicious effects of exclusionary zoning, some attempt must be made to alleviate the special plight of indigent "outsiders" adversely affected by the maladministration of land use planning. (Note, 23 Stan. L. Rev. 779-781 (1971).)

Issues unresolved by the earlier Pennsylvania rulings were presented in Commonwealth v. County of Buck, 22 Bucks Co. L. Rep. 179 (1972), in which

48. 439 Pa. 466, 268 A.2d 765 (1970).

49. "Although National Land, and this problem in general, is postured as involving the constitutional due process rights of the land-owner whose property has been zoned adversely to his best interests, it cannot realistically be detached from the rights of other people desirous of moving into the area 'in search of a comfortable place to live.'" Id. at 468 n.6, 268 A.2d at 768 n.6.

50. Under the traditional equal protection test, a statute would be upheld on review despite discriminatory character if the statutory classifications had a rational basis. Under the "new" equal protection standard, the states have been required to show some compelling interest in order to sustain a statute that makes discriminations of a suspect nature (e.g., racial or economic classifications) and infringes the exercise of a fundamental right. Under this form of review, the rights of the persons affected by the statute are balanced against the interests of the state. See Sager, supra note 33, at 774-80. "New" and "old" equal protection standards are also referred to as "active" and "inactive" review. See Developments in the Law — Equal Protection, 82 Harv. L. Rev. 1065, 1087-1132 (1969).

Pennsylvania, low-income citizens, and several housing organizations challenged zoning patterns throughout the Bucks County area as exclusionary and illegal. In addition to seeking injunctions against enforcement of the various zoning ordinances, the complainants requested the county to take specific actions to provide opportunities for low- and moderate-income housing. The Common Pleas court dismissed the case.

State litigation, particularly in New Jersey and New York, has challenged zoning ordinances which directly raised issues concerning the exclusion of the poor and minorities. The results have been mixed, but the courts seem to have joined Pennsylvania in recognizing the adverse effect of zoning that excludes low- and moderate-income people from suburban housing. The New Jersey Supreme Court sustained a variance granted by the city of Englewood to permit a low-income housing project over the objections of neighborhood residents. The court held that the variance was justified under New Jersey law, because of the desperate need for housing opportunities for low-income and minority families. Di Simone v. Greater Englewood Housing Corporation, 56 N.J. 428, 267 A.2d 31 (1970). Oakwood at Madison v. Township of Madison, 117 N.J. Super. 11 (Sup. Ct. 1971), invalidated an ordinance setting minimum lot sizes and restricting multifamily construction, on the ground that such serious restrictions could not be justified to attain a "balanced community." The court noted that exclusionary zoning policies were influential in perpetuating inner-city ghetto deterioration and congestion. In reaching a similar conclusion about another exclusionary suburban zoning practice, the court in Southern Burlington County NAACP v. Township of Mount Laurel, 119 N.J. Super. 164, 290 A.2d 465 (Sup. Ct. 1972), not only voided a restrictive zoning ordinance, but ordered the municipality to determine the existing housing needs of low- and moderate-income residents and workers in the township to estimate the number of units required, and to submit an affirmative program to meet those needs in ninety days.

Zoning provisions that, in effect, limited construction of new apartments to those in the luxury category were voided in Molino v. Mayor and Council of Borough of Glassboro, 116 N.J. Super. 195, 281 A.2d 401 (Sup. Ct. 1971). In New York, advocates of open housing have filed a number of suits contesting exclusionary zoning policies. In one case, Golden v. Ramapo, 30 N.Y.2d 359, 334 N.Y.S.2d 138, 285 N.E.2d 291 (1972), the opinion condemned in general terms local land-use policies that immunize against population growth and cripple efforts to provide regional and statewide problem-solving. The court ruled, however, that the suburban town of Ramapo could freeze development of its vacant land for as long as a generation, because the town's zoning plan was viewed as an attempt to bring about a balanced community through the efficient use of land, and to prevent the deterioration that has transformed once thriving residential communities into blighted ghettos. Opponents of exclusionary zoning have fared better in Michigan, where two appeals courts have voided restrictions on mobile home parks because of the need for low-income housing. See Bristow v. City of Woodhaven, 35 Mich. App. 205, 192

N.W.2d 322 (1971); Green v. Township of Lima, 40 Mich. App. 655, 199 N.W.2d 243 (1972). An Illinois court has held that, where certain land uses are concerned, the term "general welfare" must be defined to meet the exigencies caused by urbanized society. Lakeland Bluffs, Inc. v. County of Will, 114 Ill. App. 2d 267, 252 N.E.2d 765 (1969). A California court has held that judicial inquiry must be made into a town's objectives in barring low-cost housing projects, so as to determine whether the exclusion is discriminatory. G. and D. Holland Construction Company v. Marysville, 12 Cal. App. 3d 989, 91 Cal. Rptr. 227 (1970).

An Ohio common pleas judge found that a planning commission's refusal to approve plans for a federally subsidized housing project in a white neighborhood, would, under all the circumstances, constitute invidious discrimination against blacks in the community. The court observed that, "If only Americans of color were able to acquire housing accommodations as easily as they can purchase Cadillacs, the occasion for cases such as this would surely be rare." Lakewood Homes, Inc. v. Board of Adjustment, 258 N.E.2d 470 (Ohio 1970). The court's opinion summarizes the written objections to the project that were received by the defendant planning commission. They included:

> . . . will raise school tax levies precipitously or result in lowering of present quality of public education; will depress general property values; location is wrong — many other areas more appropriate; will result in influx of lower-income people into a higher income community and make everyone — including new arrivals — unhappy; cause congestion of traffic and people making community less safe in which to live and requiring more police for unruly people who have declared their defiance of present law; will soon cause fine community to become a slum. (258 N.E.2d at 491.)

In the Lakewood Homes case, the court, to avoid "invidious discrimination in rental of the housing project," required the builder to rent apartments to minority groups on the basis of their percentage in the population for the next twenty-one years. Rules were set for initial and subsequent vacancies, and standards for occupancy of individual units were established. Thus, the court emulated Gautreaux in establishing "benign quotas" to remedy or to avoid housing segregation. The hoped-for benefits and the wide range of practical problems involved in such arrangements were reviewed in Bittker, The Case of the Checkerboard Ordinance: An Experiment in Race Relations, 71 Yale L.J. 1387 (1962). The imposition of a benign quota does not, however, answer the objections to the housing project raised by whites in the Lakewood case. None of them mentioned race directly, and it is thus worthwhile to discuss to what extent factors other than race are involved in the opposition to either public or privately funded housing for low-income individuals.

NOTE: "NONRACIAL" MOTIVATION FOR EXCLUDING LOW-INCOME HOUSING

The careful reader of this chapter will have observed by now that not all the barriers to low-income housing, particularly public housing projects, have been erected by whites. In the public housing cases examined in the previous section, Gautreaux, El Cortez, Hicks, and Banks, it was black plaintiffs who sought relief against the construction in black areas of public housing units.

Blacks control few suburbs, but they too fear the incursion of low-income families. The town of North Hempstead in Long Island killed a federally subsidized housing program because of opposition from middle-class blacks residing in the area where the project was to be built. Two black organizations formed to oppose the project issued the by now familiar statements. They expressed concern that new families would not maintain their homes properly and that the houses might deteriorate and become rooming houses. N.Y. Times, July 24, 1970, at 27, c. 7.

The suggestion that blacks can be found liable for discriminating against other blacks presents a sociologically supportable legal issue. See E. Frazier, Black Bourgeoisie (1957); G. Marx, Protest and Prejudice (1967). One writer explains that the struggle to attain status in white society has caused some middle-class blacks to withdraw from racial issues. Thus, Harry Edwards writes:

> . . . despite their ability to empathize with the plight of downtrodden and impoverished slum-dwelling Blacks, in the past few middle-class negroes have rallied to the cause of the masses. Rather, perceiving their own well-being as highly tentative, unproven, and fragile, they have typically withdrawn from the challenge, removing themselves physically, socially, and psychologically from the ghetto. Often feeling insecure about and protective of their newly won liberation from the shackles of abject poverty or traditional welfarism, they have exhibited, as a class, a steadfast refusal to become involved in racial controversy, usually suspecting, and not without some justification, that the level of existence that they enjoyed was maintained through the tolerance and sufferance of whites as much as by their own hard work. Thus, middle-class negroes have developed feelings of superiority toward lower-class Blacks while still burdened with deep-seated feelings of insecurity. The middle-class negro has, in the past, not only sought to put forth the notion that he is certainly better off, if not better, than the lower classes of Blacks, but he has also tried to forestall any social or psychological identification with the Black masses because of his own insecurities. (Edwards, Black Students 8 (1970).)

But such situations, where blacks seek to exclude other blacks of lower income, are likely to indicate that economic, rather than racial, discrimination is at work. And, while race cannot be ignored where the exclusionary effort is by whites, it is likely that economic and social class concerns are also present.

Economist Anthony Downs sought to examine these concerns in a statement delivered to the Senate Select Committee on Equal Educational Opportunity, Part 5: De Facto Segregation and Housing Discrimination 2966 (Sept. 1, 1970). He argued that, while racism and the desire not to associate with people of lower income are strong factors motivating suburban exclusionary policies, there are other factors at work which he deemed legitimate. Educationally, most middle-class people in America want their children to attend schools in which the majority of students have characteristics which will be a good influence on their own children. This objective implies that children who do not possess the traits which parents like will somehow be screened out of the schools. Since, Downs argues, screening is illegal in public schools, the parents resort to residential screening devices, the chief of which are racial discrimination and practices which raise the cost of living in the school area. He explains that the undesirable traits perceived by middle-class people to be associated with low-income people include relatively high crime rates, high juvenile delinquency rates, high drug addiction rates, and a high illegitimacy rate, even though most low-income people do not have these attributes. Other exclusionary motivations, according to Downs, are the desire to maintain the high property value of one's home, to keep down real estate taxes, and to maintain the quality of life (e.g., safety, public comportment) in one's neighborhood — i.e., a "middle-class environment." Many whites, Downs says, confuse ethnic and socioeconomic status because such a high proportion of blacks, Puerto Ricans and Mexican-Americans live in low-income households. Thus, he believes, most white parents are unwilling to send their children to schools where blacks or Puerto Ricans are a majority or a significant minority. In such settings, whites would not be dominant in most aspects of school life.

Downs sees what is apparently an irreconcilable conflict of interest between two major groups:

> On the one hand, the relatively established middle-class has a right to protect the quality of life it has won for itself through past striving and effort. On the other hand, the presently deprived lower-income group has an equally valid right to upgrade itself by trying to gain access to many of the benefits now enjoyed mainly by members of middle- and upper-income groups. Such access requires a significant entry of low-income households into residential areas now occupied exclusively — or nearly exclusively — by middle-income and upper-income groups. (Downs, id. 2976.)

Downs believes that the conflict can be resolved because middle-class goals do not require completely excluding members of lower-income groups, so long as middle-class dominance in the neighborhood is maintained. Thus, he would advocate: (1) zoning that would provide for some low-income housing, utilizing care that such housing is placed so that low-income children will not dominate the schools they attend; (2) new public school financing arrangements, or other guarantees to suburban residents that low-income housing would not cause property taxes to rise; and (3) some form of mortgage insurance to guarantee that property values would not fall. In addition, Downs would continue litigation and other government efforts to break down barriers to low-income housing in suburban areas. He would expand low- and moderate-income housing subsidies, and require suburban communities to develop and effect plans for such housing, as a condition to receiving any federal financial aid.

QUESTIONS

1. Assume that courts will grant relief against exclusionary housing policies where there is proof of racial motivation. Does the experience of pre–Title VI district-by-district school desegregation teach us anything about how successful such litigation is likely to be, in substantially increasing the amount of low-income housing in suburban areas?

2. Anthony Downs suggests that suburban communities that refuse to prepare and implement plans for low-income housing should lose entitlement to all federal financial assistance. Could Title VI be validly employed as the basis for such a policy, if fund terminations involved programs unconnected with housing?

Racism Hypo 10
BOURGEOIS v. GHETTO EXODUS, INC.

Prodded by state and federal agencies to take its "fair share" of low-income housing, the Town Council of Suburban Dream, a middle-class residential town of 10,000 people located ten miles outside of the city of Metropolis, announced that it was seriously considering approval of the necessary zoning changes required to permit construction of a subsidized project of 100 three-family town houses. The plan called for the houses to be located on sites in and around Martin Luther King Village, a predominantly black middle-class area of Suburban Dream. This ratio was suggested by Ghetto Exodus, Inc., the nonprofit sponsors of the housing project, as one most likely to attract inner-city residents to the suburbs, and less likely to incur major opposition from white suburban residents.

But black residents of King Village, whose homes are in the $40,000 to $50,000 class, were appalled by the town council's announcement. They approved the concept of low-income housing but said that their community was an inappropriate location for the new project because schools were crowded and public facilities and services could not easily assimilate 300 new families. They also expressed the fear that the project would adversely affect property values. Urging that the project be placed in one of the neighboring communities where virtually no blacks reside, they pointed out that locating it in King Village would further racial isolation and violate national housing policy. They argued that the homes in their community were situated in a smaller space than those in other sections of Suburban Dream and that remaining open space should be used for parks and playgrounds. In response to their petitions and not inconsiderable political clout, the town council adopted what they called a "Community Control" resolution providing:

Be It Resolved That, by reason of our recognition of and sensitivity to the problems of black Americans everywhere, and especially those within our community, and our desire to be as responsive as possible to their wishes, needs, and desires, the Town Council hereby commits itself to scrutinize with every care any plan for alteration of existing housing patterns within King Village if it appears by a vote authorized by the state Referendum Law of 1920, that a majority of King Village residents are opposed to such a plan.

Shortly after this resolution was passed, the residents of King Village voted their opposition to the low-income housing plan by a 3-to-1 vote in a special referendum. Citing the referendum vote, the town council then denied the zoning changes and other approvals necessary to build the new housing.

Ghetto Exodus, Inc., together with black tenants in Metropolis public housing projects, all of whom would have been eligible for the new housing had it been approved, filed suit in federal court against the Suburban Dream City Council seeking to have the rejection of the housing project invalidated. Their suit alleges that the denial was motivated by racial discrimination by both the blacks and whites in Suburban Dream, neither of whom want lower-income blacks in their midst. They point out that the resolution and referendum set a dangerous precedent, which white communities will be able to follow to entirely exclude non–middle-class blacks from the suburbs.

Plaintiffs explain that the Ghetto Exodus project is intended to make homeowners of black tenants, and note that many King Village residents had rented apartments, often in poor areas, prior to purchasing homes in King Village. The plaintiffs deny that the new project will burden schools and other public facilities in King Village, pointing out that new middle-class housing continues to be built in King Village.

The town council, which had long valued its liberal image, was stunned by the suit and the subsequent publicity, and indicated that it was uncertain whether it should be involved in what it viewed as a "family fight" between two black groups. At this point, a group of King Village residents, led by Benjamin Bourgeois, moved to intervene as defendants in the action, urging that the referendum and vote to exclude the project from King Village be upheld as an exercise of their "devotion to democracy, not to bias, discrimination, or prejudice." They contend that to locate most of the Ghetto Exodus housing project in King Village might well lead to the destruction of the middle-class neighborhood for which they have worked so long. The district judge, finding the requisite interest and standing, granted the motion to intervene.

Law Firm A will represent the Bourgeois group of King Village.

Law Firm B will represent the Ghetto Exodus group.

Part V
RIGHTS OF EMPLOYMENT

Faced with an endless series of racial grievances and hampered by limited resources, black organizations have long differed over the setting of anti-discrimination priorities. Should emphasis be given to education, housing or police practices? Will progress in one area rather than another most help black people overcome the heritage of a slave status? The short answer is that all such discussions are academic, given the necessity of immediately opposing the worst aspects of racism across a wide spectrum of behavior patterns, and the absence of any nationally recognized leadership able to command both an all-out commitment to the elimination of racial discrimination in one area and the silent acquiescence of blacks to racism in all its other forms. Even to suggest so drastic an ordering of priorities is, however, to answer white critics who have long criticized blacks for failing to adopt just such a strategy.

But the inability to limit attention and action to one area of racial discrimination does not prevent acknowledging that, in a land where money is practically synonymous with rights, power and respect, the central obstacle in the struggle for black equality is economic. Removal of the disparity between black and white incomes would enable blacks to purchase better housing (and therefore schooling), food and health services. Family stability would improve and the number of blacks requiring income supplements would decrease. With more and better jobs, participation in politics would increase, while the incidence of crime and racist police practices would lessen.

Efforts have been made to combat employment discrimination, using principles of labor relations law, remedies contained in state, local and (since 1964) federal fair employment practices laws, and even self-help tactics. Those efforts have resulted in a quantity of litigation, the opinions and written comment about which are sufficient to fill legal texts and courses devoted exclusively to this subject. The two chapters that follow will focus on only the major areas of this rapidly growing litigation, with special attention devoted to issues where meaningful relief for black victims of job discrimination directly threatens the status of white workers. The resolution of these issues presents in clear, often dramatic, form the conflicts that occur in virtually every area of racial concern when rights sought by blacks conflict with interests whites wish to protect.

13. FEDERAL LABOR LAW AND RACIAL DISCRIMINATION

A. JOB BIAS: ITS IMPACT ON BLACK INCOME AND EQUALITY

ROSS, THE NEGRO IN THE AMERICAN ECONOMY
Employment, Race and Poverty 3, 5-6, 8
(A. Ross and H. Hill eds. 1967) *

Jobs and poverty are at the center of the racial crisis. But to understand the Negroes' economic situation today, it is necessary to begin with their place in the slave economy and to examine their experiences in the century since Emancipation, when they gradually moved out of principal slave occupations into other sectors of the economy.

During slavery, practically all Negroes were engaged in Southern agriculture or were household servants. This was still true of 87 percent in 1900 and 80 percent in 1910. But in 1960 less than 10 percent were in agriculture and 15 percent in domestic service. Approximately 10 percent were in the professional and semiprofessional occupations, 12 percent in wholesale and retail trade, 8 percent in clerical work, 20 percent in manufacturing, and 5 percent in construction. The Negroes' participation in these other sectors of the labor force was still far less than proportional, but considerable diffusion out of the original Negro activities had taken place. This movement has proceeded sporadically and irregularly since the end of slavery, however. Five basic principles appear to have governed it.

1. Competition between Negroes and various groups of white workers, particularly the poor whites in the South and the successive waves of European immigrants in the North, has been a decisive influence. While some employers have favored the Negroes, most have not, and the whites have held the upper hand. As a result, Negroes have had to move into new employment areas rather than claim their share of the already occupied territory.

2. The slave origins of the Negro, his marginal social status, his cultural deprivation, and his deficiencies in skill and education have limited the directions of his movement. As Negroes left agriculture and domestic service they took the most unskilled, unattractive, and poorly paid occupations within other types of activities. Thus while many Negroes have obtained jobs in the construction industry, for example, relatively few have become skilled trades-

* From "The Negro in the American Economy" by Arthur M. Ross in Employment, Race and Poverty edited by Arthur M. Ross and Herbert Hill, copyright © 1967 by Harcourt Brace Jovanovich, Inc. and reprinted with their permission.

men. Many have been employed in wholesale and retail trade, but few as salespeople. . . .

3. The Negro's occupational progress has been concentrated in periods of high labor demand and low unemployment: the period of rapid economic growth from 1900 to 1908, World War I, the prosperity of 1922 to 1929, World War II, and the postwar prosperity until about 1953. In these busy times the whites were able to rise into higher-status positions, leaving room for the Negroes to enter below them; and the expansion of employment created new jobs into which Negroes could move without jeopardizing or displacing their white competitors.

In periods of unemployment or economic decline, on the other hand, competition tightened up and the Negro's occupational progress halted and was sometimes reversed. Thus the Jim Crow laws and craft-union exclusivism were solidified during the depression of the 1890's. Whites took over many established "Negro jobs" during the 1930's, although overt racial conflict was held down by work relief and other New Deal social policies. These cycles of progression and retrogression are neatly indicated by the number of Negroes in the field of domestic and personal service, which has varied *inversely* with business conditions. The number increased in the 1890's, declined steadily from 1900 to the 1920's, rose during the Depression, declined again until after the Korean War, and has increased once more during the most recent decade.

OLSON, EMPLOYMENT DISCRIMINATION LITIGATION: NEW PRIORITIES IN THE STRUGGLE FOR BLACK EQUALITY

6 Harv. Civ. Rights–Civ. Lib. L. Rev. 19, 22-23 (1970)

Since World War II, the median non-white[15] family income has remained approximately fifty-five percent of that of whites, except for a slight increase in 1966-69.[16] Like a similar improvement during the Korean War,[17] this increase may reflect only temporarily favorable employment conditions brought about by the peak demands of war production.[18]

While relative measures of white/non-white income differentials have

15. In the text, the term "black" is used when data refers exclusively to blacks while the term "nonwhite" is used whenever data for blacks alone is not available or whenever the study referred to compared whites and nonwhites.

16. U.S. Bureau of Labor Statistics, Dep't of Labor Rept. No. 375, Social & Economic Status of Negroes in the U.S. — 1969, at 14 (1970). [hereinafter cited as Conditions-1969].

17. Median non-white family income rose from 53 percent of median white family income in 1951 to 57 percent in 1952 but declined back to 53 percent by 1956. Conditions-1969, at 14.

18. Non-whites have lost these relative gains during recessions, such as 1958-59, 1962-63, and 1969-70. See, e.g., P. Norgren & S. Hill, Towards Fair Employment 68-90 (1964) [hereinafter cited as Norgren & Hill]; Thurow 46-65; Council of Econ. Advisors, Annual Report — 1969 in One Year Later, supra note 2, at 13-14.

changed little, absolute measures indicate a widening gap.[19] Non-white income levels remain about thirty years behind white and there is little indication that the time lag is narrowing.[20] In constant dollars, the median non-white family income in 1966 was equal only to the median income whites had obtained in 1947.[21] "Poverty," as defined by the Social Security Administration, occurred three times as often among blacks as among whites in 1959, and three and one-half times as often in 1968.[22] In 1964-68, the number of poor families headed by a black woman increased more than one third.[23] Moreover, the economic condition of blacks is even worse than comparison of family income indicates, because the average black family is larger than the average white family.[24] As a result, while twenty-nine percent of all black families were below the "Poverty" level, thirty-five percent of all black persons were classified as poor.[25]

A. *The Second Class Worker.* Unemployment statistics document the plight of blacks; ever since the Korean War the non-white unemployment rate has remained twice that of whites.[26] In virtually every occupation, non-whites face a higher incidence of unemployment, more frequent unemployment for longer periods of time and more part-time work.[27] Moreover, non-white unemployment becomes relatively higher than that of whites as the education level increases.[28] The subemployment rate (a measure of those who worked full time for less than $3,000 a year or who were unemployed fifteen weeks or more during a year) was three times as great among non-white men as among white men in 1966.[29]

Non-whites who do find jobs also feel the effects of discrimination, for their jobs are lower status and lower paying. In 1967, among male professional workers there were proportionately less than one-half as many non-whites as

19. Conditions-1969, at 16.

20. Thurow, 14-25; R. Fein, Economic and Social Profile of the Negro American, 94 Daedalus 815, 817-24 (1965).

21. Fein, Critique, at 103.

22. Conditions-1969, at 24.

23. 93 Mon. Lab. Rev. 65 (May, 1970).

24. See, e.g., Fein, Critique, 16, at 103.

25. Conditions-1969, at 22-24.

26. Id. at 29; 93 Mon. Lab. Rev. 100 (June 1970).

27. Many of the richest black family units are not true families but rather individuals living away from home. Wetzel & Holland, Poverty Areas of our Major Cities, 89 Mon. Lab. Rev. 1105, 1109 (1966); Conditions-1969, at 32 (nonwhites have twice the long-term unemployment rate of whites).

28. In 1965, the unemployment rate among nonwhite males, 18 years and older, with an elementary education was 1.4 times that of comparable whites. But the nonwhite unemployment rate *increased* to twice that of the white males when groups with 1 to 3 years of high school and 4 years of high school or more were compared. U.S. Bureau of Labor Statistics, Dep't of Labor, Bull. No. 1511, The Negro in the United States 206 (1966).

29. U.S. Bureau of Labor Statistics, Dep't of Labor, Rep. No. 347, Recent Trends in Social and Econ. Conditions of Negroes in the U.S. 16 (1968) [hereinafter cited as conditions-1968].

whites; there were less than one-fourth as many non-white male managers and proprietors, one-fourth as many sales workers, and less than two-thirds as many craftsmen and foremen. There were nearly twice as many operatives (drivers and factory workers), however, and more than three times as many laborers.[30] The concentration of non-white workers in lower pay-lower status jobs exposes them to the greater unemployment in these job categories.[31]

The National Advisory Commission on Civil Disorders (the Kerner Commission) calculated that if the occupational distribution of non-white men in 1966 had been identical with that of the whole labor force, twenty-eight percent of the employed non-white men (about 1.3 million) would have moved up to a higher occupation. Had they received the median 1965 earned income for each occupation, non-white wages would have increased thirty percent ($4.8 billion). By contrast, if all unemployed non-white men in 1966 (about 702,000) had received the median income of non-white males, total non-white income would have increased only seventeen percent.[32] Thus, the disproportionate concentration of non-white men in low-paying occupations is a greater factor in the low level of non-white income than is unemployment.

B. The Failure of Education. A black is not able to market his education as well as a white.[33] In 1959, the non-white male college graduate earned less than the white male who never attended high school.[34] A 1966 Department of Labor analysis indicated that the income of a non-white man decreased relative to that of his white peer as their education increased.[35] In 1966, the average non-white male who had graduated from high school earned $5,188 while the white male who had graduated from high school earned forty per-

30. U.S. Bureau of Labor Statistics, Dep't of Labor, Bull. No. 1600, Handbook of Labor Statistics 46 (1968). See Norgren & Hill, 67-76; Equal Employment Opportunity Comm. [EEOC], Rep. No. 1, 1 Job Patterns for Minorities and Women in Private Industry-1966, at 3-4 (1968). Nonwhite men who hold jobs in occupations above that of operative and laborer are concentrated in seasonal industries (e.g. construction) or in the lower levels of the occupational group. See Wetzel & Holland, supra note 27.

31. Flam & Schwab, Employment & Unemployment Developments in 1969, 93 Mon. Lab. Rev. 40, 50-51 (1970).

32. Kerner Report, 254-56.

33. See text at and notes 45, 50 infra. The purpose of noting here that educational differences are an incomplete explanation is to illustrate how "common sense" reasons explaining lower incomes of blacks may be dismissed by reference to a few factual comparisons.

34. In 1959, median earnings of non-white male workers, 24-65 years old, who had completed elementary school were 62 percent of their white counterparts. This ratio rose to 70 percent when both had a high school degree, but dropped to 64.5 percent for college graduates. The nonwhite was able to raise his median income only $1,000 by completing college after high school, while the white increased his over $2,000. Hearings on Employment and Manpower, supra note 12, at 96, J.G. Maddox, The Advancing South 134 (1967). See J. Kain, Introduction to Race and Poverty 11 (J. Kain ed. 1969).

35. U.S. Bureau of Labor Statistics, Dep't of Labor, Rep. No. 332, the Social and Economic Conditions of Negroes in the U.S. 21 (1967). See Waldman, Educational Attainment of Workers, 92 Mon. Lab. Rev. 14, 21 (1969) (similar comparisons based on 1967 data.)

cent more ($7,068). The median income of non-white men over twenty-five with eight years of schooling was eighty percent of that of similar whites ($930 less). For those with four years of high school, the ratio fell to seventy-three percent ($1,880 less), and those non-whites who completed college made only sixty-six percent of the median income of comparable whites ($3,095 less). Thus, although non-whites increased their median income by completing more schooling, both the relative and absolute gap between non-white and white median incomes increased with schooling. This accentuation of median income differentials with greater schooling has been demonstrated throughout most occupations, both in the North and South.[36]

C. Effects of Job Discrimination. The income level of any individual will depend on his occupation, education (including on-the-job experience), and family background, as well as the economic conditions in the region of his residence. Insofar as income differentials between blacks and whites cannot be explained by such non-racial factors, they may be attributed to job discrimination.

Several recent studies[37] demonstrate that forty percent of median income differentials between black and white workers is the result of employment, occupational, and wage discrimination — collectively termed job discrimination. If the average black worker were hired, promoted, and paid on a par with similar white workers, his annual income would increase between $1400 and $1700, filling about forty percent of the black-white income gap.

Summarizing his study[38] of poverty[39] among non-whites, Professor Lester Thurow stated:

> In the previous analysis of distribution of income, the causes of poverty, the impact of aggregate economic policies, and the distribution of physical capital and technical progress, the conditions facing Negroes [which determine the distribution of earned

36. Siegal, On the Cost of Being a Negro, 35 Socio. Inquiry 41 (1965) [hereinafter cited as Siegal].

37. *See* Thurow 111-38; O. H. Duncan, Inheritance of Poverty or Inheritance of Race? in On Understanding Poverty Ch. 4 (D. Moynihan ed. 1969) [hereinafter cited as Inheritance of Race]; Welsh, Labor-Market Discrimination: An Interpretation of Income Differences in the Rural South, 75 J. Pol. Econ. 225 (1967) [hereinafter cited as Rural South Discrimination]; Siegal. See also Tucker, White-Nonwhite Age Differences and the Accurate Assessment of the 'Cost of Being Negro' 47 Social Forces 343 (1969).

38. Technically, Prof. Thurow assessed those factors which affect marginal productivity of labor. There is no economic reason for an employer to pay an employee more than his marginal contribution to production. The analysis asked, therefore, how much of the difference in incidence of below-poverty-income can be explained by differences in these factors between white and black work-forces.

39. Although Thurow did not analyze the difference in *median* incomes between whites and blacks, his explanation of the greater incidence of poverty among nonwhites does have broad import. The incidence of poverty among blacks is proportionally three and one half that of whites. Conditions-1969, supra note 16, at 24. Moreover, there are proportionally only half as many nonwhites (38 percent) who had incomes over $8,000. Id. at 17.

incomes] proved to be fundamentally different from conditions facing whites. No evidence can be found that the gap [between white and Negro incomes] is declining. Education[,] absence from the labor force, full-time job opportunities, and the industrial structure were significant causes of Negro poverty. *But the sheer fact of being black explained 38% of the difference between the incidence of poverty for whites and Negroes . . .*[40]

Professor Thurow estimated that the result of all forms of discrimination is that whites gain and blacks lose about $15 billion annually, about half of which is attributable to job discrimination.[41]

Job discrimination takes three forms. The first is employment discrimination, the firing or not hiring of a black worker comparable in terms of economic productivity to the white worker who is retained or hired. Differences in non-racial characteristics explain only half of the differentials in the unemployment rates.[42] Absent employment discrimination, the unemployment rate among black workers would not remain twice that of whites.[43]

Occupational discrimination is refusal to permit a qualified black worker to hold a higher status-pay position. In a detailed econometric analysis, Professor O. D. Duncan was able to explain less than half of the disparity between the occupational structures of white and non-white men by direct and indirect effects of differences in non-racial characteristics.[44] Other studies[45] have ac-

40. L. Thurow, Economics of Poverty and Discrimination, Ch. VIII, at 1 (draft no. 2, April 1967, copy in Harvard Univ., Dept. of Econ.) Accord, Thurow, supra note 11, at 111.

41. Thurow 130-43.

42. Gilman, Economic Discrimination and Unemployment, 55 Am. Econ. Rev. 1077 (1965). He assessed how much of the differences in unemployment rates could be explained by the fact that non-whites possessed in disproportionate amounts those characteristics which explain higher unemployment among white subgroups. These characteristics included: (1) occupational structure and industrial structure of employment; (2) education and experience levels; (3) age; and (4) region of employment.

43. Gillman concluded that white workers with characteristics of the average non-white worker would experience half the rate of unemployment which the non-white workforce actually experienced. Id. He also concluded that insofar as employers do not practice wage discrimination, higher unemployment rates among blacks can be expected. Where there are restraints against paying a black less for the same work as a comparably productive white, there will be a greater tendency not to hire the black or fire him more quickly. Such restraints are more likely to be found in the North e.g., union enforced wages, more mobile labor markets, and greater coverage of minimum wage legislation. Id. See text at notes 106-107 infra.

44. Inheritance of Race. Analysing a 1962 sample of employed males, Prof. Duncan concluded that differences in family background (education and occupation of family head and number of siblings) and years of schooling accounted for half of white-nonwhite occupational differences and 20 percent of median income differences. Id. at 99-100. See P. Blau & O. Duncan, American Occupational Structure (1967); Duncan, Discrimination Against Negroes, 371 Annals 85 (1966).

Recognizing that "schooling" is an imprecise measure of productivity (see note 46 infra), Duncan incorporated measures of mental ability into a similar analysis of a 1964 sample of employed males. In this analysis, he accounted for 60 percent of the occupational differences and 10 percent of median income differences. Inheritance of Race 107-09.

45. EEOC. Rep. No. 1, supra note 30, at 17. Thurow, 130-43; Lieberson & Fuguitt,

counted for only one-third of the dissimilarity between white and black occupational structures by differences between the two work forces in "years of schooling."[46]

Wage discrimination is discrimination in wages paid to black and white workers of comparable productivity in the same occupation. Professor Siegal analyzed the 1959 median incomes of men and found that as between white and non-white workmen in identical occupations, differences in schooling and region of residence explained only sixty percent of the differences in median incomes.[47] The difference in median income increased with schooling so that a white man (of the same occupation in the same region) would earn from seven hundred dollars more with an eighth grade education to thirty-eight hundred dollars more with a college degree.

Professor Duncan's comprehensive analysis of wage discrimination concluded: "At least one third [$1,300] of the income gap arises because Negro and white men in the same line of work, with the same amount of formal training, with equal ability, from families of the same size and socio-economic level, simply do not draw the same wages and salaries."[48] Effects of occupational *and* wage discrimination constituted over one-half of the income differential ($1,650).[49] By contrast, only one-fifth ($720) of the median differential could be attributed to differences in educational attainment.[50] Thus, Professor Duncan's analysis indicates that well over one-third of the income differential between whites and blacks could be eliminated by ending job discrimination with no expenditure of public funds for adult education.[51]

Negro-White Occupational Differences in the Absence of Discrimination, 72 Am. J. Sociol. 188, 197, 199 (1967).

46. "Years of Schooling" is an imperfect measure of a worker's productivity. Educational attainment would be a more precise measure of skill since a year of schooling does not produce the same increase in productivity in each student and in each school, especially in the South where there has been grossly inferior investment in black education. See J.F. Kain & J.J. Persky, The North's Stake in Southern Rural Poverty, (Discussion Paper, No. 18, Harv. Univ., Program on Regional & Urban Econ (1967).

47. Siegal 56: "To put it boldly, about two-fifths of the difference in average earnings of whites and non-whites is what it costs to be black." Accord Thurow 111-43. In an analysis of Southern rural males alone. Welch found that differences between whites and blacks in age, ownership of farm capital, years of schooling, and quality of education explained only 40 percent of the differences in median incomes. Rural South Discrimination, 238-40. Welch also found that by obtaining identical increases in schooling, the black increased income less than a third as much as the white.

48. Inheritance of Race 108 (study of 1964 male workforce, 25-34 years of age).

49. Id. at 106. In the analysis of the 1962 male workforce, wage *and* occupational discrimination accounted for 60 percent of the income differential. Id. at 98 Accord Thurow 130-43.

50. Inheritance of Race 106. In the analysis of the 1962 sample, less than 15 percent of the median income differential was explained by differences in schooling. Id. 100-102. Accord, Rural South Discrimination 237 (wage discrimination explained significantly more income differences than did differences in education.)

51. See text at and note 50 supra. Cf. Lieberson & Fuguitt, Negro-white Occupational Differences in the Absence of Discrimination, supra note 45.

Job discrimination also effects nonracial factors which determine income, thereby aggravating the black-white income disparity.[52] Because of job discrimination the black worker receives a smaller return on his investment of time and money in schooling.[53] Consequently the incentive to complete high school and acquire higher education is significantly reduced for blacks.[54]

Blacks have less on-the-job experience than whites, and this difference may have greater impact on the black-white income differential than differences in formal education.[55] If job discrimination were eliminated, however, the difference in on-the-job experience would be gradually narrowed as blacks gained access to jobs from which they have been excluded. While an increase in formal educational levels of the present black work force would require significant expenditures of public funds,[56] reductions in experience differentials could occur without the necessity of public expenditure.[57] Efforts to improve the level of education and job experience among blacks, however, will have little effect on black income if job discrimination is not eliminated.[58]

D. Residential Segregation. In 1969, seventy percent of all blacks lived in one of the 228 metropolitan areas and eighty percent of these urban blacks (55% of the total) lived in central cities.[59] In 1966 over one-third of all blacks resided within the twelve largest urban areas.[60] Eighty percent of the total black population increase from 1950-1969 occurred within the twelve central cities while ninety percent of the total white population increase in these urban areas occurred outside the central cities.[61] During 1950-69, the black population of central cities increased 5.8 million while the white population

52. For an excellent discussion of how different forms of discrimination (e.g., job, educational) are complementary and reinforce one another see Thurow 84-86, 126-38.

53. Thurow concluded that income increases for non-whites from high school and college were significantly smaller than incremental income increases for whites from similar schooling. Thurow, Occupational Distribution of the Returns to Education and Experience for Whites and Negroes, in J. Econ. Comm. Subcomm on Econ. Progress, 1 Federal Programs for Developing of Human Resources: Compendium of Papers, 90th Cong., 2nd Sess. 267, 272 (1968). Consequently, "[a]s education level rises, the Negro falls further and further behind. . . . The income gap grows as education rises and grows at an increasing rate. Discrimination hurts the better educated most". Id. at 276; Thurow 76-80. Weiss, using a more precise measure of the marginal increase in productivity from education (i.e. educational attainment) found that except for one age group (36-45) there was no relation between increases in education and income for blacks. Weiss, Effect of Education on Earnings of Whites and Blacks, supra note 11, at 154-55.

54. See Thurow 76-84.

55. Id. at 80-81, 93-95; Occupational Distribution of the Returns to Education and Experience, supra note 53.

56. See Thurow 134-37.

57. See Id. at 93-95, 134-37, 157.

58. Id. at 155, 157. See Weiss, Effect of Education on Earnings of Whites and Blacks, supra note 11, at 159.

59. Conditions-1969 at 7.

60. Kerner Report, at 243.

61. Conditions-1969 at 6; Conditions-1968 at 4.

living in central cities actually decreased.[62] The intrametropolitan residential pattern of blacks is a direct result of discrimination and the segregation of blacks into central city ghettos; it affects their employment opportunities and is the principal cause of most urban problems.

Blacks do not live in ghettos because they cannot afford to live elsewhere.[63] Rather, racial discrimination restricts residential choices of blacks to central city ghettos.[64] The two principal economic effects of residential segregation and concentration are a decrease in employment opportunities for center city residents and an increase in the cost of center city services such as education, transportation, housing and health care. In larger urban areas most new employment opportunities are located in the suburban ring outside the central city.[65] As a result, segregation of blacks into ghettos has a threefold detrimental effect upon their employment opportunities.[66] First, since most jobs are located by informal, personal contacts rather than by formal channels of communication[67] (newspaper advertisements, employment agencies), geographical isolation of blacks in ghettos seriously limits their opportunity to learn of job opportunities in the suburban ring or in other sectors of the central city. Second, the time and cost required to reach most suburban jobs, combined with the emphasis of public transportation systems on providing rush hour transportation for white-collar suburban commuters[68] may often

62. Id. "An even sharper contrast appears in the 24 urban areas with populations of over 1 million in 1960. Between 1940-1960, almost 100 percent of the increase in their white population occurred in the suburbs. Between 1950-1960, their central cities lost nearly 1½ million whites and gained more than 2 million blacks." Racial Isolation in Public Schools, supra note 1, at 11.

63. It is demonstrably false that blacks live in ghettos because they are poor: white poor live in the suburbs at 3, 4, even 20 times the rate of black poor. J. Kain & J. Persky, The Ghetto, The Metropolis and the Nation (Discussion Paper, No. 30, Harv. Univ. Program on Regional & Urban Econ. 1968); Kain & Persky, Alternatives to the Guilded Ghetto, 14 Public Interest 74 (1969).

64. E.g., Meyer, Kain & Wohl, The Urban Transportation Problem 144-165 (1965); E.g., K. & A. Taeuber, Negroes in Cities (1965).

65. Kain, Distribution and Movement of Jobs and Industry, in Metropolitan Enigma 1 (D. Wilson ed. 1967) [hereinafter cited as Kain, Distribution and Movement]; Meyer, Kain & Wohl, Urban Transportation Problem 10-50 (1965); R. Vernon, Changing Economic Function of the Central City (1959). The dispersal of manufacturing, retailing, and wholesaling firms from the central cities to suburban areas has occurred in increasing rates since WWII, and there have been corresponding shifts in location of employment. The most recent data states that in 1963, 52 percent of all manufacturing jobs in the largest 40 metropolitan areas were located outside the central cities. Kain, Distribution and Movement. Accord, Mooney, Housing Segregation, Negro Employment and Metropolitan Decentralization: Alternative Prospective, 83 Q.J. Econ 299, 300-304 (1969) (data for 25 metropolitan areas) [hereinafter cited as Mooney, Alternative Prospective].

66. Kain, Housing Segregation, Negro Employment, and Metropolitan Decentralization, 82 Q.J. Econ 175 (1968) [hereinafter cited as Kain, Housing and Negro Employment].

67. E.g., Rees, Information Networks in Labor Markets, 56 Am. Econ Rev. 559 (1966).

68. See Meyer, Urban Transportation in Metropolitan Enigma 34 (J. Wilson ed. 1967).

discourage or even prevent blacks from accepting jobs outside the ghetto. Third, the types of jobs which remain plentiful within the central city tend to be low-paying;[69] because of the greater likelihood of discrimination against blacks in positions requiring face-to-face association with customers, those white-collar and managerial positions which blacks hold are most commonly those few positions which are adjacent to ghettos.[70]

Segregation of blacks into central city ghettos restricts the type and location of their employment opportunities, and, because of the exodus of employers from the central city,[71] the total number of jobs held by blacks in larger cities may actually have been reduced.[72]

Poor employment opportunities for blacks is but one consequence of residential segregation.[73] The segregation and concentration of blacks in ghettos is responsible for failures of urban renewal, crises in urban finance,[74] urban transportation problems,[75] inadequacy of central city school systems,[76] and the failure of the cities to provide other public services.[77] Based upon his extensive research, Professor Kain argues[78] that removing discriminatory barriers to the suburbanization of the black population would increase black employment, improve prospects for urban renewal, decrease demands for expensive inbound commuter facilities, improve educational opportunities for deprived children, and ease municipal fiscal crises. The prospects for economic development in the ghetto are limited;[79] the elimination of discriminatory barriers to the suburbanization of blacks must be an important part of any strategy to end income disparity between whites and blacks.[80]

The suburbanization of the black population does not require integration of blacks into white residential neighborhoods. Many of the disadvantages of

69. See Mooney, Alternative Prospective 303-304, 309-311.

70. See Kain, Housing and Negro Employment 183-89.

71. See note 65 supra.

72. Kain, Housing and Negro Employment 179-90.

73. Id. and other studies by Prof. Kain in supra note 12, at 64-70; Ghetto, The Metropolis and the Nation, supra note 63; The Big Cities, Big Problems, 14 Challenge 5 (1966); Coping with Ghetto Unemployment, 35 J. Am. Inst. Planners 80 (1969).

74. See e.g., D. Netzer, Federal, State, and Local Finance in Metropolitan Context in Issues in Urban Economics 435-454, 459, 464 (H. Perloff & L. Wingo, Jr., eds. 1968).

75. Meyer, Urban Transportation, supra note 68 at 41-54.

76. See J. Coleman et al., Equality of Educational Opportunity, 218-74 (1966); Racial Isolation in Public Schools, supra note 1.

77. Ghetto, The Metropolis, and the Nation, supra note 63.

78. Id.

79. See note 73, supra and Brimmer, Negro in National Economy, in American Negro Reference Book (J. Davis ed. 1966); Brimmer, Economic Integration, Ebony 118 (Aug. 1970); Weaver, Beyond the Ghetto, Ebony 148 (Aug. 1970).

80. Ghetto, The Metropolis, and the Nation supra note 63, and source cited in note 73; Weaver, Beyond the Ghetto, supra note 79. The importance of eliminating obstacles to suburbanization of the black population was recently acknowledged by the U.S. Commission on Civil Rights which is considering proposing public sanctions (withholding federal assistance) to facilitate this objective. Cleveland Plain Dealer, Aug. 29, 1970 at 1, col 1.

massive central ghettos could be overcome if ghettos were replaced with small dispersed black communities.

E. Prospects for Change Without Social Intervention. The most favorable assessment of the consequences of economic growth and technological change upon relative income of blacks is that these factors will not markedly increase the gap.[81] The Department of Labor has estimated that the unemployment rate of blacks will be twice the white rate through 1975.[82] Yet, these predictions that economic growth will produce no significant change in relative economic status of blacks appear to be unduly optimistic; the present economic trend may increase the relative and absolute disadvantage of blacks.[83]

Blue collar and service occupations, in which three-quarters of all non-white males worked in 1965, are projected to require only half as many new workers as the white collar positions in which only one-sixth of all non-white males worked in 1965.[84] Because of greater discrimination in white collar positions requiring face-to-face associations,[85] blacks do not have equal opportunity to secure a white collar job.

By projecting 1958-64 rates of non-white "penetration" into higher level jobs onto the occupational requirements for 1964-75, the Department of Labor has estimated that non-white employment would grow no faster than total employment (25 percent), non-white unemployment would remain two and one-half times that of whites, and non-whites, constituting 11.3 percent of the labor force, would hold 6.5 percent of the white collar and 7.7 percent of the skilled blue collar jobs, but twenty-six percent of laboring and twenty-four percent of service positions.[86] Those blue collar and service jobs which are created increasingly will be located outside of central cities.[87] For reasons discussed earlier,[88] it will be difficult for blacks living in the ghetto to secure such suburban jobs.

81. See, e.g., Thurow ch. 2.

82. The white unemployment rate is projected to be 3 percent. U.S. Dep't of Labor, America's Industrial and Occupational Manpower Requirements, 1964-75, at 175-77 (1966) (hereinafter cited as Occupational Requirements).

83. See id.; Kerner Report 389-94; Kain, supra note 66, at 191-97; Killingsworth, Negroes in a Changing Labor Market, in Employment, Race, and Poverty, 49 (A. Ross & H. Hill eds. 1967); O. Ornati, Poverty in the Cities, in Issues in Urban Economics, supra note 74, at 335, 351; Russell, Changing Patterns in Employment of Non-white Workers, 90 Mon. Lab. Rev. 503 (1966).

84. Occupational Requirements. The entire labor force will expand in 1964-75 by 26 percent; demand for white collar workers will expand at a more rapid rate of 38 percent (11.6 million new jobs), demand for blue collar workers at the slower rate of 17 percent (3.4 million), operatives 15 percent (1.8 million) and laborers less than 3 percent (.07 million). *Id.* at 8.

85. See note 70 supra.

86. Occupational Requirements 175-77.

87. Both absolutely and relatively, most of the post-WW II growth of jobs that occurred outside the central cities and the tendency for new jobs to locate outside central city is accelerating. Kain, Distribution and Movement, supra note 65.

88. See text and notes 66-70; Kerner Report 392-93; Ornati, supra note 83, at 351-520.

In sum, there is no sound basis for reliance upon national economic growth to reduce the gap between black and white incomes. During the early 1960's, despite the federal government's efforts against poverty, the plight of blacks living in the largest ghettos worsened.[89] Accordingly, affirmative intervention is required to close the income gap.[90]

B. LABOR RELATIONS LAW REMEDIES AND RACIAL JOB BIAS

JONES, EQUAL EMPLOYMENT OPPORTUNITIES: THE PROMISES OF THE 60's — THE REALITIES OF THE 70's
2 Black L.J. 5, 10-11 (1972)

Duty of Fair Representation

The courts have imposed the duty of fair representation upon unions operating under the R.L.A.[30] and the N.L.R.A.[31] because of the special legal status which those Acts confer upon the labor organizations. Both Acts make unions which represent a majority of the employees in the craft or class, or the unit appropriate for collective bargaining, the *exclusive* representative of all such employees regardless of whether or not they are union members.[32] Thus the union is empowered by the Congressional mandate to negotiate agreements which affect the terms and conditions of employment and are binding on subject employees. The court has reasoned that such a grant of authority by Congress without a commensurate duty to exercise it fairly would run afoul of the Fifth Amendment Due Process Clause. Therefore, the courts have implied that such a duty is compelled by the R.L.A. and the N.L.R.A. to save them from constitutional challenge.

The principle, first recognized and applied by the Supreme Court in Steele [Steele v. Louisville and Nashville Railroad] is enunciated as follows:

> So long as a labor union assumes to act as the statutory representative of a craft, it cannot rightly refuse to perform the duty, which is inseparable from the power of

89. According to mid-decade census data, median family income dropped 8 percent in South Los Angeles, an area of 250,000 blacks. Similarly, in Watts, median family income decreased 2 percent. Other measures of social conditions (unemployment, number in poverty, female-headed families, etc.) also showed little improvement or worsening during this period of the longest peacetime economic expansion. Similarly, in poverty areas of Cleveland, including Hough, incidence of poverty among black families rose 28 percent and median income increased less than 3 percent. In Hough alone, however, median income declined 13 percent. More generally, the historically strong relationship between the unemployment rate and the number of families on AFDC disappeared by mid-60's: unemployment rates go down but the rates of welfare cases do not. D. Moynihan, Poverty in Cities, in Metropolitan Enigma, supra note 7, at 305-10.

90. See, e.g., Thurow 139-60; A. Batchelder, Economics of Poverty 117-192 (1966); Tobin, Raising the Incomes of the Poor, in Agenda for the Nation 77 (K. Gordon-Doubleday ed. 1969).

30. 45 U.S.C. §151 et seq. (1968).

31. 29 U.S.C. §151 et seq. (1968).

32. See Sec. 2, Fourth of the R.L.A. and Sec. 9(a) of the N.L.R.A.

representation conferred upon it, to represent the entire membership of the craft. While the statute does not deny to such a bargaining labor organization the right to determine eligibility to its membership, it does require the union, in collective bargaining and in making contracts with the carrier, to represent nonunion or minority union members of the craft without hostile discrimination, fairly, impartially, and in good faith.[33]

In a case decided the same day, Wallace Corp. v. N.L.R.B.,[34] the Court suggested such a duty under the N.L.R.A. when it stated that bargaining agents under the N.L.R.A. were: "charged with the responsibility of representing . . . (the employees') interests fairly and impartially."[35] However, the Court made it clear that the duty was to be implied from the N.L.R.A. in the 1953 case of Ford Motor Co. v. Huffman[36] and the 1955 case of Syres v. Oil Workers International Union[37] with little discussion other than a direct reference to its opinion in Steele.

Conceptually, no new or innovative theories were added to Steele from 1944 to the 1960's. Moreover, much of the innovation during the early 60's was merely an extension of the doctrine of that case. Professor Archibald Cox, former U.S. Solicitor General, is generally credited with developing the theory of the duty of fair representation, subsequently endorsed by the National Labor Relations Board and the courts as an unfair labor practice under the Taft-Hartley Act.[38] However, it was through the creative genius of the late Charles Houston, one of the many black advocates of the Howard University Law School, that the concept of the duty of fair representation later elaborated and extended by the learned professor from Harvard was added to the body of labor law.[39]

The N.L.R.B. gave early recognition to the duty of fair representation doctrine announced by the courts by threatening in a 1953 case[40] to revoke the certification of a union unless it ceased its unfair conduct immediately. In the 1962 case of Miranda Fuel Co., Inc.,[41] the Board laid down the rule that a breach of the duty of fair representation constituted an unfair labor practice, thus giving an aggrieved plaintiff an administrative forum with a free lawyer. This action by the Board was impliedly approved by the Supreme Court in the 1967 case of Vaca v. Sipes[42] and was held to be an additional remedy to that of a civil suit in the federal courts to enforce the duty.

33. 323 U.S. 192, 204 (1944).
34. 323 U.S. 248 (1944).
35. 323 U.S. 248, 255 (1944).
36. 345 U.S. 330 (1953).
37. 350 U.S. 892 (1955).
38. Cox, Duty of Fair Representation, 2 Vill. L. Rev. 151 (1957).
39. See Herring, The "Fair Representation" Doctrine: An Effective Weapon Against Union Racial Discrimination? 24 Maryland L. Rev. 113 (1964).
40. Hughes Tool Co., 104 N.L.R.B. 318 (1953).
41. 140 N.L.R.B. 181 (1962).
42. 386 U.S. 171 (1967).

The duty of fair representation clearly prevents a union from: (1) causing an employer to discriminate against an employee on an invidious basis (of which race is a prime example) in regard to discharges,[43] layoffs,[44] job classifications,[45] or other terms and conditions of employment;[46] (2) discriminatory grievance handling;[47] and (3) accepting a discriminatory contract.[48] The N.L.R.B. has decided that segregated union membership with disparate rights and benefits runs afoul of the duty.[49] But it is unsettled as to whether the duty of fair representation prevents a union from excluding minorities from membership.[50] However, if the duty is grounded on constitutional necessity, it follows that Congressional support via exclusive representation status granted by the N.L.R.A. is sufficient government involvement[51] to constitutionally taint the practice of excluding blacks from union membership as well as those mentioned above.

ROSEN, LAW AND RACIAL DISCRIMINATION IN EMPLOYMENT

Employment, Race and Poverty 487-490
(A. Ross and H. Hill, eds. 1967) *

From the very first it was clear that suits for damages and injunctive relief would lie to enforce the duty [of fair representation], and that companies that were parties to union discrimination could be joined as defendants. As initially formulated, however, the duty only covered workers subject to the Railway Labor Act; racial discrimination was prohibited only in the negotiation and drafting of formal collective bargaining agreements; and protection was available only against unions actually representing the plaintiffs. By the time the Civil Rights Act of 1964 was passed, the duty had been greatly extended. Workers subject to the National Labor Relations Act (NLRA) were also protected. The duty had to be met not only when the collective agreement was negotiated and written but also when it was administered in the grievance process. And a union was also prohibited from making agreements that dis-

43. See Rolax v. Atlantic Coastline R.R., 186 F.2d 473 (4th Cir. 1950).

44. See n. 33, supra.

45. See Brotherhood of R.R. Trainmen v. Howard, 343 U.S. 768 (1952).

46. See Local 12, United Rubber Workers (Business League of Gladsden), 150 N.L.R.B. No. 18 (1964) (Segregated lunch and work facilities).

47. See Conley v. Gibson, 355 U.S. 41 (1957).

48. See Central Ga. Ry. v. Jones, 229 F.2d 648 (5th Cir. 1965), *cert. denied,* 353 U.S. 846 (1956).

49. See Hughes Tool Co., 147 N.L.R.B. 1573 (1964).

50. But see Sovern, The N.L.R.A. & Racial Discrimination, 62 Colum. L. Rev. 563 (1962).

51. See e.g., Burton v. Wilmington Parking Authority, 365 U.S. 715 (1965). See also Betts v. Easley, 161 Kan. 459, 169 P. 2d 831 (1946).

criminatorily invaded the employment rights of workers that it did not actually represent.

Although the fair representation duty has been put to some fruitful use in particular cases, its total impact on employment discrimination has been minimized as a result of weaknesses inherent in its judicial character and limitations of its scope.[13]

The basic weaknesses of the judicially nurtured and enforced duty are interrelated. First, courts are essentially neutral agencies that do not customarily engage in prosecutional activities; they merely adjudicate claims that are brought before them on a case-by-case basis. Such adjudications are exceedingly time consuming, for extensive inquiry into the facts is necessary, and there are endless procedural ways in which proceedings can be lengthened. Moreover, attempted suits may fail without decision on the merits, for it is within the power of unfriendly judges to impose procedural and technical impediments. Second, there is no government apparatus to prosecute fair representation claims in the courts; consequently, there is no centralized enforcement of the duty. Third, lacking government prosecution, the individual Negro worker and such civil rights or other organizations as are willing to support him bear the burden of initiating and prosecuting claims and stand the risk of paying for enforcement. Because these adjudications are expensive, time consuming and precarious, suit is undertaken only by the most outraged of individuals and only in critical circumstances.[14]

13. See generally Herring, [The "Fair Representation" Doctrine: An Effective Weapon Against Union Racial Discrimination?, 24 Md. L. Rev. 113 (1964)] at 113-148. Herring engaged in careful and intense analysis of the racial fair representation cases, and he communicated with the attorneys in these cases. In an unpublished version of his article ("The Doctrine of Fair Representation in the Hands of the Courts and The National Labor Relations Board" [unpublished divisional paper, Yale Law School, 1963, on file at the Yale Law Library]), he reported that:

"In theory, the doctrine of fair representation assures Negroes that their jobs cannot be affected by unfairness on the part of their collective bargaining representatives. In fact, Negro workers have made extremely limited use of judicial coercion under the Steele standard; and when they have tried to take advantage of its apparent protection, they have secured only a slight practical amelioration of their position."

Nowhere are the weaknesses and limitations of the judicially enforced duty of fair representation more dramatically manifested than in its use to oppose harmful racial discrimination on the part of the Railroad Brotherhoods. Of particular note, the Brotherhood of Locomotive Firemen, defendant in the Steele case, has been an unsuccessful respondent in the Supreme Court in two other such cases. Until recently, nevertheless, it continued to maintain a "Caucasians only" clause in its constitution and, it is clear, it has used its lily-white policy to the extreme detriment of those Negroes who have been unfortunate enough to come within the ambit of its collective bargaining powers. As to cases that the Brotherhood of Locomotive Firemen has defended in the Supreme Court, see Steele v. Louisville & N.R.R., 323 U.S. 192 (1944); Tunstall v. Brotherhood of Locomotive Firemen, 323 U.S. 210 (1944); Graham v. Brotherhood of Locomotive Firemen, 338 U.S. 232 (1949); see also Oliphant v. Brotherhood of Locomotive Firemen, 262 F.2d 359 (6th Cir. 1958), *cert. denied,* 359 U.S. 935 (1959).

14. Sometimes, on the other hand, these difficulties have been to the advantage of plaintiffs. Instances have been reported in which allegedly discriminating parties have settled suits out of court, fearing great pecuniary expense should they lose in court.

As presently refined, the judicially enforced duty of fair representation is subject to four major limitations. First, the duty is imposed only on unions. An employer is subject to legal sanction only if he is involved with a union in discriminatory action. When there is no union functioning or seeking to function as collective bargaining agent, as is often the case in the South, or when employers discriminate unilaterally, workers are not protected.

Second, even when unions are present, it does not appear that they are obliged to resist employer discrimination or to make reasonable efforts to overcome the effects of past discrimination.

Third, since only invidious discrimination, i.e. discrimination not based on relevant differences, is prohibited, it has generally been held that a plaintiff must prove that the defendants were, in fact, motivated by race in drawing a challenged distinction. Situations often arise, however, in which the union and the employer are able to argue that distinctions were based upon other valid criteria. In such circumstances, most courts have required that the plaintiff prove that these criteria were a pretext. Under these conditions, it is exceedingly difficult to reach and remedy the more subtle discriminatory devices. In addition, although job applicants appear to be protected by the duty, difficulties of proof limit its usefulness almost exclusively to the protection of persons already employed. Two recent decisions, however, indicate a new judicial tendency toward requiring union and employer to bear the burden of demonstrating that their allegedly legitimate reasons for discriminating were, in fact, the criteria that motivated them. It is also possible that the courts could adopt a salutary rule that upon a prima facie demonstration of racial discrimination or of circumstances that give rise to a strong inference of such discrimination, e.g. in the absence or extreme underrepresentation of Negro employees or union members, the burden of proof permanently shifts and union and employer must not only go forward with the proof, but must also bear the burden of persuasion.

Fourth, probably because of the clear congressional purpose not to "impair the right of a labor organization to prescribe its own rules with respect to the acquisition or retention of membership therein," the courts have been loath to extend the statutory duty of fair representation to proscribe racial exclusion from union membership. But, unless Negroes are guaranteed equality of opportunity to become union members, there can be no such thing as fair representation, if this is to mean representation that is not differentiated according to race. Union decisional processes are political; the offices and bureaucrats respond to votes and to other political stimuli. It cannot be expected that Negroes, excluded from membership and participation in the union, will be represented equally with whites who are members and who are therefore able to participate. And, not only does exclusion adversely affect conditions of employment for Negroes, but it also renders them incapable of sharing in fringe benefits that are available within the union, e.g. death benefits, legal services and advice, and group insurance programs, and further augments their "badges of inferiority." Requirement of nondiscrimination in union membership policies will not be a full solution to union racial discrimination or apathy, but once in the union the Negro at least begins to have a fighting chance.

NOTES

1. Dean Michael Sovern has suggested that NLRB sanctions against a union found to have violated its duty of fair representation include refusal by the board to aid such unions to become or remain exclusive bargaining representatives, but he warns that the effectiveness of such actions should not be exaggerated, particularly against strong unions which do not need certification. Furthermore, Sovern points out, many small unions are uncertified and thus have nothing to lose. Even withholding of orders to bargain will not harm many unions with well-established bargaining relationships not likely to be broken off, nor are petitions for election of representatives likely to succeed against a well-entrenched union. Sovern suggests that unfair practice proceedings constitute a more viable remedy, for, when the charge is proved, the board can issue cease and desist orders directing the respondent to fulfill his obligations under the law. (M. Sovern, Legal Restraints on Racial Discrimination in Employment 154-156, 160-161 (1966).)

2. Professor James Jones finds the NLRB sanction of disestablishment a potentially more viable remedy for union discrimination than the unfair labor practice approach or decertification. Disestablishment embodies withdrawal of recognition of the union as the employee representative authorized to deal with the employer. Employer recognition of the union for purposes of dealing with grievances, labor disputes, wages, hours of work and other conditions of employment, is enjoined. Dues checkoff, arbitration and participation in the administration of pension and welfare plans would be vulnerable. While such severe sanctions have usually been aimed at "company unions," and modifications might be required to ensure that abuses by employers did not occur, Jones contends that there is constitutional authority as well as statutory support for disestablishment, particularly in egregious cases (e.g., Hughes Tool Co., 147 NLRB 1573, 56 LRRM 1289 (1964)), even though neither the NLRA nor Title VII explicitly provides for this remedy. Jones, Disestablishment of Labor Unions for Engaging in Racial Discrimination — A New Use for An Old Remedy, 1972 Wis. L. Rev. 351.

3. In Local 12, United Rubber Workers v. NLRB, 368 F.2d 12 (5th Cir. 1966), the court reviewed NLRB findings that a union had engaged in unfair labor practices by refusing to process racial grievances filed by black employees, and found that breaches in the duty of fair representation constitute an unfair labor practice. This decision, the court said, would enable aggrieved employees to avoid jurisdictional predicaments that increase litigation and delay relief, and it makes clear that the board is the appropriate body to whom such employees can look to safeguard their rights. Recognizing that

Title VII of the 1964 Civil Rights Act would afford protection against a variety of discriminatory actions, the court nevertheless stated that

> . . . there continues to exist a broad potential range of arbitrary union conduct not specifically covered by Title VII which may also violate the union's duty of fair representation. The comprehensive right of an employee to be represented fairly and in good faith by his exclusive bargaining agent clearly encompasses more than freedom from union discrimination based solely upon race, religion, and sex. (368 F.2d at 24.)

4. The question of whether an employer's policies of racial discrimination constitute an unfair labor practice for which the board can grant relief is answered in the affirmative in United Packinghouse Workers v. NLRB. Judge Wright's innovative approach to the problem provides additional insight to the always sensitive area of race and employment.

UNITED PACKINGHOUSE WORKERS v. NLRB
416 F.2d 1126 (D.C. Cir. 1969)

Before PRETTYMAN, Senior Circuit Judge, and DANAHER and WRIGHT, Circuit Judges.

J. SKELLY WRIGHT, Circuit Judge:

Farmers' Cooperative Compress is a Texas corporation engaged in processing cotton. The United Packinghouse, Food and Allied Workers, AFL-CIO was certified as representative of the company's production and maintenance employees in December 1965 after an election conducted by the National Labor Relations Board. The union and the company thereupon commenced bargaining over a contract, the sessions lasting until June 1966. On September 13, 1966, after filing unfair labor practice charges with the Board, the union struck the plant. The Board found that the company had violated Sections 8(a)(1)[1] and 8(a)(5)[2] of the National Labor Relations Act. It ordered the company to cease and desist certain practices, to bargain in good faith with the union over economic working conditions, to bargain in good faith with the union over the condition of racial discrimination against Negro and Latin American workers, and to reinstate strikers with back pay.

We have before us: (1) the company's claim that the Board's order against it was not supported by the evidence; (2) the union's claim that the Board's

1. 29 U.S.C. §158(a)(1) (1964): "It shall be an unfair labor practice for an employer —"(1) to interfere with, restrain, or coerce employees in the exercise of the rights guaranteed in section 157 of this title[.]"

29 U.S.C. §157 (1964) (§7 of the Act): "Employees shall have the right to self-organization, to form, join, or assist labor organizations, to bargain collectively through representatives of their own choosing, and to engage in other concerted activities for the purpose of collective bargaining or other mutual aid or protection . . . ."

2. U.S.C. §158(a)(5) (1964): "It shall be an unfair labor practice for an employer — "(5) to refuse to bargain collectively with the representative of his employees . . . ."

order did not go far enough — the union agrees with the Board's finding that the company's refusal to bargain over racial discrimination violates Section 8(a)(5), but the union argues that the Board should also have found that the company's practice of discrimination against Latin American and Negro employees is itself a violation of Section 8(a)(1); and (3) the Board's cross-petition for enforcement of its order as it stands.

We affirm the Board's order against the company. The particulars of the labor dispute, the unfair labor practices, and the basis for our enforcement of the Board's order are set out in Parts I and II of this opinion. In addition, without staying the enforcement of that order, in Part III we remand the case to the Board for a hearing on whether the company has a policy and practice of discrimination against its employees on account of their race or national origin. We hold that such a policy and practice violates Section 8(a)(1) of the Act. If the Board finds that the company engages in such a policy and practice, it will devise an appropriate remedy.

[In Parts I and II of the opinion, the court upholds the labor board's findings that the employer had engaged in unfair labor practices, including specifically its refusal to bargain in good faith concerning racial discrimination in job assignments and rates of pay. Such a refusal to bargain in good faith concerning terms and conditions of employment violates §8(a)(5) of the NLRA.]

III

We turn now to the question: can an employer's policy and practice of invidious discrimination against its employees on account of race or national origin violate Section 8(a)(1) of the National Labor Relations Act? When established as hereinafter discussed, we answer this question in the affirmative and remand this part of the case to the Board for further proceedings.

Preliminarily, we find that the area of racial discrimination is not new to the Board. Although we have found no cases in which an employer's policy of discrimination as such was alleged to be a violation of the Act, there is a history of union discrimination coming within the Board's jurisdiction.

That history begins with holdings by the Supreme Court that unions have a statutory duty of "fair representation," first under the Railway Labor Act, later under the National Labor Relations Act. This duty means that a union cannot discriminate against Negroes when it represents the interests of employees. [Citations omitted.]

The Board adopted the Court-enunciated doctrine of fair representation and found that its violation is a union unfair labor practice under the NLRA. [Citations omitted.] The Fifth Circuit enforced the Board's order in [Local No. 12, United Rubber Workers, 368 F.2d 12 (1966)], upholding its determination that violation of the duty of fair representation is an unfair labor practice. This court, relying on the above line of cases, has reached the same conclusion. Truck Drivers & Helpers, Local Union 568 v. N.L.R.B. . . . 379 F.2d 137 (1967). With the exception of Truck Drivers, these cases all involved racial discrimination. Thus it is apparent that the Board has not felt itself unable to examine charges of union racial discrimination to determine whether they are true, and, if true, what the effect is on the discriminated employees. No reason appears why employer discrimination is exempted from Board scrutiny.[13]

In order to hold that employer racial discrimination violates Section 8(a) (1) it must be found that such discrimination is not merely unjustified, but that it interferes with or restrains discriminated employees from exercising their statutory right to act concertedly for their own aid or protection, as guaranteed by Section 7 of the Act.[14] To be sure, Section 7 rights are not to be taken narrowly. That section protects concerted activity by workers to alleviate oppressive working conditions, regardless of whether their activity is channeled through a union, through collective bargaining, or through some other means. Morrison-Knudsen Co. v. N.L.R.B., 9 Cir., 358 F.2d 411 (1966); Salt River Valley Water Users' Ass'n v. N.L.R.B., 9 Cir., 206 F.2d 325 (1953). And racially integrated working conditions are valid objects for employee action. N.L.R.B. v. Tanner Motor Livery, Ltd., 9 Cir., 349 F.2d 1 (1965). The right to act concertedly for mutual aid obviously includes the right to act freely, without employer compulsion or deterrence against such activity. . . . Thus in the context of employer racial discrimination the question reduces to whether that discrimination inhibits its victims from asserting themselves against their employer to improve their lot.

We find that an employer's invidious discrimination on account of race or national origin has such an effect. This effect is twofold: (1) racial discrimination sets up an unjustified clash of interests between groups of workers which tends to reduce the likelihood and the effectiveness of their working in concert to achieve their legitimate goals under the Act; and (2) racial discrimination creates in its victims an apathy or docility which inhibits them from asserting their rights against the perpetrator of the discrimination. *We find that the confluence of these two factors sufficiently deters the exercise of Section 7 rights as to violate Section 8(a)(1).*

The first effect is obvious — racial discrimination sets apart the white from

13. The Board has examined employer racial discrimination in another context. It has held that an employer violates the Act if, during an election to certify a union, the employer makes flagrant appeals to racial prejudice in an attempt to defeat the union. See, e.g., Sewell Manufacturing Co., 138 N.L.R.B. 66 (1962).

14. It should be noted that no one in this case is attempting — nor could such an attempt possibly succeed — to justify racial discrimination in employment. It has always been unjustified, even before it was explicitly made illegal by Title VII of the Civil Rights Act of 1964. Neither is anyone questioning the enormous impact such discrimination has on the flow of commerce and on the allocation of economic resources in this country, perhaps best summed up by the appalling fact that as of 1963 "the Negro college graduate . . . on the average earn[ed] less in his lifetime than the white 8th grade drop out." Friedman, Racial Problems and Labor Relations: The Civil Rights Act, in T. Christensen (ed.), N.Y.U. Eighteenth Annual Conference on Labor 367, 369 (1966) (referring to Bureau of Census figures given in Senate hearings on the civil rights bill).

the Negro (and Latin American) workers. The principle of "divide and conquer" is older than the history of labor relations in this country, but that does not lessen its application here. The white workers expend their energy against the Negroes, the latter resent the whites, and neither group sees that sometimes their interests might be better served by joint action against their common employer. When white employees may suffer from upgrading the positions of Negroes, the employer's policy of discrimination inevitably sets group against group, thus frustrating the possibility of effective concerted action.

Gunnar Myrdal, in his study An American Dilemma (1944), noted this factor in employment race relations:

> When once the white workers' desires for social prestige become mobilized against the Negroes . . . when they have come to look upon Negroes as different from themselves and consequently do not feel a common labor solidarity with them, "economic interests" also will back up discrimination. . . . To give white workers a monopoly on all promotions is, of course, to give them a vested interest in job segregation.
>
> Negroes, on their side, have to try to utilize every opening, even if it means working for lower wages or under inferior working conditions. The abundance of Negro labor, kept idle because of exclusionist policies, must always be feared by white workers. If given the chance, Negroes will accept positions as "sweatshop" competitors — something which cannot fail to increase the resentment of white wage earners. . . . The Negroes react by being suspicious of the white workers and their unions. . . .
>
> The racial beliefs are conveniently at hand to rationalize prejudice and discriminatory practices. . . .
>
> Vol. 1, pp. 391-392.

The Board does not dispute Myrdal's findings. Rather, it points to other discriminations in employment, such as that based on seniority; it suggests the conflicting interests resulting from a seniority system cannot support a Section 8(a)(1) charge. This argument misses the point. First, the seniority distinction may be reasonably justified, whereas here the basis for discrimination is not only unjustified but in fact illegal. Second, we are not holding that all discrimination, even where unjustified, is by itself sufficient to make out a violation. Rather, as noted in Note 15, supra, it is the conjunction of the unreasonable and illegal discrimination with the induced docility in the discriminated group which is the basis of our unfair labor practice holding.

The conclusion that racial discrimination may impede its victims in asserting their rights seems inescapable. This docility stems from a number of factors — fear, ignorance of rights, and a feeling of low self-esteem engendered by repeated second class treatment because of race or national origin. Discrimination in employment is no different in this respect than discrimination in other spheres. In its historic decision in Brown v. Bc rd of Education of Topeka, 347 U.S. 483, 494 . . . (1954), the Supreme Court stated:

> . . . To separate [Negroes] from others of similar age and qualifications solely because of their race generates a feeling of inferiority as to their status in the community that may effect their hearts and minds in a way unlikely ever to be undone. . . .

This docility has been recognized by union leaders, businessmen, government officials and psychologists. Thus George Meany, president of the AFL-CIO, referred to the reluctance of Negro employees to file complaints under fair employment practices laws because of the fear of retaliation which accompanies racial discrimination. Senate and House hearings on equal employment bills are laced with references to the degradation, disillusionment, lack of motivation, and lessening of incentive to improve which result from racial discrimination in employment. The Civil Rights Commission has shown the debilitating effect of menial labor on Negroes, and has pointed up the reluctance of those Negroes to ask for improvement. Psychological studies have pointed out the psychologically debilitating effects of discrimination in general, and Dr. Kenneth B. Clark, especially in his book Dark Ghetto (1965), has shown how discrimination-induced self-hatred in Negro inhabitants of slums, due in good part to discrimination in employment, creates a feeling of inferiority and lack of motivation to assert themselves to change their condition. In all this, discrimination in employment thus establishes, or reinforces the effect of, discrimination in other areas — an inhibition to act for change.

Finally, this docility has been demonstrated by the record in this case. The Trial Examiner found explicitly that the policy of discrimination had this effect. His decision noted:

> The great sense of inferiority of the "Mexican" in the area . . . was shown by answers on cross-examination of the chairman of the negotiating committee, Fernando Gonzales. Although by his demeanor he impressed me as one of the natural leaders of the Latin group of employees, an impression corroborated by his selection as chairman of the negotiating committee, he was not inclined to stand up for his rights when, the morning after the first bargaining session, which he had attended, he was sent out into the cold to perform the "flagging" job. Asked on cross-examination if he asked why he was being sent out there, Gonzales replied, "You don't ask questions there, sir; you only do what you are told." . . .
>
> This same sense of inferiority and docility on the part of the "Mexican" group was further disclosed through the testimony of Polo Arias . . . . [After being transferred to a lower-paying job] he did not ask why . . . . [He testified] "in a company like that you don't ask questions, you just do what they tell you." Elaborating, a little later he repeated the substance of this answer, and added: ". . . I am a grown man and I know, you know, what you are supposed to do and what you are not supposed to do, even if you have got the right to do it." He added that he knew he would not gain anything by asking. . . .
>
> It is clear on this record, and I conclude, that the only reason Respondent paid Ruiz $1.50 an hour for seven months while he was doing a $1.80 job which five or six Anglos were concurrently paid $1.80 for performing, was because Respondent

considered Ruiz and the other minority employees as docile, cheap, labor, and in order to keep them in this condition of servitude. . . .

In the light of these considerations, we conclude that an employer's policy and practice of invidious discrimination on account of race or national origin is a violation of Section 8(a)(1). For the reasons noted above, the case is remanded to the Board for hearings on whether the company here has such a policy and practice. If the Board finds that the company does, the Board shall order an appropriate remedy.

Order affirmed; case remanded for further proceedings.

PRETTYMAN, Senior Circuit Judge:

I concur in the remand for hearings and findings. As I see it, Section 8(a)(1) of this statute makes illegal any act, policy or program of an employer which inteferes with, restrains or coerces employees in the exercise of rights given them by Section 7 of the Act. In the matter before us the complainant alleged that this employer has such a policy and program. In that situation the Board should receive the evidence and make findings. In my judgment it makes no difference what the program is called or how it is catalogued; if, in fact, by its use the employer interferes with, restrains or coerces his employees in the exercise of Section 7 rights, it is an unfair labor practice and is prohibited. I think it is neither necessary nor advisable for us at this time to explore in depth the possibilities of a program such as complainant depicts; I think we should await a finding of the facts. My brethren think otherwise. I concur in the result.

[Concurring opinions omitted.]

NOTES

1. The Supreme Court denied certiorari in the United Packinghouse Workers case *sub nom.* Farmers' Cooperative Compress v. United Packinghouse Workers, 396 U.S. 903 (1969).

2. Federal labor law encourages the voluntary and private resolution of industrial disputes through grievance and arbitration machinery. But the arbitration system which has evolved in this country has not yet been adapted sufficiently to deal with racial discrimination grievances. Professor William Gould, who has written extensively in this area, indicates that arbitration's deficiencies include the following: (1) the difficulty of obtaining an objective evaluation of the dispute if the arbitrator is chosen by the parties or party who is alleged to have discriminated; (2) the absence of black workers, as well as black managers, in positions of responsibility in labor and management; (3) the fact that the collective bargaining agreement — while sometimes containing a generalized antidiscrimination clause — often does not support the grievance which attacks discrimination; and (4) the fact that most arbitrators regard themselves as limited to the contract and not to the law — and, indeed, a substantial number of them are unequipped to survey the latter.

(See Gould, Black Power in the Unions, 79 Yale L.J. 46 (1969) and Labor Arbitration of Grievances Involving Racial Discrimination, 118 U. Pa. L. Rev. 40 (1969).)

3. The Supreme Court seems to have recognized some of the difficulties facing the black complainant. In cases alleging racial discrimination, it has created an exception to the general rule that employees must exhaust contractual grievance procedures before bringing a contract action — at least where efforts to exhaust contract remedies prove futile. See Glover v. St. Louis–San Francisco Railway Company.

QUESTIONS

Suppose that an antidiscrimination provision is included in a collective bargaining agreement, which minority group union members oppose because it is weaker than applicable FEP laws. In view of the potential conflict of interests between minority group workers and white workers, noted by Judge Wright in the Packinghouse Workers case, should the minority workers receive a "veto power" over such a provision? What if the provision is adopted over the protests of minority workers? Would such action of itself serve as the basis for an unfair representation action against the union? Against the employer? See, generally, Gould, Non-Governmental Remedies for Employment Discrimination, 20 Syracuse L. Rev. 865 (1969).

GLOVER v. ST. LOUIS–SAN FRANCISCO RAILWAY COMPANY
393 U.S. 324, 89 S. Ct. 548, 21 L. Ed. 2d 519 (1969)

Mr. Justice Black delivered the opinion of the Court.

The 13 petitioners here, eight Negroes and five white men, are all employees of the respondent railroad, whose duties are to repair and maintain passenger and freight cars in the railroad's yard at Birmingham, Alabama. They brought this action in the United States District Court against the railroad and the Brotherhood of Railway Carmen of America, which is the duly selected bargaining agent for carmen employees. The complaint alleged that all of the plaintiffs were qualified by experience to do the work of carmen but that all had been classified as carmen helpers for many years and had not been promoted. The complaint went on to allege the following explanation for the railroad's refusal to promote them:

> In order to avoid calling out Negro plaintiffs to work as Carmen and to avoid promoting Negro plaintiffs to Carmen, in accordance with a tacit understanding between defendants and a sub rosa agreement between the Frisco and certain officials of the Brotherhood, defendant Frisco has for a considerable period of time used so-called "apprentices" to do the work of Carmen instead of calling out plaintiffs to do said work as required by the Collective Bargaining Agreement as properly and customarily interpreted; and the Frisco has used this means to avoid giving

plaintiffs work at Carmen wage scale and permanent jobs in the classification of Carmen. This denial to plaintiffs of work as Carmen has been contrary to previous custom and practice by defendants in regard to seniority as far as "Upgrade Carmen" are concerned. Defendant Frisco is not calling any of plaintiffs to work as Carmen in order to avoid having to promote any Negroes to Carmen.

The complaint also claimed that each plaintiff had lost in excess of $10,000 in wages as the result of being a victim of "an invidious racial discrimination," and prayed for individual damages, for an injunction to cause the defendants to cease and desist from their discrimination against petitioners and their class and "for any further, or different relief as may be meet and proper. . . ." The respondents moved to dismiss the complaint on the ground, among others, that petitioners had not exhausted the administrative remedies provided for them by the grievance machinery in the collective bargaining agreement, in the constitution of the Brotherhood, and before the National Railroad Adjustment Board. The District Court, in an unreported opinion, sustained the motion to dismiss, and the petitioners then filed the following amendment to their complaint:

On many occasions the Negro plaintiffs through one or more of their number, have complained both to representatives of the Brotherhood and to representatives of the Company about the foregoing discrimination and violation of the Collective Bargaining Agreement. Said Negro plaintiffs have also called upon the Brotherhood to process a grievance on their behalf with the Company under the machinery provided by the Collective Bargaining Agreement. Although a representative of the Brotherhood once indicated to the Negro plaintiffs that the Brotherhood would "investigate the situation," nothing concrete was ever done by the Brotherhood and no grievance was ever filed. Other representatives of the Brotherhood told the Negro plaintiffs time and time again: (a) that they were kidding themselves if they thought they could ever get white men's jobs; (b) that nothing would ever be done for them; and (c) that to file a formal complaint with the Brotherhood or with the Company would be a waste of their time. They were told the same things by local representatives of the Company. They were treated with condescension by both Brotherhood and Company, sometimes laughed at and sometimes "cussed," but never taken seriously. When the white plaintiffs brought their plight to the attention of the Brotherhood, they got substantially the same treatment which the Negro plaintiffs received, except that they were called "nigger lovers" and were told that they were just inviting trouble. Both defendants attempted to intimidate plaintiffs, Negro and white. Plaintiffs have been completely frustrated in their efforts to present their grievances either to the Brotherhood or to the Company. In addition, to employ the purported internal complaint machinery within the Brotherhood itself would only add to plaintiffs' frustration and, if ever possible to pursue it to a final conclusion it would take years. To process a grievance with the Company without the cooperation of the Brotherhood would be a useless formality. To take the grievance before the National Railroad Adjustment Board (a tribunal composed of paid representatives from the Companies and the Brotherhoods) would consume an average time of five years, and would be completely futile under the instant circumstances where the Company and the Brotherhood are working "hand-inglove." All of these purported administrative remedies are wholly inadequate, and to require their complete exhaustion would simply add to plaintiffs' expense and frustration, would exhaust plaintiffs, and would amount to a denial of "due process of law," prohibited by the Constitution of the United States.

The District Court again sustained the motion to dismiss. The Court of Appeals affirmed the dismissal, agreeing with the opinion of the District Court and adding several authorities to those cited by the District Court, 386 F.2d 452 (C.A. 5th Cir. 1967), and we granted certiorari, 390 U.S. 1023 . . . (1968). We think that none of the authorities cited in either opinion justify the dismissal and reverse and remand the case for trial in the District Court.

It is true, as the respondents here contend, that this Court has held that the Railroad Adjustment Board has exclusive jurisdiction, under §3 First (i) of the Railway Labor Act, set out below, to interpret the meaning of the terms of a collective bargaining agreement. We have held, however, that §3 First (i) by its own terms applies only to "disputes between an employee or group of employees and a carrier or carriers." Conley v. Gibson, 355 U.S. 41, 44 . . . (1957). In Conley, as in the present case, the suit was one brought by the employees against their own union, claiming breach of the duty of fair representation, and we held that the jurisdiction of the federal courts was clear. In the present case, of course, the petitioners sought relief not only against their union but also against the railroad, and it might at one time have been thought that the jurisdiction of the Railroad Adjustment Board remains exclusive in a fair representation case, to the extent that relief is sought against the railroad for alleged discriminatory performance of an agreement validly entered into and lawful in its terms. See, e.g., Hayes v. Union Pacific R. Co., 184 F.2d 337 (C.A. 9th Cir. 1950), *cert. denied,* 340 U.S. 942 . . . (1951). This view, however, was squarely rejected in the Conley case, where we said, "[F]or the reasons set forth in the text we believe [Hayes, supra] was decided incorrectly." 355 U.S., at 44, n. 4. . . . In this situation no meaningful distinction can be drawn between discriminatory action in negotiating the terms of an agreement and discriminatory enforcement of terms that are fair on their face. Moreover, although the employer is made a party to insure complete and meaningful relief, it still remains true that in essence the "dispute" is one between some employees on the one hand and the union and management together on the other, not one "between an employee or group of employees and a carrier or carriers." Finally, the Railroad Adjustment Board has no power to order the kind of relief necessary even with respect to the railroad alone, in order to end entirely abuses of the sort alleged here. The federal courts may therefore properly exercise jurisdiction over both the union and the railroad. See also Steele v. Louisville & Nashville R. Co., 323 U.S. 192 . . . (1944).

The respondents also argue that the complaint should be dismissed because of the petitioners' failure to exhaust their remedies under the collective bargaining agreement, the union constitution, and the Railway Labor Act. . . . The Court has made clear, however, that the exhaustion requirement is subject to a number of exceptions for the variety of situations in which doctrinaire application of the exhaustion rule would defeat the overall purposes of federal labor relations policy. Thus, in Vaca [v. Sipes, 386 U.S. 171 (1967)] itself the Court stressed:

> [I]t is settled that the employee must at least attempt to exhaust exclusive grievance and arbitration procedures established by the bargaining agreement. Republic Steel Corp. v. Maddox, 379 U.S. 650, 85 S. Ct. 614, 13 L. Ed. 2d 580. However, because these contractual remedies have been devised and are often controlled by the union and the employer, they may well prove unsatisfactory or unworkable for the individual grievant. The problem then is to determine under what circumstances the individual employee may obtain judicial review of his breach-of-contract claim despite his failure to secure relief through the contractual remedial procedures. 386 U.S., at 184-185, 87 S. Ct. at 914.

The Court in Vaca went on to specify at least two situations in which suit could be brought by the employee despite his failure to exhaust fully his contractual remedies. The circumstances of the present case call into play another of the most obvious exceptions to the exhaustion requirement — the situation where the effort to proceed formally with contractual or administrative remedies would be wholly futile. In a line of cases beginning with Steele v. Louisville & Nashville R. Co., supra, the Court has rejected the contention that employees alleging racial discrimination should be required to submit their controversy to "a group which is in large part chosen by the [defendants] against whom their real complaint is made." 323 U.S., at 206, 65 S. Ct. at 234. And the reasons which prompted the Court to hold as it did about the inadequacy of a remedy before the Adjustment Board apply with equal force to any remedy administered by the union, by the company, or both, to pass on claims by the very employees whose rights they have been charged with neglecting and betraying. Here the complaint alleges in the clearest possible terms that a formal effort to pursue contractual or administrative remedies would be absolutely futile. Under these circumstances, the *attempt* to exhaust contractual remedies . . . is easily satisfied by petitioners' repeated complaints to company and union officials, and no time-consuming formalities should be demanded of them. The allegations are that the bargaining representatives of the car employees have been acting in concert with the railroad employer to set up schemes and contrivances to bar Negroes from promotion wholly because of race. If that is true, insistence that petitioners exhaust the remedies administered by the union and the railroad would only serve to prolong the deprivation of rights to which these petitioners according to their allegations are justly and legally entitled.

The judgment is reversed and the case is remanded for trial.

Reversed and remanded.

NOTE: THE ELECTION OF REMEDIES IN EMPLOYMENT CASES

Where the victim of employment discrimination attempts to utilize arbitration remedies under the contract, the Fifth Circuit has held that the ninety-day statute of limitations under Title VII is tolled. See Culpepper v. Reynolds Metals Co., 421 F.2d 888 (1970).

Thus, the complainant may often have available remedies under the contract and under the Civil Rights Statutes. Several questions arise. Must complainant elect his forum for relief at the outset? Clearly, a binding election at this point could be damaging. The complainant may file a grievance under the collective agreement before he is even aware of his Title VII rights, or he may elect the grievance procedure under the mistaken impression that the contractual protection is as broad as that provided under the statute. Conversely, he may elect the Title VII procedure only to discover that relief that might be available under the contract is for some reason barred by the statute.

Assuming that the complainant is not required to make a binding election of procedures at the outset, the more difficult question is whether he should have to make a binding election of procedures at any time. If, for example, his grievance is carried to arbitration and he loses, should he then be precluded from pursuing his Title VII remedies in federal court? On this issue the courts have divided.

The Fifth Circuit has taken a liberal view with regard to this predictable problem. In Hutchings v. U.S. Industries, 428 F.2d 303 (5th Cir. 1970), the court held that, even when the complainant had pursued the grievance arbitration machinery to a final determination, this would not constitute a binding election of remedies preventing the matter from being reviewed by a federal court. The Fifth Circuit reasoned:

> In the arbitration proceeding, then, the arbiter's role is to determine the contract rights of the employees, as distinct from the rights afforded them by enacted legislation such as Title VII. The arbitration process is a private one essentially tailored to the needs of the contracting parties, who have agreed upon this method for the final adjustment of disputes under their contract. . . .
>
> In view of the dissimilarities between the contract grievance–arbitration process and the judicial process under Title VII, it would be fallacious to assume that an employee utilizing the grievance-arbitration machinery under the contract and also seeking a Title VII remedy in court is attempting to enforce a single right in two forums. (428 F.2d at 312-313.)

The court stated that the only application of the doctrine of election of remedies in Title VII cases would be to bar the complainant from duplicate relief in the private and public forums which would result in an unjust enrichment and windfall to him. The Seventh Circuit has taken a similar position in a sex discrimination case, Bowe v. Colgate-Palmolive Company, 416 F.2d 711 (7th Cir. 1969).

In a subsequent Fifth Circuit decision, Rios v. Reynolds Metals Company, 467 F.2d 54 (1972), the employer obligation in issue under Title VII was expressly included in the arbitral process under the collective bargaining agreement, and the plaintiff had submitted his claim to arbitration and received an adverse determination. The court, noting that this issue had not been reached in the Hutchings case, supra, held to the view that the traditional willingness of courts to defer to the arbitrator's determination is not warranted when issues involve Title VII, which manifests a strong national policy against discriminatory employment practices. To further the policies of both Title VII and labor law statutes, the court held that, under limited circumstances, a district court can "defer to a prior arbitration award." In authorizing what amounts to a review of the arbitration proceeding in cases involving Title VII rights, the court set the following limitations:

> . . . First, there may be no deference to the decision of the arbitrator unless the contractual right coincides with rights under Title VII. Second, it must be plain that the arbitrator's decision is in no way violative of the private rights guaranteed by Title VII, nor of the public policy which inheres in Title VII. In addition, before deferring, the district court must be satisfied that (1) the factual issues before it are identical to those decided by the arbitrator; (2) the arbitrator had power under the collective agreement to decide the ultimate issue of discrimination; (3) the evidence presented at the arbitral hearing dealt adequately with all factual issues; (4) the arbitrator actually decided the factual issues presented to the court; (5) the arbitration proceeding was fair and regular and free of procedural infirmities. The burden of proof in establishing these conditions of limitation will be upon the respondent as distinguished from the claimant. (467 F.2d at 58.)

But the majority of a divided court in the Sixth Circuit has reached a contrary view. Dewey v. Reynolds Metal Company, 429 F.2d 324 (1970). The Supreme Court affirmed the Dewey decision by an equally divided Court, 402 U.S. 689, 91 S. Ct. 2186, 29 L. Ed. 2d 267 (1971). Dewey involved a charge of religious discrimination by an employee who was fired after he refused to work Sunday overtime, as required by the collective bargaining agreement. After an arbitrator ruled that the discharge was justified and was not on religious grounds, Dewey filed a complaint under Title VII. The Sixth Circuit reversed the district court's refusal to dismiss the suit, holding that union and management had agreed to be bound by the arbitrator's decision, and that permitting recourse from adverse arbitration would undermine the federal policy of encouraging private settlement of labor disputes.

Other courts have divided fairly evenly between the Dewey and Hutchings-Rios rationales. Compare Spann v. Kaywood Division, Joanna Western Mills Company, 446 F.2d 120 (6th Cir. 1971), with Fekete v. United States Steel Corporation, 424 F.2d 331 (3d Cir. 1970). Where complainants have elected the grievance procedure, however, and agree to a settlement offer, the tendency is to find that no public policy justifies permitting litigation under the statute. See Oubichon v. North American Rockwell Corporation, 325

F. Supp. 1033 (C.D. Cal. 1970). But the Third Circuit has held that a Title VII action was not mooted by a favorable award under a collective agreement where plaintiff was seeking an injunction against a continuing course of discrimination that was unaffected by the arbitrator's decision.

Finally, there is the question of discrimination that both is proscribed by Title VII and also constitutes an unfair labor practice under National Labor Relations Act. Should the courts defer to a ruling by the NLRB that the complaint of discrimination did not constitute an unfair labor practice? The Sixth Circuit has not taken such a position, in a case where the Title VII plaintiff's claim that he had been discharged because of his race was rejected by the NLRB. Tipler v. E.I. DuPont, 443 F.2d 125 (6th Cir. 1971). The court explained that racial discrimination violates the NLRA only if it deprives the employee of rights guaranteed by §7 of 29 U.S.C. §157, which provides in part that employees shall have the right "to self-organization, to form, join, or assist labor organizations, to bargain collectively . . . and to engage in other concerted activities. . . ." Such discrimination, however, is prohibited absolutely by Title VII, regardless of its effects on rights protected by other statutes. The Sixth Circuit distinguished its decision in Dewey by reiterating that to have allowed the Title VII suit in that case would have destroyed the efficacy of arbitration. There were no similar overriding policy considerations involved in Tipler. See, generally, Aaron, Judicial and Administrative Deference to Arbitration, 1972 Proceedings of 18th Annual Institute on Labor Law 175, 187-203.

C. FAIR EMPLOYMENT PRACTICES LAWS

HILL, THE NEW JUDICIAL PERCEPTION OF EMPLOYMENT DISCRIMINATION — LITIGATION UNDER TITLE VII OF THE CIVIL RIGHTS ACT OF 1964

43 U. Colo. L. Rev. 243-247 (1972)

After more than a decade of civil rights demonstrations and ghetto rebellions, of federal and state antidiscrimination laws and poverty programs, and after the dire warnings of various investigatory commissions, the 1970 census reports that, in virtually every category measured, blacks lagged far behind the economic status of the white population. In 1971, the Bureau of the Census reported: "while the median family income of Negro and other races as a percent of white family income has increased since 1947, the dollar gap, adjusted for price changes, has widened. The dollar gap has increased from about $2,500 in 1947 to about $3,000 in 1969."[2] Significantly, the last

2. Bureau of the Census, The Social and Economic Status of Negroes in the United States, Current Population Reports, Series P-23, No. 38, at 26 (1970).

census report also reveals that a white male with an eighth grade education earns more than a black male with a high school diploma.[3] . . .

On January 24, 1971, the United States Department of Labor reported that joblessness in urban poverty areas had increased during the previous year; by May, the national unemployment rate for blacks had reached 10 percent, and in October, 1971, the black unemployment rate increased to 10.7 percent, its highest level since November, 1963.[4] . . .

The unemployment rate for black ghetto youth during the summer of 1971 was in excess of 50 percent.[7] The rates of unemployment among black youth have reached disaster levels; if they continue, and, unfortunately, there is every reason to believe that they will, then it is necessary to conclude that a major part of a generation of ghetto youth will never enter into the labor force. Their only future will be a marginal, alienated existence, separate and unequal within American society. This is the legacy of racism and the result of past and present discrimination. This development is the single most volatile factor in causing urban unrest and holds explosive implications for the future stability of American society.

At the beginning of the decade of the 1970's, most jobs are still largely regarded as "black" or "white," and the black ones are inferior in wages and status relative to the white labor classifications. In comparison to the occupa-

3. Id. at 34.

4. N.Y. Times, May 8, 1971, at 1, col. 4; N.Y. Times, Jan. 25, 1971, at 1, col. 5; Washington Post, Nov. 5, 1971, at 1. The New York Times of October 23, 1971, in commenting editorially on the announcement that the Bureau of Labor Statistics will discontinue its quarterly reports on unemployment in poverty neighborhoods, noted: "[t]he latest such report, covering the third quarter of this year, shows a disturbing increase in joblessness among blacks, especially young blacks, while the white unemployment rate declined appreciably." The rate of unemployment as determined by the Bureau of Labor Statistics is based upon the number of persons in the labor force actively seeking work. Unfortunately, official figures do not include the significant number of unemployed persons who have been driven out of the labor force as a result of long-term joblessness and who are no longer seeking employment. Thus, many thousands of older black workers who have exhausted their unemployment insurance benefits as well as a large but undetermined number of young persons who have never entered the labor market in the first instance, are not included in official unemployment statistics which are regarded by many economists as a systematic understatement of true unemployment conditions. The problem of the "hidden unemployed" is especially acute in ghetto areas. See Wall Street Journal, Jan. 8, 1971, at 1, col. 1; N.Y. Times, July 21, 1971, at 41, col. 1.

7. N.Y. Times, May 30, 1971, at 20, col. 1. In a report on unemployment among black youth the National Urban League warned that "we are at an all-time danger level." N.Y. Times, June 24, 1971, at 45, col. 1. On December 1, 1971, the Twentieth Century Fund, in a study entitled The Job Crisis for Black Youth, reported that unemployment for young blacks has been "a disaster since 1969," and that the current situation constitutes "social dynamite." Id. at 3. Significantly, the study noted that "Official figures do not portray the extent of the problem. An additional number of the ghetto jobless are never found by the enumerators. At the very least 100,000 young black people — a most conservative estimate — have given up hope and have stopped looking for jobs."

tional and income gains of whites, blacks are on a treadmill in their inability to achieve parity with whites. Summarizing the findings of a nationwide survey covering 43,000 employers and 26 million employees, the Equal Employment Opportunity Commission[8] concluded: "Discrimination in employment is widespread and takes many forms; it can be found in almost every area, occupation group, and industry; and it has a crushing impact. In short, it is a profound condition, national in scope, and it constitutes a continuing violation of the American ideal of fair play in the private enterprise system."[9]

It is apparent that racism has become institutionalized in American industrial life. The fundamental question that must be asked is whether this nation can, by legal means, eliminate the broad pervasive patterns of job discrimination. This leads to the next question: are the legal procedures now available adequate to change or to at least significantly modify the traditional operations of a dual racial labor system?

Prior to the enactment of the Civil Rights Act of 1964 and Title VII of that Act,[10] one could have said without serious challenge that the legal machinery which this nation had devised for dealing with the problems of employment discrimination was profoundly inadequate. Indeed, the inadequacies of this machinery were so serious that any thoughtful person looking at the effects of fair employment practices legislation and law enforcement on the general problem of employment discrimination would be forced to conclude that the law was no more than an exercise in hypocrisy intended not to eliminate racial discrimination but to deceive and confuse the black worker. . . .

Racial discrimination in employment does not occur as individual random acts of bigotry; rather, it is the result of systemic patterns of practices which keep black workers as a class in a permanent state of economic and social depression. Complaints of job discrimination have traditionally been regarded as isolated phenomena, however, and limited judicial remedies have been granted accordingly.[11]

8. Hereinafter referred to as EEOC.

9. EEOC, Report No. 1, Job Patterns for Minorities and Women in Private Industry 1 (1968).

10. 42 U.S.C. §§2000e (1)-(15) (1970).

11. Alfred W. Blumrosen, former Chief of Conciliations of the EEOC, has written that "the history" of administrative civil rights agencies "is one of timidity in investigation, vacillation in decison making, and soft settlements which failed to aid the victims of discrimination and did not remedy the broader social problems. . . . A quarter century of administrative effort has failed to produce a body of law which defines discrimination. . . . The pure administrative process has proved incapable of coping with employment discrimination." A. Blumrosen, Black Employment and the Law 6 (1971). See generally J. Higbee, Development and Administration of the New York State Law Against Discrimination (1966); Blumrosen, Antidiscrimination Laws in Action in New Jersey: A Law-Sociology Study, 19 Rutgers L. Rev. 187 (1965); Frakt, Administrative Enforcement of Equal Opportunity Legislation in New Jersey, 21 Rutgers L. Rev. 442 (1967); Hill, Twenty Years of State Fair Employment Practice Commissions: A Critical Analysis With Recommendations, 14 Buff. L. Rev. 22 (1964); Minsky, FEPC in Illinois: Four Stormy Years, 41 Notre Dame Law. 152 (1965); Note, The California FEPC: Stepchild of the

It has been demonstrated over and over again that complaints of employment discrimination by aggrieved workers are not the result of occasional acts of private prejudice. Job discrimination does not occur (as spokesmen for employers and labor unions would have it) "in isolated pockets." Rather, these "pockets" reflect the operation of a racist employment system; they constitute an extensive pattern of employment practices which can be broken only by sweeping measures. Specific instances of discrimination are the product of long established employer and labor union practices involving the basic institutions of the workplace, including the collective bargaining process.

Administrative civil rights agencies do not perceive the essential nature of the problem, that complaints of job discrimination are not expressions of an aberration but are manifestations of the general condition. All too often, these agencies function as mediators rather than as law enforcement agencies, regarding themselves simply as conciliators between adversaries. They have rejected the fundamental concept that equal treatment is a legal right, not an abstraction to be negotiated away. A further reason for the dismal failure of agencies such as state civil rights commissions is that, instead of enforcing the law to effect social change, administrative agencies usually become vehicles of social control, and their leaders act primarily to advance their own bureaucratic interests. In the crucial matter of jobs, federal and state governments have failed to attack patterns of employment discrimination through enforcement of the comprehensive body of civil rights laws and regulations. The burden of doing so has, therefore, fallen upon the courts.[13]

Prior to Title VII, the public policy regarding discrimination in employment was clearly established. A large number of state laws, executive orders and court decisions had prohibited employment discrimination; however, although the law was relatively clear, it was never effectively enforced. The long established patterns of job discrimination remained intact.

The passage of Title VII of the Civil Rights Act of 1964 (printed with the 1972 Amendments in the Appendix) initiated the federal government's involvement in problems of discrimination in private employment. Its major provisions are summarized below.

State Agencies, 18 Stan. L. Rev. 187 (1965). For the history of fair employment practice law, see M. Sovern, Legal Restraints on Racial Discrimination in Employment (1966); Bonfield, The Origin and Development of American Fair Employment Legislation, 52 Iowa L. Rev. 1043 (1967); Rosen, The Law and Racial Discrimination in Employment, in Employment, Race and Poverty 479-540 (A. Ross & H. Hill eds. 1967). See also Countryman, Discrimination in Employment, in Discrimination and the Law 20 (Countryman ed. 1965).

13. See generally U.S. Commission on Civil Rights, Federal Civil Rights Enforcement Effort (1971); Hill, Whose Law — Whose Order?: The Failure of Federal Contract Compliance, in The Black Experience in American Politics (C. Hamilton ed. 1972); Jackson, Using the Law to Attack Discrimination in Employment, 8 Washb. L.J. 189 (1969); Jenkins, Study of Federal Efforts to End Job Bias: a History, a Status Report, and a Prognosis, 14 How. L.J. 259 (1968).

ROBINSON AND BALLER, EMPLOYMENT DISCRIMINATION MANUAL

Reginald Heber Smith Program 6-14 (1972)

A. OLD TITLE VII. . . .

(1) *Role of EEOC*

Title VII established the Equal Employment Opportunities Commission, an executive agency.[4] It gave EEOC the power to receive complaints of discrimination from individuals,[5] to file such complaints on behalf of individuals, to investigate such complaints,[6] and upon finding reasonable cause to believe that discrimination had occurred to conciliate the complaint by voluntary means.[7] It did not give EEOC any mandatory enforcement powers, an omission which proved fatal to EEOC's effectiveness.

(2) *Filing Procedures under Old Title VII*

Charges of discrimination filed prior to the amendment of Title VII, March 24, 1972, had to be filed with EEOC within 90 days after the occurrence of the discrimination.[8] In the case of states or municipalities which have a local fair employment practices forum for presentation of grievances, such forum could not be bypassed, and the federal charge of discrimination had to be filed within 210 days after the discriminatory incident or act.[9] The EEOC charge must designate the respondent parties responsible for the discrimination and briefly describe the circumstances surrounding the alleged discrimination.[10]

(3) *EEOC Procedures*

EEOC was directed to receive the charge of discrimination, serve copies on the named respondents, conduct an investigation, determine whether probable cause existed to believe that the act had been violated, and if so to attempt to conciliate the dispute.[11] It could refer cases to the Attorney General for litigation, but had no independent enforcement powers.[12] As a practical matter, because of insufficient staffing, EEOC in recent years was often unable to investigate or conciliate complaints promptly or effectively. Because of lack of formal enforcement powers, EEOC was also unable to bring many violators into compliance with the Act. In those cases which it did investigate, EEOC compiled an investigation report (with or without supporting documentary evidence) and rendered a decision of cause or no cause.

4. 42 U.S.C. §§2000e et seq.; 42 U.S.C. §2000e-4.
5. 42 U.S.C. §2000e-5(b) [pre-amendment].
6. Id.
7. Id.
8. 42 U.S.C. §2000e-5(e) [pre-amendment].
9. Id.
10. 42 U.S.C. §2000e-5(b) [pre-amendment].
11. Id.
12. Id.

(4) Right of Private Action

Title VII provided for the bringing of a federal court action based on violations of the Act. Private charging parties were authorized to bring action in federal district court after at least 60 days following their EEOC filing — 210 days in jurisdictions providing a local forum for such grievances (unless agency action terminated earlier).[13] In order to bring suit, the charging party had to receive a letter from EEOC authorizing suit to be brought within 30 days. . . .[14] EEOC would issue this suit letter on written demand by charging party or his attorney. 29 C.F.R. §1601.25. Suit then had to be filed within a 30 day period following receipt of the letter;[15] the period was jurisdictional.

(5) Pattern and Practice Action

The United States, by the Attorney General, was authorized to bring suit under the Act to remedy a "pattern and practice" of discrimination, where the Attorney General found such condition to exist.[16] The Justice Department's Civil Rights Division (Employment Section) has exercised this power by prosecuting a relatively small number of cases which are nearly all very large in scale and highly significant in the development of the law.

(6) Pre-filing before State Fair Employment Practices Commissions

In states and municipalities having local agencies with jurisdiction of employment discrimination complaints, [and authorization to grant relief] exhaustion of the non-federal remedies is a jurisdictional prerequisite to the federal court action.[17]

(7) Coverage

The original Act prohibited all acts or practices by any private employer or labor union having at least 25 employees or members, and engaged in an industry affecting interstate commerce.[18] In addition, it barred discriminatory referrals or other practices by federally supported state employment agencies.[19] The Act carved out a minor and partial exception for religious organizations,[20] but excluded educational institutions entirely.[21] Public employers at any level were not subject to Title VII.

B. Amended Title VII

On March 24, 1972, Title VII was amended in several significant respects. In most respects these changes became effective immediately. All substantive and procedural matters, except those relating to Title VII coverage and filing

13. 42 U.S.C. §2000e-5(f) [pre-amendment].
14. Id.
15. Id.
16. 42 U.S.C. §2000e-6 [pre-amendment].
17. 42 U.S.C. §2000e-5(e), (d).
18. 42 U.S.C. §2000e-2(a), (c).
19. 42 U.S.C. §2000e-2(b).
20. 42 U.S.C. §2000e-1.
21. Id.

procedures at the time of EEOC filings antedating March 24, 1972, are now governed by the new law.

The amended Act is substantively virtually identical to the original Act. However, certain limited procedural changes and a major expansion in coverage are included in the new Act. These principal changes (only) are indicated below.

(1) *Role of EEOC*

EEOC now has enforcement power. Upon a finding of reasonable cause and failure of conciliation, and at least 30 days after the charge is filed, EEOC may bring a federal court action to remedy the discrimination.[22] The Attorney General's pattern and practice power is gradually, over a two year period, to shift to EEOC.[23] In addition EEOC can litigate private individual and class claims. . . .

(2) *Filing Procedures*

Filing procedures remain basically unchanged, except that charging parties may resort to EEOC up to 180 days after the occurrence of the discrimination, or 300 days where a local agency has jurisdiction of such claims.[24]

(3) *EEOC Procedures*

EEOC's investigation and conciliation functions remain essentially unchanged. However, the Act places a number of time restrictions on the Commission. EEOC is directed to serve respondents with a copy of charges of discrimination within 10 days after filing.[25] Investigation is to be made promptly, and, "insofar as practicable," a finding rendered within 120 days.[26] If reasonable cause is found, conciliation or enforcement are to follow promptly.[27] Apparently the draftsmen of the Amendments envisioned that all EEOC proceedings would be completed within six months.

(4) *Right of Private Action*

The private right of action is preserved, subject to provisions designed to give EEOC a chance to obtain voluntary compliance *or* to bring its own action. The private action cannot be brought until EEOC has rendered an adverse decision or reached conciliation agreement not acceptable to the charging party, or has allowed 180 days from filing to elapse without entering any decision, or has otherwise terminated its proceedings.[28] The suing individual must, as before, obtain a letter from EEOC authorizing suit, but now suit may be filed within 90 days after receipt of that letter.[29]

If EEOC files suit, the charging party may intervene and participate as a

22. 42 U.S.C. §2000e-5(f)(1).
23. 42 U.S.C. §2000e-6.
24. 42 U.S.C. §2000e-5(e).
25. 42 U.S.C. §2000e-5(b).
26. Id.
27. Id.
28. 42 U.S.C. §2000e-5(f)(1).
29. Id.

full party to the action.[30] . . . The courts have widely and consistently held that only two procedural steps are necessary to give the federal court jurisdiction of a Title VII complaint. (1) The plaintiff must have filed a timely charge of discrimination with EEOC, naming the defendant as respondent before the commission; and (2) the plaintiff must timely file suit after receiving a right-to-sue letter from EEOC. Beverly v. Lone Star Lead Construction Co., 437 F.2d 1136 (5th Cir. 1971); Dent v. St. Louis-San Francisco Ry., 406 F.2d 399 (5th Cir. 1969); Mondy v. Crown-Zellerbach Co., 271 F. Supp. 258 (E.D. La. 1967).

None of the other procedural directives contained in Title VII rise to the level of jurisdictional prerequisites. The EEOC need not find reasonable cause, for the court's jurisdiction to be proper, Flowers v. Laborers Intl. Union, 431 F.2d 205 (7th Cir. 1970); Fekete v. United States Steel Corp., 424 F.2d 331 (3rd Cir. 1970); Beverly v. Lone Star Lead Construction Co., supra. The EEOC's failure to attempt conciliation cannot bar an otherwise proper suit, Johnson v. Seaboard Air Line R.R. Co., 405 F.2d 645 (4th Cir., 1968); Choate v. Caterpillar Tractor Co., 402 F.2d 357 (7th Cir., 1968). The EEOC charge need not be sworn, Choate v. Caterpillar Tractor Co., supra; and need not be served upon respondent, for the court's jurisdiction to be established, Holliday v. Ry. Express, 306 F. Supp. 898 (N.D. Ga. 1969). The time periods found in Title VII are not to be construed as establishing any statutes of limitations for administrative or legal action, other than the two crucial ones set forth above, Cunningham v. Litton Industries, 413 F.2d 887 (9th Cir. 1969). In general, the procedural provisions of the Act are to be construed in a non-restrictive manner, to assure that the Act works, Culpepper v. Reynolds Metals Co., 421 F.2d 888 (5th Cir. 1970).

(5) *Coverage*

The Amended Act broadens Title VII coverage in important respects. State and local governments and their agencies are now subject to Title VII on the same basis as private employers.[31, 32] Federal employment is also subject to coverage, but under an entirely different set of procedures . . . .[33] Coverage now extends to employers and unions of 15 or more employees or members, as of March 24, 1973.[34] All employment agencies and educational institutions are now fully covered,[35] but the religious organization exemption is extended to include all employees, with respect to their religion.[36] Employment of non-resident aliens is not covered.[37] The Act explicitly covers joint manage-

30. Id.

31. 42 U.S.C. §2000e-5(f)(1).

32. The exception to this rule is that the Attorney General, not EEOC, retains the right to file suit against these governmental defendants. 42 U.S.C. §2000e-5(f)(1).

33. 42 U.S.C. §2000e-16.

34. 42 U.S.C. §2000e(b).

35. 42 U.S.C. §§2000e(a), (c).

36. 42 U.S.C. §2000e-1.

37. Id.

ment-union apprenticeship committees or programs.[38] Preferences given to Indians living on or near reservations are not prohibited by the Act.[39]

(6) *Aids to Filing Suit*

The Act authorizes the district courts, in their discretion and upon application, to allow private complainants to file suit without prepayment of costs, and to provide court-appointed counsel.[40] The value of such court-appointed counsel may be dubious in many communities and in certain types of cases.

NOTES

1. The long and difficult campaign to enact federal FEP legislation (President Truman included an FEPC provision in his ill-fated 1948 Civil Rights Bill) is traced in Sape and Hart, Title VII Reconsidered: The Equal Employment Opportunity Act of 1972, 40 Geo. Wash. L. Rev. 824 (1972).

2. The enforcement provisions of the 1964 Act did not become effective until one year after the date of its enactment (§716(a),(b)). During the first year after its effective date, Title VII was applied only to covered employers of one hundred or more employees. Coverage was extended to employers of seventy-five the second year, of fifty the third year, and finally to employers of at least twenty-five in 1968, four years after its enactment (§701(b)). The deferred coverage raises no legal issue, but calls to mind both the Supreme Court's "all deliberate speed" standard of public school desegregation in Brown v. Board of Education, and the lifelong delays in some of the nineteenth-century statutes abolishing slavery in Northern states (see supra p. 35).

P. NORGREN, FAIR EMPLOYMENT PRACTICE LAWS
Employment, Race and Poverty 542
(A. Ross and H. Hill, eds. 1967) *

The statutory ban on job discrimination in Title VII is, of course, not in itself an innovation. Twenty states[2] and seven major cities[3] already had en-

38. 42 U.S.C. §2000e-2(d).
39. 42 U.S.C. §2000e-2(i).
40. 42 U.S.C. §2000e-5(f)(1).

2. The twenty states, and the years in which their laws were enacted are: New Jersey and New York (1945), Massachusetts (1946), Connecticut (1947), New Mexico, Oregon, Rhode Island, and Washington (1949), Alaska (1953), Michigan, Minnesota, and Pennsylvania (1955), Colorado and Wisconsin (1957), California and Ohio (1959), Delaware (1960), and Illinois, Kansas, and Missouri (1961).

3. Baltimore, Cleveland, Minneapolis, Philadelphia, Pittsburgh, St. Paul, and Toledo. Through special understandings with their state governments, most of the discrimination cases originating within these cities are handled by the municipal agencies.

forceable fair employment practice laws in effect before the Civil Rights Act of 1964 was passed; three additional states had laws that were for all practical purposes nonenforceable.[4] Moreover, discrimination in the Federal Civil Service had been proscribed by law since 1940.[5] That Title VII is a *Federal* measure, however, is a fact of considerable significance — especially for the nation's Negro minority. Job discrimination is already prohibited by existing laws in every industrial state in the North, and in most of the nonindustrial states as well. On the other hand, with the recent exception of Kentucky, no Southern state has yet enacted fair employment legislation of any kind and only two Southern cities have Fair Employment Practices (FEP) ordinances.[6] Since the existing FEP laws continue in effect, the main proximate result of Title VII will therefore be to bring the Southern states for the first time under a legislative ban on discrimination in the job market and the workplace.[7]

NOTES

1. Thirty-nine states (the exceptions are mainly Southern) now have state commissions or agencies which offer remedies for employment discrimination based on race or national origin. In addition, many municipalities have FEP ordinances. Coverage, authority and effectiveness vary widely, but, as the NAACP's Employment Director Herbert Hill points out in his article (supra page 742), the performance of most FEP agencies — despite the dedicated efforts of many staff and commission members — has been less than impressive. Some agencies have been little more than sham bodies, lacking the

4. Idaho (1961), and Iowa and Vermont (1963). Three additional states — Arizona, Nebraska, and Nevada — have laws that apply only to employment under state-government contracts.

5. Ramspeck Act, Title II, 54 Stat. 1211 (1940); superseded by Title I, 5 U.S.C. sec. 631a (1958).

6. In 1962, Richmond, Virginia, and El Paso, Texas, adopted FEP ordinances. In both instances, however, the ban on job discrimination is limited to municipal government employment. Two border areas — Baltimore and Delaware — have had enforceable FEP statutes since 1960.

7. Since 1941, a provision forbidding discrimination in employment has been included in most Federal procurement contracts, and five successive Presidential committees charged with administering the ban have functioned during this period. This stricture, of course, applies to Federal contract employment over the whole country. However, the various President's Committees have failed to effect a significant improvement in the racial practices of Federal contractors; and they have been especially ineffective in the South. While the currently functioning committee, established by President Kennedy in 1961, has a better record of effectiveness than its predecessors, its positive achievements in the South during the first two years of its existence were limited to a small number of plants in scattered locations, mainly branch operations of Northern-based manufacturing concerns. See President's Committee on Equal Employment Opportunity, Report to the President, November 26, 1963 (Washington: U.S. Government Printing Office, 1964), pp. 10-13; P. H. Norgren and S. E. Hill, Toward Fair Employment (New York: Columbia Univ. Press, 1964), Chapter 7.

authority, the appropriations and sometimes the will to combat even the most overt employment bias.

2. Despite criticism of their past performance, state and local FEP commissions remain important. When a Title VII violation occurs within the jurisdiction of a state or local law prohibiting the conduct and authorizing an agency to grant relief (§706(b) — now §706(c)), the complaining party is required to seek relief first under the state or local law for a period of sixty days, before the federal EEOC is permitted to act on the charge.* In view of Title VII's reliance on state and local FEP agencies, would it not be advisable even for anti-civil rights states to remedy this defensive deficiency at an early date?

3. Considering all the inherent weaknesses of the state and local counterparts to Title VII (appointed commissioners, no administrative enforcement powers, reliance on conciliation, complicated and time-consuming procedures, overburdened and underfunded staff), the larger question is why Title VII has avoided the utter failure that has marked most efforts of these agencies. In Herbert Hill's view, there were several fortuitous factors that contributed to the success it has achieved.

* Title VII provides that the aggrieved party may file with EEOC at any time after 60 days from the date proceedings are commenced, but not later than 300 days from notice of termination of the state proceedings. However, EEOC has issued procedural regulations (29 CFR 1601.12) designed to facilitate the transfer of jurisdiction. Thus, when a discrimination complaint is filed immediately with EEOC, it forwards a copy to the appropriate state agency, and then, unless notified to the contrary, EEOC automatically asserts jurisdiction after the expiration of 60 days or termination of state or local proceedings, whichever occurs earliest. This avoids the necessity for the charging party of formally resubmitting his claim to the commission. The practice was approved by the Supreme Court in Love v. Pullman Co., 404 U.S. 522, 92 S. Ct. 616, 30 L. Ed. 2d 679 (1972).

§706(b) of the 1972 Act requires the EEOC, in determining whether reasonable cause exists, "to accord substantial weight to final findings and orders made by State or local authorities." Perhaps because of this provision, EEOC has changed its former practice of deferring to any state or local agency and has issued regulations detailing the requirements that a state law must meet before EEOC must defer jurisdiction to it. Such broadly stated latitudes of authority, of course, breed litigation. In Crosslin v. Mountain States Tel. and Tel., 400 U.S. 1004, 91 S. Ct. 562, 27 L. Ed. 2d 618 (1971), the Supreme Court reversed the Ninth Circuit's dismissal of a case wherein the EEOC had refused to defer to a state agency which lacked any enforcement powers. At a minimum, the Court held that plaintiff could maintain his suit in federal court and simultaneously exhaust his state remedies whether or not EEOC erred in its failure to defer. It is likely that defendants seeking procedural defenses to Title VII litigation will continue to raise this issue. But for complainants, the important consideration is that the "substantial weight" requirement of Title VII applies only to EEOC findings of reasonable cause, and not to determinations by federal courts. It is likely, therefore, that earlier decisions, holding that a state agency's determination does not bar Title VII suits, will have continuing vitality under the 1972 Act. See, e.g., Voutsis v. Union Carbide, 452 F.2d 889 (2d Cir. 1971); Cooper v. Philip Morris, Inc., 464 F.2d 9 (6th Cir. 1972). See also Pacific Maritime Ass'n v. Quinn, 465 F.2d 108 (9th Cir. 1972), finding exhaustion of state remedies even though state agencies failed to comply with state law in processing the complaints.

Cases arising under Title VII began appearing in the federal courts by the fall of 1966, and despite some early adverse decisions by district judges, it was clear from the beginning that Title VII plaintiffs were going to fall heir to a very favorable judicial climate generated by the litigation which developed out of the school segregation cases. The mood of the courts was expressed by the Court of Appeals for the Fifth Circuit in Culpepper v. Reynolds Metal, where the court said: "Title VII of the 1964 Civil Rights Act provides us with a clear mandate from Congress that no longer will the United States tolerate this form of discrimination. It is, therefore, the duty of the courts to make sure the Act works . . . ."[26]

Given the lack of enforcement power and the apparent weaknesses of the statute, the strong antidiscrimination decisions which have developed out of Title VII litigation are surprising[31] only if the significant changes in the perception of the courts on racial matters which developed after Brown v. Board of Education are ignored. Thus, the malicious effort to gut the effectiveness of Title VII by denying the EEOC enforcement powers turned out to be of significant benefit. Instead of an inexperienced Commission of timid bureaucrats appointed for short terms and subject to political and budget pressures from hostile congressional committees and private interest groups, it is federal judges appointed for life that are making the basic law of Title VII.

Oddly enough, it was the very weakness of the statute which precluded the EEOC from following the usual pattern of the state agencies and administratively patching over employment discrimination problems. Respondents before the Commission had so little to fear in the form of administrative enforcement and so little awareness of the potential threat inherent in private litigation that they were unwilling to conciliate meritorious claims. All the forces used in the past and present to cripple and nullify state fair employment practice commissions were also mobilized against the EEOC, and a meaningful threat of court action was imperative to make Title VII administratively workable. This was accomplished by the joining of privately initiated litigation and legal support from the EEOC. Though it could not initiate litigation, under the banner of Udall v. Tallman [380 U.S. 1 (1965),] where the Supreme Court ruled that "great weight" must be given to an agency's view of the statute under which it operates, the Commission urged the courts to take a strong enforcement posture. This approach, in conjunction with aggressive private party litigation, has given birth to a new body of law which transcends anything known under previous fair employment practice law. (Hill, The New Judicial Perception of Employment Discrimination — Litigation Under Title VII of the Civil Rights Act of 1964, 43 Colo. L. Rev. 243, 251-252 (1972).)

26. 421 F.2d 888, 891 (5th Cir. 1970).

31. For a critical analysis of Title VII, see Berg, Equal Employment Opportunity Under the Civil Rights Act of 1964, 31 Brook. L. Rev. 62 (1964). For documentation regarding congressional compromises on Title VII, see EEOC, Legislative History of Titles VII and XI of the Civil Rights Act of 1964 (1966). For a discussion of these matters, see Blumrosen, Administrative Creativity: The First Year of the Equal Employment Opportunity Commission, 38 Geo. Wash. L. Rev. 695 (1970).

[For a quasi-official view of the history, development and implementation of Title VII, prepared by an EEOC staff member and a congressional aide, see Sape and Hart, Title VII Reconsidered: The Equal Employment Opportunity Act of 1972, 40 Geo. Wash. L. Rev. 824 (1972).]

NOTE: 42 U.S.C. §1981 — An Alternative to Title VII

When the Supreme Court upset the long-held view that the Civil Rights Act of 1866 applied only to state action, thereby providing a cause of action against private discrimination under 42 U.S.C. §1982 (Jones v. Alfred Mayer Co., 392 U.S. 409, 88 S. Ct. 2186, 20 L. Ed. 2d 1189 (1968), printed supra page 626), it also indicated that "the right to contract for employment [is] a right secured by 42 U.S.C. §1981 (. . . derived from §1 of the Civil Rights Act of 1866 . . .)." 392 U.S. at 442, n. 78.

In subsequent litigation, courts of appeal have construed §1981 (printed in the Appendix) as creating a cause of action for acts of racial discrimination by private employers. Brady v. Bristol-Myers, Inc., 459 F.2d 621 (8th Cir. 1972); Caldwell v. National Brewing Co., 443 F.2d 1044 (5th Cir. 1971); Young v. International Telephone and Telegraph Co., 438 F.2d 757 (3d Cir. 1971); Boudreaux v. Baton Rouge Marine Contracting Co., 437 F.2d 1011 (5th Cir. 1971); Sanders v. Dobbs Houses, Inc., 431 F.2d 1097 (5th Cir. 1970), *cert. denied,* 401 U.S. 948 (1971); Waters v. Wisconsin Steel Works, 427 F.2d 476 (7th Cir.), *cert. denied,* 400 U.S. 911 (1970); Mizell v. North Broward Hospital District, 427 F.2d 468 (5th Cir. 1970).

The argument that Congress intended Title VII to be an exclusive remedy has been rejected, but to the extent that the two statutes cover the same ground, courts have taken varying paths in search of a theory of reconciliation. The potential conflict is perhaps most acute insofar as Title VII may be said to prescribe procedures for the resolution claims of discrimination. The Seventh Circuit has taken the view that, absent a "reasonable excuse," an aggrieved party must exhaust EEOC remedies before he may bring an action under §1981. Waters, supra. The exhaustion requirement announced in Waters was based on the congressional preference for conciliation, as expressed in the legislative history of Title VII. As policy reasons for this preference, the court identified the facts that commission procedures are relatively inexpensive and uncomplicated and that they enable employers to take corrective action without being stigmatized as the result of formal judicial proceedings. The court believed that such procedures would encourage voluntary compliance. The rationale appears to ignore the EEOC's record of delay and ineffectiveness. See EEOC, 5th Annual Report 63-64 (1971). Moreover, the legislative history of Title VII has been described by courts as "chaotic" (Hall v. Werthan Bag Corp., 251 F. Supp. 184, 186 (M.D. Tenn. 1966)), and as "in such a confused state that it is of minimal value in . . . explication" (Sanchez v. Standard Brands, Inc., 431 F.2d 455, 460 (5th Cir. 1970)).

While rejecting the "reasonable excuse" test, the Third and Fifth Circuits proposed that, in the exercise of their discretion, district courts should encourage use of EEOC conciliation procedures during the pendency of §1981 actions. Young, supra; Caldwell, supra. Such restrictions on access to the courts and on the availability of final relief do not comport with the relatively unimportant place of EEOC action or nonaction in Title VII suits. See, e.g.,

Parham v. South Western Bell Tel. Co., 433 F.2d 421 (8th Cir. 1970). Nor do they comport with the fact that such restrictions are not applied in §1981 suits not related to employment contracts. Cf. Scott v. Young, 421 F.2d 143 (4th Cir.), *cert. denied* 398 U.S. 929 (1970). See also Larson, The Development of Section 1981 as a Remedy for Racial Discrimination in Private Employment, 7 Harv. Civ. Rights–Civ. Lib. L. Rev. 56, 71-73 (1972).

If plaintiffs are required to file a charge with the EEOC before bringing suit under §1981, they are perforce required to exhaust state administrative remedies where a state fair employment practices agency exists, under the provisions of 42 U.S.C. §2000e-5(b). A requirement of exhaustion of state administrative remedies, independently or precedent to exhaustion of EEOC remedies (even where state remedies are adequate), would appear to be contrary to the rationale of Monroe v. Pape (365 U.S. 167, 81 S. Ct. 473, 5 L. Ed. 2d 492 (1961), printed infra page 883), and McNeese v. Board of Education (373 U.S. 668, 83 S. Ct. 1433, 10 L. Ed. 2d 622 (1963)). Moreover, state procedures are in general no more adequate than EEOC remedies. The exhaustion doctrine has been rejected in two employment cases brought under §1981 and §1983 conjunctively. Carter v. Gallagher, 452 F.2d 315 (8th Cir. 1971), and James v. Ogilvie, 310 F. Supp. 661 (N.D. Ill. 1970). In Long v. Ford Motor Company, 352 F. Supp. 135 (E.D. Mich. 1972), there was neither state action nor exhaustion of Title VII procedures, but the court readily found for a black worker in a suit in which jurisdiction was based solely on §1981.

Another potential restriction on §1981 actions arises from the short periods of limitation applicable in Title VII suits. Under 42 U.S.C. §2000e-5(e), the action must be brought within 30 days after receipt of an EEOC right-to-sue notice; and, under §2000e-5(d), the charge of discrimination must have been filed with the EEOC within 90 days after the occurrence, or within 30 days of termination of state agency proceedings. As to whether these periods of limitation apply to §1981 actions, the Third Circuit in Young, supra, reasoned that the special considerations underlying Title VII time limitations were relevant to §1981 litigation. In deciding whether a §1981 action was barred by the 120-day period of limitation for bringing a complaint before the state fair employment practices agency, the Seventh Circuit held in Waters, supra, that the period of limitations is governed by the period provided for in the most analogous state action, and that a period of limitations for administrative remedies is based on factors not applicable to litigation in courts. Instead, the controlling statute of limitations was the general five-year statute for civil actions not otherwise provided for. As is true in civil rights litigation generally, the courts have not developed a consistent standard for determining which state statute of limitations governs §1981 actions. Compare Lazard v. Boeing Company, 322 F. Supp. 343 (E.D. La. 1971) (general statute of limitations), with Boudreaux v. Baton Rouge Marine Contracting Company, supra (contract statute of limitations) and Young, supra (common-law statute of limitations).

Further litigation will determine the scope of relief available under §1981. Both equitable relief and damages have been authorized (Young, supra; Sanders, supra; Mizell, supra), including punitive damages (Brooks v. Moss, 242 F. Supp. 531 (W.D.S.C. 1965)). The development of remedies under other provisions of the Civil Rights Statutes indicates that the courts will have the power to exercise broad discretion in granting affirmative relief.

D. PROBLEMS OF TITLE VII ENFORCEMENT

As with most regulatory measures, passage of Title VII did not ensure the immediate end of all racial discrimination in employment; but, predictably, overt refusals to hire or upgrade for racial reasons were transformed into special "qualifications" involving education, training, experience, seniority, test scores, family connections, and even arrest records and wage garnishments.

In interpreting Title VII so as to judge the substance of these qualifications, courts have developed a number of principles that appear in the cases reviewed below. Of particular importance are these rulings: statistics showing racial disparity constitute at least a prima facie case of discrimination; proof of discrimination does not include the necessity of proving intent to discriminate; qualifications that are apparently neutral but are not related to job performance are unlawful, if they create a statistical racial imbalance or perpetuate the effects of past discrimination; and relief designed to compensate for past discrimination and to cover attorneys' fees can be obtained. See National Employment Law Project, Legal Services Manual For Title VII Litigation 31-33 (rev. May 1972).

1. Job Qualification and Tests

GRIGGS v. DUKE POWER COMPANY
401 U.S. 424, 91 S. Ct. 849, 28 L. Ed. 2d 158 (1971)

[Black employees at the respondent's Dan River power-generating facility, located at Draper, North Carolina, brought a class action under Title VII, challenging the imposition of educational requirements as a condition of employment and transfer within the company. Prior to the effective date of Title VII the respondent had openly discriminated in hiring. Blacks were assigned only to the Labor Department, where the highest-paying jobs paid less than the lowest-paying jobs in the other four departments.

Beginning in 1965, the respondent ceased to restrict blacks to the Labor Department, but conditioned employment in any other department on graduation from high school and on satisfactory performance on two professionally prepared aptitude tests. Initially, completion of high school was made the prerequisite of transfer from Labor and Coal Handling to "inside" departments; then the company allowed incumbent employees who had not graduated from high school to qualify for transfer by passing the aptitude tests. The test standards were more stringent than the high school education requirement. According to the 1960 Census, only 12 percent of black males in North Carolina had graduated from high school, compared to 34 percent of white males. The aptitude tests, neither of which measured the ability to learn or perform a particular job, were among those found by the EEOC in 1966 to discriminate against blacks in that a disproportionately high number of blacks failed. In one case, 58 percent of whites passed the tests used by respondent, as compared with only 6 percent of the blacks. White employees who had been hired prior to the adoption of the educational requirements were permitted to continue working in the "inside" departments and were promoted, whether or not they had graduated from high school.]

Chief Justice BURGER delivered the opinion of the Court. . . .

The District Court had found that while the Company previously followed a policy of overt racial discrimination in a period prior to the Act, such conduct had ceased. The District Court also concluded that Title VII was intended to be prospective only and, consequently, the impact of prior inequities was beyond the reach of corrective action authorized by the Act.

The Court of Appeals was confronted with a question of first impression, as are we, concerning the meaning of Title VII. After careful analysis a majority of that court concluded that a subjective test of the employer's intent should govern, particularly in a close case, and that in this case there was no showing of a discriminatory purpose in the adoption of the diploma and test requirements. . . . The Court of Appeals noted . . . that these standards had been applied fairly to whites and Negroes alike. It held that, in the absence of a discriminatory purpose, use of such requirements was permitted by the Act. In so doing, the Court of Appeals rejected the claim that because these two requirements operated to render ineligible a markedly disproportionate number of Negroes, they were unlawful under Title VII unless shown to be job-related. We granted the writ on these claims. 399 U.S. 926.

The objective of Congress in the enactment of Title VII is plain from the language of the statute. It was to achieve equality of employment opportunities and remove barriers that have operated in the past to favor an identifiable group of white employees over other employees. Under the Act, practices, procedures, or tests neutral on their face, and even neutral in terms of intent, cannot be maintained if they operate to "freeze" the status quo of prior discriminatory employment practices.

The Court of Appeals' opinion, and the partial dissent, agreed that, on the record in the present case, "whites fare far better on the Company's alternative requirements" than Negroes. This consequence would appear to be directly traceable to race. Basic intelligence must have the means of articulation to manifest itself fairly in a testing process. Because they are Negroes, petitioners have long received inferior education in segregated schools and this Court expressly recognized these differences in Gaston County v. United States, 395 U.S. 285 . . . (1969). There, because of the inferior education received by

Negroes in North Carolina, this Court barred the institution of a literacy test for voter registration on the ground that the test would abridge the right to vote indirectly on account of race. Congress did not intend by Title VII, however, to guarantee a job to every person regardless of qualifications. In short, the Act does not command that any person be hired simply because he was formerly the subject of discrimination, or because he is a member of a minority group. Discriminatory preference for any group, minority or majority, is precisely and only what Congress has proscribed. What is required by Congress is the removal of artificial, arbitrary, and unnecessary barriers to employment when the barriers operate invidiously to discriminate on the basis of racial or other impermissible classification.

Congress has now provided that tests or criteria for employment or promotion may not provide equality of opportunity only in the sense of the fabled offer of milk to the stork and the fox. On the contrary, Congress has now required that the posture and condition of the job seeker be taken into account. It has — to resort again to the fable — provided that the vessel in which the milk is proffered be one all seekers can use. The Act proscribes not only overt discrimination but also practices that are fair in form, but discriminatory in operation. The touchstone is business necessity. If an employment practice which operates to exclude Negroes cannot be shown to be related to job performance, the practice is prohibited.

On the record before us, neither the high school completion requirement nor the general intelligence test is shown to bear a demonstrable relationship to successful performance of the jobs for which it was used. Both were adopted . . . without meaningful study of their relationship to job-performance ability. Rather, a vice president of the Company testified, the requirements were instituted on the Company's judgment that they generally would improve the overall quality of the work force.

The evidence, however, shows that employees who have not completed high school or taken the tests have continued to perform satisfactorily and make progress in departments for which the high school and test criteria are now used.[7] The promotion record of present employees who would not be able to meet the new criteria thus suggests the possibility that the requirements may not be needed even for the limited purpose of preserving the avowed policy of advancement within the Company. In the context of this case, it is unnecessary to reach the question whether testing requirements that take into account capability for the next succeeding position or related future promotion might be utilized upon a showing that such long range requirements fulfill a genuine business need. In the present case the Company has made no such showing.

The Court of Appeals held that the Company had adopted the diploma and test requirements without any "intention to discriminate against Negro employees." . . .

7. For example, between July 2, 1965, and November 14, 1966, the percentage of white employees who were promoted but who were not high school graduates was nearly identical to the percentage of nongraduates in the entire white work force.

[G]ood intent or absence of discriminatory intent does not redeem employment procedures or testing mechanisms that operate as "built-in headwinds" for minority groups and are unrelated to measuring job capability.

The Company's lack of discriminatory intent is suggested by special efforts to help the undereducated employees through Company financing of two-thirds the cost of tuition for high school training. But Congress directed the thrust of the Act to the *consequences* of employment practices, not simply the motivation. More than that, Congress has placed on the employer the burden of showing that any given requirement must have a manifest relationship to the employment in question.

The facts of this case demonstrate the inadequacy of broad and general testing devices as well as the infirmity of using diplomas or degrees as fixed measures of capability. History is filled with examples of men and women who rendered highly effective performance without the conventional badges of accomplishment in terms of certificates, diplomas, or degrees. Diplomas and tests are useful servants, but Congress had mandated the common-sense proposition that they are not to become masters of reality.

The Company contends that its general intelligence tests are specifically permitted by §703(h) of the Act. That section authorizes the use of "any professionally developed ability test" that is not "designed, intended, *or used* to discriminate because of race. . . ." (Emphasis added.)

The Equal Employment Opportunity Commission, having enforcement responsibility, has issued guidelines interpreting §703(h) to permit only the use of job-related tests.[9] The administrative interpretation of the Act by the enforcing agency is entitled to great deference. . . . Since the Act and its legislative history support the Commission's construction, this affords good reason to treat the Guidelines as expressing the will of Congress.

Section 703(h) was not contained in the House version of the Civil Rights Act but was added in the Senate during extended debate. For a period, debate revolved around claims that the bill as proposed would prohibit all testing and force employers to hire unqualified persons simply because they were part of a group formerly subject to job discrimination. Proponents of Title VII sought throughout the debate to assure the critics that the Act would have no effect on job-related tests. . . . Despite these assurances, Senator Tower of

9. EEOC Guidelines on Employment Testing Procedures, issued August 24, 1966, provide: "The Commission accordingly interprets 'professionally developed ability test' to mean a test which fairly measures the knowledge or skills required by the particular job or class of jobs which the applicant seeks, or which fairly affords the employer a chance to measure the applicant's ability to perform a particular job or class of jobs. The fact that a test was prepared by an individual or organization claiming expertise in test preparation does not, without more, justify its use within the meaning of Title VII."

The EEOC position has been elaborated in the new Guidelines on Employee Selection Procedures, 35 Fed. Reg. 12333 (August 1, 1970). These Guidelines demand that employers using tests, have available "data demonstrating that the test is predictive of or significantly correlated with important elements of work behavior comprising or relevant to the job or jobs for which Guidelines are being evaluated." Id., at §1607.4(c).

Texas introduced an amendment authorizing "professionally developed ability tests." Proponents of Title VII opposed the amendment because, as written, it would permit an employer to give any test, "whether it was a good test or not, so long as it was professionally designed. Discrimination could actually exist under the guise of compliance with the statute. Remarks of Senator Case, 110 Cong. Rec. 13504.

The amendment was defeated and two days later Senator Tower offered a substitute amendment which was adopted verbatim and is now the testing provision of §703(h). Speaking for the supporters of Title VII, Senator Humphrey, who had vigorously opposed the first amendment, endorsed the substitute amendment, stating: "Senators on both sides of the aisle who were deeply interested in Title VII have examined the text of this amendment and have found it to be in accord with the intent and purpose of that title." 110 Cong. Rec. 13724. The amendment was then adopted. From the sum of the legislative history relevant in this case, the conclusion is inescapable that the EEOC's construction of §703(h) to require that employment tests be job-related comports with congressional intent.

Nothing in the Act precludes the use of testing or measuring procedures; obviously they are useful. What Congress has forbidden is giving these devices and mechanisms controlling force unless they are demonstrably a reasonable measure of job performance. Congress has not commanded that the less qualified be preferred over the better qualified simply because of minority origins. Far from disparaging job qualifications as such, Congress has made such qualifications the controlling factor, so that race, religion, nationality, and sex become irrelevant. What Congress has commanded is that any tests used must measure the person for the job and not the person in the abstract.

The judgment of the Court of Appeals is, as to that portion of the judgment appealed from, reversed.

Mr. Justice BRENNAN took no part in the consideration or decision of this case.

NOTES

1. The technical and legal intricacies of testing issues, including the EEOC's "job-relatedness" standard adopted by the Court in Griggs (see footnote 9 of the opinion), are explained in Cooper and Sobol, Seniority and Testing Under Fair Employment Laws: A General Approach to Objective Criteria of Hiring and Promotion, 82 Harv. L. Rev. 1598 (1969). See also Note, Legal Implications of the Use of Standardized Ability Tests in Employment and Education, 68 Colum. L. Rev. 691 (1968).

2. Even prior to the Griggs decision, lower federal courts had enjoined the use of various employment tests that were not shown to be related to the jobs for which they were used. Excluded under this standard were the Wonderlic, Bennett, and SRA Non-Verbal Tests — Hicks v. Crown Zellerbach Corp., 319 F. Supp. 314 (E.D. La. 1970); the Flanagan Aptitude Test —

United States v. Local 86, Iron Workers, 315 F. Supp. 1202 (W.D. Wash. 1970), *aff'd,* 443 F.2d 544 (9th Cir. 1971); the General Aptitute Test Battery — Arrington v. Mass. Bay Transportation Authority, 306 F. Supp. 1355 (D. Mass. 1969); a civil service test — Penn v. Stumpf, 308 F. Supp. 1238 (N.D. Cal. 1970); and a union journeyman test — Dobbins v. Local 212, IBEW, 292 F. Supp. 413 (S.D. Ohio 1968).

3. Since Griggs, courts have invalidated ability tests in a growing number of cases. See, e.g., United States v. Georgia Power Co., 474 F.2d 906 (5th Cir. 1973); Moody v. Albermarle Paper Co., — F.2d — (4th Cir. 1973); Hester v. Southern Ry. Co., 349 F. Supp. 812 (N.D. Ga. 1972); United States v. Virginia Electric and Power Company, 327 F. Supp. 1034 (E.D. Va. 1971); Chance v. Board of Examiners, 330 F. Supp. 203 (S.D.N.Y. 1971), *aff'd,* 458 F.2d 1167 (2d Cir. 1972); Armstead v. Starkville Municipal Separate School District, 325 F. Supp. 560 (N.D. Miss. 1971); Fowler v. Schwarzwalder, 351 F. Supp. 721 (D. Minn. 1972); Commonwealth v. O'Neill, 348 F. Supp. 1084 (E.D. Pa. 1972). But tests were approved in Allen v. City of Mobile, 466 F.2d 122 (5th Cir. 1972) and in Davis v. Washington, 348 F. Supp. 15 (D.D.C. 1972).

4. High school education requirements have also been struck down by the lower federal courts. See United States v. Georgia Power Co., 474 F.2d 906 (5th Cir. 1973); Moody v. Albemarle Paper Co., 4 FEP cases, 561 (M.D.N.C. 1971). But see Castro v. Beecher, 459 F.2d 725, 735 (1st Cir. 1972), deeming a high school education as a "bare minimum" for successful performance of a policeman's duties.

5. Other selection devices have been held subject to the Griggs analysis. In Gregory v. Litton Systems, Inc., 316 F. Supp. 401 (C.D. Cal. 1970), the company withdrew its offer of employment to the black plaintiff after discovering that he had been arrested fourteen times for "suspicion" but was never convicted. Defendant's policy was not to hire applicants who had been arrested on a "number of occasions." In finding that defendant's use of arrest without conviction records was an unlawful employment practice under §703(a), the court cited statistics showing that although blacks constitute only 11 percent of the population, 27 percent of all arrests and 45 percent of "suspicion" arrests are of blacks. Relying on these statistics, the court held that the defendant's policy had the actual or foreseeable effect of excluding a disparate number of blacks from employment, and therefore was contrary to the basic equal employment opportunity goal of Title VII.

Similarly, a policy of barring job applicants with records of wage garnishments was voided in Johnson v. Pike Corporation, 332 F. Supp. 490 (C.D. Cal. 1971). The employer sought to justify refusal to hire persons whose wages had been garnished by pointing out the burdensome administrative problems that such persons presented for its payroll personnel. The court cited the disproportionate impact of the wage garnishment policy on nowhites, and found that the administrative difficulty complained of was not germane to the employee's ability to do the job. The court also suggested that the cycle of racial discrimination pervades all walks of life, and that Title VII requires the employers to contribute to its alleviation, even at some administrative disadvantage to himself.

QUESTIONS

1. Should the Griggs standard be applied to tests used to determine admission to professional status, such as bar examinations? Assuming, as is likely, that it is impossible to validate written examinations as currently utilized by bar examiners, and noting the higher percentage of minority applicants who fail these examinations (see Bell, Racism in American Courts: Cause for Black Disruption or Despair, 61 Cal. L. Rev. 165-199 (1973)), is there any reason why these tests should survive a judicial standard that has proved fatal to so many civil service examinations used to select policemen and firemen?

2. Eligibility for employment often depends on school achievement, measured in most schools by examinations — often of a standardized nature — which may be used both to determine which applicants are admitted and to ascertain class standing upon graduation. Assuming the lack of validation and disparate test scores among black and white students, is the Griggs standard applicable?

3. Are there occupations so important to health and safety, such as physicians and airline pilots, that society can demand standards, including tests, that require skills greater than those absolutely necessary for the job? Should the Griggs test be applied to such tests and standards even if statistics show that few blacks are able to meet them? As a job becomes more critical (either to the employer or to society), is the "business necessity" rule likely to be more frequently invoked? Should it be?

2. Seniority, Transfer and Promotion

A key question raised in Title VII litigation is the extent to which the act invalidates past discrimination continued in contemporary employment practices that are nominally neutral as to race. The problem is most frequently raised in seniority disputes between black and white workers in industrial plants where the races have been previously segregated by job and department. Similar problems are presented by the referral seniority used in the craft unions.

The difficulty (as is the case again and again in racial problems) is how to provide racial justice for blacks without interfering with the status of whites, which status is in part attributable to past discrimination against blacks. In the employment area, the question becomes how to do away with a system which has denied the black worker access to better-paying, more responsible, more satisfying, and hitherto all-white jobs.

Promotion is a particularly vexing aspect of this problem. Usually seniority lines have been separated for black and white jobs. Thus, the "competitive status" seniority of a worker for promotion and layoff is computed by the time which he has worked in the particular job and department, rather than on a plantwide or "date of entry" basis which starts from the date the worker is hired. Because of past segregation, this means that the black worker's seniority is only good in the department to which he has been confined, which usually involves the dirtiest, poorest-paid labor in the plant. But transferring to a formerly white section could cost the black employee years of seniority and expose him to long layoffs and perhaps loss of job during slow periods.

The rules evolved by federal courts to solve these problems reflect a liberal and innovative interpretation of Title VII that greatly increases the scope and effectiveness of that statute. But rights of white workers were not ignored, and the question remains of how much of the gap in employment opportunity can be closed through litigation.

LOCAL 189, UNITED PAPERMAKERS AND PAPERWORKERS, AFL-CIO v. UNITED STATES
416 F.2d 980 (5th Cir. 1969)

[The United States brought suit against the Crown Zellerbach Corporation and the union, to set aside job seniority provisions as discriminatory under Title VII. The black union and two black employees intervened on behalf of all black employees.

Jobs in the company were organized in segregated "lines of progression," with the blacks in what the court called "left-over" jobs, almost all of which paid less and had less responsibility than the lowliest white jobs. Job seniority governed promotion within each line. When a vacancy occurred, the workers in the slot immediately below it could bid for the jobs, and the worker who had worked the longest in the job slot below had priority. New employees were placed on "extra boards" and were used to fill temporary vacancies. Employees who were senior on the extra boards had priority on entry jobs at the bottom of each progression line. In the event of layoffs, those in the jobs at the bottom of the lines were "bumped back" to the boards, but had first claim to vacancies in the job category from which they had been bumped, under "rights of recall."

The company merged the extra boards in 1964, and as a result, workers who had been on the board the longest, regardless of race, had priority for entry jobs on "white" lines. However, whites who had already filled vacancies on white lines still had priority under the recall rules. In consequence, the merger did not help senior black employees, who were already in "black" lines of progression, to get into the higher-paying, more desirable white lines, but did help the relatively new black employees on the extra boards.

In 1965 a new transfer provision made it possible for black employees already in the black lines of progression to bid on entry jobs in the white lines on the basis of "mill seniority" (time worked at the mill, in contrast to time worked at a particular job). In 1966, in response to an EEOC request, the lines of progression were merged on the basis of existing pay rates. Since pay rates for black jobs were lower than for white jobs, this meant that the black lines were simply added to the bottom of the white lines. Thus, whites on the extra boards, who had rights of recall on former entry jobs, still had priority with respect to vacancies in those jobs. Moreover, promotion was still based on job seniority, so that black employees had no seniority in bidding for formerly white jobs except when competing against each other and new white employees.

In 1967, the Office of Federal Contract Compliance proposed an "A + B" seniority system, whereby an employee's seniority would be computed by adding his mill seniority to his job seniority. The company accepted, but the white union then voted to strike. The government sued to enjoin the strike as an effort to perpetuate a discriminatory seniority system, and also requested an order striking down the "A + B" system. It urged that mill experience alone be made the standard for computing seniority. The district court granted the injunction. It also concluded that job seniority "presently discriminate[s] against Negro employees at the mill whenever Negroes hired prior to January 1965 [when progression lines were merged] compete against white employees for promotion, demotion or selection for training." Reviewing the facts, the court concluded that job seniority was not necessitated by either safety or efficiency factors. It therefore ordered abolition of job seniority in favor of mill seniority "in all circumstances in which one or more competing employees is a Negro employee hired prior to January 16, 1966." The court pointed out that the abolition of job seniority did not mean that Negro employees would be able to bid on any job in the mill solely on the basis of their years with the company. They would still have to move up the lines of progression job by job, but among the competitors within the slot below a vacancy, time in the mill rather than time in the job would define seniority. The order was further qualified to provide the company with the right to require that competing employees have the fundamental qualifications necessary to fill the vacant position.

On appeal, the court considered the legality of the job seniority system at the Bogalusa Paper Mill, and the appropriate standard or guideline for identifying the seniority of employees for purposes of promotion or demotion.]

WISDOM, Circuit Judge

I

No one can quarrel with the broad proposition that Title VII operates only prospectively . . . . The central operative provision, §703(a), declares that "it *shall* be an unlawful employment practice" for an employer to discriminate. . . . The dispute is whether a seniority system based on pre-Act work credit constitutes present discrimination.

Although the effect of Title VII provoked considerable debate in Congress, the legislative history of the title is singularly uninstructive on seniority rights. Opponents of the Act warned that Title VII would destroy hard-earned seniority rights; proponents responded that it would not affect accrued seniority. In Quarles v. Philip Morris, Inc., E.D. Va. 1968, 279 F. Supp. 505, after a careful review of the legislative history, Judge John D. Butzner, Jr. concluded:

> Several facts are evident from the legislative history. First, it contains no express statement about departmental seniority. Nearly all of the references are clearly to employment seniority. None of the excerpts upon which the company and the union rely suggests that as a result of past discrimination a Negro is to have employment opportunities inferior to those of a white person who has less employment seniority. Second, the legislative history indicates that a discriminatory seniority system established before the act cannot be held lawful under the act. The history leads the court to conclude that Congress did not intend to require "reverse discrimination"; that is, the act does not require that Negroes be preferred over white employees who possess employment seniority. It is also apparent that Congress did not intend to freeze an entire generation of Negro employees into discriminatory patterns that existed before the act.

Perhaps the strongest argument for the Quarles construction of the Act is §703(h):

> Section 703(h) expressly states the seniority system must be bona fide. The purpose of the act is to eliminate racial discrimination in covered employment. Obviously one characteristic of a bona fide seniority system must be lack of discrimination. Nothing in §703(h), or in its legislative history suggests that a racially discriminatory seniority system established before the act is a bona fide seniority system under the act. Quarles v. Philip Morris, Incorporated, E.D. Va. 1968, 279 F. Supp. 505, 517.

We agree with this view.

II

The defendants assert, paradoxically, that even though the system conditions future employment opportunities upon a previously determined racial status the system is itself racially neutral and not in violation of Title VII. The translation of racial status to job-seniority status cannot obscure the hard, cold fact that Negroes at Crown's mill will lose promotions which, *but for* their race, they would surely have won. Every time a Negro worker hired under the old segregated system bids against a white worker in his job slot, the old racial classification reasserts itself, and the Negro suffers anew for his employer's previous bias. It is not decisive therefore that a seniority system may appear to be neutral on its face if the inevitable effect of tying the system to the *past* is to cut into the employees *present* right not to be discriminated against on the ground of race. The crux of the problem is how far the employer must go to undo the effects of past discrimination. A complete purge of the "but-for" effects of previous bias would require that Negroes displace white incumbents who hold jobs that, but for discrimination, the Negroes' greater mill seniority would entitle them to hold. Under this *"freedom now"* theory, allowing junior whites to continue in their jobs constitutes [an] act of discrimination.

Crown and Local 189 advance a *"status quo"* theory: the employer may satisfy the requirements of the Act merely by ending explicit racial discrimination. Under that theory, whatever unfortunate effects there might be in future bidding by Negroes luckless enough to have been hired before desegregation would be considered merely as an incident of now extinguished discrimination.

A *"rightful place"* theory stands between a complete purge of "but-for" effects [and] maintenance of the status quo. The Act should be construed to prohibit the *future awarding* of vacant jobs on the basis of a seniority system that "locks in" prior racial classification. White incumbent workers should not be bumped out of their *present* positions by Negroes with greater plan seniority; plant seniority should be asserted only with respect to new job openings. This solution accords with the purpose and history of the legislation.

Not all "but-for" consequences of pre-Act racial classification warrant relief under Title VII. For example, unquestionably Negroes, as a class, educated at all-Negro schools in certain communities have been denied skills available to their white contemporaries. That fact would not, however, prevent employers from requiring that applicants for secretarial positions know how to type, even though this requirement might prevent Negroes from becoming secretaries.

This Court recently struck down a nepotism membership requirement of a "white" union which shortly before had ceased overt discrimination. Local 53 of the International Association of Heat and Frost Insulators and Asbestos Workers v. Vogler, 5 Cir. 1969, 407 F.2d 1047. Under the nepotism rule, only the sons of members or close relatives living with members could become "improvers", and only "improvers" could be accepted into the union. Relationship to a member as a prerequisite to admission had the necessary effect of locking non-whites out of the union. The union argued that the desire to provide family security was a rational non-racial basis for the rule and that since the nepotism requirement excluded all persons unrelated to members, regardless of their race, it could not, therefore, be called a racial classification. This court held that the rule served no purpose related to ability to perform the work in the asbestos trade and that it violated Title VII:

> The District Court did no more than prevent *future* discrimination when it prohibited a continuing exclusion of Negroes through the application of an apparently neutral membership provision which was *originally* instituted at least in part because of racial discrimination and which served no significant trade-related purpose. While the nepotism requirement is applicable to black and white alike and is not on its face discriminatory, in a completely white union the present effect of its continued application is to forever deny to negroes and Mexican-Americans any real opportunity for membership.

In Vogler this Court made the point, citing Quarles, that "where necessary to insure compliance with the Act, the District Court was fully empowered to eliminate the present effects of past discrimination". Vogler, however, does not mesh completely with the facts in this case. The nepotism rule there, as the court pointed out, had scant relation to the operation of the business. It also had the inevitable effect of assuring the lily-white status of the union for all time. Nevertheless, the decision does support the position that reliance on a standard, neutral on its face, is no defense under the Act when the effect of the standard is to lock the victims of racial prejudice into an inferior position.

The controlling difference between the hypothetical typing requirement and the nepotism rule rejected in Vogler is *business necessity*. When an employer or union has discriminated in the past and when its present policies renew or exaggerate discriminatory effects, those policies must yield, unless there is an overriding legitimate, non-racial business purpose. Secretaries must be able to type. There is no way around that necessity. A nepotism rule, on the other hand, while not unrelated to the training of craftsmen, is not essential to that end. To be sure, skilled workers may gain substantial benefits from having grown up in the home of a member of the trade. It is clear, nonetheless, that the benefits secured by nepotism must give way because of its effective continuation and renewal of racial exclusion. That much was decided in Vogler.

The decisive question then is whether the job seniority standard, as it is now functioning at the Bogalusa plant, is so necessary to Crown Zellerbach's operation as to justify locking Negroes, hired before 1966, into permanent inferiority in their terms and conditions of employment. The record supports the district court's holding that job seniority is not essential to the safe and efficient operation of Crown's mill. The defendants' chief expert witness, Dr. Northrup, made it clear that he considered mill seniority "disastrous" only to the extent that it allowed *all* men in a slot to bid on the basis of their time at the mill. He stated that mill seniority in that sense would create labor unrest because its main effect would be to allow whites to "jump" other whites and Negroes to "jump" other Negroes. He also expressed fears about allowing anyone to bid on any vacancy in a line of progression, without requiring that he first advance job-by-job through the various levels below it. That problem might be solved, he stated, by imposing a residency requirement for training purposes. Dr. Northrup explicitly stated that job seniority does *not* provide the only safe or efficient system for governing promotions. . . .

The court took account of Dr. Northrup's apprehensions in fashioning its decree. In place of job security the court ordered the institution of a mill seniority system carefully tailored to assure that no employee would have a right to a job that he could not perform properly. The court's decision put the emphasis where it belongs: absent a showing that the worker has the ability to handle a particular job, the entry job is the proper beginning for any worker. Under the court's decree, employees still must move up through the various lines of progression job-by-job. As a further restraint, if a certain minimum time is needed in one job to train an employee for the next, a residency requirement may be imposed that will slow the rise of Negro employees. Under the system that is in effect at the mill now, and that is unaffected by the decree, that residency period is six months. To meet the problem of labor unrest that might result from "jumping" unrelated to racial issues, the court specifically limited its decree to instances in which Negroes hired before 1966 were among the bidders. Finally, and most importantly, both the court's decree and the existing collective bargaining agreement give Crown Zellerbach the right to deny promotions to employees who lack the ability or qualification to do the job properly.

All these precautions, we think, bear out the plaintiffs' assertion that there are satisfactory alternatives to job seniority at the Bogalusa mill. They lead us to conclude that the imposition of a system that perpetuates and renews the effects of racial discrimination in the guise of job seniority is not necessary or justified at Bogalusa. Job seniority, embodying as it does, the racially determined effects of a biased past, constitutes a form of present racial discrimination.

This case is not the first case to present to courts in this circuit the problem of dealing with a change in system that is apparently fair on its face but in fact freezes into the system advantages to whites and disadvantages to Negroes. In United States v. State of Louisiana, E.D. La. 1963, 225 F. Supp. 353, a three-judge court had before it a new citizenship test adopted by the State Board of [Voters] Registration. The test was fair on its face and, perhaps, capable of fair administration. But it was a test that white voters, almost all of whom were registered, had not had to take. It was a difficult test for eligible Negroes, most of whom were not registered. The court enjoined the State from administering the test. . . . The court said:

> The cessation of prior discriminatory practices cannot justify the imposition of new and onerous requirements, theoretically applicable to all, but practically affecting primarily those who bore the brunt of previous discrimination. An appropriate remedy therefore should undo the results of past discrimination as well as prevent future inequality of treatment. . . .

The Supreme Court affirmed, adding: "the court has not merely the power but the duty to render a decree which will so far as possible eliminate the discriminatory effects of the past as well as bar like discrimination in the future." Louisiana v. United States, 1965, 380 U.S. 145 . . . .

It might be said that in these cases the courts focussed on the unlawfulness of the prior discrimination. In Gaston County v. United States, 1969, 395 U.S. 285, . . . however, the Court's refusal to approve a voter literacy test was based on the inferior education inherent in segregated schooling. The automatic "triggering" provisions of the 1965 Voting Rights Act of 1965 had suspended Gaston County's literacy test because certain indicia chosen by Congress raised the presumption that the tests were being used to discriminate against

Negroes seeking to register. In order to reinstate its test under the Act, Gaston County had to show that it had not used the test in the preceding five years "for the purpose or with the effect of denying or abridging the right to vote on account of race or color." The district court found, as a fact, that Gaston County's Negro schools had not provided educational opportunities equal to those available to whites. That alone, said the Supreme Court, would make the imposition of a literacy test an act of continuing discrimination. Neither the fair administration of the test, nor its legitimate public purpose could save it from condemnation under the Act.

III

With specific regard to employment opportunities under Title VII, decisions by at least two district courts support our conclusion that facially neutral but needlessly restrictive tests may not be imposed where they perpetuate the effects of previous racial discrimination.

In Quarles v. Philip Morris, Inc., E.D. Va. 1968, 279 F. Supp. 505, the first case to challenge the legality of a promotion system under Title VII, the employer had segregated the races by departments at its plant. The employer desegregated the plant but prohibited transfers from one department to another. It also required that the transferor bid on vacancies according to his departmental seniority, rather than his seniority at the plant. The effect was to deny to Negroes promotion into the better paying jobs, because they could not accumulate seniority in the fabrication and warehouse departments, where the better jobs lay. Quarles, a Negro employed in the prefabrication department, could not become a truck driver, a higher-rung position in an all-white department. The court held that the new arrangement violates the statute (279 F. Supp. at 513, 519):

> The present discrimination resulting from historically segregated departments is apparent from consideration of the situation of a Negro who has worked for ten years in the prefabrication department. . . . [He is required] to sacrifice his employment seniority and take new departmental seniority based on his transfer date. Thus a Negro with ten years employment seniority transferring . . . from the prefabrication department to the fabrication department takes an entry level position with departmental seniority lower than a white employee with years less employment seniority. These restrictions upon the present opportunity for Negroes result from the racial pattern of the company's employment practices prior to January 1, 1966. The restrictions do not result from lack of merit or qualification. A transferee under any plan must satisfy ability and merit requirements regardless of his seniority. . . .
>
> The court finds that the defendants have intentionally engaged in unlawful employment practices by discriminating on the ground of race against Quarles, and other Negroes similarly situated. This discrimination, embedded in seniority and transfer provisions of collective bargaining agreements, adversely affects the conditions of employment and opportunities for advancement of the class.

In Dobbins v. Local 212, IBEW, S.D. Ohio 1968, 292 F. Supp. 413, the union had formerly excluded nonwhites from membership. The effects of this practice had been doubly serious, since the union controlled hiring referrals within a certain geographic area. After opening its apprenticeship programs and membership to Negroes the union continued to prefer applicants who had previously worked under union contracts. This preferential referral system contained no explicit racial classification or discriminatory purpose. The court looked, nonetheless, to its inevitable discriminatory effect:

> A policy of giving priority in work referral to persons who have experience under the Local's Collective Bargaining Agreement is discriminatory when competent N[egroe]s have previously been denied the opportunity to work under the referral agreement by reason of their race. 292 F. Supp. at 445.

When the defendant's conduct evidences an "economic purpose" there is no discrimination under Title VII: "The limitation of either union or apprentice membership to a number far below the number necessary for the particular trade would be a discriminatory practice and pattern in a context involving an all W[hite] union membership with a previous history of discrimination. Louisiana v. United States, 380 U.S. 145 . . . (1965). However, on a showing by a defendant that the limitation has nothing to do with any discriminatory intention but is related to reasonable economic purpose, the limitation in number is not unlawful." The court went on to hold the referral system illegal:

> Preference to union members in work referral is a violation of Title VII if that preference operates, after July, 1965, to continue to restrict the employment opportunities of N's who have been excluded from membership and work under union auspices because of their race. . . .

Nothing that we said in Whitfield v. United Steelworkers, Local 2708, 5 Cir. 1958, 263 F.2d 546, *cert. denied,* 360 U.S. 902, . . . compels a different result. In that case Negro workers challenged a plan, negotiated through collective bargaining, purporting to do away with segregated lines of progression in a steel mill. There was no issue in Whitfield as to the measure of promotion from one job to another. Quarles distinguishes Whitfield (279 F. Supp. at 518):

> Whitfield does not stand for the proposition that present discrimination can be justified simply because it was caused by conditions in the past. Present discrimination was allowed in Whitfield only because it was rooted in the Negro employees' lack of ability and training to take skilled jobs on the same basis as white employees. The fact that white employees received their skill and training in a discriminatory progression line denied to the Negroes did not outweigh the fact that the Negroes were unskilled and untrained. Business necessity, not racial discrimination, dictated the limited transfer privileges under the contract.

In Whitfield the company had organized functionally-related jobs into two separate lines of progression, Line 1 (the skilled jobs) for whites and Line 2 (the unskilled jobs) for Negroes. Advancement in a line was based on knowledge and experience acquired in the next lower job. The company opened both lines on a non-racial basis, and added that Negroes in Line 2 would in the future have preference over new whites in applying for vacancies in Line 1. Except for variations in pay, the change had the effect of merging the lines into one, with the formerly white line on top. In Whitfield, unlike the present case, the two lines were not so functionally related that experience at the top of the formerly black line could provide adequate training for the bottom jobs in the white line. The company therefore required that men moving into the formerly all-white Line 1 take a qualification test, one that the white incumbents had not been required to take. (The company had previously required 260 hours "probationary" experience instead.) Negroes objected to the test requirement on the ground that whites already working in Line 1 did not have to take the test to advance or remain in the line. The company also required, as we have said, that employees bidding into Line 1 from Line 2 start at the bottom job. Negroes in Line 2 protested that this requirement also discriminated against them because it meant that Negroes would have to take a wage cut in moving from the top job in Line 2 to the bottom job in Line 1. . . .

This Court rejected both of the plaintiff's objections. We held that the qualification test was the " 'minimum assurance' the Company could have of efficient operations", and that the company and union had gone "about as far as they could go in giving negroes a preference in filling Number 1 line vacancies, consistent with being *fair to incumbents and consistent with efficient management.*" 263 F.2d at 550 (emphasis added.) The requirement that entrants into Line 1 start at the bottom job was justified as a business necessity . . . .

In United States by Clark v. H. K. Porter Co., N.D. Ala. 1968, 296 F. Supp. 40, 90, the court rejected an attack by the Government upon "the procedure that the first man to [get] a job is the first to advance", i.e. job seniority, superimposed, as here, upon a history of racial discrimination. The court found, as a matter of fact, that it was not "permissible" to assume "on the record in this case" that

> with less than the amount of on-the-job training now acquired by reason of the progression procedure, employees could move into the jobs in the progression lines and perform those jobs satisfactorily and — more importantly — without danger of physical injury to themselves and their fellow employees. 296 F. Supp. at 91.

In other words, the record in that case, as the district court viewed it, showed that safety and efficiency, the component factors of business necessity, would not allow relaxation of the job seniority system. We see no necessary conflict between Porter's holding on this point and our holding in the present case. . . .

IV

The defendants maintain that Congress specifically exempts seniority systems such as Crown's from the operation of Title VII. In support of their assertion the defendants cite that portion of §703(h) which allows an employer to "apply different standards of compensation, or different terms, conditions, or privileges of employment *pursuant to a bone fide seniority* or merit system . . . provided that such differences are not the result of an intention to discriminate because of race, color, religion, sex, or national origin". . . .

As the court pointed out in Quarles, the treatment of "job" or "department seniority" raises problems different from those discussed in the Senate debates: "a department seniority system that has its genesis in racial discrimination is not a bone fide seniority." 279 F. Supp. at 517.

It is one thing for legislation to require the creation of *fictional* seniority for newly hired Negroes, and quite another thing for it to require that time *actually worked* in Negro jobs be given equal status with time worked in white jobs. To begin with, requiring employers to correct their pre-Act discrimination by creating fictional seniority for new Negro employees would not necessarily aid the actual victims of the previous discrimination. There would be no guaranty that the new employees had actually suffered exclusion at the hands of the employer in the past, or, if they had, there would be no way of knowing whether, after being hired, they would have continued to work for the same employer. In other words, creating fictional employment time for newly-hired Negroes would comprise preferential rather than remedial treatment. The clear thrust of the Senate debate is directed against such preferential treatment on the basis of race. That sentiment was codified in an important portion of Title VII, §703(j):

> (j) Nothing contained in this subchapter shall be interpreted to require any employer, employment agency, labor organization, or joint labor-management committee subject to this subchapter to grant preferential treatment to any individual or to any group because of the race, color, religion, sex, or national origin of such individual or group on account of an imbalance which may exist with respect to the total number or percentage of persons of any race, color, religion, sex, or national origin employed by any employer, referred or classified for employment by any employment agency or labor organization, admitted to membership or classified by any labor organization, or admitted to, or employed in, any apprenticeship or other training program, in comparison with the total number or percentage of persons of such race, color, religion, sex, or national origin in any community, State, section, or other area, or in the available work force in any community, State, section, or other area. 42 U.S.C. §2000e-2(j).

No stigma of preference attaches to recognition of time actually worked in Negro jobs as the equal of white time. The individual victims of prior discrimination in this case would necessarily be the ones — the only ones — to benefit by the institution of mill seniority, as modified in the decree. We conclude, in agreement with Quarles, that Congress exempted from the anti-discrimination requirements only those seniority rights that gave white workers preference over junior Negroes. This is not to say that Whitfield and Quarles and Title II prohibit an employer from giving compensatory training and help to the Negro workers who have been discriminated against. Title VII's imposition of an affirmative duty on employers to undo past discrimination permits compensatory action for those who have suffered from prior discrimination.

V

We find unpersuasive the argument that, whatever its operational effects, job seniority is immune under the statute because not imposed with the *intent* to discriminate. Section 703(h), quoted earlier, excludes from the strictures of Title VII different working terms dictated by "bona fide" seniority systems "provided that such differences are *not the result of an intention to discriminate because of race* . . . ." Here, however, if Crown did not intend to punish Negroes as such by reinstituting job seniority, the differences between the job status of Negroes hired before 1966 and whites hired at the same time would have to be called the "result" of Crown's earlier, intentional discrimination. Quarles put it this way:

> The differences between the terms and conditions of employment for white [*sic*] and Negroes about which plaintiffs complain are the result of an intention to discriminate in hiring policies on the basis of race before January 1, 1966. The differences that originated before the act are maintained now. The act does not condone present differences that are the result of intention to discriminate before the effective date of the act. . . . The court holds that the present differences in departmental seniority of Negroes and white [*sic*] that result from the company's intentional, racially discriminatory hiring policy before January 1, 1966 are not validated by the proviso of §703(h). 279 F. Supp. 517-518.

Section 706(g) limits injunctive (as opposed to declaratory) relief to cases in which the employer or union has "*intentionally engaged in*" an unlawful employment practice. Again, the statute, read literally, requires only that the defendant meant to do what he did, that is, his employment practice was not accidental. The relevant legislative history, quoted in the margin, bears out the language of the statute on that point.

Section 707(a) allows the Attorney General to enforce the Act only where there is a "pattern or practice of resistance to the full enjoyment of any of the rights secured by this subchapter" and where the pattern or practice "is *intended* to deny the full exercise of the rights herein described". Defendants contend that no such condition existed here. The same point arose in Dobbins. The court rejected it (292 F. Supp. at 448):

> In reviewing statutes, rules or conduct which result in the effective denial of equal rights to Negroes or other minority groups, intention can be inferred from the operation and effect of the statute or rule or from the conduct itself. The conduct of defendant in the present case "by its very nature" contains the implications of the required intent. . . .

Here, as in Dobbins, the conduct engaged in had racially determined effects. The requisite intent may be inferred from the fact that the defendants persisted in the conduct after its racial implications had become known to them. Section 707(a) demands no more. . . .

VII

Our main conclusions may be summarized as follows: (1) Crown's job seniority system carries forward the discriminatory effects integral to the company's former employment practices. (2) The safe and efficient operation of the Bogalusa mill does not depend upon maintenance of the job seniority system. (3) To the extent that Crown and the white union insisted upon carrying forward exclusion of a racially-determined class, *without business necessity,* they committed, with the requisite intent, in the statutory sense, an unfair employment practice as defined by Title VII.

The district court thoughtfully worked a decree studded with provisos to protect the employer from the imposition of unsafe or inefficient practices and at the same time prevent racial discrimination. The decree also specifically provides that job seniority may still apply to bidding between one white employee and other. By making the decree applicable only to bidding that involves Negroes hired before 1966, the district court limited the remedy to the scope of the illegal conduct. The judgment of the district court is affirmed. . . .

JONES v. LEE WAY MOTOR FREIGHT, INC., 431 F.2d 245 (10th Cir. 1970). Company policy prohibited transfers between the "city driver" and "line driver" categories. Line drivers received better pay, and line jobs were considered superior. The company hired blacks only as city drivers. Black city drivers hired prior to the effective date of the 1964 Civil Rights Act brought a Title VII action, in which they alleged that the application of the no-transfer rule to them was discriminatory because it locked them into city driving jobs. The district court denied relief.

The court of appeals held that the statistical proof established a prima facie case of discriminatory employment practices at the time plaintiffs were hired. Between 1964 and 1968 no blacks were hired as line drivers, although there were between 353 and 542 men in that category. All blacks who were hired were assigned as city drivers.

The no-transfer rule was held to Violate Title VII because it perpetuated past racial discrimination.

> Because of the company's employment policies at the time plaintiffs were hired, they were ineligible for consideration for jobs as line drivers. They were systematically relegated to the lower paying, lower status job of city driver. Now at a time when the company seems to be actively seeking Negro line drivers, plaintiffs are unable to compete for these jobs, without quitting their present jobs, because of the no-transfer policy. (431 F.2d at 248.)

According to the company, the no-transfer rule was justified by bad experience with transfers in the past, by the cost of retraining the transferee and his replacement, and by grievances which might arise from the fact that the two categories were covered by different union contracts. These claims of purported "business necessity" were rejected.

> The difficulties resulting from previous transfers, basically that the transferee had difficulty in adjustment and often required retransfer, might be largely alleviated by screening plaintiffs in the same way that prospective line drivers are interviewed. The plaintiffs' willingness to pursue this case indicates that they genuinely want to be line drivers and militates against any conclusion that the company's experience with them will be the same as it was with previous transferees.
>
> The training costs are somewhat illusory. To fill a line driver vacancy with a new hire rather than a transferee will entail as much training if not more because a transferee has some knowledge of company policy and procedure. The training of a new city driver to replace the transferee will entail some costs, but we believe that these would not be substantial enough to outweigh the detriment to the plaintiffs of permanently locking them in city drivers' jobs.
>
> Much the same might be said of the potential personnel problems occasioned by transfers and resulting from two union contracts. These may never develop. The record shows that in the case of the one city driver who was inadvertently allowed to transfer, the union sided with him when the company tried to return him to his previous job. We will not accord this contention greater weight than the plaintiffs' rights under Title VII. In short, we are not persuaded that the no-transfer policy is essential to the safe, efficient operation of the company's business. (431 F.2d at 249-250.)

UNITED STATES v. BETHLEHEM STEEL, 446 F.2d 652 (2d Cir. 1971). This Title VII litigation involved the defendant's Lackawanna, N.Y. plant. The court of appeals found that, up to the time the government began its investigation in 1967, the plant "was a microcosm of classic discrimination in the north." Reviewing the record, the court found:

> In hiring, jobs were made available to whites rather than to blacks in a number of ways. There were no fixed or reasonable objective standards and procedures for hiring; the aptitude test scores of some white applicants were fraudulently raised; some white applicants were hired without testing; and whites were given preference in summer employment. Job assignment practices were even more reprehensible. Over 80 percent of black workers were placed in 11 [of 82] departments, which contained the hotter and dirtier jobs in the plant. Blacks were excluded from higher paying and cleaner jobs. All of the defendants were aware of this racial discrimination. Even within a department the pattern continued. . . . Similar preferential treatment was given to whites in the choosing of apprentices and in the selection of supervisors. (446 F.2d at 655.)

The major issue was whether the seniority and transfer provisions of the collective bargaining agreement perpetuated the effects of past discrimination. Employee rights of promotion were based on departmental seniority.

Until 1962 transfer between departments prohibited; under the most liberal plan, adopted in 1965, a transferee lost accrued seniority for purposes of promotion and was paid at the rate of his new entry-level job.

The district court held, inter alia, that the transfer and seniority system had a discriminatory "lock-in" effect that "becomes stronger as an employee's length of service increases in a department. This means that the longer a Negro has worked in the hot and dirty department to which he was admittedly discriminatorily assigned, the more he has to lose by transfer." The defendants were ordered to establish objective criteria for promotion and hiring, and to administer apprenticeship programs in nondiscriminatory fashion. Employees in the eleven departments which had been the focus of discriminatory practices were given priority transfer rights into any other department. However, the district court refused to order that transferees be paid at a rate at least equal to the rate in their former jobs, and that transferees' employment rights should for all purposes be determined by plant, rather than departmental, seniority. The principal grounds for denial of this relief were that it was not necessary to remove deterrents to transfer and that it would unfairly affect other employees.

The court of appeals noted that, in addition to the discriminatory "lock-in effect," "a transferee to a 'white' department would never be able to reach the level of a white employee already there" under the existing system, because "the earlier discriminatory job assignment had denied him the chance to earn seniority up to [the time of transfer] in the 'white' department." 446 F.2d at 658. The district court's order was enlarged to include rate retention and seniority carry-over.

> Unless some rate retention and seniority carry-over is granted to a transferee, the incentive to transfer will remain low for the very reason that the seniority and transfer provisions of the plant were found to have perpetuated discrimination. That is, a discriminatorily assigned employee will have little incentive to transfer if he loses money or job seniority by doing so. (446 F.2d at 661.)

In analyzing the company's claims of business necessity, the court said, the

> . . . doctrine must mean more than that transfer and seniority policies serve legitimate management functions. . . . Necessity connotes an irresistible demand. . . . If the legitimate ends of safety and efficiency can be served by a reasonably available alternative system with less discriminatory effects, then the present policies may not be continued. (446 F.2d at 662.)

The goals of safety and efficiency would not be frustrated by the changes in transfer and seniority policies ordered by the district court because no one would be allowed to transfer into a job for which he was not qualified, or to transfer directly to high- or middle-level jobs. Transfer would be limited to low-skilled, entry-level positions.

The adverse impact on the morale of white employees, which defendants had feared, would be averted by the fact that transferees would lose the benefit of rate retention if they subsequently refused promotions, and by the fact that plant seniority would not be available as a means of "bumping" white employees. To the extent that rate retention and seniority carry-over might frustrate the expectations of other employees, "their hopes arise from an illegal system. Moreover, their seniority advantages are not indefeasibly vested rights but mere expectations derived from a bargaining agreement subject to modification." 446 F.2d at 663.

The district court order was modified in three other respects. First, it was extended to cover black employees who were originally discriminatorily assigned to the eleven departments but who thereafter exercised their limited right to transfer, on the ground that they had nevertheless been subject to the discriminatory effects of the departmental seniority system. Second, application of the order to white employees in the eleven departments was rejected; evidence which tended to show that "at some indeterminate time in the past certain ethnic groups congregated in certain departments . . . fell far short of proof that any of the white employees in the 11 departments were there because they could not obtain jobs elsewhere in the plant." Finally, the court of appeals agreed with the government that there was no proof that any white applicants to the apprenticeship program were rejected on account of religion, sex or national origin, and hence the district court erred in including such applicants in its order. 446 F.2d at 665.

In a subsequent aspect of this litigation, the court of appeals held that black employees who charged discrimination in defendant's method of recalling laid-off workers were not barred by res judicata or collateral estoppel from obtaining injunctive relief because the Attorney General had earlier sought and failed to obtain such relief. Williamson v. Bethlehem Steel Corporation, 468 F.2d 1201 (2d Cir. 1972).

NOTES

1. In United States v. Hayes International Corporation, 456 F.2d 112 (5th Cir. 1972), the company had adopted a rate retention–seniority carry-over transfer plan prior to the time of the final district court hearing in 1969. Under the plan, transferees were limited to entry-level jobs, although some were qualified for other jobs. In examining the record, the court of appeals found evidence that an upper-level job would not be available to black transferees so long as an employee already in the department was qualified to perform that job.

> To determine vacancies in this manner is to let the old job seniority criterion . . . in through the proverbial back door. . . . Qualified negroes with greater seniority cannot displace incumbent workers. However, they are to be given a preference for future vacant jobs absent a compelling business reason. . . . Hayes attempts to justify [the limitations on transfer] because it is necessary in times of rapid em-

ployee expansion to have experienced men rather than newcomers in the higher classified positions. While this may be considered a nonracial business purpose, we do not find it to be sufficiently overriding and compelling to outweigh the discriminatory effect it might have on the negro transferee. (456 F.2d at 117-118.)

The court also rejected the plan insofar as it precluded transfer to a technical or clerical position. The company's rationale was that, since wages in such jobs were generally lower than in the maintenance and production units and were not covered by a collective bargaining agreement, no potential black transferees would be interested. As in United States v. Bethlehem Steel, however, the court concluded that the company was required to provide incumbent black employees with only one bona fide opportunity to transfer.

2. In United States v. Local 189, United Papermakers and Paperworkers, AFL-CIO, CLC, 282 F. Supp. 39 (E.D. La. 1968), *aff'd,* 416 F.2d 980 (5th Cir. 1969), supra page 763, the district court held the job seniority system unlawful and ordered defendants to establish a system of mill seniority. In Local 189 No. 2, 301 F. Supp. 906 (E.D. La. 1969), the district court ruled, inter alia, on questions relating to "job skipping." Although the company might approve a reasonable "residency requirement," i.e., a period of time which must be served in a job before an employee might bid for a higher job in the line of progression, blacks in the affected class were held entitled to skip those jobs in the lines of progression which did not provide training and experience for the higher jobs. Where a residency requirement was reasonable, it was not to be fixed at the six months provided in the collective bargaining agreement, but was to be "fixed at the minimum time required to provide necessary training and experience for each job. . . . Any longer period would unnecessarily retard the advancement of those in the class discriminated against and would be unlawful." 301 F. Supp. at 917. Moreover, the training and experience acquired by virtue of temporary assignments were to be recognized for promotional purposes.

Any practice, system, procedure or policy that denies a member of the affected class promotion to a vacant job which he is qualified to perform, where he is senior in terms of continuous employment with the company to other eligible employees and where he has not previously waived or otherwise disqualified himself for promotion or advancement, is a "term, condition and privilege of employment" that discriminates against Negro employees on the basis of race, in violation of Sec. 703(a) of the Civil Rights Act of 1964. (301 F. Supp. at 918.)

Waivers signed by two black employees on the basis of misleading information were held invalid. See Long v. Georgia Kraft Company, 450 F.2d 557 (5th Cir. 1971), where the court referred to the relief granted in Local 189 No. 2 in ordering the district court to determine the extent to which business necessity precluded job skipping.

3. Proof that the exclusion of black truck drivers from highly paid "over the road" driving jobs (reviewed in Jones v. Lee Way Motor Freight, Inc., supra)

was not a one-company phenomenon is indicated by the frequency of court challenges to the practice. See, e.g., Belt v. Johnson Motor Lines, Inc., 458 F.2d 443 (5th Cir. 1972); United States v. Roadway Express, Inc., 457 F.2d 854 (6th Cir. 1972); Witherspoon v. Mercury Freight Lines, Inc., 457 F.2d 496 (5th Cir. 1972); Bing v. Roadway Express, Inc., 444 F.2d 687 (5th Cir. 1971).

ROBINSON v. LORILLARD CORPORATION, 444 F.2d 791 (4th Cir. 1971). Black employees brought a class action challenging the departmental seniority system established by the collective bargaining agreement. The plaintiffs had been hired at a time when the company practiced overt racial discrimination, with blacks assigned to the departments containing the lowest-paying, least desirable jobs. Interdepartmental transfers were prohibited until 1962, when the provision was amended to permit such transfers for employees willing to forfeit accrued seniority and begin as new employees in the new department. Job seniority was also abolished in the 1962 agreement, enabling the most senior interested employee in a department to fill a vacancy, regardless of what specific jobs he had previously held. The district court held that the departmental seniority system operated discriminatorily against black employees hired prior to 1962, and ordered that employees be permitted to transfer to other departments to fill vacancies, and that plant seniority be used for all purposes after a residency period of thirty days. Transferees would retain their old wage rate until they reached a position paying an equal or higher rate. Members of the affected class were also held to be entitled to back pay.

On appeal, the court rejected the company's claim that the departmental seniority system was necessary to promote "Efficiency, Economy and Morale." Judge Sobeloff first recognized that, while Title VII was intended to have prospective application only, relief may be granted to remedy present and continuing effects of past discrimination. He then listed the reasons why the company's claims lacked merit:

> First, the record is barren of any real evidence that the jobs in the formerly all-white departments are so complex and interrelated that progression through a series of jobs is necessary to efficient performance of the more difficult tasks.
>
> Second, there is direct evidence to the contrary in the fact that the seniority system ordered into effect by the District Court had been originally proposed by Lorillard in the course of negotiating the 1968 collective bargaining agreement. The District Court added only the red-circling requirement to remove the wage rate barrier to transfers. Third, Lorillard's efficiency argument is clearly inconsistent with its earlier argument that the seniority system would never have been adopted if the union had not forced it upon the company. Fourth, the order of the District Court specifically provides for a preliminary trial period on the job. If the transferee is unable to perform satisfactorily, the transfer does not become final and the employee returns to his old job.
>
> Finally, it is difficult to imagine how even the necessity for job progression could

constitute the business necessity which would justify a departmental seniority system that perpetuated the effects of prior discriminatory practices. For, after all, seniority is necessarily an inefficient means of assuring sufficient prior job experience. It may take only six months to learn a job well and become qualified for advancement. Yet the vagaries of chance may present an opportunity for advancement in only six weeks or not for six years. When some employees have been discriminatorily denied entry to the department, an alternative promotion system could advance the employee who has been discriminated against if he has the greatest employment seniority and has served a necessary minimum time in his present job or has satisfactorily established his capacity to handle the job. Such an alternative plan would accomplish the business purpose "equally well with a lesser differential racial impact."

We recognize Lorillard's point that changing the seniority system may frustrate the expectations of employees who have established departmental seniority but not employment seniority in the preferable departments. However, Title VII guarantees that all employees are entitled to the *same* expectations regardless of "race, color, religion, sex, or national origin." Where some employees now have lower expectations than their coworkers because of the influence of one of these forbidden factors, they are entitled to have their expectations raised even if the expectations of others must be lowered in order to achieve the statutorily mandated equality of opportunity. (444 F.2d at 799-800.)

BROWN v. GASTON COUNTY DYEING MACHINE COMPANY, 457 F.2d 1377 (4th Cir. 1972). A black worker trained as a welder had sought a position in this work with defendant, but was advised "that it was premature to try to place a Negro in a job as welder. . . ." A year later, on instructions from the defendant company's president, plaintiff was assigned to a welding job, but he filed a class action alleging racial discrimination in hiring, promotion, pay and other terms and conditions of employment. The district judge found that plaintiff was entitled to back pay for the period from the time he was hired until he was assigned as a welder-trainee, but refused him further relief and dismissed the suit. The court of appeals found that, while plaintiff had not proved his own Title VII claim, "the class of employees he represents is not for this reason deprived of a remedy." The court reviewed statistical evidence showing that black workers were employed in only eleven of forty-five job classifications, and generally were assigned to classifications near the bottom of the pay scale, which afforded little opportunity for advancement and were almost completely segregated. It concluded:

Here, in the absence of objective criteria applied to all workers alike, the statistics indicate that race is the only identifiable factor explaining the disparity between the jobs held by white employees and those held by black employees. . . .

Moreover, the record discloses that notices of vacancies are not posted, and news of them is passed along by word of mouth. When job classifications are as segregated as they are in this company, delay in learning about a vacancy in an all-white category may in itself discriminate against a black employee who hears of it only after it has been filled. (457 F.2d at 1383.)

The district court was ordered to retain jurisdiction of the case for a "reasonable time": if the company did not correct its discriminatory practices by the end of that period, appropriate injunctive relief was to be granted.

NOTES

1. In Rowe v. General Motors Corporation, 457 F.2d 348 (5th Cir. 1972), it was held that, against a background of plant segregation until 1962, violations of Title VII were constituted by company procedures which conditioned promotion and transfer from "hourly" jobs to salaried positions on the recommendation of the employee's supervisor, where supervisors were not required to adhere to specific, objective standards in making recommendations and where employees were not notified of promotion opportunities or of the qualifications necessary for promotion. The court approved the many affirmative steps that the defendant had taken to eliminate discrimination, but said, "the problem is not whether the employer has willingly — yea, even enthusiastically — taken steps to eliminate what it recognizes to be traces or consequences of its prior pre-Act segregation practices. . . . [T]he question is whether . . . the employer has done enough." 457 F.2d at 355. The company was ordered to post periodically, in conspicuous places throughout the plant, notices containing information regarding the qualifications of salaried jobs and the procedure for application, and to continue its practices, undertaken shortly before this action was commenced, of posting notices of training classes and of permitting employees to apply for promotion without the recommendation of their immediate supervisors.

2. The Sixth Circuit has held that departmental seniority systems are not illegal per se, but that they violate Title VII only when they tend to perpetuate the effects of historic or traditional discrimination in hiring and promotion. Thus, where a black plaintiff failed to establish that "locking" existed within the departments of defendant's plant, and failed to establish sufficient evidence concerning the traditional discrimination which the present system was alleged to have perpetuated, dismissal of the suit was affirmed. Heard v. Mueller Company, 464 F.2d 190 (6th Cir. 1972).

See also United States v. National Lead Company, 438 F.2d 935 (8th Cir. 1971), denying preliminary injunctive relief even though some vestiges of the employer's past discrimination seemed to be preserved in transfer and promotion procedures. The actual impact of such discrimination on black employees with seniority was, however, unclear.

3. In Savannah Printing Specialties & Paper Products Local Union 604 v. Union Camp Corporation, 350 F. Supp. 632 (S.D. Ga. 1972), the plaintiff union sought to require the defendant company to arbitrate the grievance of workers concerning seniority and layoff, as required by their labor agreement. The company responded that the seniority and layoff standard that it was now using was set by the Office of Federal Contracts Compliance (OFCC) acting pursuant to Executive Order 11246. Under the new policy, which

based seniority on "division" rather than the traditional "job" longevity, some workers who were laid off due to a lack of business had more seniority in their jobs, but less in their division, than workers who were retained. In ruling for the company, the court found that "Seniority and other practices violative of Title VII or Executive Order 11246 through perpetuation of racial discrimination in employment are unlawful irrespective of any conflicting provisions of a collective bargaining contract. . . ."

QUESTIONS

1. A number of writers have been highly critical of the Nixon administration's performance in the equal employment field. In comparing the Nixon record with that of previous administrations, can any substantial distinction be seen? Given the opposition of the unions and employers and the relative lack of interest of the country as a whole, would a stronger executive policy be likely to prove effective?

2. The courts have interpreted fair employment statutes liberally, and the relief contained in judicial orders has quite outdistanced anything done by the executive or probably contemplated by the Congress. And yet, without further support from other public or private sectors, how long can courts be expected to provide affirmative relief of the character obtained in the last few years? And even if enforced, would the relief granted by the courts result in widespread employment gains for blacks? In short, would the elimination of job discrimination erase or reduce substantially the economic gap between white and black workers?

3. How realistic is the answer that Professor Owen Fiss offers to this question? In his view, fair employment laws are:

> *a [limited] strategy for conferring benefits on a racial class — blacks. . . . The limited nature of this strategy is not just a function of the circumstances of politics but rather reflects a deep commitment to the values of economic efficiency and individual fairness. The most troublesome question is whether the historical legacy of the class will, or should, moderate that commitment so as to yield, through enactment or construction, a more robust strategy for law. The legacy supplies an ethical basis for the desire to improve the relative economic position of blacks, and yet it also explains why a law that does no more than prohibit discrimination on the basis of race will leave that desire, in large part, unfulfilled. (Fiss, A Theory of Fair Employment Laws, 38 U. Chi. L. Rev. 235, 313-314 (1971).)*

4. How deep is society's commitment to the values of "economic efficiency and individual fairness"? To what extent is that commitment philosophic window dressing, with little more than rhetorical value in the competitive marketplace? If indeed Fiss has missed the mark, and employers are more interested in competitive advantage and profit than in either efficiency or fairness, are blacks in a better or worse position as they seek enforcement of fair employment laws?

3. Union Discrimination

Even a cursory review of the history of the labor movement reveals that, with few exceptions, organized labor has played a major part in the massive discrimination experienced by black workers. See, e.g., The Negro and the American Labor Movement (J. Jacobson, ed. 1968). A reading of contemporary employment discrimination cases confirms that, to a far greater extent than employers, it is labor unions who pose obstacles to the goal of equal employment opportunity. Appropriately, Title VII contains specific language (§703(c)) designed to bring labor organizations and apprenticeship programs within its coverage. For example, the traditional practice of many unions of organizing segregated locals for black and white workers constitutes a specific violation of Title VII, based on which courts have not only ordered consolidation, but provided protection for the black members by permitting them to elect designated officials of the merged unions for transitional periods. See, e.g., Hicks v. Crown Zellerbach Corporation, 310 F. Supp. 536 (E.D. La. 1970).

Nevertheless, the elimination of segregated unions does not end discrimination, and, as the cases below illustrate, may lead to increased discrimination against black workers.

UNITED STATES v. INTERNATIONAL LONGSHOREMEN'S ASSOCIATION
460 F.2d 497 (4th Cir. 1972)

Before BOREMAN, Senior Circuit Judge, and BRYAN and BUTZNER, Circuit Judges.

BUTZNER, Circuit Judge:

This appeal and cross-appeal arise out of an action brought by the Attorney General under Title VII of the Civil Rights Act of 1964 to combat racial discrimination that limits employment opportunities for longshoremen in the Port of Baltimore. The district court ordered the International Longshoremen's Association, its Atlantic Coast District and two of its racially segregated locals to operate a single hiring hall, to institute a non-discriminatory seniority system, and to fill permanent vacancies in longshoreman gangs on the basis of seniority instead of race. No party has assigned error to these provisions of the court's decree, and they have been implemented pending this appeal.

The district court also ordered the merger of predominately white local 829 with predominately black local 858. The ILA, the District, and the locals appeal from this order. . . .

Local 829 was chartered in 1913, and its membership always has been predominately white. The local has no rule that excludes black workers, but an applicant must be sponsored by a member of the local and be approved by a majority of its membership. Moreover, a former president of the local, who held office after the enactment of the Civil Rights Act of 1964, told black applicants that they would have more opportunity to work if they joined the black local. Since 1960, all of the approximately 757 persons admitted to membership were white, and currently the local has only four black longshoremen among its membership of about 1,155.

Local 858 was chartered in 1914, and it has always been composed almost entirely of black persons. It also requires an applicant to be sponsored by a member and to be approved by a majority of its membership. Since 1964, it has admitted 261 black and two white persons. Currently there are only five white longshoremen in its membership of approximately 1,226.

Both locals are members of the ILA and its Atlantic Coast District. Both are parties to the same collective bargaining agreement and their members receive the same rate of pay. Both operate through a system of permanent gangs of 15 to 20 men. New members of the locals obtain work by filling temporary vacancies in a particular gang. When a permanent vacancy occurs, the gang leader selects a replacement who must be approved by other members of the gang. Gangs from both locals are assigned to ships in the Port when stevedores call the hiring halls to place job orders. When calling for gangs, the stevedores maintain a rough form of seniority based primarily on the status of the leader and the performance of his gang.

All members of local 858's gangs are black. All of 829's gangs consist of white longshoremen with two exceptions. This local has a checkerboard gang consisting of both black and white members, but black members of this gang work less desirable jobs. Another gang working out of the white local's hiring hall is composed solely of black longshoremen from both locals.

The evidence is undisputed that black and white gangs possess equal abilities and are capable of doing the same work. Gangs from both locals work for the same stevedores on the same ships and in the same hatches. Since there is no substantial difference in the locals except race, we conclude that the evidence fully substantiates the trial court's finding that the ILA chartered and maintains segregated locals in the Port of Baltimore. The presence of a few members of the opposite race in each local and the absence of racially restrictive bylaws do not invalidate the district judge's ruling.

Section 703(c) (2) of the Civil Rights Act of 1964 declares that it shall be an unlawful employment practice for a labor organization to segregate or classify its membership on the basis of race in any way which would "tend to deprive any individual of employment opportunities." The district judge found that the maintenance of the ILA's segregated locals is a per se violation of §703(c)(2). He held:

> The maintenance of separate locals for Negroes and whites performing the same duties in the same geographical area in itself would tend to deprive individual members of equal employment opportunities. As firmly established in Brown v. Board of Education, 347 U.S. 483 . . . (1954), the sanctioning of racially separate groupings in schools is inherently discriminatory, and this principle applies with equal force to cases such as the pending one where equal employment opportuni-

ties are involved. The doctrine of "separate but equal" has long since been laid to rest in other areas . . . No valid reason has been advanced by defendants for this doctrine's exhumation to justify the maintenance of racially segregated unions whose members work side by side as longshoremen. 319 F. Supp. at 741.

We agree with the district judge that the maintenance of racially segregated locals inevitably breeds discrimination that violates the Act. Racial segregation limits both black and white employees to advancement only within the confines of their races. The position that would rightfully be an employee's, but for his race, may be filled by a person of lower seniority or inferior capability because the job traditionally has been reserved for either a white person from one local or a black person from the other. Even though union officials strive in good faith to administer their duties impartially, they cannot avoid this inherent inequality, and its consequent violation of the Act. Indeed, so obvious is the discrimination that arises from segregated unions, in every case, save one, courts have ordered or approved mergers. United States v. Jacksonville Terminal Co., 451 F.2d 418 (5th Cir. 1971); Musicians' Protective Union, Local 274 v. American Federation of Musicians, 329 F. Supp. 1226 (E.D. Pa. 1971); United States v. Chesapeake & Ohio Railway Co., 3 EPD ¶8331, at 7175 (E.D. Va. 1971); Hicks v. Crown Zellerbach Corp., 319 F. Supp. 314 (E.D. La. 1970); United States v. Local 189, United Papermakers and Paperworkers, 301 F. Supp. 906 (E.D. La.), *aff'd* 416 F.2d 980 (5th Cir. 1969); Chicago Federation of Musicians, Local 10 v. American Federation of Musicians, 57 LRRM 2227 (N.D. Ill. 1964). *Contra,* United States v. International Longshoremen's Association, 334 F. Supp. 976 (S.D. Tex. 1971).

The wisdom of Judge Harvey's conclusion is illustrated by the record in this case. The evidence discloses that although there are more black gangs working in the Port than white gangs, black longshoremen work fewer hours than white longshoremen and on the average earn less money. Moreover, the black gangs traditionally work more of the "dirty" cargoes than their white counterparts.[5] The discrepancy in opportunities for work available to black and white longshoremen is due partly to the fact that most of the gearmen, mechanics, and foremen are members of the white local.[6] Since these men are not hired through the gang system, the defendants contend that the employers' preference for white workers in these classifications cannot be attributed to the union. These facts partially explain the discrimination against black longshoremen but they do not justify it. The record does not establish that black employees are unable to work satisfactorily as gearmen, mechanics, and foremen.

5. These cargoes include fish meal, bone meal, feather meal, tapioca, ore, animal hides, roots, fertilizers, and loose material requiring shoveling and manual labor.

6. The district judge found that in the contract year 1966-67, white longshoremen on the average worked 335 more hours per man than did black longeshoremen; in 1967-68, white longshoremen worked 241 more hours per man; in 1968-69, 147 more hours per man, and in 1969-70, 120 more hours per man.

Abolition of the dual hiring halls and the other reforms decreed by the district court do not eliminate the necessity of merging the locals. The ILA's failure to secure equal employment opportunities for its black members in all jobs for which they are qualified is an example of the inherent inequality that the district judge correctly concluded can be remedied only by merger. Apart from further litigation, discrimination against black workers who aspire to non-gang jobs, such as gearmen, mechanics, and foremen, can only be accomplished by bargaining with the stevedores. But the officers of the white local owe no duty to the members of the black local, and it is unrealistic to expect them to participate in hard bargaining on behalf of black longshoremen. The president of the white local, while conceding that he knew members of his local worked 300,000 hours more than members of the black local in 1968, admitted he had done nothing to correct this disparity because it was "not within my power." At best, the union's committee approaches the bargaining table with divided legal responsibilities and loyalties. However, merger of the locals will place on all bargaining representatives, not just black bargaining representatives, the statutory duty to eliminate racial discrimination throughout the Port. Steele v. Louisville & Nashville Railroad Co., 323 U.S. 192, 203 . . . (1944).

The union's officers, including the black officers of local 858, oppose merger. Their principal argument against the district court's decree is the claim that merger of the locals infringes on the workers' right to the freedom of association guaranteed them by the first amendment. This argument misapprehends the court's order. Merger will not prevent longshoremen from associating to achieve economic and political goals. The order does no more than prohibit exclusion from association on the ground of race. There is no warrant in the Constitution for a union to retain, even by majority preference, racially segregated locals that tend to deprive some black members of equal employment opportunities. The governing principles were stated by Mr. Justice Black when the Court held that right-to-work laws did not deprive union members of the protection afforded by the first amendment:

> There cannot be wrung from a constitutional right of workers to assemble to discuss improvement of their own working standards, a further constitutional right to drive from remunerative employment all other persons who will not or can not, participate in union assemblies. The constitutional right of workers to assemble, to discuss and formulate plans for furthering their own self interest in jobs cannot be construed as a constitutional guarantee that none shall get and hold jobs except those who will join in the assembly or will agree to abide by the assembly's plans. For where conduct affects the interests of other individuals and the general public, the legality of that conduct must be measured by whether the conduct conforms to valid law, even though the conduct is engaged in pursuant to plans of an assembly. Lincoln Federal Labor Union 19129 v. Northwestern Iron & Metal Co., 335 U.S. 525, 531 . . . (1949).

The district court's order does not conflict with NAACP v. Alabama, 357 U.S. 449 . . . (1958), and Thomas v. Collins, 323 U.S. 516 . . . (1945), on which the union primarily relies. These cases do not create a right in white men or black men to avoid association with persons of the other race. On the contrary they are leading authorities charting the right of all persons to associate for political and economic goals.

[Judge Bryan dissented on the merger issue. A divided court affirmed the district court's refusal to desegregate the gangs by providing for a daily shape-up system, or as an alternative reformation of each permanent gang. The district judge felt that this relief would threaten efficiency and safety. Judge Butzner, finding no valid business necessity for maintaining the segregated gangs, would have remanded the case to determine whether the earlier decree had eliminated segregated gangs, and equalized the work and wages of black and white workers.]

LOCAL 10 v. FEDERATION OF MUSICIANS, 57 LRRM 2227 (N.D. Ill. 1964). The court refused to restrain the international musicians union from imposing a trusteeship on all-white Local 10 (12,000 members), which had refused an order to merge with all-black Local 208 (1100 members). The white local objected to provisions of the merger agreement which were designed to ensure black representation on policy-making boards of the merged unit. The provisions read:

Paragraph 5 . . . provides that for the period from January 11, 1966, to January 13, 1969, the members of the merged union who are members of Local 208, as of December 1, 1965, shall elect: (1) three of the eight members of the Executive Board; (2) an Administrative Vice-President; (3) two of the eleven members of the Trial Board; (4) one of the three members of the Examining Board; and (5) specified members of persons who are to represent the merged union at various conventions. Members who were members of Local 10 as of December 1, 1965, shall elect the President, Vice-President, Recording Secretary, Financial Secretary-Treasurer, and the balance of the membership of the various boards and the balance of the delegates to the various conventions.

For the period January 14, 1969, to January 10, 1972, Paragraph 6 provides that the members who were members of Local 208 shall elect: an Administrative Vice-President and two of the seven members of the Executive Board. The remaining officials shall be elected by the entire union. . . . The plaintiffs claim that the plan will deprive the non-Negro members of the merged union of the right to vote for all officers of the merged union. (57 LRRM at 2229-2230.)

In holding that it had no jurisdiction in the case, the district judge found that Title VII had not yet taken effect, but expressed the view that the merger plan did not violate §703(c) because

The defendant's merger plan is designed to promote integration. The classification which the plan makes in voting rights for the transition period — 1966 through 1972 — is not designed to "adversely affect any member's status." Such an arrangement might be used to implement the merger of any two all-white or any two all-Negro organizations. The classification is designed to protect the interest of the smaller local. The fact that the racial make-up of two merging organizations is different is irrelevant (Id. at 2236.)

NOTES

1. Blacks have evidenced serious reservations about merging with white locals. Their concerns reflect the fear that they will not be represented on policy-making boards, and that they will lose leadership posts, dues-collecting powers and the independent status they enjoyed in the separate union. Courts have shown varying degrees of sympathy for these reservations.

In Musicians Protective Union No. 274 v. American Federation of Musicians, 329 F. Supp. 1226 (E.D. Pa. 1971), the court held that the international union could expel a black local that refused an order to merge with the white local so as to eliminate the vestiges of dual unionism in a particular geographical area. Cf. Lee v. Macon County Board of Education, 283 F. Supp. 194 (M.D. Ala. 1968), ordering that two high school athletic associations be merged and that blacks be represented in leadership positions of the merged association.

In Daye v. Tobacco Workers International Union, 234 F. Supp. 815 (D.D.C. 1964), the court granted a black local's request for a restraining order to prevent the international from imposing a trusteeship and revoking its charter because of its refusal to merge with a white local. Plaintiffs sought the relief pending action by the NLRB on an unfair labor practices complaint, charging that the merger would be discriminatory because black members would be placed behind white members on seniority lists of the merged union. The court granted the relief to preserve the status quo pending NLRB action.

In United States v. International Longshoremen's Association, 334 F. Supp. 976 (S.D. Tex. 1971), the court expressed serious doubt as to whether discrimination against black workers could best be eliminated by merging the segregated locals. The white locals argued that black locals were now getting 50 percent of the work, a much greater percentage than urged by the government under the Philadelphia Plan (see infra page 799), and would not benefit from the merger. But the court found that even under the fifty-fifty rule, blacks in several areas "have been forced to accept a diminished opportunity to earn wages, receive union benefits, work better cargo and otherwise enjoy employment opportunities solely on the basis of their race." 334 F. Supp. at 979. Negro union officials also opposed the merger, contending that, by having their own unions, blacks had been able to better themselves, to hold high positions in their locals, and to be recognized as a powerful voice for the black community. The court, after weighing all of these factors and noting the complex problems merger would bring, concluded that the government was entitled to some relief, but that merger was not the only means of removing the inequities suffered by the black local. The judge decided to certify the issue as one involving a controlling question of law, about which there is a substantial ground for difference of opinion, and urged an immediate appeal.

2. Often the advantages of membership in the white union are clear. In affirming an order requiring the Miami Police Benevolent Association to admit all black Miami police officers, the Fifth Circuit noted the many benefits of membership in the association: it performed a "public" function, and even though there was a black police association, there weren't enough blacks "to effectively raise money from the public or amongst themselves to provide benefits . . . equal to or even close to those . . . available to white officers." The black policemen were held entitled to all benefits, in that the principal source of the association's money is public contributions solicited on behalf of "the Police."

PITTSBURGH BLACK MUSICIANS v. LOCAL 60-471, AMERICAN FEDERATION OF MUSICIANS, AFL-CIO, Civ. No. 71-1008 (W.D. Pa. 1972). In Pittsburgh, the black musicians Local 471 merged with white Local 60 in 1965, under an agreement providing that for a five-year period six members of the nine-man executive board would be elected by members of Local 60, and three members by members of Local 471. Officer personnel and convention delegates were divided among members of the two unions. The merger agreement further provided:

> It is understood in December 1970, the election of officers of the merged union shall be an open election, with no mandated positions predicted on former affiliation with either Local Union, and unless changed by the members of the joined union in this 5-year period, will revert to a biennial election for all officers, at which time a President, Vice-President, Secretary Treasurer and six members of the Executive Board shall be elected. (Agreement Merging Locals 60-471, par. 6, May 17, 1965.)

At the 1970 elections, no blacks were elected. The black members filed suit complaining that discrimination in job assignments was continuing and that it justified extension of the transitional arrangement and other relief. After a lengthy investigation, the EEOC, to which the matter was referred, found reasonable cause to believe that both the local and international unions were engaged in unlawful employment practices in violation of Title VII.

In its investigation of plaintiffs' charges of discriminatory referral, the EEOC found that most musical engagements are obtained not by the musicians themselves, but by bandleaders or contractors who deal through booking agents or directly with management of establishments. The bandleaders or contractors then hire the individual musicians. The local plays no part in this hiring method, but not infrequently the local's office staff receives telephoned or other requests for referral of a certain kind of musician or musical group. While in such instances the official local policy is to send a general listing of all members and groups and not to make a specific recommendation, plaintiffs' claim that personnel recommendations are made in some of the referral requests, appears justified. Such action, the EEOC found, disadvantages black members and perpetuates the past segregation of the locals. The EEOC finding was bolstered by the fact that the local maintains an all-white office staff. Moreover, it found that few contractors (who are also members of the union) select any blacks for concerts, recording sessions, theatrical shows or other traditionally "white only" bookings. The EEOC reported that

> The Contractors explain to our investigators that very few black musicians "double-up," i.e., own or play more than one instrument, as allegedly required by a substantial number of their engagements. But the Contractors admit that in fact they are not familiar with the qualifications of very many individual black musicians, claiming that black musicians have done nothing to make themselves known to the white contractors. (EEOC Case No. YPI 3-020 (Jan. 18, 1973), page 4).

The EEOC rejected this argument, as well as the contractors' further defense that their hiring is done informally and that news about jobs is communicated among musicians and contractors by word of mouth, personal knowledge, and reputation. In response, the EEOC said,

> We believe the hiring statistics themselves, together with the Respondent's history of total segregation and this record as a whole, are enough to infer a current, intentionally discriminatory hiring pattern. . . . That inference is not rebutted by the claim, even if proven, that black musicians have not applied for work with the Contractors, since such applications justifiably would have been foreseen by the blacks as empty acts; and even if we were to assume that such applications would have been fairly considered, we would be remiss in allowing a no-applications defense where, as here, Charging Parties and their class doubtless were "chilled" out of applying by the self-induced and segregationist reputation of white contractors as a class. (Id. at 4-5.)

The contractors are obliged to take necessary steps to make themselves knowledgeable about the qualifications and availability of black musicians, to systematically inform black musicians of job openings as they arise, and to devise a formal, objective, reviewable system for selecting qualified musicians "irrespective of personal familiarity or reputation among white musicians, and to otherwise eliminate the vestiges of past discrimination." The EEOC was also critical of the local's failure to take action to end the discriminatory practices of contractors affiliated with it. "[A] labor organization may not assume a policy of benign neglect toward racial discrimination practiced by employers . . . with whom it deals. . . . Nor may a labor organization ignore discrimination by some members (here the contractors) against others."

As to the plaintiffs' claim that the proportionate black representation among the officers and staff of the local should have been extended, the EEOC found the local's refusal to agree to an extension a further "step backwards" and a signal to black musicians that the union was not concerned with their interests. While the EEOC recognized (as stated in Long v. Georgia Kraft, 455 F.2d 331 (5th Cir. 1972)) that suspension of rules governing election to union office in favor of guaranteed proportionate representation for victims of past discrimination should not be continued longer than necessary, the facts in this case certainly justified continuation of this kind of affirmative action. The union's failure to recognize this was itself a violation of Title VII. EEOC Case No. YPI 3-020 (Jan. 18, 1973).

LONG v. GEORGIA KRAFT COMPANY
455 F.2d 331 (5th Cir. 1972)

Before WISDOM, COLEMAN and SIMPSON, Circuit Judges.

WISDOM, Circuit Judge:

In this appeal we recognize the right of members of an all-black local union to protective transitional arrangements when their local is merged with a formerly all-white local, but we hold that such measures are inappropriate in this case.

For many years, International Brotherhood of Pulp, Sulphite, and Paper Mill Workers, AFL-CIO maintained segregated locals at the Krannert Division paper mill of the Georgia Kraft Company in Rome, Georgia. Local 804, with approximately 190 members at the time of the commencement of this suit, was all-white; Local 805, with approximately 80 members, was all-black. During 1969, negotiating teams from the two locals, faced with the requirements of Title VII . . . , began working toward merger of the locals. The teams representing the two locals agreed on the terms of a merger only to have the agreement rejected by the members of the two locals.

On March 10, 1970, the Equal Employment Opportunity Commission found reasonable cause to believe that the maintenance of the segregated locals violated Title VII, and merger talks began once again. The negotiating teams reached agreement in May of 1970. The agreement provided for merger of the two locals on June 1, 1970, under the following terms:

> The newly combined locals will operate under Local 804's present by-laws except for the following stipulations:
>
> 1. Members of Local 805 will select one of their members to fill the newly created office of 1st Vice-President for the remainder of 1970.
> 2. The outgoing 1st Vice-President will be appointed to the Local's Executive Board for the year 1971.
> 3. The Woodyard and Service Crew will have the right to select their Shop Stewards for their Department. The President of the Local shall have the right to appoint any additional Shop Stewards he deems necessary.

Although the members of Local 804 ratified the merger agreement, the members of Local 805 rejected it.

On August 28, 1970, the President of the International notified the two locals that merger would be accomplished by action of the International because the locals had been unable to agree on the terms of a merger. The International proposed to revoke Local 805's charter and to assign its membership, contract rights, and property to Local 804. Georgia Kraft was notified that this merger would become effective on October 1, 1970, and the Local 804 was to receive the dues check-offs for all former members of Local 805 as the new bargaining representatives of the black members.

Counsel for Local 805 wrote a letter to officials of the International demanding certain concessions in return for Local 805's approval of the merger. When his requests were not granted by the International, the members of Local 805 sought and were granted a temporary injunction stopping the merger. The members of Local 805 asked the district court to impose terms and conditions on the merger including: 1) the creation of a new office and the filling of that and other merged-Local 804 offices with former Local 805 members for an interim period, 2) interim representation of former Local 805 members on existing Local 804 committees, 3) the right of predominantly black woodyard and service crews to select their own shop stewards (shop stewards are usually appointed by the Local President), and 4) insulation of the members and funds of former-Local 805 from any liability for any award of attorney's fees.

The district court denied the requests for protective transitional measures. . . . The motion for injunctive relief, however, was granted to the extent that Local 804 was forbidden, after merger, from using the funds of Local 805 to pay attorney's fees assessed against Local 804 in the suit or to pay for costs and attorney's fees incurred by Local 804 in defending the suit. Local 804 was required to use funds on hand before the merger to satisfy the expenses. As to expenses in excess of amounts Local 804 had on hand prior to the merger, Local 804 was permitted to utilize funds collected through normal dues collection procedures from all members of the merged locals. During February 1971 the locals merged.

The black members of Local 805, appellants in this Court, ask us to reverse the decision of the district court and order the protective transitional measures. The appellants rely on two well recognized and frequently utilized doctrines in the equal employment area. First, Title VII, by its terms, allows the courts to order "such affirmative action as may be appropriate" to insure full compliance with the equal employment opportunity provisions. 42 U.S.C. §2000e-5(g). Second, this Court has repeatedly held that when it is necessary to insure full compliance with Title VII a district court is "empowered to eliminate the present effects of past discrimination". . . .

This appeal presents the question of how to "eliminate the present effects of past discrimination" in the context of the merger of two formerly segregated local unions. The appellants point out that, because of the long history of segregation in the unions and in the company, blacks have been unable to make the personal contacts and gain the prestige and respect necessary to win election to union offices. These "present effects of past discrimination" will, they argue, prevent the black members of the merged union from assuming, even to a small extent, the leadership role they enjoyed in the segregated Local 805.

The appellants urge us to follow Judge Heebe's opinion in Hicks v. Crown Zellerbach Corp., E.D. La. 1970, 310 F. Supp. 536. After finding that the maintenance of separate local unions for white and black employees at Crown Zellerbach's Bogalusa plant by the Int'l Brotherhood of Pulp, Sulphite, and Paper Mill Workers violated Title VII, Judge Heebe ordered immediate merger of the locals with "Negro participation in the leadership of [the] merged local union over a two-year transition period". 310 F. Supp. at 537. Specifically, in that case the court ordered 1) the election by the members of the formerly all-black local of a General Vice-President, a Trustee, and ten other persons to serve as stewards and members of the Executive Board of the merged union,[5] 2) an increase in the membership of the Executive Board from 83 to 95 with the twelve additional places to be filled by members of the all-black local, 3) full participation by the new officers in the supervision of the union, the negotiating committee, and the grievance committee during the transition period, and 4) representation of the formerly all-black local on all committees and delegations.

In general terms this Court has also addressed itself to this problem. In United States v. Jacksonville Terminal Co., 5 Cir. 1971, 451 F.2d 418, the Court was faced with two segregated local unions. We held: "We conclude that the District Court erred in refusing to hold that the failure to consolidate the locals violates section 703(c) of the Act, 42 U.S.C.A. §2000e-2(c). . . ."

. . . Because we recognize that transitional protective measures are a useful tool in the employment area we felt that it was necessary to discuss the subject, although we hold that such measures are inappropriate in the instant case. First, almost a year has passed since the merger of the segregated locals. During that time, the transition from two segregated locals to a fully integrated local has taken place. We are informed that Local 804 has held its election of officers. At that election, a black, former member of Local 805 was elected to one of the seven union offices.[6] In addition, the nine-member Negotiating Committee charged with negotiating the collective bargaining agreement with the employer on behalf of employees represented by Local 804, has three black members. Also, of the seventeen shop stewards appointed by the President of the Local, seven are black, former members of Local 805.[7]

5. All of these positions were specially created for the transition period and were to cease to exist after two years.

6. Local 804 has approximately 270 members; about 80 of those members are black. At the election, held in December 1971, only about seventy-five members of the Local voted; of these, only about a dozen were black. Only one black candidate was nominated by the membership, although anyone could be nominated. This black candidate was nominated by a white man and was elected. A black candidate ran for President on a write-in basis and was defeated.

7. The Shop Committee is made up of the officers and the shop stewards. This 24-member committee (7 officers and 17 stewards) has 8 black members (1 officer and 7 stewards).

In short, blacks have now attained the leadership role which over a year ago they sought through court-ordered transitional measures. The use of protective measures is addressed to the sound discretion of a court of equity. Before requiring a district court to order such relief, we must be convinced that the need for equitable relief still exists. In the case at bar, the transition has taken place. The need which once existed for transitional measures has dissipated.

Second, it must be remembered that this merger was not a court-ordered merger. The locals merged, admittedly because of the requirements of federal law, as a result of action by the International. It was, in fact, the refusal of Local 805 to ratify the terms of merger agreed upon by the negotiating teams which forced the International to intervene. This voluntary merger, rather than violating Title VII as the appellants appear to contend, brought the union into compliance with federal law. Protective transitional measures have been utilized only in the context of a court-ordered merger. This is not to say that their use is confined to such situations nor that segregated locals can escape the imposition of protective measures by effectuating a "voluntary" merger just prior to a court order. We feel, rather, that the voluntary nature of the merger in this case is an important factor to consider, along with the time lapse, in determining the need for protective transitional measures.

Although, because transition has been accomplished and the locals have voluntarily merged, we decline to order protective measures in this case, we wish to carefully note what we are *not* deciding. We do not, by our decision, imply that a district court may not, in the proper case, order protective transitional measures; nor do we imply that the case at bar, prior to transition, would not have been a proper case. Finally, we do not decide whether a district court, faced with a merger of two segregated bodies dictated by federal law, might not, in fact, be *required* to institute protective measures. . . .

NOTE: UNION NEPOTISM, REFERRAL AND OTHER EXCLUSIONARY PRACTICES

The merging of segregated union locals and the monitoring of merger agreements are not the only desegregation issues involving labor unions brought to the courts in recent years. Unions have sought to exclude minority workers and perpetuate the effects of prior exclusionary policies by using a varied and seemingly endless supply of discriminatory devices. Restricting new memberships to the sons of members, referring workers to jobs based on the length of their tenure as union members (grandfather clauses), requiring applicants to obtain written recommendations from three members and to be approved by a majority of members voting by secret ballot — all such policies have been held unlawful under Title VII. See, e.g., Local 53 International Association of Heat & Frost Workers v. Vogler, 407 F.2d 1047 (5th Cir. 1969); United States v. Local 36, Sheet Metal Workers, 416 F.2d 123 (8th Cir. 1969); United States v. International Brotherhood of Electrical Workers, Local No.

38, 428 F.2d 144 (6th Cir. 1970); United States v. Carpenters, Local 169, 457 F.2d 210 (7th Cir. 1972); United States v. Longshoremen (ILA), — F.2d — (4th Cir. 1972).

To guard against the adoption of other procedures designed to perpetuate discriminatory selection and referrals, courts have sought to formulate remedies. These include ordering unions to grant qualified minority applicants immediate membership, and to increase their size in order to correct the racial disparity in their membership. Local 53 v. Vogler, supra; Rios v. Local 638, Steamfitters, 326 F. Supp. 198 (S.D.N.Y. 1971); United States v. Ironworkers, Local 86, 315 F. Supp. 1202 (W.D. Wash. 1970), *aff'd* 443 F.2d 544 (9th Cir. 1971).

Of course, minority groups have available the right of fair representation doctrine, formulated in Steele v. Louisville and Nashville R.R. (323 U.S. 192, 65 S. Ct. 226, 89 L. Ed. 173 (1944), summarized supra page 724), but litigation based on this approach has not significantly reduced union discrimination.

Even when unions are forced to admit blacks, further court action is sometimes required to enjoin retaliatory harassment. Young v. International Telephone & Telegraph Co., 438 F.2d 757 (3d Cir. 1971); Pennsylvania v. Local Union No. 542, International Union of Operating Engineers, — F. Supp. — (E.D. Pa. Aug. 4, 1972).

Courts have issued detailed orders, appointed "Administrators" to oversee union activity under consent decrees, and held contempt hearings, but the resistance to compliance with nondiscrimination orders remains fierce, particularly from the union rank and file. In the course of an opinion approving relief against a particularly resistant union (United States v. Wood, Wire and Metal Lathers International Union, Local 46, 341 F. Supp. 694 (S.D.N.Y. 1972)), Judge Frankel included one of a substantial number of letters he had received from union members:

> We all realize we must take in minority workers. We have been reluctant to do so but it wasn't done out of hatred. Our union was started by our Grandfathers and passed on to our Fathers who passed it on to us. They built the industry to where it is, today. There are a lot of businesses, professions and other organizations that the sons follow in their Fathers' foot steps. We are accused of discrimination. Our crime was, being jealous of what we had built and taking care of our own. (341 F. Supp. at 699, n.4.)

But, while white workers and their unions deny that racism motivates their opposition to equal job opportunity for blacks, Judge Frankel in an earlier contempt proceeding against the Lathers had noticed contrary evidence in both what union witnesses said and how they said it:

> "The hardest" evidence in the record may be the combination of statistics and accumulated reports by witnesses showing specific cases of favoritism for whites and discrimination against blacks. But there are matters less quantifiable and less ob-

jective in appearance that give point and substance to the whole dreary picture. The attitude of witnesses, the bland show of innocence, the forgetfulness of things that ought to be remembered, the occasional revelations of explicitly racist sentiment, the refusal of one agent to sign the settlement agreement to enforce a regime of nondiscrimination because he thought it was "rammed down the union's throat by the government," the evidence of special and focused nastiness to black men in the hiring hall — such things betray a broad undercurrent of hostility to the decree and the commands of the law giving rise to it. (United States v. Wood, Wire and Metal Lathers, Local 46, 328 F. Supp. 429 at 437 (S.D.N.Y. 1971).)

Racism Hypo 11
BLACK MUSICIANS v. MUSICIANS UNION

Until a few years ago, union musicians belonged to segregated locals in most large cities. Merger efforts by the national union (the American Federation of Musicians) were precipitated by pressure from civil rights groups who pointed out — accurately — that the segregated locals effectively barred black musicians from virtually all the good jobs. Merger, it was hoped, would lead to a selection system based on ability rather than race.

Unfortunately, with infrequent exceptions, this did not happen. When musicians were needed for a recording session, to play with a visiting entertainer or show, at a concert, etc., the local union was called; and, according to black musicians, white musicians were notified to report for the job unless black musicians were specifically requested. As a result, most blacks received assignments only to the black-sponsored club and dance dates that they had filled prior to the merger.

Keenly aware of these problems, black musicians in segregated Local 711 refused to merge with the larger white Local 60 until the merger agreement included the following provisions:

1. No less than two of the five-member board of directors of the merged unions shall be black. Where less than two blacks are elected to the board in the annual at-large elections, the two black candidates receiving the most votes shall be seated. This provision is to be in effect for twenty years.

2. All job assignments made by the merged union will be in accordance with a "Rotation Chart." The union will not make assignments on the basis of "suitability" for the job.

3. The merged union will establish a "Compliance Fund" to ensure that the earnings gap between experienced white and black musicians is closed. For a period of five years, at the end of each year the incomes of all black musicians with five years of seniority shall be subsidized out of the Compliance Fund to the extent required to raise their incomes to $10,000.

Officials of Local 60 refused to agree to the above provisions, claiming that they lacked basis in both law and the facts of union policy. Union officials denied that their present assignment procedure was influenced by racial bias. "Assignments," they claimed "were based on the musician's training, per-

formance experience, and suitability for the job." As to the latter, the union stated that it would prove embarrassing to all concerned to send the average jazz musician (black or white) to an audition for a symphony orchestra position, and that when blacks were deemed qualified for openings, they were sent. The officials added that some jobs would not be suitable for black musicians: assigning blacks to openings with Lawrence Welk–type bands, to ethnic group gatherings (e.g. Polish weddings), or to social affairs at conservative white veterans', blue-collar, and fraternal organizations would mean that these groups would simply cease using union musicians — to the overall detriment of all union personnel. The union contended that the "suitability" policy did not violate federal Civil Rights Statutes and was specifically authorized in Title VII of the Civil Rights Act of 1964.

The black musicians responded that racial discrimination prevented them from getting formal musical training and performance experience, but that they could play as well as the white musicians who were assigned by the union to recording and concert dates. They also denied that the union's suitability criteria were condoned by Title VII or other appropriate civil rights laws. They contended that the union's past commitment to racism necessitated setting up a monitoring mechanism, to ensure that the proposed rotational assignment plan actually would alleviate the loss suffered by black musicians, through the long years of racist exclusion from the mainstream of the music world. They pointed out that white musicians had earned an average of $15,000 per year for the previous five years, while black musicians had averaged only $5000 per year during that period. They stated, "Justice requires and the union should be required to establish the Compliance Fund" described in paragraph 3 of their demands, and suggested that if assignments were fairly made, no eligible black musician should require a subsidy.

The standard merger agreement guaranteed one black seat on the board of directors for a period of five years, and contained no provision for a "Rotation Chart" or "Compliance Fund." When the international threatened to dissolve Local 711 unless it agreed to merge with Local 60 under a standard agreement, Local 711 sought injunctive relief from a federal district court to block the merger. The court has denied the black musicians' request for a temporary restraining order and denied the Musicians Union's motion to dismiss. An early hearing on the black musicians' motion for a preliminary injunction has been set.

Law Firm A will represent the black musicians.

Law Firm B will represent the Musicians Union.

4. Affirmative Remedies

It is clear that the removal of unlawful restrictions is only the first step if court orders in employment discrimination cases are to be effective. In addition, affirmative action designed to eliminate the effects of past and present discriminatory practices must be required of employers and unions.

We have discussed major examples of such action — allowing victims of past discrimination to exercise plantwide seniority, and invalidating tests, qualifications, and transfer and promotion procedures which have the effect of perpetuating discriminatory policies. But further measures may be required where such actions are inadequate to provide effective relief under federal statutes prohibiting employment discrimination.

Thus, where blacks have been excluded by the utilization of hiring sources which screen them out or do not reach them, courts may order employers and unions to adopt affirmative methods of recruitment and job vacancy notification. See United States v. Central Motor Lines, 325 F. Supp. 478 (W.D.N.C. 1972); Johnson v. Georgia Highway Express, Inc., 4 EPD ¶7753 (N.D. Ga. 1972); Lea v. Cone Mills Corporation, 301 F. Supp. 97 (M.D.N.C. 1969).

Victims of discrimination are entitled to back pay under §706(g) of Title VII, and courts have routinely granted back pay under Title VII — see, e.g., Weeks v. Southern Bell Company, 2 EPD ¶8202 (S.D. Ga. 1971); Peters v. Missouri Pacific R.R., 2 EPD ¶8274 (E.D. Tex. 1971) — and under 42 U.S.C. §1983, in public employment cases. Brown v. Gaston County Dyeing Machine Company, 457 F.2d 1377 (4th Cir. 1972), set the measure of back pay as the amount which the employee would have earned, absent the discriminatory practices, less what he did earn or could reasonably have earned in mitigation of damages. In Brown, the period of discrimination was from 1960 to 1961, a time prior to the enactment of Title VII. The court held that Brown was entitled to back pay for this period under 42 U.S.C. §1981. The 1972 Amendments to Title VII limit recovery of back pay to a period beginning no earlier than two years prior to the filing of a discrimination charge with the EEOC (§706(g)). Consider whether this limitation makes feasible, as well as just, orders granting back pay on a class basis.

Proponents of such relief maintain both that it is the only meaningful relief in many cases, and that it would serve as a potent incentive toward compliance with Title VII. See Robinson v. Lorillard Corporation, 444 F.2d 791 (4th Cir. 1971); Sprogis v. United Airlines, Inc., 444 F.2d 1194 (7th Cir. 1971), *cert. denied,* 404 U.S. 991 (1972).

Granting attorneys' fees to prevailing parties, as provided under Title VII, also furthers the enforcement function. Appellate courts have limited the discretion to deny such fees by interpreting the section liberally and suggesting that awards should ordinarily be made unless the circumstances would render them unjust. Robinson v. Lorillard Corp., supra. Standards and factors to be used in determining the amount of counsel fees are discussed in Clark v. American Marine Corporation, 320 F. Supp. 709 (E.D. La. 1970), *aff'd per curiam,* 437 F.2d 959 (5th Cir. 1971).

But while recruitment, back pay and attorneys' fees are important, courts have also granted relief designed to prevent future job bias, including specific provisions requiring preferential treatment for the victims of discrimination. For example, union job referrals have been ordered on an alternating black-white (one-for-one) basis. Local 53, International Association of Heat

& Frost Workers v. Vogler, 407 F.2d 1047 (5th Cir. 1969). See also Carter v. Gallagher, 452 F.2d 315, *modified en banc,* 452 F.2d 327 (8th Cir. 1972), requiring the Minneapolis fire department to hire one black fireman for every two whites. Employers as disparate as a trucking company and a state highway patrol have been ordered to hire one black for every white. United States v. Central Motor Lines, 325 F. Supp. 478 (W.D.N.C. 1970); NAACP v. Allen, 340 F. Supp. 703 (M.D. Ala. 1972). And a union which issues work permits for nonunion personnel has been ordered to issue a mandatory preference of 100 permits to black workers, to issue an additional 250 permits on an alternating black-white basis, and to meet specific percentage "ranges" of minority workers over a period of years. United States v. Local 46, Wood, Wire & Metal Lathers, 341 F. Supp. 694 (S.D.N.Y. 1972).

Perhaps the best-known application of preferential hiring has been the imposition of mandatory percentage "ranges" on the skilled construction trades. An early test of the most widely discussed of these, the Philadelphia Plan, is reviewed here.

CONTRACTORS ASSOCIATION OF EASTERN PENNSYLVANIA v. SECRETARY OF LABOR
442 F.2d 159 (3d Cir. 1971)

HASTIE, Chief Judge, MCLAUGHLIN and GIBBONS, Circuit Judges. GIBBONS, Circuit Judge . . .

[The association, consisting of more than eighty contractors who collectively supervise more than $150,000 of federal and federally assisted construction in the area annually, and individual contractors brought an action challenging the "Philadelphia Plan." The plan required that bidders on federally assisted projects valued at $500,000 or more, in the five-county Philadelphia area, would submit an affirmative action program, including specific goals for hiring minority group workers in six skilled crafts. The plan was promulgated under the authority of Executive Order No. 11246, which provided, inter alia, that contractors for construction of federally assisted projects shall covenant to take affirmative action to ensure nondiscriminatory hiring and conditions of employment. Pursuant to the Executive Order, on June 27, 1969, Assistant Secretary of Labor Fletcher issued an order that, because of the discriminatory practices of the craft unions on which contractors relied as their primary source for workers, definite standards for affirmative action programs were needed in the construction trades in the Philadelphia area. Public hearings were held, after which specific goals for minority hiring were established as a percentage of the total number to be employed in each of the six trades (see the table on page 800).

The percentage goals were determined by the current extent of minority group employment in each trade, the availability of minority group persons for employment, the need for training programs, the need to ensure employment for those in existing programs, and the impact of the federal plan on the

Identification of Trade	*Range of Minority Group Employment (percent)* Until 12/31/70	for 1971	for 1972	for 1973
Ironworkers	5-9	11-15	16-20	22-26
Plumbers & Pipefitters	5-8	10-14	15-19	20-24
Steamfitters	5-8	11-15	15-19	20-24
Sheetmetal workers	4-8	9-13	14-18	19-23
Electrical workers	4-8	9-13	14-18	19-23
Elevator construction workers	4-8	9-13	14-18	19-23

existing labor force. An order of September 23, 1969 specified that no bidder would be awarded a contract unless his affirmative action program contained goals falling within the prescribed range.

In November 1969 the state of Pennsylvania issued invitations to bid on the federally funded construction of a dam in one of the five counties. The secretary of agriculture ordered, as a condition of federal assistance, that each bid include a Philadelphia Plan commitment; the state then issued an addendum requiring that bids comply with the order. In support of their motion to dismiss, the Contractors Association argued that the Philadelphia Plan was illegal for a number of reasons, all of which were presented on appeal after the district court held the plan valid.]

Executive Power

The plaintiffs contend that the Philadelphia Plan is social legislation of local application enacted by the Executive without the benefit of statutory or constitutional authority. . . .

[Here, the court reviewed and distinguished cases cited on this issue by both plaintiffs and defendants. It acknowledged that the limitations of executive power have rarely been considered by the courts, and referred to the opinion of Justice Jackson in Youngstown Sheet & Tube Company v. Sawyer, 343 U.S. 579 (1952), expressing the view that executive powers may be exercised in three situations.]

1. When the President acts pursuant to an express or implied authorization of Congress, his authority is at its maximum, for it includes all that he possesses in his own right plus all that Congress can delegate. In these circumstances, and in these only, may he be said (for what it may be worth) to personify the federal sovereignty. If his act is held unconstitutional under these circumstances, it usually means that the Federal Government as an undivided whole lacks power. A seizure executed by the President pursuant to an Act of Congress would be supported by the strongest of presumptions and the widest latitude of judicial interpretation, and the burden of persuasion would rest heavily on any who might attack it.

2. When the President acts in absence of either a congressional grant or denial of authority, he can only rely upon his own independent powers, but there is a zone

of twilight in which he and Congress may have concurrent authority, or in which its distribution is uncertain. Therefore, congressional inertia, indifference or quiescence may sometimes, at least as a practical matter, enable, if not invite, measures on independent presidential responsibility. In this area, any actual test of power is likely to depend on the imperatives of events and contemporary imponderables rather than on abstract theories of law.

3. When the President takes measures incompatible with the expressed or implied will of Congress, his power is at its lowest ebb, for then he can rely only upon his own constitutional powers minus any constitutional powers of Congress over the matter. Courts can sustain exclusive presidential control in such a case only by disabling the Congress from acting upon the subject. Presidential claim to a power at once so conclusive and preclusive must be scrutinized with caution, for what is at stake is the equilibrium established by our constitutional system.

Plaintiffs contend that the Philadelphia Plan is inconsistent with the will of Congress expressed in several statutes. We deal with these statutory contentions hereinafter. Thus for the moment we may set to one side consideration of Justice Jackson's third category, and turn to category (1), action expressly or impliedly authorized, and category (2), action in which the President has implied power to act in the absence of congressional preemption. To determine into which category the Philadelphia Plan falls a review of Executive Orders in the field of fair employment practices is helpful.

The first such order, Executive Order No. 8802,[25] was signed by President Roosevelt on June 25, 1941. It established in the Office of Production Management a Committee on Fair Employment Practice, and it required that all Government contracting agencies include in all defense contracts a covenant not to discriminate against any worker because of race, creed, color, or national origin. The order contained no specific statutory reference, and describes the action "as a prerequisite to the successful conduct of our national defense production effort." In December 1941 Congress enacted "An Act to expedite the prosecution of the war effort,"[26] and on December 27, 1941, pursuant to that Act the President issued Executive Order No. 9001[27] which granted to the War and Navy Departments and the Maritime Commission broad contracting authority. This order among other provisions stated that a non-discrimination clause would be deemed incorporated by reference to all such contracts. On May 27, 1943, Executive Order No. 8802 was amended by Executive Order No. 9346[28] which established in the Office for Emergency Management of the Executive Office of the President a Committee on Fair Employment Practice. This order required the antidiscrimination clause in all government contracts rather than in defense contracts only. Still, the order was quite clearly bottomed on the President's war mobilization powers and was by its terms directed toward enhancing the pool of workers available for defense production.

25. 6 Fed. Reg. 3109, 3 C.F.R., 1938-43 Comp. 957.
26. Act of Dec. 18, 1941, ch. 593, 55 Stat. 838.
27. 6 Fed. Reg. 6787, 3 C.F.R., 1938-43 Comp. 1054.
28. 8 Fed. Reg. 7183, 3 C.F.R. 1938-43 Comp. 1280.

On December 18, 1945, President Truman signed Executive Order No. 9664,[29] which continued the Committee established by Executive Orders Nos. 8802 and 9346 "for the periods and subject to the conditions stated in the National War Agencies Appropriation Act, 1946 (Public Law 156, 79th Cong., 1st Sess., approved July 17, 1945)." On February 2, 1951, the President signed Executive Order No. 10210,[30] which transferred to the Department of Defense the contracting powers referred to in Executive Order No. 9001. The order continued the provision that a non-discrimination clause would be deemed incorporated by reference in all defense contracts. It referenced the First War Powers Act, 1941, as amended. By a subsequent series of Executive Orders, Executive Order No. 10210 was extended to other Government agencies engaged in defense related procurement. On December 3, 1951 the President signed Executive Order No. 10308,[32] creating the Committee on Government Contract Compliance, which was charged with the duty of obtaining compliance with the non-discrimination contract provisions. The statutory authorities referenced in Executive Order No. 10308 are the Defense Production Act of 1950[33] and 31 U.S.C. §691.[34] Reference to the Defense Production Act of 1950 shows that the President was still acting, pursuant to his national defense powers, to assure maximum utilization of available manpower.

President Eisenhower on August 13, 1953, by Executive Order No. 10479[35] revoked Executive Order No. 10308 and transferred the compliance functions of the Committee on Government Contract Compliance to the Government Contract Committee.[36] In this order for the first time there is no mention of defense production. For the first time the Committee is authorized to receive complaints of violations, and to conduct activities not directly related to federal procurement.[38] On September 3, 1954, by Executive Order No. 10557[39] the

29. 10 Fed. Reg. 15301, 3 C.F.R., 1943-48 Comp. 480.

30. 15 Fed. Reg. 1049, 3 C.F.R., 1949-53 Comp. 390.

32. 16 Fed. Reg. 12303, 3 C.F.R., 1949-53 Comp. 837.

33. 50 U.S.C. App. §2061 et seq.

34. This latter reference is to the source of appropriations for salaries and expenses for committee members and staff. It appears in numerous subsequent Executive Orders, but has no significance other than fiscal.

35. 18 Fed. Reg. 4899, 3 C.F.R., 1949-53 Comp. 961.

36. The new committee was composed of 15 members, 9 named by the President and one representative each from the Atomic Energy Commission, the Department of Commerce, the Department of Defense, the Department of Justice, the Department of Labor and the General Services Administration. Id. §3, as amended by Exec. Order No. 10482, 18 Fed. Reg. 4944 (Aug. 15, 1953), 3 C.F.R., 1949-53 Comp. 968.

38. "Sec. 6. The Committee shall encourage the furtherance of an educational program by employer, labor, civic, educational, religious, and other voluntary non-governmental groups in order to eliminate or reduce the basic causes and costs of discrimination in employment.

"Sec. 7. The Committee is authorized to establish and maintain cooperative relationships with agencies of state and local governments, as well as with nongovernmental bodies, to assist in achieving the purposes of this order." Id. §§6, 7.

39. 19 Fed. Reg. 5655, 3 C.F.R., 1954-58 Comp. 203.

required form of Government contract provision was revised. The new provision was much more specific, required the imposition of the contractor's obligation on his subcontractors, and required the posting of appropriate notices. The Eisenhower orders, while they did not refer to defense production and did authorize the Compliance Committee to encourage nondiscrimination outside the field of Government contracts, were still restricted in direct application to federal government procurement. While the orders do not contain any specific statutory reference other than the appropriations statute, 31 U.S.C. §690, they would seem to be authorized by the broad grant of procurement authority with respect to Titles 40 and 41.[40] No less than in the case of defense procurement it is in the interest of the United States in all procurement to see that its suppliers are not over the long run increasing its costs and delaying its programs by excluding from the labor pool available minority workmen. In the area of Government procurement Executive authority to impose non-discrimination contract provisions falls in Justice Jackson's first category: action pursuant to the express or implied authorization of Congress.

Executive Order No. 10925[41] signed by President Kennedy on March 6, 1961, among other things enlarged the notice requirements and specified that the President's Committee on Equal Employment Opportunity could by rule, regulation or order impose sanctions for violation. Coverage still extended only to federal government contracts. Significantly for purposes of this case, however, the required contract language was amended to add the provision: "The Contractor will take affirmative action to ensure that applicants are employed, and that employees are treated during employment, without regard to their race, creed, color, or national origin."[42] The Philadelphia Plan is simply a refined approach to this "affirmative action" mandate. Applied to federal procurement the affirmative action clause is supported by the same Presidential procurement authority that supports the non-discrimination clause generally.

The most significant change in the Executive Order program for present purposes occurred on June 22, 1963 when the President signed Executive Order No. 11114,[43] which amended Executive Order No. 10925 by providing that the same non-discrimination contract provisions heretofore required in all federal procurement contracts must also be included in all federally assisted construction contracts. By way of Executive Order No. 11246 issued in 1965, President Johnson transferred to the Secretary of Labor the functions formerly specified in Executive Order Nos. 10925 and 11114, and he continued both the affirmative action requirement and the coverage of federally assisted construction contracts.

While all federal procurement contracts must include an affirmative action covenant,[45] the coverage on federally assisted contracts has been extended

40. See 40 U.S.C. §486(a).
41. 26 Fed. Reg. 1977, 3 C.F.R., 1959-63 Comp. 448.
42. Id., pt. III, §301(1).
43. 28 Fed. Reg. 6485, 3 C.F.R., 1959-63 Comp. 774.
45. Section 204 of Exec. Order No. 11246 provides that the Secretary of Labor may

to construction contracts only. This choice is significant, for it demonstrates that the Presidents were not attempting by the Executive Order program merely to impose their notions of desirable social legislation on the states wholesale. Rather, they acted in the one area in which discrimination in employment was most likely to affect the cost and the progress of projects in which the federal government had both financial and completion interests. In direct procurement the federal government has a vital interest in assuring that the largest possible pool of qualified manpower be available for the accomplishment of its projects. It has the identical interest with respect to federally assisted construction projects. When the Congress authorizes an appropriation for a program of federal assistance, and authorizes the Executive branch to implement the program by arranging for assistance to specific projects, in the absence of specific statutory regulations it must be deemed to have granted to the President a general authority to act for the protection of federal interests. In the case of Executive Order Nos. 11246 and 11114 three Presidents have acted by analogizing federally assisted construction to direct federal procurement. If such action has not been authorized by Congress (Justice Jackson's first category), at the least it falls within the second category. If no congressional enactments prohibit what has been done, the Executive action is valid. Particularly is this so when Congress, aware of Presidential action with respect to federally assisted construction projects since June of 1963, has continued to make appropriations for such projects. We conclude, therefore, that unless the Philadelphia Plan is prohibited by some other congressional enactment, its inclusion as a pre-condition for federal assistance was within the implied authority of the President and his designees. We turn, then to a consideration of the statutes on which plaintiffs rely.

The Civil Rights Act of 1964

Plaintiffs suggest that by enacting Title VII of the Civil Rights Act of 1964, 42 U.S.C. §2000e et seq., which deals comprehensively with discrimination in employment, Congress occupied the field. The express reference in that statute to Executive Order No. 10925 or any other Executive Order prescribing fair employment practices for Government contractors, 42 U.S.C. §2000e-8(d), indicates, however, that Congress contemplated continuance of the Executive Order program. Moreover we have held that the remedies established by Title VII are not exclusive. Young v. International Telephone & Telegraph Co., 438 F.2d 757 (3d Cir. 1971).

But while Congress has not prohibited Presidential action in the area of fair employment on federal or federally assisted contracts, the Executive is bound by the express prohibitions of Title VII. The argument most strenu-

exempt certain contracts and purchase orders from the requirements of the order because of special circumstances in the national interest and that he may by rule or regulation exempt certain classes of contracts (1) to be performed outside the United States, (2) for standard commercial supplies or raw materials, (3) involving insubstantial amounts of money or workers, or (4) involving subcontracts below a specified tier.

ously advanced against the Philadelphia Plan is that it requires action by employers which violates the Act. Plaintiffs point to §703(j), 42 U.S.C. §2000e-2(j):

> Nothing contained in this subchapter shall be interpreted to require any employer . . . [or] labor organization . . . to grant preferential treatment to any individual or to any group because of the race . . . of such individual or groups on account of an imbalance which may exist with respect to the total number or percentage of persons of any race . . . employed . . . in comparison with the total number or percentage of persons of such race . . . in the available work force in any community . . . or other area.

The Plan requires that the contractor establish specific goals for utilization of available minority manpower in six trades in the five-county area. Possibly an employer could not be compelled, under the authority of Title VII, to embrace such a program, although §703(j) refers to percentages of minorities in an area work force rather than percentages of minority tradesmen in an available trade work force. We do not meet that issue here, however, for the source of the required contract provision is Executive Order No. 11246. Section 703(j) is a limitation only upon Title VII not upon any other remedies, state or federal.

Plaintiffs, and more particularly the union amici, contend that the Plan violates Title VII because it interferes with a bona fide seniority system. Section 703(h), 42 U.S.C. §2000e-2(h). . . . The unions, it is said, refer men from the hiring halls on the basis of seniority, and the Philadelphia Plan interferes with this arrangement since few minority tradesmen have high seniority. Just as with §703(j), however, §703(h) is a limitation only upon Title VII, not upon any other remedies.

Plaintiffs contend that the Plan, by imposing remedial quotas, requires them to violate the basic prohibitions of Section 703(a), 42 U.S.C. §2000e-2(a):

> It shall be an unlawful employment practice for an employer —
> (1) to fail or refuse to hire . . . any individual . . . because of such individual's race . . . or
> (2) to . . . classify his employees in any way which would deprive . . . any individual of employment opportunities . . . because of such individual's race. . . .

Because the Plan requires that the contractor agree to specific goals for minority employment in each of the six trades and requires a good faith effort to achieve those goals, they argue, it requires (1) that they refuse to hire some white tradsmen, and (2) that they classify their employees by race, in violation of §703(a). This argument rests on an overly simple reading both of the Plan and of the findings which led to its adoption.

The order of September 23, 1969 contained findings that although overall minority group representation in the construction industry in the five-county Philadelphia area was thirty per cent, in the six trades representation was approximately one per cent. It found, moreover, that this obvious underrepresentation was due to the exclusionary practices of the unions representing the six trades. It is the practice of building contractors to rely on union hiring halls as the prime source for employees. The order made further findings as to the availability of qualified minority tradesmen for employment in each trade, and as to the impact of an affirmative action program with specific goals upon the existing labor force. The Department of Labor found that contractors could commit to the specific employment goals "without adverse impact on the existing labor force." Some minority tradesmen could be recruited, in other words, without eliminating job opportunities for white tradesmen.

To read §703(a) in the manner suggested by the plaintiffs we would have to attribute to Congress the intention to freeze the status quo and to foreclose remedial action under other authority designed to overcome existing evils. We discern no such intention either from the language of the statute or from its legislative history. Clearly the Philadelphia Plan is color-conscious. Indeed the only meaning which can be attributed to the "affirmative action" language which since March of 1961 has been included in successive Executive Orders is that Government contractors must be color-conscious. Since 1941 the Executive Order program has recognized that discriminatory practices exclude available minority manpower from the labor pool. In other contexts color-consciousness has been deemed to be an appropriate remedial posture. [Citations omitted.]

It has been said respecting Title VII that "Congress did not intend to freeze an entire generation of Negro employees into discriminatory patterns that existed before the Act." Quarles v. Philip Morris, Inc., supra, 279 F. Supp. at 514. The Quarles case rejected the contention that existing, nondiscriminatory seniority arrangements were so sanctified by Title VII that the effects of past discrimination in job assignments could not be overcome. We reject the contention that Title VII prevents the President acting through the Executive Order program from attempting to remedy the absence from the Philadelphia construction labor of minority tradesmen in key trades.

What we have said about Title VII applies with equal force to Title VI of the Civil Rights Act of 1964, 42 U.S.C. §2000d et seq. That Title prohibits racial and other discrimination in any program or activity receiving federal financial assistance. This general prohibition against discrimination cannot be construed as limiting Executive authority in defining appropriate affirmative action on the part of a contractor.

We hold that the Philadelphia Plan does not violate the Civil Rights Act of 1964.

The National Labor Relations Act

The June 27, 1969 order, par. 8(b) provides:

> It is no excuse that the union with which the contractor has a collective bargaining agreement failed to refer minority employees. Discrimination in referral for

employment, even if pursuant to provisions of a collective bargaining agreement, is prohibited by the National Labor Relations Act and the Civil Rights Act of 1964. It is the longstanding uniform policy of OFCC that contractors and subcontractors have a responsibility to provide equal employment opportunity if they want to participate in federally involved contracts. To the extent they have delegated the responsibility for some of their employment practices to some other organization or agency which prevents them from meeting their obligations pursuant to Executive Order 11246, as amended, such contractors cannot be considered to be in compliance with Executive Order 11246, as amended, or the implementing rules, regulations and orders.

The union amici vigorously contend that the Plan violates the National Labor Relations Act by interfering with the exclusive union referral systems to which the contractors have in collective bargaining agreements bound themselves. . . . Of course collective bargaining agreements which perpetuate the effects of past discrimination are unlawful under Title VII. . . . The findings of past discrimination which justified remedial action in these cases were made in judicial proceedings, however. See 42 U.S.C. §2000e-5(g). The amici contend that the Assistant Secretary's nonjudicial finding of prior exclusionary practices is insufficient to support the Plan's implied requirement that the contractor look to other sources for employees if the unions fail to refer sufficient minority group members.

It is clear that while hiring hall arrangements are permitted by federal law they are not required. Nothing in the National Labor Relations Act purports to place any limitation upon the contracting power of the federal government. We have said hereinabove that in imposing the affirmative action requirement on federally assisted construction contracts the President acted within his implied contracting authority. The assisted agency may either agree to do business with contractors who will comply with the affirmative action covenant, or forego assistance. The prospective contractors may either agree to undertake the affirmative action covenant, or forego bidding on federally assisted work. If the Plan violates neither the Constitution nor federal law, the fact that its contractual provisions may be at variance with other contractual undertakings of the contractor is legally irrelevant. Factually, of course, that variance is quite relevant. Factually it is entirely likely that the economics of the marketplace will produce an accommodation between the contract provisions desired by the unions and those desired by the source of the funds. Such an accommodation will be no violation of the National Labor Relations Act.

The absence of a judicial finding of past discrimination is also legally irrelevant. The Assistant Secretary acted not pursuant to Title VII but pursuant to the Executive Order. Regardless of the cause, exclusion from the available labor pool of minority tradesmen is likely to have an adverse effect upon the cost and completion of construction projects in which the federal government is interested. Even absent a finding that the situation found to exist in the five-county area was the result of deliberate past discrimination, the federal interest in improving the availability of key tradesmen in the labor pool would be the same. While a court must find intentional past discrimination before it can require affirmative action under 42 U.S.C. §2000e-5(g), that section imposes no restraint upon the measures which the President may require of the beneficiaries of federal assistance. The decision of his designees as to the specific affirmative action which would satisfy the local situation did not violate the National Labor Relations Act and was not prohibited by 42 U.S.C. §2000e-5(g).

Consistency with Executive Order No. 11246

The plaintiffs argue that the affirmative action mandate of §202 of Executive Order No. 11246 is limited by the more general requirement in the same section, "The contractor will not discriminate against any employee or applicant for employment because of race, creed, color, or national origin." They contend that properly construed the affirmative action referred to means only policing against actual present discrimination, not action looking toward the employment of specific numbers of minority tradesmen.

Section 201 of the Executive Order provides:

> The Secretary of Labor shall be responsible for the administration of Parts II [Government contracts] and III [federal assistance] of this Order and shall adopt such rules and regulations and issue such orders as he deems necessary and appropriate to achieve the purposes thereof.

Acting under this broad delegation of authority the Labor Department in a series of orders of local application made it clear that it interpreted "affirmative action" to require more than mere policing against actual present discrimination. Administrative action pursuant to an Executive Order is invalid and subject to judicial review if beyond the scope of the Executive Order. . . . But the courts should give more than ordinary deference to an administrative agency's interpretation of an Executive Order or regulation which it is charged to administer. . . .

The Attorney General has issued an opinion that the Philadelphia Plan is valid, and the President has continued to acquiesce in the interpretation of the Executive Order made by his designee. The Labor Department interpretation of the affirmative action clause must, therefore, be deferred to by the courts. . . .

The Due Process Contentions

Plaintiffs urge that the Plan violates the Due Process Clause of the Fifth Amendment in several ways.

First, they allege that it imposes on the contractors contradictory duties impossible of attainment. This impossibility arises, they say, because the Plan requires both an undertaking to seek achievement of specific goals of minority employment and an undertaking not to discriminate against any qualified applicant or employee, and because a decision to hire any black employee necessarily involves a decision not to hire a qualified white employee. This is pure sophistry. The findings in the September 23, 1969 order disclosed that the specific goals may be met, considering normal employee attrition and anticipated growth in the industry, without adverse effects on the existing labor force. According to the order the construction industry has an essentially transitory labor force and is often in short supply in key trades. The complaint does not allege that these findings misstate the underlying facts.

Next the plaintiffs urge that the Plan is arbitrary and capricious administrative action, in that it singles out the contractors and makes them take action to remedy the situation created by acts of past discrimination by the craft unions. They point to the absence of any proceedings under Title VII against the offending unions, and urge that they are being discriminated against. This argument misconceives the source of the authority for the affirmative action program. Plaintiffs are not being discriminated against. They are merely being invited to bid on a contract with terms imposed by the source of the funds. The affirmative action covenant is no different in kind than other covenants specified in the invitation to bid. The Plan does not impose a punishment for past misconduct. It exacts a covenant for present performance.

Some amici urge that selection of the five-county Philadelphia area was arbitrary and capricious and without basis in fact. The complaint contains a conclusive allegation to this effect. . . . We read the allegation with respect to the five-county area as putting in issue the legal authority of the Secretary to impose a specific affirmative action requirement in any separate geographic area. The simple answer to this contention is that federally assisted construction contracts are performed at specific times and in specific places. What is appropriate affirmative action will vary according to the local manpower conditions prevailing at the time.

Finally, the plaintiffs urge that the specific goals specified by the Plan are racial quotas prohibited by the equal protection aspect of the Fifth Amendment. . . . The Philadelphia Plan is valid Executive action designed to remedy the perceived evil that minority tradesmen have not been included in the labor pool available for the performance of construction projects in which the federal government has a cost and performance interest. The Fifth Amendment does not prohibit such action.

One final point . . . . Several amici . . . contend that neither the finding of past discrimination by the craft unions made in the June 27, 1969 order nor the statistical findings as to availability of minority tradesmen, employee attrition, and industry growth made in the September 23, 1969 order should be accepted as true. . . .

We need not decide that issue, however, for in our view the data in the September 23, 1969 order revealing the percentages of utilization of minority group tradesmen in the six trades compared with the availability of such tradesmen in the five-county area, justified issuance of the order without regard to a finding as to the cause of the situation. The federal interest is in maximum availability of construction tradesmen for the projects in which the federal government has a cost and completion interest. A finding as to the historical reason for the exclusion of available tradesmen from the labor pool is not essential for federal contractual remedial action.

The judgment of the district court will be affirmed.

NOTES

1. The Supreme Court denied certiorari in the Contractors Association case, 404 U.S. 854 (1972), and other courts approved similar preferential hiring plans. See James v. Ogilvie, 310 F. Supp. 661 (N.D. Ill. 1970); Joyce v. McCrane, 320 F. Supp. 1284 (D.N.J. 1970); Carpenters v. Conforti & Eiselle, 3 F.E.P. Cases 1218 (D.N.J. 1971). The validity of government-imposed affirmative action provisions in construction contracts was also approved in Weiner v. Cuyahoga Community College District, Ohio Ct. C.P., 238 N.E.2d 839 (1968); and Ethridge v. Rhodes, 268 F. Supp. 83 (S.D. Ohio 1967).

2. Initially, there were high hopes for the Philadelphia Plan and its voluntary "hometown" plan progeny. See Note, The Philadelphia Plan: Equal Employment Opportunity in the Construction Trades, 6 Colum. J. Law & Social Problems 187 (1970). But after a year or so, another commentator concluded that the Department of Labor's efforts to seek voluntary, rather than court-ordered, "hometown" plans have limited the effectiveness of the Philadelphia-type imposed plan. Gould, Racial Discrimination, the Courts, and Construction, 11 Industrial Relations 380, 391 (1972). The same writer had concluded earlier that "voluntarism failed miserably. In Chicago, which was the AFL-CIO's highly vaunted answer to Philadelphia, the plan's promise was to recruit 3,000 minority journeymen, apprentices and on-the-job trainees. Few workers have been placed. . . ." Gould, Blacks and the General Lockout, N.Y. Times, July 17, 1971 at 23. An evaluation of both plans predicted that only the threat of racial strife would put sufficient pressure on the governments, contractors, and unions involved to achieve enforcement. Comment, The Philadelphia Plan vs. the Chicago Plan: Alternative Approaches For Integrating the Construction Industry, 1965 Nw. U.L. Rev. 642 (1970). Another writer reviewed the operation of government-sponsored voluntary plans in several large cities; he concluded that they have generally been a failure, and predicted a similar fate for the Philadelphia Plan because of major opposition from the unions and "the traditional refusal of the federal government to terminate [construction] contracts even where racial discrimination is apparent. . . ." Donegan, The Philadelphia Plan: A Viable Means of Achieving Equal Opportunity in the Construction Industry or More Pie in the Sky? 20 Kan. L. Rev. 195, 210 (1972). For an equally pessimistic view, see Jones, The Bugaboo of Employment Quotas, 1970 Wis. L. Rev. 341.

3. Executive Order 11246, 3 C.F.R. 611, 42 U.S.C. §2000e (Supp. III,

1967), is a modern version of Executive Order No. 8802, issued in June 1941 by President Roosevelt during the pre–World War II industrial mobilization. It was a response to pressure by a coalition of black groups led by A. Philip Randolph, president of the Brotherhood of Sleeping Car Porters, who threatened a major march on the nation's capital to protest racial discrimination in the growing defense industry.

The history of Executive Order 11246 and its rather disreputable enforcement record is reviewed in Note, Executive Order 11246: Anti-Discrimination Obligations in Government Contracts, 44 N.Y.U. L. Rev. 590 (1969). See also Nash, Affirmative Action Under Executive Order 11246, 46 N.Y.U.L. Rev. 225 (1971).

QUESTIONS

1. Economist John Kenneth Galbraith points out that affirmative action efforts in the fair employment field have all been directed at entry-level jobs, where white resistance based on racial hostility and the threat to economic and class status are great; while virtually nothing has been done about the fact that 96 percent of America's jobs that pay over $15,000 a year are held by white males, with women, blacks and Spanish-speaking citizens dividing the remaining 4 percent. He suggests federal legislation for a "Minorities Advancement Plan," requiring firms and federal agencies with more than two to five thousand employees to submit plans under which they will, during the next five to fifteen years (depending on firm size), recruit, train and place in their "$15,000 and over" salary hierarchy sufficient women and minorities to conform the representation of such employees with their distribution in the working force of the communities in which they operate. Galbraith, Kuh and Thurow, The Galbraith Plan to Promote the Minorities, N.Y. Times magazine, Aug. 22, 1971, at 9.

The advantages of such a plan are great, but opposition from employers and middle-class whites would likely be potent. Is there any chance that such legislation could be enacted? Given carefully drawn litigation urging such relief against a major firm under existing fair employment law, would the courts be willing to set aside the greater discretion generally given employers in filling higher-level jobs, and grant relief? What type of proof would be required to overcome the "business necessity" arguments that firms would likely advance in defense?

2. Some affirmative action advocates see potential violations of existing law in the present trend for urban-based firms to move their plants and offices to outlying areas, where blacks have great difficulty in following because of transportation difficulties and housing discrimination in the suburbs. Would legislation or litigation to halt such moves, unless employers provided transportation and housing for minority employees, be likely to receive any more consideration from Congress and the courts than the Galbraith plan? What of the "business necessity" argument here? See Blumrosen, The Duty to Plan for Fair Employment: Plant Location in White Suburbia, 25 Rutgers L. Rev. 383 (1971).

Racism Hypo 12
COMPANIES, INC. v. INNER-CITY BLACK WORKERS

Companies, Inc., a major manufacturing corporation located in a decaying section of Inner-City, has announced that in six months it plans to follow the trend of many companies, including several of its competitors, and relocate its plant in the suburbs. It has chosen, after much research, Quiet Acres, a traditional upper middle–class suburban town thirty-five miles away from Inner-City. Quiet Acres recently altered its large-lot single-residence zoning structure, to permit development of its open lands by industries willing to build new plants that blend into the landscape.

Since 1965, Companes, Inc. has recruited and hired almost 250 black workers at its 2,000-man plant. Most of the blacks perform the less skilled jobs and live in Inner-City. They fear for their jobs because many do not have cars and there is no public transportation to Quiet Acres. Complaints by the black workers about the proposed move have brought this response from Companies, Inc.:

> *This move is the result of decisions based on economic necessity, business preference and executive convenience. It was made despite, not because of, the hardship it would pose for our minority group workers. We tried to get Quiet Acres to consider altering its zoning laws to permit the construction of low-income housing, which we would sponsor, but they refused. The request that we provide transportation for black workers is not economically feasible, and would expose us to charges of reverse discrimination because we are not providing transportation for our 1750 white employees. We will miss our black workers but will not miss the crime, taxes, pollution and congestion of Inner-City.*

In fact, some of companies' black workers plan to form car pools and commute to Quiet Acres, but most have not been able to make such arrangements, and few have been able to follow the lead of most of Companies' white employees and obtain housing in or near Quiet Acres close to the new plant. A black workers' caucus, having made no progress in efforts to get Companies to reconsider its relocation decision, has filed suit in federal court under Title VII and 42 U.S.C. §1981. The suit charges that the planned relocation is a discriminatory employment practice that will have a devastating effect on the minority work force. Conceding that the move may be a business convenience for Companies, Inc., the suit asserts that it is not a business necessity as defined by recent employment cases. The black workers request the court to enjoin the move or, alternatively, to order Companies, Inc. to: (1) provide minority workers with housing near the new plant site or transportation to reach it at costs no higher than those they now pay; and (2) obtain comparable positions with other employers for those not wishing to commute or move to Quiet Acres.

Law Firm A will represent the black workers.

Law Firm B will represent Companies, Inc.

14. EMPLOYMENT DISCRIMINATION AND BLACK SELF-HELP EFFORTS

The need for militant action to overcome racism in the employment field has not escaped the black worker. Continuing opposition to fair employment laws by unions, as well as employers, has made black workers recognize that, unless they protect black interests, those interests will receive little more than lip service. Increasingly, special groups of black workers have organized "ad hoc committees" or "black caucuses" to negotiate with company and union officials a whole range of demands — increasing the number of black employees, ending discriminatory hiring qualifications, increasing training opportunities, providing transportation for black workers, and demanding upgrading of blacks to leadership positions both on the job and in union ranks. These workers are also demanding recognition of their blackness through special holidays on the birthdays of black leaders, such as Martin Luther King or Malcolm X, the serving of "soul food" in company cafeterias, the provision of all-black dressing rooms and other facilities for those who want them, etc.

As with the black college student movement in the late 1960s, pressures exerted by the black workers sometime bring results without litigation. But often the issues raised by these increasingly militant activists are presented to courts for resolution. This chapter examines the result when the rights of those resorting to direct action tactics are weighed by existing legal rules, particularly rules designed to promote the orderly settlement of labor disputes.

NATIONAL LABOR RELATIONS BOARD v. TANNER MOTOR LIVERY, LTD.
419 F.2d 216 (9th Cir. 1969)

Before Barnes, Duniway and Ely, Circuit Judges.

Duniway, Circuit Judge:

The National Labor Relations Board petitions for enforcement of its order entered after we had remanded the case to the Board for further proceedings. Initially, the Board found that Tanner had unlawfully discharged two employees for engaging in concerted activities which were protected by the National Labor Relations Act, as amended. See 148 N.L.R.B. 1402 (1964). In NLRB v. Tanner Motor Livery, Ltd., 9 Cir., 1965, 349 F.2d 1, we agreed with the Board that an attempt by two employees, acting in concert, to persuade their employer to hire Negroes was within the protection of section 7 of the

Act, 29 U.S.C. §157. We remanded to the Board for it to consider whether an employer could discharge employees who picket in support of their aims when there is an established collective bargaining representative having a contract with the employer, and the employees do not act or seek to act through that representative.

The Board on remand held that such consideration was neither essential nor necessary. It indicated that

> The employees were not acting in derogation of their established bargaining agent by seeking to eliminate what they deemed to be a morally unconscionable, if not unlawful, condition of employment. In these circumstances, we are unable to find that the Union's status as the employee's exclusive bargaining agent was infringed, imperiled, or otherwise undermined.
>
> In addition, . . . we must assume that these employees were acting in accord with, and in furtherance of, the lawful position of their bargaining agent. For the Board to find therefore, that the employee's otherwise protected concerted activities herein were rendered unprotected by virtue of an existing collective-bargaining agreement between Union and the Respondent would be offensive to public policy. [Footnotes omitted.]

A dissenter would have dismissed the complaint.

The Board's opinion obfuscates the issue somewhat, but the very troublesome question presented by this case remains: to what extent does section 9(a) (29 U.S.C. §159(a)) limit or remove the protection afforded employees by section 7? To the answering of this question the Board has contributed nothing but an ipse dixit. We therefore deem it our duty further to explore the question.

Section 7 guarantees that employees shall have the right to engage in concerted activities, but section 9(a) expresses a strong Congressional policy for an exclusive bargaining representative selected by the majority of the employees in a bargaining unit. The case is complicated by the racial character of the concerted employee activities. The employees, Abramson and Dorbin, were picketing in support of a highly desirable objective. Nonetheless, this fact should not be permitted, per se, to obscure the question. See Getman, The Protection of Economic Pressure by Section 7 of the National Labor Relations Act, 115 U. Pa. L. Rev. 1195, 1245-46, nn. 199, 200 (1967) (commenting on our prior decision in this case).

I

As we indicated in our first opinion, the desire for nondiscriminatory hiring does relate to terms and conditions of employment. Accordingly, we held that the concerted activities of Abramson and Dorbin in support of this desire would be protected by section 7 if no bargaining representative had been present. NLRB v. Tanner Motor Livery, Ltd., supra, 349 F.2d at 4. Our first opinion also noted that section 9(a)'s provision for an exclusive bargaining representative reserves the right of individual employees or groups of employees to deal with the employer regarding "grievances." But we suggested that the desire "for non-discriminatory hiring, while a proper subject for collective bargaining, may not be a proper basis for a grievance." 349 F.2d at 5. The desire relates to a condition of employment affecting the entire bargaining unit; it is not personal to Abramson or Dorbin. . . . Because it is a proper subject of bargaining between the union and the employer, the union by section 9(a) has been vested with the task of vindicating the employees' interest. Thus, the chief question presented is, to what extent does this vesting cut off minority employee rights under section 7? Further, what relevance does the existence of a collective bargaining contract have — and is it important that the contract has anti-discrimination provisions? Finally, would employees have to go through the union even in the absence of a specific anti-discrimination clause in the contract?

The leading case in this general area is NLRB v. Draper Corp., 4 Cir., 1944, 145 F.2d 199 . . . . There a union had been selected as the employees' bargaining agent and had made a collective bargaining contract with the employer. The contract expired, and a minority group of employees struck to protest delay in renegotiating the contract. The union did not sanction the strike, but neither was there any evidence of a split between the union and the "wildcat" strikers. The company fired the strikers; the Board held that the activity was protected under section 7 and that the discharges were discriminatory. The Fourth Circuit reversed, holding that a minority had "no right to take independent action to interfere with the course of bargaining which is being carried on by the duly authorized bargaining agent chosen by the majority." 145 F.2d at 203.

Draper looked for support to a concept of orderly collective bargaining in which the employer dealt with one party, the designated union. The employer was to look to the union for all demands and concerted economic activity supporting those demands. In Draper the employees had not formulated separate demands but had engaged in activity which amounted to independent unsolicited support for the union's position.

We have cited and followed Draper in situations where a minority struck without authorization from a union which had been designated as the bargaining representative. . . .

We have reached a contrary result where the employees were not represented by a union . . . .

To summarize, we believe that the Board's current position could be stated as follows: The union itself could bargain about the desire for non-discriminatory hiring. Indeed, it may be an unfair labor practice for it not to represent the employees fairly, which representation includes a requirement that it must neither practice nor tolerate racial discrimination.[3] Thus in this case it

3. See Local Union No. 12, United Rubber Workers, etc., v. NLRB, 5 Cir., 1966, 368 F.2d 12: cf. Vaca v. Sipes, 386 U.S. 171 . . . . But see NLRB v. Miranda Fuel Co., 2 Cir., 1963, 326 F.2d 172.

must be presumed that the union had adopted a position at least similar to that taken by the two individual employees. Then it must further be assumed that the strikers were acting in furtherance of the union's policies. Section 9(a) does protect majority choice against minority action. But where no interference can possibly be shown, all complaints and economic pressure should not be required to emanate from the bargaining representative. Moreover, the employer should not be allowed to benefit from the union's failure to authorize the particular type of economic action employed by the minority.

In rebuttal Tanner argues that section 9(a) provides that the selected representative shall be the exclusive representative of all employees in the unit. This exclusivity extends not only to bargaining positions but also to types of supporting activity. Draper and similar cases recognize that section 9(a) sets up a procedure for collective bargaining in which employee sentiment is aired within the union and expressed in a position adopted by a union majority. The employer can then deal with the union knowing that its position reflects shared objectives of the members. Finally, dissidents have the obligation to go first to the union to win support for their position.

The split between the positions of the parties . . . arises from two disparate views of the union as an institution. The Act does not by its terms select one view over the other, but policies expressed in the Act and Supreme Court decisions applying these policies give us some guidance beyond that provided in . . . Draper.

NLRB v. Allis-Chalmers Mfg. Co., 1967, 388 U.S. 175, . . . presented a different facet of the interplay between sections 7 and 9(a). There a union had called a strike against an employer in support of new contract demands, but some union members crossed picket lines to work during the strike. The union assessed fines of $20 to $100 against the non-strikers. The Seventh Circuit en banc found that the non-strikers' actions were protected by section 7 and accordingly held that assessment of the fines violated section 8(b)(1)(A) of the Act. The Supreme Court reversed, at least implying that "by joining a union an employee gives up or waives some of his §7 rights." The opinion of the Court found support for its decision in such interests as not wishing to limit a union's power as the exclusive bargaining agent (388 U.S. at 183-184), leaving certain internal affairs to union self-government (388 U.S. at 186-192), and recognizing the effect of the Landrum-Griffin amendments in requiring "democratic principles, fair procedures and freedom of speech . . . [in] all aspects of union affairs." (388 U.S. at 195.) These same interests support the characterization of a union as "an institution in which employee sentiment can be crystallized and expressed." Getman, supra, 115 U. Pa. L. Rev. at 1246.

Allis-Chalmers was followed in Scofield v. NLRB, 1969, 394 U.S. 423. . . . There some production employees of the Wisconsin Motor Corporation were being paid on a piecework basis. The union representing the employees had by rule imposed a ceiling on the production for which its members could accept piecework pay. Scofield and other employees exceeded the ceiling and were paid by Wisconsin for the excess. The union then imposed fines of $50 to $100 and a year's suspension from the union for violating its rule. The Court's opinion in Scofield found the piecework rule to be related to the internal affairs of the union, and accordingly relied on Allis-Chalmers and the weight which was given there to requirements for democratic union decision-making processes to uphold the union rule as applied to union members. See 394 U.S. at 429. . . .

In our view, Allis-Chalmers in particular recognizes a growing tendency to insure that an individual member's views are aired inside the union. Statutes and decisional law promote free speech and democratic decision-making processes within the union. Decisions like Allis-Chalmers and Scofield rely on these factors to give weight to a union majority's decision. In Allis-Chalmers and Scofield the Court opted for concerted *union* activity, and upheld reasonable union sanctions against union members who sought to pursue a contrary course. If the union can expect a modicum of allegiance after a majority has made a decision, then the employer should be entitled to rely on that allegiance in negotiations with the union. The Court was upholding concepts of orderly bargaining which apply from either viewpoint. . . .

The racial aspects of this case emphasize the problem of what action is proper when the intra-union processes produce a majority decision which is outside legally acceptable bounds. It is unnecessary here, and it would be premature, for us to undertake to resolve the problem of whether the minority members would then be entitled to undertake to achieve their lawful objective by dealing with the employer individually.

In sum, we conclude that Tanner's two employees, Abramson and Dorbin, had an obligation to go to the union with their desire for non-discriminatory hiring. The record does not demonstrate that they approached the union, nor does it indicate that the union gave its sanction to their actions. Thus, while their concerted activity does fall within section 7, the operation of section 9(a) deprives it of the protection to which it would otherwise be entitled.

Our decision makes immaterial the presence or absence of an anti-discrimination clause in the collective bargaining contract. Whether Abramson or Dorbin were seeking enforcement of a contract clause or seeking to instigate bargaining over such a clause, they had an obligation first to seek action by a union majority.

II

The foregoing conclusions, however, do not end the matter. Abramson was fired on July 29, ostensibly for having one accident on July 24, and another on July 25. All that he had done was first, to ask his supervisor whether he objected to hiring Negroes, to which the answer was no, second, to ask if the supervisor would consider a Negro applicant whom he knew, to which the answer was yes, third, to deny knowledge of a news broadcast criticizing Tanner's hiring policies on racial grounds, and fourth, to speak to Dorbin about that press release. Abramson was then fired. He did not picket until after he had been fired.

All that Dorbin had done was, first, to prepare press releases for a civil rights organization, second, to tell his superior, after Abramson had spoken to him, that the news broadcast was erroneous and that he had prepared a press release stating that Tanner appeared to be acting in good faith, and third, after Abramson was fired, to picket. Dorbin was then fired.

Thus Abramson was *not* fired for picketing; Dorbin was. Moreover, and more important, the employer's representative, when spoken to by Abramson and later by Dorbin, never expressed any objection to their doing so. Much less did he indicate that Tanner's position was that these were matters that should be presented to it by the union as the recognized bargaining agent, rather than by two or more employees acting independently. The manner in which each was received could well have led Abramson and Dorbin to conclude that the employer felt that what they were doing was proper, and even that it believed that they had a protected right to do it.

We think it arguable that in cases where employees, not acting through the union, initiate in a peaceful and non-disruptive manner an activity which would otherwise be protected under section 7, but is not by reason of section 9(a), the employer has a duty to tell them that the matter must be taken up through the union, and, if the employer does not do so, he has waived his right to object on that ground, so that section 7 becomes fully operative. We do not decide this question; we think it is for the Board to decide in the first instance.

Other questions lurk in this record. Abramson was not fired for picketing; Dorbin was. This raises two questions. The first assumes that there is no duty on the part of the employer to demand that the matter be taken up through the union. If so, and if the action of the employees is and remains peaceful and non-disruptive is it consistent with the objectives of the Act as embodied in sections 7 and 9(a) to say that the employer cannot fire the employees without first letting them know that he considers their activity ground for discharge if it continues?

The second question assumes a duty of the employer to demand that the matter be taken up through the union, on pain of being held to have waived the protection of section 9(a). . . . If so, how far does the "waiver" go? Is it only a waiver of the right to discipline for peaceful and non-disruptive conduct, or does it extend to picketing? If it extends to picketing, is the manner of picketing material?

There is still another question presented by the record. Was the conduct of either of the employees condoned? Tanner reinstated Dorbin on the day following his discharge. Tanner's branch manager called Dorbin and arranged a meeting. During the meeting the manager told Dorbin that his discharge had been a "mistake," and that Dorbin could begin work at his regularly scheduled time. The Board might conclude that Tanner condoned the unprotected, concerted activities in which Dorbin engaged.

The applicable standards of the doctrine of condonation were stated in NLRB v. Marshall Car Wheel & Foundry Co., 5 Cir., 1955, 218 F.2d 409, 414:

Where, as here, the strike misconduct is clearly shown, condonation may not be lightly presumed from mere silence or equivocal statements, but must clearly appear from some positive act by an employer indicating forgiveness and an intention of treating the guilty employees as if their misconduct had not occurred. . . .

The Board has not passed on this question.

The Board found that Abramson was fired for engaging in activities supporting non-discriminatory hiring, and not for having had the traffic accidents. Substantial evidence supports this determination. Abramson was never reinstated. But because Abramson and Dorbin were intimately involved in the same activity, the Board might conclude that the employer's assignment of another, fictitious reason for Abramson's discharge should not bar his reinstatement also, under the condonation doctrine. . . . The Board has not considered any of these questions.

The Board's order is vacated, and the matter is remanded to the Board for further proceedings consistent with this opinion.

NOTES

1. The Ninth Circuit's opinion on the second appeal in the Tanner case did not alter significantly its earlier unwillingness to grant protected status to discharged drivers under §7, unless they first took their request for a nondiscriminatory hiring policy to the union. Professor William Gould viewed as "unrealistic" the NLRB's assumption that the drivers' protest was in furtherance of their union's position because a contrary position by the union (one condoning discrimination in hiring) would be offensive to public policy. That assumption reflects, Gould felt, the NLRB's "inability to articulate the unique role which racial discrimination grievances play in our collective bargaining system." Writing prior to the Ninth Circuit's second opinion, Gould suggested that the evidence indicated that the union was not sympathetic with the drivers' position. While finding serious difficulties with the NLRB's rationale, he concluded:

If Tanner, despite the irrationality of its arguments, stands for the proposition that racial disputes have a unique importance in the scheme of national labor policy, it contains a holding which deserves support. Congress has, albeit through a statute which is thus far more promise than accomplishment, made clear its hostility to racial discrimination in employment. This commitment, coupled with the history of deliberate bondage and racism which has been the lot of the black worker in this country, warrants a special solicitude on the part of administrative agencies and courts. Labor stoppages arising from issues of racial discrimination should not be declared unprotected out of hand simply because they are not authorized by the union or are in defiance of the no-strike clause and peaceful procedures provided in the collective agreement. At the same time, workers and management deserve some stability in their economic affairs; the factory should not become a battlefield where economic pressure is used to settle issues unrelated to work and production. What then for the limits within which the right to strike will be protected? And what is the proper rationale to reach the laudable result inarticulately sponsored in Tanner? (Gould, Black Power in the Unions: The Impact Upon Collective Bargaining Relationships, 79 Yale L.J. 46, 63 (1969).)

2. A similar problem confronting workers for equal employment is posed by a recent Supreme Court interpretation of the Norris-LaGuardia Act, which generally bars federal courts from enjoining strikes and related activities growing out of, or involving, labor disputes. 29 U.S.C. §104. In Boys Market, Inc. v. Retail Clerks' Union, Local 770, 398 U.S. 235, 90 S. Ct. 1583, 26 L. Ed. 2d 199 (1970), a strike was called because nonunion personnel had undertaken work ordinarily reserved for union employees. The Supreme Court upheld a lower court injunction enjoining the strike, stating that an injunction may be proper where the subject matter of the dispute is covered by the compulsory arbitration provisions of the collective bargaining agreement. Such provisions are enforceable in the federal courts under the Labor Management Relations Act, 29 U.S.C. §185(a). The applicability of Boys Market to black self-help efforts is unclear. It has been suggested, however, that the holding will tend to increase judicial insensitivity to these questions: whether work stoppages in protest against racial discrimination are protected activities under the Civil Rights Acts; and whether minority group employees may act independently of the union to protect or promote their interests, despite the principle of exclusive bargaining representation. Gould, Labor Injunctions, Unions and the Judges: The Boys Market Case, 1970 S. Ct. Rev. 215, 260-261.

3. The holding in the Boys Market case is limited. It provides only that federal labor statutes do not prohibit an employer from enjoining a strike by a union where: (1) the walk-out is in breach of a no-strike provision in a collective bargaining agreement; (2) it is undisputed that the grievance in question is subject to both adjustment and arbitration under the agreement: and (3) the employer was ready to proceed with such arbitration at the time the injunction was sought and obtained to prevent irreparable injury.

But Gould's fears for its adverse implications in self-help efforts by black workers are not groundless. Note, for example, the partial reliance on Boys Market in Moore v. Sunbeam Corporation, infra. At the least, Boys Market has contributed to the courts' uncertainty about what, if any, relief should be extended to workers who use self-help, where the protest activity exceeds traditional limits of protected conduct. See Sections D and E, Chapter Seven, and Green v. McDonnell Douglas Corporation below.

GREEN v. McDONNELL-DOUGLAS CORPORATION
463 F.2d 337 (8th Cir. 1972)

Before Johnsen, Lay and Bright, Circuit Judges.

Bright, Circuit Judge.

Percy Green, a black citizen, brought this action against McDonnell-

Douglas Corporation (McDonnell) under Title VII of the Civil Rights Act of 1964, seeking relief from the latter's allegedly discriminatory conduct in denying Green employment in July 1965. Green also pressed a claim that McDonnell had discharged him from a job in August 1964 for reasons of race in violation of 42 U.S.C. §1981. The district court denied Green any relief. Green v. McDonnell-Douglas Corporation, 318 F. Supp. 846 (E.D. Mo. 1970). Green prosecutes this timely appeal. For the reasons stated below, we reverse and remand this case for further proceedings.

To place this controversy in an appropriate frame of reference, we find it necessary to examine chronologically both the underlying facts and the procedures followed in the district court. Although the immediate controversy springs from the refusal of McDonnell to employ Green on July 26, 1965, its origin lies in an earlier employment relationship. In 1956, McDonnell employed Green as a mechanic. He remained with the company continuously, except for twenty-one months of honorable military service, until he was laid off on August 28, 1964. Initially, Green's job was protected by union security, but in 1963 he transferred to a non-union position as a laboratory technician, performing work on research projects in the Electronic Equipment Division of McDonnell. In 1964, the workload decreased in the Electronic Equipment Division, and the company laid off several persons, including Green.

Green, a long-time activist in the movement to obtain equal rights for black citizens, vigorously protested his discharge as being racially motivated. He also filed formal complaints of discrimination with the President's Commission on Civil Rights, the Justice Department, the Department of the Navy, the Defense Department, and the Missouri Commission on Human Rights. As a member of CORE, and later as a member of ACTION, another civil rights organization, Green, in late 1964 and during 1965, participated in several demonstrations which were staged to call attention to McDonnell's allegedly discriminatory employment practices. These demonstrations included picketing the home of James F. McDonnell, Chairman of the Board of McDonnell; blocking a main highway access route leading to the McDonnell plant during a traffic "stall-in"; and, participating in a civil rights demonstration during which the doors of a downtown St. Louis building which housed certain McDonnell employees were locked with chains by some of the demonstrators.

On July 25, 1965, McDonnell ran an advertisement in the St. Louis, Missouri, newspapers seeking qualified electrical mechanics. The next day Green applied for one of these positions, but McDonnell, although still seeking qualified mechanics, refused to hire him. McDonnell never has disputed Green's technical ability to perform the work required in that position. Thereafter, on September 14, 1965, Green filed a formal complaint with the Equal Employment Opportunity Commission (EEOC), alleging that McDonnell had discriminated against him "because of [his] race and because of [his] persistent involvement in the Civil Rights Movement." On May 8, 1967, the EEOC determined that reasonable cause existed to believe that McDonnell had violated 42 U.S.C. §2000e-3(a) by refusing to employ Green "because of his involvement in civil rights activities." It made no determination on the allegation of racial bias.

The EEOC unsuccessfully attempted to conciliate the dispute. . . .

In a complaint filed April 15, 1968, Green alleged that McDonnell had discriminated against him by denying him employment "because of his involvement in civil rights activities."

[The court affirmed, on procedural grounds, the district court's dismissal of charges in an amended complaint asserting that plaintiff had been laid off in 1964, but reversed dismissal of charges that he had been denied employment in 1965 "because of his race and color."]

II

We now examine Green's contention that the district court erred in ruling that his participation in the "stall-in" and "lock-in" demonstrations did not fall within the protection of 42 U.S.C. §2000e-3(a). We confine our discussion here to the question whether Green's participation in the "stall-in" is a protected activity under §2000e-3(a). The record does not support the trial court's conclusion that Green "actively cooperated" in chaining the doors of the downtown St. Louis building during the "lock-in" demonstration . . . . We therefore measure the protection afforded by §2000e-3(a) against Green's admitted participation in the "stall-in."

Section 2000e-3(a), as pertinent, reads:

> It shall be an unlawful employment practice for an employer to discriminate against any of his employees or applicants for employment . . . because he has opposed any practice made an unlawful employment practice by this subchapter, or because he has made a charge, testified, assisted, or participated in any manner in an investigation, proceeding, or hearing under this subchapter.

In support of his protection argument, Green stresses the language forbidding discrimination "because [an applicant] has opposed any practice made an unlawful employment practice by this subchapter." According to Green, since the "stall-in" was a non-violent protest designed to call attention to McDonnell's allegedly discriminatory practices, this activity commands the protection of §2000e-3(a). McDonnell, on the other hand, asserts that the unlawfulness of this protest removes it from the protection of that section.

We find little relevant authority for either position. The legislative history of Title VII provides us with no guidance as to the scope of the protection afforded by §2000e-3(a), and the small body of case law surrounding that section contains little discussion on the subject. Nevertheless, we think it is clear from the language of the statute that Congress sought to protect employees and job applicants from employer retaliation for filing complaints to the EEOC. Those who have the courage to challenge discriminatory practices of an employer merit that protection. Without doubt, lawful protest also commands the same protection, but we find no suggestion that protection extends to activities which run afoul of the law. Accordingly, we agree with the district court that the "stall-in" demonstration was not a protected activity under §2000e-3(a)....

IV

. . . We cannot accept McDonnell's suggestion that it should prevail on an issue [whether McDonnell denied plaintiff employment in July 1965 "because of race and color"] that Green was not privileged to present. We cannot say that the district court's action in striking the racial discrimination claim did not hamper the preparation and presentation of Green's case, notwithstanding the commendable zeal displayed by his counsel in producing an abundant record of events and circumstances relating to Green's employment relationship with McDonnell. Additionally, as discussed in part V below, the district court failed to consider whether the reasons given by McDonnell for not rehiring Green were related to the requirements of the job. Instead, the district court simply assumed that, since the "lock-in" and "stall-in" protests were unprotected activities, McDonnell's refusal to rehire Green could not be violative of 42 U.S.C. §2000e-2(a)(1)....

We think it is clear that an applicant for employment may be entitled to the protection of §2000e-2(a)(1) even though he participates in activities which fall outside the protection of §2000e-3(a). These statutes apply to wholly different facets of the employment relationship. Section 2000e-3(a) serves peripherally in the scheme of Title VII to shield an employee or applicant from employer retaliation. Section 2000e-2(a)(1) expresses Title VII's primary promise — equal employment opportunities for all. It would be antithetical to the remedial purposes of the Act to interrelate these sections so as to construe the Act to mean that an applicant's civil rights activities which fall outside §2000e-3(a) may serve as a basis for employment disqualification without consideration of the separate standards called for by §2000e-2(a)(1).

In the light of this record, we deem it necessary to remand this case to the district court for reconsideration of the racial discrimination issue in accordance with the standards discussed below. On remand, the parties should be permitted to present such additional evidence as may be relevant to the issue.

[In response to a petition for rehearing filed by McDonnell-Douglas, the majority of the court modified Part V of the opinion, as set forth below, to make clear that plaintiff's protest activity might show lack of a responsible attitude toward performing work for the employer. The original opinion appeared to place the burden of showing unresponsiveness on defendant. The modified opinion shifts the burden to the plaintiff, to show that the decision not to rehire was racially motivated.]

V

The record shows that McDonnell has taken the position that it has the right under Title VII to make subjective hiring judgments which do not necessarily rest upon the ability of the applicant to perform the work required. Upon that hypothesis, and apparently because the pleadings did not require McDonnell to defend the charge that its refusal to rehire Green was racially motived, McDonnell rested its case upon a showing that Green had participated in unlawful civil rights activities as reasons for declining to rehire him.

Our prior decisions make clear that, in cases presenting questions of discriminatory hiring practices, employment decisions based on subjective, rather than objective, criteria carry little weight in rebutting charges of discrimination. See Moore v. Board of Education of Chidester School District No. 59, Chidester, Ark., 448 F.2d 709 (8th Cir. 1971). See also Carter v. Gallagher, 452 F.2d 315 (8th Cir., 1971). We reaffirm this principle here. "If an employment practice which operates to exclude Negroes cannot be shown to be related to job performance, the practice is prohibited." Griggs v. Duke Power Co., 401 U.S. 424 . . . (1971). In enacting Title VII, Congress has mandated the removal of racial barriers to employment. Judicial acceptance of subjectively based hiring decisions must be limited if Title VII is to be more than an illusory commitment to that end, for subjective criteria may mask aspects of prohibited prejudice. Employers seldom admit racial discrimination. Marquez v. Omaha District Sales Office, Ford Division, 440 F.2d 1157, 1162 (8th Cir. 1971). Its presence is often cloaked in generalities or vague criteria which do not measure an applicant's qualifications in terms of job requirements. Consequently, a black job applicant must usually rest his case of discrimination upon proof that he possessed the requisite qualifications to fill the position which was denied him. In this case, it is undisputed that Green possessed the requisite skills to perform the work for which he applied, and that McDonnell was seeking qualified applicants at the time it refused to hire him and continued to seek qualified applicants thereafter. Moreover, Green's prior performance with McDonnell had earned him a "satisfactory" rating.

When a black man demonstrates that he possesses the qualifications to fill a job opening and that he was denied the job which continues to remain open, we think he presents a prima facie case of racial discrimination. However, an applicant's past participation in unlawful conduct directed at his prospective employer might indicate the applicant's lack of a responsible attitude toward performing work for that employer.

Of the several civil rights protests which Green directed against McDonnell, the employer selected two, the "lock-in" and the "stall-in," as reasons for its refusal to rehire Green. Green should be given the opportunity to show that these reasons offered by the Company were pretextual, or otherwise show the presence of racially discriminatory hiring practices by McDonnell which affected its decision.

The district court did not use appropriate standards in determining whether McDonnell's refusal to hire Green was racially motivated. On remand, both parties will have the opportunity to present evidence on this matter.

The amount of lost earnings claimed by Green is not great, but the parties regard this as an important case and have devoted substantial time and energy to its litigation. Although the litigation is still not completed, we deem it appropriate to allow appellant a reasonable attorney's fee for this appeal, to be taxed as costs, upon counsel's submission of an estimate of his fee containing details of his services and time spent on this appeal. See 42 U.S.C. §2000e-5(k).

[The concurring opinion is omitted. Senior Judge JOHNSON, who had dissented from the first opinion, also dissented from its revision. Reviewing the changes, he explained his differences with the majority as follows.]

The difficulty I have with all this is that the opinion continues to adhere to the position that such unlawful acts as Green committed against McDonnell would not legally entitle McDonnell to refuse to hire him, even though no racial motivation was involved, although they would entitle and would cause it to do so in the case of white persons. In taking the position that such unlawful and immediate misdeeds do not of themselves, even though no racial motivation is involved, provide a sufficient basis for McDonnell to refuse to hire Green, the majority thus are holding, not that Green is entitled to the same opportunity as a white, but that he is entitled to one of a different and greater degree.

As indicated in my original dissent, I am not able to read Title VII of the Equal Employment Opportunity Act of 1964 as providing for such an inherently different employment opportunity or such a curbing employer prescription, nor do I believe that Congress, as a matter of respect for law adherence, would presume to impose such a requirement of business condonation upon employers in respect to the commission of unlawful acts against them, such as are here involved. And in the majority's holding that, even though no racial motivation was involved, McDonnell was not entitled to refuse to hire Green because of his unlawful misdeeds against it, but that something more than this would have to exist in the situation, I confess that I am not able to see any practical difference, so far as McDonnell's situation is concerned, between the opinion's original statement, that it must be shown that the hiring of Green would result in "disrupting plant operations" and its substituted statement that "an applicant's past participation in unlawful conduct directed at his prospective employer might indicate the applicant's lack of a responsible attitude toward performing work for that employer."

Any proof that would be possible in attempting to show that Green would be an industrial handicap to the operation of the plant, would necessarily involve opinion or subjective testimony which, as pointed out in my original dissent, the majority opinion declares to be of "little weight in rebutting charges of discrimination."

I do not desire to prolong this discussion further, except to reiterate, as noted in my original dissent, that I believe the majority have engaged in a mistaken interpretation of the holding in Griggs v. Duke Power Co., 401 U.S. 424, 431. . . . I adhere to my original dissent, with this supplemental expression added.

MOORE v. SUNBEAM CORPORATION
459 F.2d 811 (7th Cir. 1972)

STEVENS, Circuit Judge.

James Moore was discharged by Sunbeam Corporation on October 17, 1967. He claims that the corporation committed an unfair labor practice, that his union breached its duty to represent him fairly, and that he is the victim of racial discrimination proscribed by the Civil Rights Act of 1964. His appeals from adverse rulings by the Labor Board and the district court were consolidated in this court. In brief, the issues are whether the Board correctly construed the collective bargaining agreement; whether the union was required to submit Moore's grievances to arbitration; and whether Moore's civil rights claims are barred as untimely.

Although the three issues arise out of the same transaction, many factual details relate primarily to only one issue. We shall, therefore, start by considering the unfair labor practice charge which was the subject of a full evidentiary hearing before a Labor Board Trial Examiner. We shall then discuss the basis for the summary judgments entered in favor of the union and the employer, respectively, in the district court action.

I

The union represents approximately 2,400 employees in five plants operated by Sunbeam in the Chicago area. Moore, a union member, was one of approximately 1,200 employees at the main plant.

In the collective bargaining contract Sunbeam agreed to a four-stage grievance procedure, culminating, if the union so demanded, in arbitration. On its part, the union, for itself and for its members individually, broadly agreed not to strike, to picket, or to encourage any interference with orderly production.[2] During the course of his employment[3] Moore initiated several grievance

2. Article 1, paragraph 5 provided:
"5. In view of the provision for final arbitration of grievances arising under this agreement, the Union and its members, individually and collectively agree that during the term of this Agreement they will not cause, authorize, encourage, permit or take part in any strike, and the Company agrees that there shall be no lockout.

"(a) For the purpose of this Section, the term 'strike' includes a sit-down, stay in, slow-down, walk-out, curtailment of work, stoppage of work, willful refusal to perform assigned work, or other interference with work or orderly production, or picketing of the Company's plant or premises."

3. Moore was first employed by Sunbeam in May, 1962. During the ensuing five years he worked as a punch press operator, a power truck operator, and an inventory control clerk. In June, 1966, he passed a test which qualified him as a "leadman," a junior supervisory position. He attempted unsuccessfully to obtain leadman assignments in June, August, and October of 1966. He did receive leadman assignments which were not completely satisfactory between October 24, 1966, and December 14, 1966, and between December 27, 1966, and January 10, 1967. He was promoted to the position of stock clerk in August, 1967.

proceedings[4] and filed four unfair labor practice charges against Sunbeam. Apparently none of the grievances was successful. Two of the Labor Board charges were withdrawn voluntarily; the general counsel refused to issue complaints on the other two. Frustrated by his inability to obtain relief through regular channels, in February of 1967 Moore wrote to the president of Sunbeam requesting a personal interview. He was advised that the president would not set a precedent by meeting with an individual employee on a grievance matter.

On August 11, 1967, Moore again wrote to Sunbeam's president demanding a meeting with him and with the union's district representative (Janas). The letter reviewed Moore's unredressed grievances and expressed his feeling that "top management is systematically denying me the opportunity to advance to the full extent of my ability . . . only because I am a Negro." He stated that if a meeting could not be arranged, "the only alternative [is] to present my grievance to my co-workers, and the public." Surprisingly, this letter evoked no response whatsoever from Sunbeam.[7]

In late September Moore added a few paragraphs to his unanswered letter, labeled it an "Open Letter to Mr. Robert P. Gwinn, President," and made 3,500 copies for distribution to various public officials and agencies, his fellow employees, and members of the public. The added paragraphs asked for support in making equal opportunity in employment a fact and requested supporters to "refrain from buying any Sunbeam appliances . . . until justice has been served." At the end of the open letter Moore stated that he would march in front of the Sunbeam plant on October 24, 1967, "in protest of the conditions here."

On October 2, 1967, Moore gave a copy of the open letter to a fellow employee and discussed it briefly with her. Later that day the letter came to the attention of Sunbeam's Personnel Department and on October 3 Moore was suspended. He distributed his "petition" at various plant gates that day and on the next three days.

During this period he had several discussions with union representatives. On October 5 Janas prepared a grievance covering Moore's suspension; at that time Janas advised Moore that his actions violated the union contract. Accordingly, Janas responded to inquiries from union stewards by advising that the union would not sanction picketing by Moore. Moore nevertheless insisted that he would march on October 24 without union support.

4. The Trial Examiner found:

"During his 5-year tenure with Respondent, Charging Party Moore filed a number of grievances against the Company. These included grievances concerning the assignment or distribution of overtime on three occasions (1964 and 1965, prior to his passing the leadman test); over allegedly unsafe working conditions (also prior to his passing the leadman test); over an alleged improper failure to assign him as a leadman to a particular department (Dept. 133; 1966); and over a request by him for a material handler to assist him as leadman in certain manual work (Dept. 437, 1966). At least the latter two were wholly unsuccessful."

7. It was the subject of intraoffice communication within Sunbeam's management, but none of those busy executives made any reply, directly or indirectly, to Moore.

On October 11 a second stage grievance meeting regarding Moore's suspension was held. Nothing was resolved. On October 17 he was discharged. Both the discharge letter and a letter written to the union on the same day relied, in part, on the ground that Moore was seeking to encourage a strike and product boycott in violation of the union contract.

On October 24 Moore did picket for most of the day, but with almost no support from fellow employees. It is reasonably accurate to state that although he attempted to engage in collective or concerted activity, he actually conducted a one-man demonstration.

A week later a third step grievance meeting was held, but the company refused to reinstate Moore. The union subsequently rejected Moore's request for arbitration of his suspension and discharge grievance.

Thereafter, Moore filed unfair labor practice charges against both the union and the company. The charge against the union was dismissed. The general counsel issued a complaint against Sunbeam alleging that its rule against solicitation by employees was too broad and that Moore had been discharged for engaging in concerted activity protected by §7 of the Labor-Management Relations Act.

The Trial Examiner and the Board found the solicitation rule invalid, but upheld the discharge. No issue involving the rule is before us since Sunbeam has made the modification directed by the Board.

Although both the Trial Examiner and a majority of the Board concluded that Moore's activity was not protected by the Act, their reasoning was different. The Trial Examiner, stressing the individual character of Moore's campaign, found that his activity was not "concerted," and therefore not covered by the statute. The Board, stressing his expressed intentions and requests rather than his accomplishments, regarded his activity as "concerted," but prohibited by the no-strike clause of the contract. The dissenting member of the Board agreed that Moore was engaged in concerted activity, but felt that he did not violate the no-strike clause.

[1] Certain propositions of law are not disputed. There are kinds of concerted activity that are not protected by the Act. . . . Specifically, conduct which violates a no-strike clause in a collective bargaining agreement is not protected and may give rise to discharge. Atkinson v. Sinclair Refining Co., 370 U.S. 238, 246 . . . . The critical question here is whether Moore's conduct violated Article 1, Paragraph 5, of the agreement between Sunbeam and the union.

In answering this question we do not merely consider dictionary definitions of the word "strike," or even judicial interpretations of that term in other contexts. Of greater importance is the understanding of the parties who negotiated and drafted the contract before us, the interpretation of administrators who specialize in labor relations matters, and the purpose which the contractual provision was intended to serve. We thus put to one side the dissenting Board member's persuasive exposition of why Moore's conduct was not a conventional strike.

Moore had embarked on an independent effort to resolve his dispute with his employer by means other than those which the union, on his behalf, had agreed to employ. In substance, the union and its individual members had agreed to abstain from economic warfare or collective pressures during the term of the contract. To the extent that Moore's conduct can properly be viewed as concerted, it was directly opposed to the intent of the no-strike clause. He asked his co-workers to "refrain from buying any Sunbeam appliances" and for support "to obtain . . . better working conditions for all Sunbeam employees." The company, quite reasonably, viewed this overture to collective action as a violation of the employees' agreement not to encourage any interference with work or any picketing of the company's plant or premises.

Of greater significance, the union agreed with this construction of the contract. James so advised Moore in advance of the discharge, but Moore nevertheless persisted in his independent course of action. After the discharge, the union declined to submit the matter to arbitration. The union's interpretation of the scope of its own undertaking is entitled to considerable respect.

We also respect the Labor Board's appraisal of the issue. Cf. Universal Camera Corp. v. N.L.R.B., 340 U.S. 474 . . . . It might be argued that that case applies only to questions of fact decided by the Board and that we are not bound to follow the Board's construction of written instruments. It does not follow, however, that the expertise of the Board is not relevant in the interpretation of a labor contract. When, as in this case, the facts must be interpreted in connection with the contract language, the function of the Board in promoting the national labor policy is particularly important. The policy considerations discussed by the Supreme Court in N.L.R.B. v. Erie Resistor Corp., 373 U.S. 221 . . . deserve mention:

> Here, as in other cases, we must recognize the Board's special function of applying the general provisions of the Act to the complexities of industrial life [cite], and of "[appraising] carefully the interests of both sides of any labor-management controversy in the diverse circumstances of particular cases" from its special understanding of "the actualities of industrial relations." [cite] "The ultimate problem is the balancing of the conflicting legitimate interests. The function of striking that balance to effectuate national labor policy is often a difficult and delicate responsibility, which the Congress committed primarily to the National Labor Relations Board, subject to limited judicial review." 373 U.S. at 236. . . .

There is an undeniable national labor policy to promote arbitration. Textile Workers v Lincoln Mills, 353 U.S. 448 . . . . [S]ee also Boys Markets, Inc. v. Retail Clerks Local 770, 398 U.S. 235. . . . No-strike pledges constitute the quid pro quo for a binding arbitration agreement, Lincoln Mills, 353 U.S. at 455 . . . ; Boys Markets, 398 U.S. at 247-248 . . . ; United Steelworkers of America v. American Manufacturing Co., 363 U.S. 564, 567 . . . and may even be enforced by injunction notwithstanding §4 of the Norris-LaGuardia Act. Boys

Market, 398 U.S. at 249-253. . . . A no-strike pledge may even be implied. Teamsters Local 174, Teamsters, Chauffeurs, etc. v. Lucas Flour Co., 369 U.S. 95 . . . . Since the contract before us contains an express no-strike pledge, we think it is reasonable to defer to the Board's broad interpretation of that clause as applied to the facts before it. Its interpretation is entirely consistent with the national labor policy and with the union's own understanding of the agreement.

In addition to the argument that the Board misconstrued the contract, Moore argues that in any event the discharge was not predicated on his breach of contract. The record does indicate that additional factors motivated the company and the no-strike clause was not mentioned in the suspension letter on October 4. However, the discharge letter on October 17 did rely, in part, on the charge that Moore was encouraging a strike and a boycott, and the letter to the union on the same day specifically identified the relevant provision of the contract. The evidence does not support Moore's contention that his breach of the contract was a subsequently contrived justification for the October 17 discharge. On the contrary, it is clear that the Board's decision was supported by substantial evidence. On this factual question, the rule of Universal Camera, supra, is unquestionably applicable.

II

About a year after his discharge, Moore filed a three-count complaint against Sunbeam and the union. Federal jurisdiction was invoked under Title VII of the Civil Rights Act of 1964 as to count I and under §301(a) of the Labor-Management Relations Act as to counts II and III. The civil rights count is dealt with in Part III of this opinion. We here consider the two counts brought under §301 for breach of the collective bargaining agreement. Summary judgment for Sunbeam and the union was granted on both §301 counts.

The structure and allegations of the complaint make it clear that Moore was attempting to come within the §301 jurisdiction of the district court as formulated by the Supreme Court in Vaca v. Sipes, 386 U.S. 171 . . . . The Court said, "Since the employee's claim is based upon breach of the collective bargaining agreement, he is bound by terms of that agreement which govern the manner in which contractual rights may be enforced." Id. at 184. . . . The union's contract with Sunbeam contained both no-strike and binding arbitration clauses, accordingly, the Vaca decision is applicable. The Supreme Court specified two circumstances which would nevertheless permit a §301 suit: (1) when the conduct of the employer amounts to a repudiation of the contractual procedures, or (2) when the union has sole power to invoke the higher stages of the grievance procedure and *wrongfully* refuses to process the grievance. Id. at 185. . . .

Moore has not alleged that Sunbeam repudiated the contractual grievance provisions with respect to any of the incidents described in the complaint. He predicates §301 jurisdiction on only two specific incidents: a failure to promote him to a leadman position on October 24, 1966; and the suspension and discharge in October, 1967. In his deposition, two additional specific matters are discussed: the failure to assign him appropriate leadman work when he held that position in department 437 from October 25, 1966, to December 14, 1966; and his allegedly improper transfer from a leadman position to power truck operator on January 10, 1967. Moore testified that grievances were instituted and processed as to the October 24, 1966, incident and as to his work assignment between October 25 and December 14. These grievances were not, however, carried to arbitration. No grievance was filed as to the January 10 transfer; Moore clearly failed to exhaust contractual remedies on that issue. Finally, as indicated in part I of this opinion, the suspension and discharge issue was taken through the third step grievance procedure. Sunbeam did not repudiate the contractual procedure either as to specific incidents mentioned in the complaint or as to those discussed by Moore in his deposition.

Moore's only possibility of coming within the Vaca standards, therefore, is to establish a wrongful refusal on the part of the union to take the grievances to arbitration. The Supreme Court held in Vaca that a union has no mandatory obligation to submit every employee claim to arbitration. 386 U.S. at 191-192 . . . . A labor contract must be construed in its totality. Unfortunately, Moore has not placed before us a complete copy of the contract in question; he merely quotes portions of it in his complaint. However, we are assuming that the contract contained a no-strike clause and a clause making the grievance procedure exclusive, with binding arbitration at the discretion of the union. Thus, part of the consideration for management's agreeing to the entire contract package was that it could rely on the union to screen grievances and demand arbitration only on those which the union in good faith thought meritorious. Moore, in accepting the benefits of the labor agreement also had to accept its burdens — in this case he had no choice but to rely on the grievance procedure specified, which included the provision that the union could decide whether or not to demand arbitration.

The Supreme Court in Vaca left no doubt that a union owes its members a duty of fair representation, but that opinion also makes it clear that the union may exercise discretion in deciding whether a grievance warrants arbitration. Even if an employee claim has merit, a union may properly reject it unless its action is arbitrary or taken in bad faith. 386 U.S. at 193 . . . . In this case we believe the union properly evaluated the merits of Moore's claims and can find no basis for the charge that it did not fairly represent him simply because it terminated the grievance proceedings at the third stage and did not demand arbitration of his claims, which were dubious at best.

The summary judgment dismissing Moore's §301 claims is affirmed.

[The portion of the opinion reviewing plaintiff's §301(a) and Title VII claims is omitted. The court held that Moore's EEOC complaint was filed too late to permit review of the primary incidents of discrimination which occurred before May 22, 1967. The case was remanded, however, for consideration of the claim of "continuing harassment" after May 22.]

NOTES

1. Rightfully or not, many black workers share Mr. Moore's distrust of the unions to which they belong and of the grievance procedures in the collective bargaining agreements to which they have been bound. Nor is the sense that fairness and justice will prevail any greater when arbitration procedures are invoked. Exhaustion of these procedures is not required, where the union and company have exhibited extreme hostility to black workers who seek their contractual remedies. Glover v. St. Louis–San Francisco Railway Company, 393 U.S. 324 (1969), printed supra page 736. But even in the absence of such hostility, Gould argues that several factors render normal arbitration procedures inadequate to handle fairly grievances involving charges with elements of racial discrimination. He writes:

> One difficulty with submitting racial discrimination grievances to arbitration is that the union and employer, who select the arbitrator, are quite often both alleged to have participated in the discrimination. While impartial arbitration has an integrity which makes it superior to devices such as labor-management committees, it is difficult to ignore its responsiveness to the parties to the agreement under which the arbitration takes place. Black workers and their allies have no standing to intervene in the arbitration proceeding, and, moreover, it is labor and management — not rebellious minority employees — who will decide whether the arbitrator is selected to arbitrate in the future. This is not to cast ethical aspersions on arbitrators, but only to highlight an institutional fact of life: each arbitration process serves those who have created it.
>
> This responsiveness of the arbitrator to the labor-management team precludes the formulation of "affirmative action" remedies for black workers. Even where a contract contains a no-discrimination clause, as well as a separability provision which provides that an illegal clause does not taint the remainder of the contract, it is doubtful that an effective remedy can be formed which does not controvert some expectation of the parties.
>
> Arbitrators are also reluctant to rely on public laws such as Title VII in issuing awards since they have no particular competence in this realm. Indeed, the Supreme Court's requirement that the arbitrator maintain a measure of fidelity to the contract terms gives legal justification to this rationale. Even in those instances where there is a clear conflict between civil rights legislation and the privately negotiated contract, the existing arbitration system does not impel optimism as to the arbitrators' reaction. This recognition of the conflicting roles forced upon the union where racial cleavages within the membership have resulted in strife of various types and the black workers' distrust of the union where racial grievances have existed for some time with the union's passive or active cooperation has serious implications for labor law policy beyond the realm of arbitration. (Gould, Black Power in the Unions: The Impact Upon Collective Bargaining Relationships, 79 Yale L.J. 46, 55 (1969).)

2. But the status of black workers in this country makes them more, not less, likely to assume racial motives for adverse actions by unions, employers and grievance officials. Assuming that Moore's charges against Sunbeam were not

justified, how can a standard be devised to enable accurate distinction of the crank from the many legitimate victims of discrimination, whose complaints receive no more consideration than did Moore's?

HOTEL EMPLOYERS ASSOCIATION
47 Lab. Arb. 873 (1966)

Decision of Arbitrators

Burns, Arbitrator: — Hotel Employers Association of San Francisco (herein called the "association" or the "hotels") and San Francisco Local Joint Executive Board of the Hotel and Restaurant Employees and Bartenders International Union, AFL-CIO, representing hotel employee unions named in the agreement (herein called the "union") are parties to a collective bargaining agreement effective July 1, 1964, until June 30, 1969 (herein referred to as the "agreement" or "collective bargaining agreement"). This agreement was in full force and effect during all of the times relevant to this proceeding.

Under date of July 26, 1966, the union filed with the Hotel Industry Adjustment Board established by the agreement a complaint . . . .

[In summary, the complaint alleged that the association had entered into an agreement with civil rights groups concerning wages, hours and other terms and conditions of employment covered in the collective bargaining agreement. The union sought a cease and desist order and damages. In response, the association claimed that it had been forced by civil rights picketing and demonstrations to sign the agreement, and that the union had "stood idly by" during the protest. A hearing was held, following which Mr. Burns reviewed the evidence.]

The association and its members have had collective bargaining relations with the Local Joint Executive Board and its constituent unions for many years. The Hilton Hotel in San Francisco, one of a nationwide chain of hotels, is a member of the association.

Since 1937 the union has been the sole collective bargaining representative of all employees covered by the agreement. Successive collective bargaining agreements have been entered by the parties since 1937. The current agreement is the result of negotiations and Adjustment Board proceedings since 1937. The agreement (some of the provisions being set forth above) relating to wages, hours, seniority, pensions, health protection, sick leave, apprenticeship standards, protection against unjust discharge and unfair treatment, and other working conditions. Over the years the association has represented its member hotels and the union has represented the craft unions of the hotel workers employed in the classifications covered by the agreement.

In the spring of 1964 the Sheraton Palace Hotel in San Francisco, a member of the association, was subjected to mass picketing, demonstrations, sit-ins, blockade, and other conduct by large numbers of persons. Portions of the hotel were occupied by the mob. There was damage to hotel property and interference with its business. These activities were sponsored by so-called civil rights groups and their leaders. The professed goal was more jobs for Negroes. Arising out of these events was an agreement dated March 7, 1964 (herein sometimes referred to as the "1964 civil rights agreement") between the association and an "Ad Hoc Committee to End Discrimination." The 1964 civil rights agreement was endorsed, ratified and approved by the United San Francisco Freedom Movement, San Francisco Baptist Ministers Union, CORE and the Conference on Religion and Race. It provided that the policy of the association was that the selection and promotion of employees were to be determined solely on the basis of qualification without reference to race or color, that information was to be disseminated concerning the equal opportunity policy of the hotels, that all boycotting, picketing and demonstrations would cease on March 7, 1964, that no hiring quota was established, and that the term of the agreement was until March 7, 1966. Significantly it was provided that this agreement was subject to and limited by state and federal law and applicable collective bargaining agreements and any provision which conflicted therewith was "deemed excised therefrom."

Whatever may have been the effect of the 1964 civil rights agreement, the specific provision (above quoted) excising from the agreement provisions in conflict with collective bargaining agreements made it clear that the 1964 agreement did not impinge upon or conflict with collective bargaining agreements. The record does not disclose what, if anything, was done under the 1964 civil rights agreement.

The 1964 civil rights agreement by its terms expired on March 7, 1966.

[In March 1966, minority group workers at the Hilton Hotel began reporting grievances to Local 283 of the union. A union representative attempted to negotiate these grievances and, although he experienced some success, the difficulties culminated in a walkout and picketing. Civil rights groups again entered the negotiations, with the aim of securing a new agreement with the association. During subsequent negotiations on a new civil rights agreement, picketing continued and protest leaders threatened more serious activity. The record also indicates that the San Francisco police chief advised the president of the association that he lacked the manpower to protect the hotel in case of violence, advising that "if anything was triggered at the Hilton Hotel it would be the signal for a city-wide race riot." Furthermore, during this period the city Human Rights Commission arbitrated the dismissal of several hotel maids who had walked out in protest of conditions. The commission determined that the maids should be returned to work with full seniority, back pay and other benefits. The commission then worked with civil rights groups and the association to complete the 1966 agreement. The union was barred from participating in the final negotiating sessions.]

Opinion

The 1966 civil rights agreement is unlawful. It is void and unenforceable for numerous reasons. The civil rights groups representing a very few employees acted as labor organizations within the meaning of the law and entered with the association a collective bargaining agreement purporting to be a civil rights agreement. They had no right to do so. The 1966 civil rights agreement is in conflict with and purports to supersede the collective bargaining agreement between the union which represents the employees and the association. The 1966 civil rights agreement is unlawful and contrary to public policy and provides for discrimination in favor of one group of employees against other employees. It purports to interfere with and supersede the vested rights of the employees of the hotels granted to them by the collective bargaining agreement which was made for their benefit by the union and the association. The 1966 civil rights agreement was procured through threat of force against the association and its members and under menace and duress. We shall discuss the reasons for the foregoing conclusions.

By section 1 of the agreement the association has recognized the union as the sole representative for collective bargaining purposes of all employees falling within the jurisdiction of the union except for certain excluded employees not involved here. There is no question concerning the validity and scope of the agreement between the union and the association. It is now and has been during all of the times involved in this proceeding binding on the association and its members and upon the union and the employees represented by the union.

Section 9(a) of the National Labor Relations Act as amended (29 U.S.C., sec. 159) provides that representatives designated or selected for the purposes of collective bargaining by the majority of employees in the appropriate unit shall be the exclusive representatives of all employees in such unit for purposes of bargaining with respect to rates of pay, wages, hours of employment, and other conditions of employment. The affirmative duty on the employer to bargain collectively with the chosen representative of his employees imposes a correlative duty not to bargain with any other employee representatives. [Citations omitted.]

The association bargained with, recognized and entered an agreement with the civil rights groups. The civil rights groups acted as labor organizations and were for the purposes of the agreement which they forced upon the association labor organizations within the meaning of the law. . . .

An organization to be a labor organization need not designate itself as such. There are many decisions of the courts and National Labor Relations Board . . . which hold that an agency or group or committee which deals or offers to deal with employers on terms or conditions of employment is a labor organization. . . .

The civil rights groups which entered the agreement with the association acted on behalf of the maids at the Hilton Hotel, participated in arbitration proceedings with respect to these grievances, and bargained over a period of weeks with the Hilton Hotel and the association concerning terms and conditions of employment of some of the employees of the hotel. The civil rights group had no right to represent or purport to represent employees of the hotels with respect to terms or conditions of employment since the union was the authorized bargaining representative. The hotels through the association and the Hilton Hotel joined in these negotiations and proceedings and entered an agreement with the civil rights groups which is a collective bargaining agreement in everything but name. The agreement was not valid or lawful since the union was the authorized bargaining representative. . . . The association should not have bargained with the civil rights groups concerning terms and conditions of employment.

Conflict with Contract

The invalidity of the 1966 civil rights agreement is further demonstrated by its conflict with the particular provisions of the collective bargaining agreement between the association and the union.

[Here the opinion reviews the conflicting provisions in the 1966 civil rights agreement and the collective bargaining agreement, in such areas as seniority rights, recruitment and hiring policies, racial quotas, arbitration procedures, racial breakdown of jobs, and affirmative action programs. The opinion found that none of these protections against discrimination were necessary, in that there was no discrimination against blacks or other minority groups and the union had successfully represented blacks in grievances brought to it.]

Public Policy

The purpose and effect of the 1966 civil rights agreement are to establish a preference for Negroes and other minority groups in the hotel industry in San Francisco and thereby to discriminate against non-Negroes and those who do not belong to some minority group. The purpose and effect are unlawful. Discrimination against any individual in hiring or discharging or with respect to compensation, terms, conditions, or privileges of employment because of such individual's race, color, religion, sex, or national origin is unlawful under Federal law . . . . The 1966 civil rights agreement is against public policy of the United States and State of California. It is contrary to the statutes made and provided to prevent discrimination in employment. On this ground alone the 1966 civil rights agreement is illegal and therefore void and unenforceable.

There is no question whatsoever that the 1966 civil rights agreement was procured by force, threats of force, menace, duress and unlawful means. The brief review of the evidence which we have set forth above establishes without question that the Hilton Hotel in particular was unlawfully picketed by representatives of the civil rights group and all the hotel members of the association were threatened with invasion of the hotel premises and destruction of hotel property by the "troops," a euphemism for hoodlums, which Mr. Bradley threatened to call. The Association was given the choice of executing the 1966 civil rights agreement or having the hotels, beginning with the Hilton Hotel, suffer the attack by mobs which the Chief of Police said he could not control. Under the point of a gun most people will surrender their property or, if demanded, execute and deliver a document. The analogy is apposite except that the threat was by a mob and not one robber. The representatives of the association and its member hotels had well in mind the invasion of the Sheraton-Palace Hotel in the spring of 1964 and the consequent occupation and destruction of property in that hotel. The threats were not idle ones and the hotels knew that they could be and would be implemented without protection from the public authorities. It is indeed a sad commentary on the status of affairs in San Francisco when the Chief of Police informs a citizen that he is unable to protect his person or property against unlawful attack and destruction by mob actions and both the Mayor of the city and the Governor of the state are unavailable to take such further action as may be indicated to assure protection to persons and property of the residents of this city.

The association had no choice except to sign the agreement. The circumstances of its inducement and execution make the 1966 civil rights agreement voidable and unenforceable. Whether voidable or void, the question of the validity of the agreement has been submitted to this Adjustment Board and the arbitration board finds that on this ground as well the 1966 civil rights agreement is void and unenforceable because it was executed as the direct result of unlawful duress and coercion and threats of unlawful action.

The attorneys for the parties in their briefs have discussed at length the legal procedures and steps which the association could have taken against the civil rights group through criminal and injunction actions to prevent the implementation of the threats of force, violence, and other unlawful action by the civil rights group. Whether or not civil proceedings by way of injunction or criminal proceedings would have been effective is a matter of doubt. If the police department and other public authorities stated that they are unable to protect property from mob action, the police could not enforce an injunction or have much if any effect in arresting the rioters. The circumstances under which the 1966 civil rights agreement was entered explain the reasons for the execution by the association but such circumstances do not validate the agreement. On the contrary, they invalidate it.

The union did not participate in or consent to the execution of the 1966 civil rights agreement. Except for the invitation to attend the meeting held on May 24, 1966, and the meeting of July 22, 1966, the union was not asked to attend the several meetings or to participate in the drafting or execution of the 1966 civil rights agreement. The association, through its president, pointed out at each of the meetings that the association had a collective bargaining agreement that it was bound to observe and was told that "we don't give a damn about the union and the collective bargaining agreement. That is your problem". When the union did appear at the July 22, 1966, meeting the Human Rights Commission representatives indicated that it was mediating between the civil rights group and the association and the union representatives were invited to leave the meeting. It was after the union representatives had left the meeting that the 1966 civil rights agreement was executed.

The union urges that it was ready and willing to exert its influence and that of organized labor to assist the association in the protection of the collective bargaining agreement and made known its readiness to do so to the association as well as to the Human Rights Commission. There is nothing in the record which indicates that the union or any of its representatives acquiesced in the 1966 civil rights agreement or any of the provisions thereof which conflict with the collective bargaining agreement and the rights of the union and the hotel employees under that agreement. Nor is the conduct of the union the basis of an estoppel against the union to assert the invalidity of the 1966 civil rights agreement. The union took no action, and did not fail to take any action, which led or would be calculated to lead the association to believe that it was waiving any of the rights of the union or the employees under the collective bargaining agreement or that it would consent to its infringement, modification or change by the 1966 civil rights agreement or any other document. It is doubtful under the circumstances of this case whether the union had the obligation to do anything or that it had the right to waive the rights of the employees. Under the law the union had no right to consent to any document such as the 1966 civil rights agreement. . . .

Remedy

We now come to the matter of the remedy. . . .

The complaint requests the Adjustment Board to find the association in violation of the agreement, to issue an order requiring the employers to cease and desist from the conduct, and to set aside and give no force and effect to the agreement. The complaint states arbitrable questions and disputes within the meaning of the collective bargaining agreement.

Accordingly the Adjustment Board finds and concludes that the remedy requested in the complaint as amended should be granted. . . .

THE EMPORIUM AND WESTERN ADDITION COMMUNITY ORGANIZATION

192 N.L.R.B. (No. 19), 77 L.R.R.M. 1669 (1971)

Before Miller, Chairman; Fanning, Brown, Jenkins, and Kennedy, Members.

The employer operates retail stores in California. This case concerns The Emporium, the employer's department store in San Francisco.

The employer is a party to a multi-employer contract with Department Store Employees Union. This contract contains a no-strike, no-lockout clause, and a clause (Section 21(E)) prohibiting discrimination in employment based on race, color, creed, national origin, age, or sex. Section 5(b) of the contract provides for submission of "any act . . . that is interfering with the faithful performance of this agreement" to an adjustment board.

In April 1968, it became the union's "official" position that there was discrimination against minority-race employees at the store. On April 11, the union sent the multi-employer bargaining agent and several union members copies of a letter stating that "discrimination does exist and . . . this discrimination is directed against the Negro employees and the more senior employees. . . ." It was agreed that the employer would "look into the matter" of discrimination and see what could be done to "improve conditions."

In May Johnson, the union's chief executive officer, met with 10 employees. The main topic of the meeting concerned Russell Young, a Negro; it was claimed that he had been passed over for a promotion which instead had gone to an "outsider." Since Young was leaving on his vacation, it was agreed to take the matter up at a later meeting.

Another meeting was held on September 3, attended by representatives of the Fair Employment Practices Committee (FEPC) and the EEOC. Several union members were present, including Tom Hawkins and James Joseph Hollins, who also had attended prior meetings. The union advised that it intended to submit grievances concerning racial discrimination to the adjustment board.

On September 4, the union sent the multi-employer bargaining agent a letter alleging violations of Section 5(b) and 21(E) of the agreement and asking for arbitration.

On October 16, the adjustment board met. Four employees, including Hawkins and Hollins, stated that they would not participate as individuals, but only as a group; they stated that they objected to prosecuting grievances on an individual basis and wanted the matter of racial discrimination presented as an issue affecting all employees belonging to minority races. They also insisted on meeting with the employer's president, and refused to go ahead with the adjustment board hearing. The four of them left the meeting.

Hollins told the employer's president that he wanted to discuss what was happening with regard to minority employees. The president replied that the employer's personnel director attended to such matters. Hollins declined to take up the matter with the personnel director.

On October 22, Hollins, Hawkins, and two or three other employees held a press conference with regard to what they viewed as the employer's discriminatory racial policies.

On Saturday, November 2, Hawkins, Hollins, and at least two other employees began picketing in front of the Emporium on their own time. They gave passersby pamphlets headed, "Beware Emporium Shoppers, Boycott is on." These pamphlets read as follows:

> *For years at The Emporium black, brown, yellow and red people, have worked at the lowest jobs, at the lowest levels. Time and time again we have seen intelligent hard working brothers and sisters denied promotions and basic respect.*
>
> *The Emporium is a 20th century colonial plantation. The brothers and sisters are being treated the same way as our brothers are being treated in the slave mines of South Africa.*
>
> *Whenever the racist pig at The Emporium injures or harms a black sister or brother, they injure and insult all black people. The Emporium must pay for these insults. Therefore, we encourage all of our people to take their money out of this racist store, until black people have full employment and are promoted justly through-out The Emporium.*

We welcome the support of our brothers and sisters from the churches, unions, sororities, fraternities, social clubs, Afro-American Institute, Black Panther Party, W.A.C.O. and the Poor People's Institute.

On November 7, the employer notified Hawkins and Hollins in writing that they would be discharged if they continued to engage in such acts or to make public statements which were untrue and were intended to injure The Emporium's reputation.

On November 9, Hollins and Hawkins again picketed The Emporium on their own time, handing out pamphlets which were identical in all material respects to the pamphlets distributed on November 2.

On November 11, the employer discharged Hollins and Hawkins for their distribution of "Boycott Emporium" literature on November 9.

[*Text from trial examiner's decision adopted by Board*] "What we have here is a group of four employees who set out on their own to rectify what they in good faith considered working conditions unfair to minority employees. Apparently, they were self-appointed for there is no evidence that they were elected or in any way designated by minority employees generally to represent them, they alone walked out of the September 3 meeting, and it does not appear that they were joined in their picketing activities by other Emporium employees. We are concerned with only two of them, Hollins and Hawkins, the other two not being named in the complaint. It matters not whether we as individuals approve or disapprove their conduct, for if we approved it in toto there would still remain the issue of whether their activities ran counter to the bargaining agreement by which the Respondent was bound and had the effect of requiring, if their demands were to be met, that the Respondent bargain on two fronts when it was required by law to bargain on only one. On the entire evidence I am convinced that their activities did run counter to the bargaining agreement and did have that effect.

"Aside from the clause outlawing racial and other discrimination, the bargaining agreement set up a comprehensive procedure for the adjustment and arbitration of grievances. The Union was bound to follow those procedures and so was the Respondent. The picketing employees were not satisfied to follow those procedures, but in the words of the Union's president, wanted something 'dramatic.' The Union declined to submit to their demands that grievances be prosecuted on a store-wide rather than an individual basis, or to endorse their resort to the 'dramatic' by way of picketing and the distribution of accusatory pamphlets. There is no basis in the evidence for a finding that the Union approved, endorsed, or in any way connived in the action taken by the four employees. They were told that the Union would consider it illegal for it to engage in such activities, but they could do what they pleased as individuals. Obviously, the Union could not stop them from acting as individuals, and beyond attempting to persuade them against the course they took, was powerless to prevent it. It would be absurd to say that because they and the Union had a common ultimate objective, these four employees were somehow implementing or strengthening the Union in its position. They were acting outside the agreement and contrary to the Union's advice and urging. All the evidence indicates that the Union, their duly designated bargaining representative, was endeavoring in every way available to it under the agreement to adjust any and all cases of racial discrimination brought to its attention, and in at least one and apparently two cases had brought about the desired adjustment. It is also evident that it was prepared to resort to arbitration to enforce its position that racial discrimination in conditions of employment existed in Respondent's store, and was handicapped in proceeding by the four employees' refusal to assist or to be represented by the Union in the matter.

"The evidence further establishes that this was no mere presentation of a grievance, but nothing short of a demand that the Respondent bargain with the picketing employees for the entire group of minority employees. This is shown by Hollins' meeting with Respondent's president, Batchelder, in which he told the latter that he wanted to 'discuss what was happening among minority employees,' his later insistence that those picketing would be satisfied with nothing less than a meeting with Batchelder, and Hawkins' testimony that those picketing were seeking to 'talk to the top management to get better conditions for The Emporium,' that those picketing were seeking to accomplish their objectives through 'group talk and through the president if we could talk to him.' It is further clear that the Respondent never refused to have an informal discussion with these employees and referred them to Respondent's personnel director for such discussions, and that they scorned such talks and insisted on negotiating directly with Batchelder.

"In sum, to extend the protection of the Act to the two employees named in the complaint would seriously undermine the right of employees to bargain collectively through representatives of their own choosing, handicap and prejudice the employees' duly designated representative in its efforts to bring about a durable improvement in working conditions among employees belonging to racial minorities, and place on the Employer an unreasonable burden of attempting to placate self-designated representatives of minority groups while abiding by the terms of a valid bargaining agreement and attempting in good faith to meet whatever demands the bargaining representative put forth under that agreement. Therefore, aside from the issue of whether the picketing employees engaged in invective and incitation to boycott which denied them protection in their concerted activities, . . . I would dismiss the complaint in this proceeding."

[*Text from Board's decision*] "Unlike our dissenting colleague, Member Jenkins, we conclude that the record before us neither requires nor allows findings as to two matters which were not alleged or litigated but which, nevertheless, are assumed as facts and supply the foundation of his dissent, specifically: (1) that Respondent was engaged in a pattern or practice of racial discrimination, and (2) that the Union's efforts to remedy that supposed discrimination were so limited that the Union breached its duty of fair representation and should forfeit its status as the exclusive representative of employees in the bargaining unit. Furthermore, since those issues were not litigated, any factual findings with respect to them could not properly be made upon this record. Thus the sole issue presented for decision on this record is whether the conduct of the discharged employees was unprotected because in derogation of the duly designated exclusive bargaining representative. For the reasons stated by the Trial Examiner, we agree that the actions of the discharged employees in abandoning the contractual grievance procedure and seeking to initiate direct negotiations with Respondent by picketing and boycott activities were not protected by the Act."

Complaint is dismissed.

JENKINS, Member, dissenting:

[Text] "Respondent, The Emporium, operates a department store in the San Francisco area. It has a collective-bargaining agreement with the Union, containing a clause prohibiting racial discrimination. Respondent discharged two Black employees for orderly picketing and leafletting of Respondent's store in protest of alleged racial discrimination respecting promotions and other terms and conditions of employment.

"Over six months before the picketing and leafletting began, the Union had alleged The Emporium had violated the nondiscrimination clause, and had sought to pursue individual cases of alleged discrimination through the grievance and arbitration procedure established by the collective-bargaining agreement. Some employees, including those discharged, considered that the alleged discrimination problem affected all black, brown, yellow, and red employees. They objected to the Union's limiting grievances to individual cases as being too slow, narrow, and ineffective as a remedy, and asked the Union to seek grievance adjustment, and arbitration if necessary, of the broad question of all phases of discriminatory treatment of all Black and other minority employees. The Union declined, and the picketing and leafletting resulted.

"The question thus presented is whether concerted activity by employees protesting the existence of all forms of alleged racial discrimination loses its protection under the Act because the Union representing the employees has taken a position in support of eliminating some, but not all, phases of the alleged discrimination.[3]

3. It will be noted, contrary to the statement in . . . the majority opinion, that I have set forth the facts as involving "alleged" discrimination, and have refrained from any indication of the merit (or lack of it) in the protesting employees' assertions that Respondent engaged in racial discrimination. If the employees were of the opinion that such discrimination existed, and protested, this suffices (in the absence of additional factors such as those subsequently considered in the text) to make their activities concerted and concerned with terms and conditions of their employment, and thus brings such activities within the protection of Section 7. It is on this principle, and on these facts, that my subsequent analysis and discussion is based — as I had thought was clear. While it would make no difference in my conclusions whether the Union agreed or disagreed with the

"The Trial Examiner found that the picketing and leafletting lost its protection, primarily for two reasons: (1) The Union is the exclusive representative of the employees under the Act; the Act entitles the Employer to deal only with the Union rather than bargain on two fronts; thus the picketing and leafletting undermined the Union's exclusive representation of the employees; and (2) the Union had made substantial and good-faith efforts to achieve an orderly solution to the problem within the collective-bargaining processes.[4]

"Neither of these reasons withstands scrutiny.

"The union's right to be the exclusive representative of the employees originates in the principle of collective bargaining established by the Act. This principle requires that the representative of the employees present a single set of demands or goals covering all employees, and that whatever bargain is struck with the representative by the employer be applicable to all employees, so that the employer need bargain neither with splinter groups of employees nor with individual employees, and may not undermine the union by doing so. This in turn implies that the union must have the power to balance and adjust the legitimate competing claims within the employee groups, and that whatever adjustment is arrived at fairly by the union and its membership forecloses individual or splinter-group assertion of conflicting positions. It was these considerations of balances, adjustment, and exclusive representation which the Trial Examiner applied to find that the leafletting and picketing here were unprotected.

"This application rests upon a serious misconception. Union action preempts or forecloses individual employee action only in those cases where the balancing of competing *legitimate* interests of employees is involved. In the case of racial discrimination, no such balancing is permitted. A union cannot permit a little, or a lot, of racial discrimination against one group in order to obtain something in a different area from the employer, for a different group of employees. Such 'balancing' has been unlawful since Steele v. Louisville & Nashville Railroad Co., 323 U.S. 192, 15 LRRM 708. . . .

---

protesters, I note further that the Union also was of the opinion that Respondent practiced racial discrimination.

4. The third ground relied on by the Trial Examiner, that the discharged employees were only "self-styled" representatives of others, does not warrant further consideration here, for it is plain the activity was concerted and related to conditions of employment. I do not suppose my colleagues to rely on this ground.

The Trial Examiner's inference that the protesting employees, by seeking a meeting with the Employer's president, were thereby seeking to "bargain" for all minority employees apart from the Union appears unfounded. Their desire to talk to Respondent's president, far from evincing a desire to "bargain," merely reflected a traditional opinion shared by Blacks and often enforced by actual experience that only the president or "boss" of the company can effect permanent solutions to problems involving racial discrimination. Apart from this consideration, there is no rule of law which requires an employee to adjust his grievance with a lower ranking official or which transforms a grievance when presented to the president of a company into collective bargaining. Nor is there any reason why a grievance may not pertain to a group rather than an individual complaint and accordingly be resolved on a group rather than an individual basis.

"The principles of Steele have been uniformly followed, refined, and broadly applied in a long line of cases since then. . . . These cases all make it clear that a union's obligation under this Act is to refrain from actions which permit discrimination on arbitrary or invidious grounds. This duty to refrain, as explicitly stated in Steele, includes the duty not to engage in, permit, or tolerate provisions in bargaining agreements, or practices under or outside such agreements, which constitute or permit such invidious discrimination. It follows from this that whenever union conduct falls short of this obligation, it cannot preempt or foreclose the concerted action of employees, outside the collective-bargaining relationship, directed toward doing the very thing which the union itself is obligated to do. If this were not so, we would face the grave constitutional questions concerning the validity of the union's representation which the Court noted in Steele.

"As this Board pointed out in Tanner Motor Livery, Ltd., 166 NLRB 551, 65 LRRM 1502, the union is required, by its duty of fair representation and by constitutional considerations, to support the elimination of racial discrimination; consequently, the protest of racial discrimination in employment *cannot* be in opposition to or at cross-purposes with the union's position . . . .[5]

"To hold otherwise would permit a union to control the scope, direction, pace, and degree of elimination of racial discrimination, of which any voluntary tolerance by the union breaches its duty of fair representation. The only permissible collective bargaining concerning racial discrimination is its elimination.

"No court has permitted the existence of a collective-bargaining agreement to stay its hand in ordering an employer to eliminate discrimination. Further, employers can ultimately change existing collective-bargaining agreement provisions which have discriminatory effects and may do so free from the threat of a strike. . . . As to discriminatory practices which are not derived from or are not inherent in the collective-bargaining agreement, employers are not only free unilaterally to eliminate such discrimination, but are duty-bound to do so. They cannot be heard to protest that their failure to eliminate discriminatory practices or to treat with employees who concertedly protest such practices is in derogation of the exclusive representative states of the

5. The Ninth Circuit, in remanding Tanner, did so on the ground that the protesting employees had not first sought to pursue their cause through the union, 419 F.2d 216, 72 LRRM 2886. In the present case the employees did request or demand that the Union pursue the broad overall grievance and it was only after the Union declined to do so that they began the picketing and leafletting. The court left standing the Board's finding that employees who engaged in concerted protests of an employer's racially discriminatory practices were entitled to the protection of Section 7 of the Act.

In the recent case of Washington State Service Employees State Council No. 18, 188 NLRB No. 141, 76 LRRM 1467, this Board held that the protection accorded to such protests in Tanner Motor extended even to protests which occurred outside the immediate employer-employee relationship. As this recent decision clearly demonstrates, the right to engage in such activities stands on a different footing from the collective-bargaining relationship.

union. Nor may they shift their responsibility under the national labor policy to eliminate all racial discrimination to the union by making such illegal discrimination a matter solely within the jurisdiction of a grievance-arbitration procedure, thereby placing the burden largely on the union and providing themselves with a ready defense to any and all concerted activities by their employees to directly eliminate discriminatory practices. If a union position in favor of the elimination of *some* but not all racial discrimination can foreclose concerted employee activity to remove *all* racial discrimination, collective bargaining on this subject is converted from a shield protecting employees against racial discrimination into a sword by which such protection can be cut down or cut back. . . . Thus the victims of discrimination have a right under the Act to sue both the employer and their union in order to end the discrimination. If union inactivity to end discrimination cannot cause such extreme measures by the employees to lose them the protection of the Act, plainly that protection cannot be lost by the employees' efforts at persuasion here.

"Accordingly, the principle of exclusive representation by the union cannot preclude the picketing and leafletting the employees engaged in here, nor deprive such activity of protection under the Act.

"In addition to having made a 'tardy assumption' of its responsibilities in this area in the past, the Board here, by holding the concerted conduct of the employees to be unprotected and thus sanctioning their discharge, places itself in the position of participating in and aiding and abetting the continuance of those phases of racial discrimination which the Union elected not to try to remedy. In Independent Metal Workers Union, Local No. 1 (Hughes Tool Company), 147 NLRB 1573, 56 LRRM 1289, the Board stated that it 'cannot validly render aid under Section 9 of the Act' to a labor organization which discriminates racially. Yet here, the Board as an organ of the Government, by withdrawing its protection from these employees who are protesting racial discrimination, is breaching its constitutional and statutory obligation not to aid or permit such discrimination. Brown v. Board of Education, 347 U.S. 483; Shelley v. Kraemer, 334 U.S. 1.

"The Trial Examiner also relied upon the Union's good-faith efforts to achieve an orderly solution to the problem within the collective-bargaining relationship as a ground for finding that the concerted activity outside union channels was unprotected.

"This position misconceives the problem. The question is not whether the Union moved as vigorously or as effectively as it reasonably could have. It may have done so. The Employer's economic power and the desire to retain economic benefits of racial discrimination may impose severe limitations on a union's ability to make progress on this front. Indeed, there is no intimation in this case that the Union had the ability to do substantially more than it had undertaken to do, and the Employer's prompt retaliation by discharging the picketing and leafletting employees suggests that perhaps the Union may have been exerting the full range of its power and ability to eliminate racial discrimination.[6]

"The union's own judgment of its capabilities with regard to the pace and scope of eliminating the discrimination may result from its own fair estimate of the realities[7] and in that sense may not be grounded in bias or hostility. But the absence of subjective bias or animus is irrelevant to the duty of fair representation, and it does not follow from the absence of hostility by the union that the employees cannot themselves then take action under the protection of the Act in support of the complete elimination of racial discrimination. The right to be free from racial discrimination in employment does not arise solely from this statute creating union representation but, as Steele held, is in substantial part based upon the Constitution which requires the exclusive representative under this Act to refrain from tolerating racial discrimination respecting terms and conditions of employment. In this respect, it is analogous to the employer's freedom of speech to oppose union's, or the union's freedom of speech in handbilling: There are some respects in which it cannot be circumscribed or limited by the Act or by this Board. One of these is the freedom from limiting the protection of the Act by union preemption through the union's assertion of a lesser opposition to racial discrimination than the protesting employees assert. If the employees cannot engage in concerted activity to eliminate racial discrimination entirely after the union has declined to try to do so, a union interested in retaining discrimination can preempt the field by moving only at a snail's pace, or in token areas.

6. The reverse, of course, may also be true, with the union rather than the employer exercising the greater power and resisting the elimination of discrimination. The existence of racial discrimination does not automatically imply that both the union and employer have committed violations of the Act, though this may be true in some cases. The issue can be resolved by charging both with violations, ascertaining through the hearing process which was the responsible party, and holding it liable for the remedy.

The preceding portion of this footnote and the paragraph in the text to which this note is appended make it plain, contrary to the statement of the majority . . . that I make no assumption that the Union here has breached its duty of fair representation; rather, the reverse is true. The further statement . . . that I also assume or infer that because of this breach the Union should forfeit its status as bargaining representative is gratuitous. I have suggested no such proposal, either explicitly or implicitly.

7. It hardly follows from this, of course, that the Trial Examiner was correct in his conclusion that the Union was *in fact* "endeavoring in every way available to it under the agreement to adjust any and all cases of racial discrimination brought to its attention." The record shows an unexplained time lag between May and September when the Union apparently did nothing. At the May meeting, the disenchanted employees asked for a delay only until the return of employee Young who was about to go on vacation. In addition, there is no evidence that the Union actually investigated the merits of the numerous complaints Johnson received from approximately 40 employees who attended the April 3 meeting. Indeed, there is evidence in the record that throughout the summer various employees expressed to Johnson frustration at the delay and implored him to take action. It is apparent that the delay engendered suspicion of the motives of the Union and that the frustrations built up during the summer months contributed to the discriminatees' resort to the activities for which they were discharged.

"Finally, the doctrine enunciated by the Court in Steele has been embraced by the Congress in the enactment of Title VII of the Civil Rights Act of 1964, so that the national labor policy itself specifically forbids racial discrimination in the terms and conditions of employment, and its existence is unlawful. The Act we administer must be read consistently with other Federal statutes which establish the national labor policy. Textile Workers Union of America, AFL-CIO v. Lincoln Mills, 353 U.S. 448, 456-458, 40 LRRM 2118. To withdraw the protection of this Act from these employees whose concerted protest was in furtherance of the national labor policy, merely because their Union stopped short of assuming its full obligations under the statute, is contrary to the express purpose of Congress and to the national policy itself.

"Consequently, the employee's handbilling and leafletting remained concerted activity and protected under Section 7 of the Act, and the discharge of the employees for such activity violated Section 8(a)(1). Accordingly, I think we are required to reverse the Trial Examiner and find the discharges to be unlawful."

[The dissenting opinion of Member Brown is omitted.]

NOTES

1. While evidently not adopted by the NLRB, the trial examiner's decision in the Emporium case (NLRB-TXD-(SF)-154-69) Case No. 20-CA-5304, Oct. 24, 1969) contained a lengthy discussion of the significance under the act of language used by the discharged employees.

Given good faith in their picketing activities, the next problem is whether Hawkins and Hollins took themselves out of the protection of the Act by the invective they used both orally and in the pamphlets they distributed, coupled with a call for a boycott by a minority race. To recapitulate, the invective in question accused The Emporium of discrimination in working conditions accorded their minority employees, called it a "20th Century Colonial Plantation," equated its treatment of Negro employees with the "Slave Mines of South Africa," employed the term "Racist Pig" in referring to Respondent, and made this appeal: "Wherefore, we encourage all of our people to take their money out of this racist store, until black people have full employment and are promoted justly throughout the Emporium."

A certain amount of name-calling and exaggeration has been found permissible when occurring in collective bargaining sessions, and in strike and picketing cases. At times the use of abusive epithets has been ascribed to "animal exuberance" or termed "spontaneous." This cannot apply here. Before there had been any picketing the employees in question held a press and radio conference in which they used substantially the same language, and made substantially the same appeal. In short, whatever else may be said of the character of the total performance, it was premeditated, deliberate, made with an intent to do harm to Respondent's business, unless and until the Respondent made what those picketing would regard as an appropriate response.

Attention has also been paid in the decisions to the environment in which the abusive conduct takes place, on or off the job, during or outside working hours, etc. Here the conduct occurred off the job and on the employees' own time. Had they while on the job, singly or concertedly, without immediate provocation addressed their supervisors or officers of management as "racist pigs," and been discharged therefor, I hardly think their employer would be faced with a complaint issued by this agency.[10] It seems to me that the employer suffers far greater injury when such accusations and abusive terms are addressed to the general public and used as incitation to boycott.

The General Counsel would distinguish this case from cases in which the protection of the Act was denied those acting concertedly because they attacked the Employer's product and such attack was unrelated to a labor dispute and unaccompanied by an appeal for public support. N.L.R.B. v. Electrical Workers, 346 U.S. 464; Patterson-Sargent, 115 NLRB 225, 38 LRRM 1134. The cases, as the General Counsel contends, are distinguishable. Here there was no attack on the quality of Respondent's merchandise, the attack was related to a labor dispute, and it was accompanied by an appeal to the public. I would be reluctant to assume, however, that because verbal assaults are related to a labor dispute and attack an employer's reputation rather than the employer's merchandise, anything goes.[11] With a department store which must depend to a substantial degree on the patronage of minority groups, I should think the verbal assault in such terms as "racist pig" and "colonial plantation" would have a graver potential than an attack on the store's merchandise, and the public would be in no better position to determine the truth or falsity of the accusations.

It is further observed that misstatements of fact, where not deliberately or maliciously false, do not remove an employee engaged in concerted activities from the protection of the Act, and I have already found that Hawkins and Hollins *believed* that Respondent was engaging in discriminatory practices relating to minorities. I have some question in my mind whether when a basis for the employer's discharge action is the untruthfulness of the employee's verbal assault, as it is here, we can dispose of the matter so summarily, but the decisions point in that direction. Schnell Tool & Die Corp., 144 NLRB No. 52; Tracy Towing Line, Inc., 166 NLRB No. 9, 65 LRRM 1575; Bowling Green Manufacturing Co., 169 NLRB No. 15, 67 LRRM 1125; Home Restaurant Drive-In, 127 NLRB 635. Cf. Bowling Green Mfg. Co. v. N.L.R.B., (C.C.A. 6, No. 18491), 72 LRRM 2301, reversing 169 NLRB No. 15, 67 LRRM 1124. And where the decisions lead I must follow.

10. Such language if accompanied by, say, a hefty shove, a poke in the nose or a kick in the posterior, would almost certainly deprive the offending employee of the protection of the Act no matter how great his good faith motivation, but on the theory (I presume) that "sticks and stones may break my bones but words can never harm me," we must distinguish between the use of epithets and corporeal assault, no matter how flagrant the former or how minor the latter, when we are dealing with strike or picket line activities. Language found permissible by the Board includes such choice epithets as "wop-bastard," "ignorant s-o-b," "scabby bastard," "goddam bastards," etc., but the line is drawn at "indecent and obscene suggestions relating to biological and bodily functions" and language ascribing "the capability of committing an act so foul as to be unmentionable." Efro Manufacturing Company, 108 NLRB 245, 249; Nutone, Inc., 112 NLRB 1153, 1171-1173; American Tool Works Company, 116 NLRB No. 247; Longview Furniture Company, 110 NLRB 1734, 1738 (in which the Board sets forth its rationale). . . .

11. As the Bard put it, "Who steals my purse steals trash, 'twas something, nothing, 'twas mine, 'tis his . . . but he who filches from me my good name robs me of that which not enriches him but makes me poor indeed."

Returning to the language of the pamphlets itself, the General Counsel correctly observes that such terms as "racist pig" have become terms of common usage in the "contemporary civil rights struggle." (Parenthetically, it is noted that as adjudicators under the Act we do not belong in the contemporary civil rights struggle. Congress did not put us there.) I do not know, however, that the currency of this and like terms make them any the less terms of obliquy, or less damaging to the prestige of a department store such as The Emporium. I assume that there gravity depends a good deal on who is at the receiving end, and how great the potential for injury. Here, I think the gravity is substantial and the protential for injury considerable.

2. The decisions in Hotel Employers Association and The Emporium, supra, point up the difficulties of relying on labor law procedures and personnel to resolve civil rights issues competently. The problem becomes particularly acute when self-help efforts to effect relief from discriminatory practices apparently threaten traditional labor relations concepts contained in collective bargaining agreements. Would the decision makers in the above two cases have a broader view of the racial issues if: (1) civil rights groups could have intervened in the arbitration hearing? (2) the discharged workers in The Emporium had available a special committee (including civil rights, as well as union and employer, representatives) to receive complaints of racial discrimination? What issues might the minority group workers in Hotel Employers Association raise if they could get their case into court?

3. The teaching of the preceding cases is that a few workers attempting to effect change by self-help methods in what they perceive as racist policies are likely to be discharged for their efforts, with little expectation that the courts will be able or willing to provide relief. Where large numbers of minority group workers engage in the protest activity, the chances of change are greater, and unlike the Hotel Employers Association case, such changes can be affirmed by the courts.

CENTRAL CONTRACTORS ASSOCIATION v. LOCAL UNION NO. 46

312 F. Supp. 1388 (W.D. Wash. 1969)

LINDBERG, Chief Judge

Findings of Fact

1. The plaintiff Central Contractors Association is a non-profit Washington corporation organized to involve inner city contractors and craftsmen in more construction jobs.

Tyree E. Scott is a black contractor and Chairman of the Central Contractors Association.

The other plaintiffs are black workers who were employed on construction jobs at the King County Administration Building site and the Harborview Hospital project in Seattle.

2. Defendants are labor organizations representing employees engaged in the construction industry, an industry affecting commerce.

3. On or about August 29, 1969, persons demonstrated at the Harborview Hospital job site in an effort to obtain more jobs in the construction industry for black workers. The job was closed down for approximately six hours for fear that the demonstration might lead to injury.

4. On September 2, 1969, both the Harborview and the King County Administration Building jobs were closed down due to pressure exerted by persons demanding more jobs for minority workers in the construction industry and on these two jobs.

On that date, during demonstrations, led by the Central Contractors Association, acts of intimidation occurred, involving, among others, the driving of a truck through a locked gate into the construction site, creating a condition of hazard to life and property from the confrontation created.

5. Various state, county, city, federal and other contracting agencies have required "affirmative action programs" for the purpose of increasing employment opportunities for minority, non-white employees. King County, as well as many other agencies are obligated under Executive Order 11246, §301 "to assist and cooperate actively . . . in obtaining . . . compliance . . . with these contract provisions." According to the evidence, there appears to be a disproportionate ratio of such employees by each of the defendant unions actually employed on construction sites.

6. On September 6, 1969, Kings County Executive John D. Spellman — pursuant to negotiations between city, county, federal officials, Associated General Contractors and the Central Contractors Association — required and directed Cawdrey & Vemo, Inc., and Sellen Construction Company, by change orders under and within the scope of their respective construction contracts with such County for construction and additions to Harborview Hospital and the King County Administration Building, to: "Hire one trainee or apprentice for each four journeymen employed in each trade union craft jurisdiction on this job and to institute an appropriate program for training persons so hired in conformance with the contract between King County and Seattle Model City Program dated September 6, 1969."

Such change orders were not signed by the contractors.

7. Pursuant to such change orders said contractors or their subcontractors, hired persons, some of whom are plaintiffs herein, each of whom after being hired presented his written notice of employment . . . to the appropriate defendant union, excepting Local 302 of the International Union of Operating Engineers, in which craft no trainee was hired.

8. On September 8, 1969, both the Harborview and King County jobs reopened. Thereafter, commencing on or about September 9, 1969, each of defendant unions, with the exception of the Painters Locals, caused its membership to leave such construction sites, as a result of which the Harborview Hospital project was forced to close on September 10, 1969, and the King County Administration Building was forced to close on September 11, 1969.

9. Each of the defendant unions is a party to a collective bargaining agreement with Cawdrey & Vemo, Inc., and Sellen Construction Company, or their respective subcontractors, each of which contains a no-strike, no-lockout provision and arbitration procedures for the resolution of disputes. None of the defendant unions have presented any grievance and there is no labor dispute between defendant unions and any employer.

10. The appropriate bargaining agents for Cawdrey & Vemo, Inc., and Sellen Construction Company and their respective subcontractors have since at least September 5, 1969, sought to bargain in good faith to amend, alter or otherwise change existing collective bargaining agreements, if necessary, to accommodate trainees.

11. This controversy arises out of allegations of discrimination on the part of defendant unions in that they have not cooperated in the past in attempts to place black workers on jobs under their agreements, that their present efforts are still not sufficient. The labor walkoffs of September 10 and 11, were at least in part motivated by the presence of black trainees employed by the contractors and subcontractors as referred to in Finding 7 herein.

12. The plaintiffs have filed charges with the Equal Employment Opportunities Commission, the National Labor Relations Board, and the Washington State Board Against Discrimination. Neither the National Labor Relations Board, the Equal Employment Opportunity Commission nor the Washington State Board against Discrimination have acted or refused to act on the charges filed with them, nor have any of these agencies sought injunctive relief from this Court as a result of the charges pending before them.

13. The current situation cannot be allowed to continue. Irreparable damage is occurring, including serious delay in construction of much needed public buildings, substantial loss of wages, impairment of contractual rights, probable loss of government financing, and danger of civil strife.

[Conclusions of Law omitted.]

Order

Upon the foregoing Findings of Fact and Conclusions of Law a preliminary injunction shall be entered as follows:

Ordered that:

1. The defendants are enjoined and restrained from discriminating against members of minority races in violation of the provisions of 42 U.S.C., §1981 and that in the implementation of this Order, the following shall apply: . . .

(b) All minority applicants shall be entitled to be represented at any and all hiring hall or apprenticeship proceedings by persons of their choosing to assist them in their efforts to qualify for dispatch or apprenticeship. Provided, however, that such applicants shall not be entitled to assistance during the administering of apprenticeship tests or examinations.

(c) The Defendants shall proceed forthwith and with all possible speed to complete all aspects of the Outreach Program to qualify minority applicants who do not otherwise qualify for apprenticeship or dispatch. The progress of this program shall be reported to the Court within (30) days.

(d) Pending the implementation of the Outreach Program and report to the Court, which shall be made within thirty (30) days of this date, the named plaintiffs shall be returned to their former positions at the Harborview Hospital and King County Administrative Building jobs.

2. That the defendants be ordered to cease and desist from any work stoppage at the Harborview construction site and the King County Administration Building.

3. The Plaintiffs, their agents and representatives, and all other persons having knowledge of this Order are enjoined and restrained from any acts of violence or force or threats of violence or force in connection with any construction work at Harborview Hospital and King County Administration Building.

NOTE

Work stoppages designed to perpetuate racially discriminatory practices have also been enjoined in other cases. See, e.g., State v. Baugh, 2 FEP Cases 271 (W.D. Wash. 1969); United States v. Local 189, United Papermakers and Paperworkers, 282 F. Supp. 39 (E.D. La. 1968); Central Contractors Assn. v. Local 46 IBEW, 2 FEP Cases 189 (W.D. Wash. 1969); United States v. Building and Construction Trades Council of St. Louis, 271 F. Supp. 447 (E.D. Mo. 1966).

Racism Hypo 13
THE BLACK CAUCUS v. EMPLOYER AND UNION (THE DISMISSAL SUIT)

Employer is a medium-size manufacturing firm with approximately one thousand workers, some 10 percent of whom are black. Union has an exclusive bargaining agreement with Employer, provisions of which agreement provide, inter alia:

a. There shall be no strike, picketing, or lockout during the life of this agreement.

b. No person shall be discriminated against in regard to hiring, tenure of employment, or job status by reason of race, color, creed, national origin, age, or sex.

c. Any act of Employer, Union, or any employee that is interfering with the faithful performance of this agreement must be referred to the arbitration board (consisting of two representatives of Employer, two representatives of Union, and one arbitrator agreed to by both) for such action as the arbitration board deems proper and is permissive within this agreement.

In the last few years, both Employer and Union have achieved commendable records in the civil rights area. Pursuant to ∫b of the bargaining agreement, and in compliance with applicable federal civil rights laws, Employer attempted to eliminate prior employment policies which admittedly discriminated against blacks. Union cooperated with Employer's actions and, as a result, the following affirmative steps were taken: the number of black employees was increased, opportunities for upgrading were made available, and blacks were given supervisory positions in Union as well as Employer.

A number of black employees remained unsatisfied with the above actions. They began meeting as a "Black Caucus" to determine additional steps which Employer and Union should take to eliminate "lasting traces of racism."

The Black Caucus demanded that Employer and Union establish a one-million-dollar "Reparations Fund," the money to be used in the financing of a newly organized community black school. The caucus supported its demands with a study estimating that discriminatory practices by Employer and Union during the period from 1954 until 1964 had cost black workers and their families at least ten million dollars in lost wages and economic opportunities. They stated that the reparations fund (which they acknowledged would make a substantial dent in both the Employer and Union treasuries) was necessary, to atone for their past racist actions and to ensure that black youth would have the educational backgrounds required to obtain the increasingly technical jobs at Employer. They asserted that this demand could be justified under existing legal precedent.

Black Caucus refused a Union-Employer request that the reparations fund demand be submitted to the arbitration board provided for by the exclusive bargaining contract. They called for a special arbitration panel to hear all racially oriented grievances, by Employer, Union and the Caucus, with representatives to be chosen by each of the three parties. Employer and Union rejected this plan. Despite warnings that their activity was interfering with production and outside the ambit of a labor dispute, Black Caucus members distributed leaflets throughout the plant urging other workers — black and white — to support the reparations demand. Three Caucus workers, apprehended passing out literature during working hours, were discharged because their activity was deemed disruptive, because it violated the terms of the collective bargaining agreement, and because it endangered further efforts to improve conditions for black workers. Union refused to initiate grievance procedures on behalf of the three men for similar reasons.

Caucus has filed suit on behalf of the three men under applicable federal labor law provisions, Title VII and 42 U.S.C. ∫1981. They seek reinstatement and back pay.

Law Firm A will represent Black Caucus in a hearing on a motion to dismiss filed by Employer.

Law Firm B will represent Employer and Union.

Racism Hypo 14
EMPLOYER v. BLACK CAUCUS (THE INJUNCTION SUIT)

Three days after the denial of the preliminary injunction prayed for by the Black Caucus in Racism Hypo 13, ninety-five black workers went out on strike and began picketing Employer's plant, in response to the discharge of the three Black Caucus members. Their picket signs urged other workers not to cross the picket lines and to stay off the job until the three workers were rehired.

On the same day, Caucus leaders appeared on a local television station's news program and charged that Employer and Union were "hypocritically racist." The two organizations were called "dangerously racist institutions."

The next day, Caucus leaders were served with copies of a temporary restraining order secured by Employer from the appropriate federal district court. It enjoined Caucus from further picketing, statements and activity resulting in harm and injury to the company's name and business reputation.

Ten days later, a hearing was had on Employer's motion for a permanent injunction. Union did not join Employer in its suit but refused to provide funds needed by Caucus for legal fees.

After hearing the evidence and arguments from both sides, the court handed down the following findings, opinion, and order:

NEUTER, J. — *The plaintiff's complaint alleges continued picketing of plaintiff's plant by Black Caucus in violation of the collective bargaining agreement covering the striking workers and the prayer is for a permanent injunction in the same terms as the temporary restraining order issued by this court ten days ago. Defendant's answer entered a general denial as to all relevant matters.*

Upon plaintiff's motion for a permanent injunction, a hearing was had at which evidence was taken and oral arguments made. On the basis of those proceedings and the briefs and record herein, the court made the following findings of fact and law:

FINDINGS OF FACT

(1) Employer and Union currently have a collective bargaining agreement covering all employees, including the striking members of Black Caucus;

(2) Section (a) of the agreement is a clause forbidding strikes during the life of the agreement;

(3) Section (c) of the agreement is a clause requiring arbitration of disagreements arising under the agreement;

(4) The agreement is currently in full force;

(5) Under the agreement, the Arbitration Board consists of two representatives of Employer, two representatives of Union, and one impartial party;

(6) No black man or black worker or member of Black Caucus has ever served on the Arbitration Board;

(7) There are twenty posts in Union hierarchy; one is held by a black man; no member of Union's five-man governing board is black;

(8) Ninety-five members of Caucus were, up to the issuance of this court's temporary restraining order, picketing Employer's plant;

(9) Caucus intends to resume its picketing if the order of this court is withdrawn; and

(10) Employer was irreparably harmed by Caucus's picketing in that:

(a) a small but undetermined number of workers who were not members of Black Caucus refused to cross the picket lines;

(b) a number of deliveries to Employer's plant were not made because drivers would not cross Caucus picket lines; and

(c) Employer's reputation suffered on account of the charges made by the leaders of Black Caucus;

for none of which does Employer have an adequate remedy at law.

CONCLUSIONS OF LAW

(1) This case arises under the laws of the United States and this court has jurisdiction to hear suits for violation of contracts of the type involved herein pursuant to §301 of the Labor Management Relation Act of 1947, 61 Stat. 156, 29 U.S.C. §185; Textile Workers Union v. Lincoln Mills of Alabama, 353 U.S. 448, 77 S. Ct. 923, 1 L. Ed. 2d 972 (1957);

(2) This court has jurisdiction to issue an injunction pursuant to §301 of the Labor Management Relations Act of 1947, 61 Stat. 156, 29 U.S.C. §185; cf. Boys Market, Inc. v. Retail Clerk's Union, Local 770, 397 U.S. 235, 90 S. Ct. 1583, 26 L. Ed. 199 (1970);

(3) The Caucus picketing was in violation of Section (a) of the agreement; and

(4) Ordinary principles of equity warrant the issuance of an injunction in this case. Cf. Boys Market, supra. This court will not withhold its injunction in favor of a defendant who has not exhausted his remedies under the contract (Section (c)) or in other administrative proceedings available to him. (Civil Rights Act of 1964, §703, 42 U.S.C. §2000e-2 (1964).)

WHEREFORE, let the permanent injunction issue in the same terms as the temporary restraining order herein.

Law Firm A will represent Employer at the oral argument of the Black Caucus's appeal.

Law Firm B will represent Black Caucus, urging reversal of the district court's final order.

Part VI
RIGHT TO JUSTICE

15. REMEDIES FOR SUMMARY PUNISHMENT

A. PROTECTION VIA CRIMINAL PENALTIES

In the final analysis, law has failed the black man, less because it was inadequate than because when he needed it most, for his physical safety, it deserted him entirely. Laws requiring his children to attend segregated schools posed an onerous handicap to his development; laws that required segregation in public facilities constituted a humiliation to his spirit. But it was the absolute refusal of the law to protect his person that is responsible for the subjugation of blacks. That process began immediately after the Civil War, but eased for a period during Reconstruction when Civil Rights Statutes were enacted and federal troops were present (if not always effective). Then, when it was clear that the withdrawal of these protections would spell death to many blacks and the worst form of oppression to all, they were withdrawn.

The story of the oppression of blacks by force has been told in literally hundreds of reports, histories, narratives and studies, many of which are excerpted or cited in Emerson, Haber and Dorsen, II Political and Civil Rights in the United States 996-1012 (student ed. 1967). There were the organized terror groups, the Ku Klux Klan, the White Camellias and the White League. There were also the lynchings, sometimes carried out by organized groups, but more frequently the work of ad hoc mobs. R. Ginzburg, in One Hundred Years of Lynchings (1969), has compiled a partial listing of the approximately 5000 blacks lynched in the United States since 1859. Ginzburg reprints hundreds of newspaper reports of lynchings, the reading of which almost, but not quite, explains how one presidential commission could report that murders in which the victims were riddled with bullets constituted some "of the less brutal lynchings of the past years [because] [t]he victims in these cases were not mutilated or burned. . . ." To Secure These Rights, Report of the President's Committee On Civil Rights (1947), excerpted in Emerson, Haber and Dorsen, supra, at 997.

In addition to the lynchings, hundreds of blacks lost their lives in what are generally referred to as "race riots," but which in most instances were simply racial massacres. One of the bloodiest of these occurred in 1917 in East St. Louis, Illinois. Estimates of the number of blacks killed range from 40 to 200, and nearly 6000 were driven from their homes. Petitions and protests, including in 1917 an NAACP-sponsored silent march down Fifth Avenue in New York, in which 10,000 persons protested against brutalities and lynchings, received major press coverage, but had little effect on lynchers and rioters, and little more on the nation. The Congress never enacted an antilynching law, although efforts, made by liberal congressmen, date back to 1922. In that year, a Senate filibuster killed a House-passed measure that would have punished not only lynchers, but state officers who made no reasonable effort to prevent lynching; further, it would have required the county where the murder occurred to pay the victim's family $10,000. P. Bergman, The Chronological History of the Negro in America 403 (1969).

But in the absence of any legal deterrent, whites needed neither the cover of an organization nor the group support of a mob to murder or brutalize blacks. And, while no statistics could be maintained on such crimes, it is likely that the number of blacks who were victims of random, arbitrary white violence far exceeded those who lost their lives in riots or mob attacks. Immediately after the Civil War,

> Native whites undertook to "manage" or "control" the freedmen as they were handled when slaves. If the freedmen objected, they were beaten or killed. Referring to South Carolina, an authority said: "The pecuniary value which the individual Negro formerly represented having disappeared, the maiming and killing of them seemed to be looked upon by many as one of those venial offenses which must be forgiven to the outraged feelings of a wronged and robbed people." "E. H. Johnson, a Virginia clergyman, killed a Negro soldier in 1865." According to the Richmond Inquirer on November 3, 1866, "J. C. Johnston, a law student of Lexington charged with killing a freedman, was acquitted." For a trivial reason, one Queensbury, a planter in Louisa County, killed a Negro in his employ. Because of slight misunderstandings, R. N. Eastham of Rappahannock, and Washington Alsworth of Lunenburg killed Negroes in their service. On November 24, 1866, the Inquirer reported that Dr. James Watson, "one of the most respectable gentlemen of Rockbridge County," killed a Negro for driving into his vehicle. These criminals were not punished. (C. Woodson and C. Wesley, The Negro In Our History 394 (1922).)

The efforts of the Reconstruction Congresses to combat white lawlessness, together with the wildly varying Supreme Court interpretations given the statutes enacted for this purpose, are recounted in the following cases.

UNITED STATES v. PRICE
383 U.S. 787, 86 S. Ct. 1152, 16 L. Ed. 2d 267 (1966)

Mr. Justice Fortas delivered the opinion of the Court. . . .

The indictments allege assaults by the accused persons upon the rights of the asserted victims to due process of law under the Fourteenth Amendment. The indictment in No. 59 charges 18 persons with violations of 18 U.S.C. §241 (1964 ed.). In No. 60, the same 18 persons are charged with offenses based upon 18 U.S.C. §242 (1964 ed.). These are among the so-called civil rights statutes which have come to us from Reconstruction days, the period in our history which also produced the Thirteenth, Fourteenth, and Fifteenth Amendments to the Constitution.

The sole question presented in these appeals is whether the specified statutes make criminal the conduct for which the individuals were indicted. It is an issue of construction, not of constitutional power. We have no doubt of "the power of Congress to enforce by appropriate criminal sanction every right guaranteed by the Due Process Clause of the Fourteenth Amendment." United States v. Williams, 341 U.S. 70, 72. . . .[2]

The events upon which the charges are based, as alleged in the indictments, are as follows: On June 21, 1964, Cecil Ray Price, the Deputy Sheriff of Neshoba County, Mississippi, detained Michael Henry Schwerner, James Earl Chaney and Andrew Goodman in the Neshoba County jail located in Philadelphia, Mississippi. He released them in the dark of that night. He then proceeded by automobile on Highway 19 to intercept his erstwhile wards. He removed the three men from their automobile, placed them in an official automobile of the Neshoba County Sheriff's office, and transported them to a place on an unpaved road.

These acts, it is alleged, were part of a plan and conspiracy whereby the three men were intercepted by the 18 defendants, including Deputy Sheriff Price, Sheriff Rainey and Patrolman Willis of the Philadelphia, Mississippi, Police Department. The purpose and intent of the release from custody and the interception, according to the charge, were to "punish" the three men. The defendants, it is alleged, "did wilfully assault, shoot and kill" each of the three. And, the charge continues, the bodies of the three victims were transported by one of the defendants from the rendezvous on the unpaved road to the vicinity of the construction site of an earthen dam approximately five miles southwest of Philadelphia, Mississippi.

These are federal and not state indictments. They do not charge as crimes the alleged assaults or murders. The indictments are framed to fit the stated federal statutes, and the question before us is whether the attempt of the

2. Cf. Mr. Justice Holmes in United States v. Mosley, 238 U.S. 383, 386 . . . (a federal voting rights case under an earlier version of §241): "It is not open to question that this statute is constitutional. . . ." The source of congressional power in this case is, of course, §5 of the Fourteenth Amendment, which reads: "The Congress shall have power to enforce, by appropriate legislation, the provisions of this article."

There are three "Williams" cases arising from the same events. The first, with no bearing on the present appeal is United States v. Williams, 341 U.S. 58 . . . involving a prosecution for perjury. The second, United States v. Williams, 341 U.S. 70 . . . was a prosecution for violation of §241; it will be referred to hereinafter as Williams I. The third, Williams v. United States, 341 U.S. 97 . . . was a prosecution for violation of §242; it will be referred to as Williams II.

draftsman for the Grand Jury in Mississippi has been successful: whether the indictments charge offenses against the various defendants which may be prosecuted under the designated federal statutes.

We shall deal first with the indictment in No. 60, based on §242 of the Criminal Code and then with the indictment in No. 59, under §241. We do this for ease of exposition and because §242 was enacted by the Congress about four years prior to §241. Section 242 was enacted in 1866; §241 in 1870.

I. No. 60

Section 242 defines a misdemeanor, punishable by fine of not more than $1,000 or imprisonment for not more than one year, or both. So far as here significant, it provides punishment for "Whoever, under color of any law, statute, ordinance, regulation, or custom, willfully subjects any inhabitant of any State . . . to the deprivation of any rights, privileges, or immunities secured or protected by the Constitution or laws of the United States. . . ."

The indictment in No. 60 contains four counts, each of which names as defendants the three officials and 15 nonofficial persons. The First Count charges, on the basis of allegations substantially as set forth above, that all of the defendants conspired "to wilfully subject" Schwerner, Chaney and Goodman "to the deprivation of their right, privilege and immunity secured and protected by the Fourteenth Amendment to the Constitution of the United States not to be summarily punished without due process of law by persons acting under color of the laws of the State of Mississippi." This is said to constitute a conspiracy to violate §242, and therefore an offense under 18 U.S.C. §371 (1964 ed.). The latter section, the general conspiracy statute, makes it a crime to conspire to commit any offense against the United States. The penalty for violation is the same as for direct violation of §242 — that is, it is a misdemeanor.

On a motion to dismiss, the District Court sustained this First Count as to all defendants. As to the sheriff, deputy sheriff and patrolman, the court recognized that each was clearly alleged to have been acting "under color of law" as required by §242.[5] As to the private person, the District Court held that "[I]t is immaterial to the conspiracy that these private individuals were not acting under color of law" because the count charges that they were conspiring with persons who were so acting. See United States v. Rabinowich, 238 U.S. 78, 87. . . .

The court necessarily was satisfied that the indictment, in alleging the arrest, detention, release, interception and killing of Schwerner, Chaney and Goodman, adequately stated as the purpose of the conspiracy, a violation of §242, and that this section could be violated by "wilfully subject[ing the victims] . . . to the deprivation of their right, privilege and immunity" under the Due Process Clause of the Fourteenth Amendment.

5. This is settled by our decisions in Screws v. United States, 325 U.S. 91, 107-113, and Williams II, 341 U.S., at 99-100.

No appeal was taken by the defendants from the decision of the trial court with respect to the First Count and it is not before us for adjudication.

The Second, Third and Fourth Counts of the indictment in No. 60 charge all of the defendants, not with conspiracy, but with substantive violations of §242. Each of these counts charges that the defendants, acting "under color of the laws of the State of Mississippi," "did wilfully assault, shoot and kill" Schwerner, Chaney and Goodman, respectively, "for the purpose and with the intent" of punishing each of the three and that the defendants "did thereby wilfully deprive" each "of rights, privileges and immunities secured and protected by the Constitution and the laws of the United States" — namely, due process of law.

The District Court held these counts of the indictment valid as to the sheriff, deputy sheriff and patrolman. But it dismissed them as against the nonofficial defendants because the counts do not charge that the latter were "officers in fact, or de facto in anything allegedly done by them 'under color of law.'"

We note that by sustaining these counts against the three officers, the court again necessarily concluded that an offense under §242 is properly stated by allegations of willful deprivation, under color of law, of life and liberty without due process of law. We agree. No other result would be permissible under the decisions of this Court. Screws v. United States, 325 U.S. 91 . . . ; Williams II.[6]

But we cannot agree that the Second, Third or Fourth Counts may be dismissed as against the nonofficial defendants. Section 242 applies only where a person indicted has acted "under color" of law. Private persons, jointly engaged with state officials in the prohibited action, are acting "under color" of law for purposes of the statute. To act "under color" of law does not require that the accused be an officer of the State. It is enough that he is a willful participant in joint activity with the State or its agents.[7]

In the present case, according to the indictment, the brutal joint adventure was made possible by state detention and calculated release of the prisoners by an officer of the State. This action, clearly attributable to the State, was

6. ". . . where police take matters in their own hands, seize victims, beat and pound them until they confess, there cannot be the slightest doubt that the police have deprived the victim of a right under the Constitution. It is the right of the accused to be tried by a legally constituted court, not by a kangaroo court." Williams II, 341 U.S., at 101.

7. "Under color" of law means the same thing in §242 that it does in the civil counterpart of §242, 42 U.S.C. §1983 (1964 ed.). Monroe v. Pape, 365 U.S. 167, 185, 212 (majority opinion). . . . Recent decisions of this Court which have given form to the "state action" doctrine make it clear that the indictments in this case allege conduct on the part of the "private" defendants which constitutes "state action," and hence action "under color" of law within §242. In Burton v. Wilmington Parking Authority, 365 U.S. 715, we hold that there is "state action" whenever the "State has so far insinuated itself into a position of interdependence [with the otherwise 'private' person whose conduct is said to violate the Fourteenth Amendment] . . . that it must be recognized as a joint participant in the challenged activity, which, on that account, cannot be considered to have been so 'purely private' as to fall without the scope of the Fourteenth Amendment." 365 U.S., at 725.

part of the monstrous design described by the indictment. State officers participated in every phase of the alleged venture: the release from jail, the interception, assault and murder. It was a joint activity, from start to finish. Those who took advantage of participation by state officers in accomplishment of the foul purpose alleged must suffer the consequences of that participation. In effect, if the allegations are true, they were participants in official lawlessness, acting in willful concert with state officers and hence under color of law. . . .

Accordingly, we reverse the dismissal of the Second, Third and Fourth Counts of the indictment in No. 60 and remand for trial.

II. No. 59

No. 59 charges each of the 18 defendants with a felony — a violation of §241. This indictment is in one count. It charges that the defendants "conspired together . . . to injure, oppress, threaten and intimidate" Schwerner, Chaney and Goodman "in the free exercise and enjoyment of the right and privilege secured to them by the Fourteenth Amendment to the Constitution of the United States not to be deprived of life or liberty without due process of law by persons acting under color of the laws of Mississippi." The indictment alleges that it was the purpose of the conspiracy that Deputy Sheriff Price would release Schwerner, Chaney and Goodman from custody in the Neshoba County jail at such time that Price and the other 17 defendants "could and would intercept" them "and threaten, assault, shoot and kill them." The penalty under §241 is a fine of not more than $5,000, or imprisonment for not more than 10 years, or both.

Section 241 is a conspiracy statute. It reads as follows:

> If two or more persons conspire to injure, oppress, threaten, or intimidate any citizen in the free exercise or enjoyment of any right or privilege secured to him by the Constitution or laws of the United States, or because of his having so exercised the same; or
>
> If two or more persons go in disguise on the highway, or on the premises of another, with intent to prevent or hinder his free exercise or enjoyment of any right or privilege so secured —
>
> They shall be fined not more than $5,000 or imprisoned not more than ten years, or both.

The District Court dismissed the indictment as to all defendants. In effect, although §241 includes rights or privileges secured by the Constitution or laws of the United States without qualification or limitation, the court held that it does not include rights protected by the Fourteenth Amendment.

It will be recalled that in No. 60 the District Court held that §242 included the denial of Fourteenth Amendment rights — the same right to due process involved in the indictment under §241. Both include rights or privileges secured by the Constitution or laws of the United States. Neither is qualified or limited. Each includes, presumably, *all* of the Constitution and laws of the

United States. To the reader of the two sections, versed only in the English language, it may seem bewildering that the two sections could be so differently read.

But the District Court purported to read the statutes with the gloss of Williams I. In that case, the only case in which this Court has squarely confronted the point at issue, the Court did in fact sustain dismissal of an indictment under §241. But it did not, as the District Court incorrectly assumed, hold that §241 is inapplicable to Fourteenth Amendment rights. The Court divided equally on the issue. Four Justices, in an opinion by Mr. Justice Frankfurter, were of the view that §241 "only covers conduct which interferes with rights arising from the substantive powers of the Federal Government" — rights "which Congress can beyond doubt constitutionally secure against interference by private individuals." 341 U.S., at 73, 77 . . . . Four other Justices, in an opinion by Mr. Justice Douglas, found no support for Mr. Justice Frankfurter's view in the language of the section, its legislative history, or its judicial interpretation up to that time. They read the statute as plainly covering conspiracies to injure others in the exercise of the Fourteenth Amendment rights. They could see no obstacle to using it to punish deprivations of such rights. Dismissal of the indictment was affirmed because Mr. Justice Black voted with those who joined Mr. Justice Frankfurter. He did so, however, for an entirely different reason — that the prosecution was barred by res judicata — and he expressed no view on the issue whether "§241, as applied, is too vague and uncertain in scope to be consistent with the Fifth Amendment." Williams I thus left the proper construction of §241, as regards its applicability to protect Fourteenth Amendment rights, an open question.

In view of the detailed opinions in Williams I, it would be supererogation to track the arguments in all of their intricacy. On the basis of an extensive re-examination of the question, we conclude that the District Court erred; that §241 must be read as it is written — to reach conspiracies "to injure . . . any citizen in the free exercise or enjoyment of any right or privilege secured to him by the Constitution or laws of the United States . . ."; that this language includes rights or privileges protected by the Fourteenth Amendment; that whatever the ultimate coverage of the section may be, it extends to conspiracies otherwise within the scope of the section participated in by officials alone or in collaboration with private persons; and that the indictment in No. 59 properly charges such a conspiracy in violation of §241. We shall confine ourselves to a review of the major considerations which induce our conclusion.

1. There is no doubt that the indictment in No. 59 sets forth a conspiracy within the ambit of the Fourteenth Amendment. Like the indictment in No. 60, supra, it alleges that the defendants acted "under color of law" and that the conspiracy included action by the State through its law enforcement officers to punish the alleged victims without due process of law in violation of the Fourteenth Amendment's direct admonition to the States.

The indictment specifically alleges that the sheriff, deputy sheriff and a patrolman participated in the conspiracy; that it was a part of the "plan and purpose of the conspiracy" that Deputy Sheriff Price, "while having [the three victims] . . . in his custody in the Neshoba County Jail . . . would release them from custody at such time that he [and others of the defendants] . . . could and would intercept [the three victims] . . . and threaten, assault, shoot and kill them."

This is an allegation of state action which, beyond dispute, brings the conspiracy within the ambit of the Fourteenth Amendment. It is an allegation of official, state participation in murder, accomplished by and through its officers with the participation of others. It is an allegation that the State, without the semblance of due process of law as required of it by the Fourteenth Amendment, used its sovereign power and office to release the victims from jail so that they were not charged and tried as required by law, but instead could be intercepted and killed. If the Fourteenth Amendment forbids denial of counsel, it clearly denounces denial of any trial at all.

As we have consistently held "The Fourteenth Amendment protects the individual against *state action,* not against wrongs done by *individuals.*" Williams I, 341 U.S., at 92 . . . (opinion of Douglas, J.). In the present case, the participation by law enforcement officers, as alleged in the indictment, is clearly state action, as we have discussed, and it is therefore within the scope of the Fourteenth Amendment.

2. The argument, however, of Mr. Justice Frankfurter's opinion in Williams I, upon which the District Court rests its decision, cuts beneath this. It does not deny that the accused conduct is within the scope of the Fourteenth Amendment, but it contends that in enacting §241, the Congress intended to include only the rights and privileges conferred on the citizen by reason of the "substantive" powers of the Federal Government — that is, by reason of federal power operating directly upon the citizen and not merely by means of prohibitions of state action. As the Court of Appeals for the Fifth Circuit in Williams I, relied upon in the opinion below, put it, "the Congress had in mind the federal rights and privileges which appertain to citizens as such and not the general rights extended to all persons by the . . . Fourteenth Amendment." 179 F.2d 644, 648. We do not agree.

The language of §241 is plain and unlimited. As we have discussed, its language embraces *all* of the rights and privileges secured to citizens by *all* of the Constitution and *all* of the laws of the United States. There is no indication in the language that the sweep of the section is confined to rights that are conferred by or "flow from" the Federal Government, as distinguished from those secured or confirmed or guaranteed by the Constitution. We agree with the observation of Mr. Justice Holmes in United States v. Mosley, 238 U.S. 383, 387-388, . . . that

> The source of this section in the doings of the Ku Klux and the like is obvious, and acts of violence obviously were in the mind of Congress. Naturally Congress put forth all its powers. . . . [T]his section dealt with Federal rights, and with all Federal rights, and protected them in the lump . . . [It should not be construed so] as to

deprive citizens of the United States of the general protection which on its face §19 [now §241] most reasonably affords.[8]

We believe, with Mr. Justice Holmes, that the history of the events from which §241 emerged illuminates the purpose and means of the statute with an unmistakable light. We think that history leaves no doubt that, if we are to give §241 the scope that its origins dictate, we must accord it a sweep as broad as its language. We are not at liberty to seek ingenious analytical instruments for excluding from its general language the Due Process Clause of the Fourteenth Amendment — particularly since the violent denial of legal process was one of the reasons motivating enactment of the section.[9]

Section 241 was enacted as part of what came to be known as the Enforcement Act of 1870, 16 Stat. 140.[10] The Act was passed on May 31, 1870, only a few months after ratification of the Fifteenth Amendment. In addition to the new §241, it included a re-enactment of a provision of the Civil Rights Act of 1866 which is now §242. The intended breadth of §241 is emphasized by contrast with the narrowness of §242 as it then was.[11] Section 242 forbade the deprivation, "under color of any law," of "any right secured or protected by this act." The rights protected by the Act were narrow and specific: "to make and enforce contracts, to sue, be parties, give evidence, and to the full and equal benefit of all laws and proceedings for the security of person and property as is enjoyed by white citizens [and to] be subject to like punishment, pains, penalties, taxes, licenses, and exactions of every kind, and none other." Act of May 31, 1870, §16, 16 Stat. 144, re-enacting with minor changes Act of April 9, 1866, §1, 14 Stat. 27. Between 1866 and 1870 there was much agitated criticism in the Congress and in the Nation because of the continued denial of rights to Negroes, sometimes accompanied by violent assaults. In response to the demands for more stringent legislation Congress enacted the

8. See also Mr. Justice Rutledge, concurring in result, in Screws v. United States, 325 U.S. 91, 120.

9. It would be strange, indeed, were this Court to revert to a construction of the Fourteenth Amendment which would once again narrow its historical purpose — which remains vital and pertinent to today's problems. As is well known, for many years after Reconstruction, the Fourteenth Amendment was almost a dead letter as far as the civil rights of Negroes were concerned. Its sole office was to impede state regulation of railroads or other corporations. Despite subsequent statements to the contrary, nothing in the records of the congressional debates or the Joint Committee on Reconstruction indicates any uncertainty that its objective was the protection of civil rights. See Stampp, The Era of Reconstruction, 1865-1877, 136-137 (1965).

10. The official title is "An Act to enforce the Right of Citizens of the United States to vote in the several States of this Union, and for other Purposes."

11. The substantial difference in coverage of the two sections as they were in the Act of 1870 precludes the argument that §241 should be narrowly construed to exclude Fourteenth Amendment rights because otherwise it would have been duplicative of §242 taken in conjunction with the general conspiracy statute, 18 U.S.C. §371. If, as we hold, §241 was intended to cover all Fourteenth Amendment rights, it was far broader in 1870 than was §242. For other reasons for rejecting the duplication argument, see the opinion of Mr. Justice Douglas in Williams I, 341 U.S., at 88, n. 2.

Enforcement Act of 1870. Congress had before it and re-enacted §242, which was explicitly limited as we have described. At the same time, it included §241 in the Act using broad language to cover not just the rights enumerated in §242, but all rights and privileges under the Constitution and laws of the United States.

It was not until the statutory revision of 1874 that the specific enumeration of protected rights was eliminated from §242. The section was then broadened to include as wide a range of rights as §241 already did: "any rights, privileges, or immunities, secured or protected by the Constitution or laws of the United States." The substantial change thus effected was made with the customary stout assertions of the codifiers that they had merely clarified and reorganized without changing substance. Section 241 was left essentially unchanged, and neither in the 1874 revision nor in any subsequent re-enactment has there been the slightest indication of a congressional intent to narrow or limit the original broad scope of §241. It is clear, therefore, that §241, from original enactment through subsequent codifications, was intended to deal, as Mr. Justice Holmes put it with conspiracies to interfere with "Federal rights, and with all Federal rights." We find no basis whatsoever for a judgment of Solomon which would give to the statute less than its words command.

The purpose and scope of the 1866 and 1870 enactments must be viewed against the events and passions of the time. The Civil War had ended in April 1865. Relations between Negroes and whites were increasingly turbulent. Congress had taken control of the entire governmental process in former Confederate States. It had declared the governments in 10 "unreconstructed" States to be illegal and had set up federal military administrations in their place. Congress refused to seat representatives from these States until they had adopted constitutions guaranteeing Negro suffrage, and had ratified the Fourteenth Amendment. Constitutional conventions were called in 1868. Six of the 10 States fulfilled Congress' requirements in 1868, the other four by 1870.

For a few years "radical" Republicans dominated the governments of the Southern States and Negroes played a substantial political role. But countermeasures were swift and violent. The Ku Klux Klan was organized by southern whites in 1866 and a similar organization appeared with the romantic title of the Knights of the White Camellia. In 1868 a wave of murders and assaults was launched including assassinations designed to keep Negroes from the polls. The States themselves were helpless, despite the resort by some of them to extreme measures such as making it legal to hunt down and shoot any disguised man.

Within the Congress pressures mounted in the period between the end of the war and 1870 for drastic measures. A few months after the ratification of the Thirteenth Amendment on December 6, 1865, Congress, on April 9, 1866, enacted the Civil Rights Act of 1866, which, as we have described, included §242 in its originally narrow form. On June 13, 1866, the Fourteenth Amendment was proposed, and it was ratified in July 1868. In February 1869 the Fifteenth Amendment was proposed, and it was ratified in February 1870. On May 31, 1870, the Enforcement Act of 1870 was enacted.

In this context, it is hardly conceivable that Congress intended §241 to apply only to a narrow and relatively unimportant category of rights.[18] We cannot doubt that the purpose and effect of §241 was to reach assaults upon rights under the entire Constitution, including the Thirteenth, Fourteenth and Fifteenth Amendments, and not merely under part of it.

This is fully attested by the only statement explanatory of §241 in the recorded congressional proceedings relative to its enactment. We refer to the speech of Senator Pool of North Carolina who introduced the provisions as an amendment to the Enforcement Act of 1870.* . . . He urged that the section was needed in order to punish invasions of the newly adopted Fourteenth and Fifteenth Amendments to the Constitution. He acknowledged that the States as such were beyond the reach of the punitive process, and that the legislation must therefore operate upon individuals. He made it clear that "It matters not whether those individuals be officers or whether they are acting upon their own responsibility." We find no evidence whatever that Senator Pool intended that §241 should not cover violations of Fourteenth Amendment rights, or that it should not include state action or actions by state officials.

We conclude, therefore, that it is incumbent upon us to read §241 with full credit to its language. Nothing in the prior decisions of this Court or of other courts which have considered the matter stands in the way of that conclusion.

The present application of the statutes at issue does not raise fundamental questions of federal-state relationships. We are here concerned with allegations which squarely and indisputably involve state action in direct violation of the mandate of the Fourteenth Amendment — that no State shall deprive any person of life or liberty without due process of law. This is a direct, traditional concern of the Federal Government. It is an area in which the federal interest has existed for at least a century, and in which federal participation has intensified as part of a renewed emphasis upon civil rights. Even as recently as 1951, when Williams I was decided, the federal role in the establishment and vindication of fundamental rights — such as the freedom to travel, nondiscriminatory access to public areas and nondiscriminatory educational facilities — was neither as pervasive nor as intense as it is today. Today, a decision interpreting a federal law in accordance with its historical design,

18. See, for example, United States v. Waddell, 112 U.S. 76 (right to perfect a homestead claim); United States v. Classic, 313 U.S. 299 (right to vote in federal elections); Logan v. United States, 144 U.S. 263 (right to be secure from unauthorized violence while in federal custody); In re Quarles, 158 U.S. 532 (right to inform of violations of federal law). Cf. also United States v. Cruikshank, 92 U.S. 542, 552; Hague v. Committee for Industrial Organization, 307 U.S. 496 (opinion of Roberts, J.); Collins v. Hardyman, 341 U.S. 651, 660.

* The Court printed the senator's remarks in an appendix to its opinion to show that he clearly intended §241 to cover Fourteenth Amendment rights.

to punish denials by state action of constitutional rights of the person can hardly be regarded as adversely affecting "the wise adjustment between State responsibility and national control . . . ." Williams I, 341 U.S., at 73 . . . (opinion of Frankfurter, J.). In any event, the problem, being statutory and not constitutional, is ultimately, as it was in the beginning, susceptible of congressional disposition.

Reversed and remanded.

Mr. Justice BLACK concurs in the judgment and opinion of the Court except insofar as the opinion relies upon [the Williams decisions].

UNITED STATES v. GUEST
383 U.S. 745, 86 S. Ct. 1170, 16 L. Ed. 2d 239 (1966)

Mr. Justice STEWART delivered the opinion of the Court.

The six defendants in this case were indicted by a United States grand jury in the Middle District of Georgia for criminal conspiracy in violation of 18 U.S.C. §241 (1964 ed.). . . . [D]efendants moved to dismiss the indictment on the ground that it did not charge an offense under the laws of the United States. The District Court sustained the motion and dismissed the indictment as to all defendants and all numbered paragraphs of the indictment. . . .

I

The first numbered paragraph of the indictment, reflecting a portion of the language of §201(a) of the Civil Rights Act of 1964, 42 U.S.C. §2000a(a) (1964 ed.), alleged that the defendants conspired to injure, oppress, threaten, and intimidate Negro citizens in the free exercise and enjoyment of: "The right to the full and equal enjoyment of the goods, services, facilities, privileges, advantages, and accommodations of motion picture theaters, restaurants, and other places of public accommodation." The District Court held that this paragraph of the indictment failed to state an offense against rights secured by the Constitution or laws of the United States. The court found a fatal flaw in the failure of the paragraph to include an allegation that the acts of the defendants were motivated by racial discrimination, an allegation the court thought essential to charge an interference with rights secured by Title II of the Civil Rights Act of 1964. The court went on to say that, in any event, 18 U.S.C. §241 is not an available sanction to protect rights secured by that title because §207(b) of the 1964 Act, 42 U.S.C. §2000a-6(b) (1964 ed.), specifies that the remedies provided in Title II itself are to be the exclusive means of enforcing the rights the title secures.

[The district court's ruling on this issue was held not reviewable by the Supreme Court.]

II

The second numbered paragraph of the indictment alleged that the defendants conspired to injure, oppress, threaten, and intimidate Negro citizens of the United States in the free exercise and enjoyment of: "The right to the equal utilization, without discrimination upon the basis of race, of public facilities in the vicinity of Athens, Georgia, owned, operated or managed by or on behalf of the State of Georgia or any subdivision thereof."

Correctly characterizing this paragraph as embracing rights protected by the Equal Protection Clause of the Fourteenth Amendment, the District Court held as a matter of statutory construction that 18 U.S.C. §241 does not encompass any Fourteenth Amendment rights, and further held as a matter of constitutional law that "any broader construction of §241 . . . would render it void for indefiniteness." 246 F. Supp., at 486. In so holding, the District Court was in error, as our opinion in United States v. Price, 383 U.S. 787 . . . decided today, makes abundantly clear.

To be sure, Price involves rights under the Due Process Clause, whereas the present case involves rights under the Equal Protection Clause. But no possible reason suggests itself for concluding that §241 — if it protects Fourteenth Amendment rights — protects rights secured by the one Clause but not those secured by the other. We have made clear in Price that when §241 speaks of "any right or privilege secured . . . by the Constitution or laws of the United States," it means precisely that.

Moreover, inclusion of Fourteenth Amendment rights within the compass of 18 U.S.C. §241 does not render the statute unconstitutionally vague. Since the gravamen of the offense is conspiracy, the requirement that the offender must act with a specific intent to interfere with the federal rights in question is satisfied. Screws v. United States, 325 U.S. 91 . . . ; United States v. Williams, 341 U.S. 70 . . . (dissenting opinion). And the rights under the Equal Protection Clause described by this paragraph of the indictment have been so firmly and precisely established by a consistent line of decisions in this Court, that the lack of specification of these rights in the language of §241 itself can raise no serious constitutional question on the ground of vagueness or indefiniteness.

Unlike the indictment in Price, however, the indictment in the present case names no person alleged to have acted in any way under the color of state law. The argument is therefore made that, since there exist no Equal Protection Clause rights against wholly private action, the judgment of the District Court on this branch of the case must be affirmed. On its face, the argument is unexceptionable. The Equal Protection Clause speaks to the State or to those acting under the color of its authority.

In this connection, we emphasize that §241 by its clear language incorporates no more than the Equal Protection Clause itself; the statute does not purport to give substantive, as opposed to remedial, implementation to any rights secured by that Clause. Since we therefore deal here only with the bare terms of the Equal Protection Clause itself, nothing said in this opinion goes to the question of what kinds of other and broader legislation Congress might constitutionally enact under §5 of the Fourteenth Amendment to implement that Clause or any other provision of the Amendment.[9]

9. Thus, contrary to the suggestion in Mr. Justice Brennan's separate opinion, nothing

It is a commonplace that rights under the Equal Protection Clause itself arise only where there has been involvement of the State or of one acting under the color of its authority. The Equal Protection Clause "does not . . . add any thing to the rights which one citizen has under the Constitution against another." United States v. Cruikshank, 92 U.S. 542, 554-555 . . . . As Mr. Justice Douglas more recently put it, "The Fourteenth Amendment protects the individual against *state action,* not against wrongs done by *individuals.*" United States v. Williams, 341 U.S. 70, 92 . . . (dissenting opinion). This has been the view of the Court from the beginning. . . . It remains the Court's view today. See, e.g., Evans v. Newton, 382 U.S. 296 . . . ; United States v. Price, 383 U.S. 787 . . . .

This is not to say, however, that the involvement of the State need be either exclusive or direct. In a variety of situations the Court has found state action of a nature sufficient to create rights under the Equal Protection Clause even though the participation of the State was peripheral, or its action was only one of several co-operative forces leading to the constitutional violation. . . .

This case, however, requires no determination of the threshold level that state action must attain in order to create rights under the Equal Protection Clause. This is so because, contrary to the argument of the litigants, the indictment in fact contains an express allegation of state involvement sufficient at least to require the denial of a motion to dismiss. One of the means of accomplishing the object of the conspiracy, according to the indictment, was "By causing the arrest of Negroes by means of false reports that such Negroes had committed criminal acts." In Bell v. State of Maryland, 378 U.S. 226 . . . three members of the Court expressed the view that a private businessman's invocation of state police and judicial action to carry out his own policy of racial discrimination was sufficient to create Equal Protection Clause rights in those against whom the racial discrimination was directed. Three other members of the Court strongly disagreed with that view, and three expressed no opinion on the question. The allegation of the extent of official involvement in the present case is not clear. It may charge no more than co-operative private and state action similar to that involved in Bell, but it may go considerably further. For example, the allegation is broad enough to cover a charge of active connivance by agents of the State in the making of the "false reports," or other conduct amounting to official discrimination clearly sufficient to constitute denial of rights protected by the Equal Protection Clause. Although it is possible that a bill of particulars, or the proof if the case goes to trial, would disclose no co-operative action of that kind by officials of the State, the allegation is enough to prevent dismissal of this branch of the indictment.

III

The fourth numbered paragraph of the indictment alleged that the defendants conspired to injure, oppress, threaten, and intimidate Negro citizens of

---

said in this opinion has the slightest bearing on the validity or construction of Title III or Title IV of the Civil Rights Act of 1964, 42 U.S.C. §§2000b, 2000c (1964 ed.).

the United States in the free exercise and enjoyment of: "The right to travel freely to and from the State of Georgia and to use highway facilities and other instrumentalities of interstate commerce within the State of Georgia."

The District Court was in error in dismissing the indictment as to this paragraph. The constitutional right to travel from one State to another, and necessarily to use the highways and other instrumentalities of interstate commerce in doing so, occupies a position fundamental to the concept of our Federal Union. It is a right that has been firmly established and repeatedly recognized. In Crandall v. State of Nevada, 6 Wall. 35 . . . , invalidating a Nevada tax on every person leaving the State by common carrier, the Court took as its guide the statement of Chief Justice Taney in the Passenger Cases, 7 How. 283, 492: "For all the great purposes for which the Federal government was formed, we are one people, with one common country. We are all citizens of the United States; and, as members of the same community, must have the right to pass and repass through every part of it without interruption, as freely as in our own States." See 6 Wall., at 48-49.

Although the Articles of Confederation provided that "the people of each State shall have free ingress and regress to and from any other State,"[14] that right finds no explicit mention in the Constitution. The reason, it has been suggested, is that a right so elementary was conceived from the beginning to be a necessary concomitant of the stronger Union the Constitution created.[15] In any event, freedom to travel throughout the United States has long been recognized as a basic right under the Constitution. [Citations omitted.]

In Edwards v. People of State of California, 314 U.S. 160 . . . invalidating a California law which impeded the free interstate passage of the indigent, the Court based its reaffirmation of the federal right of interstate travel upon the Commerce Clause. This ground of decision was consistent with precedents firmly establishing that the federal commerce power surely encompasses the movement in interstate commerce of persons as well as commodities. [Citations omitted.] It is also well settled in our decisions that the federal commerce power authorizes Congress to legislate for the protection of individuals from violations of civil rights that impinge on their free movement in interstate commerce. [Citations omitted.]

Although there have been recurring differences in emphasis within the Court as to the source of the constitutional right of interstate travel, there is no need here to canvass those differences further. All have agreed that the right exists. Its explicit recognition as one of the federal rights protected by what is now 18 U.S.C. §241 goes back at least as far as 1904. United States v. Moore, C.C., 129 F. 630, 633. We reaffirm it now.[17]

14. Art. IV, Articles of Confederation.

15. See Chafee, Three Human Rights in the Constitution of 1787, at 185 (1956).

17. As emphasized in Mr. Justice Harlan's separate opinion, §241 protects only against interference with rights secured by other federal laws or by the Constitution itself. The right to interstate travel is a right that the Constitution itself guarantees, as the cases cited in the text make clear. Although these cases in fact involved governmental interference with the right of free interstate travel, their reasoning fully supports the conclusion

This does not mean, of course, that every criminal conspiracy affecting an individual's right of free interstate passage is within the sanction of 18 U.S.C. §241. A specific intent to interfere with the federal right must be proved, and at a trial the defendants are entitled to a jury instruction phrased in those terms. Screws v. United States, 325 U.S. 91, 106-107 . . . . Thus, for example, a conspiracy to rob an interstate traveler would not, of itself, violate §241. But if the predominant purpose of the conspiracy is to impede or prevent the exercise of the right of interstate travel, or to oppress a person because of his exercise of that right, then, whether or not motivated by racial discrimination, the conspiracy becomes a proper object of the federal law under which the indictment in this case was brought. Accordingly, it was error to grant the motion to dismiss on this branch of the indictment.

For these reasons, the judgment of the District Court is reversed and the case is remanded to that court for further proceedings consistent with this opinion.

Reversed and remanded.

[Justice Clark, with whom Justice Black and Justice Fortas joined, concurred, expressing the view that the Court avoided the question of whether Congress has the power to punish private conspiracies that interfere with Fourteenth Amendment rights. He felt that §5 of the amendment gave Congress the power to punish all conspiracies, whether or not there is the element of state action which interferes with Fourteenth Amendment rights.

Justice Harlan concurred in Parts I and II, but dissented from the affirmance of the indictment under §241. Based on earlier decisions under the Commerce and Privileges and Immunities Clauses, he concluded that §241 protects the right to travel only against state interference. He acknowledged that the Due Process Clause is the source of a right to travel, but as a fundamental substantive right, he found it speaks only to governmental action. He doubted that the Constitution was intended "to create certain rights of private individuals against other private individuals." Interference with "private vigilantes" should be "remedied by the exercise of state authority or by appropriate federal legislation." 383 U.S. at 772.

Justice Brennan, with whom the Chief Justice and Justice Douglas joined, concurred in part and dissented in part. He felt that the Court in

---

that the constitutional right of interstate travel is a right secured against interference from any source whatever, whether governmental or private. In this connection, it is important to reiterate that the right to travel freely from State to State finds constitutional protection that is quite independent of the Fourteenth Amendment.

We are not concerned here with the extent to which interstate travel may be regulated or controlled by the exercise of a State's police power acting within the confines of the Fourteenth Amendment. See Edwards v. People of State of California, 314 U.S. 160, 184 (concurring opinion); People of State of New York v. O'Neill, 359 U.S. 1, 6-8. Nor is there any issue here as to the permissible extent of federal interference with the right within the confines of the Due Process Clause of the Fifth Amendment. Cf. Zemel v. Rusk, 381 U.S. 1; Aptheker v. Secretary of State, 378 U.S. 500; Kent v. Dulles, 357 U.S. 116.

Part II had misconstrued §241. He felt that §241 did reach private conspiracies which interfered with the rights secured by the Constitution, and that §241 was a valid exercise by Congress under §5 of the Fourteenth Amendment. He thought that the Court limited too narrowly the coverage of §241, which, he felt, was "secured" by the Constitution itself, along with all those areas that Congress should choose to describe as being protected.

"Viewed in its proper perspective, §5 . . . [is] a positive grant of legislative power, authorizing Congress to exercise its discretion in fashioning remedies to achieve civil and political equality for all citizens. . . . I can find no principle of federalism nor word of the Constitution that denies Congress power to determine that in order adequately to protect the right to equal utilization of state facilities, it is also appropriate to punish other individuals — not state officers themselves and not acting in concert with state officers — who engage in the same brutal conduct for the same misguided purpose." 383 U.S. at 784.]

NOTES

1. On August 4, 1964, following a search of several weeks, the FBI found the bodies of three missing civil rights workers, two of whom, Michael H. Schwerner and Andrew Goodman, were white, and one, James E. Chaney, black. The discovery climaxed a nation's horror and concern at what all feared had happened when the three were reported missing, following their release from the Neshoba County jail. The details of the deaths, while far from pleasant, showed that these were not the least humane lynchings in the history of this most unhappy American pastime. The difference, of course, was that white blood was shed in the cause of blacks. The act came during a period of shocking assassinations — Medgar Evers, NAACP field secretary, in Mississippi in June 1963, and President John Kennedy in November 1963 — and the nation's guilt and outrage manifested itself in widespread demands that the guilty be prosecuted. Suddenly, the concern about federal intrusion on states' rights was cast aside (as it had been during the decade after the Civil War) both by the country and, as the Price opinion reflects, by the Supreme Court.

It was not until October 20, 1967 that Deputy Sheriff Price was convicted with six others in a federal district court (N.Y. Times, Oct. 21, 1967 at 1, c. 8), and subsequently sentenced to six years in prison on December 29, 1967 (N.Y. Times, Dec. 30, 1967 at 1, c. 4). Sheriff Rainey was acquitted on all charges. There was no attempt on the part of state officials to bring criminal charges against Price and Rainey.

2. The murder of Mrs. Viola Liuzzo, a white civil rights worker, on March 26, 1965 on an Alabama highway, also raised a national furor. The federal government was able to successfully obtain a conviction under the 1870 Civil Rights Statute. Three members of the Ku Klux Klan, William Eaton, Eugene Thomas and LeRoy Wilkins, Jr., were all found guilty on December 3, 1965.

N.Y. Times, Dec. 4, 1965 at 1, c. 3. However, there were no convictions in state court trials for the murder of Mrs. Liuzzo. LeRoy Wilkins' first trial ended on May 8, 1965 with a hung jury (N.Y. Times, May 8, 1965 at 1, c. 2); he was acquitted at the second trial on October 22, 1965 (N.Y. Times, Oct. 22, 1965 at 1, c. 4).

3. Eugene Thomas was acquitted by a jury of eight blacks and four whites on September 28, 1966. N.Y. Times, Sept. 28, 1966 at 1, c. 7. The third member of the group, William Eaton, died of a heart attack before he could be brought to trial. N.Y. Times, Sept. 28, 1966 at 1, c. 7. At both the Wilkins and Thomas trials, the jury refused to believe the testimony of an FBI informer who swore he was in the car with the three Klansmen when they gunned Mrs. Liuzzo down.

The failure to convict Eaton, Thomas and Wilkins of murder charges was cushioned by the successful federal prosecutions. Blacks in Mississippi will not forget the aftermath of the murder of Medgar Evers on June 12, 1963. Evidence was introduced at the trial of Byron de la Beckwith which showed that he was the owner of the gun used in the murder and that he had asked a number of persons to pinpoint Evers' house for him. The first all-white jury deadlocked, with a majority favoring an acquittal. N.Y. Times, Feb. 8, 1964 at 1, c. 2. A second prosecution ended in a hung jury again. N.Y. Times, April 18, 1964 at 1, c. 1. There was no third prosecution, and de la Beckwith at one point soon after considered running for lieutenant governor of Mississippi.

4. The opinion in United States v. Price enables a comparison of the more liberal interpretation of §§241 and 242 given in that case, with the stringently restrictive reading given the provisions in the earlier cases therein cited. The sections had been little used for decades after the Supreme Court, in the post-Reconstruction era, had invalidated certain portions of the Civil Rights Acts outright, and severely limited the scope of possible protection provided by those sections that remained.

UNITED STATES v. CRUIKSHANK, 92 U.S. 542, 23 L. Ed. 588 (1876), arose out of a tragedy known both as the Grant Parish Massacre and the Colfax Massacre. In Louisiana during the elections of 1872 there were numerous disputes over the results of local elections. In the town of Colfax, where an election dispute over the positions of sheriff and judge had arisen, the sheriff, on the governor's orders, seized a building which was to be used as the courthouse. The seizure was made with the assistance of a posse of blacks. Rumors spread that the blacks were about to attack local whites, and on April 15, 1873 the courthouse was burned down and the blacks were shot as they came out. The governor took no action, but the Department of Justice investigator secured evidence, and ninety-six people were indicted under the Civil Rights Act of 1870 (now 18 U.S.C. §241). The Justice Department succeeded in arresting nine of them. They were found not guilty of murder but guilty of conspiracy to prevent blacks from the free exercise and enjoyment of rights and privileges granted and secured by the Constitution, including the rights to assemble peacefully for lawful purposes, to bear arms, vote, and not be placed in fear of bodily harm for voting. H. Cummings and C. McFarland, Federal Justice, Ch. XII 230 (1937).

The Supreme Court reversed as to each count of the indictment:

— Considering first the right "peaceably to assemble for lawful purposes," the Court found that the First and Fourteenth Amendments to the Constitution provide protection against interference with the right by Congress, but that otherwise the state must protect its citizens in this regard.

— The Court acknowledged that the statute would be applicable to protect the right "peaceably to assemble for the purpose of petitioning Congress for a redress of grievances," if defendants had been charged with halting a meeting the purpose of which was to petition the federal government for a redress of grievances. But the Court found that the indictment charged an offense by showing merely that defendants conspired to prevent a meeting for any lawful purpose whatever, and thus the statute was not applicable.

— The Court held that the "right to bear arms for a lawful purpose" was protected only against congressional interference.

— The right not to be deprived of life and liberty without due process of law, the Court said, was the "very highest duty of the States. . . . It is no more the duty or within the power of the United States to punish for a conspiracy to falsely imprison or murder within a State, than it would be to punish for false imprisonment or murder itself."

— The Court conceded that the "Fourteenth Amendment prohibits a State from depriving any person of life, liberty, or property, without due process of law; but," the court explained, "this adds nothing to the rights of one citizen as against another. It simply furnishes an additional guaranty against any encroachment by the States upon the fundamental rights which belong to every citizen as a member of society. . . ." 92 U.S. at 554.

— As to the charge that defendants had intended to prevent and hinder citizens of African descent and persons of color in the free exercise and enjoyment of their rights and privileges under state and federal law, which rights and privileges are enjoyed by white persons, the Court responded, "There is no allegation that this was done because of the race or color of the persons conspired against." The Court reiterated that the Fourteenth Amendment meant that the federal government had the obligation to ensure that the states did not interfere with constitutional rights, but that the states and not the federal government had the duty to intercede when one individual interfered with the constitutional rights of others.

NOTES

1. In United States v. Reese, 92 U.S. 214, 23 L. Ed. 563 (1876), two inspectors of a municipal election in Kentucky refused to receive and count in the election the vote of a black citizen. An action was brought under provi-

sions of the Civil Rights Acts which prohibited interference with the right to vote. The Supreme Court held that the provisions were unconstitutional because they prohibited all interference with the right to vote, and that this was beyond the scope of the Fifteenth Amendment, which prohibited only interference based on race, color or previous condition of servitude.

2. In United States v. Harris, 106 U.S. 629, 1 S. Ct. 601, 27 L. Ed. 290 (1883), twenty men seized four prisoners held by a county deputy sheriff in Tennessee, and beat them severely, killing one of them. The Court ruled that, absent a finding of state action, an action under the provision of the Civil Rights Act which prohibited deprivation of equal protection of laws or equal privileges and immunities under the law could not stand. "It was never supposed that the section under consideration conferred on Congress the power to enact a law which would punish a private citizen for an invasion of the rights of his fellow citizen. . . ." 106 U.S. at 644.

Justice Harlan dissented in Harris and also in Baldwin v. Franks, 120 U.S. 678, 7 S. Ct. 656, 32 L. Ed. 766 (1887), in which the Court, citing Harris, directed the release of a defendant arrested for assaulting Chinese citizens and driving them out of a California town. The Court found that the Chinese citizens were protected under a treaty which might have afforded basis for federal protection, but the provision was deemed too broadly worded.

3. During this period, the Court also severely limited civil remedies under the Civil Rights Acts. See Civil Rights Cases, 109 U.S. 3, 3 S. Ct. 18, 27 L. Ed. 835 (1883), printed supra page 200. The Court did sustain the validity of provisions prohibiting the exclusion of blacks from state juries, finding that the action of a judge charged with such exclusion was state action. Ex parte Virginia, 100 U.S. 339, 25 L. Ed. 676 (1880). A state statute excluding blacks from jury duty was held a violation of the Fourteenth Amendment; this afforded grounds for removal of the case to a federal court under the removal statutes. Strauder v. West Virginia, 100 U.S. 303, 25 L. Ed. 664 (1880). See also Virginia v. Rives, 100 U.S. 313, 25 L. Ed. 667 (1880).

In Ex parte Yarbrough, 110 U.S. 651, 4 S. Ct. 152, 28 L. Ed. 274 (1884), the Court ruled that a Ku Klux Klansman, who had forcefully prevented a black from voting in a congressional election in Georgia, was found to have violated a Civil Rights Act. The provision, §5508 (a predecessor of 18 U.S.C. §241), was sustained as a valid exercise of the federal power to control elections which emanated from Art. 1, §4 of the Constitution. This was held to be the case also in Ex parte Siebold, 100 U.S. 371, 25 L. Ed. 717 (1880). However, in James v. Bowman, 190 U.S. 127, 23 S. Ct. 678, 47 L. Ed. 979 (1903), the Court ruled that another act of Congress, §5507, which covered all elections, was invalid. It held that the Fifteenth Amendment applied only to interference by states and that Art. 1, §4 extended to federal authorities and to federal elections.

The Civil Rights Statutes were held to provide protection to a black who was attacked on a homestead on United States land. The statutes were said to protect the constitutional right to cultivate and enjoy that land. United

States v. Waddell, 112 U.S. 76, 5 S. Ct. 35, 28 L. Ed. 673 (1884). In Logan v. United States, 144 U.S. 263, 12 S. Ct. 617, 36 L. Ed. 429 (1892), the Court held that prisoners who had been attacked while in the custody of a federal marshall had the constitutionally protected right to be safe while in United States custody. The Court stated, "The United States, having the absolute right to hold such prisoners, has an equal duty to protect them, while so held, against assault or injury from any quarter."

NOTE: FEDERAL ENFORCEMENT POLICY OF CIVIL RIGHTS ACTS

Initially, there was a major effort by the federal government in the post–Civil War period to enforce the Civil Rights Acts, in the hope that this would break the violent resistance to black citizenship. Thousands of prosecutions were brought, but only about 20 percent resulted in convictions. As the cases reviewed above indicate, the Supreme Court reversed some of them, and by their voiding of some provisions and restrictive interpretation of others, discouraged vigorous enforcement. See Carr, Federal Protection of Civil Rights 40-55 (1947). By the end of the nineteenth century, the statutes were seldom used. Some revisions were made in the predecessors of §§241 and 242 in 1909, but during the next thirty years, no cases involving §242 and only four cases under the predecessor of §241 reached the Supreme Court, none of them involving racial issues. In the lower courts, a typical case was Smith v. United States, 157 Fed. 721 (8th Cir. 1907), involving the forceful taking of some blacks from Tennessee to Missouri, where they were made to work, beaten, and denied wages. The white defendants were found guilty of conspiracy to deprive citizens of their right to be free from slavery and involuntary servitude.

There was some increase in civil rights activity in the Department of Justive after Attorney General Frank Murphy created a Civil Section there in 1939. United States v. Classic, 313 U.S. 299, 61 S. Ct. 1031, 85 L. Ed. 1368 (1941), upheld an indictment under §§241 and 242 against election officials who made a false count in a federal primary election. §241 was held an appropriate sanction for election officials who studied ballot boxes in federal elections. United States v. Saylor, 322 U.S. 385, 64 S. Ct. 1001, 88 L. Ed. (1944). But caution and restraint remained the key elements in the federal government's enforcement policy. Moderation, though, impressed neither the lawbreakers (as the statistics on lynching indicate) nor those members of the Supreme Court who viewed any prosecution under the Civil Rights Statutes with the gravest suspicion. Thus in Screws v. United States, summarized infra, Justice Roberts, dissenting for himself and Justices Frankfurter and Jackson, reviewed the Justice Department's assurances that its policy was moderate and remained concerned.

The Department of Justice has established a policy of strict self-limitation with regard to prosecutions under the civil rights acts. When violations of such statutes are reported, the Department requires that efforts be made to encourage state officials to take appropriate action under state law. To assure consistent observance of this policy in the enforcement of the civil rights statutes, all United States Attorneys have been instructed to submit cases to the Department for approval before prosecutions or investigations are instituted. The number of prosecutions which have been brought under the civil rights statutes is small. No statistics are available with respect to the number of prosecutions prior to 1939, when a special Civil Rights Section was established in the Department of Justice. Only two cases during this period have been reported: United States v. Buntin, 10 Fed. 730 (C.C.S.D. Ohio), and United States v. Stone, 188 Fed. 836 (D. Md.). Since 1939, the number of complaints received annually by the Civil Rights Section has ranged from 8,000 to 14,000, but in no year have prosecutions under both Sections 20 and 19, its companion statute, exceeded 76. In the fiscal year 1943, for example, 31 full investigations of alleged violations of Section 20 were conducted, and three cases were brought to trial. In the following fiscal year there were 55 such investigations, and prosecutions were instituted in 12 cases.

Complaints of violations are often submitted to the Department by local law enforcement officials who for one reason or another may feel themselves powerless to take action under state law. It is primarily in this area, namely, where the official position of the wrongdoers has apparently rendered the State unable or unwilling to institute proceedings, that the statute has come into operation. . . .

But such a "policy of strict self-limitation" is not accompanied by assurance of permanent tenure and immortality of those who make it the policy. Evil men are rarely given power; they take it over from better men to whom it had been entrusted. There can be no doubt that this shapeless and all-embracing statute can serve as a dangerous instrument of political intimidation and coercion in the hands of those so inclined. (325 U.S. at 159-160.)

In SCREWS v. UNITED STATES, 325 U.S. 91, 65 S. Ct. 1031, 89 L. Ed. 1495 (1945), the Court dealt with an action arising out of what Justice Douglas called a "shocking and revolting episode in law enforcement." Robert Hall, a black, was arrested at his home late at night by Screws, the sheriff of Baker County in Georgia, and two other law officers, on a warrant charging Hall with the theft of a tire. Between the time he was arrested and placed in jail, Hall was beaten by the officers with their fists and with a solid bar blackjack eight inches long and weighing two pounds, until he was unconscious. He died soon after his arrest.

An indictment was brought under §20 (now 242), charging that the defendants, acting under the color of state law, had "willfully" deprived the prisoner of the right not to be deprived of life without due process of law, the right to be given a trial, and the right to be punished in accordance with the laws of Georgia, and that the denial of these rights was in violation of the Fourteenth Amendment.

Defendants appealed from the guilty verdict returned by the jury in the federal district court. They argued that: (1) §20 was unconstitutional under the Due Process Clause of the Fifth Amendment because it was too vague and indefinite, and (2) the section requiring that their conduct was "under color of law" excludes their assault, which was not authorized by state law but rather was in itself a violation of state law. The majority of the Court rejected both arguments, although five members of the Court voted to return the case to the district court for a new trial, with more specific instruction respecting the kind of intent required under the statute.

Justice Douglas, speaking for the majority in rejecting defendants' "color of law" argument, conceded that, based on prior cases, a violation of local law does not necessarily mean that federal rights have been invaded even when a prisoner is assaulted, injured or murdered.

> It is only state action of a "particular character" that is prohibited by the Fourteenth Amendment and against which the Amendment authorized Congress to afford relief. . . . In the present case, as we have said, the defendants were officers of the law who had made an arrest and by their own admissions made the assault in order to protect themselves and to keep the prisoner from escaping, i.e., to make the arrest effective. That was a duty they had under Georgia law. United States v. Classic [referred to supra page 877] is, therefore, indistinguishable from this case so far as "under color of" state law is concerned. In each officers of the State were performing official duties; in each the power which they were authorized to exercise was misused. We cannot draw a distinction between them unless we are to say that §20 is not applicable to police officers. But the broad sweep of its language leaves no room for such an exception. . . . (325 U.S. at 109-110.)

Justices Roberts, Frankfurter, and Jackson, in dissent, challenged the majority holding that the defendants had been acting under the color of state law. In their view, the federal government could intervene only when a specific state statute or an officer of the state acting under a state statute violated an individual's constitutional rights. They argued that a state official who was violating his own state law in his actions was not acting under the color of state law.

They also voiced concern about the overriding broadness of the statute. Since the statute did not specify what constitutional rights were protected, the dissenters argued that any time a state official did something wrong he was subject to a criminal action under the Civil Rights Statute. To the point that the federal statute was needed because local officials might not act because of personal or political reasons, the dissenters responded: "If it be significantly true that crimes against local law cannot be locally prosecuted, it is an ominous sign indeed. In any event, the cure is a reinvigoration of State responsibility. It is not an undue incursion of remote federal authority into local duties with consequent debilitation of local responsibility. . . ." 325 U.S. at 160-161.

Justice Murphy would have affirmed. In his dissent, he said there was no "reasonable doubt" that defendants knew their actions violated due process. He saw no real issue of warning, since "the Constitution, §20 and their own consciences" told them that they lacked any authority to take human life unnecessarily without due process in law. Justice Murphy felt that the really significant question was "whether law enforcement officers and those entrusted with authority shall be allowed to violate with impunity the clear constitutional rights of the inarticulate and the friendless." He continued:

> Too often unpopular minorities, such as Negroes, are unable to find effective refuge from the cruelties of bigoted and ruthless authority. States are undoubtedly capable of punishing their officers who commit such outrages. But where, as here, the states are unwilling for some reason to prosecute such crimes the federal government must step in unless constitutional guarantees are to become atrophied. . . . (325 U.S. at 138.)*

QUESTIONS

1. The Justice Department's cautious policy about initiating prosecutions for violations of §§241 and 242 was based on the view (generally admirable for a prosecutor) that only those cases should be brought in which conviction was almost certain. Applying that standard to civil rights cases, however, meant that in addition to evidence of guilt (which might be substantial), consideration had to be given to the small likelihood that a jury would convict, and it can be presumed that many cases were dropped for this reason. Would there have been a deterrent effect on civil rights violations if the government had prosecuted cases where the evidence justified such actions, even if juries refused to convict out of sympathy with the defendants' acts? Can prosecutions ever be justified on such a basis?

2. The penalties for violating 18 U.S.C. §§241 and 242 were substantially increased in Title I of the 1968 Civil Rights Act. Those convicted of violating §241 can be fined up to $10,000 and imprisoned up to ten years or both. Penalties for violations of §242 are fines of not more than $1000 or sentences up to one year. Under both sections, a term of years or for life can be imposed if death is caused by the prohibited conduct. The newer 18 U.S.C. §245 carries penalties roughly approximate to the early sections. Is it likely that the heavier penalties will serve as an added deterrent to civil rights violations, or will they merely make convictions harder to obtain?

3. The difficulty of obtaining convictions for civil rights violations is not limited to the South. Northern cities which passed ordinances in the 1930s and 1940s providing criminal penalties for racial discrimination in public accommodations found that district attorneys would seldom prosecute the unpopular cases, and that when they did, juries generally refused to convict. Subsequent civil rights laws substituted injunctive relief and money damages for criminal provisions, and this procedure was followed in the Civil Rights Act of 1964 (see Appendix). If federal civil rights statutes dropped criminal provisions and relied entirely on injunctive relief and money damages to the victims from both defendants and the county where the violation occurred,

* On retrial, following remand of the Screws case, defendants were acquitted by the jury. See R. Carr, Federal Protection of Civil Rights 114 (1947).

as in the antilynching bill passed by the House in 1922, would serious racial violence be deterred?

4. In their dissent in the Screws case, Justices Roberts, Frankfurter and Jackson asserted that the ominous symptom of crimes against local law not being locally prosecuted could be "cured" not by reliance on "remote federal authority," which merely debilitates local responsibility, but by "a reinvigoration of State responsibility." Assuming that the justices were aware of the history of nonenforcement of the law in racial cases, might they have suggested how such "reinvigoration of State responsibility" be achieved? Was their prescription a responsible one, to be taken seriously in 1945? Would it be worthy of serious consideration if made today?

NOTE: 18 U.S.C. §245 (1970)

18 U.S.C. §245, which is set out in full in the Appendix, establishes criminal liability for willful interference by force or threat of force with enumerated rights and activities. The measure, enacted as part of the Civil Rights Act of 1968, incorporates in substantial part the criminal provisions of the comprehensive civil rights legislation proposed by the Johnson administration in 1966, but defeated in the Senate because of opposition to the housing provisions.

A significant difference between the 1966 proposal and §245 is that the former would not have predicated liability on willfulness. §245 proscribes willful interference with any person who has voted, campaigned for office or acted as an election official; participated in any federal program; applied for or obtained federal employment; or served as a petit or grand juror. Also prohibited is interference on account of race, color, religion or national origin with anyone who has attended any public school; participated in any state program; applied for or obtained employment, private or state; served as a juror; used the facilities of interstate commerce or such public facilities as hotels, restaurants and theaters. Another subsection protects lawful participation in speech and assembly for the purpose of opposing discrimination or encouraging others to do so. Other provisions may be intended to prevent "reverse discrimination" and interference by civil rights organizations with law enforcement (see subsections B4 and C).

The penalty for violations of civil rights resulting in death is set at "imprisonment for any term of years or for life." This conforms §245 with similar penalties contained in the amended provisions of §§241 and 242, previously discussed. It also provides for sentences up to ten years and fines up to $10,000 if bodily injury results from the prohibited activity. Otherwise, penalties under the section are limited to sentences to one year and fines of not more than $1000. §345(b)(c). The section reflects a continued recognition of potential federal-state friction because of civil rights prosecutions. The effort to mitigate this conflict seriously limits the scope of protection that §245 provides civil rights victims. Thus, (a)(1) provides that no prosecution may be initiated under the section unless the Attorney General (or his deputy) certifies in writing that in his judgment a prosecution by the United States "is in the public interest and necessary to secure substantial justice." The certification function may not be delegated and appears to ensure a pre-prosecution bureaucracy similar to that described in Screws v. United States. Further, it is made clear that §245 does not limit state jurisdiction over offenses or lessen the responsibility of states for prosecuting violations of local law that are also violations of the section. Protection is not provided to those who are "aiding, abetting, or inciting other persons to riot or to commit any act of physical violence upon any individual or against any real or personal property in furtherance of a riot." §245(a)(5). And finally, no law enforcement officer will be considered in violation of the section for "lawfully carrying out the duties of his office . . . or [for] lawfully enforcing ordinances and [the] laws . . ." §245(c).

There have been few reported federal prosecutions under §245. The necessity of proving willful intent to deny civil rights is a likely obstacle. It was, however, overcome in United States v. Price, 464 F.2d 1217 (5th Cir. 1972), where the court affirmed a conviction under the section. Defendant had stopped George Smith, the black victim, who was driving with friends to a government recreational area; he directed at Smith vulgar expletives containing direct racial slurs, and then blocked his way, knocked him to the ground, beat him unconscious and threw him in a lake. The court termed "frivolous" defendant's assertion that, while the victim's race may have provoked the fight, the altercation only incidentally occurred on federal property and could have happened anywhere: "Here the circumstances under which defendant assaulted Smith were fully known to him and it is clear that the natural and probable consequences of his acts were to prevent Smith from enjoying the recreational facilities." 164 F.2d at 1218.

Attempts by activists to utilize §245 as a source of substantive rights have failed. In Hill v. Commonwealth of Pennsylvania, 439 F.2d 1016 (3rd Cir. 1971), *cert. denied,* 404 U.S. 985 (1972), members of the Black Construction Coalition, while protesting the lack of equal employment in Pittsburgh, were arrested for assault, unlawful assembly and inciting to riot. They argued that, because they were engaged in activities designed to secure federally protected rights, §245 immunized them from prosecution. This argument was rejected. Removal was denied on the ground that a clear prediction could not be made that the federal rights relied upon would be unenforceable in the state courts.

People v. Horelick, 424 F.2d 697 (2d Cir. 1970), *cert. denied,* 398 U.S. 939 (1970), involved teachers charged with trespassing and resisting arrest for entering a school building during the Ocean Hill–Brownville teachers strike. The court held that defendants were not relieved by §245 of the duty to obey the orders of law enforcement officers, simply because their conduct constituted a protest against alleged denial of equal protection. In Dodge v. Nakai, 298 F. Supp. 17 (D. Ariz. 1968), §245 was held not to provide jurisdiction of an action by a legal services organization seeking to secure entry to an Indian reservation, against tribal officers who had barred the organization's director from the reservation.

Prosecutions involving conduct prohibited by §245 are, perhaps because of the difficulties described above, more likely to be brought under the more general provision of §241. See, e.g., Hayes v. United States, 464 F.2d 1252 (5th Cir. 1972). There, the court denied postconviction relief to defendants. They had been convicted under §241 and sentenced to ten years and $10,000 under one count, and one year and $1000 under another, for bombing school buses used to transport black students to desegregated schools. What factors likely caused the government to seek indictments in the Hayes case under §241 rather than §245?

B. PROTECTION VIA CIVIL REMEDIES

The Reconstruction Civil Rights Acts contained, in addition to criminal provisions, authorization for victims of racial violence to seek damages and injunctive relief in federal courts. The history and recent revitalization of the two most important of the surviving sections, 42 U.S.C. §§1983 and 1985(3), are covered in some detail here. The opinion in Monroe v. Pape, set out below, traces the development of §1983, the most frequently used of all federal civil rights provisions, while Griffin v. Breckenridge, infra, gives §1985(3) the only reading likely to provide protection against the type of violence so rampant in the South at the time of its enactment.

MONROE v. PAPE
365 U.S. 167, 81 S. Ct. 473, 5 L. Ed. 2d 492 (1961)

Mr. Justice Douglas delivered the opinion of the Court.

This case presents important questions concerning the construction of R.S. §1979, 42 U.S.C. §1983, . . . which reads as follows:

> Every person who, under color of any statute, ordinance, regulation, custom, or usage, of any State or Territory, subjects, or causes to be subjected, any citizen of the United States or other person within the jurisdiction thereof to the deprivation of any rights, privileges, or immunities secured by the Constitution and laws, shall be liable to the party injured in an action at law, suit in equity, or other proper proceeding for redress.

The complaint alleges that 13 Chicago police officers broke into petitioners' home in the early morning, routed them from bed, made them stand naked in the living room, and ransacked every room, emptying drawers and ripping mattress covers. It further alleges that Mr. Monroe was then taken to the police station and detained on "open" charges for 10 hours, while he was interrogated about a two-day-old murder, that he was not taken before a magistrate, though one was accessible, that he was not permitted to call his family or attorney, that he was subsequently released without criminal charges being preferred against him. It is alleged that the officers had no search warrant and no arrest warrant and that they acted "under color of the statutes, ordinances, regulations, customs and usages" of Illinois and of the City of Chicago. . . .

The City of Chicago moved to dismiss the complaint on the ground that it is not liable under the Civil Rights Acts nor for acts committed in performance of its governmental functions. All defendants moved to dismiss, alleging that the complaint alleged no cause of action under those Acts or under the Federal Constitution. The District Court dismissed the complaint. The Court of Appeals affirmed, 272 F.2d 365. . . . The case is here on a writ of certiorari. . . .

I

Petitioners claim that the invasion of their home and the subsequent search without a warrant and the arrest and detention of Mr. Monroe without a warrant and without arraignment constituted a deprivation of their "rights, privileges, or immunities secured by the Constitution" within the meaning of R.S. §1979. It has been said that when 18 U.S.C. §241, 18 U.S.C.A. §241, made criminal a conspiracy "to injure, oppress, threaten, or intimidate any citizen in the free exercise or enjoyment of any right or privilege secured to him by the Constitution," it embraced only rights that an individual has by reason of his relation to the central government, not to state governments. United States v. Williams, 341 U.S. 70 . . . . Cf. United States v. Cruikshank, 92 U.S. 542 . . . ; Ex parte Yarbrough, 110 U.S. 651 . . . ; Guinn v. United States, 238 U.S. 347 . . . . But the history of the section of the Civil Rights Act presently involved does not permit such a narrow interpretation.

Section 1979 came onto the books as §1 of the Ku Klux Act of April 20, 1871. 17 Stat. 13. It was one of the means whereby Congress exercised the power vested in it by §5 of the Fourteenth Amendment to enforce the provisions of that Amendment. Senator Edmunds, Chairman of the Senate Committee on the Judiciary, said concerning this section: "The first section is one that I believe nobody objects to, as defining the rights secured by the Constitution of the United States when they are assailed by any State law or under color of any State law, and it is merely carrying out the principles of the civil rights bill, [Act of Apr. 4, 1866, 14 Stat. 27] which has since become a part of the Constitution," viz., the Fourteenth Amendment.

Its purpose is plain from the title of the legislation, "An Act to enforce the Provisions of the Fourteenth Amendment to the Constitution of the United States, and for other Purposes." 17 Stat. 13. Allegation of facts constituting a deprivation under color of state authority of a right guaranteed by the Fourteenth Amendment satisfies to that extent the requirement of R.S. §1979. . . . So far petitioners are on solid ground. For the guarantee against unreasonable searches and seizures contained in the Fourth Amendment has been made applicable to the States by reason of the Due Process Clause of the Fourteenth Amendment. . . .

II

There can be no doubt at least since Ex parte Virginia, 100 U.S. 339, 346-347 . . . that Congress has the power to enforce provisions of the Fourteenth Amendment against those who carry a badge of authority of a State and represent it in some capacity, whether they act in accordance with their authority or misuse it. . . . The question with which we now deal is the narrower one of whether Congress, in enacting §1979, meant to give a remedy to parties deprived of constitutional rights, privileges and immunities by an official's abuse of his position. . . .We conclude that it did so intend.

It is argued that "under color of" enumerated state authority excludes acts of an official or policeman who can show no authority under state law, state custom, or state usage to do what he did. In this case it is said that these policemen, in breaking into petitioners' apartment, violated the Constitution and laws of Illinois. It is pointed out that under Illinois law a simple remedy is offered for that violation and that, so far as it appears, the courts of Illinois are available to give petitioners that full redress which the common law affords for violence done to a person; and it is earnestly argued that no "statute, ordinance, regulation, custom or usage" of Illinois bars that redress.

The Ku Klux Act grew out of a message sent to Congress by President Grant on March 23, 1871, reading:

> A condition of affairs now exists in some States of the Union rendering life and property insecure and the carrying of the mails and the collection of the revenue dangerous. The proof that such a condition of affairs exists in some localities is now before the Senate. That the power to correct these evils is beyond the control of State authorities I do not doubt; that the power of the Executive of the United States, acting within the limits of existing laws, is sufficient for present emergencies is not clear. Therefore, I urgently recommend such legislation as in the judgment of Congress shall effectually secure life, liberty, and property, and the enforcement of law in all parts of the United States. . . .

The legislation — in particular the section with which we are now concerned . . . had three main aims.

First, it might, of course, override certains kinds of state laws. . . .

Second, it provided a remedy where state law was inadequate. That aspect of the legislation was summed up as follows by Senator Sherman of Ohio:

> . . . it is said the reason is that any offense may be committed upon a negro by a white man, and a negro cannot testify in any case against a white man, so that the only way by which any conviction can be had in Kentucky in those cases is in the United States courts, because the United States courts enforce the United States laws by which negroes may testify.

But the purposes were much broader. The *third* aim was to provide a federal remedy where the state remedy, though adequate in theory, was not available in practice. The opposition to the measure complained that "It overrides the reserved powers of the States," just as they argued that the second section of the bill "absorb[ed] the entire jurisdiction of the States over their local and domestic affairs."

This Act of April 20, 1871, sometimes called "the third 'force bill,'" was passed by a Congress that had the Klan "particularly in mind." The debates are replete with references to the lawless conditions existing in the South in 1871. There was available to the Congress during these debates a report, nearly 600 pages in length, dealing with the activities of the Klan and the inability of the state governments to cope with it. This report was drawn on by many of the speakers. It was not the unavailability of state remedies but the failure of certain States to enforce the laws with an equal hand that furnished the powerful momentum behind this "force bill." Mr. Lowe of Kansas said:

> While murder is stalking abroad in disguise, while whippings and lynchings and banishment have been visited upon unoffending American citizens, the local administrations have been found inadequate or unwilling to apply the proper corrective. Combinations, darker than the night that hides them, conspiracies, wicked as the worst of felons could devise, have gone unwhipped of justice. Immunity is given to crime, and the records of the public tribunals are searched in vain for any evidence of effective redress.

Mr. Beatty of Ohio summarized in the House the case for the bill when he said:

> . . . certain States have denied to persons within their jurisdiction the equal protection of the laws. The proof on this point is voluminous and unquestionable. . . . [M]en were murdered, houses were burned, women were outraged, men were scourged, and officers of the law shot down; and the State made no successful effort to bring the guilty to punishment or afford protection or redress to the outraged and innocent. The State, from lack of power or inclination, practically denied the equal protection of the law to these persons.

While one main scourge of the evil — perhaps the leading one — was the Ku Klux Klan, the remedy created was not a remedy against it or its members but against those who representing a State in some capacity were *unable* or *unwilling* to enforce a state law. . . .

There was, it was said, no quarrel with the state laws on the books. It was their lack of enforcement that was the nub of the difficulty. . . .

Although the legislation was enacted because of the conditions that existed in the South at that time, it is cast in general language and is as applicable to Illinois as it is to the States whose names were mentioned over and again in the debates. It is no answer that the State has a law which if enforced would give relief. The federal remedy is supplementary to the state remedy, and the latter need not be first sought and refused before the federal one is invoked.

Hence the fact that Illinois by its constitution and laws outlaws unreasonable searches and seizures is no barrier to the present suit in the federal court.

We had before us in United States v. Classic [313 U.S. 299] . . . 18 U.S.C. §242 . . . which provides a criminal punishment for anyone who "under color of any law, statute, ordinance, regulation, or custom" subjects any inhabitant of a State to the deprivation of "any rights, privileges, or immunities secured or protected by the Constitution or laws of the United States." . . . In an opinion written by Mr. Justice (later Chief Justice) Stone, in which Mr. Justice Roberts, Mr. Justice Reed, and Mr. Justice Frankfurter joined, the Court ruled, "Misuse of power, possessed by virtue of state law and made possible only because the wrongdoer is clothed with the authority of state law, is action taken 'under color of' state law." Id., 313 U.S. 326 . . . .

That view of the meaning of the words "under color of" state law, 18 U.S.C. §242 . . . was reaffirmed in Screws v. United States, 325 U.S. [91], 108-113. . . . The acts there complained of were committed by state officers in performance of their duties, viz., making an arrest effective. It was urged there, as it is here, that "under color of" state law should not be construed to duplicate in federal law what was an offense under state law. . . . It was said there, as it is here, that the ruling in the Classic case as to the meaning of "under color of" state law was not in focus and was ill-advised. . . . It was argued there, as it is here, that "under color of" state law included only action taken by officials pursuant to state law. . . . We rejected that view. . . . We stated: "The construction given §20 [18 U.S.C. §242, 18 U.S.C.A. §242] in the Classic case formulated a rule of law which has become the basis of federal enforcement in this important field. The rule adopted in that case was formulated after mature consideration. . . ."

We conclude that the meaning given "under color of" law in the Classic case and in the Screws and Williams cases was the correct one; and we adhere to it. . . .

So far, then, the complaint states a cause of action. There remains to consider only a defense peculiar to the City of Chicago.

III

The City of Chicago asserts that it is not liable under §1979. We do not stop to explore the whole range of questions tendered us on this issue at oral argument and in the briefs. For we are of the opinion that Congress did not undertake to bring municipal corporations within the ambit of §1979.

[Justice Douglas reviewed the legislative history on the issue.]

It is said that doubts should be resolved in favor of municipal liability because private remedies against officers for illegal searches and seizures are conspicuously ineffective, and because municipal liability will not only afford plaintiffs responsible defendants but cause those defendants to eradicate abuses that exist at the police level. We do not reach those policy considerations. Nor do we reach the constitutional question whether Congress has the power to make municipalities liable for acts of its officers that violate the civil rights of individuals.

The response of the Congress to the proposal to make municipalities liable for certain actions being brought within federal purview by the Act of April 20, 1871, was so antagonistic that we cannot believe that the word "person" was used in this particular Act to include them. Accordingly we hold that the motion to dismiss the complaint against the City of Chicago was properly granted. But since the complaint should not have been dismissed against the officials the judgment must be and is reversed.

Reversed.

Mr. Justice HARLAN, whom Mr. Justice STEWART joins, concurring.

Were this case here as one of first impression, I would find the "under color of any statute" issue very close indeed. However, in Classic and Screws this Court considered a substantially identical statutory phrase to have a meaning which, unless we now retreat from it, requires that issue to go for the petitioners here.

[Justice Harlan's extended discussion of his conclusion is omitted, as is Justice Frankfurter's lengthy dissent. He joined the Court's conclusion that the action could not be maintained against the City of Chicago.]

NOTES

1. Monroe v. Pape is a valuable precedent for those seeking relief under §1983. Its conclusion that acts of state officials are committed "under color of law" even when in clear violation of state law, serves to continue the very necessary fiction of Ex parte Young (209 U.S. 123, 28 S. Ct. 441, 52 L. Ed. 714 (1908)), that a suit against a state official is not a suit against the state and thus barred by the Eleventh Amendment, where it is alleged that the official is enforcing an unconstitutional act. In doing so, the official is "stripped of his official or representative character and is subject in his person to the consequences of his individual conduct." 209 U.S. at 159-160.

2. But getting into court is one thing, effecting relief is another. Monroe holds that Congress did not intend to include municipalities within the word "person" as used in §1983. A few courts have sought to mitigate the result of this interpretation, which insulates the government from financial liability for the actions of its officials and removes the prime incentive for effective governmental control of police misconduct. Thus, MacArthur v. Pennington, 253 F. Supp. 420 (E.D. Tenn. 1963), held that a municipality waived its immunity under §1983 to the extent that it was covered by liability insurance. But in Wilcher v. Gain, 311 F. Supp. 754 (N.D. Cal. 1970), where the black community sought redress for alleged brutalities committed by members of the Oakland Police Force, the court found that the rationale in Monroe extends even to states which have provided for municipal liability, and that this result is not affected by reliance on 42 U.S.C. §1988, providing generally that federal courts, in enforcing Civil Rights Acts, may use "that combination of

federal law, common law, and state law as will be best 'adopted to the object' of the civil rights laws." (§1988 does permit the application of state rules of liability to redress deprivation of federal rights protected against interference by private persons, as under 42 U.S.C. §§1981, 1982, Sullivan v. Little Hunting Park, 396 U.S. 229, 90 S. Ct. 400 (1969).) Of course, where a municipality has waived immunity, there is less need for a federal civil rights statute by victims of police brutality.

3. The exclusion of municipalities from liability for damages under §1983 does not bar effective injunctive relief, but such relief is rare in police misconduct cases, in the absence of shocking facts and a sympathetic court. Thus, in Anderson v. Nosser, 456 F.2d 835 (5th Cir. 1972), the plaintiff civil rights demonstrators were arrested and taken to a state penitentiary, where they were placed in maximum security and subjected to various abuses, including deprivation of their clothing and the essentials of hygiene. The court held that a clear case of summary punishment without due process of law had been made out. However, liability was limited to those officials, the police chief and the prison superintendent, who were directly responsible for the arrest and detention of the plaintiffs.

NOTE: THE FEDERAL INJUNCTION AS A REMEDY FOR UNCONSTITUTIONAL POLICE CONDUCT

78 Yale L.J. 143

For a century, the federal Constitution has guaranteed to all persons in the United States the rights to "due process" and "equal protection" at the hands of state and local police. Recent Supreme Court decisions have greatly expanded the content of these constitutional guarantees. But despite recent efforts by federal courts to define and enforce these rights, constitutional violations by the police remain commonplace.[4]

4. "Only occasional and more flagrant abuses come to the attention of the courts, and then only those where the search and seizure yields incriminating evidence and the defendant is at least sufficiently compromised to be indicted. If the officers raid a home, an office, or stop and search an automobile but find nothing incriminating, this invasion of the personal liberty of the innocent too often finds no practical redress. There may be, and I am convinced that there are, many unlawful searches of homes and automobiles of innocent people which turn up nothing incriminating, in which no arrest is made, about which courts do nothing, and about which we never hear." Brinegar v. United States, 338 U.S. 160, 181 (1949) (Jackson, J., dissenting).

Though there are of course no statistics on police violations of constitutional rights, most observers believe that such violations are very numerous, especially in certain areas of large cities. See, e.g., Report of the National Advisory Commission on Civil Disorders 299-305 (1968) [hereinafter cited as Commission on Civil Disorders]; President's Commission on Law Enforcement and Administration of Justice: Task Force Report: The Police 178-89 (1967) [hereinafter cited as Task Force Report]; W. LaFave, Arrest 437-82 (1965); Note, Philadelphia Police Practice and the Law of Arrest, 100 U. Pa. L. Rev. 1182 (1952). Fifteen years ago, unconstitutional arrests in the United States were estimated to number several million per year. Hall, Police and Law in a Democratic Society, 28 Ind. L.J. 133, 152, 154 (1953).

The vast majority of police transgressions are acts of harassment and bullying which never lead to prosecutions — unwarranted arrests, illegal searches, unreasonable disruptions of harmless conduct, verbal insults. Such violations leave no visible scars; the victim usually does not suffer bodily injury or loss of property. Yet to the individual victim these acts constitute serious intrusions upon his privacy, dignity, and security. Where the police violations fall evenly upon residents of a community, everyone's security is threatened. Where, as is often the case, police misconduct focuses largely on classes of people who are politically powerless to protect themselves, the Constitution's promise of equal protection is mocked, and a community is divided into those whom the police protect and those whom the police victimize. Such police misconduct, unredressed and undeterred, has often been blamed for the frustrations which have recently erupted into violence in many large American cities.

Normally, actual or potential victims of legal wrongs can look to the courts for relief. But where police abuse is the wrong, courts have seemed largely powerless to help.[8] Neither criminal prosecutions nor civil tort actions for individual acts of police misconduct have been frequent or successful enough to have significant deterrent force.[9] The exclusionary rule, applicable to the states since 1961, can work only where the police are developing a case for prosecution and hence has no effect on violations whose only purpose is harassment.[11]

8. The powerlessness of the courts has caused some observers to favor the creation of civilian review boards to hear citizen complaints of police misconduct. See, e.g., Burger, Who Will Watch the Watchman? 14 Am. U.L. Rev. 1 (1964). This remedy, defeated in a referendum in New York City in November 1966, N.Y. Times, Nov. 10, 1966, at 32, col. 6, and rejected by the Newark city government in early 1968, N.Y. Times, Mar. 1, 1968, at 1, col. 7, has been applied in only a few cities. One factor to be weighed against civilian review boards is that the boards seem to draw strong and sometimes not very rational opposition from policemen's organizations. This strong opposition raises the possibility that creation of such boards might have a substantial adverse effect on police department morale and initiative. The FBI report on riots in 1964 blamed civilian review boards for making police too passive. N.Y. Times, Sept. 27, 1964, at 82, col. 1. On the general subject of police departments' complaint review machinery, see Note, The Administration of Complaints by Civilians Against the Police, 77 Harv. L. Rev. 499 (1964); Task Force Report 200-02.

9. Criminal prosecutions are infrequent partly because prosecutors work closely and "on the same side" with offending policemen. The many barriers to recovery of worthwhile tort damages from policemen are discussed in Foote, Tort Remedies for Police Violations of Individual Rights, 39 Minn. L. Rev. 493 (1955). On the general inadequacy of possible criminal and tort liabilities as deterrents for police violations of constitutional rights, see Task Force Report, 31-32; W. LaFave, Arrest 411-27 (1965).

11. The inadequacies of the exclusionary rule as a means of enforcing constitutional restraints even on police action directed at obtaining evidence for trial have been almost universally recognized. See, e.g., Task Force Report 31; W. LaFave, Arrest 427-35, 488 (1965); J. Skolnick, Justice Without Trial 211-29 (1966); Burger, Who Will Watch the Watchman? 14 Am. U.L. Rev. 1 (1964); LaFave & Remington, Controlling the Police: The Judge's Role in Making and Reviewing Law Enforcement Decisions, 63 Mich. L. Rev. 987 (1965).

NOTES

1. In the Yale Law Journal Note it is suggested that the injunctive remedy has not been fully utilized and that it could prove an effective means of preventing police malfeasance. However, the Note relies heavily on Lankford v. Gelston, 364 F.2d 197 (4th Cir. 1966), one of the few cases in recent judicial history where a court actually ordered the police to stop a deliberate policy of unconstitutional searches. By the time the Fourth Circuit decided the Lankford case, the searches had, for the most part, been stopped. The Note suggests, however, that it would be possible for the courts to utilize the injunction to order a police commission to rectify constitutional abuses, and suggests further that the court order would give more strength to a police commissioner who was seriously attempting to rectify misconduct problems within his department. Remedial steps might be ordered, including the creation of an undercover squad to gather evidence of police misconduct and the establishment of disciplinary hearings within the police department. Courts could, if necessary, utilize the contempt power to enforce those orders.

In theory, such remedies are available, but experience indicates that, even in cases of serious police misconduct, courts are reluctant to exercise injunctive powers against police activities. The Yale proposal is criticized in Note, Use of §1983 to Remedy Unconstitutional Police Conduct: Guarding the Guards, 5 Harv. Civ. Rights–Civ. Lib. L. Rev. 104 (1970). As an alternative means of obtaining compliance with an injunctive order, the Harvard Note suggests that the court appoint an impartial "monitor" empowered to investigate allegations of misconduct, urge police to alter their behavior and report continued wrongdoing to the court. Id. at 110-119. But the problem under either plan is the reluctance of courts to grant injunctive relief.

2. On May 28, 1970, in response to a failure of the New York City Police Department to protect antiwar demonstrators from attacks by construction workers, Federal District Judge Motley ordered the New York City Police Department to provide such protection for the antiwar demonstrations scheduled during the upcoming Memorial Day weekend, and to have her order read to every policeman who would be on duty during that period. Belknap v. Leary, 314 F. Supp. 574 (S.D.N.Y. 1970). The order was overruled the following day, as an abuse of discretion, by an emergency meeting of the court of appeals, which held that one failure by the police — which had been promptly criticized by the mayor and police officials — did not justify injunctive relief. Belknap v. Leary, 427 F.2d 496 (2d Cir. 1970).

3. Where money damages are sought, Monroe's conclusion as to municipalities and other state agencies bars access to the only source of funds likely to be adequate where serious harm has occurred. Under a more recent Supreme Court decision, Pierson v. Ray, the liability of the officers themselves is limited to factual situations — such as found in Monroe v. Pape, where the conduct entirely belies a claim of "good faith."

PIERSON v. RAY, 386 U.S. 547, 87 S. Ct. 1213, 18 L. Ed. 2d 288 (1967). An integrated group of fifteen Episopal ministers was arrested and charged with breach of the peace while attempting to use segregated facilities at an interstate bus terminal in Jackson, Mississippi. Convicted before a municipal police justice, they appealed, and on a trial de novo the charges were either reversed or dropped. The group then sought damages against the arresting officers and the trial judge, based on both 42 U.S.C. §1983 and common-law grounds of false arrest and imprisonment. A federal jury found for respondents on both counts, and the Fifth Circuit affirmed as to the judge's immunity from liability under both §1983 and common law for his actions as a member of the judiciary. As to the police officers, the court reluctantly concluded that under Monroe v. Pape they would be liable in a suit under §1983 for an unconstitutional arrest, even if they acted in good faith and with probable cause in making the arrest, under a state statute that several years later was declared unconstitutional. The court held that the police officers would not be liable under the common-law counts if they had probable cause to believe that the statute had been violated. The Fifth Circuit reversed and remanded for a new trial on the §1983 claim, at which trial the court held that the ministers could not recover if it were proved that they went to Mississippi anticipating that they would be illegally arrested.

The Supreme Court granted review and, after finding that judges were immune at common law for acts committed within their judicial jurisdiction, concluded that §1983 had not altered this settled principle of law. Similarly, as to the police officers, the Court noted that, while the common law had never granted police officers an absolute and unqualified immunity, the prevailing view in this country is that a peace officer who arrests someone with probable cause is not liable for false arrests simply because the innocence of the suspect is later proved. Speaking for the Court, Chief Justice Warren said,

> A policeman's lot is not so unhappy that he must choose between being charged with dereliction of duty if he does not arrest when he has probable cause, and being mulcted in damages if he does. . . . the same consideration would seem to require excusing him from liability for acting under a statute that he reasonably believes to be valid but that was later held unconstitutional on its face or as applied. (386 U.S. at 555.)

Distinguishing Monroe v. Pape, the Court held "that the defense of good faith and probable cause, which the Court of Appeals found available to the officers in the common-law action for false arrests and imprisonment, is also available to them in the action under §1983." 386 U.S. at 557. However, in this case petitioners claimed that the police officers arrested them solely for attempting to use the "White Only" waiting room, that no crowd was present, and that no one threatened violence or seemed about to cause a disturbance. The officers, on the other hand, claimed that serious disorder and violence threatened. The Court found that the jury's verdict for the police officers was influenced by the admission of irrelevant and prejudicial evidence, and remanded the case for a new trial. In remanding the case, the Court stated that petitioners were not barred from recovering damages because they had anticipated arrest.

Justice Douglas dissented on the judicial immunity point, stating: "I do not think that all judges, under all circumstances, no matter how outrageous their conduct, are immune from suit under 17 Stat. 42 U.S.C. §1983." 386 U.S. at 558-559.

NOTES

1. Counsel for petitioners (Carl Rachlin, Esq.) has reported that no attempt was made to retry the cases following the Supreme Court's decision. B. Bittker, The Case For Black Reparations 42, n. 44 (1973). Assuming that counsel's decision not to seek a new trial was based on a conclusion that the Supreme Court had erected a standard for police liability under §1983 that would be impossible to meet, was his conclusion justified?

2. In Pierson v. Ray, including judicial officials within the traditional shield of sovereign immunity against §1983 attacks was no real surprise. But extending this immunity to police officers, where they acted in good faith and with probable cause in making an arrest under a statute they believed to be valid, so effectively limits the scope of §1983 relief that, in the absence of the truly shocking case, the possibility of recovery is little better than under the state's common-law tort remedies.

3. In the "shocking" case, however, the chances of a favorable recovery remain better in a federal action, as illustrated in the decision in Jenkins v. Averett infra. Judge Sobeloff, inter alia, construes Pierson v. Ray as not requiring proof of bad motive or evil intent for relief under §1983.

4. The defense of judicial immunity has been held not to be available in actions for equitable relief under the Civil Rights Statutes. In Littleton v. Berbling, 468 F.2d 389 (7th Cir. 1972), black citizens of Cairo, Illinois sought to enjoin state judges from discriminating against their class in setting bonds, sentencing, and assessing court costs; and to enjoin the state's attorney from abusing his authority by refusing to prosecute whites who committeed crimes against blacks. The court held that "The legislative history of [§§1981 and 1983] . . . makes clear that Congress meant to eliminate judicial immunity of state judges, at least as to suits seeking injunctive relief." It was further held that the "exceptional circumstances" of Younger v. Harris had been met, and injunctive relief was therefore warranted. The court of appeals provided guidelines for the trial judge, who was directed to grant relief if plaintiffs were able to prove their allegations at trial. It suggested:

> An initial decree might set out the general tone of rights to be protected and require only periodic reports of various types of aggregate data on actions on bail and

sentencing and dispositions of complaints. Nevertheless, we have complete confidence in the district court's ability to set up further guides as required and if necessary to consider individual decisions. Difficulty of formulating a remedy if a complaint is proved following a trial cannot be grounds for dismissing the complaint ab initio. We cannot so easily belittle the powers of a court of equity nor the ability of district judges who have grappled with difficult remedies before, e.g., school desegregation orders, railroad reorganizations.

We also are not unmindful of the possibility of a substantial additional burden being placed on the federal judiciary by our decision. However, if it can be alleged and proved, and the sweep of our decision is to be no broader, that the state officials consistently, designedly and egregiously have, under color of law, deprived an entire group of citizens of their civil rights, then the additional burden will necessarily have to be assumed. The civil rights of all persons, too often merely words in a constitutionally inspired century-old statute, deserve no lesser implementation than here accorded them. (468 F.2d at 389.)

JENKINS v. AVERETT
424 F.2d 1228 (4th Cir. 1970)

SOBELOFF, Circuit Judge:

The subject matter of this appeal is an occurrence in Asheville, North Carolina, on August 5, 1967. On that night, appellant, Robert Jenkins, an 18-year-old black youth, was shot by F. W. Averett, appellee, a white Asheville police officer. Jenkins had committed no crime nor was he ever charged with one. Subsequently, he sued Averett in the United States District Court to recover damages for violation of his constitutional rights under 42 U.S.C. §1983 and for assault and battery under a pendent claim based upon the law of North Carolina. The District Court rejected the section 1983 claim but found defendant liable in the state cause of action. The assessment of compensatory damages, however, was limited to out-of-pocket expenses, in the amount of $448.00. Nothing was allowed for pain and suffering.

I. FACTUAL SETTING

A. *The Evidence*

Between midnight and 1:00 a.m., on the night in question, Jenkins was walking home from a club in the company of three or four other Negro boys. They had not proceeded far when they were overtaken by a car filled with white boys who hurled racial taunts as they sped past. The automobile returned in short order. This time one white boy got out and threw a tire tool, which hit one of Jenkins' companions on the leg.

The tire tool, which became the focal point of ensuing events, and later of this litigation, is a metal bar with a bend or crook. Its length is about 18 inches. Plaintiff retrieved the thrown tool and pursued the automobile on foot by himself. After rounding a street corner he lobbed the bar at the speeding vehicle, but missed. His adversaries, however, evidently noting that he was now alone, stopped and began to pelt him with beer bottles.

Jenkins retreated around the corner to enlist his colleagues. He was joined by his friends and approximately ten other Negro boys who happened upon the scene. They rushed the seven or eight white boys, who now scurried away.

It was at this point, while the group of black youths was still milling about, that the squad car containing appellee Averett and his partner, Officer Bumpus, pulled up across the street. They had come in response to a radio call addressed to another police patrol. When the boys saw the police they began to scatter. It was Jenkins who sought to restrain them, admonishing that having done no wrong they should not run. Finally, when the last boy, whom Jenkins had grabbed by the arm, broke away, Jenkins as well flew. He still had the tire tool, and according to his version, ran with it in his hand.

When the police first arrived they perceived no wrongdoing. But Averett claims that he saw Jenkins stuff something into his pants leg before bounding off and that across the concededly fairly well lit street it looked to him like a gun. Officer Bumpus saw neither gun nor tool. According to his testimony, what he saw appeared to him like a boy tucking his shirt in.

The officers in their automobile went in pursuit of Jenkins. Jenkins thinks he was selected simply because he was the last to leave the scene. Averett says that the young man was singled out for pursuit because he was a suspected gun wielder. At any rate Jenkins ran some distance. In fact, for six blocks he outran the police car which, according to Averett, was moving at a fast pace. Averett claims that all along the implement was concealed in Jenkins' trousers. He offers no explanation of how a man could run, indeed run so well, with a long metal bar in his pants leg.

The squad car finally caught up with appellant when he darted down a narrow lane. The police vehicle turned in and Jenkins, according to defendant's testimony, was caught against a wall in the squad car's headlights and "almost under the street light." Significantly, Averett acknowledges that the tool was now out and visibily in plaintiff's hand. But even with the aid of the street light and the direct beam of the headlights, Averett, we are told, still could not discern that the tire tool was not a gun.

Jenkins now reversed direction and came back toward the car in order to turn out of the street. He passed Bumpus' (the driver's) side of the police vehicle and continued to run. Averett got out, drew and cocked his pistol, and then chased his quarry about 60 feet. Averett says that as he ran he continued to be unable to espy the character of the article in Jenkins' hand. The officer yelled "halt" and Jenkins halted, apparently in the light. According to all the witnesses, including Averett, Jenkins then dropped the tire tool and turned to face his pursuer. The tool made a distinct noise upon falling that was heard all around, and even Averett recalls that it dropped. Only a few feet away, and two or three seconds later, Averett relates, he lowered his gun, and in doing so accidentally pulled the trigger, putting a hole through Jenkins' thigh.

The appellant maintains that the shooting was deliberate. Indeed he testified that after he was shot, appellee took aim again, but by that time Bumpus, who had now also left the police car, appeared, and Averett then lowered the gun.

The two officers placed the wounded man in the back of the police car. Jenkins claims that Averett said, "You better be glad my gun wasn't pointed at your God damned belly or you would have been dead." The policeman admits having said that his captive was indeed lucky that the shot did not hit him in the stomach. At trial, Bumpus corroborated this milder version although in his pretrial deposition he had disclaimed any memory of such a statement.

Jenkins was not taken to the hospital immediately. Instead, although admittedly not according to police procedure, the officers drove to the police station first so that Averett could report in and ask for "advice" on what to do about the bleeding boy in his custody. Averett concedes that this could have been accomplished as well by radio.

B. The Findings of the District Court

The District Judge generally credited defendant's story. He found that Averett suspected that Jenkins had a gun. He also found that Averett did not intend to shoot plaintiff. On the other hand, the District Judge found that defendant was grossly or culpably negligent. This finding is well supported by the record. Therefore, as will presently appear, there is no need to examine the other findings.

II. The State Claim

The District Judge held in favor of the plaintiff on the pendent state claim for assault and battery. Acknowledging that ordinarily intent is a necessary element in assault and battery, the court relied on the principle that gross or culpable negligence may supply that intent. . . . Since use of the unnecessary force was correctly found by the court below to amount to gross or culpable negligence, the imposition of liability on this count is affirmed.

III. The Federal Claim

The District Judge was of the opinion that Jenkins should not prevail under federal law. We do not agree, and hold that plaintiff has established the elements of recovery under 42 U.S.C. §1983.

A. The Constitutional Deprivation

The constitutional right to be free from unreasonable interference by police officers is incontrovertible. The Constitution has long been interpreted to embrace security from "arbitrary intrusion by the police." [Citations omitted.]

It is likewise clear that this shield covers the individual's physical integrity. Injuries arbitrarily inflicted by the police are constitutionally cognizable and remediable. [Citations omitted.]

As the District Court recognized, our plaintiff was subjected to the reckless use of excessive force. The wound he suffered was a result of unreasonable — or, to use the apt terminology of the District Court, "gross or culpable" — conduct of the defendant police officer. This arbitrary action was a constitutional violation.

The dissent maintains that arbitrariness is not the same as negligence. We agree. . . . Our affirmance of state liability is on the premise that the "gross or culpable" finding is the equivalent of a finding of arbitrariness. We propose at this juncture only to utilize the same finding in applying federal law.

Thus, we emphatically reject the spectre raised in the dissent that our opinion contemplates a constitutional remedy for all state-perpetrated negligence. Our concern here is with the raw abuse of power by a police officer — as found by the District Judge — and not with simple negligence on the part of a policeman or any other official. . . . We have no occasion to speculate about cases that are not before us.

B. The Relevance of Intent to Injure Under Section 1983

Having established the deprivation of a secured right, plaintiff asserts that his injury is redressible under section 1983. The District Judge, however, denied relief under this section, accepting defendant's claim that he did not intend to shoot plaintiff and deeming that to be a defense.

A simple answer is that if intent is required, it may be supplied, for federal purposes, by gross and culpable negligence, just as it was supplied in the common law cause of action. Pierson v. Ray, 386 U.S. 547 . . . (1967), discussed infra.

More fundamentally, however, after a constitutional violation has been made out, a showing of intent to injure is not a further prerequisite to recovery under section 1983. There is no longer room to doubt that one need not prove bad motive or evil intent to avail himself of the section 1983 remedy.

The actual words of the statute evince a design, without qualification, to compensate the deprivation of constitutional rights under color of law. . . .

Pierson v. Ray, 386 U.S. 547 . . . (1967), preserving to section 1983 defendants certain common law immunities, does not detract from our conclusion, but supports it. That case did not introduce into the statute an absolute shield from liability for non-malicious acts; it held only that defenses continue to exist where they existed in parallel common law causes. The lower court had imposed liability on police officers who made arrests founded upon probable cause under a statute valid when invoked but subsequently declared unconstitutional. Under the common law the officers could have defended on the basis of good faith reliance on the statute. . . . Pierson held that common law immunities retain vitality in a section 1983 action if they could have been utilized in the cognate state action. But having been properly held liable in the common law analogue, Averett obviously can mount no such defense to the federal suit.

IV. Damages

A. Compensatory

The District Judge limited damages to out-of-pocket expenses totaling $448.00. The award is inadequate. Indisputably, pain and suffering which accompany personal injury should be compensated. . . .

The evidence demonstrates that the bullet hole (six inches in depth) made by the shot caused considerable pain. The wound required constant redressing and the administration of pain-relieving drugs. Furthermore, Jenkins, a young man of some athletic ability, was prevented, because of the injury, from taking his place in scholastic athletic endeavors during his senior year of high school. On remand the court will make an award sufficient to redress fairly all the consequences of the gun wound, including pain and suffering.

B. Punitive

The court below found "no evidence in this record which would justify the awarding of punitive damages." That holding may have been influenced by the supposition that the section 1983 claim should be denied. We express no view as to the appropriateness of punitive damages in this case. That question will remain open on remand.

[The opinion of Judge Bryan, concurring in part and dissenting in part, is omitted.]

NOTES

1. §1983 of Title 42 not only authorizes actions to redress conduct under color of state law alleged to be in violation of state law, as in Monroe v. Pape, but also may be used to challenge state statutes or ordinances deemed in conflict with federally protected rights. Because §1983 is by its terms limited to acts done under color "of any state or territory," it does not apply to acts done under color of federal law. Gregoire v. Biddle, 177 F.2d 579 (2d Cir. 1949), *cert. denied,* 339 U.S. 949 (1950); Norton v. McShane, 332 F.2d 855 (5th Cir. 1964).

2. Generally, §1983 is not available to redress private conduct. In Adickes v. S. H. Kress & Company, 398 U.S. 144, 90 S. Ct. 1598, 26 L. Ed. 2d 142 (1970), however, the Supreme Court held that damages might be recovered against a private store that denied service on the basis of race, if such action were proved to have been "under color of any . . . custom or usage, of any state. . . ." The plaintiff, a white volunteer teacher at a "freedom school" for black children in Mississippi, sought service in defendant's store restaurant with six of her students. A waitress took the students' orders but refused to serve petitioner because she was a white person in the company of blacks. Upon leaving the store, the teacher was arrested by local police and charged with vagrancy. In her federal suit, she alleged that defendant's refusal had been pursuant to

a custom of the community to segregate races in public eating places. The district court directed a verdict in favor of the store, and the court of appeals affirmed. The Supreme Court reversed. In an opinion by Justice Harlan, it was held that plaintiff could recover under §1983 if she could prove that the discrimination she suffered was with knowledge of, and pursuant to, a custom having the force of law by virtue of persistent official practices. Such a custom, the opinion said, might be shown through evidence of intentional police toleration of violence or threats of violence against sit-in demonstrators, or through direct police harassment involving groundless arrests on any charges. The majority rejected petitioner's contention (adopted by Justice Brennan) that the customs of the people, in addition to the customs of state officials, amounted to state action for purposes of §1983.

As pointed out in a review of the case, 84 Harv. L. Rev. 71, 81 (1970), Justice Harlan characterized the question in Adickes as being whether an individual who discriminates "under the *compulsion* of state law," 398 U.S. at 170 (emphasis added), violates the fourteenth amendment. But in recent years, the Court has found state action not only when segregation was compelled, but when it was encouraged by statute.

The value of the Adickes opinion is further reduced by two disclaimers in the majority opinion's final footnote, 398 U.S. at 174, n. 44:

First, the note suggests that a suit for damages may not be a "proper proceeding" under §1983 when the private discriminator is compelled by state law to discriminate.

Second, citing Pierson v. Ray, the majority states that it does not decide what, if any, defenses might be available to an action under §1983. Pierson held that a reasonable belief in the constitutionality of a statute under which arrests are made absolves police officers of liability for damages. Assuming that private individuals can raise similar defenses, a plaintiff would have the almost impossible task of proving that the individual acted with knowledge of, and pursuant to, a statute or custom, while having reason to know the statute or custom was unconstitutional. 84 Harv. L. Rev. at 82.

3. The state action requirement of §1983 has always been a particularly vexing limitation to civil rights lawyers, because it shielded "private action" which simply could not have been performed without help from the state. Shelley v. Kraemer, 334 U.S. 1, 68 S. Ct. 836, 92 L. Ed. 1161 (1948), was welcomed precisely because it recognized the assistance provided by courts to enforce racially restrictive covenants, and barred this assistance. The restrictive covenants remained "valid," but their breach could not be remedied in the courts.

But, as Henry v. First National Bank of Clarksdale, 444 F.2d 1300 (5th Cir. 1971), printed supra page 333, shows, efforts to find state action in private individuals who use the courts to further activities deemed by plaintiffs to infringe their rights, have not been successful. The distinction in Henry, that relief in Shelley came after a final court order was entered, seems an irrelevant distinction; and to refer the plaintiffs to state court remedies is, of course, to ignore the whole purpose of §1983. But such a referral is predictable where, as in Henry, the court is willing to presume that race and Mississippi's antipathy toward the NAACP are not factors worthy of consideration.

4. A problem when §1983 is used as the basis for a suit for damages is the absence of a time-limiting provision for the initiation of the action. The general policy in such situations is to apply state statutes of limitation, but this still leaves unresolved issues of potentially crucial importance.

The basic policy and the reasons supporting it are set forth in Willis v. Reddin, 418 F.2d 702 (9th Cir. 1969), infra. See also Franklin v. City of Marks, 439 F.2d 665 (5th Cir. 1971). In a suit challenging the validity of the city's de-annexation ordinance, a statutory ten-day period for appeal from the de-annexation decree was held only a procedural limitation to the de-annexation process, and not a true statute of limitations. The state's six-year "catch-all" statute of limitation was deemed the correct one for application in the case. See also Wilcher v. Gain, 311 F. Supp. 754 (N.D. Cal. 1970).

In Mizell v. North Broward Hospital District, 427 F.2d 468 (5th Cir. 1970) (rehearing en banc), the defendant hospital asserted that the plaintiff's suit for suspension of his surgical privileges was barred by a three-year state statute of limitations. Plaintiff maintained that the state statute tolled because, during all of its period, he had been seeking relief in state administrative procedures. The court, speaking through Judge Tuttle, agreed:

> Having in mind the salutary rule that under our system of federalism aggrieved persons should be encouraged to utilize state procedures before appealing to the federal courts . . . we are persuaded that in cases arising under the Constitution or laws of the United States, a federal rule on tolling a state statute of limitations (when applicable) should be observed, if such rule clearly carries out the intent of Congress or of the constitutional principle at stake. (427 F.2d at 474.)

5. In Brazier v. Cherry, 293 F.2d 401 (5th Cir. 1961), *cert. denied*, 368 U.S. 921 (1961), the cause of action for damages created by §1983 was held to survive the death of the victim.

GRIFFIN v. BRECKENRIDGE, 403 U.S. 88, 91 S. Ct. 1790, 29 L. Ed. 2d 338 (1971). Griffin involved a group of blacks who, while driving along a Mississippi highway, were mistaken by whites for civil rights workers. The whites used their pickup truck to force the blacks' car to stop, ordered them out, and beat them seriously with iron clubs.

The blacks brought an action under 42 U.S.C. §1985(3), which authorizes the recovery of damages when two or more persons conspire or attempt to deprive any person or group of persons of the equal protection of the laws or equal privileges and immunities under the laws. (For full text of section, see Appendix.)

The district court, relying on Collins v. Hardyman, 341 U.S. 651, 71 S. Ct. 937, 95 L. Ed. 1253 (1950), dismissed the complaint. In Collins, the action had been brought by a group of whites against another group of whites who broke up a political meeting about the Marshall Plan. There the Supreme Court held that §1985(3) applied only to conspiracies involving state action, which had not been alleged in Griffin. The Fifth Circuit upheld the district court on the same ground, although expressing "serious doubts" as to the "continued validity" of Collins after United States v. Guest, 383 U.S. 745 (1966), supra page 868, and Jones v. Mayer Co., 392 U.S. 409 (1968), supra page 626.

Justice Stewart, writing for the entire Court, reversed the lower court's decision. The Court reviewed Collins and concluded that it need not now decide whether that case had been decided correctly on its facts, but that "in the light of the evolution of decisional law . . . many of the constitutional problems there perceived simply do not exist." 403 U.S. at 95-96.

Examination of the statute on its face showed that it is applicable to the conduct of private persons. While §1985(3) speaks in Fourteenth Amendment language of actions depriving persons of equal protection of the laws, "there is nothing inherent in the phrase that requires the action working the deprivation to come from the state." And, granting the section the broad sweep accorded Civil Rights Statutes in recent years — citing United States v. Price and Jones v. Mayer Co. — the Court construed the provision to reach private conduct. A further review of both its judicial and legislative history justified this conclusion.

The Court cautioned that the section is not to be read as a federal tort law. To avoid the "constitutional shoals" that would lie in the path of interpreting §1985(3) too broadly, full effect must be given "to the congressional purpose — by requiring, as an element of the cause of action, the kind of invidiously discriminatory motivation stressed by the sponsors . . . there must be some racial, or perhaps otherwise class-based, invidiously discriminatory animus behind the conspirators' action." 403 U.S. at 102.

Turning to the allegations in the complaint, the Court found that it adequately charged defendants with conspiring to deprive plaintiffs of their right to travel, a federal right under the Constitution, and also that it subjected them to involuntary servitude. "We can only conclude that Congress was wholly within its powers under §2 of the Thirteenth Amendment in creating a statutory cause of action for Negro citizens who have been the victims of conspiratorial, racially discriminatory private action aimed at depriving them of the basic rights that the law secures to all free men." 403 U.S. at 105.

Justice Harlan concurred, but felt it "unnecessary to rely on the right of interstate travel as a premise for justifying federal jurisdiction under §1985(3)."

NOTES

1. In Action v. Gannon, 450 F.2d 1227 (8th Cir. 1971), summarized supra page 361, Griffin was interpreted to establish the liability of black activists

who had disrupted plaintiff's church services with demands that reparations be made to the black community and that other conditions be met. The district court had premised liability on §1985(3), on the grounds that it reached the "conspiracy" of the defendants because Congress had power, under §5 of the Fourteenth Amendment, to protect the plaintiff's First Amendment rights of free exercise of religion. The court granted injunctive relief, declaring that defendant's First Amendment rights were limited to nondisruptive expressions of opinion and to peaceful, nonobstructive pamphleting and picketing on public property.

2. In Dombrowski v. Dowling, 459 F.2d 190 (7th Cir. 1972), the plaintiff, a white lawyer, alleged that the owner of an office building and his agent had conspired to deprive him of equal enjoyment of the facilities of a place of public accommodation, in refusing to rent space to him because a substantial number of his clients were black. The district court granted summary judgment in the plaintiff's favor on the grounds that §1985(3) reaches private conspiracy. The court of appeals reversed and remanded, holding that only interests which are protected against infringement "under color of state law" within the meaning of §1983 are also protected by §1985(3) against infringement by private conspiracy. If the building in question was not a public facility within the meaning of the 1964 Civil Rights Act, the plaintiff's Fourteenth Amendment rights had not been violated by "a discriminatory business decision," 459 F.2d at 196, because there was no state involvement in the discrimination. The plaintiff had no standing under the Thirteenth Amendment, nor had his right to interstate travel been violated. However, the court also held that, under 42 U.S.C. §2000(b)(4), the building might be considered a public facility; the district court was instructed to hear evidence to determine whether the statutory definition was applicable.

3. In United States v. Original Knights of the Ku Klux Klan, 250 F. Supp. 330 (E.D. La. 1965), the activities of the Klan were enjoined. The court based jurisdiction on provisions of the Civil Rights Acts of 1957 and 1964, concluding that the defendants' acts of intimidation and harassment violated specific rights protected against interference by private persons by civil rights measures (e.g., the right to vote, the right to equal enjoyment of public facilities and the right to equal employment opportunities). After Griffin, a cause of action for equitable relief from such unlawful acts should be available under §1985(3).

NOTE ON EXTRAORDINARY RELIEF

Injunctions. Subsequent cases vitiated the promise of Dombrowski v. Pfister, that 28 U.S.C. §2283 would not bar injunctive relief where "statutes have an overbroad sweep [and thus] the assumption that defense of a criminal prosecution will generally answer ample vindication of constitutional rights is unfounded." 380 U.S. 479, 486, 85 S. Ct. 1116, 1121, 14 L. Ed. 22, 28 (1965). In Cameron v. Johnson, 390 U.S. 611, 88 S. Ct. 1335, 20 L. Ed. 2d 182 (1968), appellants had been arrested under an antipicketing statute enacted by the Mississippi legislature. The arrest came after the appellants had been demonstrating peacefully and with the acquiescence of the police for nearly three months. The Supreme Court affirmed denial of injunctive relief, on the ground that, in enforcing the statute, state officials were not acting in bad faith. The circumstances in which injunctive relief would be appropriate were further limited by the principle of federalism adverted to in Younger v. Harris (401 U.S. 37, 91 S. Ct. 746, 27 L. Ed. 2d 669 (1971)), which requires that the plaintiff show "great and immediate injury" going beyond the injury normally incident to criminal prosecution, including the "chilling effect" on First Amendment rights. In the absence of bad faith, harassment, or possibly other "extraordinary circumstances" or "unusual situations," injunctive relief may not be granted. 401 U.S. at 54-55. Moreover, declaratory relief is inappropriate where a state criminal proceeding is pending and injunctive relief is not warranted under Younger. Samuels v. Mackell, 401 U.S. 66, 91 S. Ct. 764, 27 L. Ed. 2d 688 (1971). These doctrines were applied in Boyle v. Landry, 401 U.S. 77, 91 S. Ct. 758, 27 L. Ed. 2d 696 (1971), to deny relief to black organizations who sought an end to police harassment under allegedly invalid statutes. In Donohoe v. Duling, 330 F. Supp. 308 (E.D. Va. 1971), *aff'd* 465 F.2d 196 (4th Cir. 1972), an action to enjoin police surveillance of protest demonstrations, relief was denied on the ground that there was no evidence that any of the plaintiffs had, in fact, been deterred from exercising their First Amendment rights. Although 42 U.S.C. §1983 is an express exception to 28 U.S.C. §2283 (see Mitchum v. Foster, 407 U.S. 225, 92 S. Ct. 2151, 32 L. Ed. 705 (1972)), the principles of equity, comity and federalism nevertheless require that Younger standards be met in a §1983 action for equitable relief, where a state proceeding is pending.

Removal. The scope of removal under 28 U.S.C. §1443 (see Appendix), another form of relief which might be termed "extraordinary," has also been narrowly construed. §1443(1) provides for the removal by the defendant from state court to federal district court, of civil or criminal actions "against any person who is denied or cannot enforce in the courts of such State a right under any law providing for the equal civil rights of citizens of the United States, or of all persons within the jurisdiction thereof."

In Georgia v. Rachel, 384 U.S. 780, 86 S. Ct. 1783, 16 L. Ed. 2d 925 (1966), the defendants sought removal of prosecutions for trespass arising out of restaurant sit-ins. The Supreme Court held that removal may be had under §1443(1) upon an allegation in the removal petition that the prosecutions were initiated after petitioners were asked to leave solely for racial reasons. In such case, the mere pendency of prosecutions would enable a federal court to make a firm prediction that petitioners would be denied their rights in the state courts. Because §203 of the 1964 Civil Rights Act prohibits attempts to punish an individual for seeking service in restaurants, the burden of prosecution would itself constitute the denial of the right conferred by the Civil Rights Act.

A seemingly more restrictive standard was set forth in City of Greenwood v. Peacock, 384 U.S. 808, 86 S. Ct. 1800, 16 L. Ed. 2d 944 (1966), where removal was sought by blacks who were being prosecuted, under various inciting-to-riot and disturbing-the-peace statutes, for conduct connected with a voter registration drive. The Court held that removal was not permissible, on the ground that no explicit federal or state law provided a clear basis for predicting that the defendants would be unable to enforce their rights in state courts. "[N]o federal law confers an absolute right on private citizens . . . to obstruct a public street. . . ." The fact that federal civil rights had been denied by state officials in advance of trial did not provide a basis for removal.

In Hill v. Commonwealth, 439 F.2d 1016 (3d Cir. 1971), members of the Black Construction Coalition were charged with assault, unlawful assembly, and inciting to riot as a result of their protest against racially biased employment policies. Removal was denied in reliance on Peacock, supra, on the ground that there was no basis for predicting that defendant's rights would be unenforceable in state courts. Although 18 U.S.C. §245 prohibited attempts to interfere with the assertion of civil rights, the statute did not immunize the defendants from prosecution for the type of conduct with which they were charged. Removal was denied on similar grounds in Schoen v. Sulton, 297 F. Supp. 538 (D. Md. 1969). Defendants, an interracial married couple, sought to remove a suit to enjoin a nuisance brought by their neighbors, who alleged that defendants constantly disturbed the entire neighborhood by bickering, arguing and assaulting other residents. Defendants sought removal on the grounds that the suit violated their right under 42 U.S.C. §§1982 and 3617 to enjoy their property and that it was motivated by racial prejudice. The court analogized the case to Peacock, supra, saying that "no federal law permits a man to disturb and harass his neighbors and no federal law prohibits a neighbor from suing a neighbor to enjoin a nuisance." Moreover, the defendants had neither alleged nor shown that their federal rights would be denied by the Maryland courts. The court noted that, if it were to grant defendants' request for an evidentiary hearing on this question, it would, in effect, have to decide the merits of the case in deciding whether there was sufficient basis for removal.

Judge Brown, dissenting in Perkins v. Mississippi, 455 F.2d 7 (5th Cir. 1972), argued that the right of removal can be enforced only through an extensive evidentiary hearing going to the question of the state's motivation in prosecuting the defendants. In Perkins, defendants were civil rights workers arrested for a variety of misdemeanors, including reckless driving, resisting arrest, and possession of concealed weapons, while returning from a civil rights demonstration in another county. The majority credited the district court testimony of the police officers and denied removal on the ground that defendants were not arrested because of their exercise of constitutional rights. On the basis of a close analysis of Peacock and Rachel, Judge Brown urged that proof of invidious motivation not be limited to a showing that the conduct charged is immunized against prosecution by federal statute. Removal should also be permitted where "though ostensibly resulting from conduct entirely unrelated to the previous exercise of a Federally protected right [arrest and prosecution] were nevertheless motivated exclusively by conduct protected against State Criminal prosecution by Federal law." 455 F.2d at 30. Otherwise, "effective vindication of Federal rights through the removal remedy [may] be effortlessly circumnavigated by the simple expedient of holding the spurious arrest in abeyance until *after* [*sic*] the right has been exercised and the innocent defendant has begun to engage in 'unprotected activity.'" 455 F.2d at 31-32.

In a somewhat similar case, the Fourth Circuit affirmed the remand of two removal petitions filed by two civil rights activists charged by the state with rioting at two stores. Petitioners claimed that they were engaged in lawful civil rights marches, demonstrations, boycotts and other protest activity. Conceding that the factual dispute between the state and petitioners could not be resolved without a hearing, the court interpreted Peacock as directing the courts away from hearings in such cases. Peacock rather than Rachel was applied, because the court saw no great probability that a federal right would be denied if the prosecution was not removed. As the court viewed it:

> A white storekeeper may lawfully order Negro persons in his store to discontinue destruction of his property whether or not he is racially prejudiced. He may not, however, for racial reasons lawfully order nonviolent persons to leave. As an exercise in probability prediction, we may confidently assert that there is a far greater probability that a trespass warrant will be flawed by a policy of invidious discrimination than that a riot warrant will be similarly invalidated. This is so because the riot warrant will be valid if violence (the essential element) occurred, whereas the trespass warrant may be void even though presence over the protest of the owner (the essential element) is admitted. This is so, in turn, because peaceful presence is protected and violence is not. Race, color, or creed may well be a sufficient defense to a charge of trespass, but are wholly irrelevant to a charge of rioting. (Frinks v. North Carolina, 468 F.2d 639, 643 (1972).)

In dissent, Judge Sobeloff charged,

> The majority would have a district court summarily dismiss a removal petition without an evidentiary hearing whenever the state has alleged a crime of which violence is an element. A petitioner is thereby denied the opportunity to vindicate his contention that, by means of a bogus prosecution, the state is attempting to mete out punishment for the exercise or attempted exercise of rights secured by the public accommodations section of the Civil Rights Act of 1964. The state prosecutor is permitted to attach a convenient tag to a defendant's conduct, and this labeling, rather than what the individual was actually doing, becomes the test of removability. (468 F.2d at 645.)

He contended that Rachel and not Peacock was controlling, in that in the instant case, as in Rachel, petitioners alleged violation of rights guaranteed by the public accommodations act, which explicitly provides that no person shall "punish or attempt to punish any persons for exercising or attempting to exercise any right or privilege" secured by the act. §203(c). He concluded that petitioners met the two-prong test of Rachel, and that the conflict between the allegations in the removal petition and those in the criminal indictment justifies a hearing to resolve the conflict, and not dismissal of the petition.

Habeas Corpus. Pretrial relief from bad faith arrest or prosecution is apparently not available under 28 U.S.C. §2254, the federal habeas corpus statute.

In Brown v. Rayfield, 320 F.2d 96 (5th Cir. 1963), *cert. denied,* 375 U.S. 902 (1963), a pretrial application for habeas relief where petitioners were arrested for parading without a permit during a peaceful civil rights protest march, it was held that under §2254 exhaustion of state remedies was required, although by the terms of the statute the limitations of §2254 apply only to postconviction petitions for writ of habeas corpus. This interpretation was again applied in Hillegas v. Sams, 349 F.2d 859 (5th Cir. 1965), where the petitioner, a white civil rights worker, was arrested for refusing to leave the county courthouse and was confined pending trial. Judge Brown, in a separate opinion, argued on historical grounds and by analogy from Dombrowski v. Pfister and Peacock v. Greenwood that a federal habeas corpus was an appropriate remedy: "[W]e have now passed the point where Federal Courts can refuse to hear evidence in support of a factually detailed claim that a state criminal prosecution has been initiated to effectuate racially motivated denial of constitutional rights. . . . [T]he situation is 'extraordinary' and therefore calls for extraordinary relief."

NOTE: SUITS BASED DIRECTLY ON CONSTITUTIONAL AMENDMENTS

As the materials in this section have shown, the individual relying on §§1983 or 1985(3) to recover damages for the violation of his constitutional rights faces many obstacles, but he nevertheless travels a more certain path than if his suit were against federal officers, whose actions are not covered by either provision.

For a long time, it has been clear that a complaint alleging such violations should not be dismissed. The Supreme Court in 1946 held that a suit for damages against federal agents alleged to have invaded plaintiff's Fourth Amendment rights stated a constitutional claim within the jursdiction conferred by 28 U.S.C. §1331(a). Bell v. Hood, 327 U.S. 678, 66 S. Ct. 773, 90 L. Ed. 939 (1946). While finding that the claim for damages "arises" under the Constitution in the strictly procedural sense that the district court must "entertain the suit," the Court, however, specifically declined to decide whether it "arises" in the substantive sense that it states a federal claim for which relief could be granted. On remand, the district court, faced with the tough substantive question, concluded that the suit did not state a federal claim for relief. Bell v. Hood, 71 F. Supp. 813 (S.D. Cal. 1947).

The Supreme Court was presented with the substantive issue for the first time in Bivens v. Six Unknown Named Agents of the Fed. Bur. Narcotics, 403 U.S. 388, 91 S. Ct. 1999, 29 L. Ed. 2d 619 (1971). A majority found that violation of Fourth Amendment rights by federal agents is in itself an actionable offense, for which the agents can be held personably liable in damages.

The Bivens decision is potentially important. It presents possibilities for more effective damages suits against state officers based solely on the Thirteenth or Fourteenth Amendments, in cases involving violations of rights for which remedies under existing civil rights legislation are either nonexistent or inadequate. To raise but one question: might a federal court, in an appropriate case based on the Fourteenth Amendment, permit damages against a municipality whose officials have violated plaintiff's equal protection or due process rights, under circumstances indicating that the governmental unit approved or condoned such violations? §1983 does not permit such recovery, under Monroe v. Pape supra, and the policy factors, based on sovereign immunity and Eleventh Amendment considerations, will pose serious obstacles. However, considering that individuals seeking damages for police brutality, bureaucratic harassment, and political oppression are unable to obtain effective relief in damages under existing law, the results in cases such as United States v. Price and United States v. Guest indicate that, in a shocking situation, the argument would receive serious attention.

Racism Hypo 15
LAW v. COMMUNITY TRIAL, ET AL.

John Law is a white policeman, who for a number of years has been assigned to the black community. His work there has been quite effective when judged by the number of persons he has arrested for burglary, armed robbery, gambling, use of narcotics and other crimes that afflict the ghetto area. Recently, while in a platoon of policemen seeking to restore order during a destructive outbreak in the ghetto, John Law shot and killed a black youth in front of a clothing store that had just been looted. He ran when Law ordered him to halt. According to testimony Law gave at a police inquiry into the shooting, he had intended only to fire a warning shot over the youth's head, but other black youths attacked him at that point and ruined his aim.

Further testimony at the inquiry indicated that the victim had not looted the store, but in fact had been quite obviously attempting to dissuade other black youths from going into the store when the policemen arrived. The young man ran, according to eyewitnesses who knew him, because he feared the police would not believe that he was not involved in the looting. They said that Law shot the youth deliberately and that his story of being attacked by unarmed blacks was preposterous on its face.

The black community was greatly incensed when an inquest and a police inquiry found that the killing was accidental and that no charges would be filed against Law. An ad hoc community group was organized. After a review of remedies provided by federal and state law, all of which it concluded were worthless, the group decided to hold a "Community Trial" to determine Law's guilt. This was done, and in a well-attended and highly publicized session, a number of witnesses testified that Law's action was intentional, deliberate and unjustified. Law and other appropriate police officials were invited to testify but refused. Following the trial, the "jury," composed of leading citizens of the black community, found John Law guilty of murder and urged the district attorney to take action.

In the days that followed, placards were placed throughout the ghetto with pictures of Law, under which was the caption: "Wanted — Guilty of Murder." The community group authorized these posters. It did not, however, support or condone the series of threatening phone calls to which Law was then subjected, both at the police station and his home. In addition, the group said Law's claims that snipers fired on him during his tour of duty in the ghetto were lies. Law was subsequently transferred, both because he was in danger and because police officials feared that his presence was contributing to growing tensions in the area.

As a result of all this, Law has filed a suit for injunction and damages in federal court, basing jurisdiction on 42 U.S.C. §§1981, 1983, and 1985(3). He named as defendants those persons participating in the community trial. He was certain that the trial and the program of harassment that followed it exceeded First Amendment bounds and constituted both libel and an interference with his means of livelihood. In his suit, Law stated again that the shooting was accidental and that his record in the black community reflected the kind of police protection that the black community needs, and he believes, wants. In the trial court, Law was granted an injunction prohibiting Community Trial leaders from further distribution of the "Wanted" placards and from other similar actions, and was awarded a total of $10,000 in damages from the named defendants. The defendants are appealing.

Law Firm A will represent the Community Trial leaders in the appeal.

Law Firm B will represent John Law in the appeal.

(Both sides should review the cases and materials in Chapter 7.)

C. FAIR HEARINGS FOR STUDENTS

DIXON v. ALABAMA STATE BOARD OF EDUCATION, 294 F.2d 150 (5th Cir. 1961). The six plaintiffs were expelled from Alabama State College, a state-owned institution, without notice or hearing. Between February 25 and March 1, 1960, black students at the college had engaged in a series of civil rights demonstrations, including a sit-in, a march and a sing-in. All of the plaintiffs had participated in at least one of these events, but, in instructing the college president to expel them, the Board of Education did not assign specific grounds for its action. School regulations authorized expulsion for willful disobedience of school rules, failure to meet academic standards, and conduct "prejudicial to the school." The plaintiffs brought an action for injunctive relief. The district court dismissed the complaint, and the court of appeals reversed, holding that due process required that a student at a state college or university not be expelled without notice and hearing.

The court began with the premise that "[w]henever a governmental body acts to injure an individual, the Constitution requires that the act be consonant with due process of law. The minimum procedural requirements necessary to satisfy due process depend upon the circumstances and the interests of the parties involved." 294 F.2d at 155. In the court's view, the balance weighed heavily in favor of plaintiffs: "It requires no argument to demonstrate that education is vital, and indeed, basic to civilized society. Without sufficient education the plaintiffs would not be able to earn an adequate livelihood, to enjoy life to the fullest, or to fulfill as completely as possible the duties and responsibilities of good citizens." 294 F.2d at 157. Further sources of harm were identified: even if other colleges were open to the plaintiffs, their studies would be interrupted at midterm, and it was likely that the plaintiffs would be prejudiced in their attempts to gain admission to any other college. In contrast, the government's interests involved no considerations of danger to the public or to the national security that would justify the failure to adhere to at least minimal standards of due process. Earlier cases holding that college students were not entitled to due process before expulsion were distinguished, on the grounds that either they involved a private institution, where the relationship between the student and the school was one of contract and where procedural rights had been waived, or there was a question whether the hearing that had been provided was adequate.

The court concluded by setting forth the standards regarding notice and hearing that state colleges would be required to meet. Students should be apprised of "the specific charges and grounds which, if proved, would justify expulsion under the regulations of the Board of Education." 294 F.2d at 158. Although the type of hearing required would depend upon the circumstances of each case, more than an "informal interview" would be necessary where misconduct was charged.

> In such circumstances, a hearing which gives the Board or the administrative authorities of the college an opportunity to hear both sides in considerable detail is best suited to protect the rights of all involved. This is not to imply that a full-dress judicial hearing, with the right to cross-examine witnesses, is required. . . . Nevertheless, the rudiments of an adversary proceeding may be preserved without encroaching upon the interests of the college [in maintaining an atmosphere consonant with its educational functions]. (294 F.2d at 159.)

The "rudiments of an adversary proceeding" were to include advance notice of the names of witnesses against the student and a statement of the facts to which each testifies; an opportunity to appear before the board, or at least before an administrative official, and present a defense by way of oral testimony or affidavits of witnesses; and a statement of the board's findings and decision.

NOTES

1. Dixon was preceded by a long line of cases that denied procedural rights to students. Several theories were advanced in support of such holdings: (1) Schools, whether public or private, stand in loco parentis and thus have inherent authority to discipline. (2) The relationship between a student and a privately owned school is a matter of contract, and the school may condition admission upon a promise to abide by school regulations and upon waiver, express or implied, of procedural rights. (3) Education is a privilege, not a right, and therefore due process requirements do not apply, even in the case of a student at a state-owned or state-supported school. Dixon was compatible, however, with later Supreme Court decisions that have discredited the privilege-right distinction and given wider application to due process requirements. In the school discipline cases that followed, Dixon was frequently taken as the starting point.*

2. The Dixon decision represents another instance where blacks, using the courts to combat racial discrimination, have established new precedents that strengthen the rights of all citizens — in this case, students who traditionally were powerless to defend against arbitrary and even malicious actions of school officials. The issue remains, though, of whether the procedural rights found in Dixon can be translated into substantive value for students, in cases where protest activity is deemed disruptive by school officials whose broad authority to discipline students is not directly limited by the Dixon case.

KNIGHT v. STATE BOARD OF EDUCATION, 200 F. Supp. 174 (M.D. Tenn. 1961), was an action for injunctive relief by students dismissed without notice or hearing from a state college, under a regulation prescribing prompt dismissal of any student convicted on charges of "personal misconduct." During summer vacation the plaintiffs had participated in freedom rides and had

* Due process requirements have not been extended to disciplinary hearings at private schools or universities. Neither the tax-exempt status of schools, nor regulation by the state, nor the "public function" of education is considered to involve "state action" within the meaning of the Fourteenth Amendment. Browns v. Mitchell, 409 F.2d 593 (10th Cir. 1969); Bright v. Isenbarger, 314 F. Supp. 1382 (N.S. Ind. 1970); Grossner v. Trustees of Columbia University, 287 F. Supp. 535 (S.D.N.Y. 1968).

In Powe v. Miles and Alfred University, 407 F.2d 73 (2d Cir. 1969), the court found "state action" at a private college with respect to students at its Ceramics School, which by statute operated "on behalf of the state," but relief was denied on the merits. But in Coleman v. Wagner College, 429 F.2d 1120 (2d Cir. 1970), students seeking reinstatement pending hearing on suspension for sitting in at a dean's office were held entitled to a district court hearing, to prove that a statute requiring that the college file its disciplinary regulations with the state represented a state intrusion into disciplinary policies of private colleges, subjecting application of such policies to constitutional limitations.

been arrested and convicted of disorderly conduct in Mississippi. The court held that, where the fact of conviction alone was not clearly indicative of misconduct that reflected dishonor on the school, notice and hearing were required.

DUE v. FLORIDA A & M UNIVERSITY, 233 F. Supp. 396 (N.D. Fla. 1963). Plaintiffs had been suspended because of their contempt convictions for disobeying a state court order restraining demonstrations. Relief was denied on the ground that the Dixon requirements had been met. The plaintiffs were telephoned and asked to appear that same day before a disciplinary committee, which informed them of the charges and interrogated them. The plaintiffs made no request for witnesses or counsel, and no transcript was made. The court held that neither representation by counsel nor a transcript was necessary, and that the suspension was valid because it was supported by the evidence and was based on a clearly stated school regulation, which defined misconduct to include conviction for violation of any law.

NOTES

1. There was no discussion in Knight or Due of the possibility that the conduct for which sanctions were imposed was protected by the First Amendment. Compare Hammond v. South Carolina State College, 272 F. Supp. 947 (D.S.C. 1967), where students were suspended for participating in peaceful demonstrations, in violation of a school regulation requiring prior approval of such demonstrations by the college president. The court enjoined the suspensions, finding that the regulation was an unconstitutional prior restraint. See also Dickey v. Alabama State Board of Education, 273 F. Supp. 613 (M.D. Ala. 1967), where a student editor of the school newspaper was suspended because he refused to substitute an editorial on raising dogs in North Carolina for his own editorial on academic freedom, in which he had criticized members of the state legislature. The court ordered the plaintiff reinstated, holding that a school regulation prohibiting editorials critical of the governor or legislature of Alabama was an unreasonable prior restraint on First Amendment rights. The advantage of a decision extending constitutional protection to the activity, as opposed to simply requiring the adherence of due process standards before the activity can be punished, is obvious.

2. Adherence to the principles set forth in Dixon has often been little more than perfunctory, and many courts have manifested unwillingness to go beyond minimal notice and hearing requirements. In Davis v. Ann Arbor Public Schools, 313 F. Supp. 1217 (E.D. Mich. 1970), suspension of a black student for repeated lateness, truancy and other misconduct was upheld, although neither formal notice nor hearing had been provided. The court held that the student and his mother were fully aware of the reasons for suspension, and that the student was heard in answer by virtue of several telephone conferences between his mother and school officials. See also Schiff v. Hannah,

282 F. Supp. 381 (W.D. Mich. 1968); Hobson v. Bailey, 309 F. Supp. 1393 (W.D. Tenn. 1970); Tate v. Board of Education, 453 F.2d 375 (8th Cir. 1972).

3. Kelley v. Metropolitan Board of Education, 293 F. Supp. 485 (M.D. Tenn. 1968), extended the Dixon due process requirements to the suspension of an all-black high school from an interscholastic athletic program, as a result of misconduct following a basketball game. The only specific standards set forth were that the student body was to be given notice and that school officials were to be provided with an opportunity to be heard. In Williams v. Dade County School Board, 441 F.2d 299 (5th Cir. 1971), plaintiff was suspended for ten days for participating in a "mob." No hearing was held, but plaintiff's parents were invited to confer with the principal at an informal meeting. A thirty-day suspension followed the conference. The district court denied relief, but the court of appeals reversed, holding that the conference between plaintiff's parents and the principal did not meet the requirements of Dixon. The court distinguished Banks v. Board of Public Instruction, 314 F. Supp. 285 (S.D. Fla. 1970), *vacated sub nom.* Board of Public Instruction v. Richardson, 401 U.S. 988, 91 S. Ct. 1223, 28 L. Ed. 2d 526 (1971), where a ten-day suspension without hearing was upheld, on the ground that the more serious punishment imposed here required notice and hearing.

4. Schools sometimes voluntarily offer due process standards that exceed minimal requirements. See, e.g., Buttny v. Smiley, 281 F. Supp. 280 (D. Colo. 1968); Moore v. Student Affairs Commission of Troy State University, 284 F. Supp. 725 (M.D. Ala. 1968); Jones v. State Board of Education, 279 F. Supp. 150 (M.D. Tenn. 1969). In each case, students were permitted counsel at their hearings. But where the minimal standards have been satisfied, challenges to disciplinary proceedings are usually rejected. In Madera v. Board of Education, 386 F.2d 778 (2d Cir. 1969), a charge of delinquency was filed in family court against a student who had been suspended from school. Prior to the family court hearing, the student's parents were notified that there would be a "guidance conference" with the school superintendent. Although such a conference might result in placement in a detention home or a school for socially maladjusted students, and although the parents could be prosecuted for failure to consent to such placement, the court of appeals, reversing the district court, held that the parents were not entitled to have counsel present at the conference, because it was not a criminal proceeding. In Barker v. Hardway, 283 F. Supp. 228 (S.D.W. Va.), *aff'd,* 399 F.2d 638 (4th Cir. 1968), plaintiffs were students expelled from a state college for participation in a disruptive demonstration following a football game. They received suspension notices and were advised of their right to an appeal hearing, but they refused to proceed with hearing when their requests for the presence of counsel were denied. The district court dismissed the action, holding that due process requirements had been met by notice and opportunity for hearing, and that the right to counsel did not apply because the disciplinary committee had a "purely" investigative function. That is, the committee could only make recommendations to the college president, who alone had adjudicative au-

thority. The court of appeals affirmed, on the grounds that due process had been provided and that plaintiffs' claims of a right to counsel were rendered moot by virtue of the "plenary de novo hearing" with counsel in district court.

5. A challenge to suspension for possession of marihuana, on the ground that the search of plaintiff's dormitory room violated the Fourth Amendment, was rejected in Moore v. Student Affairs Commission of Troy State University, 284 F. Supp. 725 (M.D. Ala. 1968). The court held that, when a regulation or action by school authorities is necessary in aid of the school's power to maintain discipline, it will be presumed to be reasonable; and that here the search, pursuant to a regulation authorizing inspection of rooms, was lawful because it was based on a "reasonable belief" that the room was being used for an illegal purpose. Compare Caldwell v. Cannady, 340 F. Supp. 835 (N.D. Tex. 1972), where a high school student expelled for possession of marihuana was ordered reinstated, because, among other reasons, the search of his car — in which the marihuana was found — was warrantless, although the policemen who conducted the search had had ample time and opportunity to obtain a warrant.

6. Courts have been particularly unresponsive to claims that disciplinary proceedings violated standards of fairness because of bias on the part of the trier. Wasson v. Trowbridge, 382 F.2d 807 (2d Cir. 1967), was an action for a stay of expulsion by a cadet at the Merchant Marine Academy. The district court denied relief, and the court of appeals remanded, in part to provide the plaintiff with an opportunity to show prior bias-producing contact with the case by members of the disciplinary board. On remand, 285 F. Supp. 936 (E.D.N.Y. 1968), it was held that the plaintiff had failed to produce such evidence, although distinctions between command, investigatory and adjudicatory functions were unclear.

In Zanders v. Louisiana State Board of Education, 281 F. Supp. 747 (W.D. La. 1968), plaintiffs were expelled without noticc from an all-black state college for participation in an obstructive demonstration. After the court issued a temporary restraining order, a disciplinary hearing was held at which the college presented no evidence. The temporary restraining order was enlarged and a full hearing was held before the Board of Education; again, all the plaintiffs were expelled. Relief was denied on the grounds that the second hearing had met due process requirements and cured any prejudice resulting from the first hearing; that the plaintiffs' conduct was not protected by the First Amendment; and that, without proof of actual bias, the fact that board counsel acted as both prosecutor and adviser to the board did not violate due process. See also Jones v. State Board of Education, 279 F. Supp. 190 (M.D. Tenn. 1969), *aff'd*, 397 U.S. 31, 90 S. Ct. 779, 25 L. Ed. 2d 27 (1970), where students who had been indefinitely suspended for such disruptive conduct as interrupting meetings were denied reinstatement, on the grounds, inter alia, that the fact that two members of the disciplinary committee testified against the plaintiffs was not a denial of due process, absent a showing of bias. See also Esteban v. Central Missouri State College, 277 F. Supp. 649 (W.D. Mo.

1967), *cert. denied,* 398 U.S. 965 (1970), where the court set out detailed procedural standards to be followed in school disciplinary proceedings, including a requirement that the hearing be held before the president of the college, who was the only person with authority to suspend or expel. In Winnick v. Manning, 460 F.2d 545 (2d Cir. 1972), the plaintiff had been suspended from the University of Connecticut for participating in disruption of an examination, as a protest against the 1970 invasion of Cambodia and the slayings at Kent State. He alleged that the suspension hearing was invalid because of bias on the part of the trier, the associate dean of students. This claim was rejected on the grounds that the evidence did not show such "prior official contact with [the] case as to give rise to a presumption of bias," and that bias could not be predicated upon the view that the dean had an interest in upholding order by virtue of his official position. Id. at 548. But see Caldwell v. Cannady, supra note 5, where another reason for the student's reinstatement was that members of the school board, before whom the expulsion hearing was held, had participated in both prosecutorial and adjudicatory functions.

7. In some jurisdictions, the Dixon concept of fairness had been interpreted to require that interim suspension (i.e., suspension pending full administrative hearing) may not be imposed without a preliminary hearing, unless it can be shown that it is impossible or unreasonably difficult to accord such a hearing. Even then, interim suspension is justified only where the continued presence of the student threatens the well-being and safety of the college and its residents. In Stricklin v. Regents, 297 F. Supp. 416 (W.D. Wis. 1969), the suspended plaintiffs, who were charged with participation in violent disorders, were ordered reinstated pending hearing. The university appealed the order, but the appeal was dismissed as moot because in the meantime a full hearing had been held and the students expelled. 420 F.2d 1257 (7th Cir. 1970). Compare Buck v. Carter, 308 F. Supp. 1246 (W.D. Wis. 1970), an action for reinstatement pending full hearing, where the plaintiffs, university students, had been suspended for invading a fraternity house and physically attacking the occupants. Immediately after the incident, plaintiffs were called to a meeting with the university president, who suspended them pending hearing. Relief was denied on the ground that, since none of the plaintiffs specifically denied participation, the meeting with the president satisfied the requirements of a preliminary hearing. See also Williams v. Dade County School Board, 441 F.2d 299 (5th Cir. 1970), holding that suspension may not be imposed without a prior hearing where the suspension is for a substantial period of time and the need for summary action is not overriding.

MARZETTE v. McPHEE, 294 F. Supp. 562 (W.D. Wis. 1968). As the cases discussed above indicate, courts tend to give short shrift to due process claims where the students raising them have been involved in disruptive protest. The Marzette decision is an exception. There, seven black students at Wisconsin State University, Oshkosh, had been suspended after allegedly taking part in a student protest that involved a building take-over, serious property damage, and the imprisonment of the university president in his office with two vice-presidents. The district judge, concerned for the students' motivation (referred to supra page 371), extended a close review of the suspension notices received by the students. The court concluded that the suspensions violated the students' due process rights and ordered early hearings as an alternative to immediate reinstatement. The court also quoted with approval the following summary of procedural safeguards recognized by the courts since the Dixon case:

> (a) the student charged with an infraction has been furnished with a written statement of the charge adequately in advance of a hearing to enable him to prepare (e.g., 10 days);
>
> (b) the student thus charged "shall be permitted to inspect in advance of such hearing any affidavits or exhibits which the college intends to submit at the hearing";
>
> (c) the student is "permitted to have counsel present at the hearing to advise [him]";
>
> (d) the student is "permitted to hear the evidence presented against [him]," or at least the student should be given the names of the witnesses against him and an oral or written report on the facts to which each witness testifies;
>
> (e) the student or his attorney may question at the hearing any witness who gives evidence against him;
>
> (f) those who hear the case "shall determine the facts of each case solely on the evidence presented at the hearing";
>
> (g) "the results and findings of the hearing should be presented in a report open to the student's inspection";
>
> (h) "either side may, at its own expense, make a record of the events at the hearing." (Van Alstyne, The Student As University Resident, 45 Denver L.J. 582, 593-594 (1968).)

TINKER v. DES MOINES INDEPENDENT SCHOOL DISTRICT, 393 U.S. 503, 89 S. Ct. 733, 21 L. Ed. 2d 731 (1969). Petitioners were junior and senior high school students who decided during Christmas vacation to wear black armbands to school as a means of expressing their opposition to the Vietnam War. Having learned about the plan prior to the reopening of the school session, school authorities adopted a rule that any student who wore an armband and refused to remove it when requested to do so would be suspended until he returned without the armband. Petitioners were suspended for violation of the regulation, and they brought an action for declaratory and injunctive relief.

The Supreme Court held that, absent "facts which might reasonably have led school authorities to forecast substantial disruption or material interference with school activities" (393 U.S. at 514), and with no disruption actually occurring, the prohibition of armbands was an unjustifiable restriction on First Amendment rights. It was noted also that the regulation extended only to armbands, although other students wore political campaign buttons and some even wore the Iron Cross, traditionally a symbol of Nazism. "Clearly, the prohibition of expression of one particular opinion, at least without evidence that it is necessary to avoid material and substantial interference with schoolwork and discipline, is not constitutionally permissible." 393 U.S. at 511.

> In our system, state-operated schools may not be enclaves of totalitarianism. School officials do not possess absolute authority over their students. Students in school as well as out of school are "persons" under our Constitution. They are possessed of fundamental rights which the State must respect, just as they themselves must respect their obligations to the State. In our system, students may not be regarded as closed-circuit recipients of only that which the State chooses to communicate. They may not be confined to the expression of those sentiments that are officially approved. In the absence of a specific showing of constitutionally valid reasons to regulate their speech, students are entitled to freedom of expression of their views. . . . A student's rights, therefore, do not embrace merely the classroom hours. When he is in the cafeteria, or on the playing field, or on the campus during the authorized hours, he may express his opinions, even on controversial subjects like the conflict in Vietnam, if he does so without "materially and substantially interfer[ing] with . . . appropriate discipline in the operation of the school" and without colliding with the rights of others. . . . But conduct by the student, in class or out of it, which for any reason — whether it stems from time, place, or type of behavior — materially disrupts classwork or involves substantial disorder or invasion of the rights of others, is, of course, not immunized by the constitutional guaranty of freedom of speech. (393 U.S. at 511-513.)

The court drew on Burnside v. Byars, 363 F.2d 744 (5th Cir. 1966), where a school rule prohibiting the wearing of "freedom buttons" was struck down as an "arbitrary and unreasonable" infringement on the rights of expression of high school students. The same court held in Blackwell v. Issaquena County Board of Education, 363 F.2d 749 (5th Cir. 1966), that an identical rule was valid where the wearing of buttons caused "an unusual degree of commotion, boisterous conduct, a collision with the rights of others," and general disruption of school routine. The court contrasted the facts of Burnside, where the buttons provoked only "mild curiosity." The Fifth Circuit purported to apply a standard of "reasonableness": "It is not for us to consider whether such rules are wise or expedient but merely whether they are a reasonable exercise of the power and discretion of school authorities." 363 F.2d at 748.

NOTES

1. In theory, the Tinker standard imposes a heavier burden on school authorities, that is, the responsibility of showing that a rule trenching on First Amendment rights was justified in the circumstances. But because Tinker looks primarily to the actual impact of conduct, the usual practice of lower courts has been to sanction disciplinary action whenever the conduct in question results in disruption. There has been no apparent serious attempt by the lower courts to balance the students' rights of expression against the

interests of the state in preventing and punishing conduct that interferes with discipline.

Thus, in Hobson v. Bailey, 309 F. Supp. 1393 (W.D. Tenn. 1970), participation by a student in school boycotts that were part of the civil rights movement was held to be properly subject to disciplinary action because of the "disruptive effect" of her repeated absences. Although the procedure initially followed in suspending the student had not met minimum due process standards, a postsuspension hearing before the Board of Education cured any defects, even though the student was not given prior notice of the charges. The student was reinstated on the basis of her good academic record and the hardships involved in transferring to another high school.

2. The "no disruption" standard has been particularly hard on black students protesting what they deem are racist activities in desegregated schools. In Tate v. Board of Education, 453 F.2d 975 (8th Cir. 1972), an action for injunctive relief by students who were suspended for five days was dismissed for lack of a substantial federal question. The students had walked out of a pep rally when "Dixie" was played, an act that was "deemed disruptive" by school authorities. 453 F.2d at 977. The court distinguished Tinker on the ground that here the conduct of the students was not "akin to 'pure speech,'" and relied on Blackwell in holding that reasonable prior restraints on First Amendment rights are within the inherent power of school officials, where necessary to prevent breakdown of order. Due process standards were not violated, the court reasoned, because the penalty was mild; students were advised of the charges and given "an opportunity for an informal hearing," which consisted of the offer by the principal, immediately after suspension was imposed, to answer questions. The court concluded with a recital of the history of "Dixie," intended to show that the song was not a "badge of slavery, [and] that the playing of the tune [had not] constituted officially sanctioned racial abuse." 453 F.2d at 982. See also Caldwell v. Craighead, 432 F.2d 213 (6th Cir. 1970), where an action for injunctive relief by a school band member who had refused to play "Dixie" and by his mother, who claimed she was discharged from her job as a teacher's aide in retaliation, was dismissed as moot because the plaintiffs had moved to another city.

3. In Black Students of North Fort Myers Junior-Senior High School v. Williams, 335 F. Supp. 820 (M.D. Ala. 1971), students who had been suspended, under a school policy of automatic suspension for participation in demonstrations, were reinstated because due process standards had been violated. The plaintiffs had walked out of school to protest the program planned for the celebration of Negro History Week; the court assumed that the plaintiffs had "failed in the burden which is theirs of establishing the facts relevant to their First Amendment claim for relief," because the parties had agreed that "no further facts remain to be litigated." Id. at 824. See also Hull v. Weems, 2 Race Rel. L. Sur. 4 (N.D. Miss. 1970), where black students had been suspended for walking peacefully out of school, after the principal rejected their petition for redress of grievances. They were reinstated on due

process grounds, but their claims of First Amendment protection were not recognized.

4. Tinker has been followed in cases which, like Tinker itself, involve conduct "closely akin to 'pure speech.'" 393 U.S. at 505. Miller v. Shuker, 307 F. Supp. 27 (E.D.N.Y. 1969), was a class action by a black high school student seeking to enjoin school officials from requiring him to leave the classroom during recital of the Pledge of Allegiance. The plaintiff refused to say the pledge because he believed that "with liberty and justice for all" was untrue. The court granted the requested relief, citing Tinker, and held that a student may select whatever form of expression he chooses, so long as it does not materially infringe on the rights of other students or disrupt school activities.

In Sullivan v. Houston Independent School District, 307 F. Supp. 1328 (S.D. Tex. 1969), the plaintiff high school students were expelled without a hearing because they published and distributed, on school grounds, a newspaper that was critical of school authorities. Their activities did not have any disruptive effect. The court held that, unless there is unreasonable interference with normal school routine, such conduct is protected by the First Amendment. The defendants were enjoined, in the absence of precise and narrowly drawn regulations, from imposing serious disciplinary sanctions on students who publish and distribute newspapers on or off school grounds, where there is no substantial disruption with school operations, and from expelling or suspending students without compliance with minimal due process standards. See also Dunn v. Tyler, 327 F. Supp. 528 (E.D. Tex. 1971), where black students were indefinitely suspended without a hearing, for walking peacefully out of school in protest against an administrative decision to limit the number of black cheerleaders. A school regulation authorized suspension for participation in demonstrations. White students who had walked out were readmitted. The court ordered the plaintiffs reinstated, holding that the plaintiffs had been denied due process and that the school regulation was overbroad in that it was not limited to activities likely to cause substantial disruption. Cf. Milton v. Young, 328 F. Supp. 88 (E.D. Tenn. 1971), where suspension from a recently integrated school of a white student for wearing a confederate flag shoulder patch was held valid, because of the disruptive potential of his conduct in the circumstances. The school regulation under which the action was taken (prohibiting the wearing of "provocative symbols" on clothing) was held impermissibly vague and overbroad.

5. There is no generally accepted view as to the applicability of the "void for vagueness" and overbreadth doctrines to school and college regulations. See Soglin v. Kaulman, 295 F. Supp. 978 (W.D. Wis. 1968), where students were suspended for participating in an obstructive demonstration, under school regulations permitting only nondisruptive demonstrations and authorizing suspension for "misconduct." The court held that the vagueness and overbreadth doctrines were applicable "in some measure" to university disciplinary regulations, and that the regulations here were impermissibly vague

and overbroad. However, the court refused to enjoin permanently the use of the misconduct regulation, and stated that it would rule on the applicability of the vagueness and overbreadth doctrines to school and college regulations on a case-by-case basis. But see Esteban v. Central Missouri State College, 415 F.2d 1077 (8th Cir. 1969), where suspended students, after a court-ordered hearing, 277 F. Supp. 649 (W.D. Mo. 1967), were again suspended for their participation in "riots." The district court denied relief, and the court of appeals affirmed, holding that the demonstrations were not protected by the First Amendment, and that the school regulations that had been applied, which prohibited "unruly" and "unlawful" demonstrations, were valid, measured not by the standards of specificity governing criminal statutes, but by their reasonableness in the academic context.

SCOTT v. ALABAMA BOARD OF EDUCATION, 300 F. Supp. 163 (M.D. Ala. 1969). The 1960 expulsions from Alabama State College, reversed by the Dixon case, supra, resulted from student sit-ins, parades and protests. Almost a decade later, Alabama State College students were still being expelled for demonstrations at the college.* They filed suit, alleging violation of both due process and First Amendment rights. The college officials filed a counterclaim, charging that the students had:

> (1) Refused to quit the campus after being dismissed or suspended as students; (2) Intimidated students desiring to attend classes and prevented their attendance at classes; (3) Intimidated faculty members desiring to conduct classes; (4) Damaged college property; and (5) Otherwise disrupted the orderly operation of Alabama State College as an educational institution. (300 F. Supp. at 165.)

Applying the standard set in Dixon, the district court found:

> The evidence reflects that approximately 80 students were served with formal statements of charges. Each of these statements was on a form letter listing 11 charges growing out of the "demonstration." Those charges which were deemed applicable to the addressee were marked with a prominent "X." The letter advised the students that hearings would be held on April 17, 1969, at which time they would be afforded an opportunity to be heard and to present witnesses in their defense.
>
> The hearings were later rescheduled for April 23, 1969. At that time, counsel for plaintiffs, representing some 50 of the students charged, objected to the statement of charges on the ground that the charges were unduly vague and did not advise students specifically of the acts they were alleged to have committed. When counsel's request that the charges be made more definite was denied, he and plaintiffs, on his advice, dramatically refused to participate in the hearings.

* Actually, nine students from the college were suspended in April 1965 after taking part in campus demonstrations. The students brought suit for readmission pending a trial, but the action was dismissed after the students were readmitted "under undisclosed conditions." Dickerson v. Alabama State Board of Education, 10 Race Rel. L. Rep. 1003 (M.D. Ala. 1965).

The hearings were held as scheduled before an Ad Hoc Faculty-Student Committee. This Committee heard the evidence against each student charged, made specific findings with respect to each charge, and made recommendations to President Watkins of an appropriate disposition of each case. As a result, it appears that 7 students were dismissed from the college, 43 were indefinitely suspended, 21 were found not guilty, and 3 cases were disposed of otherwise. Those who were dismissed or suspended were offered an opportunity to have their cases reviewed by President Watkins. Of those who exercised that opportunity, at least eight had their indefinite suspensions reduced to special probation. (300 F. Supp. at 165.)

Considering the plaintiffs' contention that the charges were vague, the court agreed that some of the charges lacked the specificity required to enable a student to adequately prepare defenses against them, but felt that certain other charges, "when viewed in the circumstances of the case, make quite clear the basis upon which the college proposes to take disciplinary action." It rejected plaintiffs' argument that one vague charge, like one bad apple, spoils the entire barrel, holding that Dixon requires only the rudimentary elements of fair play.

Plaintiffs challenged the impartiality of the committee which heard the evidence, but the court found that "this Committee was selected in a reasonable fashion considering the emotional circumstances which tended to render nearly everyone at the college at least mildly partisan."

Turning to the First Amendment, the court took the view that, if a student was found guilty of a specific charge of conduct not protected by the First Amendment, his suspension or dismissal could stand even though activities in other charges might be protected. A demonstration including the takeover of the college dining hall was held not protected. It was not symbolic speech, and did not achieve protected status simply because it was largely peaceful and nonviolent and involved little if any destruction of college property. In entering a broad injunction against further demonstrations, the court said:

> There seems to be a tendency in this country — and it is especially prevalent among students — toward the view that if one only believes strongly enough that his cause is right, then one may use in advancing that cause any means that seem effective at the moment, whether they are lawful or unlawful and whether or not they are consistent with the interests of others. The law, of course, cannot and does not take that position, and those who do must not expect to receive substantive protection from the law; to the contrary, they must expect to be punished when they violate laws and college regulations which are part of a system designed to protect the rights and interests of all. (300 F. Supp. at 168.)

QUESTIONS

1. Did the court in Scott undercut the gains in due process won by students in Dixon, when it (a) found that, if some of several charges were sufficiently clear, all charges were not invalidly vague? (b) asserted that the review committee was fairly selected, "considering the emotional circumstances" rendering nearly everyone on campus "mildly partisan"? (c) held students facing expulsion responsible for the consequences of their attorney's decision to boycott the hearing?

2. To what extent does the whole concept of "fair hearing" turn on the presence of an impartial hearing body, i.e., a tribunal removed sufficiently from direct interest in the outcome that neither party can reasonably charge bias? Is the presence of such a tribunal more or less important in a student dismissal case than in a major felony trial?

3. In criminal cases, findings of guilt — as opposed to considerations of clemency — are seldom altered by evidence that the defendant's unlawful behavior was caused by his environment. Is it more feasible and appropriate in student than criminal cases to consider whether the actions or inactions of college officials served as a provocation for the student demonstrations?

4. Does the rule in Tinker do any more than face black student protesters with the dilemma observed in Chapter Seven? That is, does it extend First Amendment protection only to those persons whose activities don't upset anyone? Remember that racial issues in this society tend to be inherently upsetting. Are campus protests, even with the protection of Dixon, a form of "ultra-hazardous activity"?

5. Suppose that students involved in a disruptive campus protest are facing a hearing before faculty members who refuse to consider possible school responsibility. The students object to the hearing in these words: "We assert that, as the hearing is presently structured, there is no reasonable chance that those of us found to have participated in the protest can be exonerated. This hearing is, in fact, a sentencing procedure, at which, in a kind of demeaning quasi-judicial confessional, we can acknowledge our guilt, pledge repentence, and thereby seek absolution for our transgressions from the very persons against whom our protest was aimed." Is the student objection well taken? Can it be incorporated into an argument that courts will take seriously?

Racism Hypo 16
BLACK STUDENT UNION v. DIXIE UNIVERSITY

Dixie University is a prestigious state school in a deep South state. It first admitted black students in 1965, after a long court battle and after HEW threatened to cut off federal funds. The school now has an enrollment of 200 blacks, 2 percent of its 10,000 students.

For more than a year, the black students have been meeting with Dixie officials, seeking the following: the establishment of a black studies program; the recruitment, with adequate scholarship aid, of more black students so that in five years there will be at least 1000 black students at the college (blacks constitute approximately 30 percent of the state's population); the hiring of black faculty and administrators; and the setting up of a "Racism

Review Board," which would be an impartial group of faculty and students, to review and recommend action on a variety of complaints by black students alleging instances of racially biased behavior by teachers, students, and administrative personnel.

University officials steadfastly maintained that all the black student suggestions were "under consideration," but took no action on them. This spring, the twenty black seniors, despairing of obtaining change at Dixie University through meetings with its officials, decided to boycott and picket the baccalaureate sermon. That event is traditionally held the evening before graduation, at the famed Dixie Chapel, and is attended by all graduating students, their parents, and distinguished alumni, many of whom use the occasion to make large gifts to the school. To dramatize their protest, the black seniors welded shut the locks to all the chapel doors, a fact discovered only an hour before the service was scheduled to begin.

Unwilling to damage the beautiful, hand-carved doors of the chapel, and unable to open the locks without many hours of work, Dixie officials reluctantly canceled the service. Many of the "Old Grads" were horrified; they called for the immediate expulsion of all black students and threatened to withhold all further contributions until disruptive blacks were banned for good. Repairs on the chapel locks cost $1000; the potential lost alumni contributions amounted to perhaps $50,000.

University officials immediately suspended the twenty black seniors, refusing to grant their degrees. Two weeks later, hearings were held that complied with the notice and all other due process requirements for such hearings established by the court in Marzette v. McPhee, supra. Acting on the recommendations of a panel of senior faculty members, who heard and evaluated the testimony, Dixie expelled the black seniors.

The panel dismissed as "nonsense" the students' contention that they had acted to gain public attention and publicity for their demands, after vain efforts to get stories about their problems and the university's inaction into the local news media and into the school newspaper.

Following the expulsions, there were widespread but peaceful protests by black and white students. In the wake of these protests, which received national attention, Dixie University announced changes in personnel, curriculum and programs greatly similar to those initially suggested by the black students.

As the result of all the above, the black seniors filed suit in federal court for their immediate readmission and granting of degrees. In support of their motion for injunctive relief, they repeated legal arguments made and rejected by the faculty panel at their hearing, including (1) the university's refusal to permit black students or black community leaders on the hearing panel, (2) the university's failure to assess the fairness of the penalties in the light of the school's "racist policies of provocation," and (3) the university's refusal to eliminate racist policies until forced to do so by "radical student action." The district court upheld the expulsions and summarily rejected all the points raised by the black students. The case is now on appeal.

Firm A, representing the black students, seeks to have the district court's dismissal of the case reversed, with directions that the students be readmitted and granted their degrees, and with all references to the suspension and expulsion expunged from their records. In the alternative, they seek a full hearing on the defenses rejected summarily by the district court.

Firm B, representing the university, seeks to have the district court's dismissal order affirmed. Indeed, university officials have been pressured by alumni and other conservative forces to argue on appeal that the elaborate hearing process in the Marzette case is not constitutionally required. They will state, though, that the expulsions were fully justified by the students' conduct, which violated state laws and university regulations similar to those set out in the Marzette opinion.

D. THE RIGHTS OF BLACK PRISONERS

Despite the popular myths that tend to be perpetuated by some of the mass media, the state and federal prisons in this country are not filled with blacks. However, the number of blacks and other nonwhites in most prisons does represent a disproportionately high percentage of the minority group population.

There is now a wealth of evidence that crime is not a function of race, that it is closely related to poverty, ignorance and disease, all of which blacks have experienced in very full measure.* But until the increase in interest in prison reform — sparked by an epidemic of prison riots — there was little public concern about conditions in the country's prisons, despite endless studies which concluded with monotonous regularity that the nation's correctional institutions fail at rehabilitation and are eminently successful in breeding recidivism, brutality and despair. The discussion of prison reform has been transformed into action in some areas, and the courts, sensing the need for change, have slowly re-examined their former "hands-off" attitude toward at least the most shocking of prison practices.†

* When the crime reports and prison population are broken down along class lines, the difference in frequency of criminal behavior between lower-class whites and lower-class blacks is much lower than the difference between the total black and total white population. The remaining difference is explainable by such variables as police discrimination toward blacks, discrimination in the sentencing process, differences in treatment inside prison, differences in education and job opportunities, the effect of migratory patterns on criminal behavior, etc. See, e.g., Race, Crime, and Justice (C. Reasons and J. Kuykendall, eds. 1972); M. Wolfgang, Crime and Race — Conceptions and Misconceptions (1964); The Sociology of Crime and Delinquency (M. Wolfgang, L. Savitz and N. Johnston, eds., 2d ed. 1970).

† Until the 1960s federal courts took the position that internal prison matters were not issues appropriate for judicial determination. The right of access to the courts (Ex parte

It would be surprising if racism, which at least indirectly is responsible for putting so many blacks on a path that leads to crime, disappeared once people arrive inside prison walls. Racial segregation of prison facilities is no longer valid. See Washington v. Lee, 263 F. Supp. 327 (M.D. Ala. 1966), *aff'd* 390 U.S. 333, 88 S. Ct. 994, 19 L. Ed. 2d 1212 (1968). But courts recognize that, in some instances, "prison security and discipline necessitates segregation of the races for a limited period." 263 F. Supp. at 331, 390 U.S. at 334 (concurring opinion). This exception is likely used to justify a good deal of continuing segregation. One district judge refused to enjoin segregation in a county jail, finding that "this practice was a consequence of the good faith judgment of correctional personnel in discharging their primary responsibility of providing for the safety of the prisoners in their charge, as well as to provide for the safety of the jail personnel, and other members of the public. . . ." United States v. Wyandotte County, Kansas, 343 F. Supp. 1189, 1204 (D. Kan. 1972).

But whether or not prison facilities are segregated (testimony in the Wyandotte case indicated that black inmates preferred segregation), there is a growing stream of litigation presenting issues of arbitrary action, denial of basic due process, and brutality. Black prisoners, particularly Black Muslims, have filed a number of suits charging violation of their First Amendment freedom of religion rights. Prison officials have reacted negatively to militant black prisoners generally, and have been particularly hostile to inmates of the Black Muslim religion, perceiving its black supremacy doctrines as a threat to prison discipline.* In Knuckles v. Prasse, 302 F. Supp. 1036 (E.D. Pa. 1969), the court found that prison officials did not permit Black Muslim pris-

---

Hull, 312 U.S. 546, 61 S. Ct. 640, 85 L. Ed. 1034 (1941)) has been vindicated through expansion of the habeas corpus remedy to include relief from unconstitutional conditions of confinement. Wilwording v. Swenson, 404 U.S. 249, 92 S. Ct. 407, 30 L. Ed. 2d 418 (1971). See also Fay v. Noia, 372 U.S. 391, 83 S. Ct. 822, 9 L. Ed. 837 (1963); Townsend v. Sain, 372 U.S. 293, 83 S. Ct. 745, 9 L. Ed. 2d 770 (1963); Sanders v. United States, 373 U.S. 1, 83 S. Ct. 1068, 10 L. Ed. 2d 148 (1963); and interpretation of 42 U.S.C. §1983 and 28 U.S.C. §1361, the federal mandamus statute, to create causes of action for deprivation of prisoners' constitutional rights, Cooper v. Pate, 378 U.S. 546, 84 S. Ct. 1733, 12 L. Ed. 2d 1030 (1964); Long v. Parker, 390 F.2d 816 (3d Cir. 1968). Recognition of remedies is correlative with a substantive shift. In Price v. Johnston, 334 U.S. 266, 285, 68 S. Ct. 1049, 1060 (1948), the Supreme Court expressed the prevailing attitude of judicial restraint: "Lawful incarceration brings about the necessary withdrawal or limitation of many privileges and rights, a retraction justified by the considerations underlying our penal system." Two decades later, in striking down a Tennessee prison regulation that forbade "jailhouse lawyering" where the state provided no other source of legal assistance, the Court stated that "where paramount federal constitutional or statutory rights supervene . . . state regulations applicable to inmates of prison facilities . . . may be invalidated." Johnson v. Avery, 393 U.S. 483, 486, 89 S. Ct. 747, 749, 21 L. Ed. 2d 718, 721-722 (1969). See also Wilwording v. Swenson, supra.

* See A. Haley, Autobiography of Malcolm X (1964); E. Cleaver, Soul On Ice (1968); G. Jackson, Soledad Brother: The Prison Letters of George Jackson (1970). See also Note, Black Muslims in Prison: Of Muslim Rites and Constitutional Rights, 62 Colum. L. Rev. 1488 (1962).

oners to hold religious services, receive the assistance of a Muslim minister, subscribe to Muslim periodicals, correspond with Elijah Muhammad, wear Muslim medals, or be provided with a pork-free diet, "because defendants believe that the presence and activities of Muslims in prison creates a dangerous situation." The court agreed in large part, on the basis that it was not "unreasonable or irrational" to infer that Muslim teachings would encourage defiance of authority and aggressive behavior. See also Wilson v. Prasse, 463 F.2d 109 (3rd Cir. 1972). The court held that plaintiffs were entitled to visits from Muslim ministers who espoused nonviolent doctrines and to monitored services conducted by such ministers, but upheld the right of prison officials to deny access to Muslim publications. There was evidence in the Knuckles case that Black Muslim prisoners had, on one occasion, engaged in physical violence against other inmates. See also Jones v. Willingham, 248 F. Supp. 791 (D. Kan. 1965).

Courts have been less tolerant to unsubstantiated rationalizations for denying or infringing the right to practice the Black Muslim religion, in part because of the tradition that religion serves the goal of rehabilitation. See, e.g., Brown v. Peyton, 437 F.2d 1228 (4th Cir. 1971). In Barnett v. Rogers, 410 F.2d 995 (D.C. Cir. 1969), the court of appeals instructed the district court to focus on the questions of whether any compelling state interest could be shown to justify denial of a request for one pork-free meal a day, and whether the prison food service program could be administered in a fashion that involved less restriction on the free exercise of religion. The action was remanded to the district court for a second time. Other courts have adopted the standard of compelling state interest and least restrictive means. See Rowland v. Sigler, 327 F. Supp. 821 (D. Neb. 1971), *aff'd. sub nom.* Rowland v. Jones, 452 F.2d 1005 (8th Cir. 1971), and Brown v. Peyton, supra, in contrast to the "reasonableness" test applied in Knuckles. But see Williford v. California, 217 F. Supp. 245 (N.D. Cal. 1963), where the determination of prison authorities that "Muslim activities pose a threat to peaceable and orderly behavior" was held to be conclusive.

The right to free exercise of religion has been circumscribed not only by what are perceived to be inherent necessities for maintenance of security and discipline, but also by judicial reliance on equal protection theories in defining the scope of the right. In Walker v. Blackwell, 411 F.2d 23 (5th Cir. 1969), it was held that the petitioners were not entitled to listen to the weekly national radio broadcast of Elijah Muhammad, although other religious programs were broadcast on the two channels of the prison radio system which played continuously. "[P]etitioners failed to demonstrate any denial of equal protection. From the evidence presented, we cannot determine that any religious programming was being directed at other denominations or religions, as opposed to forming a part of the balanced program desired by the warden for the whole prison population." 411 F.2d at 27. See also Cruz v. Beto, 405 U.S. 319, 92 S. Ct. 1079, 31 L. Ed. 2d 263 (1972); Long v. Parker, 390 F.2d 816 (3rd Cir. 1968). Petitioners in Walker v. Blackwell were also denied the right to after-sunset pork-free meals during the month of Ramadan, on the ground that "considerations of security and administrative expense outweigh[ed] whatever constitutional deprivation" was involved. The right to receive the newspaper *Muhammad Speaks* was upheld on the ground that the copies before the court were not inflammatory, with the qualification that in the event of an inflammatory effect, the warden was entitled to take appropriate action "to avoid imminent prison violence." 411 F.2d at 29.

Modes of analysis similar to those developed in the area of religious practice have been applied to the right to correspond with others and the right to receive nonreligious publications. The right to receive black periodicals was upheld on equal protection grounds in Jackson v. Godwin, 400 F.2d 529 (5th Cir. 1968). See also Owens v. Brierley, 452 F.2d 640 (3rd Cir. 1971), and Rowland v. Sigler, supra. In contrast, the right to receive a newsletter from an association of ex-convicts was cast in terms of the absence of a demonstrated compelling state interest related to a "clear and present danger of a breach of prison discipline." Fortune Society v. McGinnis, 319 F. Supp. 901, 904 (S.D.N.Y. 1970). For the most part, however, inmates' mailing rights remain severely restricted in terms of the amount of correspondence permitted, the necessity for prior approval by authorities, and the degree of censorship practiced. See Jacob, Prison Discipline and Inmate Rights, 5 Harv. Civ. Rights–Civ. Lib. L. Rev. 227, 238-240.

The expounding of standards like "compelling state interest" and "clear and present danger" may have little practical effect, given the broad discretion that remains to prison authorities. See Fox, First Amendment Rights of Prisoners, 63 J. Crim. L.C. & P.S. 162, 177-178 (1972). The most direct efforts to limit that discretion have been made in challenges to prison disciplinary procedures, beginning with the recognition that certain forms of punishment so far exceed the bounds of human decency as to violate the Eighth Amendment. See, e.g., Jackson v. Bishop, 404 F.2d 571 (8th Cir. 1968), proscribing further use of the strap; and Knuckles v. Prasse, supra, holding, inter alia, that disciplinary segregation for two and one-half days in cells lacking the fundamentals of hygiene constituted cruel and unusual punishment. The Supreme Court has held that modes of punishment in prison are a proper subject for judicial review. Haines v. Kerner, 404 U.S. 519, 92 S. Ct. 594, 30 L. Ed. 2d 652 (1972). In Holt v. Sarver, 300 F. Supp. 825 (E.D. Ark. 1969), *aff'd,* 442 F.2d 304 (8th Cir 1971), certain living conditions at a state prison farm were themselves held to violate the Eighth Amendment. Specifically, the state had violated constitutional mandates by not providing guards in open sleeping areas to prevent murders and assaults, and by failing to correct conditions of overcrowding, lack of hygiene facilities, and lack of opportunity for exercise. The court declined to become directly involved in supervising the necessary changes, but retained jurisdiction to allow prison authorities to formulate a workable plan.

Other courts have intervened more directly to require that standards of procedural fairness be met before sanctions are imposed for misconduct, and to correct conditions of confinement. In Sostre v. Rockefeller, 312 F. Supp. 863 (S.D.N.Y. 1970), the plaintiff was a state prisoner who had been actively involved in earlier efforts to reform the penal system. See Pierce v. LaVallee, 293 F.2d 233 (2d Cir. 1961); Sostre v. McGinnis, 334 F.2d 906 (2d Cir. 1964), *cert. denied,* 379 U.S. 892, 85 S. Ct. 168, 13 L. Ed. 2d 96 (1964).

The lengthy appellate decision in the Sostre case, printed below, provides ample basis for discussion of several underlying issues in black prisoner cases: (1) Is it only fear of a prison uprising that prompted prison officials to consign Sostre to such severe punishment? (2) Were the penalties imposed on Sostre designed to protect prison security or break his spirit, and do you get the impression that officials deemed the latter was required to ensure the former? (3) Do the Second Circuit Court's frequent expressions of concern about interference with prison disciplinary policies explain its refusal to affirm the relief granted by the district court? To justify noninterference, was it necessary for the court to minimize the horrors of Sostre's ordeal? (4) What message did the Second Circuit's opinion likely convey to prison authorities?

SOSTRE v. McGINNIS
442 F.2d 178 (2d Cir. 1971)

Before LUMBARD, Chief Judge, WATERMAN, Senior Circuit Judge, and MOORE, FRIENDLY, SMITH, KAUFMAN, HAYS, ANDERSON and FEINBERG, Circuit Judges.

Irving R. KAUFMAN, Circuit Judge:

We voted to hear the initial argument of this appeal en banc, a procedure we reserve for extraordinary circumstances, so that we might give plenary review to a complex of urgent social and political conflicts persistently seeking solution in the courts as legal problems, a phenomenon de Tocqueville commented upon many years ago. Democracy in America, vol. I. at 290 (Vintage ed. 1945). The elaborate opinion and order below raise important questions concerning the federal constitutional rights of state prisoners which neither Supreme Court precedent nor our own past decisions have answered. The sparse authority from other courts is for the most part either inconclusive or conflicting.

I. PROCEEDINGS BELOW AND JURISDICTION

This is an appeal from an order entered May 14, 1970, by Judge Motley, sitting in the Southern District of New York, 312 F. Supp. 863, which granted plaintiff Martin Sostre punitive and compensatory damages against defendants Follette and McGinnis as well as a wide variety of injunctive relief. . . . At the time Sostre filed his handwritten complaint, he was incarcerated in New York's Green Haven Prison (now called Green Haven Correctional Facility), serving a sentence of thirty to forty years for selling narcotics, followed by thirty days further imprisonment for contempt of court, imposed on him March 18, 1968. The original defendants included the Governor of New York as well as the State Commissioner of Correction, appellant McGinnis; the Warden of Green Haven, Harold W. Follette, who died shortly before the opinion below was entered. . . .

II. Facts

A. Circumstances of Sostre's Commitment to Punitive Segregation

On June 25, 1968, Warden Follette ordered that Sostre be committed . . . to "solitary confinement" (the words in the statute) or "punitive segregation" (the term adopted by Judge Motley and by the parties on appeal, which we will use for that reason and also because he was not as isolated in his segregation as "solitary" would imply). The parties vigorously disagree as to the considerations that motivated Follette to inflict this punishment.

On June 25, 1968, the day he put Sostre in segregation, Follette called Sostre to his office. At this meeting, Follette questioned Sostre about his attempt that morning to mail to an attorney, Miss Joan Franklin of the National Association for the Advancement of Colored People, a letter with handwritten legal papers attached, including a motion for use in the trial of Mrs. Geraldine Robinson. Mrs. Robinson is described by Judge Motley and the parties on appeal as Sostre's "codefendant." Although she was joined with Sostre in the indictment which resulted in Sostre's imprisonment, they were not tried together. Follette told Sostre "he must confine his legal activities to his own incarceration" and accordingly that the motion would not be mailed. Follette explained that he objected to Sostre's attempt to "practice law" without a license. Sostre believed that he had a right to mail legal papers in behalf of Mrs. Robinson and refused to assure Follette, as Follette requested, that he would discontinue attempting to mail such documents through normal prison channels.

During the same interview, Follette questioned Sostre about a reference to an organization known as "R.N.A.," mentioned by Sostre in his letter to Miss Franklin and to which Sostre had referred in earlier correspondence. "R.N.A." in fact referred to the Republic of New Africa, which Sostre identified at the trial before Judge Motley as a black liberation or black separatist organization. Sostre disputed Follette's testimony that Sostre had lied about R.N.A. at the June 25 interview by persistently claiming at that time that it was a "federal agency . . . 'Recovery National Administration' or something like this." Sostre did admit, as Follette asserted at trial, that after responding to a few questions Sostre refused to discuss R.N.A. further. The plaintiff's justification for his silence was that Follette had persisted in labelling R.N.A. a "subversive organization." Sostre "clammed up," as he testified, to avoid antagonizing Follette by further explaining or defending R.N.A.

Follette testified without contradiction that the organization known as the Republic of New Africa was of sufficient concern to him to have been the object of an investigation before the interview with Sostre. Follette feared that "this organization was a cloak for an attempt to organize prison inmates for riot and insurrection," based on information obtained from the F.B.I. and the New York State and Buffalo City Police. "[T]he possibility of insurrection at Green Haven" was a "major fear" to Follette at all times, but particularly so in June, 1968. Security at the prison had been weakened, in Follette's view, by an exceptionally high turnover of correction officers, approaching a rate of about fifty percent each year. An influx of new officers had not yet been cleared through the New York State Identification and Intelligence System. Moreover, Sostre had exacerbated Follette's concern with the possibility of major disorder because of a statement in a letter that Sostre had written to his sister, dated May 19, 1968: "As for me, there is no doubt in my mind whatsoever that I will be out soon, either by having my appeal reversed in the courts or by being liberated by the Universal Forces of Liberation." This sentence is included in a broad indictment of militarism and oppression in this country and a prediction that "the power structure" would soon be overthrown.

Follette insists that his decision to commit Sostre to segregation reflected (1) Sostre's declared intent to defy Folette's order by preparing legal papers for his co-defendant; (2) his intransigence about R.N.A.; (3) the allusion in the letter to his sister to his impending liberation. Rule 54 of the "Inmate's Rule Book," a publication of the New York Department of Correction issued to each prisoner when he arrives at Green Haven, limits inmate correspondence to "their own personal matters." Follette interpreted this as proscribing the sending of legal papers in behalf of a co-defendant. Sostre's refusal to discuss R.N.A. and his persistence about Mrs. Robinson's legal papers both violated Rule 5 of the Inmate Rule Book which requires that an inmate obey orders "promptly and fully," pending whatever appeal he may wish to take to higher authority. In addition, his silence violated Rule 12, enjoining inmates to answer "fully and truthfully" all questions put by prison officials. In sum, Follette assigned as his motive for Sostre's punishment the fact that Sostre's "whole attitude was one of defiance, of flatly refusing . . . to conduct himself as a proper inmate within the rules, regulations and laws set down by the State of New York and the Department of Correction." Section 140 of the New York Correction Law authorized Follette, by its terms in his unfettered discretion, to commit Sostre to segregation when "necessary . . . to produce [his] entire submission and obedience" and to keep him there "until he shall be reduced to submission and obedience."

Judge Motley disbelieved each of Follette's asserted motives for punishing Sostre, crediting instead Sostre's testimony that Follette was motivated by Sostre's threat to sue Follette over his withholding the motion papers intended for Mrs. Robinson. Additionally, Judge Motley attributed to Follette an intent to punish Sostre because of his earlier activism in bringing litigation related to the practice of the Black Muslim religion in New York prisons and "because he is, unquestionably, a black militant who persists in writing and expressing his militant and radical ideas in prison." Judge Motley held that the summary meeting with Warden Follette which resulted in Sostre's commitment to segregation did not afford due process of law to Sostre before his "liberty" was taken.

Apart from the events of the June 25 interview, Judge Motley also dismissed as one of Follette's reasons for continuing Sostre's incarceration in segregated confinement several items of "contraband" which Follette claimed were the fruit of a search of Sostre's cell conducted immediately after he entered segregation. These items consisted of (1) two small (3 inches by 5 inches) pieces of heavy black emery paper covered with an abrasive material like sand which, according to Follette, could be flaked off and in some manner attached to a string to fashion an instrument capable of sawing through cell bars; (2) six tables of contents torn from issues of the Harvard Law Review and stamped by prison officials to indicate that the books, Sostre's personal property, were not to circulate to other prisoners; (3) a letter dated June 10, 1968, from the Appellate Division of the Supreme Court of New York addressed to a fellow-prisoner of Sostre's, Juan Moline, a Puerto Rican, which Sostre later explained he was translating for Moline from English into Spanish. Judge Motley believed Sostre's testimony that he had never seen the pieces of emery paper before they were introduced by defendants at trial. 312 F. Supp. at 869. The other contraband indicated that Sostre had violated prison rules by circulating his law periodicals to other prisoners and by giving a fellow-prisoner legal assistance without first securing the Warden's permission. The Court below not only declined to find that these activities motivated the punishment of Sostre, but held in addition that Sostre's activities were protected by the Fourteenth Amendment.

B. Conditions of Punitive Segregation

Sostre remained confined in punitive segregation for twelve months and eight days, until Judge Motley restrained his continued punishment pendente lite on July 2, 1969. By regulation, Sostre lost the opportunity to earn 124⅓ days of good behavior credit while he was segregated.[5] We cannot avoid setting forth the precise conditions of Sostre's long confinement with some particularity because Judge Motley found as a matter of law, that (1) in view of those conditions, Sostre's punishment — or any confinement in segregation under similar conditions for longer than 15 days — was "cruel and unusual" under the Eighth Amendment; (2) this absolute rule aside, Judge Motley held that the penalty inflicted upon Sostre was so disproportionate to the offenses charged against him that his segregation would have been cruel and unusual even crediting each of Follette's assigned justifications for it. We

5. New York State prisoners may earn a maximum of ten days "good behavior time" credit each month, thereby advancing both the date the prisoner will be eligible for parole and the date he is entitled as of right to be "conditionally released" (that is, released from custody subject to parole conditions). Prison authorities may restore good behavior time withheld or revoked. . . .

cannot approve these conclusions. Our reasons for refusing to do so are based in part on undisputed facts in the record which do not appear in Judge Motley's otherwise entirely accurate description of Sostre's segregated environment. The following account draws upon those undisputed facts which do not appear in the opinion below, as well as thosewhich do, in an effort to present the whole fabric.

1. Isolation from Human Contact

Although for four months only one other prisoner was confined with Sostre in his small "segment" of five cells, the entire punitive segregation unit at Green Haven housed on the average about 15 prisoners at any one time. During the period between June 28, 1967, and September 18, 1968, 179 prisoners were held in segregation for a total of 8,960 days. From September 19, 1968 to July 3, 1969, when Sostre was there, a total of 79 inmates were segregated at Green Haven. Of these, about ten percent were held in "protective" segregation. This term is used to describe those who are segregated from the general population to protect them from harm rather than as punishment. Those prisoners were incarcerated in cells entirely separately from Sostre's cell in the punitive segregation unit. The other prisoners were confined in cells near Sostre's, so that he would have been able to communicate with them, albeit with some difficulty depending on the distance between Sostre and the other prisoners. We are informed of an incident where one prisoner brought to solitary and placed in another group of cells committed suicide. Sostre was able to communicate with this inmate and indeed was able to dictate a legal document to him.

Finally, although we do not doubt that "the crux of the matter is human isolation," as Judge Motley observed, Sostre aggravated his isolation by refusing to participate in a "group therapy" program offered each inmate in segregation beginning October or November 1968. "Therapy" sessions were conducted in groups of about eight per class, generally one each week or ten days, under the guidance of a "recreation supervisor," Sergeant Louis Profera. Profera had been trained in group counseling in a six month, 40-hour course by a psychiatrist at the New York State Vocational Institution. Special rules for punitive segregation posted in the segregation unit provided that inmates in punitive segregation would be "returned to the general population after demonstrating their willingness to accept and adhere to the institutional rules and regulations as shown by their participation in group counselling sessions. . . . Refusal to participate in group counselling is indicative of the inmate's unwillingness to accept and abide by the rules and regulations of the institution." Profera's favorable recommendation generally resulted in a prisoner's release from segregation. Although one prisoner who testified at trial returned to the general population without participating in group therapy, there is no doubt that there was significant pressure to participate. Expert witnesses at trial disagreed as to whether coercion would increase or decrease the efficacy of group therapy.

2. Other Conditions of Sostre's Segregated Confinement

Judge Motley heard extensive testimony describing such important details as Sostre's diet, his opportunity for exercise, the hygienic conditions of his cell, and the possibility for intellectual stimulation. It can hardly be questioned that his life in segregation was harsher than it would have been in the general population, but neither was it clearly unendurable or subhuman or cruel and inhuman in a constitutional sense.

Thus, Sostre would not be served seconds of the main course upon his demand; but there was no testimony that he would have had that privilege in the general population. He was denied the dessert that would have been available to the general population; but apart from the dessert his diet still consisted of 2800 to 3300 calories a day. Sostre remained in his cell at all times except for a brief period once each week to shave and shower. An hour of exercise with four or five other prisoners in a small, enclosed yard, open to the sky was a daily routine. But the record reveals that Sostre refused this privilege because he would not submit to a "strip search." Officials testified that it was necessary to subject prisoners to such an examination each time they entered the exercise yard to prevent them from concealing on their bodies small bits of wire or other material suitable for use as a weapon.

Hygienic conditions were at least minimally adequate to permit Sostre to remain clean and healthy. Thus, Sostre was allowed to shave and shower with hot water once each week. The furnishings of his normal-sized (6 ft. x 8 ft.) cell included a toilet and a face bowl with running cold water, and he was provided with soap and a towel.

The strictures on Sostre's intellectual fare were severe. He could not buy or receive books, magazines or newspapers, and his access to the prison's library collection was limited to a selection among approximately thirty-five volumes, mostly "shoot-em-ups" as Sostre described them, chosen by the prison guards. Still, light from a single bulb, controlled by the guards and usually turned on early in the morning and off at 10 p.m., was adequate for reading. And although he could not attend school or watch television, as could the inmates in the general population, any material related to the law requested by him would be brought to his cell.

3. Length of Segregated Confinement

Pursuant to the usual practice at Green Haven, Sostre was sentenced to "solitary" confinement for an indefinite period. According to New York Correction Law Section 140, "submissiveness" was to be the touchstone for his release. Follette testified that Sostre could have returned to the general population either by successful participation in group therapy or by agreeing to live by the rules of the prison. Sostre's contention is that he refused to agree to obey rules that he considered an infringement of his constitutional rights.

C. Censorship and Possession of Literature

Defendant Follette censored Sostre's correspondence with Joan Franklin of the NAACP, the attorney of record representing Sostre on appeal from his conviction. Follette regularly excised from letters passing between Sostre and Miss Franklin "objectionable" material — anything which "in his judgment was not relevant to Sostre's appeal." In accordance with Rule 47 of the Inmate Rule Book which restricts inmates' correspondence to persons on an approved mailing list, Warden Follette in late September, 1968, refused to forward a letter from Sostre to the United States Post Office Inspector, in which Sostre complained of Green Haven's practice of not returning to prisoners receipts for certified mail. The district judge found that each of these actions violated Sostre's First Amendment right to freedom of speech.

About August 3, 1969, a month after his release from segregation, Sostre was deprived of the use of the prison exercise yard and the privilege of attending movies because he possessed "inflammatory racist literature" in his cell. The literature consisted of articles written by Sostre himself on paper properly in his possession. Most of the articles consisted of extracts from magazines and newspapers which Sostre was also permitted to have and read in his cell. The extracts included quotations from Mao Tse Tung, poetry written by a prison inmate, the names of the officers, the party program, and rules of conduct of the Black Panther Party; the officers and oath of allegiance of the Republic of New Africa; a "program" for Black Student Unions; and the poem "If We Must Die," by Claude McKay. In addition, guards found in Sostre's cell an article which he had written himself, entitled "Revolutionary Thoughts." The district court found that Sostre's punishment for possessing this material constituted another infringement of his freedom of expression.[8]

III. The District Court's Order

Upon these findings which we have necessarily sketched, Judge Motley on May 14, 1970, entered the following order, which because of its complexity and importance to the questions we must decide, we reproduce in full. The district court subsequently granted a stay of its order pending appeal as to the bracketed portions. A stay as to the remainder of the order was denied.

It is now ordered, that defendants Follette, McGinnis and Mancusi, their employees, agents, successors, and all persons in active concert and participation with them be, and they are hereby, perpetually enjoined and restrained from:

1) Returning plaintiff to punitive segregation for charges previously preferred against him;

2) Placing plaintiff in punitive segregation or subjecting him to any other punishment as a result of which he loses accrued good time credit or is unable to earn good time credit, without:

8. On the date Sostre was released from segregation he was punished by confinement to his cell for several days, ostensibly because "dust" was found on his cell bars. Although Judge Motley found that this punishment represented "retaliation for his legal success," no relief was predicated on this finding and hence the incident need not concern us further.

a. giving him, in advance of a hearing, a written copy of any charges made against him, citing the written rule or regulation which it is charged he has violated;

b. granting him a recorded hearing before a disinterested official where he will be entitled to cross-examine his accusers and to call witnesses on his own behalf;

c. granting him the right to retain counsel or to appoint a counsel substitute;

d. giving him, in writing, the decision of the hearing officer in which is briefly set forth the evidence upon which it is based, the reasons for the decision, and the legal basis for the punishment imposed.[9]

[3) Censoring, refusing to mail or refusing to give to Sostre: 1) Any communication between Sostre and the following — (a) any court; (b) any public official or agency; (c) any lawyer; (d) his co-defendant in the criminal matter pending against him; and, 2) Any letter relating to any legal matter to or from any other inmate who requests the assistance of Sostre in translating that letter into English.]

4) Punishing Sostre for sharing with other inmates his law books, law reviews, and other legal materials, and from refusing to permit Sostre to assist any other inmate in any legal matter as long as defendants have not provided any court approved alternative means of legal assistance for such inmates.

[5) Punishing Sostre for having in his possession political literature and for setting forth his political views orally or in writing, except for violation of reasonable rules approved by the court regulating freedom of speech.]

[It is further ordered that the above named defendants submit, within 90 days from the date of this order, for approval by this court, proposed rules and regulations governing the following:

1) the receipt, distribution, discussion and writing of political literature;

2) all future disciplinary charges and hearings with respect thereto where the possible punishments include solitary confinement, punitive segregation or any other segregation, and any other punishment in connection with which there is loss of, or inability to earn, good time credit.]

It is further ordered that the above named defendants and their agents credit plaintiff with the 124⅓ days of good time credit which he was unable to earn while wrongfully incarcerated in punitive segregation from June 25, 1968 to July 2, 1969.

[It is further ordered that the plaintiff, Martin Sostre, recover of the defendants, Warden Follette, and Commissioner McGinnis the sum of $13,020.00.]

9. A panel of this court on July 10, 1970, expedited the appeal and granted a further stay of subparagraph 2 to the extent that it was limited to placing Sostre in punitive segregation for more than three days at any one time or a total of more than ten days, pending the hearing of this appeal.

IV. Punishment for Political Beliefs and Legal Activities

The question as to the propriety of withdrawing from incarcerated individuals constitutional privileges enjoyed by citizens of the community, although troublesome, is not new to the courts. It is clear that in many respects the constitutionally protected freedoms enjoyed by citizens-at-large may be withdrawn or constricted as to state prisoners, so far as "justified by the considerations underlying our penal system." [Citations omitted.] Accordingly, Sostre's lengthy confinement to segregation violated due process of law if, as the district court found, Warden Follette inflicted the punishment either because of Sostre's militant political ideas or his litigation, past or threatened, against Follette or other state officials.

Sostre does not shrink from characterizing himself as a "jailhouse lawyer" and the record before us does justice to this label, as does the history of Sostre's earlier period of confinement in New York prisons from 1952-64 following his first conviction for selling narcotics. It is not unreasonable to suppose, as the district court apparently did, that Warden Follette was aware of Sostre's Black Muslim activities during that period; of his solitary confinement in Attica Prison for four years, resulting from his religious activism; and of his success in securing through earlier litigation before this court the recognition of certain constitutional liberties for state prisoners. See Pierce v. LaVallee, 293 F.2d 233 (2d Cir. 1961); Sostre v. McGinnis, 334 F.2d 906 (2d Cir.), *cert. denied*, 379 U.S. 892 . . . (1964). Sostre's version of his June 25, 1968, interview with Follette, if believed, was a proper basis for Judge Motley's conclusion that Follette committed Sostre to segregation, if not in retaliation for his black militancy or past litigation, then at least to squelch Sostre's threat to take Follette to court over his censorship of Sostre's correspondence. Some substantiation for Sostre's account might be inferred from Follette's summary commitment of Sostre, without following the practice described in the New York Department of Correction's Employees' Rule Book (Rule 8.4), requiring trial by a "disciplinary officer or court."

On this evidence, we cannot conclude that the district judge was "clearly erroneous" in attributing improper motives to Follette, affording as we must "due regard . . . to the opportunity of the trial court to judge of the credibility" of Sostre and Follette, F.R. Civ. P. 52(a). . . . On the other hand, McGinnis was not privy to Follette's interview with Sostre. The record is barren of any justification for attributing to him, in sanctioning Sostre's continued confinement, any more sinister motive than appropriate deference to the judgment of Warden Follette. McGinnis on the record before us, had no reason to suspect Follette of other than proper motivation.

V. Cruel and Unusual Punishment

A reflection of maturing sensitivity in this country to the condition of some of our prisons may be seen in the district court's finding that deprivations such as Sostre endured for a year may not again be inflicted on New York State prisoners for longer than fifteen days, and only then for serious violations of prison rules. Otherwise, Judge Motley held, such punishment would run ashoal of the Eighth Amendment prohibition of cruel and unusual punishment, as applied to the states through the due process guarantee of the Fourteenth Amendment, Robinson v. California, 370 U.S. 660 . . . (1962).

We respect the outrage, given form and content by scholarly research and reflection, that underlay the expert testimony at trial of Sol Rubin, for many years Counsel for the National Council on Crime and Delinquency, and Dr. Seymour Halleck, a psychiatrist at the University of Wisconsin with long experience in state correctional practices. Mr. Rubin testified that Sostre's segregated environment was degrading, dehumanizing, conducive to mental derangement, and for these reasons "a gross departure" from enlightened and progressive contemporary standards for the proper treatment of prison inmates. Dr. Halleck feared that the isolation from human contact in punitive segregation might cause prisoners to hallucinate and to distort reality. Long-term isolation might have so serious an impact, in fact, as to "destroy" a person's "mentality." Dr. Halleck singled out for particular censure Green Haven's "group therapy" program, whose compulsory aspects he found repugnant to effective treatment of participants and indeed inconsistent with minimal standards of professionalism among trained group counsellors.

Nor would candor permit us to dismiss these opinions as aberrational among those views revealed in relevant sources referred to us by counsel or known to us through our own research. To the contrary, it would not be misleading to characterize many of the opinions of plaintiff's experts as fairly representative of the perspective of adherents to the "new penology," . . . the thrust of whose doctrine may be gauged by the preference for the adjective "correctional" rather than "penal" as more accurately indicating the proper function of a prison system. The rapidly rising standards in the field of penology and corrections that Mr. Rubin referred to in his testimony are reflected in a growing preoccupation with institutional strictures and techniques designed to "reintegrate" prisoners with society or, in the jargon of the experts, to "provide . . . motivation for acquiring a conventional role in a non-delinquent setting." Conjugal visiting, daytime work or educational-release programs, vocational training, half-way houses, and inmate publication of prison newspapers are some of the vanguard weapons in the "modern" approach to prison administration. The key concepts are access and involvement of prisoners with the free society "on the outside." Anathema to this perspective are perhaps more traditional practices which subject prisoners to deprivation, degradation, subservience, and isolation, in an attempt to "break" them and make them see the error of their ways. It is suggested by many observers that such techniques are counter-productive, tending only to instill in most prisoners attitudes hostile to rehabilitation, summarized by one author as "doubt, guilt, inadequacy, diffusion, self-absorption, apathy [and] despair."

We do not question, either, the relevance to an inquiry under the Eighth

Amendment of opinions which may represent a progressing sense of humaneness as well as a new calculation as to the efficacy of penal practices. . . . For a federal court, however, to place a punishment beyond the power of a state to impose on an inmate is a drastic interference with the state's free political and administrative processes. It is not only that we, trained as judges, lack expertise in prison administration. Even a lifetime of study in prison administration and several advanced degrees in the field would not qualify us *as a federal court* to command state officials to shun a policy that they have decided is suitable because to us the choice may seem unsound or *personally* repugnant. As judges we are obliged to school ourselves in such objective sources as historical usage . . . practices in other jurisdictions . . . and public opinion . . . before we may responsibly exercise the power of judicial review to declare a punishment unconstitutional under the Eighth Amendment.

Accordingly, we have in the past declined to find an Eighth Amendment violation unless the punishment can properly be termed "barbarous" or "shocking to the conscience." . . . Although the conditions Sostre endured were severe, we cannot agree with the district court that they were "so foul, so inhuman, and so violative of basic concepts of decency," . . . as to require that similar punishments be limited in the future to any particular length of time. Nor can we agree that Sostre's own long confinement — however contrary such prolonged segregation may be to the views of some experts — would have been "cruel and unusual" had Sostre in fact been confined for the reasons asserted by Warden Follette, rather than on account of his beliefs and litigiousness.

It is undisputed on this appeal that segregated confinement does not itself violate the Constitution. . . . Indeed, we learn that a similar form of confinement is probably used in almost every jurisdiction in this country and has been described as one of "the main traditional disciplinary tools" of our prison systems. . . . Plaintiff has directed our attention to currently operative rules in other jurisdictions which limit the duration of segregated confinement, and to several commentaries recommending or approving such rules. In several states, however, incarceration in segregated cells seems to be for an indefinite period, as it is in New York. The federal practice appears to be that prisoners shall be retained in solitary "for as long as necessary to achieve the purposes intended," sometimes "indefinitely." Furthermore, "willful refusal to obey an order or demonstrated defiance of personnel acting in line of duty may constitute sufficient basis for placing an inmate in segregation." Such analogous practices do not impel us to the conclusion that the Eighth Amendment forbids indefinite confinement under the conditions endured by Sostre for all the reasons asserted by Warden Follette until such time as the prisoner agrees to abide by prison rules — however counter-productive as a correctional measure or however personally abhorrent the practice may seem to some of us.

In arriving at this conclusion, we have considered Sostre's diet, the availability in his cell of at least rudimentary implements of personal hygiene, the opportunity for exercise and for participation in group therapy, the provision of at least some general reading matter from the prison library and of unlimited numbers of law books, and the constant possibility of communication with other segregated prisoners. These factors in combination raised the quality of Sostre's segregated environment several notches above those truly barbarous and inhumane conditions heretofore condemned by ourselves and by other courts as "cruel and unusual."[27] See Ford v. Board of Managers, 407 F.2d 937 (3rd Cir. 1969) (no running water or wash bowl; bread and water diet except one regular meal each third day; held constitutional); Landman v. Peyton, 370 F.2d 135 (4th Cir. 1966), *cert. denied*, 388 U.S. 920 . . . (1967); Knuckles v. Prasse, 302 F. Supp. 1036 (E.D. Pa. 1969) (400 days segregation held constitutional).

Finally, we cannot agree with Judge Motley that even if New York might in an appropriate case subject a prisoner to the conditions of Sostre's segregated confinement, had Follette's motives been as he described them, the punishment would in any event have been unconstitutionally disproportionate to the offense. Were we to rule otherwise, we would deny to prison authorities the power to use an entirely constitutional means of discipline in response not only to a credible threat to the security of the prison, but in response to a prisoner's refusal to answer appropriate questions put by prison authorities and to obey valid prison regulations.[28]

VI. Procedural Due Process

A divergence of perspectives similar to those we have seen in considering the Eighth Amendment issue is presented in another form by the district court's order that Sostre may not be punished in the future in such a way as to forfeit earned "good time" credit or to lose the chance to earn such credit unless he has (a) written notice of the charges against him; (b) a recorded hearing before a disinterested official with a chance to cross-examine adverse witnesses and call witnesses in his own behalf; (c) the right to retain counsel or counsel substitute; and unless (d) a written decision is rendered.[29]

27. E.g., Wright v. McMann, 387 F.2d 519, 521 (2d Cir. 1967) (complaint alleged cell encrusted with excrement; plaintiff entirely naked 11 days, then clad only in thin underwear; windows open throughout subfreezing night; prisoner slept on concrete floor; no soap, towel, or toilet paper); Hancock v. Avery, 301 F. Supp. 786 (M.D. Tenn. 1969) (virtually no light or ventilation; hole for wastes flushed irregularly by guards; no soap, towel, or toilet paper; two meals of bread, one full meal); Jordan v. Fitzharris, 257 F. Supp. 674 (N.D. Calif. 1966) (conditions similar to Hancock and in addition prisoner slept naked on concrete floor). . . .

28. We stress the seriousness of the multiple offenses charged against Sostre by Warden Follette . . . and express no view as to the constitutionality of such segregated confinement as Sostre experienced if it were imposed for lesser offenses. Specifically, we express no view as to the constitutionality of such segregated confinement if it had been imposed on account of any one or any combination of the offenses charged against Sostre other than all of them.

29. Judge Foley of the Northern District of New York has adopted the procedural

Sostre presses upon us a variety of cases, relied upon by the district court and said to be analogous to this case, in which federal courts have required states to square corners before exacting a penalty by following procedures similar to those mandated by Judge Motley.

[Here, the court reviews the relevance of due process requirements in Goldberg v. Kelly, 397 U.S. 254 (1970) (requiring minimal procedural safeguards in welfare termination cases); Escalera v. New York City Housing Authority, 425 F.2d 853 (2d Cir. 1970) (requiring due process hearing procedures prior to eviction of "privilege" of residing in public housing project); and Mempa v. Rhay, 389 U.S. 128 (1967) (counsel required in deferred sentencing proceedings). The court concludes that Sostre was entitled to due process of law before he was punished for an infraction of prison rules, but doubts that due process requirements of a formal trial type are necessary. The court feared that such requirements might make prison discipline more difficult and might prove destructive of proper prison atmosphere and rehabilitative ends. The court noted that little research was available on the subject of prison disciplinary procedures, and that reforms undertaken in other states had not gone as far as the safeguards required by Judge Motley's injunction.]

We therefore find ourselves in disagreement with Judge Motley's conclusion that each of the procedural elements incorporated in her mandatory injunction are necessary constitutional ingredients of every proceeding resulting in serious discipline of a prisoner. In thus rejecting Judge Motley's conclusions, however, we are not to be understood as disapproving the judgment of many courts that our constitutional scheme does not contemplate that society may commit lawbreakers to the capricious and arbitrary actions of prison officials. If substantial deprivations are to be visited upon a prisoner, it is wise that such action should at least be premised on facts rationally determined. This is not a concept without meaning. In most cases it would probably be difficult to find an inquiry minimally fair and rational unless the prisoner were confronted with the accusation, informed of the evidence against him . . . and afforded a reasonable opportunity to explain his actions. [Citations omitted.]

---

aspect of Judge Motley's order. Wright v. McCann, 257 F. Supp. 739 (N.D.N.Y. 1966), *on rehearing after remand* 387 F.2d 519 (2d Cir. 1967). In Carothers v. Follette, 314 F. Supp. 1014 (S.D.N.Y. 1970), Judge Mansfield approved aspects of these procedures, remarking that "any serious charge" would require such "essential elements of fundamental procedural fairness" as "an opportunity to present evidence before a relatively objective tribunal."

[The court noted that defendants appended to their brief on appeal new rules and regulations recently promulgated by the New York Department of Correction, effective October 19, 1970. These governed, among other things, inmate discipline in all state correctional institutions which, the court said, "appear to provide some new procedural safeguards." The court considered it inappropriate to comment on the constitutional adequacy of the new procedures because they were adopted after the events before it on the Sostre appeal.]

VII. Rights of Communication and Expression

A. Correspondence

The distaste with which some observers view prolonged segregated confinement attaches as well to that kind of isolation flowing from restrictions on and censorship of prisoners' correspondence: "The harm censorship does to rehabilitation cannot be gainsaid. Inmates lose contact with the outside world and become wary of placing intimate thoughts or criticisms of the prison in letters. The artificial increase of alienation from society is ill advised."

The values commonly associated with free expression — an open, democratic marketplace of ideas, the self-development of individuals through self-expression, the alleviation of tensions by their release in harsh words rather than hurled objects — these values that we esteem in a free society do not turn to dross in an unfree one. "Letter writing keeps the inmate in contact with the outside world, helps to hold in check some of the morbidity and hopelessness produced by prison life and isolation, stimulates his more natural and human impulses, and otherwise may make contributions to better mental attitudes and reformation." Palmigiano v. Travisono, 310 F. Supp. 857 (D.R.I. Aug. 24, 1970). Suppression of diversity and dissenting views is probably not less apt in a prison than elsewhere to hasten the stagnation and bureaucratization of the institution that indulges in it. . . .

Whatever wisdom there might be in such reflection, we cannot say with requisite certitude that the traditional and common practice of prisons in imposing many kinds of controls on the correspondence of inmates, lacks support in any rational and constitutionally acceptable concept of a prison system. [Citations omitted.] We note that Sostre did not contest the validity of Warden Follette's action in striking the name of his sister from the list of Sostre's authorized correspondents after it was learned that he was using letters addressed to his sister as vehicles for unauthorized correspondence. . . . Discipline and prison order are sufficient interests to justify such regulation incidental to the content of prisoners' speech. . . .

Sui generis in both logic and the case law, however, are letters addressed to courts, public officials, or an attorney when a prisoner challenges the legality of either his criminal conviction or the conditions of his incarceration. [Citations omitted.] It would be inappropriate on constitutional grounds, ironic, and irrational to permit drastic curtailment of constitutional rights in the name of punishment and rehabilitation, while denying prisoners a full opportunity to pursue their appeals and postconviction remedies. The generous scope of discretion accorded prison authorities also heightens the importance of permitting free and uninhibited access by prisoners to both administrative and judicial forums for the purpose of seeking redress of grievances against state officers. The importance of these rights of access suggests the need for guidelines both generous and specific enough to afford protection against the reality or the chilling threat of administrative infringement.

Thus, we do not believe it would unnecessarily hamper prison administration to forbid prison authorities to delete material from, withhold, or refuse to mail a communication between an inmate and his attorney, see Burns v. Swensen, 430 F.2d 771 (8th Cir., Aug. 31, 1970) (protecting correspondence with the ACLU), or any court, or any public official, unless it can be demonstrated that a prisoner has clearly abused his rights of access. Obviously, the transmittal of contraband or laying plans for some unlawful scheme would constitute such an abuse. In addition, if it were clear that a prisoner's recitation of complaints about his confinement in otherwise protected correspondence were a mere pretext to accomplish his sole motivating purpose of communicating instead about restricted matters, then prison officials may block the inmate's scheme by deleting that portion of such a communication unrelated to the complaints. In such a case, the need to restrain the abuse outweighs the danger that prison authorities may by inadvertence or design hamper the prisoner's access.

On the other hand, if a communication is properly intended to advance a prisoner's effort to secure redress for alleged abuses, no interest would justify deleting material thought by prison authorities to be irrelevant to the prisoner's complaint. The danger that an official will improperly substitute his judgment for that of the correspondent's then preponderates. For similar reasons, prison officials may not withhold, refuse to mail, or delete material from otherwise protected communications merely because they believe the allegations to be repetitious, false, or malicious. See Nolan v. Scafati, 430 F.2d 548 (1st Cir. 1970) (absent some countervailing interest other than that prisoner's letter contained "lies," authorities may not prevent inmate from seeking legal assistance); Fulwood v. Clemmer, 206 F. Supp. 370, 377 (D.D.C. 1962) (right to seek redress of grievances was abridged by punishment for alleged false accusations about prison conditions in prisoner's letter of complaint to public officials).

Accordingly, we agree with Judge Motley that it was improper for Warden Follette to delete material from correspondence between Sostre and his attorney merely because Follette thought the material irrelevant to Sostre's appeal of his conviction. We believe it was also improper for Follette to refuse to mail a letter of complaint to the Postal Inspector. We leave a more precise delineation of the boundaries of this protection for future cases. We need only add that when we say there may be cases which will present special circumstances that *would* justify deleting material from, withholding, or refusing to mail communications with courts, attorneys, and public officials, we necessarily rule that prison officials may open and read all outgoing and incoming correspondence to and from prisoners.

B. Prison Legal Aid

Johnson v. Avery, 393 U.S. 483 . . . (1969), instructs that states must permit prisoners to help fellow inmates prepare habeas corpus petitions, subject to reasonable regulation, absent a sufficient showing by the state that through some other means it provides prisoners with an adequate substitute for the "jailhouse lawyer." [Citations omitted.] The failure of any such showing in this case makes it mandatory that New York permit prisoner aid to the extent required by Johnson. Johnson's explicit permission to states reasonably to regulate this right, however, validates the Green Haven rule requiring prisoners to apply to the Warden for permission to help other inmates with legal activities. There would be a violation of Johnson only if the Warden denied permission, or if the conditions on which he granted it were unreasonable.

Since Sostre never requested permission, there is no cause for an injunction to enforce the Johnson rule. We assume that permission would be granted as a matter of course, subject only to reasonable conditions. Nor can we consider unreasonable the Green Haven rule forbidding prisoners from sharing their personal law books with one another. This regulation would not prohibit Sostre, for example, from recommending legal source material to other inmates. We do not see how they would be unduly burdened by being required to acquire the books through prison officials rather than directly from Sostre. See Gilmore v. Lynch, supra (upholding prison rule prohibiting jailhouse lawyers from keeping in their cells legal material pertaining to other prisoners). In a closely related situation, we held that a prisoner could be refused permission to keep "law books" in his cell where there was no allegation he was denied use of the prison library. Williams v. Wilkins, 315 F.2d 396, 397 (2d Cir. 1963). We cannot ignore the concern of prison officials that strong-willed inmates might exact hidden and perhaps non-monetary fees in return for nominally free privileges at the inmates' private lending library.

C. Possession of Literature and Mere Expression of Beliefs

Our holding that prisoners may not be punished for their beliefs carries the necessary corollary that we may not permit punishment for the mere expression of those beliefs. One can hardly speak of beliefs apart from their expression, cf. Fulwood v. Clemmer, 206 F. Supp. 370 (D.D.C. 1962). In the absence of arbitrariness or discrimination . . . we do not say on this record that Warden Follette would have exceeded his legitimate authority if he had confiscated the writings that guards found in Sostre's cell following his release from segregation. Whatever doubts we might have as to the wisdom of seizing an inmate's political writings, we would not lightly overturn a warden's judgment that possession of the writings might subvert prison discipline if there existed the risk of their circulation among other prisoners.

However, Sostre was *punished* simply for putting his thoughts on paper, with no prior warning and no hint that he intended to spirit the writings outside his cell. To sanction such punishment, even though in the judgment of prison officials the writings were "inflammatory" and "racist," as in the instant case, would permit prison authorities to manipulate and crush thoughts under the guise of regulation. The intimidating threat of future similar punishment would chill a wide range of prisoner expression, not limited to that expression which Follette might in fact deem dangerous enough to discipline.

The danger of undetected discriminatory punishment of ideas is particularly acute in the absence of statutory standards to guide the exercise of Follette's discretion. See, e.g., Cox v. Louisiana, 379 U.S. 536, 556-557 (1965); Schneider v. State, 308 U.S. 147 (1939). Any real threat to prison security that Sostre's possession of his writings might have posed could have been met by confiscation rather than punishment. See Shelton v. Tucker, 364 U.S. 479 (1960).

VIII. Conclusion

A. Injunction

1. . . . All of the elements of due process recited by the district court are not necessary to the constitutionality of every disciplinary action taken against a prisoner. In light of this, we reverse the district court insofar as it enjoined defendants and others from so disciplining Sostre that he loses accrued good time credit or is unable to earn good time credit without full compliance with all the procedural steps set forth in Judge Motley's injunction. We do not thereby imply that discipline in New York prisons may be administered arbitrarily or capriciously. We would not lightly condone the absence of such basic safeguards against arbitrariness as adequate notice, an opportunity for the prisoner to reply to charges lodged against him, and a reasonable investigation into the relevant facts — at least in cases of substantial discipline. However, as consideration of Sostre's case does not properly raise any question whether New York prisons regularly or systematically ignore minimal due process requirements, we must reverse the order of the district court that defendants submit for its approval, proposed rules and regulations governing future disciplinary actions. In this connection, we note that New York State has recently promulgated rules and regulations governing prison discipline which appear to give inmates new procedural protections.

2. The refusal to mail Sostre's letter to the Post Office Inspector, complaining of prison practices, clearly infringed Sostre's Fourteenth Amendment rights. We also affirm Judge Motley's order insofar as it enjoins defendants Follette and McGinnis, their employees, agents, successors, and all persons in active concert and participation with them, from deleting material from, refusing to mail or refusing to give to Sostre: (1) Any communication between Sostre and the following — (a) any court; (b) any public official or agency; or (c) any lawyer — with respect to either his criminal conviction or any complaint he may have concerning the administration of the prison where he is incarcerated. We reverse, however, insofar as Judge Motley enjoined nonarbitrary restraint of communication between Sostre and his codefendant in the criminal matter pending against him.

3. There is no cause for an injunction to enforce the principles announced in Johnson v. Avery, supra, since no infractions of those principles have been shown. Johnson v. Avery permitted reasonable rules regulating the conduct of inmates in assisting other inmates in legal proceedings. Sostre has not

proved that the rules regulating his right to assist other prisoners in their legal affairs were unreasonable and that his punishment was for violating such rules. Therefore, we must reverse the district court insofar as it enjoined interference with Sostre's translation of letters of fellow-inmates since he had failed to comply with the rule requiring that he seek permission of the warden. For the same reason, we reverse the injunction against punishing Sostre for sharing with other inmates his law books, law reviews, and other legal materials, and from refusing to permit Sostre to assist any other inmate in any legal matter.

4. We have held that Sostre was improperly punished for possession of constitutionally protected literature. We perceive no reason, however, to set *political* speech apart from other kinds of constitutionally protected speech. We therefore modify the district court order so as to enjoin defendants Follette and McGinnis, their employees, agents, successors, and all persons in active concert and participation with them, from punishing Sostre for having literature in his possession and for setting forth his views orally or in writing, except for violation of reasonable regulations. We do not hereby enjoin officials from taking reasonable measures to prevent prisoners from inciting disturbances and otherwise to protect the security and order of New York prisons, consistent with prisoners' rights to freedom of expression. Also we do not believe that there is any need for the extraordinary procedure requiring defendants to submit rules and regulations governing the receipt, distribution, discussion and writing of political literature for the approval of the district court.

5. We have no reason to conclude that New York prison officials will not abide by the constitutional rights of prisoners as we define them today. We have refused to set aside Judge Motley's findings that Warden Follette unlawfully committed Sostre to segregated confinement because of his legal activities and beliefs. Warden Follette, however, is deceased and we perceive no threat that others will duplicate his improper conduct. Accordingly, we vacate that portion of the district court order which enjoined defendants and others from returning Sostre to punitive segregation for charges previously preferred against him.

B. Good Time Credit

Since we have held that Sostre was unlawfully confined to punitive segregation on account of his political beliefs and legal activities, we agree with Judge Motley's order requiring Sostre to be credited with 124⅓ days of earned "good time." Sostre may not be penalized because of his time in segregation by remaining incarcerated longer or by becoming eligible for parole later than he otherwise would. We do not consider the argument that Sostre may not have earned the credit even if he had remained in the general population to be of substance. Whether he would or would not have earned it is pure speculation. Since Sostre's constitutional rights have been violated, we resolve the doubt in his favor. Moreover, this is the only feasible way to ensure that Sostre is not again unlawfully penalized by arbitrary action.

C. Money Damages

All parties seem to agree upon two principles with which we also are in accord. First, Section 1983 authorizes recovery of compensatory, and, in an appropriate case, punitive damages against an individual for the unjustifiable violation of constitutional rights "under color" of state law. Monroe v. Pape, 365 U.S. 167 . . . (1961). . . . This liability, however, is entirely personal in nature intended to be satisfied out of the individual's own pocket. Moreover, the doctrine of sovereign immunity, as codified by the Eleventh Amendment, bars the exaction of a fine from a state treasury without the state's consent, at least on account of tortious actions committed by its agents under the circumstances of this case. Larson v. Domestic & Foreign Corp., 337 U.S. 682 . . . (1949); Westberry v. Fisher, 309 F. Supp. 12 (D. Me. 1970).

It follows from these principles that although Sostre was entitled to compensatory damages against Warden Follette,[52] Follette's successor as warden, who had no part whatsoever in Follette's wrongful conduct against Sostre, incurred no personal money responsibility upon Follette's death. We note also that no application was made in the court below to substitute any party who could be held responsible to assume Follette's obligation to Sostre, Rule 25, F. R. Civ. P., if such a party existed. Accordingly, there is no party before us against whom appropriately to award damages.

In any event, we are persuaded to reverse the award of punitive damages. Warden Follette's improper conduct in segregating Sostre so far as appears reflected no pattern of such behavior by himself or by other officials. The deterrent impact of a punitive award would be of minimal use.

It is appropriate, lest our action today be misunderstood, that we disclaim any intent by this decision to condone, ignore, or discount the deplorable and counter-productive conditions of many of this country's jails and prisons. We strongly suspect that many traditional and still widespread penal practices, including some which we have touched on in this case, take an enormous toll, not just of the prisoner who must tolerate them at whatever price to his humanity and prospects for a normal future life, but also of the society where prisoners return angry and resentful. Nevertheless, we would forget at our peril and at the peril of our free governmental process, that we are federal judges reviewing decisions made in due course by officers of a sovereign state. We have interpreted and applied the law as it appears to us in light of circumstance and principle. We do not doubt the magnitude of the task ahead before our correctional systems become acceptable and effective from a

52. Judge Motley awarded $25.00 compensatory damages per day for every day that Sostre spent in segregation (372 days) or a total of $9,300. In view of the conditions of Sostre's segregation, which we have described, this amount is not unreasonable. In addition, she awarded $3,270 in punitive damages.

correctional, social and humane viewpoint, but the proper tools for the job do not lie with a remote federal court. The sensitivity to local nuance, opportunity for daily perseverance, and the human and monetary resources required lie rather with legislators, executives, and citizens in their communities. See, Amsterdam, The Supreme Court and the Rights of Suspects in Criminal Cases, 45 N.Y.U.L. Rev. 785, 810 (1970).

[Chief Judge Lumbard concurred, but saw no need to express views on state policies regarding the withholding or withdrawing of good-time credit. On this subject, Judge Waterman felt it was the court's duty to set basic standards on good-time credit, and to strike any practice that does not conform to at least minimally acceptable levels of due process.

Judge Smith concurred in most of Judge Kaufman's opinion, but dissented from the majority's failure to find that the record supported a finding that Sostre's segregation for more than one year was cruel and unusual punishment. He would have also found defendant McGinnis, State Commissioner of Correction, civilly liable for compensatory damages, since he was aware of Sostre's long segregation and did nothing to terminate it, although empowered to do so. Judge Feinberg also concurred in most of the majority's opinion, but dissented on the cruel and unusual punishment issue as well as the reversal as to defendant McGinnis. In his view, Sostre's long confinement was unjustified, cruel and unusual, and could not be justified even if his offenses were "serious." He also found that Sostre's punishment contained a "vindictive flavor." Judge Hays, with whom Judge Moore concurs, dissented from the affirmance of any grant of injunctive relief or damages. He reviewed the authorities indicating that prisoners' rights can be sharply circumscribed, and that matters of prison discipline should not be disturbed when they are supported by evidence and do not result in shocking deprivations of fundamental human rights.]

NOTES

1. In 1965, Martin Sostre opened a bookstore in the ghetto of Buffalo, where he sold black literature. He incurred the enmity of local police when, during the June 1969 riots in that city, he provided a refuge for young blacks. Two weeks later he was arrested on a narcotics charge. Unable to raise bail ($25,000 property bond or $12,000 cash), he spent eight months in jail prior to trial; at the trial (having refused representation by the public defender) he represented himself, refused to recognize the trial as legitimate, and asked no questions, confining himself to speeches to his followers, who filled the courtroom. He was found guilty and later sentenced to thirty to forty-one years. V. Copeland, The Crime of Martin Sostre 11-28 (1970).

2. A sense of what Sostre felt to be the object of his solitary confinement is contained in his testimony at the district court hearing: "I never went to the yard," he explained, "because I wouldn't subject myself to their searches.

You have to strip, bend over, be searched — that is undergo a rectal examination by the guard, like in the service — every time you go out and come back in. That is merely harassment because we [in solitary] have nothing. They will never dehumanize me." As to the group therapy, Sostre reported that Sergeant Lowery tried to recruit him, "but within a few minutes of his being there, it got into politics. I told him, how can you help me, if you are the one who is oppressing me?" Sostre explained that he refused to take therapy on the ground that its purpose was to make him bend down mentally to the guards, just as they expected him to bend over physically for the "rectal examination." V. Copeland, supra at 176-177.

3. Courts are probably incapable of supervising the day-to-day operations of prisons, but in Marse v. Travisono, 310 F. Supp. 857 (D.R.I. 1970), and Clutchette v. Procunier, 328 F. Supp. 767 (N.D. Cal. 1971), detailed factual inquiries into prison conditions in general and disciplinary procedures in particular were made. The court order in Marse was preceded by negotiations between the parties, which resulted in a draft of proposed regulations governing disciplinary and classification procedures. The proposal was distributed to all prisoners, after which the court heard testimony from prisoners who objected to certain provisions. The proposed rules were adopted as the court's interim decree, but the court retained jurisdiction for eighteen months and reviewed all reclassifications. The new rules set forth the purposes of the classification process, the degree of control to which prisoners in each classification category could be subjected, the standards governing reclassification, and the procedures to be followed in reclassifications and disciplinary proceedings. Reclassification could not be based on misconduct unless a finding unfavorable to the inmate had been made at a disciplinary hearing. No disciplinary action could be taken without a written charge by a prison officer or employee, a preliminary investigation of the charge by a superior officer, prior notice of hearing, and a hearing at which the inmate could present evidence and be assisted by a classification counselor. Disciplinary board decisions were to be based on substantial evidence, and the record was to contain a summary of the evidence and an explanation of the decision. The decision in Clutchette, supra, was even more far-reaching, though less detailed. Prisoners were held to have the rights, to cross-examination of witnesses against them, to the assistance of counsel in cases which could be referred to the state courts for trial, and to at least counsel substitute in all other cases. Defendants were enjoined from disciplining inmates until constitutional requirements were met.

4. In Gates v. Collier, 349 F. Supp. 881 (N.D. Miss. 1972), the court ordered the correction of a long list of deplorable conditions — including racial segregation, mail censorship, corporal punishment of inmates, unsanitary barracks, use of inmates as guards, etc. — at Mississippi's state penitentiary at Parchman. Some relief was granted immediately, and the court scheduled a conference of all parties, open to the public, to review how best

to improve housing and other basic physical facilities. The court noted the availability of federal funds, but warned:

> Nevertheless, the state must move to bring all aspects of the penitentiary operation in conformity with constitutional principles if it is to continue the use of Parchman as a place of incarceration of criminals, and this court is obliged to make certain that such steps are not only begun with reasonable promptitude but are fully carried out. (349 F. Supp. at 897.)

16. JURY DISCRIMINATION

It would require a miracle to effectively screen from the jury room all of the beliefs based on racial myths and fears that social scientists have found permeate society (see Chapter Three). And so it is not surprising to find that, notwithstanding the sworn promise of impartiality, the specific instructions to view the facts objectively, and the undoubtedly earnest efforts by many jurors, studies show that racial considerations do influence jury decisions.

In the major jury study by H. Kalven and H. Zeisel, The American Jury, 1966, the influence of racist thinking on jury decisions was found in several cases where the juries (and judges) held blacks to a less strict standard of conduct when the victim was also black. The book quotes a judge who presided in such a case, where the black defendant was acquitted: "If this had been a white man he would have been convicted. Negroes in cases of this type receive more than equal rights; juries seem to think its okay for them to cut, if it's another colored person that is cut." The American Jury at 341. A study based on interviews with 225 jurors, conducted in the mid-1950s, shows clearly that many persons brought their racial prejudices to the jury box. As one juror reported: "Niggers have to be taught to behave. I feel that if he hadn't done that, he'd done something else probably even worse and that he should be put out of the way for a good long while." Broeder, The Negro in Court, in Race, Crime, and Justice 301 (C. Reasons and J. Kuykendall, eds. 1972).

Perhaps a better and certainly more obvious proof of jury discrimination is the statistics of jury performance in racial cases. For example, the fear on the part of whites that black men pose a serious threat to white women was reviewed in Chapter Six. The manifestation of such fears in jury decisions can be read in statistics prepared by the U.S. Bureau of Prisons for the years 1930-1962; of 446 persons found guilty and executed for rape in the United States, 339 were black, 45 were white, and 2 were of other races. These figures prompted a detailed study of rape convictions in twelve Southern states (virtually all of the states which authorized the death penalty for rape are Southern), and resulted in findings that, compared to other rape defendants, blacks convicted of raping white women were disproportionately found guilty and sentenced to death. Despite the introduction of this data in support of an argument that the application of the death penalty to blacks charged with rape constituted cruel and unusual punishment, the courts have refused to find that Southern juries practice racial discrimination in rape cases. See Maxwell v. Bishop, 398 F.2d 138 (8th Cir. 1968); Moorer v. South Carolina, 368 F.2d 458 (4th Cir. 1966). For a review of racial disparities in sentencing and other aspects of the criminal justice system, see Bell, Racism in American Courts: Cause for Black Disruption or Despair? 61 U. Cal. L. Rev. 165 (1973).

Of course, the longstanding policy of excluding blacks from juries — particularly where blacks are charged with crimes against whites — is based, in substantial part, on the expectation that an all-white jury will return a verdict that accords with racial standards and views held by the white community.

Except in the most outrageous cases, in which racial prejudice so reduced the trial to a "mask, — that counsel, jury, and judge were swept to the fatal end by an irresistible wave of public passion . . ." (Moore v. Dempsey, 261 U.S. 86, at 91, 43 S. Ct. 265, at 266, 67 L. Ed. 543, at 545 (1923)), the Supreme Court has chosen to handle the problem of racism in jury decisions in an oblique and generally ineffective manner. The Court, for example, agreed to review the Maxwell v. Bishop case, supra, but not on the validity of death penalties for blacks convicted of raping white women. 393 U.S. 997 (1968). See also Rudolph v. Alabama, 375 U.S. 889, 84 S. Ct. 155, 11 L. Ed. 2d 119 (1963). As the opinion in Swain v. Alabama, set forth below, indicates, the Supreme Court has adhered to the standard set in the 1880s that black defendants are entitled to be tried by juries from which members of their race have not been systematically excluded. While theoretically available to every criminal defendant, the procedural defense is usually pursued only where the defendant is involved in controversial activities, like civil rights, or where he is charged with a serious offense, such as rape or murder. The defense has served to win reversals and new trials in Southern jurisdictions where jury discrimination is blatantly obvious, and has provided federal courts with a means to ameliorate, or at least delay, the harshest aspects of Southern racial justice — particularly in those rape cases where the record raises substantial question as to whether the alleged criminal assault was not, in reality, simple seduction. See, e.g., the "Scottsboro Boys" cases, Powell v. Alabama, 287 U.S. 45, 53 S. Ct. 55, 77 L. Ed. 158 (1932), and Norris v. Alabama, 294 U.S. 587, 55 S. Ct. 579, 79 L. Ed. 1074 (1935); and Giles v. Maryland, 386 U.S. 66, 87 S. Ct. 793, 17 L. Ed. 2d 737 (1967); United States ex rel. Montgomery v. Ragen, 86 F. Supp. 382 (N.D. Ill. 1949).

The jury discrimination cases are reviewed below in Swain v. Alabama, a decision that many critics believe substantially increased the difficulty of obtaining such reversals.

SWAIN v. ALABAMA

380 U.S. 202, 85 S. Ct. 824, 13 L. Ed. 2d 759 (1965)

Mr. Justice White delivered the opinion of the Court.

The petitioner, Robert Swain, a Negro, was indicted and convicted of rape in the Circuit Court of Talladega County, Alabama, and sentenced to death. His motions to quash the indictment, to strike the trial jury venire and to declare void the petit jury chosen in the case, all based on alleged invidious discrimination in the selection of jurors, were denied. . . .

In support of his claims, petitioner invokes the constitutional principle announced in 1880 in Strauder v. State of West Virginia, 100 U.S. 303 . . . where the Court struck down a state statute qualifying only white people for jury duty. Such a statute was held to contravene the central purposes of the Fourteenth Amendment: "exemption from unfriendly legislation against [Negroes] distinctively as colored, — exemption from legal discriminations, implying inferiority in civil society, lessening the security of their enjoyment of the rights which others enjoy. . . ." 100 U.S., at 308. Although a Negro defendant is not entitled to a jury containing members of his race, a State's purposeful or deliberate denial to Negroes on account of race of participation as jurors in the administration of justice violates the Equal Protection Clause. Ex parte State of Virginia, 100 U.S. 339 . . . ; Gibson v. State of Mississippi, 162 U.S. 565. . . . This principle was further elaborated in Carter v. State of Texas, 177 U.S. 442 . . . where, in respect to exclusion from grand juries, the Court said: Whenever by any action of a state, whether through its legislature, through its courts, or through its executive or administrative officers, all persons of the African race are excluded, solely because of their race or color, from serving as grand jurors in the criminal prosecution of a person of the African race, the equal protection of the laws is denied. . . ." Further, "[j]urymen should be selected as individuals, on the basis of individual qualifications, and not as members of a race." Cassell v. State of Texas, 339 U.S. 282, 286 . . . (opinion of Mr. Justice Reed, announcing judgment). Nor is the constitutional command forbidding intentional exclusion limited to Negroes. It applies to any identifiable group in the community which may be the subject of prejudice. Hernandez v. State of Texas, 347 U.S. 475. . . .

But purposeful discrimination may not be assumed or merely asserted. . . . It must be proven, . . . the quantum of proof necessary being a matter of federal law. . . . It is not the soundness of these principles, which is unquestioned, but their scope and application to the issues in this case that concern us here.

I

We consider first petitioner's claims concerning the selection of grand jurors and the petit jury venire. The evidence was that while Negro males over 21 constitute 26% of all males in the county in this age group, only 10 to 15% of the grand and petit jury panels drawn from the jury box since 1953 have been Negroes, there having been only one case in which the percentage was as high as 23%. In this period of time, Negroes served on 80% of the grand juries selected, the number ranging from one to three. There were four or five Negroes on the grand jury panel of about 33 in this case, out of which two served on the grand jury which indicted petitioner. Although there has been an average of six to seven Negroes on petit jury venires in criminal cases, no Negro has actually served on a petit jury since about 1950. In this case there were eight Negroes on the petit jury venire but none actually served, two being exempt and six being struck by the prosecutor in the process of selecting the jury.

It is wholly obvious that Alabama has not totally excluded a racial group from either grand or petit jury panels, as was the case in Norris v. State of Alabama, 294 U.S. 587 . . . ; Hill v. State of Texas, 316 U.S. 400 . . . ; Patton v. State of Mississippi, 332 U.S. 463 . . . ; Hernandez v. State of Texas, 347 U.S. 475 . . . ; and Reece v. State of Georgia, 350 U.S. 85. . . . Moreover, we do not consider an average of six to eight Negroes on these panels as constituting forbidden token inclusion within the meaning of the cases in this Court. Thomas v. State of Texas, 212 U.S. 278 . . . ; Akins v. State of Texas, 325 U.S. 398 . . . ; Avery v. State of Georgia, 345 U.S. 559. . . . Nor do we consider the evidence in this case to make out a prima facie case of invidious discrimination under the Fourteenth Amendment.

Alabama law requires that the three jury commissioners in Talladega County place on the jury roll all male citizens in the community over 21 who are reputed to be honest, intelligent men and are esteemed for their integrity, good character and sound judgment. . . . In practice, however, the commissioners do not place on the roll all such citizens, either white or colored. A typical jury roll at best contains about 2,500 names, out of a total male population over 21, according to the latest census, of 16,406 persons. Each commissioner, with the clerk's assistance, produces for the jury list names of persons who in his judgment are qualified. The sources are city directories, registration lists, club and church lists, conversations with other persons in the community, both white and colored, and personal and business acquaintances.

Venires drawn from the jury box made up in this manner unquestionably contained a smaller proportion of the Negro community than of the white community. But a defendant in a criminal case is not constitutionally entitled to demand a proportionate number of his race on the jury which tries him nor on the venire or jury roll from which petit jurors are drawn. State of Virginia v. Rives, 100 U.S. 313, 322-323 . . . ; Gibson v. State of Mississippi, 162 U.S. 565 . . . ; Thomas v. State of Texas, 212 U.S. 278, 282 . . . ; Cassell v. State of Texas, 339 U.S. 282. . . . Neither the jury roll nor the venire need be a perfect mirror of the community or accurately reflect the proportionate strength of every identifiable group. "Obviously the number of races and nationalities appearing in the ancestry of our citizens would make it impossible to meet a requirement of proportional representation. Similarly, since there can be no exclusion of Negroes as a race and no discrimination because of color, proportional limitation is not permissible." Cassell v. State of Texas, 339 U.S. 282, 286-287 . . . (opinion of Mr. Justice Reed, announcing judgment). We cannot say that purposeful discrimination based on race alone is satisfactorily proved by showing that an identifiable group in a community is underrepresented by as much as 10%. . . . Here the commissioners denied that racial considerations entered into their selections of either their contacts in the community or the names of prospective jurors. There is no evidence that the commissioners applied different standards of qualifications to the Negro community than they did to the white community. Nor was there any meaningful attempt to demonstrate that the same proportion of Negroes qualified under the standards being administered by the commissioners. It is not clear from the record that the commissioners even knew how many Negroes were in their respective areas, or on the jury roll or on the venires drawn from the jury box. The overall percentage disparity has been small, and reflects no studied attempt to include or exclude a specified number of Negroes. Undoubtedly the selection of prospective jurors was somewhat haphazard and little effort was made to ensure that all groups in the community were fully represented. But an imperfect system is not equivalent to purposeful discrimination based on race.[5] We do not think that the burden of proof was carried by petitioner in this case.

II

Petitioner makes a further claim relating to the exercise of peremptory challenges to exclude Negroes from serving on petit juries.

In Talladega County the petit jury venire drawn in a criminal case numbers about 35 unless a capital offense is involved, in which case it numbers about 100. . . . After excuses and removals for cause, the venire in a capital case is reduced to about 75. The jury is then "struck" — the defense striking two veniremen and the prosecution one in alternating turns, until only 12 jurors remain. . . . This essentially is the Alabama struck-jury system, applicable in all criminal cases and available in civil cases. . . . In this case, the six Negroes available for jury service were struck by the prosecutor in the process of selecting the jury which was to try petitioner.

In the trial court after the jury was selected, petitioner moved to have the jury declared void on Fourteenth Amendment grounds. Among other things the motion alleged:

> (4) That because of the systematic and arbitrary method of selecting the names of qualified male citizens, negro male citizens, by the Jury Commission of Talladega County, Alabama, the State can, and did in this case, readily strike members of the negro race and that there were only six negroes remaining on the final venire in this cause, in violation of the Fourteenth Amendment of the Constitution of the United States and also the Constitution of the State of Alabama . . . .

The main thrust of the motion according to its terms was the striking of the six Negroes from the petit jury venire. No evidence was taken, petitioner

5. "'It may be that the jury commissioners did not give the negro race a full pro rata with the white race in the selection of the grand and petit jurors in this case, still this would not be evidence of discrimination. If they fairly and honestly endeavored to discharge their duty, and did not in fact discriminate against the negro race in the selection of the jury lists, then the Constitution of the United States has not been violated.'" Thomas v. State of Texas, 212 U.S. 278, 283. . . .

apparently being content to rely on the record which had been made in connection with the motion to quash the indictment. We think the motion, seeking as it did to invalidate the alleged purposeful striking of Negroes from the jury which was to try petitioner, was properly denied. . . .

Alabama contends that its system of peremptory strikes — challenges without cause, without explanation and without judicial scrutiny — affords a suitable and necessary method of securing juries which in fact and in the opinion of the parties are fair and impartial. This system, it is said, in and of itself, provides justification for striking any group of otherwise qualified jurors in any given case, whether they be Negroes, Catholics, accountants or those with blue eyes. Based on the history of this system and its actual use and operation in this country, we think there is merit in this position.

[The Court here reviews, in minute detail, the historical background and current use of the peremptory challenge and struck juries in England and the United States.]

In contrast to the course in England, where both peremptory challenge and challenge for cause have fallen into disuse, peremptories were and are freely used and relied upon in this country, perhaps because juries here are drawn from a greater cross-section of a heterogeneous society. The voir dire in American trials tends to be extensive and probing, operating as a predicate for the exercise of peremptories, and the process of selecting a jury protracted. The persistence of peremptories and their extensive use demonstrate the long and widely held belief that peremptory challenge is a necessary part of trial by jury. See Lewis v. United States, 146 U.S. 370, 376. . . . Although "[t]here is nothing in the Constitution of the United States which requires the Congress [or the States] to grant peremptory challenges," Stilson v. United States, 250 U.S. 583, 586 . . . , nonetheless the challenge is "one of the most important of the rights secured to the accused," Pointer v. United States, 151 U.S. 396, 408. . . . The denial or impairment of the right is reversible error without a showing of prejudice, Lewis v. United States, supra; Harrison v. United States, 163 U.S. 140 . . . ; cf. Gulf, Colorado & Santa Fe R. Co. v. Shane, 157 U.S. 348. . . . "[F]or it is, as Blackstone says, an arbitrary and capricious right, and it must be exercised with full freedom, or it fails of its full purpose." Lewis v. United States, 146 U.S., at 378. . . .

The function of the challenge is not only to eliminate extremes of partiality on both sides, but to assure the parties that the jurors before whom they try the case will decide on the basis of the evidence placed before them, and not otherwise. In this way the peremptory satisfies the rule that "to perform its high function in the best way 'justice must satisfy the appearance of justice.'" In re Murchison, 349 U.S. 133, 136. . . . Indeed the very availability of peremptories allows counsel to ascertain the possibility of bias through probing questions on the voir dire and facilitates the exercise of challenges for cause by removing the fear of incurring a juror's hostility through examination and challenge for cause. Although historically the incidence of the prosecutor's challenge has differed from that of the accused, the view in this country has been that the system should guarantee "not only freedom from any bias against the accused, but also from any prejudice against his prosecution. Between him and the state the scales are to be evenly held." Hayes v. State of Missouri, 120 U.S. 68, 70. . . .

The essential nature of the peremptory challenge is that it is one exercised without a reason stated, without inquiry and without being subject to the court's control. . . . While challenges for cause permit rejection of jurors on a narrowly specified, provable and legally cognizable basis of partiality, the peremptory permits rejection for a real or imagined partiality that is less easily designated or demonstrable. . . . It is often exercised upon the "sudden impressions and unaccountable prejudices we are apt to conceive upon the bare looks and gestures of another," . . . upon a juror's "habits and associations," . . . or upon the feeling that "the bare questioning [a juror's] indifference may sometimes provoke a resentment." . . . It is no less frequently exercised on grounds normally thought irrelevant to legal proceedings or official action, namely, the race, religion, nationality, occupation or affiliations of people summoned for jury duty. For the question a prosecutor or defense counsel must decide is not whether a juror of a particular race or nationality is in fact partial, but whether one from a different group is less likely to be. It is well known that these factors are widely explored during the voir dire, by both prosecutor and accused. . . . This Court has held that the fairness of trial by jury requires no less. . . . Hence veniremen are not always judged solely as individuals for the purpose of exercising peremptory challenges. Rather they are challenged in light of the limited knowledge counsel has of them, which may include their group affiliations, in the context of the case to be tried.

With these considerations in mind, we cannot hold that the striking of Negroes in a particular case is a denial of equal protection of the laws. In the quest for an impartial and qualified jury, Negro and white, Protestant and Catholic, are alike subject to being challenged without cause. To subject the prosecutor's challenge in any particular case to the demands and traditional standards of the Equal Protection Clause would entail a radical change in the nature and operation of the challenge. The challenge, pro tanto, would no longer be peremptory, each and every challenge being open to examination, either at the time of the challenge or at a hearing afterwards. The prosecutor's judgment underlying each challenge would be subject to scrutiny for reasonableness and sincerity. And a great many uses of the challenge would be banned.

In the light of the purpose of the peremptory system and the function it serves in a pluralistic society in connection with the institution of jury trial, we cannot hold that the Constitution requires an examination of the prosecutor's reasons for the exercise of his challenges in any given case. The presumption in any particular case must be that the prosecutor is using the State's challenges to obtain a fair and impartial jury to try the case before the court. The presumption is not overcome and the prosecutor therefore subjected to examination by allegations that in the case at hand all Negroes were removed from the jury or that they were removed because they were Negroes. Any other result, we think, would establish a rule wholly at odds with the peremptory challenge system as we know it. Hence the motion to strike the trial jury was properly denied in this case.

III

Petitioner, however, presses a broader claim in this Court. His argument is that not only were the Negroes removed by the prosecutor in this case but that there never has been a Negro on a petit jury in either a civil or criminal case in Talladega County and that in criminal cases prosecutors have consistently and systematically exercised their strikes to prevent any and all Negroes on petit jury venires from serving on the petit jury itself. This systematic practice, it is claimed, is invidious discrimination for which the peremptory system is insufficient justification.

We agree that this claim raises a different issue and it may well require a different answer. We have decided that it is permissible to insulate from inquiry the removal of Negroes from a particular jury on the assumption that the prosecutor is acting on acceptable considerations related to the case he is trying, the particular defendant involved and the particular crime charged. But when the prosecutor in a county, in case after case, whatever the circumstances, whatever the crime and whoever the defendant or the victim may be, is responsible for the removal of Negroes who have been selected as qualified jurors by the jury commissioners and who have survived challenges for cause, with the result that no Negroes ever serve on petit juries, the Fourteenth Amendment claim takes on added significance. Cf. Yick Wo v. Hopkins, 118 U.S. 356. . . . In these circumstances, giving even the widest leeway to the operation of irrational but trial-related suspicions and antagonisms, it would appear that the purpose of the peremptory challenge is being perverted. If the State has not seen fit to leave a single Negro on any jury in a criminal case, the presumption protecting the prosecutor may well be overcome. Such proof might support a reasonable inference that Negroes are excluded from juries for reasons wholly unrelated to the outcome of the particular case on trial and that the peremptory system is being used to deny the Negro the same right and opportunity to participate in the administration of justice enjoyed by the white population. These ends the peremptory challenge is not designed to facilitate or justify.

We need pursue this matter no further, however, for even if a State's systematic striking of Negroes in the selection of petit juries raises a prima facie case under the Fourteenth Amendment, we think it is readily apparent that the record in this case is not sufficient to demonstrate that the rule has been violated by the peremptory system as it operates in Talladega County. . . .

The difficulty with the record before us, perhaps flowing from the fact that it was made in connection with the motion to quash the indictment, is that it does not with any acceptable degree of clarity, show when, how often, and under what circumstances the prosecutor alone has been responsible for striking those Negroes who have appeared on petit jury panels in Talledega County. The record is absolutely silent as to those instances in which the prosecution participated in striking Negroes, except for the indication that the prosecutor struck the Negroes in this case and except for those occasions when the defendant himself indicated that he did not want Negroes on the jury. Apparently in some cases, the prosecution agreed with the defense to remove Negroes. There is no evidence, however, of what the prosecution did or did not do on its own account in any cases other than the one at bar.[31] In one instance the prosecution offered the defendant an all-Negro jury but the defendant in that case did not want a jury with any Negro members. There was other testimony that in many cases the Negro defendant preferred an all-white to a mixed jury. One lawyer, who had represented both white and Negro defendants in criminal cases, could recall no Negro client who wanted Negroes on the jury which was to try him. The prosecutor himself, who had served since 1953, said that if the Negro defendant wanted Negroes on the jury it would depend "upon the circumstances and the conditions and the case and what I thought justice demanded and what [it] was in that particular case," and that striking is done differently depending on the race of the defendant and the victim of the crime. These statements do not support an inference that the prosecutor was bent on striking Negroes, regardless of trial-related considerations. The fact remains, of course, that there has not been a Negro on a jury in Talladega County since about 1950. But the responsibility of the prosecutor is not illuminated in this record. There is no allegation or explanation, and hence no opportunity for the State to rebut, as to when, why and under what circumstances in cases previous to this one the prosecutor used his strikes to remove Negroes. In short, petitioner has not laid the proper predicate for attacking the peremptory strikes as they were used in this case. Petitioner has the burden of proof and he has failed to carry it.

A dissent asserts that a showing that there are qualified Negroes and that

31. The prosecutor testified that on occasion he would ask defense counsel if he wanted Negroes on the jury; if the defense did not, and the prosecutor agreed, "what we do then is just to take them off. Strike them first." The record makes clear that this was not a general practice and the matter was not explored further:

"Q. Let me ask you this. You stated that the defendants generally do not want a negro to serve on a jury that is sworn to try him?

"A. I didn't say that. I didn't — they generally didn't want it. I said in the past there has been occasion here where that has happened.

"Q. Have there been any cases where they did want negroes to serve on juries in their behalf?

"A. I wouldn't know if there has been. Not to my knowledge, because I am not representing defendants. I am representing the State. Do you see what I mean?

"Q. Yes.

"A. In other words, that would be between attorney and client, privileged, and I wouldn't know what they wanted. You would have to ask these defense attorneys about that."

none have served makes out a prima facie case of purposeful discrimination on the part of the State and that the continued vitality of Strauder v. State of West Virginia, 100 U.S. 303 . . . , as well as "a practical accommodation" between the constitutional right of equal protection and the statutory right of peremptory challenge, requires application of such a rule here. Where discrimination is said to occur in the selection of veniremen by state jury commissioners, "proof that Negroes constituted a substantial segment of the population . . . that some Negroes were qualified to serve as jurors, and that none *had been called* for jury service over an extended period of time . . . constitute[s] prima facie proof of the systematic exclusion of Negroes from jury service," Hernandez v. State of Texas, 347 U.S. 475, 480 . . . , as does proof "that no Negro had served on a criminal court *grand or petit jury* for a period of thirty years," Patton v. State of Mississippi, 332 U.S. 463, 466. . . . (Emphasis added.) See also Norris v. State of Alabama, 294 U.S. 587 . . . ; Harper v. State of Mississippi, 251 Miss. 699, 171 So.2d 129 (1965). Total exclusion of Negroes by the state officers responsible for selecting names of jurors gives rise to a fair inference of discrimination on their part, an inference which is determinative absent sufficient rebuttal evidence. But this rule of proof cannot be woodenly applied to cases where the discrimination is said to occur during the process of peremptory challenge of persons called for jury service. Unlike the selection process, which is wholly in the hands of state officers, defense counsel participate in the peremptory challenge system, and indeed generally have a far greater role than any officers of the State. It is for this reason that a showing that Negroes have not served during a specified period of time does not, absent a sufficient showing of the prosecutor's participation, give rise to the inference of systematic discrimination on the part of the State. The ordinary exercise of challenges by defense counsel does not, of course, imply purposeful discrimination by state officials. This is not to say that a defendant attacking the prosecutor's use of peremptory challenges over a period of time need elicit an admission from the prosecutor that discrimination accounted for his rejection of Negroes, any more than a defendant attacking jury selection need obtain such an admission from the jury commissioners. But the defendant must, to pose the issue, show the prosecutor's systematic use of peremptory challenges against Negroes over a period of time. . . . We see no reason, except for blind application of a proof standard developed in a context where there is no question of state responsibility for the alleged exclusion, why the defendant attacking the prosecutor's systematic use of challenges against Negroes should not be required to establish on the record the prosecutor's conduct in this regard, especially where the same prosecutor for many years is said to be responsible for this practice and is quite available for questioning on this matter.[32] Accordingly the judgment is affirmed.

32. We also reject the assertion that the method of selecting veniremen in Talladega County, with its lower proportion of Negroes on the venire list, when considered with the system of peremptory strikes establishes a prima facie case of discrimination. Absent a

Affirmed.

Mr. Justice HARLAN, concurring.

In joining the opinion of the Court I deem it appropriate to emphasize my understanding that the Court reserves, and does not decide, the question which in Part III of its opinion it finds not presented by the record in this case.

Mr. Justice BLACK concurs in the result.

Mr. Justice GOLDBERG, with whom The Chief Justice and Mr. Justice DOUGLAS join, dissenting.

In 1880 this Court, in Strauder v. State of West Virginia, 100 U.S. 303 . . . , one of the first cases applying the Fourteenth Amendment to racial discrimination, held that under the Equal Protection Clause, a State cannot systematically exclude persons from juries solely because of their race or color. Since Strauder and until today this Court has consistently applied this constitutional principle. . . .

The principles and reasoning upon which this long line of decisions rests are sound. The need for their reaffirmation is present. The United States Commission on Civil Rights in its 1961 Report, Justice 103, after exhaustive study of the practice of discrimination in jury selection, concluded that "[t]he practice of racial exclusion from juries persists today even though it has long stood indicted as a serious violation of the 14th amendment." It is unthinkable, therefore, that the principles of Strauder and the cases following should be in any way weakened or undermined at this late date particularly when this Court has made it clear in other areas, where the course of decision has not been so uniform, that the States may not discriminate on the basis of race. . . .

Regrettably, however, the Court today while referring with approval to Strauder and the cases which have followed, seriously impairs their authority and creates additional barriers to the elimination of jury discrimination practices which have operated in many communities to nullify the command of the Equal Protection Clause. This is evident from an analysis of the Court's holding as applied to the facts which are virtually undisputed.

Petitioner, a 19-year-old Negro, was indicted in Talladega County for the rape of a 17-year-old white girl, found guilty, and sentenced to death by an all-white jury. The petitioner established by competent evidence and without contradiction that not only was there no Negro on the jury that convicted and sentenced him, but also that no Negro within the memory of persons now living has ever served on any petit jury in any civil or criminal case tried in Talladega County, Alabama. Yet, of the group designated by Alabama as generally eligible for jury service in that county, 74% (12,125) were white and 26% (4,281) were Negro.

Under well-established principles this evidence clearly makes out "a prima

---

showing of purposeful exclusion of Negroes in the selection of veniremen, which has not been made, the lower proportion of Negroes on the venire list sheds no light whatsoever on the validity of the peremptory strike system or on whether the prosecutor systematically strikes Negroes in the county. Moreover, the constitutional issue in regard to the prosecutor's systematic use of strikes against Negroes remains much the same whatever the number of Negroes on the venire list.

facie case of the denial of the equal protection which the Constitution guarantees." . . .

Alabama here does not deny that Negroes as a race are excluded from serving on juries in Talladega County. The State seeks to justify this admitted exclusion of Negroes from jury service by contending that the fact that no Negro has ever served on a petit jury in Talladega County has resulted from use of the jury-striking system, which is a form of peremptory challenge. While recognizing that no Negro has ever served on any petit jury in Talladega County, that the method of venire selection was inadequate, that the prosecutor in this case used the peremptory challenge system to exclude all Negroes as a class, and that the systematic misuse by the State of a peremptory challenge system to exclude all Negroes from all juries is prohibited by the Fourteenth Amendment, the Court affirms petitioner's conviction on the ground that petitioner has "failed to carry" his burden of proof. The Court holds this because it believes the record is silent as to whether the State participated in this total exclusion of all Negroes in previous cases; it would require petitioner specifically to negative the possibility that total exclusion of Negroes from jury service in all other cases was produced solely by the action of defense attorneys.

I cannot agree that the record is silent as to the State's involvement in the total exclusion of Negroes from jury service in Talladega County. The Alabama Supreme Court found that "Negroes are commonly on trial venires but are always struck by attorneys in selecting the trial jury." . . . In response to a question concerning the operation of the jury-striking system, the Circuit Solicitor, the state prosecuting attorney, stated:

> Sometimes, it depends on who is involved in a case. We have been very fortunate in this county, we have not had any white against black or black against white. If we have — where we have a situation arising in a case such as that, in the cases that we have had — we have had no capital felonies, but, we strike a jury different from what if it was two white men involved or two colored men.

This statement, it seems to me, plainly indicates that, at the very least, the State — "we" — participates, in Talladega County, in employing the striking or peremptory challenge system to exclude Negroes from jury service in cases where white men are involved.

Also, the state prosecuting attorney testified as follows:

> Many times I have asked Mr. Love for instance, I would say there are so many colored men on this jury venire, do you want to use any of them, and he would say, my client doesn't want them, or we don't see fit to use them. And then if I didn't see fit to use them, then we would take them off. We would strike them first or take them off. . . .
>
> If I am trying a case for the State, I will ask them what is their wish, do they want them [Negro jurors], and they will as a rule discuss it with their client, and then they will say, we don't want them. If we are not going to want them, if he

doesn't want them, and if I don't want them, what we do then is just take them off. Strike them first.

These quotations show either that the State "many times" abandons even the facade of the jury-striking system and agrees with the defense to remove all Negroes as a class from the jury lists even before the striking begins, or that pursuant to an agreement the State directly participates in the striking system to remove Negroes from the venire. Indeed the Court recognizes that "[a]pparently in some cases, the prosecution agreed with the defense to remove Negroes." . . . The Court, however, goes on to state that "[t]he record makes clear that this was not a general practice. . . ." With all deference, it seems clear to me that the record statement quoted by the Court to support this conclusion, cuts against rather than in favor of the Court's statement and inference that the general practice was not to exclude Negroes by agreement between the prosecution and defense or by the State acting alone. The prosecutor, in the quoted statement, denied that he had stated that Negro defendants "generally do not want" Negroes to serve on juries and stated that there had only "been occasion here when that has happened." . . . Since it is undisputed that no Negro has ever served on a jury in the history of the county, and a great number of cases have involved Negroes, the only logical conclusion from the record statement that only on occasion have Negro defendants desired to exclude Negroes from jury service, is that in a good many cases Negroes have been excluded by the state prosecutor, either acting alone or as a participant in arranging agreements with the defense.[2]

Moreover, the record shows that in one case, the only one apparently in the history of the county where the State offered Negroes an opportunity to sit on a petit jury, the state prosecutor offered a Negro accused an all-Negro jury where the case involved an alleged crime against another Negro. The offer was refused but it tends to confirm the conclusion that the State joins in systematically excluding Negroes from jury service because it objects to any mixing of Negro and white jurors and to a Negro sitting in a case in which a white man is in any way involved.

Furthermore, the State concededly is responsible for the selection of the jury venire. As the Court recognizes, . . . the evidence showed that while Negroes represent 26% of the population generally available to be called for

2. I believe that the record shows that agreement between the State and the defense to exclude Negroes has occurred "many times." The Court itself admits that at least "in some cases, the prosecution agreed with the defense to remove Negroes." Ante, at 838. It concludes, however, that this is not sufficient on the ground that "[t]here is no evidence, however, of what the prosecution did or did not do *on its own account* in any cases other than the one at bar." Ibid. (Emphasis added.) This Court, however, has never held in any case involving racial discrimination under the Fourteenth Amendment that such discrimination is unconstitutional only if it is brought about by the State acting *alone*. The test which has been applied is whether the State "to some significant extent . . . has been . . . involved." Burton v. Wilmington Parking Authority, 365 U.S. 715, 722. See Peterson v. City of Greenville, 373 U.S. 244; Lombard v. State of Louisiana, 373 U.S. 267.

jury service in Talladega County, Negroes constituted a lesser proportion, generally estimated from 10% to 15%, of the average venire. The Alabama Supreme Court noted that under state law "the jury commission is required to keep a roll containing the names of all male citizens living in the county who possess the qualifications prescribed by law and who are not exempted by law from serving on juries," . . . and, in fact, this had not been done in Talladega County. The Alabama Supreme Court concluded that the method of jury selection in Talladega County was "not exhaustive enough to insure the inclusion of all qualified persons," . . . and this Court admits it is "imperfect," . . . and that "[v]enires drawn from the jury box made up in this manner unquestionably contained a smaller proportion of the Negro community than of the white community." . . . It may be, for the reasons stated by the Court, that this "haphazard" method of jury selection standing alone as an alleged constitutional violation does not show unlawful jury discrimination. However, this method of venire selection cannot be viewed in isolation and must be considered in connection with the peremptory challenge system with which it is inextricably bound. When this is done it is evident that the maintenance by the State of the disproportionately low number of Negroes on jury panels enables the prosecutor, alone or in agreement with defense attorneys, to strike all Negroes from panels without materially impairing the number of peremptory challenges available for trial strategy purposes.

Finally, it is clear that Negroes were removed from the venire and excluded from service by the prosecutor's use of the peremptory challenge system in this case and that they have never served on the jury in any case in the history of the county. On these facts, and the inferences reasonably drawn from them, it seems clear that petitioner has affirmatively proved a pattern of racial discrimination in which the State is significantly involved, cf. Burton v. Wilmington Parking Authority, 365 U.S. 715, 722. . . .

There is, however, a more fundamental defect in the Court's holding. Even if the Court were correct that the record is silent as to state involvement in previous cases in which Negroes have been systematically excluded from jury service, nevertheless, it is undisputed that no Negro has ever served on any petit jury in the history of Talladega County. Under Norris, Patton and the other cases discussed above, it is clear that petitioner by proving this made out a prima facie case of unlawful jury exclusion. The burden of proof then shifted to the State to prove, if it could, that this exclusion was brought about for some reason other than racial discrimination in which the State participated. . . .

Despite the fact that the petitioner therefore has made out what is, under the settled decisions of this Court, a prima facie case of jury exclusion which the State has not rebutted, the Court today affirms petitioner's conviction because, according to the Court, petitioner has "failed to carry" his burden of proof. . . . The Court concedes that if this case involved exclusion of Negroes from jury panels, under Norris and Patton a prima facie case of unconstitutional jury exclusion would be made out. However, the Court argues that because this case involved exclusion from the jury itself and not from the jury venire, the burden of proof on a defendant should be greater. This distinction is novel to say the least.

The Court's jury decisions, read together, have never distinguished between exclusion from the jury panel and exclusion from the jury itself. Indeed, no such distinction can be drawn. The very point of all these cases is to prevent that deliberate and systematic discrimination against Negroes or any other racial group that would prevent them, not merely from being placed upon the panel, but from serving on the jury. The Court quotes from Hernandez v. State of Texas, supra, to show that the prima facie rule applies only where no Negro "*had been called* for jury service," ante, at 839, but such a view is rejected by Patton's statement of the rule, for Patton held that a prima facie case was made out when it was shown that "no Negro had *served* on a criminal court grand or petit jury for a period of thirty years." 332 U.S., at 466. . . . (Emphasis added.) And, Patton is confirmed by our very recent cases. Eubanks v. State of Louisiana [356 U.S. 584 (1958)], and Arnold v. North Carolina [376 U.S. 773 (1964)], which also speak only in terms of jury "service" and jury "duty." [*Sic*] "The exclusion of otherwise eligible persons from jury *service* solely because of their ancestry or national origin is discrimination prohibited by the Fourteenth Amendment." Hernandez v. State of Texas, supra, 347 U.S., at 479. . . . (Emphasis added.)

The rule of exclusion set forth in these cases is a highly pragmatic one. It is designed to operate in jury cases so that once the defendant has made a showing of total exclusion, the burden of going forward with the evidence is placed upon the State, the party in the better position to develop the facts as to how the exclusion came about. The defendant is a party to one proceeding only, and his access to relevant evidence is obviously limited. The State is a party to all criminal cases and has greater access to the evidence, if any, which would tend to negative the State's involvement in discriminatory jury selection. . . .

Finally, the Court's reasoning on this point completely overlooks the fact that the total exclusion of Negroes from juries in Talladega County results from the interlocking of an inadequate venire selection system, for which the State concededly is responsible, and the use of peremptory challenges. All of these factors confirm my view that no good reason exists to fashion a new rule of burden of proof, which will make it more difficult to put an end to discriminatory selection of juries on racial grounds and will thereby impair the constitutional promise of "Equal Protection of the Laws," made effective by Strauder and the cases which follow it. By undermining the doctrine of the prima facie case while paying lip service to Strauder the Court today allies itself with those "that keep the word of promise to our ear and break it to our hope."

The Court departs from the long-established burden of proof rule in this area, and imposes substantial additional burdens upon Negro defendants such as petitioner, because of its view of the importance of retaining inviolate the right of the State to use peremptory challenges. I believe, however, that the preference granted by the Court to the State's use of the peremptory challenge is both unwarranted and unnecessary.

[Justice Goldberg quotes Blackstone to the effect that the purpose of the peremptory challenge was to confer a benefit on defendants.]

While peremptory challenges are commonly used in this country both by the prosecution and by the defense, we have long recognized that the right to challenge peremptorily is not a fundamental right, constitutionally guaranteed, even as applied to a defendant, much less to the State. Stilson v. United States, 250 U.S. 583. . . . This Court has sanctioned numerous incursions upon the right to challenge peremptorily. Defendants may be tried together even though the exercise by one of his right to challenge peremptorily may deprive his codefendant of a juror he desires or may require that codefendant to use his challenges in a way other than he wishes. . . . A defendant may be required to exercise his challenges prior to the State, so that some may be wasted on jurors whom the State would have challenged. Pointer v. United States, 151 U.S. 396. . . . Congress may regulate the number of peremptory challenges available to defendants by statute and may require codefendants to be treated as a single defendant so that each has only a small portion of the number of peremptories he would have if tried separately. Stilson v. United States, supra. In Stilson this Court stated, "There is nothing in the Constitution of the United States which requires the Congress to grant peremptory challenges to defendants in criminal cases; trial by an impartial jury is all that is secured." 250 U.S., at 586. . . . The Fourteenth Amendment would impose no greater obligation upon the States. Today this Court reverses Stilson's maxim, in effect holding that "There is nothing in the Constitution of the United States which requires the State to grant trial by an impartial jury so long as the inviolability of the peremptory challenge is secured."

Were it necessary to make an absolute choice between the right of a defendant to have a jury chosen in conformity with the requirements of the Fourteenth Amendment and the right to challenge peremptorily, the Constitution compels a choice of the former. Marbury v. Madison . . . settled beyond doubt that when a constitutional claim is opposed by a nonconstitutional one, the former must prevail. But no such choice is compelled in this situation. The holding called for by this case, is that where as here, a Negro defendant proves that Negroes constitute a substantial segment of the population, that Negroes are qualified to serve as jurors, and that none or only a token number has served on juries over an extended period of time, a prima facie case of the exclusion of Negroes from juries is then made out; that the State, under our settled decisions, is then called upon to show that such exclusion has been brought about "for some reason other than racial discrimination," Patton v. State of Mississippi, supra, 332 U.S., at 466 . . . ; and that the State wholly fails to meet the prima facie case of systematic and purposeful racial discrimination by showing that it has been accomplished by the use of a peremptory challenge system unless the State also shows that it is not involved in the misuse of such a system to prevent all Negroes from ever sitting on any jury. Such a holding would not interfere with the rights of *defendants* to use peremptories, nor the right of the State to use peremptories as they normally and traditionally have been used.

It would not mean, as the Court's prior decisions, to which I would adhere make clear, that Negroes are entitled to proportionate representation on a jury. . . . Nor would it mean that where systematic exclusion of Negroes from jury service has not been shown, a prosecutor's motives are subject to question or judicial inquiry when he excludes Negroes or any other group from sitting on a jury in a particular case. Only where systematic exclusion has been shown, would the State be called upon to justify its use of peremptories or to negative the State's involvement in discriminatory jury selection.

This holding would mean, however, that a conviction cannot stand where, as here, a Negro defendant, by showing widespread systematic exclusion, makes out a prima facie case of unconstitutional discrimination which the State does not rebut. Drawing the line in this fashion, in my view, achieve a practical accommodation of the constitutional right and the operation of the peremptory challenge system without doing violence to either.

I deplore the Court's departure from its holdings in Strauder and Norris. By affirming petitioner's conviction on this clear record of jury exclusion because of race, the Court condones the highly discriminatory procedures used in Talladega County under which Negroes never have served on any petit jury in that county. By adding to the present heavy burden of proof required of defendants in these cases, the Court creates additional barriers to the elimination of practices which have operated in many communities throughout the Nation to nullify the command of the Equal Protection Clause in this important area in the administration of justice. . . .

I would be faithful to the teachings of this Court in its prior jury exclusion cases and the view, repeatedly expressed by this Court, that distinctions between citizens solely because of their race, religion, or ancestry, are odious to the Fourteenth Amendment. . . .

Applying these principles, I would reverse. This, of course, would "not mean that a guilty defendant must go free." Patton v. State of Mississippi, 332 U.S., at 469. . . . For, as the Court pointed out in Patton v. State of Mississippi, supra, 322 U.S., at 469 . . . , the State, if it so desired, could retry petitioner by a jury "selected as the Constitution commands."

NOTES

1. The Court's statement in Swain that blacks were underrepresented on the venire by 10 percent is in error. Since blacks constituted 26 percent of those eligible by age for jury service, but only 10 to 15 percent on the venire list, the disparity was in fact close to 50 percent. In Whitus v. Georgia, 385 U.S. 545, 87 S. Ct. 643, 17 L. Ed. 2d 599 (1967), the Court found that the disparity between the percentage of blacks on the tax digest (27.1), and that

of the grand jury venire (9.1) and the petit jury venire (7.8), strongly indicated that the jury commissioners utilized opportunities in the selection process to discriminate. The Court noted that the mathematical probability of having seven blacks on a venire chosen from a jury list, 27 percent of which consisted of the names of black persons, was only 0.000006, but did not base its holding on statistical analysis. Rather, the defendant's murder convictions were set aside for the second time because the same jury selection procedure had been used in the second trial as had resulted in discrimination in the first.

Based on a record revealing serious disparities between blacks on tax digests and those serving in juries, the Court followed Whitus in Jones v. Georgia, 389 U.S. 23, 19 L. Ed. 2d 25, 88 S. Ct. 4 (1967), and rejected the Georgia Supreme Court's effort to distinguish the two cases on a presumption that because "public officers are presumed to have discharged their sworn official duties . . . we can not assume that the jury commissioners did not eliminate prospective jurors on the basis of their competency to serve, rather than because of racial discrimination."

In Alexander v. Louisiana, 405 U.S. 625, 92 S. Ct. 1221, 31 L. Ed. 2d 536 (1972), the Court again declined to rely solely on statistical improbability. From a population that was 21 percent black, a grand jury list was compiled that was 14 percent black. But only 5 percent of the grand jury venire was black, and there were no blacks on the grand jury that indicted the petitioner. The probability of such a result, had the grand jurors been chosen randomly, was one in 20,000. The holding that the petitioner had made out a prima facie case of discrimination, which the state failed to overcome, was based also on the finding that jury selection procedures were not racially neutral.

2. While, as these cases indicate, judges are willing to rely on intuitive notions of probability in deciding whether the absence of blacks from the jury selection process can be attributed to racial discrimination, they are much more reluctant to apply more advanced mathematical techniques, which are necessary in jury cases where blacks are neither entirely excluded nor included on only a token basis. In these "underrepresentation" cases, courts have not been able to articulate a rationale that defines what is meant by the oft stated notion that *some* blacks should have been chosen, when in fact some blacks *were* chosen. This problem, as Mr. Finkelstein suggests below, can be solved by the use of mathematical tests.

FINKLESTEIN, THE APPLICATION OF STATISTICAL DECISION THEORY TO THE JURY DISCRIMINATION CASES
80 Harv. L. Rev. 338, 350-353 (1966)

The mathematical test which can be used to determine the existence of discrimination is based on the probability that, as veniremen are selected, any given venireman will be a Negro. This probability is usually derived from the proportion of adult Negro males to the total adult male population. In each jury case, however, it has been urged that these population figures are misleading and that the absence of Negroes from venires or juries reflects a lack of literacy, of integrity, or of other qualifications required of jurors. Statistical methods can be fruitfully used here to determine the percentages of Negroes and whites it would be necessary to assume disqualified in order to account for the observed numbers of Negroes on venires. Whether these percentages are consistent with the education, status, and general qualifications of the Negro and white populations is a question which the Court can approach with some confidence since it resembles other factual issues underlying constitutional claims.

The Court has taken a similar but nonquantitative approach to the qualifications issue in the cases we have discussed. In the exclusion cases, the contention that the absence of Negroes from juries could be explained by their lack of qualifications was rejected because it involved the assumption (so the Court believed) that virtually the entire Negro population was unqualified.[47] "[A] race [cannot] be proscribed as incompetent for service."[48] Similar reasoning appears in the underrepresentation cases. In Speller v. Allen,[49] for example, the Court held that a discrepancy of thirty-one points between the percentage of Negroes on venires and the percentage on tax lists from which the venires were drawn could not be explained by the clerk's disqualification of Negroes for poor moral character. "It would not be assumed," the Court held, "that in Vance County there is not a much larger percentage of Negroes with qualifications of jurymen."[50] The same method of reasoning, using mathematical techniques, will be adopted here.

In certain situations it is impossible to determine whether the number of Negroes appearing on a series of venires or juries is consistent or inconsistent with the qualifications of the Negro population. This may occur when there is inadequate evidence concerning qualifications or when persons selected for service may be excused on grounds other than lack of qualifications. Those called for grand jury service, for instance, may be excused on grounds of economic hardship. Another example is the appearance of Negroes on petit juries (as distinguished from jury panels). Although in Swain the Supreme Court stated that the prosecution may not use peremptory strikes to exclude Negroes systematically, there remains a broad area of discretion in the use of such strikes or challenges which makes it virtually impossible to determine from population statistics, however carefully refined, the probability that a Negro will appear on a petit jury.

While in such cases it is not possible to use a statistical analysis based on the failure to select a greater number of Negroes, it is possible, at least in the case of venires and grand juries, to determine whether the number of Negroes

47. Patton v. Mississippi, 332 U.S. 463, 468 (1947).
48. Brown v. Allen, 344 U.S. 443, 471 (1953).
49. 344 U.S. 443 (1953).
50. Id. at 481.

selected, which I shall call the *distribution* of Negroes, is consistent with randomness. To take a crude example, the appearance of a series of grand juries alternately 100% and 0% Negro would excite our suspicions as to the selection process whatever the probability of selecting a Negro or white juror. Statistical decision theory provides a measure of the extent to which a given distribution differs from the theoretical or expected random distribution and a test of the significance of such difference. The test will indicate, within mathematically determined limits of accuracy, whether the nature of the observed distribution is so at variance with the expected distribution that the hypothesis of random selection ought to be rejected. . . .

In concluding that probability theory can usefully be applied to these problems, it has been assumed that the intuitive idea of probability used by the Court is conceptually similar to the mathematical definition used by the statisticians. Although the premises of the legal argument remain obscure, the assumption is a reasonable one, since the intuitive content of the mathematical definition is the common idea of probability. Thus the mathematical notion of an event with a probability of, say, 0.1 corresponds to the practical notion of an event that occurs on the average of once in every ten trials.[52] *

52. For a nontechnical discussion see Nagel, The Meaning of Probability, in 2 The World of Mathematics 1398 (J. Newman ed. 1956).

* Using a similar statistical approach to that advocated by Finkelstein, Professor Jerome Kirk of the University of California analyzed data compiled on the selection of grand jurors with Spanish surnames for several California counties. In a letter explaining how conventional statistical methods were used to compute the proportion of people with Spanish surnames who must be disqualified in order to account for the observed numbers of jurors with Spanish surnames, he wrote:

"The standard procedure for arriving at conclusions by statistical methods is called, as you probably know, 'hypothesis testing.' This is done by assuming something to be true and deducing the likelihood of observing any given outcome on the basis of that assumption. If the likelihood (according to that assumption, or 'null hypothesis') of observing what *actually has* been observed is sufficiently *low,* we conclude that the assumption is false: 'rejecting the null hypothesis,' we accept its contrary. It is conventional in natural and social science to reject null hypotheses which have probabilities of less than one in twenty of yielding the observed data. Thus, 'type I error' (i.e. — in this application — error of which the state, rather than the plaintiff, has standing to complain, viz. a finding of discrimination where there is none in fact) occurs one in twenty times.

"The null hypothesis in the case at hand is that every person in some population is equally likely to be on a grand jury. (This population is the population of *eligibles;* it is all residents of the county not legally disqualified by virtue of age, transience, or any other characteristic. I am not qualified to state how nearly it is the total adult population.) If this is the case, it is easy to see that if p% of the eligible population have Spanish surnames, 95% of the samples of N grand jurors will have at least $p - 1.645[p(100 - p)/N]^{1/2}\%$ members with Spanish surnames, since $[p(100 - p)/N]^{1/2}\%$ is the standard error of the proportion.

"From this observation, all that is necessary is to estimate p from the data, add to it 1.645 times its standard error, and we have *the largest percentage of eligibles having Spanish surnames consistent both with the assumption that there is no discrimination and with the observed data.* Wherever the percentage of eligibles exceeds this figure, the conclusion that there is de facto discrimination is inescapable. . . ." Letter dated May 28, 1968

NOTES

1. Despite their apparent relevancy to jury discrimination problems, courts have been reluctant to rely on mathematical computations, which require a knowledge of the subject that may be beyond the training of many jurists. In the absence of an acceptable mathematical formula, the standards in Swain v. Alabama have been relied on to reject jury discrimination claims in several courts. The cases are cited in United States v. Carlton, 456 F.2d 207 (5th Cir. 1972). The law review commentators generally have been quite critical of the Swain decision. A compilation of comment and an all encompassing analysis of jury discrimination problems can be found in Kuhn, Jury Discrimination: The Next Phase, 41 S. Cal. L. Rev. 235 (1968). In general, the writers point out that in cases prior to Swain — notwithstanding standards requiring only that defendants make out a prima facie case of jury discrimination, before the burden was switched to the state to rebut the charge — convictions were in fact usually reversed only where either complete exclusion of blacks or obvious tokenism was shown. In Swain, the Court not only rejected what seemed clear statistical proof of exclusion of blacks, but also virtually removed the prosecutor's use of the peremptory challenge as a source of jury discrimination, by requiring that defendant show that, over an indefinite period of time, the prosecutor has been responsible for the exclusion of blacks by his use of the peremptory challenge. The difficulty of meeting this burden is compounded by the Court's failure to provide more explicit standards of proof. At least in terms of access to evidence, it would seem more appropriate to follow the traditional approach to burden of proof problems; and, where all blacks are peremptorily challenged by the prosecutor, require the state to come forward with evidence to show that it has not contributed to discrimination in jury selection and composition, whether through abuse of the peremptory challenge or by other means.

2. The commentators' criticisms of Swain have been borne out by experience. Thus, in overruling a motion by black defendants in a federal case that the government discriminatorily used its peremptory challenges to remove blacks from the trial jury, the court observed, "In the six years which have passed since Swain, we have not found a single instance in which a defendant has prevailed on this issue." United States v. Pearson, 448 F.2d 1207, 1217-1218 (5th Cir. 1971). In the Pearson case, the only written records available were the prosecutor's retained notes, covering only the period during the week that Pearson and his codefendant were tried. Reviewing these notes, the court concluded "that the Government permitted Negroes to remain on the jury when the defendant was white, and challenged as many Negroes as possible . . . when the defendant was black." The Justice Department refused to admit the prosecutor to testify as to his mental processes in exercising his peremptory challenges. The court ruled that Swain permitted the

---

from Jerome Kirk to Don B. Kates, Jr., in Mexican Americans and the Administration of Justice in the Southwest, U.S. Comm. on Civil Rights, 131 (Mar. 1970).

prosecutor to be questioned only as to his conduct, not his thought processes, and observed that a contrary ruling on this question might require the prosecutor to testify as to whether he had committed a crime. (Title XVIII, §243 prohibits the exclusion of jurors on account of race or color.) In a footnote, the court suggested that "A rule requiring the keeping of a simple factual record by the court clerk or actual systematic keeping of such a record by the prosecutor, by defense counsel, or by some association would alleviate the difficulty." 448 F.2d at 1218, note 26.

3. The Supreme Court's reluctance to interfere with the use of the peremptory challenge is based in part on the sound premise that attorneys must be allowed to exercise their discretion in removing jurors for valid, trial-related reasons. But, according to one writer, the Court's conclusion that the occasional striking of black jurors by defense attorneys absolves the state of involvement in jury discrimination, ignores "the fact that racial discrimination is built into and pervades the entire power structure of southern society, and that the defense attorney in the vast majority of cases is himself a member of the white power structure." Comment, Swain v. Alabama: A Constitutional Blueprint for the Perpetuation of the All-White Jury, 52 Va. L. Rev. 1157 at 1162 (1966). The same writer charges that in Swain the Court "blind[ed] itself to the continuing total white control of the processes of justice in most of the South." Id. at 1159.

4. Any attempt to supervise the prosecution's use of the peremptory challenge would, of course, pose administrative problems. Application of the exclusionary rule could be easily circumvented, by prosecutors who let enough blacks remain on juries in unimportant cases to preclude a finding of tokenism. It has been suggested that a better approach would be to require more adequate representation of blacks on the venire, thus making it more difficult for prosecutors to remove all blacks from juries. Note, Fair Jury Selection Procedures, 75 Yale L.J. 322 at 325 (1965). Again, the purpose of such a requirement could be undermined by state legislation increasing the number of peremptory challenges available to the prosecutor. Moreover, the absence of a nondiscriminatory source of names of prospective jurors might preclude adequate representation on the venire. Even voter lists might not be sufficiently representative, despite the impact of the 1965 Voting Rights Act. See Broadway v. Culpepper, 439 F.2d 1253 (5th Cir. 1971).

QUESTIONS

1. Is the reluctance of courts to rely on mathematical experts in jury discrimination cases involving underrepresentation reasonable? Are there alternative methods by which defense counsel can show jury discrimination in such cases?

2. Consider the court's suggestion in United States v. Pearson, supra, that court clerks, prosecutors, or defense counsel maintain records of the race of persons peremptorily challenged. Could courts where jury discrimination has been found in the past be required to keep such records?

3. *Might jury challenges be better made in affirmative suits by citizens alleging denial of their right not to be excluded from jury service on a racial basis? In reading the cases that follow, consider whether plaintiffs, most of whom are not facing criminal prosecution, proved more successful in achieving real reform in jury selection practices.*

CARTER v. JURY COMMISSION of GREENE COUNTY, 396 U.S. 320, 90 S. Ct. 518, 24 L. Ed. 2d 549 (1970). Carter, and its companion case Turner v. Fouche, summarized below, were the first affirmative jury challenges to reach the Supreme Court.

Black citizens of Greene County, Alabama brought a class action against officials who administered the state jury selection laws, alleging systematic exclusion of blacks from grand and petit juries, and seeking declaratory and injunctive relief, including an order requiring that all eligible blacks be placed on the jury rolls and that the jury commissioners be appointed on a nondiscriminatory basis. The district court enjoined systematic exclusion of blacks and ordered that a new jury list be filed within sixty days, but refused to enjoin enforcement of the challenged statutes or to order appointment of new jury commissioners.

The Supreme Court recognized the standing of the plaintiffs to bring suit:

> People excluded from juries because of their race are as much aggrieved as those indicted and tried by juries chosen under a system of racial exclusion. . . . Once the State chooses to provide grand and petit juries . . . it must hew to federal constitutional criteria in ensuring that the selection of membership is free of racial bias. (396 U.S. at 329-330.)

Nevertheless, the statute which provided that in the jury box be placed names of citizens who are "generally reputed to be honest and intelligent and are esteemed in the community for their integrity, good character and sound judgment," 396 U.S. at 232, was not deemed invalid on its face. The Court pointed out that the statute did not mention any race, nor was there any evidence that it was racially motivated. "[T]he Constitution does not forbid the States to prescribe relevant gratifications for their jurors. The States remain free to confine the selection to citizens, to persons meeting specified qualifications of age and educational attainment, and to those possessing good intelligence, sound judgment, and fair character." 396 U.S. at 332.

The Court also rejected the contention that the district court should have ordered the appointment of blacks to the jury commission. The fact that for many years no blacks had served on the commission did not constitute a prima facie case of exclusion because of race. "The appellants are no more entitled to proportional representation by race on the jury commission than on any particular grand or petit jury." 396 U.S. at 339. The decree of the district court was affirmed, with leave to the appellants to seek modification as changed circumstances might justify.

Justice Black concurred, in a brief opinion in which he stressed his belief that the Court did not have the power to compel appointment of members of any particular group to a body appointed by the State Governor. Justice Douglas, dissenting in part, took the position that only a biracial jury commission would ensure nondiscriminatory jury selection.

TURNER v. FOUCHE, 396 U.S. 346, 90 S. Ct. 532, 24 L. Ed. 2d 567 (1970). In a companion case to Carter v. Jury Commission of Greene County, a black student and her father, on behalf of black citizens of Taliaferro County, Georgia, challenged the system by which juries and school boards are selected. The jury commission, appointed by the circuit judge, is responsible for selection of the grand jury, which in turn names the members of the school board, who are required to be freeholders. The plaintiffs alleged systematic underrepresentation of blacks on the grand jury and sought a declaration that the state constitutional and statutory scheme was invalid, an injunction prohibiting enforcement of those provisions, the appointment of a receiver for the school system and a master to select grand jurors, and damages. The district court ordered compilation of a new jury list, which included forty-four blacks and seventy-seven whites, but refused to strike down the state provisions. In its final judgment, the district court permanently enjoined the jury commissioners from systematically excluding blacks from the grand jury system.

The challenged constitutional and statutory provisions gave discretion to the circuit court judge to exclude from the jury commission anyone he did not think "discreet," and empowered the jury commissioners to exclude from grand jury service those they did not think "upright" and "intelligent." The Supreme Court agreed with the district court that this scheme was "not inherently unfair, or necessarily incapable of administration without regard to race." 396 U.S. at 355.

On the other hand, under long established tests for racial discrimination in the composition of juries, error was found in the district court's determination that the new jury list had been properly compiled. Only 37 percent of the names on the new list were black, in contrast to 60 percent of the population of the county. "In the absence of a countervailing explanation by the appellees, we cannot say that the underrepresentation reflected in these figures is so insubstantial as to warrant no corrective action by a federal court. . . ." 396 U.S. at 329. The district court should have responded to the disqualification of 171 of 178 blacks for lack of "intelligence" or "uprightness," and to the jury commission's lack of information regarding 225 names on the county voting list. These facts amounted to a prima facie case of discrimination, because "the disparity originated, at least in part, at the one point in the selection process where the jury commissioners invoked their subjective judgment rather than objective criteria." 396 U.S. at 360.

The freehold requirement for school board membership was struck down on the ground that it was unrelated to any state interest. "It cannot be seriously argued that a citizen in all other respects qualified to sit on a school board must also own real property if he is to participate responsibly in educational decisions. . . . Nor does the lack of ownership of realty establish a lack of attachment to the community and its educational values." 396 U.S. at 363-364.

The district court judgment was vacated and the case remanded for further proceedings.

NOTES

1. Following the Supreme Court decisions in Carter and Turner, the Fifth Circuit indicated its uncertainty as to whether substantial statistical disparities were "sufficient to raise an inference of discrimination." Black v. Curb, 422 F.2d 656 (1970). But the failure of jury commissioners to comply strictly with the provisions of a prior court order, to compile a new jury list representing a cross-section of the county's population, was held to constitute a prima facie case not satisfactorily overcome by the defendants. "[T]he method by which the numbers were reached condemns the result." Id. at 659. See also Stephens v. Cox, 449 F.2d 657 (4th Cir. 1971).

2. In Broadway v. Culpepper, 439 F.2d 1253 (1971), the Fifth Circuit relied on state law in holding that a grand jury roll, drawn from voter registration lists that were 37 percent black in a county where the population over twenty-one was 52 percent black, did not constitute a representative cross-section of the adult population. The basis for this holding was that the method of obtaining names for the jury list — namely, sending questionnaires to persons whose names were on the voter list — was inadequate, because only 60 percent of the questionnaires were returned and there was not proof that "the composition of the 40 percent remnant is comparable to the 60 percent available." 439 F.2d at 1257. Significantly, the voter registration list itself (37 percent black, 63 percent white) did not reflect the actual composition of the population. At issue also was the same statutory standard that the Supreme Court had upheld in Turner, requiring that the jury commissioners compile a list of "intelligent and upright citizens." The Fifth Circuit took the view that the existence of such a subjective standard required very close supervision of selection methods by the federal courts, and a detailed showing by the state of the reasons for disqualification of potential jurors.

3. In earlier affirmative challenges to jury selection procedures, the Fifth Circuit granted relief on the basis of statistical disparities and the use of nonrepresentative sources, Pullum v. Greene, 396 F.2d 251 (5th Cir. 1968), and on the failure of jury commissioners to comply with their affirmative duties to familiarize themselves with the qualifications of eligible jurors and to follow a course of conduct that would not operate discriminatorily. Salary v. Wilson, 415 F.2d 467 (5th Cir. 1969).

In the Salary case, evidence indicated that, while blacks potentially available for jury service in the area constituted 55 percent of the population during 1966 and 1967, the names of blacks on the jury rolls selected during those two years amounted to only 7 and 12.9 percent, respectively, of the total number of names on the rolls. The Fifth Circuit consolidated the appeal in Salary v. Wilson with Smith v. Goodwyn, an individual action filed by a black woman charged with murder in the Bessemer district of Alabama. She sought declaratory and injunctive relief to protect her against prosecution, on the ground that the indictment returned against her was void because it was a product of the unconstitutional jury selection system complained of in Salary. However, the Fifth Circuit affirmed the district court's dismissal of the Smith case, declaring that "The normal and most appropriate method for appellant Smith to question the validity of the indictment against her in the operation of the jury selection system . . . is in any criminal prosecution that may be brought against her in the state courts." The court concluded that, since it would assume the state officials' compliance with the order in Salary to reconstitute the jury roll and box in a proper manner, no exceptional circumstances existed to warrant the interposition of a federal court in a state criminal prosecution.

NOTE, THE CASE FOR BLACK JURIES
79 Yale L.J. 531 (1970)

Because of the way the jury functions and the extent of racial prejudice in this country, increased participation cannot involve token numbers of blacks. The charade of one or two blacks per jury may appease the white conscience, but it cannot alter discriminatory jury decisions. Although the minimum number of jurors necessary to resist a majority bent on conviction is a matter of conjecture, studies have suggested that the number is at least three. In other contexts even greater numbers of black jurors would be needed to offset racial prejudice.[30]

Tokenism must be avoided not only in the matter of numbers, but also in control of the jury selection process.[31] When the white majority controls selection, we can expect the selection of black jurors who reflect as much as possible the values of that majority.[32] This process may bring to the jury box a black person who is so eager to dissociate himself from the rest of his race that he decides against black people to appear impartial, or one who comes

30. The actual composition of juries constituted with regard to the principles here suggested involves a different kind of analysis, one that studies in a perhaps more statistical fashion how a jury actually operates, in terms of shifting coalitions, majorities, and the like. A good starting point is Note, Instructing Deadlocked Juries, 78 Yale L.J. 100 (1968).

31. Equally important as numbers is the temperament and economic and political situation of the juror. While on a particular case one very aggressive black man serving as a juror might be of little value, in the same case a jury of twelve black ultra-conservatives might be worth even less.

32. Of course, more than simple control of the jury selection process is involved. Black people are under complete political and economic control in many, if not most parts of the country. Physical intimidation is brought to bear when these subtler methods of control prove ineffective. Cf. United States v. Guest, 383 U.S. 745 (1966); United States v. Price, 383 U.S. 787 (1966); and Wilkins v. United States, 376 F.2d 552, 557 (5th Cir. 1967).

to the jury box under the assumption that he will perform as the white majority dictates.

These, then, are the parameters of the remedy. The jury system must be structured to produce a substantial number of blacks on juries trying cases directly affecting the interests of black litigants or of the black community.[33] In addition, there must be a pool of black veniremen large enough to allow the selection of jurors who are not white-controlled. Both of these conditions are necessary to ensure the appearance and reality of a jury system which works for blacks just as it does for whites. . . .

The Supreme Court considers equal protection to be equal opportunity rather than equal results. Though it has never considered the question on its merits, the Court seems to disapprove of considerations of race in bringing about a significant number of black jurors. It has acknowledged the value of juries representative of the community, but has allowed juries to be rendered unrepresentative by qualification barriers that have little to do with the jury function. Possible conflict between the interest of criminal defendants or civil litigants and the community have been inadequately resolved. In jury discrimination cases, the Court has never squarely considered the full range of problems black people face — problems requiring juries which represent black people.

Brooks [see infra page 978] and other Fifth Circuit cases have recognized that the significant question is whether there *are* blacks on juries, and not how legitimate is the means by which black people are excluded. The Court will find that meaningful black representation in race-related cases is constitutionally compelled when it accepts one or both of two principles. First, when black people are not represented on juries, the black community and the black criminal defendant or civil litigant are denied the equal protection of the laws; any process which results in the absence of black jurors is constitutionally suspect. While random selection may in some cases suffice,[80] any method of restricting jury service which is adopted creates a consequent obligation to ensure that that method does not result in the absence of blacks from juries. Second, in state criminal cases, any black defendant tried by a jury which does not significantly represent black people is denied a fair trial. The acceptance of either or both of these principles presumes that the Court will remove the hurdles it has set up. But whether black representation be achieved by constitutional command or legislative or administrative innova-

33. In addition to the obvious case involving a black person as litigant, criminal defendant, or victim, there are also cases not directly involving blacks in which there might be an interest — a few years ago, we might have used the example of a white civil rights worker. Cf., e.g., Rabinowitz v. United States, 366 F.2d 34 (5th Cir. 1966).

80. Random selection, of course, is satisfactory in very few situations; by ignoring important distinctions, it may work severe injustice. A randomly assessed tax would ignore disparities between rich and poor in ability to pay the tax. And wherever a system is structured to reach a desired end, randomness will be inadequate. If we wished to increase the numbers of blacks in college by providing scholarship aid, we would not distribute aid without regard to the race of the recipient.

tion, another, and equally crucial, question will remain: how large should the black presence be? Not "whether black jurors," but "how *many*?"

The number of blacks on juries is crucial both to the black litigant or criminal defendant and to the black community. It is true that a black defendant accused of a crime against a black victim would favor an all-white jury,[81] which would probably be more lenient toward him than toward a white defendant accused of a like crime against a white victim. But this is not a valid argument against black juries. The interests of the community are not here pitted against a legitimate interest of the defendant. No defendant has the right to profit by discrimination against his race.[83] Equally important as numbers of blacks on the jury is that whites do not control the selection process. Purposeful inclusion, though it properly ignores specious arguments against considering race in the solution of a racial problem, leaves control of the jury selection process in white hands.[84]

It is possible to solve the problem of both numbers and control. In Northern urban areas, jury districts could be redrawn so that each black community would constitute a jury district, or vicinage, the other vicinages being predominantly white. Juries drawn from vicinages duplicating the boundaries of the black community would be by natural consequence all-black.[85] In the Black Belt counties of the rural South, however, the black and white communities are not so readily distinguishable, and the problems outlined would not be solved simply by reconstituting jury districts. Here we would do better to require that every jury be proportionately representative of the black *population* in the vicinage.[86] In most cases this would yield juries that are at least three-quarters black.[87]

81. There are civil analogs. A black tortfeasor might get off with a very small settlement when his victim was black, because the jury sympathy which goes with large settlements — or a finding for the plaintiff at all — would be lacking. [See H. Kalven and H. Zeisel, The American Jury, referred to supra page 949.]

83. Certainly not all black defendants accused of a crime against another black will desire an all-white jury. The . . . New Haven Black Panther trial, in which fourteen members of the Black Panther party [were] accused of the murder of one Alex Rackley, a black man, may be an example. If an all-white jury were constituted for this trial, and were the outcome *not* lenient, we could safely say that result proceeded from antipathy towards the Panthers rather than from concern for the safety of black citizens.

84. The basic difference between white jury commissioners purposefully including Uncle Toms on a jury, and a system which, taking race into account, seeks an automatic black representation in meaningful numbers, is that of control.

85. The reconstitution of jury districts would produce the desired result, of course, only so long as other qualifications for jury service do not operate unjustly against blacks. The present constitution of Southern districts, for example, is already suitable to the vicinage proposal, but other qualifications and practices keep blacks off juries.

86. Not black voters, or blacks with a high school education, but black population. Of course, nearly all qualification hurdles — which have very little to do with the function of the jury . . . and which too often are unfairly applied or have inequitable results . . . — would have to be eliminated.

87. Greene County, Alabama, for example, is 81.3% black.

The problem of numbers and control could be solved in the federal context by dividing federal jury districts into sub-districts paralleling the proposed state jury districts in the North,[88] and paralleling counties (that is, existing state jury districts) in the South. Legal problems that black people face tend to arise where they live and carry on their daily business. By requiring that juries trying civil cases be drawn from the community where the cause of action arose,[89] and in criminal cases where the crime occurred, we could ensure that civil and criminal law for black people would be administered by substantially all-black juries.

This solution would not help the small number of black defendants accused of crimes committed outside the black community, in the North, or outside Black Belt counties in the South. But a great many more black defendants, to say nothing of the black community, suffer as a result of the existing system. The proposed system will ensure some all-white as well as all-black juries. The present system, however, ensures white juries and no black ones; it does not even ensure individual black *jurors*. To those concerned (perhaps in earnest) that this alternative may perpetuate racial polarization, it can be pointed out that as the society becomes less racist — if it ever does — the different vicinages become less all-white or all-black. The vicinage solution goes directly past the "racism in reverse" argument, and puts the burden of eradicating racism in this country squarely where it belongs. As society itself becomes less racially polarized, so will juries. Call it a test of good faith.

We might consider another alternative[90] which does not raise the problems posed by redrawing jury districts. We could establish a formula that makes the number of black jurors dependent upon both the degree to which race is central to the decision and the number of jurors necessary to bring about an equitable result. The formula follows the pattern of an ideal modern legislature, and requires that those interests most clearly affected by an issue play the major role in its resolution. A labor bill in Congress, for example, draws the AFL-CIO and NAM, but rarely the National Rifle Association. Serious problems arise, however, when we consider that interest representation would have to be restricted by the size of the jury and the number of jurors necessary

88. Jurors would be called, as in the state system, from the district where the cause of action arose. Federal jury districts would have to be subdivided, because when the area or vicinage from which prospective jurors come becomes too large to draw in a way such that it is nearly all-black, the resulting jury is no different from that of the present system.

89. In some cases — torts for example — the problem of defining the site of the cause of action would be easier than in others. The use of standard procedural techniques, such as change of venue, would have to be carefully scrutinized to ensure that the purposes of the reform are not defeated.

90. One other alternative can be dismissed out of hand: proportional representation of blacks on all juries in all cases, race-related or not, with respect to their percentage of the total population. It would yield only one black on every jury, and it would be impossible to ensure complete proportional representation of all elements of the community. (E.g., we'd need a half-Chinese, half-Indian juror).

to acquit, to convict, or to get a hung jury would have to be determined. Neither of these tasks would be easy,[91] and on balance the disadvantages of this formula would probably outweigh its benefits. The vicinage mechanism is much to be preferred. Discussion of how such districts would be drawn, and other questions of implementation, are topics for further analysis.[92] But it should be remembered that in the best sense, the Constitution is both "color-blind and color-conscious."

> How . . . is this constitutional imperative to be achieved in a society that still bears the ugly scars of decades of racial segregation with all of its discriminations? For it is in this social structure — not that of some hoped-for idyllic state when the last vestige of this invidious distinction has gone away — that the constitutional ideal must be made to work.[94]

It is in that society, with its cities torn apart by racial disorder, with lawlessness and violence plaguing the black community — that black juries are of such critical importance.

BROOKS v. BETO
366 F.2d 1 (5th Cir. 1966)

[The Court of Appeals for the Fifth Circuit, covering as it does much of the South, has decided more racial cases than any other appellate court, and as a result many of its opinions reflect a depth of understanding of racial problems seldom equaled by other courts. The very long opinion in Brooks v.

91. For the difficulty of estimating the number of jurors needed to achieve a particular result, see note 30 and accompanying text supra. Permutations and combinations with respect to interest representation could easily be pushed into the absurd, given the limited size of the jury.

92. The Borough of Manhattan would divide fairly easily into jury districts following natural community lines. We might draw lines to constitute five districts: Harlem-East Harlem; The East Side from the eighties to the thirties, and Central Park; the West Side from the seventies to the beginning of Harlem and all the way uptown west of Amsterdam; the West Side from 50th Street to the Village; and the Lower East Side. The first and fifth districts would be predominantly black and Puerto Rican, the second mostly white with a sprinkling of black professionals, the third and fourth black, Puerto Rican, and "ethnic white." Jury districts would have to be small enough, of course, to register the effects of shifts in population. Whites moving into a black area, blacks moving into a white area, or simple expansion of the ghetto and the consequent creation of new black areas would show up in the composition of juries drawn from a particular district. One undesirable result would be that the first groups of blacks moving into a previously white jury district would have only proportional representation to protect them. This is insufficient in many cases. . . . But this result is administratively preferable to constantly redrawing district lines. This is merely to concretize the proposal: obviously such an exercise cannot be fully undertaken within the scope of this Note. See United States v. Board of Education, 372 F.2d 836, 876 (5th Cir. 1966).

94. Gibson, Racial Discrimination on Grand Juries, 3 Baylor L. Rev. 29, 38 et seq. (1950).

Beto, illustrates how difficult it is to give affirmative meaning to the constitutional prohibition against jury discrimination. It is one thing to say that blacks cannot be systematically excluded from juries. It is quite another to determine how and by what method they should be included, and to determine what that inclusion means in terms of a real remedy for systematic exclusion.

Here, the purposeful inclusion of two blacks on a grand jury panel of twelve (the basis of petitioner's constitutional claim) not only was deemed appropriate and sufficient to affirm the conviction, but, in the majority's view, justified rejection of an earlier decision (Collins v. Walker, 329 F.2d 100 (5th Cir. 1964)), which reversed the conviction where the grand jury had five blacks and seven whites. The opinion is long, but reading it will provide a better understanding of how difficult it will be to achieve jury selection standards that minimize the effects of society's racism toward black defendants, without broadening current jury discrimination standards far beyond anything courts are likely to adopt. And yet Brooks signifies the willingness of some courts to grapple with the problem. The Supreme Court denied certiorari, 386 U.S. 975, 87 S. Ct. 1169, 18 L. Ed. 2d 135 (1967), which action, coming the year after Swain, reflects at least the unreadiness of the Court to insist on an across-the-board application of the traditional standard, reiterated in Swain, barring systematic exclusion.]

Before TUTTLE, Chief Judge, and BROWN, WISDOM, GEWIN, BELL, THORNBERRY and COLEMAN, Circuit Judges.

John R. BROWN, Circuit Judge:

II

Before examining the details as to why or how it came about, it sharpens the focus to state broadly that in the operation of the grand jury selection machinery in this case, two members of the list (who subsequently became two members of the panel) were selected because, among other reasons, they were Negroes.

The Petitioner, Brooks, a Negro, was convicted in 1960 after a jury trial before Judge A. A. Dawson, 86th Judicial District, Van Zandt County, Texas, for raping a white woman. Petitioner was originally indicted in August 1959 by an all white grand jury impaneled under a system that concededly excluded Negroes for racial reasons. Van Zandt County, located in the eastern part of Texas, had a population of about 25,000 of which approximately 10% were Negroes. Although the state trial Judge, in giving the statutorily required instructions to the Grand Jury Commissioners, had apparently instructed them from term-to-term that they were not to exclude jurors because of race, historically Van Zandt County had never had a Negro serve as a member of a grand or petit jury.

The significance of all of this was apparently brought sharply to Judge Dawson's attention by the January 1960 decision of the Texas Court of Criminal Appeals in Stoker v. State, Tex. Cr. App., 1960, 331 S.W.2d 310, in which a criminal conviction was reversed and the indictment dismissed because over the past 50 years no Negro had been included in the grand jury list. Aware that Jury Commissioners had not carried out their instructions to select persons for the list without racial discrimination, and thus that the indictment of Petitioner would not pass muster under Stoker, Judge Dawson appointed five new Jury Commissioners, one of whom, Mrs. Betty Smith, was a Negro. Judge Dawson, as his later testimony revealed, included Mrs. Smith on the new Commission for the purpose of complying with the mandate of the Court of Criminal Appeals in Stoker . . . . This new Jury Commission then proceeded to select and put upon the list 16 prospective jurors, two of whom were Negroes. Those two Negroes were among the 12 on the panel chosen by Judge Dawson. It was this grand jury which subsequently re-indicted Petitioner.

On the basis of that second indictment, Petitioner was brought to trial. His court-appointed counsel moved to quash the indictment because there had been impermissible inclusion of Negroes on the grand jury. An evidentiary hearing was held by Judge Dawson which included testimony from him and one of the Jury Commissioners, Cooley. The motion was denied, Brooks was tried and found guilty. On direct appeal, the Texas Court of Criminal Appeals, on rehearing, Judge Davidson dissenting, rejected this claim of unconstitutional racial inclusion. Brooks v. State, Tex. Crim. App., 1960, 342 S.W.2d 439, on rehearing, 1961, 342 S.W.2d 442. . . .

The upshot of this is, we think, that we must treat this case as one in which a substantial element of a collective body purposely selected two members for the list for the reason, among others, that they were Negroes. . . . Judge Dawson knew better than anyone else that the infirmity of the former grand jury was the total absence of any Negro on the list or panel — a result completely consistent with the historical pattern of that county. He knew also that this result had obtained over the years despite his recurring instructions to each new Jury Commission against racial discrimination. Suppose Judge Dawson had contented himself merely with repeating those instructions to a new Jury Commission made up solely of white persons of the white race. Suppose also that this new Jury Commission had once again filed its list of 16 persons none of whom were Negroes. Holding that such historical statistics effectively serve the role of making out a prima facie case, United States v. Wyman, 5 Cir., 1962, 304 F.2d 53, 65-66; Smith v. State of Texas, supra [311 U.S. 128, 1940]; Hill v. State of Texas, supra [316 U.S. 400, 1942]; Hernandez v. State of Texas, supra; Eubanks v. State of Louisiana, 1958, 356 U.S. 584, and for that matter our very recent en banc cases, make it quite plain that the constitutional mortality rate for such a grand jury list would have been high. For once again, against the historical pattern and the 90/10 racial composition of the county, all there would have been is the repeated protestations, unctuous or otherwise, of Judge and Jury Commissioners that the selections were made in good faith without regard to race or color. But judicial history demonstrates that such protestations would simply not destroy the prima facie case based on the historical statistics. Anticipating as he would be bound to do that the second of such grand juries would fare no better than the former one, Judge Dawson would have been required to ignore its indictments too. Then what? Was he to repeat this process against the hope that someday, someway, one of these Jury Commissions — aware of constitutional imperatives only as they obtained definitive instruction from the Court — would select a list with one or more Negroes on it?

Faced with this problem which was both practical and of profound importance to a community naturally concerned simultaneously about its peace and welfare and the protection of society through the constitutional prosecution of offenders, one obvious thing was open. And this Judge Dawson did. Breaking with history, he named for the first time a Negro to the Jury Commission. If — and there is no real if any more — the law is to see what all others see, Bailey v. Drexel Furniture Co., 1922, 259 U.S. 20, 37 . . . , is not the law large enough to acknowledge that Judge Dawson expected this to bring forcibly to the attention of all of the Jury Commissioners the vital meaning of his instructions against racial discrimination? Is it to the discredit of Mrs. Smith that, besides having all of the statutory qualifications for a Jury Commissioner, Art. 333, she was a Negro? What better way would there be to make certain that the Jury Commission, as an entity, is made aware of the names and availability of potential jurors, and especially those of a significant element of the community who historically had been ignored?

And what of the action of the Jury Commission and its members? Was it not entitled to consider Mrs. Smith, the Negro, both as a reminder of the court-instructed duty not to discriminate on account of race and, at the same time, as the most likely adviser as to the source of prospective Negroes qualified for jury selection? And assuming — a matter discussed in Part V — that there was an obligation on the Commission to make certain that in the list of 16 there was a fair representation of the community, how was this to be done without consciously thinking in terms of race when that community has, as a significant element, 10% Negroes who had, up to that time, been ignored as the victims of unconstitutional discrimination?

These are, as we have said, practical problems encountered inescapably in making a color-blind Constitution work. How well do these intellectually honest practical responses jibe with the Constitution? With the law and its obligations?

V

In answering these questions, we know first that it is a constitutional imperative that the jury, grand or trial, fairly represent the community.

> It is part of the established tradition in the use of juries as instruments of public justice *that the jury be a body truly representative of the community.* For racial discrimination to result in the exclusion from jury service of otherwise qualified groups not only violates our Constitution and the laws enacted under it but is at war with our basic concepts of a democratic society and a representative government.

Smith v. State of Texas, supra, 311 U.S. at 130. . . . (Emphasis added.) . . .

And this concept imposes the corollary duty described in Avery v. State of Georgia, 345 U.S. 559, 561 . . . :

The Jury Commissioners, and the other officials responsible for the selection of this panel, were under a constitutional duty to follow a procedure — "a course of conduct" — which would not "operate to discriminate in the selection of jurors on racial grounds." Hill v. Texas [1942], 316 U.S. 400, 404 [62 S. Ct. 1159, 1161, 86 L. Ed. 1559]. If they failed in that duty, then this conviction must be reversed — no matter how strong the evidence of petitioner's guilt. That is the law established by decisions of this Court spanning more than seventy years of interpretation of the meaning of "equal protection."

Similarly, see Akins v. State of Texas, supra, 325 U.S. at 403. . . .

The cases — the long, long line of cases borne of a century's struggle against this evil of race discrimination — make quite clear that this duty is not one to be exercised in the abstract. On the contrary, it is the reality of the world, indeed, at times the segregated world, which must be kept in mind. As with the problem dealt with by us here, the constitutional imperative is the by-product of experience in finding a practicable means of overcoming the evil consistent with constitutional demands.

Thus in many of these cases, answering the strong prima facie case made by startling statistics, the jury officials have made two principal replies. The first has generally been that of protestation of innocence and good faith. But the Courts have consistently held that statistics speak louder than the jury commissioners. . . .

The second, often a part of the first as an effort to bolster the sometimes unctuous claim of good faith, is the truthful assertion of the fact that more, or some, Negroes could not have been selected because the jury officials did not know of them, know who or where they were and hence knew no qualified persons from whom choices could be made.

But the law has never contented itself with any such hollow, shallow ignorance. To the contrary, the law — the very demands of the Constitution — so developed as to place a specific, tangible, identifiable burden on jury-choosing officials. It is not enough to choose from those they see. They must uncover the source of competent jury prospects from all significantly identifiable elements of the community. Innocent ignorance is no excuse. It neither shields the jury's action — verdict or indictment — from scrutiny, nor does it justify the half-hearted, obviously incomplete performance of duty by the officials.

The Court has long been aware of this see-no-evil — hear-no-evil — find-no-evil approach. Thus Mr. Justice Black stated for a unanimous Court in Smith v. State of Texas, supra, 311 U.S. at 132 . . . :

Where jury commissioners limit those from whom grand juries are selected to their own personal acquaintance, discrimination can arise from commissioners who knew no negroes as well as from commissioners who know but eliminate them. If there has been discrimination, whether accomplished ingeniously or ingenuously, the conviction cannot stand. . . .

We have adhered to this principle in United States ex rel. Seals v. Wiman, supra, 304 F.2d at 65-67; Scott v. Walker, supra, 358 F.2d at 573, and Davis v. Davis, supra, 361 F.2d at 773, where prima facie cases on the statistics became conclusive with the revelation that the commissioners had failed in "their duty to familiarize themselves fairly with the qualifications of the eligible jurors of the county." Cassell v. State of Texas, supra, 339 U.S. at 289. . . .

But inaction, evidenced by the statistics or by the commissioners' admissions that they have failed to acquaint themselves with the qualifications of Negroes, cannot be cured by the symbolic or mechanical action which some commissioners defensively resort to. Pointing to the presence of Negroes on the lists or juries, these officials assert compliance with their constitutional duty. However, guarding against sophisticated as well as simple-minded discrimination, Lane v. Wilson, 1939, 307 U.S. 268, 275 . . . , the Courts have been alert to discover from the commissioners' statements, thought to be self-serving, either ill-motivated or misguided action. On the one hand, the attempt by commissioners to avoid the prima facie case arising from total exclusion by systematically including a token number of Negroes is sure to be condemned. . . . On the other hand, though the Courts in speaking of the commissioners' duty to familiarize themselves with the qualifications of members of significant racial groups have emphasized that proportional representation is not required, the good faith but misguided effort of commissioners who failed to heed this caveat and aim mechanically at proportional representation will likewise be condemned as a form of exclusion in the guise of limited inclusion. Cf. Cassell v. State of Texas, supra, 339 U.S. at 286-287. . . ; Swain v. State of Alabama, supra, 380 U.S. at 208. . . . In short, neither symbolic nor proportional representation is permitted. Representation must be the product of either "the operation of an honest exercise of relevant judgment or the uncontrolled caprices of chance." Cassell v. State of Texas, supra, 339 U.S. at 291 . . . (Frankfurter, J., concurring).

Thus, the queries are answered: the Constitution requires (a) a fair cross section and (b) to attain that cross section, jury selectors must become acquainted with that community's human resources, which is to say, significant elements — significant racial elements — of that community. That cannot be done without a conscious recognition of that element's existence.

VI

Thus we are brought face-to-face with our prior decision in Collins v. Walker, 5 Cir., 1964, 329 F.2d 100, on rehearing, 1964, 335 F.2d 417, *cert. denied,* 379 U.S. 901. . . . What we declared the legal principles to be, rather than the result reached in that particular case, is the decisive thing. In a variety of ways, we declared that purposeful *inclusion* of Negroes in a grand jury list of twenty discriminated against a Negro accused and hence the indictment returned by a grand jury drawn from that list was constitutionally invalid.

Involved in Collins was grand jury selection procedures in Jefferson Davis Parish, Louisiana. Under the Louisiana statutes then effective, the Jury Commissioners were to compile a general venire list of 300 persons from which they were to select the names of 20 citizens qualified to serve as grand jurors. Once the Commissioners have compiled this 20-man "list of grand jurors," the Judge selects one as the foreman and 11 more are drawn at random by the sheriff to form the grand jury of 12. But the list of grand jurors was selective, not at random or by chance.

At the time of the alleged commission of the offense by Collins, the current grand jury had no Negroes on it. The Jury Commissioners thereupon selected a new list of grand jurors. The several Jury Commissioners, apparently acting independently, purposely included some persons because they were Negroes, so that out of the 20 on the list of grand jurors, six were Negroes. In drawing of the 11 names (besides the foreman), the names of five of these six Negroes were drawn, making the composition of the grand jury seven white persons and five Negroes. On this finding the Court, speaking through Judge Rives, had this to say:

> Six Negroes were deliberately included in this list of twenty because of their race. When to this circumstance is added the additional facts then known to the jury commissioners that the grand jury to be chosen from that list of twenty was to consider whether to return an indictment against Collins, and that no other case was scheduled to be considered by that grand jury, the conclusion becomes inescapable that in the organization of the grand jury which indicted Collins there was discrimination against him because of his race or color. 329 F.2d at 105.

This Court finally concluded that this broad and sweeping result was compelled by Cassell v. State of Texas, 1949, 339 U.S. 282. . . . Its reasoning is reflected by its synthesis of that 3-1-3-1 decision:

> . . . As further observed in Cassell, the grand-jury commissioners for 21 consecutive lists subsequent to the Hill case had limited Negroes in the list of 16 selected for grand jury service to not more than 1 on each grand jury. 339 U.S. at [282] 285, 286. . . . Mr. Justice Reed said that, "If, notwithstanding this caution by the trial court judges, commissioners should limit proportionally the number of Negroes selected for grand-jury service, such limitation would violate our Constitution. Jurymen should be selected as individuals, on the basis of individual qualifications, and not as members of a race." 339 U.S. 286. ". . . the Constitution requires only a fair jury selected without regard to race. Obviously the number of races and nationalities appearing in the ancestry of our citizens would make it impossible to meet a requirement of proportional representation. Similarly, since there can be no exclusion of Negroes as a race and no discrimination because of color, proportional limitation is not permissible." 339 U.S. 286, 287. "Proportional racial limitation is therefore forbidden. An accused is entitled to have charges against him considered by a jury in the selection of which there has been neither inclusion nor exclusion

because of race." 339 U.S. 287. Chief Justice Vinson and Justices Black and Clark concurred in the opinion of Mr. Justice Reed. Justices Burton and Minton concurred in the opinion of Mr. Justice Frankfurter, who said: "It (the Constitution) does command that no State purposefully make jury service turn on color." 339 U.S. 291. "The basis of selection cannot consciously take color into account." 339 U.S. 295. Mr. Justice Clark, also concurring, recognized the holding that there must be no "purposeful systematic limitation of the number of Negroes on grand juries," 339 U.S. 296; and "that representation on the grand jury by race in proportion to population is not permissible for there must be 'neither inclusion nor exclusion because of race.'" 339 U.S. 298. Mr. Justice Jackson dissented on the ground that the defendant had not been harmed by the method of selection of the grand jury. 339 U.S. 305, 335 F.2d 419-420.

That this result came only after a struggle with great difficulty is revealed not only by the number of opinions and the sharp division among the Judges.[27] But it is more vividly revealed by the Court's efforts to reconcile that result — this outright, flat, categorical prohibition against *conscious* consideration of persons by race — with (a) the demand that the jury be a fair representation of the community and (b) the obligation of the jury-selecting agency to acquaint itself with significant racial elements. . . .

Our problem, then, essentially is whether Cassell and the other cases so heavily relied on in Collins permit or require this principle announced in Collins. . . .

VIII

With Collins unsupported by its assumed reading of Cassell and the individual statements of the several Justices, we return to the beginning: the law not only permits, it mandatorily imposes its dual requirement — (1) fair representation and (2) the duty to know significant, identifiable elements of the community which have been the object of state discrimination.

How then is this constitutional imperative to be achieved in a society that still bears the ugly scars of decades of racial segregation with all of its discriminations? For it is in this social structure that the problem arises. And it is in this social structure — not that of the hoped for idyllic state when the last vestige of this invidious distinction has gone away — that the constitutional ideal must be made to work. The answer is clear.

To fairly represent the community, there must be an awareness of the make-up of that community. Even random selection from broad lists, such as voter registration records, city directories, tax rolls, public utility customer lists, and the like, inescapably requires a basic preliminary test: do each, or all, or some, give a true picture of the community and its components? Of course that condition precedent may be satisfied only by testing this "sample" against the known components — racial, economic, sociological, educational,

27. Three by Judge Rives for the Court, one special concurrence by Judge Jones, a special concurrence by Judge Dawkins, and a dissent by Judge Dawkins.

etc. It is inevitable, therefore, that jury selectors be *conscious* of those components. And where identifiable racial groups are significant elements, that means there must be an awareness of race as such.

But even more subjective is the demand that jury selectors make themselves acquainted with, not just the class, but the members of it in order to determine the identity and availability of individuals who have the qualifications for potential jurors and whose presence is required in the "universe" to assure fair community representation. Here again noncontroversial distinctions illustrate the process. In a municipality where, as is frequent, geographical areas — precincts, wards, sections — reflect significant groups, such as laborers, highly educated professionals or executives, those of lower incomes, the wealthy, or the like, jury selectors must first "know" that community. But they must also "know" the internal structure of such area groupings sufficiently to be able to determine identity and availability of those qualified to serve.

There are, of course, a variety of ways of going about this. One, obviously, is fairly to place on the juror-selecting body persons from or closely identifiable with such groups. The selectors thus serve the dual role as selectors and as the source of indispensable information. Another, broadly, is the establishment of a more or less systemized procedure for contacting responsible members or organizations within the class to obtain names or lists of names of those likely to be available and qualified. But whether one or the other, or some other variation, the process has a single end: to know the availability of persons in that class. The subject of scrutiny is that class. It is people within that class who are the object of the search. In the look and in the discovery, it is membership in that class which is the decisive thing.

When that class is a racial group and, moreover, a racial group which historically has been the object or victim of state-generated discrimination, the selectors can perform their constitutionally-imposed duty only by being *conscious* of that class. This means they must be conscious of that race. And they must be conscious that the system contrived or followed by them has as its conscious aim the supplying of persons of that race for inclusion in the "universe." In a setting where the presence of the Negro race in the community structure sets in motion the constitutional duty to know, a juror selector could fulfill that duty only by being aware of that race and the steps reasonably needed to assure representation of that race in the "universe" from which jurors are obtained. Not only may he do so, he must. Thus the conscientious Judge instructing the juror selector group would be on sound ground in formally charging the body in terms of the dual constitutional imperative discussed at length in Part V. Surely, the selectors would be within their rights in following such instructions. How then can it be said that conscientiously to do what the Constitution demands makes the result bad because race has been consciously considered to assure that race has not been the basis of discrimination?

That this perhaps poses difficulties in administration is not decisive. Few there are of the guaranties so vital to real freedom which do not daily pose troublesome problems — accommodating society's need for protection from the lawless with securing Fourth, Fifth and Sixth Amendment rights to the accused, or the First Amendment guaranty of free press, with the Fifth, Sixth and Fourteenth Amendment right of a fair trial, or the like. As in these difficult areas of constitutional rights, this one, too, is complex. The dual requirements making awareness of race inevitable must be met, but this must never, simply never, be done as the means of discrimination. It must never, simply never, be applied to secure proportional representation. It must never, simply never, be applied to secure a predetermined or fixed limitation.

Although there is an apparent appeal to the ostensibly logical symmetry of a declaration forbidding race consideration in both exclusion and inclusion, it is both theoretically and actually unrealistic. Adhering to a formula which in words forbids conscious awareness of race in inclusion postpones, not advances, the day when this terrible blight of racial discrimination is exterminated. The challenge is to assure constitutional equality now. This often means, as it did in this case, eradication of the evils of the past. That evil of racial exclusion cannot be ignored. It must be reckoned with in terms which permit, indeed assure, equality for the immediate future. The evil and the evil practices are not theoretical. They are realities. The law's response must therefore be realistic.

Thus the solution to this problem, as in many other aspects of civil rights, comes from experience born of the rich history of the struggles of the past decade. This Court has not hesitated to fashion judicial remedies to the realities to assure actual enjoyment of the constitutional ideals. In voter registration cases, for example, history taught us much. History taught us that it is not enough to forbid discrimination in the future. Sanctioning, indeed requiring, the use of freeze orders to wipe out the effects of past discrimination, we described this process of living law:

> Like decisions in other fields, this was but new material out of which, with much coming later, and in the best Anglo-American juridical tradition, we synthesize principles and sanctions which experience demonstrates are needed. This experience has been rich, abundant in volume, and instructive. From it we have learned that it is unrealistic to suppose that the evils of decades of flagrant racial discrimination can be overcome by purging registration rolls of white voters. From it we have also learned that unless there is some appropriate way to equalize the present with the past, the injunctive prohibitions even in the most stringent, emphatic, mandatory terms forbidding discrimination in the future, continues for many years a structure committing effective political power to the already registered whites while excluding Negroes from this vital activity of citizenship. . . . This experience has taught us also that if the constitutional ideal of voter rights free of racial distinctions — now over a century old — is to be effectively achieved, the relief required becomes successively more exacting as successive cases come to us. United States v. Ward (Louisiana), 5 Cir., 1965, 349 F.2d 795, 802.

Similarly, history — a long ten years of history — taught us that in school segregation cases time made increasingly more stringent sanctions essential.

. . . And the conscious awareness of race in extinguishing racial discrimination in jury service, no more than in eradicating racial exclusion in school attendance, does not itself become the instrument of racial discrimination. . . .

This is the law's response to the problem of today. Today we are dealing with the remnants of a segregated society being compelled to alter its ways to stamp out for all time this invidious distinction. As success is achieved and the constitutional ideal of a prejudiceless society is attained, the law will surely have both the capacity for and the duty of molding its relief to that hoped for situation. . . .

Affirmed.

Wisdom, Circuit Judge (concurring in the result):

I regret that I cannot go all the way with the majority of the Court.

Since a state may abolish grand juries without violating the Fourteenth Amendment, a state has considerable latitude in the type of grand jury system it may establish. Texas uses a small handpicked grand jury venire of sixteen. The system dictates the result the Court reached here; given the system, I concur in the result.

I applaud Judge Brown's eloquent apologia — but not when he discusses Collins v. Walker. I see no reason whatever for the Court to reach out and bootlessly overrule Collins.

I cannot accept the Court's premise that "the heart of the matter, the question facing us is whether we should adhere to Collins v. Walker." The result in Collins is right, dead right. Assuming the constitutionality generally of the Texas jury system, the result in Brooks is right, dead right. On principle, as I see it, Collins is not in conflict with Brooks. The facts in Collins compelled a different result from that reached in Brooks.

I. On principle, Collins is not inconsistent with Brooks.

The Texas grand jury system is based on handpicking sixteen veniremen. Obviously, in such a limited selection process the jury commissioners cannot meet the constitutional requirement that the jury represent a cross-section of the community without consciously selecting persons because of their race, color, economic standing, sex, and religion. To sustain the constitutionality of such a system, the Court must treat the Constitution as color-conscious.

The Louisiana jury system has three stages, three jury lists (except in Orleans Parish): (1) a "general venire" of 300 (the "jury box" or "jury wheel") selected by the jury commissioners from the parish at large and intended to represent a cross-section of the parish; (2) a grand jury venire of 20 selected (under the law in effect when Collins was indicted) by the commissioners from the general venire;[2] and (3) the jury panel of twelve, the foreman selected by the district judge and the other eleven drawn at random.

2. Under the spur of Collins, the Louisiana statutes were amended to provide for random drawing of the individual grand jury venires. Acts 1964, No. 161, §1; LSA-R.S. 15:180.

In Orleans Parish, as a matter of custom, there was and is a preliminary stage, a fourth list, a card index or pool of 40,000 names from which the jury commissioners select a general venire or jury box of 750.

Texas has only two stages: (1) the commissioners handpick 16 for the venire; (2) the jury is drawn from the list of 16. The Louisiana general venires of 300 and 750, not the grand jury venire of 20, should be equated with the Texas list of 16.

Louisiana jury commissioners consciously include Negroes in the general venires of 300 and 750, just as the Texas commissioners did in their list of 16 from which the Brooks grand jury was chosen. As a matter of fact, the record in Collins shows that in Jefferson Davis Parish, where Collins was indicted and tried, the commissioners regularly and deliberately included a number of Negroes on the general venire of 300.[3] Their inadvertent failure to do so in selecting the general venire for the grand jury sitting when Collins was arrested led the commissioners to make a departure from the jury system that opens the door to abuse.

Collins approves the conscious inclusion of Negroes on the general venire. On principle, therefore, Collins, in terms, is consistent with the conscious selection of Negroes approved in Brooks. Thus, Judge Rives said in the last Collins opinion:

> *[I]t may be that the "general venire list" of three hundred persons is required to reflect a suitable cross-section of the population,* and *that the jury commissioners have an affirmative duty to include qualified Negroes in that list.* If such a requirement and duty have once been met in compiling the "general venire list" no repetition is necessary or even allowed in the selection of the list of twenty "therefrom." Certainly, as to the list of twenty, the basis of selection cannot consciously take race or color into account. There may be a very real distinction in this respect between the "general venire list" of three hundred and the "list of grand jurors" consisting of the names of twenty citizens selected "therefrom." (Emphasis added.) 335 F.2d at 420.

II. The facts in Collins are completely different from the facts in Brooks and compelled the holding the Court reached.

At the time Collins was arrested there were no Negroes on the grand jury then empanelled for six months in Jefferson Davis Parish. There were none on the grand jury venire, for each commissioner assumed that the other commissioners would include Negroes and took no action himself. For this reason, instead of presenting Collins for indictment before the grand jury then sitting the parish officials *held him in jail for five months, then empanelled a new grand jury.* The new grand jury was drawn at random, as required by law,

3. The record shows that the trial judge had from time to time instructed the jury commissioners "to just be careful that there should be both white and colored members on the jury"; the clerk of the district court had instructed "that there should be some colored representation on each grand jury." 329 F.2d at 103.

from a venire of 20 selected from the general venire of 300. The venire of 20 included six Negroes who were intentionally selected because they were Negroes; five served on the grand jury.

The significant fact in Collins, distinguishing it from Brooks, is that the commissioners used the jury system in a way that is inherently dangerous to the fairness of the system and prejudicial to the accused, giving him standing to challenge his indictment.[4] By holding Collins in jail for five months until a new grand jury could be selected, the parish, in effect, maintained an all-white grand jury for white accuseds and a mixed jury for Negro accuseds. By treating Collins differently from other defendants because of his race, the state violated the equal protection clause.

We may assume that the commissioners were actuated by benevolent motives. The effect, however, was not necessarily benign. The second grand jury was empanelled *after* the crime and arrest of Collins. It is fair to infer that the five who served on the special jury were under the pressure of believing that they had been chosen because of their color and for the purpose of indicting Collins. The departure from the system as it was established by law and practiced in the parish presented the opportunity for undetectable "fundamental unfairness", in the sense that term was used in Betts v. Brady, 1942, 316 U.S. 455. The apparent tailoring of the jury selection to one particular case necessarily raises a suspicion of jury packing. It taints the integrity of the indictment and the reliability of the verdict. In distinguishing Collins on the facts, Judge Connally characterized the procedure as "salting" the jury for "a particular case":

> I am convinced that the Court [in Collins] was further of the view that this new grand jury was literally "loaded" with negroes purely as a defensive measure against a later charge of racial discrimination; *and that this grand jury was chosen in this fashion for the express purpose of considering an indictment against Collins alone. . . .* 241 F. Supp. at 745-746.

When courts discuss fundamental rights, some of which might be described as absolutes, it is difficult to avoid lapses into overbroad pronouncements. If the language in Collins is overbroad, we should cut the language down to size. But it is unthinkable that we should give our blessing to the method of jury selection at issue in Collins.

III. Brooks should be limited to the facts it presents.

The Texas grand jury may not be a blue-ribbon jury, but it wears a broad and bright blue stripe. There is historical justification for the system. And if a state wants a superior grand jury, one that carries prestige, and is capable of bringing competent presentments on county jails, county hospitals, and other

4. See Comment, The Defendant's Challenge to a Racial Criterion in Jury Selection: A Study in Standing, Due Process and Equal Protection, 74 Yale L. Jour. 919 (1965); Note, 78 Harv. L. Rev. 1658 (1965); Note, 50 Iowa L. Rev. 619 (1965).

local agencies, much can be said for a small, handpicked, elite grand jury venire.[5] But it is no great shakes as an example of the "basic concepts of a democratic society and a representative government" extolled in Smith v. State of Texas.

As I read Brooks, the Texas system would not be workable without quotas or proportional representation for minority groups. Even if the Texas system is not unconstitutional by contemporary equal protection and due process standards — there is grave doubt in my mind — it is anachronistic, a creaky sort of a vehicle to carry the great bundle of principles that constitute Brooks.

I do not follow the majority's view that the selection of two, and no more, Negroes, both chosen because of their race, cures the past evils of a discriminatory jury system. In these circumstances benign quota creates the appearance, not the reality, of non-discrimination. The effect here is to set a limit to the number of Negroes selected for the venire, thereby systematically excluding consideration of additional qualified Negroes. In such a system, the Jury Commission must concern itself less with the general fairness of the jury process than with the composition of each grand jury. This is exactly the opposite of the principle that it is the fairness of the method of selection that is important; a defendant is not entitled to have the members of his group or class represented on the particular jury that indicts or tries him. The only check is the good faith of the commissioners. The grand jury is virtually autonomous and the jury commissioners' selections depend on their subjective judgments. I do not question the good faith of Texas jury commissioners. I have no doubt that in Collins the district judge and the jury were also in good faith. I suggest, however, that the Texas system and others like it are made to order for subtle but effective discrimination in the guise of token integration. Brooks licenses such systems.

In view of the nature of the Texas grand jury system, the invitation it offers for abuse, and the general invidiousness of racial classification, I would limit the question in Brooks as narrowly as possible. As I see it, Brooks held only that in a jury system based on a small, handpicked grand jury venire of 16 the commissioners did the only thing they could do to select a cross-section of the community: they knowingly selected two Negroes because of their race. Thus limited, it is not necessary to overrule Collins: in an analogous situation, the Jury Commission for Jefferson Davis Parish consciously selected Negroes for its general venire.

The Court itself carefully limited its holding in Collins.[6] Collins does not

5. Vanderbilt, Judges and Jurors 62-66 (1958); Vanderbilt, Minimum Standards of Judicial Administration 185 (1949); Orfield, Criminal Procedure from Arrest to Appeal 146 (1947).

6. "We limited our holding in the present case as follows: 'The only list of importance to the decision of this case is the list of twenty from which the foreman was selected and the other eleven grand jurors drawn.' 329 F.2d 105. The question of whether it would be a denial of equal protection of the laws to intentionally include names of persons selected on the basis of individual qualifications and also on the basis of race in the 'general venire

mean that all standards or classifications based on race or color are unconstitutional. Each case depends on the facts. The Collins rationale that there should be no racial exclusion or inclusion on the grand jury venire of 20[7] is not inconsistent with taking race into consideration in selecting the general venire of 300 or *perhaps* to correct imbalance in housing or employment. . . .

[The concurring opinion of Judge Gewin criticizes language in the majority opinion that muddies the standards of jury selection clarified by Swain. Concurring only in the result, Judge Bell expresses the fear that the settled constitutional doctrine that a jury list must reflect a fair cross-section of the community (Glasser v. United States, 315 U.S. 60, 85-86 (1942)) will be fragmented by obiter dicta in the majority opinion into a "dual requirement — (1) fair representation and (2) the duty to know significant, identifiable elements of the community which have been the object of state discrimination." Application of such doctrine will prove "a fertile new ground for postponing the execution of sentences. . . . In the future careful counsel will not only test the jury list to make certain that it reflects a fair cross-section of the community: they will test the knowledge and activities of the jury commissioners."]

NOTES

1. Interestingly enough, Judge Bell's concurring opinion objects to the potential of Brooks v. Beto to better achieve the immediate tactical goal of jury discrimination challenges — reversal of convictions. As indicated previously, challenges to the racial composition of the jury are seldom raised and almost never taken seriously in cases other than those where the defendant faces death or long imprisonment. Not surprisingly, the challenges generally have received careful and lengthy judicial attention (whether or not convictions are reversed) where black defendants have faced execution for rape of white women. But the goal of a jury from which blacks have not been systematically excluded (particularly a petit jury, not, as in Brooks and Collins, a grand jury which can indict without a unanimous verdict) assumes that either the presence of blacks or their nonintentional exclusion will bring about a "fair" jury, i.e., one not tainted by racism. But does not the mere statement of the proposition serve to refute it? Can the achievement of such a jury either eliminate racist considerations in whites or relieve blacks of pressures resulting from racism?

---

list' of three hundred is not here before us and is not decided." Collins v. Walker, 1964, 335 F.2d 417 at 420-421.

7. It was a close question in my mind whether to dissent or to concur in the result reached in Brooks. I concluded not to dissent because the petitioner did not directly attack the statutory scheme; and because on four occasions the United States Supreme Court has had the Texas jury system under consideration, although never on the precise issue Brooks raises. As I see it, given the Texas statutory scheme, the jury commissioners had no alternative. They could provide representative juries only by intentionally including Negroes. . . .

2. Defense attorneys have developed elaborate sets of voir dire questions designed to uncover conscious and unconscious racism in prospective jurors. See Minimizing Racism in Jury Trials (A. Ginger, ed. 1969). Of course, such procedures require time, dozens (sometimes hundreds) of prospective jurors, and a judge with more patience than can be expected in cases other than those of cause célèbre proportions. Indeed, some judges believe that such questioning implies that they condone racial prejudice in their courts. A black lawyer, seeking to raise the racial issue with a prospective juror in a Bronx, New York court, was held in contempt and fined $50. Wechsler, "Whose Contempt?" N.Y. Post, Aug. 31, 1972 at 31. The contempt conviction was reversed by order of a unanimous Appellate Division Court on Oct. 13, 1972.

HAM v. SOUTH CAROLINA, 409 U.S. 524, 93 S. Ct. 848, 35 L. Ed. 2d 46 (1973). The conviction on a marihuana possession charge of a young, bearded, black civil rights worker was reversed, based on the trial court's refusal to ask prospective jurors questions relating to possible racial prejudice against the defendant during the voir dire examination. The majority found no constitutional violation in the trial court's refusal to examine jurors as to their prejudice against beards and the possibility that they were influenced by allegedly adverse pretrial publicity.

Speaking for the majority, Justice Rehnquist wrote:

The dissenting justices in the Supreme Court of South Carolina thought that this Court's decision in Aldridge v United States, 283 US 308 . . . (1931), was binding on the State. There a Negro who was being tried for the murder of a white policeman requested that prospective jurors be asked whether they entertained any racial prejudice. This Court reversed the judgment of conviction because of the trial judge's refusal to make such an inquiry. Chief Justice Hughes, writing for the Court, stated that the "essential demands of fairness" required the trial judge under the circumstances of that case to interrogate the veniremen with respect to racial prejudice upon the request of counsel for a Negro criminal defendant.

The Court's opinion relied upon a number of State court holdings throughout the country to the same effect, but it was not expressly grounded upon any constitutional requirement. Since one of the purposes of the Due Process Clause of the Fourteenth Amendment is to insure these "essential demands of fairness," e.g., Lisenba v California, 314 US 219, 236 . . . (1941), and since a principal purpose of the adoption of the Fourteenth Amendment was to prohibit the States from invidiously discriminating on the basis of race, Slaughter-House Cases, 83 US (16 Wall) 36 . . . (1872), we think that the Fourteenth Amendment required the judge in this case to interrogate the jurors upon the subject of racial prejudice. South Carolina law permits challenges for cause, and authorizes the trial judge to conduct voir dire examination of potential jurors. The State having created this statutory framework for the selection of juries, the essential fairness required by the Due Process Clause of the Fourteenth Amendment requires that under the facts shown by this record the petitioner be permitted to have the jurors interrogated on the issue of racial bias. . . .

We agree with the dissenting justices in the Supreme Court of South Carolina that the trial judge was not required to put the question in any particular form, or to ask any particular number of questions on the subject, simply because requested to do so by petitioner. The Court in Aldridge was at pains to point out, in a context where its authority within the federal system of courts allows a good deal closer supervision than does the Fourteenth Amendment, that the trial court "had a broad discretion as to the questions to be asked," 283 US, at 310 . . . . The discretion as to form and number of questions permitted by the Due Process Clause of the Fourteenth Amendment is at least as broad. In this context either of the brief, general questions urged by the petitioner would appear sufficient to focus the attention of prospective jurors to any racial prejudice they might entertain. . . . (35 L. Ed. at 50.)

Justices Douglas and Marshal concurred with the majority as to the constitutional necessity of inquiring into the possibility of racial prejudice, but dissented as to the finding that due process standards did not require inquiry about the defendant's beard or other factors important to his right to a fair trial.

NOTES

1. In the deep South, where blacks have long been excluded from jury service, there are indications that their inclusion — even in substantial numbers — will not result in major changes in jury outcomes. One civil rights attorney, Melvyn Leventhal of Jackson, Mississippi (Interview, Oct. 1972), reports that in several Mississippi counties, including Holmes, Madison, Cohoma and Jefferson, where blacks constitute as much as 75 percent of the population, the juries in recent years regularly have contained from seven to twelve blacks and never less than six. And yet these black juries are as likely to convict as all-white juries — even in cases involving racial issues where the criminal charges are "suspect."

2. In Jackson, members of the nationalist group Republic of New Africa (RNA) have been indicted for the death of a policeman who was killed in August 1971 during an early morning police raid on RNA headquarters. Mr. Leventhal reported that the juries in the first three trials contained, respectively, two, four and three blacks. In each case, the defendants were found guilty and sentenced to life. Lawyers report that black jurors are opposed to crime and tend to rely heavily on the prosecutor, whom they perceive as the law's representative. They explain that blacks, most of them serving on juries for the first time, are like the enlisted man sitting on a military court-martial. Both tend to bend over backwards to prove that they are fair, that they are "worthy" of the privilege of jury service. In the case of militants such as the RNA members, there may even be resentment toward such black "outsiders," whose rhetoric and threats are making life harder for those blacks who hoped for decreased racial tensions after the long civil rights struggle.

QUESTIONS

1. Would courts likely become more or less responsive to requests by blacks for reversal of their convictions, based on jury discrimination, if juries containing blacks regularly returned acquittals or were hung by black members?

2. What is the likely effect on courts of the indication that juries, even with three and four blacks, are willing to convict black defendants whose trials have political overtones? What is the likely effect on defense counsel?

NOTE ON RIGHT OF WHITE DEFENDANTS TO NONDISCRIMINATORY JURIES

The observation that rules designed to protect blacks from racial discrimination often serve to broaden the rights of whites, has had unexpected impact in the jury discrimination area. Following the Supreme Court's reversal of the dismissal and remand for trial of federal indictments against those charged with killing three civil rights workers in Neshoba County, Mississippi in the summer of 1964 (United States v. Price, 383 U.S. 787, supra page 868), defendants filed motions in the district court to dismiss the indictments, because the grand jury which returned them did not represent a fair cross-section of the citizens in the district, as required by Rabinowitz v. United States. On finding that the jury lists contained the names of no women, very few blacks and no Indians, and that no effort had been made to purge the lists of names supplied by registrars in various counties in the district, the court dismissed the indictments, but without prejudice to further action by a new and properly compiled grand jury.

In Rabinowitz v. United States, 366 F.2d 34 (5th Cir. 1966), the appellant, a white field worker for SNCC, was convicted of perjury before a federal grand jury that was investigating the use of pressure tactics on whites. Appellants in the companion case, Jackson v. United States, 366 F.2d 34, were blacks convicted of perjury in the same circumstances. Although no question was raised by the appellees as to Rabinowitz's standing to raise the question of exclusion of blacks from the jury list, the court noted that even a litigant not a member of the excluded class could challenge departures from the statutory scheme, because of the importance to a democratic system of a broadly based jury selection system.

The convictions were reversed, with direction that the indictments were to be dismissed. The court held that the purpose of the federal statute was to ensure that juries "reflect a fair cross-section of the community" by lowering standards of qualification, and that by applying "broad and vague subjective tests" of good character, intelligence and ability to understand the cases, the jury commissioners had defeated that purpose. "If a fair cross-section is consistently lacking, then, without more, it is established that the commissioners have failed in their duty." 366 F.2d at 58. In these cases, 34.5 percent of the voting population was black, but only 5.9 percent of those on the jury list were black.

In Peters v. Kiff, 407 U.S. 493, 92 S. Ct. 2163, 33 L. Ed. 2d 83 (1972), the Supreme Court for the first time considered a white defendant's challenge to the exclusion of blacks from grand and petty juries. The defendant had been convicted of burglary in Muscogee County, Georgia. Justice Marshall, in an opinion joined by Justices Douglas and Stewart, concluded that defendant is denied due process of law by subjecting him to indictment and trial by grand and petit juries that are plainly illegal in their composition, even if there is no showing of actual bias in the tribunal. In explaining his position, Justice Marshall said that the risk of bias resulting from illegally selected juries is not limited to blacks or perhaps white civil rights workers (Allen v. State, 110 Ga. App. 56, 62, 137 S.E.2d 711, 715 (1964), alternative holding).

> But the exclusion from jury service of a substantial and identifiable class of citizens has a potential impact that is too subtle and too pervasive to admit of confinement to particular issues or particular cases. First, if we assume that the exclusion of Negroes affects the fairness of the jury only with respect to issues presenting a clear opportunity for the operation of race prejudice, that assumption does not provide a workable guide for decision in particular cases. For the opportunity to appeal to race prejudice is latent in a vast range of issues, cutting across the entire fabric of our society.
>
> Moreover, we are unwilling to make the assumption that the exclusion of Negroes has relevance only for issues involving race. When any large and identifiable segment of the community is excluded from jury service, the effect is to remove from the jury room qualities of human nature and varieties of human experience, the range of which is unknown and perhaps unknowable. It is not necessary to assume that the excluded group will consistently vote as a class in order to conclude, as we do, that their exclusion deprives the jury of a perspective on human events that may have unsuspected importance in any case that may be presented.
>
> It is in the nature of the practices here challenged that proof of actual harm, or lack of harm, is virtually impossible to adduce. For there is no way to determine what jury would have been selected under a constitutionally valid selection system, or how that jury would have decided the case. Consequently it is necessary to decide on principle which side shall suffer the consequences of unavoidable uncertainty. . . . In light of the great potential for harm latent in an unconstitutional jury-selection system, and the strong interest of the criminal defendant in avoiding that harm, any doubt should be resolved in favor of giving the opportunity for challenging the jury to too many defendants, rather than giving it to too few. (407 U.S. at 503-504.)

Justice White, joined by Justices Brennan and Powell, concurred in the judgment, but suggested that the strong statutory policy of the criminal provision in an 1875 Civil Rights Act, 18 U.S.C. §243, barring exclusion of any citizen on account of race, be invoked to set aside the defendant's conviction. Chief Justice Burger, with Justices Blackmun and Rehnquist, dissented, asserting that defendant had failed to show that his conviction resulted from the denial of federally secured rights. The dissenters were particularly concerned that defendant first raised his claim on habeas corpus several months after his conviction was affirmed on appeal.

NOTES

1. The interest of blacks in having the jury discrimination rule made applicable to white defendants is reflected by the fact that an amicus brief urging reversal was filed by the NAACP Legal Defense and Educational Fund, Inc.

2. Significantly, the majority of the Supreme Court in Peters v. Kiff were not deterred by the fact that defendant had raised the jury discrimination issue neither prior to trial nor on appeal. At one point, such failure was considered a fatal waiver of the right.

3. Labat v. Bennett, 365 F.2d 698 (5th Cir. 1966), presented the question of whether a procedural default under state law could be converted into "a relinquishment of [the] substantive federal right" to a constitutionally selected grand jury. A Louisiana statute required that objections to the grand jury be raised before the expiration of the third judicial day after the end of the grand jury's term, or before trial, whichever was earlier. Under the terms of the statute, petitioners' pretrial motion to quash the indictments because of systematic exclusion of blacks from the jury venire and from the grand jury came too late. The court held that there had been no waiver, on the ground that, where neither petitioner had had effective and timely assistance of counsel, there was no "intentional relinquishment of a known right [or] deliberate by-passing of a known procedural requirement." 365 F.2d at 710. See also Hamilton v. Watkins, 436 F.2d 1323 (5th Cir. 1970). The convictions were reversed because the systematic exclusion of the names of daily wage earners from the jury wheel (general venire) operated discriminatorily as to race, and the state had not come forward with a constitutionally acceptable explanation for the disproportionately small numbers of blacks on venires.

The court notes that, as to the state's waiver contention, there certainly was not the "intentional relinquishment or abandonment of a known right or privilege" required by Fay v. Noia, 372 U.S. 391, 83 S. Ct. 822, 9 L. Ed. 2d 837 (1963). However, it added with some pride, "This Court, before and after Fay v. Noia, has consistently taken a jaundiced view of waiver in habeas proceedings in which the state has relied on the petitioner's failing to make a timely objection to the exclusion of Negroes from juries." 365 F.2d at 708, n. 14. The first of several cases cited by the court is United States ex rel. Goldsby v. Harpole.

UNITED STATES ex rel. GOLDSBY v. HARPOLE
263 F.2d 71 (5th Cir. 1959)

[Obviously, the rules in Swain v. Alabama and even Brooks v. Beto do not represent the final statements on the question of jury discrimination. And it is likely that future developments will result from litigation rather than legislation. Formulating the new principles will require the lawyering skills exhibited by George N. Leighton in what has become one of the classic cases in the civil rights field: an excellent example of how an able lawyer can structure arguments that a sensitive court can use to effect at least temporary relief against clear injustice.]

Before Rives, Brown, and Wisdom, Circuit Judges.

Rives, Circuit Judge.

On September 4, 1954, Bryant Nelms, a white man, and Mrs. Moselle McCorkle Nelms, his wife, were shot by one or more Negroes firing from an automobile after Nelms had ordered the Negroes to leave his gasoline filling station and dairy bar near Vaiden, Mississippi. Mrs. Nelms was killed. Later that same day, Robert Lee Goldsby and several other Negroes in an automobile with him were apprehended and lodged in jail. There was evidence to the effect that a .32 caliber bullet was removed from the body of Mrs. Nelms; that a pistol was obtained by the sheriff from appellant's possession when he was arrested; that the two were sent to the F.B.I. Laboratory in Washington, D.C.; and that there a ballistics examination identified the bullet as having been fired from appellant's pistol.

On his preliminary trial, the appellant was represented by Messrs. Tighe and Tighe, a law firm of Jackson, Mississippi. On November 8, 1954, a Grand Jury of the Second Judicial Circuit of Carroll County, Mississippi, indicted the appellant for the murder of Mrs. Nelms. By that time, an aunt who lived in Gary, Indiana, had employed George N. Leighton, Esquire, a Negro attorney of Chicago, Illinois, to defend the appellant. Mr. Leighton appeared with him on his arraignment, the same day that the indictment was returned. A plea of not guilty was entered. The attorney requested and the court granted time for the preparation of motions necessary to raise certain constitutional questions.

November 10th, allowing a lapse of two days, was set as the date of trial. Before that time the attorney had ready for filing a motion to quash the indictment on the ground that Negroes had been systematically excluded from the grand jury, a motion for change of venue, and a petition for removal of the case to the federal court. Before they could be filed, however, appellant's brother and a different aunt had employed John W. Prewitt, Esquire, a white attorney of Vicksburg, Mississippi. Mr. Prewitt told these relatives of appellant that he could not work with the Negro attorney, Mr. Leighton. They informed Leighton of their employment of Prewitt and requested Leighton's withdrawal. Leighton promptly advised the District Attorney and thereafter the court that he was withdrawing from the case. The motions which he had prepared were never filed.

The court then appointed Luther Ringgold, Esquire, a white attorney of Winona, Mississippi, to defend the appellant. Mr. Ringgold informed the court that relatives had employed Mr. Prewitt, and both Ringgold and Prewitt defended the appellant skillfully and ably, with the possible exception that they failed to raise the points that Negroes were systematically excluded from the grand jury and from the petit jury. The appellant was convicted and sentenced to death. On appeal to the Supreme Court of Mississippi, his conviction was affirmed.

Attorneys Ringgold and Prewitt took no further action and have not since appeared in the case. Attorney Leighton re-entered the case and applied for a writ of certiorari to the Supreme Court of the United States, actually urging for the first time the systematic exclusion of Negroes from the grand jury and from the petit jury. Certiorari was denied by the Supreme Court of the United States. The Supreme Court of Mississippi then fixed the date of appellant's execution for February 24, 1956.

Three days theretofore, on February 21, 1956, Mr. Leighton filed for the appellant in the Supreme Court of Mississippi a petition for writ of error coram nobis, or, in the alternative, habeas corpus, asserting for the first time in the State courts the systematic exclusion of Negroes from the jury lists. The Supreme Court of Mississippi held that the denial of certiorari by the United States Supreme Court was res judicata of the question, and that the application came too late since no objection to the validity of the juries had been made at the time of trial.

Attorney Leighton again petitioned for certiorari to the Supreme Court of the United States. The Clerk of the Supreme Court requested the Attorney General of Mississippi to file a response, stating, "The response should discuss particularly the issues of systematic exclusion of negroes from the grand and petit jury panel and the state procedure for raising this question in a post conviction proceeding." Such a response was of course filed. The Supreme Court denied certiorari. The Supreme Court of Mississippi again set a date for execution, this time for February 12, 1957.

On January 29, 1957, Attorney Leighton filed for the appellant a petition for writ of habeas corpus in the United States District Court for the Northern District of Mississippi, Greenville Division. Honorable Allen Cox, United States District Judge, after hearing argument but without waiting for an answer, denied the petition on the same day that it was filed and also denied a certificate of probable cause.

On February 8, 1957, a motion for stay of execution was denied by Honorable Wayne G. Borah, a Judge of this Court. On February 11, 1957, the Honorable Earl Warren, Chief Justice of the United States, granted a stay of execution "until petitioner has had an opportunity to exhaust his federal rights in this proceeding." This Court thereafter heard the appeal from the decision of Judge Cox and reversed and remanded the cause for a hearing of the evidence.

Upon remand the case was heard at a special session of the court before Honorable Claude F. Clayton, United States District Judge. At the conclusion of the evidence and after hearing argument, Judge Clayton denied the petition, expressing his views in an oral opinion as follows:

Third: The proof fails to meet the burden, as I understand it, of showing a "systematic and willful" exclusion of any member of the Negro race from jury service in that county.

Fourth: [Reviewing the record showing that petitioner had been represented by counsel at every stage of the prosecution,] the Court could not do otherwise than conclude, as a matter of law, that ample opportunity was afforded this petition to raise in the courts of the State of Mississippi, the constitutional question involved in this hearing, and undoubtedly if the question of the absence of Negroes from the grand jury and the absence of Negroes from the petit jury had been presented in the Circuit Court of Carroll County by a proper motion to quash, such a motion would have been sustained. . . .

The opportunity was there, the decision was made by competent counsel of the family's employment and of the Court's appointment not to raise that question and not to invoke that issue in the lawsuit.

Under these circumstances, the Court is of the opinion that the petitioner understandingly, in connection with his counsel, waived whatever right he may have had to present any question with respect to the composition of the jury, and that he, therefore, is barred from raising the question here or prevailing on that question being raised in this Court. . . .

Judge Clayton refused to issue a certificate of probable cause, and the Supreme Court of Mississippi again set a date for execution, this time for May 29, 1958. On May 27, 1958, the Chief Justice of the United States again granted a stay of execution "until the petitioner has had an opportunity to exhaust his federal rights in this habeas corpus proceeding." Upon consideration, we now grant a certificate of probable cause.

The present appeal is from Judge Clayton's decision and presents the questions of whether Negroes were systematically excluded from the grand jury and from the petit jury, and whether those objections were waived as to both the grand jury and the petit jury, when not taken on the trial. In so far as it pertains to those issues, the documentary evidence and the testimony of each of the witnesses are summarized at some length in an appendix to this opinion.

I. Were Negroes Systematically Excluded from the Grand Jury and the Petit Jury or from Either?

. . .

In the present case, the naked figures prove startling enough. According to the 1950 United States Census, Carroll County, Mississippi, had a population of 15,448 persons, of which 8,836 or more than fifty-seven per cent were nonwhite, predominantly Negroes. Of the nonwhite population, 1,949 were males twenty-one years of age and over. The median school years completed by the nonwhite population of Carroll County, twenty-five years of age and over, were 5.2 years. Yet none of the officials called as witnesses — the Circuit Clerk, the Chancery Clerk, the Sheriff, the ex-Sheriff who had served for twenty years, the District Attorney, or the Circuit Judge — could remember any instance of a Negro having been on a jury list of any kind in Carroll County.[18]

We cannot assume that Negroes, the majority class in Carroll County, had en masse, or in any substantial numbers, voluntarily abstained from registering as electors[18a] and, by such action, had rendered themselves ineligible for jury duty. If the registration officials freely and fairly registered qualified Negroes as electors, that fact rested more in the knowledge of the State. The burden was on appellee, as the State's representative, to refute the strong prima facie case developed by the appellant. The only Negroes ever proved registered as electors in Carroll County were two who had died before 1954.

We have called the figures startling, but we do not feign surprise because we have long known that there are counties not only in Mississippi, but in the writer's own home State of Alabama, in which Negroes constitute the majority of the residents but take no part in government either as voters or as jurors. Familiarity with such a condition thus prevents shock, but it all the more increases our concern over its existence.[21] When, in a proper case such

18. That is true even if full weight be given to the testimony of several of the officials to the effect that they were unable accurately to distinguish between whites and Negroes. That testimony tends to negative the sharp distinction between whites and Negroes habitually drawn in nearly all parts of the South. We would expect that distinction to be no less definite in Mississippi in the light of the decision of the Mississippi Supreme Court to the effect that ". . . descendants of Africans are classed as members of the colored race, regardless of the admixture, as long as there is an appreciable amount of negro blood found." Moreau v. Grandich, 1917, 114 Miss. 560.

18a. As has been said, in Mississippi, to be eligible for jury duty one must be a qualified elector.

21. Situations like that were disturbing at a much earlier period of our Country's life. In 1832, more than a century and a quarter ago, de Tocqueville wrote:

"I said one day to an inhabitant of Pennsylvania: 'Be so good as to explain to me how it happens that in a state founded by Quakers, and celebrated for its toleration, free blacks are not allowed to exercise civil rights. They pay taxes; is it not fair that they should vote?"

" 'You insult us,' replied my informant, 'if you imagine that our legislators could have committed so gross an act of injustice and intolerance.'

" 'Then the blacks possess the right of voting in this country?'

" 'Without a doubt.'

" 'How come it, then, that at the polling-booth this morning I did not perceive a single Negro?'

" 'That is not the fault of the law. The Negroes have an undisputed right of voting, but they voluntarily abstain from making their appearance.'

" 'A very pretty piece of modesty on their part!' rejoined I.

" 'Why, the truth is that they are not disinclined to vote, but they are afraid of being maltreated; in this country the law is sometimes unable to maintain its authority without the support of the majority. But in this case the majority entertains very strong prejudices against the blacks, and the magistrates are unable to protect them in the exercise of their legal rights.'

" 'Then the majority claims the right not only of making the laws, but of breaking the laws it has made?' "

as this, there is added to our common knowledge proof that some of the Negro citizens are qualified educationally and by other legal standards but are excluded from serving as jurors solely because of their race or color, the courts must declare the maintenance of such a condition violative of the Constitution and must not tolerate its longer continued existence.

In our opinion, the appellant proved a strong prima facie case that Negroes were systematically excluded from the grand jury and from the petit jury, and that case was not refuted by the State.

II. Were Objections to Systematic Exclusion of Negroes Effectively Waived?

The more serious questions are whether objections to the systematic exclusion of Negroes from the grand jury and to a like exclusion from the petit jury were waived when they were not made at the trial.

In deciding those questions, we should understand exactly the nature of the right under consideration. Usually the discrimination has been condemned as a denial of the equal protection of the laws. It has been indicated, however, that under certain circumstances it may constitute also a denial of due process of law.

The denial of the equal protection of the laws is especially marked when the defendant is a Negro and the victim is a white person; that is when the right is viewed narrowly and strictly from the viewpoint of the accused. Looking at it more broadly from the interest of the public in the administration of justice, systematic exclusion of Negroes from juries can result in inadequate protection of law-abiding Negroes against the criminal elements of their own race. The necessity for protection may not be brought close enough home to white jurors to prevent them from being too lenient with Negroes who commit crimes against other Negroes. The Constitution provides to law-abiding Negroes also the safeguard that members of their race shall not be systematically excluded from juries. The denial of the equal protection of the laws extends also to civil cases in which the lists of jurors are drawn from a jury box from which the names of Negroes have been systematically excluded. Thus, the right is one of broad significance closely and vitally connected with the proper administration of justice in both civil and criminal cases. . . .

Usually it is clear, and in the present case especially so, that, regardless of its composition, any grand jury would insist that the accused be brought to trial. When it comes to the actual trial, however, the decision of whether to submit to trial before a jury in the selection of which the defendant's race has been systematically excluded presents a problem fraught with far more serious consequences. The apprehended existence of prejudice was one inducement which led to the adoption of the Fourteenth Amendment. Sys-

---

Democracy in America by Alexis de Tocqueville, Vol. 1, Chapter 15, page 261, quoted by Professor Roland M. Harper of the University of Alabama in his letter to the Editor of the Montgomery Advertiser published December 17, 1958.

tematic exclusion of members of a defendant's race from a trial jury would, we think, be violative both of the equal protection clause and of the due process clause of the Fourteenth Amendment. . . .

The United States Constitution does not guarantee to a defendant in a State court a trial before a jury in which his race is proportionately represented, nor a trial before a jury composed in any part of members of his race, nor even to a jury trial at all, if other defendants are not accorded a jury trial. It does assure him of equal treatment under the law and that, so long as the State elects to accord jury trials, it must not systematically exclude from jury service qualified persons of his race. "An accused is entitled to have charges against him considered by a jury in the selection of which there has been neither inclusion nor exclusion because of race." Cassell v. State of Texas, supra, 339 U.S. at page 287. . . .

The fact that the prohibition is aimed at a system often makes it practically inadvisable for a defendant in a particular case to raise the issue. If Negroes were placed upon the list or venire, their names might easily be stricken before the particular jury was selected and impaneled. To a single defendant, then, the principle involved is often of doubtful or no value and he may forego seeking its protection, though it cannot be denied that from a broader, overall consideration, the long-continued, systematic and arbitrary exclusion of qualified Negro citizens from service on juries solely because of their race or color deprives every Negro of the equal protection of the law.

Morover, the very prejudice which causes the dominant race to exclude members of what it may assume to be an inferior race from jury service operates with multiplied intensity against one who resists such exclusion. Conscientious southern lawyers often reason that the prejudicial effects on their client of raising the issue far outweigh any practical protection in the particular case. Many extertain the view expressed by Mr. Justice Jackson concurring in the result in Shepherd v. State of Florida, 1951, 341 U.S. 50, 55 . . . :

> . . . I do not see, as a practical matter, how any Negro on the jury would have dared to cause a disagreement or acquittal. The only chance these Negroes had of acquittal would have been in the courage and decency of some sturdy and forthright white person of sufficient standing to face and live down the odium among his white neighbors that such a vote, if required, would have brought. To me, the technical question of discrimination in the jury selection has only theoretical importance.

Such courageous and unselfish lawyers as find it essential for their clients' protection to fight against the systematic exclusion of Negroes from juries sometimes do so at the risk of personal sacrifice which may extend to loss of practice and social ostracism.

As Judges of a Circuit comprising six states of the deep South, we think that it is our duty to take judicial notice that lawyers residing in many southern jurisdictions rarely, almost to the point of never, raise the issue of systematic exclusion of Negroes from juries. The Supreme Court of Mississippi has said that, "We have the right to make use of knowledge of the popular and general customs of the people of this State, and public conditions therein." Moore v. Grillis, 1949, 205 Miss. 865, 39 So. 2d 505, 508. . . . A like authority and duty is vested in this Court.

The evidence in this case . . . fairly considered shows no waiver by the appellant himself but at most by his counsel without his express authority. In ordinary procedural matters, the defendant in a criminal case is bound by the acts or nonaction of his counsel. That might extend to the waiver of the objection that Negroes were systematically excluded from the grand jury. In noncapital cases, it might extend to a like waiver as to the petit jury. It might extend to such a waiver even in capital cases, where the record affirmatively shows that the particular jury was desired by defendant's counsel after conscientious consideration of that course of action which would be best for the client's cause.

In this case, neither of the petitioner's trial attorneys has appeared or has been called to testify to any reason for waiving his client's constitutional right to a legally constituted trial jury, and no good reason appears otherwise from the record. The very heinousness of the crime and the weight of the physical evidence made it all the more necessary that the defendant's constitutional rights be not lightly or unadvisedly surrendered. The State trial judge testified that, "had such a motion been made and proved, that would have been sustained." . . . However strong might be the evidence of guilt, there was a possibility that a nondiscriminatory jury might not impose capital punishment. That chance was waived by defendant's counsel, so the District Court held.

If for any reason beyond the defendant's control, upon his trial for murder, the defendant did not have the effective representation of counsel at the time of a purported waiver by such counsel without consulting the client of the right to be tried before a legally constituted jury, such waiver can be given no effect.

Even in handling civil litigation, there are limitations upon the implied authority of an attorney to make decisions for his client. Few, if any, would argue that, without consulting his client, an attorney has implied authority to submit his cause to arbitration, or to any but a legally constituted tribunal. When not merely the client's property but his life is at stake, it is all the more essential that an attorney should advise with his client before waiving objections to a trial jury unconstitutionally and discriminatorily constituted.

The Negro lawyer was ready and willing to raise the issue of systematic exclusion of Negroes from the juries. The white lawyer, who was retained, refused to join with the Negro lawyer in the defense of appellant. When, upon request of the appellant's relatives, the Negro lawyer had left the case, the white lawyers failed to raise the issue. When the white lawyers had finished with the trial of the case, that issue was left as the only one that could save the appellant's life. The Negro lawyer then took over and raised the issue. . . .

The conditions giving rise to serious doubt as to whether the failure to make the objection at the trial constituted a voluntary and intelligent waiver of appellant's constitutional rights are all matters for which the State of Mississippi must bear responsibility. It is in a poor position to insist upon waiver. Upon this record, we hold that the appellant's constitutional right to be tried before a petit jury from which Negroes have not been systematically excluded has not been effectively waived by counsel authorized to make such waiver. . . .

Racism Hypo 17
UNITED STATES EX REL. NATIONALIST v. DIXIE PRISON

Jomo K. Nationalist is the brother of appellant in Racism Hypo 5, and he holds greatly similar views about American racism. He agrees with Julius Lester's article, The Necessity For Separation, supra page 108, that blacks have no future in America; and he joined the Pioneers for Black Liberation (PBL), a nationalist group whose goal is the obtaining "through any means possible" of large sections of what are now Southern states.

The first step in the PBL plan was the purchase of two large, adjoining farms in Magnolia, a deep South state. This precipitated major organized hostility and violence from local whites, quite similar to that experienced by the Black Muslims in Alabama. The PBL warned local whites that they were not nonviolent and would protect their property with force.

In an early morning raid by heavily armed state and local police (assertedly to serve subpoenas on PBL members for a Magnolia legislative committee investigating subversive groups within the state), shooting broke out and a local police officer was killed. Nationalist and three other PBL members were indicted, tried separately, convicted of murder and sentenced to life in the state prison farm, headed by the notorious superintendent, Dixie Prison.

The state of Magnolia has a grand jury selection procedure similar to the Texas process reviewed in Brooks v. Beto, and four blacks were on the sixteen-man grand jury that indicted the PBL members. The petit jury was selected by the Alabama "struck jury" system described in Swain v. Alabama. While the petit jury venire of seventy-five (after excuses and removals for cause) was 25 percent black (a proportion roughly half of the proportion of blacks in the county eligible for jury duty), the prosecutor struck all but two blacks, both of whom were elderly men who had worked as sharecroppers all their lives on a large plantation owned by a state senator, whose antebellum views on the race question were well known. Fearing that their status would affect their judgment, Nationalist's counsel (a local black lawyer) struck both blacks, with the result that Nationalist was convicted by an all-white jury. The other

PBL members were tried by juries with either no blacks or only one black member. Defense counsel raised no issue as to the validity of the grand or petit juries in these cases.

Having exhausted his direct appeals, Nationalist, with new counsel (a national black lawyers' group), sought reversal of his conviction through a federal habeas corpus petition asserting that: (1) the grand jury that indicted him included a selected number of token blacks rather than a true cross-section of the community, in violation of his Fourteenth Amendment rights; and (2) the selection of the petit jury by the "struck jury" system deprived him of his constitutional right to a fair jury, the achievement of which required, in Magnolia, an opportunity to ascertain the depth of racist views of those who were seated on the jury.

Counsel explained that, while these issues were not raised at his trial, Nationalist had not waived them, and that his local attorney, while willing to raise the issue of systematic exclusion, could not be expected to charge all prospective white jurors with harboring racist beliefs so deep that it would be impossible to give defendant an unbiased trial. The presence of a few or even several blacks on the petit jury, Nationalist claims, is irrelevant to the issue of racism in whites, which serves to dictate their outlook on such cases and to pressure black jurors into a similar position.

Counsel for Nationalist maintain that they will prove their case through social science testimony and studies at the hearing on the habeas corpus petition.

The state responded to the petition with a summary of the Supreme Court and Fifth Circuit jury discrimination cases. The state pointed with pride to the progress it had made in placing blacks on grand and petit juries. Recalling a time less than a decade earlier when no blacks had served on juries, the state acknowledged that this situation had been wrong, but noted that jury verdicts of "guilty" in cases with racial issues were being returned as regularly now as when blacks were excluded — a fact attributable, the state suggested, to the respect for law and order held by black as well as white citizens. The state argued that petitioner's position, if adopted, would endanger progress by subjecting all prospective jurors to lengthy psychoanalytic questioning about beliefs that they themselves might not be aware of.

The district judge, after reviewing the papers filed by both sides and hearing oral argument, refused to hold an evidentiary hearing, and denied the petition. He said that petitioner's arguments had no constitutional support and that they sought to hold jurors to standards of fairness and objectivity not required by law and impossible to attain in fact. Nationalist appealed.

Law Firm A will represent Jomo K. Nationalist on appeal.

Law Firm B will represent the state of Magnolia.

APPENDIX

In CONGRESS, July 4, 1776
A DECLARATION
By the REPRESENTATIVES of the
UNITED STATES OF AMERICA,
In General Congress Assembled

When in the Course of human Events, it becomes necessary for one People to dissolve the Political Bands which have connected them with another, and to assume among the Powers of the Earth, the separate and equal Station to which the Laws of Nature and of Nature's God entitle them, a decent Respect to the Opinions of Mankind requires that they should declare the causes which impel them to the Separation.

We hold these Truths to be self-evident, that all Men are created equal, that they are endowed by their Creator with certain inalienable Rights, that among these are Life, Liberty, and the Pursuit of Happiness. That to secure these Rights, Governments are instituted among Men, deriving their just Powers from the Consent of the Governed. That whenever any Form of Government becomes destructive of these Ends, it is the Right of the People to alter or to abolish it, and to institute new Government, laying its Foundation on such Principles and organizing its Powers in such Form as to them shall seem most likely to effect their Safety and Happiness. Prudence, indeed, will dictate that Governments long established should not be changed for light and transient Causes; and accordingly all Experience hath shown, that Mankind are more disposed to suffer, while Evils are sufferable, than to right themselves by abolishing the Forms to which they are accustomed. But when a long Train of Abuses and Usurpations, pursuing invariably the same Object, evinces a Design to reduce them under absolute Despotism, it is their Right, it is their Duty, to throw off such Government, and to provide new Guards for their future Security. — Such has been the patient Sufferance of these Colonies; and such is now the Necessity which constrains them to alter their former Systems of Government. The History of the present King of Great-Britain is a History of repeated Injuries and Usurpations, all having in direct Object the Establishment of an absolute Tyranny over these States. To prove this, let Facts be submitted to a candid World. . . . [The long list of grievances is omitted.]

LINCOLN'S PRELIMINARY EMANCIPATION PROCLAMATION (SEPTEMBER 22, 1862)

A Proclamation, 22 September 1862

I, Abraham Lincoln, President of the United States of America, and commander-in-chief of the army and navy thereof, do hereby proclaim and declare that hereafter, as heretofore, the war will be prosecuted for the object of practically restoring the constitutional relation between the United States and each of the States, and the people thereof, in which States that relation is or may be suspended or disturbed.

That it is my purpose, upon the next meeting of Congress, to again recommend the adoption of a practical measure tendering pecuniary aid to the free acceptance or rejection of all slave States, so called, the people whereof may not then be in rebellion against the United States, and which States may then have voluntarily adopted, or thereafter may voluntarily adopt, immediate or gradual abolishment of slavery within their respective limits; and that the effort to colonize persons of African descent with their consent upon this continent or elsewhere, with the previously obtained consent of the governments existing there, will be continued.

That on the first day of January, in the year of our Lord one thousand eight hundred and sixty-three, all persons held as slaves within any State or designated part of a State the people whereof shall then be in rebellion against the United States, shall be then, thenceforward, and forever free; and the Executive Government of the United States, including the military and naval authority thereof, will recognize and maintain the freedom of such persons, and will do no act or acts to repress such persons, or any of them, in any efforts they may make for their actual freedom.

That the Executive will, on the first day of January aforesaid, by proclamation designate the States and parts of States, if any, in which the people thereof, respectively, shall then be in rebellion against the United States; and the fact that any State, or the people thereof, shall on that day be in good faith represented in the Congress of the United States by members chosen thereto at elections wherein a majority of the qualified voters of such State shall have participated, shall, in the absence of strong countervailing testimony, be deemed conclusive evidence that such State, and the people thereof, are not then in rebellion against the United States.

That attention is hereby called to an Act of Congress entitled "An Act to make an additional article of war," approved 13 March 1862, and which Act is in the words and figures following:

Be it enacted by the Senate and House of Representatives of the United States of America in Congress assembled, That hereafter the following shall be promulgated as an additional article of war, for the government of the army of the United States, and shall be obeyed and observed as such:

Article. — All officers or persons in the military or naval service of the United States are prohibited from employing any of the forces under their respective commands for the purpose of returning fugitives from service or labor who may have escaped from any person to whom such service or labor is claimed to be due; and any officer who shall be found guilty by a court martial of violating this article shall be dismissed from the service.

Sec. 2. And be it further enacted, That this Act shall take effect from and after its passage.

Also to the ninth and tenth sections of an Act entitled "An Act to suppress insurrection, to punish treason and rebellion, to seize and confiscate property of rebels, and for other purposes," approved 17 July 1862, and which sections are in the words and figures following:

Sec. 9. And be it further enacted, That all slaves of persons who shall hereafter be engaged in rebellion against the Government of the United States, or who shall in any way give aid or comfort thereto, escaping from such persons and taking refuge within the lines of the army; and all slaves captured from such persons or deserted by them, and coming under the control of the Government of the United States; and all slaves of such persons found *on* [or] being within any place occupied by rebel forces and afterwards occupied by the forces of the United States, shall be deemed captives of war, and shall be forever free of their servitude, and not again held as slaves.

SEC. 10. And be it further enacted, That no slave escaping into any State, Territory, or the District of Columbia, from any other State, shall be delivered up, or in any way impeded or hindered of his liberty, except for crime, or some offense against the laws, unless the person claiming said fugitive shall first make oath that the person to whom the labor or service of such fugitive is alleged to be due is his lawful owner, and has not borne arms against the United States in the present rebellion, nor in any way given aid and comfort thereto; and no person engaged in the military or naval service of the United States shall, under any pretense whatever, assume to decide on the validity of the claim of any person to the service or labor of any other person, or surrender up any such person to the claimant, on pain of being dismissed from the service.

And I do hereby enjoin upon and order all persons engaged in the military and naval service of the United States to observe, obey, and enforce, within their respective spheres of service, the Act and sections above recited.

And the Executive will in due time recommend that all citizens of the United States who shall have remained loyal thereto throughout the rebellion shall (upon the restoration of the constitutional relation between the United States and their respective States and people, if that relation shall have been suspended or disturbed) be compensated for all losses by Acts of the United States, including the loss of slaves.

In witness whereof, I have hereunto set my hand and caused the seal of the United States to be affixed.

Done at the city of Washington, this twenty-second day of September, in the year of our Lord one thousand
[L.S.] eight hundred and sixty-two, and of the independence of the United States and eighty-seventh.

ABRAHAM LINCOLN

THE EMANCIPATION PROCLAMATION

January 1, 1863

BY THE PRESIDENT OF THE UNITED STATES OF AMERICA:

A Proclamation.

Whereas, on the twentysecond day of September, in the year of our Lord one thousand eight hundred and sixty two, a proclamation was issued by the President of the United States, containing, among other things, the following, to wit:

That on the first day of January, in the year of our Lord one thousand eight hundred and sixty-three, all persons held as slaves within any State or designated part of a State, the people whereof shall then be in rebellion against the United States, shall be then, thenceforward, and forever free; and the Executive Government of the United States, including the military and naval authority thereof, will recognize and maintain the freedom of such persons, and will do no act or acts to repress such persons, or any of them, in any efforts they may make for their actual freedom.

That the Executive will, on the first day of January aforesaid, by proclamation, designate the States and parts of States, if any, in which the people thereof, shall on that day be, in good faith, represented in the Congress of the United States by members chosen thereto at elections wherein a majority of the qualified voters of each State shall have participated, shall in the absence of strong countervailing testimony, be deemed conclusive evidence that such State, and the people thereof, are not then in rebellion against the United States.

Now, therefore, I, Abraham Lincoln, President of the United States, by virtue of the power in me invested as Commander-in-Chief, of the Army and Navy of the United States in time of actual armed rebellion against authority and government of the United States, and as a fit and necessary war measure for suppressing said rebellion, do, on this first day of January, in the year of our Lord one thousand eight hundred and sixty three, and in accordance with my purpose so to do publicly proclaimed for the full period of one hundred days, from the day first above mentioned, order and designate as the States and parts of States wherein the people thereof respectively, are this day in rebellion against the United States, the following, to wit:

Arkansas, Texas, Louisiana, (except the Parishes of St. Bernard, Plaquemines, Jefferson, St. Johns, St. Charles, St. James Ascension, Assumption, Terrebonne, Lafourche, St. Mary, St. Martin, and Orleans, including the City of New-Orleans) Mississippi, Alabama, Florida, Georgia, South-Carolina, North-Carolina, and Virginia, (except the fortyeight counties designated as West Virginia, and also the counties of Berkley, Accomac, Northampton, Elizabeth-City, York, Princess Ann, and Norfolk, including the cities of Norfolk and Portsmouth), and which excepted parts are, for the present, left precisely as if this proclamation were not issued.

And by virtue of the power, and for the purpose aforesaid, I do order and declare that all persons held as slaves within said designated States, and parts of States, are, and henceforward shall be free; and that the Executive government of the United States, including the military and naval authorities thereof, will recognize and maintain the freedom of said persons.

And I hereby enjoin upon the people so declared to be free to abstain from all violence, unless in necessary self-defence; and I recommend to them that, in all cases when allowed, they labor faithfully for reasonable wages.

And I further declare and make known that such persons of suitable condition, will be received into the armed service of the United States to garrison forts, positions, stations, and other places, and to man vessels of all sorts in said service.

And upon this act, sincerely believed to be an act of justice, warranted by the Constitution, upon military necessity, I invoke the considerate judgment of mankind, and the gracious favor of Almighty God.

In witness whereof, I have hereunto set my hand and caused the seal of the United States to be affixed.

Done at the City of Washington, this first day of January, in the year of our Lord one thousand eight hundred and sixty three, and of the Independence of the United States of America the eighty-seventh.

By the President: ABRAHAM LINCOLN

WILLIAM H. SEWARD, Secretary of State

THIRTEENTH AMENDMENT (1865)

SECTION 1. Neither slavery nor involuntary servitude, except as a punishment for crime whereof the party shall have been duly convicted, shall exist within the United States, or any place subject to their jurisdiction.

SECTION 2. Congress shall have power to enforce this article by appropriate legislation.

FOURTEENTH AMENDMENT (1868)

SECTION 1. All persons born or naturalized in the United States, and subject to the jurisdiction thereof, are citizens of the United States and of the State wherein they reside. No State shall make or enforce any law which shall abridge the privileges or immunities of citizens of the United States; nor shall any State deprive any person of life, liberty, or property, without due process of law; nor deny to any person within its jurisdiction the equal protection of the laws.

SECTION 2. Representatives shall be apportioned among the several States according to their respective numbers, counting the whole number of persons in each State, excluding Indians not taxed. But when the right to vote at any election for the choice of electors for President and Vice President of the United States, Representatives in Congress, the Executive and Judicial officers of a State, or the members of the Legislature thereof, is denied to any of the male inhabitants of such State, being twenty-one years of age, and citizens of the United States, or in any way abridged, except for participation in rebellion, or other crime, the basis of representation therein shall be reduced in the proportion which the number of such male citizens shall bear to the whole number of male citizens twenty-one years of age in such State.

SECTION 5. The Congress shall have power to enforce, by appropriate legislation, the provisions of this article.

FIFTEENTH AMENDMENT (1870)

SECTION 1. The right of citizens of the United States to vote shall not be denied or abridged by the United States or by any State on account of race, color, or previous condition of servitude.

SECTION 2. The Congress shall have power to enforce this article by appropriate legislation.

18 UNITED STATES CODE §§241-243, 245 (1970)

§241. Conspiracy against rights of citizens.

If two or more persons conspire to injure, oppress, threaten, or intimidate any citizen in the free exercise or enjoyment of any right or privilege secured to him by the Constitution or laws of the United States, or because of his having so exercised the same; or

If two or more persons go in disguise on the highway, or on the premises of another, with intent to prevent or hinder his free exercise or enjoyment of any right or privilege so secured —

They shall be fined not more than $10,000 or imprisoned not more than ten years, or both; and if death results, they shall be subject to imprisonment for any term of years or for life. (June 25, 1948, ch. 645, 62 Stat. 696; Apr. 11, 1968, Pub. L. 90-284, title I, §103(a), 82 Stat. 75.)

§242. Deprivation of rights under color of law.

Whoever, under color of any law, statute, ordinance, regulation, or custom, willfully subjects any inhabitant of any State, Territory, or District to the deprivation of any rights, privileges, or immunities secured or protected by the Constitution or laws of the United States, or to different punishments, pains, or penalties, on account of such inhabitant being an alien, or by reason of his color, or race, than are prescribed for the punishment of citizens, shall be fined not more than $1,000 or imprisoned not more than one year, or both; and if death results shall be subject to imprisonment for any term of years or for life. (June 25, 1948, ch. 645, 62 Stat. 696; Apr. 11, 1968, Pub. L. 90-284, title I, §103(b), 82 Stat. 75.)

§243. Exclusion of jurors on account of race or color.

No citizen possessing all other qualifications which are or may be prescribed by law shall be disqualified for service as grand or petit juror in any court of the United States, or of any State on account of race, color, or previous condition of servitude; and whoever, being an officer or other person charged with any duty in the selection or summoning of jurors, excludes or fails to summon any citizen for such cause, shall be fined not more than $5,000. (June 25, 1948, ch. 645, 62 Stat. 696.)

§245. Federally protected activities.

(a) (1) Nothing in this section shall be construed as indicating an intent on the part of Congress to prevent any State, any possession or Commonwealth of the United States, or the District of Columbia, from exercising jurisdiction over any offense over which it would have jurisdiction in the absence of this section, nor shall anything in this section be construed as depriving State and local law enforcement authorities of responsibility for prosecuting acts that may be violations of this section and that are violations of State and local law. No prosecution of any offense described in this section shall be undertaken by the United States except upon the certification in writing of the Attorney General or the Deputy Attorney General that in his judgment a prosecution by the United States is in the public interest and necessary to secure substantial justice, which function of certification may not be delegated.

(2) Nothing in this subsection shall be construed to limit the authority of Federal officers, or a Federal grand jury, to investigate possible violations of this section.

(b) Whoever, whether or not acting under color of law, by force or threat of force willfully [injures], intimidates or interferes with, or attempts to injure, intimidate or interfere with —

(1) any person because he is or has been, or in order to intimidate such person or any other person or any class of persons from —

(A) voting or qualifying to vote, qualifying or campaigning as a candidate for elective office, or qualifying or acting as a poll watcher, or any legally authorized election official, in any primary, special, or general election;

(B) participating in or enjoying any benefit, service, privilege, program, facility, or activity provided or administered by the United States;

(C) applying for or enjoying employment, or any perquisite thereof, by any agency of the United States;

(D) serving, or attending upon any court in connection with possible service, as a grand or petit juror in any court of the United States;

(E) participating or in enjoying the benefits of any program or activity receiving Federal financial assistance; or

(2) any person because of his race, color, religion or national origin and because he is or has been —

(A) enrolling in or attending any public school or public college;

(B) participating in or enjoying any benefit, service, privilege, program, facility or activity provided or administered by any State or subdivision thereof;

(C) applying for or enjoying employment, or any perquisite thereof, by any private employer or any agency of any State or subdivision thereof, or joining or using the services or advantages of any labor organization, hiring hall, or employment agency;

(D) serving, or attending upon any court of any State in connection with possible service, as a grand or petit juror;

(E) traveling in or using any facility of interstate commerce, or using any vehicle, terminal, or facility or any common carrier by motor, rail, water, or air;

(F) enjoying the goods, services, facilities, privileges, advantages, or accommodations of any inn, hotel, motel, or other establishment which provides lodging to transient guests, or of any restaurant, cafeteria, lunchroom, lunch counter, soda fountain, or other facility which serves the public and which is principally engaged in selling food or beverages for consumption on the premises, or of any gasoline station, or of any motion picture house, theater, concert hall, sports arena, stadium, or any other place of exhibition or entertainment which serves the public, or of any other establishment which serves the public and (i) which is located within the premises of any of the aforesaid establishments or within the premises of which is physically located any of the aforesaid establishments, and (ii) which holds itself out as serving patrons of such establishments; or

(3) during or incident to a riot or civil disorder, any person engaged in a business in commerce or affecting commerce; including, but not limited to, any person engaged in a business which sells or offers for sale to interstate travelers a substantial portion of the articles, commodities, or services which it sells or where a substantial portion of the articles or commodities which it sells or offers for sale have moved in commerce; or

(4) any person because he is or has been, or in order to intimidate such person or any other person or any class of persons from —

(A) participating, without discrimination on account of race, color, religion or national origin, in any of the benefits or activities described in subparagraphs (1)(A) through (1)(E) or subparagraphs (2)(A) through (2)(F); or

(B) affording another person or class of persons opportunity or protection to so participate; or

(5) any citizen because he is or has been, or in order to intimidate such citizen or any other citizen from lawfully aiding or encouraging other persons to participate, without discrimination on account of race, color, religion or national origin, in any of the benefits or activities described in subparagraphs (1)(A) through

(1)(E) or subparagraphs (2)(A) through (2)(F), or participating lawfully in speech or peaceful assembly opposing any denial of the opportunity to so participate —

shall be fined not more than $1,000, or imprisoned not more than one year, or both; and if bodily injury results shall be fined not more than $10,000, or imprisoned not more than ten years, or both; and if death results shall be subject to imprisonment for any term of years or for life. As used in this section, the term "participating lawfully in speech or peaceful assembly" shall not mean the aiding, abetting, or inciting of other persons to riot or to commit any act of physical violence upon any individual or against any real or personal property in furtherance of a riot. Nothing in subparagraph (2)(F) or (4)(A) of this subsection shall apply to the proprietor of any establishment which provides lodging to transient guests, or to any employee acting on behalf of such proprietor, with respect to the enjoyment of the goods, services, facilities, privileges, advantages, or accommodations of such establishment if such establishment is located within a building which contains not more than five rooms for rent or hire and which is actually occupied by the proprietor as his residence.

(c) Nothing in this section shall be construed so as to deter any law enforcement officer from lawfully carrying out the duties of his office; and no law enforcement officer shall be considered to be in violation of this section for lawfully carrying out the duties of his office or lawfully enforcing ordinances and laws of the United States, the District of Columbia, any of the several States, or any political subdivision of a State. For purposes of the preceding sentence, the term "law enforcement officer" means any officer of the United States, the District of Columbia, a State, or political subdivision of a State, who is empowered by law to conduct investigations of, or make arrests because of, offenses against the United States, the District of Columbia, a State, or a political subdivision of a State. (Added Pub. L. 90-284, title I, §101(a), Apr. 11, 1968, 82 Stat. 73.)

28 UNITED STATES CODE §§1343, 1443, 1446-1448, 2283 (1970)

§1343. Civil rights and elective franchise.

The district courts shall have original jurisdiction of any civil action authorized by law to be commenced by any person:

(1) To recover damages for injury to his person or property, or because of the deprivation of any right of privilege of a citizen of the United States, by any act done in furtherance of any conspiracy mentioned in section 1985 of Title 42;

(2) To recover damages from any person who fails to prevent or to aid in preventing any wrongs mentioned in section 1985 of Title 42 which he had knowledge were about to occur and power to prevent;

(3) To redress the deprivation, under color of any State law, statute, ordinance, regulation, custom or usage, of any right, privilege or immunity secured by the Constitution of the United States or by any Act of Congress providing for equal rights of citizens or of all persons within the jurisdiction of the United States;

(4) To recover damages or to secure equitable or other relief under any Act of Congress providing for the protection of civil rights, including the right to vote.

(June 25, 1948, ch. 646, 62 Stat. 932; Sept. 3, 1954, ch. 1263, §42, 68 Stat. 1241; Sept. 9, 1957, Pub. L. 85-315, part III, §121, 71 Stat. 637.)

§1443. Civil rights cases.

Any of the following civil actions or criminal prosecutions commenced in a State court may be removed by the defendant to the district court of the United States for the district and division embracing the place wherein it is pending:

(1) Against any person who is denied or cannot enforce in the courts of such State a right under any law providing for the equal civil rights of citizens of the United States, or of all persons within the jurisdiction thereof;

(2) For any act under color of authority derived from any law providing for equal rights, or for refusing to do any act on the ground that it would be inconsistent with such law.

(June 25, 1948, ch. 646, 62 Stat. 938.)

§1446. Procedure for removal.

(a) A defendant or defendants desiring to remove any civil action or criminal prosecution from a State court shall file in the district court of the United States for the district and division within which such action is pending a verified petition containing a short and plain statement of the facts which entitle him or them to removal together with a copy of all process, pleadings and orders served upon him or them in such action.

(b) The petition for removal of a civil action or proceeding shall be filed within thirty days after the receipt by the defendant, through service or otherwise, of a copy of the initial pleading setting forth the claim for relief upon which such action or proceeding is based, or within thirty days after the service of summons upon the defendant if such initial pleading has then been filed in court and is not required to be served on the defendant, whichever period is shorter.

If the case stated by the initial pleading is not removable, a petition for removal may be filed within thirty days after receipt by the defendant, through service or otherwise, of a copy of an amended pleading, motion, order or other paper from which it may first be ascertained that the case is one which is or has become removable.

(c) The petition for removal of a criminal prosecution may be filed at any time before trial.

(d) Each petition for removal of a civil action or proceeding, except a petition in behalf of the United States, shall be accompanied by a bond with good and sufficient surety conditioned that the defendant or defendants will pay all costs and disbursements incurred by reason of the removal proceedings should it be determined that the case was not removable or was improperly removed.

(e) Promptly after the filing of such petition and bond the defendant or defendants shall give written notice thereof to all adverse parties and shall file a copy of the petition with the clerk of such State court, which shall effect the removal and the State court shall proceed no further unless and until the case is remanded.

(f) If the defendant or defendants are in actual custody on process issued by the State court, the district court shall issue its writ of habeas corpus, and the marshal shall thereupon take such defendant or defendants into his custody and deliver a copy of the writ to the clerk of such State court. (June 25, 1948, ch. 646, 62 Stat. 939; May 24, 1949, ch. 139, §83, 63 Stat. 101; Sept. 29, 1965, Pub. L. 89-215, 79 Stat. 887.)

§1447. Procedure after removal generally.

(a) In any case removed from a State court, the district court may issue all necessary orders and process to bring before it all proper parties whether served by process issued by the State court or otherwise.

(b) It may require the petitioner to file with its clerk copies of all records and proceedings in such State court or may cause the same to be brought before it by writ of certiorari issued to such State court.

(c) If at any time before final judgment it appears that the case was removed improvidently and without jurisdiction, the district court shall remand the case, and may order the payment of just costs. A certified copy of the order of remand shall be mailed by its clerk to the clerk of the State court. The State court may thereupon proceed with such case.

(d) An order remanding a case to the State court from which it was removed is not reviewable on appeal or otherwise, except that an order remanding a case to the State court from which it was removed pursuant to section 1443 of this title shall be reviewable by appeal or otherwise. (June 25, 1948, ch. 646, 62 Stat. 939; May 24, 1949, ch. 139, §84, 63 Stat. 102; July 2, 1964, Pub. L. 88-352, title IX, §901, 78 Stat. 266.)

§1448. Process after removal.

In all cases removed from any State court to any district court of the United States in which any one or more of the defendants has not been served with process or in which the service has not been perfected prior to removal, or in which process served proves to be defective, such process or service may be completed or new process issued in the same manner as in cases originally filed in such district court.

This section shall not deprive any defendant upon whom process is served after removal of his right to move to remand the case. (June 25, 1948, ch. 646, 62 Stat. 940.)

§2283. Stay of State court proceedings.

A court of the United States may not grant an injunction to stay proceedings in a State court except as expressly authorized by Act of Congress, or where necessary in aid of its jurisdiction, or to protect or effectuate its judgments. (June 25, 1948, ch. 646, 62 Stat. 968.)

42 UNITED STATES CODE §§1981-1986, 1988 (1970)

§1981. Equal rights under the law.

All persons within the jurisdiction of the United States shall have the same right in every State and Territory to make and enforce contracts, to sue, be parties, give evidence, and to the full and equal benefit of all laws and proceedings for the security of persons and property as is enjoyed by white citizens, and shall be subject to like punishment, pains, penalties, taxes, licenses, and exactions of every kind, and to no other.

R.S. §1977. Derivation. Act May 31, 1870, c. 114, §16, 16 Stat. 144.

§1982. Property rights of citizens.

All citizens of the United States shall have the same right, in every State and Territory, as is enjoyed by white citizens thereof to inherit, purchase, lease, sell, hold, and convey real and personal property.

R.S. §1978. Derivation. Act April 9, 1866, c. 31, §1.

§1983. Civil action for deprivation of rights.

Every person who, under color of any statute, ordinance, regulation, custom, or usage, of any State or Territory, subjects, or causes to be subjected, any citizen of the United States or other person within the jurisdiction thereof to the deprivation of any rights, privileges, or immunities secured by the Constitution and laws, shall be liable to the party injured in an action at law, suit in equity, or other proper proceeding for redress.

R.S. §1979. Derivation. Act April 20, 1871, c. 22, §1, 17 Stat. 13.

§1984. Same; review of proceedings.

All cases arising under the provisions of this Act in the courts of the United States shall be reviewable by the Supreme Court of the United States, without regard to the sum in controversy, under the same provisions and regulations as are provided by law for the review of other causes in said court.

Mar. 1, 1875, c. 114, §5, 18 Stat. 337.

§1985. Conspiracy to interfere with civil rights — Preventing officer from performing duties.

(1) If two or more persons in any State or Territory conspire to prevent, by force, intimidation, or threat, any person from accepting or holding any office, trust, or place of confidence under the United States, or from discharging any duties thereof; or to induce by like means any officer of the United States to leave any State, district, or place, where his duties as an officer are required to be performed, or to injure him in his person or property on account of his lawful discharge of the duties of his office, or while engaged in the lawful discharge thereof, or to injure his property so as to molest, interrupt, hinder, or impede him in the discharge of his official duties;

Obstructing justice; intimidating party, witness, or juror

(2) If two or more persons in any State or Territory conspire to deter, by force, intimidation, or threat, any party or witness in any court of the United States from attending such court, or from testifying to any matter pending herein, freely, fully, and truthfully, or to injure such party or witness in his person or property on account of his having so attended or testified, or to influence the verdict, presentment, or indictment of any grand or petit juror in any such court, or to injure such juror in his person or property on account of any verdict, presentment, or indictment lawfully assented to by him, or of his being or having been such juror; or if two or more persons conspire for the purpose of impeding, hindering, obstructing, or defeating, in any manner, the due course of justice in any State or Territory, with intent to deny to any citizen the equal protection of the laws, or to injure him or his property for lawfully enforcing, or attempting to enforce, the right of any person, or class of persons, to the equal protection of the laws;

Depriving persons of rights or privileges

(3) If two or more persons in any State or Territory conspire or go in disguise on the highway or on the premises of another, for the purpose of depriving, either directly or indirectly, any person or class of persons of the equal protection of the laws, or of equal privileges and immunities under the laws; or for the purpose of preventing or hindering the constituted authorities of any State or Territory from giving or securing to all persons within such State or Territory the equal protection of the laws; or if two or more persons conspire to prevent by force, intimidation, or threat, any citizen who is lawfully entitled to vote, from giving his support or

advocacy in a legal manner, toward or in favor of the election of any lawfully qualified person as an elector for President or Vice President, or as a Member of Congress of the United States; or to injure any citizen in person or property on account of such support or advocacy; in any case of conspiracy set forth in this section, if one or more persons engaged therein do, or cause to be done, any act in furtherance of the object of such conspiracy, whereby another is injured in his person or property, or deprived of having and exercising any right or privilege of a citizen of the United States, the party so injured or deprived may have an action for the recovery of damages, occasioned by such injury or deprivation, against any one or more of the conspirators.

R.S. §1980. Derivation. Acts July 31, 1861, c. 33, 12 Stat. 284; April 20, 1871, c. 22, §2, 17 Stat. 13.

§1986. Same; action for neglect to prevent.

Every person who, having knowledge that any of the wrongs conspired to be done, and mentioned in section 1985 of this title, are about to be committed, and having power to prevent or aid in preventing the commission of the same, neglects or refuses so to do, if such wrongful act be committed, shall be liable to the party injured, or his legal representatives, for all damages caused by such wrongful act, which such person by reasonable diligence could have prevented; and such damages may be recovered in an action on the case; and any number of persons guilty of such wrongful neglect or refusal may be joined as defendants in the action; and if the death of any party be caused by any such wrongful act and neglect, the legal representatives of the deceased shall have such action therefor, and may recover not exceeding $5,000 damages therein, for the benefit of the widow of the deceased, if there be one, and if there be no widow, then for the benefit of the next of kin of the deceased. But no action under the provisions of this section shall be sustained which is not commenced within one year after the cause of action has accrued.

R.S. §1981. Derivation. Act April 20, 1871, c. 22, §6, 17 Stat. 15.

§1988. Proceedings in vindication of civil rights.

The jurisdiction in civil and criminal matters conferred on the district courts by the provisions of this chapter and Title 18, for the protection of all persons in the United States in their civil rights, and for their vindication, shall be exercised and enforced in conformity with the laws of the United States, so far as such laws are suitable to carry the same into effect; but in all cases where they are not adapted to the object, or are deficient in the provisions necessary to furnish suitable remedies and punish offenses against law, the common law, as modified and changed by the constitution and statutes of the State wherein the court having jurisdiction of such civil or criminal cause is held, so far as the same is not inconsistent with the Constitution and laws of the United States, shall be extended to and govern the said courts in the trial and disposition of the cause, and, if it is of a criminal nature, in the infliction of punishment on the party found guilty.

R.S. §722. Derivation. Acts April 9, 1866, c. 31, §3, 14 Stat. 27; May 31, 1870, c. 114, §18, 16 Stat. 144.

CIVIL RIGHTS ACT OF 1964

Title II. — Public Accommodations

§2000a. Prohibition against discrimination or segregation in places of public accommodation.

(a) Equal access.

All persons shall be entitled to the full and equal enjoyment of the goods, services, facilities, privileges, advantages, and accommodations of any place of public accommodation, as defined in this section, without discrimination or segregation on the ground of race, color, religion, or national origin.

(*b*) *Establishments affecting interstate commerce or supported in their activities by State action as places of public accommodation; lodgings; facilities principally engaged in selling food for consumption on the premises; gasoline stations; places of exhibition or entertainment; other covered establishments.*

Each of the following establishments which serves the public is a place of public accommodation within the meaning of this subchapter if its operations affect commerce, or if discrimination or segregation by it is supported by State action:

(1) any inn, hotel, motel, or other establishment which provides lodging to transient guests, other than an establishment located within a building which contains not more than five rooms for rent or hire and which is actually occupied by the proprietor of such establishment as his residence;

(2) any restaurant, cafeteria, lunchroom, lunch counter, soda fountain, or other facility principally engaged in selling food for consumption on the premises, including, but not limited to, any such facility located on the premises of any retail establishment; or any gasoline station;

(3) any motion picture house, theater, concert hall, sports arena, stadium or other place of exhibition or entertainment; and

(4) any establishment (A) (i) which is physically located within the premises of any establishment otherwise covered by this subsection, or (ii) within the premises of which is physically located any such covered establishment, and (B) which holds itself out as serving patrons of such covered establishment.

(*c*) *Operations affecting commerce; criteria; "commerce" defined.*

The operations of an establishment affect commerce within the meaning of this subchapter if (1) it is one of the establishments described in paragraph (1) of subsection (b) of this section; (2) in the case of an establishment described in paragraph (2) of subsection (b) of this section, it serves or offers to serve interstate travelers of a substantial portion of the food which it serves, or gasoline or other products which it sells, has moved in commerce; (3) in the case of an establishment described in paragraph (3) of subsection (b) of this section, it customarily presents films, performances, athletic teams, exhibitions, or other sources of entertainment which move in commerce; and (4) in the case of an establishment described in paragraph (4) of subsection (b) of this section, it is physically located within the premises of, or there is physically located within its premises, an establishment the operations of which affect commerce within the meaning of this subsection. For purposes of this section, "commerce" means travel, trade, traffic, commerce, transportation, or communication among the several States, or between the District of Columbia and any State, or between any foreign country or any territory or possession and any State or the District of Columbia, or between points in the same State but through any other State or the District of Columbia or a foreign country.

(*d*) *Support by State action.*

Discrimination or segregation by an establishment is supported by State action within the meaning of this subchapter if such discrimination or segregation (1) is carried on under color of any law, statute, ordinance, or regulation; or (2) is carried on under color of any custom or usage required or enforced by officials of the State or political subdivision thereof; or (3) is required by action of the State or political subdivision thereof.

(e) Private establishments.

The provisions of this subchapter shall not apply to a private club or other establishment not in fact open to the public, except to the extent that the facilities of such establishment are made available to the customers or patrons of an establishment within the scope of subsection (b) of this section. (Pub. L. 88-352, title II, §201, July 2, 1964, 78 Stat. 243.)

§2000a-1. Prohibition against discrimination or segregation required by any law, statute, ordinance, regulation, rule or order of a State or State agency.

All persons shall be entitled to be free, at any establishment or place, from discrimination or segregation of any kind on the ground of race, color, religion, or national origin, if such discrimination or segregation is or purports to be required by any law, statute, ordinance, regulation, rule, or order of a State or any agency or political subdivision thereof. (Pub. L. 88-352, title II, §202, July 2, 1964, 78 Stat. 244.)

§2000a-2. Prohibition against deprivation of, interference with, and punishment for exercising rights and privileges secured by section 2000a or 2000a-1 of this title.

No person shall (a) withhold, deny, or attempt to withhold or deny, or deprive or attempt to deprive any person of any right or privilege secured by section 2000a or 2000a-1 of this title, or (b) intimidate, threaten, or coerce, or attempt to intimidate, threaten, or coerce any person with the purpose of interfering with any right or privilege secured by section 2000a or 2000a-1 of this title, or (c) punish or attempt to punish any person for exercising or attempting to exercise any right or privilege secured by section 2000a or 2000a-1 of this title. (Pub. L. 88-352, title II, §203, July 2, 1964, 78 Stat. 244.)

§2000a-3. Civil actions for injunctive relief.

(a) Persons aggrieved; intervention by Attorney General; legal representation; commencement of action without payment of fees, costs, or security.

Whenever any person has engaged or there are reasonable grounds to believe that any person is about to engage in any act or practice prohibited by section 2000a-2 of this title, a civil action for preventive relief, including an application for a permanent or temporary injunction, restraining order, or other order, may be instituted by the person aggrieved and, upon timely application, the court may, in its discretion, permit the Attorney General to intervene in such civil action if he certifies that the case is of general public importance. Upon application by the complainant and in such circumstances as the court may deem just, the court may appoint an attorney for such complainant and may authorize the commencement of the civil action without the payment of fees, costs, or security.

(b) Attorney's fees; liability of United States for costs.

In any action commenced pursuant to this subchapter, the court, in its discretion, may allow the prevailing party, other than the United States, a reasonable attorney's fee as part of the costs, and the United States shall be liable for costs the same as a private person.

(c) State or local enforcement proceedings: notification of State or local authority; stay of Federal proceedings.

In the case of an alleged act or practice prohibited by this subchapter which occurs in a State, or political subdivision of a State, which has a State or local law prohibiting such act or practice and establishing or authorizing a State or local authority to grant or seek relief from such practice or to institute criminal proceedings with respect thereto upon receiving notice thereof, no civil action may be brought under subsection (a) of this section before the expiration of thirty days after written notice of such alleged act or practice has been given to the appropriate State or local authority by registered mail or in person, provided that the court may stay proceedings in such civil action pending the termination of State or local enforcement proceedings.

(d) References to Community Relations Service to obtain voluntary compliance; duration of reference; extension of period.

In the case of an alleged act or practice prohibited by this subchapter which occurs in a State, or political subdivision of a State, which has no State or local law prohibiting such act or practice, a civil action may be brought under subsection (a) of this section: *Provided,* That the court may refer the matter to the Community Relations Service established by subchapter VIII of this chapter for as long as the court believes there is a reasonable possibility of obtaining voluntary compliance, but for not more than sixty days: *Provided further,* That upon expiration of such sixty-day period, the court may extend such period for an additional period, not to exceed a cumulative total of one hundred and twenty days, if it believes there then exists a reasonable possibility of securing voluntary compliance. (Pub. L. 88-352, title II, §204, July 2, 1964, 78 Stat. 244.)

§2000a-4. Community Relations Service; investigations and hearings; executive session; release of testimony; duty to bring about voluntary settlements.

The Service is authorized to make a full investigation of any complaint referred to it by the court under section 2000a-3(d) of this title and may hold such hearings with respect thereto as may be necessary. The Service shall conduct any hearings with respect to any such complaint in executive session, and shall not release any testimony given therein except by agreement of all parties involved in the complaint with the permission of the court, and the Service shall endeavor to bring about a voluntary settlement between the parties. (Pub. L. 88-352, title II, §205, July 2, 1964, 78 Stat. 244.)

§2000a-5. Civil actions by the Attorney General.

(a) Complaint.

Whenever the Attorney General has reasonable cause to believe that any person or group of persons is engaged in a pattern or practice of resistance to the full enjoyment of any of the rights secured by this subchapter, and that the pattern or practice is of such a nature and is intended to deny the full exercise of the rights herein described, the Attorney General may bring a civil action in the appropriate district court of the United States by filing with it a complaint (1) signed by him (or in his absence the Acting Attorney General), (2) setting forth facts pertaining to such pattern or practice, and (3) requesting such preventive relief, including an application for a permanent or temporary injunction, restraining order or other order against the person or persons responsible for such pattern or practice, as he deems necessary to insure the full enjoyment of the rights herein described.

(*b*) *Three-judge district court for cases of general public importance: hearing, determination, expedition of action, review by Supreme Court; single-judge district court: hearing, determination, expedition of action.*

In any such proceeding the Attorney General may file with the clerk of such court a request that a court of three judges be convened to hear and determine the case. Such request by the Attorney General shall be accompanied by a certificate that, in his opinion, the case is of general public importance. A copy of the certificate and request for a three-judge court shall be immediately furnished by such clerk to the chief judge of the circuit (or in his absence, the presiding circuit judge of the circuit) in which the case is pending. Upon receipt of the copy of such request it shall be the duty of the chief judge of the circuit or the presiding circuit judge, as the case may be, to designate immediately three judges in such circuit, of whom at least one shall be a circuit judge and another of whom shall be a district judge of the court in which the proceeding was instituted, to hear and determine such case, and it shall be the duty of the judges so designated to assign the case for hearing at the earliest practicable date, to participate in the hearing and determination thereof, and to cause the case to be in every way expedited. An appeal from the final judgment of such court will lie to the Supreme Court.

In the event the Attorney General fails to file such a request in any such proceeding, it shall be the duty of the chief judge of the district (or in his absence, the acting chief judge) in which the case is pending immediately to designate a judge in such district to hear and determine the case. In the event that no judge in the district is available to hear and determine the case, the chief judge of the district, or the acting chief judge, as the case may be, shall certify this fact to the chief judge of the circuit (or in his absence, the acting chief judge) who shall then designate a district or circuit judge of the circuit to hear and determine the case.

It shall be the duty of the judge designated pursuant to this section to assign the case for hearing at the earliest practicable date and to cause the case to be in every way expedited. (Pub. L. 88-352, title II, §206, July 2, 1964, 78 Stat. 245.)

§2000a-6. Jurisdiction; exhaustion of other remedies; exclusiveness of remedies; assertion of rights based on other Federal or State laws and pursuit of remedies for enforcement of such rights.

(a) The district courts of the United States shall have jurisdiction of proceedings instituted pursuant to this subchapter and shall exercise the same without regard to whether the aggrieved party shall have exhausted any administrative or other remedies that may be provided by law.

(b) The remedies provided in this subchapter shall be the exclusive means of enforcing the rights based on this subchapter, but nothing in this subchapter shall preclude any individual or any State or local agency from asserting any right based on any other Federal or State law not inconsistent with this subchapter, including any statute or ordinance requiring nondiscrimination in public establishments or accommodations, or from pursuing any remedy, civil or criminal, which may be available for the vindication or enforcement of such right. (Pub. L. 88-352, title II, §207, July 2, 1964, 78 Stat. 245.)

Title III. — Public Facilities

§2000b. Civil actions by the Attorney General.

(*a*) *Complaint; certification; institution of civil action; relief requested; jurisdiction; impleading additional parties as defendants.*

Whenever the Attorney General receives a complaint in writing signed by an individual to the effect that he is being deprived of or threatened with the loss of his right to the equal protection of the laws, on account of his race, color, religion, or national origin, by being denied equal utilization of any public facility which is owned, operated, or managed by or on behalf of any State or subdivision thereof, other than a public school or public college as defined in section 2000c of this title, and the Attorney General believes the complaint is meritorious and certifies that the signer or signers of such complaint are unable, in his judgment, to initiate and maintain appropriate legal proceedings for relief and that the institution of an action will materially further the orderly progress of desegregation in public facilities, the Attorney General is authorized to institute for or in the name of the United States a civil action in any appropriate district court of the United States against such parties and for such relief as may be appropriate, and such court shall have and shall exercise jurisdiction of proceedings instituted pursuant to this section. The Attorney General may implead as defendants such additional parties as are or become necessary to the grant of effective relief hereunder.

(*b*) *Persons unable to initiate and maintain legal proceedings.*

The Attorney General may deem a person or persons unable to initiate and maintain appropriate legal proceedings within the meaning of subsection (a) of this section when such person or persons are unable, either directly or through other interested persons or organizations, to bear the expense of the litigation or to obtain effective legal representation, or whenever he is satisfied that the institution of such litigation would jeopardize the personal safety, employment, or economic standing of such person or persons, their families, or their property. (Pub. L. 88-352, title III, §301, July 2, 1964, 78 Stat. 246.)

§2000b-1. Liability of United States for costs and attorney's fee.

In any action or proceeding under this subchapter the United States shall be liable for costs, including a reasonable attorney's fee, the same as a private person. (Pub. L. 88-352, title III, §302, July 2, 1964, 78 Stat. 246.)

§2000b-2. Personal suits for relief against discrimination in public facilities.

Nothing in this subchapter shall affect adversely the right of any person to sue for or obtain relief in any court against discrimination in any facility covered by this subchapter. (Pub. L. 88-352, title III, §303, July 2, 1964, 78 Stat. 246.)

§2000b-3. "Complaint" defined.

A complaint as used in this subchapter is a writing or document within the meaning of section 1001, Title 18. (Pub. L. 88-352, title III, §304, July 2, 1964, 78 Stat. 246.)

Title IV. — Public Education

§2000c. Definitions.

As used in this subchapter —

(a) "Commissioner" means the Commissioner of Education.

(b) "Desegregation" means the assignment of students to public schools and within such schools without regard to their race, color, religion, or national origin, but "desegregation" shall not mean the assignment of students to public schools in order to overcome racial imbalance.

(c) "Public school" means any elementary or secondary educational institution, and "public college" means any institution of higher education or any technical or vocational school above the secondary school level, provided that such public school or public college is operated by a State, subdivision of a State, or governmental agency within a State, or operated wholly or predominantly from or through the use of governmental funds or property, or funds or property derived from a governmental source.

(d) "School board" means any agency or agencies which administer a system of one or more public schools and any other agency which is responsible for the assignment of students to or within such system.

(Pub. L. 88-352, title IV, §401, July 2, 1964, 78 Stat. 246.)

§2000c-1. Survey and report of educational opportunities.

CODIFICATION

Section, Pub. L. 83-352, title IV, §402, July 2, 1964, 78 Stat. 247, which authorized the Commissioner to conduct a survey and make a report to the President and the Congress within two years of July, 1964 concerning the availability of educational opportunities for minority group members, has been omitted as executed.

§2000c-2. Technical assistance in preparation, adoption, and implementation of plans for desegregation of public schools.

The Commissioner is authorized, upon the application of any school board, State, municipality, school district, or other governmental unit legally responsible for operating a public school or schools, to render technical assistance to such applicant in the preparation, adoption, and implementation of plans for the desegregation of public schools. Such technical assistance may, among other activities, include making available to such agencies information regarding effective methods of coping with special educational problems occasioned by desegregation, and making available to such agencies personnel of the Office of Education or other persons specially equipped to advise and assist them in coping with such problems. (Pub. L. 88-352, title IV, §403, July 2, 1964, 78 Stat. 247.)

§2000c-3. Training institutes; stipends; travel allowances.

The Commissioner is authorized to arrange, through grants or contracts, with institutions of higher education for the operation of short-term or regular session institutes for special training designed to improve the ability of teachers, supervisors, counselors, and other elementary or secondary school personnel to deal effectively with special educational problems occasioned by desegregation. Individuals who attend such an institute on a full-time basis may be paid stipends for the period of their attendance at such institute in amounts specified by the Commissioner in regulations, including allowances for travel to attend such institute. (Pub. L. 88-352, title IV, §404, July 2, 1964, 78 Stat. 247.)

§2000c-4. Grants for inservice training in dealing with and for employment of specialists to advise in problems incident to desegregation; factors for consideration in making grants and fixing amounts, terms, and conditions.

(a) The Commissioner is authorized, upon application of a school board, to make grants to such board to pay, in whole or in part, the cost of —

(1) giving to teachers and other school personnel inservice training in dealing with problems incident to desegregation, and

(2) employing specialists to advise in problems incident to desegregation.

(b) In determining whether to make a grant, and in fixing the amount thereof and the terms and conditions on which it will be made, the Commissioner shall take into consideration the amount available for grants under this section and the other applications which are pending before him; the financial condition of the applicant and the other resources available to it; the nature, extent, and gravity of its problems incident to desegregation; and such other factors as he finds relevant. (Pub. L. 88-352, title IV, §405, July 2, 1964, 78 Stat. 247.)

§2000c-5. Payments; adjustments; advances or reimbursement; installments.

Payments pursuant to a grant or contract under this subchapter may be made (after necessary adjustments on account of previously made overpayments or underpayments) in advance or by way of reimbursement, and in such installments, as the Commissioner may determine. (Pub. L. 88-352, title IV, §406, July 2, 1964, 78 Stat. 248.)

§2000c-6. Civil actions by the Attorney General.

(a) Complaint; certification; notice to school board or college authority; institution of civil action; relief requested; jurisdiction; transportation of pupils to achieve racial balance; judicial power to insure compliance with constitutional standards; impleading additional parties as defendants.

Whenever the Attorney General receives a complaint in writing —

(1) signed by a parent or group of parents to the effect that his or their minor children, as members of a class of persons similarly situated, are being deprived by a school board of the equal protection of the laws, or

(2) signed by an individual, or his parent, to the effect that he has been denied admission to or not permitted to continue in attendance at a public college by reason of race, color, religion, or national origin,

and the Attorney General believes the complaint is meritorious and certifies that the signer or signers of such complaint are unable, in his judgment, to initiate and maintain appropriate legal proceedings for relief and that the institution of an action will materially further the orderly achievement of desegregation in public education, the Attorney General is authorized, after giving notice of such complaint to the appropriate school board or college authority and after certifying that he is satisfied that such board or authority has had a reasonable time to adjust the conditions alleged in such complaint, to institute for or in the name of the United States a civil action in any appropriate district court of the United States against such parties and for such relief as may be appropriate, and such court shall have and shall exercise jurisdiction of proceedings instituted pursuant to this section, provided that nothing herein shall empower any official or court of the United States to issue any order seeking to achieve a racial balance in any school by requiring the transportation of pupils or students from one school to another or one school district to another in order to achieve such racial balance, or otherwise enlarge the existing power of the court to insure compliance with constitutional standards. The Attorney General may implead as defendants such additional parties as are or become necessary to the grant of effective relief hereunder.

(b) Persons unable to initiate and maintain legal proceedings.

The Attorney General may deem a person or persons unable to initiate and maintain appropriate legal proceedings within the meaning of subsection (a) of this section when such person or persons are unable, either directly or through other interested persons or organizations, to bear the expense of the litigation or to obtain effective legal representation; or whenever he is satisfied that the institution of such litigation would jeopardize the personal safety, employment, or economic standing of such person or persons, their families, or their property.

(c) "Parent" and "complaint" defined.

The term "parent" as used in this section includes any person standing in loco parentis. A "complaint" as used in this section is a writing or document within the meaning of section 1001, Title 18. (Pub. L. 88-352, title IV, §407, July 2, 1964, 78 Stat. 248.)

§2000c-7. Liability of United States for costs.

In any action or proceeding under this subchapter the United States shall be liable for costs the same as a private person. (Pub. L. 88-352, title IV, §408, July 2, 1964, 78 Stat. 249.)

§2000c-8. Personal suits for relief against discrimination in public education.

Nothing in this subchapter shall affect adversely the right of any person to sue for or obtain relief in any court against discrimination in public education. (Pub. L. 88-352, title IV, §409, July 2, 1964, 78 Stat. 249.)

§2000c-9. Classification and assignment.

Nothing in this subchapter shall prohibit classification and assignment for reasons other than race, color, religion, or national origin. (Pub. L. 88-352, title IV, §410, July 2, 1964, 78 Stat. 249.)

Title VI. — Nondiscrimination in Federally Assisted Programs

§601. No person in the United States shall, on the ground of race, color, or national origin be excluded from participation in, be denied the benefits of, or be subjected to discrimination under any program or activity receiving Federal financial assistance. [July 2, 1964, P.L. 88-352, Title VI, §601, 78 Stat. 252, 42 U.S.C. §2000d.]

§602. Each Federal department and agency which is empowered to extend Federal financial assistance to any program or activity, by way of grant, loan, or contract other than a contract of insurance or guaranty, is authorized and directed to effectuate the provisions of section 2000d of this title with respect to such program or activity by issuing rules, regulations, or orders of general applicability which shall be consistent with achievement of the objectives of the statute authorizing the financial assistance in connection with which the action is taken. No such rule, regulation, or order shall become effective unless and until approved by the President. Compliance with any requirement adopted pursuant to this section may be effected (1) by the termination of or refusal to grant or to continue assistance under such program or activity to any recipient as to whom there has been an express finding on the record, after opportunity for hearing, of a failure to comply with such requirement, but such termination or refusal shall be limited to the particular political entity, or part thereof, or other recipient as to whom such a finding has been

made and, shall be limited in its effect to the particular program, or part thereof, in which such noncompliance has been so found, or (2) by any other means authorized by law: *Provided, however,* That no such action shall be taken until the department or agency concerned has advised the appropriate person or persons of the failure to comply with the requirement and has determined that compliance cannot be secured by voluntary means. In the case of any action terminating, or refusing to grant or continue, assistance because of failure to comply with a requirement imposed pursuant to this section, the head of the Federal department or agency shall file with the committees of the House and Senate having legislative jurisdiction over the program or activity involved a full written report of the circumstances and the grounds for such action. No such action shall become effective until thirty days have elapsed after the filing of such report. [July 2, 1964, P.L. 88-352, Title VI, §602, 78 Stat. 252, 42 U.S.C. §2000d-1.]

§603. Any department or agency action taken pursuant to section 2000d-1 of this title shall be subject to such judicial review as may otherwise be provided by law for similar action taken by such department or agency on other grounds. In the case of action, not otherwise subject to judicial review, terminating or refusing to grant or to continue financial assistance upon a finding of failure to comply with a requirement imposed pursuant to section 2000d-1 of this title, any person aggrieved (including any State or political subdivision thereof and any agency of either) may obtain judicial review of such action in accordance with section 1009 of Title 5, and such action shall not be deemed committed to unreviewable agency discretion within the meaning of that section. [July 2, 1964, P.L. 88-352, Title VI, §603, 78 Stat. 253, 42 U.S.C. §2000d-2.]

§604. Nothing contained in this subchapter [Title] shall be construed to authorize action under this subchapter [Title] by any department or agency with respect to any employment practice of any employer, employment agency, or labor organization except where a primary objective of the Federal financial assistance is to provide employment. [July 2, 1964, P.L. 88-352, Title VI, §604, 78 Stat. 253, 42 U.S.C. §2000d-3.]

§605. Nothing in this subchapter [Title] shall add to or detract from any existing authority with respect to any program or activity under which Federal financial assistance is extended by way of a contract of insurance or guaranty. [July 2, 1964, P.L. 88-352, Title VI, §605, 78 Stat. 253, 42 U.S.C. §2000d-4.]

Title VII. — Equal Employment Opportunity (Selected Portions)

(Act of July 2, 1964, P.L. 88-352, 42 U.S.C.A. §§2000e–2000e-17, effective July 2, 1965. as amended March 24, 1972, P.L. 92-261, 86 Stat. 103, Equal Employment Opportunity Act of 1972.)

DEFINITIONS

§701, 2000e. For the purposes of this title —

(a) The term "person" includes one or more individuals, governments, governmental agencies, political subdivisions, labor unions, partnerships, associations, corporations, legal representatives, mutual companies, joint-stock companies, trusts, unincorporated organizations, trustees, trustees in bankruptcy, or receivers. [As amended March 24, 1972, P.L. 92-261, Sec. 2.]

(b) The term "employer" means a person engaged in an industry affecting commerce who has fifteen or more employees for each working day in each of twenty or more calendar weeks in the current or preceding calendar year, and any agent of such a person, but such term does not include (1) the United States, a corporation wholly owned by the Government of the United States, an Indian tribe, or any department or agency of the District of Columbia subject by statute to procedures of the competitive service (as defined in section 2102 of Title 5 of the United States Code), or (2) a bona fide private membership club (other than a labor organization) which is exempt from taxation under section 501(c) of the Internal Revenue Code of 1954, except that during the first year after the date of enactment of the Equal Employment Opportunity Act of 1972, persons having fewer than twenty-five employees (and their agents) shall not be considered employers. [As amended March 24, 1972, P.L. 92-261, Sec. 2.]

(c) The term "employment agency" means any person regularly undertaking with or without compensation to produce employees for an employer or to procure for employees opportunities to work for an employer and includes an agent of such a person. [As amended March 24, 1972, P.L. 92-261, Sec. 2.]

(d) The term "labor organization" means a labor organization engaged in an industry affecting commerce, and any agent of such an organization, and includes any organization of any kind, any agency, or employee representation committee, group, association, or plan so engaged in which employees participate and which exists for the purpose, in whole or in part, of dealing with employers concerning grievances, labor disputes, wages, rates of pay, hours, or other terms or conditions of employment, and any conference, general committee, joint or system board, or joint council so engaged which is subordinate to a national or international labor organization.

(e) A labor organization shall be deemed to be engaged in an industry affecting commerce if (1) it maintains or operates a hiring hall or hiring office which procures employees for an employer or procures for employees opportunities to work for an employer, or (2) the number of its members (or, where it is a labor organization composed of other labor organizations or their representatives, if the aggregate number of the members of such other labor organization) is (A) twenty-five or more during the first year after the date of enactment of the Equal Employment Opportunity Act of 1972, or (B) fifteen or more thereafter, and such labor organization —

(1) is the certified representative of employees under the provisions of the National Labor Relations Act, as amended, or the Railway Labor Act, as amended;

(2) although not certified, is a national or international labor organization or a local labor organization recognized or acting as the representative of employees of an employer or employers engaged in an industry affecting commerce; or

(3) has chartered a local labor organization or subsidiary body which is representing or actively seeking to represent employees of employers within the meaning of paragraph (1) or (2); or

(4) has been chartered by a labor organization representing or actively seeking to represent employees within the meaning of paragraph (1) or (2) as the local or subordinate body through which such employees may enjoy membership or become affiliated with such labor organization; or

(5) is a conference, general committee, joint or system board, or joint council

subordinate to a national or international labor organization, which includes a labor organization engaged in an industry affecting commerce within the meaning of any of the preceding paragraphs of this subsection. [As amended March 24, 1972, P.L. 92-261, Sec. 2.]

(f) The term "employee" means an individual employed by an employer, except that the term "employee" shall not include any person elected to public office in any State or political subdivision of any State by the qualified voters thereof, or any person chosen by such officer to be on such officer's personal staff, or an appointee on the policy making level or an immediate adviser with respect to the exercise of the constitutional or legal powers of the office. The exemption set forth in the preceding sentence shall not include employees subject to the civil service laws of a State government, governmental agency or political subdivision. [As amended March 24, 1972, P.L. 92-261, Sec. 2.] . . .

Employer practices

§703, 2000e-2. (a) It shall be an unlawful employment practice for an employer —

(1) to fail or refuse to hire or to discharge any individual, or otherwise to discriminate against any individual with respect to his compensation, terms, conditions, or privileges of employment, because of such individual's race, color, religion, sex, or national origin; or

(2) to limit, segregate, or classify his employees or applicants for employment in any way which would deprive or tend to deprive any individual of employment opportunities or otherwise adversely affect his status as an employee, because of such individual's race, color, religion, sex, or national origin. [As amended March 24, 1972, P.L. 92-261, Sec. 8.]

Employment agency practices

(b) It shall be an unlawful employment practice for an employment agency to fail or refuse to refer for employment, or otherwise to discriminate against, any individual because of his race, color, religion, sex, or national origin, or to classify or refer for employment any individual on the basis of his race, color, religion, sex, or national origin.

Labor organization practices

(c) It shall be an unlawful employment practice for a labor organization —

(1) to exclude or to expel from its membership, or otherwise to discriminate against, any individual because of his race, color, religion, sex, or national origin;

(2) to limit, segregate, or classify its membership or applicants for membership, or to classify or fail or refuse to refer for employment any individual, in any way which would deprive or tend to deprive any individual of employment opportunities, or would limit such employment opportunities or otherwise adversely affect his status as an employee or as an applicant for employment, because of such individual's race, color, religion, sex, or national origin; or

(3) to cause or attempt to cause an employer to discriminate against an individual in violation of this section. [As amended March 24, 1972, P.L. 92-261, Sec. 8.]

Training programs

(d) It shall be an unlawful employment practice for any employer, labor organization, or joint labor-management committee controlling apprenticeship or other training or retraining, including on-the-job training programs to discriminate against any individual because of his race, color, religion, sex, or national origin in admission to, or employment in, any program established to provide apprenticeship or other training.

Businesses with personnel qualified on basis of religion, sex, or national origin; educational institutions with personnel of a particular religion

(c) Notwithstanding any other provision of this title, (1) it shall not be an unlawful employment practice for an employer to hire and employ employees, for an employment agency to classify, or refer for employment any individual, for a labor organization to classify its membership or to classify or refer for employment any individual, or for an employer, labor organization, or joint labor-management committee controlling apprenticeship or other training or retraining programs to admit or employ any individual in any such program, on the basis of his religion, sex, or national origin in those certain instances where religion, sex, or national origin is a bona fide occupational qualification reasonably necessary to the normal operation of that particular business or enterprise, and (2) it shall not be an unlawful employment practice for a school, college, university, or other educational institution or institution of learning to hire and employ employees of a particular religion if such school, college, university, or other educational institution or institution of learning is, in whole or in substantial part, owned, supported, controlled, or managed by a particular religion or by a particular religious corporation, association, or society, or if the curriculum of such school, college, university, or other educational institution or institution of learning is directed toward the propagation of a particular religion.

Communists excluded from coverage

(f) As used in this title, the phrase "unlawful employment practice" shall not be deemed to include any action or measure taken by an employer, labor organization, joint labor-management committee, or employment agency with respect to an individual who is a member of the Communist Party of the United States or of any other organization required to register as a Communist-action or Communist-front organization by final order of the Subversive Activities Control Board pursuant to the Subversive Activities Control Act of 1950.

National security as an exemption to coverage

(g) Notwithstanding any other provision of this title, it shall not be an unlawful employment practice for an employer to fail or refuse to hire and employ any individual for any position, for an employer to discharge any individual from any position, or for an employment agency to fail or refuse to refer any individual for employment in any position, or for a labor organization to fail or refuse to refer any individual for employment in any position, if —

(1) the occupancy of such position, or access to the premises in or upon which any part of the duties of such position is performed or is to be performed, is subject to any requirement imposed in the interest of the national security of the United States under any security program in effect pursuant to or administered under any statute of the United States or any Executive order of the President; and

(2) such individual has not fulfilled or has ceased to fulfill that requirement.

Seniority or merit system; quantity or quality of production; ability tests; compensation based on sex and authorized by minimum wage provisions

(h) Notwithstanding any other provision of this title, it shall not be an unlawful employment practice for an employer to apply different standards of compensation, or different terms, conditions, or privileges of employment pursuant to a bona fide seniority or merit system, or a system which measures earnings by quantity or quality of production or to employees who work in different locations, provided that such differences are not the result of an intention to discriminate because of race, color, religion, sex, or national origin, nor shall it be an unlawful employment practice for an employer to give and to act upon the results of any professionally developed ability test provided that such test, its administration or action upon the results is not designed, intended or used to discriminate because of race, color, religion, sex or national origin. It shall not be an unlawful employment practice under this title for any employer to differentiate upon the basis of sex in determining the amount of the wages or compensation paid or to be paid to employees of such employer if such differentiation is authorized by the provisions of section 6(d) of the Fair Labor Standards Act of 1938, as amended (29 U.S.C. 206(d)).

Businesses or enterprises extending preferential treatment to Indians

(i) Nothing contained in this title shall apply to any business or enterprise on or near an Indian reservation with respect to any publicly announced employment practice of such business or enterprise under which a preferential treatment is given to any individual because he is an Indian living on or near a reservation.

Preferential treatment not to be granted on account of existing number or percentage imbalance

(j) Nothing contained in this title shall be interpreted to require any employer, employment agency, labor organization, or joint labor-management committee subject to this title to grant preferential treatment to any individual or to any group because of the race, color, religion, sex, or national origin of such individual or group on account of an imbalance which may exist with respect to the total number or percentage of persons of any race, color, religion, sex, or national origin employed by any employer, referred or classified for employment by any employment agency or labor organization, admitted to membership or classified by any labor organization, or admitted to, or employed in, any apprenticeship or other training program, in comparison with the total number or percentage of persons of such race, color, religion, sex, or national origin in any community, State, section, or other area, or in the available work force in any community, State, section, or other area.

Other unlawful employment practices — Discrimination for making charges, testifying, assisting, or participating in enforcement proceedings

§704, 2000e-3. (a) It shall be an unlawful employment practice for an employer to discriminate against any of his employees or applicants for employment, for an employment agency, or joint labor-management committee controlling apprenticeship or other training or retraining, including on-the-job training programs, to discriminate against any individual, or for a labor organization to discriminate against any member thereof or applicant for membership, because he has opposed any practice made an unlawful employment practice by this title, or because he has

made a charge, testified, assisted, or participated in any manner in an investigation, proceeding, or hearing under this title. [As amended March 24, 1972, P.L. 92-261, Sec. 8.]

Printing or publication of discriminatory notices or advertisements

(b) It shall be an unlawful employment practice for an employer, labor organization, employment agency, or joint labor-management committee controlling apprenticeship or other training or retraining, including on-the-job training programs, to print or publish or cause to be printed or published any notice or advertisement relating to employment by such an employer or membership in any classification or referral for employment by such a labor organization, or relating to any classification or referral for employment by such an employment agency, or relating to admission to, or employment in, any program established to provide apprenticeship or other training by such a joint labor-management committee, indicating any preference, limitation, specification, or discrimination, based on race, color, religion, sex, or national origin, except that such a notice or advertisement may indicate a preference, limitation, specification, or discrimination based on religion, sex, or national origin when religion, sex, or national origin is a bona fide occupational qualification for employment. [As amended March 24, 1972, P.L. 92-261, Sec. 8.]

Equal Employment Opportunity Commission

§705, 2000e-4. (a) There is hereby created a Commission to be known as the Equal Employment Opportunity Commission, which shall be composed of five members, not more than three of whom shall be members of the same political party. Members of the Commission shall be appointed by the President by and with the advice and consent of the Senate for a term of five years. Any individual chosen to fill a vacancy shall be appointed only for the unexpired term of the member whom he shall succeed, and all members of the Commission shall continue to serve until their successors are appointed and qualified, except that no such member of the Commission shall continue to serve (1) for more than sixty days when the Congress is in session unless a nomination to fill such vacancy shall have been submitted to the Senate, or (2) after the adjournment sine die of the session of the Senate in which such nomination was submitted. The President shall designate one member to serve as Chairman of the Commission, and one member to serve as Vice Chairman. The Chairman shall be responsible on behalf of the Commission for the administrative operations of the Commission, and, except as provided in subsection (b), shall appoint, in accordance with the provisions of title 5, United States Code, governing appointments in the competitive service, such officers, agents, attorneys, hearing examiners, and employees as he deems necessary to assist it in the performance of its functions and to fix their compensation in accordance with the provisions of chapter 51 and subchapter III of chapter 53 of title 5, United States Code, relating to classification and General Schedule pay rates: Provided, That assignment, removal, and compensation of hearing examiners shall be in accordance with sections 3105, 3344, 5362, and 7521 of title 5, United States Code. [As amended March 24, 1972, P.L. 92-261, Sec. 8.] . . .

Enforcement provisions

§706, 2000e-5. (a) The Commission is empowered, as hereinafter provided, to prevent any person from engaging in any unlawful employment practice as set

forth in section 703 or 704 of this title. [As amended March 24, 1972, P.L. 92-261, Sec. 4.]

State or local enforcement provisions

(b) Whenever a charge is filed by or on behalf of a person claiming to be aggrieved, or by a member of the Commission, alleging that an employer, employment agency, labor organization, or joint labor-management committee controlling apprenticeship or other training or retraining, including on-the-job training programs, has engaged in an unlawful employment practice, the Commission shall serve a notice of the charge (including the date, place and circumstances of the alleged unlawful employment practice) on such employer, employment agency, labor organization, or joint labor-management committee (hereinafter referred to as the "respondent") within ten days, and shall make an investigation thereof. Charges shall be in writing under oath or affirmation and shall contain such information and be in such form as the Commission requires. Charges shall not be made public by the Commission. If the Commission determines after such investigation that there is not reasonable cause to believe that the charge is true, it shall dismiss the charge and promptly notify the person claiming to be aggrieved and the respondent of its action. In determining whether reasonable cause exists, the Commission shall accord substantial weight to final findings and orders made by State or local authorities in proceedings commenced under State or local law pursuant to the requirements of subsections (c) and (d). If the Commission determines after such investigation that there is reasonable cause to believe that the charge is true, the Commission shall endeavor to eliminate any such alleged unlawful employment practice by informal methods of conference, conciliation, and persuasion. Nothing said or done during and as a part of such informal endeavors may be made public by the Commission, its officers or employees, or used as evidence in a subsequent proceeding without the written consent of the persons concerned. Any person who makes public information in violation of this subsection shall be fined not more than $1,000 or imprisoned for not more than one year, or both. The Commission shall make its determination on reasonable cause as promptly as possible and, so far as practicable, not later than one hundred and twenty days from the filing of the charge or, where applicable under subsection (c) or (d), from the date upon which the Commission is authorized to take action with respect to the charge. [As amended March 24, 1972, P.L. 92-261, Sec. 4.]

Notification of state or local authority

(c) In the case of an alleged unlawful employment practice occurring in a State, or political subdivision of a State, which has a State or local law prohibiting the unlawful employment practice alleged and establishing or authorizing a State or local authority to grant or seek relief from such practice or to institute criminal proceedings with respect thereto upon receiving notice thereof, no charge may be filed under subsection (a) by the person aggrieved before the expiration of sixty days after proceedings have been commenced under the State or local law, unless such proceedings have been earlier terminated, provided that such sixty-day period shall be extended to one hundred and twenty days during the first year after the effective date of such State or local law. If any requirement for the commencement of such proceedings is imposed by a State or local authority other than a requirement of the filing of a written and signed statement of the facts upon which the proceeding is based, the proceeding shall be deemed to have been commenced for the purposes of this subsection at the time such statement is sent by registered mail to the appropriate State or local authority. [As amended March 24, 1972, P.L. 92-261, Sec. 4.]

Notification of state or local authority

(d) In the case of any charge filed by a member of the Commission alleging an unlawful employment practice occurring in a State or political subdivision of a State which has a State or local law prohibiting the practice alleged and establishing or authorizing a State or local authority to grant or seek relief from such practice or to institute criminal proceedings with respect thereto upon receiving notice thereof, the Commission shall, before taking any action with respect to such charge, notify the appropriate State or local officials and, upon request, afford them a reasonable time, but not less than sixty days (provided that such sixty-day period shall be extended to one hundred and twenty days during the first year after the effective day of such State or local law), unless a shorter period is requested, to act under such State or local law to remedy the practice alleged. [As amended March 24, 1972, P.L. 92-261, Sec. 4.]

Time for filing charges

(e) A charge under this section shall be filed within one hundred and eighty days after the alleged unlawful employment practice occurred and notice of the charge (including the date, place and circumstances of the alleged unlawful employment practice) shall be served upon the person against whom such charge is made within ten days thereafter, except that in a case of an unlawful employment practice with respect to which the person aggrieved has initially instituted proceedings with a State or local agency with authority to grant or seek relief from such practice or to institute criminal proceedings with respect thereto upon receiving notice thereof, such charge shall be filed by or on behalf of the person aggrieved within three hundred days after the alleged unlawful employment practice occurred, or within thirty days after receiving notice that the State or local agency has terminated the proceedings under the State or local law, whichever is earlier, and a copy of such charge shall be filed by the Commission with the State or local agency. [As amended March 24, 1972, P.L. 92-261, Sec. 4.]

Civil action by Commission, Attorney General or person aggrieved

(f) (1) If within thirty days after a charge is filed with the Commission or within thirty days after expiration of any period of reference under subsection (c) or (d), the Commission has been unable to secure from the respondent a conciliation agreement acceptable to the Commission, the Commission may bring a civil action against any respondent not a government, governmental agency, or political subdivision named in the charge. In the case of a respondent which is a government, governmental agency, or political subdivision, if the Commission has been unable to secure from the respondent a conciliation agreement acceptable to the Commission, the Commission shall take no further action and shall refer the case to the Attorney General who may bring a civil action against such respondent in the appropriate United States district court. The person or persons aggrieved shall have the right to intervene in a civil action brought by the Commission or the Attorney General in a case involving a government, governmental agency, or political subdivision. If a charge filed with the Commission pursuant to subsection (b) is dismissed by the Commission, or if within one hundred and eighty days from the filing of such charge or the expiration of any period of reference under subsection (c) or (d), whichever is later, the Commission has not filed a civil action under this section or the Attorney General has not filed a civil action in a case involving a government, governmental agency, or political subdivision, or the Commission has not entered into a conciliation agreement to which the person aggrieved is a party, the Commission, or the Attorney General in a case involving a government, governmental agency, or political subdivision, shall so notify the person aggrieved and within ninety days after the giving of such notice a civil action may be brought against the respondent named in the charge (A) by the person claiming to be aggrieved or (B) if such charge was filed by a member of the Commission, by any person whom the charge alleges was aggrieved by the alleged unlawful employment practice. Upon application by the complainant and in such circumstances as the court may deem just, the court may appoint an attorney for such complainant and may authorize the commencement of the action without the payment of fees, costs, or security. Upon timely application, the court may, in its discretion, permit the Commission, or the Attorney General in a case involving a government, governmental agency, or political subdivision, to intervene in such civil action upon certification that the case is of general public importance. Upon request, the court may, in its discretion, stay further proceedings for not more than sixty days pending the termination of State or local proceedings described in subsections (c) or (d) of this section or further efforts of the Commission to obtain voluntary compliance. [As amended March 24, 1972, P.L. 92-261, Sec. 4.]

(2) Whenever a charge is filed with the Commission and the Commission concludes on the basis of a preliminary investigation that prompt judicial action is necessary to carry out the purposes of this Act, the Commission, or the Attorney General in a case involving a government, governmental agency, or political subdivision, may bring an action for appropriate temporary or preliminary relief pending final disposition of such charge. Any temporary restraining order or other order granting preliminary or temporary relief shall be issued in accordance with rule 65 of the Federal Rules of Civil Procedure. It shall be the duty of a court having jurisdiction over proceedings under this section to assign cases for hearing at the earliest practicable date and to cause such cases to be in every way expedited. [As added March 24, 1972, P.L. 92-261, Sec. 4.]

(3) Each United States district court and each United States court of a place subject to the jurisdiction of the United States shall have jurisdiction of actions brought under this title. Such an action may be brought in any judicial district in the State in which the unlawful employment practice is alleged to have been committed, in the judicial district in which the employment records relevant to such practice are maintained and administered, or in the judicial district in which the aggrieved person would have worked but for the alleged unlawful employment practice, but if the respondent is not found within any such district, such an action may be brought within the judicial district in which the respondent has his princpal office. For purposes of sections 1404 and 1406 of title 28 of the United States Code, the judicial district in which the respondent has his principal office shall in all cases be considered a district in which the action might have been brought. [As added March 24, 1972, P.L. 92-261, Sec. 4.]

(4) It shall be the duty of the chief judge of the district (or in his absence, the

acting chief judge) in which the case is pending immediately to designate a judge in such district to hear and determine the case. In the event that no judge in the district is available to hear and determine the case, the chief judge of the district, or the acting chief judge, as the case may be, shall certify this fact to the chief judge of the circuit (or in his absence, the acting chief judge) who shall then designate a district or circuit judge of the circuit to hear and determine the case. [As added March 24, 1972, P.L. 92-261, Sec. 4.]

(5) It shall be the duty of the judge designated pursuant to this subsection to assign the case for hearing at the earliest practicable date and to cause the case to be in every way expedited. If such judge has not scheduled the case for trial within one hundred and twenty days after issue has been joined, that judge may appoint a master pursuant to rule 53 of the Federal Rules of Civil Procedure. [As added March 24, 1972, P.L. 92-261, Sec. 4.]

Injunctions; appropriate affirmative action, back pay

(g) If the court finds that the respondent has intentionally engaged in or is intentionally engaging in an unlawful employment practice charged in the complaint, the court may enjoin the respondent from engaging in such unlawful employment practice, and order such affirmative action as may be appropriate, which may include, but is not limited to, reinstatement or hiring of employees, with or without back pay (payable by the employer, employment agency, or labor organization, as the case may be, responsible for the unlawful employment practice), or any other equitable relief as the court deems appropriate. Back pay liability shall not accrue from a date more than two years prior to the filing of a charge with the Commission. Interim earnings or amounts earnable with reasonable diligence by the person or persons discriminated against shall operate to reduce the back pay otherwise allowable. No order of the court shall require the admission or reinstatement of an individual as a member of a union, or the hiring, reinstatement, or promotion of an individual as an employee, or the payment to him of any back pay, if such individual was refused admission, suspended, or expelled, or was refused employment or advancement or was suspended or discharged for any reason other than discrimination on account of race, color, religion, sex, or national origin or in violation of section 704(a). [As amended March 24, 1972, P.L. 92-261, Sec. 4.]

Proceedings by Commission to compel compliance with judicial orders

(i) In any case in which an employer, employment agency, or labor organization fails to comply with an order of a court issued in a civil action brought under this section, the Commission may commence proceedings to compel compliance with such order. [As amended March 24, 1972, P.L. 92-261, Sec. 4.]

Appeals

(j) Any civil action brought under this section, and any proceedings brought under subsection (i) shall be subject to appeal as provided in sections 1291 and 1292, title 28, United States Code. [As amended March 24, 1972, P.L. 92-261, Sec. 4.]

Attorney's fee; liability of Commission and United States for costs

(k) In any action or proceeding under this title the court, in its discretion, may allow the prevailing party, other than the Commission or the United States, a reasonable attorney's fee as part of the costs, and the Commission and the United States shall be liable for costs the same as a private person.

Civil actions by the Attorney General

§707, 2000e-6. (a) Whenever the Attorney General has reasonable cause to believe that any person or group of persons is engaged in a pattern or practice of resistance to the full enjoyment of any of the rights secured by this title, and that the pattern or practice is of such a nature and is intended to deny the full exercise of the rights herein described, the Attorney General may bring a civil action in the appropriate district court of the United States by filing with it a complaint (1) signed by him (or in his absence the Acting Attorney General), (2) setting forth facts pertaining to such pattern or practice, and (3) requesting such relief, including an application for a permanent or temporary injunction, restraining order or other order against the person or persons responsible for such pattern or practice, as he deems necessary to insure the full enjoyment of the rights herein described.

Jurisdiction

(b) The district courts of the United States shall have and shall exercise jurisdiction of proceedings instituted pursuant to this section, and in any such proceeding the Attorney General may file with the clerk of such court a request that a court of three judges be convened to hear and determine the case. Such request by the Attorney General shall be accompanied by a certificate that, in his opinion, the case is of general public importance. A copy of the certificate and request for a three-judge court shall be immediately furnished by such clerk to the chief judge of the circuit (or in his absence, the presiding circuit judge of the circuit) in which the case is pending. Upon receipt of such request it shall be the duty of the chief judge of the circuit or the presiding circuit judge, as the case may be, to designate immediately three judges in such circuit, of whom at least one shall be a circuit judge and another of whom shall be a district judge of the court in which the proceeding was instituted, to hear and determine such case, and it shall be the duty of the judges so designated to assign the case for hearing at the earliest practicable date, to participate in the hearing and determination thereof, and to cause the case to be in every way expedited. An appeal from the final judgment of such court will lie to the Supreme Court.

In the event the Attorney General fails to file such a request in any such proceeding, it shall be the duty of the chief judge of the district (or in his absence, the acting chief judge) in which the case is pending immediately to designate a judge in such district to hear and determine the case. In the event that no judge in the district is available to hear and determine the case, the chief judge of the district, or the acting chief judge, as the case may be, shall certify this fact to the chief judge of the circuit (or in his absence, the acting chief judge) who shall then designate a district or circuit judge of the circuit to hear and determine the case.

It shall be the duty of the judge designated pursuant to this section to assign the case for hearing at the earliest practicable date and to cause the case to be in every way expedited.

Transfer of functions to Commission

(c) Effective two years after the date of enactment of the Equal Employment Opportunity Act of 1972, the functions of the Attorney General under this section shall be transferred to the Commission, together with such personnel, property, records, and unexpended balances of appropriations, allocations, and other funds employed, used, held, available, or to be made available in connection with such functions unless the President submits, and neither House of Congress vetoes, a reorganization plan pursuant to chapter 9 of title 5, United States Code, inconsistent with the provisions of this subsection. The Commission shall carry out such functions in accordance with subsections (d) and (e) of this section. [As added March 24, 1972, P.L. 92-261, Sec. 5.]

(d) Upon the transfer of functions provided for in subsection (c) of this section, in all suits commenced pursuant to this section prior to the date of such transfer, proceedings shall continue without abatement, all court orders and decrees shall remain in effect, and the Commission shall be substituted as a party for the United States of America, the Attorney General, or the Acting Attorney General, as appropriate. [As added March 24, 1972, P.L. 92-261, Sec. 5.]

(e) Subsequent to the date of enactment of the Equal Employment Opportunity Act of 1972, the Commission shall have authority to investigate and act on a charge of a pattern or practice of discrimination, whether filed by or on behalf of a person claiming to be aggrieved or by a member of the Commission. All such actions shall be conducted in accordance with the procedures set forth in section 706 of this Act. [As added March 24, 1972, P.L. 92-261, Sec. 5.]

Effect on state laws

§708, 2000e-7. Nothing in this title shall be deemed to exempt or relieve any person from any liability, duty, penalty, or punishment provided by any present or future law of any State or political subdivision of a State, other than any such law which purports to require or permit the doing of any act which would be an unlawful employment practice under this title. [July 2, 1964, P.L. 88-352, Title VII, §708, 78 Stat. 262, 42 U.S.C. §2000c-7.]

Investigations

§709, 2000e-8. (a) In connection with any investigation of a charge filed under section 706, the Commission or its designated representative shall at all reasonable times have access to, for the purposes of examination, and the right to copy any evidence of any person being investigated or proceeded against that relates to unlawful employment practices covered by this title and is relevant to the charge under investigation.

Cooperation with state and local agencies

(b) The Commission may cooperate with State and local agencies charged with the administration of State fair employment practices laws and, with the consent of such agencies, may, for the purpose of carrying out its functions and duties under this title and within the limitation of funds appropriated specifically for such purpose, engage in and contribute to the cost of research and other projects of mutual interest undertaken by such agencies, and utilize the services of such agencies and their employees, and, notwithstanding any other provision of law, pay by advance or reimbursement such agencies and their employees for services rendered to assist the Commission in carrying out this title. In furtherance of such cooperative efforts, the Commission may enter into written agreements with such State or local agencies and such agreements may include provisions under which the Commission shall refrain from processing a charge in any cases or class of cases specified in such agreements or under which the Commission shall relieve any person or class of persons in such State or locality from requirements imposed under this section. The Commission shall rescind any such agreement whenever it determines that the agreement no longer serves the interest of effective enforcement of this title. [As amended March 24, 1972, P.L. 92-261, Sec. 6.]

Execution, retention, and preservation of records

(c) Every employer, employment agency, and labor organization subject to this title shall (1) make and keep such records relevant to the determinations of whether unlawful employment practices have been or are being committed, (2) preserve such records for such periods, and (3) make such reports therefrom as the Commission shall prescribe by regulation or order, after public hearing, as reasonable, necessary, or appropriate for the enforcement of this title or the regulations or orders thereunder. The Commission shall, by regulation, require each employer, labor organization, and joint labor-management committee subject to this title, which controls an apprenticeship or other training program to maintain such records as are reasonably necessary to carry out the purposes of this title, including, but not limited to, a list of applicants who wish to participate in such program, including the chronological order in which applications were received, and to furnish to the Commission upon request, a detailed description of the manner in which persons are selected to participate in the apprenticeship or other training program. Any employer, employment agency, labor organization, or joint labor-management committee which believes that the application to it of any regulation or order issued under this section would result in undue hardship may apply to the Commission for an exemption from the application of such regulation or order, and, if such application for an exemption is denied, bring a civil action in the United States district court for the district where such records are kept. If the Commission or the court, as the case may be, finds that the application of the regulation or order to the employer, employment agency, or labor organization in question would impose an undue hardship, the Commission or the court, as the case may be, may grant appropriate relief. If any person required to comply with the provisions of this subsection fails or refuses to do so, the United States district court for the district in which such person is found, resides, or transacts business, shall, upon application of the Commission, or the Attorney General in a case involving a government, governmental agency or political subdivision, have jurisdiction to issue to such person an order requiring him to comply. [As amended March 24, 1972, P.L. 92-261, Sec. 6.]

Consultation and coordination between Commission and interested State and Federal agencies

(d) In prescribing requirements pursuant to subsection (c) of this section, the Commission shall consult with other interested State and Federal agencies and shall endeavor to coordinate its requirements with those adopted by such agencies. The Commission shall furnish upon request and without cost to any State or local agency charged with the administration of a fair employment practice law information obtained pursuant to subsection (c) of this section from any employer, employment agency, labor organization, or joint labor-management committee subject to the jurisdiction of such agency. Such information shall be furnished on condition that it not be made public by the recipient agency prior to the institution of a proceeding under State or local law involving such information. If this condition is violated by a recipient agency, the Commission may decline to honor subsequent requests pursuant to this subsection. [As amended March 24, 1972, P.L. 92-261, Sec. 6.]

Prohibited disclosures; penalties

(e) It shall be unlawful for any officer or employee of the Commission to make public in any manner whatever any information obtained by the Commission pursuant to its authority under this section prior to the institution of any proceeding under this title involving such information. Any officer or employee of the Commission who shall make public in any manner whatever any information in violation of this subsection shall be guilty of a misdemeanor and upon conviction thereof, shall be fined not more than $1,000, or imprisoned not more than one year.

Investigatory powers, conduct of hearings

§710, 2000e-9. For the purpose of all hearings and investigations conducted by the Commission or its duly authorized agents or agencies, section 11 of the National Labor Relations Act (49 Stat. 455; 29 U.S.C. 161) shall apply. [As amended March 24, 1972, P.L. 92-261, Sec. 7.] . . .

Posting of notices, penalties

§711, 2000e-10. (a) Every employer, employment agency, and labor organization, as the case may be, shall post and keep posted in conspicuous places upon its premises where notices to employees, applicants for employment, and members are customarily posted a notice to be prepared or approved by the Commission setting forth excerpts from or, summaries of, the pertinent provisions of this title and information pertinent to the filing of a complaint.

(b) A willful violation of this section shall be punishable by a fine of not more than $100 for each separate offense.

Veterans' special rights or preference

§712, 2000e-11. Nothing contained in this title shall be construed to repeal or modify any Federal, State, territorial, or local law creating special rights or preference for veterans. . . .

Employment discrimination prohibited in Federal Government

§717, 2000e-16. (a) All personnel actions affecting employees or applicants for employment (except with regard to aliens employed outside the limits of the United States) in military departments as defined in section 102 of title 5, United States Code, in executive agencies (other than the General Accounting Office) as defined in section 105 of title 5, United States Code (including employees and applicants for employment who are paid from nonappropriated funds), in the United States Postal Service and the Postal Rate Commission, in those units of the Government of the District of Columbia having positions in the competitive service, and in those units of the legislative and judicial branches of the Federal Government having positions in the competitive service, and in the Library of Congress shall be made free from any discrimination based on race, color, religion, sex, or national origin. [As added March 24, 1972, P.L. 92-261, Sec. 11.]

Civil Service Commission, enforcement powers

(b) Except as otherwise provided in this subsection, the Civil Service Commission shall have authority to enforce the provisions of subsection (a) through appropriate remedies, including reinstatement or hiring of employees with or without back pay, as will effectuate the policies of this section, and shall issue such rules, regulations, orders and instructions as it deems necessary and appropriate to carry out its responsibilities under this section. The Civil Service Commission shall —

(1) be responsible for the annual review and approval of a national and regional equal employment opportunity plan which each department and agency and each appropriate unit referred to in subsection (a) of this section shall submit in order to maintain an affirmative program of equal employment opportunity for all such employees and applicants for employment;

(2) be responsible for the review and evaluation of the operation of all agency equal employment opportunity programs, periodically obtaining and publishing (on at least a semiannual basis) progress reports from each such department, agency, or unit; and

(3) consult with and solicit the recommendations of interested individuals, groups, and organizations relating to equal employment opportunity.

The head of each such department, agency, or unit shall comply with such rules, regulations, orders, and instructions which shall include a provision that an employee or applicant for employment shall be notified of any final action taken on any complaint of discrimination filed by him thereunder. The plan submitted by each department, agency, and unit shall include, but not be limited to —

(1) provision for the establishment of training and education programs designed to provide a maximum opportunity for employees to advance so as to perform at their highest potential; and

(2) a description of the qualifications in terms of training and experience relating to equal employment opportunity for the principal and operating officials of each such department, agency, or unit responsible for carrying out the equal employment opportunity program and of the allocation of personnel and resources proposed by such department, agency, or unit to carry out its equal employment opportunity program.

With respect to employment in the Library of Congress, authorities granted in this subsection to the Civil Service Commission shall be exercised by the Librarian of Congress. [As added March 24, 1972, P.L. 92-261, Sec. 11.]

(c) Within thirty days of receipt of notice of final action taken by a department, agency, or unit referred to in subsection 717(a), or by the Civil Service Commission upon an appeal from a decision or order of such department, agency, or unit on a complaint of discrimination based on race, color, religion, sex or national origin, brought pursuant to subsection (a) of this section, Executive Order 11478 or any succeeding Executive orders, or after one hundred and eighty days from the filing of the initial charge with the department, agency, or unit or with the Civil Service Commission on appeal from a decision or order of such department, agency, or unit until such time as final action may be taken by a department, agency, or unit, an employee or applicant for employment, if aggrieved by the final disposition of his complaint, or by the failure to take final action on his complaint, may file a civil action as provided in section 706, in which civil action the head of the department, agency, or unit, as appropriate, shall be the defendant. [As added March 24, 1972, P.L. 92-261, Sec. 11.]

(d) The provisions of section 706(f) through (k), as applicable, shall govern civil actions brought hereunder. [As added March 24, 1972, P.L. 92-261, Sec. 11.]

(e) Nothing contained in this Act shall relieve any Government agency or official of its or his primary responsibility to assure nondiscrimination in employment as required by the Constitution and statutes or of its or his responsibilities under Executive Order 11478 relating to equal employment opportunity in the Federal Government. [As added March 24, 1972, P.L. 92-261, Sec. 11.]

Procedure for denial, withholding, termination, or suspension of Government contracts

§718, 2000e-17. No Government contract, or portion thereof, with any employer, shall be denied, withheld, terminated, or suspended, by any agency or officer of the United States under any equal employment opportunity law or order, where such employer has an affirmative action plan which has previously been accepted by the Government for the same facility within the past twelve months without first according such employer full hearing and adjudication under the provisions of title 5, United States Code, section 554, and the following pertinent sections: Provided, That if such employer has deviated substantially from such previously agreed to affirmative action plan, this section shall not apply: Provided further, That for the purposes of this section an affirmative action plan shall be deemed to have been accepted by the Government at the time the appropriate compliance agency has accepted such plan unless within forty-five days thereafter the Office of Federal Contract Compliance has disapproved such plan. [As added March 24, 1972, P.L. 92-261, Sec. 13.]

VOTING RIGHTS ACT OF 1965, 42 UNITED STATES CODE (1970)

SUBCHAPTER I. — GENERALLY

§1971. Voting rights.

(*a*) *Race, color, or previous condition not to affect right to vote; uniform standards for voting qualifications; errors or omissions from papers; literacy tests; agreements between Attorney General and State or local authorities; definitions.*

(1) All citizens of the United States who are otherwise qualified by law to vote at any election by the people in any State, Territory, district, county, city, parish, township, school district, municipality, or other territorial subdivision, shall be entitled and allowed to vote at all such elections, without distinction of race, color, or previous condition of servitude; any constitution, law, custom, usage, or regulation of any State or Territory, or by or under its authority, to the contrary notwithstanding.

(2) No person acting under color of law shall —

(A) in determining whether any individual is qualified under State law or laws to vote in any election, apply any standard, practice, or procedure different from the standards, practices, or procedures applied under such law or laws to other individuals within the same county, parish, or similar political subdivision who have been found by State officials to be qualified to vote;

(B) deny the right of any individual to vote in any election because of an error or omission on any record or paper relating to any application, registration, or other act requisite to voting, if such error or omission is not material in determining whether such individual is qualified under State law to vote in such election; or

(C) employ any literacy test as a qualification for voting in any election unless (i) such test is administered to each individual and is conducted wholly in writing, and (ii) a certified copy of the test and of the answers given by the individual is furnished to him within twenty-five days of the submission of his request made within the period of time during which records and papers are required to be retained and preserved pursuant to sections 1974 to 1974e of this title: *Provided, however,* That the Attorney General may enter into agreements with appropriate State or local authorities that preparation, conduct, and maintenance of such tests in accordance with the provisions of applicable State or local law, including such special provisions as are necessary in the preparation, conduct, and maintenance of such tests for persons who are blind or otherwise physically handicapped, meet the purposes of this subparagraph and constitute compliance therewith.

(3) For purposes of this subsection —

(A) the term "vote" shall have the same meaning as in subsection (e) of this section;

(B) the phrase "literacy test" includes any test of the ability to read, write, understand, or interpret any matter.

(*d*) *Intimidation, threats, or coercion.*

No person, whether acting under color of law or otherwise, shall intimidate, threaten, coerce, or attempt to intimidate, threaten, or coerce any other person for the purpose of interfering with the right of such other person to vote or to vote as he may choose, or of causing such other person to vote for, or not to vote for, any candidate for the office of President, Vice President, presidential elector, Member of the Senate, or Member of the House of Representatives, Delegates or Commissioners from the Territories or possessions, at any general, special, or primary election held solely or in part for the purpose of selecting or electing any such candidate.

(*c*) *Preventive relief; injunction; rebuttable literacy presumption; liability of United States for costs; State as party defendant.*

Whenever any person has engaged or there are reasonable grounds to believe that any person is about to engage in any act or practice which would deprive any other person of any right or privilege secured by subsection (a) or (b) of this section, the Attorney General may institute for the United States, or in the name of the United States, a civil action or other proper proceeding for preventive relief, including an application for a permanent or temporary injunction, restraining order, or other order. If in any such proceeding literacy is a relevant fact there shall be a rebuttable presumption that any person who has not been adjudged an incompetent and who has completed the sixth grade in a public school in, or a private school accredited by, any State or territory, the District of Columbia, or the Commonwealth of Puerto Rico where instruction is carried on predominantly in the English language, possesses sufficient literacy, comprehension, and intelligence to vote in any election. In any proceeding hereunder the United States shall be liable for costs the same as a private person. Whenever, in a proceeding instituted under this subsection any official of a State or subdivision thereof is alleged to have committed any act or practice constituting a deprivation of any right or privilege secured by subsection (a) of this section, the act or practice shall also be deemed that of the State and the State may be joined as a party defendant and, if, prior to the institution of such proceeding, such official has resigned or has been relieved of his office and no successor has assumed such office, the proceeding may be instituted against the State.

(*d*) *Jurisdiction; exhaustion of other remedies.*

The district courts of the United States shall have jurisdiction of proceedings instituted pursuant to this section and shall exercise the same without regard to whether the party aggrieved shall have exhausted any administrative or other remedies that may be provided by law.

(*e*) *Order qualifying person to vote; application; hearing; voting referees; transmittal of report and order; certificate of qualification; definitions.*

In any proceeding instituted pursuant to subsection (c) of this section in the event the court finds that any person has been deprived on account of race or color of any right or privilege secured by subsection (a) of this section, the court shall upon request of the Attorney General and after each party has been given notice and the opportunity to be heard make a finding whether such deprivation was or is pursuant to a pattern or practice. If the court finds such pattern or practice, any person of such race or color resident within the affected area shall, for one year and thereafter until the court subsequently finds that such pattern or practice has ceased, be entitled, upon his application therefor, to an order declaring him qualified to vote, upon proof that at any election or elections (1) he is qualified under State law to vote, and (2) he has since such finding by the court been (a) deprived of or denied under color of law the opportunity to register to vote or otherwise to qualify to vote, or (b) found not qualified to vote by any person acting under color of law. Such order shall be effective as to any election held within the longest period for which such applicant could have been registered or otherwise qualified under State law at which the applicant's qualifications would under State law entitle him to vote.

Notwithstanding any inconsistent provision of State law or the action of any State officer or court, an applicant so declared qualified to vote shall be permitted to vote in any such election. The Attorney General shall cause to be transmitted certified copies of such order to the appropriate election officers. The refusal by any such officer with notice of such order to permit any person so declared qualified to vote to vote at an appropriate election shall constitute contempt of court.

An application for an order pursuant to this subsection shall be heard within ten days, and the execution of any order disposing of such application shall not be stayed if the effect of such stay would be to delay the effectiveness of the order beyond the date of any election at which the applicant would otherwise be enabled to vote.

The court may appoint one or more persons who are qualified voters in the judicial district, to be known as voting referees, who shall subscribe to the oath of office required by Revised Statutes, section 1757; to serve for such period as the court shall determine, to receive such applications and to take evidence and report to the court findings as to whether or not any election or elections (1) any such applicant is qualified under State law to vote, and (2) he has since the finding by the court heretofore specified been (a) deprived of or denied under color of law the opportunity to register to vote or otherwise to qualify to vote, or (b) found not qualified to vote by any person acting under color of law. In a proceeding before a voting referee, the applicant shall be heard ex parte at such times and places as the court shall direct. His statement under oath shall be prima facie evidence as to his age, residence, and his prior efforts to register or otherwise qualify to vote. Where proof of literacy or an understanding of other subjects is required by valid provisions of State law, the answer of the applicant, if written, shall be included in such report to the court; if oral, it shall be taken down stenographically and a transcription included in such report to the court.

Upon receipt of such report, the court shall cause the Attorney General to transmit a copy thereof to the State attorney general and to each party to such proceeding together with an order to show cause within ten days, or such shorter time as the court may fix, why an order of the court should not be entered in accordance with such report. Upon the expiration of such period, such order shall be entered unless prior to that time there has been filed with the court and served upon all parties a statement of exceptions to such report. Exceptions as to matters of fact shall be considered only if supported by a duly verified copy of a public record or by affidavit of persons having personal knowledge of such facts or by statements or matters contained in such report; those relating to matters of law shall be supported by an appropriate memorandum of law. The issues of fact and law raised by such exceptions shall be determined by the court or, if the due and speedy administration of justice requires, they may be referred to the voting referee to determine in accordance with procedures prescribed by the court. A hearing as to an issue of fact shall be held only in the event that the proof in support of the exception disclose the existence of a genuine issue of material fact. The applicant's literacy and understanding of other subjects shall be determined solely on the basis of answers included in the report of the voting referee.

The court, or at its direction the voting referee, shall issue to each applicant so declared qualified a certificate identifying the holder thereof as a person so qualified.

Any voting referee appointed by the court pursuant to this subsection shall to the extent not inconsistent herewith have all the powers conferred upon a master by rule 53(c) of the Federal Rules of Civil Procedure. The compensation to be allowed to any persons appointed by the court pursuant to this subsection shall be fixed by the court and shall be payable by the United States.

Application pursuant to this subsection shall be determined expeditiously. In the case of any application filed twenty or more days prior to an election which is undetermined by the time of such election, the court shall issue an order authorizing the applicant to vote provisionally: *Provided, however,* That such applicant shall be qualified to vote under State law. In the case of an application filed within twenty days prior to an election, the court, in its discretion, may make such an order. In either case the order shall make appropriate provision for the impounding of the applicant's ballot pending determination of the application. The court may take any other action, and may authorize such referee or such other person as it may designate to take any other action, appropriate or necessary to carry out the provisions of this subsection and to enforce its decrees. This subsection shall in no way be construed as a limitation upon the existing powers of the court.

When used in the subsection, the word "vote" includes all action necessary to make a vote effective including, but not limited to, registration or other action required by State law prerequisite to voting, casting a ballot, and having such ballot counted and included in the appropriate totals of votes cast with respect to candidates for public office and propositions for which votes are received in an election; the words "affected area" shall mean any subdivision of the State in which the laws of the State relating to voting are or have been to any extent administered by a person found in the proceeding to have violated subsection (a) of this section; and the words "qualified under State law" shall mean qualified according to the laws, customs, or usages of the State, and shall not, in any event, imply qualifications more stringent than those used by the persons found in the proceeding to have violated subsection (a) in qualifying persons other than those of the race or color against which the pattern or practice of discrimination was found to exist.

(*f*) *Contempt; assignment of counsel; witnesses.*

Any person cited for an alleged contempt under this Act shall be allowed to make his full defense by counsel learned in the law; and the court before which he is cited or tried, or some judge thereof, shall immediately, upon his request, assign to him such counsel, not exceeding two, as he may desire, who shall have free access to him at all reasonable hours. He shall be allowed, in his defense to make any proof that he can produce by lawful witnesses, and shall have the like process of the court to compel his witnesses to appear at his trial or hearing, as is usually granted to compel witnesses to appear on behalf of the prosecution. If such person shall be found by the court to be financially unable to provide for such counsel, it shall be the duty of the court to provide such counsel.

(*g*) *Three-judge district court: hearing, determination, expedition of action, review by Supreme Court; single-judge district court: hearing, determination, expedition of action.*

In any proceeding instituted by the United States in any district court of the United States under this section in which the Attorney General requests a finding of a pattern or practice of discrimination pursuant to subsection (e) of this section the Attorney General, at the time he files the complaint, or any defendant in the proceeding, within twenty days after service upon him of the complaint, may file with the clerk of such court a request that a court of three judges be convened to hear and determine the entire case. A copy of the request for a three-judge court shall be immediately furnished by such clerk to the chief judge of the circuit (or in his absence, the presiding circuit judge of the circuit) in which the case is pending. Upon receipt of the copy of such request it shall be the duty of the chief judge of the circuit or the presiding circuit judge, as the case may be, to designate immediately three judges in such circuit, of whom at least one shall be a circuit judge and another of whom shall be a district judge of the court in which the proceeding was instituted, to hear and determine such case, and it shall be the duty of the judges so designated to assign the case for hearing at the earliest practicable date, to participate in the hearing and determination thereof, and to cause the case to be in every way expedited. An appeal from the final judgment of such court will lie to the Supreme Court.

In any proceeding brought under subsection (c) of this section to enforce subsection (b) of this section, or in the event neither the Attorney General nor any defendant files a request for a three-judge court in any proceeding authorized by this subsection, it shall be the duty of the chief judge of the district (or in his absence, the acting chief judge) in which the case is pending immediately to designate a judge in such district to hear and determine the case. In the event that no judge in the district is available to hear and determine the case, the chief of the circuit (or, in his absence, the acting chief judge of the district, or the acting chief judge, as the case may be, shall certify this fact to the chief judge) who shall then designate a district or circuit judge of the circuit to hear and determine the case.

It shall be the duty of the judge designated pursuant to this section to assign the case for hearing at the earliest practicable date and to cause the case to be in every way expedited. (R.S. §2004; Sept. 9, 1957, Pub. L. 85-315, pt. IV, §131, 71 Stat. 637; May 6, 1960, Pub. L. 86-449, title VI, §601, 74 Stat. 90; July 2, 1964, Pub. L. 88-352, title I, §101, 78 Stat. 241; Aug. 6, 1965, Pub. L. 89-110, §15, 79 Stat. 445.)

Derivation

Act May 31, 1870, ch. 114, §1, 16 Stat. 140.

§1972. Interference with freedom of elections.

No officer of the Army, Navy, or Air Force of the United States shall prescribe or fix, or attempt to prescribe or fix, by proclamation, order, or otherwise, the qualifications of voters in any State, or in any manner interfere with the freedom of any election in any State, or with the exercise of the free right of suffrage in any State. (R.S. §2003.)

Derivation

Act Feb. 25, 1865, ch. 52, §1, 13 Stat. 437.

Subchapter I-A. — Enforcement of Voting Rights

Subchapter Referred to in Other Sections

This subchapter is referred to in section 1973aa-4 of this title.

§1973. Denial or abridgement of right to vote on account of race or color through voting qualifications or prerequisites.

No voting qualification or prerequisite to voting, or standard, practice, or procedure shall be imposed or applied by any State or political subdivision to deny or abridge the right of any citizen of the United States to vote on account of race or color. (Pub. L. 89-110, title I, §2, Aug. 6, 1965, 79 Stat. 437.)

§1973a. Proceeding to enforce the right to vote.

(*a*) *Authorization by court for appointment of federal examiners.*

Whenever the Attorney General institutes a proceeding under any statute to enforce the guarantees of the fifteenth amendment in any State or political subdivision the court shall authorize the appointment of Federal examiners by the United States Civil Service Commission in accordance with section 1973d of this title to serve for such period of time and for such political subdivisions as the court shall determine is appropriate to enforce the guarantees of the fifteenth amendment (1) as part of any interlocutory order if the court determines that the appointment of such examiners is necessary to enforce such guarantees or (2) as part of any final judgment if the court finds that violations of the fifteenth amendment justifying equitable relief have occurred in such State or subdivision: *Provided,* That the court need not authorize the appointment of examiners if any incidents of denial or abridgement of the right to vote on account of race or color (1) have been few in number and have been promptly and effectively corrected by State or local action, (2) the continuing effect of such incidents has been eliminated, and (3) there is no reasonable probability of their recurrence in the future.

(*b*) *Suspension of use of tests and devices which deny or abridge the right to vote.*

If in a proceeding instituted by the Attorney General under any statute to enforce the guarantees of the fifteenth amendment in any State or political subdivision the court finds that a test or device has been used for the purpose or with the effect of denying or abridging the right of any citizen of the United States to vote on account of race or color, it shall suspend the use of tests and devices in such State or political subdivisions as the court shall determine is appropriate and for such period as it deems necessary.

(c) *Retention of jurisdiction to prevent commencement of new devices to deny or abridge the right to vote.*

If in any proceeding instituted by the Attorney General under any statute to enforce the guarantees of the fifteenth amendment in any State or political subdivision the court finds that violations of the fifteenth amendment justifying equitable relief have occurred within the territory of such State or political subdivision, the court, in addition to such relief as it may grant, shall retain jurisdiction for such period as it may deem appropriate and during such period no voting qualification or prerequisite to voting, or standard, practice, or procedure with respect to voting different from that in force or effect at the time the proceeding was commenced shall be enforced unless and until the court finds that such qualification, prerequisite, standard, practice, or procedure does not have the purpose and will not have the effect of denying or abridging the right to vote on account of race or color: *Provided,* That such qualification, prerequisite, standard, practice, or procedure may be enforced if the qualification, prerequisite, standard, practice, or procedure has been submitted by the chief legal officer or other appropriate official of such State or subdivision to the Attorney General and the Attorney General has not interposed an objection within sixty days after such submission, except that neither the court's finding nor the Attorney General's failure to object shall bar a subsequent action to enjoin enforcement of such qualification, prerequisite, standard, practice, or procedure. (Pub. L. 89-110, title I, §3, Aug. 6, 1965, 79 Stat. 437.)

§1973b. Suspension of the use of tests or devices in determining eligibility to vote.

(a) *Action by state or political subdivision for declaratory judgment of no denial or abridgement; three-judge district court; appeal to Supreme Court; retention of jurisdiction by three-judge court.*

To assure that the right of citizens of the United States to vote is not denied or abridged on account of race or color, no citizen shall be denied the right to vote in any Federal, State, or local election because of his failure to comply with any test or device in any State with respect to which the determinations have been made under subsection (b) of this section or in any political subdivision with respect to which such determinations have been made as a separate unit, unless the United States District Court for the District of Columbia in an action for a declaratory judgment brought by such State or subdivision against the United States has determined that no such test or device has been used during the ten years preceding the filing of the action for the purpose or with the effect of denying or abridging the right to vote on account of race or color: *Provided,* That no such declaratory judgment shall issue with respect to any plaintiff for a period of ten years after the entry of a final judgment of any court of the United States, other than the denial of a declaratory judgment under this section, whether entered prior to or after the enactment of this subchapter, determining that denials or abridgments of the right to vote on account of race or color through the use of such tests or devices have occurred anywhere in the territory of such plaintiff.

An action pursuant to this subsection shall be heard and determined by a court of three judges in accordance with the provisions of section 2284 of Title 28 and any appeal shall lie to the Supreme Court. The court shall retain jurisdiction of any action pursuant to this subsection for five years after judgment and shall reopen the action upon motion of the Attorney General alleging that a test or device has been used for the purpose or with the effect of denying or abridging the right to vote on account of race or color.

If the Attorney General determines that he has no reason to believe that any such test or device has been used during the ten years preceding the filing of the action for the purpose or with the effect of denying or abridging the right to vote on account of race or color, he shall consent to the entry of such judgment.

(*b*) *Required factual determinations necessary to allow suspension of compliance with tests and devices; publication in Federal Register.*

The provisions of subsection (a) of this section shall apply in any State or in any political subdivision of a state which (1) the Attorney General determines maintained on November 1, 1964, any test or device, and with respect to which (2) the Director of the Census determines that less than 50 per centum of the persons of voting age residing therein were registered on November 1, 1964, or that less than 50 per centum of such persons voted in the presidential election of November 1964. On and after August 6, 1970, in addition to any State or political subdivision of a State determined to be subject to subsection (a) of this section pursuant to the previous sentence, the provisions of subsection (a) of this section shall apply in any State or any political subdivision of a State which (i) the Attorney General determines maintained on November 1, 1968, any test or device, and with respect to which (ii) the Director of the Census determines that less than 50 per centum of the persons of voting age residing therein were registered on November 1, 1968, or that less than 50 per centum of such persons voted in the presidential election of November 1968.

A determination or certification of the Attorney General or of the Director of the Census under this section or under section 1973d or 1973k of this title shall not be reviewable in any court and shall be effective upon publication in the Federal Register.

(*c*) *Definition of test or device.*

The phrase "test or device" shall mean any requirement that a person as a prerequisite for voting or registration for voting (1) demonstrate the ability to read, write, understand, or interpret any matter, (2) demonstrate any educational achievement or his knowledge of any particular subject, (3) possess good moral character, or (4) prove his qualifications by the voucher of registered voters or members of any other class.

(*d*) *Required frequency, continuation and probable recurrence of incidents of denial or abridgement to constitute forbidden use of tests or devices.*

For purposes of this section no State or political subdivision shall be determined to have engaged in the use of tests or devices for the purpose or with the effect of denying or abridging the right to vote on account of race or color if (1) incidents of such use have been few in number and have been pomptly and effectively corrected by State or local action, (2) the continuing effect of such incidents has been eliminated, and (3) there is no reasonable probability of their recurrence in the future.

(*e*) *Completion of requisite grade level of education in American-flag schools in which the predominant classroom language was other than English.*

(1) Congress hereby declares that to secure the rights under the fourteenth amendment of persons educated in American-flag schools in which the predominant

classroom language was other than English, it is necessary to prohibit the States from conditioning the right to vote of such persons on ability to read, write, understand, or interpret any matter in the English language.

(2) No person who demonstrates that he has successfully completed the sixth primary grade in a public school in, or a private school accredited by, any State or territory, the District of Columbia, or the Commonwealth of Puerto Rico in which the predominant classroom language was other than English, shall be denied the right to vote in any Federal, State, or local election because of his inability to read, write, understand, or interpret any matter in the English language, except that in States in which State law provides that a different level of education is presumptive of literacy, he shall demonstrate that he has successfully completed an equivalent level of education in a public school in, or a private school accredited by, any State or territory, the District of Columbia, or the Commonwealth of Puerto Rico in which the predominant classroom language was other than English. (Pub. L. 89-110, title I, §4, Aug. 6, 1965, 79 Stat. 438; Pub. L. 91-285, §§3, 4, June 22, 1970, 84 Stat. 315.)

§1973c. Alteration of voting qualifications and procedures; action by state or political subdivision for declaratory judgment of no denial or abridgment of voting rights; three-judge district court; appeal to Supreme Court.

Whenever a State or political subdivision with respect to which the prohibitions set forth in section 1973b(a) based upon determinations made under the first sentence of section 1973b(b) of this title are in effect shall enact or seek to administer any voting qualification or prerequisite to voting, or standard, practice, or procedure with respect to voting different from that in force or effect on November 1, 1964, or whenever a State or political subdivision with respect to which the prohibitions set forth in section 1973b(a) of this title based upon determinations made under the second sentence of section 1973b(b) of this title are in effect shall enact or seek to administer any voting qualification or prerequisite to voting, or standard, practice, or procedure with respect to voting different from that in force or effect on November 1, 1968, such State or subdivision may institute an action in the United States District Court for the District of Columbia for a declaratory judgment that such qualification, prerequisite, standard, practice, or procedure does not have the purpose and will not have the effect of denying or abridging the right to vote on account of race or color, and unless and until the court enters such judgment no person shall be denied the right to vote for failure to comply with such qualification, prerequisite, standard, practice, or procedure: *Provided,* That such qualification, prerequisite, standard, practice, or procedure may be enforced without such proceeding if the qualification, prerequisite, standard, practice, or procedure has been submitted by the chief legal officer or other appropriate official of such State or subdivision to the Attorney General and the Attorney General has not interposed an objection within sixty days after such submission, except that neither the Attorney General's failure to object nor a declaratory judgment entered under this section shall bar a subsequent action to enjoin enforcement of such qualification, prerequisite, standard, practice, or procedure. Any action under this section shall be heard and determined by a court of three judges in accordance with the provisions of section 2284 of Title 28 and any appeal shall lie to the Supreme Court. (Pub. L. 89-110, title I, §5, Aug. 6, 1965, 79 Stat. 439; Pub. L. 91-285, §5, June 22, 1970, 84 Stat. 315.)

§1973d. Federal voting examiners; appointment.

Whenever (a) a court has authorized the appointment of examiners pursuant to the provisions of section 1973a(a) of this title, or (b) unless a declaratory judgment has been rendered under section 1973b(a) of this title, the Attorney General certifies with respect to any political subdivision named in, or included within the scope of, determinations made under section 1973b(b) of this title that (1) he has received complaints in writing from twenty or more residents of such political subdivision alleging that they have been denied the right to vote under color of law on account of race or color, and that he believes such complaints to be meritorious, or (2) that in his judgment (considering, among other factors, whether the ratio of nonwhite persons to white persons registered to vote within such subdivision appears to him to be reasonably attributable to violations of the fifteenth amendment or whether substantial evidence exists that bona fide efforts are being made within such subdivision to comply with the fifteenth amendment), the appointment of examiners is otherwise necessary to enforce the guarantees of the fifteenth amendment, the Civil Service Commission shall appoint as many examiners for such subdivision as it may deem appropriate to prepare and maintain lists of persons eligible to vote in Federal, State, and local elections. Such examiners, hearing officers provided for in section 1973g(a) of this title and other persons deemed necessary by the Commission to carry out the provisions and purposes of this subchapter shall be appointed, compensated, and separated without regard to the provisions of any statute administered by the Civil Service Commission, and service under this subchapter shall not be considered employment for the purposes of any statute administered by the Civil Service Commission, except the provisions of section 9 of the Act of August 2, 1939, as amended, prohibiting partisan political activity: *Provided,* That the Commission is authorized, after consulting the head of the appropriate department or agency, to designate suitable persons in the official service of the United States, with their consent, to serve in these positions. Examiners and hearing officers shall have the power to administer oaths. (Pub. L. 89-110, title I, §6, Aug. 6, 1965, 79 Stat. 439.)

§1973e. Examination of applicants for registration.

(*a*) *Form of application; requisite allegation of non-registration.*

The examiners for each political subdivision shall, at such places as the Civil Service Commission shall by regulation designate, examine applicants concerning their qualifications for voting. An application to an examiner shall be in such form as the Commission may require and shall contain allegations that the applicant is not otherwise registered to vote.

(*b*) *Placement of eligible voters on official lists; transmittal of lists.*

Any person whom the examiner finds, in accordance with instructions received under section 1973g(b) of this title, to have the qualifications prescribed by State law not inconsistent with the Constitution and laws of the United States shall promptly be placed on a list of eligible voters. A challenge to such listing may be made in accordance with section 1973g(a) of this title and shall not be the basis for a prosecution under section 1973j of this title. The examiner shall certify and transmit such list, and any supplements as appropriate, at least once a month, to the offices of the appropriate election officials, with copies to the Attorney General and the attorney general of the State, and any such lists and supplements thereto transmitted during the month shall be available for public inspection on the last business day of the month and in any event not later than the forty-fifth day prior to any election. The appropriate State or local election official shall place such names on the official voting list. Any person whose name appears on the examiner's list shall be entitled and allowed to vote in the election district of his residence unless and until the appropriate election officials shall have been notified that such person has been removed from such list in accordance with subsection (d) of this section: *Provided,* That no person shall be entitled to vote in any election by virtue of this subchapter unless his name shall have been certified and transmitted on such a list to the offices of the appropriate election officials at least forty-five days prior to such election.

(*c*) *Certificate of eligibility.*

The examiner shall issue to each person whose name appears on such a list a certificate evidencing his eligibility to vote.

(*d*) *Removal of names from list by examiners.*

A person whose name appears on such a list shall be removed therefrom by an examiner if (1) such person has been successfully challenged in accordance with the procedure prescribed in section 1973g of this title, or (2) he has been determined by an examiner to have lost his eligibility to vote under State law not inconsistent with the Constitution and the laws of the United States. (Pub. L. 89-110, title I, §7, Aug. 6, 1965, 79 Stat. 440.)

§1973f. Observers at elections; assignment; duties; reports.

Whenever an examiner is serving under this subchapter in any political subdivision, the Civil Service Commission may assign, at the request of the Attorney General, one or more persons, who may be officers of the United States, (1) to enter and attend at any place for holding an election in such subdivision for the purpose of observing whether persons who are entitled to vote are being permitted to vote, and (2) to enter and attend at any place for tabulating the votes cast at any election held in such subdivision for the purpose of observing whether votes cast by persons entitled to vote are being properly tabulated. Such persons so assigned shall report to an examiner appointed for such political subdivision, to the Attorney General, and if the appointment of examiners has been authorized pursuant to section 1973a(a) of this title, to the court. (Pub. L. 89-110, title I, §8, Aug. 6, 1965, 79 Stat. 441.)

§1973g. Challenges to eligibility listings.

(*a*) *Filing of challenge; supplementary affidavits; service upon person challenged; hearing; review.*

Any challenge to a listing on an eligibility list prepared by an examiner shall be heard and determined by a hearing officer appointed by and responsible to the Civil Service Commission and under such rules as the Commission shall by regulation prescribe. Such challenge shall be entertained only if filed at such office within the State as the Civil Service Commission shall by regulation designate, and within ten days after the listing of the challenged person is made available for public inspection, and if supported by (1) the affidavits of at least two persons having personal knowledge of the facts constituting grounds for the challenge, and (2) a certification that a copy of the challenge and affidavits have been served by mail or in person upon the person challenged at his place of residence set out in the application. Such challenge shall be determined within fifteen days after it has been filed. A petition for review of the decision of the hearing officer may be filed in the United States court of appeals for the circuit in which the person challenged resides within fifteen days after service of such decision by mail on the person petitioning for review but no decision of a hearing officer shall be reversed unless clearly erroneous. Any person listed shall be entitled and allowed to vote pending final determination by the hearing officer and by the court.

(*b*) *Rules and regulations by Civil Service Commission.*

The times, places, procedures, and form for application and listing pursuant to this subchapter and removals from the eligibility lists shall be prescribed by regulations promulgated by the Civil Service Commission and the Commission shall, after consultation with the Attorney General, instruct examiners concerning applicable State law not inconsistent with the Constitution and laws of the United States with respect to (1) the qualifications required for listing, and (2) loss of eligibility to vote.

(*c*) *Subpena power of Civil Service Commission; contempt.*

Upon the request of the applicant or the challenger or on its own motion the Civil Service Commission shall have the power to require by subpena the attendance and testimony of witnesses and the production of documentary evidence relating to any matter pending before it under the authority of this section. In case of contumacy or refusal to obey a subpena, any district court of the United States or the United States court of any territory or possession, or the District Court of the United States for the District of Columbia, within the jurisdiction of which said person guilty of contumacy or refusal to obey is found or resides or is domiciled or transacts business, or has appointed an agent for receipt of service of process, upon application by the Attorney General of the United States shall have jurisdiction to issue to such person an order requiring such person to appear before the Commission or a hearing officer, there to produce pertinent, relevant, and nonprivileged documentary evidence if so ordered, or there to give testimony touching the matter under investigation; and any failure to obey such order of the court may be punished by said court as a contempt thereof. (Pub. L. 89-110, title I, §9, Aug. 6, 1965, 79 Stat. 441.)

§1973h. Poll taxes.

(*a*) *Congressional finding and declaration of policy against enforced payment of poll taxes as a device to impair voting rights.*

The Congress finds that the requirement of the payment of a poll tax as a precondition to voting (i) precludes persons of limited means from voting or imposes unreasonable financial hardship upon such persons as a precondition to their exercise of the franchise, (ii) does not bear a reasonable relationship to any legitimate State interest in the conduct of elections, and (iii) in some areas has the purpose or effect of denying persons the right to vote because of race or color. Upon the basis of these findings, Congress declares that the constitutional right of citizens to vote is denied or abridged in some areas by the requirement of the payment of a poll tax as a precondition to voting.

(*b*) *Authority of Attorney General to institute actions for relief against enforcement of poll tax requirement.*

In the exercise of the powers of Congress under section 5 of the fourteenth amendment and section 2 of the fifteenth amendment, the Attorney General is authorized and directed to institute forthwith in the name of the United States such actions, including actions against States or political subdivisions, for declaratory judgment or injunctive relief against the enforcement of any requirement of the payment of a poll tax as a precondition to voting, or substitute thereof enacted after November

1, 1964, as will be necessary to implement the declaration of subsection (a) of this section and the purposes of this section.

(c) *Jurisdiction of the three-judge district courts; appeal to Supreme Court.*

The district courts of the United States shall have jurisdiction of such actions which shall be heard and determined by a court of three judges in accordance with the provisions of section 2284 of Title 28 and any appeal shall lie to the Supreme Court. It shall be the duty of the judges designated to hear the case to assign the case for hearing at the earliest practicable date, to participate in the hearing and determination thereof, and to cause the case to be in every way expedited.

(d) *Post-payment of poll taxes in the event of a judicial declaration of constitutionality.*

During the pendency of such actions, and thereafter if the courts, notwithstanding this action by the Congress, should declare the requirement of the payment of a poll tax to be constitutional, no citizen of the United States who is a resident of a State or political subdivision with respect to which determinations have been made under secion 1973b(b) of this title and a declaratory judgment has not been entered under section 1973b(a) of this title, during the first year he becomes otherwise entitled to vote by reason of registration by State or local officials or listing by an examiner, shall be denied the right to vote for failure to pay a poll tax if he tenders payment of such tax for the current year to an examiner or to the appropriate State or local official at least forty-five days prior to election, whether or not such tender would be timely or adequate under State law. An examiner shall have authority to accept such payment from any person authorized by this subchapter to make an application for listing, and shall issue a receipt for such payment. The examiner shall transmit promptly any such poll tax payment to the office of the State or local official authorized to receive such payment under State law, together with the name and address of the applicant. (Pub. L. 89-110, title I, §10, Aug. 6, 1965, 79 Stat. 442.)

§1973i. Prohibited acts.

(a) *Failure or refusal to permit casting or tabulation of vote.*

No person acting under color of law shall fail or refuse to permit any person to vote who is entitled to vote under any provision of this subchapter or is otherwise qualified to vote, or willfully fail or refuse to tabulate, count, and report such person's vote.

(b) *Intimidation, threats, or coercion.*

No person, whether acting under color of law or otherwise, shall intimidate, threaten, or coerce, or attempt to intimidate, threaten, or coerce any person for voting or attempting to vote, or intimidate, threaten, or coerce, at attempt to intimidate, threaten, or coerce any person for urging or aiding any person to vote or attempt to vote, or intimidate, threaten, or coerce any person for exercising any powers or duties under section 1973a(a), 1973d, 1973f, 1973g, 1973h or 1973j(e) of this title.

(c) *False information in registering or voting; penalties.*

Whoever knowingly or willfully gives false information as to his name, address or period of residence in the voting district for the purpose of establishing his eligibility to register or vote, or conspires with another individual for the purpose of encouraging his false registration to vote or illegal voting, or pays or offers to pay or accepts payment either for registration to vote or for voting shall be fined not more than $10,000 or imprisoned not more than five years, or both: *Provided, however,* That this provision shall be applicable only to general, special, or primary elections held solely or in part for the purpose of selecting or electing any candidate for the office of President, Vice President, presidential elector, Member of the United States Senate, Member of the United States House of Representatives, Delegate from the District of Columbia, or Resident Commissioner of the Commonwealth of Puerto Rico.

(*d*) *Falsification or concealment of material facts or giving of false statements in matters within jurisdiction of examiners or hearing officers; penalties.*

Whoever, in any matter within the jurisdiction of an examiner or hearing officer knowingly and willfully falsifies or conceals a material fact, or makes any false, fictitious, or fraudulent statements or representations, or makes or uses any false writing or document knowing the same to contain any false, fictitious, or fraudulent statement or entry, shall be fined not more than $10,000 or imprisoned not more than five years, or both. (Pub. L. 89-110, title I, §11, Aug. 6, 1965, 79 Stat. 443; Pub. L. 91-405, title II, §204(e), Sept. 22, 1970, 84 Stat. 853.)

§1973j. Same; civil and criminal sanctions.

(*a*) *Depriving or attempting to deprive persons of secured rights.*

Whoever shall deprive or attempt to deprive any person of any right secured by section 1973, 1973a, 1973b, 1973c, 1973e, or 1973h of this title or shall violate section 1973i(a) of this title, shall be fined not more than $5,000, or imprisoned not more than five years, or both.

(*b*) *Destroying, defacing, mutilating, or altering ballots or official voting records.*

Whoever, within a year following an election in a political subdivision in which an examiner has been appointed (1) destroys, defaces, mutilates, or otherwise alters the marking of a paper ballot which has been cast in such election, or (2) alters any official record of voting in such election tabulated from a voting machine or otherwise, shall be fined not more than $5,000, or imprisoned not more than five years, or both.

(*c*) *Conspiring to violate or interfere with secured rights.*

Whoever conspires to violate the provisions of subsection (a) or (b) of this section, or interferes with any right secured by section 1973, 1973a, 1973b, 1973c, 1973e, 1973h, or 1973i(a) of this title shall be fined not more than $5,000, or imprisoned not more than five years, or both.

(*d*) *Civil action by Attorney General for preventive relief; injunctive and other relief.*

Whenever any person has engaged or there are reasonable grounds to believe that any person is about to engage in any act or practice prohibited by section 1973, 1973a, 1973b, 1973c, 1973e, 1973h, 1973i, or subsection (b) of this section, the Attorney General may institute for the United States, or in the name of the United States, an action for preventive relief, including an application for a temporary or permanent injunction, restraining order, or other order, and including an order directed to the State and State or local election officials to require them (1) to permit persons listed under this subchapter to vote and (2) to count such votes.

(*e*) *Proceeding by Attorney General to enforce the counting of ballots of registered and eligible persons who are prevented from voting.*

Whenever in any political subdivision in which there are examiners appointed pursuant to this subchapter any persons allege to such an examiner within fortyeight hours after the closing of the polls that notwithstanding (1) their listing under this subchapter or registration by an appropriate election official and (2) their eligibility to vote, they have not been permitted to vote in such election, the examiner shall forthwith notify the Attorney General if such allegations in his opinion appear to be well founded. Upon receipt of such notification, the Attorney General may forthwith file with the district court an application for an order providing for the marking, casting, and counting of the ballots of such persons and requiring the inclusion of their votes in the total vote before the results of such election shall be deemed final and any force or effect given thereto. The district court shall hear and determine such matters immediately after the filing of such application. The remedy provided in this subsection shall not preclude any remedy available under State or Federal law.

(f) Jurisdiction of district courts; exhaustion of administrative or other remedies unnecessary.

The district courts of the United States shall have jurisdiction of proceedings instituted pursuant to this section and shall exercise the same without regard to whether a person asserting rights under the provisions of this subchapter shall have exhausted any administrative or other remedies that may be provided by law. (Pub. L. 89-110, title I, §12, Aug. 6, 1965, 79 Stat. 443; Pub. L. 90-284, title I, §103(c), Apr. 11, 1968, 82 Stat. 75.)

§1973k. Termination of listing procedures; basis for termination; survey or census by Director of the Census.

Listing procedures shall be terminated in any political subdivision of any State (a) with respect to examiners appointed pursuant to clause (b) of section 1973d of this title whenever the Attorney General notifies the Civil Service Commission, or whenever the District Court for the District of Columbia determines in an action for declaratory judgment brought by any political subdivision with respect to which the Director of the Census has determined that more than 50 per centum of the nonwhite persons of voting age residing therein are registered to vote, (1) that all persons listed by an examiner for such subdivision have been placed on the appropriate voting registration roll, and (2) that there is no longer reasonable cause to believe that persons will be deprived of or denied the right to vote on account of race or color in such subdivision, and (b), with respect to examiners appointed pursuant to section 1973a(a) of this title, upon order of the authorizing court. A political subdivision may petition the Attorney General for the termination of listing procedures under clause (a) of this section, and may petition the Attorney General to request the Director of the Census to take such survey or census as may be appropriate for the making of the determination provided for in this section. The District Court for the District of Columbia shall have jurisdiction to require such survey or census to be made by the Director of the Census and it shall require him to do so if it deems the Attorney General's refusal to request such survey or census to be arbitrary or unreasonable. (Pub. L. 89-110, title I, §13, Aug. 1965, 79 Stat. 444.)

§1973l. Enforcement proceedings.

(a) Criminal contempt.

All cases of criminal contempt arising under the provisions of this subchapter shall be governed by section 1995 of this title.

(b) Jurisdiction of courts for declaratory judgment, restraining orders, or temporary or permanent injunction.

No court other than the District Court for the District of Columbia or a court of appeals in any proceeding under section 1973g of this title shall have jurisdiction to issue any declaratory judgment pursuant to section 1973b or 1973c of this title or any restraining order or temporary or permanent injunction against the execution or enforcement of any provision of this subchapter or any action of any Federal officer or employee pursuant hereto.

(c) Definitions.

(1) The terms "vote" or "voting" shall include all action necessary to make a vote effective in any primary, special, or general election, including, but not limited to, registration, listing pursuant to this subchapter, or other action required by law prerequisite to voting, casting a ballot, and having such ballot counted properly and included in the appropriate totals of votes cast with respect to candidates for public or party office and propositions for which votes are received in an election.

(2) The term "political subdivision" shall mean any county or parish, except that where registration for voting is not conducted under the supervision of a county or parish, the term shall include any other subdivision of a State which conducts registration for voting.

(d) Subpenas.

In any action for a declaratory judgment brought pursuant to section 1973b or 1973c of this title, subpenas for witnesses who are required to attend the District Court for the District of Columbia may be served in any judicial district of the United States: *Provided,* That no writ of subpena shall issue for witnesses without the District of Columbia at a greater distance than one hundred miles from the place of holding court without the permission of the District Court for the District of Columbia being first had upon proper application and cause shown. (Pub. L. 89-110, title I, §14, Aug. 6, 1965, 79 Stat. 445.)

§1973m. Study by Attorney General and Secretary of Defense of discriminatory practices affecting voting rights of Armed Forces personnel. [omitted]

§1973n. Impairment of voting rights of persons holding current registration.

Nothing in this subchapter shall be construed to deny, impair, or otherwise adversely affect the right to vote of any person registered to vote under the law of any State or political subdivision. (Pub. L. 89-110, title I, §17, Aug. 6, 1965, 79 Stat. 446.)

§1973o. Authorization of appropriations.

There are hereby authorized to be appropriated such sums as are necessary to carry out the provisions of this subchapter. (Pub. L. 89-110, title I, §18, Aug. 6, 1965, 79 Stat. 446.)

§1973p. Separability of provisions.

If any provision of this subchapter or the application thereof to any person or circumstances is held invalid, the remainder of the subchapter and the application of the provision to other persons not similarly situated or to other circumstances shall not be affected thereby. (Pub. L. 89-110, title I, §19, Aug. 6, 1965, 79 Stat. 446.)

Subchapter I-B. — Supplemental Provisions

§1973aa. Application of prohibition to other States; definition of "test or device".

(a) Prior to August 6, 1975, no citizen shall be denied, because of his failure to comply with any test or device, the right to vote in any Federal, State, or local election conducted in any State or political subdivision of a State as to which the provisions of section 1973b(a) of this title are not in effect by reason of determinations made under section 1973b(b) of this title.

(b) As used in this section, the term "test or device" means any requirement that a person as a prerequisite for voting or registration for voting (1) demonstrate the ability to read, write, understand or interpret any matter, (2) demonstrate any educational achievement or his knowledge of any particular subject, (3) possess good moral character, or (4) prove his qualifications by the voucher of registered voters or members of any other class. (Pub. L. 89-110, title II, §201, as added Pub. L. 91-285, §6, June 22, 1970, 84 Stat. 315.)

§1973aa-1. Residence requirements for voting.

(a) Congressional findings.

The Congress hereby finds that the imposition and application of the durational residency requirement as a precondition to voting for the offices of President and Vice President, and the lack of sufficient opportunities for absentee registration and absentee balloting in presidential elections —

(1) denies or abridges the inherent constitutional right of citizens to vote for their President and Vice President;

(2) denies or abridges the inherent constitutional right of citizens to enjoy their free movement across State lines;

(3) denies or abridges the privileges and immunities guaranteed to the citizens of each State under article IV, section 2, clause 1, of the Constitution;

(4) in some instances has the impermissible purpose or effect of denying citizens the right to vote for such officers because of the way they may vote;

(5) has the effect of denying to citizens the equality of civil rights, and due process and equal protection of the laws that are guaranteed to them under the fourteenth amendment; and

(6) does not bear a reasonable relationship to any compelling State interest in the conduct of presidential elections.

(b) Congressional declaration: durational residency requirement, abolishment; absentee registration and balloting standards, establishment.

Upon the basis of these findings, Congress declares that in order to secure and protect the above-stated rights of citizens under the Constitution, to enable citizens to better obtain the enjoyment of such rights, and to enforce the guarantees of the fourteenth amendment, it is necessary (1) to completely abolish the durational residency requirement as a precondition to voting for President and Vice President, and (2) to establish nationwide, uniform standards relative to absentee registration and absentee balloting in presidential elections.

(c) Prohibition of denial of right to vote because of durational residency requirement or absentee balloting.

No citizen of the United States who is otherwise qualified to vote in any election for President and Vice President shall be denied the right to vote for electors for President and Vice President, or for President and Vice President, in such election because of the failure of such citizen to comply with any durational residency requirement of such State or political subdivision; nor shall any citizen of the United States be denied the right to vote for electors for President and Vice President, or for President and Vice President, in such election because of the failure of such citizen to be physically present in such State or political subdivision at the time of such election, if such citizen shall have complied with the requirements prescribed by the law of such State or political subdivision providing for the casting of absentee ballots in such election.

(*d*) *Registration: time for application; absentee balloting; time of application and return of ballots.*

For the purposes of this section, each State shall provide by law for the registration or other means of qualification of all duly qualified residents of such State who apply, not later than thirty days immediately prior to any presidential election, for registration or qualification to vote for the choice of electors for President and Vice President or for President and Vice President in such election; and each State shall provide by law for the casting of absentee ballots for the choice of electors for President and Vice President, or for President and Vice President, by all duly qualified residents of such State who may be absent from their election district or unit in such State on the day such election is held and who have applied therefor not later than seven days immediately prior to such election and have returned such ballots to the appropriate election official of such State not later than the time of closing of the polls in such State on the day of such election.

(*e*) *Change of residence; voting in person or by absentee ballot in State of prior residence.*

If any citizen of the United States who is otherwise qualified to vote in any State or political subdivision in any election for President and Vice President has begun residence in such State or political subdivision after the thirtieth day next preceding such election and, for that reason, does not satisfy the registration requirements of such State or political subdivision he shall be allowed to vote for the choice of electors for President and Vice President, or for President and Vice President, in such election, (1) in person in the State or political subdivision in which he resided immediately prior to his removal if he had satisfied, as of the date of his change of residence, the requirements to vote in that State or political subdivision, or (2) by absentee ballot in the State or political subdivision in which he resided immediately prior to his removal if he satisfies, but for his nonresident status and the reason for his absence, the requirements for absentee voting in that State or political subdivision.

(*f*) *Absentee registration requirement.*

No citizen of the United States who is otherwise qualified to vote by absentee ballot in any State or political subdivision in any election for President and Vice President shall be denied the right to vote for the choice of electors for President and Vice President, or for President and Vice President, in such election because of any requirement of registration that does not include a provision for absentee registration.

(*g*) *State or local adoption of less restrictive voting practices.*

Nothing in this section shall prevent any State or political subdivision from adopting less restrictive voting practices than those that are prescribed herein.

(*h*) *Definition of "State."*

The term "State" as used in this section includes each of the several States and the District of Columbia.

(i) False registration, and other fraudulent acts and conspiracies: application of penalty for false information in registering or voting.

The provisions of section 1973i(c) of this title shall apply to false registration, and other fraudulent acts and conspiracies, committed under this section. (Pub. L. 89-110, title II, §202, as added Pub. L. 91-285, §6, June 22, 1970, 84 Stat. 316.)

§1973aa-2. Judicial relief; civil actions by the Attorney General; three-judge district court; appeal to Supreme Court.

Whenever the Attorney General has reason to believe that a State or political subdivision (a) has enacted or is seeking to administer any test or device as a prerequisite to voting in violation of the prohibition contained in section 1973aa of this title, or (b) undertakes to deny the right to vote in any election in violation of section 1973aa-1 of this title, he may institute for the United States, or in the name of the United States, an action in a district court of the United States, in accordance with sections 1391 through 1393 of Title 28, for a restraining order, a preliminary or permanent injunction, or such other order as he deems appropriate. An action under this subsection shall be heard and determined by a court of three judges in accordance with the provisions of section 2282 of Title 28 and any appeal shall be to the Supreme Court. (Pub. L. 89-110, title II, §203, as added Pub. L. 91-285, §6, June 22, 1970, 84 Stat. 317.)

§1973aa-3. Penalty.

Whoever shall deprive or attempt to deprive any person of any right secured by section 1973aa or 1973aa-1 of this title shall be fined not more than $5,000, or imprisoned not more than five years, or both. (Pub. L. 89-110, title II, §204, as added Pub. L. 91-285, §6, June 22, 1970, 84 Stat. 317.)

§1973aa-4. Separability of provisions.

If any provision of subchapters I-A to I-C of this chapter or the application of any provision thereof to any person or circumstance is judicially determined to be invalid, the remainder of subchapters I-A to I-C of this chapter or the application of such provision to other persons or circumstances shall not be affected by such determination. (Pub. L. 89-110, title II, §205, as added Pub. L. 91-285, §6, June 22, 1970, 84 Stat. 318.)

SUBCHAPTER I-C — REDUCING VOTING AGE TO EIGHTEEN IN FEDERAL, STATE, AND LOCAL ELECTIONS

§1973bb. Congressional declaration and findings; prohibition of denial of right to vote because of age.

(a) The Congress finds and declares that the imposition and application of the requirement that a citizen be twenty-one years of age as a precondition to voting in any primary or in any election —

(1) denies and abridges the inherent constitutional rights of citizens eighteen years of age but not yet twenty-one years of age to vote — a particularly unfair treatment of such citizens in view of the national defense responsibilities imposed upon such citizens;

(2) has the effect of denying to citizens eighteen years of age but not yet twenty-one years of age the due process and equal protection of the laws that are guaranteed to them under the fourteenth amendment of the Constitution; and

(3) does not bear a reasonable relationship to any compelling State interest.

(b) In order to secure the constitutional rights set forth in subsection (a) of this section, the Congress declares that it is necessary to prohibit the denial of the right to vote to citizens of the United States eighteen years of age or over. (Pub. L. 89-110, title III, §301, as added Pub. L. 91-285, §6, June 22, 1970, 84 Stat. 318.)

§1973bb-1. Prohibition of denial of right to vote because of age.

Except as required by the Constitution, no citizen of the United States who is otherwise qualified to vote in any State or political subdivision in any primary or in any election shall be denied the right to vote in any such primary or election on account of age if such citizen is eighteen years of age or older. (Pub. L. 89-110, title III, §302, as added Pub. L. 91-285, §6, June 22, 1970, 84 Stat. 318.)

§1973bb-2. Enforcement.

(a) Civil actions by the Attorney General; jurisdiction; three-judge district court; appeal to Supreme Court; expedition of cases.

(1) In the exercise of the powers of the Congress under the necessary and proper clause of section 8, article I of the Constitution, and section 5 of the fourteenth amendment of the Constitution, the Attorney General is authorized and directed to institute in the name of the United States such actions against States or political subdivisions, including actions for injunctive relief, as he may determine to be necessary to implement the purposes of this subchapter.

(2) The district courts of the United States shall have jurisdiction of proceedings instituted pursuant to this subchapter, which shall be heard and determined by a court of three judges in accordance with the provisions of section 2284 of Title 28, and any appeal shall lie to the Supreme Court. It shall be the duty of the judges designated to hear the case to assign the case for hearing and determination thereof, and to cause the case to be in every way expedited.

(b) Penalty.

Whoever shall deny or attempt to deny any person of any right secured by this subchapter shall be fined not more than $5,000 or imprisoned not more than five years, or both. (Pub. L. 89-110, title III, §303, as added Pub. L. 91-285, §6, June 22, 1970, 84 Stat. 318.)

§1973bb-3. Definition of "State."

As used in this subchapter the term "State" includes the District of Columbia. (Pub. L. 89-110; title III, §304, as added Pub. L. 91-285, §6, June 22, 1970, 84 Stat. 319.)

§1973bb-4. Effective date.

The provisions of this subchapter shall take effect with respect to any primary or election held on or after January 1, 1971. (Pub. L. 89-110, title III, §305, as added Pub. L. 91-285, §6, June 22, 1970, 84 Stat. 319.)

SUBCHAPTER II. — FEDERAL ELECTION RECORDS

§1974. Retention and preservation of records and papers by officers of elections; deposit with custodian; penalty for violation.

Every officer of election shall retain and preserve, for a period of twenty-two months from the date of any general, special, or primary election of which candidates for the office of President, Vice President, presidential elector, Member of the Senate, Member of the House of Representatives, or Resident Commissioner from the Commonwealth of Puerto Rico are voted for, all records and papers which come into his possession relating to any application, registration, payment of poll tax, or other act requisite to voting in such election, except that, when required by law, such records and papers may be delivered to another officer of election and except that, if a State or the Commonwealth of Puerto Rico designates a custodian to retain and preserve these records and papers at a specific place, then such records and papers may be deposited with such custodian, and the duty to retain and preserve any record or paper so deposited shall devolve upon such custodian. Any officer of election or custodian who willfully fails to comply with this section shall be fined not more than $1,000 or imprisoned not more than one year, or both. (Pub. L. 86-449, title III, §301, May 6, 1960, 74 Stat. 88.)

§1974a. Theft, destruction, concealment, mutilation, or alteration of records or papers; penalties.

Any person, whether or not an officer of election or custodian, who willfully steals, destroys, conceals, mutilates or alters any record or paper required by section 1974 of this title to be retained and preserved shall be fined not more than $1,000 or imprisoned not more than one year, or both. (Pub. L. 86-449, title III, §302, May 6, 1960, 74 Stat. 88.)

§1974b. Demand for records or papers by Attorney General or representative; statement of basis and purpose.

Any record or paper required by section 1974 of this title to be retained and preserved shall, upon demand in writing by the Attorney General or his representative directed to the person having custody, possession, or control of such record or paper, be made available for inspection, reproduction, and copying at the principal office of such custodian by the Attorney General or his representative. This demand shall contain a statement of the basis and the purpose therefor. (Pub. L. 86-449, title III, §303, May 6, 1960, 74 Stat. 88.)

§1974c. Disclosure of records or papers.

Unless otherwise ordered by a court of the United States, neither the Attorney General nor any employee of the Department of Justice, nor any other representative of the Attorney General, shall disclose any record or paper produced pursuant to this subchapter, or any reproduction or copy, except to Congress and any committee thereof, governmental agencies, and in the presentation of any case or proceeding before any court or grand jury. (Pub. L. 86-449, title III, §304, May 6, 1960, 74 Stat. 88.)

§1974d. Jurisdiction to compel production of records or papers.

The United States district court for the district in which a demand is made pursuant to section 1974b of this title, or in which a record or paper so demanded is located, shall have jurisdiction by appropriate process to compel the production of such record or paper. (Pub. L. 86-449, title III, §305, May 6, 1960, 74 Stat. 88.)

§1974e. Definitions.

As used in this subchapter, the term "officer of election" means any person who, under color of any Federal, State, Commonwealth, or local law, statute, ordinance, regulation, authority, custom, or usage, performs or is authorized to perform any function, duty, or task in connection with any application, registration, payment of poll tax, or other act requisite to voting in any general, special, or primary election at which votes are cast for candidates for the office of President, Vice President, presidential elector, Member of the Senate, Member of the House of Representatives, or Resident Commissioner from the Commonwealth of Puerto Rico. (Pub. L. 86-449, title III, §306, May 6, 1960, 74 Stat. 88.)

FAIR HOUSING ACT OF 1968, 42 UNITED STATES CODE §§3601 ET SEQ. (1970)

SUBCHAPTER I. — GENERALLY

§3601. Declaration of policy.

It is the policy of the United States to provide, within constitutional limitations, for fair housing throughout the United States. (Pub. L. 90-284, title VIII, §801, Apr. 11, 1968, 82 Stat. 81.)

Federally Protected Activities; Penalties

Penalties for violations respecting federally protected activities not applicable to and not affecting activities under this subchapter, see section 101(b) of Pub. L. 90-284, set out as a note under section 245 of Title 18, Crimes and Criminal Procedure.

§3602. Definitions.

As used in this subchapter —

(a) "Secretary" means the Secretary of Housing and Urban Development.

(b) "Dwelling" means any building, structure, or portion thereof which is occupied as, or designed or intended for occupancy as, a residence by one or more families, and any vacant land which is offered for sale or lease for the construction or location thereon of any such building, structure, or portion thereof.

(c) "Family" includes a single individual.

(d) "Person" includes one or more individuals, corporations, partnerships, associations, labor organizations, legal representatives, mutual companies, joint-stock companies, trusts, unincorporated organizations, trustees, trustees in bankruptcy, receivers, and fiduciaries.

(e) "To rent" includes to lease, to sublease, to let and otherwise to grant for a consideration the right to occupy premises not owned by the occupant.

(f) "Discriminatory housing practice" means an act that is unlawful under section 3604, 3605, or 3606 of this title.

(g) "State" means any of the several States, the District of Columbia, the Commonwealth of Puerto Rico, or any of the territories and possessions of the United States. (Pub. L. 90-284, title VIII, §802, Apr. 11, 1968, 82 Stat. 81.)

§3603. Effective dates of certain prohibitions.
(a) Application to certain described dwellings.

Subject to the provisions of subsection (b) of this section and section 3607 of this title, the prohibitions against discrimination in the sale or rental of housing set forth in section 3604 of this title shall apply:

(1) Upon enactment of this subchapter, to —

(A) dwellings owned or operated by the Federal Government;

(B) dwellings provided in whole or in part with the aid of loans, advances, grants, or contributions made by the Federal Government, under agreements entered into after November 20, 1962, unless payment due thereon has been made in full prior to April 11, 1968;

(C) dwellings provided in whole or in part by loans insured, guaranteed, or otherwise secured by the credit of the Federal Government, under agreements entered into after November 20, 1962, unless payment thereon has been made in full prior to April 11, 1968: *Provided,* That nothing contained in subparagraphs (B) and (C) of this subsection shall be applicable to dwellings solely by virtue of the fact that they are subject to mortgages held by an FDIC or FSLIC institution; and

(D) dwellings provided by the development or the redevelopment of real property purchased, rented, or otherwise obtained from a State or local public agency receiving Federal financial assistance for slum clearance or urban renewal with respect to such real property under loan or grant contracts entered into after November 20, 1962.

(2) After December 31, 1968, to all dwellings covered by paragraph (1) and to all other dwellings except as exempted by subsection (b) of this section.

(b) Exemptions.

Nothing in section 3604 of this title (other than subsection (c)) shall apply to —

(1) any single-family house sold or rented by an owner: *Provided,* That such private individual owner does not own more than three such single-family houses at any one time: *Provided further,* That in the case of the sale of any such single-family house by a private individual owner not residing in such house at the time of such sale or who was not the most recent resident of such house prior to such sale, the exemption granted by this subsection shall apply only with respect to one such sale within any twenty-four month period: *Provided further,* That such bona fide private individual owner does not own any interest in, nor is there owned or reserved on his behalf, under any express or voluntary agreement, title to or any right to all or a portion of the proceeds from the sale or rental of, more than three such single-family houses at any one time: *Provided further,* That after December 31, 1969, the sale or rental of any such single-family house shall be excepted from the application of this chapter only if such house is sold or rented (A) without the use in any manner of the sales or rental facilities or the sales or rental services of any real estate broker, agent, or salesman, or of such facilities or services of any person in the business of selling or renting dwellings, or of any employee or agent of any such broker, agent, salesman, or person and (B) without the publication, posting or mailing, after notice, of any advertisement or written notice in violation

of section 3604(c) of this title; but nothing in this proviso shall prohibit the use of attorneys, escrow agents, abstractors, title companies, and other such professional assistance as necessarily to perfect or transfer the title, or

(2) rooms or units in dwellings containing living quarters occupied or intended to be occupied by no more than four families living independently of each other, if the owner actually maintains and occupies one of such living quarters as his residence.

(c) *Same; business of selling or renting dwellings defined.*

For the purposes of subsection (b) of this section, a person shall be deemed to be in the business of selling or renting dwellings if —

(1) he has, within the preceding twelve months, participated as principal in three or more transactions involving the sale or rental of any dwelling or any interest therein, or

(2) he has, within the preceding twelve months, participated as agent, other than in the sale of his own personal residence in providing sales or rental facilities or sales or rental services in two or more transactions involving the sale or rental of any dwelling or any interest therein, or

(3) he is the owner of any dwelling designed or intended for occupancy by, or occupied by, five or more families.

(Pub. L. 90-284, title VIII, §803, Apr. 11, 1968, 82 Stat. 82.)

§3604. Discrimination in the sale or rental of housing.

As made applicable by section 3603 of this title and except as exempted by sections 3603(b) and 3607 of this title, it shall be unlawful —

(a) To refuse to sell or rent after the making of a bona fide offer, or to refuse to negotiate for the sale or rental of, or otherwise make unavailable or deny, a dwelling to any person because of race, color, religion, or national origin.

(b) To discriminate against any person in the terms, conditions, or privileges of sale or rental of a dwelling, or in the provisions of services or facilities in connection therewith, because of race, color, religion, or national origin.

(c) To make, print, or publish, or cause to be made, printed, or published any notice, statement, or advertisement, with respect to the sale or rental of a dwelling that indicates any preference, limitation or discrimination based on race, color, religion, or national origin, or an intention to make any such reference, limitation, or discrimination.

(d) To represent to any person because of race, color, religion, or national origin that any dwelling is not available for inspection, sale, or rental when such dwelling is in fact so available.

(e) For profit, to induce or attempt to induce any person to sell or rent any dwelling by representations regarding the entry or prospective entry into the neighborhood of a person or persons of a particular race, color, religion, or national origin.

(Pub. L. 90-284, title VIII, §804, Apr. 11, 1968, 82 Stat. 83.)

§3605. Discrimination in the financing of housing.

After December 31, 1968, it shall be unlawful for any bank, building and loan association, insurance company or other corporation, association, firm or enterprise whose business consists in whole or in part in the making of commercial real estate loans, to deny a loan or other financial assistance to a person applying therefor for the purpose of purchasing, constructing, improving, repairing, or maintaining a dwelling, or to discriminate against him in the fixing of the amount, interest rate, duration, or other terms or conditions of such loan or other financial assistance, because of the race, color, religion, or national origin of such person or of any person associated with him in connection with such loan or other financial assistance or the purposes of such loan or other financial assistance, or of the present or prospective owners, lessees, tenants, or occupants of the dwelling or dwellings in relation to which such loan or other financial assistance is to be made or given: *Provided,* That nothing contained in this section shall impair the scope or effectiveness of the exception contained in section 3603(b) of this title. (Pub. L. 90-284, title VIII, §805, Apr. 11, 1968, 82 Stat. 83.)

§3606. Discrimination in the provision of brokerage services.

After December 31, 1968, it shall be unlawful to deny any person access to or membership or participation in any multiple-listing service, real estate brokers' organization or other service, organization, or facility relating to the business of selling or renting dwellings, or to discriminate against him in the terms or conditions of such access, membership, or participation, on account of race, color, religion, or national origin. (Pub. L. 90-284, title VIII, §806, Apr. 11, 1968, 82 Stat. 84.)

§3607. Religious organization or private club exemption.

Nothing in this subchapter shall prohibit a religious organization, association, or society, or any nonprofit institution or organization operated, supervised or controlled by or in conjunction with a religious organization, association, or society, from limiting the sale, rental or occupancy of dwellings which it owns or operates for other than a commercial purpose to persons of the same religion, or from giving preference to such persons, unless membership in such religion is restricted on account of race, color, or national origin. Nor shall anything in this subchapter prohibit a private club not in fact open to the public, which as an incident to its primary purpose or purposes provides lodgings which it owns or operates for other than commercial purpose, from limiting the rental or occupancy of such lodgings to its members or from giving preference to its members. (Pub. L. 90-284, title VIII, §807, Apr. 11, 1968, 82 Stat. 84.)

§3608. Administration.

(a) Authority and responsibility.

The authority and responsibility for administering this Act shall be in the Secretary of Housing and Urban Development.

(b) Delegation of authority; appointment of hearing examiners; location of conciliation meetings; administrative review.

The Secretary may delegate any of his functions, duties, and powers to employees of the Department of Housing and Urban Development or to boards of such employees, including functions, duties, and powers with respect to investigating, conciliating, hearing, determining, ordering, certifying, reporting, or otherwise acting as to any work, business, or matter under this chapter. The persons to whom such delegations are made with respect to hearing functions, duties, and powers shall be appointed and shall serve in the Department of Housing and Urban Development in compliance with sections 3105, 3344, 5362, and 7521 of Title 5. Insofar as possible, conciliation meetings shall be held in the cities or other localities where the discriminatory housing practices allegedly occurred. The Secretary shall by rule prescribe such rights of appeal from the decisions of his hearing examiners to other hearing examiners or to other officers in the Department, to boards of officers or to himself, as shall be appropriate and in accordance with law.

(*c*) *Cooperation of Secretary and executive departments and agencies in administration of housing and urban development programs and activities to further fair housing purposes.*

All executive departments and agencies shall administer their programs and activities relating to housing and urban development in a manner affirmatively to further the purposes of this subchapter and shall cooperate with the Secretary to further such purposes.

(*d*) *Functions of Secretary.*

The Secretary of Housing and Urban Development shall —

(1) make studies with respect to the nature and extent of discriminatory housing practices in representative communities, urban, suburban, and rural, throughout the United States;

(2) publish and disseminate reports, recommendations, and information derived from such studies;

(3) cooperate with and render technical assistance to Federal, State, local, and other public or private agencies, organizations, and institutions which are formulating or carrying on programs to prevent or eliminate discriminatory housing practices;

(4) cooperate with and render such technical and other assistance to the Community Relations Service as may be appropriate to further its activities in preventing or eliminating discriminatory housing practices; and

(5) administer the programs and activities relating to housing and urban development in a manner affirmatively to further the policies of this subchapter.

(Pub. L. 90-284, title VIII, §808 (a), (c) — (e), Apr. 11, 1968, 82 Stat. 84, 85.)

§3609. Education and conciliation; conferences and consultations: reports.

Immediately after April 11, 1968, the Secretary shall commence such educational and conciliatory activities as in his judgment will further the purposes of this subchapter. He shall call conferences of persons in the housing industry and other interested parties to acquaint them with the provisions of this subchapter and his suggested means of implementing it, and shall endeavor with their advice to work out programs of voluntary compliance and of enforcement. He may pay per diem, travel, and transportation expenses for persons attending such conferences as provided in section 5703 of Title 5. He shall consult with State and local officials and other interested parties to learn the extent, if any, to which housing discrimination exists in their State or locality, and whether and how State or local enforcement programs might be utilized to combat such discrimination in connection with or in place of, the Secretary's enforcement of this subchapter. The Secretary shall issue reports on such conferences and consultations as he deems appropriate. (Pub. L. 90-284, title VIII, §809, Apr. 11, 1968, 82 Stat. 85.)

§3610. Enforcement.

(*a*) *Person aggrieved; complaints; copy; investigation; informal proceedings; violations of secrecy; penalties.*

Any person who claims to have been injured by a discriminatory housing practice or who believes that he will be irrevocably injured by a discriminatory housing practice that is about to occur (hereafter "person aggrieved") may file a complaint with the Secretary. Complaints shall be in writing and shall contain such information and be in such form as the Secretary requires. Upon receipt of such a complaint the Secretary shall furnish a copy of the same to the person or persons who allegedly committed or are about to commit the alleged discriminatory housing practice.

Within thirty days after receiving a complaint, or within thirty days after the expiration of any period of reference under subsection (c) of this section, the Secretary shall investigate the complaint and give notice in writing to the person aggrieved whether he intends to resolve it. If the Secretary decides to resolve the complaint, he shall proceed to try to eliminate or correct the alleged discriminatory housing practice by informal methods of conference, conciliation, and persuasion. Nothing said or done in the course of such informal endeavors may be made public or used as evidence in a subsequent proceeding under this subchapter without the written consent of the persons concerned. Any employee of the Secretary who shall make public any information in violation of this provision shall be deemed guilty of a misdemeanor and upon conviction thereof shall be fined not more than $1,000 or imprisoned not more than one year.

(*b*) *Complaint; limitations; answer; amendments; verification.*

A complaint under subsection (a) of this section shall be filed within one hundred and eighty days after the alleged discriminatory housing practice occurred. Complaints shall be in writing and shall state the facts upon which the allegations of a discriminatory housing practice are based. Complaint may be reasonably and fairly amended at any time. A respondent may file an answer to the complaint against him and with the leave of the Secretary which shall be granted whenever it would be reasonable and fair to do so, may amend his answer at any time. Both complaints and answers shall be verified.

(*c*) *Notification of State or local agency of violation of State or local fair housing law; commencement of State or local law enforcement proceedings; certification of circumstances requisite for action by Secretary.*

Wherever a State or local fair housing law provides rights and remedies for alleged discriminatory housing practices which are substantially equivalent to the rights and remedies provided in this title, the Secretary shall notify the appropriate State or local agency of any complaint filed under this subchapter which appears to constitute a violation of such State or local fair housing law, and the Secretary shall take no further action with respect to such complaint if the appropriate State or local law enforcement official has, within thirty days from the date the alleged offense has been brought to his attention, commenced proceedings in the matter, or, having done so, carries forward such proceedings with reasonable promptness. In no event shall the Secretary take further action unless he certifies that in his judgment, under the circumstances of the particular case, the protection of the rights of the parties or the interests of justice require such action.

(*d*) *Commencement of civil actions; State or local remedies available; jurisdiction and venue; findings; injunctions; appropriate affirmative orders.*

If within thirty days after a complaint is filed with the Secretary or within thirty days after expiration of any period of reference under subsection (c) of this section, the Secretary has been unable to obtain voluntary compliance with this subchapter, the person aggrieved may, within thirty days thereafter, commence a civil action in any appropriate United States district court, against the respondent named in the complaint, to enforce the rights granted or protected by this subchapter, insofar as such rights relate to the subject of the complaint: *Provided,* That no such civil action may be brought in any United States district court if the person aggrieved has a judicial remedy under a State or local fair housing law which provides rights and remedies for alleged discriminatory housing practices which are substantially equivalent to the rights and remedies provided in this subchapter. Such actions may be brought without regard to the amount in controversy in any United States district court for the district in which the discriminatory housing practice is alleged to have occurred or be about to occur or in which the respondent resides or transacts business. If the court finds that a discriminatory housing practice has occurred or is about to occur, the court may, subject to the provisions of section 3612 of this title, enjoin the respondent from engaging in such practice or order such affirmative action as may be appropriate.

(*e*) *Burden of proof.*

In any proceeding brought pursuant to this section, the burden of proof shall be on the complainant.

(*f*) *Trial of action; termination of voluntary compliance efforts.*

Whenever an action filed by an individual, in either Federal or State court, pursuant to this section or section 3612 of this title, shall come to trial the Secretary shall immediately terminate all efforts to obtain voluntary compliance. (Pub. L. 90-284, title VIII, §810, Apr. 11, 1968, 82 Stat. 85.)

§3611. Evidence.

(*a*) *Investigations; access to records, documents, and other evidence; copying; searches and seizures; subpenas for Secretary; interrogatories; administration of oaths.*

In conducting an investigation the Secretary shall have access at all reasonable times to premises, records, documents, individuals, and other evidence or possible sources of evidence and may examine, record, and copy such materials and take and record the testimony or statements of such persons as are reasonably necessary for the furtherance of the investigation: *Provided, however,* That the Secretary first complies with the provisions of the Fourth Amendment relating to unreasonable searches and seizures. The Secretary may issue subpenas to compel his access to or the production of such materials, or the appearance of such persons, and may issue interrogatories to a respondent, to the same extent and subject to the same limitations as would apply if the subpenas or interrogatories were issued or served in aid of a civil action in the United States district court for the district in which the investigation is taking place. The Secretary may administer oaths.

(*b*) *Subpenas for respondent.*

Upon wrtten application to the Secretary, a respondent shall be entitled to the issuance of a reasonable number of subpenas by and in the name of the Secretary to the same extent and subject to the same limitations as subpenas issued by the Secretary himself. Subpenas issued at the request of a respondent shall show on their face the name and address of such respondent and shall state that they were issued at his request.

(*c*) *Compensation and mileage fees of witnesses.*

Witnesses summoned by subpena of the Secretary shall be entitled to the same witness and mileage fees as are witnesses in proceedings in United States district courts. Fees payable to a witness summoned by a subpena issued at the request of a respondent shall be paid by him.

(*d*) *Revocation or modification of petition for subpena; good reasons for grant of petition.*

Within five days after service of a subpena upon any person, such person may petition the Secretary to revoke or modify the subpena. The Secretary shall grant the petition if he finds that the subpena requires appearance or attendance at an unreasonable time or place, that it requires production of evidence which does not relate to any matter under investigation, that it does not describe with sufficient particularity the evidence to be produced, that compliance would be unduly onerous, or for other good reason.

(*e*) *Enforcement of subpena.*

In case of contumacy or refusal to obey a subpena, the Secretary or other person at whose request it was issued may petition for its enforcement in the United States district court for the district in which the person to whom the subpena was addressed resides, was served, or transacts business.

(*f*) *Violations; penalties.*

Any person who willfully fails or neglects to attend and testify or to answer any lawful inquiry or to produce records, documents, or other evidence, if in his power to do so, in obedience to the subpena or lawful order of the Secretary, shall be fined not more than $1,000 or imprisoned not more than one year, or both. Any person who, with intent thereby to mislead the Secretary, shall make or cause to be made any false entry or statement of fact in any report, account, record, or other document submitted to the Secretary pursuant to his subpena or other order, or shall willfully neglect or fail to make or cause to be made full, true, and correct entries in such reports, accounts, records, or other documents, or shall willfully mutilate, alter, or by any other means falsify any documentary evidence, shall be fined not more than $1,000 or imprisoned not more than one year, or both.

(*g*) *Attorney General to conduct litigation.*

The Attorney General shall conduct all litigation in which the Secretary participates as a party or as amicus pursuant to this Act. (Pub. L. 90-284, title VIII, §811, Apr. 11, 1968, 82 Stat. 87.)

§3612. Enforcement by private persons.

(*a*) *Civil action; Federal and State jurisdiction; complaint; limitations; continuance pending conciliation efforts; prior bona fide transactions unaffected by court orders.*

The rights granted by sections 3603, 3604, 3605, and 3606 of this title may be enforced by civil actions in appropriate United States district courts without regard to the amount in controversy and in appropriate State or local courts of general jurisdiction. A civil action shall be commenced within one hundred and eighty days after the alleged discriminatory housing practice occurred: *Provided, however,* That the court shall continue such civil case brought pursuant to this section or section 3610(d) of this title from time to time before bringing it to trial if the court believes that the conciliation efforts of the Secretary or a State or local agency are likely to result in satisfactory settlement of the discriminatory housing practice complained of in the complaint made to the Secretary or to the local or State agency and which practice forms the basis for the action in court: *And provided, however,* That any sale, encumbrance, or rental consummated prior to the issuance of any court order issued under the authority of this Act, and involving a bona fide purchaser, encumbrancer, or tenant without actual notice of the existence of the filing of a complaint or civil action under the provisions of this Act shall not be affected.

(*b*) *Appointment of counsel and commencement of civil actions in Federal or State courts without payment of fees, costs, or security.*

Upon application by the plaintiff and in such circumstances as the court may deem just, a court of the United States in which a civil action under this section has been brought may appoint an attorney for the plaintiff and may authorize the commencement of a civil action upon proper showing without the payment of fees, costs, or security. A court of a State or subdivision thereof may do likewise to the extent not inconsistent with the law or procedures of the State or subdivision.

(c) *Injunctive relief and damages; limitation; court costs; attorney fees.*

The court may grant as relief, as it deems appropriate, any permanent or temporary injunction, temporary restraining order, or other order, and may award to the plaintiff actual damages and not more than $1,000 punitive damages, together with court costs and reasonable attorney fees in the case of a prevailing plaintiff: *Provided,* That the said plaintiff in the opinion of the court is not financially able to assume said attorney's fees. (Pub. L. 90-284, title VIII, §812, Apr. 11, 1968, 82 Stat. 88.)

§3613. Enforcement by the Attorney General; issues of general public importance; civil action; Federal jurisdiction; complaint; preventive relief.

Whenever the Attorney General has reasonable cause to believe that any person or group of persons is engaged in a pattern or practice of resistance to the full enjoyment of any of the rights granted by this subchapter, or that any group of persons has been denied any of the rights granted by this subchapter and such denial raises an issue of general public importance, he may bring a civil action in any appropriate United States district court by filing with it a complaint setting forth the facts and requesting such preventive relief, including an application for a permanent or temporary injunction, restraining order, or other order against the person or persons responsible for such pattern or practice or denial of rights, as he deems necessary to insure the full enjoyment of the rights granted by this subchapter. (Pub. L. 90-284, title VIII, §813, Apr. 11, 1968, 82 Stat. 88.)

§3614. Expedition of proceedings.

Any court in which a proceeding is instituted under section 3612 or 3613 of this title shall assign the case for hearing at the earliest practicable date and cause the case to be in every way expedited. (Pub. L. 90-284, title VIII, §814, Apr. 11, 1968, 82 Stat. 88.)

§3615. Effect on State laws.

Nothing in this subchapter shall be construed to invalidate or limit any law of a State or political subdivision of a State, or of any other jurisdiction in which this subchapter shall be effective, that grants, guarantees, or protects the same rights as are granted by this subchapter; but any law of a State, a political subdivision, or other such jurisdiction that purports to require or permit any action that would be a discriminatory housing practice under this subchapter shall to that extent be invalid. (Pub. L. 90-284, title VIII, §815, Apr. 11, 1968, 82 Stat. 89.)

§3616. Cooperation with State and local agencies administering fair housing laws; utilization of services and personnel; reimbursement; written agreements; publication in Federal Register.

The Secretary may cooperate with State and local agencies charged with the administration of State and local fair housing laws and, with the consent of such agencies, utilize the services of such agencies and their employees and, notwithstanding any other provision of law, may reimburse such agencies and their employees for services rendered to assist him in carrying out this subchapter. In furtherance of such cooperative efforts, the Secretary may enter into written agreements with such State or local agencies. All agreements and terminations thereof shall be published in the Federal Register. (Pub. L. 90-284, title VIII, §816, Apr. 11, 1968, 82 Stat. 89.)

§3617. Interference, coercion, or intimidation; enforcement by civil action.

It shall be unlawful to coerce, intimidate, threaten, or interfere with any person in the exercise or enjoyment of, or on account of his having exercised or enjoyed, or on account of his having aided or encouraged any other person in the exercise or enjoyment of, any right granted or protected by section 3603, 3604, 3605, or 3606 of this title. This section may be enforced by appropriate civil action. (Pub. L. 90-284, title VIII, §817, Apr. 11, 1968, 82 Stat. 89.)

§3618. Authorization of appropriations.

There are hereby authorized to be appropriated such sums as are necessary to carry out the purposes of this subchapter. (Pub. L. 90-284, title VIII, §818, Apr. 11, 1968, 82 Stat. 89.)

§3619. Separability of provisions.

If any provision of this subchapter or the application thereof to any person or circumstances is held invalid, the remainder of the subchapter and the application of the provision to other persons not similarly situated or to other circumstances shall not be affected thereby. (Pub. L. 90-284, title VIII, §819, Apr. 11, 1968, 82 Stat. 89.)

SUBCHAPTER II. — PREVENTION OF INTIMIDATION

§3631. Violations; bodily injury; death; penalties.

Whoever, whether or not acting under color of law, by force or threat of force willfully injures, intimidates or interferes with, or attempts to injure, intimidate or interfere with —

(a) any person because of his race, color, religion or national origin and because he is or has been selling, purchasing, renting, financing, occupying, or contracting or negotiating for the sale, purchase, rental, financing or occupation of any dwelling, or applying for or participating in any service, organization, or facility relating to the business of selling or renting dwellings; or

(b) any person because he is or has been, or in order to intimidate such person or any other person or class of persons from —

(1) participating, without discrimination on account of race, color, religion or national origin, in any of the activities, services, organizations or facilities described in subsection (a) of this section; or

(2) affording another person or class of persons opportunity or protection so to participate; or

(c) any citizen because he is or has been, or in order to discourage such citizen or any other citizen from lawfully aiding or encouraging other persons to participate, without discrimination on account of race, color, religion or national origin, in any of the activities, services, organzations or facilities described in subsection (a) of this section, or particpating lawfully in speech or peaceful assembly opposing any denial of the opportunity to so participate —

shall be fined not more than $1,000, or imprisoned not more than one year, or both; and if bodily injury results shall be fined not more than $10,000, or imprisoned not more than ten years, or both; and if death results shall be subject to imprisonment for any term of years or for life. (Pub. L. 90-284, title IX, §901, Apr. 11, 1968, 82 Stat. 89.)

HIGHER EDUCATION AMENDMENTS OF 1972

Title VIII — General Provisions Relating to the Assignment or Transportation of Students, 20 U.S.C.A. (Supp. 1973)

§1651. Prohibition against assignment or transportation of students to overcome racial imbalance

No provision of this Act shall be construed to require the assignment or transportation of students or teachers in order to overcome racial imbalance.
Pub. L. 92-318, Title VIII, §801, June 23, 1972, 86 Stat. 371.

§1652. Prohibition against use of appropriated funds for busing

(a) No funds appropriated for the purpose of carrying out any applicable program may be used for the transportation of students or teachers (or for the purchase of equipment for such transportation) in order to overcome racial imbalance in any school or school system, or for the transportation of students or teachers (or for the purchase of equipment for such transportation) in order to carry out a plan of racial desegregation of any school or school system, except on the express written voluntary request of appropriate local school officials. No such funds shall be made available for transportation when the time or distance of travel is so great as to risk the health of the children or significantly impinge on the educational process of such children, or where the educational opportunities available at the school to which it is proposed that any such student be transported will be substantially inferior to those opportunities offered at the school to which such student would otherwise be assigned under a nondiscriminatory system of school assignments based on geographic zones established without discrimination on account of race, religion, color, or national origin.

(b) No officer, agent, or employee of the Department of Health, Education, and Welfare (including the Office of Education), the Department of Justice, or any other Federal agency shall, by rule, regulation, order, guideline, or otherwise (1) urge, persuade, induce, or require any local education agency, or any private nonprofit agency, institution, or organization to use any funds derived from any State or local sources for any purpose, unless constitutionally required, for which Federal funds appropriated to carry out any applicable program may not be used, as provided in this section, or (2) condition the receipt of Federal funds under any Federal program upon any action by any State or local public officer or employee which would be prohibited by clause (1) on the part of a Federal officer or employee. No officer, agent, or employee of the Department of Health, Education, and Welfare (including the Office of Education) or any other Federal agency shall urge, persuade, induce, or require any local education agency to undertake transportation of any student where the time or distance of travel is so great as to risk the health of the child or significantly impinge on his or her educational process; or where the educational opportunities available at the school to which it is proposed that such student be transported will be substantially inferior to those offered at the school to which such student would otherwise be assigned under a nondiscriminatory system of school assignments based on geographic zones established without discrimination on account of race, religion, color, or national origin.

(c) An applicable program means a program to which the General Education Provisions Act applies.
Pub. L. 92-318, Title VIII, §802, June 23, 1972, 86 Stat. 371.

§1653. Judicial orders postponed pending court appeals; expiration date

Notwithstanding any other law or provision of law, in the case of any order on the part of any United States district court which requires the transfer or transportation of any student or students from any school attendance area prescribed by competent State or local authority for the purposes of achieving a balance among students with respect to race, sex, religion, or socioeconomic status, the effectiveness of such order shall be postponed until all appeals in connection with such order have been exhausted or, in the event no appeals are taken, until the time for such appeals has expired. This section shall expire at midnight on January 1, 1974.

Pub. L. 92-318, Title VIII, §803, June 23, 1972, 86 Stat. 372.

§1654. Intervention authorization in implementation of court orders

A parent or guardian of a child, or parents or guardians of children similarly situated, transported to a public school in accordance with a court order, may seek to reopen or intervene in the further implementation of such court order, currently in effect, if the time or distance of travel is so great as to risk the health of the student or significantly impinge on his or her educational process.

Pub. L. 92-318, Title VIII, §804, June 23, 1972, 86 Stat. 372.

§1655. Uniform rules of evidence of racial discrimination

The rules of evidence required to prove that State or local authorities are practicing racial discrimination in assigning students to public schools shall be uniform throughout the United States.

Pub. L. 92-318, Title VIII, §805, June 23, 1972, 86 Stat. 372.

§1656. Prohibition against official or court orders to achieve racial balance or insure compliance with constitutional standards applicable to entire United States

The proviso of section 407(a) of the Civil Rights Act of 1964 providing in substance that no court or official of the United States shall be empowered to issue any order seeking to achieve a racial balance in any school by requiring the transportation of pupils or students from one school to another or one school district to another in order to achieve such racial balance, or otherwise enlarge the existing power of the court to insure compliance with constitutional standards shall apply to all public school pupils and to every public school system, public school and public school board, as defined by Title IV, under all circumstances and conditions and at all times in every State, district, territory, Commonwealth, or possession of the United States regardless of whether the residence of such public school pupils or the principal offices of such public school system, public school or public school board is situated in the northern, eastern, western, or southern part of the United States.

Pub. L. 92-318, Title VIII, §806, June 23, 1972, 86 Stat. 373.

INDEX